W9-AWW-096

Cover Girl	http://www.covergirl.com/
Daniel Swarovski Corp.	http://www.swarovski.com/
DealerNet	http://dealernet.com/
Dell Computer Corp.	http://www.dell.com/
Discovery Channel	http://www.discovery.com/
Disney Corp.	http://www.disney.com/
Domino's Pizza, Inc.	http://www.dominos.com/
DreamShop	http://www.dreamshop.com
Duracell Corp.	http://www.duracell.com/
E-Lab LLC	http://www.elab.com/
Eastman Chemical Co.	http://www.eastman.com/
Eastman Kodak Co.	http://www.kodak.com/
EB World	http://www.ebworld.com/
Edmark Corp.	http://www.edmark.com/
ESSENCE Online	http://www.essence.com/
Eveready/Energizer Battery Co.	http://www.eveready.com/
Federal Express	http://www.fedex.com/
Ford WorldWide Connection	http://www.ford.com/
Fortune Brands, Inc.	http://www.ambrands.com/
Frito Lay, Inc.	http://www.fritolay.com/
Fruit of the Loom, Inc.	http://www.fruit.com/
GATX Logistics, Inc.	http://www.gatx.inter.net/
General Motors Corp.	http://www.gm.com/
Globalstar LP	http://www.globalstar.com/
Godiva Chocolatier	http://www.godiva.com/
The Goodyear Tire & Rubber Co.	http://www.goodyear.com/
Hallmark Cards, Inc.	http://www.hallmark.com/
Helmsley Hotels	http://www.helmsleyhotels.com/
Hewlett-Packard Co.	http://www.hewlett-packard.com/
Hilton Hotels Corp.	http://www.hilton.com/
Home Depot, Inc.	http://www.homedepot.com/
Hot Hot Hot	http://www.hot.presence.com/
Hyatt Hotels & Resorts	http://www.hyatt.com/
iflowers	http://www.iflowers.com/
IKEA	http://www.netvigator.com/ikea/
Industry.net	http://www.industry.net/
Intercollegiate Communications (Student Union)	http://www.studentunion.com/

CONTEMPORARY MARKETING wired

Ninth Edition

CONTEMPORARY MARKETING wired

Ninth Edition

Louis E. Boone
Ernest G. Cleverdon Chair of Business and Management
University of South Alabama

David L. Kurtz
The R. A. and Vivian Young Chair of Business Administration
University of Arkansas

The Dryden Press
Harcourt Brace College Publishers
Fort Worth Philadelphia San Diego New York Orlando Austin San Antonio
Toronto Montreal London Sydney Tokyo

Publisher	George Provol
Acquisitions Editor	Bill Schoof
Executive Product Manager	Lisé Johnson
Developmental Editor	Tracy L. Morse
Project Editor	Kathryn M. Stewart
Production Manager	Carlyn Hauser
Art Director	Bill Brammer
Cover Image	Cover photography courtesy of Mark Humphries

ISBN: 0-03-018597-1

Library of Congress Catalog Card Number: 97-67635

Address for Orders
The Dryden Press, 6277 Sea Harbor Drive, Orlando, FL 32887
1-800-782-4479

Address for Editorial Correspondence
The Dryden Press, 301 Commerce Street, Suite 3700, Fort Worth, TX 76102

Web-site address
http://www.hbcollege.com

Printed in the United States of America

7 8 9 0 1 2 3 4 5 6   032   9 8 7 6 5 4 3 2 1

The Dryden Press
Harcourt Brace College Publishers

To the late G. E. Kiser:
War hero, mentor, and friend

The Dryden Press Series in Marketing

Assael
Marketing

Avila, Williams, Ingram, and LaForge
The Professional Selling Skills Workbook

Bateson
Managing Services Marketing: Text and Readings
Third Edition

Blackwell, Blackwell, and Talarzyk
Contemporary Cases in Consumer Behavior
Fourth Edition

Boone and Kurtz
Contemporary Marketing[WIRED]
Ninth Edition

Churchill
Basic Marketing Research
Third Edition

Churchill
Marketing Research: Methodological Foundations
Sixth Edition

Czinkota and Ronkainen
Global Marketing

Czinkota and Ronkainen
International Marketing
Fifth Edition

Czinkota and Ronkainen
International Marketing Strategy: Environmental Assessment and Entry Strategies

Dickson
Marketing Management
Second Edition

Engel, Blackwell, and Miniard
Consumer Behavior
Eighth Edition

Futrell
Sales Management: Teamwork, Leadership, and Technology
Fifth Edition

Grover
Theory & Simulation of Market-Focused Management

Ghosh
Retail Management
Second Edition

Hassan and Blackwell
Global Marketing: Managerial Dimensions and Cases

Hoffman/Bateson
Essentials of Services Marketing

Hutt and Speh
Business Marketing Management: A Strategic View of Industrial and Organizational Markets
Sixth Edition

Ingram, LaForge, and Schwepker
Sales Management: Analysis and Decision Making
Third Edition

Lewison
Marketing Management: An Overview

Lindgren and Shimp
Marketing: An Interactive Learning System

Krugman, Reid, Dunn, and Barban
Advertising: Its Role in Modern Marketing
Eighth Edition

Oberhaus, Ratliffe, and Stauble
Professional Selling: A Relationship Process
Second Edition

Parente, Vanden Bergh, Barban, and Marra
Advertising Campaign Strategy: A Guide to Marketing Communication Plans

Rosenbloom
Marketing Channels: A Management View
Fifth Edition

Sandburg
Discovering Your Marketing Career CD-ROM

Schaffer
Applying Marketing Principles Software

Schellinck and Maddox
Marketing Research: A Computer-Assisted Approach

Schnaars
MICROSIM

Schuster and Copeland
Global Business: Planning for Sales and Negotiations

Shimp
Advertising, Promotion, and Supplemental Aspects of Integrated Marketing Communications
Fourth Edition

Talarzyk
Cases and Exercises in Marketing

Terpstra and Sarathy
International Marketing
Seventh Edition

Weitz and Wensley
Readings in Strategic Marketing Analysis, Planning, and Implementation

Zikmund
Exploring Marketing Research
Sixth Edition

Harcourt Brace College Outline Series

Peterson
Principles of Marketing

Preface

The new edition of our best-selling *Contemporary Marketing* text is wired for twenty-first-century marketing. And now more than ever you'll want to plug into this marketing powerhouse!

In our ninth edition, *Contemporary Marketing*^{WIRED} continues to add to its collection of precedent-setting firsts. More than a million students have been introduced to the dynamic world of marketing through *Contemporary Marketing*. And after reading this sampling of our many firsts, we hope you'll understand why *Contemporary Marketing* continues to rank first with instructors and students alike.

- The **FIRST** marketing text written specifically for the student—rather than the professor—featuring a clear, concise style that readers can readily understand and enjoy.
- The **FIRST** marketing text based on marketing research and written the way instructors actually teach the course.
- The **FIRST** text to integrate computer applications into each chapter.
- The **FIRST** text to employ extensive pedagogy—such as boxed features—to breathe life into exciting real-world concepts and issues of marketing.
- The **FIRST** text to introduce end-of-chapter video cases tied to professionally produced video segments.
- The **FIRST** text to offer services and international chapters early and to thoroughly integrate those topics throughout the textbook with literally hundreds of examples.
- The **FIRST** text to include a separate chapter on quality and customer satisfaction.
- The **FIRST** text to utilize multimedia technology to integrate all components of the principles of marketing ancillary program—*Contemporary Marketing* laser discs linked to videos, overhead transparencies, and material from the text—enabling instructors to custom create exciting, energetic lecture presentations.

NEW! for the Ninth Edition

Contemporary Marketing^{WIRED} is the **FIRST** to integrate a true technology emphasis throughout the text and package. The ninth edition incorporates the technology theme into every facet: opening vignettes, chapter concepts, end-of-chapter assignments, boxed features, cases, and innovatively packaged items. The text applies today's technology—the Internet, CD-ROM, and multimedia—to traditional as well as emerging marketing concepts. Creative assignments and exercises give students hands-on experience in applying technological advances to real marketing issues. Engaging in-text examples now include company Web addresses and students can glean additional information and insight from *Contemporary Marketing's* own home page.

The improvements to the new edition are so extensive and so far-reaching that even the title of the text has been modified to *Contemporary Marketing*^{WIRED}. The change reflects not simply a new edition, but a new approach to the marketing discipline.

NEW TECHNOLOGY EMPHASIS

NEW! Student Preface

A new high-tech student preface details the new emphasis *Contemporary Marketing*^{WIRED} places on technology and gives directions to the Boone & Kurtz home page and other Internet resources.

NEW! Technology-Based Chapter Openers

Innovative chapter opening vignettes illustrate current marketing technology in action and link real-world scenarios to chapter concepts. Each vignette describes how an actual company has applied technology to its competitive advantage. The marketing research chapter (Chapter 6) opens with descriptions of Internet and Web databases, while the retailing coverage chapter (Chapter 15) begins with discussions of the virtual store and the advertising chapter (Chapter 18) with cyberspace media.

MORE! Technology in Marketing Research

Coverage of technology in marketing research has been expanded to include more examples of high-tech tools and more coverage of how computers are used to support marketing decision systems, including marketing databases, data warehouses, and decision support systems.

NEW! 'netWork Technology Exercises

End-of-chapter 'netWork applications give students hands-on experience employing the Internet in marketing-related exercises. These cutting-edge exercises:

- Contain problems that require students to locate data on different Web sites.

- Include computer exercises that can be completed at the *Contemporary Marketing*[WIRED] Web site.
- Incorporate follow-up assignments enabling students to further research in-text examples on Dryden Web locations.

NEW! Video Case Web-Site Questions

End-of-chapter video case questions include exercises that require students to visit a specific Web site related to the company or the concepts covered in the video in order to obtain the information necessary to solve the application.

KEY CONTENT CHANGES

NEW! Early Emphasis on the Internet and Relationship Marketing

Chapter 1, "Developing Relationships through Customer Focus, Quality, Technology, and Ethical Behavior," has been completely revised and revamped, reflecting the text's newly integrated emphasis on technology. Students are immediately introduced to hot topics such as the Internet, virtual marketing, and interactive marketing. The chapter also discusses relationship marketing, the increasing influence of global marketing, and the role of ethics and social responsibility in building customer relationships.

NEW! Relationship Marketing Chapter

An entire chapter has been devoted to relationship marketing, including coverage of database marketing, strategic alliances, co-marketing, co-branding, and dedicated sales forces. Coverage of this increasingly important marketing topic begins early in the text in Chapter 1 before the in-depth discussion in Chapter 10. Relationship marketing is also integrated throughout the text.

NEW! Integrated Communications Approach to Advertising and Promotion

The advertising and promotion chapter has been completely rewritten and revised to emphasize an integrated marketing communications approach, reflecting emerging trends in the field. A new Chapter 17, "Integrated Marketing Communications" also details the importance of the Internet's role in the promotional mix, including discussions of methods for determining the effectiveness of using Web sites. Sponsorship as a promotional tool and expanded coverage of direct marketing are also included in Chapter 17.

EXPANDED! Value and Customer Satisfaction

Chapter 2, "Creating Value through Customer Satisfaction and Quality," has been completely reorganized to focus on the importance of value and customer satisfaction to marketing. Quality is presented as a part of customer satisfaction, rather than vice versa. Value is shown as the link between quality and customer satisfaction and the path leading to successful customer relationships.

REORGANIZED! Product Chapters

Chapters 11 and 12 have been reorganized, with Chapter 11 focusing on product strategies and Chapter 12 emphasizing brand management and new product planning. As a result, the product line and product mix sections are now in Chapter 11, and the consumer adoption process is part of the new product introduction section in Chapter 12.

REVISED! Physical Distribution Chapter

The physical distribution chapter (Chapter 16) has been thoroughly revised and retitled "Logistics and Value Chain Management." Terminology and chapter content have been updated and particular attention is devoted to the contemporary concept of the value chain. By grouping all the distribution and wholesaling sections, this chapter now focuses more on distribution as it relates to the overall marketing strategy. The chapter also covers direct selling. The importance of managing channel relationships is now part of the expanded section on Channel Leadership and Management in Chapter 14.

EXPANDED! Direct Selling and Direct Marketing Coverage

The new edition includes expanded discussions of direct selling as a separate channel in Chapter 14, while discussions of direct mail are presented in the context of direct marketing in Chapter 18.

EXPANDED! Ethics Emphasis

Beginning early in the text (Chapter 1) with a section on "Ethics and Social Responsibility: Doing Well by Doing Good," the ninth edition emphasizes how ethical behavior promotes lasting customer relationships and leads to marketplace success. In addition to each chapter's ethical controversy boxes, Chapter 3 includes discussions of marketing's role in society, marketing ethics, and social responsibility. Special attention is also given to ethics in promotion, with new sections in Chapters 17, 18, and 19.

KEY PEDAGOGICAL CHANGES

NEW! "Marketing Hall of Fame" and "Marketing Hall of Shame" Boxes

Each chapter contains "Marketing Hall of Fame" and "Marketing Hall of Shame" boxes that detail actual marketing strategies that scored big as well as those that flopped. Presented in a punchy, eye-grabbing format, these stories give students an inside view of the results of actual marketing decisions.

NEW! "Solving an Ethical Controversy" Boxes

Real-world ethics and diversity issues are integrated with chapter concepts in this exciting new boxed feature that appears in every chapter. These topics are an excellent springboard for classroom discussion and debate.

NEW! Questions for Critical Thinking

Included in each "Marketing Hall of Fame" and "Marketing Hall of Shame" boxed feature are "Questions for Critical Thinking" that reflect the text's emphasis on critical-thinking applications. These exercises help students develop analytical skills while considering specific business scenarios.

NEW! "Briefly Speaking" Cut-Ins

Intriguing, unusual, and entertaining marketing facts are featured in each chapter in unique "Briefly Speaking" cut-in quotes.

NEW! Microsoft Continuing End-of-Part Case

A continuing, end-of-part case on Microsoft is fully integrated with chapter concepts, implementing new topics and issues as students learn them.

NEW! "Marketing Dictionary"

A student-friendly "Marketing Dictionary" defines key terms as they appear in the text and provides a list of definitions for each two-page spread.

NEW! End-of-Chapter Achievement Check Summaries

Each chapter contains an "Achievement Check Summary" section that uniquely reinforces chapter concepts by reviewing chapter highlights with quiz-like true/false and short multiple-choice questions. This question and answer format provides a more interactive and creative method for reviewing key chapter concepts.

UNPARALLELED RESOURCE PACKAGE

NEW! Boone & Kurtz Home Page

Using the *Contemporary Marketing*^{WIRED} Web site, professors and students can gain additional information, resources, and firsthand experience surfing the Net. Featuring in-text graphics and illustrations, the **Boone & Kurtz home page** is completely integrated with text topics as well as end-of-chapter exercises and video cases, many of which require readers to look up information at this or other Web sites. The home page is also the address for additional material integrated with the end-of-chapter computer exercises. The Boone & Kurtz home page is located on the Dryden World Wide Web site at

http://www.dryden.com/mktng/boone/

Home Page content is provided by Rosemary Ramsey, Eastern Kentucky University.

The Boone and Kurtz Web site includes the following features:

- "Incorporating the Internet into Your Basic Marketing Class" for professors
- "Teaching Resources" section for professors
- Short summaries of articles with accompanying supporting exercises
- Integration with end-of-chapter 'netWork applications
- Additional chapter review exercises
- "Career Communications" section for students
- Integration with the *Discovering Your Marketing Career CD-ROM*
- Integration with end-of-chapter video cases
- Chat area for students and professors
- Many, many more additional resources

NEW! World Wide Web Directory

Giving readers even more practice cruising the World Wide Web, online addresses are included for companies and organizations highlighted in extended-text examples, focus boxes, opening vignettes, and photo illustrations. Readers are also referred to Web sites to gain additional insight on chapter material, such as secondary data discussion in marketing research and competitive analysis relating to marketing planning. Addresses are spotlighted in the text with a special eye-catching design. In addition, company Web addresses are listed alphabetically on the endpapers of the text.

NEW! PowerPoint/CD-ROM Media Active Presentation Software

Classroom lectures and discussions come to life with this innovative presentation tool. Extremely professor-friendly and organized by chapter, this program enables instructors to custom design their own multimedia classroom presentations, using overhead transparencies, figures, tables, and graphs from the text as well as completely new material from outside sources. Content is provided by Rajiv Vaidyanathan, University of Minnesota-Duluth.

NEW! CD-ROM: *Discovering Your Marketing Career*

This innovative, student-friendly software package helps students learn about and assess their compatibility with marketing careers. In one comprehensive, multimedia CD-ROM, students receive broad guidance and practical advice on everything from clarifying the depth of their interest in a particular marketing career to preparing and implementing an effective job search strategy.

Students complete questionnaires regarding their preferences both for marketing-related job activities as well as such career factors as work environment, compensation, and career advancement. The program matches student responses to specific marketing careers. Students then view a customized video summarizing what their responses reveal about how well the career suits them, and then read a detailed report explaining how each of their responses may or may not indicate a good career match.

Through videos, audios, and extensive textual content, comprehensive career profiles present a detailed, up-to-date picture of actual job responsibilities, career paths, and skills required to be successful. Students are also advised on current compensation levels and associations, directories, books, and other relevant information for finding out more about the marketing career of interest. Career profiles were compiled following extensive interviews with professionals from such prominent companies as AT&T, General Electric, Ogilvy & Mather, J. Walter Thompson, Walt Disney, Coca-Cola, Microsoft, General Mills, Johnson & Johnson, Procter & Gamble, Neiman Marcus, Wal-Mart, Sears, Kmart, Digital Equipment Corporation, and IBM. Content for the program is provided by Eric Sandburg, Career Design Software.

The CD-ROM includes a free copy of the student version of *Career Design,* the landmark career planning software program based on the work of John Crystal, the major contributor to the most widely read career text of all time, *What Color is Your Parachute?* by Richard N. Bolles.

NEW! Internet Marketing Connection

Available through The Dryden Press Web site, students owning a copy of the *Discovering Your Marketing Career* CD-ROM included in *Contemporary Marketing*^{WIRED} can download the **Internet Marketing Connection**, an online guide to a wide range of marketing links. This innovative resource is run from the student's favorite Web browser, enabling the user to read the description of a marketing link and then click on the link to immediately visit that Internet location. Although topics may change according to current availability on Web sites, these are representative of the links:

- Global marketing
- Direct marketing
- Business-to-business marketing
- Sports marketing
- Database marketing
- Marketing issues related to ethics, quality, social responsibility, and cultural diversity
- Marketing through strategic alliances and co-branding
- Relationship marketing

Students can also link to Web sites where they can identify marketing job opportunities in the career fields covered in *Discovering Your Marketing Career.* The **Internet Marketing Connection** is updated regularly to ensure links are current. Visit The Dryden Press Web site at

http://www.dryden.com/mktng/careercd/

for the latest version.

UPDATED and EXPANDED! Custom Videos

Integrating the ninth edition's new technology emphasis, this exciting, innovative video package adopts a problem-resolution approach to video segments, which are tied directly to chapter concepts and even includes art and graphics from the text. Custom-produced for *Contemporary Marketing*^{WIRED}, the videos were created in partnership with successful, well-known companies, giving students a real-world perspective of how firms meet the challenges of the marketplace.

The videos illustrate such themes as quality, customer satisfaction, brand equity, relationship marketing, teamwork, product revitalization, regulation, and ethics.

Additionally, many segments conclude with career profiles of people featured in the videos. These real-world marketers discuss their career paths, marketing successes, key managerial skills, and the role of marketing, as well as offer personal advice to students. The video career profiles are coordinated with Dryden's *Discovering Your Marketing Career* CD-ROM. Approximately half of the videos are completely new, while the others have been thoroughly revised and updated.

The 21 videos (each approximately 15 minutes) include the following:

Chapter 1 A Search Engine Named Yahoo! (Yahoo!)
Chapter 2 Pursuing a Lofty Goal (Wainwright Industries, Inc.)
Chapter 3 Riding on the Information Superhighway (AT&T)
Chapter 4 Building a Global Competitive Advantage (Whirlpool Corporation)
Chapter 5 Growing Pains (Kropf Fruit Company)
Chapter 6 Taking the Path of Customer Focus (Walker Information)
Chapter 7 Targeting the Business Traveler (Marriott International)
Chapter 8 Beating Baldness (Pharmacia & Upjohn Company, Inc.)
Chapter 9 Creating Kitchens to Please Partners (Delfield Corporation)
Chapter 10 Launching Tommy: The New American Fragrance (Tommy Hilfiger)
Chapter 11 Serving the Needs of Golf Professionals (Slazenger USA)
Chapter 12 The Boulevard Cruiser (Cadillac)
Chapter 13 Changing to Help Others Change (Andersen Consulting)
Chapter 14 Choosing Channels (Next Door Foods)
Chapter 15 Renewing Retailing (Kmart)
Chapter 16 Leveraging the Links of Logistics (Dow Chemical)
Chapter 17 Flying High—From Nearby Skies (Cherry Capital Airport)
Chapter 18 Creating Advertising That Charms, Disarms, and Delivers (W.B. Doner Ad Agency)
Chapter 19 Selling the Free-Standing Insert (Valassis Communication, Inc.)
Chapter 20 Pricing a Lifesaver (Second Chance)
Chapter 21 Combating Competition in the Cookie Market (Archway Cookies)

Media Instructor's Manual

The **Media Instructor's Manual** provides further teaching support for each of the 21 videos. Tips on using the *Contemporary Marketing* videos, outlines for each video case, descriptions, case topics, video running times, and organizations discussed are included. Also included are teaching notes for the **Transparency Acetates** and the **PowerPoint CD-ROM.** A detailed description of the *Discovering Your Marketing Career* CD-ROM and information on *MICROSIM, Applying Marketing Principles Software,* and *The Marketing Game* is here as well.

Instructor's Resource Manual

Boone & Kurtz's precedent-setting **Instructor's Resource Manual** has been completely revised and revamped to provide an even more innovative and powerful teaching tool. The ninth edition **Instructor's Resource Manual** includes the following:

- Suggested class schedules
- Ideas for more than 100 term paper topics
- Suggestions for obtaining guest speakers for your classes
- **NEW!** Ideas on how to use the Internet and technology in your class
- Changes in the new ninth edition
- New chapter coverage
- New features
- **NEW!** Internet addresses for each chapter
- Annotated learning goals
- Key terms
- Lecture outlines
- **NEW!** Answers to the "Achievement Check Summary" sections
- Answers to review questions
- Answers to discussion questions
- **NEW!** Answers to 'netWork technology exercises
- Answers to video case questions (cases to accompany each video are placed at the end of each text chapter)
- **NEW!** Answers to "Questions for Critical Thinking" box questions
- Guest speaker suggestions
- **NEW!** Answers to Microsoft continuing end-of-part case questions

Test Bank

Available in computerized and printed formats, this completely revised and updated **Test Bank** offers more than 4,000 questions—the most of any principles text—

including application and knowledge-based multiple-choice, true/false, short-answer, and essay questions. Each question is keyed to specific chapter learning objectives and level of difficulty. Students will also be tested on their knowledge of the "Marketing Hall of Fame," "Marketing Hall of Shame," and "Solving an Ethical Controversy" boxed material. This new **Test Bank** has also been thoroughly reviewed by 21 professors to ensure an accurate, high-quality product. **Test Bank** authors include Amy Enders, Northampton Community College, William Rice, California State University—Fresno and Ken Lawrence, New Jersey Institute of Technology.

Computerized Test Bank

Available in PC-, Windows-, and Macintosh-compatible formats, the computerized version of the printed test bank enables instructors to preview and edit test questions, as well as add their own. The tests and answer keys can also be printed in "scrambled" formats.

RequesTest and Online Testing Service

The Dryden Press makes test planning quicker and easier than ever with this program. Instructors can order test masters by question number and criteria over a toll-free telephone number. Test masters will be mailed or faxed within 48 hours. Dryden can provide instructors with software to install their own online testing program, allowing tests to be administered over network or individual terminals. This program offers instructors greater flexibility and convenience in grading and storing test results.

Study Guide

Designed to enhance student understanding and provide additional practical application of chapter content, this comprehensive learning tool includes chapter outlines, experiential exercises, self-quizzes, cases, short-answer questions, computer and Internet application problems, crossword puzzles, marketing plan exercises, term projects, and solutions to study questions. The **Study Guide** was written by Tom O'Connor, University of New Orleans.

Overhead Transparencies

Full-color **Transparency Acetates** have been created with striking graphic illustrations and advertisements. The **Transparency Acetates** are described in detail in the **Media Instructor's Manual.**

Marketing Simulations

MICROSIM, a marketing simulation game created by Professor Steven Schnaars, Baruch College, and *Applying Marketing Principles,* written by Professor Robert Schaffer, California State Polytechnic—Pomona, enhance classroom participation and give students hands-on experience applying chapter concepts to real-world marketing issues.

NEW! *The Marketing Game*

An innovative new Windows-based computer simulation by Robert Schaffer has been added to the *Contemporary Marketing*^{WIRED} package. *The Marketing Game* is a traditional simulation game with some novel twists. The underlying model is based on the digital camera industry and will help students develop their marketing skills within the framework of an evolving product life cycle.

Large classes can play *The Marketing Game* in solitaire mode, with each student competing against computer-generated opponents. This option greatly reduces classroom game management problems and allows instructors to provide their students with a computer simulation experience that they would otherwise be unable to implement. Because of its link to the Internet, there also is an option to allow competitive play between teams of students at different universities.

The Dryden Press will provide complimentary supplements or supplement packages to those adopters qualified under our adoption policy. Please contact your sales representative to learn how you may qualify. If as an adopter or potential user you receive supplements you do not need, please return them to your sales representative or send them to:

ATTN: Returns Department
Troy Warehouse
465 South Lincoln Drive
Troy, MO 63379

ACKNOWLEDGMENTS

The authors gratefully acknowledge the following colleagues who reviewed all or part of the manuscript in previous editions:

Keith Absher
Kerri L. Acheson
Zafar U. Ahmed
M. Wayne Alexander
Linda Anglin
Paul Arsenault
Dub Ashton
Tom F. Badgett
Joe K. Ballenger
Wayne Bascom
Richard D. Becherer
Tom Becker
Richard F. Beltramini
Robert Bielski
Carol C. Bienstock
Roger D. Blackwell
Jocelyn C. Bojack
Michele D. Bunn
Les Carlson
Robert Collins
Elizabeth Cooper-Martin
Deborah L. Cowles
Howard B. Cox
John E. Crawford
Michael R. Czinkota
Kathy Daruty
Gilberto De Los Santos
Carol W. DeMoranville
Fran DePaul
Gordon Di Paolo
John G. Doering
Jeffrey T. Doutt
Sid Dudley
John W. Earnest
Phillip E. Egdorf
Sandra M. Ferriter
Dale Fodness
Gary T. Ford
Michael Fowler
Sam Fullerton
Ralph M. Gaedeke
G.P. Gallo
Nimish Gandhi
Sheryl A. Gatto
Robert Georgen
Don Gibson
David W. Glascoff
James Gould
Donald Granbois
Paul E. Green
William Green
Blaine Greenfield
Matthew Gross
Robert F. Gwinner
Raymond M. Haas
John H. Hallaq
Cary Hawthorn
E. Paul Hayes
Hoyt Hayes
Debbora Heflin-Bullock
John (Jack) J. Heinsius
Sanford B. Helman
Nathan Himelstein
Robert D. Hisrich
Ray S. House
George Housewright
Michael D. Hutt
Gregory P. Iwaniuk
Don L. James
David Johnson
Eugene M. Johnson
James C. Johnson
Harold H. Kassarjian
Bernard Katz
Stephen K. Keiser
Michelle Keller
J. Steven Kelly
James H. Kennedy
Charles Keuthan
Maryon King
Randall S. Kingsbury
Donald L. Knight
Linda S. Koffel
Philip Kotler
Terrence Kroeten
Martha Laham
L. Keith Larimore
Edwin A. Laube
Francis J. Leary, Jr.
Mary Lou Lockerby
Paul Londrigan
Lynn J. Loudenback
David L. Loudon
Dorothy Maass
James C. Makens
Lou Mansfield
James McCormick
Carl McDaniel
James McHugh
Faye McIntyre
H. Lee Meadow
William E. (Gene) Merkle
John D. Milewicz
Robert D. Miller
Laura M. Milner
Harry J. Moak
J. Dale Molander
John F. Monoky
James R. Moore
Thomas M. Moran
Susan Logan Nelson
Colin F. Neuhaus
Robert T. Newcomb
Jacqueline Z. Nicholson
Robert O'Keefe
Sukgoo Pak
Eric Panitz
Dennis D. Pappas
Constantine Petrides
Barbara Piasta
Dennis D. Pitta
Barbara Pletcher
Carolyn E. Predmore
Arthur E. Prell
Bill Quain
Thomas C. Reading
Gary Edward Reiman
Arnold M. Rieger
C. Richard Roberts
Patrick J. Robinson
William C. Rodgers
William H. Ronald
Bert Rosenbloom
Barbara Rosenthal
Carol Rowery
Ronald S. Rubin
Rafael Santos
Dennis W. Schneider
Larry J. Schuetz
Bruce Seaton
Howard Seigelman
Jack Seitz
Steven L. Shapiro
F. Kelly Shuptrine
Carol S. Soroos
A. Edward Spitz
Miriam B. Stamps
William Staples
David Steenstra
Bruce Stern
Robert E. Stevens
Kermit Swanson
G. Knude Swenson
Cathy Owens Swift
Clint B. Tankersley
Ruth Taylor
Donald L. Temple
Vern Terpstra

Ann Marie Thompson
Howard A. Thompson
John E. Timmerman
Rex Toh
Dennis H. Tootelian
Fred Trawick
Richard Lee Utecht
Rajiv Vaidyanathan
Toni Valdez
Dinoo T. Vanier
Gayle D. Wasson
Fred Weinthal
Susan B. Wessels
John J. Whithey
Robert J. Williams
Nicholas C. Williamson
Cecilia Wittmayer
Van R. Wood
Julian Yudelson
Robert J. Zimmer

The ninth edition and its ancillaries were no exception when it came to benefiting from quality reviewer comments. The authors are indebted to the following colleagues for their willingness to help in creating another innovative edition of *Contemporary Marketing*:

Bruce Allen, *Central Michigan University*
Allen Appell, *San Francisco State University*
Amardeep Assar, *York College*
Thomas Becker, *University of South Alabama*
James Camerius, *Northern Michigan University*
John Carmichael, *Union County College*
Jacob Chacko, *University of North Dakota*
Kathy Daruty, *Pierce College*
Grant Davis, *University of South Alabama*
Michael Elliot, *University of Missouri—St. Louis*
Amy Enders, *Northampton Community College*
Bob Farris, *Mt. San Antonio College*
Lori Feldman, *Purdue University—Calumet*
Edward Friese, *Okaloosa-Walton Community College*
Ivan Figeroa, *Miami-Dade Community College*
Meryl Gardner, *University of Delaware*
John Grant, *Southern Illinois University*
Betty Jean Hebel, *Madonna University*
Nathan Hemelstein, *Essex County College*
Donald Howard, *Augusta State University*
James Jeck, *North Carolina State*
Candida Johnson, *Holyoke Community College*
Russell Laczniak, *Iowa State University*
Edwin Laube, *Macomb Community College*
Ken Lawrence, *New Jersey Institute of Technology*
James Lollar, *Radford University*
Warren Martin, *University of Alabama—Birmingham*
Michael McGinnis, *University of South Alabama*
Mohan Menon, *University of South Alabama*
Banwari Mittal, *Northern Kentucky University*
Tom O'Connor, *University of New Orleans*
Eric Panitz, *Ferris State University*
Rosemary Ramsey, *Eastern Kentucky University*
Cathy Rich-Duval, *Merrimack College*
Glen Riecken, *East Tennessee State University*
Don Ryktarsyk, *Schoolcraft College*
Duane Schecter, *Muskegon Community College*
Mike Simone, *Delaware Valley College*
Ricardo Singson, *California State University—Hayward*
Norman Smothers, *California State University—Hayward*
James Spiers, *Arizona State University*
Robert Stevens, *Northeast Louisiana University*
Frank Titlow, *St. Petersburg Junior College*
Rajiv Vaidyanathan, *University of Minnesota—Duluth*
Peter Vander Haeghen, *Coastline Community College*
Donald Weinrauch, *Tennessee Tech*
Debbora Whitson, *California State Polytechnic—Pomona*
Kathy Wilder, *Delta State University*

We are grateful to Marlene Bellamy—whose contribution to the ninth edition was invaluable. Special thanks go to our research assistants—Jeanne Bartimus and Jamie Campbell. Their good cheer and perseverance was a constant source of inspiration to the authors.

We would also like to thank our good friends at The Dryden Press. Bill Schoof, our editor; Tracy Morse, our development editor; and Lisé Johnson, our product manager, who were a valued part of this edition. Our sincere thanks goes to each of them.

Other Dryden Press contributors to *Contemporary Marketing*[WIRED] were Kathryn Stewart, our project editor; Bill Brammer, art director; Carlyn Hauser, production manager; Nancy Moudry, photo research; Doris Milligan, permissions editor; and Adele Krause, picture and rights editor. Thanks so much for your efforts on our behalf.

Louis E. Boone
David L. Kurtz

To the Student

Marketing has gone high-tech. And never has there been a more exciting time to study this dynamic field. New technological advances have created an industry of endless opportunities—limited only by a marketer's creativity.

The ninth edition of *Contemporary Marketing*^{WIRED} is wired for the new high-tech advances, integrating a technology emphasis throughout the text and package. Internet, CD-ROM, multimedia—these are some of the new tools you'll use to learn about traditional and emerging marketing concepts and issues.

For example, *Contemporary Marketing*^{WIRED} has an especially strong connection to the Internet, including its own student-friendly site on the World Wide Web. The Internet offers countless exciting opportunities for marketers. With Boone & Kurtz, you'll learn firsthand what an effective marketing tool this—and other high-tech applications—can be, as well as experience the intricacies of effectively navigating the Information Superhighway.

The Internet is literally the application of all marketing principles:

1. The Internet is all about advertising—from advertising goods and services to creating an image through the home page.
2. Many companies gather data over the Net—practical information about competitors, suppliers, and customers. Many firms include questionnaires on the Web for data gathering.
3. Companies can test-market new ideas or product/service enhancements over the Net.
4. Home pages often include e-mail addresses or links, offering another avenue for helpful information.
5. Legal issues are reviewed on the Web. Issues such as product liability or the Communications Decency Act may be investigated. There are also mechanisms for reporting consumer complaints to various agencies.
6. The Web opens the door to international companies or governments. It is especially insightful to investigate legal issues regarding marketing in other countries.
7. Many special-interest groups have home pages. Ethical and environmental issues, for example, are frequently reviewed.
8. The Web is a unique channel for distributing goods, services, and information.
9. Direct access to producers by consumers may significantly change the nature of selling.
10. The Internet may be used for job searches. Many companies post job openings on their homes pages. There are also several online job search services.

As you can see, the applications are endless. And *Contemporary Marketing*^{WIRED} is your direct link to marketing innovation. Visit the Boone & Kurtz *Contemporary Marketing*^{WIRED} Web site at

http://www.dryden.com/mktng/boone/

STUDENT GLOSSARY OF HELPFUL INTERNET TERMS

Bookmark. A browser feature that places selected URLs in a file for quick access.

FTP (file transfer protocol). A tool for transferring files between computers on the Internet, often used to transfer large files of statistics, scientific experiments, and full-text articles.

Gopher. A text-based Internet search engine developed by the University of Minnesota that provides subject access to files on the Internet through menus.

Home page. The first hypertext document displayed on a Web server. A home page is often a menu page with information about the developer and links to other sites.

HTML (hypertext markup language). Code in which World Wide Web documents are written and presented.

HTTP (hypertext transfer protocol). The protocol used by the Web to transfer hypertext documents.

Hypertext. Documents that contain links to other documents, allowing the user to jump from one document to another.

URL (uniform resource locator). Web address that gives the exact location of an Internet resource.

Usenet. A group of systems that enable users to exchange discussion on specific topics through newsgroups.

World Wide Web (WWW). A hypertext-based system for finding and accessing Internet resources.

HOW TO GET ONLINE

Learning to use the basic tools will make surfing the Net more profitable and enjoyable for you. Each site has an address, which is referred to as a URL, or uniform resource locator. Using a URL is a fast way to get to a site. Setting a bookmark makes getting to a useful site at a later time even faster. If you do not know a specific URL, you can use any of the various search engines (Yahoo!, Infoseek, etc.) available to conduct a search.

YOUR PERSONAL WORLD WIDE WEB DIRECTORY

Contemporary Marketing^WIRED^ provides students with an in-text World Wide Web directory. Online addresses are included in the textbook for companies and organizations highlighted in extended-text examples, focus boxes, opening vignettes, and photo illustrations. Company Web addresses are also listed alphabetically on the endpapers (inside front and back cover pages) of the text.

For additional resources, you can reach the Boone & Kurtz *Contemporary Marketing*^WIRED^, Ninth Edition home page at

http://www.dryden.com/mktng/boone

Because the Internet is a constantly changing network of networks, no subject list is ever complete. Each day, addresses change, new sites are added, and old sites disappear without warning. Following is a list of search engines and private data sources that provide links to numerous other sites relating to marketing and business.

SEARCH ENGINES

If you don't know the URL for a site, you can use various search engines to perform a keyword search by developer or subject name. As with everything on the Internet, these search tools change daily and new features are constantly added. The following search engines can help track down online information on a variety of topics:

Search.com (http://www.search.com/). This site gives access to more than 300 specialized indexes and search engines.

Metacrawler (http://www.metacrawler.com/). This tool submits your query to nine of the top search engines at once.

Altavista (http://altavista.digital.com/). This service provides one of the largest search indexes on the Web.

Infoseek Guide (http://www.infoseek.com/). This search index includes millions of listings.

Yahoo! (http://www.yahoo.com/). This useful search index divides reference sites into logical groups.

Government Data Sources

U.S. Census Bureau (http://www.census.gov/). This site provides free access to many census data reports and tables, including international census data from many countries.

U.S. Bureau of Economic Analysis (http://www.bea.doc.gov/). This site provides national and regional economic information, including gross domestic product by industry.

U.S. Bureau of Labor Statistics (http://stats.bls.gov/). This site gives access to the BLS survey of consumer expenditures, a report on how U.S. consumers spend their money.

Department of Commerce/STAT-USA (http://www.stat-usa.gov/). This subscription-based site provides access to hundreds of government-sponsored marketing research studies and other statistical information.

FedWorld (http://www.fedworld.gov/). This site provides a central access point for locating government information. If you need data from the government but don't know where to find it, start here.

PRIVATE DATA SOURCES

Knight-Ridder Information (http://www.dialog.com/). This extensive database provides access to thousands of marketing research reports, industry and competitor information, and trade publications. Although it proves itself an excellent source for secondary data of all types, a typical search can be expensive. Knowledge index, available on CompuServe, provides access to many of the Dialog databases for an hourly fee.

Lexis-Nexis (http://www.lexis-nexis.com/). This is another extensive—and expensive—database of directories, trade publications, and legal information.

HOW TO CITE INTERNET SITES

If you plan to use the information you have retrieved from the Internet in a research paper or in homework assignments, you need to know how to cite the information correctly. Although formats are still being developed for the various types of electronic documents, new editions of most of the accepted style manuals have a section on citing electronic resources, including the Internet.

The University of Michigan's Internet Public Library has a list with links to recommended electronic information citation guides at

http://www.ipl.org/classroom/userdocs/internet/citing.html

Another useful site

http://www.uvm.edu/~xli/reference/estyles.html

offers citation formats based on the forthcoming book by Li & Crane, *Electronic Styles: An Expanded Guide to Citing Information,* according to the American Psychological Association and the Modern Language Association styles.

CD-ROM: *Discovering Your Marketing Career*

This innovative, student-friendly software package helps you learn about and assess your compatibility with marketing careers. This comprehensive, multimedia CD-ROM offers broad guidance and practical advice on everything from selecting a career path to implementing an effective job search strategy. And it's completely integrated with Boone & Kurtz's home page.

After asking you questions regarding specific job activities and such factors as work environment, compensation and career advancement, the program matches your preferences to specific marketing careers. A customized video and detailed report give detailed insight into your responses and subsequent career match.

Comprehensive career profiles present a detailed, up-to-date picture of actual job responsibilities, career paths and skills required to be successful. Information is also available on current compensation levels and associations, directories, books, and other relevant information for researching the marketing career of interest.

Career profiles were compiled following extensive interviews with professionals from such prominent companies as AT&T, General Electric, Ogilvy & Mather, J. Walter Thompson, Walt Disney, Coca-Cola, Microsoft, General Mills, Johnson & Johnson, Procter & Gamble, Neiman Marcus, Wal-Mart, Sears, Kmart, Digital Equipment Corporation, and IBM.

Also included on the CD-ROM is a free copy of the student version of *Career Design,* a career planning software program based on the work of John Crystal, the major contributor to *What Color is Your Parachute?* by Richard N. Bolles.

Internet Marketing Connection

Available through The Dryden Press' Web site, students owning a copy of the CD-ROM included in *Contemporary Marketing*^{WIRED} can download the **Internet Marketing Connection,** an online guide to a wide range of marketing links. Operated from your favorite Web browser, this innovative tool enables you to read the description of a marketing link and then click on the link to immediately visit that Internet location. Following is just a sampling of topics:

- Global marketing
- Direct marketing
- Business-to-business marketing
- Sports marketing
- Database marketing
- Marketing issues related to ethics, quality, social responsibility, and cultural diversity
- Marketing through strategic alliances and co-branding
- Relationship marketing

You can also link to Web sites where you can identify marketing job opportunities in the career fields covered in *Discovering Your Marketing Career.* The **Internet Marketing Connection** is updated regularly to ensure links are current. Visit The Dryden Press' Web site at

http://www.dryden.com/mktng/careercd

for the latest version.

About the Authors

Louis E. Boone (Ph.D.) holds the Ernest G. Cleverdon Chair of Business and Management at the University of South Alabama. He formerly chaired the Divisions of Management and Marketing at the University of Tulsa and has taught marketing in Australia, Greece, and the United Kingdom.

Dr. Boone is a prolific researcher and writer. In addition to authoring numerous marketing and business texts and computer simulation games, he is author of *Quotable Business,* published by Random House. His current research focuses on event and sports marketing. Dr. Boone's research has been published in such journals as the *Journal of Marketing, Journal of Business Strategy, Journal of Retailing, Business Horizons, Journal of Business Research, Journal of Business of the University of Chicago, Journal of Personal Selling & Sales Management, Journal of Marketing Education, Business,* and *Sport Marketing Quarterly*. He has served as president of the Southwestern Marketing Association and vice president of the Southern Marketing Association.

David L. Kurtz (Ph.D.) is the R.A. and Vivian Young Chair of Business Administration at the University of Arkansas. Dr. Kurtz has also taught at Seattle University, Eastern Michigan University, Davis & Elkins College, and Australia's Monash University.

Dr. Kurtz has authored or co-authored 30 books and more than 100 articles, cases, and papers. His recent work has appeared in such publications as the *Journal of Marketing, Journal of Retailing, Journal of Business Research,* and numerous other well-known journals.

Contents in Brief

Contents

CHAPTER 3 The Marketing Environment, Ethics, and Social Responsibility 78

CHAPTER 4 Global Dimensions of Marketing 114

Marketing Hall of Shame
Phone Fiasco

Solving an Ethical Controversy
Is it Fair to Force Suppliers to Use Electronic Data Interchange?

OPENING VIGNETTE
Online Grocery Shopping with Peapod

Marketing Hall of Fame
The Saturn Homecoming Party

Marketing Hall of Shame
Rubbermaid's Worst Relationship Decision

Solving an Ethical Controversy
Should Relationship Marketers Have Access to Confidential Database Information?

PART 4
PRODUCT STRATEGY

OPENING VIGNETTE
How Plantronics Headed for Success

Marketing Hall of Fame
How CNS Helped Americans "Breathe Right"

CHAPTER 14 Distribution 462

PART 5
DISTRIBUTION STRATEGY

OPENING VIGNETTE
Software Direct

Marketing Hall of Fame
Arrow Shoots to the Top

Marketing Hall of Shame
Marketers Flunk College Distribution

Solving an Ethical Controversy
Are Retailer Slotting Allowances Fair?

CHAPTER 15 Retailing 496

OPENING VIGNETTE
Net Profits: Virtually Attainable?

Marketing Hall of Fame
Old Navy Sets a New Course for the Gap

Marketing Hall of Shame
Retail Failures: Who's Next?

Solving an Ethical Controversy
Should Retailers Pay More Attention to Their Ethical Conduct?

CHAPTER 16 Logistics and Value Chain Management 528

OPENING VIGNETTE
Federal Express: The Logical Choice

Marketing Hall of Fame
A Salute for Wal-Mart

CHAPTER 20 Price Determination 686

PART 7
PRICING STRATEGY

OPENING VIGNETTE
Long-Distance Phone Wars Go Local

Marketing Hall of Fame
Beanie Babies—Creating Markets by Creating Shortages

Marketing Hall of Shame
The Price of Price Fixing

Solving an Ethical Controversy
Does Cost-Plus Pricing Injure the Terminally Ill?

CHAPTER 21 Managing the Pricing Function 716

OPENING VIGNETTE
Why Gasoline Prices Just Keep Going Up

Marketing Hall of Fame
Trendmasters: Succeeding by Delivering Full Markups

Marketing Hall of Shame
Marketing in Japan, Where the Prices Are Insane!

Solving an Ethical Controversy
Rock 'n' Roll's Holy War

APPENDIX Careers in Marketing A-1

PART 1

THE CONTEMPORARY MARKETING ENVIRONMENT

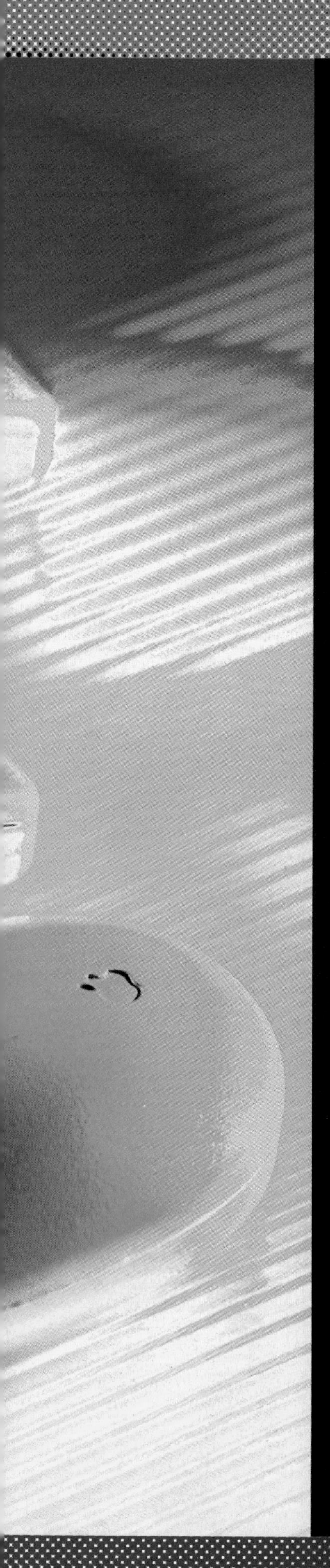

Chapter 1
Developing Relationships through Customer Focus, Quality, Technology, and Ethical Behavior

Chapter 2
Creating Value through Customer Satisfaction and Quality

Chapter 3
The Marketing Environment, Ethics, and Social Responsibility

Chapter 4
Global Dimensions of Marketing

dryden
landsend.
border
annie
800flow
flowers
asqc.co
circu
godiva
colgate

CHAPTER 1

DEVELOPING RELATIONSHIPS THROUGH CUSTOMER FOCUS, QUALITY, TECHNOLOGY, AND ETHICAL BEHAVIOR

Home
Back
Forward
Current URL:
Page complete
FedEx
SOUTHWEST AIRLINES
Home
Back
Forward
Page complete
GODIVA
Chocolatier
Shop

Chapter Objectives

1. Explain how marketing creates utility through the exchange process.
2. Contrast marketing activities during the four eras in the history of marketing.
3. Define the marketing concept and its relationship to marketing myopia.
4. Describe the five types of nontraditional marketing.
5. Identify the basic elements of a marketing strategy and the environmental characteristics that influence strategy decisions.
6. Outline the changes in the marketing environment due to technology and relationship marketing.
7. Highlight the universal functions of marketing.
8. Demonstrate the relationship between ethical business practices and marketplace success.
9. List three reasons for studying marketing.

Hot Hot Hot's Cool Spot on the Net

To boost sales of their spicy sauces and foods, the owners of a food boutique in Pasadena, California, turned to the hottest new advertising locale: a site on the World Wide Web—an appropriate choice for a store named Hot Hot Hot. Like many other pint-sized businesses that contemplate online marketing, Hot Hot Hot faced monumental challenges.

Operating out of a tiny, 300-square-foot storefront with limited financial resources, Perry and Monica Lopez couldn't spend much on a flashy Web site. Nor could they gamble on a medium that would produce meager results. The couple fretted about whether to roll the dice on cyberspace marketing or simply advertise with a traditional catalog. The Internet won when one of their regular customers, the owner of a Web service company, offered to help.

Netscape: Hot Hot Hot Welcome
Back
Forward
Home
Reload
Images
Open
Print
Find
Stop
Netscape
Location: http://www.hot.presence.com/
What's New?
Search
News Groups
Directory
Mail
Help
HOTHOTHOT
Welcome to Hot Hot Hot,
the Net's coolest hot sauce shop!
(brought to you by Presence)
We want to welcome you to the Internet's first "Culinary Headshop!" Here you'll find fiery foodstuffs you never thought existed. Please come in and browse!
We have over 100 products of fire and the list is always growing. With names like Bats Brew, Nuclear Hell, and Ring of Fire, we're sure you'll find something you like.
TOP 5% OF ALL WEB SITES
LYCOS
If you're a first time user of this catalog, you may be interested in taking a look at:
catalog instructions or
an introduction from the owners

Hot Hot Hot spent $20,000 creating the site—a major financial commitment for a retailer whose first-year sales reached only $150,000. With so much at stake, the Lopezes needed an attention-grabbing, easy-to-use site based on interactive marketing techniques that would attract customer attention and generate business.

Rather than bombard shoppers with information about all of their 450 products, the entrepreneurs became brutal online editors. "We could have added all kinds of information and products," recalls Monica, "but that costs money. Does it increase sales or just create more pages for the user to weed through? In a small business, you need to see a return." The site showcased just 125 products, organizing them alphabetically and by ingredients, heat level, and country of origin. The site design anticipated customers' impatience with long delays downloading graphics to their computer screens. Instead of presenting detailed product labels to categorize the spicy selections, the design featured colorful banners with eye-catching motifs like flames, chili peppers, and hot sauce bottles. Limited color palettes also helped to speed downloads. Vivid flames on each page provided visual continuity, and control elements allowed customers to move quickly and easily between pages.

http://www.hot.presence.com/

Even with ruthless editing, the site expanded to 20 pages. The Lopezes spent three months developing pages and testing for glitches and ease of use with all major Web browsers. To encourage repeat visits and customer involvement, the site also features a sauce of the month, contests, articles from *Chile Pepper* magazine, and a "What's New" page. A key function gathers customer feedback. For example, the popular four-sauce gift pack resulted from a customer's suggestion. To allay customer security concerns, the store offers a toll-free telephone number to take orders from those who don't want to send credit card numbers online. Staff members also confirm orders via e-mail.

Cybermarketing paid off quickly for Hot Hot Hot; sales doubled to $300,000 in the 18 months following its Web site debut. Over 1,000 customers still cruise the Web site each day—many from Switzerland, Brazil, New Zealand, and other far-away spots. Their purchases account for 20 percent of total revenue.

Hot Hot Hot illustrates how computer-based marketing can help entrepreneurial upstarts tap into new markets and succeed on limited budgets. After paying off the site's $20,000 start-up cost, the retailer now devotes 5 percent of all online sales revenue to monthly Web site maintenance.

It's all been worth the investment for the Lopezes. "So many people know about us," Monica marvels. "People come into the store because of the site. It's incredible." Through interactive marketing, the company has eliminated many of the traditional barriers to entering a national or global market.

As the Lopezes learned, a Web site allows a small company to compete with larger rivals, reach a wider customer base, and target new customer groups. Immediate availability of current product information encourages impulse purchases. Another major advantage is the low cost of setting up and updating a Web page compared to a print catalog. As Craig Danuloff, president of Seattle-based software developer iCat Corp., points out, "On the Internet, Wal-Mart can't make much more of a fancier store than a general store can."

Because the medium is still in its infancy, it is difficult to know just what determines the success of one attempt at cyberspace marketing and the failure of another. Today's ads are "primitive," according to Tim Brady, marketing director at Yahoo!, a directory that indexes thousands of Internet sites. They remind him of TV spots in the 1950s when a model would walk onto a stage holding a sign that simply said "Buy Coke." "Three years from now," Brady predicts, "We'll look back and say, 'I can't believe what we put up.'"[1]

CHAPTER OVERVIEW

Like Hot Hot Hot, today's organizations—giant multinational firms and small boutiques, profit-oriented and not-for-profit—stand on the threshold of new marketing frontiers. Advances in communications technology allow them to supply information to consumers faster and through more media channels than ever before, including broadcast media, print, telecommunications, online computer services, and the Internet. Today's companies offer consumers more product choices and more places to buy, from shopping malls, mail-order catalogs, and television home shopping channels to virtual stores accessed through online services.

The technology revolution is changing the rules of marketing at the dawn of the twenty-first century. The combined power of telecommunications and computer technology create inexpensive, global networks that transfer voice messages, text, graphics, and data within seconds. These sophisticated technologies create new types of products, and they also demand new approaches to marketing existing products.

Communications technology also contributes to the globalization of today's marketplace, where companies manufacture, buy, and sell across national borders. You can eat at McDonald's or drink Coca-Cola almost anywhere in the world, while Japanese and Korean companies manufacture most of the consumer electronics products sold in the United States and Canada. The Reebok sneakers in your closet today might have come from designers in the United States and assembly plants in China that use cushioning material made in California and soles from South Korea; your next pair may be assembled in Vietnam or India.[2] Toyota manufactures cars in Marysville, Ohio; many General Motors models are assembled in Canada. Products and components routinely cross international borders, but global marketing also requires knowledge to tailor products to regional tastes. Wal-Mart's São Paulo, Brazil, store stocks local grocery favorites like dried codfish, Guarana soda, and manioc flour as well as Revlon cosmetics and Fisher-Price toys.[3]

This rapidly changing business landscape creates new challenges for companies. They must react quickly to shifts in consumer tastes and other market dynamics. Fortunately, information technologies give organizations fast, new ways to interact and develop long-term relationships with their customers and suppliers. In fact, such links have become a core element of marketing.

Every company must serve consumer needs to succeed. Marketing strategies provide the tools by which businesspeople identify and analyze customers' needs and then inform them about how the company can meet those needs. Tomorrow's market leaders will be companies who can effectively harness the vast amounts of customer feedback and respond with solutions to consumer needs.

Contemporary Marketing explores the strategies that allow companies to succeed in today's interactive marketplace. This chapter sets the stage for the entire text, examining the meaning of *marketing* and its importance for all organizations. Initial sections describe the development of marketing, from early times to today's focus on relationship marketing, and its contributions to society. Later sections introduce the variables defined by a marketing strategy and discuss the impact of the technology revolution on future marketing strategies.

WHAT IS MARKETING?

Production and marketing of goods, services, and causes are the essence of economic life in any society. All organizations perform these two basic functions to satisfy their commitments to society, their customers, and their owners. They create a benefit that economists call **utility**—the want-satisfying power of a good or service. Table 1.1 describes the four basic kinds of utility—form, time, place, and ownership utility.

Form utility is created when the firm converts raw materials and component inputs into finished goods and services. By combining glass, plastic, metals, circuit boards, and other components, RCA creates a television set and Sony makes a camcorder. With fabric, thread, wood, springs, and down feathers, Ethan Allen produces a sofa. The television show *Friends* starts with writers, actors, scripts, director, producer, technical crew, and sound stage. Although marketing provides important inputs that specify consumer and audience preference, the organization's production function is responsible for the actual creation of form utility.

Marketing creates time, place, and ownership utilities. *Time* and *place utility* occur when consumers find goods and services available when and where they want to purchase them. Overnight courier services like Federal Express and Airborne Express emphasize time utility; vending machines focus on providing place utility for people buying newspapers, snacks, and soft drinks. The transfer of title to goods or services at the time of purchase creates *ownership utility*.

The two promotional messages shown in Figure 1.1 illustrate marketing's ability to create time, place, and ownership utility. The GTE Airfone in front of an air traveler's

Marketing Dictionary

utility Want-satisfying power of a good or service.

Table 1.1 Four Types of Utility

Type	Description	Examples	Organizational Function Responsible
Form	Conversion of raw materials and components into finished goods and services	Prudential life insurance policy; Boeing 767 aircraft	Production[a]
Time	Availability of goods and services when consumers want them	Federal Express' guarantee of package delivery by 10:30 a.m. the next day; DHL Worldwide Delivery Service	Marketing
Place	Availability of goods and services at convenient locations	Espresso/snack carts in office buildings and shopping malls; Pizza Hut outlets in Moscow, Melbourne, and Minneapolis	Marketing
Ownership (possession)	Ability to transfer title to goods or services from marketer to buyer	Retail sales (in exchange for currency or credit card payment)	Marketing

[a]Marketing provides inputs related to consumer preferences, but the actual creation of form utility is the responsibility of the production function.

seat allows him or her to make calls, send e-mail messages, retrieve voice mail, and even surf the Internet from 35,000 feet above the earth. A customer purchases the service by swiping a credit card along a special reader that activates the phone. The second ad emphasizes the ability of service-provider Federal Express to generate time, place, and possession utility by quickly, safely, and dependably shipping packages ranging in weight from a few ounces to over 500 pounds. The image of the Thai temple illustrates FedEx's ability to deliver as easily to Bangkok as to Boston.

To survive, all organizations must create utility. Designing and marketing want-satisfying goods, services, and ideas is the foundation for the creation of utility. However, the importance of marketing in an organization's success has only recently been recognized. This has been particularly evident in eastern European nations converting from state-controlled to market-driven business ventures. Management author Peter F. Drucker emphasized the importance of marketing in his classic book, *The Practice of Management:*

> If we want to know what a business is, we have to start with its purpose. And its purpose must lie outside the business itself. In fact, it must lie in society since a business enterprise is an organ of society. There is one valid definition of business purpose: to create a customer.[4]

How does an organization create a customer? Professors Joseph Guiltinan and Gordon Paul explain it this way:

> Essentially, "creating" a customer means identifying needs in the marketplace, finding out which needs the organization can profitably serve, and developing an offering to convert potential buyers into customers. Marketing managers are responsible for most of the activities necessary to create the customers the organization wants. These activities include:
>
> - Identifying customer needs
> - Designing goods and services that meet those needs
> - Communicating information about those goods and services to prospective buyers
> - Making the goods or services available at times and places that meet customers' needs
> - Pricing goods and services to reflect costs, competition, and customers' ability to buy
> - Providing for the necessary service and follow-up to ensure customer satisfaction after the purchase.[5]

A Definition of Marketing

Ask five people to define the term *marketing,* and five definitions are likely to follow. Continuous exposure to advertising and personal selling leads most respondents to link marketing and selling, or to think that marketing activities start once goods and services have been produced. But marketing also involves analyzing customer needs, securing information needed to design and produce goods or services that match buyer expectations, and creating and maintaining relationships with customers and suppliers. It applies not only to profit-oriented firms but also to thousands of not-for-profit organizations that offer goods and services.

Figure 1.1 **Marketing: Creating Time, Place, and Ownership Utility**

Check Voicemail,
Return Calls,
E-Mail,
Surf The 'Net,
Whatever.
Airfone® Service Makes The Most Of Your Flight Time.
There's a phone in the seat in front of you. And, until you land, its sole purpose is to give you a fast, affordable way to keep up with your world. Even when you're six miles above it.
GTE
It's Amazing What We Can Do Together.®

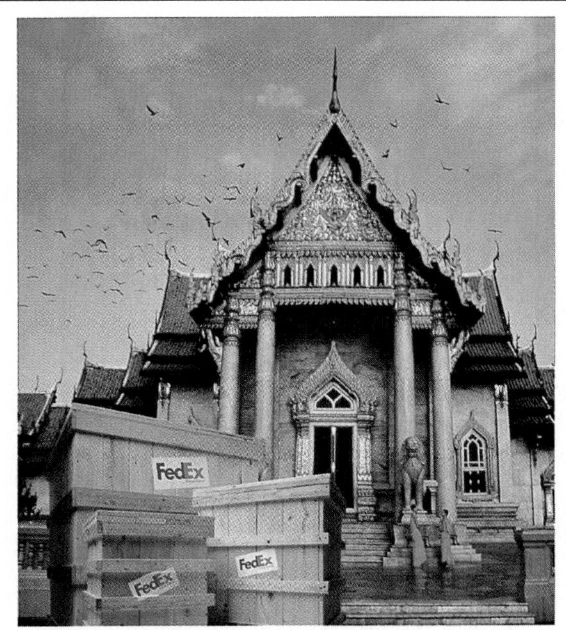
FedEx
Our international service.
Available in small, medium and large.
No matter what kind of cargo you're shipping, no one takes it over there like FedEx®. From a few ounces to shipments over 500 pounds. Just call 1-800-247-4747®, and we'll make shipping overseas as easy as shipping next door. Our most important package is yours®.
FedEx
Federal Express

Today's definition takes these factors into account. **Marketing** is the process of planning and executing the conception, pricing, promotion, and distribution of ideas, goods, services, organizations, and events to create and maintain relationships that will satisfy individual and organizational objectives.

The expanded concept of marketing activities permeates all organizational functions. It assumes that the marketing effort will proceed in accordance with ethical practices and that it will effectively serve the interests of both society and the organization. The concept also identifies the marketing variables—product, price, promotion, and distribution—that combine to provide customer satisfaction. In addition, it assumes that the organization begins by identifying and analyzing the consumer segments that it will later satisfy through its production and marketing activities. In other words, the customer, client, or public determines the marketing program. The concept's emphasis on creating and maintaining relationships is consistent with the focus in business on long-term, mutually satisfying sales, purchases, and other interactions with customers and suppliers. Finally, it recognizes that marketing concepts and techniques apply to not-for-profit organizations as well as to profit-oriented businesses, as shown in the advertisements in Figure 1.2. Godiva, an international marketer renowned for its high-quality chocolates, targets lovers of sweets who are willing to pay high prices for top-of-the-market products. The "big gun" ad is intended to force homeowners to think about the dangers of having handguns accessible to children. The message created by the not-for-profit organization Cease Fire includes a description of a tragic incident involving a handgun.

Today's Global Marketplace

Countries can no longer limit their economic views to events within their own national borders. The interdependence

Marketing Dictionary

marketing Process of planning and executing the conception, pricing, promotion, and distribution of ideas, goods, services, organizations, and events to create and maintain relationships that satisfy individual and organizational objectives.

Figure 1.2 **Marketing Concepts Applied by Profit-Oriented and Not-for-Profit Organizations**

SOME BUNNY TO LOVE.
Nothing becomes a habit like a rabbit from Godiva. Except of course our chicks and eggs. So why not lavish someone with one of our luscious gifts? And make Easter simply the best thing about spring. Hop in or call 1-800-9-GODIVA.
GODIVA
Chocolatier

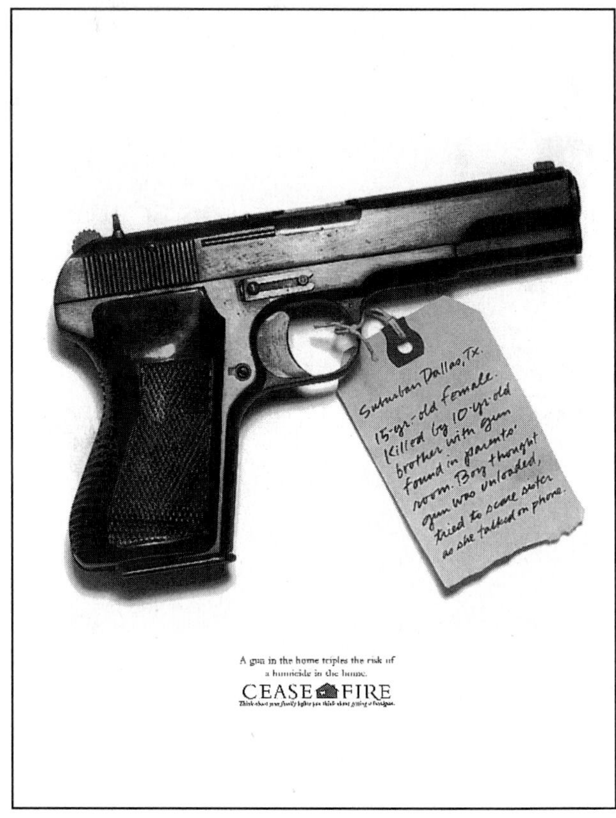
Suburban Dallas, Tx.
15-yr-old female killed by 10-yr-old brother with gun found in parents' room. Boy thought gun was unloaded, tried to scare sister as she talked on phone.
A gun in the home triples the risk of a homicide in the home.
CEASE FIRE

of the world's economies is a reality. A recession in Europe affects business strategies in North America and the Far East. To remain competitive, companies must continually search for the most efficient manufacturing sites and most lucrative markets for their products. The global economy is currently expanding at an annual rate of about 4 percent. The U.S. share of world exports continues to increase; it reached 13 percent in 1996, up from 11 percent in 1993.[6] Marketers now find tremendous opportunities serving customers not only in traditional industrialized nations but also in Latin America and emerging economies in eastern Europe and Asia, where rising standards of living create increased customer demand for the latest goods and services.

Briefly speaking

"If I had my life to live over again, I would elect to be a trader of goods rather than a student of science. I think barter is a noble thing."

Albert Einstein (1879–1955)
American physicist

Expanding operations beyond the U.S. market gives domestic companies access to almost 6 billion international customers. This explains why over 80 percent of Coca-Cola sales are generated outside the United States. Two-thirds of Gillette's sales and 54 percent of Boeing's aircraft business come from non-U.S. customers. Ford Motor Co. is well-positioned to benefit from Russian consumers' love affair with cars. The Russian auto market, currently one-tenth the size of the U.S. market, is expected to generate 4 million car sales annually by 2000. Ford now has over 30 car dealerships there, plus auto assembly and component-part plants in nearby Hungary, Poland, and the former Soviet republic of Belarus. This region represents a major strategic market for Ford, whose products are increasingly familiar sights on Russian highways. In Moscow, even the police ride around in big Ford Crown Victorias.[7]

Service firms, too, are major global players. Both CitiCorp and McDonald's generate about half of their revenues abroad. Technology products are also popular U.S. exports. Compaq sells half of its computers outside the United States, and software giant Microsoft gets 40 percent of its revenues from beyond North America. The importance of the global marketplace is clear in the ACDelco ad in Figure 1.3. The company makes over 65,000 parts that fit over 95 percent of the world's vehicles.

The United States is also an attractive market for foreign competitors because of its size and the high standards of living that American consumers enjoy. Companies like Matsushita, BMW, Benetton, and Sun Life of Canada operate production, distribution, service, and retail facilities here. Foreign ownership

Figure 1.3 ACDelco: Global Supplier of Auto and Truck Parts

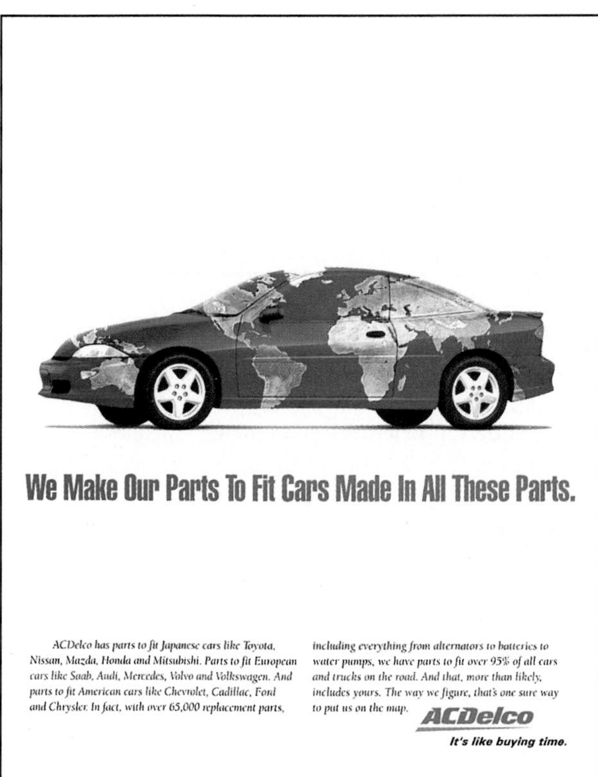

We Make Our Parts To Fit Cars Made In All These Parts.
ACDelco has parts to fit Japanese cars like Toyota, Nissan, Mazda, Honda and Mitsubishi. Parts to fit European cars like Saab, Audi, Mercedes, Volvo and Volkswagen. And parts to fit American cars like Chevrolet, Cadillac, Ford and Chrysler. In fact, with over 65,000 replacement parts, including everything from alternators to batteries to water pumps, we have parts to fit over 95% of all cars and trucks on the road. And that, more than likely, includes yours. The way we figure, that's one sure way to put us on the map.
ACDelco
It's like buying time.

of U.S. companies has increased, as well. Pillsbury, MCA, and Firestone Tires are some well-known firms with foreign parents. Even American-dominated industries like computer software must contend with foreign competition. While U.S. firms still hold about 75 percent of the market, European companies are quickly gaining market share. They currently supply about 18 percent of the $100 billion worldwide market for packaged software.

Global markets may be the same or similar to those used in domestic markets. Rather than creating a different promotional campaign for each country where they sell Pringles chips, Procter & Gamble marketers used the same ad—with spectacular results. Nearly everything in the U.S.-made ads—the rap music themes, the young people dancing, and the tag line, "Once you pop, you can't stop"—was the same. As a result, P&G had to boost production to handle the global demand.[8]

In other instances, domestic marketing strategies may need significant changes to meet customer needs abroad. Product names may have different connotations in other countries. Rolls Royce renamed its Silver Mist model Silver Shadow before exporting it to Germany, because *Mist* means manure or rubbish in German.[9] Companies eager to sell to new markets, like the 100 million middle-class consumers in China or shoppers in the former Soviet Union, must study buying habits carefully to identify the best opportunities and discover cultural differences and regional preferences.

THE ORIGINS OF MARKETING

The essence of marketing is the **exchange process,** in which two or more parties give something of value to each other to satisfy felt needs. In many exchanges, people trade tangible goods, such as a magazine, a compact disk, or a pair of shoes, for money. In others, they trade intangible services such as child care, a haircut, or a concert performance. In still others, people may donate funds or time to a Red Cross office, a church or synagogue, or a local recycling center.

The marketing function is both simple and direct in a subsistence-level economy. For example, assume that a primitive society consists solely of Person A and Person B. Assume also that the elements of their standard of living are food, clothing, and shelter. The two live in adjoining caves on a mountainside. They weave their own clothes and independently tend their own fields. They can subsist with only a minimal standard of living.

Person A is an excellent weaver but a poor farmer, whereas Person B is an excellent farmer but a poor weaver. In this situation, it would be wise for each to specialize in the work that he or she does best. The net result would be greater total production of both clothing and food. In other words, specialization and division of labor would lead to a production surplus. But neither Person A nor Person B would be any better off until each had traded the product of his or her individual labor, thereby creating the exchange process.

Exchange is the origin of marketing activity. In fact, marketing has been described as the process of creating and resolving exchange relationships. When people need to exchange goods, they naturally begin a marketing effort. As Wroe Alderson, a leading marketing theorist, has pointed out, "It seems altogether reasonable to describe the development of exchange as a great invention which helped to start primitive man on the road to civilization."[10]

While the cave dweller example is simplistic, it reveals the essence of the marketing function. A complex, industrial society has a more complicated exchange

Marketing Dictionary

exchange process Activity in which two or more parties give something of value to each other to satisfy perceived needs.

Table 1.2 Four Eras in the History of Marketing

Era	Approximate Time Period[a]	Prevailing Attitude
Production	Prior to 1920s	"A good product will sell itself."
Sales	Prior to 1950s	"Creative advertising and selling will overcome consumers' resistance and convince them to buy."
Marketing	Since 1950s	"The consumer is king! Find a need and fill it."
Relationship	Began in 1990s	"Long-term relationships with customers and other partners lead to success."

[a]In the United States and other highly industrialized economies

process, but the basic concept is the same: Production is not meaningful until a system of marketing has been established. Perhaps publisher Red Motley's adage sums it up best: "Nothing happens until somebody sells something."

FOUR ERAS IN THE HISTORY OF MARKETING

Although marketing has always been a part of business, its importance has varied greatly. Table 1.2 identifies four eras in the history of marketing: (1) the production era, (2) the sales era, (3) the marketing era, and (4) the relationship era.

The Production Era

Until about 1925, most firms—even those operating in highly developed economies in western Europe and North America—focused narrowly on production. Manufacturers stressed production of quality products and then looked for people to purchase them. The history of Pillsbury provides an excellent example of a production-oriented company. Here is how the company's former chief executive officer, the late Robert J. Keith, described Pillsbury during its early years:

> We are professional flour millers. Blessed with a supply of the finest North American wheat, plenty of water power, and excellent milling machinery, we produce flour of the highest quality. Our basic function is to mill high-quality flour, and, of course, we must hire [salespeople] to sell it, just as we hire accountants to keep our books.[11]

The prevailing attitude of this era held that a good product (one with high physical quality) would sell itself. This **production orientation** dominated business philosophy for decades; indeed, business success was often defined solely in terms of production victories.

Although marketing had emerged as a functional activity within the business organization even prior to the twentieth century, management's preoccupation with production continued for quite some time. In fact, the production era did not reach its peak until the early part of this century. Henry Ford's mass-production line exemplifies this orientation. Ford's slogan, "They [customers] can have any color they want, as long as it's black," reflected the prevalent attitude toward marketing. Production shortages and intense consumer demand ruled the day. It is easy to understand how production activities took precedence.

The essence of the production era resounds in a statement made over 100 years ago by the philosopher Ralph Waldo Emerson: "If a man writes a better book, preaches a better sermon, or makes a better mousetrap than his neighbor, though he builds his house in the woods, the world will make a beaten path to his door." However, a better mousetrap is no guarantee of success, and marketing history is full of miserable failures despite better mousetrap designs. In fact, over 80 percent of new products fail. Last year, 22,000 new products were introduced; over 18,000 of them are no longer on store shelves.[12] Inventing the greatest new product is not enough. That product must also solve a perceived marketplace need. Otherwise, even the best-engineered, highest-quality product will fail.

The Sales Era

Between 1925 and the early 1950s, production techniques in the United States and other highly industrialized nations became more sophisticated and output grew. Thus, manufacturers began to increase their emphasis on effective sales forces to find customers for their output. In this era, firms attempted to match their output to the potential number of customers who would want it. Companies with a **sales**

orientation assume that customers will resist purchasing goods and services not deemed essential and that the task of personal selling and advertising is to convince them to buy.

Although marketing departments began to emerge from the shadows of production, finance, and engineering during the sales era, they tended to remain in subordinate positions. Many chief marketing executives held the title of sales manager. Here is how Pillsbury described itself during the sales era:

> We are a flour-milling company, manufacturing a number of products for the consumer market. We must have a first-rate sales organization which can dispose of all the products we can make at a favorable price. We must back up this sales force with consumer advertising and market intelligence. We want our sales representatives and our dealers to have all the tools they need for moving the output of our plants to the consumer.[13]

But selling is only one component of marketing. As Theodore Levitt has pointed out, "Marketing is as different from selling as chemistry is from alchemy, astronomy from astrology, chess from checkers."[14]

The Marketing Era

Personal incomes and consumer demand for goods and services dropped rapidly during the Great Depression of the early 1930s, thrusting marketing into a more important role. Organizational survival dictated that managers pay close attention to the markets for their goods and services. This trend ended with the outbreak of World War II, when rationing and shortages of consumer goods became commonplace. The war years, however, created only a pause in an emerging trend that shifted a company's business focus from products and sales to customers' needs.

Emergence of the Marketing Concept The marketing concept, a crucial change in management philosophy, can be explained best by the shift from a **seller's market**—one with a shortage of goods and services—to a **buyer's market**—one with an abundance of goods and services. When World War II ended, factories stopped manufacturing tanks and ships and started turning out consumer goods again, a type of activity that had, for all practical purposes, stopped in early 1942.

The advent of a strong buyer's market created the need for a **consumer orientation** in businesses. Companies had to market goods and services, not just produce and sell them. This realization has been identified as the emergence of the marketing concept. The recognition of this concept and its dominant role in business dates from 1952, when General Electric's *Annual Report* heralded a new management philosophy:

> [The concept] introduces the [marketer] at the beginning rather than at the end of the production cycle and integrates marketing into each phase of the business. Thus, marketing, through its studies and research, will establish for the engineer, the design and manufacturing [person], what the customer wants in a given product, what price he [or she] is willing to pay, and where and when it will be wanted. Marketing will have authority in product planning, production scheduling, and inventory control, as well as in sales, distribution, and servicing of the product.[15]

Marketing would no longer be regarded as a supplemental activity performed after completion of the production process. The marketer would play the lead role in product planning, for example. Marketing and selling would no longer be synonymous terms.

The fully developed **marketing concept** is a companywide consumer orientation with the objective of achieving

Marketing Dictionary

production orientation Business philosophy stressing efficiency in producing a quality product, with the attitude toward marketing that "a good product will sell itself."

sales orientation Business assumption that consumers will resist purchasing nonessential goods and services with the attitude toward marketing that only creative advertising and personal selling can overcome consumers' resistance and convince them to buy.

seller's market Marketplace characterized by a shortage of goods and/or services.

buyer's market Marketplace characterized by an abundance of goods and/or services.

consumer orientation Business philosophy incorporating the marketing concept that emphasizes first determining unmet consumer needs and then designing a system for satisfying them.

marketing concept Companywide consumer orientation with the objective of achieving long-run success.

Figure 1.4 **Applying the Marketing Concept in the Health-Insurance Market**

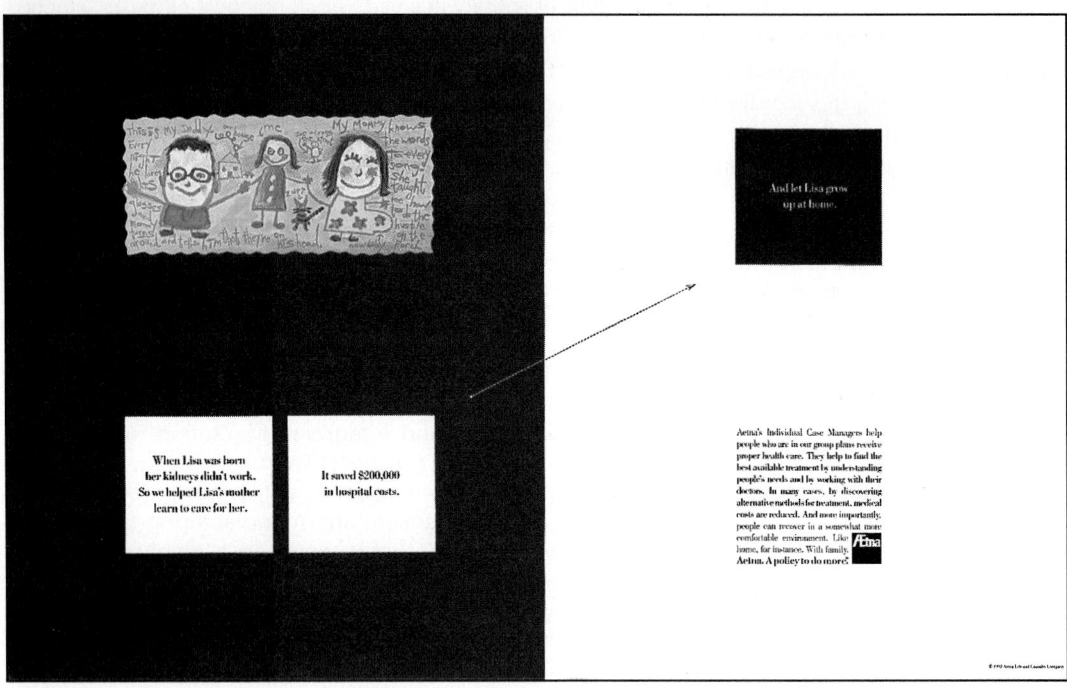
When Lisa was born
her kidneys didn't work.
So we helped Lisa's mother
learn to care for her.
It saved $200,000
in hospital costs.
And let Lisa grow
up at home.
Aetna's Individual Case Managers help people who are in our group plans receive proper health care. They help to find the best available treatment by understanding people's needs and by working with their doctors. In many cases, by discovering alternative methods for treatment, medical costs are reduced. And more importantly, people can recover in a somewhat more comfortable environment. Like home, for instance. With family.
Aetna. A policy to do more.
Ætna

long-run success. The key words are *companywide consumer orientation.* All facets of the organization must contribute first to assessing and then to satisfying customer wants and needs. The effort is not something to be left only to marketers. Accountants working in the credit office and engineers designing products also play important roles. The words *with the objective of achieving long-run success* differentiate the concept from policies of short-run profit maximization. Since the firm's continuity is an assumed component of the marketing concept, companywide consumer orientation will lead to greater long-run profits than managerial philosophies geared toward reaching short-run goals.

A strong market orientation—the extent to which a company adopts the marketing concept—generally improves market success and overall performance. It also has a positive effect on new-product development and the introduction of innovative products. Companies that implement market-driven strategies better understand their customers' experiences, buying habits, and needs. They can, therefore, design products with advantages and levels of quality compatible with customer requirements. Another benefit is that customers more quickly accept the new products.[16]

Aetna's Individual Case Manager program, described in the advertisement in Figure 1.4, illustrates the striking difference between the production era and today's consumer orientation. Rather than the production-era philosophy that one policy or treatment fits all, Aetna marketers focus on the individual attention the company pays to policyholders for its group health plan. The ad also tries to allay consumer concerns about the growing impersonalization of health care. Despite the millions of people covered by Aetna's policies, the company strives to find the "best available treatment by understanding people's needs." This personal approach sends policyholders the message that they are longtime partners with Aetna and that they will receive the right type of care for their individual health needs, while reducing medical costs.

The Relationship Era

The 1990s marked the beginning of the fourth era in marketing history. Organizations carried the marketing era's customer orientation one step further by focusing on establishing and maintaining relationships with both customers and suppliers. This effort represented a major shift from the traditional concept of marketing as a simple exchange between buyer and seller. *Relationship marketing,* by contrast, involves long-term, value-added relationships developed over time with customers and suppliers. *Strategic alliances* and partnerships with vendors and retailers play major roles in relationship marketing. Packaged-goods giant Procter & Gamble has contracts with giant retailers such as Wal-Mart and Safeway to automatically replenish their inventories of Head & Shoulders, Crest, Tide, and other personal-care and household products. Computerized systems track withdrawals from customers' warehouses, allowing P&G to ship 40 percent of its orders automatically, cutting paperwork and inventory costs and holding the line on retail prices. A recent Coopers & Lybrand study of fast-growing firms revealed that participants in such collaborative relationships generated almost 25 percent more sales than independent firms. Teaming up with potential buyers of their products also reduced the risk of new-product introductions.[17] We will discuss the concept of relationship marketing in detail later in the chapter.

Converting Needs to Wants

Figure 1.5 Frito-Lay: Converting Needs to Wants

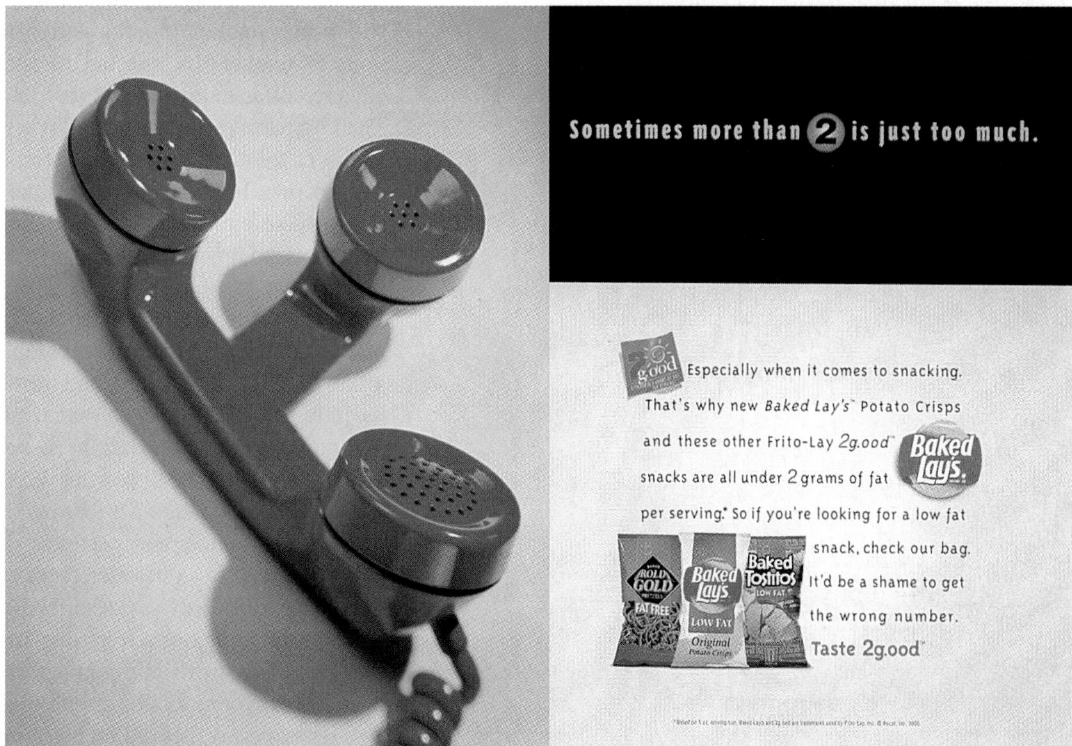
Sometimes more than 2 is just too much.
Especially when it comes to snacking.
That's why new Baked Lay's Potato Crisps and these other Frito-Lay 2g.ood snacks are all under 2 grams of fat per serving.* So if you're looking for a low fat snack, check our bag. It'd be a shame to get the wrong number.
Taste 2g.ood
Baked Lay's
Rold Gold
Baked Tostitos
Low Fat
Original Potato Crisps

Every consumer must acquire goods and services on a continuing basis to fill certain needs. Everyone must satisfy the fundamental needs for food, clothing, a home, and transportation by purchasing things or, in some instances, temporarily using rented property and hired or leased transportation. By focusing on the *benefits* resulting from these goods and services, effective marketing converts needs to wants. A need for clothing may be translated into a desire (or want) for designer clothes. The need for a vacation may become the desire to take a Caribbean cruise or to go backpacking in the Rocky Mountains. In Figure 1.5, snack-food giant Frito-Lay strives to convert a basic need—satisfying hunger—to a specific desire for its snacks. The company is promoting the benefits of its new line of healthy snack foods, developed in response to today's emphasis on low-fat diets. With Rold Gold pretzels, Baked Lay's potato crisps, and Baked Tostitos tortilla chips, consumers can still have their favorite snack foods while limiting their fat intake.

Companies that adopt the marketing concept focus on providing solutions to customer problems. They promote product benefits rather than features to show the added value that customers will receive from the product. For example, car salespeople emphasize powerful engines, ABS brakes, and air bags as safety benefits, while office products dealers promote reliable, high-speed copiers and printers for the time savings and low maintenance costs they offer to companies.

AVOIDING MARKETING MYOPIA

The emergence of the marketing concept has not been devoid of setbacks. One troublesome problem led Harvard Business School professor Theodore Levitt to coin the term *marketing myopia.* According to Levitt, **marketing myopia** is management's failure to recognize the scope of its business. Product-oriented rather than customer-oriented management endangers future growth. Levitt cites many service industries—dry cleaning, electric utilities, movies, and railroads—as examples of marketing myopia.

To avoid marketing myopia, companies must broadly define organizational goals oriented toward consumer needs. This approach can help a company stand out from its competitors, even in a crowded industry. Southwest Airlines took on major air carriers like Delta, American, and United with an irreverent, unconventional approach. Despite its lack of amenities like assigned seating, checked baggage, and food service, the airline has racked up increasing passenger miles and profits. It views itself not as an airline but as a transportation company, an important

Marketing Dictionary

marketing myopia Term coined by Theodore Levitt in his argument that executives in many industries fail to recognize the broad scope of their businesses. (According to Levitt, future growth is endangered when executives lack a marketing orientation.)

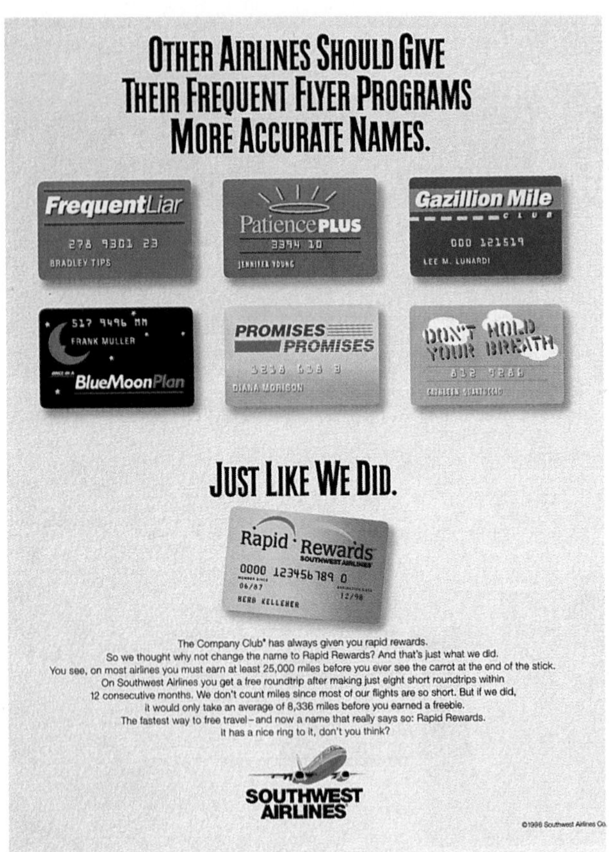
OTHER AIRLINES SHOULD GIVE THEIR FREQUENT FLYER PROGRAMS MORE ACCURATE NAMES.
FrequentLiar
PatiencePLUS
Gazillion Mile CLUB
BlueMoonPlan
PROMISES PROMISES
DON'T HOLD YOUR BREATH
JUST LIKE WE DID.
Rapid · Rewards
SOUTHWEST AIRLINES
0000 123456789 0
HERB KELLEHER
The Company Club® has always given you rapid rewards.
So we thought why not change the name to Rapid Rewards? And that's just what we did.
You see, on most airlines you must earn at least 25,000 miles before you ever see the carrot at the end of the stick.
On Southwest Airlines you get a free roundtrip after making just eight short roundtrips within
12 consecutive months. We don't count miles since most of our flights are so short. But if we did,
it would only take an average of 8,336 miles before you earned a freebie.
The fastest way to free travel—and now a name that really says so: Rapid Rewards.
It has a nice ring to it, don't you think?
SOUTHWEST AIRLINES
©1996 Southwest Airlines Co.

Low-cost tickets, efficient customer service, and a dose of humor provide a profitable mix for Southwest Airlines. Southwest's self-proclaimed "home gate" can be reached via the Internet address shown below.

distinction for an air carrier specializing in short flights of about 400 miles lasting just over an hour. Southwest's main competitor, however, is not another airline but the automobile.

Southwest defines itself not just as a transportation provider but also as a people-pleasing company. Its corporate culture rewards humor as well as hard work and efficiency. This principle also appears in the company's ads for its frequent flyer program and Web site ticket-ordering service.

http://www.iflyswa.com/

Passengers eagerly await flight attendants' greetings, which may include nonregulation messages, like invitations to smokers to "file out to our lounge on the wing, where you can enjoy our feature film, *Gone with the Wind.*" The company regards its employees as key assets, and it sponsors frequent events that promote camaraderie. Employees own 10 percent of the airline's stock, and this ownership stake builds staff loyalty and pride in serving customers as company representatives. These programs pay off. Jobs at the airline are hard to get. In a recent year, 124,000 people applied for about 5,500 openings. Unlike many companies, Southwest labor and management groups get along very well, and the discount air carrier was recently named to *Fortune* magazine's most admired corporation list. The firm has been profitable almost every year, even during the disastrous 1990 to 1994 period when the industry recorded a net loss of $12.5 billion.[18]

Revlon founder and president Charles Revson understood the need for a broader focus on benefits rather than on products. As Revson described it, "In our factory we make perfume; in our advertising we sell hope." Table 1.3 illustrates how firms in a number of other industries have overcome myopic thinking with marketing-oriented business descriptions focused on consumer need satisfaction.

EXTENDING THE TRADITIONAL BOUNDARIES OF MARKETING

Until fairly recently, marketing focused primarily on exchanges of goods and services between individuals and businesses. Today, both profit-oriented and not-for-profit organizations recognize universal needs for marketing and its importance to their success. A television advertisement for Little Caesar's pizza may be followed by a "Save the Children" public-service announcement, a political message by a congressional candidate, or a ticket offer for a traveling art exhibit.

Table 1.3 Avoiding Marketing Myopia by Focusing on Benefits Provided by the Organization

Company	Myopic Description	Marketing-Oriented Description
MCI	"We are a telephone company."	"We are a communications company."
American Airlines	"We are in the airline business."	"We are in the transportation business."
Merrill Lynch	"We are in the stock brokerage business."	"We are in the financial services business."
Nintendo	"We are in the video game business."	"We are in the entertainment business."

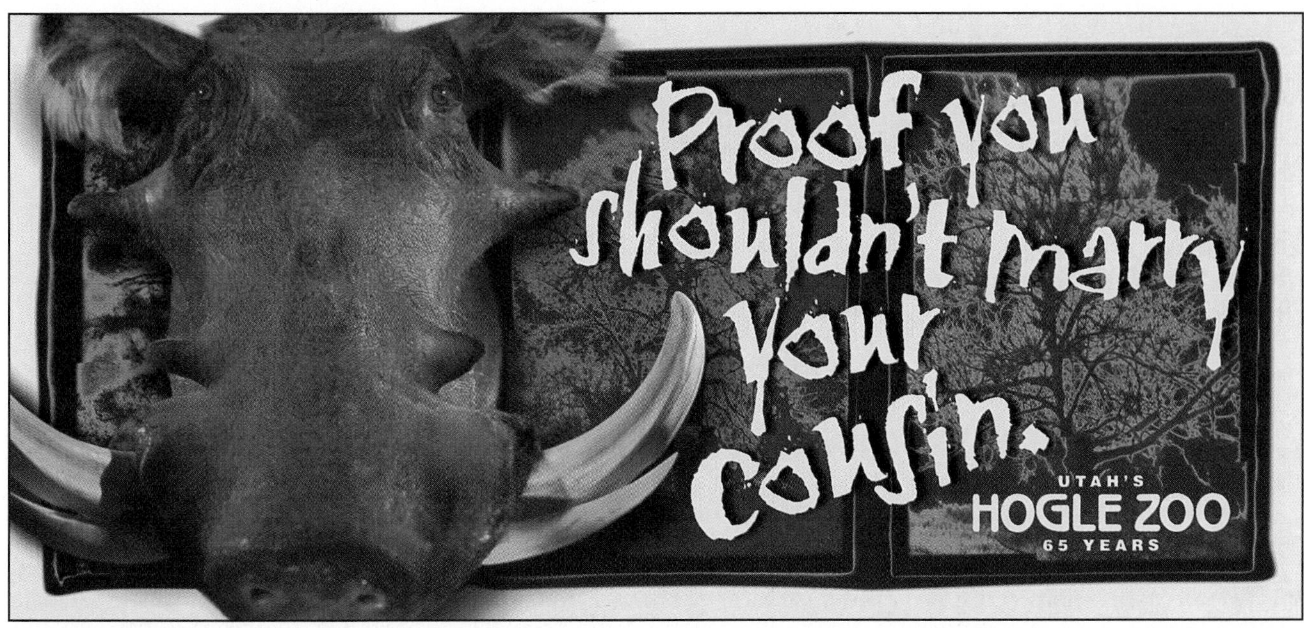
Proof you shouldn't marry your cousin.
UTAH'S
HOGLE ZOO
65 YEARS

To entice Salt Lake City residents to buy tickets to the Hogle Zoo's new warthog exhibit, zoo marketers turned to humor in this ad.

Marketing in Not-for-Profit Organizations

In the large and growing not-for-profit sector, two of every three organizations now operating were formed since 1960.[19] The 1.2 million not-for-profit organizations operating in the United States employ almost 11 million people (including volunteers) and generate an estimated $300 billion in revenues each year.

Not-for-profit organizations operate in both public and private sectors. Federal, state, and local government units and agencies derive revenues from tax collection to pursue service objectives that are not keyed to profitability targets. The U.S. Department of Defense, for example, protects the nation's borders; a state's department of natural resources regulates conservation and environmental programs; the local animal-control officer enforces ordinances that protect people and animals.

The private sector has an even more diverse array of not-for-profit organizations, including art institutes, the Florida State University football team, labor unions, hospitals, private schools, the American Cancer Society, the Rotary Club, and local youth organizations. Some, like Florida State's football team, may generate surplus revenue that can pay for other university activities, but the organization's primary goal is to win football games.

In some not-for-profits, adopting the marketing concept means forming a partnership with a for-profit company to promote the not-for-profit's message or image. A partnership between Walt Disney Co. and the Royal Canadian Mounted Police produced expensive leather jackets, golf balls, toys, and diaper bags emblazoned with Mountie logos for sale in outlets from Florida's Epcot Center to Banff National Park in the Canadian Rockies. The marketing and licensing arrangement accomplished two goals for Canada's famed national police: It cracked down on tasteless, tacky misuse of Mountie-related symbols, and it generated revenue for community policing projects. So far, the joint venture has generated profits for both parties, ending any concerns of a "Mickey Mouse" operation.[20]

Not-for-profits may form alliances with profit-seeking firms for the benefit of both. Consider some current examples:

- The Arthritis Foundation recently signed a $1 million deal with the makers of Tylenol to sell painkillers with the foundation's name on the boxes.
- American Express and other companies agreed to donate portions of their sales to the restoration of the Statue of Liberty and Ellis Island.
- The American Cancer Society has endorsed NicoDerm antismoking patches and Florida orange juice in exchange for $4 million in contributions.[21]

The diversity of not-for-profit organizations suggests the presence of numerous organizational objectives other than profitability. In addition to organizational goals, not-for-profits differ from profit-seeking firms in other ways.

MARKETING HALL OF SHAME

The Worst "Better Mousetrap" Marketing Decision

In the early 1960s, Chester M. Woolworth, president of the nation's largest mousetrap producer, introduced a better mousetrap. Sure to be a winner, the new brown, plastic model featured a completely sanitary design, cost only a few cents more than the commonplace wood mousetrap, and never missed. But despite thorough research, Woolworth's better mousetrap failed as a new-product venture. His designers created a quality product—but they forgot how their customers would make purchase decisions and use the product.

Why was this product a loser? Men bought and set most of the new plastic mousetraps. Often, however, they forgot to check the trap the next morning, so that the task of disposing of the dead mouse fell to women. With the traditional wood trap, this undesirable task was simple: They swept both trap and mouse into a dustpan. But the new trap looked too expensive to throw away, so women chose to eject the mouse and clean the trap for reuse—very unpleasant jobs. Soon, the traditional wood version replaced the supposedly better mousetrap.

The moral of the mousetrap story is obvious: Without effective marketing, a quality product will fail. As Mr. Woolworth said, "Fortunately, Mr. Emerson made his living as a philosopher, not a company president."

Woolworth's mousetrap would be right at home with more than 60,000 products on the shelves of Ithaca, New York's New Product Showcase and Learning Center. These once-new consumer products—from condiments to coffee, personal care to pet products, health items to home cleaners—represent over $6 billion in new-product development costs. Representatives of consumer-product companies like Procter & Gamble, Johnson & Johnson, Gillette, Kraft, General Foods, and a host of others visit the Showcase to consult with Robert McMath, founder and director of this unique collection, and see why others have failed. As he says, "We provide product developers with a hands-on opportunity to study what's happened in the past and to learn from others' mistakes."

Some ideas sound great until you try them. PepsiCo attempted to capitalize on the trend for clear,

Characteristics of Not-for-Profit Marketing

Not-for-profit organizations encounter a special set of characteristics that influence their marketing activities. Like profit-seeking firms, not-for-profits may market tangible goods and/or intangible services. The U.S. Postal Service, for example, offers stamps (a tangible good) and mail delivery (an intangible service).

For one important distinction between not-for-profits and profit-oriented companies, profit-seeking businesses tend to focus their marketing on just one public: their customers. Not-for-profit organizations, however, must often market to multiple publics, which complicates decision making regarding the correct markets to target. Many deal with at least two major publics—their clients and their sponsors—and often many other publics, as well. Political candidates, for example, target both voters and campaign contributors. A college targets prospective students as clients of its marketing program, but it also markets to current students, parents of students, alumni, faculty, staff, local businesses, and local government agencies.

A second distinguishing characteristic of not-for-profit marketing is that a customer or service user may wield less control over the organization's destiny than would be true for customers of a profit-seeking firm. A government employee may be far more concerned with the opinion of a member of the legislature's appropriations committee than with that of a service user. Further, not-for-profit organizations often possess some degree of monopoly power in a given geographic area. An individual contributor might object to the United Fund's inclusion of a crisis center among its beneficiary agencies, but that agency still receives a portion of the person's total contribution.

In another potential problem, a resource contributor, such as a legislator or financial backer, may interfere with the marketing program. It is easy to imagine a political candidate harassed by financial supporters who want to replace an unpopular campaign manager (the primary marketing position in a political campaign).

Perhaps the most commonly noted feature of the not-for-profit organization is its lack of a *bottom line*—business jargon referring to the overall profitability measure of

light-tasting carbonated beverages with Crystal Pepsi. It flopped miserably, because consumers said it didn't taste the same and expected their colas to be brown. Other ideas that consumers rejected include jalapeño soda and aerosol versions of mustard and toothpaste. Products that have a gimmick, such as Thirsty Pup bottled water for dogs, typically have a high failure rate. Hard-to-understand products also fall into this category. Consumers who bought Wine and Dine gourmet dinner mixes often drank the wine in the package, not realizing it was a recipe ingredient, and hated its salty taste. Poor timing leads to losers, too. Nabisco's 1974 introduction of Baker Tom's Baked Catfood, a feline health food, was ten years ahead of its time.

Packaging mistakes can doom a product, as well. "Mess with consumers' notions of packaging at your peril," McMath cautions. Compact disk look-alike packaging for bubble gum was one such disaster. Kids bought the gum and then tried to put it into their parents' CD players. Like Chester Woolworth, the product development team failed to anticipate consumer reaction to packaging.

http://www.showlearn.com/

QUESTIONS FOR CRITICAL THINKING

1. **How might Mr. Woolworth's marketing team have avoided its problems with the new mousetrap?**
2. **Describe some products that have failed, and discuss the reasons that they were not successful with customers.**
3. **Many companies have recently introduced canned nutritional milkshake products targeted to consumers 45 and older. For example, Mead Johnson advertises its Boost Nutritional Energy Drink as "rocket fuel" for your body. Discuss why you think these products will succeed or fail.**

Sources: PepsiCo Annual Report, downloaded from http://www.pepsi.com/, March 27, 1997; Jan Alexander, "Failure, Inc." *World Business,* May/June 1996, pp. 46–47; James Dao, "From a Collector of Turkeys, a Tour of a Supermarket Zoo," *New York Times,* September 24, 1995, pp. 12–13; and Chester M. Woolworth, "So We Made a Better Mousetrap," *The President's Forum,* Fall 1962, pp. 26–27.

performance. Profit-seeking firms measure profitability in terms of sales and revenues. While not-for-profit organizations may attempt to maximize their return from specific services, they usually substitute less exact goals, such as service-level standards, for overall evaluation criteria. As a result, it is often difficult to set marketing objectives that are aligned specifically with overall organizational goals. However, in recent years, not-for-profit groups have been under increased pressure to develop more cost-effective ways to provide services. They are also being held accountable for administrative costs.

A final characteristic of a typical not-for-profit is the lack of a clear organizational structure. Not-for-profit organizations often respond to constituencies that they serve, but these usually are less exact than, for example, the stockholders of a profit-oriented corporation. Not-for-profit organizations often have multiple organizational structures. A hospital might have an administrative structure, a professional organization consisting of medical personnel, and a volunteer organization that dominates the board of trustees. These people may sometimes work at cross-purposes and disagree with the organization's marketing strategy.

While profit-seeking firms may share some of these characteristics, they are particularly prevalent in not-for-profit organizations. However, all organizations, both profit seekers and not-for-profit groups, must develop marketing strategies to satisfy the needs and wants of consumers.

Nontraditional Marketing

As marketing gained acceptance as a generic activity, its application broadened far beyond its traditional boundaries. In some cases, broader appeals focus on causes, events, individuals, organizations, and places in the not-for-profit sector. In other instances, they encompass diverse groups of profit-seeking individuals, activities, and organizations. Table 1.4 lists and describes five major categories of nontraditional marketing: person marketing, place marketing, cause marketing, event marketing, and organization marketing.

Table 1.4 Categories of Nontraditional Marketing

Type	Brief Description	Examples
Person marketing	Marketing efforts designed to cultivate the attention, interest, and preference of a target market toward a person	Celebrities such as Jay Leno, Michael Jordan, Barbra Streisand; political candidates such as "Jorgenson for Congress"
Place marketing	Marketing efforts designed to attract visitors to a particular area; improve consumer images of a city, state, or nation; and/or attract new business	Virginia: The Bottom Line State; Sea World: Let the Adventure Begin; Las Vegas: Open 24 Hours
Cause marketing	Identification and marketing of a social issue, cause, or idea to selected target markets	Just Say No; Buckle Up for Safety
Event marketing	Marketing of sporting, cultural, and charitable activities to selected target markets	March of Dimes WalkAmerica; Davis Cup tennis matches
Organization marketing	Marketing efforts of mutual-benefit organizations, service organizations, and government organizations that seek to influence others to accept their goals, receive their services, or contribute to them in some way	United Way Brings Out the Best in All of Us; Army: Be All You Can Be; Boys & Girls Clubs: The Positive Place for Kids

Person Marketing One category of nontraditional marketing, **person marketing,** refers to efforts designed to cultivate the attention, interest, and preferences of a target market toward a person. Campaigns for political candidates and the marketing of celebrities are examples of person marketing. In political marketing, candidates target two markets: They attempt to gain the recognition and preference of voters and the financial support of donors. Increasing numbers of campaign managers are using computerized marketing research techniques to identify voters and donors and then design advertising to reach those markets. Other promotional efforts include personal handshakes, political rallies, fund-raising dinners, and publicity.

Highly successful sports celebrities such as Michael Jordan, Tiger Woods, and Shaquille O'Neal earn huge endorsement fees from marketers seeking to link the athletes' images to their brands. Nike and Titleist gave Woods a $40 million endorsement contract before the Stanford golfing champion won his first professional tournament. But no athlete has succeeded better in marketing himself as a brand than the youthful, talented, likable O'Neal. Even though he has succeeded on the basketball court with the Orlando Magic and the Los Angeles Lakers, recorded two successful rap music albums, and starred in motion pictures, O'Neal has been even more impressive as a celebrity endorser. Here is how his manager describes this versatile star:

> Shaq has such a unique persona. He's incredibly powerful and big; he's 7-foot-1, 315 pounds, but he loves kids, and relates to them. He wants to encourage young people to access their potential in academics, in sports, in every area of their lives.[22]

To maintain a consistent image, Shaq and his manager have developed a plan for deciding on projects. The plan includes:

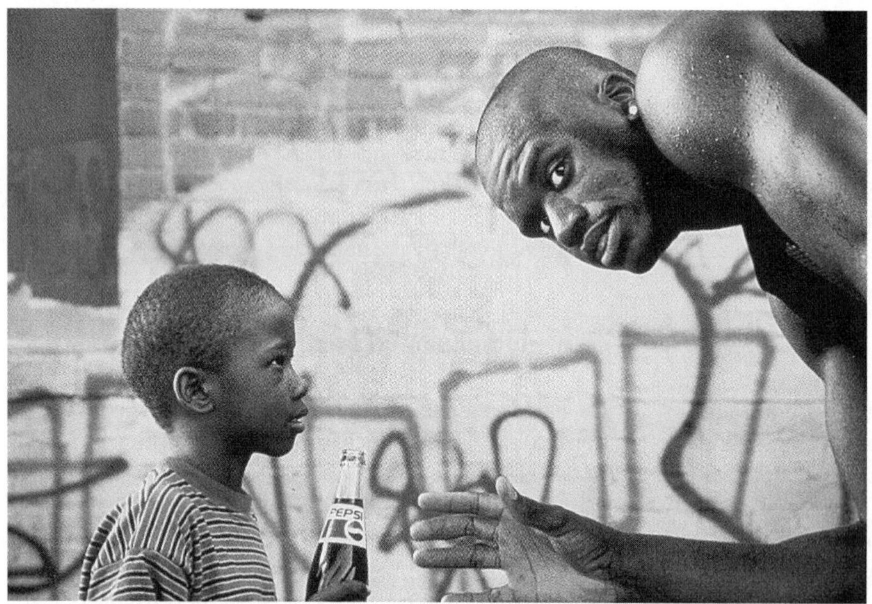
PEPSI

Person marketing pays off as Shaq projects his image in this Pepsi "Playground" ad. When the last bottle of Pepsi ends up in the hands of a young boy, Shaq flashes his megabucks smile and goes for the bottle. "Don't even think about it," the tiny tyke deadpans.

- *Motion pictures:* kid-friendly roles filled with physical humor such as the crime-fighting comic-book superhero in *Steel* are fine, but roles in more adult-oriented action films are avoided for now.
- *Product endorsements:* Pepsi's "Be Young, Have Fun" slogan matches the Shaq image; so, too, does Reebok's "Prepare to Win" campaign.
- *TV programming:* recent hosting of Nickelodeon's *Sports Theater with Shaquille O'Neal* on the image-conscious, kid-centric cable network is consistent with his kid-friendly image.

Place Marketing Another category of nontraditional marketing is **place marketing,** which attempts to attract customers to particular areas. Cities, states, and countries publicize their tourist attractions to lure vacation travelers. They also promote themselves as good locations for businesses. Place marketing has become more important in the world economy, where localities compete for economic advantage, increased employment, trade, and investment. Organizations as varied as Tokyo Disneyland, the Monterey, California Aquarium, the Mall of America in Minnesota, state economic development commissions, and the Los Angeles Port Authority apply place marketing techniques to attract visitors, residents, and new businesses to their areas. Their strategies include promoting positive images; marketing special attractions like Egypt's pyramids, the Grand Canyon, and Paris's Eiffel Tower; highlighting efficient transportation infrastructures and communication systems; and stressing the quality of available education, low crime rates, clean air and water, and cultural and recreational opportunities. Place marketing also fills promotional messages with positive perceptions of visitors as well as people who live in the area.[23]

Figure 1.6 illustrates how nations seek to attract international businesses. The Invest in Denmark ad informs prospective businesses of the country's ideal location, low corporate tax rate, and flexible labor laws that make it easy to distribute products to customers throughout Europe.

Many U.S. states and cities launch marketing campaigns to attract new business, foreign investment, and exports. They also spend considerable amounts to promote tourism. Total annual state promotional spending exceeds $400 million. Illinois' $32 million budget leads the way, followed by Hawaii ($25 million), Texas ($21 million), and South Carolina ($19 million).[24] Place marketing also includes sporting activities sponsored to attract visitors. License plates encourage people to "Ski Utah." Cities construct new professional sports stadiums and compete to host football's Super Bowl. Prestigious tournaments like the British Open and Masters in golf and the U.S. Open and Wimbledon in tennis help create positive images and attract visitors for their areas. In fact, golf has become a featured component of many place marketing programs due to its universal appeal to a lucrative market segment and its role as a corporate recreation activity.[25]

Figure 1.6 Place Marketing: Denmark

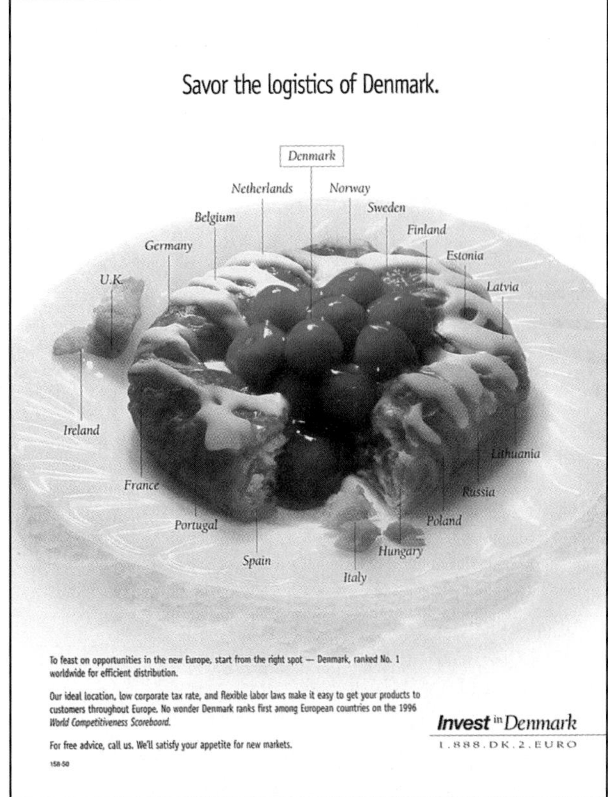
Savor the logistics of Denmark.
Denmark
Netherlands
Norway
Sweden
Belgium
Finland
Germany
Estonia
U.K.
Latvia
Ireland
Lithuania
France
Russia
Portugal
Poland
Spain
Hungary
Italy
To feast on opportunities in the new Europe, start from the right spot — Denmark, ranked No. 1 worldwide for efficient distribution.
Our ideal location, low corporate tax rate, and flexible labor laws make it easy to get your products to customers throughout Europe. No wonder Denmark ranks first among European countries on the 1996 World Competitiveness Scoreboard.
For free advice, call us. We'll satisfy your appetite for new markets.
158-50
Invest in Denmark
1.888.DK.2.EURO

Cause Marketing A third category of nontraditional marketing, **cause marketing,** refers to the identification

Marketing Dictionary

person marketing Marketing efforts designed to cultivate the attention, interest, and preference of a target market toward a person (typically a political candidate or celebrity).

place marketing Marketing efforts to attract people and organizations to a particular geographic area.

cause marketing Identification and marketing of a social issue, cause, or idea to selected target markets.

Figure 1.7 Event Marketing: *Rent* on Broadway

RENT
RENT book, music and lyrics by
JONATHAN LARSON
NEDERLANDER THEATRE NYC
directed by MICHAEL GREIF

and marketing of a social issue, cause, or idea to selected target markets. Cause marketing covers a wide range of issues, including literacy, physical fitness, gay and lesbian rights, family planning, prison reform, control of overeating, environmental protection, elimination of birth defects, prevention of child abuse, gun control, and punishment of drunk driving.

The California Department of Health Services stressed family and community themes in its successful antismoking campaign that resulted in a measurable decline in cigarette smoking. The goal was to reduce the social acceptability of smoking by tailoring messages to demographic segments. To reach African-American markets, the department developed ads that pictured well-known entertainers like Sammy Davis Jr. and Sarah Vaughan who died from smoking-related diseases. For Asian-Americans, the central theme was family values, while the effort directed toward youths took a different approach. Because so many young people think they are invincible, the health theme wasn't as effective as focusing on appearance and peer acceptance.[26]

Event Marketing **Event marketing** refers to the marketing of sporting, cultural, and charitable activities to selected target markets. It also includes the sponsorship of such events by firms seeking to increase public awareness and bolster their images by linking themselves and their products to the events. The hit Broadway play *Rent* proved to be not only an artistic success but a financial one, as well, due in large part to the application of marketing strategies. For years, industry experts grew increasingly concerned about the aging of the typical theater-goer, wondering how to attract younger audiences in the future. The play tells the story of an HIV-positive musician and his dancer girlfriend surviving on society's fringes—a story that appeals to a nontraditional theater audience of young people.

The innovative, highly realistic play, depicted in the advertisement shown in Figure 1.7, succeeded in its goal of attracting a youthful audience, but marketing was necessary to overcome several stumbling blocks. One was the ticket price, which typically reaches $75 for a hit musical. *Rent* marketers decided to hold tickets in the first two rows until the day of the performance and then sell them for $20. This not only attracted budget-minded buyers; it also produced long lines in front of the theater every day, adding to the event's excitement. Merchandising agreements resulted in specialized *Rent* boutiques set up in Bloomingdale's where fans could buy T-shirts, halter tops, and black vinyl pants similar to those worn in the play.[27]

Sports sponsorships have gained effectiveness in increasing brand recognition, enhancing image, boosting purchase volume, and increasing popularity with sports fans in demographic segments corresponding to sponsor business goals. Between 1988, when it first became an Olympic sponsor, through the 1996 summer games, Visa's brand awareness grew from 52 to 75 percent.[28] The role of sponsorship in a firm's marketing program is discussed in detail in Chapter 17.

Organization Marketing The category of nontraditional marketing called **organization marketing** in this book involves attempts to influence others to accept the goals of, receive the services of, or contribute in some way to an organization. Organization marketing includes mutual-benefit organizations (churches, labor unions, and political parties), service organizations (colleges and universities, hospitals, and museums), and government organizations (military services, police and fire departments, and the U.S. Postal Service).

As cultural organizations encounter declining public funding for the arts and rising competition from other entertainment forms, they respond by actively marketing their programs. The Edgewood Symphony Orchestra, a community ensemble serving the Pittsburgh area, conducted a phone survey to find out how residents viewed the orchestra's contribution to the city, their musical preferences, and similar information. The orchestra's marketing campaign and news releases centered on changes resulting from this feedback, bringing its programs to the attention of a larger audience. Complimentary tickets were mailed to survey respondents with copies of the season brochure. Attendance at concerts increased substantially, as did the number of season subscriptions and public awareness of the organization.[29]

The 80 classical theaters in North America also develop marketing plans and search out new sponsorship ideas to attract audiences. "Irreverence, youth, sex, passion, and fun sell Shakespeare these days," says Jan Powell, artistic director of Portland, Oregon's Tygres Heart Shakespeare Company. This new company promotes itself by staging sword fights at benefit dinners. The Utah Shakespeare Festival chose "Let's Play" as its successful slogan. It appealed to two very different target audiences: Mormons, who felt it related to family entertainment, and Las Vegans, who thought it related to casinos.[30]

ELEMENTS OF A MARKETING STRATEGY

Although the product at the center of a marketing campaign may consist of a tangible good or an intangible service, a cause, event, person, place, or organization, success in the marketplace always depends on an effective marketing strategy. The basic elements of a marketing strategy consist of (1) the target market, and (2) the marketing mix variables of product, distribution, promotion, and price that combine to satisfy the needs of the target market. The outer circle in Figure 1.8 lists environmental characteristics that provide the framework within which marketing strategies are planned.

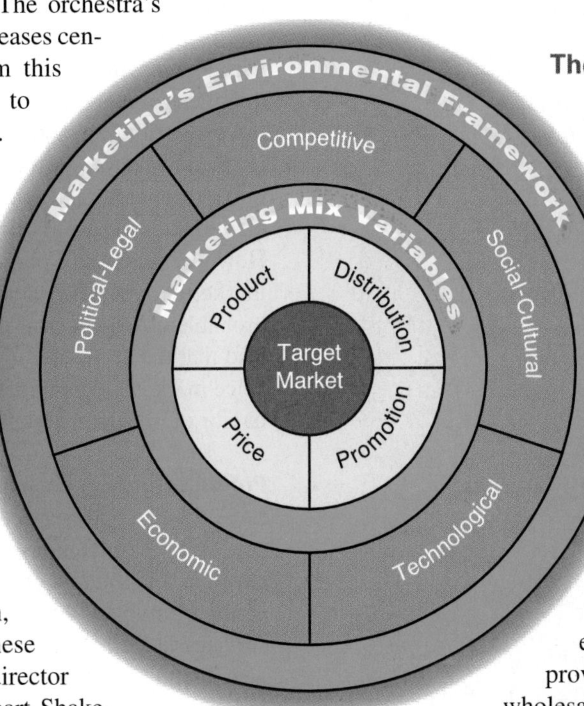
Marketing's Environmental Framework
Competitive
Political-Legal
Social-Cultural
Economic
Technological
Marketing Mix Variables
Product
Distribution
Price
Promotion
Target Market

Figure 1.8

Elements of a Marketing Strategy and Its Environmental Framework

The Target Market

Marketing activities focus on the consumer. Therefore, a market-driven organization begins its overall strategy with a detailed description of its **target market:** the group of people toward whom the firm decides to direct its marketing efforts.

JCPenney serves a target market consisting of consumers purchasing for themselves and their families. Other companies, such as General Dynamics Corp., market most of their products to government purchasers. Still other firms provide goods and services to retail and wholesale buyers. In every instance, however, marketers should delineate their target markets as specifically as possible. Consider the following examples:

- Swimwear manufacturer Authentic Fitness targets women over 35, who spend the most for swimwear, by designing a line of suits using figure-slimming materials.
- Retailer Target customizes merchandise in each store to local customer demographics; even stores in the same metropolitan area may carry very different products.

Marketing Dictionary

event marketing The marketing of sporting, cultural, and charitable activities to selected target markets.

organization marketing Marketing by mutual-benefit organizations, service organizations, and government organizations intended to influence others to accept their goals, receive their services, or contribute to them in some way.

target market Group of people toward whom a firm markets its goods, services, or ideas with a strategy designed to satisfy their specific needs and preferences.

Figure 1.9 **Elements of the Michelin Product Strategy**

Introducing better wet traction than any rain tire.
But why would we stop there?
At Michelin, we believe a tire that's just good in the rain isn't good enough. Introducing the new Michelin X-One. It not only gives you the best wet traction of any rain tire, but also gives you legendary Michelin control in snow, sun, or any driving condition. And it is engineered to last so long that it comes with a 6-year unlimited mileage tread life warranty.* So why buy a tire that's just good in the rain, when you can buy one that's good in any weather?
MICHELIN X-ONE
BECAUSE SO MUCH IS RIDING ON YOUR TIRES.
*LIMITED warranty. Exclusions apply. See dealer for details.

▼ The target market for the Saab 900 convertible consists of well-educated professionals and managers aged 30 to 40 years old with household incomes over $50,000 who want a high-performance car that is fun to drive.

Although considerations about identification and satisfaction of a target market are relevant to every chapter in this text, three chapters in Part 3 focus specifically on this subject. Consumer behavior is the subject of Chapter 7. Chapter 8 is devoted to the analysis of business-to-business marketing. Methods of segmenting markets are analyzed in Chapter 9.

> **Briefly speaking**
>
> "There is only one boss, the customer, and he can fire everybody in the company, from the chairman down, simply by spending his money elsewhere."
>
> Sam Walton (1918–1992)
> Founder, Wal-Mart stores

Marketing Mix Variables

After marketers select a target market, they direct company activities toward profitably satisfying that segment. Although they must manipulate thousands of variables to reach this goal, marketing decision making can be divided into four strategies: product, pricing, distribution, and promotion strategies. The total package forms the **marketing mix**—the blending of the four strategy elements to fit the needs and preferences of a specific target market. Each strategy is a variable in the mix. While the fourfold classification is useful in study and analysis, a particular *combination* of these variables determines marketing success.

Figure 1.8 illustrates the focus of the marketing mix variables on the central choice of consumer or organizational target markets. In addition, decisions about product, price, distribution, and promotion are affected by the environmental factors in the outer circle of the figure. Unlike the controllable marketing mix elements, the environmental variables frequently lie outside the control of marketers. However, they may play a major role in the success of a marketing program, and marketers must consider their probable effects even if control remains impossible. Note also that the consumer is not a marketing mix component, since marketers have little or no control over the future behavior of present and potential consumers.

Product Strategy In marketing, the word *product* means more than a good, service, or idea. Product is a broad concept that also encompasses the satisfaction of all consumer needs in relation to a good, service, or idea. Thus, **product strategy** involves more than just deciding what goods or services the firm should offer to a group of consumers. It also includes making decisions about customer service, package design, brand names, trademarks, warranties, product life cycles, positioning, and new-product development. Many of these elements are illustrated in the Michelin ad shown in Figure 1.9. It emphasizes the X-One tire's ability to provide outstanding traction in rain through a humorous visual reference to Noah's ark. It also describes the product's other qualities, such as excellent control in any driving conditions and six-year unlimited mileage warranty. At the same time, it also sends the message that your most valued passenger—your child—will be safe riding in a car equipped with Michelin tires. This message enhances Michelin's image as a company that cares about its customers.

Southern California clothing manufacturer No Fear has caught the attention of the teenage boys with its "in-your-face attitude wear." No Fear sees itself not as an apparel company but as a company that sells confidence and self-esteem to teen boys. It has carefully crafted this image through products, many with slogans that promote an attitude "You are what you fear." The company's product strategy seeks to create items that project a "cool" identity for the wearer. Originally popular with niche groups like surfers and bikers, No Fear clothing is now worn by both boys and girls. No Fear clothing and decals send the message that they have taken control of their lives.[31]

Three chapters in Part 4 deal with product strategy.

Chapter 11 introduces the basic elements of product strategy, Chapter 12 discusses product mix decisions and new-product planning, and Chapter 13 focuses on strategies for marketing services.

Pricing Strategy One of the most difficult areas of marketing decision making, **pricing strategy,** deals with the methods of setting profitable and justifiable prices. It is closely regulated and subject to considerable public scrutiny.

One of the many factors that influence a marketer's pricing strategy is competition. The computer industry provides an example where price can be a determining factor in the purchase decision. To gain market share, Compaq Computer Corp. lowered prices up to 28 percent in 1996. These price cuts produced a ripple effect and started a price war. Competitors like IBM, Dell, Digital, and Hewlett-Packard also dropped prices, in some cases as much as 30 percent. At stake was Compaq's leadership position in the PC server market. (Servers are especially powerful computers that connect desktop PCs to networks.) About two months later, Compaq announced another set of price cuts, again to protect market share, triggering a similar response from the other players in the market. Such price wars expose a firm to serious dangers. Slashing prices and offering new dealer incentives to increase revenues are effective only when they generate enough new sales to offset the per-unit revenue decline produced by the price cuts. Otherwise, such moves simply erode a company's profitability. Compaq executives were willing to take that risk in an attempt to lock up more of the market before competitors introduced comparable models.[32]

Pricing strategy is the subject of Part 7. Chapter 20 analyzes the elements involved in determining prices and Chapter 21 examines the management aspect of pricing.

Distribution Strategy Marketers develop **distribution strategies** to ensure that consumers find their products available in the proper quantities at the right times and places. Distribution decisions involve modes of transportation, warehousing, inventory control, order processing, and selection of marketing channels. Marketing channels are made up of institutions such as retailers and wholesalers—all those involved in a product's movement from producer to final consumer.

Technology is opening up new channels of distribution for some industries. For example, software, a product made up of digital data files, is ideally suited to electronic distribution. Major players like Netscape, Sun Microsystems, and Microsoft Corp. already distribute their programs and upgrades over the Internet. These companies are expected to distribute 50 percent of their software electronically by 2000. Both consumers and the software companies like the move to the Net. Customers no longer have to wait for updates. Without packaging and shipping, companies can lower their prices.

Distribution strategy is covered in Part 5. Topics include channel strategy and wholesaling (Chapter 14), retailing (Chapter 15), and logistics and physical distribution (Chapter 16).

Promotional Strategy Promotion is the communication link between sellers and buyers. Organizations use many different means of sending messages about their goods, services, and ideas. They may communicate messages directly through salespeople or indirectly through advertisements and sales promotions. Highly creative advertisements like the one in Figure 1.10 can even provide a form of demonstration. Wrangler's Shadow Canyon line of jeans is competing with such well-known brands as Levi's by emphasizing the product's authenticity and ruggedness under extreme conditions. The striking photo almost allows the viewer to feel the mud-soaked clothing of the fallen cowboy.

In developing a **promotional strategy,** marketers blend together the various elements of promotion to communicate most effectively with their target market. Many companies use an approach called *integrated marketing communications* to coordinate all promotional activities so

Marketing Dictionary

marketing mix Blending the four strategy elements of marketing decision making—product, price, distribution, and promotion—to satisfy chosen consumer segments.

product strategy Element of marketing decision making involved in developing the right good or service for the firm's customers, including package design, branding, trademarks, warranties, product life cycles, and new-product development.

pricing strategy Element of marketing decision making dealing with methods of setting profitable and justifiable prices.

distribution strategy Element of marketing decision making concerned with activities and marketing institutions that get the right good or service to the firm's customers.

promotional strategy Element of marketing decision making that involves appropriate blending of personal selling, advertising, and sales promotion to communicate with and seek to persuade potential customers.

Figure 1.10 Advertising as Part of the Wrangler Promotional Strategy

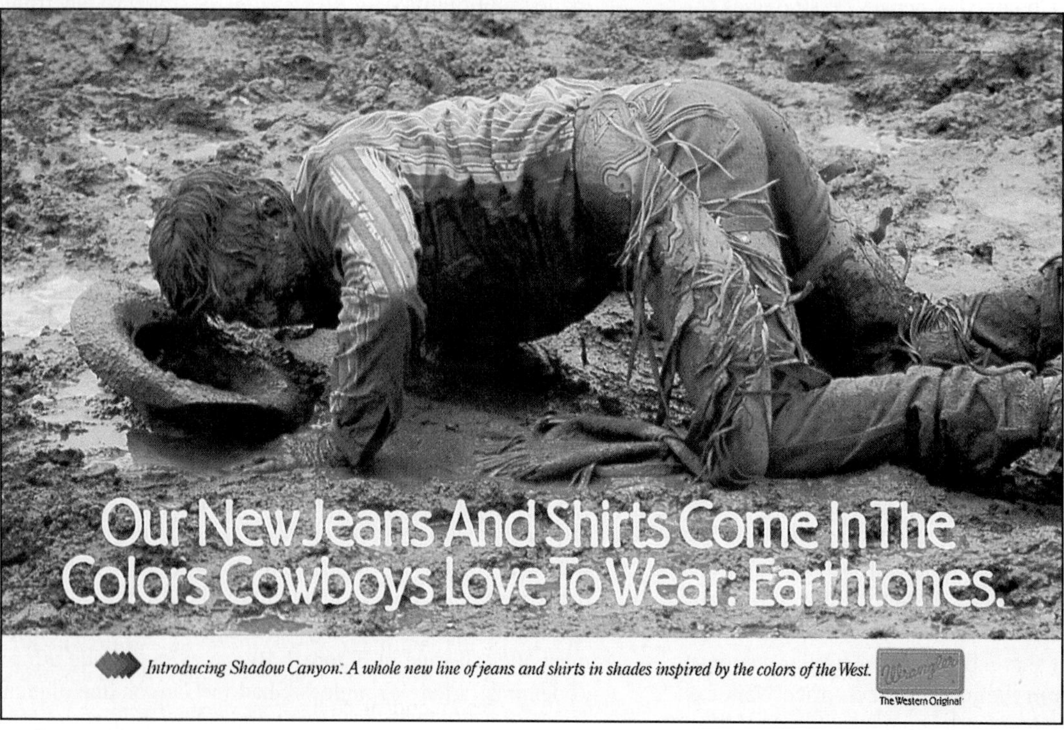
Our New Jeans And Shirts Come In The Colors Cowboys Love To Wear: Earthtones.
Introducing Shadow Canyon: A whole new line of jeans and shirts in shades inspired by the colors of the West.
Wrangler
The Western Original

that the consumer receives a unified and consistent message. National Westminster Bank (NatWest) developed a campaign that emphasized customer service to distinguish itself from banks that promote rates and products. Its slogan, "We'll go out of our way for you," told customers about its high level of personal service. Music played an unusual role in the campaign. NatWest offered free CDs and tapes to existing and potential customers when they met with bank representatives, filled out questionnaires, and provided other information about personal financial issues. This information formed the basis of the bank's future contacts with the customers, which included targeted mailings and phone calls. Survey respondents could also enter a sweepstakes to win a CD player, and bank managers handed out free concert tickets to employees and customers. Television ads, direct mail, and in-bank interactive displays were also part of the promotional strategy. The campaign made consumers feel good about the bank, leading to a significant increase in credit card and loan applications—as well as an award as one of the year's ten best promotions.[33]

Integrated marketing communications and promotional strategy are examined in Part 6. The concepts are introduced in Chapter 17. Chapter 18 deals with advertising, sales promotion, and public relations. Personal selling and sales management are the topics of Chapter 19.

The Marketing Environment

Marketers do not make decisions about target markets and marketing mix variables in a vacuum. They must take into account the dynamic nature of the five dimensions of the marketing environment shown in Figure 1.8: competitive, political–legal, economic, technological, and social–cultural dimensions. Changing government legislation about formerly regulated industries creates new opportunities for many companies. The Telecommunications Act of 1996, for example, increased competition in phone service by allowing long-distance carriers to offer local phone service and the regional Baby Bell companies to offer long-distance and cellular services. Because brand awareness is an important factor in this market, long-distance carriers like AT&T, Sprint, and MCI responded with major marketing campaigns promoting the advantages of a single carrier for all communications services. The Baby Bells explored ways to package long-distance calls with other services, like cellular phones, and implemented customer service programs to improve their images. Additional competition will come from cable television companies, which are upgrading their networks to handle phone traffic.[34]

Marketing decisions must account for an increasingly international business environment. They must recognize the important fact that 77 percent of the world's population lives in developing countries rather than industrialized nations. The economy of the developing world is expanding rapidly—about 6 percent annually—and its consumers and businesses represent a huge potential market for U.S. firms. Marketing strategies for these areas must be tailored to local conditions like market size, degree of economic liberalization, and residents' annual incomes. Nations that are expected to be the most promising global markets during the next ten years include Mexico, Argentina, India, and China. The buying power of consumers depends on annual incomes and accumulated savings. In developing countries, income growth has fueled the demand for imported products. For example, shipments of U.S. goods to China, Singapore, and Mexico were up considerably in 1996.

Companies like Whirlpool Corp. view Asia as the next marketing frontier. The appliance giant established itself as a top player in the European market by acquiring Philips Electronics' appliance business; a similar strategy underlies its move into Asian markets. With majority ownership stakes in six joint ventures, Whirlpool offers locally produced refrigerators, washing machines, air conditioners, and microwave ovens to Indian and Chinese customers. The company is betting that Asia's rapid economic growth and low appliance usage—in less than 10 percent of homes—will make it the largest appliance market in the world. Also, Chinese consumers have more income to spend than their salaries might indicate, because the government and private employers cover most or all housing, health care, and education costs.[35]

Two more important characteristics in the contemporary marketing environment include cultural diversity and ethical concerns. Every chapter in this book contains detailed examples that explore the impact of these factors.

Dimensions of the marketing environment are discussed in more depth in Chapter 3. The significance of these dimensions in the global marketplace is presented in Chapter 4. The marketing environment is important because it provides a framework for all marketing activity. It influences the development of marketing plans and forecasts, which are described in Chapter 5, and the process of marketing research, the subject of Chapter 6. Marketers consider the environmental dimensions when they study consumer and organizational buying behavior, the topics of Chapters 7 and 8, respectively, and when they develop segmentation and relationship strategies, covered in Chapters 9 and 10.

Quality and Customer Satisfaction

Chapter 2 is entirely devoted to discussing the importance of quality and customer satisfaction, both in the United States and in global markets. Consumers in developing markets are just as interested in quality, performance, and customer satisfaction as those in industrialized nations. Mass media have educated them about the best brands, products, and services, and improved technology has made top-quality products available around the world. A big part of Whirlpool's Asian strategy is to raise quality levels of appliances manufactured there, while at the same time keeping up with demand. Tests showed that comparable Chinese-made units had only about half the life expectancies of Whirlpool's U.S. appliance models. The company is investing $9 billion over a five-year period to improve engineering and testing facilities at its Raybo plant in Shenzen, China. "Until we have a product that we feel represents a modern, upscale product, we're not going to put the Whirlpool name on it," says William Marohn, Whirlpool's president and chief operating officer.[36]

As this example shows, quality is a vital ingredient in global business success. Chapter 2 discusses ways in which companies can promote quality goods and services and describes strategies for measuring and increasing customer satisfaction.

Critical Thinking and Creativity

The challenges presented by today's complex and technologically sophisticated marketing environment require critical thinking skills and creativity from marketing professionals. *Critical thinking* refers to the process of determining the authenticity, accuracy, and worth of information, knowledge, claims, and arguments. Critical thinkers react skeptically to what they hear or see. They do not take information at face value and simply *assume* that it is accurate; they analyze the data themselves and develop their own opinions and conclusions. Developing critical thinking skills is emphasized throughout the text in such forms as critical thinking questions at the end of each focus box and special end-of-chapter questions.

Likewise, creativity is an extremely valuable skill for marketers. It helps them to develop novel solutions to perceived marketing problems. Leonardo da Vinci conceived his idea for a helicopter after watching leaves twirl in the wind. Swiss engineer George de Mestral noticed that burrs stuck to his wool socks because of their tiny hooks, and invented Velcro.

Creativity is particularly important in the creation of promotional messages. Figure 1.11 uses irreverent humor in communicating the lifetime guarantee of backpacks made by Massachusetts-based Eastpak Corp. The ad proved so popular among the firm's teenage and young-adult target market that Eastpak now sells posters of it.

THE TECHNOLOGY REVOLUTION IN MARKETING

As we witness the dawn of a new century, we also enter into a new era in communication, considered by some as unique as the fifteenth-century invention of the printing press or the first radio and television broadcasts early in the twentieth century. **Technology** is the business application

Marketing Dictionary

technology Application to business of knowledge based on scientific discoveries, inventions, and innovations.

Figure 1.11 Creative Communication of a Product Guarantee

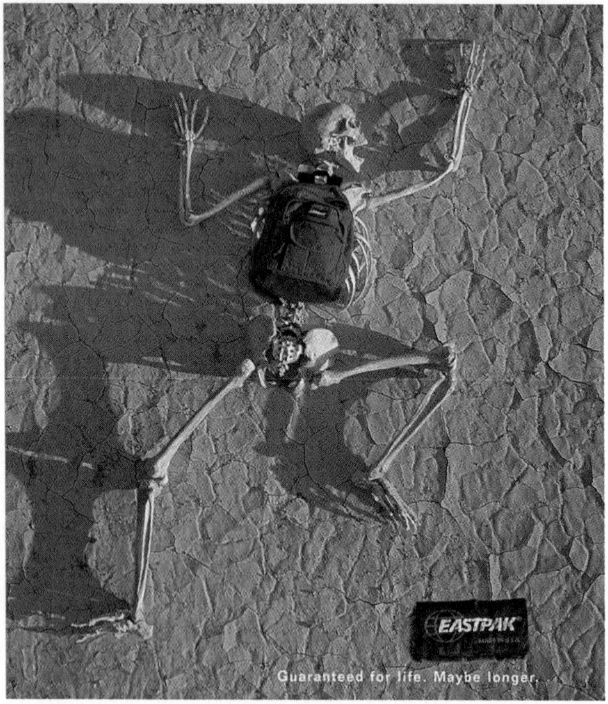
EASTPAK
Guaranteed for life. Maybe longer.

of knowledge based on scientific discoveries, inventions, and innovations. Interactive multimedia technologies such as computer networks, videoconferencing, online services and the Internet, interactive kiosks, CD-ROM catalogs, and personal digital assistants have revolutionized the way people store, distribute, retrieve, and present information. As John Sculley, former CEO of Apple Computer, observed, interactive multimedia represents "a tool of a near tomorrow that, like the printing press, will empower individuals, unlock worlds of knowledge, and forge a new community of ideas.[37]

Computer networks and other telecommunications technologies link employees, suppliers, and customers in different locations through the public Internet or in-house intranets. People with diverse skills now work together in "virtual departments" to develop new products. The technique of efficient consumer response (ECR) uses scanner technology to connect manufacturers with retailers and customers, filling orders quickly with minimum investment in inventory and even adjusting production automatically in response to changes in expected purchase patterns.

These technological advances are revolutionizing marketing. Companies can reach specific groups of customers in a variety of ways, from hotels' in-house television channels targeting guests to toll-free telephone numbers and in-store videos with point-of-purchase product demonstrations. Now that about 40 percent of all U.S. households have personal computers, online services and the Internet offer a new medium over which companies can market products and offer customer service. Marketing and sales departments can maintain and quickly access vast databases with information about customers and their buying patterns. They can develop targeted marketing campaigns and zoned advertising programs for consumers within a certain distance from a store and even specific city blocks.

Shoppers can visit kiosks in shopping malls that feature video displays, discount coupons, and product information for a variety of merchants. They can browse through a CD-ROM product catalog on their computers or conduct specific searches to quickly find desired items. Surfing the World Wide Web or online services is another way to get product information and order merchandise from catalogs. Firms can quickly update this information at minimal cost.

Technological innovations create whole new industries as well as new products within existing industries. Just five years ago, the Internet was an obscure computer network used mainly by researchers and educators. Today, it offers organizations and individuals a new, efficient way to communicate and access information. This industry is growing geometrically each year and includes the firms that provide the infrastructure (hardware and software) as well as new types of businesses. For example, financial services companies provide security for electronic transactions, and certain advertising agencies specialize in Internet-related promotions.

These and other technological developments play an important role in every phase of marketing, as you will see throughout the text. Each chapter begins with a case that illustrates how companies use technology to develop more effective marketing strategies. We also include many examples of the impact of technology on marketing, along with Web addresses of many featured companies so you can visit their home pages. Every chapter ends with a number of *'netWork* assignments that let you explore the Internet and take advantage of its capabilities in solving marketing problems. The text has been expanded through the creation of the Boone & Kurtz Home Page, which contains

http://www.dryden.com/mktng/boone/

additional case materials, up-to-date reports of recent marketing developments, and updates on people and organizations featured in the text.

As an example of the effect of the technological revolution on marketing consider two key developments: interactive marketing and the Internet.

Interactive Marketing

Interactive media technologies combine computers and telecommunications resources to create software that users can direct themselves. They allow people to digitize reports and drawings and transmit them, quickly and inexpensively, over phone lines, coaxial cables, or fiberoptic cables. They can subscribe to personalized news services that deliver article summaries on specified topics directly to their fax machines or computers. They can telecommute via e-mail, voice mail, fax, videoconferencing, and computer networks; pay bills using online banking services; and use online resources to get information about everything from investments to a local retailer's special sale, day-care facilities, and local entertainment activities for the upcoming weekend.[38]

Companies are now using interactivity in their marketing programs, as well. **Interactive marketing** refers to buyer-seller communications in which the customer controls the amount and type of information received from a marketer. This technique provides immediate access to key product information when the consumer wants it. "Every time you involve the consumer, you bring [him or her] closer to a sale," explains one advertising specialist.[39] Interactive techniques have been used for more than a decade; point-of-sale brochures and coupon dispensers are a simple form of interactive advertising. But today the term also includes two-way electronic communication using a variety of media such as the Internet, CD-ROM disks, and virtual reality kiosks.

Interactive marketing frees communications between marketers and their customers from the limits of the traditional, linear, one-way messages to passive audiences using broadcast or print ads. Now customers come to companies for information, creating opportunities for one-to-one marketing. For example, each customer who visits a Web site has a different experience, based on the pathway of links he or she chooses to follow. Interactive marketing can also allow many-to-many exchanges, where consumers can communicate with each other using e-mail or electronic bulletin boards.

Interactivity involves more than just moving from one section of a CD-ROM or Web page to another. These electronic conversations establish innovative relationships between users and the technology, providing customized information based on users' interests and levels of understanding. Interactive technologies support almost limitless exchanges of information. People gain access to chosen programs and services via their personal computers and telephones, and they can purchase products not only from stores but also via television or the Internet.

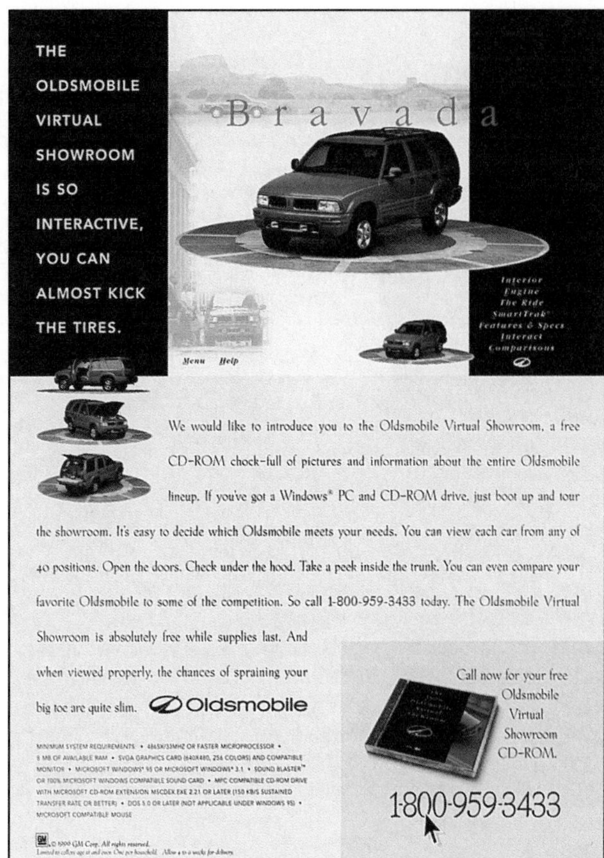
THE OLDSMOBILE VIRTUAL SHOWROOM IS SO INTERACTIVE, YOU CAN ALMOST KICK THE TIRES.
Bravada
Interior
Engine
The Ride
SmartTrak
Features & Specs
Interact
Comparisons
Menu
Help
We would like to introduce you to the Oldsmobile Virtual Showroom, a free CD-ROM chock-full of pictures and information about the entire Oldsmobile lineup. If you've got a Windows® PC and CD-ROM drive, just boot up and tour the showroom. It's easy to decide which Oldsmobile meets your needs. You can view each car from any of 40 positions. Open the doors. Check under the hood. Take a peek inside the trunk. You can even compare your favorite Oldsmobile to some of the competition. So call 1-800-959-3433 today. The Oldsmobile Virtual Showroom is absolutely free while supplies last. And when viewed properly, the chances of spraining your big toe are quite slim.
Oldsmobile
Call now for your free Oldsmobile Virtual Showroom CD-ROM.
1-800-959-3433

For the automobile shopper too reluctant (or too busy) to visit the Oldsmobile showroom, interactive marketing offers the next best thing in the form of a free CD-ROM. The "Virtual Showroom" offers a self-directed tour, permitting the car shopper to open any door, peer under the hood and in the trunk, ask questions, and get answers about options, financing, and all of the topics that arise during an actual visit to a dealership.

Customers become active participants in the interactive marketplace, controlling the amount and type of information they receive with the push of a button or click of a mouse. At Intouch Group's iStations, interactive kiosks in over 200 retail music stores, customers can listen to 30-second music samples from a huge selection of CDs, searching by artist and album. The kiosks also carry ads from companies like Toyota, Levi's, Coca-Cola, and Kraft; they even dispense discount coupons. Users of iStation who register and provide

Marketing Dictionary

interactive marketing Buyer-seller communications in which the customer controls the amount and type of information received from a marketer through such channels as the Internet, CD-ROM disks, interactive 800 telephone numbers, and virtual reality kiosks.

MARKETING HALL OF FAME

The Best Snake-Shaped Product Ever Made

To an outsider, Black & Decker Corp.'s new SnakeLight flashlight might have seemed at first like a marketing nightmare. While the typical flashlight costs about as much as a Big Mac dinner, the venerable consumer products company wanted to sell its improved model for $30. "Until the SnakeLight came into the market, the average price of a flashlight was somewhere around $5," observed John Venema, product general manager at Black & Decker's U.S. Household Products Group. "Selling a $30 flashlight in large quantities was not a small challenge."

But the product succeeded. Well over 1 million SnakeLights have been sold since its rollout for the 1994 holiday season, and the numbers keep rising.

http://www.blackanddecker.com/

The design of the pricey flashlight turned out to be an instant hit with consumers.

Unlike other flashlights, the SnakeLight provides a bendable handle. Its 2-foot, flexible cord will attach to just about anything; you can wrap it around a pole, a chain-link fence, or even your neck. You can even bend it into the shape of a snake and place it on a desk. The flashlight's main selling point is the handle that frees the user from holding it, allowing both hands to accomplish a task.

The SnakeLight was hardly a product fluke. Black & Decker, the world's largest producer of power tools and accessories, is known for its scrupulous attention to consumer needs. In fact, two of the firm's biggest

demographic information receive discount coupons. Retailers can also connect to the company's World Wide Web site, expanding the number of available CDs to over

http://www.worldwidemusic.com/

40,000. Web site visitors can join a music club, rate the albums, and provide other types of feedback to the company. "We'll be able to determine who is coming to the site, and target the advertising accordingly," says chief executive officer Josh Kaplan.[40]

Interactive marketing can transform and enhance customer relationships. Interactive promotions put the customer in control. They can easily get product information, tips on product usage, and answers to customer service questions; they can also tell the company what they like or dislike about a product, and they can just as easily click the Exit button and move on to another area. The challenge is attracting and holding consumer attention. Marketing departments and advertising agencies must develop new strategies based on interactive marketing techniques to build lasting customer relationships. Subsequent chapters will show how companies are successfully using interactive techniques in their marketing campaigns.

The Internet

Most of today's discussion of interactive marketing centers on the Internet. The **Internet** is an all-purpose global network composed of some 48,000 different networks around the globe that, within limits, lets anyone with access to a personal computer send and receive images and data anywhere. It grows at a phenomenal rate of 10 percent a week. Over 35 million Americans used the Internet or an online service in the past three months. Regular users—those who connect to the Internet for more than two hours per week—now number over 20 million. While the Internet is not yet a mass medium, it has moved beyond a fad. Businesses are entering the Net at the rate of 500 to 1,000 per day.[41] Some people use the Internet only for electronic mail (e-mail), while others spend hours online participating in newsgroups (discussion forums), gathering product information, performing sophisticated research, transferring data files, and downloading software.

The Internet provides an efficient way to find and share information, but until recently most people outside universities and government agencies found it difficult to

strengths are marketing and new-product development. One technique that helps Black & Decker executives to put a fresh face on traditional products like staplers and saws is rubbing elbows with customers to find out what they really need. For instance, Black & Decker officials shed their business suits when they visit home improvement centers, which are crawling with just their types of customers.

"When Black & Decker executives come to our stores, it's not a coat-and-tie thing," says Denny Ryan, a senior vice president of Home Depot in Atlanta. "It's like they have an orange apron on, same as our associates; they really work the aisles."

In the case of the SnakeLight, the company developed the flashlight after it discovered that 75 percent of consumers wanted both hands free when they used a flashlight. Black & Decker, however, couldn't just depend on a novel product to generate big sales; the firm developed a complete marketing campaign.

SnakeLight was positioned as a "task" light with catchy advertising. During the commercials, the song "The Wanderer" played while the SnakeLight appeared in different situations demonstrating how it could be used.

For an encore, Black & Decker will unveil other versions of its smash hit. There's already a SnakeFan that offers similar benefits.

QUESTIONS FOR CRITICAL THINKING

1. **Does Black & Decker apply the marketing concept? Use specific examples in your answer.**
2. **Discuss why the SnakeLight succeeded. Refer to the Web site listed on page 19 for ideas and suggestions on what helps a product succeed.**

Sources: Corporate profile of Black & Decker, downloaded from Black & Decker Web site, http://www.blackanddecker.com/, January 6, 1997; Leah Richard, "SnakeLight," *Advertising Age,* June 26, 1996, p. S2; "Black & Decker," *Hoover's Company Profile Database* (Austin, Tex.: Reference Press, 1996), downloaded from America Online May 20, 1996; and Jonathan Friedland, "Shoppers Talk, Black & Decker Listens, Profits," *Wall Street Journal,* January 9, 1995, pp. B1, B6.

use and learn. This changed in 1993 with the advent of browser technology that provides point-and-click access to the **World Wide Web (WWW** or **Web).** The Web is actually an interlinked collection of graphically rich information sources within the larger Internet. Web sites provide *hypermedia* resources, a system allowing storage of and access to text, graphics, audio, and video in so-called *pages* linked to each other in a way that integrates these different media elements. When a user clicks on a highlighted word or picture (icon), the browser converts the click to computer commands and brings the requested new information—text, photograph, chart, song, or movie clip—to the user's computer.

Today the Web is the most popular area of the Internet; the number of Web sites grew from less than 100 in 1993 to over 100,000 in 1996. It continues to double every two months.[42]

Compared to traditional media, the hypermedia resources of the Web offer a number of advantages. Data moves in seconds, without the user noticing that several computers in different locations combine to fulfill a request. Interactive control allows users to quickly access other information resources through related pages, either at the same or other sites, and easily navigate through documents. Because it is dynamic, Web site sponsors can easily keep information current. Finally, multimedia capacities increase the attractiveness of hypermedia documents.[43]

How Marketers Use the Web

Companies are rushing to establish themselves on the World Wide Web. It offers marketers a powerful, yet affordable way to reach customers across town or overseas, at almost any time, with interactive messages. The Pillsbury Bake-Off Web site is designed to spread the word

Marketing Dictionary

Internet An all-purpose global network composed of some 48,000 different networks around the globe that, within limits, lets anyone with access to a personal computer send and receive images and data anywhere.

World Wide Web (WWW or **Web)** An interlinked collection of graphically rich information sources within the larger Internet.

Figure 1.12 Selections from Pillsbury's Web Site

Netscape: Pillsbury Bake-Off Contest: The Scoop
Back
Forward
Home
Reload
Images
Open
Print
Find
Stop
Netscape
Location: http://www.bakeoff.com/bakeoff/scoop.html
What's New?
Search
News Groups
Directory
Mail
Help
PILLSBURY
Bake-Off
CONTEST
The Way America Cooks Today
HOMEPAGE
THE SCOOP
RECIPES
DOUGHBOY STUFF
HOW TO ENTER
CONTENTS
47 Years of America's Best-Loved Contest.
What's It All About?
For nearly a half-century, American cooks have been striving for the title of America's best amateur cook. Every two years, The Pillsbury Bake-Off Contest awards that "crown" to one talented cook whose original creation somehow emerges as truly superior. What is it that makes this contest the granddaddy of them all?
The first contest.
It all began in 1949 at the elegant Waldorf-Astoria Hotel in New York City, and contestants became overnight celebrities. So popular was the contest that Pillsbury executives decided to repeat it the next year.
Document: Done.

about the popular cooking competition to a wider audience than conventional media reach.

The company's strategy calls for modernizing the contest and giving it a fresh image. "Since our first contest, the Bake-Off has reflected the times. These are fast-paced, high-tech times, and we want the Bake-Off to be part of today's more digitally aware lifestyle," says Diane Slayton, Pillsbury group promotions director.[44] As Figure 1.12 shows, visitors to the site find an online kitchen with winning recipes—complete with downloadable color photos—from current and past contests, contest trivia, sweepstakes, a Pillsbury Doughboy video, and merchandise offers.

The online techniques that companies like Pillsbury and Hot Hot Hot use to market their businesses fall into four broad categories: interactive brochures, virtual storefronts, information clearinghouses, and customer service tools.[45]

- *Interactive brochures* that provide company, product, and service information are among the most popular high-tech marketing applications. These range from simple, one-page electronic flyers to multimedia presentations. In addition to the standard product, company, and shareholder information, the Colgate-Palmolive site has Kid's World, an area designed to teach children about good dental care. Children can visit the No-Cavities Clubhouse, color pictures in a story book, and send e-mail to the Tooth Fairy.[46]

http://www.colgate.com/
http://www.mtsobek.com/

- Mountain Travel-Sobek, an adventure travel agency, uses its Web site to publish "Hot News," a weekly online newsletter with trip descriptions and travel information like the political climates in various countries. Almost 80,000 people read "Hot News" each month.
- Founder Richard Bangs likes the low cost of electronic marketing literature. "Can you imagine if we tried to mail these every week? Now I just push one button, and 'Hot News' goes to everybody," he says. He attributes a large part of the company's 37 percent increase in business to its "media experiments."[47]
- The **virtual storefront** takes the interactive brochure one step further and allows customers to view and order merchandise. At the Godiva Chocolate site, consumers can read about the history of chocolate, browse through product offerings, and then place orders.

http://www.godiva.com/
http://www.nordstrom-pta.com/

- Web stores can be stand-alone operations, like Godiva and Hot Hot Hot, or grouped in *cybermalls* with links to 30 to 100 participating retailers. Some use popular national retailers to "anchor" the malls and draw traffic. Among the cyberstores at MCI Marketplace are Borders Books and Music, Day-Timers, Hammacher Schlemmer, L'Eggs, The Mac Zone, Nordstrom, and PC Zone.
- *Information clearinghouses* provide in-depth product information. Consumers can ask questions and get online answers, and companies can hold virtual meetings (online conferences) and

sponsor discussion groups. British firm Accelerated Learning Systems maintains an online journal with articles of interest to educators.

- The Web can also be a *customer service tool.* Consumers can order catalogs and refer to lists of frequently-asked customer questions with answers. Shoppers can send questions to company representatives and place service orders online. Federal Express lets customers download package tracking software from its Web site.
- This customer service feature is surprisingly popular and cost effective. Sun Microsystems saves $250,000 each quarter in toll-free phone calls from customers who go directly to its Web site for product information, updates, and documentation.[48]

Regardless of the type of information on its Web site, a marketer first must attract consumers to visit. One way to generate traffic is to advertise on other heavy-traffic sites. Directories and search engines, such as Yahoo!, Excite, and Alta Vista, prove especially helpful in pointing users toward Web sites. Traffic to the Federal Express site increased 40 percent after it placed such an ad. Links from other Web sites also bring visitors. Car-rental firm Rent-a-Wreck of America links about 500 other travel-related sites, listing any site it feels will add value for its customers.[49]

Despite the hype about the Web and how it can transform business, the fact remains that this medium is still in its embryonic stages. While some hail it as the first major change in marketing and advertising since commercial television, no one can yet predict whether it will have an impact as great as that of TV. Properly used, the Internet and WWW should prove to be powerful tools to promote connections, build associations, deliver information, and create online communities.

To date, few companies have made money on the Internet. The primary beneficiaries have been firms marketing Net-related goods or services—for example, computer networking equipment; software such as access, browser, Web page authoring, and e-mail programs; consultants and Web page creators; Internet access and online service providers like PsiNet, Netcom, America Online, and CompuServe; and companies offering sites where companies can advertise. But the Net brings strong potential for profits; Web-related goods and services generated revenues of over $700 million in 1995, with another $1.5 billion to commercial online services and access providers. By 2000, the total is expected to top $45 billion. Of that, spending for Web advertising, now about $75 million, should jump to $2.6 billion.[50]

Why
just surf
when you can
ski?
http://www.SkiNet.com
For the seriously cool skier.

***Ski Magazine* and *Skiing Magazine* use print ads to attract consumers to their SkiNet Web site.**

As the Web evolves, marketers need to explore its capabilities and learn the best ways to use it effectively as an extension of other communications media. Among the questions marketers need to ask are:

- What types of goods and services can be successfully marketed on the Web?
- What characteristics make a successful Web presentation?
- Does the Net offer a secure way to process customer orders?
- How will the Net affect traditional store-based and non-store retailing and distribution?
- What is the best use of this technology in a

Marketing Dictionary

virtual storefront Form of interactive media that allows customers to view and order merchandise.

SOLVING AN ETHICAL CONTROVERSY

Should the Government Regulate Internet Advertisers?

One of the most volatile issues confronting advertisers who embrace the Internet to market their products is consumer privacy. Marketers see their ability to collect consumer data on this new advertising frontier as a powerful way to respond to customers' needs. Consumer advocates, however, worry that the Internet is just another insidious way that marketers can violate individuals' privacy rights.

There is little debate that firms are collecting a great deal of personal information about their customers. Some corporations sponsor contests that require Internet users to divulge their e-mail addresses or names. On Perrier's World Wide Web site, for instance, visitors who reveal how much sparkling water they drink are eligible to win a year's supply of Perrier. On another Web site, a music retailer offers $1 off each purchase if visitors fill out a questionnaire.

What remains controversial is what these inquisitive companies can do with all this potentially valuable data. Armed with such information about its customers, corporations have the opportunity to improve their products and marketing strategies to generate heftier profits. But companies can also raise cash by selling this information to third parties. In fact, the sale of consumer profiles has mushroomed into a multi-billion dollar industry.

PRO

1. **Consumers need government protection because they are no match for clever marketers. A disturbing 80 percent of U.S. respondents to a Harris Poll agreed that they had lost control over how their personal information is disseminated by corporate America. But at the same time, 59 percent said they had tried to fight back by refusing to provide information they thought was too personal or unnecessary.**
2. **While advertisers feel justified in passing along personal information unless the consumer explicitly forbids it, consumer advocates disagree. "The burden has to be on the company to get the consumer's permission," says David Banisar of the Electronic Privacy Information Center in Washington, D.C.**
3. **Some materials should be off limits to advertisers. Such data should include public records concerning home ownership,**

specific firm's marketing strategy: promotion, image building, sales?

As forthcoming chapters discuss specific marketing topics, we will revisit the Internet and look for answers to these and other questions.

FROM TRANSACTION-BASED MARKETING TO RELATIONSHIP MARKETING

As marketing enters the twenty-first century, a significant change is taking place in the way companies interact with customers. The traditional view of marketing as a simple exchange process—a concept that might be termed *transaction-based marketing*—is being replaced by a different, longer-term approach.

Traditional marketing strategies focused on attracting customers. The goal was to identify prospects, convert them to customers, and complete sales transactions. But today's marketers realize that, although it remains important, attracting new customers is only an intermediate step in the marketing process. Marketing efforts must focus on establishing and maintaining mutually beneficial relationships with existing customers. These efforts must expand to include suppliers and employees, as well.

This concept, called **relationship marketing,** refers to the development, growth, and maintenance of long-term, cost-effective exchange relationships with individual customers, suppliers, employees, and other partners for mutual benefit. It broadens the scope of external marketing relationships to include suppliers, customers, and referral sources. In relationship marketing, the term *customer* takes on new meaning. Employees serve customers within an organization as well as outside it; individual employees and their departments are customers of and suppliers to each other. They must apply the same high standards of customer satisfaction to intradepartmental relationships as they do to external customer relationships. Relationship marketing recognizes the critical importance of *internal marketing* to the success of *external marketing* plans. Programs that improve customer service inside a company also raise productivity and staff

car loans, driver's license information, and medical records.

CON

1. **Advertisers argue that it is premature to enact laws that would tighten the noose around their cyberspace data collecting. "Let's not create new rules for a new medium before the medium develops," says John Kamp of the Association of Accredited Advertising Agencies. "If you write them first, they almost always have unintended consequences."**
2. **Voluntary controls imposed by the advertising industry itself offer the best way to handle privacy concerns. One trade group, the Coalition for Advertising-supported Information and Entertainment, recently developed its own Internet privacy goals. The coalition's guidelines suggest that marketers reveal their identities and make only "appropriate" use of personal information.**
3. **Let consumers—not the government—decide whether they want information about themselves passed along to direct marketing circles. Many companies now offer consumers the option of being excluded from marketing lists when they sign up for services or register products.**

Summary

Advertisers believe that a freer flow of information about consumers' likes and dislikes through the Internet will bring about only better, more personalized service to customers. The industry compares its services to the personal touch of a luxury hotel that presents handwritten notes to its repeat customers.

But opponents see a darker side to the rush for cyberspace consumer profiles. "Soon," says Marc Rotenberg, head of the Electronic Privacy Information Center, "you won't be able to drop a piece of e-mail without someone knowing about it, someone selling it, someone buying it."

Sources: Steven Brier, "There's No Guarantee of Privacy on the Internet," *New York Times,* January 13, 1997, downloaded from http://www.nyt.com/, March 4, 1997; Sally Goll Beatty, "Consumer Privacy on the Internet Goes Public," *Wall Street Journal,* February 12, 1996, p. B3; Bruce Horovitz, "Out in Cyberspace, You're Often Not Alone," *USA Today,* December 19, 1995, p. 2A; and Bruce Knecht, "Is Big Brother Watching Your Dinner and Other Worries of Privacy Watchers," *Wall Street Journal,* November 11, 1995, pp. B1, B3.

morale, resulting in better customer relationships outside the firm.

Relationship marketing gives a company new opportunities to gain a competitive edge by moving customers up a loyalty hierarchy from *new customers* to *regular purchasers,* then to *loyal supporters* of the company and its goods and services, and finally to *advocates* who not only buy the company's products but recommend them to others.[51] By converting indifferent customers into loyal ones, companies generate repeat sales. The cost of maintaining existing customers is far below the cost of finding new ones, and these loyal customers are profitable ones. A study of over 100 service firms showed that a 5 percent reduction in customer defection rates improved profits anywhere from 25 to 85 percent.[52]

Programs to encourage customer loyalty are not new. Walt Disney Co. formed its Magic Kingdom Club in 1957 to offer special Disneyland discounts to employees of nearby companies. Today, the club operates around the world, and offers members discounts at more than 27,000 participating organizations; in addition, over 6 million cardholders receive a special magazine, ticket and merchandise discounts, and special discounts with Disney partners like Delta Airlines and National Car Rental. Through the Magic Kingdom Club, Disney communicates frequently with members, encouraging them and their families to visit the theme parks more often, stay longer, and select Disney resorts for lodging. The club program also allows Disney to gather a wealth of demographic and membership behavior information.[53]

The Magic Kingdom Club is an example of one firm creating and maintaining good customer relationships as vital strategic weapons. By identifying current purchasers,

Marketing Dictionary

relationship marketing Development and maintenance of long-term, cost-effective exchange relationships with individual customers, suppliers, employees, and other partners for mutual benefit.

Figure 1.13 **The Disneyland–Delta Air Lines Strategic Alliance**

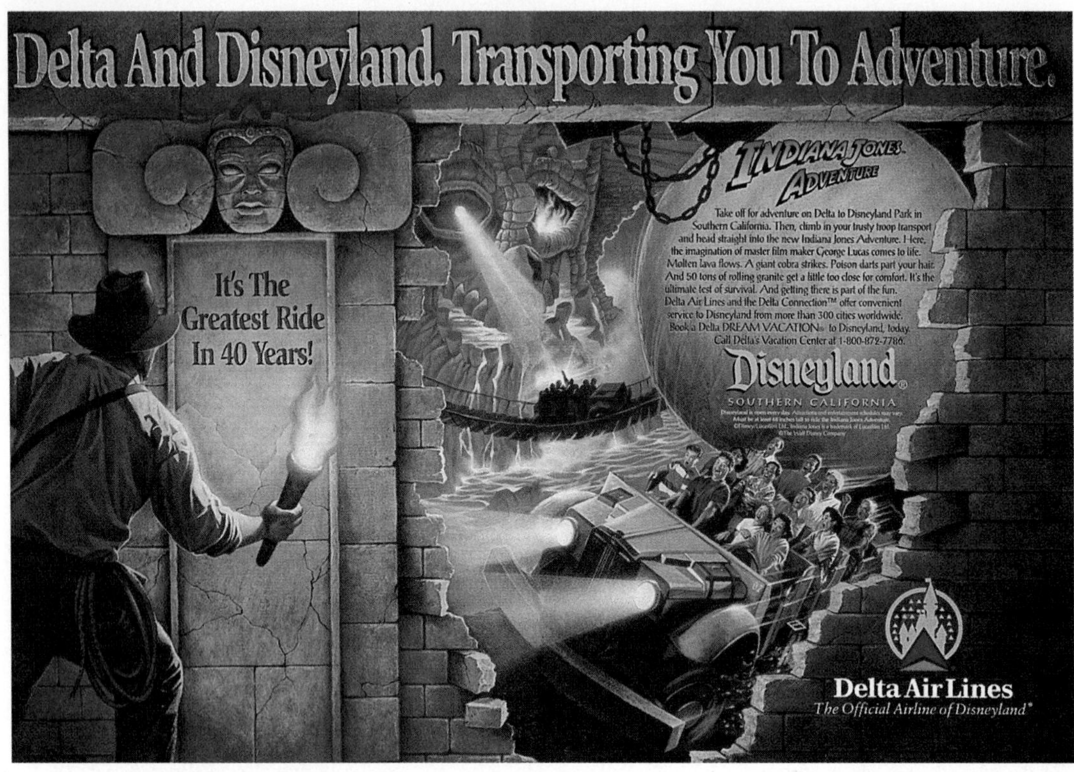
Delta And Disneyland. Transporting You To Adventure.
It's The Greatest Ride In 40 Years!
Indiana Jones Adventure
Take off for adventure on Delta to Disneyland Park in Southern California. Then, climb in your trusty troop transport and head straight into the new Indiana Jones Adventure. Here, the imagination of master film maker George Lucas comes to life. Molten lava flows. A giant cobra strikes. Poison darts part your hair. And 50 tons of rolling granite get a little too close for comfort. It's the ultimate test of survival. And getting there is part of the fun. Delta Air Lines and the Delta Connection™ offer convenient service to Disneyland from more than 300 cities worldwide. Book a Delta DREAM VACATION to Disneyland, today. Call Delta's Vacation Center at 1-800-872-7786.
Disneyland
SOUTHERN CALIFORNIA
Delta Air Lines
The Official Airline of Disneyland

studying their buying habits and preferences, and maintaining positive relationships with them, organizations efficiently target their best customers. In fact, most companies find that the bulk of their profits come from a small group of highly loyal, heavy-user customers, increasing the importance of a customer-driven marketing strategy.

Effective relationship marketing relies heavily on information technologies such as computer databases that record customers' tastes, price preferences, and lifestyles along with the increase of electronic communications. This technology helps companies become one-to-one marketers that gather customer-specific information and provide individually customized goods and services. The firms target their marketing programs to appropriate groups, rather than relying on mass-marketing campaigns. "Successful companies get their product to conform to the needs of the customer. . . . This sense that the market has shifted control to the consumer is profound. It will never be reversed," says Barry Sullivan, corporate vice president for Electronic Data Systems.[54]

Companies who study their customers' preferences and react accordingly gain distinct competitive edges. Waldenbooks' Preferred Reader program gives members a 10 percent discount on all purchases and targets those who spend at least $100 a year. (The annual membership fee is $10.) Tracking purchases also provides valuable information about customer preferences. The retailer then responds by notifying customers of such events as the publication dates of a favorite author's next novel or when the writer will be autographing books in local stores.[55]

Firms in the service industry, from retailers to hotels to airlines, are among the leaders in relationship marketing. Their staff members have many opportunities to meet customers personally and build loyalty and repeat business. Rewards for frequent buyers of a firm's goods or services, such as hotel programs that reward frequent visitors with free room stays and other travel discounts, are another form of relationship marketing.

Developing Partnerships and Strategic Alliances

Relationship marketing doesn't apply just to individual consumers and employees, however. It also affects a wide range of other markets, including business-to-business relationships with the company's suppliers and distributors as well as other types of corporate partnerships. In the past, companies have often viewed their suppliers as adversaries against whom they must fiercely negotiate prices, playing one off against the other. This attitude is much less prevalent today, however, as companies find benefits from collaborative relationships.

The formation of **strategic alliances**—partnerships that create competitive advantages—is also on the rise. These take many forms, from product development partnerships that involve shared costs for research and development and marketing to vertical alliances where one company provides a product or component to another firm, which distributes or sells it under its own brand. Figure 1.13 illustrates how the Delta Air Lines and Disneyland partnership creates a strategic advantage for both firms. By jointly marketing the Disneyland theme park as a vacation destination, both firms benefit through increased sales of airline tickets, gate admissions, and merchandise.

Table 1.5 Eight Universal Marketing Functions

Marketing Function	Description
A. EXCHANGE FUNCTIONS	
1. Buying	Ensuring that product offerings are available in sufficient quantities to meet customer demands
2. Selling	Using advertising, personal selling, and sales promotion to match goods and services to customer needs
B. PHYSICAL DISTRIBUTION FUNCTIONS	
3. Transporting	Moving products from their points of production to locations convenient for purchasers
4. Storing	Warehousing products until needed for sale
C. FACILITATING FUNCTIONS	
5. Standardizing and grading	Ensuring that product offerings meet established quality and quantity control standards of size, weight, and other product variables
6. Financing	Providing credit for channel members (wholesalers and retailers) or consumers
7. Risk taking	Dealing with uncertainty about consumer purchases resulting from creation and marketing of goods and services that consumers may purchase in the future
8. Securing marketing information	Collecting information about consumers, competitors, and channel members (wholesalers and retailers) for use in making marketing decisions

One of the most popular forms of strategic alliance is the affinity credit card program. Airline industry leaders like American, United, and Delta build brand loyalty among air travelers by offering awards for frequent travel. They have also established cooperative relationships with hotel chains, auto-rental companies, long-distance telephone firms, and credit-card companies to jointly market their services.

Co-marketing and licensing arrangements are also popular alliances. Kraft Foods teamed up with Viacom's Nickelodeon cable network to jointly promote kid-related brands. Kraft launched a $10 million promotional campaign that aired during Nickelodeon's afternoon programming block. Nickelodeon characters and logos appeared on a variety of Kraft products, from Oscar Meyer hot dogs to Post cereals and Jell-O molds in the shapes of cartoon characters. This co-marketing program put the "Nick" name on about 300 million Kraft packages.[56]

Clearly, relationship building begins early in the marketing process and applies to many areas. It begins with the development of quality products that meet customer needs and continues with the provision of excellent customer service during and after the purchase process. Relationship building also includes programs that encourage repeat purchases and foster customer loyalty. Chapter 10 explores the many facets of this important topic in greater depth.

COSTS AND FUNCTIONS OF MARKETING

Firms must spend money to create time, place, and ownership utilities. Numerous attempts have been made to measure marketing costs in relation to overall product costs and service costs, and most estimates have ranged between 40 and 60 percent. On the average, one-half of the costs involved in a product such as Pizza Hut pizza, an ounce of Joy perfume, a pair of Calvin Klein jeans, or even a European vacation can be traced directly to marketing. These costs are not associated with fabrics, raw materials and other ingredients, baking, sewing, or any of the other production functions necessary for creating form utility. What, then, does the consumer receive in return for this 50 percent marketing cost? What functions does marketing perform?

As Table 1.5 reveals, marketing is responsible for the performance of eight universal functions: buying, selling, transporting, storing, standardizing and grading, financing, risk taking, and securing marketing information. Some

Marketing Dictionary

strategic alliance Partnership between organizations that creates competitive advantages.

functions are performed by manufacturers, others by retailers, and still others by marketing intermediaries called *wholesalers.*

Buying and selling, the first two functions shown in Table 1.5, represent *exchange functions. Buying* is important to marketing on several levels. Marketers must determine how and why consumers buy certain goods and services. To be successful, they must seek to understand consumer behavior. In addition, retailers and other intermediaries must seek out products that will appeal to their customers. Since they generate time, place, and ownership utilities through these purchases, they must anticipate consumer preferences for purchases to be made several months later. *Selling* is the second half of the exchange process. It involves advertising, personal selling, and sales promotion in an attempt to match the firm's goods and services to consumer needs.

Transporting and storing are *physical distribution functions. Transporting* involves the physical movement of goods from the seller to the purchaser. *Storing* involves warehousing goods until they are needed for sale. Manufacturers, wholesalers, and retailers all typically perform these functions.

The final four marketing functions—standardizing and grading, financing, risk taking, and securing market information—are often called *facilitating functions* because they assist the marketer in performing the exchange and physical distribution functions. Quality and quantity control *standards* and *grades,* frequently set by federal or state governments, reduce the need for purchasers to inspect each item. Specific tire sizes, for example, permit buyers to request needed sizes and to expect uniform sizes.

Financing is another marketing function, because buyers often need access to funds in order to finance inventories prior to sales. Manufacturers often provide financing for their wholesale and retail customers. Some types of wholesalers perform similar functions for their retail customers. Finally, retailers frequently permit their customers to buy on credit.

The seventh function, *risk taking,* is part of most ventures. Manufacturers create goods and services based on research and their belief that consumers need them. Wholesalers and retailers acquire inventory based on similar expectations of future consumer demand. Entrepreneurial risk takers accommodate these uncertainties about future consumer behavior when they market goods and services.

The final marketing function involves *securing marketing information.* Marketers gather information to meet the need for decision-oriented input about customers—who they are, what they buy, where they buy, and how they buy. By collecting and analyzing marketing information, marketers also seek to understand why consumers purchase some goods and services and reject others.

ETHICS AND SOCIAL RESPONSIBILITY: DOING WELL BY DOING GOOD

In recent years, headlines have publicized unethical conduct by several well-known businesses. The U.S. Department of Justice investigated allegations of global price-fixing and other illegal activities by agribusiness giant Archer-Daniels-Midland. Bausch & Lomb came under fire for accounting and ethical abuses, including inflating sales, using fake invoices, and pressuring distributors to take unwanted inventory. Talk-show hostess Kathy Lee Gifford was the subject of allegations that her line of clothing was manufactured by ill-paid workers operating in sweatshop conditions.

Despite these and other alleged breaches of ethical standards, most businesspeople do follow ethical practices. Over half of all major corporations now offer ethics training to employees, and most corporate mission statements include pledges to protect the environment, contribute to communities, and improve workers' lives. In some cases, only media attention and pressure from consumers motivate companies to implement social responsibility programs. In response to rising antismoking sentiment in the United States, Philip Morris launched a marketing campaign aimed at reducing smoking by youths. With ads like the one shown in Figure 1.14, the company communicates its position on underage smoking and promotes its Action Against Access program to prevent cigarette sales to minors.

Such programs often produce benefits like improved customer relationships, increased employee loyalty, marketplace success, and improved financial performance. Finast, a Cleveland-based retail chain, is one company that has discovered a way to do well by doing good. Instead of following the all-too-common approach of simply closing marginal outlets located in the inner city, Finast has chosen a different path. Five new Finast superstores recently opened in inner-city Cleveland; another six nearby stores have been remodeled. Two-thirds of the stores are profitable, and sales are growing rapidly despite higher costs to the company for additional services like security guards. Finast even installed calculators on grocery carts so that customers wouldn't come to the checkout lane with more items than they could afford; this step reduced the costly need to restock the unwanted products. By providing customers with a wide selection of quality products, Finast saw its profits rise as shoppers bought more produce, meat, and fish, which carry higher margins than packaged goods.[57]

Many companies sponsor community-based programs. Price/Costco warehouse stores around the country participate in a variety of programs like Youth Business

Figure 1.14 Philip Morris "Action Against Access" Promotional Message

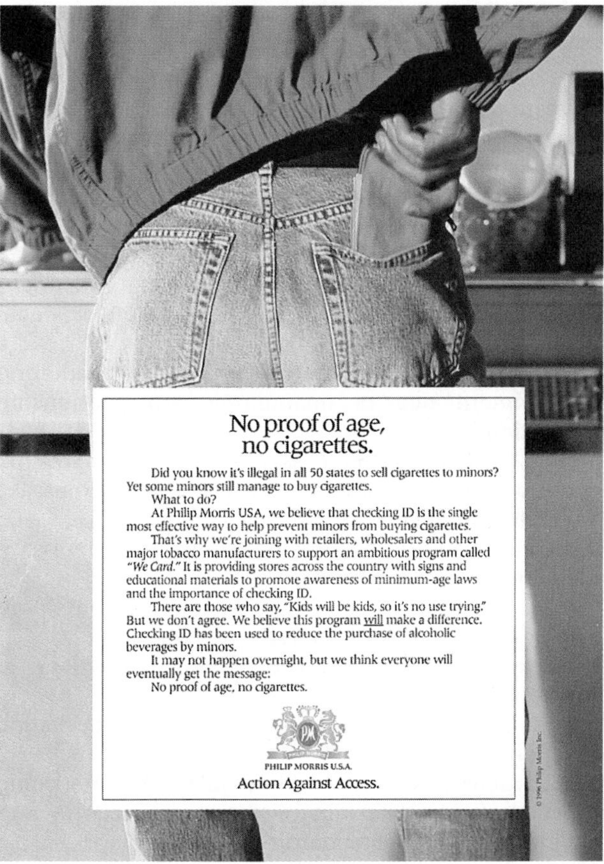
No proof of age,
no cigarettes.
Did you know it's illegal in all 50 states to sell cigarettes to minors? Yet some minors still manage to buy cigarettes.
What to do?
At Philip Morris USA, we believe that checking ID is the single most effective way to help prevent minors from buying cigarettes.
That's why we're joining with retailers, wholesalers and other major tobacco manufacturers to support an ambitious program called "We Card." It is providing stores across the country with signs and educational materials to promote awareness of minimum-age laws and the importance of checking ID.
There are those who say, "Kids will be kids, so it's no use trying." But we don't agree. We believe this program will make a difference. Checking ID has been used to reduce the purchase of alcoholic beverages by minors.
It may not happen overnight, but we think everyone will eventually get the message:
No proof of age, no cigarettes.
PHILIP MORRIS U.S.A.
Action Against Access.
© 1996 Philip Morris Inc.

Day, which introduces students to the expectations of the workplace. In San Diego, the stores hosted Special Occasions trade shows to raise funds for the Children's Miracle Network. Through its partnership with a local elementary school, employees at the Silverdale, Washington Price/Costco outlet touched the lives of the students and their families, most of whom live at the poverty level. In addition to providing gifts like backpacks, Halloween pumpkins, and holiday food baskets, employees serve as tutors and mentors for students and teach them about the jobs at the store.[58]

Because ethics and social responsibility are important topics to marketers, each chapter in this book includes an experiential exercise called "Solving an Ethical Controversy." For example, this chapter's feature presents pro and con arguments about whether government should regulate advertising on the Internet to protect consumer privacy. Chapter 3 will discuss ethics and social issues in greater detail.

THE STUDY OF MARKETING

Marketing is a pervasive element in contemporary life. In one form or another, it reaches every person. This chapter concludes with a list of three of the most important things for students to know about marketing:

1. Marketing costs passed on to consumers may account for the largest percentage of their personal expenditures. As pointed out earlier, approximately 50 percent of the total cost for the average product pays for marketing.

   Cost alone, however, does not indicate the value of marketing. The living standards of citizens in highly developed nations are in large part a function of their countries' efficient marketing systems. When considered in this perspective, the costs of marketing seem reasonable. For example, marketing expands sales, thereby spreading fixed production costs over more units of output and reducing total output costs. Reduced costs offset many marketing costs.

2. Many students have a good chance of becoming marketers. Marketing-related occupations account for 25 to 30 percent of the jobs in the typical highly industrialized nation. History has shown that the demand for effective marketers is not affected by cyclical economic fluctuations.

   A recent survey by executive recruiter Korn/Ferry International revealed that the best route to the top of the corporate ladder begins in marketing. The reasons why three of every eight CEOs are chosen from a company's marketing division: an increasingly global economy and the fight for worldwide market share demands proven market leaders to lead the battle. Finance, which had long dominated as the top career path for senior executives, fell to third place with executives who had completed international assignments in second.[59]

3. Marketing provides an opportunity to contribute to society as well as to an individual company. Marketing decisions affect everyone's welfare. Opportunities to advance to more responsible decision-making positions come sooner in marketing than in most occupations. (Societal aspects of marketing are covered in detail in later chapters.)

Why study marketing? The answer is simple: Marketing influences numerous facets of daily life as well as the future careers and economic well-being of almost everybody, to some degree. It is little wonder that marketing is now one of the most popular fields of academic study.

ACHIEVEMENT CHECK SUMMARY

Reread the learning goals that follow, and consider the questions for each goal. Answering these questions will reinforce your grasp of the most important concepts in the chapter and allow you to check how well you have achieved these learning goals. Where a blank appears before a question, answer with *T* or *F;* for multiple-choice questions, circle the letter of the correct answer.

Objective 1.1: Explain how marketing creates utility through the exchange process.

1. ___ Utility is the want-satisfying power of a good or service.
create exchanges of value to satisfy perceived needs.

2. ___ The marketing function creates form utility when it assembles a product, such as a television set, from component parts.

3. ___ Marketing is defined as a series of activities that

Objective 1.2: Contrast marketing activities during the four eras in the history of marketing.

1. ___ Product marketing was a major activity during the production era.

2. ___ Which of the following strategies did not form part of the sales era?

a. Companies rely on sales forces and advertising to convince customers to buy.

b. Marketing activities begin after the completion of the production process.

c. Product benefits are a primary focus of the marketing strategy.

3. ___ The relationship era emphasizes the importance of acquiring new customers.

Objective 1.3: Define the marketing concept and its relationship to marketing myopia.

1. ___ In a buyer's market, supply exceeds demand.

2. ___ The marketing concept requires an organization to orient all of its activities toward the consumer.

3. ___ Focusing narrowly on a product rather than customer needs helps a company to grow.

Objective 1.4: Describe the five types of nontraditional marketing.

1. ___ A campaign by Disneyland to attract new visitors is an example of organization marketing.

2. ___ Only not-for-profit organizations use person, place, cause, event, and organization marketing.

3. ___ The Mormon Church, Metropolitan Museum of Art, U.S. Air Force, and Cedars-Sinai Hospital would be most likely to use:

a. person marketing
b. place marketing
c. cause marketing
d. event marketing
e. organization marketing

Objective 1.5: Identify the 0basic elements of a marketing strategy and the environmental characteristics that influence strategy decisions.

1. ___ The first step in developing a marketing strategy is to: (a) create a product to sell; (b) select a target market; (c) develop a pricing strategy; (d) design a promotional campaign.

2. ___ Product strategy, pricing strategy, distribution strategy, and promotional strategy are components of the marketing environment.

3. ___ Compaq Computer decided to reduce its prices in response to changes in the political–legal environment.

Objective 1.6: Outline the changes in the marketing environment due to technology and relationship marketing.

1. ___ Companies should replace traditional marketing communications channels with new technologies like CD-ROM and the World Wide Web.

2. ___ A television advertising campaign is an example of interactive marketing.

3. ___ The main reason companies use the World Wide Web is to provide customer service.

Objective 1.7: Highlight the universal functions of marketing.

1. ___ Buying and selling are categorized as facilitating functions.

2. ___ Quality control is an example of the marketing function of: (a) risk taking; (b) storing; (c) securing market information; (d) standardizing and grading.

3. ___ Some wholesalers perform the financing function for their retail customers.

Objective 1.8: Demonstrate the relationship between ethical business practices and marketplace success.

1. ___ The cost of social responsibility and ethical conduct generally exceeds the business value they create.

2. ___ Environmental protection measures like pollution control and recycling are the responsibility of government, not business.

Objective 1.9: List three reasons for studying marketing.

1. ___ Marketing costs may account for about 25 percent of a consumer's personal expenditures.

2. ___ Efficient marketing systems raise a country's standard of living.

Students: See the solutions section located on page S-1 to check your responses to the Achievement Check Summary.

Key Terms

utility
marketing
exchange process
production orientation
sales orientation
seller's market

buyer's market
consumer orientation
marketing concept
marketing myopia
person marketing
place marketing
cause marketing
event marketing
organization marketing
target market
marketing mix
product strategy
pricing strategy
distribution strategy
promotional strategy
technology
interactive marketing
Internet
World Wide Web
virtual storefront
relationship marketing
strategic alliance

Review Questions

1. Identify the types of utility created by marketing. What types are created in each example?
   a. One-day bicycle rental outlet
   b. One-hour photo processing store
   c. Busch Gardens amusement park
   d. annual New Orleans Jazz and Heritage Festival
   e. factory outlet shopping mall
2. Relate the definition of *marketing* to the concept of the exchange process.
3. Discuss the production and sales eras. How does the marketing era differ from the previous eras?
4. How does relationship marketing expand the marketing concept?
5. Explain the concept of marketing myopia. Why is this problem likely to occur? What steps can reduce the likelihood of its occurrence?
6. Explain the concepts of person marketing and event marketing. Contrast them with marketing of a consumer product such as magazines. Why is cause marketing more difficult than place, event, or organization marketing?
7. What type of not-for-profit marketing does each example represent?
   a. American Medical Association advertisement
   b. "Buy Recycled and Save" slogan
   c. "Taiwan. Lighting the way to business in Asia." TV commercial
   d. "Feinstein for Senator" campaign
   e. Special Olympics appeal
   f. Smithsonian Institution catalog
   g. University of Hawaii brochure
   h. Junior Achievement banquet
8. Identify the major variables of the marketing mix. Briefly contrast the mix variables in not-for-profit marketing with those involved in profit-oriented marketing.
9. What are the components of the marketing environment? Why are these characteristics not separate from the marketing mix? Is the target market a component of the marketing mix? Briefly describe some technological innovations that are changing the marketing environment.
10. Categorize the following marketing functions as exchange functions, physical distribution functions, or facilitating functions. Choose a local retail store, and give an example of how it performs each of these eight functions:
    a. Buying
    b. Financing
    c. Securing marketing information
    d. Standardizing and grading
    e. Selling
    f. Risk taking
    g. Storing
    h. Transporting

Discussion Questions

1. Identify two firms that you feel reflect the philosophies of each of the following eras. Defend your answers.
   a. Production era
   b. Sales era
   c. Marketing era
   d. Relationship era
2. How would you explain marketing and its importance in the economy to someone not familiar with the subject? Identify the product and the consumer market for each of the following organizations:
   a. Local public broadcasting television station
   b. American Leukemia Society
   c. Fat-free snack foods
   d. Orlando Magic basketball team
3. Describe an experience you had as a customer in which a company used relationship marketing techniques to build customer loyalty.
4. Do you think the World Wide Web is an effective marketing tool? Why or why not? How will the Web and other technological advances affect the way you select and purchase goods in the future?
5. Can a profit-seeking company realistically expect to "do well by doing good"? Explain your answer, using examples.

'netWork

1. The Internet's success as a marketing tool is determined by its ability to provide more utility than traditional advertising or store visits. Visit one of the leading Internet market research sites

http://www.nielsenmedia.com/

and use the information you find to describe the firms likely to be most successful in marketing on the Internet. Which are likely to encounter the most difficulties with Internet marketing?

2. Visit one of the Internet malls such as

http://Internet-mall.com/ or http://www.21stcenturyplaza.com/

Critically evaluate this approach to marketing. What recommendations would you make to improve this shopping experience?

3. The Internet is already spawning new products and even entire new industries. For instance, a remote control mouse device for Web browsing is now available

http://www.logitech.com/

What marketing utilities are promised for purchasers of this product? In your opinion, is this product likely to prove a marketplace success? Why or why not?

VIDEO CASE 1

A SEARCH ENGINE NAMED YAHOO!

Rare is the Net surfer who remains unacquainted with "Yet Another Hierarchical Officious Oracle," better known as Yahoo! With 170,000 new pages daily joining the 90 million pages already on the World Wide Web, search engines like Yahoo! have become indispensable tools to help Web travelers navigate through the Internet and find information. On a typical day, 2 million visitors will access the Yahoo! site.

Yahoo! creators Jerry Yang and David Filo trace the beginnings of their company to 1994 when, as Ph.D. students at Stanford, they started compiling lists of their favorite Web pages. This activity led to the creation of a free directory called *David's Guide to the World Wide Web.* The enthusiastically positive response from people who used the directory convinced Yang and Filo to turn their hobby into a business. They conducted market research by asking other Internet surfers for suggestions, and they developed customized software to locate, identify, and edit material stored on the Internet. Then they launched Yahoo! "My dad used to call us yahoos," says Filo, "which is fitting since the Internet is a wild frontier."

The explosive growth of the Internet coupled with corresponding increases in the number of users created a need for a search engine like Yahoo! "Somebody could create a great Web page about soccer," explains Filo, "but nobody would know it was there. What we did was organize the Web for people." When a user clicks on Yahoo!, the screen displays an alphabetized list of topics ranging from *entertainment* to *social sciences.* Clicking on a topic button such as entertainment calls up another list with subcategories like books, comics, and television. Keeping in mind their target market of young Internet users, most under 35, Yang and Filo decided to create a separate series of "cool links," as well. This feature, labeled "the coolest stuff on the Web," enabled Yahoo! users to quickly connect with exciting Web pages like the FBI's Ten Most Wanted list and NASA's space shuttle information.

Yang and Filo's marketing plan specified sources of revenues that would ensure profitability. To encourage use of the site, Yahoo! does not charge users for the service itself. Instead, the firm generates revenues from advertising and licensing fees paid by online services. A Yahoo! advertiser pays a fee for each *impression,* that is, every time a computer loads a Web page with its ad.

A major event in Yahoo's success occurred when Netscape chose to replace Netscape Destinations with Netscape Guide by Yahoo! This move made Yahoo! the default directory for the company's Netscape Communicator Web browser suite. When Navigator users click on the Guide button, they are automatically routed to Yahoo! and offered a choice of eight of the most popular information categories on the Web.

Even though they pioneered search engine technology, Yang and Filo realized that others could easily duplicate their service. They knew that their long-term success depended on adding customer value to what was otherwise a commodity-type product. Indeed, competitors such as Excite, Lycos, and Infoseek quickly entered the new industry. As Yang put it, "If we are a tools company, we are not going to survive. Microsoft will just take over our space. If we are a publication, like a *Fortune* or a *Time,* and we create brand loyalty, then we have a sustainable business."

Yang and Filo decided to create brand loyalty by moving Yahoo! toward becoming a media company. First, they formed an alliance with the Japanese media conglomerate Softbank and launched two brand extensions: a print and online magazine called *Yahoo! Internet Life* and a personal computer information center on the Web called *Yahoo! Computing.* In partnership with such publishers as Fodor's and the *Village Voice,* Yahoo! is also creating online city guides for New York, Chicago, Los Angeles, Boston, San Francisco, and Dallas/Fort Worth.

The goal of these targeted geographic metro guides and online magazines is to transform the Yahoo! Web site into a *destination* that tempts each visitor to browse several pages instead of just typing in a keyword on the first page. The metro guides are excellent advertising vehicles, since they match local advertisers with targeted audiences within specific regions.

Another Yahoo! alliance aimed at strengthening the company's drive to become a media company involves MTV Music Television. The two first recently launched a co-branded venture called *MTV Yahoo! Unfurled,* a combination of music-related editorials and an online guide to other music sites on the Web. "We're partnering with Yahoo! because it's the search engine that's really built a brand name for themselves," says MTV executive Matt Farber. "We both understand the importance of branding, and that's essential to our partnership." Because the MTV and Yahoo! target audiences share a number of demographic characteristics, the alliance is expected to attract new users for each company. "We're partnering to fill the gaps in each of our sites,"says Yahoo! Director of Production Tim Brady. "To retain music users, we need to offer more than just music lists."

Yahoo! has invested over $50 million in advertising designed to promote its brand. The firm recently launched its "Do You Yahoo?" campaign with ads in such magazines as *Wired, Red Herring,* and *Fortune* backed by local radio commercials. Sales offices in major U.S. cities also seek additional advertisers on the Yahoo! Web site.

The list of Yahoo! online services continues to grow. *Yahooligans* is an online directory for children, and *Beatrice's Web guide* is targeted at women. The company has also moved into narrowcasting, an electronic delivery service for customized information, by launching *My Yahoo!* This service delivers content update from a user's favorite Web sites and news about new sites that relate to the user's personal interests.

With $8.6 million in annual revenues, Yahoo! continues to adapt to the Internet's ever-changing environment. By sponsoring and participating in a variety of community programs, Yang and Filo's company helps to promote the development of Internet education and programming. Yahoo! is connecting classrooms to the Internet, providing free educational seminars, and offering promotional exposure for not-for-profit organizations on its Web sites.

Questions

1. Peter Drucker defined the purpose of business as creating a customer. How has Yahoo! created a customer as implied by Drucker's definition? What is the firm doing to avoid marketing myopia in marketing its services?

2. Relate the concepts of the target market, marketing mix, and the marketing environment to this case.

3. The fourth era in marketing's history focuses on relationship marketing. Give examples that illustrate how Yahoo! is embracing this concept.

4. Yahoo! generates a sizable portion of its total revenues from advertising. Visit the Yahoo! home page at

   http://www.yahoo.com/

   and review the ads and the advertisers whose messages appear there. Evaluate the ads in comparison with traditional ads appearing in magazines and on billboards, radio, and television. What motivated these advertisers to select this medium for their messages?

Source: "Netscape and Yahoo! to Launch Netscape Guide by Yahoo!, March 19, 1997.

CHAPTER 2

CREATING VALUE THROUGH CUSTOMER SATISFACTION AND QUALITY

Back
Forward
Home
Reload
Images
Open
Print
Location: http://circuitcity.pic.net/index.html
What's New?
What's Cool?
Destinations
Net Search
Product Info!
Hot News!
Computer Answer Web, Car Stereo
NEW! Camcorder Guide. NEW!
CIRCUIT CITY RACING
Store Locator!
Find your nearest Circuit City store or RoadShop Installation Center.
Jobs!
We're growing and have job openings in many areas.
JOBS
Welcome To The World's First Internet Bank
WIN A CRUISE!!
click here to visit SFNB-ATLANTA
SFNB
Send Deposits To: Security First Network Bank P.O. Box 191427 Atlanta, GA 31119-9954
SECURITY FIRST NETWORK BANK
why sfnb?
information
demonstration
apply
CEO's letter
account access
Customer Service
Security
Rates
Demo
Customers
Information
MACRO*WORLD™ financial research
www.sfnb.com
Location: http://www.helmsleyhotels.com/
What's New?
What's Cool?
Destinations
Net Search
People
SAY WHAT YOU WILL
SHE RUNS A HELLUVA HOTEL
NOTHING ORDINARY ABOUT IT.
TACO BELL
Home
http://www.theborder.co
What's Cool?

Chapter Objectives

1. Explain the relationships between value, customer satisfaction, and quality.
2. Identify the major components of customer satisfaction.
3. List the goals of internal marketing.
4. Explain the primary methods by which marketers measure customer satisfaction.
5. Outline the historical development of the quality movement.
6. Discuss the roles of top management and employees in implementing total quality management (TQM).
7. Outline the objectives of a marketing audit.
8. Explain the benchmarking process and its role in improving a marketing strategy.
9. Describe how an organization can work toward continuous improvement in its marketing activities.
10. Explain how marketing managers can deliver value to customers by balancing the marketing mix elements.

Virtual Banking

A customer at Security First Network Bank sees the usual sights during a visit to the institution's lobby—tellers, promotional materials, and an imposing security guard. But no one ever has to wait in line for a teller's help. Lines don't exist. In fact, the bank has no real lobby.

Security First is the nation's first bank to operate exclusively in cyberspace. It can serve customers who live in Alaska, Florida, or anywhere in between. Location doesn't matter as long as they have access to computers and modems.

Security First is a trailblazing operation, but it's certainly not a fluke. More and more banks are coaxing their customers to conduct business anywhere but in bank lobbies. Over 1 million households, or 10 percent of all U.S. households with online connections, use those links to conduct banking transactions, and that number is expected to grow to 10 million by 2001.

Welcome To The World's First Internet Bank
WIN A CRUISE!!
click here to visit SFNB-ATLANTA
why sfnb?
information
demonstration
apply
CEO's letter
account access
MACRO*WORLD financial research
SFNB
Send Deposits To: Security First Network Bank P.O. Box 191427 Atlanta, GA 31119-9954
SECURITY FIRST
NETWORK BANK
Customer Service
Security
Rates
Demo
Customers
Information
www.sfnb.com
All content © 1995-1996, Security First Network Bank [Security First Technologies | E-Mail]
Equal Housing Lender | Member FDIC
FDIC

The reasons are simple. Foremost, banking by computer, telephone, or automated teller machine (ATM) makes economic sense for financial institutions. Customers who don't need access to tellers and other face-to-face amenities save banks lots of money. As walk-in and drive-through traffic falls, banks can close down branches or cancel expansion plans. In something of a chain reaction, the need for tellers and other branch employees also declines.

In the past, many banks prided themselves on their attentive customer service. The branch manager often knew many of the customers who walked through the lobby, and tellers greeted regulars by name. Changes in the business raise a big question: Will the impersonal nature of electronic banking create a customer satisfaction success or a fiasco? So far, preliminary studies attempting to assess the risk have found a mixed bag of results.

http://www.sfnb.com/

Banks have encountered resistance trying to convince older customers to adopt these high-tech alternatives; these customers have been banking the same way for decades. Younger customers, however, have provided a much more receptive market.

Bank marketers cite plenty of persuasive arguments to convince patrons that nontraditional banking offers quicker and more convenient service. Customers find ATMs conveniently located in supermarkets and airports. They can transfer funds, check account balances, or inquire about deposits at any hour of the day or night through their telephones or computers. What's more, they never have to leave home or the office to do it.

Security First has competed with California-headquartered Wells Fargo Bank, another major player in cyberbanking. "We think retail banking customers are looking for the same things as they're looking for in the rest of their lives—value and convenience," says Joe Stiglich, head of Wells Fargo's retail banking operations. His company, a pioneer in technology applications, is committed to finding new and better ways to satisfy its customers. But it also has major incentives for pushing customers into nontraditional banking. Wells Fargo must spend $50,000 to establish a tiny outpost in a supermarket staffed by one or two employees, compared to $4 million to open a branch with 6,000 to 7,000 square feet of space. For every 2 million transactions moved from the bank lobby to a telephone operator, the company saves about $15 million, or $7.50 a transaction.

While banking by phone and computer channels great savings directly to a financial institution's bottom line, it can involve some tricky marketing tasks. This is especially true when banking executives try to modify consumers' behavior by assessing stiff fees to those who insist on personally visiting bank facilities. In one extreme case, the Bank of Chicago started charging customers $3 per visit to deal with a real, live banker; the fee reflected the actual cost of the service. This move may have boosted revenues, but it proved to be a public relations nightmare and a customer satisfaction disaster.

Virtual banking will catch on only if bank marketers convince customers that online banking is safe and reliable. Security is the number one concern; customers fear that online transactions fail to protect their financial information. Banks will also have to maintain high standards of customer satisfaction and service quality. Automatic payment systems have created minimal problems, but customers who pay bills electronically often wonder when—and if—the payments actually arrive. While some businesses prefer to receive electronic payments from consumers, others who are not yet equipped to handle these exchanges find that they increase processing costs.

Both online financial services and traditional banks that add electronic services are finding that they can't take customer service for granted in their highly competitive market. Security First set up an Internet call center to provide fast, personalized service. Customers cite lack of the personal touch as one of their biggest complaints about virtual banking. The call center tracks which customer service rep handles each call and then connects customers with the same reps when they call back.

Despite the marketing and technological challenges, Dudley Nigg, a Wells Fargo executive vice president, predicts that electronic banking efforts will continue to increase in popularity. "Online banking is the Holy Grail," he says. "Today technology is on an express. If you're not on the train, I don't know how you'll catch it."[1]

CHAPTER OVERVIEW

The success with which a company satisfies customers by providing high-quality goods and services can make or break its chances of prospering in today's competitive global marketplace. In one recent survey of chief executive officers, 47 percent listed customer satisfaction as the main goal of their businesses.[2] However, like the banks mentioned in the opening vignette, many U.S. companies have found that satisfying customers can be a tricky proposition, requiring a careful balance between customer needs, quality, and the firm's financial performance.

These issues reinforce the importance of the marketing concept, which Chapter 1 described as a companywide consumer orientation. Increasingly, companies are implementing the marketing concept by involving employees from every business function in the process of understanding and satisfying customer needs and wants. Businesses cannot afford to ignore one important demand—the craving of today's customers for high-quality goods and services. Truly customer-focused firms commit themselves to managing their own business activities by constantly assessing and satisfying their customers' definitions of quality and value. The end result is a mutually beneficial relationship between a business and its customers.

This chapter discusses the role of customer satisfaction and quality programs in building competitive advantage. It begins by examining the components of customer satisfaction and the methods by which businesses measure their success at meeting—and exceeding—customer expectations. The chapter then focuses on the issues that arise and the tools that contribute to the discipline of total quality management. Finally, it considers how marketers can design the elements of the marketing mix to build and reinforce customer value and satisfaction.

THE IMPORTANCE OF SATISFYING CUSTOMERS

A typical business loses half of its customers every five years.[3] The underlying reason for many customer defections is simple: The customers were not satisfied with the value they received from the firm.

Today's savvy customers want the satisfaction of acquiring more than ordinary goods and services. They demand more than just a fair price; they are seeking added value. **Value** is the customer's perception of the balance between the quality of goods or services that a firm provides and their price. A **value-added** good or service gives the customer increased worth by delivering more than expected—some benefit of personal significance to the customer, such as unanticipated product features.

Quality describes the degree of excellence or superiority of an organization's goods and services. This broad term encompasses both the tangible and intangible characteristics of a good or service. Applied technically, *quality* can refer to physical product traits, such as durability and reliability. It also includes the intangible components of **customer satisfaction,** the ability of a good or service to meet or exceed buyer needs and expectations. The true measure of quality determines whether a business has satisfied its customers. As author and quality management consultant A. V. Feigenbaum notes, "Quality is what your customer says it is—not what you say it is. To find out about your quality, ask your customer."[4]

As long as customers feel that they have received value, that is, good quality for a fair price, they are likely to remain satisfied with and continue their relationship with the firm. However, when customers perceive an inequitable balance between quality and price, they will become dissatisfied and start to look for opportunities to abandon their relationship with the business.

The value-added services that guests enjoy at the five different hotels in the Helmsley Hotel chain in New York add up to customer satisfaction. Feedback from satisfied guests, shown in Figure 2.1, focuses on both amenities included in the physical accommodations and the professional capabilities of hotel employees. These factors combine to create added value and increase the likelihood of repeat business among these satisfied customers.

http://www.helmsleyhotels.com/

Marketing Dictionary

value The customer's perception of the balance between the quality of goods or services that a firm provides and their prices.

value-added Increased worth of a good or service resulting from added features, lower price, enhanced customer service, a strengthened warranty, or other marketing mix improvements that increase customer satisfaction.

quality The degree of excellence or superiority of an organization's goods and services.

customer satisfaction The result of a good or service meeting or exceeding the buyer's needs and expectations.

Figure 2.1 Helmsley's Attempt to Create Value through Customer Satisfaction and Quality

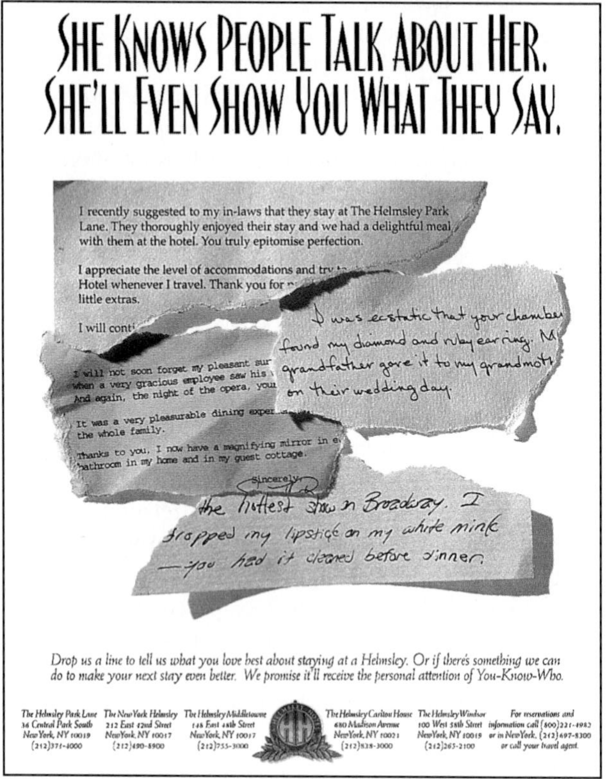
SHE KNOWS PEOPLE TALK ABOUT HER.
SHE'LL EVEN SHOW YOU WHAT THEY SAY.
I recently suggested to my in-laws that they stay at The Helmsley Park Lane. They thoroughly enjoyed their stay and we had a delightful meal with them at the hotel. You truly epitomise perfection.
I appreciate the level of accommodations and
Hotel whenever I travel. Thank you for
little extras.
I was ecstatic that your chamber
found my diamond and ruby ear ring. My
grandfather gave it to my grandmother
on their wedding day.
I will not soon forget my pleasant
when a very gracious employee saw his
And again, the night of the opera, your
It was a very pleasurable dining
the whole family.
Thanks to you, I now have a magnifying mirror in
bathroom in my home and in my guest cottage.
Sincerely
the hottest show on Broadway. I
dropped my lipstick on my white mink
—you had it cleaned before dinner.
Drop us a line to tell us what you love best about staying at a Helmsley. Or if there's something we can do to make your next stay even better. We promise it'll receive the personal attention of You-Know-Who.
The Helmsley Park Lane 36 Central Park South New York, NY 10019 (212)371-4000
The New York Helmsley 212 East 42nd Street New York, NY 10017 (212)490-8900
The Helmsley Middletowne 148 East 48th Street New York, NY 10017 (212)755-3000
The Helmsley Carlton House 680 Madison Avenue New York, NY 10021 (212)838-3000
The Helmsley Windsor 100 West 58th Street New York, NY 10019 (212)265-2100
For reservations and information call (800)221-4982 or in New York, (212)697-8300 or call your travel agent.

Marketers benefit in several ways when they can maintain stable relationships with their customers. First, it is more expensive to acquire new customers than to serve existing customers. In fact, the cost of acquiring new customers is five times greater than the expense of keeping old ones.[5] Firms that must constantly replace customers incur higher marketing costs than those that maintain ongoing relationships with established groups of loyal customers. Long-term customers also tend to purchase more frequently than new buyers, require less service, and respond less sensitively to price.

Satisfied customers frequently recruit new customers for a firm.[6] Dissatisfied customers, on the other hand, can have disastrous effects on a firm's image and sales. Studies show, for instance, that 95 percent of dissatisfied customers don't complain directly to the company, but each one ends up telling 11 friends and/or business acquaintances about the negative experience.[7] Obviously, the ultimate results of customer satisfaction are growth in market share, increased profitability, and success in the marketplace.

One of McDonald's main marketing goals, for instance, is to increase the frequency of current customers' visits to its restaurants. The firm's research shows that loyal customers who eat in its restaurants three to five times a week account for 77 percent of its total sales. By building customer loyalty, McDonald's hopes to boost revenues.[8] Chapter 10 will look at other examples of the link between customer satisfaction and relationship marketing.

Components of Customer Satisfaction

What does pickle and ketchup king H.J. Heinz have in common with The Coca-Cola Co., Cadillac, and United Parcel Service? They're all companies that scored at the top of a recent consumer study to measure customer satisfaction. At the bottom of the list—the Internal Revenue Service.[9]

These results emerged from the annual American Customer Satisfaction Index (ACSI) study. Developed by the University of Michigan and the American Society of Quality Control, the study tracks customer satisfaction across a broad range of industries and companies. Table 2.1 shows recent ACSI ratings for the highest-scoring firms in various industries. Among many findings, the ACSI results point out one critical element in satisfying customers: Know what your customers want, need, and expect.

On the surface, this advice seems like a simple suggestion. Many companies have discovered, however, that pinpointing customer expectations isn't always a straightforward job. Marketing executives sometimes fall into the trap of believing that they already know what will satisfy customers without actually asking the customers themselves. This can be a dangerous assumption.

Harley-Davidson is one company that discovered this risk the hard way. The motorcycle manufacturer's global brand name meant independence, freedom, and power in dozens of languages. It also carried a powerful image and even more powerful customer loyalty in the heavyweight bike market. This freedom, independence, and power image is reflected in the ad shown in Figure 2.2.

Seeking to capitalize on this strong brand name, Harley management greatly increased output, in the process suffering noticeable declines in quality. So many bikes left the factory with leaky crankcases that Harley owners shared an inside joke: "Harleys don't leak oil; they just mark their spot."

Harley-Davidson narrowly avoided bankruptcy. By the early 1990s, the company had returned to profitability through numerous product improvements, customer service innovations such as guaranteed trade-in allowances, and employee involvement in the production and quality-enhancement programs. Regular meetings with current owners, would-be owners, and owners of other motorcycle brands provide information that helps Harley marketers to assess customer satisfaction. The results have been so successful that today's new customer is likely to have come from a two-year waiting list to buy a new Hog.[10]

Applebee's Restaurants is another U.S.-based business that has enjoyed marketplace success and rapid expansion in recent years. However, its managers committed

Table 2.1 Industry Leaders in Customer Satisfaction

Product Category	Company	Score
Food processing	H.J. Heinz	90
Automobiles	Cadillac	88
Parcel delivery	UPS	87
Soft drinks	Coca-Cola	87
Personal care and cleaning	Dial; Procter & Gamble[a]	85
Household appliances	Whirlpool	85
Consumer electronics	Zenith	84
Long-distance telephone service	AT&T	83
Department stores	Nordstrom	83
Gasoline—service stations	Texaco	82
Supermarkets	Publix	82
Apparel	Liz Claiborne	81
Beer	Anheuser-Busch	79
Athletic shoes	Nike	77
Personal computers	Hewlett-Packard	77
Airlines	Southwest	76
Fast-food restaurants	Wendy's International	73
National Average		72
Category Ranked Lowest in Customer Satisfaction		
Government agencies	Internal Revenue Service	50

[a]First-place tie.

the firm to maintain quality—and what they labeled *world-class service*—even in the face of this growth. But they didn't simply assume that they knew what world-class service meant to the typical Applebee's customer. Instead, the firm polled over 2,000 guests to pinpoint the reasons they gave for making repeat visits. Applebee's executives found that, while food ranked as the most important component of customer satisfaction, other, more subtle characteristics also played roles in satisfying customers. For example, a smiling host or hostess who greeted guests at the door proved an important secondary way of satisfying customers, as did fast service. From this research, Applebee's developed a list of the critical ingredients needed to satisfy its guests: atmosphere, personality, performance, lightning speed, and excellent food.[11]

When marketers at CNA Insurance Cos. decided to improve customer satisfaction, they also began by pinpointing customer needs. They interviewed decision makers for insurance purchases at different-sized businesses to learn about how these buyers would decide whether to renew or cancel their group insurance policies. CNA also makes regular site visits to get input from customers in different industries. As a result of this research, the insurance giant has identified specific steps it needs to take to ensure that its offerings meet customer expectations.[12]

Internal Marketing

So far, this chapter has discussed customer satisfaction in terms of **external customers**—people or organizations that buy or use another firm's goods or services. However,

Marketing Dictionary

external customer A person or organization that buys or uses another firm's goods or services.

Figure 2.2 **The Link between Customer Satisfaction and Quality at Harley-Davidson**

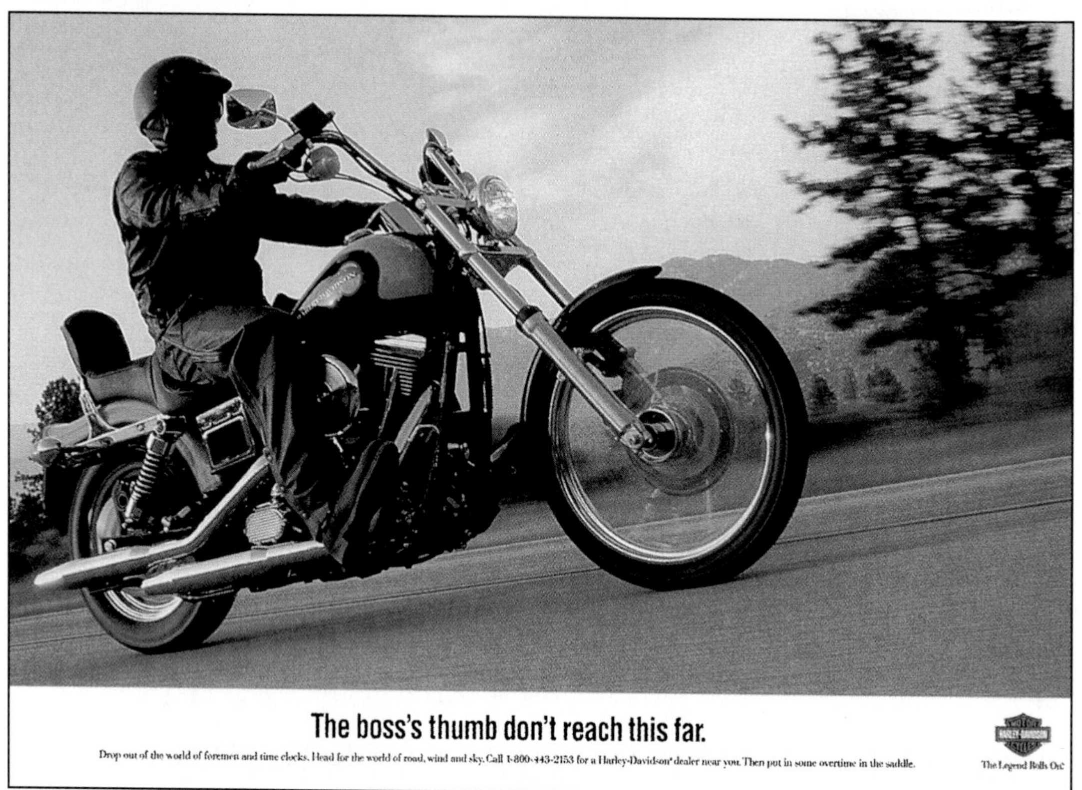
The boss's thumb don't reach this far.
Drop out of the world of foremen and time clocks. Head for the world of road, wind and sky. Call 1-800-443-2153 for a Harley-Davidson® dealer near you. Then put in some overtime in the saddle.
The Legend Rolls On

as noted in Chapter 1, marketing in an organization concerned with quality must also address messages to **internal customers**—employees or departments within an organization whose job performance depends on the work of other employees or departments. For example, a person processing an order for a new piece of equipment is the internal customer of the salesperson who completed the sale, just as the person who bought the product is the salesperson's external customer. Although the order processor might never directly encounter an external customer, his or her performance can have a direct impact on the overall value the firm delivers to the marketplace.

Internal marketing involves managerial actions that help all members of an organization understand, accept, and fulfill their respective roles in implementing its marketing strategy. An internal marketing program shows employees how their work aids the firm's marketing strategy and contributes to customer satisfaction. Internal marketing also encourages employees to view coworkers as internal customers. This orientation motivates them to deliver high-quality goods and services to their coworkers. They want to help fellow employees do their jobs well, and add further value throughout the marketing process.

Employee knowledge and involvement is an important goal of internal marketing. Companies that excel at satisfying customers emphasize the priority of keeping their employees informed about organizational goals and strategies as well as customer needs. Employees also need tools to address customer requests and problems in a timely manner. Often, the marketing department is part of the conduit disbursing this information throughout the organization.

In working toward this end, some companies are introducing intranets to aid communications flows between departments and functional areas. An **intranet** is an internal network that conforms to Internet standards in order to support two-way organizational communications, Businesses can send information, distribute technical data, and support team processes through intranets. Glaxo Wellcome's 6,000 employees can access the company's intranet from their desktop computers. On this network, they can find everything from internal online conferences, research data, and software applications to personal home pages of their fellow employees at distant work sites.[13]

Employee satisfaction is another critical objective of internal marketing. Employees can seldom, if ever, satisfy customers if they themselves are unhappy. Dissatisfied employees are likely to spread negative word-of-mouth messages to relatives, friends, and acquaintances, and these reports can affect purchasing behavior. Satisfied employees often buy their employer's goods and services, sending a powerful message to potential customers.[14]

http://www.tacobell.com/

For this reason, some companies set up internal promotion programs to complement their external advertising and marketing campaigns. Taco Bell supported its "Run for the Border" advertising campaign with an internal program designed to inform employees about the campaign and their own roles in promoting it.[15]

Figure 2.3 **Building Employee Satisfaction through Messages Featuring Their Contributions to Product Quality**

"THERE ISN'T A PERSON ON THIS PLANET WHO NEEDS TO DRIVE A GM VEHICLE IN ORDER TO LIVE."
There are at least four things in life that are truly indispensable: food, air, shelter, love. But people can always find a way to muddle through without General Motors products. This is how GMC Truck Division head Roy Roberts explains what satisfying today's customer is about to his team: "Build something so right for your customers, they can't imagine living without it." This strikes us as a pretty good definition. After all, General Motors cars and trucks, no matter how much we labor over their creation, have something the "four indispensables" don't. Competition.
General Motors

General Motors ads, such as the one shown in Figure 2.3, describe the contributions of several GM employees to product quality and their importance in the firm's marketplace success. This ad features the head of the GMC Truck Division carrying a message that emphasizes the need to satisfy today's customer to avoid losing sales to GM competitors. Such ads communicate to two groups: prospective customers and GM employees, who feel acknowledged for their indispensable work.

The internal marketing process can also reach suppliers. By educating suppliers and enlisting their participation in adding value for an organization's end customers, the firm can avoid many problems with external customer satisfaction. Chrysler Corp., for example, operates a program to involve suppliers in product development and process improvement. Chrysler has improved communications and built trust with its suppliers by including them in design, problem-solving, and team planning programs. Chrysler credits these efforts with helping the company achieve its highest market share in 25 years.[16]

MEASURING CUSTOMER SATISFACTION

Customer satisfaction is not a static concept. Many internal and external events can quickly change a satisfied customer into a dissatisfied one. Companies that commit themselves to satisfying customers must institute a system to continually monitor and measure how well they perform the task. Figure 2.4 shows the three main steps involved in this process: understanding customer needs, obtaining customer feedback, and instituting an ongoing program to measure customer satisfaction.

Understanding Customer Needs

When they try to measure customer satisfaction, marketers must keep in mind that there may be gaps, or differences between expected quality and perceived quality of the firm's goods and services. Such gaps can produce favorable or unfavorable impressions. A product may be better

Marketing Dictionary

internal customer An employee or department within an organization whose job performance depends on the work of another employee or department.

internal marketing Management actions that help all members of an organization to understand and accept their respective roles in implementing its marketing strategy.

intranet An internal network that conforms to Internet standards in order to support two-way organizational communications.

Figure 2.4 **Three Steps to Measure Customer Satisfaction**

Customer Satisfaction
Ongoing Measurement
Customer Feedback
Understanding Customer Needs

than expected or worse than expected. To avoid unfavorable gaps, marketers need to keep in touch with current and potential customers. Companies must look beyond traditional performance measures and explore the factors that determine purchasing behavior in order to formulate customer-based missions, goals, and performance standards. Chapter 13 will discuss these gaps in more detail as they relate to marketing for services.

Clearly, knowledge of what customers need, want, and expect is a central concern of a company focused on customer satisfaction. This information is also a vital first step in setting up a system to measure customer satisfaction. Marketers must carefully monitor the characteristics that really matter to customers. They must remain constantly alert to new elements that might affect customer satisfaction.

"We view a customer who is complaining as a real blessing in disguise. He or she is someone we can re-sell."

Louis Carbone
Vice President,
National Car Rental

Obtaining Customer Feedback

For the second step in measuring customer satisfaction, marketers must compile feedback from customers regarding present performance. In a sense, this action captures a snapshot of how well the firm currently meets customer expectations. This information can be gathered in two ways: reactive and proactive methods.

Most firms rely on reactive methods to monitor customer feedback. These arrangements can include toll-free customer-service telephone lines or systems to track customer complaints. Increasingly, firms are monitoring exchanges on Usenet and other online discussion groups as a means of tracking customer comments and attitudes about the value they receive. Some companies hire *mystery shoppers,* professionals who visit or call businesses posing as customers and evaluate the service they receive by filling out questionnaires. A mystery shopper is typically a disinterested party who brings no prior experience with the company. These unbiased appraisals are usually conducted biannually or quarterly to monitor employees, diagnose problem areas in customer service, and measure the impact of employee training.

Columbia, one of the nation's leading health-care providers, conducts regular patient surveys to gather feedback that helps the firm to build on its strengths and identify ways of improving its services. As the ad copy in Figure 2.5 states, attention to customer satisfaction has resulted in 30 Columbia hospitals among the top 100 in the United States along with "satisfied" or "very satisfied" ratings from 95 percent of its patients.

Taco Bell has incorporated a toll-free telephone hot line as part of its customer satisfaction efforts. Signs prominently display the 800 number inside each restaurant and at drive-through windows. Hot-line calls reach guest relations representatives who have been trained to quickly resolve customer complaints and problems. Many customers receive personalized follow-up letters or telephone calls from the unit managers. The company also tracks complaints to spot developing issues that might affect customer satisfaction.[17]

Any method that helps customers to complain benefits a firm. Customer complaints offer an organization opportunities to overcome problems and prove its commitment to service. Customers often have greater loyalty to a company after a conflict has been resolved than if they had never complained at all. Businesses benefit from treating complaints as welcome resources and opportunities to gain innovative ideas for improvement.

Many firms also use proactive methods to assess customer satisfaction. These include visiting clients, calling them, or sending out written surveys. Xerox gathers information by mailing approximately 60,000 customer satisfaction surveys per month to its customers, and AT&T's Universal Credit Card division calls 2,500 customers every month to measure quality in the company's nine most important areas of service performance. Pizza Hut calls 50,000 customers each week to ask about their experiences at the restaurant chain's units. Many car dealers call or send surveys to customers asking them to rate the service they received, either in purchase situations or service visits.

Figure 2.5 Measuring Customer Satisfaction at Columbia Healthcare

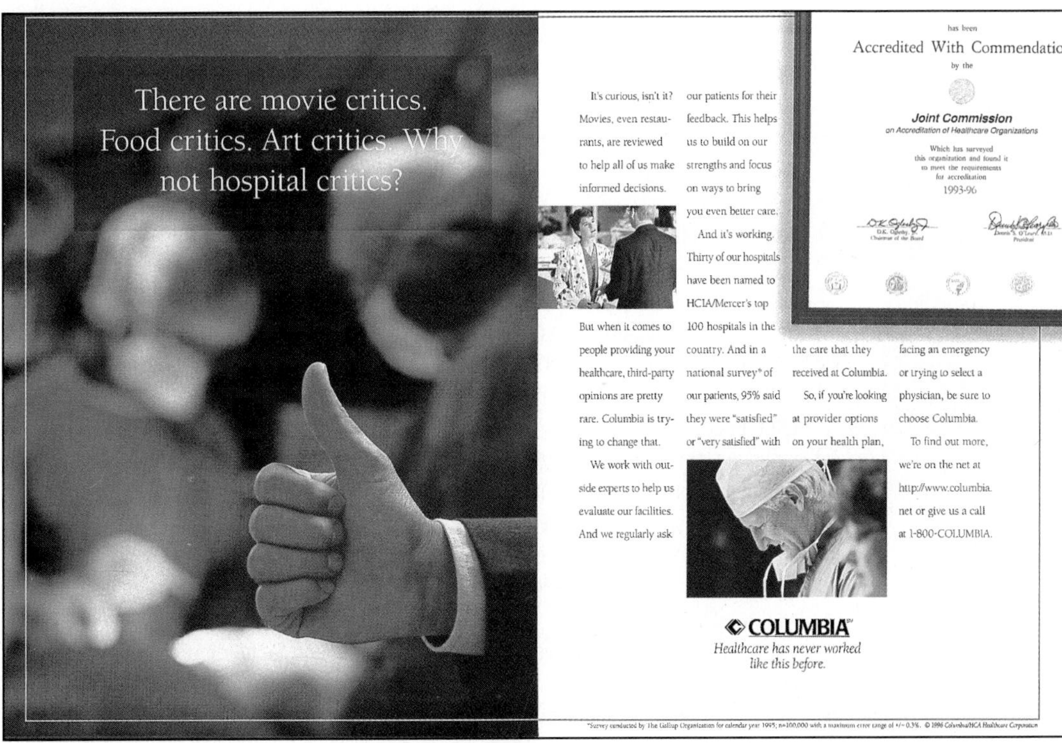
There are movie critics. Food critics. Art critics. Why not hospital critics?
It's curious, isn't it? Movies, even restaurants, are reviewed to help all of us make informed decisions.
But when it comes to people providing your healthcare, third-party opinions are pretty rare. Columbia is trying to change that.
We work with outside experts to help us evaluate our facilities. And we regularly ask our patients for their feedback. This helps us to build on our strengths and focus on ways to bring you even better care.
And it's working. Thirty of our hospitals have been named to HCIA/Mercer's top 100 hospitals in the country. And in a national survey* of our patients, 95% said they were "satisfied" or "very satisfied" with the care that they received at Columbia.
So, if you're looking at provider options on your health plan, facing an emergency or trying to select a physician, be sure to choose Columbia.
To find out more, we're on the net at http://www.columbia.net or give us a call at 1-800-COLUMBIA.
has been
Accredited With Commendatio
by the
Joint Commission
on Accreditation of Healthcare Organizations
Which has surveyed this organization and found it to meet the requirements for accreditation
1993-96
COLUMBIA
Healthcare has never worked like this before.
*Survey conducted by The Gallup Organization for calendar year 1995; n=100,000 with a maximum error range of +/- 0.3%. © 1996 Columbia/HCA Healthcare Corporation

Customer satisfaction surveys have provided successful tools for Circuit City. The chain posts computer printouts of survey tabulations in training rooms and throughout each store. Comparisons with the scores of other Circuit City stores promote healthy competition. As part of its LTC (Love the Customer) program, the company also solicits customer feedback through comment cards, exit interviews, and follow-up phone calls. Employees concentrate on improving low scores, and prizes and awards acknowledge their efforts.

http://www.circuitcity.com/

Customer Satisfaction Measurement Programs

Once a company identifies priorities that determine customer satisfaction and gathers feedback on present performance, its next step is to initiate an ongoing **customer satisfaction measurement (CSM) program.** The CSM system provides a procedure for tracking customer satisfaction over time. Rather than just a snapshot of how the firm performs at a particular moment, ongoing measurement allows the firm to identify changes in customer attitudes and satisfaction and to develop action plans for improvement. Such programs can become quite sophisticated, sometimes requiring the aid of outside consultants.

While most customer satisfaction measurement programs focus on tracking the satisfaction levels of current customers, some companies have gained valuable insights by tracking the dissatisfaction that leads customers to abandon their products for those of competitors. Some customer defections are only partial; customers remain somewhat satisfied with a business but not completely satisfied. Such attitudes may lead them to take some of their business elsewhere. Studying the underlying causes of customer defections, even partial defections, can provide useful tools for identifying problem areas that need repair.[18]

Marketing Dictionary

customer satisfaction measurement (CSM) program A set of ongoing procedures for measuring customer feedback against customer satisfaction goals and developing an action plan for improvement.

Figure 2.6 Applying Total Quality Management

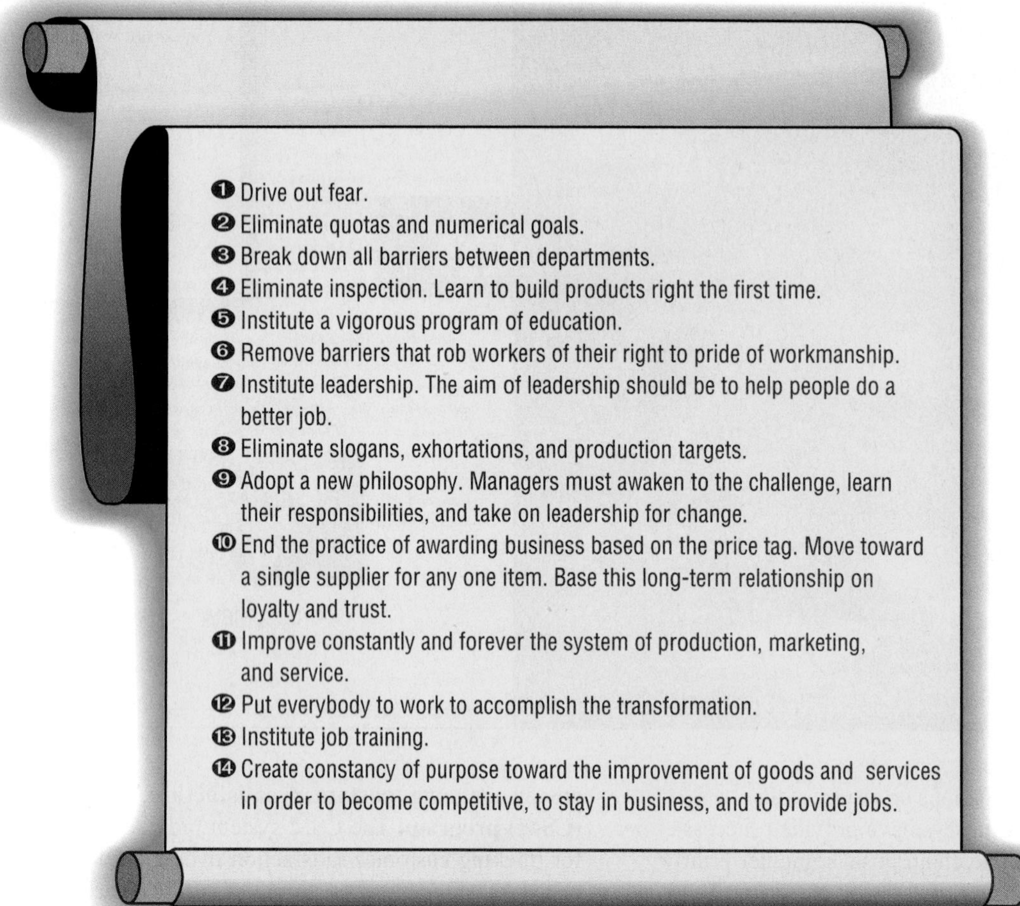
❶ Drive out fear.
❷ Eliminate quotas and numerical goals.
❸ Break down all barriers between departments.
❹ Eliminate inspection. Learn to build products right the first time.
❺ Institute a vigorous program of education.
❻ Remove barriers that rob workers of their right to pride of workmanship.
❼ Institute leadership. The aim of leadership should be to help people do a better job.
❽ Eliminate slogans, exhortations, and production targets.
❾ Adopt a new philosophy. Managers must awaken to the challenge, learn their responsibilities, and take on leadership for change.
❿ End the practice of awarding business based on the price tag. Move toward a single supplier for any one item. Base this long-term relationship on loyalty and trust.
⓫ Improve constantly and forever the system of production, marketing, and service.
⓬ Put everybody to work to accomplish the transformation.
⓭ Institute job training.
⓮ Create constancy of purpose toward the improvement of goods and services in order to become competitive, to stay in business, and to provide jobs.

MicroScan, a manufacturer of automated medical instruments, offers an example of successful use of this kind of information. The firm's managers felt that they had made an exceptional effort to improve product quality, and positive customer feedback supported this conclusion. When market research specialists interviewed former customers who had moved all or some of their business to MicroScan's competitors, however, a different picture emerged. These customers expressed doubts about the reliability of MicroScan's instruments and indicated a dislike for certain features. Further, they felt that MicroScan had not responded effectively to their concerns and complaints.

As a result of these findings, MicroScan committed additional resources to correct the shortcomings identified by its former customers. It redesigned its customer-service system to speed up corrections of equipment and delivery problems. Within two years, MicroScan had risen to become the industry leader with increased profits, as well.[19]

The MicroScan story highlights the importance of turning customer feedback into action. Merely measuring customer satisfaction—or in MicroScan's case, dissatisfaction—seldom affects a company's long-term success. To obtain true competitive advantage, the firm must continually strive to turn customer input into strategies that solve problems, enhance value, and satisfy customers. As more businesses recognize this fact, they are fueling a growing movement toward quality improvement, both in the United States and in other industrialized nations. The next part of this chapter focuses on some specific strategies and tactics that business organizations can implement to improve quality.

THE QUALITY MOVEMENT

Organizations worldwide are applying quality theories, principles, and methods to every business function. This movement, called **total quality management (TQM),** involves all employees in a firm to continually improve products and work processes with the goal of achieving customer satisfaction and world-class performance. In a total quality organization, marketers develop products that people want to buy; engineers design products to work the way customers want to use them; production workers build quality into every product they produce; salespeople deliver what they promise customers; information systems experts apply technology to ensure that the firm fills customer orders correctly and on time; financial specialists help to determine prices that give customers value.

The quality movement started in the United States during the 1920s as an attempt to improve product quality by improving the manufacturing process itself. Walter Shewhart, a physicist at AT&T Bell Laboratories, pioneered an innovative approach called **statistical quality control** that employed statistical techniques to locate and measure quality problems on production lines. Using the principles of statistics and probability, Shewhart developed control charts to identify variations in the manufacturing process that could generate defective products. By controlling these variations, this innovative method built quality into the production process rather than relying on inspectors to remove defective output at the end of the production line.

Figure 2.7 How Quality Improvements Benefit an Organization

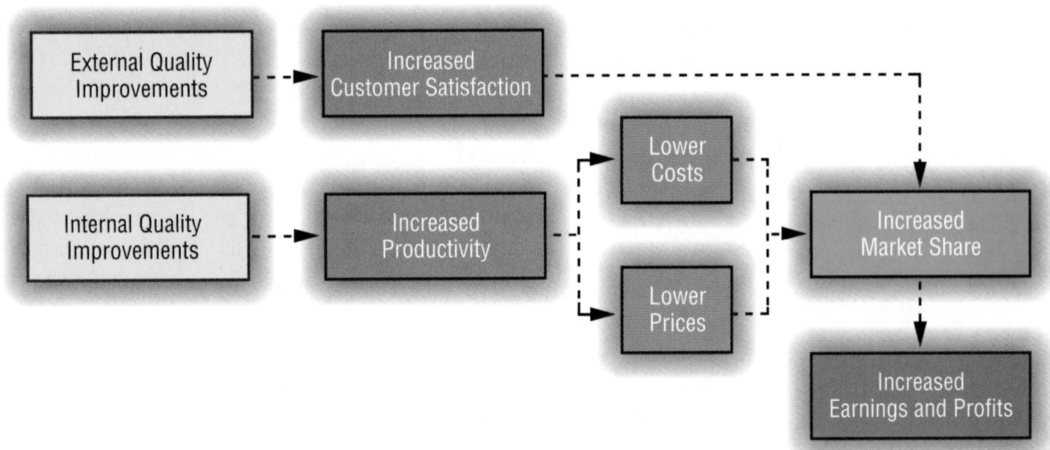
External Quality Improvements
Increased Customer Satisfaction
Internal Quality Improvements
Increased Productivity
Lower Costs
Lower Prices
Increased Market Share
Increased Earnings and Profits

W. Edwards Deming, a statistician who worked with Shewhart, helped to popularize Shewhart's quality control methods in the United States and abroad. One of the best-known descriptions of total quality management is Deming's 14 Points for Quality Improvement. Figure 2.6 offers specific advice to marketers seeking to include quality as a key ingredient throughout the organization. Note that these points encourage managers to view their organizations as systems that direct the knowledge and skills of all employees toward improving quality. Managers are responsible for communicating the goals of total quality management to all staff members and for encouraging workers to improve themselves and take pride in their work.

Research determines customer needs and wants. Based on this information, the company designs and redesigns functional, dependable goods and services. It removes defects by steadily reducing process variations. Organizations build relationships of loyalty and trust with suppliers to improve incoming materials and decrease costs. A true competitive advantage results when organizations move beyond continuous improvement to practice continuous product innovation. As Deming said, "Better quality and lower prices with a little ingenuity in marketing will create a market."[20] Figure 2.7 shows how quality improvements affect an organization, both internally and externally.

Two other pioneers in statistical quality control techniques were Joseph Juran and A. V. Feigenbaum. Juran's work helped to expand quality control from a production technique to a broader orientation that could encompass all business processes and support systems involved in producing and marketing goods and services. A. V. Feigenbaum authored an influential book entitled *Total Quality Control* that introduced the idea of total employee involvement in a companywide push for quality.

Other important contributions to the quality movement came from Japan, where the interest in quality developed among business leaders trying to rebuild that country's industrial base after World War II. Sony, Honda, Toshiba, Nippon Steel, Hitachi, and hundreds of other Japanese firms implemented statistical quality control and the other ideas and practices of total quality management. To show the country's appreciation for Deming, the Japanese government created the Deming Prize, which recognizes companies that produce high-quality goods and services. Today it remains Japan's most coveted industrial award.

Marketing Dictionary

total quality management (TQM) An effort to involve all employees in a firm to continually improve products and work processes with the goal of achieving customer satisfaction and world-class performance.

statistical quality control A set of methods for applying statistical techniques to locate and measure quality problems in production and marketing activities.

MARKETING HALL OF SHAME

Customer Satisfaction Fiascoes

The customer is always right. In the world of business, this old adage is as true today as it was when some clever person long ago summed up the principles of customer satisfaction.

Obviously, keeping customers happy and satisfied is crucial to the livelihood of any business. Disgruntled patrons won't return. A business that alienates enough people will not leave much of a company for new prospects to visit. This idea may seem too basic for a college textbook, but it's forgotten all the time in the real world.

Take the day a distinguished-looking gentleman wearing blue jeans walked into a bank to complete a transaction. The customer was told that the person who could help him was out of the office that day. Preparing to leave, the man asked the teller to validate his parking ticket. She declined, explaining that bank policy allowed validation only for someone who completed a transaction. When the customer urged her to make an exception, she refused to budge.

By now quite incensed, the man proceeded to complete a transaction the bank would soon terribly regret. The unhappy customer was John Akers, the chairman of IBM. He withdrew all the money in his account—$1.5 million.

If you think this event represents an isolated incidence of customer dissatisfaction, think again. Just ask the 53 passengers who were traveling from Dallas to Phoenix on an America West jet. After half an hour in the air, the plane abruptly turned around and landed back in Dallas. The plane had not suffered any mechanical problems; it simply returned to pick up members of the Anaheim Angels baseball team, whose chartered America West plane had been grounded for mechanical problems.

As the passengers disembarked, they had to pass the waiting team members ready to board. The grounded customers sat for two hours while ticket agents scrambled to get them aboard a different airline's flight.

Not surprisingly, those evicted travelers responded with fury. One wrote a letter to the company's chief executive officer that began, "Dear Village Idiot, May your airline go belly up as soon as possible so a more qualified group can assume your routes." Making the customer relations fiasco even worse,

The TQM concept of *continuous improvement* was an outgrowth of Japanese quality efforts. This concept, called *kaizen* in Japanese, refers to the process of constantly studying and improving work activities. A later section of the chapter will discuss continuous improvement in more detail.

Worldwide Quality Programs

During the 1980s, the quality revolution picked up speed in U.S. organizations. The campaign to improve quality found leadership in large manufacturing firms like Ford, Xerox, and Motorola that had lost market share to Japanese competitors. Then smaller companies that supplied parts to large firms began to recognize quality as a requirement for success. Today, a commitment to quality has spread to service industries, not-for-profit organizations, government agencies, and educational institutions.

As part of the nation's quality improvement campaign, Congress established the Malcolm Baldrige National Quality Award in 1987 to recognize excellence in quality management. Named after late Secretary of Commerce Malcolm Baldrige, the award is the highest national recognition for quality that a U.S. company can receive. The award works toward promoting quality awareness, recognizing quality achievements of U.S. companies, and publicizing successful quality strategies. Each year, only two applicants can win awards in each of three categories: manufacturing, services, and small business.

Figure 2.8 lists criteria for these awards and the number of points that a firm can earn by meeting each criterion. Award winners may publicize and advertise receipt of the award provided they agree to share information about their quality strategies with other U.S. organizations. Winners of the award include such corporate giants as Xerox Business Products and Systems in the manufacturing category and Federal Express in the services category, as well as small companies like the relatively unknown Globe Metallurgical, Inc.

The quality movement has also spread to European countries. The European Union's **ISO 9000** standards define international criteria for quality management and quality assurance. These standards were developed by the

the hostile letter was widely reported in the media.

At least, the airline did what it could to make amends. A representative personally contacted each passenger to apologize, and each received a voucher for an unspecified amount.

"We inconvenienced 53 very important passengers, and we're truly sorry," said America West representative Gus Whitcomb, who was still hearing from angry passengers days after the incident. "We made a mistake. There's no other way to explain it. It was a well-intentioned decision to make sure everybody got where they were going."

Customers are not feeling insulted only on the ground or in the air these days. In this ever-evolving technological age, corporations are also irritating customers in cyberspace. An increasing number of companies are setting up World Wide Web sites that include e-mail addresses to accept customers' questions and comments. This step makes a lot of sense for companies that want to maintain good relations with their technically adept and often relatively affluent customers. But troubles arise when e-mail goes unanswered, as it often does.

The *Wall Street Journal* recently sent e-mail inquiries to two dozen corporate Web sites that included those of Coca-Cola, McDonald's, PepsiCo, IBM, and Eastman Kodak Co. The experiment yielded dismal results. Nine never responded, while many others sent standard responses that didn't answer the questions posed in the original e-mails. Only three companies answered adequately within one day.

"It's important to be fast. It's a fast medium," says Larry Dale, a marketing specialist working on Ford's Web site. "Some of these people might well be sitting at their PC, waiting for a return e-mail."

QUESTIONS FOR CRITICAL THINKING

1. **America West was contractually bound to provide transportation to the California Angels. If you were in charge, what would you have done to keep everyone satisfied?**
2. **In the case of the rude banker, how can a company help employees understand the importance of following rules without being rigid?**
3. **How badly do you think highly publicized public relations gaffs hurt a company?**

Sources: Steve Lohr, "Beyond Consumers, Companies Pursue Business-to-Business Net Commerce," *New York Times,* April 28, 1997, downloaded from http://www.nyt.com/, May 2, 1997; Thomas E. Weber, "Many Queries Seem to E-vade Cyber Queries," *San Diego Union-Tribune,* October 31, 1996, p. E1; "No Angels," *USA Today,* October 2, 1996, p. C1; H. G. Reza, "Heaven Can Wait," *Los Angeles Times,* October 2, 1996, pp. C1, C7; and "Life in the Fast Lane," *Inc.,* September 1996.

International Standards Organization in Switzerland to ensure consistent quality among products manufactured and sold throughout the nations of the European Union (EU).

Many European companies now require suppliers to complete ISO certification as a condition of doing business with them. To become ISO certified, a company must undergo an on-site audit that includes inspection of the firm's facilities to ensure that documented quality procedures are in place and that all employees understand and follow those procedures. A firm meets ISO requirements by maintaining an ongoing process, typically covering a 14-month period, during which periodic audits verify conformance. Once granted certification, the firm frequently must ensure that its suppliers are also ISO certified. Clearly, ISO 9000 will soon be a minimum requirement for firms doing business in Europe. Competitors in non-EU countries, concerned over threats of exclusion from this huge market, have moved quickly to implement ISO 9000 standards.

TQM IN ACTION

TQM is an ongoing process that involves all functions of the organization. Effective TQM programs generally include five key components: (1) top management involvement, (2) employee involvement, (3) conducting a marketing audit, (4) benchmarking, and (5) continuous improvement. The next few sections examine how each of these components can lead to an organizationwide quality culture.

Marketing Dictionary

ISO 9000 A set of standards for quality management and quality assurance developed by the International Standards Organization in Switzerland for countries in the European Union (EU).

Figure 2.8 Malcolm Baldrige National Quality Award Criteria

Criteria	Description	Points
Customer and Market Focus	The effectiveness of systems to determine customer and market requirements and enhance customer satisfaction	80
Leadership	The senior executives' success in creating and sustaining a quality culture	110
Strategic Planning	The effectiveness of integrating quality requirements into business plans	80
Information and Analysis	The effectiveness of information collection and analysis for quality improvement and planning	80
Human Resource Development and Management	The success of efforts to develop and realize the full potential of the workforce for quality	100
Process Management	The effectiveness of systems and processes for assuring the quality of all operations	100
Business Results	The results in quality achievement and quality improvement, demonstrated through quantitative measures	450

Involving Top Management

Effective TQM programs begin with the involvement of top managers who believe in the importance of quality and customer satisfaction. Many TQM programs fail because top managers delegate these responsibilities to quality assurance departments. TQM can succeed only if senior managers play integral roles in setting strategy, allocating resources, and evaluating results. According to Charles Aubrey, president of the American Society for Quality Control, top managers "must take a strategic view of quality: setting priorities, identifying what's most critical to the success of the enterprise, and focusing improvement efforts on the customer. These are decisions that only top management can make."[21]

Studies of Baldrige Award winners reveal that these companies attribute their market achievements to senior managers who instill quality values into daily operations; these organizational leaders also train, empower, and involve all employees in improvement efforts and integrate systems and processes throughout their entire companies. Often, top executives maintain deep involvements in customer contact activities.

For example, at ADAC Laboratories, a 1996 winner of the Baldrige Award, customer focus is a core value that starts at the very top of the organization. All of the company's executives spend at least 25 percent of their time with customers. They personally answer customer phone calls and invite customers to attend the company's weekly quality meetings.[22]

Senior executives at the Defense Systems & Electronics Group of Texas Instruments, another Baldrige Award winner, are also actively involved in steering the quality process. The company's quality design improvement team, which plans and evaluates quality and customer satisfaction, is directly chaired by the company's president.[23]

Involving Employees

An important tool for boosting customer satisfaction and promoting companywide quality is **employee involvement**—an emphasis on motivating employees to boost their job performance and to participate actively in quality initiatives. Employee involvement seeks to unleash the energy, creativity, and talents of all employees. Bringing out employees' best qualities makes them feel good about themselves and their work. It also gives them a sense of ownership, so they take pride in their work.

The Dutch electronics firm Philips created a global advertising campaign around the theme "Let's make things better" to motivate its employees to improve their work and to emphasize the quality of the company's products to consumers. The ads, such as the one shown in Figure 2.9, describe employees' involvement in marketing products designed to satisfy consumer needs. TQM programs usually seek to involve employees in the quality process through empowerment, training, and teamwork.

Figure 2.9 Philips: Involving Employees in Promoting Companywide Quality

A finished product
doesn't mean our work is over.
Let's make things better.
Anne-Marie Visse, Sales Representative Lighting.
Ivry Sur Seine, France.
At Philips, when a product is finished, my work is just beginning.
My name is Anne-Marie Visse. I am a Sales Representative for consumer products at Philips Lighting and I collaborate on a daily basis with distributors.
My role consists of guaranteeing the regular presence of Philips Lighting Products at the greatest number of point of sale locations, and on the best displays, backed by original promotions.
This makes sure that as the world's biggest lighting company, our products are not only the best, but are seen in all the best places.
PHILIPS
PHILIPS

Employee Empowerment **Empowerment** is the practice of giving employees authority to make decisions about their work without supervisory approval. Empowered employees gain increased authority and responsibility for implementing the organization's mission and strategy. For example, empowered assembly-line workers can stop the production process and fix problems as they detect them. In marketing, an empowered salesperson can resolve a customer complaint without authorization from a superior.

Empowerment taps the brain power of all employees to find better ways of doing their jobs and executing ideas. A U.S. Labor Department report found that empowered employees tend to generate higher profits for their companies than workers without such programs produce.[24] Additionally, employee job satisfaction has been found to be higher at firms committed to empowering employees.[25]

Empowerment can also make a highly effective contribution to a strategy for satisfying customers. Customers appreciate dealing with an employee who has the authority to handle a transaction or a complaint efficiently without checking with a supervisor. Such excellent service leaves a lasting impression and personally ties the customer to the company.

Sears is one organization that has garnered rewards from empowering employees. In the early 1990s, the retailer had suffered a severe decline in customer loyalty. Consumers complained that stores seemed unresponsive, poorly staffed, and stocked with inferior merchandise. As part of Sears' efforts to provide increased value to customers, the company delegated authority to individual stores and departments so employees could make their own decisions about how these units should function; they reported their changes to the home office afterward. As a result, store employees can now take prompt action to fix problems. For example, when one customer complained about cluttered aisles to employees of one Sears store, he was surprised to find the aisles clear and straight on a return visit only two weeks later. "I was elated," the shopper said about his experience. "I'm the customer, and what I think means something."[26]

Marketing Dictionary

employee involvement Motivating employees to improve their job performance through internal marketing, empowerment, training, and teamwork.

empowerment Giving employees authority to make decisions about their work without supervisory approval.

MARKETING HALL OF FAME

Quality and Customer Satisfaction Meet at Lands' End

When Lands' End Inc. tapped Michael J. Smith to become the company's next chief executive officer in late 1994, the move must have seemed like quite a gamble to many observers. After all, Smith was only 34 years old. Further, he had never worked for any other company; he had landed a job at the Dodgeville, Wisconsin direct marketing institution following a stint there as a college intern.

But 12 years later, the Lands' End board of directors decided they wanted an insider at the helm. The company had seemed to lose its focus during the four-year tenure of outsider William End, who had brought in seven new divisional vice presidents. The new faces, along with changes in management techniques and a parade of outside consultants, only served to alienate many employees in the tightly knit corporate culture. "People trusted me and knew I did not have any hidden agendas," Smith recalls.

The company's decision to bypass other, more experienced executives and fill the slot with Smith has paid tremendous benefits. After a bumpy start, profits, sales, and morale are up. Wall Street analysts are including the catalog retailing giant on their lists of recommended securities to purchase. So far, Smith is enjoying much of the credit for the turnaround.

Smith's success is amazing, considering that he took over during one of the worst periods in the company's 33-year history. Consumer demand for apparel had plummeted, mailing costs had jumped, and, with little warning, paper prices had doubled.

But Smith survived by focusing on the company's mantra, "Make it as good as you can. Improve it whenever possible." Instead of downsizing and cheapening the product, Smith did the opposite. He improved the quality of the clothing and sweetened employee benefits. Paying more attention to customer service in a troubled time only made sense. "Our customers will pay for great-quality products" sold by employees who coddle them, Smith observes.

Smith succeeded by taking Lands' End back to its roots: providing high-quality, timeless fashions along with the best customer service in the industry. In one move, Smith refined some of the company's classic clothes. The company strengthened seams on mesh knit shirts and added fleece to the pockets of squall jackets. When employees told Smith that the children's snow boots weren't water-

Employee Training The importance of quality and plans for achieving it should influence integrated employee training programs. Properly trained employees need to know more than just how to perform their job duties; they also need complete information about the organization's goals, strategies, and tactics. Additionally, their training must prepare them to recognize and fill all customer needs and expectations.

Teaching employees technical skills for measuring and monitoring the quality of their work is another aspect of training. Technical training varies depending on employees' jobs, but it generally involves learning how to use such quality tools as statistical quality control and problem-solving methods.

Employee training can generate large financial payoffs. Motorola, for instance, estimates that it earns $30 for every dollar it invests in employee training. Another firm, Edy's Grand Ice Cream, says its training efforts have boosted productivity 57 percent while reducing inventories 66 percent. The net result has been an 830 percent increase in sales volume.[27]

Teamwork The final component of employee involvement in TQM is teamwork. A *team* is a small number of people with complementary skills who commit themselves to a common purpose. The team members set their own performance goals and hold themselves mutually accountable. By working collectively, a team of employees reach higher performance levels than they could achieve working separately; they also respond more quickly and thoroughly to customer needs. Depending on the objective of their tasks, teams can range in size from several employees in one work area to hundreds of employees from different company facilities around the world.

A **quality circle** is a group of employees from one work area or department who meet regularly to identify and solve problems. Quality circles pervade the 1990s workplace. As part of its employee empowerment efforts, for example, Sears instituted Town Hall Meetings at each store. During these gatherings, employees are encouraged to discuss obstacles they encounter in serving customers; they then develop solutions that will enable them to provide better service. For example, in a recent Town Hall

proof, he pulled them from the catalog. That decision left the company holding $500,000 worth of boots. After some customers received defective turtlenecks, Smith sent apologetic letters to 200,000 buyers and offered free replacements.

All this attention to the consumer has not gone unnoticed. In a survey of 100 senior managers of American companies, Lands' End was voted the most customer-sensitive of all catalog retailers.

Smith is treating employees just as royally. He's added such employee benefits as adoption assistance and mental health referrals, as well as health benefits for part-time workers. Why the perks during tough times in the intensely competitive apparel-catalog business? "If people feel squeezed, they won't treat the customer as well," says Smith, who wears only Lands' End clothes.

In another move, Smith realigned the management structure for all the company's catalogs so that each one could operate autonomously, with its own profit and loss statements. The change, he says, fit in with the company's culture, which values independence.

Overall, Smith has tightened the company's financial and inventory operations, sharpened the focus of its catalogs, and reduced supplier costs. As an example, analysts say that the company has done a better job of selecting and negotiating with suppliers. In some cases, Lands' End has managed to improve the quality of its merchandise while lowering its costs.

http://www.landsend.com/

With customer service the company's top priority, Smith has put international expansion and further acquisitions on hold for now. Whether this strategic decision will stunt future growth remains to be seen.

QUESTIONS FOR CRITICAL THINKING

1. **Do you think that a decision to place so much emphasis on customer service can ever backfire? Analysts worry, for instance, that concentrating on customer service rather than on expansion into overseas markets and acquisitions will hurt profits in the long run.**
2. **What does the Lands' End experience tell you about the importance of customer service?**

Sources: Company profile from Lands' End Web site, downloaded from http://www.landsend.com/, February 3, 1997; Robert Berner, "Catalog Retailer Dumps Outsiders, Prospers under Home-Grown Management," *Wall Street Journal,* August 30, 1996, p. B3; Susan Chandler, "Lands' End Looks for Terra Firma," *Business Week,* July 8, 1996, pp. 130–131; and Susan Chandler, "Lands' Endgame," *Business Week,* December 19, 1994, p. 42.

Meeting, employees mentioned difficulties communicating with Spanish-speaking customers. In the course of the meeting, a participant proposed a solution that solved the problem. The store's manager would maintain a list of employees who speak foreign languages so other employees could call on them for help in serving non-English-speaking customers.[28]

Two other types of teams can play important roles in quality and customer satisfaction efforts: cross-functional teams and self-managed teams. A **cross-functional team** joins employees from different departments to work together on a specific project, such as developing a new product or solving a particular problem. Cross-functional teams often participate in new-product development. They are discussed in more detail in Chapter 11.

A **self-managed team** is a group of employees who work with little or no supervision. Team members schedule their own work, learn to do other employees' jobs, and accept responsibility for the quality of their work and accountability for results. At Eastman Kodak Co., the Zebras—1,500 employees who make black-and-white film—work in self-managed teams that are responsible for making hundreds of types of film for Kodak's Health Sciences Division. Zebras control everything from scheduling production to developing new products—a Zebra specialty.

Marketing Dictionary

quality circle A small group of employees from one work area or department who meet regularly to identify and solve problems.

cross-functional team A group of employees from different departments who work together on a specific project.

self-managed team A group of employees who work with little or no supervision.

Figure 2.10 A Sample Marketing Audit Outline

Customer Philosophy

Does management recognize the importance of designing the company to serve the needs and wants of chosen markets?

0 ❑ Management primarily thinks in terms of selling current and new products to whoever will buy them.
1 ❑ Management thinks in terms of serving a wide range of markets and needs with equal effectiveness.
2 ❑ Management thinks in terms of serving the needs and wants of well-defined markets chosen for their long-growth and profit potential for the company.

Does management develop different offerings and marketing plans for different segments of the market?

0 ❑ No.
1 ❑ Somewhat.
2 ❑ To a good extent.

Does management take a whole marketing system view (suppliers, channels, competitors, customers, environment) in planning its business?

0 ❑ No. Management concentrates on selling and servicing its immediate customers.
1 ❑ Somewhat. Management takes a long view of its channels, although the bulk of its effort goes to selling and servicing the immediate customers.
2 ❑ Yes. Management takes a whole marketing systems view, recognizing the threats and opportunities created for the company by changes in any part of the system.

Integrated Marketing Organization

Is there high-level marketing integration and control of the major marketing functions?

0 ❑ No. Sales and other marketing functions are not integrated at the top and there is some unproductive conflict.
1 ❑ Somewhat. There is formal integration and control of the major marketing functions but less than satisfactory coordination and cooperation.
2 ❑ Yes. The major marketing functions are effectively integrated.

Does marketing management work well with management in research, manufacturing, purchasing, physical distribution, and finance?

0 ❑ No. There are complaints that marketing is unreasonable in the demands and costs it places on other departments.
1 ❑ Somewhat. The relations are amicable although each department pretty much acts to serve its own power interest.
2 ❑ Yes. The departments cooperate effectively and resolve issues in the best interest of the company as a whole.

How well organized is the new product development process?

0 ❑ The system is ill-defined and poorly handled.
1 ❑ The system formally exists but lacks sophistication.
2 ❑ The system is well-structured and professionally staffed.

The Marketing Audit

A **marketing audit** is a thorough, objective evaluation of an organization's marketing philosophy, goals, policies, tactics, practices, and results. A marketing audit can help identify weaknesses in a company's efforts to satisfy customers and continuously improve quality. Managers must be willing to conduct periodic marketing audits of their plans—and to accept the objective results of these evaluations.

A periodic audit should both identify the tasks that the organization performs well and reveal its weaknesses. Periodic review, criticism, and self-analysis are crucial to the vitality of any organization. They provide particularly critical guidance for a function as diverse and dynamic as marketing. Marketing audits generate especially valuable insight about areas in which managerial perceptions differ sharply from reality.

Methods of conducting marketing audits are almost as diverse as the firms that apply them. Some audits follow informal procedures; others involve elaborate checklists, questionnaires, profiles, tests, and related research instruments. Figure 2.10 presents a sample marketing audit outline that assesses an organization's marketing effectiveness according to five variables: consumer philosophy, integrated mar-

Adequate Marketing Information

When were the latest marketing research studies of customers, buying influences, channels, and competitors conducted?

0 ❑ Several years ago.
1 ❑ A few years ago.
2 ❑ Recently.

How well does management know the sales potential and profitability of different market segments, customers, territories, products, channels, and order sizes?

0 ❑ Not at all.
1 ❑ Somewhat.
2 ❑ Very well.

What effort is expended to measure the cost-effectiveness of different marketing expenditures?

0 ❑ Little or no effort.
1 ❑ Some effort.
2 ❑ Substantial effort.

Strategic Orientation

What is the extent of formal marketing planning?

0 ❑ Management does little or no formal marketing planning.
1 ❑ Management develops an annual marketing plan.
2 ❑ Management develops a detailed annual marketing plan and a careful long-range plan that is updated annually.

What is the quality of the current marketing strategy?

0 ❑ The current strategy is not clear.
1 ❑ The current strategy is clear and represents a continuation of traditional strategy.
2 ❑ The current strategy is clear, innovative, data-based, and well–reasoned.

What is the extent of contingency thinking and planning?

0 ❑ Management does little or no contingency thinking.
1 ❑ Management does some contingency thinking, although little formal contingency planning.
2 ❑ Management formally identifies the most important contingencies and develops contingency plans.

Operational Efficiency

How well is the marketing thinking at the top communicated and implemented down the line?

0 ❑ Poorly.
1 ❑ Fairly well.
2 ❑ Successfully.

Is management doing an effective job with marketing resources?

0 ❑ No. The marketing resources are inadequate for the job to be done.
1 ❑ Somewhat. The marketing resources are adequate, but they are not employed optimally.
2 ❑ Yes. The marketing resources are adequate and are deployed efficiently.

Does management show a good capacity to react quickly and effectively to on-the-spot developments?

0 ❑ No. Sales and market information is not very current and management reaction time is slow.
1 ❑ Somewhat. Management receives fairly up-to-date sales and market information; management reaction time varies.
2 ❑ Yes. Management has installed systems yielding highly current information and fast reaction time.

keting organization, adequate marketing information, strategic orientation, and operational efficiency. The final score can range from 30 points (superior marketing effectiveness) to 0 (absolute ineffectiveness) or anywhere in between.[29]

Marketing audits reveal information applicable to all organizations—large or small, not-for-profit or profit-oriented. Audits are particularly valuable exercises when performed for the first time or

Marketing Dictionary

marketing audit A thorough, objective evaluation of an organization's marketing philosophy, goals, policies, tactics, practices, and results.

Figure 2.11 The Benchmarking Process

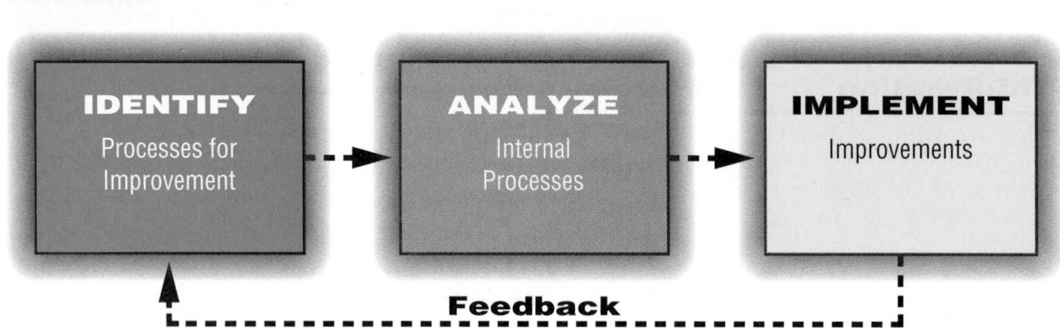
IDENTIFY
Processes for Improvement
ANALYZE
Internal Processes
IMPLEMENT
Improvements
Feedback

when conducted after having been discontinued for several years. While not all firms complete marketing audits, an increasing number are recognizing their importance in evaluating strategies to maintain competitiveness and profitability.

Benchmarking against the Best

What do marketers mean when they ask for *high quality?* Would a 99 percent defect-free rate satisfy this priority? Firms in several industries pursue zero defects as a very real goal. After all, consider the intolerable results of even a 99.9 percent error-free performance standard: In the United States, 18 commercial air carriers would crash every day, the U.S. Postal Service would lose 17,000 pieces of mail each hour, doctors would perform 500 incorrect surgical operations each week, and financial institutions would deduct $24.8 million from the wrong accounts every hour.

Most quality-conscious marketers rely on an important tool called **benchmarking** to set performance standards. This method for creating a world-class marketing operation seeks to identify how business leaders achieve superior marketing performance levels in their industries and to develop a system for continuously comparing and measuring performance against outstanding performers. The technique involves learning how the world's best goods and services are designed, produced, and marketed. The purpose of benchmarking is to achieve superior performance that results in a competitive advantage in the marketplace.

Xerox Corp. pioneered benchmarking in the United States two decades ago when it compared its own manufacturing costs for photocopying machines against the costs of Japanese and domestic competitors. The comparison revealed that competitors were selling their copiers at prices equal to Xerox's cost. After analyzing competitors' manufacturing processes, product components, and costs, Xerox set new targets to achieve those higher standards. By the early 1980s, Xerox had adopted benchmarking companywide as a key component of its drive for quality in all products and processes.[30]

A typical benchmarking process involves three main activities: identifying processes that need improvement, comparing internal processes against similar activities of industry leaders, and implementing changes for better quality. As Figure 2.11 shows, the process continuously repeats itself, since vigilant companies continue to search for and identify areas that need improvement, even after implementing changes. This ongoing devotion helps these firms to ensure that they remain market leaders.

Identifying Processes for Improvement The benchmarking process begins when a firm identifies a process or practice it wants to improve, such as new-product design or customer service. The bench marking project should focus on **critical success factors,** that is, product and process characteristics that most powerfully affect efforts to gain competitive advantage and achieve long-term success. One firm's critical success factors might center on satisfying customers with superior service; another might focus on rapidly bringing products to the marketplace.

A survey conducted by The Benchmarking Exchange (TBE) identified the business processes chosen most often for benchmarking studies: human resources, information systems, purchasing, and customer service. The study noted a relatively recent trend toward inclusion of customer service processes such as help desks, service departments, and customer satisfaction in benchmarking studies.[31]

After deciding what activities to benchmark, a firm must identify recognized performance leaders. The company may consider divisions or departments within its own organization or look externally to competitors and leading firms in other industries. For example, Xerox has benchmarked its billing and collection processes against those of American Express, its quality processes against those of Florida Power and Light, and its warehousing and distribution operations against those of L. L. Bean, Hershey Foods, and Mary Kay Cosmetics.

Southwest Airlines pointed to an ability to service planes quickly while maintaining high safety standards as a critical success factor. Southwest chose an unusual but logical operation as a benchmark: the Indianapolis 500. After studying how pit crews service race cars quickly, Southwest applied the knowledge it gained to improve the performance of its own maintenance crews.[32]

AT&T, Harley Davidson, and the Department of Energy have recently visited Chrysler's Auburn Hills, Michigan, facilities to learn about the carmaker's supply-chain management techniques. By benchmarking Chrysler's best practices in supplier relations, these organizations hoped to study how to involve their suppliers early in the product-design process to get ideas about cost savings and technological innovation in new materials and parts. Many suppliers contributed to the design of the Plymouth Prowler, the 1930s-style roadster shown in the ad in Figure 2.12. Alcoa, one supplier on the design team, developed a special aluminum alloy for the car's body parts, allowing the Prowler to be built with an all-aluminum body.

Figure 2.12 **Using Chrysler as a Benchmark of Best Practices in Supplier Relations**

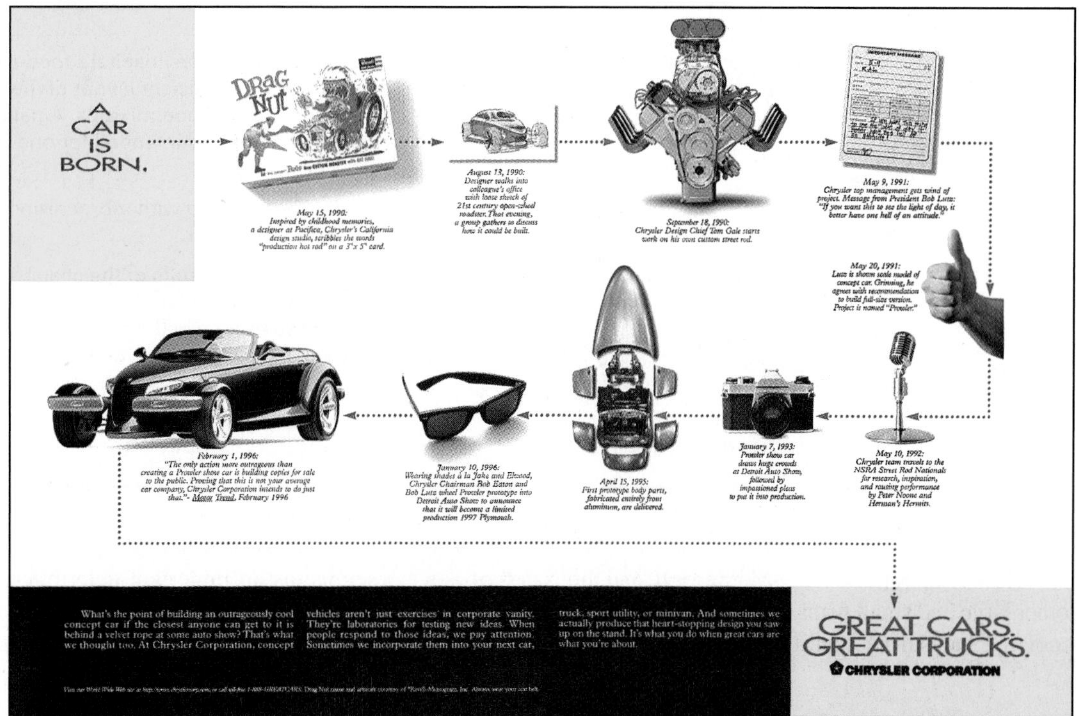
A CAR IS BORN.
DRAG NUT
May 15, 1990: Inspired by childhood memories, a designer at Pacifica, Chrysler's California design studio, scribbles the words "production hot rod" on a 3"x 5" card.
August 13, 1990: Designer walks into colleague's office with loose sketch of 21st century open-wheel roadster. That evening, a group gathers to discuss how it could be built.
September 18, 1990: Chrysler Design Chief Tom Gale starts work on his own custom street rod.
May 9, 1991: Chrysler top management gets wind of project. Message from President Bob Lutz: "If you want this to see the light of day, it better have one hell of an attitude."
May 20, 1991: Lutz is shown scale model of concept car. Grinning, he agrees with recommendation to build full-size version. Project is named "Prowler."
May 10, 1992: Chrysler team travels to the NSRA Street Rod Nationals for research, inspiration, and rousing performance by Peter Noone and Herman's Hermits.
January 7, 1993: Prowler show car draws huge crowds at Detroit Auto Show, followed by impassioned pleas to put it into production.
April 15, 1995: First prototype body parts, fabricated entirely from aluminum, are delivered.
January 10, 1996: Wearing shades à la Jake and Elwood, Chrysler Chairman Bob Eaton and Bob Lutz wheel Prowler prototype into Detroit Auto Show to announce that it will become a limited production 1997 Plymouth.
February 1, 1996: "The only action more outrageous than creating a Prowler show car is building copies for sale to the public. Proving that this is not your average car company, Chrysler Corporation intends to do just that."- Motor Trend, February 1996
What's the point of building an outrageously cool concept car if the closest anyone can get to it is behind a velvet rope at some auto show? That's what we thought too. At Chrysler Corporation, concept vehicles aren't just exercises in corporate vanity. They're laboratories for testing new ideas. When people respond to those ideas, we pay attention. Sometimes we incorporate them into your next car, truck, sport utility, or minivan. And sometimes we actually produce that heart-stopping design you saw up on the stand. It's what you do when great cars are what you're about.
GREAT CARS. GREAT TRUCKS.
CHRYSLER CORPORATION

Analyzing Internal Processes Benchmarking requires two types of analyses: internal and external studies. Before a company can compare its own processes with those of another firm, it must first analyze internal activities to determine their strengths and weaknesses. This preparation establishes a baseline for comparison. External analysis then gathers information about the benchmarking partner to discover the basis of its high reputation. A comparison of the results of the analysis provides an objective standard for planning improvements.

Implementing Improvements Firms use benchmark findings to implement many kinds of improvements. They set new performance goals, change current processes by adapting the best practices of benchmark partners, and measure the progress of those new work practices. Benchmarking analysts should communicate results to employees so that everyone understands the reasons for change, the opportunities for improvement, their roles in implementing changes, and the impact of these changes on the organization's overall marketing strategy.[33]

Bell Atlantic, for example, benchmarked the performance and processes of its customer service telephone centers against those of service centers at AT&T, Delta Air Lines, and GE Credit. The Bell Atlantic executives discovered that centralization seemed to improve the efficiency and effectiveness of customer service centers. As a result, Bell Atlantic consolidated its 374 customer service centers into just 54 sites.[34]

Today, benchmarking is a major component of many quality programs. Xerox conducts benchmarking studies in each of the more than 100 countries where it operates.

Marketing Dictionary

benchmarking Process in which an organization continuously compares and measures itself against business leaders anywhere in the world to learn how it could improve performance.

critical success factor Product or process characteristic that most powerfully affects efforts to gain competitive advantage and achieve long-term success.

Table 2.2 Applying the PDCA Cycle at Florida Hospital

Step	Description	Example
Planning	Analyze work to determine what changes might improve it	Employees analyzed the hospital's food-service operations and found that the inefficient layout of the cafeteria's tray lines sometimes led to food mix-ups. A patient on a restricted diet might receive a tray intended for one on a regular diet and vice versa.
Doing	Implement needed changes	The staff experimented with reorganizing the tray lines to reduce the chances of error.
Checking	Observe effects of the changes	They measured the results of the change, and found that, complaints about the food fell from 12 percent to 2 percent. Overall patient satisfaction with the food increased, even though the meals themselves tasted the same as they always had.
Acting	Finalize changes in work activities to protect the improvements	The new tray line setup was made into a permanent arrangement.

AT&T, Metropolitan Life, IBM, Marriott, and thousands of other large and small firms use benchmarking as a standard tool for measuring quality. Increased interest in benchmarking has spawned a number of associations, councils, and consulting firms that provide a variety of benchmarking services. For example, the American Productivity and Quality Center has organized an International Benchmarking Clearinghouse that offers training, a database of the best practices, and conferences to help members share information.

http://www.metlife.com/

Working toward Continuous Improvement

The goal of continuous improvement is a critical aspect of any TQM program. **Continuous improvement** is the process of constantly studying and making changes in work activities to improve their quality, timeliness, efficiency, and effectiveness. Continuous improvement helps a firm to produce value-added goods and services that meet customer needs, and it supports innovations that exceed customer expectations. This process must be ongoing, since customers' needs, wants, and expectations are always changing. The quality of work processes determines much about the quality of the resulting goods and services, and strong processes can give marketers a highly competitive advantage.

Table 2.2 shows how the marketing department at Florida Hospital Medical Center in Orlando used a popular sequence called the **PDCA cycle** to implement continuous improvement. A recent marketing audit identified food service as an important determinant of patients' attitudes toward hospitals; the same study found that 12 percent of Florida Hospital's patients had complained about the food. Management applied the PDCA cycle—a step-by-step process of planning, doing, checking, and acting—to help resolve the problem.

In the *planning* step, employees analyze their work and determine what changes might improve it. In the *doing* step, they try out the changes. During the *checking* step, they observe the effects of the changes. The final *acting* step finalizes changes in work activities to bring about improvement. Throughout the cycle, employees are encouraged to view their work activities as ways to enhance customer satisfaction.

Reducing Cycle Time Continuous improvement efforts focus on improving quality and customer satisfaction by reducing cycle time, reducing variations, and eliminating waste. **Cycle time** is the time required to complete a work process or activity from beginning to end. For instance, cycle time might measure the time it takes to design a car, handle a customer complaint, or create a marketing brochure. Continuous improvement can reduce cycle time by simplifying work processes, eliminating steps that do not add value to the product, and forming cross-functional teams. The drive to reduce cycle time serves two main goals: to bring new products quickly to the marketplace and to reduce the time it takes to produce and deliver goods and services to customers. Sears, for example, required its managers to comply with 50,000 pages of rules and regulations governing every action and decision. As part of its quality-improvement efforts, Sears replaced the old manager's manual with a slim, 16-page pamphlet. The change sought to develop a streamlined culture where all associates could quickly and independently respond to changing market conditions.[35]

Reducing Variation All work processes, goods, and services produce some degree of variation. Variation can result from causes like poor market research, faulty machinery or outdated technology, inadequately trained employees, inefficient work procedures, and defective parts and materials from suppliers. Quality programs train employees to apply statistical controls and problem-solving methods in a way that reduces variations. The goal is to reach the highest possible performance standard, so customers can depend on consistently high quality each time they purchase a firm's goods or services. Effective work processes build quality into a product by reducing variations in production activities that could cause errors. This focus on cause allows for much more cost-effective intervention than inspecting finished products to spot defects and correct problems.

Tennessee-based Elo TouchSystems, for example, was losing $3 million a year, because a 25 percent defect rate plagued its touch-sensitive computer screens for products like automated teller machines. The company was forced to inspect each screen as it was produced—a costly and time-consuming effort. By applying statistical quality control methods, however, Elo cut its defect rate to only 1 percent. These control methods allowed the company to identify the variables in the production process that were affecting product quality instead of relying on inspection at the end of the production lines.[36]

Variation can be reduced in service environments as well. For example, Southwestern Bell received a number of complaints from large customers about errors on service orders and response time to service calls. The company developed a set of 15 alterations to its customer service function. After a five month test, Southwestern Bell was able to isolate the changes that would most effectively improve service levels. The modifications, including weekly meetings for customer service representatives and changing the length of employee training, helped the company provide more consistent service.[37]

Figure 2.13 Eliminating Waste through Physical Inspection

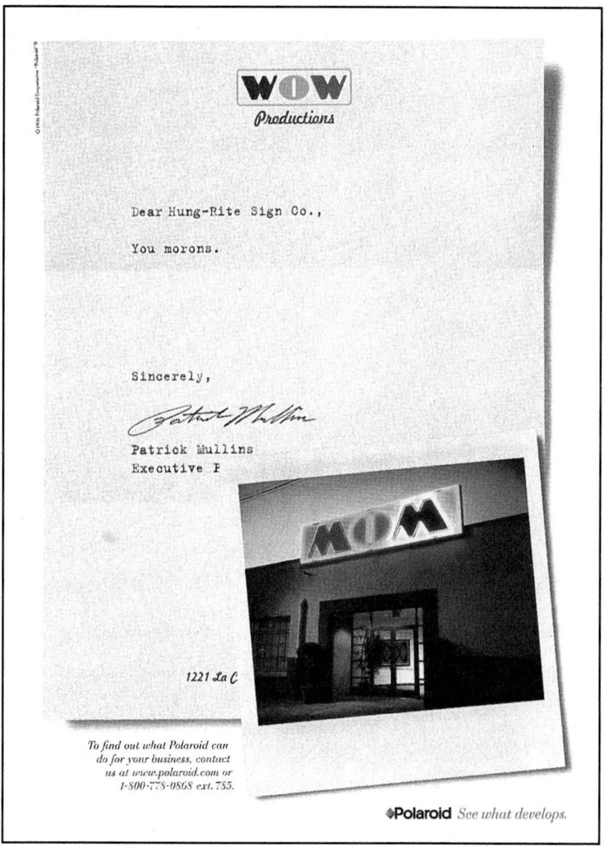
WOW
Productions
Dear Hung-Rite Sign Co.,
You morons.
Sincerely,
Patrick Mullins
Executive P
MOM
To find out what Polaroid can do for your business, contact us at www.polaroid.com or 1-800-778-0868 ext. 785.
Polaroid See what develops.

Eliminating Waste When work processes are continually improved to do things right the first time, customers benefit by receiving high-quality goods and services at lower prices. Economical production and marketing of products that satisfy customers forces a quality-oriented company to concentrate on eliminating waste. The humorous Polaroid ad shown in Figure 2.13 brings to mind a frequently repeated question: "Why is there never enough time to do a job right, but always time enough to do it over?" The sign company personnel should easily have recognized their mistake before the customer's inspection alerted them to the need for correction.

Quality consultants estimate that most companies pay a substantial cost for not doing things right the first time, often as much as 25 percent to 30 percent of sales revenues. The costs associated with poor quality, such as scrap, rework, and loss of customers, are called the **cost of quality.** The cost of quality has both internal and external dimensions. Most internal costs of quality are measurable; examples include discarding unusable parts, reworking defective parts, inspecting and discarding faulty goods,

Marketing Dictionary

continuous improvement Process of constantly studying and making changes in work activities; called *kaizen* in Japan.

PDCA cycle Continuous improvement sequence of planning, doing, checking, and acting.

cycle time The time required to complete a work process or activity from beginning to end.

cost of quality The total of costs associated with poor quality such as scrap, rework, and loss of customers.

Figure 2.14 Creating a Quality Image through Product Guarantees

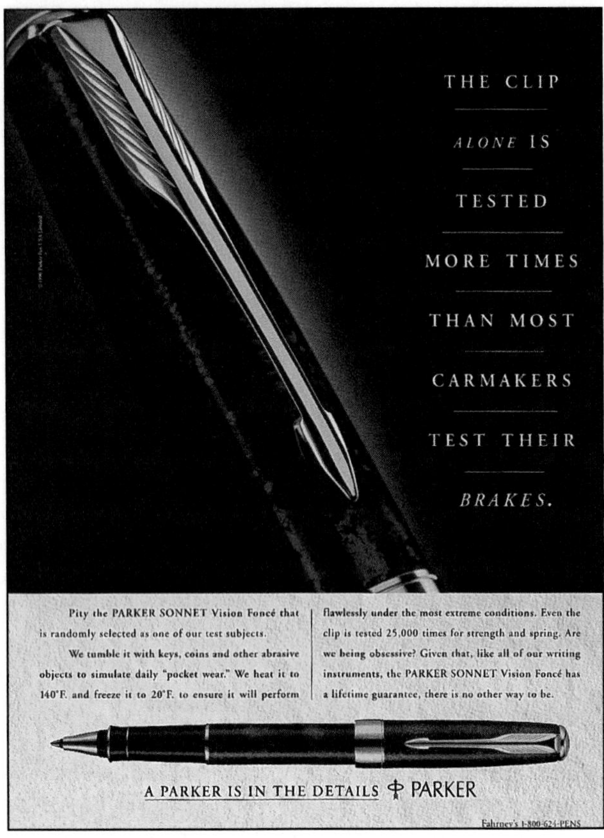
THE CLIP
ALONE IS
TESTED
MORE TIMES
THAN MOST
CARMAKERS
TEST THEIR
BRAKES.
Pity the PARKER SONNET Vision Foncé that is randomly selected as one of our test subjects.
We tumble it with keys, coins and other abrasive objects to simulate daily "pocket wear." We heat it to 140°F. and freeze it to 20°F. to ensure it will perform flawlessly under the most extreme conditions. Even the clip is tested 25,000 times for strength and spring. Are we being obsessive? Given that, like all of our writing instruments, the PARKER SONNET Vision Foncé has a lifetime guarantee, there is no other way to be.
A PARKER IS IN THE DETAILS
PARKER
Fahrney's 1-800-624-PENS

redesigning poor-quality products, and retraining employees. External costs are more difficult to measure. They include lost sales, missed marketing opportunities, frequent repairs, negative word-of-mouth advertising, bad publicity, and loss of customers to competitors.

TQM IN THE GLOBAL MARKETPLACE

U.S. firms are realizing that superior quality in goods and services can raise their reputations and expertise, leading to new opportunities in global markets. The poor quality of Russian goods and services, for example, has created market opportunities for American entrepreneurs in Moscow.

Implementing TQM in foreign subsidiaries can sometimes challenge domestically developed skills, though. Consider the case of Milliken's European division. In the U.S. market, the textile manufacturer was recognized for its quality initiatives, culminating in its receipt of the Malcolm Baldrige Award in 1989. The company's European division had eight plants, each serving its own markets with its own management team and products. That division's executives believed that continuous improvement initiatives would raise costs to unacceptable levels. Their quality programs focused on work inspection and handling customer complaints rather than on finding better processes.

Before the division could move toward a quality focus, the parent company had to change these attitudes. The European division also had to change its relationships with customers, employees, and suppliers, moving from adversarial to a more supportive association based on mutual satisfaction. This change required a new emphasis on listening to customers, working with suppliers, and finding processes for continuous improvement. Workers needed training to take more active roles in the division's quality commitment. As a result of these and other changes, Milliken's European division is now providing quality and customer satisfaction comparable to the award-winning parent company.[38]

DELIVERING CUSTOMER VALUE

As discussed earlier, the priority of delivering value to customers defines a core strategy that can help firms build competitive advantage. When a company pursues the goal of nourishing a culture of quality and customer satisfaction, it must design its marketing mix to support this decision. Chapter 1 defined the marketing mix as the blending of the four strategic elements of marketing decision making—product, distribution, promotion, and price—to satisfy a specific target market. This section examines how each strategic element contributes to customer perceptions of value.

Product Strategy

Delivering value to customers depends on providing goods and services that meet or exceed customers' quality expectations. The discussion of TQM has explained how marketplace winners organize teams of employees to design quality into both goods and services. Doing so requires making product strategy decisions that correctly identify and satisfy the needs and desires of a target market.

Customers of 3Com Corp., for instance, recently reported satisfaction with the company much higher than the norm for other computer equipment manufacturers. The main reason given by customers for their high satisfaction was the attention 3Com had paid to producing quality products that are easy to install and use. Customers said these features provided them with high "value for the dollar."[39]

In the fiercely competitive market for prestige writing instruments, Parker offers a lifetime guarantee as a key element in its product strategy. The advertisement in Figure 2.14 promises potential buyers that the Parker Sonnet has undergone extensive—and grueling—quality tests designed to ensure that its owners receive outstanding value.

Figure 2.15 **International On-Time Delivery as a Source of Added Value for Customers**

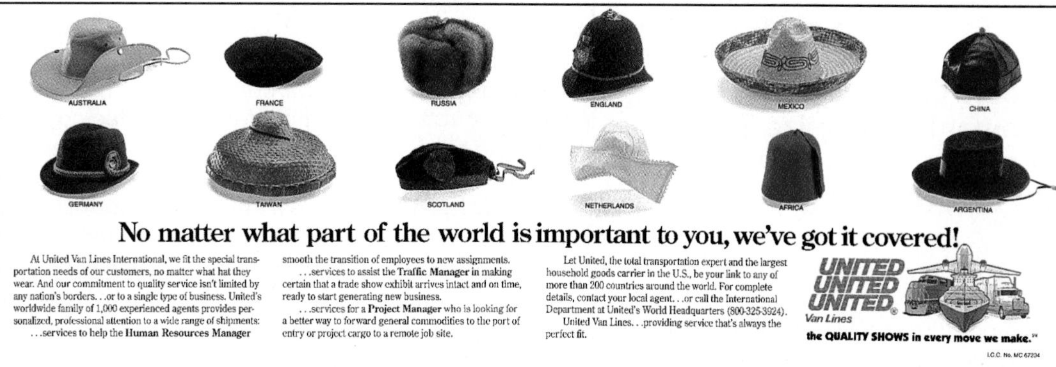
AUSTRALIA
FRANCE
RUSSIA
ENGLAND
MEXICO
CHINA
GERMANY
TAIWAN
SCOTLAND
NETHERLANDS
AFRICA
ARGENTINA
No matter what part of the world is important to you, we've got it covered!
At United Van Lines International, we fit the special transportation needs of our customers, no matter what hat they wear. And our commitment to quality service isn't limited by any nation's borders. . .or to a single type of business. United's worldwide family of 1,000 experienced agents provides personalized, professional attention to a wide range of shipments:
. . .services to help the Human Resources Manager smooth the transition of employees to new assignments.
. . .services to assist the Traffic Manager in making certain that a trade show exhibit arrives intact and on time, ready to start generating new business.
. . .services for a Project Manager who is looking for a better way to forward general commodities to the port of entry or project cargo to a remote job site.
Let United, the total transportation expert and the largest household goods carrier in the U.S., be your link to any of more than 200 countries around the world. For complete details, contact your local agent. . .or call the International Department at United's World Headquarters (800-325-3924).
United Van Lines. . .providing service that's always the perfect fit.
UNITED UNITED UNITED Van Lines
the QUALITY SHOWS in every move we make.℠
I.C.C. No. MC 67234

In addition to emphasizing quality, marketers can align their product strategies with their attempts to provide value by working toward mass customization. **Mass customization** seeks to provide customers with high-quality, competitively priced goods and services tailor-made to their specifications or needs. Oxford Health Systems, a Connecticut health maintenance organization, uses mass customization techniques to add value for its 800,000 members. At the core of Oxford's program is the company's computer database system, which identifies customer health service needs as they change and allows Oxford employees to custom-design a treatment plan for each member. For example, when a member notifies her Oxford representative that she is pregnant, the information is immediately passed on to Oxford employees. An Oxford nurse telephones the mother-to-be to assess her need for services during the course of her pregnancy and to set up a service plan designed to accommodate any special health concerns.[40]

In most cases, mass customization requires extensive support from technology. Databases, such as Oxford's patient-information system, often provide essential tools to support mass customization. Manufacturing industries depend on production technologies that allow rapid responses to customer specifications. Because of this heavy reliance on technology, mass customization can become an expensive product strategy. Marketers must carefully weigh the benefits of adapting this strategy to maximize value for customers against its costs. Mass customization is also a relationship marketing strategy, as Chapter 10 will explain.

Distribution Strategy

A firm can enhance value for customers by developing a customer-focused distribution strategy that delivers the right goods and services to customers at the right place and at the right time. MacGregor Golf Company has turned its distribution strategy into a tool to assure value for retail customers. When Kmart, The Sports Authority, or another retailer places an order from MacGregor, the firm's computer system automatically sends a confirmation to the customer and forwards the order to MacGregor's shipping department. The retailer can easily change the order at the last minute simply by entering the new data through a direct link with MacGregor's computer system. Besides increasing MacGregor's order volume by more than 25 percent, this distribution strategy has also strengthened the firm's relationships with retailers who know they can rely on MacGregor to get merchandise on their shelves in a hurry. As a result, they can effectively serve their own customers.[41]

Other companies are also developing innovative distribution methods to give added value to their customers. G&F Industries, a small manufacturer of plastic molding, maintains a distribution support employee on full-time duty in the plant of its largest customer, Bose Corp. The employee is responsible for assisting Bose production planning and making sure that G&F immediately fills Bose's supply needs. The measure has shortened Bose's production cycle and allowed the customer to eliminate expensive inventory of G&F products. G&F has forged a close relationship with Bose by providing value-added distribution support.[42]

As the chapter's opening vignette illustrates, banks are using the most up-to-date technology to change their distribution strategies. Instead of relying on bricks-and-mortar branches, banks allow customers to access their accounts via ATMs, 24-hour telephone lines, and even the Internet.

As the ad in Figure 2.15 explains, United Van Lines, the largest household-goods transporter in the United States, has expanded its services to meet the increasingly

Marketing Dictionary

mass customization Providing high-quality, competitively priced goods and services tailor-made to customers' specifications or needs.

SOLVING AN ETHICAL CONTROVERSY

Should Credit Card Companies Penalize Their Best Customers in Pursuit of Profits?

In the old days, credit card companies prized customers who faithfully paid their bills on time and maintained immaculate credit ratings. That attitude may no longer persist. Credit card providers are beginning to take steps that make their best customers feel unwelcome. GE Capital Services made headlines recently when it announced that card holders who paid off their balances every month would have to pay a $25 annual fee for their GE Rewards MasterCard.

If this snub seems strange, the industry cites solid financial reasons for the shift in thinking. The most conscientious credit card customers are, in one sense, bad for business. These people pay off their balances every month, leaving little opportunity for the card issuers to make money by imposing high interest rates. Prompt payers cost the industry $400 million annually in foregone interest payments, estimates James J. Daly, editor of the Chicago-based newsletter *Credit Card Management.*

Should Credit Card Companies Charge Fees to Their Best Customers?

PRO

1. **In an era when stockholders demand ever higher earnings, companies must do what they can to strengthen revenues. Card issuers, especially those that offer cash rebates and other financial incentives, must naturally assess fees to the least profitable card holders. These card holders just happen to be the most conscientious payers.**

   Rebate card issuers must struggle even harder than others to make money when customers quickly pay off their charges. "If it is a no-annual-fee card, that leaves two sources of revenue: interest income and interchange," says industry analyst Moshe A. Orenbuch. "And if the person doesn't borrow, you're down to just one: interchange." Most issuers earn 1.3 percent to 1.4 percent of charged purchase amounts in interchange income paid by merchants. For a card, such as the GE Rewards MasterCard, that gives out financial rewards for purchases, Orenbuch says, it is "virtually impossible to make any money."
2. **More than just the best customers are feeling the heat. Debt-ridden borrowers are also experiencing higher expenses. Some card companies are shortening their no-interest grace periods from 25 or 30 days to 20 days. They are hiking fees for late payments and charging for services that they once offered for free.**

global needs of its customers. Moving beyond its typical highway-transportation mission, the firm's 1,000 agents can now handle the moving needs of an employee who is transferred overseas or make certain that a trade-show exhibit arrives in Frankfort, Tokyo, or Tucson intact and on time, ready to start generating new business.

Promotional Strategy

Careful management of promotional activities such as personal selling, support services, advertising, and public relations can also help to increase customer perceptions of the benefits they receive from a firm. Any type of promotional strategy must deliver accurate messages to consumers. On one hand, promotional activities can help to educate customers about the value-added benefits they'll receive by purchasing a specific product. On the other hand, if a firm's promotional activities promise more than a good or service actually provides, customers will rapidly become dissatisfied with both the product and the firm.

Salespeople can play important roles in managing customer expectations, as anyone who's ever encountered a used car salesperson can confirm. One survey of consumers found that buying a car is "the most anxiety-provoking and least satisfying of any retail experiences." Customers walk away doubting their purchases. "The feeling that you got taken bothers you," said one car buyer of her experience. In response, some car dealers are changing the way they sell. Used-car superstore CarMax trains salespeople to avoid high-pressure sales tactics. Salespeople are paid by salary instead of commission. Potential customers

3. **Drastic measures are necessary because an increasing number of customers are acting responsibly. In 1990, 29 percent of Americans paid their credit card bills on time, while today 36 percent do.**

CON

1. **Encouraging consumers to stay out of debt offers opportunities that prove just as lucrative as traditional business for card-holding companies. Not long after GE Capital announced its new policy, Cleveland's Key Bank U.S.A. unveiled a credit card that actually rewards people for fiscally responsible behavior. Customers who make big payments on their bills each month pay a lower interest rate than those who pay only the minimum. With strong response to the new card, the bank is making money because 90 percent of the customers are carrying balances compared with the in-dustry average of 70 percent.**
2. **With credit card delinquencies at a 15-year high, it is ethically bankrupt to encourage Americans to sink further into debt. Companies that avoid tempting consumers are acting as good corporate citizens. "I have nothing but praise for the Key Bank card," said Ruth Susswein, director of Bankcard Holders of America, a consumer group. "It is working to assist consumers and rewarding them for paying off their debt."**
3. **Alienating customers with sterling repayment records could backfire. If these customers walk away, a firm might replace them with card carriers who bring checkered credit histories. Card companies need to worry just as much about bad credit risks that can also hurt their profitability.**

Summary

While other card companies have resisted following GE Capital's lead, some observers speculate that others in the industry will increasingly reward big debtors and punish those who avoid carrying balances. Citibank, for example, hikes its interest rate for customers when their balances fall below $2,500. Any Citibank customer whose balance exceeds $2,500 enjoys a lower interest rate. Says Robert McKinley, president of a credit card research company, "The GE and Citibank strategy is probably going to win out over (Key Bank's) nice-guy strategy."

Sources: Joseph Weber, "A Hard Blow for Easy Credit," *Business Week,* March 31, 1997, p. 39; Martha Nolan McKenzie, "Bank's Credit Card Rewards Holders Who Are Fiscally Prudent," *San Diego Union-Tribune,* November 3, 1996, p. I–2; and Kerry Capell, "Dunned if You Do, Dunned if You Don't," *Business Week,* September 23, 1996, pp. 130–131.

may freely browse and research prices on touch-screen computers. In one survey, CarMax earned a 98 percent customer satisfaction rating, a far cry from the used-car sales routine of old.[43]

Promotional activities can also help customers get the highest possible value out of their purchases by providing training and support services. Yamaha Corp. of America marketers found that improving their customer service practices helps to reduce defects and improve customer satisfaction. The company automated its phone-support function to promptly direct customers to engineers who can address service and product problems.[44]

Other companies are finding that the Internet can help them to add value through promotional strategies. Millipore, a manufacturer of high-technology purification systems for research and manufacturing applications, successfully uses the Internet to provide value-added information to customers. Millipore's customers are mainly engineers and scientists who require a great deal of information, both before and after they buy, about the technical specifications of the firm's products. Millipore has developed a Web site that allows prospective and current customers to interact directly with the company for technical, application, product, and ordering information. Millipore customers can visit the site's database to search the company's product catalog; they can also receive technical assistance from Millipore's service department. Millipore sees this site as a strategic tool for both promoting its products and providing value-added information to customers. The Web site has provided added benefits for the company by helping it promote to and serve its international customers.[45]

Figure 2.16 **Emphasizing Performance Quality as Part of a Value-Pricing Strategy**

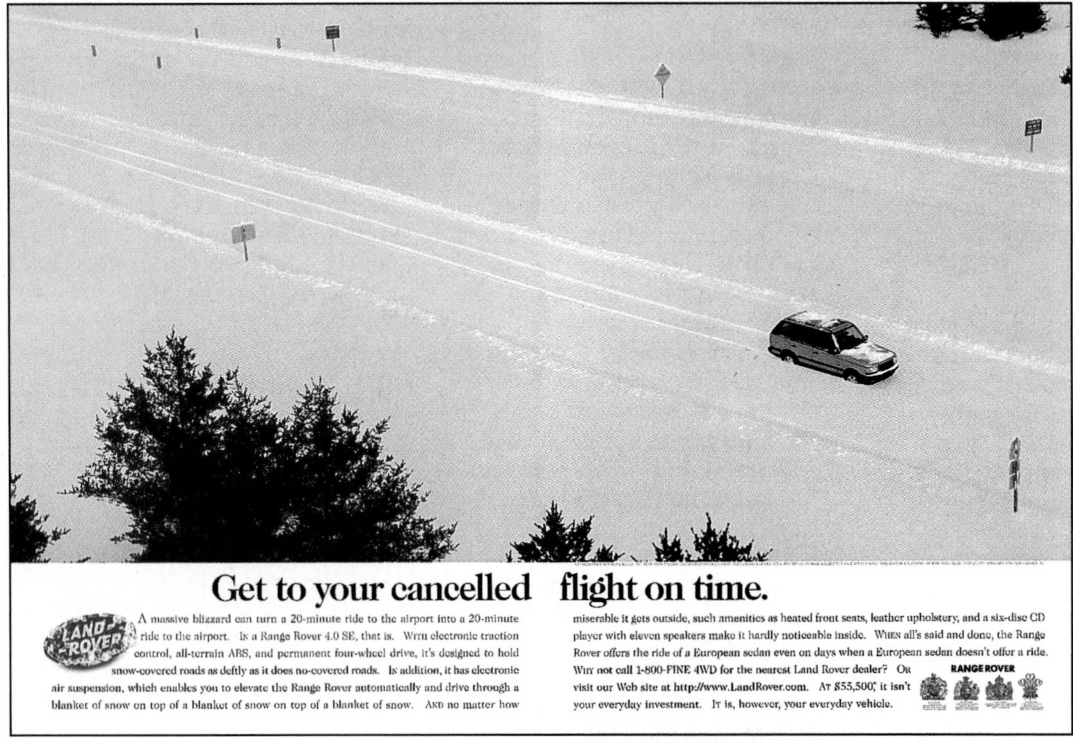
Get to your cancelled flight on time.
LAND-ROVER
A massive blizzard can turn a 20-minute ride to the airport into a 20-minute ride to the airport. In a Range Rover 4.0 SE, that is. With electronic traction control, all-terrain ABS, and permanent four-wheel drive, it's designed to hold snow-covered roads as deftly as it does no-covered roads. In addition, it has electronic air suspension, which enables you to elevate the Range Rover automatically and drive through a blanket of snow on top of a blanket of snow on top of a blanket of snow. And no matter how miserable it gets outside, such amenities as heated front seats, leather upholstery, and a six-disc CD player with eleven speakers make it hardly noticeable inside. When all's said and done, the Range Rover offers the ride of a European sedan even on days when a European sedan doesn't offer a ride. Why not call 1-800-FINE 4WD for the nearest Land Rover dealer? Or visit our Web site at http://www.LandRover.com. At $55,500,* it isn't your everyday investment. It is, however, your everyday vehicle.
RANGE ROVER

Pricing Strategy

Customers perceive value when they believe that a company has provided quality goods and services at fair prices. Consumers need not settle for anything less than the right products at the right prices. Pinpointing the correct value-pricing strategy can require complex analysis. Once again, marketers must understand customer attitudes and motivations to find the right price. Customers may willingly pay relatively high prices for goods that they feel provide exceptional attributes. In some industries, however, the traditional idea that higher prices mean better quality is changing as quality levels rise while prices fall. As a result, organizations often work to lower their production costs and pass the savings on to consumers in the form of lower prices.

Marketers at Land Rover realize that the Range Rover 4.0 SE, with a retail sticker price of $55,500, isn't an everyday expense. To convince top-of-the-line car buyers to seriously consider their brand over alternatives from BMW, Lexus, or Mercedes in the same price range or a Jeep Grand Cherokee at two-thirds the price, Land Rover must emphasize value-added features like dependability, comfort, and a host of amenities. The ad shown in Figure 2.16 uses humor to emphasize the four-wheel-drive vehicle's ability to perform under conditions too adverse for almost every other vehicle.

Another company with a successful value-pricing strategy is Southwest Airlines. As other airlines have struggled with rising costs, Southwest Airlines has kept operating costs dramatically under industry standards. The company flies only one type of jet to cut maintenance and pilot training costs. Passengers aren't served meals and cannot reserve seats. Employees are paid by the trip, not by the hour. As a result, Southwest spends approximately seven cents per mile for each seat, while larger airlines such as United and American spend thirteen cents. By keeping operating costs low, Southwest has held air fares at or below those charged by competing airlines. Southwest customers don't mind the lack of amenities; they're willing to sacrifice onboard meals for fare savings. Southwest has correctly identified the value equation between pricing and service.[46]

> **Briefly speaking**
>
> "Quality in a product or service is not what the supplier puts in. It is what the customer gets out and is willing to pay for. A product is not quality because it is hard to make and costs a lot of money, as manufacturers typically believe. This is incompetence. Customers pay only for what is of use to them and gives them value. Nothing else constitutes quality."
>
> **Peter Drucker (1909–)**
> **American business philosopher**

ACHIEVEMENT CHECK SUMMARY

Reread the learning goals that follow, and consider the questions for each goal. Answering these questions will reinforce your grasp of the most important concepts in the chapter and allow you to check how well you have achieved these learning goals. Where a blank appears before a question, answer with *T* or *F;* for multiple-choice questions, circle the letter of the correct answer.

Objective 2.1: Explain the relationships between value, customer satisfaction, and quality.

1. ___ Value is the customer's perception of the balance between price and quality.

2. ___ A firm can acquire new customers less expensively than keeping existing customers.

3. ___ Quality refers only to the physical characteristics of a good.

Objective 2.2: Identify the major components of customer satisfaction.

1. ___ Business executives can usually figure out what will satisfy customers by brainstorming during executive meetings.

2. ___ To satisfy customers, businesses must pinpoint what prospective buyers want, need, and expect.

3. ___ The best way to find out what customers expect is (a) determine what competitors are doing; (b) study market trends and statistics; (c) ask customers directly.

Objective 2.3: List the goals of internal marketing.

1. ___ Only employees who interact directly with customers can influence customer satisfaction.

2. ___ Internal marketing efforts help employees to support each other.

3. ___ Communicating with employees about customer needs helps a business to reach its objectives.

Objective 2.4: Explain the primary methods by which marketers measure customer satisfaction.

1. ___ Businesses must verify that they measure the right things when they track customer satisfaction.

2. ___ The only way to measure customer satisfaction is to conduct regular customer surveys.

3. ___ Studying the reasons behind customer defections can help a firm to improve customer satisfaction.

4. ___ Measurement must combine with action in order to fully meet customer expectations.

Objective 2.5: Outline the historical development of the quality movement.

1. ___ The quality movement started in Japan.

2. ___ Shewhart's method of statistical quality control encourages businesses to improve assembly-line inspection methods.

3. ___ The Baldrige Award (a) recognizes quality Japanese products; (b) is given to U.S. companies with superior quality programs; (c) is awarded only to manufacturing firms.

4. ___ *Kaizen* is a Japanese term for value-added quality.

5. ___ To do business in Europe, manufacturers need to comply with ISO 9000 standards.

Objective 2.6: Discuss the roles of top management and employees in implementing total quality management (TQM).

1. ___ Senior managers must take an active role in the quality management process.

2. ___ Empowerment initiatives provide financial resources to departments so that employees can improve productivity.

3. ___ A quality circle is a method of organizing the work space in an office so employees can interact effectively.

Objective 2.7: Outline the objectives of a marketing audit.

1. ___ A marketing audit seeks to identify weaknesses in a firm's efforts to satisfy customers.

2. ___ Marketing audits most effectively identify weaknesses in large, multinational companies.

Objective 2.8: Explain the benchmarking process and its role in improving a marketing strategy.

1. ___ The factors that are most important in gaining competitive advantage are called (a) critical success factors; (b) benchmarking factors; (c) marketing mix factors.

2. ___ Benchmarking is the process of measuring a firm's performance and comparing it against competitors' results.

3. ___ Firms usually choose to benchmark against other firms in their industries.

4. ___ The ultimate goal of benchmarking is to improve processes for enhanced quality and customer satisfaction.

Objective 2.9: Describe how an organization can work toward continuous improvement in its marketing activities.

1. ___ Continuous improvement requires that businesses constantly study and make changes in work activities to improve quality.

2. ___ Statistical control reduces cycle time.

3. ___ A firm can inspect finished products for defects more cost-effectively than it can change a plant's operating processes.

4. ___ Eliminating waste is important to customer satisfaction because (a) customers are worried about environmental concerns; (b) waste can contribute to higher prices; (c) cycle times fall dramatically when a firm eliminates waste.

Objective 2.10: Explain how marketing managers can deliver value to customers by balancing the marketing mix elements.

1. ___ A manufacturer of men's shirts designs and produces shirts that are tailor-made to the individual measurements and desires of customers. This is an example of (a) customer quality; (b) mass customization; (c) mass production.

2. ____ Marketers must ensure the accuracy of promotional messages because (a) inaccurate messages may lead to false customer expectations; (b) advertising is expensive; (c) competitors may use the messages in benchmarking.
3. ____ To find the right pricing strategies, companies must understand customer attitudes and motivations.
4. ____ A good distribution strategy can satisfy customers by making the right product available when and where they need it.

Students: See the solutions section located on page S-1 to check your responses to the Achievement Check Summary.

Key Terms

value
value added
quality
customer satisfaction
external customer
internal customer
internal marketing
intranet
customer satisfaction measurement (CSM) program
total quality management (TQM)
statistical quality control
ISO 9000
employee involvement
empowerment
quality circle
cross-functional team
self-managed team
marketing audit
benchmarking
critical success factor
continuous improvement
PDCA cycle
cycle time
cost of quality
mass customization

Review Questions

1. Explain the relationship between quality and customer satisfaction.
2. Distinguish between external customers and internal customers.
3. Explain the role of buyer feedback in achieving customer satisfaction. What are the primary methods of securing such feedback?
4. How does total quality management help an organization to compete?
5. Summarize the contribution(s) made by each of the following pioneers of TQM: Walter Shewhart, W. Edwards Deming, Joseph Juran, and the International Standards Organization in Switzerland.
6. Identify and briefly explain five strategies that promote successful quality management efforts in marketing.
7. How can managers encourage employee involvement?
8. What criteria are likely to characterize a good benchmarking partner?
9. What are the goals of continuous improvement?
10. Summarize the ways in which quality improvements can affect each element of the marketing mix in both domestic and international markets.

Discussion Questions

1. According to one study, nearly half of the subscribers to online service providers such as America Online and CompuServe plan to switch to new service providers within a year. Reasons given for wanting to switch include desire for faster service (25 percent), preference for flat monthly fees (20 percent), and availability of local dial-in access. Assuming that service providers can find new customers to replace lost subscribers, should they still worry about this trend? Why? What actions would you recommend?
2. Apply the continuous improvement principle to a service or procedure at your college or university. Does this service currently satisfy customers as much as it could? If not, why not? How might you reduce the gap between actual and desired service levels?
3. Describe a situation in which you as a customer experienced poor quality in either a good or a service. How did this experience affect your feelings toward the company? What advice would you give to that company's managers?
4. Identify a firm in your city or state that you consider to be a world-class competitor in each of the following marketing mix elements:
   a. product
   b. distribution
   c. promotion
   d. price
   Briefly defend your choice.
5. You've been chosen to design and staff a 400-room hotel in New York City. Explain how you would apply the concepts and tactics discussed in this chapter to attract repeat visitors to the hotel. How would your plans affect the hotel's financial performance?

'netWork

1. Many companies have started measuring customer satisfaction via the Internet. Go to Polaroid's home page,

http://www.polaroid.com/

and access the Customer Survey screen. Evaluate the usefulness of the instrument. Does it measure customer satisfaction? By just placing this instrument on the Web, does Polaroid make customers feel that the firm cares about them?

2. Many research firms research topics related to customer satisfaction for client companies. One such research provider is Custom Research Interactive (CRI). Not only does this firm evaluate other firms' customer satisfaction levels, but it also has won the Malcolm Baldrige Quality Award itself, which depends heavily on satisfied customers. Go to the CRI home page located at

http://www.cresearch.com/

How does the firm provide customer satisfaction research to its clients? Why are its customers so satisfied?

3. J. D. Power and Associates is an international marketing information firm that provides consulting services on collecting consumer opinions and customer satisfaction data in the auto, airline, and personal computer industries. Go to the company's home page

http://www.jdpower.com/

What firms rank at the top of these three industries, according to the data you find there? How were these leaders chosen? Do you agree with the decisions? How would you change Power's research methods?

VIDEO CASE 2

PURSUING A LOFTY GOAL

"If you want to build a truly great company . . . you need a road map to twenty-first-century success in an organization," says Don Wainwright. "You need lofty goals."

Don Wainwright is chairman of Wainwright Industries, a contract manufacturer that produces precision components and subassembled systems for the automotive, aerospace, home security, and information processing industries. Founded in 1947 by the Wainwright family, the company has production facilities in Missouri. In 1994, Wainwright won the Malcolm Baldrige National Quality Award in small business for ". . . excellence in quality management."

The seven Baldrige criteria provided the road map Wainwright used for its journey to quality, customer satisfaction, and self-assessment. The journey began during the 1980s after General Motors, a major Wainwright customer, told its 400 suppliers that due to pressure from foreign competition in the auto industry, GM would cut the number of its suppliers in half and demand higher-quality products from suppliers it kept. To keep GM as a customer, Wainwright set a lofty goal of becoming a world-class supplier.

Management realized that to achieve its lofty goal it had to change its relationship with employees from one based on mistrust to one based on trust. During an employee meeting, Don Wainwright admitted that in the past management had not trusted employees to make decisions. He said management had been wrong in making decisions for employees and in telling them how to do their jobs. He pledged his support in sharing information with employees, asking them for their suggestions about how to improve their jobs, and empowering them to make decisions about improving quality. He asked them to " . . . pull together as team members and make this company go forward."

Wainwright then launched a training program to give employees the skills they needed to accomplish the firm's new expectations. Training included teaching employees basic math and vocabulary skills, as well as such interpersonal skills as problem solving, constructive feedback, how to listen, and the importance of information sharing.

Benchmarking played a key role in the development of Wainwright's quality program. Wainwright employees met with previous Baldrige Award winners to learn about their best practices. They adopted a customer-satisfaction measurement system from Solectron Corp. and a suggestion program from Milliken & Company.

Each month Wainwright sends a report card to its customers and asks them for a customer satisfaction grade of A, B, C, or D—for 100 percent, 90 percent, 50 percent, or 0 percent satisfaction, respectively. The grading system allows customers to be teachers. From customer feedback, employees learn what customers like and dislike. They look at problems as opportunities for improvement.

Employees grade their managers in the same way that customers grade Wainwright. Employee customer departments also rate their internal supplier departments on a quarterly basis. Wainwright posts all internal and external customer satisfaction ratings in Mission Control, a conference room open to all employees.

Also displayed in Mission Control are the company's strategic operating indicators, which Wainwright developed by asking employees what was important to them. They are, in order of importance,

1. Safety
2. Internal Customer Satisfaction
3. External Customer Satisfaction
4. Quality
5. Business Performance

These indicators are continuously measured, benchmarked, and improved, helping Wainwright bridge the gap between its goals and day-to-day operations.

Wainwright's quality drive has focused all employees on working together to satisfy customers. The firm has been honored by General Motors, Ford, and IBM for supplier excellence. For employees, the difference between being told what to do and being able to make changes and improvements has resulted in pride in their work, a sense of ownership, and increased job satisfaction. Their suggestions for continuous improvement have helped Wainwright enhance customer satisfaction by lowering customer reject rates. Wainwright has reduced scrap and rework costs and cut operating expenses 35 percent during the past five years and has passed the savings on to customers.

Employee involvement has changed the role of management. Managers now have time to spend on planning for the future, developing partnerships with major customers, and identifying new business opportunities. By satisfying customers, Wainwright has experienced tremendous growth in market share, sales revenue, and net profits, evolving from a struggling supplier to a $30 million company positioned for continued success in the twenty-first century.

Questions

1. Which marketing mix elements are most affected by Wainwright's quality drive?
2. Describe how Wainwright used the Baldrige criteria listed in Figure 2.8 as a road map for quality improvement.
3. Are report cards an effective way to measure internal and external customer satisfaction? Explain your answer.
4. The process of becoming a Baldrige Award recipient has been called "the best, most cost-effective, and comprehensive business health audit you can get." Review the National Institute of Standards and Technology Web site at

   http://www.quality.nist.gov/

   before answering the following questions:

   a. Identify the different categories in which the Baldrige Award is given.

   b. Describe the application and review process for firms seeking the Baldrige Award.

   c. What are the positive outcomes of receiving this award?

   d. In what ways do you feel Wainwright Industries has benefited from receiving the Baldrige Award?

Source: Telephone interview with Carol Anderson, Wainwright Accounts Receivable, May 16, 1997; and Michael Verespej, "America's Best Plants: Wainwright Industries," *Industry Week,* October 21, 1996, pp. 72–74.

CHAPTER 3

THE MARKETING ENVIRONMENT, ETHICS, AND SOCIAL RESPONSIBILITY

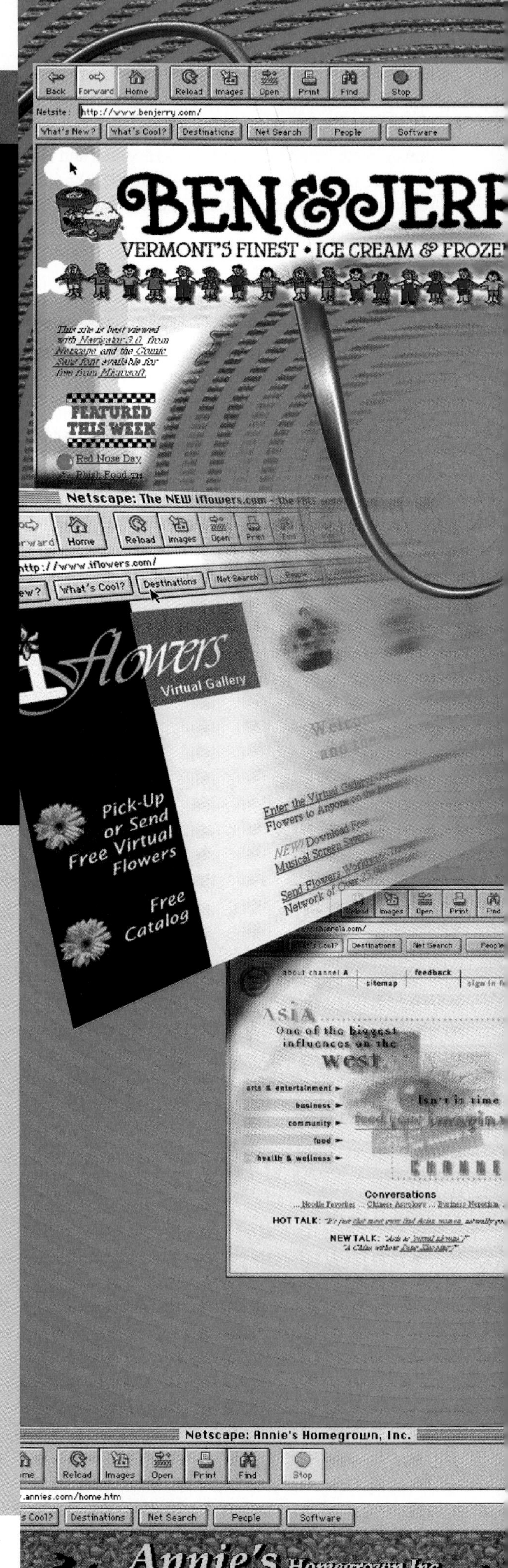

Back
Forward
Home
Reload
Images
Open
Print
Find
Stop
Netsite: http://www.benjerry.com/
What's New?
What's Cool?
Destinations
Net Search
People
Software
BEN&JERR
VERMONT'S FINEST • ICE CREAM & FROZE
FEATURED THIS WEEK
Red Nose Day
Netscape: The NEW iflowers.com
http://www.iflowers.com/
iflowers
Virtual Gallery
Pick-Up or Send Free Virtual Flowers
Free Catalog
Enter the Virtual Gallery
NEW! Download Free Musical Screen Savers!
Send Flowers Worldwide
about channel A
sitemap
feedback
ASIA
One of the biggest influences on the west.
arts & entertainment
business
community
food
health & wellness
Conversations
HOT TALK:
NEW TALK:
Netscape: Annie's Homegrown, Inc.
annies.com/home.htm
Annie's Homegrown Inc.

Chapter Objectives

1. Identify the five components of the marketing environment.
2. Explain the types of competition that marketers face and the steps they take to develop competitive strategies.
3. Describe how government and other groups regulate marketing activities and how marketers can influence the political-legal environment.
4. Outline the economic forces that affect marketing decisions and consumer buying power.
5. Explain the impact of the technological environment on a firm's marketing activities.
6. Explain how the social-cultural environment influences marketing.
7. Describe the role of marketing in society, and name the two major social issues in marketing.

The Green Consumer

In the early 1990s, decisions seemed to come easily enough for environmentally concerned consumers. "Every time you opened your wallet, you cast a vote 'for' or 'against' the planet," recalls Joel Makower, editor of *The Green Business Letter.* "Paper or plastic? Cloth or disposable? Biodegradable? Ozone friendly?"

The drive to make the environment better through shopping choices demonstrated an admirable, though rather naive spirit, Makower and other experts suggest. Choices considered black and white back then were really anything but straightforward decisions. Take the environmentalists' argument against plastic grocery bags. Shoppers would request brown-paper bags because they envisioned landfills overflowing with plastic. Actually, plastic comprises only 9 percent of municipal solid waste, while paper and cardboard take up four times as much dump space.

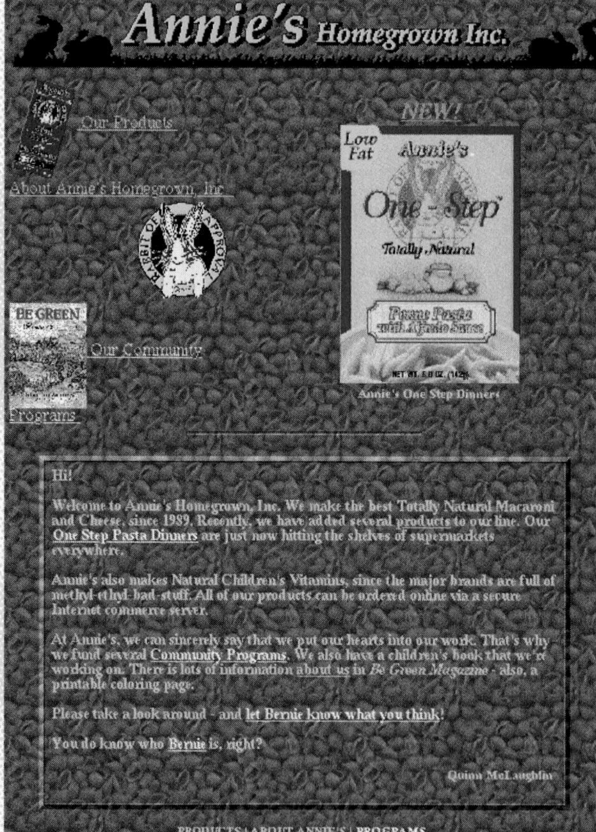
Annie's Homegrown Inc.
Our Products
About Annie's Homegrown, Inc.
BE GREEN
Our Community
Programs
NEW!
Low Fat
Annie's
One-Step
Totally Natural
Annie's One Step Dinners
Hi!
Welcome to Annie's Homegrown, Inc. We make the best Totally Natural Macaroni and Cheese, since 1989. Recently, we have added several products to our line. Our One Step Pasta Dinners are just now hitting the shelves of supermarkets everywhere.
Annie's also makes Natural Children's Vitamins, since the major brands are full of methyl-ethyl-bad-stuff. All of our products can be ordered online via a secure Internet commerce server.
At Annie's, we can sincerely say that we put our hearts into our work. That's why we fund several Community Programs. We also have a children's book that we're working on. There is lots of information about us in Be Green Magazine - also, a printable coloring page.
Please take a look around - and let Bernie know what you think!
You do know who Bernie is, right?
PRODUCTS | ABOUT ANNIE'S | PROGRAMS

Of course, revelations like these only confused consumers who wanted to help the environment but were no longer sure how to do it. Attempting to dispel some of the confusion, the Federal Trade Commission stepped in with regulations for recycling claims. Companies must now follow specific guidelines whenever they make claims about whether a product is biodegradable or appropriate for recycling.

Yet some consumers still want to practice green shopping. The Internet offers one way for businesses to reach out to this market segment. In fact, the World Wide Web is increasingly becoming an essential tool for green marketers. The upscale consumer profiles of many Internet users match quite nicely with many suggested profiles for environmentally concerned consumers. For example, ice cream maker Ben & Jerry's Homemade, Inc. and Annie's Homegrown Inc., a maker of All Natural Pasta, both mix advertising messages with environmental

http://www.benjerry.com/
http://www.annies.com/

news. Their Web pages include a mix of current environmental and social information, games, and activities to entertain green shoppers with information for ordering the companies' products.

By peddling green products, companies can profit while protecting the environment. Perhaps more importantly, some marketers are now instituting green business practices intended to enhance their revenues and perhaps their reputations. For example, Anheuser-Busch, America's largest brewery, has saved 21 million pounds of aluminum annually by slimming the diameter of its beer can by one-eighth inch.

Indeed, researchers from Carnegie-Mellon University argue that the brewing giant's actions illustrate the best way for corporations to fulfill their green responsibilities. The real emphasis in recycling should center on designing products with easily salvaged and reused parts.

Baxter International, the Illinois-based manufacturer and marketer of medical products, typifies this trend. Baxter advises scores of hospitals to help them structure their internal programs for pollution reduction and recycling. It's no wonder Baxter's green programs are popular. Federal environmental regulations for medical centers, which filled 470 pages in 1972, bulged at 10,000 pages in 1990.

"Several customers sought corporate partners to be part of their environmental program and today we enjoy a lion's share of their business because of our efforts to assist them with waste audits, and establishing a recycling program," says Rene Welch, a Baxter senior marketing manager. Baxter is also constantly trying to identify products that generate unnecessary waste. After learning that physicians at one medical center discarded unused trays included with surgical packs, Baxter marketers conducted a study to determine whether other users followed similar practices. When the study concluded that customers rarely used the trays, the company eliminated them from the packs.

Baxter's numerous green initiatives have encouraged clients to buy more of its products, helped it to win new accounts, and even attracted the interest of other ecologically conscious firms. Over 25 percent of Baxter's customers request its help on environmental issues, and its commitment to the environment attracts a growing number of potential customers. When Evangelical Health Systems issued a request for proposals to complete a multimillion-dollar project, it asked bidders questions like, "Is your company's environmental program a strategy or an afterthought?" Baxter's leadership in environmental issues and well-defined programs provided an advantage that helped it to win this major account.[1]

CHAPTER OVERVIEW

Industry competition, legal constraints, the impact of technology on product design, and social concerns are some of the many important conditions that shape the business environment. This chapter examines the forces that define marketing's external environment. It also discusses the social role of marketing and looks at the nature of marketers' responsibilities, both to business and to society at large.

Members of every organization need to think seriously about the environments in which they operate and the roles that they play in society. All firms must identify, analyze, and monitor external forces and assess their potential impacts on those firms' goods and services. Although external forces frequently operate outside the marketing manager's control, decision makers still must consider those influences together with the variables of the marketing mix in developing the firm's marketing plans and strategies.

This chapter begins by describing five forces in marketing's external environment: competitive, political-legal, economic, technological, and social-cultural forces, as shown in Figure 3.1. These forces provide the critical frame of reference within which marketers formulate their decisions. The chapter also discusses the responses of marketers to society in general through socially responsible and ethical behavior.

ENVIRONMENTAL SCANNING AND ENVIRONMENTAL MANAGEMENT

Marketers must carefully and continually monitor crucial trends and developments in the business environment. **Environmental scanning** is the process of collecting information about the external marketing environment to identify and interpret potential trends. This activity then seeks to analyze the collected information and determine whether identified trends represent opportunities or threats to the company. This judgment, in turn, allows a firm to determine the best response to a particular environmental change.

Environmental scanning is a vital component of effective environmental management. **Environmental management** is the effort to attain organizational objectives by predicting and influencing the firm's competitive, political-legal, economic, technological, and social-cultural environments. This influence can result from a number of activities by the firm's management. For example, they may exercise political power by joining political action committees (PACs) to lobby legislators and contribute to the campaigns of sympathetic politicians as a way of achieving desired modifications of regulations, laws, or tariff restrictions.

Political-Legal Environment
Competitive Environment
Social-Cultural Environment
Economic Environment
Technological Environment
Product
Pricing
Promotion
Distribution
Target Market

Figure 3.1

Elements of the Marketing Mix within an Environmental Framework

The development of a global marketplace has complicated environmental scanning and environmental management. These processes may now need to track political developments, economic trends, and cultural influences anywhere in the world. To compete in the global arena, many firms are forming alliances with foreign companies that can help to provide this intelligence.

Industries that once operated entirely within national borders now compete against global rivals. Even telecommunications and electric utility companies are opening up new markets through alliances. The merger of British Telecommunications (BT) and MCI gave BT an entry into the U.S. market after eight years of trying. BT set the stage for this merger by purchasing 20 percent of MCI in 1993. It also undertook joint ventures with MCI to sell telecommunications services to multinational companies and to develop the first global Internet backbone network.

Electric utilities are also looking overseas for higher earnings. Dominion Resources, the Virginia-based utilities company, recently purchased a British firm, East Midlands Electricity. East Midlands joined a number of other subsidiaries owned by this aggressively expanding utility. In addition to natural gas utilities in Australia, Canada, and several U.S. cities, Dominion owns electricity-related businesses in six U.S. states and several Latin American countries.[2]

Through successful research and development efforts, firms may influence changes in their own technological environments. A research breakthrough may lead to reduced production costs or a technologically superior new product. While the marketing environment may exceed the confines of the firm and its marketing

Marketing Dictionary

environmental scanning The process of collecting information about the external marketing environment in order to identify and interpret potential trends.

environmental management An effort to attain organizational objectives by predicting and influencing the firm's competitive, political-legal, economic, technological, and social-cultural environments.

Figure 3.2 Color Copiers and Digital Cameras: Competition for Photo Processors and Traditional Cameras

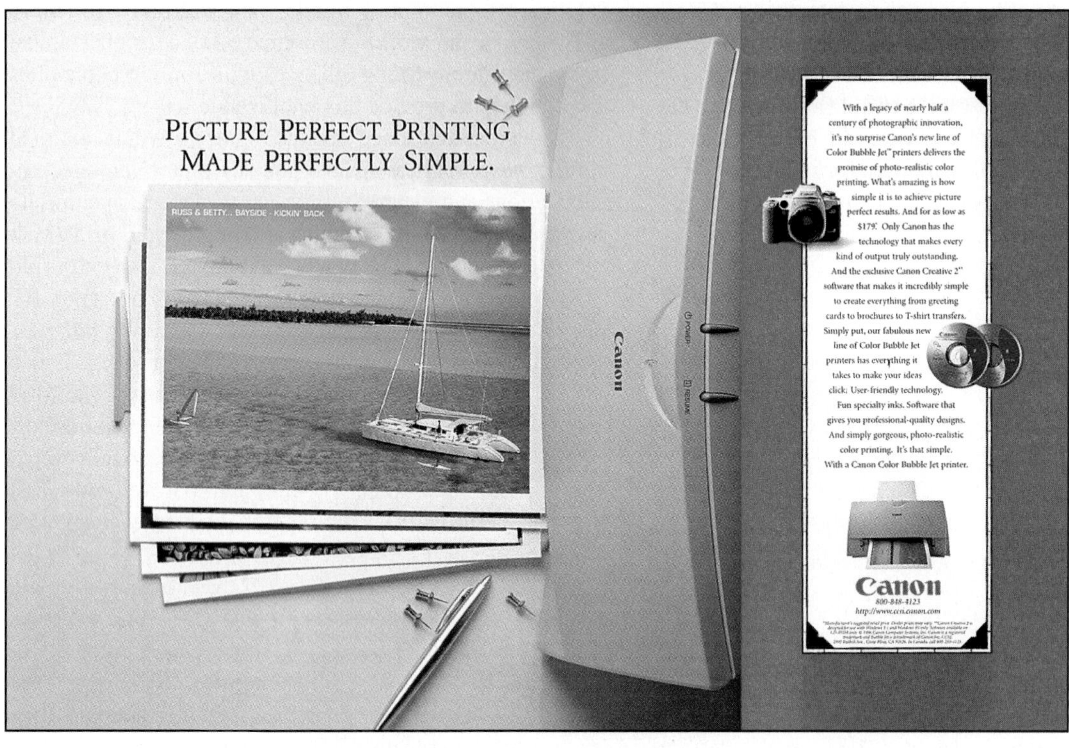
PICTURE PERFECT PRINTING
MADE PERFECTLY SIMPLE.
RUSS & BETTY... BAYSIDE - KICKIN' BACK
Canon
With a legacy of nearly half a century of photographic innovation, it's no surprise Canon's new line of Color Bubble Jet™ printers delivers the promise of photo-realistic color printing. What's amazing is how simple it is to achieve picture perfect results. And for as low as $179.* Only Canon has the technology that makes every kind of output truly outstanding. And the exclusive Canon Creative 2** software that makes it incredibly simple to create everything from greeting cards to brochures to T-shirt transfers. Simply put, our fabulous new line of Color Bubble Jet printers has everything it takes to make your ideas click: User-friendly technology. Fun specialty inks. Software that gives you professional-quality designs. And simply gorgeous, photo-realistic color printing. It's that simple. With a Canon Color Bubble Jet printer.
Canon
800-848-4123
http://www.ccsi.canon.com

mix components, effective marketers continually seek to predict its impact on marketing decisions and to modify its conditions whenever possible.

In addition to its effect on current marketing decisions, the dynamic marketing environment demands that managers at every level continually reevaluate marketing decisions in response to changing conditions. Even modest environmental shifts can alter the results of marketing decisions.

THE COMPETITIVE ENVIRONMENT

The interactive exchange in the marketplace as organizations vie with one another to satisfy customers creates the **competitive environment.** Marketing decisions by each individual firm influence consumer responses in the marketplace. They also affect the marketing strategies of competitors. As a consequence, decision makers must continually monitor competitors' marketing activities—their products, channels, prices, and promotions.

Few organizations enjoy monopoly positions in the marketplace. Utilities, such as natural gas, electricity, water, and cable television services, accept considerable regulation from local authorities, who control such marketing elements as rates, service levels, and geographic coverage; in exchange, the utilities gain exclusive rights to serve particular groups of consumers. Further, utilities no longer enjoy total monopoly protection within their territories. Other firms, such as manufacturers of pharmaceutical products, sometimes achieve temporary monopolies as a result of patents. By increasing competition, deregulation also has changed the nature of the telecommunications industry. Consumers receive constant streams of solicitations from long-distance telephone companies, providing almost daily evidence of the increased competition in a formerly monopolized industry.

Types of Competition

Marketers actually face three types of competition. Their most direct competition occurs among marketers of similar products, as when Allstate competes with other insurance companies. Competitors in the personal computer industry include IBM, Apple, Compaq, Dell, and NEC of Japan. The American Red Cross competes with United Way, among others, for charitable contributions.

A second type of competition involves products that users can substitute for one another. In the transportation industry, Amtrak competes with auto-rental services, airlines, and bus services. In the business of delivering business documents, overnight express mail services and messenger services compete with facsimile (fax) machines. The spread of fax machines has put a huge dent in the business of transportation companies such as Federal Express and courier services. However, fax machines are already beginning to lose business to electronic communications via the Internet and videoconferencing, a technology that combines video, audio, and electronic mail elements with shared access to documents in a personal computer network.

A change such as a price increase or an improvement in a product's capabilities can directly affect demand for substitute products. A major drop in the cost of solar energy would adversely affect the demand for such energy products as heating oil, electricity, and natural gas.

The introduction of affordable digital cameras signals the beginning of a new era of picture-taking and developing. The new devices take pictures without film and store images as electronic data until users download them into computer systems. The new filmless cameras from Canon, Kodak, Casio, and others provide instant gratification for consumers by eliminating the wait for developing. They also save money on film and processing and open up ways to manipulate photo images on the computer.

As Figure 3.2 shows, the new color printers from Canon, Hewlett-Packard, Lexmark, and Epson produce remarkably accurate photo images, just slightly less sharp than those made by traditional development labs. Currently priced at $350 and under, these printers are expected to become even more affordable in coming months. By allowing consumers to convert their home computer systems into personal photo labs, these innovations also threaten sales of traditional cameras and film.[3]

The final type of competition occurs among all other organizations that compete for consumers' purchases. Traditional economic analysis views competition as a battle among companies in a single industry or among firms that produce substitute goods and services. Marketers must, however, accept the argument that all firms compete for a limited pool of discretionary buying power. *Competition* in this sense means that a Ford Mustang competes with a Colorado ski vacation, and a Smashing Pumpkins compact disk competes with a ticket to a New York Yankees game for buyers' entertainment dollars.

Because the competitive environment often determines the success or failure of a product, marketers must continually assess competitors' marketing strategies. A firm must carefully monitor new product offerings with technological advances, price reductions, special promotions, or other competitive variations, and the firm's marketing mix may require adjustments to counter these changes.

Among the first purchasers of any new product are the producing company's competitors. Careful analysis of its elements—physical components, performance attributes, packaging, retail price, service requirements, and estimated production and marketing costs—allows rival marketers to forecast the new offering's likely competitive impact. They may need to adjust one or more of their own marketing mix components in order to compete with the new market entry.

Developing a Competitive Strategy

Every firm's marketers must develop an effective strategy for dealing with its competitive environment. One company may compete in a broad range of markets in many areas of the world. Another may specialize in particular market segments, such as those determined by customers' geographic, age, or income characteristics. Determining a competitive strategy involves answering three questions:

1. Should we compete?
2. If so, in what markets should we compete?
3. How should we compete?

The answer to the first question depends on the firm's resources, objectives, and expectations for the market's profit potential. A firm may decide not to pursue or continue operating a potentially successful venture that does not mesh with its resources, objectives, or profit expectations. In recent years, Monsanto has sold its familiar textiles and chemical-oriented businesses to focus on its high-growth, high-profitability agricultural and biotechnology divisions. Semiconductor manufacturer Texas Instruments auctioned off its defense electronics business unit, which makes missile sensors and radar and night-vision systems, to an aircraft company where the unit made a better fit.[4]

Answering the second question—in what markets should we compete?—requires marketers to acknowledge their limited resources (sales personnel, advertising budgets, product development capabilities, and the like). They must accept responsibility for allocating these resources to the areas of greatest opportunity.

Some companies gain access to markets through acquisitions. Staples, the second-largest office supplies superstore, is attempting to acquire its bigger competitor Office Depot. Both companies hope to join forces and end their rivalry. "We're a lot happier to be together with Staples than to compete with them," said Office Depot CEO David Fuente. The combined companies, with 1,100 stores in 47 states and ten countries, would control about 10 percent of this $150 billion market.[5]

PSINet, an Internet service provider, sold its consumer accounts to go after business users seeking fast and reliable service. After investing $150 million to upgrade its system with the latest technology, the high-tech firm also broke

Marketing Dictionary

competitive environment The interactive exchange in the marketplace influenced by actions of marketers of directly competitive products, marketers of products that can substitute for one another, and other marketers competing for the same consumers' purchasing power.

Figure 3.3 **The 800-Flowers Competitive Strategy: Using the Internet to Increase Sales**

Netscape: 1-800-FLOWERS - Welcome to Our Store
Back
Forward
Home
Reload
Images
Open
Print
Find
Stop
Location: http://www.800flowers.com/
What's New?
What's Cool?
Handbook
Net Search
Net Directory
Software
FEATURE of the day
Fruits, Sweets & Treats
Click to Order
Fresh Idea...
Need a practical gift? Fruits & sweets are suitable for anyone, on any occasion!
Home Page
Email Us
US Customer Service
International Customer Service
Awards and Honors
Best Viewed With:
Microsoft Internet Explorer
1-800-FLOWERS
a fresh APPROACH TO living & giving
Browse our selection of more than 150 floral & gift products -- perfect for all occasions. It's fast, easy, & secure! Your 100% satisfaction is guaranteed & our Customer Service associates are available 24 hours a day.
ONLINE shopping
EVENTS AND HAPPEN!NGS
Here's what's new, fun, & entertaining.
CONTESTS AND FUN STUFF
Enter to win... or simply to have some fun with us.
fresH THOUGHTS
Our very own e-zine on living with flowers, including fresh tips for home decorating, lifestyle, & entertaining.
100% of 8K

ranks with the industry's emerging low-price, flat-rate pricing strategy. Instead of apologizing for higher rates, PSINet offered guarantees of unprecedented service levels. After all, marketers reasoned, business customers who use the Net for critical applications cannot afford lapses in service—and they are willing to pay for superior performance.[6]

Answering the third question—how should we compete?—requires marketers to make product, pricing, distribution, and promotional decisions that give their firm a competitive advantage in the marketplace. Firms can compete on a variety of claims, including product quality, price, and customer service. For example, retailer Nordstrom Inc. has gained a competitive advantage by providing superior customer service, while retailer Wal-Mart competes by providing low prices.

Firms may also compete by exceeding the efficiency of their rivals. For example, many firms downsize to reduce costs. DuPont Co. recently reduced its workforce by 2,800 jobs in the process of consolidating its nylon business and upgrading its plants with new technology. These strategies are designed to give DuPont, the inventor of nylon fiber, an edge in a competitive market.[7]

The Internet has added a new set of answers to the question of how to compete. For example, new outlets for the flower-delivery industry have blossomed on both the World Wide Web and online services. Florists maintain over 200 electronic storefronts ranging from mom-and-pop growers with individual Web pages to cyber-flower shops hosting major sites on the Internet Shopping Network and America Online. With sales stable at about $13 billion, industry participants face keen competition as they try to distinguish themselves from other bloom purveyors. No longer do FTD and 800-Flowers have any advantage in telephone or online orders. Consumers visiting iFlowers can surf the Web to find a local florist anywhere in the country and place an order.

http://www.iflowers.com/

Companies need to create strong identities to compete effectively in cyberspace. FTD developed a consistent image, forging its identity in everything from its logo to wrapping paper. It even changed its toll-free number from 800-SEND-FTD to 800-FTD-BLOOM in an attempt to project a "softer" image. The company designs its sales presentations to increase the number of electronic orders. 800-FLOWERS, through 130 retail stores of its own and partnerships with 1,600 florists, gets $20 million, or 8 percent of its total revenues, from electronic sales. To increase that income, the company has become involved in numerous interactive projects. In addition to its colorful Web site, shown in Figure 3.3, it has established its presence on the major online services and developed CD-ROMs.[8]

http://www.800flowers.com/

Time-Based Competition

With increased international competition and rapid changes in technology, a steadily growing number of firms are using time as a strategic competitive weapon. A **time-based competition** strategy seeks to develop and distribute goods and services more quickly than competitors. The flexibility and responsiveness of a time-based strategy enables the firm to improve product quality, reduce costs, and expand the variety of its products to cover new market segments, and enhance customer satisfaction.

No industry relies more heavily on time-based competition than the computer and software industries. As users demand more computing power and speed, competitors have substantially reduced the time they require to develop new-generation chips. Researchers work simultaneously on several generations of their firm's technology rather than waiting for the release of one product to start on the next. Software upgrades now reach retail shelves every 6 to 12 months, rather than once every year or two. Announcements of new products and revisions of existing ones tempt consumers to wait for promised product releases. Some proposed products never materialize, giving rise to the term *vaporware*.

The Internet is a major battleground for time-based competitors. In recognition of the speed of change in this arena, companies count time in "Internet Years," periods of several months. Microsoft has targeted reducing product development time as a corporate priority, particularly in its battle with Netscape for dominance in the World Wide Web browser market. Each company released the final version of its browser—Microsoft's Internet Explorer 3.0 and Netscape's Navigator 3.0—in mid-August 1996. Both had Version 4.0 in private testing two months later, and in public testing by the end of the same year.[9]

THE POLITICAL-LEGAL ENVIRONMENT

Before you play the game, learn the rules! No one should start playing a new game without first understanding the rules, yet some businesspeople exhibit remarkably limited knowledge about marketing's **political-legal environment**—the laws and their interpretations that require firms to operate under certain competitive conditions and to protect consumer rights. Ignorance of laws, ordinances, and regulations or failure to comply with them can result in fines, embarrassing negative publicity, and possibly expensive civil damage suits.

Marketing Dictionary

time-based competition A strategy of developing and distributing goods and services more quickly than competitors can achieve.

political-legal environment A component of the marketing environment defined by laws and their interpretations that require firms to operate under certain competitive conditions and to protect consumer rights.

Businesspeople need considerable diligence to understand the legal framework for their marketing decisions. Numerous laws and regulations affect those decisions, many of them vaguely stated and inconsistently enforced by a multitude of different authorities. The existing U.S. legal framework was constructed piecemeal, often in response to concerns over monetary issues.

Regulations enacted at the federal, state, and local levels affect marketing practices, as do the actions of independent regulatory agencies. These requirements and prohibitions touch on all aspects of marketing decision making—designing, labeling, packaging, distributing, advertising, and promoting goods and services. To cope with the vast, complex, and changing political-legal environment, many large firms maintain in-house legal departments; small firms often seek professional advice from outside attorneys. All marketers, however, should be aware of the major regulations that affect their activities.

Government Regulation

The history of government regulation in the United States can be divided into four phases. The first phase was the antimonopoly period of the late ninteenth and early twentieth centuries. During this era, major laws such as the Sherman Antitrust Act, Clayton Act, and Federal Trade Commission Act were passed to maintain a competitive environment by reducing the trend toward increasing concentration of industry power in the hands of a small number of competitors. The second phase, aimed at protecting competitors, emerged during the Depression Era of the 1930s, when independent merchants felt the need for legal protection against competition from larger chain stores. Federal legislation enacted during this period included the Robinson-Patman Act and the Miller-Tydings Resale Price Maintenance Act.

The third regulatory phase focused on consumer protection. Although the objective of consumer protection underlies most laws—with good examples including the Sherman Act, FTC Act, and Federal Food and Drug Act—many of the major consumer-oriented laws have been enacted during the past 40 years. The fourth phase, industry deregulation, began in the late 1970s and has continued to the present. During this phase, government has worked to increase competition in such industries as telecommunications, utilities, transportation, and financial services by discontinuing many regulations and permitting firms to expand their service offerings to new markets.

The newest regulatory frontier is cyberspace. The Federal Trade Commission is investigating ways to police the Internet and online services. The immediate goal focuses on protecting consumers who buy goods and services online from fraud and deceptive advertising. Privacy and intellectual property issues are another big concern. However, the FTC's initial wait-and-see attitude has favored self-regulation. "I don't believe we know enough to regulate now," said Commissioner Christine Varney. This hesitation has not stopped the FTC and state regulators from searching out fraudulent schemes, however, like self-employment scams and supposedly casual chat-room comments about products that are actually promotions by company representatives. The Securities and Exchange Commission is investigating possible manipulation of stock prices through chat rooms and bulletin boards.

Privacy may present the most difficult enforcement challenge, because the technology changes so quickly. By tracking users' visits to various Web sites, marketers can learn a lot about users. Such knowledge of consumer Net habits may cross the lines of individual privacy rights.[10]

Table 3.1 lists and briefly describes the major federal laws that affect marketing. Later chapters discuss additional legislation affecting specific marketing practices, such as product development, packaging, labeling, product warranties, and franchise agreements.

Marketers must also monitor state and local laws that affect their industries. Many states, for instance, allow sales of hard liquor only in liquor stores; such laws limit the distribution of low-alcohol cocktails made with rum, vodka, whiskey, and bourbon. California's stringent regulations for automobile emissions require special pollution control equipment on cars sold in the state.

Government Regulatory Agencies

Federal, state, and local governments have established regulatory agencies to enforce laws. At the federal level, the Federal Trade Commission (FTC) wields the broadest powers of any agency to influence marketing activities. It has the authority to enforce laws regulating unfair business practices, and it can take action to stop false and deceptive advertising. Other agencies operate within narrower mandates. The Federal Communications Commission, for example, regulates wire, radio, and television communications. The Surface Transportation Board (STB) monitors interstate rates of railroads as well as some trucking activities. Other federal regulatory agencies include the Food and Drug Administration, the Consumer Products Safety Commission, the Federal Power Commission, and the Environmental Protection Agency.

The FTC applies several procedures to enforce laws. It may issue a consent order through which a business accused of violating a law can agree to voluntary compliance without admitting guilt. If a business refuses to comply with an FTC request, the agency can issue a cease-and-desist order, which gives a final demand to stop an illegal practice. Firms often challenge cease-and-desist orders in court. The FTC can require advertisers to provide additional information about products in their advertisements,

Table 3.1 Major Federal Laws Affecting Marketing

Date	Law	Description
A. LAWS MAINTAINING A COMPETITIVE ENVIRONMENT		
1890	Sherman Antitrust Act	Prohibits restraint of trade and monopolization; identifies a competitive marketing system as national policy goal
1914	Clayton Act	Strengthens the Sherman Act by restricting such practices as price discrimination, exclusive dealing, tying contracts, and interlocking boards of directors where the effect "may be to substantially lessen competition or tend to create a monopoly"
1914	Federal Trade Commission Act (FTC)	Prohibits unfair methods of competition; establishes the Federal Trade Commission, an administrative agency that investigates business practices and enforces the FTC Act
1938	Wheeler-Lea Act	Amends the FTC Act to outlaw additional unfair practices; gives the FTC jurisdiction over false and misleading advertising
1950	Celler-Kefauver Antimerger Act	Amends the Clayton Act to include major asset purchases that will decrease competition in an industry
1975	Consumer Goods Pricing Act	Prohibits pricing maintenance agreements among manufacturers and resellers in interstate commerce
1980	FTC Improvement Act	Gives the Senate and House of Representatives joint veto power over FTC trade regulations; limits FTC power to regulate unfairness issues
B. LAWS REGULATING COMPETITION		
1936	Robinson-Patman Act	Prohibits price discrimination in sales to wholesalers, retailers, or other producers; prohibits selling at unreasonably low prices to eliminate competition
1937	Miller-Tydings Resale Price Maintenance Act	Exempts interstate fair trade contracts from compliance with antitrust requirements
1993	North American Free Trade Agreement (NAFTA)	International trade agreement between Canada, Mexico, and the United States designed to facilitate trade by removing tariffs and other trade barriers among the three nations
C. LAWS PROTECTING CONSUMERS		
1906	Federal Food and Drug Act	Prohibits adulteration and misbranding of foods and drugs involved in interstate commerce; strengthened by the Food, Drug, and Cosmetic Act (1938) and the Kefauver-Harris Drug Amendment (1962)
1939	Wool Products Labeling Act	Requires identification of the type and percentage of wool used in products
1951	Fur Products Labeling Act	Requires identification of the animal from which a fur product was derived
1953	Flammable Fabrics Act	Prohibits interstate sale of flammable fabrics
1958	National Traffic and Safety Act	Provides for creation of safety standards for automobile tires

(continued)

and it can force firms using deceptive advertising to correct earlier claims with new promotional messages. The FTC sometimes requires firms to give refunds to consumers misled by deceptive advertising.

The FTC and U.S. Justice Department can stop mergers if they believe the proposed acquisitions will reduce competition by discouraging new companies from entering the field. In recent years, these agencies have taken a harder line on proposed mergers, especially in the computer, telecommunications, financial services, and health-care sectors. For example, the Justice Department keeps close tabs on software giant Microsoft to make sure that it does not use its market clout to unfair advantage. Recently, the department blocked Microsoft's acquisition of financial software developer Intuit. A current review of Microsoft's Internet activities seeks to prevent strategies like building its Web browser into the Windows operating system from penalizing rivals' products.

Table 3.1 Major Federal Laws Affecting Marketing, continued

Date	Law	Description
1958	Automobile Information Disclosure Act	Prohibits automobile dealers from inflating factory prices of new cars
1966	Child Protection Act	Outlaws sale of hazardous toys; 1969 amendment adds products posing electrical, mechanical, or thermal hazards
1966	Fair Packaging and Labeling Act	Requires disclosure of product identification, name and address of manufacturer or distributor, and information on the quality of contents
1967	Federal Cigarette Labeling and Advertising Act	Requires written health warnings on cigarette packages
1968	Consumer Credit Protection Act	Truth-in-lending law requiring disclosure of annual interest rates on loans and credit purchases
1970	Fair Credit Reporting Act	Gives individuals access to their credit records and allows them to change incorrect information
1970	National Environmental Policy Act	Establishes the Environmental Protection Agency to deal with various types of pollution and organizations that create pollution
1971	Public Health Cigarette Smoking Act	Prohibits tobacco advertising on radio and television
1972	Consumer Product Safety Act	Created the Consumer Product Safety Commission, which has authority to specify safety standards for most products
1975, 1977	Equal Credit Opportunity Act	Bans discrimination in lending practices based on sex and marital status (1975) and race, national origin, religion, age, or receipt of payments from public assistance programs (1977)
1990	Nutrition Labeling and Education Act	Requires food manufacturers and processors to provide detailed information on the labeling of most foods
1990	Children's Television Act	Limits the amount of advertising to be shown during children's television programs to no more than 10.5 minutes per hour on weekends and not more than 12 minutes per hour on weekdays
1991	Americans with Disabilities Act (ADA)	Protects the rights of people with disabilities; makes discrimination against the disabled illegal in public accommodations, transportation, and telecommunications
1993	Brady Law	Imposes a five-day waiting period and a background check before a gun purchaser can take possession of the gun
D. LAWS DEREGULATING SPECIFIC INDUSTRIES		
1978	Airline Deregulation Act	Grants considerable freedom to commercial airlines in setting fares and choosing new routes
1980	Motor Carrier Act and Staggers Rail Act	Significantly deregulates trucking and railroad industries by permitting them to negotiate rates and services
1996	Telecommunications Act	Significantly deregulates the telecommunications industry by removing barriers to competition in local and long-distance phone and cable television markets

In health care, economies of scale inspire many mergers as companies try to lower costs by consolidating administrative functions. The FTC refrains from objecting unless companies use their leverage to raise prices. For example, in 1996 it blocked a merger between the Rite Aid and Revco drugstore chains due to fears that the size of the combined company could give it unacceptable power over employee insurance plans during price negotiations for prescription drugs.[11]

Other recent antitrust investigations have involved more traditional cases. The Justice Department investigated claims that Frito-Lay, the snack food unit of PepsiCo, pressured retailers not to carry competing brands. The FTC accused Toys 'R' Us of abusing its size advantage by raising toy prices and limiting competition through exclusive deals for custom products with manufacturers. Publicity surrounding the charges hurt the company's image and resulted in a temporary loss of market share.[12]

Despite the increased attention that some companies receive from antitrust regulators, others have more leeway. This freedom is particularly helpful for companies that compete in global markets. Regulators recognize that mergers can improve U.S. companies' ability to maintain their market positions against those of their foreign competitors.[13]

Figure 3.4 Deregulation: Enabling an Electric Utility to Go Global

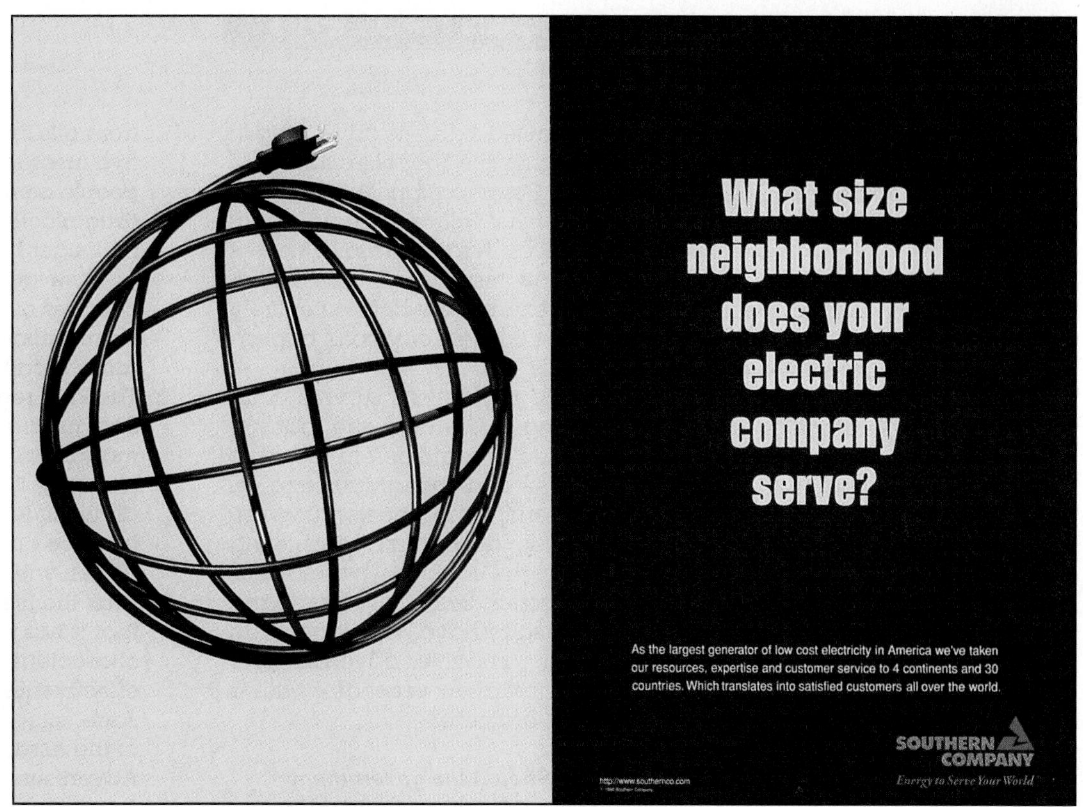
What size neighborhood does your electric company serve?
As the largest generator of low cost electricity in America we've taken our resources, expertise and customer service to 4 continents and 30 countries. Which translates into satisfied customers all over the world.
SOUTHERN COMPANY
Energy to Serve Your World
http://www.southernco.com

Removing regulation also affects the marketing environment. Deregulation of the telecommunications and utilities industries has changed the competitive picture considerably. For example, utilities have lost exclusive rights to operate within specific territories. In 1993, natural gas distributors gained the right to send gas via local pipelines, similar to the way long-distance phone companies use local lines, and compete with other companies around the country. The Archdiocese of Chicago saved $8 million by purchasing gas from Houston's Enron Corp. rather than its local utilities. Customers of KN Energy in southeastern Wyoming can choose from among 12 competing gas suppliers. In response to the competition, KN reduced its rates. Other companies are joining the nationwide battle for customers. PanEnergy Pipeline of Houston fields over 100 salespeople in the Northeast. Another approach is the development of "branded" natural gas by joint ventures between natural gas companies and major oil companies like Tejas Gas/Shell and PanEnergy/Mobil.[14] The ad in Figure 3.4 describes one result of these trends, as Southern Company, a U.S.-based electric utility, has expanded its service to 30 countries on four continents.

This kind of restructuring in the utility industry after 90 years of monopoly will affect many different sectors. If power costs drop the expected 20 percent due to deregulation of the generation process, businesses and individuals will have more money to spend on other things. Competition will improve efficiency in what had become a complex and inefficient market. Mergers between utility companies will consolidate the industry.[15]

The latest round of deregulation brought the passage of the Telecommunications Act of 1996. This law removed barriers between the businesses of local and long-distance phone companies and cable companies. It allowed the seven regional Bell operating companies and GTE Corp. to offer long-distance service; at the same time, long-distance companies—such as AT&T, MCI, and Sprint, which together control over 90 percent of this market—gained authority to offer local service. Cable companies can offer phone service, and phone companies can get into the cable business. The change promises huge rewards for competitive winners. Just capturing 20 percent of the local calling market, for example, would be worth $15 billion to $20 billion per year to AT&T.

Other Regulatory Forces

Marketing activities also feel the effects of activities by public and private consumer interest groups and self-regulatory organizations. Consumer interest groups have mushroomed in the past 25 years. Today hundreds of these organizations operate at the national, state, and local levels. Groups such as the National Coalition against Misuse of

SOLVING AN ETHICAL CONTROVERSY

Will Further Government Regulation of the Tobacco Industry Reduce Tobacco Consumption?

The first chinks in Big Tobacco's armor were apparent in 1997 as word surfaced that Philip Morris and RJR Nabisco were quietly negotiating with antismoking advocates. Some reports stated that the industry was willing to pay out $300 billion over 25 years to smokers, rein in advertising and promotions, and drop its legal battle to prevent regulation of tobacco by the Food and Drug Administration.

The $45-billion tobacco industry, which spends roughly $6 billion a year on advertising and promotion, even proposed to put its two greatest pitchmen—the Marlboro Man and Joe Camel—permanently out of business in exchange for the right to continue in business. Some major restrictions were already imposed in 1997 when the U.S. Food and Drug Administration cracked down on cigarette advertising aimed at teenagers. The regulations dramatically limited cigarette advertising in magazines like *Sports Illustrated, TV Guide, Cosmopolitan, Rolling Stone,* and others with significant youth audiences. Also, tobacco billboards are now restricted to black-and-white text and are banned entirely within 1,000 feet of schools or playgrounds.

If the regulations survive court challenges, the cigarette industry will need to use different tactics to reach its audience. Marketing on the Internet and underwriting aggressive direct-mail marketing campaigns could be two obvious approaches. Both Philip Morris and RJR already have Web pages, and smaller companies advertise cigarettes and allow purchases with a click of a mouse.

Should the government expand regulation of the tobacco industry to reduce tobacco consumption or otherwise hurt the tobacco giants?

PRO

1. **The rebellious and cool image of smoking results primarily from alluring ads. These seductive messages hook young people on the highly addictive drug nicotine. If teenagers are no longer bombarded with positive smoking messages, the chances of them resisting the temptation should increase dramatically.**
2. **The FDA regulations would limit cigarette ads in many magazines to black-and-white text only. This change should diminish teenagers' interest in tobacco's marketing messages. "When you drain the blood and suck the life out of an ad so that it has no attention-getting characteristics, you lose its effectiveness," says Daniel L. Jaffe, executive vice president of the Association of National Advertisers.**
3. **Some also see positive signs that the advertising community, which has always allied itself with Big Tobacco, is having second thoughts about the marriage. A group of advertising professionals has launched a campaign to prod Madison**

Pesticides seek to protect the environment. People for Ethical Treatment of Animals (PETA) is an activist group opposing product testing on animals. Other groups attempt to advance the rights of minorities, elderly Americans, and other special-interest causes. The power of these groups has also grown. Pressure from antialcohol groups has resulted in proposed legislation requiring health warnings on all alcohol ads and tightening regulations of alcoholic beverage advertising.

Self-regulatory groups represent industry's attempts to set guidelines for responsible business conduct. The Council of Better Business Bureaus is a national organization devoted to consumer service and business self-regulation. The council's National Advertising Division (NAD) works to promote truth and accuracy in advertising. It reviews and advocates voluntary resolutions of advertising-related complaints between consumers and businesses. If NAD fails to resolve a complaint, an appeal can reach the National Advertising Review Board, which is composed of advertisers, ad agency representatives, and public members. In addition, many individual trade associations set business guidelines and codes of conduct, actively encouraging members' voluntary compliance.

In 1936, the Distilled Spirits Council of the United States (DISCUS) imposed a voluntary ban on radio advertising for liquor, followed by a similar ban on television ads in 1948. This ban remained in effect until June 1996, when Seagram aired an ad for its Crown Royal whiskey on a Corpus Christi, Texas, television station. Seagram objected to the ban, claiming that it gave beer and wine companies, which can advertise on radio and television, an unfair advantage. The manager of one Corpus Christi liquor chain said that sales of Seagram's Crown Royal and Chivas Regal brands jumped 15 percent after the ads began, although he could not be sure whether the ads or the publicity about them drove the sales increase.[16]

Avenue into developing cigarette ads that won't entice kids.

CON

1. Cigarette companies are clever marketers. Big Tobacco can implement many strategies to circumvent FDA rules. Just look at results in other countries that have passed laws to crack down on cigarette ads. An advertising ban in Hong Kong triggered a music-based promotional campaign called "Marlboro Red Hot Hits" in magazines and a "Salem Attitude" clothing line. In countries such as China and Thailand, cigarette companies have formed travel and music booking agencies as promotional devices.
2. The FDA crackdown on cigarette advertising may actually boost cigarette companies' profits. The chief goal of today's advertising is to capture market share from competitors. If the ads stop, the companies will no longer sponsor expensive promotional campaigns to fight off their rivals. What has happened in Canada, where cigarette advertising has been banned for five years, could very well occur here. Imperial Tobacco, which controls 65 percent of Canada's market, saw operating profits more than double, largely due to the cutback in advertising costs.
3. The change will have a negligible effect, because the tobacco industry has sharply reduced its advertising in magazines and on billboards in recent years. In 1970, for instance, tobacco was the biggest ad category for magazines, representing almost 11 percent of their ad dollars. Today, tobacco ads represent only three percent of magazine revenues. "Our tobacco advertisements have been falling off since the early '80s, when it made up about 30 percent to 50 percent of our revenues. Today, it is only about 10 percent to 15 percent," says Chris Carr, a vice president of Gannett Outdoor.

Summary

The question remains whether tobacco giants can bounce back from federal restrictions, as they have in the past. But if they focus on Internet marketing, they might find tough barriers against breaking in, warns Nick Rothenberg, the chief executive officer of W3-design, a Los Angeles Web-site developer. "We'd be very reticent to do anything that's directly supportive of the large-scale tobacco industry," he says. "The major players (Web developers) are very, very reticent to step into this territory. There's no lack of participation on the Web of the alcohol industry, but for whatever reason, we just don't see any similar movement among tobacco."

Sources: Daniel Kadlec, "The $300 Billion Question," *Time,* May 12, 1997, p. 66; Jason Vest, "They Came A Long Way, Baby," *U.S. News & World Report,* April 28, 1997, p.54; Lisa Brownlee, "Ad Executives Break Ranks over Tobacco," *Wall Street Journal,* November 13, 1996, pp. B1, B8; and Vivienne Walt, "Tobacco Industry Absence Creates a Smoke-Free Zone," *Wall Street Journal Interactive Edition,* November 9, 1996, downloaded from http://www.wsj.com/, November 14, 1996.

Critics ranging from President Clinton to Mothers Against Drunk Driving criticized the move. At first other liquor distillers upheld the ban, afraid that a public backlash might lead to restrictions on beer and wine ads. In November 1996, however, the Council agreed to level the playing field and dropped its broadcast advertising ban. DISCUS research showed that the lack of advertising contributed to the perception that there was a big difference between spirits and wine or beer, whereas single servings have about the same alcohol content.

FCC chairman Reed Hundt called the DISCUS decision "disappointing for parents and dangerous for our kids." The group countered with assurances that they will advertise as responsibly on the air as they have in print, using no children or cartoon characters in ads. However, ABC, CBS, and NBC continued their policies of refusing to accept liquor ads.[17]

As mentioned earlier, government regulation of the online world poses a challenge. Favoring self-regulation as the best starting point, the FTC has sponsored a Privacy Initiative for consumers, advertisers, online companies, and others as a way to develop voluntary industry privacy guidelines. The Interactive Services Association is also working on its own privacy standards.

Controlling the Political-Legal Environment

Most marketers comply with laws and regulations. However, noncompliance can scar a firm's reputation and hurt profits. Recall how Toys 'R' Us lost market share after the FTC accused it of violating antitrust regulations. Other companies fight regulations they consider unjust. The regional Bell operating companies filed lawsuits to protect their turf against competition from long-distance carriers and cable companies, while GTE claimed that deregulation of local phone service violated the constitution.[18]

Other companies have jumped in to take advantage of new opportunities. For example, Furst Group is a long-distance phone company with no lines or equipment. It buys blocks of long-distance time from major carriers at greatly reduced rates and then resells this service by the minute at a discount, becoming a distributor, or *switchless reseller.* Now the regional Bells and long-distance carriers are competing aggressively to keep their customers. They are also working with resellers, who provide a way to retain small business customers that would otherwise choose other options.[19]

Consumer groups and political action committees may try to influence the outcome of proposed legislation or change existing laws by engaging in political lobbying or boycotts. Many industry groups, trade associations, and corporations also apply pressure to legislators and regulators through political lobbying and political action committees. Lobbying groups frequently enlist the support of customers, employees, and suppliers to assist their efforts.

THE ECONOMIC ENVIRONMENT

The overall health of the economy influences how much consumers spend and what they buy. This relationship also works the other way. Consumer buying plays an important role in the economy's health; indeed, consumer outlays perennially make up some two-thirds of overall economic activity. Since all marketing activity is directed toward satisfying consumer wants and needs, marketers must understand how economic conditions influence consumer buying decisions.

Marketing's **economic environment** consists of forces that influence consumer buying power and marketing strategies. They include the stage of the business cycle, inflation, unemployment, resource availability, and income.

Business Cycles

Historically, the U.S. economy has tended to follow a cyclical pattern consisting of four stages: prosperity, recession, depression, and recovery. No depressions have occurred in the United States since the 1930s, and many economists argue that society is capable of preventing future depressions through intelligent use of various economic policies. Good decision making should ensure that a recession would give way to a period of recovery rather than sinking further into depression.

Consumer buying differs in each stage of the business cycle, and marketers must adjust their strategies accordingly. In times of prosperity, consumer spending maintains a brisk pace. Marketers respond by expanding product lines, increasing promotional efforts and expanding distribution in order to raise market share, and raising prices to widen their profit margins. During periods of prosperity, buyers often seem willing to pay high prices for premium versions of well-known brands.

During recessions, however, consumers frequently shift their buying patterns to emphasize basic, functional products that carry low price tags. They spend more at hardware stores, auto parts stores, and do-it-yourself centers and less on restaurant meals and nonessential products such as convenience foods. Sales of low-priced, black-and-white-label generic grocery products and private-label goods rise. During recessions, marketers should consider lowering prices, eliminating marginal products, improving customer service, and increasing promotional outlays to stimulate demand. They may also launch value-priced products likely to appeal to cost-conscious buyers.

Consumer spending sinks to its lowest level during a depression. The last true depression in the United States occurred during the 1930s. Although the possibility of a return to depression always persists, experts see only a slim likelihood of another severe depression. Through its monetary and fiscal policies, the federal government attempts to control such extreme fluctuations in the business cycle.

In the recovery stage of the business cycle, the economy emerges from recession and consumer purchasing power increases. While consumers' *ability* to buy increases, however, caution often restrains their *willingness* to buy. Remembering the tough times of recession, they may prefer to save than to spend or buy on credit. During the recovery of the early 1990s, for instance, U.S. consumers paid down their debts for car and bank loans and borrowed less on their credit cards. With lower principal and interest payments, they actually had higher levels of disposable income to spend, but cautious decisions continued to limit spending. Usually, as a recovery strengthens, consumers become more indulgent, buying convenience products and relatively pricey goods and services such as lawn care help and ServiceMaster's residential cleaning service illustrated in Figure 3.5.

This pattern did indeed characterize the mid-1990s as the economy edged toward recovery. Economic growth, as measured by the change in gross domestic product (GDP), continued its upward trend. Businesses invested more capital in equipment and construction as economic activity increased. Sales of new single-family homes and cars rebounded as consumer confidence in the economy increased. These purchases produced a ripple effect in related sectors. For example, the demand for housing led to higher sales of wallpaper, carpet, furniture, appliances, and similar home-related items.[20]

However, consumers not only spent more, but they also charged many purchases. Once again, the level of credit card debt climbed, due in part to the flood of attractive card offers stuffing consumers' mail boxes. Consumer debt rose faster than income, delinquent credit card payments reached new highs, and personal bankruptcy filings

Figure 3.5 Increased Spending for a Convenience Service during the Recovery Stage

ServiceMASTER
When Our Van Is Outside Your Home Is Clean Inside.
The bright yellow ServiceMaster van delivers over 45 years of heavy-duty cleaning experience right to your front door. Every ServiceMaster van comes equipped with highly-trained professionals, the latest equipment and exclusive cleaning solutions. Together they get your furniture, carpeting, windows and draperies their cleanest. It's the easiest, most hassle-free cleaning experience you'll ever have. Before you know it, your home will be spotless. Guaranteed. Or we'll do it again, no questions asked.
So for a home that's deep-down clean, check the phone book for your local ServiceMaster professional or call 1-800-WE SERVE. That bright yellow van will make you feel good inside.
Call 1-800-WE SERVE any time for our free Cleaning Tips Guide.
ServiceMASTER.
1-800-WE SERVE.

showed sharp increases. Credit card issuers, which had courted new borrowers with tempting offers of low introductory interest rates and various reward programs, found themselves suffering from consumers' inability to keep spending within reasonable—and repayable—limits when handed still more plastic cards. In response, these firms reduced their unsolicited mailings and adopted stricter approval guidelines.[21]

Recovery remains a difficult stage for businesses just climbing out of recession, since it requires them to earn profits while trying to gauge uncertain consumer demand. Many try to cope by holding down administrative costs as much as possible. Some trim payrolls and close down branch offices. Others cut back on employees' business travel budgets or explore the least expensive travel options. Some industries struggle more than others during recovery periods; travel and casual dining often remain weak, since consumers view these services as unnecessary luxuries.

Business cycles, like other aspects of the economy, are complex phenomena that seem to defy the control of marketers. Success depends on flexible plans that can be adjusted to satisfy consumer demands during the various business cycle stages.

Inflation

A major constraint on consumer spending can affect any stage of the business cycle. *Inflation* devalues money by reducing the products it can buy through persistent price increases. Inflation would restrict purchases less severely if income were to keep pace with rising prices, but often it does not. Inflation increases marketers' costs, such as expenditures for wages and raw materials, and the resultant higher prices may therefore negatively affect sales.

The rate of inflation in the United States soared to double digits in the late 1970s and early 1980s, reaching 13.6 percent in 1980. However, the inflation rate dropped to 3 percent during 1991 and hovered near that level through 1997. Many economists predicted that similarly low levels would continue into the twenty-first century. At these low levels, inflation may not affect the economy as strongly in the future as it has in the past.

Inflation makes consumers conscious of prices, especially during periods of high inflation. This influence can lead to three possible outcomes, all important to marketers: (1) consumers can elect to buy now, in the belief that prices will rise later (an argument that automobile dealers often cite in their commercial messages); (2) they can decide to alter their purchasing patterns; and (3) they can postpone certain purchases.

Unemployment

Unemployment is defined as the proportion of people in the economy who do not have jobs and are actively looking for work. Unemployment rises during recessions and declines in the recovery and prosperity stages of the business cycle. Like inflation, unemployment affects marketing by modifying consumer behavior. Unless unemployment insurance, personal savings, and union benefits effectively offset lost earnings, unemployed people have relatively little income to spend. Even if these protections completely compensate people for lost earnings, their buying behavior is still likely to change. Instead of buying, they may choose to build their savings.

Marketing Dictionary

economic environment Forces that influence consumer buying power and marketing strategies, including the state of the business cycle, inflation, unemployment, resource availability, and income.

Figure 3.6 **Online Service Designed for the Mature Market**

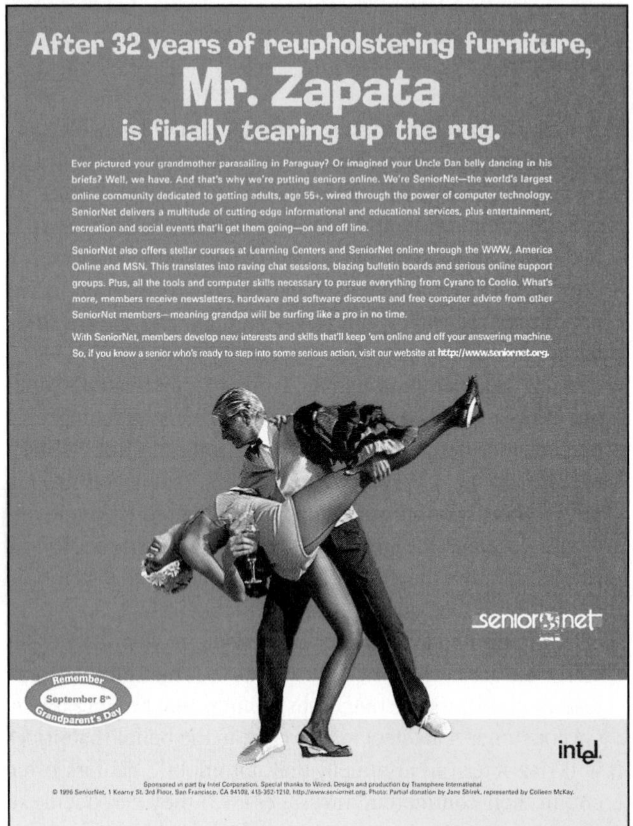
After 32 years of reupholstering furniture,
Mr. Zapata
is finally tearing up the rug.
Ever pictured your grandmother parasailing in Paraguay? Or imagined your Uncle Dan belly dancing in his briefs? Well, we have. And that's why we're putting seniors online. We're SeniorNet—the world's largest online community dedicated to getting adults, age 55+, wired through the power of computer technology. SeniorNet delivers a multitude of cutting-edge informational and educational services, plus entertainment, recreation and social events that'll get them going—on and off line.
SeniorNet also offers stellar courses at Learning Centers and SeniorNet online through the WWW, America Online and MSN. This translates into raving chat sessions, blazing bulletin boards and serious online support groups. Plus, all the tools and computer skills necessary to pursue everything from Cyrano to Coolio. What's more, members receive newsletters, hardware and software discounts and free computer advice from other SeniorNet members—meaning grandpa will be surfing like a pro in no time.
With SeniorNet, members develop new interests and skills that'll keep 'em online and off your answering machine. So, if you know a senior who's ready to step into some serious action, visit our website at http://www.seniornet.org.
seniornet
Remember
September 8th
Grandparent's Day
intel

Unemployment rose during the 1991 recession and continued to climb during the early stages of the recovery. After peaking near 8 percent in 1992, it declined steadily, reaching about 5 percent today. This low level of unemployment contributed to the increase in spending of the middle 1990s.

Briefly speaking

"It's a recession when your neighbor loses his job. It's a depression when you lose your own."

Harry S. Truman (1884–1972)
32nd president of the United States

Income

Income is another important determinant of marketing's economic environment, because it influences consumer buying power. By studying income statistics and trends, marketers can estimate market potential and develop plans for targeting specific market segments. For example, U.S. household incomes have grown in recent years; coupled with a low rate of inflation, this increase has boosted purchasing power for millions of American households. For marketers, a rise in income represents a potential for increasing overall sales. However, marketers are most interested in *discretionary income,* the amount of money that people have to spend after they have paid for necessities such as food, clothing, and housing.

Changes in average earnings powerfully affect discretionary income. Workers' earnings rose slightly in the first part of 1994 but then dropped and showed almost no growth until 1996, when they climbed steadily upward. In that year, real pay (adjusted for inflation) was 1.3 percent higher than the year before, the largest increase for many years.[22]

Consumers' discretionary incomes vary greatly by age group and household type. Bureau of the Census statistics show that older people, for example, one of the fastest growing segments of the overall population, also have significant buying power, even compared to other groups with higher incomes. Contributing to elderly consumers' buying power are smaller household sizes and freedom from regular mortgage payments.

This trend has led to the increasingly frequent appearance of mature models in ads promoting goods, services, and ideas. A growing number of firms are offering specialized products, such as the SeniorNet online service described in Figure 3.6, or creating special incentives designed to attract this once-neglected market.[23]

Resource Availability

Resources are not unlimited. Shortages—temporary or permanent—can result from several causes. Brisk demand may bring in orders that exceed manufacturing capacity or outpace the response time required to gear up a production line. A shortage may also reflect a lack of raw materials, component parts, energy, or labor. Regardless of the cause, shortages require marketers to reorient their thinking.

One reaction is **demarketing,** the process of reducing consumer demand for a product to a level that the firm can reasonably supply. Oil companies, for example, publicize tips on how to cut gasoline consumption, and utility companies encourage homeowners to install insulation to reduce heating costs. Many cities discourage central business district traffic by raising parking fees and violation penalties and promoting mass transit and car pooling.

A shortage presents marketers with a unique set of challenges. They may have to allocate limited supplies, a sharply different activity from marketing's traditional objective of expanding sales volume. Shortages may require marketers to decide whether to spread limited supplies over all customers, leaving none totally satisfied, or to limit purchases by some customers so that the firm can completely satisfy others.

In 1994, the paper industry was faced with reduced demand for its products, leading to growing inventories and record low prices. Marketers searched for ways to increase business. When the situation reversed a few months later, shortages of all types of paper pushed prices through the roof. Newspapers could not get enough newsprint, forcing them to cut back on advertising pages.

Shortages in human resources also affect companies. During the recession of the early 1990s, high-quality employees inundated small businesses with resumes in the aftermath of corporate downsizing. As the recovery progressed, however, large companies began to rebuild their workforces. To compete, small firms had to increase wages and improve benefits packages. Wichita Tool Co. in Kansas turned down $700,000 in orders because the firm lacked enough skilled workers to handle the load. To remedy the situation, the company raised wages 10 percent and joined a training alliance. Still, sales continued to drop. Other companies turn to automated equipment to counter the employee shortage. Brookdale Plastics Inc. of Minneapolis replaced 15 jobs with new molding machinery, at a cost of $500,000. Even that investment was not enough. Orders climbed to the point where the company's lead times doubled, creating a major obstacle to satisfying customers.[24]

Companies today have devised several ways to deal with increased demand for fixed amounts of resources. Reynolds Metal Company seeks to supplement the dwindling supply of aluminum through its recycling programs, including cash-paying vending machines. Such "reverse" vending machines allow recyclers to insert empty cans and receive money, stamps, and/or discount coupons for merchandise or services.

The International Economic Environment

In today's global business climate, marketers must also monitor the economic environments of other nations. Just as in the United States, a recession in Europe or Japan changes buying habits. Because Europe recovered more slowly than the United States from the 1991 recession, exports of American-made products suffered for several years.

Changes in foreign currency rates compared to the U.S. dollar also affect marketing decisions. In 1995, a peso crisis in Mexico created havoc with plans of marketers drawn to that country by the growth of its middle-class consumer sector. Devaluation of the peso, very high inflation (50 to 70 percent during one two-month period), and government limits on wage increases reduced purchasing power and discretionary income.

These conditions spurred manufacturers of a variety of products to develop new strategies. Many of them chose to reposition their brands for the changed economic climate. Because U.S. products became more expensive, some produced more goods within Mexico rather than importing them as a way to keep prices down. Ford postponed the introduction of a new import model, and Kraft cut margins on imported cereals. Apple Computer eased credit for dealers and ran seminars to stimulate demand. Maybelline sent out delivery trucks more often, because retailers didn't want to hold inventory at the high interest rates, preferring instead to run out of stock. By 1997, the government's austerity program had reduced inflation and renewed foreign confidence in the ability of Mexico's economy to recover from its worst recession in 60 years.[25]

THE TECHNOLOGICAL ENVIRONMENT

The **technological environment** represents the application to marketing of discoveries in science, inventions, and innovations. New technology results in new goods and services for consumers; it also improves existing products, strengthens customer service, and often reduces prices through new, cost-efficient production and distribution methods. Technology can quickly make products obsolete—calculators, for example, wiped out the market for slide rules—but it can just as quickly open up new marketing opportunities.

As discussed in Chapter 1, technology is revolutionizing the marketing environment. Technological innovations create not just new products but also whole new industries. The Internet is transforming the way companies promote and distribute products. Among the new business categories developing as a result of the Net's success are Web page designers, new types of software firms, interactive advertising agencies, and companies like CyberCash and First Virtual that allow customers to make secure financial transactions over the Web. Industrial and medical use of lasers, superconductor transmission of electricity, wireless communications products, seeds and plants enhanced by biotechnology, and genetically engineered proteins that fight disease are just a few more examples of technological advances.

Technology can sometimes address social concerns. In 1997, General Motors introduced the EV1, the world's first

Marketing Dictionary

demarketing The process of reducing consumer demand for a good or service to a level that the firm can supply.

technological environment The application to marketing of discoveries in science, inventions, and innovations.

Figure 3.7 Applying Technology to Address a Social Concern

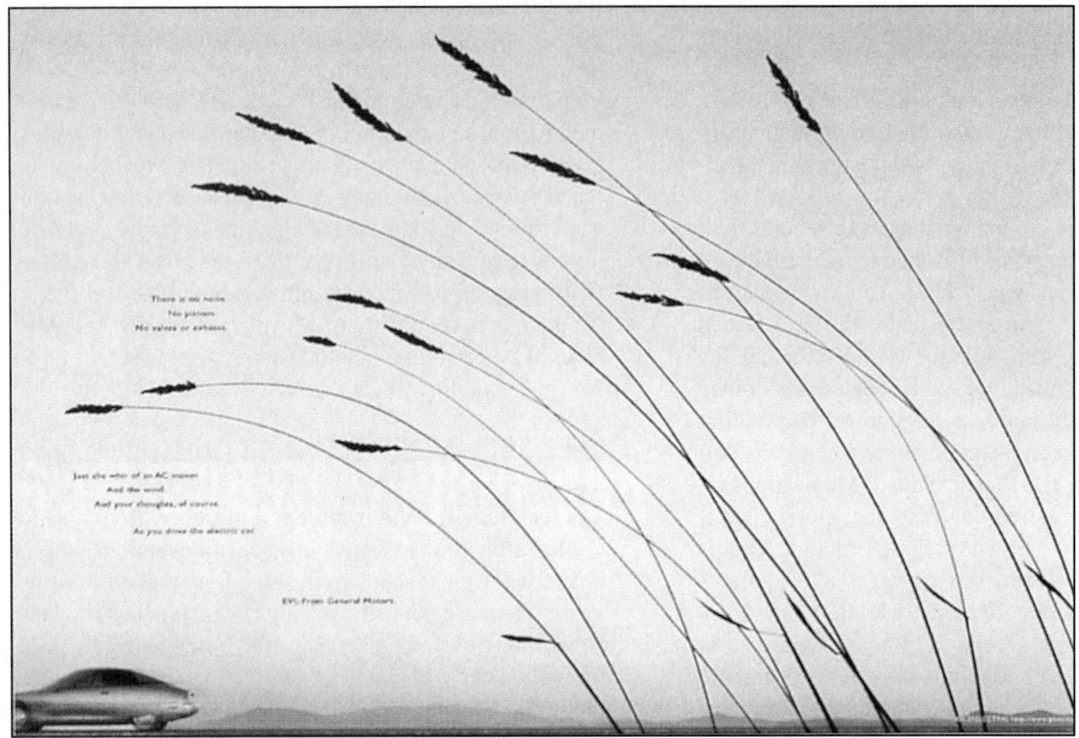

commercially produced electric car. This innovation represented, in part, a response to consumer demands for smog-free air and in part an accommodation of California mandates requiring auto manufacturers to develop electric cars. The project also was intended to enhance GM's image as an environmentally conscious technology leader. Even though the auto giant invested $350 million and six years in developing the car, GM marketers had developed realistic expectations about its limited market size. They simply hoped to build a market that might become profitable some time in the next century.

The new car suffers from several technical limitations—two-person capacity, top speed of 80 miles per hour, a range of 70 to 80 miles followed by 3 to 12 hours of recharging, and a price tag so high that the EV1 is available only by lease. These drawbacks severely limit the model's market potential. In addition, the lease price and $50-per-month payment for charger rental add up to $530 to $690 a month, more than a Lexus ES300 costs. Initially, GM is marketing the EV1 through Saturn dealerships in four markets: Los Angeles, San Diego, Phoenix, and Tucson. An $8 million multimedia promotional launch included humorous theater and TV spots and print ads. Figure 3.7 shows a selection from the car's 40-page Web site, which gives the campaign international reach.[26]

Industry, government, colleges and universities, and other not-for-profit institutions all play roles in the development of new technology. In the United States, research and development efforts by private industry represent a major source of technological innovation. Intel channels over one-third of its profits back into research and development of new microprocessor chips. This investment enables the market leader to produce innovations such as its Pentium and P6 chips, which incorporate over 4 million transistors and carry out more than 200 million software instructions per second (mips). The firm's MMX-P6 chips add special multimedia capabilities, and Intel CEO Andrew Grove predicts that by 2011 chips able to handle 100,000 mips will be on the market.[27]

Another major source of technology is the federal government, including the military services. In fact, many consumer products that people take for granted today originated as military projects. Examples include air bags (originally Air Force ejection seats), scratch-resistant sunglasses (developed first as visors for space helmets), digital computers (first designed to calculate artillery trajectories), and microwave ovens (a derivative of radar systems).

Although the United States has long led the world in research, competition from rivals in Japan and Europe has intensified in recent years. For the past two decades, the United States has pioneered development of personal computers, networking systems, and Internet technology. Japanese firms focused on industries where they could capitalize on their demonstrated ability to transfer technologies into commercial products. For instance, American firms developed the technology for videocassette recorders, but two Japanese companies, Sony and JVC, commercialized the invention into one of the most successful new products of the past two decades.

Japanese manufacturers are now challenging U.S. firms by moving quickly into digital consumer electronics like small, powerful digital camcorders and multimedia PCs for the home entertainment market. The digital video disk is another Japanese-developed product that provides better picture quality than videotapes and laser disks.[28] To remain at the leading edge, American firms have taken steps to improve technology transfers from university and military researchers to private companies.

Figure 3.8 **Applying Technology to Develop Innovative Products**

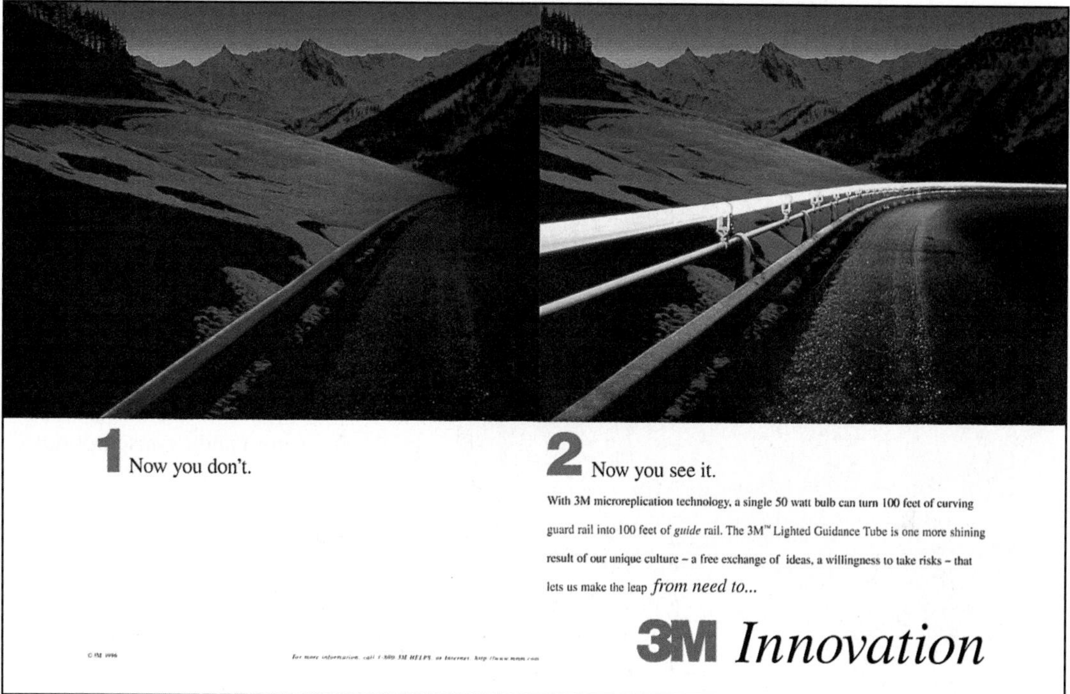
1 Now you don't.
2 Now you see it.
With 3M microreplication technology, a single 50 watt bulb can turn 100 feet of curving guard rail into 100 feet of *guide* rail. The 3M™ Lighted Guidance Tube is one more shining result of our unique culture – a free exchange of ideas, a willingness to take risks – that lets us make the leap *from need to...*
3M *Innovation*

Applying Technology

Marketers must closely monitor the technological environment for a number of reasons. For one, creative applications of new technologies give a firm a definite competitive edge. 3M Company's success as an innovator stems from its ability to apply new technologies in developing new products. For example, 3M used microreplication technology to create the lighted guide rail shown in the ad in Figure 3.8.

Marketers who monitor new technology and successfully apply it may also enhance customer service. Breakthroughs in electronic communications have brought consumers the convenience of in-home shopping and 24-hour banking at automated teller machines. Some restaurants accelerate their service by equipping serving staff with palmtop computers that transmit patrons' orders to the kitchen receivers.

The banking industry has embraced many technical developments. Banks will spend over $5 billion on new technology, 20 percent of it to support online banking. Retail customers are not the only ones to benefit. For example, Boston University likes to receive online payments of student loans. Automatic electronic transfers reduce the chance that borrowers will miss payments. Wells Fargo's Business Gateway on CompuServe is designed exclusively to serve small businesses. The site helps users to transfer funds, review account balances, and check on the status of transactions.[29]

Freightliner Corp., a Portland, Oregon-based unit of the German automotive firm Daimler-Benz AG, has adopted new technology as aggressively as any truck manufacturer. The firm made this strategy pay off, grabbing the top spot in the king-size truck market in 1992 and increasing its market share ever since. In the late 1980s, Freightliner began to integrate technology into its entire business operations. Computer networks link dealers to company headquarters. This system simplifies the customer ordering process by replacing a thick catalog showing thousands of options with an easy-to-use database. The network also speeds parts ordering.

Although the system is expensive, it provides solid benefits. Sales at the Portland dealership tripled and the size of the sales staff dropped from seven to five following installation of the system. Customers also feel more satisfied, because diagrams help them to make sure that they get the right parts for their trucks. Freightliner also uses computers to aid inventory control, reducing the parts stocks required in its fleet shops, and to speed up production at assembly plants.[30]

Subsequent chapters will discuss how companies apply technology to marketing in more detail—for example, databases, electronic data interchange, and interactive promotional techniques.

THE SOCIAL-CULTURAL ENVIRONMENT

As a nation, the United States is becoming older and more affluent. The birthrate is falling, and subculture populations are rising. People express concerns about the environment, buying ecologically friendly products that reduce pollution. They value the time spent at home with family

Figure 3.9 Designing Products for a Culturally Diverse Marketplace

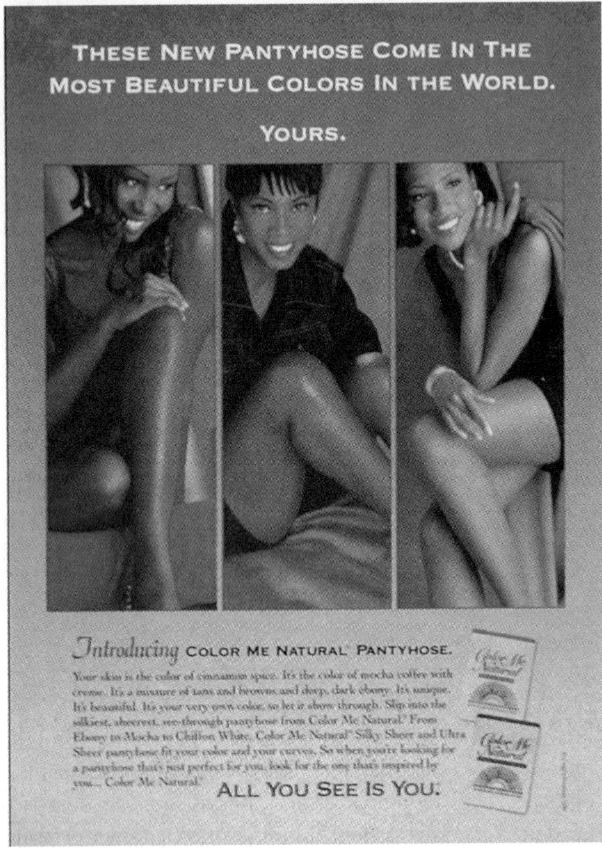
THESE NEW PANTYHOSE COME IN THE MOST BEAUTIFUL COLORS IN THE WORLD.
YOURS.
Introducing COLOR ME NATURAL® PANTYHOSE.
Your skin is the color of cinnamon spice. It's the color of mocha coffee with creme. It's a mixture of tans and browns and deep, dark ebony. It's unique. It's beautiful. It's your very own color, so let it show through. Slip into the silkiest, sheerest, see-through pantyhose from Color Me Natural.® From Ebony to Mocha to Chiffon White, Color Me Natural® Silky Sheer and Ultra Sheer pantyhose fit your color and your curves. So when you're looking for a pantyhose that's just perfect for you, look for the one that's inspired by you... Color Me Natural.®
ALL YOU SEE IS YOU.®

and friends, watching videos and eating microwaved snacks. These types of events help to shape marketing's **social-cultural environment**—the relationship between marketing and society and its culture.

Marketers must cultivate sensitivity to society's changing values and to demographic shifts such as population growth and age distribution changes. These changing variables affect consumers' reactions to different products and marketing practices. For example, people are more health conscious today than they were ten years ago. They watch their diets, eating lots of fruits and vegetables and limiting fat consumption. As a result, both food companies and restaurants have added low-fat or fat-free versions of many items. Fast-food chains Taco Bell and Dunkin' Donuts now include healthier foods on their menus. Taco Bell developed its Border Light meals after consumer groups like The Center for Science in the Public Interest criticized the chain's high-fat meals. The Light Taco has 5 fat grams, versus 11 in the original, and the Seven-Layer Burrito's 21 grams of fat were cut to 10. Company representative Jonathan Blum attributed the success of Border Light products to their great taste, coming close to the original products. Likewise, Dunkin' Donuts added low-fat muffins, with only 1.5 grams of fat, to its menu list. The company hoped to attract customers who would not ordinarily patronize a donut shop.[31]

Candy manufacturers are also taking note of consumer interest in low-fat foods. Hershey Foods, best-known for its chocolate products, acquired several nonchocolate candy brands like Twizzlers licorice, Jolly Rancher hard candies, Good & Plenty licorice candies, and Jujyfruits. These products have given Hershey something it needed: low-fat or fat-free candies that satisfy consumers' sweet cravings. While a Hershey milk chocolate bar has 13 grams of fat, Jolly Rancher and Good & Plenty have none. The addition of these complementary product types has helped the country's leading chocolate maker to adapt and meet changing consumer tastes in order to maintain its share of increasing candy consumption: Consumers now eat over 23 pounds each year.[32]

Another social-cultural trend has raised the importance of cultural diversity. The United States is a mixed society composed of various submarkets, each with its unique values and cultural characteristics and its own age distribution, places of residence, consumer preferences, and purchasing behavior. Some companies find it highly profitable to target these submarkets. Firms have found success selling many different products, from ethnic foods to music, to small, well-defined groups of customers. Even on the vast World Wide Web, companies can reach specific demographic markets.

Channel A is an interactive site designed to attract Asian-Americans with a mix of information about Asia, politics, and cultural and social news, as well as products and services. Designed to serve as a medium for entertaining and educating the various Asian ethnic groups and bringing them closer together, Channel A will reach an economically desirable market. This group shows a higher percentage of Web usage than average—40 percent—and a higher-than-average household income. "We want to be what MTV is to music, what CNN is to world news, and what the Home Shopping Network is to retail," said Steve Chin, executive editor.[33] Chapter 7 looks closer at demographic considerations of market segmentation, and Chapter 8 considers how social and cultural trends influence consumer behavior.

http://www.channela.com/

Creative marketers at L'eggs recognize the growing importance of cultural diversity by making fleshtone hosiery in many shades for the U.S. population of the twenty-first century. L'eggs meets this need by offering a wide variety of product choices. The Color Me Natural advertisement in Figure 3.9 offers a palette of shades that includes Ebony, Mocha, and Chiffon White to reflect the cultural diversity of today's marketplace.

Importance in International Marketing Decisions

The social-cultural context often exerts a more pronounced influence on marketing decision making in the international sphere than in the domestic arena. Learning about cultural and social differences among countries proves a paramount condition for a firm's success abroad. Marketing strategies that work in the United States often fail when directly applied in other countries. In many cases, marketers must redesign packages and modify products and advertising messages to suit the tastes and preferences of different cultures.

Even a seemingly simple marketing strategy, like that for Ben & Jerry's Homemade, Inc. in the United Kingdom, may yield surprising results. In the U.S. market, the premium ice cream company implemented an unconventional, limited-marketing strategy and a business philosophy of "caring capitalism." Its genuine image, all-natural product of high quality, playful attitude, social consciousness, and low-key founders appealed to the American public. This approach, however, did not travel well across the Atlantic. Häagen-Dazs preceded Ben & Jerry's by five years in the U.K. market, effectively using high-profile advertising to promote the brand as the ultimate, super-premium ice cream. Although Ben & Jerry's marketers hoped to capitalize on their U.S. counterculture image, they discovered that British consumers were largely unaware of their existence. This problem was compounded by their late arrival in the British Isles. The firm originally had planned an inexpensive product launch, but it found itself funding a high-priced venture based on product sampling to improve brand awareness. Costs increased further when the company had to expand the number of "scoop shops" and "scoop carts" dispensing Ben & Jerry's ice cream to British buyers.[34] Chapter 4 continues the discussion of the social-cultural aspects of international marketing.

Consumerism

Changing social values have led to the consumerism movement. Today everyone—marketers, industry, government, and the public—is acutely aware of the impact of consumerism on the nation's economy and general well-being.

JUSTICIA
AHORA

Hispanic and African-American consumer activists picketed Texaco's refinery in Wilmington, California, to protest the company's racial discrimination policies. The sign's Spanish text reads, "We want justice now."

Consumerism has been defined as a social force within the environment designed to aid and protect buyers by exerting legal, moral, and economic pressures on business.[35] This definition sums up society's demand that organizations apply the marketing concept.

In recent years, marketers have witnessed increasing consumer activism. Animal-rights activists have demonstrated against furriers and firms that test their products on animals. Marketers of canned tuna have received harsh criticism for selling fish caught by nets that also trap and kill dolphins.

Boycotts are another effective consumerist technique. The number of boycotts against various companies has risen in recent years. Even the threat of a boycott can bring results. When a former Texaco executive released secretly recorded audio tapes in which company officials belittled African-Americans, civil rights activists called for a boycott and picketed Texaco gas stations. A day later, Texaco settled a two-year-old discrimination lawsuit for $176 million and agreed to increase the percentage of minorities on its staff from 23 percent to 29 percent by 2000.[36]

But firms do not fulfill all consumer demands. A competitive marketing system emerges from the individual

Marketing Dictionary

social-cultural environment The component of the marketing environment defined by the relationship of marketers to society and its culture.

consumerism A social force within the environment designed to aid and protect buyers by exerting legal, moral, and economic pressures on businesses and government.

MARKETING HALL OF SHAME

Benetton's Ads: More's the Pity

Any company that launches an advertising campaign clearly wants attention, but just about all companies shy away from the wrong kind of notoriety. When clever ads turn controversial, most companies scurry for cover.

But some firms create exceptions. No doubt, Benetton, the Italian apparel maker, is one of the most notable examples. Critics around the globe have complained bitterly about Benetton's inflammatory and manipulative advertisements. But the complaints have seemed to encourage ever more shocking ads from this unusual, family-run company.

While most firms in the clothing business rarely stray from image advertising, Benetton has made its name ignoring this approach. Instead, Benetton's ads exploit the consumer's sense of pity, according to detractors. In the same vein, Calvin Klein, another provocative marketer, has been accused of exploiting underage sex, as well as drug use, in its advertisements.

The Benetton ads have focused on such social issues as racism, ethnic violence, the war in Bosnia, and social taboos—all without a sweater in sight. Benetton's slick advertisements have captured images like a priest and nun kissing, dying AIDS patients, and Palestinian refugees. One recent ad campaign showed a blood-stained T-shirt seared with a bullet hole and a pair of camouflage pants. The uniform belonged to a slain Bosnian soldier. Only the company's logo in the corner gave consumers any hint of who sponsored the ad.

Ironically, notes Luciano Benetton, the man behind the global apparel network, the company's most controversial ad was actually meant to celebrate life. The advertisement showed a newborn baby with its umbilical cord still attached. "This was the most highly boycotted of all the publicity campaigns we ever did and yet we thought it was optimistic," says Benetton, who doesn't shrink from exploiting images of himself. He once posed nude in a charity ad campaign for the homeless.

The company cites twofold goals for its highly charged ads: to gener-

actions of competing firms. The U.S. economic system requires that firms achieve reasonable profit objectives. Business cannot meet all consumer demands and still generate enough profits to remain viable. This choice defines one of the most difficult dilemmas facing society today. Given these constraints, what should buyers have a right to expect from the competitive marketing system?

The most frequently quoted statement of **consumer rights** was made by President John F. Kennedy in 1962. While this list does not amount to a definitive statement, it offers good rules of thumb that explain basic consumer rights:

1. *The right to choose freely.* Consumers should be able to choose among a range of goods and services.
2. *The right to be informed.* Consumers should have access to enough education and product information to make responsible buying decisions.
3. *The right to be heard.* Consumers should be able to express legitimate complaints to appropriate parties—that is, sellers, consumer assistance groups, and city or state consumer affairs offices.
4. *The right to be safe.* Consumers should feel assured that the goods and services they purchase will not cause injuries in normal use. Product designs should allow average consumers to use them safely.

These rights have formed the conceptual framework of much of the consumerist legislation passed in the first 40 years of the movement. However, the question of how best to guarantee these rights remains unanswered.

The social-cultural environment for marketing decisions at home and abroad is expanding in scope and importance. Today no marketer can initiate a strategic decision without taking into account the society's norms, values, culture, and demographics. Marketers must understand how these variables affect their decisions. The constant influx of social input requires that marketing managers focus on addressing these questions instead of concerning themselves only with the standard marketing tools. Some firms have created a new position—manager of public policy research—to study the changing social environment's future impact on their operations.

MARKETING'S ROLE IN SOCIETY

The five environments described so far in the chapter do not completely capture the role that marketing plays in so-

ate discussions of serious social issues and to heighten brand awareness in a unique way. "People's expectations and tolerance levels are changing," says Peter Fressola, director of communications for Benetton in North America. "They're starved for something new and different to shake us from complacency. Benetton represents the fringe of a new kind of advertising."

In some respects, Benetton is trying to achieve the same objectives as any other company—sales messages that leap out in an already saturated market. "What Benetton has done—perhaps in the most spectacular way—is react to the new conditions of the marketplace," suggests Sut Jhally, author of several advertising books and professor at the University of Massachusetts. In addition to incredible competition among rival messages, today's ads must strain to reach fragmented and increasingly disaffected audiences. "It no longer has anything to do with sweaters, it has to do with cutting through the clutter."

Growing evidence shows, however, that Benetton's controversial ads have hurt the company's bottom line. A European recession, as well as the ad furor, is blamed for virtually flat sales. German retailers sued the clothing maker, alleging that the ads have turned shoppers away in droves. Store owners in France and Spain are also complaining. The shocking ads have triggered numerous boycotts. Even some Benetton family members are themselves disenchanted with the ads.

No other advertisers have tried to mimic Benetton's marketing approach, and for solid reasons. "You'll find that most advertisers don't try to shock people," says Karen King, associate professor of advertising at the University of Georgia. "Getting attention is not necessarily selling a product."

QUESTIONS FOR CRITICAL THINKING

1. **Do you think that Benetton's strategy works? If so, do you think advertisers in general are too timid?**
2. **Who would be the most attracted to Benetton's ads? Why? What market segment would disapprove of them?**

Sources: Benetton Advertising page, http://www.benetton.com/benetton-web/advertising, downloaded April 4, 1997; Kirsten A. Conover, "Advertisers Aim to Cut Through Media Clutter," *Christian Science Monitor,* May 31, 1996, p. 12; Lawrence Van Gelder, "Levi Drops Its 'Nice Pants' ads in New York City," *San Diego Union-Tribune,* September 27, 1995, p. A1; John Rossant, "The Faded Colors of Benetton," *Business Week,* April 10, 1995; and Shelley Donald Coolidge, "Thriving on Controversy," *Christian Science Monitor,* May 26, 1994, p. 9.

ciety itself and the consequent effects and responsibilities of marketing activities. Marketing's activities within society in general and in connection with various public issues invite constant scrutiny by the public. In fact, marketing may typically seem to mirror changes in the entire business environment. Because marketing determines the final interface between a business enterprise and the society in which it operates, marketers often carry much of the responsibility for dealing with various social issues affecting their firms.

Marketing operates in an environment external to the firm. It reacts to that environment and, in turn, feels environmental influences. Relationships with customers, employees, the government, vendors, and society as a whole form the basis of the social issues that confront contemporary marketers. While these concerns often grow out of the exchange process, they produce effects coincidental to the primary sales and distribution functions of marketing. Marketing's relationship to its external environment has a significant effect on the firm's eventual success. Marketing must continually find new ways to deal with the social issues facing the competitive system.

The competitive marketing system is a product of a general drive for materialism. However, it is important to note that materialism developed from the priorities of society itself. Most of U.S. culture, with its acceptance of the work ethic, traditionally has looked favorably on the acquisition of wealth. The motto of this philosophy seems to be "more equals better." A better life has been defined in terms of more physical possessions, although that definition seems to be changing.

Evaluating the Quality of Life

One recurring theme runs through the arguments of marketing's critics: Materialism, as exemplified by the competitive marketing system, leads people to concern themselves only with the quantities of life and to ignore its quality. Traditionally, a firm held a reputation as socially

Marketing Dictionary

consumer rights As stated by President Kennedy in 1962, the consumer's right to choose freely, to be informed, to be heard, and to be safe.

responsible in the community if it provided employment for its residents and contributed to its economic base. Employment, wages, bank deposits, and profits—the traditional measures of business's social contributions—are quantity indicators. But what about air, water, and cultural pollution? Should workers tolerate the boredom and isolation of mass assembly lines? Should future generations accept the depletion of natural resources? Charges of organizational neglect in these areas go largely unanswered simply because businesspeople have not developed reliable indicators with which to measure a firm's contribution to the quality of life.

Criticisms of the Competitive Marketing System

A critic's indictment of the competitive marketing system would cite at least the following complaints:

1. Marketing costs are too high.
2. The marketing system is inefficient.
3. Marketers and the business system commit collusion and price fixing.
4. Firms deliver poor product quality and service.
5. Consumers receive incomplete, false, and/or misleading information.
6. The marketing system produces health and safety hazards.
7. Marketers persuasively promote unwanted and unnecessary products to those who least need them.

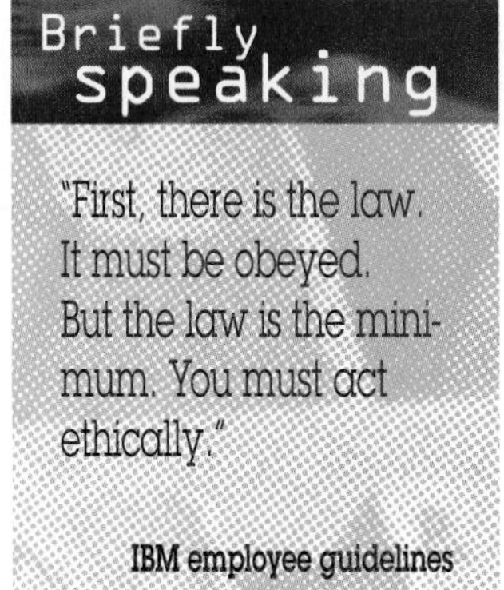
Briefly
speaking
"First, there is the law. It must be obeyed. But the law is the minimum. You must act ethically."
IBM employee guidelines

Almost anyone could cite specific examples that confirm these charges. Because each person applies a somewhat different set of values, a fair judgment should recognize that each one evaluates the performance of the marketing system according to personal experience within an individual frame of reference.

Bearing this condition in mind and taking the system as a whole, everyone can form his or her own evaluation of the success or failure of the competitive marketing system in serving consumers' needs. Most people will likely arrive at the uncomfortable and somewhat unsatisfying conclusion that the system usually works quite adequately, although some aspects would improve with changes.

CURRENT ISSUES IN MARKETING

Marketers face many diverse social issues. The current issues in marketing can be divided into two major subjects: marketing ethics and social responsibility. While the overlap and classification problems are obvious, the framework provides a foundation for systematically studying these issues.

Marketing Ethics

Environmental influences have directed increased attention toward **marketing ethics**—marketers' standards of conduct and moral values. Ethics concern matters of right and wrong, the decisions of individuals and firms to do what is morally right. A discussion of marketing ethics highlights the types of problems that individuals face in their roles as marketers. Considerations of such problems should precede any suggestions for improvements in the marketing system. Increased recognition of the importance of marketing ethics is evident from the growing number of full-time corporate ethics officers in such organizations as Dun & Bradstreet, American Express, Dow Corning, Texas Instruments, and even the Internal Revenue Service.

"Corporations are beginning to realize that ethics initiatives can help reduce risk and limit liability," said W. Michael Hoffman, executive director of the Ethics Officers' Association. According to an Ethics Resource Center survey, about 60 percent of U.S. companies operate formal ethics programs, and about 33 percent have set up special ethics offices. A recent survey reported in *Training* magazine found that 38 percent of American organizations offer ethics training.[37]

Some issues in marketing ethics lack clear-cut answers. The issue of cigarette advertising, for example, has divided the ranks of advertising executives. Can ethical advertisers promote a product that, while legal, imposes known health hazards on users? Can they ethically justify the huge profits they earn from that promotion? Should the industry self-regulate its advertising to prevent encouraging kids to start smoking?

Some advertising executives have formed the Initiative on Tobacco Marketing to Children and sponsored a unique ad campaign. Aimed not at consumers but at other advertisers, the program was designed to promote voluntary restrictions on tobacco ads. One ad featured a picture of a young teen with padlocked eyes and the tag line, "We can't close their eyes. Can we open ours?" The copy urged other advertisers to take responsibility for the messages they create and to stop marketing tobacco products to kids. Other advertising executives respond by questioning whether these attempts to voluntarily regulate another industry's products amount to collusion and restraint of trade.[38]

People develop standards of ethical behavior based on their own systems of values. Their individual ethical be-

Figure 3.10 American Marketing Association's Code of Ethics

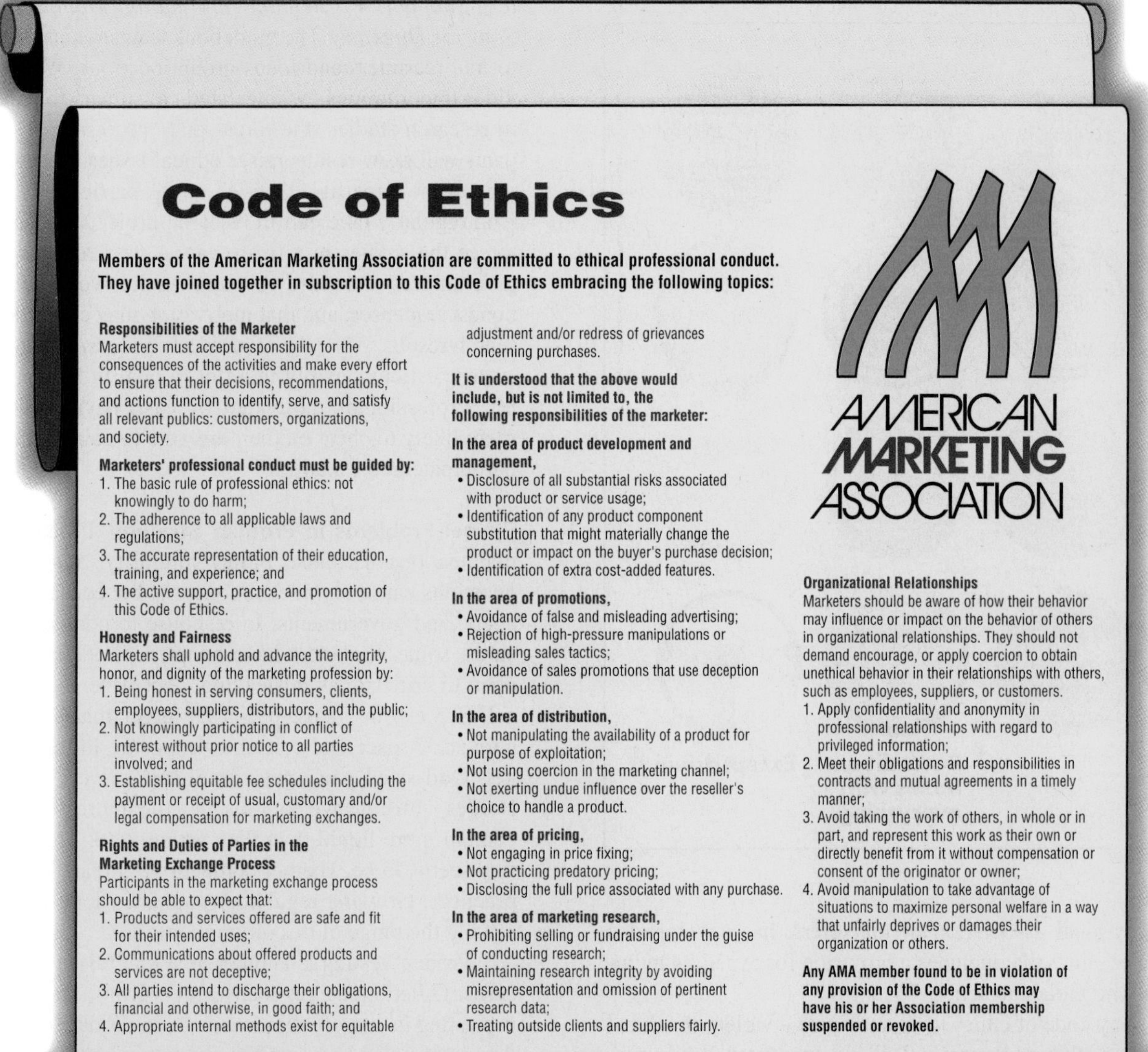

Code of Ethics

Members of the American Marketing Association are committed to ethical professional conduct. They have joined together in subscription to this Code of Ethics embracing the following topics:

Responsibilities of the Marketer

Marketers must accept responsibility for the consequences of the activities and make every effort to ensure that their decisions, recommendations, and actions function to identify, serve, and satisfy all relevant publics: customers, organizations, and society.

Marketers' professional conduct must be guided by:

1. The basic rule of professional ethics: not knowingly to do harm;
2. The adherence to all applicable laws and regulations;
3. The accurate representation of their education, training, and experience; and
4. The active support, practice, and promotion of this Code of Ethics.

Honesty and Fairness

Marketers shall uphold and advance the integrity, honor, and dignity of the marketing profession by:

1. Being honest in serving consumers, clients, employees, suppliers, distributors, and the public;
2. Not knowingly participating in conflict of interest without prior notice to all parties involved; and
3. Establishing equitable fee schedules including the payment or receipt of usual, customary and/or legal compensation for marketing exchanges.

Rights and Duties of Parties in the Marketing Exchange Process

Participants in the marketing exchange process should be able to expect that:

1. Products and services offered are safe and fit for their intended uses;
2. Communications about offered products and services are not deceptive;
3. All parties intend to discharge their obligations, financial and otherwise, in good faith; and
4. Appropriate internal methods exist for equitable adjustment and/or redress of grievances concerning purchases.

It is understood that the above would include, but is not limited to, the following responsibilities of the marketer:

In the area of product development and management,

- Disclosure of all substantial risks associated with product or service usage;
- Identification of any product component substitution that might materially change the product or impact on the buyer's purchase decision;
- Identification of extra cost-added features.

In the area of promotions,

- Avoidance of false and misleading advertising;
- Rejection of high-pressure manipulations or misleading sales tactics;
- Avoidance of sales promotions that use deception or manipulation.

In the area of distribution,

- Not manipulating the availability of a product for purpose of exploitation;
- Not using coercion in the marketing channel;
- Not exerting undue influence over the reseller's choice to handle a product.

In the area of pricing,

- Not engaging in price fixing;
- Not practicing predatory pricing;
- Disclosing the full price associated with any purchase.

In the area of marketing research,

- Prohibiting selling or fundraising under the guise of conducting research;
- Maintaining research integrity by avoiding misrepresentation and omission of pertinent research data;
- Treating outside clients and suppliers fairly.

AMERICAN
MARKETING
ASSOCIATION

Organizational Relationships

Marketers should be aware of how their behavior may influence or impact on the behavior of others in organizational relationships. They should not demand encourage, or apply coercion to obtain unethical behavior in their relationships with others, such as employees, suppliers, or customers.

1. Apply confidentiality and anonymity in professional relationships with regard to privileged information;
2. Meet their obligations and responsibilities in contracts and mutual agreements in a timely manner;
3. Avoid taking the work of others, in whole or in part, and represent this work as their own or directly benefit from it without compensation or consent of the originator or owner;
4. Avoid manipulation to take advantage of situations to maximize personal welfare in a way that unfairly deprives or damages their organization or others.

Any AMA member found to be in violation of any provision of the Code of Ethics may have his or her Association membership suspended or revoked.

liefs help them to deal with ethical questions that arise in their personal lives. However, a work situation may generate serious conflicts with those beliefs. Individual ethics may differ from an employer's organizational ethics. An individual may strongly favor industry participation in developing a recycling program for industrial waste, but his or her firm may dismiss the venture as an unprofitable expense.

How can people resolve these conflicts? The development of and adherence to professional ethical standards may provide a third basis of authority. These standards should derive from a concept of professionalism that transcends both organizational and individual ethics. A professional peer association can exercise collective oversight to limit a marketer's individual behavior. As Figure 3.10 shows, the American Marketing Association, the major

Marketing Dictionary

marketing ethics Marketers' standards of conduct and moral values.

Figure 3.11 Promoting Responsible Consumption of Alcoholic Beverages

diet Coke
MISE EN BOUTEILLE A LA SOURCE
Perrier
FRANCE
Schweppes
Tonic Water
Ocean spray
Sprite
Minute Maid
Orange Soda
Coca-Cola CLASSIC
BACARDI
Bacardi rum mixes with everything.
Except driving.

international association of marketers, has developed a code of ethics that includes a provision for expelling members who violate its tenets.

Any code of ethics must anticipate a variety of ethical problems that marketers will likely encounter. While promotional matters tend to receive the greatest attention, ethical issues also relate to marketing research, product strategy, distribution strategy, and pricing.

Ethical Problems in Marketing Research Marketing research has received criticism for alleged invasions of personal privacy. People today value their individual identities more strongly than ever before. Personal privacy is important to most consumers, so it has become a public issue. As databases have proliferated and marketers have more freely rented address lists and other information, public concern about threats to personal privacy has increased. Chapter 10 will return to the issue of privacy.

Recruiting and paying people to participate in marketing research studies creates another ethical concern for market researchers. Ads offering consumers $25 an hour to shop or $100 per hour for their opinions appear with toll-free phone numbers in local shopper publications and in e-mail messages. Callers to these numbers receive invitations to send $25 for a publication, *Focus Group and Mystery Shoppers Participant Information Manual and Nationwide Directory.* The guidebook teaches consumers how to find recruiters and focus group locations. While it provides opportunities for interested consumers to participate in research studies, the threat that "professional" participants will skew results raises ethical issues for researchers who want impartial, "naive" study participants. People who regularly take part in research projects are less likely to see the studies in a fresh way. A paid respondent may give answers intended to secure more work rather than honest responses, and that motivation may compromise research results. Also, the manual advises respondents to answer questions flexibly in order to qualify for many studies. Professionals motivated by cash payments may be more likely to cheat on their answers to gain invitations to participate in the studies.[39]

Ethical Problems in Product Strategy Product quality, planned obsolescence, brand similarity, and packaging questions cause significant concerns for consumers, managers, and governments. In response to competitive pressures, some marketers have adopted packaging practices open to criticism as misleading, deceptive, and/or unethical. Some firms make packages larger than necessary to gain shelf space and consumer exposure in the supermarket. Odd-sized packages complicate price comparisons. Bottles with concave bottoms give the impression that they contain more liquid than they actually do. The real question seems to be whether competitive threats justify these practices. Growing regulatory mandates appear to be narrowing the range of discretion in this area.

Product testing is another area that raises ethical concerns. Gillette receives many letters from school children protesting its use of rabbits and rats in product testing. Students have also boycotted the company's products. These early reactions could affect Gillette's long-term sales if they lead people to avoid its products in later years. Chairman Alfred Zeien expresses concern that uninformed teachers give children the wrong idea of the reasons for the tests. Some consumers criticize the research as unnecessary because it does not cure or prevent disease. Before a company releases a product for public use, however, it must test the ingredients for safety. Consumers would raise a different kind of uproar if a new shampoo's ingredient caused blindness or allergies. Animal testing may be the only way to assess these possibilities. Still, Gillette has spent $4 million to find alternatives to animal testing and reduced the amount of its animal testing.[40]

Ethical Problems in Distribution Strategy A firm's channel strategy should anticipate two kinds of ethical questions:

1. What degree of control should the firm exert over its channel?

2. Should a company distribute its products in marginally profitable outlets that lack alternative sources of supply?

The question of control typically arises in relationships between manufacturers and franchised dealers. Should the parent organization coerce an automobile dealership, a gas station, or a fast-food outlet to purchase parts, materials, and supplementary services? What is the proper degree of control in the channel of distribution?

The second question concerns marketers' responsibility to serve unsatisfied market segments, even if it foresees only slight profit potential. Should marketers maintain retail stores in low-income areas, ensure supplies for users of limited amounts of the firm's product, or keep up locations in declining rural markets? These questions are difficult to resolve, because they often involve individuals rather than broad segments of the general public. An important first step is to ensure that the firm consistently enforces its channel policies.

Ethical Problems in Promotional Strategy Promotion gives rise to more ethical questions than other components of the marketing mix. Personal selling has always attracted ethical criticism. Early traders, pack peddlers, greeters, drummers, and today's used-car salespeople, for example, have all been accused of marketing malpractice ranging from exaggerating product merits to outright deceit. Gifts and bribes are common ethical abuses. Advertisers have responded to criticism for sexist messages by showing women in varied situations, especially in nontraditional work roles such as bus driver, bank officer, and heavy-equipment operator. Similarly, marketers of alcoholic beverages try to deflect criticism by promoting responsible consumption of their products through advertisements such as the Bacardi Imports message in Figure 3.11.

Advertisements stating that consumers would pay "zero interest" on purchases led to suits against four retailers by authorities in 12 states. Best Buy, Tandy, CompUSA, and Montgomery Ward paid a total of $925,000 and agreed to improve disclosure of financing terms in their ads. The states claimed that the term zero interest makes customers think that they will pay no interest under any circumstances. In fact, this claim held true only if customers paid in full for their purchases during specified time periods, typically one year. Any missed payments resulted in interest due for the entire zero-interest period.[41] Chapters 17, 18, and 19 discuss promotional ethics in greater detail.

Ethical Problems in Pricing Pricing is probably the most thoroughly regulated aspect of a firm's marketing strategy. As a result, most unethical pricing behavior also violates the law. Some gray areas remain, however, in pricing ethics. For example, should some customers pay premium prices for merchandise to offset high distribution costs in their areas? Do marketers have any obligation to warn customers of impending changes in price, discount, or return policies? A marketer must deal with all of these queries in developing a professional ethic.

Social Responsibility

In a general sense, **social responsibility** demands that marketers accept an obligation to give equal weight to profits, consumer satisfaction, and social well-being in evaluating their firm's performance. They must recognize the importance of relatively qualitative consumer and social benefits as well as the quantitative measures of sales, revenue, and profits by which firms have traditionally measured marketing performance.

Social responsibility allows for easier measurement than marketing ethics. Government legislation can mandate socially responsible actions. Consumer activism can also promote social responsibility by business.

Actions alone determine social responsibility, and a firm can behave responsibly, even under coercion. For example, government requirements may *force* firms to take socially responsible actions in matters of environmental policy, deceptive product claims, and so forth. Also, consumers, through their power to repeat or withhold purchases, may *force* marketers to provide honest and relevant information, fair prices, and so forth. Ethically responsible behavior, on the other hand, requires more than appropriate actions; ethical intentions must also motivate those actions.[42]

The locus for socially responsible decisions in organizations has always been an important issue. Who should accept specific accountability for the social effects of marketing decisions? Responses range from the district sales manager to the marketing vice-president, the firm's CEO, and even the board of directors. Probably the most valid assessment holds that *all marketers,* regardless of their stations in the organization, remain accountable for the social aspects of their decisions.

When a fire destroyed Malden Mills' textile manufacturing plant, CEO Aaron Feuerstein kept the company's

Marketing Dictionary

social responsibility The collection of marketing philosophies, policies, procedures, and actions intended primarily to enhance society's welfare.

Figure 3.12 Polartec: Product Success for a Socially Responsible Marketer

Loves bloody elbows.
Digs chain-grease calves.
Craves road-rash hips.
Detests a sweaty midriff.
Polartec® fabric pulls sweat away from your skin and disperses it evenly so it evaporates quickly. Keeping your skin drier than with any other fabric available. With over 100 other Climate Control Fabrics™, Polartec keeps you cool when it's hot, warm when it's cold, dry when you sweat. So you can perform at your peak. Look for the label.
MALDEN MILLS
POLARTEC®
BELIEVE IN WHAT YOU WEAR.

3,000 employees on the payroll while he rebuilt the business. Feuerstein acknowledged both humanitarian and businesslike motives for the decision. He viewed the firm's loyal workforce as an essential source of competitive advantage, and he recognized his responsibility to keep it intact during his troubled period. One of the last textile producers in Lawrence, Massachusetts, Malden is the developer and exclusive producer of the Polartec climate control fabrics shown in Figure 3.12.

After three months, most employees had returned to work in a temporary facility set up in a warehouse. Those without jobs continued to receive assistance. Feuerstein accepted a responsibility to the company beyond a requirement to make money for the shareholders—even though his family holds all the stock. "I consider our workers an asset, not an expense," he said. "I have a responsibility to the worker. . . . I have an equal responsibility to the community." Even though the salary continuance program cost the firm several million dollars, the effect of retaining employee loyalty justified the expense. A few weeks after the fire, the company was producing 230,000 yards of fabric per week, compared to 130,000 before. Lands' End, a major customer for Polartec products, told Malden's story in its December catalog and publicly supported Feuerstein's actions.[43]

Marketing's Social Responsibilities The concept of business's social responsibility traditionally has concerned managers' relationships with customers, employees, and stockholders. Managers felt responsibility for providing quality products at reasonable prices for customers, adequate wages and decent working environments for employees, and acceptable profits for stockholders. Only occasionally did the concept extend to relations with the government and rarely to the general public.

Today, the responsibility concept extends to cover the entire social framework. A decision to temporarily delay the installation of a pollution control device may satisfy the traditional sense of responsibility. Customers would continue to receive an uninterrupted supply of the plant's products, employees would not face layoffs, and stockholders would still receive reasonable returns on their investments in the company. Contemporary business ethics, however, would not accept this choice as a socially responsible decision.

Similarly, a firm that markets foods with low nutritional value may satisfy the traditional concept of responsibility, but such behavior raises questions in the contemporary perspective. This principle does not imply that all firms should distribute only foods of high nutritional value; it means merely that the previous framework for evaluation is no longer considered comprehensive in terms of either scope or time.

Contemporary marketing decisions must consider the entire societal framework, not only in the United States but also throughout the world. Marketing decisions must also account for their eventual, long-term effects and for their results for future generations. Consumer groups have criticized some companies for buying from foreign suppliers that employ children or prison convicts as laborers, damage the environment, or force employees to work in dangerous conditions. Inputs produced by cheap, foreign labor in developing countries have attracted wide publicity as consumers have learned about poor conditions in overseas apparel manufacturing factories. Both Wal-Mart and Kmart now follow new policies for dealing with foreign contract labor. JCPenney refuses to buy from ShinWon Honduras, a South Korean subcontractor's Honduran plant, unless the firm makes improvements like installing emergency exits and fire extinguishers. To comply with Reebok and Sears policies of not buying from plants using underage workers, a supplier company laid off teenagers. American manufacturers like Levi's, Reebok, and Gap regularly inspect contractors' facilities to check on labor conditions and product quality.[44]

Marketers can apply many methods to help their companies behave in socially responsible ways. Chapter 1 discussed cause marketing through which companies promote social causes by sponsoring programs that persuade people to support particular activities or priorities. Socially responsible marketing involves campaigns that encourage people to adopt socially beneficial behaviors, like driving safely and eating nutritious food. Such campaigns can help society and the firm's bottom line, too.

Eveready Battery marketers identified a problem that had largely escaped attention: One-third of all smoke detectors don't work because of missing or dead batteries. Nonfunctioning smoke detectors contribute substantially to deaths, injuries, and damage from fires. The company developed its "Change Your Clock, Change Your Battery" campaign to educate consumers about the importance of regularly replacing smoke detector batteries. Cosponsored by the International Association of Fire Chiefs, the advertising campaign generated lots of media coverage—and it also boosted battery sales.[45]

Marketing and Ecology Ecology—the relationship between organisms and their natural environments—has become one of the most important aspects of marketing in the 1990s. Many industry and government leaders rank environmental effects as the biggest challenge facing business. Environmental concerns of garbage disposal, acid rain, depletion of the ozone layer, global warming, and contamination of the air and water span the globe. These priorities influence all areas of marketing decision making from product planning to public relations. Marketers must address several ecological aspects of their businesses: planned obsolescence, pollution, recycling waste materials, and resource conservation.

The initial ecological problem facing marketing was *planned obsolescence*—intentional manufacturing of products with limited durability. Some products become obsolete when technological improvements allow better alternatives. Others, however, reach physical obsolescence due to intentional design features that make them wear out within short periods of time. Marketers have responded to consumer demand for convenience by offering extremely short-lived products such as disposable diapers, pens, razors, and cameras. In other products, such as those in the fashion industry, rapid changes in design produce obsolescence.

Planned obsolescence has always represented a significant ethical question for marketers. On one side, firms need to turn over products to maintain sales and employment; on the other, they need to ensure product quality and durability. In the process, they must wrestle with the practical question whether consumers really want or can afford increased durability. Many buyers prefer to change styles often and knowingly accept products that will quickly age. Increased durability has an implicit cost that may prevent some people from affording a product.

Pollution is a broad term that covers a number of circumstances. It usually implies something unclean. Public concern about polluting such natural resources as water and air has reached critical proportions in some areas. The marketing system annually generates billions of tons of packaging materials, such as glass, metal, paper, and plastics, that add to the world's growing piles of trash and waste.

Figure 3.13 **Phillips Petroleum's Recycling Efforts to Conserve Natural Resources**

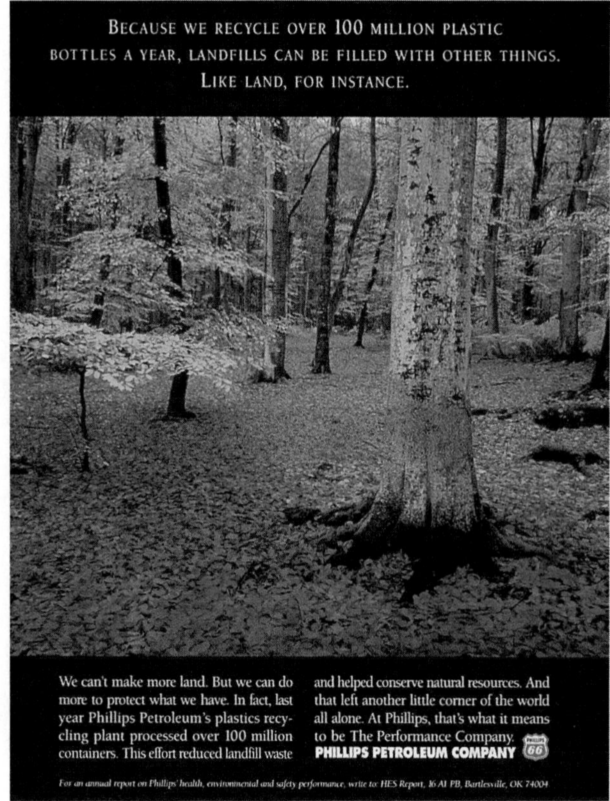
BECAUSE WE RECYCLE OVER 100 MILLION PLASTIC BOTTLES A YEAR, LANDFILLS CAN BE FILLED WITH OTHER THINGS. LIKE LAND, FOR INSTANCE.
We can't make more land. But we can do more to protect what we have. In fact, last year Phillips Petroleum's plastics recycling plant processed over 100 million containers. This effort reduced landfill waste and helped conserve natural resources. And that left another little corner of the world all alone. At Phillips, that's what it means to be The Performance Company.
PHILLIPS PETROLEUM COMPANY
66
For an annual report on Phillips' health, environmental and safety performance, write to: HES Report, 16 A1 PB, Bartlesville, OK 74004

Recycling—processing used materials for reuse—is another important aspect of ecology. The underlying rationale of recycling holds that reprocessed materials can benefit society by saving natural resources and energy as well as by alleviating major causes of environmental pollution. The ad in Figure 3.13 describes how Phillips Petroleum recycles plastics to reduce landfill waste and to help conserve natural resources.

Many companies respond to consumers' growing concern about ecological issues by practicing **green marketing**—production, promotion, and reclamation of environmentally sensitive products. This trend seeks to address conditions like the fact that less than 5 percent of the

Marketing Dictionary

green marketing Production, promotion, and reclamation of environmentally sensitive products.

MARKETING HALL OF FAME

Big Business in Cash from Trash

When you think of junked cars, you probably envision rusty hulks piled as high as the eye can see in landfills all across America. Think again. U.S. companies are arguably the most efficient recyclers of vehicle parts in the world. When measured by weight, American companies reuse 75 percent of nearly every car after its last gasp through a multibillion-dollar recycling effort.

Much like ants at a picnic, thousands of auto recycling outfits devour as much of an auto carcass as possible. Some 12,000 recyclers strip the cars of any valuable parts—alternators, starters, and engines—and refurbish them for resale. Roughly 200 auto shredders get what's left. The metal skeletons are shredded into steel fragments and shipped to steel makers as materials for new car bodies. The Ford Synthesis 2010 goes even further. Its all-aluminum shell is 100 percent recyclable.

The massive car recycling business is just one example of marketplace payoffs from green manufacturing practices. An insatiable demand for recyclables in this country—everything from car parts to yesterday's newspapers to soda bottles—has drawn corporate America's interest toward recycling. This situation represents a complete change from a few years ago, when only Sierra Club types were heralding the practice.

Ironically, one of the industries that has benefited from the recycling boom is the major trash haulers, which were among its most vocal critics. Just a few years ago, these companies strongly resisted any outside attempts to force them to institute curbside recycling programs. But now they are reaping the benefits of an explosion in the price of and demand for everyday bundled trash.

One of the biggest winners is Browning-Ferris Industries, the nation's second-largest waste-handling company. Over a four-year period, it has seen revenues from recycling soar from a modest $32 million to $359 million.

Browning-Ferris benefited when technology finally caught up with environmentalists' fervor for recy-

world's population resides in the United States, but American consumers generate one-fourth of the carbon dioxide produced worldwide.

Green marketing takes many forms. Discount retailer Wal-Mart is testing designs for ecologically sensitive store facilities that will reduce energy demands and consumption of natural resources. Lumber for a prototype store in Lawrence, Kansas, came from second-growth timber that was selectively harvested rather than clear-cut. The building's skylights combine with electronic daylight sensors that can dim or brighten fluorescent lights, depending on the amount of natural light available at a particular time. This system, combined with well-insulated windows, minimizes heating and cooling demands. The air-conditioning system uses relatively inexpensive, off-peak electricity to make ice, which cools the store during summer days, and the lighted sign out front is solar-powered. While the new store cost 10 percent to 20 percent more than conventional designs to build, Wal-Mart managers hope to recoup much of the cost through savings on energy and other expense items. Explains architect Kirsten Childs, "By using less energy through resource conservation, by improving air quality, you can save money, you can raise productivity, and you can reduce absenteeism."[46]

Another form of green marketing seeks to develop new uses and create new markets for recycled materials. At the same Kansas Wal-Mart store, the parking lot is paved with recycled asphalt. A pond collects runoff, which later irrigates the store's landscaping of native shrubs and other plants. The store also contains a recycling center—the first one in town. All over the country, new Wal-Mart outlets are built with recycled asphalt, steel, and plastic. New stores in California have specially designed joists that use half the wood required for standard joists. This change reduces wood requirements by 6,500 cubic feet—about 87 trees—to build each store.[47]

Recently, more than two dozen large U.S. companies formed a voluntary group, the "Buy Recycled Business Alliance," to develop and expand markets for recycled products. For one major goal, the alliance seeks to encourage suppliers to expand offerings of recycled raw materials and boost the recycled content in finished items. The group includes such well-known corporations as McDonald's,

cling. Between 1988 and 1992, the number of curbside recycling programs skyrocketed from 1,042 to over 5,400 as environmentalists and local officials worried about shrinking landfill space. The economic incentive, however, took a while to catch up with the idealistic fervor. Americans became quite good at tossing soda cans and newspapers in recycling bins, but the technology could not yet take advantage of this brand-new resource. A glut of garbage quickly developed, depressing the prices of recyclables even further.

But the market eventually caught up. More than 85 recently built paper mills using recycling technology have created a huge market for used paper goods. Foreigners have also fueled the demand for discarded materials. In an attempt to cope with a polyester shortage, Asian buyers began bidding up the prices in the used bottle market, creating a bidding war for Pepsi-Cola and Mountain Dew empties.

Also heating up the market for discarded materials is American ingenuity. More and more product designs now call for these castoffs. For instance, Wellman, Inc., has developed a process that transforms soda bottles into a soft polyester fiber suitable for clothing and sensuously smooth upholstery fabrics. The company's velvet sells for $12 a yard and up. Since Wellman started producing the fiber in 1993, the firm has used more than 2 billion old soda bottles. It's not hard to see why. The material to recover a couch requires 200 2-liter bottles. One square yard of polyester carpet consumes 36 plastic soda bottles, fiberfill for one sleeping bag uses up 35 bottles, and a polyester T-shirt requires five.

QUESTIONS FOR CRITICAL THINKING

1. **If recyclable trash becomes too expensive, do you think its price will discourage new commercial applications?**
2. **Some customers balk when Xerox tries to sell them refurbished photocopiers with the same warranty as a new machine. Do you think this resistance to "retread" products will last? How can companies overcome it?**

Sources: Mitchel Benson, "Recycling Overhaul Is Proposed," *Wall Street Journal,* April 23, 1997, p. CA2; David Fischer, "Turning Trash into Cash," *U.S. News & World Report,* July 17, 1996, p. 43; "Our Environment," *Better Homes and Gardens,* January 1996, p. 56; James P. Miller, "Plastic Soda Bottles Treasured Material," *Mobile Register,* July 7, 1995, p. 5F; and Gene Bylinsky, "Manufacturing for Reuse," *Fortune,* February 6, 1995, pp. 102–112.

Sears, 3M, Coca-Cola, Rubbermaid, United Parcel Service, and BankAmerica.[48]

CONTROLLING THE MARKETING SYSTEM

When the marketing-oriented economic system does not perform as well as people would like, they attempt to change it. The adjustments intend to make it serve needs better by producing and distributing goods and services in a fairer way. Most people believe that the system works sufficiently well to require no drastic changes and that relatively minor adjustments can achieve a fair distribution.

People try to control or influence the direction of the marketing system and rid it of imperfections in four major ways: (1) helping the competitive market system to operate in a self-correcting manner, (2) educating consumers, (3) increasing regulation, and (4) encouraging political action. The competitive market system operates to allocate resources and to provide most of the products that consumers purchase to satisfy felt needs. While some complain about the system, most of the goods and services they purchase or use flow through it with little difficulty. Competition works if the conditions of many buyers and sellers and other technical requirements of the free-market economic model allow it to do so. Market participants have attempted—sometimes with limited success—to restore competition where monopolies have reduced it.

Combined with the free-market system, consumer education can lead to wise choices. As products become increasingly complex, diverse, and plentiful, consumers also need new tools to make wise decisions. Educational programs and other efforts by parents, schools, business, government, and consumer organizations all contribute to a better system. A responsible marketing philosophy should encourage consumers to voice their opinions. Such comments can result in significant improvements in sellers' goods and services.

The marketing concept must include social responsibility as a primary function of any marketing organization. Social and profit goals are compatible, but they require aggressive implementation of an expanded marketing concept. All companies must articulate explicit criteria for responsible decision making. This is truly marketing's greatest challenge.

ACHIEVEMENT CHECK SUMMARY

Reread the learning goals that follow, and consider the questions for each goal. Answering these questions will reinforce your grasp of the most important concepts in the chapter and allow you to check how well you have achieved these learning goals. Where a blank appears before a question, answer with *T* or *F*; for multiple-choice questions, circle the letter of the correct answer.

Objective 3.1: Identify the five components of the marketing environment.
1. ___ The process by which organizations that market goods or services seek to satisfy their markets is called (a) environmental management; (b) scanning the environment; (c) the competitive environment; (d) demarketing.
2. ___ Laws to determine competitive conditions and protect consumer rights are part of the political-legal environment.
3. ___ The social-cultural environment refers to the relationship between the marketer, society, and technology.

Objective 3.2: Explain the types of competition that marketers face and the steps they take to develop competitive strategies.
1. ___ The competition between cable television movie channels, rental videos, and movie theaters is an example of (a) direct competition; (b) competition among substitute goods or services; (c) competition among all organizations that compete for consumers' dollars.
2. ___ When a firm decides whether to compete, it evaluates its resources, objectives, and profit potential.
3. ___ Decisions about the four *P*s help marketers to choose the markets in which their firm will compete.

Objective 3.3: Describe how government and other groups regulate marketing activities and how marketers can influence the political-legal environment.
1. ___ Government regulation of marketing activities is a recent development that began with laws passed around 1950.
2. ___ The FTC uses consent orders and cease-and-desist orders to enforce laws regarding unfair business practices and false or misleading advertising.
3. ___ A consumer boycott is an example of self-regulation.

Objective 3.4: Outline the economic forces that affect marketing decisions and consumer buying power.
1. ___ Consumers' buying habits remain constant regardless of the stage of the business cycle.
2. ___ During periods of high inflation, consumers are likely to buy many luxury goods.
3. ___ Discretionary income is more important to marketers than total income.

Objective 3.5: Explain the impact of the technological environment on a firm's marketing activities.
1. ___ Technological advances tend to raise product prices.
2. ___ Technology transfer from the military to private companies is one source of new-product development.
3. ___ Marketers who apply technology creatively gain a competitive advantage for their firm.

Objective 3.6: Explain how the social-cultural environment influences marketing.
1. ___ Shifts in social values influence consumer attitudes toward products.
2. ___ The consumerism movement brings legal, moral, and economic pressures on businesses to act in socially responsible ways.
3. ___ President Kennedy's statement of consumer rights includes all but one of the following: (a) the right to choose freely; (b) the right to be informed; (c) the right to the lowest price for a product; (d) the right to be safe.

Objective 3.7: Describe the role of marketing in society, and name the two major social issues in marketing.
1. ___ Marketers are often responsible for developing strategies that shape their firm's position on social issues.
2. ___ *Marketing ethics* refers to standards of conduct and moral values that govern decisions regarding products, research, distribution, promotion, and pricing.
3. ___ A company that focuses on boosting sales and increasing profits meets today's definition of corporate social responsibility.

Students: See the solutions section located on page S-1 to check your responses to the Achievement Check Summary.

Key Terms

environmental scanning
environmental management
competitive environment
time-based competition
political-legal environment
economic environment
demarketing
technological environment
social-cultural environment
consumerism
consumer rights
marketing ethics
social responsibility
green marketing

Review Questions

1. Briefly describe each of the five components of the marketing environment. Give an example of each.
2. Explain the types of competition that marketers face. What steps must they complete to develop a competitive strategy?

3. Government regulation in the United States has evolved in four general phases. Identify each phase and give an example of laws enacted during that time.
4. Give an example of a federal law affecting:
   a. product strategy
   b. pricing strategy
   c. distribution strategy
   d. promotional strategy
5. Explain the methods the Federal Trade Commission uses to protect consumers. Which of these methods seems the most effective to you?
6. What major economic forces affect marketing decisions? How does each of these forces produce its effect?
7. Identify the ways in which the technological environment and the social-cultural environment affect marketing activities. Cite examples of both.
8. What arguments does consumerism assert to indict the competitive marketing system? Critically evaluate these arguments.
9. Describe the ethical problems related to:
   a. marketing research
   b. product strategy
   c. distribution strategy
   d. promotional strategy
   e. pricing strategy
10. Identify and briefly explain the major avenues through which people can resolve contemporary issues facing the marketing system. Cite relevant examples.

Discussion Questions

1. Give examples to show how each of the environmental variables discussed in this chapter might affect the following firms:
   a. Amway products
   b. The Sharper Image catalog sales
   c. local cable TV franchise
   d. Amtrak
   e. local YMCA
   f. Olive Garden restaurant
2. Classify the following laws as (1) assisting in maintaining a competitive environment, (2) assisting in regulating competitors, (3) regulating specific marketing activities, or (4) deregulating industries. Justify your classifications, and identify the marketing mix variables(s) most affected by each law.
   a. Miller-Tydings Act
   b. Staggers Rail Act
   c. Clayton Act
   d. Robinson-Patman Act
3. Cite two instances in which developments in the technological environment have produced positive benefits for marketers. Give two instances of harmful impacts of the technological environment on companies' marketing operations.
4. Should the United States government impose regulations on advertising of alcoholic beverages? Explain.
5. Identify a critical social issue confronting your local community. How does this issue affect marketers in your area? Discuss.

'netWork

1. The growing emphasis on social responsibility in marketing is a major focal point of this chapter. Go to

http://www.bsr.org/

and evaluate information there to answer the following questions: What purpose does BSR serve? Why do business decision makers need such an organization? What future activities will the organization likely undertake?

2. Should Internet services function like any other service available to consumers, providing access to those who can afford it? On the other hand, should everyone have Internet access through some type of government funding? Debate these positions.

3. The Office of Environmental Management within the U.S. Department of Energy (DOE) works to ensure worker safety and health in the nation's nuclear energy industry. It also manages and plans budgets, monitors legal and compliance issues dealing with environmental effects, and works to minimize waste at both nuclear and nonnuclear-related cleanup sites. Go to

http://www.em.doe.gov/

and study the latest consumer and environmental issues under investigation by this government agency. Write a report about what you find.

VIDEO CASE 3

RIDING ON THE INFORMATION SUPERHIGHWAY

Telecommunications firms are among the strongest proponents of development projects for the information superhighway—the huge and rapidly evolving pathway that links telecommunications and data resources to businesses, not-for-profit organizations, and individual households. To ensure America's long-term economic competitiveness, AT&T, along with many other U.S. firms, competes fiercely to design, build, manage, and service the various components that make up the information pipeline. As a global telecommunications leader, AT&T intends to maintain a conspicuous presence on the superhighway by turning technology into useful services that customers want and selling those services at reasonable prices.

To compete successfully in today's global market, AT&T CEO Robert Allen has restructured the firm into three separate global corporations:

- The new AT&T, a company focused on offering customers a full menu of communications and information services
- Lucent Technologies, Inc., a company producing telecommunications equipment and systems, software, and products, with research activities conducted by Bell Laboratories
- NCR, a company concentrating on transaction-intensive computer systems and services

The company intended the restructuring to reduce the size and complexity of its operations. By operating not as one large company but as three smaller, more manageable companies, each can pursue its own business strategy and react quickly to marketplace changes. According to Allen, "Our decision to restructure was driven by seismic shifts in customer needs, technology, and public policy. Make no mistake about it, these are fundamental changes. They offer unprecedented new opportunities for us, but they also carry the threat of washing away any company that chooses to cling to the status quo and ignore the power of these changing conditions."

Customers clamor ever more loudly for information goods and services with global reach due to worldwide economic growth, technological advances, and the declining cost of information technology. Residential customers and businesses, from multinationals involved in global commerce to work-at-home entrepreneurs, are driving the expanding demand for new, customized services that combine voice, data, image, facsimile, and online transmissions.

Public policy changes continue to reshape the competitive landscape. For example, the Telecommunications Act of 1996 allows long-distance companies and local telephone service firms to enter each other's markets. Although still dominated by state-owned monopolies, the global phone industry is also changing as nations continue to privatize and deregulate their phone markets.

The pace of change in this already-competitive landscape is intensifying dramatically as new firms enter the telecommunications industry and existing competitors broaden their service offerings. For example, in the interactive multimedia business, the diverse list of suppliers includes phone companies such as AT&T, cable TV franchises, computer firms, wireless cellular service providers, and publishing and entertainment giants. Technology is evolving so rapidly that the life spans of new technologies have decreased over the last ten years from a five-year average to less than 24 months. The Internet and its graphical interface, the World Wide Web, is changing the way businesses interact with customers.

The new AT&T wants to base its strategy on delivering a bundle of services to customers over the information superhighway. A market leader in some services and a new player in others, the company is focusing on five areas: long-distance calls, local calls, wireless communications, online (Internet) services, and access to home entertainment. Allen says, "Our future is a long distance from long distance. We're moving to a full menu of communications and information services."

The U.S. leader in residential long-distance phone service with a 65 percent market share, AT&T is strengthening its position by adding new features such as the AT&T One Rate plan, a simplified pricing structure that lets consumers make direct-dialed long-distance calls to anyone, any time, anywhere in the United States for 15 cents a minute. As a new competitor in the local market, AT&T has announced its intention to provide local phone service in all 50 states. It plans to offer local calling either by reselling network capacity purchased from local providers or by building its own infrastructure.

Already the largest U.S. wireless service provider, AT&T has acquired 23 licenses to offer personal communications services. This technology resembles wireless services, but it operates at another radio frequency to extend its reach to more than 80 percent of the U.S. population. Its WorldNet Service has enabled the company to begin competing as an Internet service provider. The company's home entertainment delivery system makes it the first national communications company to bring consumers programming choices from DirecTV and U.S. Satellite Broadcasting. The AT&T Universal Card, a combination credit, ATM, and calling card, provides customers with a convenient payment option for many of its services.

Global markets offer major growth opportunities for AT&T. "What's important," says Allen, "is that we expand as quickly as possible around the world." AT&T is implementing this vision by forming partnerships, strategic alliances, and consortiums to market telecommunications services to businesses and consumers worldwide. A consortium led by AT&T and GTE owns 40 percent of CANTV, a phone company in Venezuela. AT&T formed a joint venture with Unisource, a consortium owned by Dutch KPN, Spanish Telefonica, Swedish Telia, and Swiss BTT. AT&T's WorldPartners alliance includes Kokusai Denshin Denwa (Japan's largest international carrier), Singapore Telecom, and other Asian carriers. According to Victor Pelson, head of global operations, AT&T's biggest competitor in the international arena is Concert, an alliance formed by MCI and British Telecommunications PLC.

AT&T is also designing easy-to-use services for international travelers. Its WorldConnect service allows customers to place calls to and from more than 75 countries over company-owned lines. WorldPlus service allows travelers to set up AT&T accounts to pay for local calls in more than 40 countries.

With its financial strength, global reach, strong brand name, and new freedom from regulation, AT&T is poised to be a big player on the information highway. "Our decision to restructure reflects our determination to shape and lead the dramatic changes that have already begun in the worldwide market for communications and information services—a market that promises to double in size before the turn of the new century," says Allen.

Questions

1. What forces in marketing's external environment influenced Allen's decision to restructure AT&T?
2. Which of the three types of competition discussed in the chapter text do AT&T marketers face?
3. Give examples of AT&T's actions to manage its new environment.
4. AT&T is developing and enhancing services in long-distance calling, local calling, wireless communications, Internet services, and home entertainment. Based on information from the company's home page,

   http://www.att.com/

   give a brief description of each service area. Find companies on the Web that offer competing services, and compare AT&T's products to those of its competitors. For each service area, which company would you choose? Why?

Sources: Telephone interview with AT&T Corporate Executive Office, May 13, 1997; *AT&T Quarterly Shareowners Report,* October 17, 1996; *AT&T Special Report to Shareowners,* September 1996; Andrew Kupfer, "What, Me Worry?" *Fortune,* September 30, 1996, pp. 121–124; and "Intelligent Networking Will Rule the World," *Industry Week,* August 19, 1996.

CHAPTER 4

GLOBAL DIMENSIONS OF MARKETING

http://www.nike.com
Discovery Online
http://www.discovery.com/
Discovery CHANNEL
Site at a Glance
What's On TV
Discovery Channel
The Learning Channel
Animal Planet
What's Online
Search Our Site
This way to MSN
The Rollercoaster Mind
Try and Catch the Wind
http://www.duracell.c
DURACELL.com
The Coppertop
Battery Info
The Company
New Products & Technology
http://www.globalstar.com/
Globalstar
System Description
Corporate Overview
Meet Our Partners
http://www.dominos.com/
Domino's Pizza
WORLD OF SOLUTIONS
Rubbermaid
CORPORATE
online shopping
HOME PRODUCTS
LITTLE TIKES
GRACO

Chapter Objectives

1. Describe the importance of international marketing from the perspectives of the individual firm and the nation.
2. Identify the major components of the environment for international marketing.
3. Compare alternative strategies for entering international markets.
4. Differentiate between a global marketing strategy and a multidomestic marketing strategy.
5. Describe the marketing mix strategies that international marketers implement.
6. Explain the attractiveness of the U.S. market as a target for foreign marketers.

The Discovery Channel Ventures Abroad

The Discovery Channel loves couch potatoes, and it finds them lounging in living rooms and dens around the world. The cable channel that brings viewers upscale, educational programming has turned into a global television pioneer.

Just three years after Discovery Communications marketers decided to create a global television brand, they had expanded their signal to reach more than 87 million subscribers in 90 far-flung countries from New Zealand to Saudi Arabia. If those numbers seem staggering, The Discovery Channel considers them just a beginning. John Hendricks, Discovery's founder, predicts that in just seven years, the company's revenue in Asia alone will surpass what it earns serving the U.S. market.

Take your eyes off him.
Take your eyes off him.
Take your eyes off him.
We know 30 million viewers in Latin America just like you.

high as ours, you can bet
we've got their attention.
Would you like to borrow
it for :30? If you've got
something to sell, you've
got somewhere to buy.
Call Cathleen Pratt-Kerrigan
in New York at 212-751-2220, x5121
or Fernando Barbosa in Miami at 305-461-4710, x4211.

"The twenty-first century will be recognized as the global century," says Domenick Fioravanti, the firm's senior vice president of international networks. "We will all prosper on the back of technology that barely existed two decades ago."

Discovery maintains such tremendous growth by identifying huge pools of future customers. In Latin America, fewer than one in six households with television sets currently receives cable or satellite services, compared to nearly 75 percent in the United States. The number of households hooked to cable in the emerging markets is spiraling upward. In Brazil, for instance, more than 50,000 households sign up for cable every month. When a viewer in Argentina or India plugs into cable, Discovery marketers want to make certain that the new viewer can see their channel. After all, the company makes money in two ways: selling advertising time and charging monthly fees to cable subscribers.

Paving the way for Discovery's international success, friendly foreign officials anxiously await Western-style programming. "Regulators and legislators in countries like Mexico, Chile, and Peru will grant you special concessions if you do business in their countries," says Jimena Urquijo, analyst at Kagan World Media in Carmel, California. "They want your money and your expertise. They are determined to modernize."

As viewers in the emerging markets gain sophistication in their television habits, they will inevitably

demand higher-quality programming. This trend, too, can work to Discovery Channel's advantage. Many local and national companies currently lack capabilities to provide this higher level of professional programming. Discovery's reputation smooths its entry into these new markets. That was certainly the case in Asia, says Kevin John McIntyre, vice president and general manager of Discovery Channel Asia. "Viewers know it is what they want to see and what their children can see," he says.

http://www.discovery.com/

The Discovery Channel has invested a great deal of resources in delivering quality shows. The channel doesn't simply air what Americans are watching on their sets. In fact, a familiar slogan guides the actions of Discovery executives overseas: "Think globally, act locally." Market research helps Discovery tailor its programming to local needs. For instance, Discovery marketers learned that Mexicans like programs about architecture and history, Australians prefer science and technology shows, and Chinese viewers enjoy learning more about military technology.

Discovery doesn't skimp when developing these shows. "It can be done cheaper, but then you're creating a service that will not be around," says Dawn McCall, senior vice president of Discovery Latin America-Iberia. "The customers today are more sophisticated and they know quality."

When Discovery launched its global network, officials realized that the move would not earn immediate profits. At this point, only Discovery Channel-Europe is breaking even. But the company believes that its investment in laying the groundwork will pay off handsomely in the future. "Cable overseas is not for the faint of heart," acknowledges Fioravanti. "This is not a get-rich-quick scheme. You have to build a revenue stream from a subscriber base and gradually a revenue stream from ad sales."[1]

CHAPTER OVERVIEW

Like The Discovery Channel, unprecedented legions of U.S. and foreign companies are crossing national boundaries in search of new markets and profits. International trade now accounts for 25 percent of the U.S. gross domestic product (GDP), compared to 5 percent 25 years ago. Exports of U.S. manufactured goods exceed $450 billion, 50 percent more than in 1990. "We are without question the world's premier export engine," says Stuart E. Eizenstat, undersecretary of commerce for international trade.[2]

International trade can be divided into **exporting**—marketing domestically produced goods and services abroad—and **importing**—domestic purchases of goods and services produced in foreign countries. International trade is vital to a nation and its marketers for several reasons. Trade expands markets, creates opportunities for production and distribution economies, allows companies to explore growth opportunities in other nations, and makes them less dependent on economic conditions in their home nations. Many also find that global marketing and international trade can help them to meet customer demand, reduce costs, and provide valuable information on potential markets around the world.

North American firms view international trade with special attention, because the U.S. and Canadian economies represent mature markets for many products. Outside North America, however, marketers find a different world. Rapidly growing economies in many parts of Asia, Latin America, Europe, and the Middle East open up new markets for U.S. goods. Consumers in these areas have money to spend, and foreign companies need American goods and services. Exports of high-tech products accounted for 30 percent of U.S. GDP growth since 1985. In some categories—computer equipment, semiconductors, aircraft, software, and entertainment—exports represent almost half of total sales.[3]

International trade also builds employment. Each billion-dollar increment of export sales supports about 14,200 jobs—an average number that varies considerably by industry. Your next job, in fact, might involve global marketing, since export-related jobs play important roles in the U.S. economy. Over 11 million U.S. workers—about 10 percent of the total workforce—produce goods or provide services for export, a 75 percent increase in the last decade. Besides a growing source of employment, careers in this sector often promise lucrative pay and benefits. Wages and benefits in firms producing goods for export average 10 percent more than those at comparable nonexporting plants.[4]

International marketers implement the basic marketing concepts described in Chapters 1 and 2. However, transactions that cross national boundaries encounter an additional set of environmental factors. For example, differences in laws, economic conditions, cultural and business norms, and consumer preferences often demand variations in strategies. Companies that want to market their products worldwide must reconsider each of the marketing variables (product, promotion, price, and distribution) in terms of the global marketplace. To succeed in global marketing, managers should answer some basic questions:

- How will our idea/good/service fit into the international market?
- What adjustments will we have to make?
- What threats will we face from global competition?
- How can we turn these threats into opportunities?
- What strategic alternatives will work in global markets?[5]

Chapter 4 explores the world of international marketing and the answers that companies have given to these questions. First, it considers the importance and characteristics of the global marketplace. Then it examines the international marketing environment, the trend toward multinational economic integration, and the steps through which most firms enter the global marketplace. Finally, the chapter looks at how a firm's marketers develop an international marketing mix.

THE IMPORTANCE OF GLOBAL MARKETING

Most U.S. companies, both large and small, are rapidly acknowledging the necessity of global marketing. The demand for foreign products in the fast-growing economies of Asia and other Pacific Rim nations offers one example of the benefits of global thinking. In a recent year, U.S. exports to Asia rose 37 percent to about $200 billion—almost twice the country's exports to Europe. In a survey by South China Marketing Research, 85 percent of respondents agreed that Western products offer better quality, 75 percent think they last longer, and 70 percent consider them better values than locally produced alternatives.[6]

As a result, overseas sales are important revenue sources for many U.S. firms. In fact, since 1986 U.S. exports have grown an average of 10.5 percent each year. Table 4.1 shows the top ten categories of U.S. exports. Strong export products include agricultural products, computers and office equipment, and electrical machinery. Among the leading U.S. players in the global market (companies that derive the largest portions of their revenues from exports) are Boeing, Intel, Motorola, Caterpillar, and Sun Microsystems.

Perhaps the ultimate symbol of a global marketer is The Coca-Cola Co. Now selling in 195 countries, the soft-drink giant generates $4 of every $5 in its annual revenues and profits outside the United States. It even looks outside the U.S. market for new-product ideas. Surge, Coke's newly launched brand designed to compete with PepsiCo's popular Mountain Dew, was first marketed in Norway under the brand name *Urge*.

Not only do international markets account for most of Coca-Cola's sales and profits, but they also continue to generate most of the firm's sales growth. Although U.S. sales are rising only about 4 percent a year, sales in China, India, and Indonesia double every three years. In India, the company wants to make Coke drinkers out of a nation that now prefers tea and mineral water. Coca-Cola conveys a

Marketing Dictionary

exporting Marketing domestically produced goods and services in foreign countries.

importing Domestic purchases of goods, services, and raw materials produced in foreign countries.

Table 4.1 Top Ten U.S. Exports and Imports

Major Export Product	Amount (billions)	Major Import Product	Amount (billions)
1. Agricultural products	$54.9	1. Computers and office equipment	$62.8
2. Electrical machinery	53.1	2. Crude oil	42.8
3. Computers and office equipment	36.4	3. Clothing	39.5
4. General industrial machinery	24.4	4. Telecommunications equipment	34.4
5. Motor vehicle parts	23.4	5. Agricultural products	29.3
6. Specialized industrial machinery	23.3	6. Cars produced in Canada	24.4
7. Power generating equipment	21.9	7. General industrial machinery	24.1
8. Telecommunications equipment	19.0	8. Cars produced in Japan	21.1
9. Scientific instruments	18.6	9. Power generating equipment	20.5
10. Chemicals—organic	16.6	10. Motor vehicle parts	20.1

local image by sponsoring World Cup Cricket and filling its advertisements with images of Indian cricket fans. CEO Roberto Goizueta also considers Indonesia a "soft-drink paradise." Its 200 million residents are mostly Muslims, whose religion prohibits drinking alcohol. The large, young population of Latin America has also attracted Coca-Cola's attention as a target for future growth. In Brazil, advertising with the theme "Mom Knows Everything," shown in Figure 4.1, is aimed at supermarket-shopping mothers, who account for 80 percent of Coke's $3.5 billion Brazilian sales.[7]

Electronics is another industry in which global marketing plays a prominent role. Semiconductor manufacturer Intel earns 55 percent of its revenues and 37 percent of its profits outside the United States. "The U.S. is less and less the focus of our marketing," says Andrew Grove, Intel's CEO. The company's global strategy reflects a deliberate move away from developed countries to emerging economies like Latin America and India.[8]

It's not just Fortune 500 firms that benefit from exporting. According to a Coopers & Lybrand survey, small businesses that export goods and services report faster growth than those that don't: about 31 percent compared to 25 percent for domestically limited companies. Advances in computer and telecommunication technologies allow these firms to market their products overseas.[9]

While large organizations enjoy advantages through stronger distribution systems, financial resources, and political clout, small businesses are making inroads in their own ways. Opportunities for personal contact with top executives often appeal to foreign businesses. Red Spot Paint & Varnish Co., Inc. is an Evansville, Indiana, paint and coating company whose international sales now represent 20 percent of its $90 million in annual revenues. Recently, President Charles Storm guided a tour of the company's research and development facility and hosted a dinner for the president of an Argentinean firm. At stake was a $100,000-per-year contract for specialty coatings—small by a large company's standards but important to Red Spot.

Red Spot stepped up its foreign marketing program in 1988 and now sells in 15 countries, with Vietnam and India its next target markets. New products, such as abrasion-resistant coatings for auto headlamps, help it to gain international sales. The company's persistence also contributes to its success. It continued sales calls for seven years before winning an initial order from a German auto parts manufacturer.[10]

http://www.redspot.com/

Just as some firms depend on foreign sales for revenue, others rely on inputs of raw materials from abroad to feed their domestic manufacturing operations. A furniture company's purchase of South American mahogany is an example. Along with exports, Table 4.1 also shows the top U.S. imports, including computers and office equipment, crude oil, and clothing. Since 1986, U.S. imports have grown about 7 percent per year.

While the United States trades hundreds of thousands of products with many countries, its major trading partners are Canada, Japan, Mexico, Germany, and the United Kingdom. Until recently, sales by U.S. marketers in the European Union exceeded purchases there. However, the sluggish European recovery from recession has limited purchases from U.S. companies, adjusting exports and imports to about the same level.

Figure 4.1 **Coca-Cola: The World's Leading Global Brand**

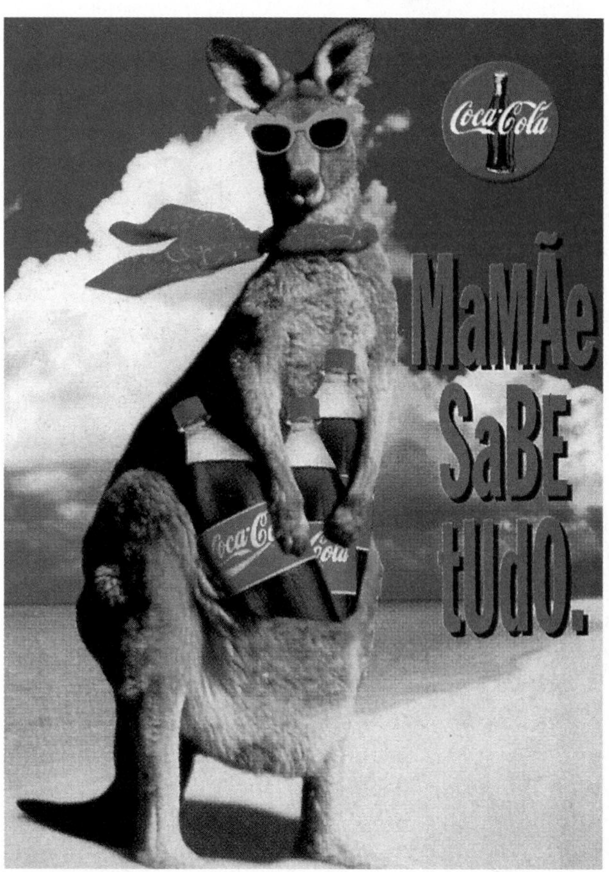
Coca-Cola
MaMÃe
SaBE
tUdO.

Service and Retail Exports

In addition to agricultural products and manufactured goods, U.S. firms are also big exporters of services and retailing. While the United States runs a trade deficit in tangible products of about $170 billion a year, it enjoys a trade surplus in services of about $70 billion. In fact, U.S. service providers lead the world in exports of their products. Of approximately $210 billion in U.S. service exports in a recent year, over half came from travel and tourism—money spent by foreign nationals visiting the United States.

The most profitable U.S. service exports are business and technical services such as engineering, accounting, computing, legal services, and entertainment. Other service exports involve technologies developed by U.S. firms that earn royalties and licensing fees from users abroad. The roughly 400,000 foreign students enrolled in American colleges and universities pump another $5 billion a year into the U.S. service economy.

Some service exporters are household names: American Express, AT&T, Citibank, Walt Disney, Wal-Mart, Allstate Insurance, and Federal Express. U.S. airlines earn 25 percent of their revenues from their international routes. Restaurants and retailers are also branching out overseas. Starbucks launched its first venture outside North America in Japan, the third-largest coffee consuming country behind the United States and Germany. Retailers ranging from Victoria's Secret, Foot Locker, and the Gap to Office Depot, Toys 'R' Us, and Price/Costco warehouse clubs are opening stores around the world at a fast pace. U.S. retailers do especially well in Asia, where consumers like the convenience and wide selection of American-made products that they provide. Foreign customers also favor products associated with American lifestyles, such as Timberland's rugged outdoor apparel.[11]

Other service exporters are smaller companies, including many software firms that have found overseas markets receptive to their products. Hyperion Software of Stamford, Connecticut, a designer and producer of financial reporting software for large business applications, earns half of its revenues from overseas sales. While Hyperion maintains a direct sales force in North America, it sells through independent local distributors in foreign markets. San Diego-based StarGuide Digital Networks exports both goods (satellite communications equipment) and services (air time on satellites) to major Japanese companies.

The U.S. entertainment industry is another major exporter. Foreign movie audiences spend over $5 billion a year to see U.S. films like *The Lion King,* advertised to Japanese audiences by the poster in Figure 4.2. U.S. television programs and cable networks also reach huge international audiences. Viewers in Japan, Europe, and India watch MTV and CNN, while *Baywatch* is one of the most popular syndicated television shows in the world. The Children's Television Workshop recently launched a Chinese version of *Sesame Street,* called *Zhima Jie,* in partnership with Shanghai television.[12]

Major U.S. entertainment studios derive increasing percentages of their revenues from foreign sales, as multiscreen cinema complexes, cable and satellite television, and video rental stores appear overseas. Blockbuster Video's non-U.S. rental outlets now outnumber the firm's U.S. properties, and they generate more profits than their American counterparts. About 35 percent of Time Warner/Turner Broadcasting revenues come from overseas markets, while Viacom and Disney-Capital Cities/ABC earn 30 percent abroad. However, marketers cannot easily predict which American films will be hits abroad. Audiences in Italy loved *The Scarlet Letter* with Demi Moore, but those in Taiwan hated it.[13]

The Walt Disney Co. is one of the world's most popular providers of entertainment, selling experiences at Euro Disney and Tokyo Disneyland along with movies, videos, toys, and related products. China has become a big market for Disney. Movies like *The Hunchback of Notre Dame, Forrest Gump,* and *Toy Story* draw audiences to Chinese

Figure 4.2 The Entertainment Industry: An Important Component of U.S. Exports

PICTURES PRESENTS
THE
LION KING
ライオン・キング

theaters. Over 400,000 Chinese listeners tune in to a radio program called *It's a Small World,* and another 150,000 read Disney's monthly Chinese-language cartoon magazine. Consumers also eagerly buy stationery and clothing with Disney characters.[14]

Still another class of service exporters, U.S. fast-food franchisers, are opening outlets throughout the world at an increasing rate. In addition to its 12,000 U.S. outlets, McDonald's sells burgers in over 6,000 restaurants in 91 countries, and its non-U.S. operations are expanding about three times faster than those in the United States. By 2001, McDonald's plans to increase its presence in Australia, for example, from 560 to over 880 outlets as it strives to become that country's leading fast-food retailer. It will locate outlets in airports, gas stations, and retail stores. Over 8,000 Pizza Hut and KFC restaurants are currently operating in non-U.S. locations. Some 1,200 Domino's Pizza outlets serve customers in 46 countries.

Each company adapts its menus to local tastes. McDonald's restaurants make burgers from kosher beef in Israel, sell beer in Germany, and include Cadbury chocolate sticks in ice cream cones sold in Britain. Japanese diners can choose from such unusual Pizza Hut toppings as corn, barbecued beef, sautéed burdock root, tuna, apple, teriyaki chicken, rice, and squid. KFC includes a spicy Zinger chicken burger on its menu in Singapore restaurants.[15]

Benefits of Going Global

Besides generating additional revenue, firms expand their operations outside their home countries to gain other benefits, including new insights into consumer behavior, opportunities for alternative distribution strategies, and advance notice of new products. By setting up foreign offices and production facilities, firms may learn new marketing techniques and gain invaluable experience. Global marketers typically position themselves to compete effectively with foreign rivals. Companies involved in global marketing also enjoy advantages in hiring skilled employees.

Rubbermaid, Inc., for example, discovered that European consumers have different ideas than Americans about their houseware products. Neutral colors appeal to U.S. buyers, while southern Europeans like red, and those in Holland like white. Europeans are also fussier about garbage cans and want tight-fitting lids. In addition, they consider plastic furniture an inferior product. Until Rubbermaid marketers started paying attention to the messages

http://www.rubbermaid.com/

coming from international consumers, they were unable to compete with Tupperware and European manufacturers of household goods. Rubbermaid expanded by buying two companies in France and Poland, and it began designing and manufacturing products especially for the European market. By addressing local needs, it moved into second place in the market, behind Curver, a Dutch firm.

Selling Little Tykes swing sets and playhouses in the international marketplace presented another problem for Rubbermaid. Because toy stores didn't want to give up space to display the large toys, Rubbermaid changed its distribution method. The company rents space in malls to showcase the toys and ships purchases directly to consumers.[16]

Some marketers discover significant product innovations in competitors' offerings in foreign markets. Consumer products giant Procter & Gamble assumed that its Pampers brand was the world's best disposable diaper. When P&G began marketing in Japan in the 1980s, how-

Even though this TV spot shows how patrons enjoy McDonald's in a far-flung location such as a one-horse Mexican town, the fast-food giant recognizes the need to adapt its menus and ingredients to appeal to local tastes. Vegetarian burgers are offered in parts of India; some Australian outlets include beets as a condiment; beer can be purchased in German outlets; and wine is on the menu in French McDonald's restaurants.

ever, it learned to its surprise that Japanese manufacturers made a disposable diaper that fit better and absorbed more moisture. P&G researchers studied this technology, leading to a number of modifications in their product. The improvements propelled Pampers to its current position as the world's leading disposable diaper. Similarly, the popularity of Campbell's low-fat cream soups in the United Kingdom convinced the company to market the products in the United States.[17]

Since firms must perform the marketing functions of buying, selling, transporting, storing, standardizing and grading, financing, risk taking, and obtaining market information in both domestic and global markets, some may question the wisdom of treating international marketing as a distinct subject. After all, international marketing is marketing; a firm performs the same functions and works toward the same objectives in domestic or international marketing. As the chapter will explain, however, both similarities and differences influence strategies for international and domestic marketing.

THE INTERNATIONAL MARKETPLACE

Today, few U.S. firms limit themselves to their own country's customers and suppliers, never venturing outside the domestic market. Even if a firm deals primarily with the U.S. market, a huge group of customers in its own right, decision makers may look overseas for raw materials or component parts or compete with foreign rivals in the firm's home market. Marketers who venture abroad find the international marketplace far different from the domestic one. Market sizes, buyer behavior, and marketing practices all vary. To succeed, international marketers must do their homework and carefully evaluate all market segments in which they expect to compete.

Market Size

In 1865, the world population reached 1 billion. It has now swollen to 6 billion. Although the United States has attained one of the highest standards of living in world history, creating a huge market for many products in the process, its population is dwarfed by those of countries such as India and China. One-fifth of the world's population—1.2 billion people—lives in China, for example, but only one-twentieth resides in the United States.

A prime determinant of market size is population growth. At the current growth rate of 1.5 percent a year, the world's population will approach 9 billion by 2025. A review of these projections produces some important contrasts. The population of relatively well-developed countries, currently about 1.3 billion, is growing at about 0.4 percent a year. By contrast, less developed countries contain 4.7 billion people, and that figure is rising at an annual rate of almost 2 percent.

Nearly 80 percent of the world's population now lives in less developed nations, a figure that will top 90 percent by 2025. Africa is growing fastest at 2.8 percent a year, followed by Latin America at 1.9 percent and Asia at 1.7 percent. Average birth rates are dropping around the world due to family planning efforts, but the rate remains high in Africa (six children per woman), and Indian women average 3.4 children. Even faster declines in death rates fuel continued growth. European birth rates have fallen considerably, and couples there now average only 1.5 children. This change could create economic challenges as the age distribution shifts due to the low birth rate.[18]

The world marketplace is increasingly an urban marketplace. By 2000, almost 50 percent of its people will live in large cities. This growth swells cities: 39 of them currently have populations of 5 million or more. Mexico City, whose population of 18 million ranks it as the world's largest city, is expected to grow to 31 million by 2010. Increased urbanization will expand the need for transportation, housing, machinery, and services there and elsewhere.

The growing size and urbanization of the international marketplace does not mean that all foreign markets offer the same potential. Another important influence on market potential is a nation's economic development stage. A

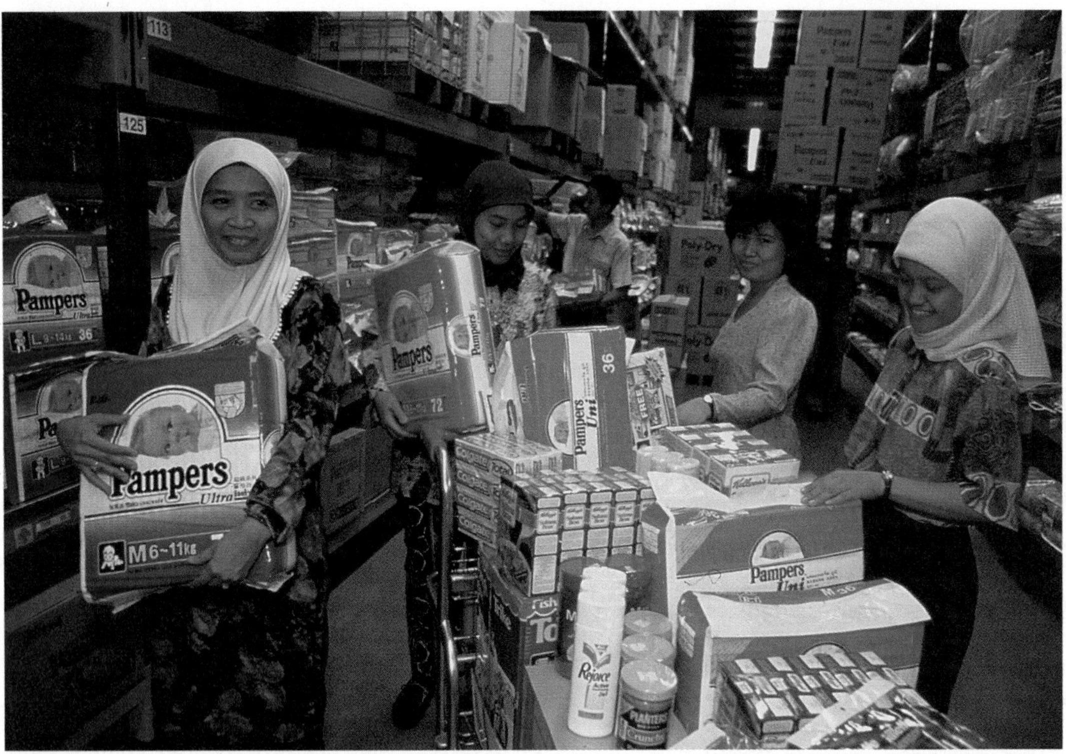
Pampers
Ultra
M6~11kg
Pampers Uni
36
Rejoice

P&G's Pampers, the leading U.S. disposable diaper, also ranks highest around the world. These Asian shoppers are buying the American product in a Dutch-owned store. Makro, Southeast Asia's biggest store group, operates the warehouse store in Malaysia's capital city of Kuala Lumpur.

subsistence economy offers a different environment than that of a newly industrialized country or an industrial nation. In a *subsistence economy,* most people engage in agriculture and earn low per-capita incomes, supporting few opportunities for international trade. In a *newly industrialized country,* such as Brazil and South Korea, growth in manufacturing creates demand for consumer products and industrial goods such as high-tech equipment. The *industrial nations,* including the United States, Japan, and western Europe, trade manufactured goods and services among themselves and export to less developed countries. Although these wealthy countries account for just a small percentage of the world's population, they produce over half of its output.

As a nation develops economically, an increasingly affluent, educated, and cosmopolitan middle class emerges. India's middle class includes nearly 300 million people, a number larger than the entire population of the United States. International marketers see similar growth in middle-income households in the booming East Asian economies like China, Thailand, Singapore, South Korea, Hong Kong, Malaysia, and Indonesia, as well as in Mexico and South America. These new, middle-class consumers have both the desire for consumer goods, including luxury and leisure goods and services, and money to pay for them.

Buyer Behavior

Buyer behavior differs among nations and often among market segments within a country. Marketers must carefully match their marketing strategies to local customs, tastes, and living conditions. At the same time, they must look for economies of scale. Only flexible firms can operate efficiently and also satisfy local consumer preferences. Globally minded marketers often look for global synergies—the similarities that underlie more obvious differences—when choosing the most promising countries in which to expand.

Food companies face some of the biggest challenges. H. J. Heinz Co. changes its ketchup recipe for different markets. It limits the sweetness of the product in Belgium and Holland, because consumers use ketchup as a pasta sauce. Domino's Pizza allows local managers to develop new flavors for their customers. These include mayo jaga (mayonnaise and potato) in Tokyo and pickled ginger in India.

Local preferences and customs influence more than the characteristics of the product itself. Domino's had to reconfigure its delivery systems when it ventured abroad. Knocking on doors is considered rude behavior in Britain, while Japanese house numbers don't follow logical patterns. Domino's outlets in Japan therefore rely on detailed maps to find customers' houses. A delivery in Kuwait may reach the door of a limousine rather than a home. Lack of

http://www.dominos.com/

phone service didn't stop the company from serving customers in Iceland. Domino's joined forces with a Reykjavik drive-in movie theater. Customers use their turn signals to summon a theater employee with a cellular phone, who helps them to order reindeer-sausage pizzas for delivery to their cars.

Even a simple product can surprise marketers. When Pillsbury decided to market its Green Giant vegetables overseas, it started with canned corn. However, it discovered that consumers use this basic item very differently in different countries. The French add it to salads, the British top sandwiches and pizza with corn, Japanese children eat it as a snack, and Koreans put it on ice cream. Pillsbury marketers, therefore, developed Green Giant ads for each locale that showed the corn used in these ways.

Packaging also merits attention. Not only did PepsiCo's Frito-Lay unit develop cheeseless Cheetos to accommodate Asian tastes, but it sold them in small packages for about 12 cents. The resulting product appealed strongly to children with little money to spend.[19]

Sometimes, international marketers change local buyer behavior by introducing successful marketing strategies from other countries. The new Bangkok Tower Records superstore is many times larger than the typical Thai music retail outlet. By stocking both Thai and U.S. recordings, including many not available elsewhere in Thailand, the store has attracted young customers and defined buying tapes and CDs as a fashionable pastime in this city of 6 million.[20]

Briefly speaking

"Xenophobia doesn't benefit anybody unless you're playing high-stakes Scrabble."

Dennis Miller (1953–)
American comedian

Failure to adapt to local preferences can lead to costly trouble. Many U.S. companies discovered this principle the hard way when they began selling products in Japan. U.S. car manufacturers, for example, found that unless an American car placed the steering wheel on the right, Japanese consumers would not buy it. Although American car companies are now producing right-hand-drive vehicles, European automakers like BMW, Volkswagen, and Daimler-Benz learned this lesson early and have captured a larger share of the market.[21]

Snapple was introduced to Japan in 1994, posting strong initial sales as consumers were attracted to the novel labels and the bottle shape. After trying the fruit-flavored and tea-flavored beverages, however, consumers didn't buy them again. Sugary and sticky formulations didn't appeal to local tastes, and the fruit sediment and murky look were turnoffs. Local managers suggested offering different flavors of Snapple and filtering out the sediment, but by then consumers had switched to other brands and stores didn't want to carry the product.[22]

Differences in buying patterns require marketing executives to complete considerable research before entering a foreign market. Sometimes the marketer's own organization or a U.S.-based research firm can provide needed information. In other cases, only a foreign-based marketing research organization can tell marketers what they need to know. Whoever conducts the research, investigators must focus on five different areas before advising a company to enter a foreign market:

1. *Demand.* Do foreign consumers need the company's good or service?
2. *Competition.* How do supplies currently reach the market?
3. *Economic environment.* What is the state of the nation's economic health?
4. *Social-cultural environment.* How do cultural factors affect business opportunities?
5. *Political-legal environment.* Do any legal restrictions complicate entering the market?

THE INTERNATIONAL MARKETING ENVIRONMENT

As in domestic markets, the environmental forces discussed in Chapter 3 powerfully influence the development of international marketing strategies. Marketers must pay close attention to economic, social-cultural, and political-legal influences when they venture abroad.

International Economic Environment

As noted earlier, an increasing number of China's 1.2 billion consumers are eagerly buying Western consumer products, from Cheetos to Cokes to Pert shampoo. Receptive to advertising, the Chinese are becoming very brand conscious. India's 950 million consumers present another huge marketing opportunity. The growing middle classes of both countries make them even more attractive as targets for Western marketers.

While such prospects might tempt American firms, they must first consider the economic conditions of business in China, India, and anywhere else. A nation's size, per-capita income, and stage of economic development determine its prospects as a host for international business expansion. Nations with low per-capita incomes may be poor markets for expensive industrial machinery, but good ones for agricultural hand tools. These nations cannot afford the technical equipment that powers an industrialized society. Wealthier countries may offer prime markets for many U.S. industries, particularly those producing

Figure 4.3 **Transportation Systems: Important Components of a Nation's Infrastructure**

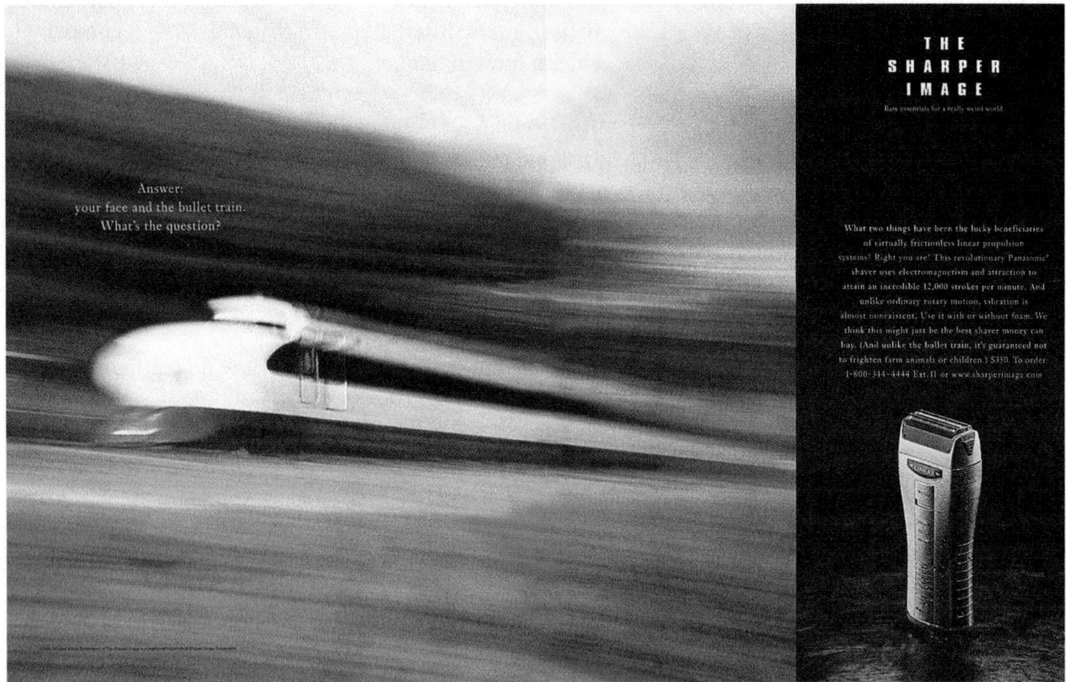
Answer:
your face and the bullet train.
What's the question?
THE SHARPER IMAGE
Bare essentials for a really weird world
What two things have been the lucky beneficiaries of virtually frictionless linear propulsion systems? Right you are! This revolutionary Panasonic® shaver uses electromagnetism and attraction to attain an incredible 12,000 strokes per minute. And unlike ordinary rotary motion, vibration is almost nonexistent. Use it with or without foam. We think this might just be the best shaver money can buy. (And unlike the bullet train, it's guaranteed not to frighten farm animals or children.) $350. To order: 1-800-344-4444 Ext.11 or www.sharperimage.com

consumer goods and services and advanced industrial products.

In India, for example, the median household income is only $480. Economic reforms have improved the country's standard of living somewhat, but most Indians have very few Western conveniences. Only 2 percent own cars, 4 percent have running hot water, and 7 percent have phones. Color television and refrigerator ownership run a bit higher at 12 percent.

Successful marketing in India requires an understanding of how the economy affects Indian consumers. Both rich and poor Indians practice frugal buying habits and spend as little as possible at one time. They prefer small packages with low prices, even though larger packages may offer more economical purchases. Even the wealthy are price-conscious consumers. Nestlé S.A. improved its market penetration by reducing package sizes and then pricing more than half of its food products under 25 rupees (about 70 cents). For example, sales of Maggi instant noodles tripled after Nestlé reduced the price from 19 cents to 14 cents a package. Recycling is a way of life in India. Although that country is the world's largest market for razor blades, disposable razors sell very poorly because the idea of throwing them away mystifies typical Indians.[23]

Another important economic characteristic is a country's **infrastructure.** *Infrastructure* refers to a nation's communications systems (television, radio, print media, telecommunications), transportation networks (paved roads, railroads, airports), and energy facilities (power plants, gas and electric utilities). An inadequate infrastructure may constrain marketers' plans to manufacture, promote, and distribute goods and services. Wal-Mart opened its first Chinese Sam's Club stores in Shenzhen, near the Hong Kong border, in 1996. Eager shoppers soon packed the outlets, breaking display cases in an effort to purchase chickens and buying the entire stock of big-screen televisions in one hour. But building stores in China is not an easy process. Not only did the company face construction delays, but it also had problems getting enough telephone lines and making its computerized inventory system work.[24]

Consumers outside the United States rely much more heavily than American consumers on rail transportation. High-speed rail systems, such as France's TGV and Japan's fleet of bullet trains shown in Figure 4.3, move passengers at speeds exceeding 200 miles per hour. A fan attending the 1998 Winter Olympics in Nagano, Japan, can enjoy a comfortable side trip to Tokyo's Disneyland via this fast, direct rail connection.

A communications network is another vital component of a nation's infrastructure. Phone lines gain increasing importance as computer networks spread to link people and businesses all over the world. Yet for every 100 people, India has 1 phone line; China, 2; Mexico, 9; and Russia, 16; the United States has 59.[25] Clearly, companies planning to open offices in other countries must consider the implications of limited communications services.

http://www.globalstar.com/

Such infrastructure limitations create opportunities as well as problems. Globalstar, a San Jose, California-based telecommunications company, negotiated a contract with the Chinese government to include the country in its global satellite network. Globalstar's system will send calls from its satellites through gateways in China, providing phone services to about 500,000 Chinese villages currently without access to telephone lines.[26]

Changes in exchange rates can also complicate international marketing. An **exchange rate** is the price of one nation's currency in terms of another country's currency. Fluctuations in exchange rates can make a nation's currency more valuable or less valuable compared to those of other nations. For example, Japan's traditional price advantage over domestic competitors in the United States eroded during the early 1990s primarily due to two factors: increasingly competitive U.S. companies and the rising value of the yen in comparison to the U.S. dollar. By the mid-1990s, however, the yen had depreciated by as much as 40 percent, once again reducing the cost of Japanese goods in the U.S. market. The shift allowed Toyota to drop the price of its popular 1997 Camry model in an effort to boost its share of the U.S. market and compete with domestic models.[27]

Russian and many eastern European currencies are considered *soft* currencies; people who hold these currencies cannot readily convert them into such *hard* currencies as the U.S. dollar, British pound, Japanese yen, and German mark. Rather than taking payment in soft currencies, international marketers doing business in countries that issue them may resort to barter, accepting such commodities as oil, timber, or even alcoholic beverages as payment for exports.

Like the U.S. economy, those of other industrialized nations experience business cycles that affect marketing strategies. Japan enjoyed a huge boom in economic activity during the 1980s and early 1990s. Its consumer electronics, automobiles, and semiconductors were acknowledged market leaders. Japanese companies invested heavily overseas, buying real estate like Rockefeller Center and entertainment companies like Universal Studios. However, the recession that began in 1992 brought an end to the country's growth. Japanese gross domestic product has grown less than 1 percent per year since then, land values have fallen drastically, and manufacturing production has slumped. Consumer spending, which represents 60 percent of the nation's economic activity, dropped sharply as the economy stalled.

Despite government attempts to correct the deteriorating economic situation, Japanese wages and the cost of living are twice comparable figures in the United States. Many manufacturers are moving jobs overseas to lower-cost labor markets elsewhere in Asia. By 1998, Toyota completed 65 percent of the assembly work for its automobiles outside Japan. The nation's highly publicized lifetime-employment programs actually apply to only 20 percent of the population, and climbing unemployment levels threaten the rest. Such changes have further reduced consumer spending and made Japan a less attractive marketplace for both its own and foreign marketers.[28]

For another change in the Japanese economy, the farming sector has seriously declined. Few young people are interested in agricultural careers, and no one seems eager to take the places of retiring farmers. As farm production declines, Japan must import more food. This need creates opportunities for foreign companies to supply food products to Japanese buyers. In fact, Japan has become the single largest market for U.S. farmers and food processors, accounting for over $12 billion in U.S. agricultural exports.[29]

International Social-Cultural Environment

Before entering a foreign market, marketers should study all aspects of that nation's culture, including language, education, religious attitudes, and social values. Western goods and services may encounter differing degrees of consumer resistance abroad due to variations in cultural values.

The Middle East, for example, stirs together diverse cultures and ideologies. Marketers cannot assume homogeneous attitudes among all Arab or Israeli consumers. Although growing numbers of consumers view television through broadcasts, cable services, and satellite dishes, many still follow old traditions.

Respect for cultural beliefs and religious customs is an essential precaution for marketers, especially when their messages portray women. In many Middle Eastern countries, women in ads must wear veils or cover their arms and upper torsos from view. The differences between the U.S. ad for Guerlain's Champs-Elysées perfume and its more sedate Middle Eastern version illustrate the steps that marketers must take in order to promote their messages in countries outside the United States.

Israel's ultra-orthodox Jews, with their large families, form an attractive segment for marketers, because they buy

Marketing Dictionary

infrastructure A nation's basic conditions in transportation networks, communication systems, and energy facilities.

exchange rate The price of one nation's currency in terms of another country's currency.

MARKETING HALL OF FAME

Avon Succeeds without Ringing the Bell

Not so long ago, the good fortunes of Avon Products, Inc., depended upon the hospitality of American homemakers. But now these women are no longer answering the doorbell. Their busy careers don't leave time to entertain Avon ladies carrying thick catalogs stuffed with pictures of the latest lipsticks and colognes.

Avon is also fighting the allure of superstores like Wal-Mart, with plentiful inventories of cheap and immediately available cosmetics. Why order through a catalog and wait days for lipsticks to arrive? In addition, a recent fashion trend has led many younger women to use less makeup, rejecting the well-groomed look for messy grunge instead.

Avon made the smart decision—to look beyond its own backyard. By thinking globally, it exponentially broadened its market. Almost 95 percent of all women live outside the United States and Canada. Avon had peddled its wares in western Europe for some time but ignored much of the rest of the world. That changed in 1990, when Avon representatives began selling in emerging markets—places as remote as the Brazilian Amazon basin and Siberia.

So far, the move has yielded impressive results. While annual Avon sales in the United States have slumped, emerging markets now produce 38 percent of the firm's total revenues and 49 percent of its pretax profit. "We see great promise in these markets," says Avon CEO James E. Preston. "And we feel the growth rate is sustainable."

To generate robust sales, Avon had to do more than simply establish beachheads in exotic places. It became acquainted with local customs and adapted its practices according to its new insights. For example, Avon quickly learned that Chinese and Russian customers are suspicious of door-to-door saleswomen. Instead, Avon established showrooms in the Orient where women can sample beauty aids and ask questions of representatives. Russian Avon representatives sell the products in parks, offices, and beauty shops.

The firm also created new products to fit local tastes. For instance, a lightening cream developed for Asian women has been a huge success.

Emerging markets represent logistical challenges to any multinational company. Inadequate roads and bridges, shaky communica-

more food, clothing, and jewelry than other Israelis. To reach these consumers, however, marketers must follow their rules, which forbid images of women in advertisements. Anything perceived as an insult may result in a well-organized boycott. Because this group prohibits television viewing, marketers rely on ads run in synagogue newsletters or in magazines that serve that specific population. Even banks may not publicly display video screens. When Visa began showing a video series in banks, some customers threatened to boycott the branches unless they stopped playing the videos.

Language also plays an important role in international marketing. Marketers must make sure to not only use the right language for a country but also correctly translate their communications and convey the intended meaning. Abbreviations and slang words and phrases may also cause misunderstandings when marketing abroad. A German or Italian consumer may not understand American ads with references to *Catch-22* situations or including abbreviations like *ASAP.*

Toyota had to rename its MR2 car in France, because the name sounds like a French swear word. Ocean Spray ran into problems marketing its cranberry juice drinks overseas, because foreign languages include no words for *cranberry.* Another problem resulted from the company name, Ocean Spray. Many foreigners associated it with a perfume, not a drink, complicating the firm's effort to gain consumer awareness.[30]

International Political-Legal Environment

Political conditions often influence international marketing. Consider the effect of political turmoil in Bosnia, Peru, Zaire, and Korea. Such political unrest sometimes results in acts of violence, such as destruction of a firm's property. Middle Eastern terrorists have targeted U.S. companies' offices abroad. IBM and American Express have been subject to terrorist threats and attacks. As a result, many Western firms have set up internal *political risk assessment*

tion systems, and a lack of local retailers to provide dependable distribution channels can deter newcomers. But Avon nimbly sidesteps these hurdles with its army of local saleswomen. "It's a big advantage for us," says Susan Kropf, Avon's vice president for eastern Europe. "We don't need an infrastructure." In China, where cosmetics demand is rising 20 percent a year, Avon avoids poor roads and unreliable mail service by using stores as distribution points for its sales representatives.

Of course, Avon isn't the only cosmetics maker trying to export the all-American look. One of its chief rivals, Mary Kay Cosmetics Inc., has scattered 25,000 reps throughout Russia and the former Soviet republics. Procter & Gamble's Max Factor brand is selling bright-colored makeup in Latin America and pushing Vidal Sassoon shampoos in the Far East. Meanwhile, women in South Africa are snatching up Maybelline's specially formulated, high-humidity face makeup.

"It's the Westernization of the world," says William Steele, a Dean Witter analyst who follows the cosmetics industry. "There is a clamoring for these products." Susan Kropf agrees. Just two years after opening, Avon's small Hungarian office was overseeing an army of 25,000 sales reps in Hungary, the Czech Republic, Slovakia, and Poland.

Why have women overseas embraced American cosmetics with so much enthusiasm? Kropf thinks she knows. "Let's just say the contrast between what they used to stand in line for and modern Western products is unbelievable. It's like advancing 100 years."

QUESTIONS FOR CRITICAL THINKING

1. **Sales to emerging markets now make up 38 percent of Avon's revenues. Do you think this component will represent the majority of the firm's sales some day? Why?**
2. **As competition from other American cosmetics makers grows, what marketing strategies should Avon follow to maintain its momentum?**

Sources: "Avon Reports First Quarter Earnings Per Share Up 11% on 7% Sales Increase," Avon Products, Inc., April 23, 1997, downloaded from http://www.prnewswire.com/, on May 20, 1997; Dyan Machan, "The Makeover," *Forbes*, December 2, 1996, pp. 135–140; Alessandra Stanley, "There Are More than 15,000 Avon Ladies in Russia, and Not One of Them Rings the Doorbell," *San Diego Union-Tribune*, September 1, 1996, pp. 1–2; Paulette Thomas, "Cosmetics Makers Offer World's Women an All-American Look with Local Twists," *Wall Street Journal*, May 8, 1995, pp. B1, B6; and Veronica Byrd, "The Avon Lady of the Amazon," *Business Week*, October 24, 1994, pp. 93–96.

(PRA) units or turned to outside consulting services to evaluate the political risks of the marketplaces in which they operate.

The legal environment for U.S. firms operating abroad results from three forces: (1) international law, (2) U.S. law, and (3) legal requirements of host nations. International law emerges from the treaties, conventions, and agreements that nations formulate. The U.S. government has agreed to many **friendship, commerce, and navigation (FCN) treaties** with other governments. These agreements set terms for various aspects of commercial relations with other countries, such as the right to conduct business in the treaty partner's domestic market. Other international business agreements concern worldwide standards for various products, patents, trademarks, reciprocal tax agreements, export controls, international air travel, and international communications. The International Monetary Fund lends foreign exchange to nations that require it in order to conduct international trade. These agreements facilitate the whole process of world marketing. However, companies do not enact international laws, governments do. Therefore, marketers include special provisions in contracts to define specific conditions such as which country's courts have jurisdiction.

The force in the international legal environment, U.S. law, includes various trade regulations, tax laws, and import/export requirements that affect international marketing. One important law, the *Export Trading Company Act*

Marketing Dictionary

friendship, commerce, and navigation (FCN) treaty An international agreement that sets terms for many aspects of commercial relations among nations.

Champs-Elysées.
La vie est plus belle quand on l'écrit soi-même
GUERLAIN
PARIS
(Life is best played without a script)

Champs-Elysées.
La vie est plus belle quand on l'écrit soi-même
GUERLAIN
PARIS

Guerlain Paris addresses marketing and cultural differences in these similar Champs-Elysées perfume ads. Acknowledging strict dress codes for women in many Middle Eastern countries, the model's clothing on the right has been changed to a more conservative look than that shown in the American ad on the left.

of 1982, created exemptions from antitrust regulations that allow companies to form export groups that cooperate to offer a variety of products to foreign buyers. The law seeks to help foreign buyers to connect with U.S. exporters. It also allows banks to participate directly in such ventures by financing trading activities. Although export trading companies offer many benefits to U.S. companies, relatively few firms have joined forces in these cooperative ventures.

A controversial 1996 law, the *Helms-Burton Act,* tried to impose trade sanctions against Cuba. Under this law, U.S. companies and citizens can sue foreign companies and their executives that use expropriated U.S. assets to do business in Cuba. The law also denies U.S. visas to executives at firms facing suits for violating the act.

The legislation has not successfully curtailed foreign investment in Cuba. In the months following its passage, foreign companies launched over 40 new ventures there, including plans by Canada Leisure to build 11 hotels. "This is an unacceptable intrusion into the trade and foreign policy of other countries," claimed Art Eggleton, Canada's trade minister. Even some U.S. companies with properties seized by the Cuban government in its revolution oppose the Helms-Burton act, citing new obstacles to their efforts to reenter Cuba.[31]

The *Foreign Corrupt Practices Act of 1977* prohibits U.S. businesspeople from bribing foreign officials in soliciting new or repeat sales abroad, producing a major impact on international marketing. The act also mandates that firms install adequate accounting controls to monitor internal compliance. A violation can result in a $1 million fine for the firm and a $10,000 fine and five years' imprisonment for the individuals who pay the bribe. This law has stirred controversy, mainly because it fails to clearly define *bribery.* The 1988 *Trade Act* amended the law to include more specific statements about prohibited practices.

Finally, legal requirements of host nations affect the political-legal environment in which foreign marketers operate. International marketers generally recognize the importance of obeying legal requirements, since even the slightest violation could cloud the future of international trade.

Some nations limit foreign ownership in their business sectors. India raised the limit on any foreigner's investment in an Indian company from 40 percent to 51 percent to encourage joint ventures. Unilever, Glaxo, Hoechst, Philips Electronics, and Ciba Corp., among other companies, have taken majority control of existing joint ventures under liberalized foreign ownership policies that permit 100 percent ownership in some situations. To attract foreign investors, India has altered other laws as well, eliminating requirements for licenses for most imports and allowing foreign institutions to trade on Indian stock exchanges. These and other legal changes stimulated dramatic increases in U.S. investment in Indian businesses. Hewlett-Packard India has benefitted from a drop in the time needed to receive parts from the United States from 87 to 15 days, and companies like Baskin-Robbins and McDonald's are opening retail outlets there. However, resentment toward foreign companies has once again started to grow. Many Indian companies, unhappy with 20 percent interest rates, want to shift back to a more protectionist economy. The local companies fear losing ground to stronger foreign rivals with better financing options.[32]

Many types of host-country legal requirements can affect the actions of foreign marketers. Global producers and marketers must not only maintain required minimum quality levels of all the countries in which they operate, but they must also comply with numerous local regulations. For example, the European Union (EU) has introduced a standardized system of ecological information on labels for certain products. Other European regulations deal with information and privacy issues. The Data Protection Act in the United Kingdom, for instance, restricts the applications of computer-generated lists by direct marketers for promotional campaigns. In addition, the European Union's General Directive on Data Protection includes guidelines for companies that market goods and services in all 15 EU nations about how and when they should disclose to consumers their practices for storing, processing, and using customer information.

Legal requirements of host countries can create unexpected hurdles. Retail outlets in Japan cannot distribute discount coupons or sell copyrighted products at discount prices. The Japanese government also sets different testing standards for imports than for domestic goods. Stricter tests encourage companies to sell locally produced products. Rather than performing individual tests on each different size of Thai-produced plastic containers and their lids, as required by law, Japanese retailer Mr. Max opted to sell Japanese containers even though they cost considerably more.[33]

Host-country laws can also affect how marketers advertise their products. The Malaysian government prohibits cigarette advertising, and other Asian governments restrict it. To get around these limitations, cigarette makers license their brand names to other products, such as clothing, travel agencies, and television shows. The Benson & Hedges Bistro in Kuala Lumpur features walls painted the same color as the cigarette package. The Camel brand name has also become one of the most popular international clothing brands in Malaysia. As these and other examples throughout the chapter show, marketers must carefully study local legislation affecting their specific industries.[34]

Trade Barriers Assorted trade barriers form an important part of the political-legal environment for global marketing. These barriers fall into two major categories: **tariffs**—taxes levied on imported products—and *administrative,* or *nontariff, barriers.* Some tariffs impose taxes per pound, gallon, or unit; others are calculated according to the values of imported products. Administrative barriers, more subtle than tariffs, work in a variety of ways such as customs barriers, quotas on imports, unnecessarily restrictive standards for imports, and export subsidies. Because the GATT and WTO agreements (discussed later in the chapter) eliminated tariffs on many products, countries now frequently substitute nontariff barriers to boost exports and control flows of imported products.

Trade barriers vary by industry and country. In a recent Coopers & Lybrand survey, American and Asian high-tech companies named tariffs as the top barrier to entering global markets. Their European counterparts ranked "buy local" policies as their top barrier.[35] The Bank of Boston ran into trouble with tariffs when it upgraded its trading systems in Boston and wanted to use the same Sun Microsystems workstations to revamp its trading floor in São Paulo, Brazil. That country's import tariffs doubled the bank's hardware and software costs. In fact, Brazilian tariffs and taxes on computer equipment account for 82 percent of those products' costs. The bank had to choose between paying the tariffs and purchasing Brazilian-assembled hardware, which was not covered under Sun's service and support agreement.

Tariffs Tariffs can be classified as either revenue or protective tariffs. Revenue tariffs serve the purpose of raising funds for the importing government. Most early U.S. government revenue came from this source. *Protective*

Marketing Dictionary

tariff A tax levied on imported goods.

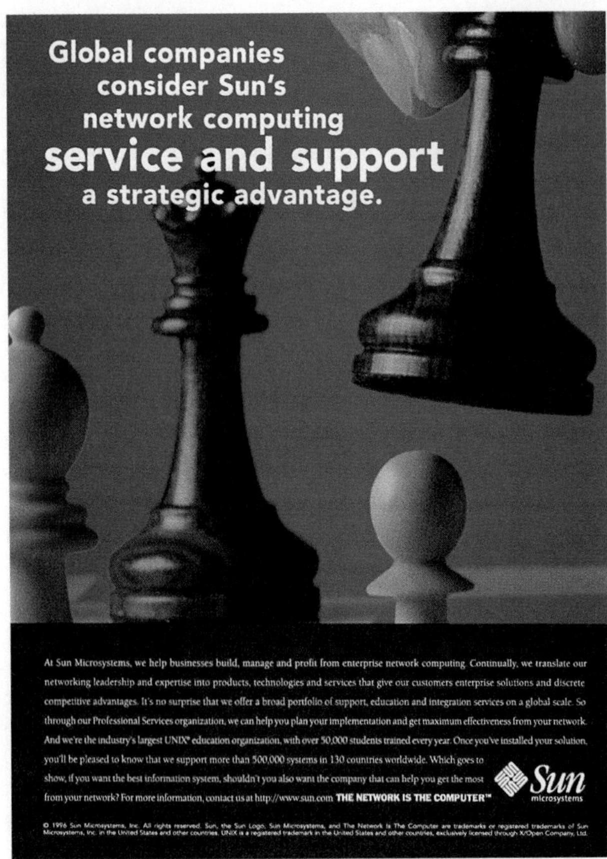
Global companies consider Sun's network computing service and support a strategic advantage.
At Sun Microsystems, we help businesses build, manage and profit from enterprise network computing. Continually, we translate our networking leadership and expertise into products, technologies and services that give our customers enterprise solutions and discrete competitive advantages. It's no surprise that we offer a broad portfolio of support, education and integration services on a global scale. So through our Professional Services organization, we can help you plan your implementation and get maximum effectiveness from your network. And we're the industry's largest UNIX® education organization, with over 50,000 students trained every year. Once you've installed your solution, you'll be pleased to know that we support more than 500,000 systems in 130 countries worldwide. Which goes to show, if you want the best information system, shouldn't you also want the company that can help you get the most from your network? For more information, contact us at http://www.sun.com THE NETWORK IS THE COMPUTER™
Sun microsystems
© 1996 Sun Microsystems, Inc. All rights reserved. Sun, the Sun Logo, Sun Microsystems, and The Network Is The Computer are trademarks or registered trademarks of Sun Microsystems, Inc. in the United States and other countries. UNIX is a registered trademark in the United States and other countries, exclusively licensed through X/Open Company, Ltd.

American high-tech firms like Sun Microsystems face high tariffs when exporting equipment to developing countries determined to protect their own fledgling technology industries.

tariffs usually set higher taxes than revenue tariffs in order to raise the retail prices of imported products to match or exceed those of similar domestic products. Some countries selectively impose tariffs to discourage certain consumption practices and reduce access to their local markets. For example, U.S. tariffs discourage imports of luxury goods like Rolex watches and expensive foreign liquors.

In the past, government officials commonly believed that a country should protect its infant industries by imposing tariffs to keep out foreign-made products. Some foreign goods still entered, but the high tariffs helped domestic products to compete in price. Recent arguments claim that high tariffs protect employment and profits in domestic industries.

In 1988, the U.S. Congress passed the Omnibus Trade and Competitiveness Act to remedy what it perceived as unfair international trade conditions. Under the law's so-called *Super 301* provisions, the U.S. government can now single out countries that unfairly impede trade by U.S. businesses within their borders. If these countries fail to open their markets within 18 months, the law requires retaliation in the form of U.S. tariffs or quotas on the offenders' imports into this country.

Governments can also enact tariffs to gain bargaining clout with other countries, but they risk adversely affecting the fortunes of domestic companies. Over 70 percent of the world's silk comes from China, and silk clothing is one of that country's vital exports. A recent threat of a 100 percent U.S. tariff on silk apparel imports from China gained the attention of the Chinese trade negotiators and also threatened to bankrupt many U.S. importers of Chinese silk clothing for sale to retailers like Lands' End, L. L. Bean, and JCPenney. The Chinese dependence on selling a single product to a mass market that can turn to substitutes made the negotiators especially vulnerable. However, the U.S. trade representatives withdrew the tariff threat when they reached agreement on intellectual property rights with the Chinese.[36]

In 1996, the 125 member countries of the World Trade Organization agreed to abolish tariffs on 500 high-technology products such as computers, software, calculators, fax machines, and related goods by 2000. Eliminating these tariffs could save as much as $100 million annually for IBM. To get European Union representatives to support the information-technology proposal—which was more important to the United States and Canada than to Europe—U.S. negotiators agreed to cut tariffs on expensive liquor imports.[37]

Administrative Barriers Nations implement a variety of strategies other than tariffs to keep out imports. In Japan, for example, pharmaceutical companies must apply for permits to import drugs. They must wait an average of four years to receive approval, by which time a Japanese drug firm may already have a local version of the product on the market. Japan's restrictive testing requirements for imports, mentioned earlier, also create obstacles. One Japanese distributor subjected a portable boat made by a California company to safety tests that included filling it with 600 pounds of concrete and dropping it 20 feet into the water three times. To the distributor's surprise, the boat passed the test.

Customs regulations can also create trade barriers. France tried to protect its manufacturers of videocassette recorders by requiring all imported VCRs to pass through one customs station at Poitiers. Located in the middle of the country, the station was hard to reach, open only a few days each week, and staffed by only a few customs officials who insisted on inspecting individual packages. This totally legal system caused major delays in processing VCR imports.[38]

Other forms of trade restrictions include import quotas and embargoes. An **import quota** limits the number of units of products in a certain category that can cross a country's border. The quota acts to protect domestic industry and employment and to preserve foreign exchange. The ultimate quota is an **embargo**—a complete ban on imports of a product. Since 1960, the United States has maintained an embargo against Cuba in protest of Fidel Castro's dictatorship and policies such as expropriation of property and disregard for human rights. Not only does the United States not allow Cuban exports (especially cigars and sugar—the island's best-known products) to enter the country, but U.S. companies cannot make investments in Cuba. However, many leading U.S. executives oppose the embargo. They complain about losing the opportunity to develop the Cuban market, while foreign rivals establish production and marketing facilities there.[39]

Foreign trade regulations may also include exchange controls imposed through a central bank or government agency. **Exchange controls** require firms that gain foreign exchange by exporting to sell foreign currencies to the central bank or another agency, and importers must buy foreign currencies from the same organization. The exchange control authority can then allocate, expand, or restrict foreign exchange to satisfy national policy.

Demands for protection against foreign imports are common in all countries, particularly during periods of economic uncertainty. Firms ask for protection against sales losses, and unions seek to preserve their members' jobs. But overall, as the next section will show, trade restrictions are losing ground to a long-term trend in the direction of free trade among nations.

Dumping The practice of selling a product in a foreign market at a lower price than it commands in the producer's domestic market is called **dumping.** Critics of free trade often argue that foreign governments give substantial support to their own exporting companies. Government support may permit these firms to extend their export markets by offering lower prices abroad. In retaliation for this kind of interference with free trade, the United States adds import tariffs to products that foreign firms dump on U.S. markets to bring their prices in line with those of domestically produced products. However, businesses often complain that charges of dumping must undergo a lengthy investigative and bureaucratic procedure before the government assesses import duties.

A U.S. firm that perceives a threat to its business from dumping can file a complaint with the U.S. International Trade Commission. If the ITC confirms a claim of dumping, it can assess fines that in theory equalize the prices of the goods in question. Between 1990 and 1995, nearly 300 such cases were filed; the ITC rejected about half of these claims.

MULTINATIONAL ECONOMIC INTEGRATION

A noticeable trend toward multinational economic integration has developed since the end of World War II. Countries can gain the benefits of integrating their economies in several ways. In the simplest, they can establish a *free-trade area* in which participating nations agree to maintain free trade of goods among themselves, abolishing all tariffs and trade restrictions. A *customs union* establishes a free-trade area plus a uniform tariff for trade with nonmember nations. A *common market* extends a customs union by seeking to reconcile all government regulations affecting trade.

GATT and the World Trade Organization

The year 1997 marked the 50th anniversary of the **General Agreement on Tariffs and Trade (GATT),** a 117-nation trade accord that has promoted several rounds of major tariff negotiations, substantially reducing worldwide tariff levels. In 1994, a seven-year series of conferences, called the *Uruguay Round,* culminated in one of the biggest victories for free trade in decades. The new accord's partial opening of world trade, which took effect in 1995, is expected to expand the U.S. economy by $1 trillion by 2000, creating as many as 2 million new jobs.

The Uruguay Round cut average tariffs by one-third, or more than $700 billion. Its major victories include the following changes:

Marketing Dictionary

import quota An administrative trade restriction that limits the number of units of a certain good that can enter a country for resale.

embargo An administrative trade restriction that imposes a complete ban on imports of a specified product.

exchange control An administrative trade restriction that controls access to foreign currencies.

dumping The controversial trade practice of selling a product in a foreign market at a lower price than it commands in the producer's domestic market.

General Agreement on Tariffs and Trade (GATT) An international trade accord that has helped to reduce worldwide tariffs.

SOLVING AN ETHICAL CONTROVERSY

Should Congress Eliminate U.S. Laws Forbidding Corporate Bribery?

U.S. law definitely prohibits offering a foreign official a bribe to secure a lucrative contract overseas—or does it? In much of the world, the answer is no. In France and Germany, bribes to foreign intermediaries are considered legitimate business expenses. In fact, companies' tax returns often list *Bribes* as deductible expenses in these countries. Organizations elsewhere in Europe, as well as Asia, hand out payoffs to muscle their way into new markets.

In a global economy all-too-frequently influenced by bribery, the United States stands virtually alone among the major powers. The Foreign Corrupt Practices Act forbids American companies from offering money under the table to obtain contracts. This restriction, corporate executives grumble, puts them at a distinct disadvantage. A U.S. Department of Commerce report reinforced that belief, concluding that foreign companies undercut U.S. firms by distributing questionable payments. In one recent year, U.S. intelligence agents tracked down 100 cases of bribery that cost American businesses $45 billion.

Do U.S. Laws Forbidding Organizational Bribery Unfairly Restrict International Marketers?

PRO

1. **Antibribery laws place U.S.-based global marketers at an unfair disadvantage. Among countless examples, consider the experience of Houston-based Enron Corp. Enron spent several hundred million dollars building a power-plant project in India, only to have a state government delay its completion for four years. Privately, officials said the biggest foreign investment project ever in India was mothballed because Enron paid no bribes. Eventually, the project got back on track, but only after extremely costly delays.**
2. **The antibribery statutes prove ineffective as people skirt them, anyway. Instead of blatantly paying off officials, American companies offer legal inducements. For instance, Chubb Corp., which wants to sell insurance in China, has donated $1 million to a Shanghai university to establish an insurance education program. Chubb filled the board of directors with Chinese officials who will decide whether the insurer can operate in their country. "You try to show them this is a two-way street," says Vice Chairman Percy Chubb III, who notes that his company has spent millions on similar endeavors overseas.**
3. **American companies will suffer even worse financial penalties as bribery spreads in international business. "With**

- Reduction of farm subsidies, which opened new markets for U.S. exports
- Increased protection for patents, copyrights, and trademarks
- Inclusion of services under international trading rules, creating opportunities for U.S. financial, legal, and accounting firms
- Phasing out import quotas on textiles and clothing from developing nations, a move that will benefit U.S. retailers and consumers, because quotas currently increase clothing prices by $15 billion

A key outcome of the GATT talks was establishment of the **World Trade Organization (WTO),** a 125-member organization that succeeds GATT. The WTO oversees GATT agreements, mediates disputes, and continues the effort to reduce trade barriers throughout the world. Unlike GATT provisions, WTO decisions are binding.

To date, however, the WTO has made only slow progress toward its major policy initiatives—liberalizing world financial services, telecommunications, and maritime markets. Trade officials have not agreed on a basic direction for the WTO. Its activities have focused more on complaint resolution than on removing global trade barriers. The WTO has reached over 60 decisions, including one ordering the Japanese to stop taxing European Union (EU) vodka at higher rates than Japanese liquor and two others prohibiting the United States from requiring stricter emissions standards for imported gasoline and imposing a quota on Costa Rican underwear.

Big differences between developed and developing areas of the globe create a major roadblock to WTO progress. These conflicts became apparent at the first WTO meeting in Singapore in 1996. Asian nations want other countries to lift trade barriers on their manufactured goods, but they also want to protect their own telecommunications companies. In addition, they oppose monitoring of corruption and

Asia emerging as a market, the opportunity for corruption is probably greater than it's ever been," says Robert C. Broadfoot, a founder of Political & Economic Risk Consulting Ltd. in Hong Kong.

CON

1. **The statutes need no changes, because disgruntled Americans wildly exaggerate incidences of organizational bribery. "Each time we win a deal, it's because of dirty tricks," says a sarcastic official with Airbus Industrie, a European consortium that makes commercial airplanes. "Each time Boeing wins, it's because of a better product."**
2. **The necessity to bribe officials should actually decrease as the current enthusiasm for privatization and free trade gains strength. What's more, says John Cavanagh, a fellow at the Institute for Policy Studies in Washington, "There are fewer corrupt dictators with an entourage of yes-men you have to get through to get the contract."**
3. **The premise that Americans should feel free to bribe foreign companies because their competitors do it is a morally bankrupt argument. Instead, America should exert its influence to clean up everybody else's act. For example, the U.S. government tried to apply pressure to Asian nations through the World Trade Organization during the recent Asia-Pacific Economic Cooperation Summit in Manila.**

Summary

Congress probably will not repeal America's overseas anticorruption laws. A movement to encourage the rest of the world to play by American rules has proven much more successful, however. In June 1997, trade ministers from 29 leading global trading nations approved a pact to bar payoffs and kickbacks by their companies. This agreement would force companies based in these nations to follow rules similar to those governing U.S.-based firms.

Under the accord, each of the 29 industrialized nations agreed to introduce laws in their national legislatures by April 1998 that would subject their companies to criminal penalties for bribing foreign officials while soliciting business. Even though the accord is a major breakthrough, its signers do not include the fast-growing nations of the developing world. But as General Electric executive Fritz Heiman points out, "The 29 [signees] are the home bases of practically every major international company around the world. So [this] is really the key step in addressing the whole supply side in international bribery."

A continuing challenge will be to monitor the actions taken by the signers of the accord to ensure that they follow through on their pledges to provide effective legislation and enforcement.

Sources: Paul Blustein, "Pact to Bar Bribery Is Reached: Major Nations Agree to U.S. Request," *Washington Post,* May 24, 1997, p. F1; and "Just Say No to Bribery," *Business Week,* July 29, 1996, p. 43.

labor practices by outsiders. The United States wants free trade for telecommunications, more controls on corruption, and establishment of international labor standards. European members want standard rules on foreign investments and removal of restrictions on profit repatriation, but they express less concern than the United States with worker rights.

China's entrance into the WTO is another big issue. China wants to join under the less restrictive terms permitted for developing nations. The United States, concerned about its growing trade deficit with China, favors stronger criteria because China plays such a huge role in world trade. The European Union, however, would give China more leeway to encourage it to become a WTO member. Clearly, until members can resolve these philosophical differences, the WTO will achieve limited effectiveness.[40]

The NAFTA Accord

Creation of the WTO followed the 1993 approval by the United States, Canada, and Mexico of the **North American Free Trade Agreement (NAFTA).** This agreement

Marketing Dictionary

World Trade Organization (WTO) A 125-member organization that succeeds GATT in overseeing trade agreements, mediating disputes, and reducing trade barriers; unlike GATT provisions, WTO decisions are binding.

North American Free-Trade Agreement (NAFTA) An accord to remove trade barriers among Canada, Mexico, and the United States.

Figure 4.4 U.S. Trade Balance with NAFTA Partners

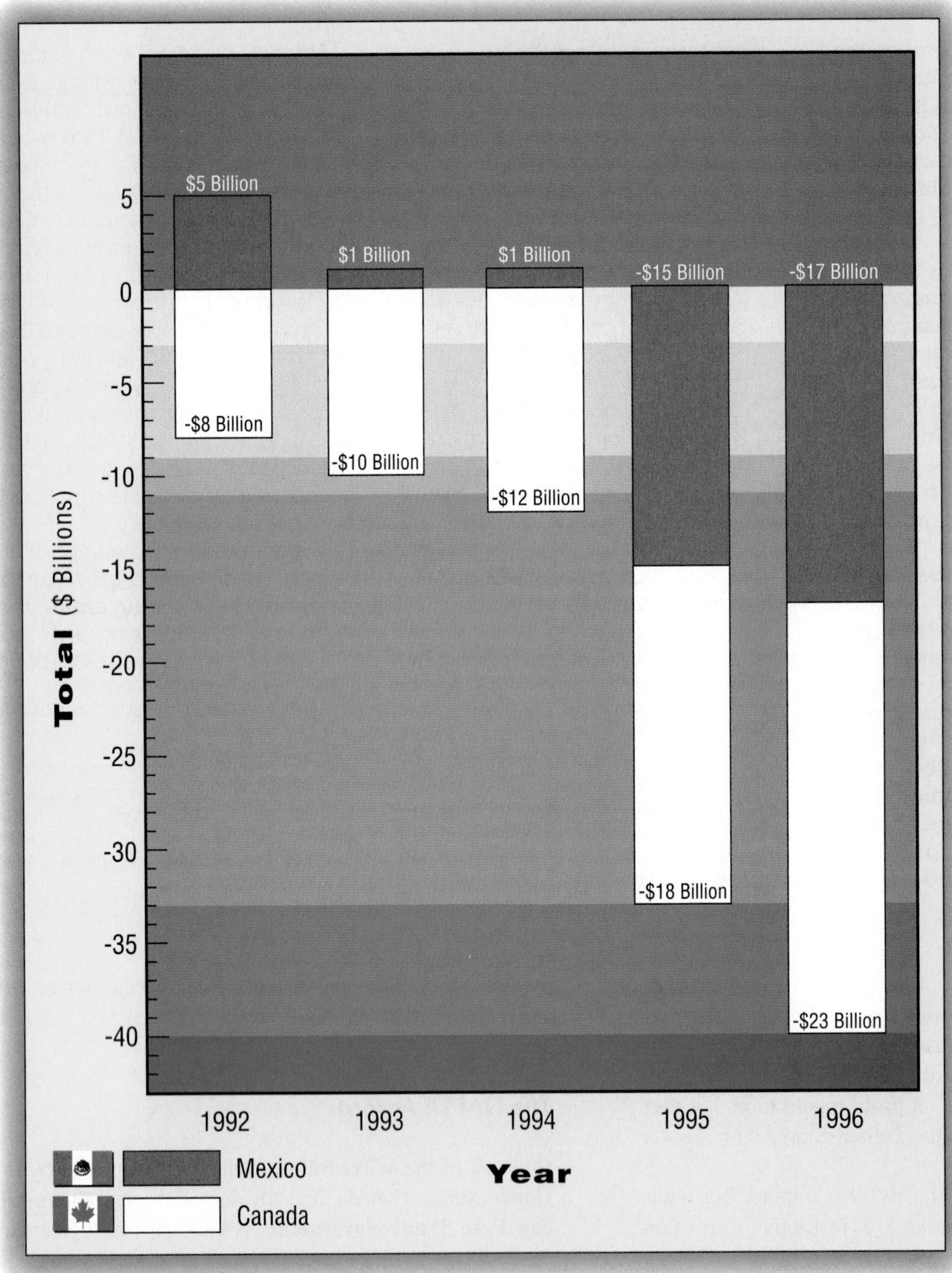
$5 Billion
$1 Billion
$1 Billion
-$15 Billion
-$17 Billion
-$8 Billion
-$10 Billion
-$12 Billion
-$18 Billion
-$23 Billion
5
0
-5
-10
-15
-20
-25
-30
-35
-40
Total ($ Billions)
1992
1993
1994
1995
1996
Year
Mexico
Canada

removes, over a 14-year period, trade restrictions among the three nations. The NAFTA accord brings together 390 million people and a combined gross domestic product of $7.9 trillion, creating by far the world's largest free-trade zone. It marked the first step in the creation of a free-trade zone covering the entire western hemisphere—850 million people, representing a $12 trillion annual market by 2005.

NAFTA is not the only western hemisphere trade bloc. Canada and Chile have reached a free-trade agreement. Also, the MERCOSUR customs union, composed of Brazil, Argentina, Paraguay, Uruguay, Chile, and Bolivia, is another group with which the United States may have to negotiate.

NAFTA has produced mixed initial results. Trade among the three NAFTA partners has increased 25 percent since 1993, and U.S.-Mexican trade is up 62 percent. The number of cross-border investments between U.S. and Canadian firms has also increased. For one example, Nike acquired Canstar Sports, a hockey equipment manufacturer.

However, the U.S. merchandise trade gap with its two NAFTA partners has increased steadily since 1992, as Figure 4.4 shows. By 1996, the combined deficit was about $40 billion—four times the pre-NAFTA 1993 level. (Figures that include trade in services move the U.S.-Canadian trade relationship closer to balance however.) These deficits result from economic conditions in Canada and Mexico. Canada's sluggish economy and the weak Canadian dollar slowed imports and increased exports. In addition, U.S. auto manufacturers moved production north of the border.

Mexico's recession and the devaluation of the peso helped its own products to compete with imports. Also, its exports, including petrochemicals, steel, and farm products, became more attractive to buyers in the United States and elsewhere. Inflation reached about 27 percent in 1996, and unemployment also rose slightly. As a result, many of Mexico's 85 million consumers struggled to afford necessities, much less imported goods.

As Mexico's economy has revived, U.S. exports there have increased. Both U.S. and Japanese car manufacturers have established large production facilities in Mexico that export about 1 million cars a year, mostly to the U.S. market. However, opening up Mexico's economy has had another effect: a shift away from reliance on U.S. goods. Many U.S. observers hoped that Mexico would buy mainly from its northern neighbor. Instead, growing numbers of Mexican companies now purchase parts and other industrial inputs from suppliers in Europe and Asia.

Before NAFTA, the U.S. government imposed a 32 percent tariff on brooms made at this Mexican factory, where workers earn about $2.30 an hour. Since NAFTA eliminated the tariff, the company's exports have doubled. But sales for U.S. broom makers, which pay employees four to five times more per hour, have dropped about 25 percent each year.

These early trends concern some experts, but the agreement may be too new to know whether they are signs of future problems. NAFTA's opponents claim that free-trade policies send American jobs and factories overseas to low-wage nations.[41]

Briefly
speaking

"Poor Mexico. So far from God and so close to the United States."

Porfirio Diaz (1830–1915)
President of Mexico

NAFTA's Effect on Jobs NAFTA was supposed to create jobs and raise wages in all three participating nations. Yet an estimated 88,000 U.S. workers claim that they lost jobs due to imports from Canada and Mexico. These claims mask the difficulty of determining accurately NAFTA's effect on jobs in the three countries. Current job loss statistics do not group figures by reason, so they do not reveal whether changes have resulted from NAFTA, currency devaluation, automation, or other causes.

Critics initially worried that Mexico, with its relatively low wages, posed the primary threat to U.S. jobs, especially in the auto industry. But Mexican auto-industry employment actually dropped 13 percent since 1989. Even though the decline in the value of the peso is bringing auto jobs back, technological improvements will reduce the number of workers the industry needs. Displaced workers will find comparatively low-wage assembly jobs for auto parts, electronics, and other products in *maquiladoras* located near the U.S. border. Auto-industry jobs also rose in the United States, but the new positions emphasized low-paying parts work, rather than high-paying assembly jobs.

Canada has been the real winner in the race for auto jobs. It has gained 28,000 high-wage jobs, bringing the total number of workers employed in Canadian assembly plants by U.S. auto manufacturers to 60,000. The employers incur one-third lower total labor costs for Canadian workers than they must pay in the United States; the difference results from lower employee health-care costs and the weaker Canadian dollar. Since 1989, Canadian auto exports to the United States have doubled, making Canada the leading car exporter to the United States.

NAFTA, hailed by its supporters as a win-win-win accord, was supposed to bring the three partners closer together. In theory, reduced trade barriers should boost

Figure 4.5 **The Cost of Protectionism**

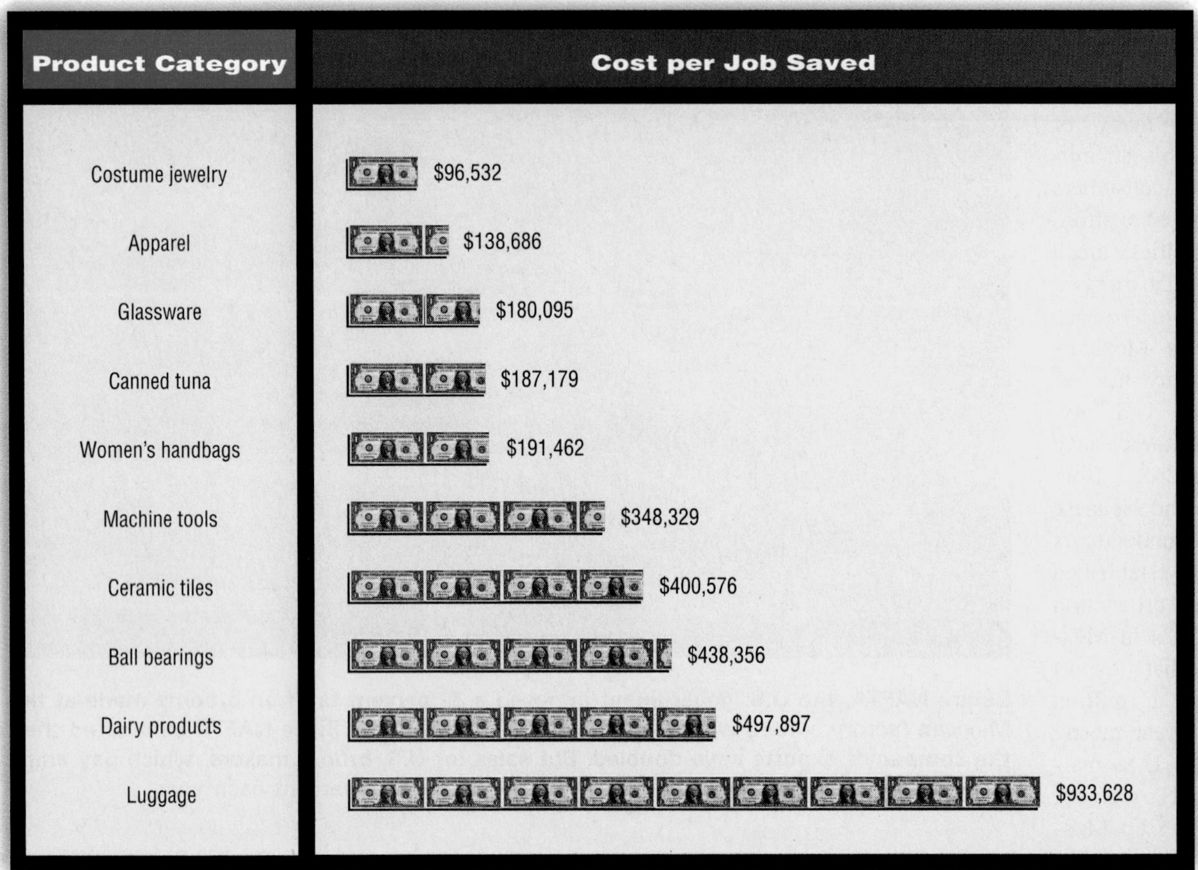

Product Category	Cost per Job Saved
Costume jewelry	$96,532
Apparel	$138,686
Glassware	$180,095
Canned tuna	$187,179
Women's handbags	$191,462
Machine tools	$348,329
Ceramic tiles	$400,576
Ball bearings	$438,356
Dairy products	$497,897
Luggage	$933,628

market efficiency over time. While the three governments consider it a success, the industries under attack continue to complain. Florida produce growers, for example, petitioned President Clinton to stop cheaper Mexican vegetable imports.[42]

Protectionism, the Economy, and Jobs

Some politicians argue passionately that trade protectionism helps a nation's economy, but most economists strongly support free trade. A recent study shows a strong association between free trade and economic growth. Between 1970 and 1990, developing nations with open economies averaged annual growth of 4.5 percent, compared to less than 1 percent per year in closed economies. Developed countries that allowed free trade grew an average 2.3 percent, versus 0.7 percent for countries that blocked trade. Changing from closed to open economies resulted in more than 1 percent increases in annual growth.

Another study, by the McKinsey Global Institute, found that trade restrictions in the United States and Germany generally hurt manufacturing productivity, because managers in protected industries hesitated to modernize operations. Global competition, the report concluded, stimulates productivity advances.[43]

Protection may save some jobs in protected industries, but at a high cost. As Figure 4.5 shows, annual consumer costs per American job saved range from almost $100,000 in the costume jewelry industry to nearly $1 million in the luggage industry. The Institute for International Economics estimates that tariffs and other import barriers cost a typical U.S. household $720 per year. Another study, conducted by the St. Louis-based Center for the Study of American Business, determined that trade barriers did save jobs for the steel industry. But for every job saved, more than two jobs in steel-using U.S. industries were lost—protectionism cost the economy more jobs than it saved.

Critics of NAFTA and other free-trade agreements contend that low wages in developing countries push down wages for U.S. workers. However, the Commerce Department estimates that, excluding oil, imports of goods from

Mexico and other developing or newly industrialized countries represent less than 5 percent of the total U.S. economy. Also, comparisons between wages in different countries may mislead. Although workers in one nation may receive less pay, they often achieve lower productivity. A Federal Reserve Bank of San Francisco study found *unit labor costs,* costs after adjustments for productivity, in Mexico averaged 75 percent of the U.S. level. Other low-wage countries produced unit labor costs equal to or higher than those in the United States.[44]

The European Union

The best-known example of free trade within a multinational economic community comes from the *European Union (EU),* a customs union that is moving in the direction of a full economic union. The EU combines 15 countries, 350 million people, and a gross domestic product of $5 trillion to form a huge common market. In addition to the 15 member nations from Western Europe, several former Soviet republics and other eastern European countries have applied for admission to the EU.

The EU member nations intend eventually to remove all barriers to free trade among themselves, making a shipment of products between England and Spain as easy and painless as a similar shipment between New Jersey and Pennsylvania. Economic integration also involves a drive to standardize regulations and requirements that businesses must meet. Instead of learning and complying with 15 sets of standards to operate throughout Europe, companies will have to comply with just one. This change should lower the costs of doing business in Europe by allowing firms to take advantage of economies of scale.

In some ways, the EU is making definite progress toward its economic goals. Recall its emerging standard for ecological information on labels to certify that products are manufactured according to certain environmental standards; in addition, the EU is creating guidelines governing marketers' use of customer information. Marketers can also protect trademarks throughout the entire EU with a single application and registration process. The Community Trademark (CTM) system simplifies doing business and eliminates having to register with each member country, although applicants do not always win easy approval.[45]

Yet marketers still face challenges when selling their products in the EU. Differences in customs, taxes, and currencies create obstacles, and no uniform postal system serves all member nations. Mail moves extremely slowly between countries. In fact, the Federation of European Direct Marketing is pushing for modernization and integration of postal systems. A firm cannot set up one toll-free number for several countries, either, because each country has its own codes and numbers for its telephone system.[46]

GOING GLOBAL

A strategy for entering the international marketplace is becoming an important part of a firm's overall marketing strategy. Most large companies already participate in global commerce, and many small businesses recognize the need to investigate opportunities for marketing their products overseas. No firm can easily step into global markets, and all must complete careful evaluation and preparation. The chapter has mentioned many differences in business practices and regulations in foreign markets, and the social-cultural environment presents new challenges, as well.

The first step toward successful global marketing is to secure top management's support. Without the enthusiastic support of senior executives, export efforts usually fail. The advocate for going global must explain and promote the potential of foreign markets and facilitate the global marketing process.

The next important step is to research the export process and potential markets. The U.S. Department of Commerce sponsors a toll-free hotline (1-800-872-8723) for an information service that describes the various federal export programs. Trade counselors at 68 district offices offer export advice, computerized market data, and names of contacts in over 60 countries. Firms can use some services free of charge, while others are available at a reasonable cost. These services include:

- *National Trade Data Bank.* This large database, updated monthly, provides market reports on foreign demand for specific products. Marketers can get it at Commerce Department district offices or by subscription.
- *Agent/Distributor Services.* This search service helps companies locate overseas distributors for their products.

http://www.cnewsusa.com/

- *Commercial News USA.* This monthly export catalog-magazine promotes U.S. products and services to 100,000 international buyers in over 150 countries. An electronic version of *Commercial News USA* now appears on the World Wide Web. This site helps foreign importers find American companies.

Figure 4.6 **Levels of Involvement in International Marketing**

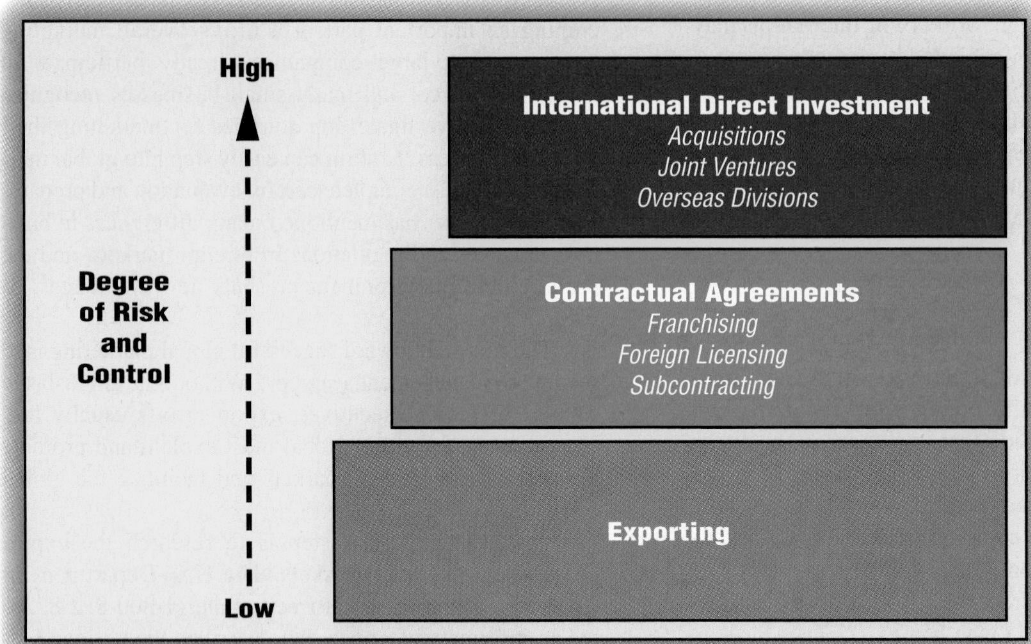
High
Degree of Risk and Control
Low
International Direct Investment
Acquisitions
Joint Ventures
Overseas Divisions
Contractual Agreements
Franchising
Foreign Licensing
Subcontracting
Exporting

- *Catalog and Video Shows.* This service sponsors catalog shows at U.S. consulates and embassies that display companies' catalogs and demonstration videos. Shows focus on particular industries, such as medical supplies and marine equipment.
- *Matchmaker Missions.* These government-sponsored visits help U.S. marketers in specific industries to meet potential customers in foreign countries.
- *Trade Shows.* Commerce Department-sponsored trade shows in other countries set up effective forums for companies to collect market information and meet customers.

Another good information source, TradePoint USA, helps companies analyze foreign markets. This Columbus, Ohio, not-for-profit service gives access to print and online resources. Its Internet service, I-Trade, provides country data, international news, the National Trade Databank, and trade and country reports from several sources.

Strategies for Entering International Markets

Once marketers have completed their research, they may choose among three basic strategies for entering international markets: exporting; contractual agreements like franchising, licensing, and subcontracting; and international direct investment. As Figure 4.6 shows, the level of risk increases with greater involvement, as does the firm's degree of control over its international marketing. Firms often combine more than one of these entry strategies. L. L. Bean subcontracts with a Japanese company to handle its product returns, and it also maintains a direct investment in several Japanese retail outlets in partnership with Matsushita.[47]

Exporting, the most common form of international marketing, involves a continuous effort to market a firm's merchandise to customers abroad. Many firms export their products as the first step in reaching foreign markets. Success in exporting often encourages them to move on to other entry strategies.

First-time exporters can reach foreign customers through one or more of three alternatives: export-trading companies, export-management companies, and offset agreements. An *export trading company (ETC)* buys products from domestic producers and resells them abroad. While manufacturers surrender control over marketing and distribution to the ETC, it helps them to export through a relatively simple and inexpensive channel, in the process providing feedback about the overseas market potential of their products.

The second option, an *export management company (EMC),* provides the first-time exporter with expertise in locating foreign buyers, handling necessary paperwork, and ensuring that its goods meet local labeling and testing laws. However, the manufacturer retains more control over the export process when it deals with an EMC than if it were to sell the goods outright to an export trading company. Smaller firms can get assistance with administrative needs such as financing and paperwork from large EMC contractors.

The final option, entering a foreign market under an *offset agreement,* teams a small firm with a major international company. The smaller firm essentially serves as a subcontractor on a large foreign project. This entry strategy provides new exporters with international experience, supported by the assistance of the primary contractor in such areas as international transaction documents and financing.

Contractual Agreements As a firm gains sophistication in international marketing, it may enter contractual agreements that provide several flexible alternatives to exporting. Both large and small firms can benefit from these methods. Franchising and foreign licensing, for example, are good ways to take services abroad. Subcontracting may set up either production facilities or services. Sponsorships are another form of international contractual marketing agreements. For example, Nike boosted its role as a global brand by signing a $200 million, ten-year sponsorship agreement with the Brazilian national soccer team, one of the world's best teams. Nike hopes to strengthen its cultural ties to Hispanics and soccer fans through the agreement. In a similar deal, rival Reebok is sponsoring the Argentinean team in a $60 million, five-year deal.[48]

http://www.nike.com/

Franchising A **franchise** is a contractual arrangement in which a wholesaler or retailer (the franchisee) agrees to meet the operating requirements of a manufacturer or other franchiser. The franchisee receives the right to sell the franchiser's products under its brand name, as well as a variety of marketing, management, and business services. As mentioned earlier, fast-food companies have actively franchised their products around the world.

For one advantage, franchising reduces risks by offering a proven concept. Also, standardized operations reduce costs, promote operating efficiencies, and provide internationally recognized credibility. However, the success of an international franchise depends on its willingness to balance these standard practices with sensitivity to local customs. McDonald's, Pizza Hut, and Domino's are all expanding into India with special menus that feature lamb, chicken, and vegetarian items, in deference to Hindu and Muslim customers who do not eat beef and pork. Mrs. Fields cookies is also expanding globally through franchising. With 30 stores in six Asian countries, the company plans to open 150 more by 2000. Its cookie recipes change by market. In Indonesia, for example, the cookies contain cashew nuts, a local product.[49]

California-based Gold's Gym has set up 500 franchisees around the world. Young entrepreneur Jake Weinstock and two business partners, another American and a Russian, opened a state-of-the-art fitness facility in Moscow. The Moscow Gold's Gym offers members access to Astroturf tennis courts, a Nike-sponsored basketball court, the latest weight-training machines, and a tanning salon. With its high level of customer service, the outlet attracts both Russian businesspeople and Western expatriates. Weinstock believes that his local partner added critical momentum to move the project through the Russian bureaucracy, develop a local contact network, and tailor the facility to its local clientele.[50]

Foreign Licensing A second type of contractual agreement, **foreign licensing,** helps a firm to go global in a different way. Such an agreement grants foreign marketers the right to distribute a firm's merchandise or use its trademark, patent, or process in a specified geographic area. These arrangements usually set certain time limits. Toy maker Hasbro, Inc. has entered foreign licensing agreements with several manufacturers in Japan and Latin America. The foreign firms carry out local production of popular Hasbro toys such as the Playskool brand shown in the ad in Figure 4.7.

Licensing offers several advantages over exporting, including access to local partners' marketing information and distribution channels and protection from various legal barriers. Because licensing does not require capital outlays, many firms, both small and large, regard it as an attractive entry strategy. Like franchising, licensing allows a firm to quickly enter a foreign market with a known product or concept. The arrangement also may provide entry into a market that government restrictions close to imports or international direct investment.

Fila Sports, an Italian sports apparel marketer, launched its line of athletic shoes in India through a licensing agreement with Moja Shoes, a New Delhi footwear manufacturer. Fila receives a royalty from Moja for any Fila shoes sold in India. Because India restricts shoe manufacturing to small, local firms, Moja also produces shoes

Marketing Dictionary

franchise A contractual arrangement in which a wholesaler or retailer (the franchisee) agrees to make some payment and to meet the operating requirements of a manufacturer or other franchiser in exchange for the right to market the franchiser's goods or services under its brand name.

foreign licensing A contractual agreement that grants foreign marketers the right to distribute a firm's merchandise or use its trademark, patent, or process in a specified geographic area for a specified time period.

Figure 4.7 Going Global through Foreign Licensing Agreements

PLAYSKOOL
KEEPS ME STEADY!
In-Line Skates
Playskool makes learning to in-line skate fun, easy and extra cool!
Fits shoe sizes 6-12.
1 Extra balance wheel setting.
2 Forward only wheel lock.
3 Unlock the wheels and go!
3 yrs and up
PLAYSKOOL
MAKES ME A HITTER!
1-2-3 Baseball™
The best batting instructor a preschooler ever had!
U.S. Patent Pending
1 Kids start hitting off the tee.
2 Next, kids hit a popped up ball.
3 Your kid is ready for a real pitch!
3 yrs and up
PLAYSKOOL
GETS ME ON 2-WHEELS!
1-2-3 Bike™
More beginners go with Playskool, because it's the fastest way to 2 Wheels... in fun primary colors, too.
1 Wide wheels for extra balance.
2 Wheels turn in as kids progress.
3 Wheels off for 2-wheeling fun!
2 yrs and up
Playskool Makes Playing like the BIG KIDS easy as
1
2
3
Questions? Call: 1-800-PLAYSKL

for Sierra Industrial Enterprises, the Indian licensee for Nike.[51]

Subcontracting A third type of contractual agreement, *subcontracting,* takes a firm's products to global markets by hiring local companies to produce the firm's goods or services. Local subcontractors can offer advice that prevents mistakes involving local culture and regulations. A manufacturer might subcontract with a local company to produce its goods or contract with a foreign distributor to handle its products abroad or provide customer service. Manufacturing within a foreign country can avoid import duties, and potential cost savings may help the product to compete with local offerings.

U.S. mail-order companies have found that subcontracting order fulfillment and customer service to local companies usually costs less and speeds up delivery. The resulting increase in customer satisfaction attracts repeat orders. Prestige International is a Japanese company that operates call centers serving such catalogers as Hanna Andersson and Nieman Marcus. It develops customized software to duplicate the U.S. client's customer service and database systems, trains representatives, and handles other operational issues. Prestige also contracts with 70 percent of Japan's credit-card issuers, giving catalog firms an additional medium through which to promote their products by placing ads in monthly bill mailings and in cardholder magazines.[52]

International Direct Investment

A firm that adopts the third strategy for entering international markets, the one with the greatest involvement and risk, makes direct investments in foreign companies or in production and marketing facilities abroad. Worldwide foreign direct investment has tripled since 1991 to about $325 billion, with 80 percent going to Asia. U.S.-owned foreign companies generate annual sales twice the amount of U.S. exports.[53]

Direct investment can take several forms. For example, an American company can acquire an existing firm in a country where it wants to do business, or it can set up an independent division outside U.S. borders with responsibility for production and marketing in a country or geographic region. Foreign sales offices, overseas marketing subsidiaries, and foreign offices of U.S. advertising agencies are also examples of direct investment.

Companies may also engage in international marketing by forming **joint ventures,** in which they share the risks, costs, and management chores of the foreign operation with one or more partners. These partnerships usually join the investing companies with nationals of the host countries.

Some companies open their own facilities overseas. For example, Singapore is developing an industrial park in Suzhou, China, with the infrastructure to support manufacturing facilities. RJR Nabisco has built a Ritz cracker factory in the industrial park, Eli Lilly has set up a drug manufacturing facility, Samsung Electronics has built a semiconductor plant, and Siemens Electronics makes hearing aids there. Malaysian locations have also attracted production facilities of high-tech companies like Seagate, a U.S. disk drive manufacturer, and semiconductor companies such as Intel, Motorola, and Texas Instruments.[54]

Service companies also establish foreign operations. After Germany deregulated its insurance market in 1994,

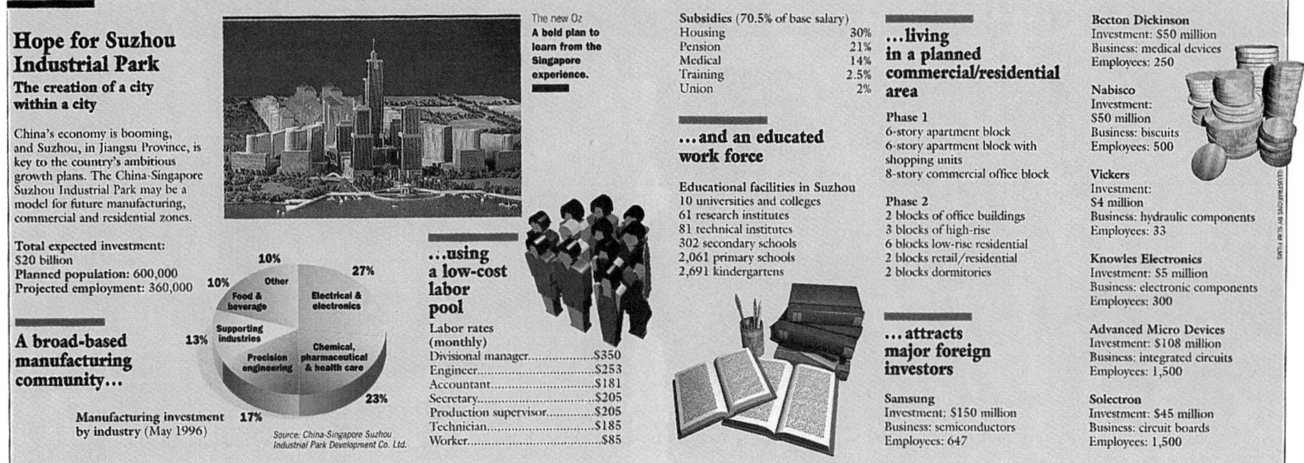
Hope for Suzhou Industrial Park
The creation of a city within a city
China's economy is booming, and Suzhou, in Jiangsu Province, is key to the country's ambitious growth plans. The China-Singapore Suzhou Industrial Park may be a model for future manufacturing, commercial and residential zones.
Total expected investment: $20 billion
Planned population: 600,000
Projected employment: 360,000
The new Oz
A bold plan to learn from the Singapore experience.
A broad-based manufacturing community...
10% Other
10% Food & beverage
27% Electrical & electronics
13% Supporting industries
23% Chemical, pharmaceutical & health care
17% Precision engineering
Manufacturing investment by industry (May 1996)
Source: China-Singapore Suzhou Industrial Park Development Co. Ltd.
...using a low-cost labor pool
Labor rates (monthly)
Divisional manager..........$350
Engineer..........$253
Accountant..........$181
Secretary..........$205
Production supervisor..........$205
Technician..........$185
Worker..........$85
Subsidies (70.5% of base salary)
Housing 30%
Pension 21%
Medical 14%
Training 2.5%
Union 2%
...and an educated work force
Educational facilities in Suzhou
10 universities and colleges
61 research institutes
81 technical institutes
302 secondary schools
2,061 primary schools
2,691 kindergartens
...living in a planned commercial/residential area
Phase 1
6-story apartment block
6-story apartment block with shopping units
8-story commercial office block
Phase 2
2 blocks of office buildings
3 blocks of high-rise
6 blocks low-rise residential
2 blocks retail/residential
2 blocks dormitories
...attracts major foreign investors
Samsung
Investment: $150 million
Business: semiconductors
Employees: 647
Becton Dickinson
Investment: $50 million
Business: medical devices
Employees: 250
Nabisco
Investment: $50 million
Business: biscuits
Employees: 500
Vickers
Investment: $4 million
Business: hydraulic components
Employees: 33
Knowles Electronics
Investment: $5 million
Business: electronic components
Employees: 300
Advanced Micro Devices
Investment: $108 million
Business: integrated circuits
Employees: 1,500
Solectron
Investment: $45 million
Business: circuit boards
Employees: 1,500
ILLUSTRATIONS BY SLIM FILMS

Allstate Insurance invested $100 million in its German operations with plans to become one of the country's top ten insurers by 2000. Allstate sells auto policies through telemarketing, which allows the insurer to price its product about 30 percent lower than companies with agents. In another first for the German market, Allstate added a risk classification feature that gives lower rates for certain categories and safe-driver discounts.[55]

Other American companies find that joint ventures simplify the process of doing business abroad. SyQuest Technology, Inc., a U.S. manufacturer of computer hard drives, formed a joint venture with Legend Group, China's largest manufacturer and distributor of computer systems. Both are contributing capital to the alliance, which manufactures hard drives in China and holds exclusive distribution rights for SyQuest products there. The joint venture brings benefits to both companies. SyQuest gains entrance to and instant market presence in the world's largest consumer market; it also expands its manufacturing capacity. Legend gains access to SyQuest's training, technology, and manufacturing skills. Legend's expertise in low-cost, high-volume manufacturing will help SyQuest to improve production efficiency.[56]

Although joint ventures offer many advantages, foreign investors have encountered problems in several Asian countries. A continuing building boom could lead to overcapacity in the automotive, semiconductor, consumer electronics, and chemical processing industries. Export growth is slowing, while costs are climbing as wages rise faster than productivity levels. Firms must search for skilled workers in some markets; unemployment in Malaysia, for example, is down to 2 percent. Most of the region's infrastructure is very poor and corruption is common, causing many investors to stay away.[57]

While growth rates have not matched those of countries in Asia, central European nations (especially Poland, Hungary, and the Czech Republic) have also drawn increasing foreign investment. Consumer demand is growing at 15 percent a year there, compared to only 3 percent in western Europe. In Hungary, for example, IBM recently spent $40 million to expand its disk drive factory, and GE Capital owns a one-fourth interest in Budapest Bank. The bank plans to call on GE Capital's expertise to increase its consumer finance operations. U.S. firms are not the only ones that see the market potential for international direct investments in central Europe. Korea's Daewoo Motors purchased 70 percent of Polish automaker FSO, and Matsushita, the Japanese electronics giant, is building a $66 million television factory in the Czech Republic. E. Le Clerc, a French firm, opened a huge shopping mall in Warsaw that enjoyed immediate success, and the firm expects to build 50 more throughout Poland.[58]

From Multinational Corporation to Global Marketer

A **multinational corporation** is a firm with significant operations and marketing activities outside its home country. Examples of multinationals include General Electric, Siemens, and Mitsubishi in heavy electrical equipment; and Timex, Seiko, and Citizen in watches. Table 4.2 lists

Marketing Dictionary

joint venture An agreement in which a firm shares the risks, costs, and management of a foreign operation with one or more partners, who are usually citizens of the host country.

multinational corporation A firm with significant operations and marketing activities outside its home country.

Table 4.2 Ten Largest U.S.-Based Multinationals

	Foreign Revenue (percentage of total)	Foreign Net Profits (percentage of total)	Foreign Assets (percentage of total)
Exxon	78.8%	76.5%	59.0%
General Motors	29.0	53.9	26.9
IBM	62.8	85.4	55.3
Mobil	66.4	69.2	61.7
Ford Motor	30.5	14.0	28.4
Texaco	56.1	69.2	46.5
Citicorp	59.3	57.9	57.6
Philip Morris	34.2	24.3	36.2
Chevron	45.6	24.0	44.5
General Electric	25.5	13.4	26.0

the ten largest U.S.-based multinationals, showing not only the percentage of revenues each derives from foreign operations but also the percentage of net profits and assets attributed to these operations. Note that six of the ten receive more than half of their net profits from overseas sales.

Since they first began to influence international business in the 1960s, multinationals have evolved in some important ways. First, these companies are no longer exclusively U.S. based. Today it is as likely for a multinational to be based in Japan, Germany, or Great Britain as in the United States. Second, multinationals no longer think of their foreign operations as mere outsourcing appendages to carry out design, production, and engineering ideas conceived at home. Instead, they encourage constant exchanges of ideas, capital, and technologies among all of their global operations.

Many multinationals, including IBM, Gillette, and Xerox, have spread their operations so far that they now generate more than half of their sales abroad. Also, multinationals often employ huge foreign workforces relative to their American staffs. Over half of Ford and IBM employees work at locations outside the United States.

These workforces no longer function merely as sources of cheap labor. On the contrary, many multinationals center technically complex activities in locations throughout the world. Texas Instruments, for example, does much of its research, development, design, and manufacturing in east Asia. In fact, U.S. multinationals now bring increasing streams of product innovations back to the United States from their foreign facilities.

Multinational corporations, based in both the United States and foreign countries, are investing in overseas operations at a rapid pace. In a recent year, these outlays rose 40 percent to $315 billion, most of it spent in big, industrial economies rather than developing nations. Of the $315 billion, only $100 billion went to developing countries, with China getting $38 billion. U.S. corporations, the largest investors, spent $96 billion in direct investments.[59]

Multinationals have become global organizations that reflect the interdependence of world economies, the growth of international competition, and the globalization of world markets. Procter & Gamble, the 12th-largest U.S. multinational, illustrates this kind of global strategy. The company derives half of its revenues and one-third of its net profits from foreign operations; it holds 43 percent of its assets overseas. P&G's Tide detergent has become a market leader in Canada, Saudi Arabia, and Morocco as well as in the United States, and it sells well in Russia and China, too. Joy dishwashing liquid leads the market in Japan. The company's Head & Shoulders, Oil of Olay, and Old Spice brands have also achieved growing global popularity.

As Figure 4.8 illustrates, P&G's international marketing strategies resemble its domestic programs. This German ad for Clearasil acne medicine focuses on benefits by showing the distorted face of a worried, pimple-plagued teenager in a before-and-after illustration that emphasizes the satisfaction of the Clearasil user.

Procter & Gamble implements a variety of marketing strategies in its international operations. It acquires major local brands to supplement its own production facilities around the world. Recently, it bought the two leading bleach brands in Latin America, Lavan San and Magia Blanca, to enter the $600 million Latin American market for this laundry product. Among its new manufacturing facilities are plants in Belgium, Brazil, China, the Philippines, Thailand, and Vietnam.

P&G regards its role as a global citizen as a serious obligation and supports charities and social programs in communities around the world. The firm's gifts include donations to antidrug programs and sponsorship of educational programs in the United Kingdom and the Czech Republic; Project Hope, which builds schools in rural China; and the Girl's Literacy program in India.[60]

DEVELOPING AN INTERNATIONAL MARKETING STRATEGY

Like domestic firms, international marketers must follow the steps in the marketing planning process (described in Chapter 5). They should assess organizational strengths and weaknesses, study environmental conditions, set marketing objectives, select target markets, and develop marketing mixes that will satisfy their chosen targets.

In developing a marketing mix, an international competitor's marketers may choose between two alternative approaches: a global marketing strategy or a multidomestic marketing strategy. A **global marketing strategy** defines a standard marketing mix and implements it with minimal modifications in all foreign markets. This approach brings the advantage of economies of scale in production and marketing activities. Procter & Gamble follows a global marketing strategy for Pringles potato chips, its leading export brand. The company sells one product with a consistent formulation in every country. Unlike Frito-Lay's Cheetos snacks, which come in flavors geared to local tastes, P&G meets 80 percent of worldwide demand with only six flavors of Pringles. The brand relies on one package design throughout the world. This standard saves money by allowing large-scale production and reinforces the brand's image. Also, similar advertising around the world features the slogan, "Once you pop, you can't stop." P&G intends all of these tactics to build strong global brand equity for Pringles.[61]

A global strategy can effectively market some goods and services to certain market segments that are common to many nations. The approach works especially well for products with strong, universal appeal, such as Coca-Cola. The global strategy can also effectively appeal to upscale consumers everywhere. Seagram's global billboard advertising campaign promotes its Chivas Regal scotch.

Most firms would like to follow the lead of P&G and The Coca-Cola Co. and implement global marketing strategies. For one benefit, a standard marketing mix limits costs. Most firms, however, must practice market segmentation outside their home markets and tailor their marketing mixes to fit the unique needs of customers in specific countries. This **multidomestic marketing strategy** assumes that differences between the market characteristics and competitive situations in specific nations require firms to customize their marketing decisions to effectively reach individual marketplaces. (This strategy is sometimes mistakenly called *multinational* marketing. In fact, a multinational corporation may combine both strategies in its international marketing.)

Many marketing experts feel that most products demand multidomestic marketing strategies to give them realistic global marketing appeals. They cite differences

Figure 4.8 German Promotion for Procter & Gamble's Clearasil

Das Gefühl, einen Pickel
zu kriegen, ist oft hart.
It works!
Clearasil

Marketing Dictionary

global marketing strategy A standardized marketing mix with minimal modifications that guides marketing decisions in all of a firm's domestic and foreign markets.

multidomestic marketing strategy A program of market segmentation that identifies specific foreign markets and tailors the marketing mix to match specific traits in each nation.

Figure 4.9 **Alternative International Product and Promotional Strategies**

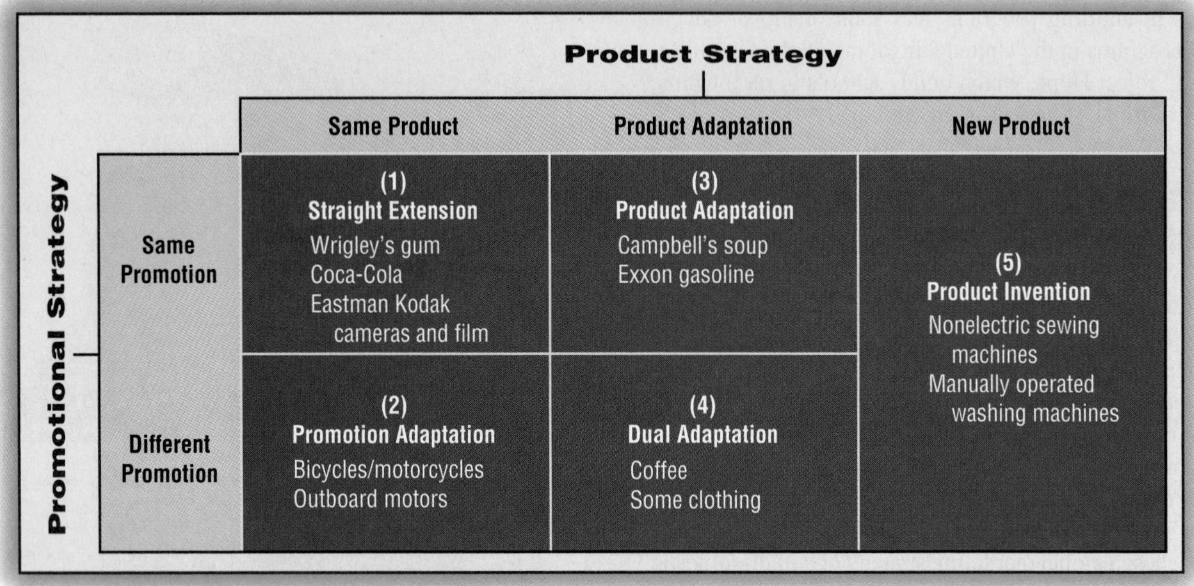
Product Strategy
Same Product
Product Adaptation
New Product
Promotional Strategy
Same Promotion
Different Promotion
(1) Straight Extension
Wrigley's gum
Coca-Cola
Eastman Kodak cameras and film
(3) Product Adaptation
Campbell's soup
Exxon gasoline
(5) Product Invention
Nonelectric sewing machines
Manually operated washing machines
(2) Promotion Adaptation
Bicycles/motorcycles
Outboard motors
(4) Dual Adaptation
Coffee
Some clothing

among societies that prevent successful widespread globalization of marketing strategies. Marketers should base this decision on their own products and the countries they want to serve. Specific situations may allow them to standardize some parts of the marketing process while they must customize others. For example, they may market standard products, but promotions or packages may change.

Companies practice multidomestic marketing for a variety of reasons, both bad and good. Many carry over regional strategies from old, decentralized international marketing organizations. Clearly, continuity with the past is not the best standard for marketing decisions. Because a multidomestic strategy raises costs as compared with a global strategy, marketers should vary their strategies between markets only when the incremental revenues that the changes generate exceed their incremental expenses. This principle is particularly important for marketers of consumer nondurable goods.

A company's strategy choices can determine its success in international markets. For example, the two leading battery companies, Duracell and Eveready, compete using different international marketing strategies. Duracell has established a global brand produced in European manufacturing facilities. Eveready did not consolidate under its Energizer brand but kept its many local brands and production facilities.

http://www.duracell.com/
http://www.eveready.com/

Because alkaline batteries are a product that can be marketed successfully using a standardized approach, the global advertising and brand strategy paid off. Overseas sales generate 50 percent of Duracell's revenues, and the company controls 42 percent of the worldwide alkaline battery market, compared to Eveready's 24 percent. Duracell also has a technological advantage and introduced appealing innovations like freshness dating and built-in power gauges on packages. Eveready subsequently decided to follow Duracell's lead and consolidate its alkaline battery brands, but it still lags its rival. Now that Duracell has saturated the European market, it is pushing into China. Its large Chinese plant will provide a good distribution point for the rest of Asia. It gains another benefit through cost advantages, because the Chinese government charges no tariffs on locally produced batteries.[62]

International Product and Promotional Strategies

International marketers can choose among five strategies for matching their product and promotion decisions to the needs of a specific foreign market. As Figure 4.9 indicates, the strategies differ in their arrangements to extend domestic product and promotional strategies into international markets or to adapt one or both to meet each target market's unique requirements.

A firm typically follows a one-product, one-message **straight extension** strategy as part of a global marketing strategy like Coca-Cola's. This strategy permits economies of scale in production and marketing. Also, successful im-

Figure 4.10 **Promotion Adaptation Strategy in International Marketing**

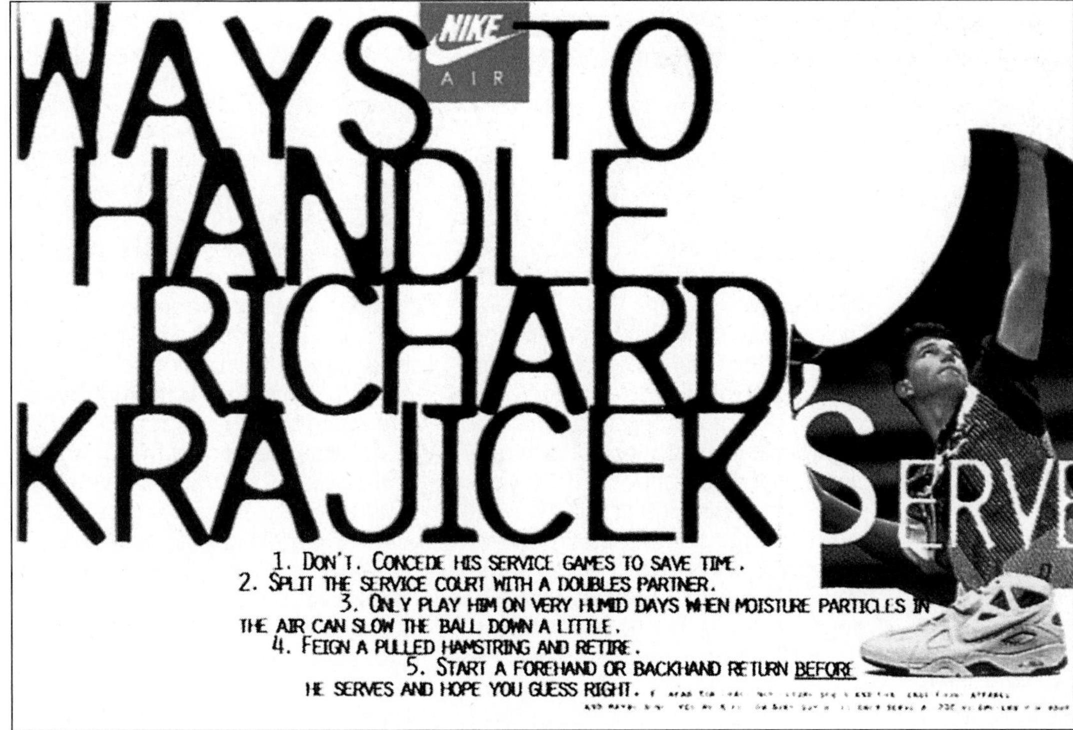
NIKE
AIR
WAYS TO HANDLE RICHARD KRAJICEK'S SERVE
1. DON'T. CONCEDE HIS SERVICE GAMES TO SAVE TIME.
2. SPLIT THE SERVICE COURT WITH A DOUBLES PARTNER.
3. ONLY PLAY HIM ON VERY HUMID DAYS WHEN MOISTURE PARTICLES IN THE AIR CAN SLOW THE BALL DOWN A LITTLE.
4. FEIGN A PULLED HAMSTRING AND RETIRE.
5. START A FOREHAND OR BACKHAND RETURN BEFORE HE SERVES AND HOPE YOU GUESS RIGHT.

plementation creates universal recognition of a product for consumers from country to country.

Other strategies call for **product adaptation, promotion adaptation,** or both. While bicycles, motorcycles, and outboard motors primarily form part of the market for recreational vehicles in the United States, they may represent important basic transportation modes in other nations. Consequently, producers of these products may adapt their promotional messages even if they sell the product without changes.

Nike markets tennis shoes in Europe through methods similar to those it uses in the United States; minor promotional adaptations accommodate language differences and attitudes toward particular celebrities in specific markets. As Figure 4.10 illustrates, European ads shy away from such U.S. stars as Andre Agassi, Michael Chang, and Pete Sampras. Instead, this ad, which appeared throughout Europe, features the deadly 125-mph serve of Dutch tennis player Richard Krajicek.

In contrast, Exxon successfully applied its promotional theme "Put a Tiger in Your Tank" in dozens of nations, even though it reformulated the gasoline to adapt to varying weather conditions and engine specifications in different countries. Sometimes, international marketers must change both the product and the promotional message in a **dual adaptation** strategy to meet the unique needs of specific international markets. Coffee marketers, such as Nestlé with its Nescafe brand, develop different blends and promotional campaigns to match consumer preferences in different countries.

Recall the discussion earlier in the chapter about the effect of cultural values in the Middle East on promotional strategies. A country's government regulations may also influence promotional strategy. China's tough advertising laws prohibit exaggerated claims and comparative advertising. For example, Anheuser-Busch couldn't market Budweiser beer under its slogan "King of Beers," because regulators considered the statement an exaggeration; ads could describe Bud as America's favorite beer only if the company offered statistics to prove the claim.[63]

Marketing Dictionary

straight extension An international product and promotional strategy that introduces the same product marketed in the home market to a foreign market using the same promotional strategy.

product adaptation An international product and promotional strategy that calls for product modifications to suit a foreign market, but no changes in promotional strategy.

promotion adaptation An international product and promotional strategy that introduces a product without changes to a foreign market supported by a unique promotional strategy targeted to that new market.

dual adaptation An international product and promotional strategy that modifies both product and promotional strategies to suit individual foreign markets.

MARKETING HALL OF SHAME

Piracy Is Not the Sincerest Form of Flattery

Microsoft Corp., America's software Goliath, spent years successfully squashing competitors that challenged its supremacy in the computer world. But thousands of miles away in rural Chinese hamlets, cunning outlaws are easily outfoxing Microsoft.

Every year, Chinese criminals illegally reproduce billions of dollars worth of American software, music, and movies in small, often nameless factories. By some estimates, these secretive counterfeiting operations produce 54 million illegal software packages each year, cutting deeply into the revenues of American corporations like Microsoft. "This is costing us tens of millions of dollars outside China," laments Bill Gates, Microsoft's founder and chief executive officer.

Redmond, Washington-based Microsoft unleashed an army of attorneys to tackle the problem. Yet one of Microsoft's legal triumphs illustrates the frustrations of navigating China's Byzantine court system. Microsoft registered a win when it pursued a trademark-infringement case in China's two-year-old Intellectual Property Tribunal of the Beijing Intermediate People's Court. But the legal award—a paltry $2,600—will barely cover one attorney's round-trip ticket from Seattle to Beijing. The result could have been worse; in a similar trademark infringement suit, victorious Disney pocketed $91.

Unfortunately, suing heads the list of the few legal options through which American companies can fight Chinese outlaws. "We never had any illusions that if we spent zillions of dollars bringing cases, we could stop the piracy," says Eric H. Smith, president of the Washington-based International Intellectual Property Alliance. "But part of our strategy is to test the system."

Whether they like it or not, American marketers must rely primarily upon the U.S. government's diplomatic efforts to bring true relief. The federal government has repeatedly mentioned trade sanctions against China, but so far it has

In the final strategy alternative, **product invention,** a firm may decide to develop an entirely different product to take advantage of a unique foreign market opportunity. For example, to match user needs in developing nations, an appliance manufacturer might introduce a hand-powered washing machine even though such products became obsolete in industrialized countries many years ago.

Distribution Strategy

Distribution is a vital aspect of overseas marketing. Marketers must set up proper channels and anticipate extensive physical distribution problems. Foreign markets may offer poor transportation systems and warehousing facilities or none at all. International marketers must adapt promptly and efficiently to these situations in order to profit from overseas sales.

A distribution decision involves two steps. First, the firm must decide on a method of entering the foreign market. Second, it must determine how to distribute the product within the foreign market through that entry channel.

Distribution decisions balance many factors, including the nature of the firm's products, consumer tastes and buying habits, market competition, and transportation options. The Coca-Cola Co. wanted to improve sales of its juice unit's products in Europe through better distribution. It formed a jointly owned and operated company with Groupe Danone of France to distribute Minute Maid orange juice in European supermarkets. This move essentially duplicates its U.S. strategy to create alliances with large dairy networks in the foreign markets. Coca-Cola can also expand into the higher-priced refrigerated juice market using existing production facilities and delivery networks. Most of its investment will pay for marketing programs to encourage Europeans to boost their consumption of orange juice, which lags that of Americans. The agreement will improve Minute Maid's competitive position against Seagram's Tropicana brand, which has been making inroads into global markets.[64]

Pricing Strategy

Pricing can critically affect the success of an overall marketing strategy for foreign markets. Considerable competitive, economic, political, and legal constraints often limit pricing decisions. Global marketers can succeed only if they thoroughly understand these requirements.

Companies must adapt their pricing strategies to local markets and change them when conditions change. Until recently, foreign products carried premium prices in Japan. A wool sweater from J. Crew, with a U.S. price of $48, sold for $130 in Japan. But as Japan's recession turned many lo-

hesitated to follow through on the threats. China signed an accord with the U.S. government promising to tightly regulate compact disk plants, but American firms have every reason to question China's sincerity. A raid on a laser disk factory organized by Chinese authorities and Microsoft Corp. found no copyright monitors on duty as required. What's more, no codes on the disks identified where they were manufactured, and workers were producing CD-ROMs on three unauthorized presses.

Under increasing American pressure, the Chinese government has made some genuine efforts to stem the piracy. It tormented Chinese retailers, who sell the contraband, with some 3,200 raids that uncovered 2 million unauthorized CDs. In one highly publicized case, the confiscated CDs were crushed by a road-paving machine.

Efforts to corral the manufacturers of this contraband, however, have yielded less success. Remote counterfeiting factories, often the sole enterprises in small villages, inspire pride in the locals. What's more, these renegades are backed by groups that extract kickbacks, such as the People's Liberation Army. "It's a cash issue," says a Clinton administration official. "For a relatively modest investment, localities can achieve big gains."

If left unchecked, these lawless entrepreneurs can cause unknown amounts of economic damage. At this point, software companies like Microsoft are watching with dread as some counterfeiters turn their focus from music to software. One Chinese disk, retailing for as little as $5, can hold dozens of software titles worth $10,000.

QUESTIONS FOR CRITICAL THINKING

1. **Can you suggest any solutions to this massive counterfeiting problem?**
2. **Some believe that the U.S. government should impose trade sanctions on China to protest its lackluster crackdown on counterfeiters. Do you think this action would ultimately reduce the counterfeiting trade? Why?**

Sources: "Global Study Shows Increase in Software Units Pirated," May 7, 1997, Software Publishers Association, downloaded from http://www.spa.org/, May 14, 1997; Joyce Barnathan, "A Pirate under Every Rock," *Business Week,* June 17, 1996, pp. 50–51; Susan Moffatt, "China's Crackdown on CD Counterfeiting: Too Little, Too Late?" *Fortune,* March 3, 1996, p. 32; and Linda Himelstein, "See You in Chinese Court," *Business Week,* February 27, 1995, p. 48.

cal consumers into bargain shoppers, companies had to cut prices there. Faced with increased competition from the Gap and Eddie Bauer, J. Crew dropped its sweater price to $72, 150 percent of the U.S. price—the same "fair pricing" policy practiced by the other stores. General Electric slashed prices on its refrigerators up to 70 percent.[65]

In an important development for international pricing strategy, commodity marketing organizations have periodically tried to control prices through collective action. The Organization of Petroleum Exporting Countries (OPEC) is the best example of this kind of collective export organization, but many others mirror OPEC's efforts for various products.

Countertrade In a growing number of nations, the only way a marketer can gain access to foreign markets is through **countertrade—**a form of exporting in which a firm barters products rather than selling them for cash. Less developed nations sometimes impose countertrade requirements when they lack sufficient foreign currency to attain goods and services they want or need from exporting countries. These countries allow sellers to exchange their products only for domestic products as a way to control their balance-of-trade problems.

Countertrade became popular in the 1980s, when companies wanted to do business with the former USSR and eastern European countries. Those governments did not allow exchanges of hard currency, so this form of barter facilitated trade. PepsiCo made one of the largest countertrades ever when it exchanged $3 billion of Pepsi Cola for Russian Stolichnaya vodka and a freighter and tankers from the former Soviet Union.

Estimating the actual volume of countertrade as a percentage of world trade is difficult, but the American Countertrade Association puts the figure at about 25 percent. Countertraders include large multinational firms like General Electric and PepsiCo. Almost half of the Fortune 500 companies now practice countertrade in response to increasing global competition. Although countertrade is still

Marketing Dictionary

product invention An international product and promotion strategy to develop a new product supported by a new promotional strategy to take advantage of a unique foreign opportunity.

countertrade A form of exporting in which sellers barter their goods and services rather than exchanging them for cash.

Figure 4.11 **The Honda Accord: Made in America**

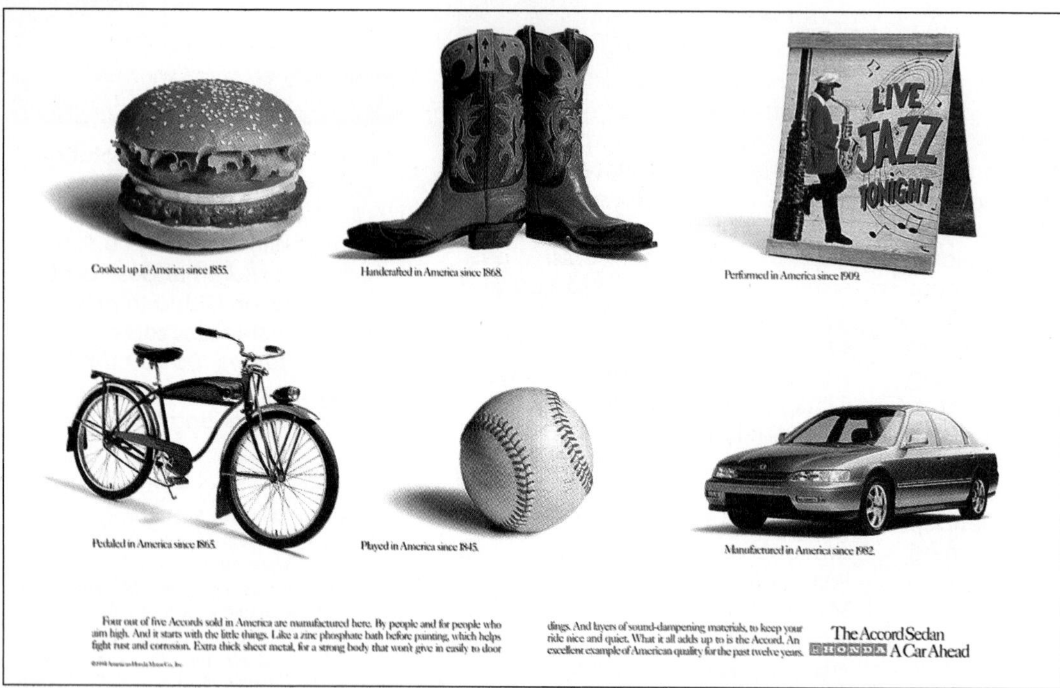
LIVE
JAZZ
TONIGHT
Cooked up in America since 1855.
Handcrafted in America since 1868.
Performed in America since 1909.
Pedaled in America since 1865.
Played in America since 1845.
Manufactured in America since 1982.
Four out of five Accords sold in America are manufactured here. By people and for people who aim high. And it starts with the little things. Like a zinc phosphate bath before painting, which helps fight rust and corrosion. Extra thick sheet metal, for a strong body that won't give in easily to door dings. And layers of sound-dampening materials, to keep your ride nice and quiet. What it all adds up to is the Accord. An excellent example of American quality for the past twelve years.
The Accord Sedan
HONDA A Car Ahead

Figure 4.11 claims that Honda's Marysville, Ohio, assembly plant turns out four of every five Accords sold in America.

Steadily climbing foreign ownership of U.S. assets now totals well over $1 trillion. Annual investments peaked in 1988 at almost $73 billion but then dropped through the early 1990s to just over $15 billion in 1992. Today, foreign investment in the United States has risen to about $60 billion a year. Acquisitions account for about 85 percent of the total, with the rest funding launches of new companies. Foreign drug companies have actively acquired U.S. pharmaceutical companies for their research capabilities and to achieve economies of scale in worldwide production. European banks are also acquiring U.S. financial institutions to gain access to U.S. capital markets.[67]

The leading countries in terms of foreign investments in U.S. assets are the United Kingdom, the Netherlands, and Japan. Among the foreign investments that recently attracted public attention, Hoechst AG of Germany spent $7.1 billion to purchase U.S. drug manufacturer Marion Merrill Dow. Also, Canada's Seagram Co. purchased 80 percent ownership of entertainment conglomerate MCA from Japan's Matsushita Electric Industrial for $5.7 billion, and British Telecom acquired MCI for over $20 billion. Other major U.S. companies owned by foreign firms include:

- Columbia Pictures and Universal Studios, owned by Sony Corp. (Japan)
- Pillsbury, Burger King, Heublein, Pearle Vision, and Pet Inc., owned by Grand Metropolitan (United Kingdom)
- A&W Brands and Dr Pepper/Seven Up Cos., owned by Cadbury Schweppes (United Kingdom)
- Maybelline and Cosmair cosmetics, owned by L'Oréal (a French company owned by the Swiss conglomerate Nestlé S.A.)

growing at 10 to 12 percent a year, its rate of increase has slowed. One reason is improved economic conditions in other countries—for example, in Latin America—that allow buyers to pay cash.

Small companies also engage in countertrade. Cross Pointe Paper, a Wisconsin paper manufacturer, found itself with about 400 tons of its Woodland brand earth-tone, textured paper because consumer tastes moved toward brighter colors. Using the services of countertrade broker Atwood Richards, Cross Pointe exchanged the paper for $400,000 in credits. The broker sold the paper in Asia, where earth tones remained popular. Cross Pointe, in turn, exchanged its credits for wood fiber and filler it needed to make its papers.[66]

THE UNITED STATES AS A TARGET FOR INTERNATIONAL MARKETERS

Foreign marketers regard America as an inviting target. It offers a large population, high levels of discretionary income, political stability, a generally favorable attitude toward foreign investment, and relatively well-controlled economic ills.

Among the best-known industries where foreign manufacturers have established U.S. production facilities is automobiles. Most of the world's leading auto companies have built assembly facilities in the United States: BMW in South Carolina, Toyota in Kentucky, Nissan in Tennessee, Honda in Ohio, and Mercedes-Benz in Alabama. The ad in

- ▼ Stop & Shop, BI-LO, First National, and Tops supermarkets, owned by Royal Ahold (Netherlands)
- ▼ Brown & Williamson Tobacco, owned by B.A.T. Industries (United Kingdom)
- ▼ Citgo Petroleum, owned by Petróleos de Venezuela (Venezuela)[68]

Among the many companies expanding in the U.S. market is Shiseido, Japan's largest cosmetics company. Its major overseas push requires a boost in manufacturing capacity, so it has added a fourth U.S. factory. Shiseido's global strategy includes acquiring local brands and developing new brands for overseas markets; the firm intends to raise overseas sales to 25 percent of its total by 2000. The company will focus on skin care and makeup in the U.S. market and perfume products in Europe.[69]

Foreign multinationals will probably continue to invest in U.S. assets as they seek to produce goods locally and control channels of distribution. Honda now generates 42 percent of its revenues from the United States, and Seagram gets 81 percent. Belgium's Delhaize supermarkets earn about 65 percent of total revenues from the Food Lion grocery chain.[70]

ACHIEVEMENT CHECK SUMMARY

Reread the learning goals that follow, and consider the questions for each goal. Answering these questions will reinforce your grasp of the most important concepts in the chapter and allow you to check how well you have achieved these learning goals. Where a blank appears before a question, answer with *T* or *F;* for multiple-choice questions, circle the letter of the correct answer.

Objective 4.1: Describe the importance of international marketing from the perspectives of the individual firm and the nation.
1. ___ When companies import, they purchase goods and services from overseas companies.
2. ___ International trade has a minimal effect on the growth of GDP and employment in the United States.
3. ___ Because buyers behave similarly in most industrialized countries, firms can use the same strategies for international and domestic marketing.
Objective 4.2: Identify the major components of the environment for international marketing.
1. ___ The exchange rate in a foreign country can influence a firm's pricing strategy.
2. ___ Companies must comply with the same laws in the United States and in foreign countries where they operate.
3. ___ A quota on the number of cars the United States can sell in Brazil is an example of (a) a revenue tariff; (b) a protective tariff; (c) an administrative barrier; (d) an embargo.
Objective 4.3: Compare alternative strategies for entering international markets.
1. ___ Most companies first enter international markets by entering contractual agreements.
2. ___ When Compaq Computer arranges with a Taiwanese firm to produce components used in its computers, it engages in (a) exporting; (b) foreign licensing; (c) direct investment; (d) subcontracting.
3. ___ The rate of international direct investment by U.S. multinational corporations is decreasing.
Objective 4.4: Differentiate between a global marketing strategy and a multidomestic marketing strategy.
1. ___ Because The Coca-Cola Co. believes that tastes around the world are sufficiently homogeneous to allow the effective use of standard marketing strategies everywhere, it practices global marketing.
2. ___ By selling different-sized packages of Cheetos in Asia and in the United States, PepsiCo practices multidomestic marketing.
3. ___ A company should choose a multidomestic strategy if (a) it has already created a regional, decentralized international marketing organization; (b) it produces consumer goods; (c) the added revenues of the move will cover the added expenses; (d) it costs less than global marketing.
Objective 4.5: Describe the marketing mix strategies that international marketers implement.
1. ___ Pringle's global marketing strategy using the standard slogan "Once you pop, you can't stop" is an example of promotion adaptation.
2. ___ When U.S. automakers produce cars, trucks, and sport-utility vehicles with the steering wheels on the right side for sale in the United Kingdom and Japan, they are (a) implementing a straight extension strategy; (b) introducing a new product; (c) adapting their products to meet local needs.
3. ___ *Countertrade* refers to pricing terms that allow buyers to pay for goods in currencies other than those of their own countries.
Objective 4.6: Explain the attractiveness of the U.S. market as a target for foreign marketers.
1. ___ Because the United States is considered a mature market for many goods, foreign investors no longer want to acquire businesses here.

2. ___ One reason foreign companies like to invest in the United States is to improve channels of distribution.
3. ___ The U.S. business environment is hostile to foreign investment.

Students: See the solutions section located on page S-1 to check your responses to the Achievement Check Summary.

Key Terms

exporting
importing
infrastructure
exchange rate
friendship, commerce, and navigation (FCN) treaty
tariff
import quota
embargo
exchange control
dumping
General Agreement on Tariffs and Trade (GATT)
World Trade Organization (WTO)
North American Free-Trade Agreement (NAFTA)
franchising
foreign licensing
joint venture
multinational corporation
global marketing strategy
multidomestic marketing strategy
straight extension
product adaptation
promotion adaptation
dual adaptation
product invention
countertrade

Review Questions

1. Why is the global marketplace so important to international marketers? Cite examples of highly successful competitors in the global market. Why do you think these firms succeed?
2. How does the international marketplace differ from the domestic marketplace? In your answer, specifically examine differences in market sizes and buyer behavior.
3. Name the major variables in the global marketing environment. Explain how each influences marketing decision making.
4. List the components of the political-legal environment for U.S. firms operating abroad. Specifically discuss FCN treaties, the Export Trade Act of 1982, and the Foreign Corrupt Practices Act.
5. What major barriers inhibit international trade? Explain how a government can manipulate trade restrictions to either restrict or stimulate international marketing activities. Also explain the role of the WTO.
6. Explain the practice of dumping. Why does dumping sometimes occur?
7. Describe the process through which the world moves toward growing economic interdependence. Relate this trend to the emergence of free-trade pacts in North America and Europe.
8. Identify the basic market-entry strategies in international business. What factors should guide marketers' selection of an entry strategy?
9. Outline the basic premises behind the operation of a multinational corporation. Why have many of these organizations become global firms?
10. Differentiate between a global marketing strategy and a multidomestic marketing strategy. In what ways is the international marketing mix most likely to differ from a marketing mix for the domestic market?

Discussion Questions

1. Relate specific environmental considerations to each of the following aspects of a firm's international marketing mix:
   a. brands and warranties
   b. advertising
   c. distribution channels
   d. discounts to intermediaries
   e. placement of comparative advertising
2. Give a hypothetical or actual example of a firm operating at each of the following levels of international marketing:
   a. exporting
   b. franchising
   c. foreign licensing
   d. joint venture
   e. acquisition
3. As marketers develop strategies to sell their goods and services in China, they must choose product and promotional strategies. Give examples of products that you would market using (a) straight extension; (b) product adaptation; and (c) promotion adaptation. Explain why you chose each strategy.
4. As a major exporter of citrus fruit, Israel wants to increase its market share in Europe. The Citrus Marketing Board of Israel hires local ad agencies to differentiate its agricultural commodities and create a brand identity. Through market research, it has identified consumer taste preferences in different countries. For example, the French prefer Jaffa Sunrise grapefruit with its red color. The campaign uses the slogan "Passes au Rouge" ("Move over to Red"). The British perceive oranges as hard to peel, so ads stress the ease of peeling Israeli-grown oranges. At home, the board takes an entirely different approach. Since younger Israelis consider oranges old-fashioned, domestic ads counter this image by featuring young, attractive models and using the tagline, "Strip an orange." Describe how local environmental conditions might affect marketing campaigns. Discuss the overall marketing strategy and specific marketing mix strategies of the Israeli Citrus Marketing Board.
5. Some people argue for limits on foreign investment in the United States. Would you support a plan that would limit an investment by foreign firms or individuals in a particular firm to some specified amount? Do other nations have a right to limit American investments in their countries? Explain your answer.

'netWork

1. Many companies have decided to "go international." Obviously, this strategic decision requires employees to travel outside the United States. The U.S. Department of State maintains a home page that provides useful information for international business travelers at

http://travel.state.gov/

Visit that home page, and critically evaluate the information it provides. What information would give especially pertinent support to an international marketer? What additional information should the Web site offer?

2. Controversy continues to swirl around the NAFTA international trade agreement. Go to the NAFTA home page at

http://iepnt1.itaiep.doc.gov/nafta/nafta2.htm/

and evaluate the advice it offers for doing business in Canada and/or Mexico. If you were a U.S. business specializing in perishable consumer products (perhaps Ben & Jerry's), would you choose to market your products in Canada or Mexico? Justify your response.

3. Global communications over the Internet must obviously involve many languages. Several software publishers offer programs that translate Web page information into various languages. Go to

http://www.accentsoft.com/

and determine what services and programs the company offers. What problems and opportunities might these programs create for a company? Should U.S. marketers consider the activities of these programs when designing their Web advertising?

VIDEO CASE 4

BUILDING A GLOBAL COMPETITIVE ADVANTAGE

Within a few months after becoming CEO of Whirlpool Corp. in 1987, David Whitwam met with his senior managers to plot a strategy for securing future company growth. At the time, Whirlpool was the market leader among U.S. appliance makers, but it generated only weak sales outside North America. Operating in a mature market, it faced the same low profit margins as major competitors like General Electric and Maytag.

Whitwam and his management team explored several growth options, including diversifying into other industries experiencing more rapid growth, such as furniture or garden products; restructuring the company financially; and expanding vertically and horizontally. The group sharpened its focus to consider opportunities for expanding the appliance business beyond North American markets. After all, the basics of managing the appliance business and the product technologies are similar in Europe, North America, Asia, and Latin America. As Whitwam put it, "We were very good at what we did. What we needed was to enter appliance markets in other parts of the world and learn how to satisfy different kinds of customers."

Whirlpool industry data predicted that, over time, appliance manufacturing would become a global industry. As Whitwam saw it, his company had three options: "We could ignore the inevitable—a decision that would have condemned Whirlpool to a slow death. We could wait for globalization to begin and then try to react, which would have put us in a catch-up mode, technologically and organizationally. Or we could control our own destiny and try to shape the very nature of globalization in our industry. In short, we could force our competitors to respond to us."

Whitwam and his team chose the third option and set out on a mission to make Whirlpool "one company worldwide." They aimed much higher than simply marketing products or operating around the globe. For decades, Whirlpool had sold some appliances in other countries to buyers who could afford them. Whitwam wanted to expand this reach by establishing a vision of a company that could leverage global resources to gain a long-term competitive advantage. In his words, this effort meant "having the best technologies and processes for designing, manufacturing, selling, and servicing your products at the lowest possible costs. Our vision at Whirlpool is to integrate our geographical businesses wherever possible, so that our most advanced expertise in any given area—whether it's refrigeration technology, or distribution strategy—isn't confined to one location or one division. We want to be able to take the best capabilities we have and leverage them in all of our operations worldwide."

As its first step in transforming a largely domestic operation into a global powerhouse, Whirlpool purchased the European appliance business of Dutch consumer-goods giant Philips Electronics. Philips had been losing market share for years running its European operations as independent regional companies that made different appliances for individual markets. "When we bought this business," Whitwam recalls, "we had two automatic washer designs, one built in Italy and one built in Germany. If you as a consumer looked at them, they were basically the same machines. But there wasn't anything common about those two machines. There wasn't even a common screw."

The Whirlpool strategy called for reversing the decline in European market share and improving profitability by changing product designs and manufacturing processes and by switching to centralized purchasing. The change reorganized the national design and research staffs inherited from Philips into European product teams that worked closely with Whirlpool's U.S. designers. Redesigned models shared more parts, and inventory costs fell when Whirlpool consolidated warehouses from 36 to 8. The transformation trimmed Philips's list of 1,600 suppliers by 50 percent, and it converted the national operations to regional companies.

Whitwam believed that the drive to become one company worldwide required making Whirlpool a global brand—a formidable task in Europe, where the name was not well-known. The company rebranded the Philips product lines, supported by a $135 million pan-European advertising campaign that initially presented both the Philips and Whirlpool names and eventually converted to Whirlpool alone.

Another important component of the Whirlpool global strategy—product innovation—sought to develop superior products based on consumer needs and wants. "We have to provide a compelling reason other than price for consumers to buy Whirlpool-built products," says Whitwam. "We can do that only by understanding the consumer better than anyone else does and then translating our understanding into clearly superior product designs, features, and after-sales support. Our goal is for consumers to prefer the Whirlpool brand because it offers greater overall value than competing products."

One successful product innovation led to the Whirlpool Crispwave microwave oven. Extensive research with European consumers revealed a desire for a microwave that could brown and crisp food. In response, Whirlpool engineers designed the VIP Crispwave, which can fry crispy bacon and cook a pizza with a crisp crust. The new microwave proved successful in Europe, and Whirlpool later introduced it in the United States.

Whirlpool's global strategy includes a goal to become the market leader in Asia, which will be the world's largest appliance market in the twenty-first century. In 1988, it began setting up sales and distribution systems in Asia to help it serve Asian markets and to make the firm more familiar with those markets and potential customers. The company established three regional offices: one in Singapore to serve Southeast Asia, a second in Hong Kong to handle the Chinese market, and a Tokyo office for Japan. Through careful analysis, Whirlpool marketers sought to match specific current products with Asian consumers. They studied existing and emerging trade channels and assessed the relative strengths and weaknesses of competitors in the Asian markets. The company set up joint ventures with five Asian manufacturers for four appliance lines with the highest market potential: refrigerators, washers, air conditioners, and microwave ovens. With a controlling interest in each of the joint ventures, the newly global company confidently expects to excel in the world's fastest-growing market.

Whirlpool has come a long way since embarking on its global strategy. Revenues have doubled to more than $8 billion. The company now reaches markets in more than 140 countries, leading the markets in both North America and Latin America. Whirlpool is number three in Europe and the largest Western appliance company in Asia. For building its integrated global network, "Whirlpool gets very high marks," says an industry analyst. "They are outpacing the industry dramatically."

Questions

1. Relate Whirlpool's strategy to the chapter's discussions of alternative global marketing strategies.
2. How might the international marketplace trends discussed in the chapter affect Whirlpool's expansion strategy?
3. Explain how changes in Whirlpool's economic, social-cultural, and political-legal environments might affect its marketing strategy.
4. Whirlpool offers different combinations of product lines to customers in different parts of the world. Visit the whirlpool Web site at:

   http://www.whirlpool.com/

   Review the list of countries where Whirlpool currently operates. Do its products carry the Whirlpool brand name in each country? How might the Internet help the company to increase global brand recognition of the Whirlpool name?

Sources: Portions of this video case were researched from material downloaded from http://www.whirlpool.com/, April 16, 1997.

Part 1 Microsoft Corp.: Becoming the World's Largest Marketer of Computer Software

Authors' Note

Each of the seven parts in *Contemporary Marketing* ends with a case study about Microsoft. The continuing case study of this dominant firm will help you to understand how marketing provides an opportunity to contribute to society and to an individual organization. It will also demonstrate how one company identifies customer needs and satisfies them by developing and executing product, distribution, promotion, and pricing strategies. By focusing on the growth of Microsoft and the enormous success it has achieved in such a comparatively short time, the continuing case will help you integrate the marketing concepts presented throughout the text.

When people talk about Microsoft Corp. and its CEO, William H. Gates III, they tend to speak in superlatives. "I think he's got to be the world's best visionary businessman," offers PeopleSoft Inc. CEO Dave Duffield. Advanced Manufacturing Research executive Bruce Richardson says, "He's probably the savviest guy in recognizing a trend and being able to act on it. He's a genius in recognizing the commercial appeal of things."

> *"I personally believe that Microsoft is the most powerful economic force in the United States," says Eric Schmidt, chief technology officer of Sun Microsystems*

In his early 40s, Bill Gates is credited with a rare combination of technical expertise and marketing acumen, qualities that have made him an extraordinarily effective leader for Microsoft. His status as a global technology pacesetter brought him a recent invitation to address the World Economic Forum, an annual gathering of the world's most powerful business and political leaders. Fiercely competitive, Gates pushes his company hard to win in the marketplace. His energetic drive to succeed has made him the richest person in America with a net worth estimated at $18 billion.

Shares of Microsoft, the world's largest personal computer software company, carry a total stock-market value of $80 billion. Each year since its founding, the company has experienced robust growth in sales and revenues by developing and marketing new products that have led the evolution in personal computing. Over 20,000 employees currently draw paychecks from Microsoft, and the firm generates annual sales of almost $18 billion.

Microsoft's phenomenal success has made the firm the target of recurring charges of unfair competition. These charges have resulted in investigations of Microsoft's pricing, marketing, and management practices by the Federal Trade Commission, the U.S. Department of Justice, and the European Union. These probes have not yet adversely affected the software giant, but one writer promises, "there will always be a new gunslinger on hand, eager to test Microsoft's mettle."

The Visionaries

Bill Gates and Paul Allen met in 1968 as students at Seattle's Lakeside prep school, where they learned computer programming skills. They talked about forming their own software company one day, believing that computers would become as commonplace in people's homes as TVs. The computers would need software, and Gates and Allen intended to supply it. In 1975, the pair founded the company that would allow them to achieve their vision: A computer on every desk and in every home, all running Microsoft software.

Evolving computer technology helped Gates and Allen to realize their vision. In the 1950s, the computer industry was dominated by IBM and other giant companies that produced large, expensive mainframe computers.

Figure 1 **Microsoft Revenues and Workforce: 1976–1997**

Revenue Figures			Number of Employees
1976	$22	thousand	7
1981	$16	million	130
1986	$198	million	1,442
1991	$1.8	billion	8,226
1996	$8.7	billion	20,561
1997	$10	billion	21,298

During the next decade, the development of the semiconductor resulted in development of the smaller and less expensive minicomputer. Intel's introduction of the world's first microprocessor moved computers into their next evolutionary step.

The market that Gates and Allen had anticipated for their software arrived when a New Mexico-based company MITS used Intel's 8080 microprocessor chip in the Altair, the world's first personal computer. After reading the featured article "World's First Microcomputer Kit to Rival Commercial Models" in a 1975 issue of *Popular Electronics,* Gates and Allen saw their opportunity. It took them six weeks to develop their BASIC computer-language program for the Altair. A formal licensing agreement with MITS followed, and Gates joined the MITS president on a public relations tour across the United States to promote the Altair PC and Microsoft's first software product.

When asked recently about the secret to Microsoft's success, Gates admitted that luck played a part. However, he singled out the founders' original vision as the most important element. In his words:

> We glimpsed what lay beyond that Intel 8080 chip and then acted on it. We asked, "What if computing were nearly free?" We believed there would be computers everywhere because of cheap computing power and great new software that would take advantage of it. We set up shop betting on the former and producing the latter when no one else was. . . . We got there first, and our early success gave us the chance to hire smart people. We built a worldwide sales force and used the revenue it generated to find new products. From the beginning we set off down a road that was headed in the right direction.

Building the Business

Microsoft set up offices in Albuquerque in 1975 and started assembling a team of programmers to develop new products for this new type of computer. Known as the Microkids, the programmers were young, creative people with high IQs, high energy levels, and a shared passion for computers. The firm implemented a product strategy focused on expanding its product line by anticipating market needs and then gaining a competitive advantage by releasing a new product before rivals could. As Allen recalls, "Every time there was a new language we thought was going to be popular, we'd see that as another possible market for our software technology."

Gates took personal command of marketing for Microsoft software. Through personal sales calls and attendance at trade shows, he persuaded business customers to package his software together with their equipment.

Gates also signed licensing contracts to supply a version of BASIC for Tandy Corp.'s new TRS-80 and Apple Computer's Apple II. These deals targeted the OEM market, made up of original equipment manufacturers that included Microsoft software as a component in their personal computer packages. "Our basic business strategy was to charge a price so low that microcomputer makers couldn't [produce] the software internally that cheap," says Gates.

By licensing the firm's software at extremely low prices, Microsoft marketers planned to generate profits by selling in large volume. "We adapted our programming languages, such as our version of BASIC, to each machine," says Gates. "We were very responsive to all the hardware manufacturers' requests. We didn't want to give anyone a reason to look elsewhere. We wanted choosing Microsoft software to be a no-brainer."

The strategy worked. Most of Microsoft's revenues

during its early years came from arrangements with OEMs. Ads by the PC marketers often mentioned that Microsoft programming languages accompanied their equipment, and that recognition helped Microsoft's BASIC to become an industry standard.

Gates wanted to ensure that Microsoft's competitive advantage would carry around the globe. In 1977, he entered the Japanese market by signing an agreement with Kuzuhiko Nishi as Microsoft's Far East representative. "I went into Japan only two years after I started Microsoft knowing that in terms of working with hardware companies, that was a great place to be," he recalls. "A lot of great research goes on there. And also it was the most likely source of competition other than the U.S. itself."

At the end of 1978, Gates and Allen moved their growing company to the Seattle area. The following year they set up a consumer products division to develop applications software, laying the foundation for Microsoft's future growth. Software Arts had just introduced its VisiCalc electronic spreadsheet program, and MicroPro had begun selling its WordStar word-processing program. "What we realized was that we needed to be in those markets," said Steve Smith, who joined the company in 1979 as its first marketing director.

The Eighties: A Decade of Explosive Growth

When IBM debuted its entry into the personal computer market in 1981, it included Microsoft's BASIC language program and applications software such as the game Adventure along with a version of MS-DOS, the Microsoft Disk Operating System. Development teams from IBM and Microsoft collaborated on the project for one year prior to the launch of the IBM PC. Since the MS-DOS licensing agreement with IBM did not grant exclusive rights to the software, over the next three years, over 200 PC manufacturers entered into similar agreements, making the operating system the industry standard.

In 1982, Microsoft expanded its marketing base outside the United States by opening its first European sales and marketing office in the United Kingdom. Propelled by expansion in foreign markets and the introduction of new products, Microsoft was experiencing explosive growth. It had more than 200 employees and revenues approaching $25 million by year's end.

The entire personal computer industry was growing so fast that *Time* magazine replaced its annual "Person of the Year" for 1983 with a feature on the PC as "The Machine of the Year." Microsoft was poised to compete in every area of personal computing software. It marketed an operating system—the software that determines the basic functions of the computer, applications products that help users to perform specific tasks, and language tools that programmers need to develop software.

At the 1983 Comdex computer trade show, Microsoft introduced its new word-processing application, Microsoft Word, which would compete with MicroPro's WordStar with 50 percent of the word-processing market at that time. Microsoft's product development team incorporated new graphical user interface (GUI) concepts into Word, such as menus activated by clicks of a mouse. This user-friendly pointing device was new to most attendees, but it would play a major role in Microsoft's next generation of products: Windows. In marketing the Microsoft line of applications software, Gates knew the importance of creating consumer demand for the packages at retail outlets. A $3.5 million promotional campaign supported the launch of Word, including distribution of 450,000 demonstration diskettes in issues of *PC World* magazine.

During 1983, Microsoft continued to expand internationally by establishing subsidiaries in Australia, France, Germany, and South Korea. During that year, Allen left Microsoft after being diagnosed with Hodgkin's disease. He has since recovered and participates actively in professional sports organizations, a high-tech movie production facility, and a Jimi Hendrix museum, in addition to continuing service on the Microsoft board of directors.

Gates realized in the early 1980s that GUI operating systems and applications defined the future of mass-market computing. He explains:

> I didn't believe we would be able to retain our position at the forefront of the software industry if we stuck with MS-DOS, because MS-DOS was character-based. I believed that in the future interfaces would be graphical and that it was essential for Microsoft to move beyond MS-DOS and set a new standard in which pictures and fonts (typefaces) would be part of an easier-to-use interface. In order to realize our vision, PCs had to be made easier to use—not only to help existing customers, but also to attract new ones who wouldn't take the time to learn to work with a complicated interface.

Gates assembled a team of programmers to work on designing the new operating system. The result was Windows 3.1, which was introduced in 1992 and became the new market standard for IBM-compatible PCs.

Anticipating the success of Apple's innovative Macintosh, Gates signed an agreement with Apple Computer to develop several software products for the new PC model. When Apple introduced the Mac in 1984, it came loaded with Microsoft applications, including desktop utilities such as an alarm clock and a calculator.

Throughout the 1980s, Microsoft continued to expand its line with new products and updated versions of older ones. In early 1986, the company moved its headquarters from Seattle to suburban Redmond, Washington. In March of that same year, its stock was listed on the New York

Stock Exchange, and the NASDAQ. By the end of the decade, 4,000 Microsoft employees were designing and marketing products that generated annual revenues of more than $800 million.

Extending the Vision

Microsoft continues to extend its reach into every niche of computing and information technology. Starting as a one-product company, it now markets more than 200 products, from organizational networking systems to software products designed especially for children such as Writer and Fine Artist. By playing a major role in creating the market for personal computers, Microsoft has touched the lives of millions of students, business and home users, and employees throughout the world. In his book *The Road Ahead,* Gates shares his vision of the new age of communications technology:

> We are all beginning another great journey. . . . There is never a reliable map for unexplored territory, but we can learn important lessons from the creation and evolution of the $120 billion personal computer industry. The PC—its evolving hardware, business applications, online systems, Internet connections, electronic mail, multimedia titles, authoring tools, and games—is the foundation for the next revolution. One important lesson Microsoft has learned is that customers have become more demanding about product quality and on-time delivery. In the past, Microsoft has missed delivery deadlines and shipped products with defects due in part to the extreme complexity of the software development process. A major focus of Microsoft during the 1990s is improving its ability to deliver reliable products on time.

Focusing on Satisfying Customers

The technical excellence of such Microsoft products as Windows, PowerPoint presentation software, Microsoft Office for Windows, and Windows NT 3.5 has gained wide recognition in the form of both consumer purchases and industry awards. Since its beginning, the firm has applied numerous quality-management techniques in developing its products.

Microsoft forms small teams of employees from different functional areas to work on development projects. The teams work closely with customers and suppliers, listening to their suggestions for improvements. Market-focused and flexible, the teams are empowered to make decisions and adapt quickly to changing customer needs and market conditions. Team members continually test their products throughout the development process.

A major current focus commits Microsoft to enhance value through quality and customer satisfaction. A Product Improvement Group was formed in 1991 to organize customer feedback and deliver information needed to permit development teams to fix problems, add features, and design products customers really want. The group set up the Microsoft Wish Line to encourage customers to call the company to suggest the features and functions they want.

"One of the reasons our products are so successful is that everybody takes responsibility for them," says a development manager for Word. "You own this thing, you make it great, you're responsible for it."

Microsoft also hires an outside consulting firm to conduct an annual End-User Customer Satisfaction Benchmark Survey. The survey compares Microsoft against its key competitors on product offerings, product support service, and overall satisfaction. Telephone surveys also seek input from customers who call in for product support.

Sharing Its Success

To support its belief that information is the real source of wealth, Microsoft contributes software and funds to a number of educational institutions. In a typical year, the firm donates over $11 million in cash and software worth another $62 million to charitable organizations worldwide. Microsoft partnered with the American Library Association in introducing Libraries Online, a program designed to provide information technology to underfunded libraries. The Microsoft National Scholarship program provides financial assistance for college-bound women and minority students who show a passion for technology and the ability to make a difference in the software industry.

In addition, Gates has dipped into his personal fortune to provide $15 million for a new computer center at Harvard. Another $34 million gift went to the University of Washington and $6 million to Stanford. Gates and Allen have donated $2.2 million to Lakeside, the school where they met and learned programming, for a new science and math center.

Microsoft created the Microsoft Volunteer Program (MVP) to support community work performed by its employees. MVP encourages grass-roots volunteer activities by matching interested employees with volunteer service opportunities. Through KidReach, Microsoft promotes children's access to technology in Canada. The Microsoft Scholar Program trains unemployed information technology professionals in Europe. A computer literacy program for disadvantaged children is offered through Martha's Table in Washington, D.C. In the United States and

Canada, Microsoft matches the charitable gifts of its employees. Microsoft's wide-ranging environmental programs include conservation, reuse, and recycling activities. For example, employees working at Microsoft facilities throughout the Puget Sound headquarters region recycle more than 3,200 tons of materials that would otherwise end up in a landfill.

Questions

1. Business philosopher Peter Drucker identifies the one valid definition of business purpose as creating a customer. Relate Drucker's statement to Bill Gates' vision for Microsoft. Identify the firm's target market and discuss how Microsoft applies each of the marketing mix elements in its marketing strategy.
2. Explain how Microsoft creates value for its customers through quality and customer satisfaction. How does the company measure customer satisfaction?
3. How has Microsoft managed the elements of its external marketing environment?
4. What type of international marketing strategy does Microsoft implement? Identify some modifications that products would need in certain foreign countries.

PART 2

MARKETING PLANNING, INFORMATION, AND SEGMENTATION

CHAPTER 5

MARKETING PLANNING AND FORECASTING

SEARS
explore the many sides of Sears
Spring '97
Netscape: IBM Corp
http://www.ibm.com/
IBM NEWS
PRODUCTS
SUPPORT
LEAD STORY
bandwidth
breakthroughs
Why the web won't collapse
Netscape: World Of Coca-Cola Pavilion
http://www.cocacola.com/
Welcome to The World of Coca-Cola.
(A lot like the real thing in Atlanta but no standing in line.)
Netscape: Borders on the Web
http://www.borders.com/
BORDERS
MUSIC·CAFE
About Borders
Disney.com Home Page
Best of the Web
Web Gallery
Product News

Chapter Objectives

1. Distinguish between strategic planning and tactical planning.
2. Explain how marketing plans differ at various levels in an organization.
3. Identify the steps in the marketing planning process.
4. Describe the concept of SWOT analysis and its four major elements: leverage, problems, constraints, and vulnerabilities.
5. Explain how the strategic business unit concept, the market share/market growth matrix, the market attractiveness/business strength matrix, and spreadsheet analysis can be used in marketing planning.
6. Identify the major types of forecasting methods.
7. Explain the steps in the forecasting process.

Entertainment in Cyberspace: Planning for the Twenty-First Century

Imagine a vacation day that begins with a morning's browse through the galleries at New York's Metropolitan Museum of Art. Afterward, you play a Nintendo-style game against an opponent who lives half a globe away. Later, you pepper Shaquille O'Neal, the Los Angeles Lakers basketball star, with questions about his performance. Tired from your whirlwind day, you finally relax by watching the hottest music videos from your favorite rock singers.

If this schedule sounds preposterous, it isn't. Anybody can cram all of these activities and more into just one day on the screen of a computer hooked up to the Internet. In fact, many cyberspace experts predict that the Internet will become America's playground in the twenty-first century. The giants in the film, music, and toy industries are busily planning new developments including Web sites to keep us entertained.

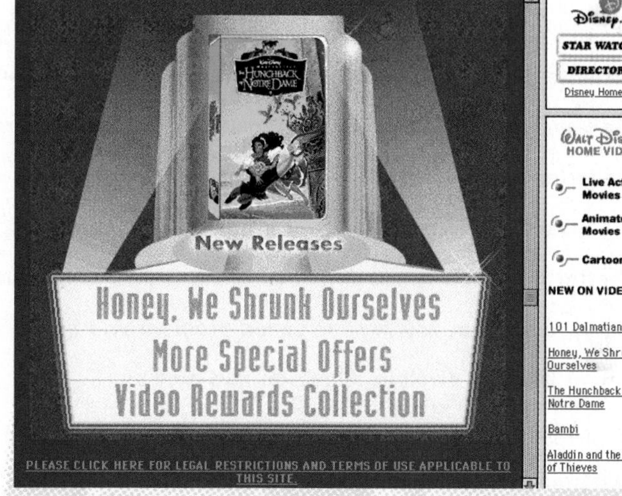
New Releases
Honey, We Shrunk Ourselves
More Special Offers
Video Rewards Collection
PLEASE CLICK HERE FOR LEGAL RESTRICTIONS AND TERMS OF USE APPLICABLE TO THIS SITE.
Disney.com
STAR WATCH
DIRECTORY
Disney Home Video
Walt Disney HOME VIDEO
Live Action Movies
Animated Movies
Cartoons
NEW ON VIDEO!
101 Dalmatians
Honey, We Shrunk Ourselves
The Hunchback of Notre Dame
Bambi
Aladdin and the King of Thieves

Even in the technology's infancy, it offers plenty to keep a cybercruiser amused. Extremely popular sports sites allow fans to chat electronically with stars like O'Neal. Museums download images of their extensive art holdings onto home pages. Kids can preview the hottest new electronic games on their computers.

Not surprisingly, big business has identified some solid financial reasons for entertaining us online. First, companies rush into cyberspace because they fear falling behind competitors in the high-tech race. Marketing executives, however, also love the Internet's demographics. So far, the medium connects them to mostly young and affluent users. One way to keep these desirable customers coming back is to fill their Internet experiences with fun. After grabbing the attention of these online customers, marketers can bombard them with all sorts of promotional messages.

Executives at the Disney Company, for example, see the Internet as a fun way to peddle more products connected with Mickey Mouse and the other members of the growing Disney gang. "We're taking the long-term view," says Dennis Hightower, president of Walt Disney Television and Telecommunications. "The Internet can become a fruitful foothold strategy to acquaint both children and parents to the Disney brand, and begin to build loyalty at an early age." At the main Disney site, created by the Disney Online subsidiary, users can link to a wide assortment of pages with information,

graphics, and video and audio clips on Disney movies, home videos, software products, television shows, books, and theme parks. They can also order merchandise from the online store.

Other companies and institutions have followed similar strategies. For instance, the Whitney Museum of Art, the Pushkin Museum in Moscow, and many others welcome cyberguests with access to their cultural amenities and their gift shops. At the site for Time Warner's Elektra Entertainment Group, a visitor can listen to his or her favorite singer's new song, see the music video, and then instantly order the recording. Kids can sample the latest electronic games from Time Warner's CD-ROM games division through its own site. After kids sign on, the stripe-shirted Waldo, of the *Where's Waldo* books, greets them. If kids like the games they try, their parents can order copies from their computers.

http://www.disney.com/

Industry executives predict success for this type of Internet commerce sugar-coated with entertainment. "Everybody needs and wants to be entertained and informed," says Lee Bailey, president of Bailey Broadcasting in Los Angeles. "People will come online looking for the same things that they look for off line."

Online entertainment will probably get its biggest boost when the Internet's infrastructure can better meet the speed demands of the video game format. In fact, some enthusiastic industry insiders predict that solving the speed problem will finally transform the Internet into a major entertainment medium rivaling television and movies.

What can people expect when they log on in the future? Consumers will enjoy "the ability to interact with people in a more compelling manner, with better graphics as well as with real-time audio and video, versus having to download something," predicts Rick Spence of Dataquest, which follows the computer industry. "That makes for much richer experiences, because the entertainment business isn't based only on text, but on pictures and audio too."[1]

CHAPTER OVERVIEW

- Will a change in the time and date of a performance affect concert attendance?
- Should the company assign its own sales personnel or independent agents to serve a new territory?
- Should the company offer discounts to cash customers? How would credit customers react to this policy?

These questions illustrate the thousands of major and minor decisions that a marketing manager regularly faces. The marketplace changes continually in response to emerging consumer expectations, technological developments, competitors' actions, economic trends, and political-legal events, as well as product innovations and pressures from channel members. Although the causes of these changes often lie outside the marketing manager's control, effective planning can anticipate many of them. Indeed, effective planning often means the difference between success and failure.

Table 5.1 Coca-Cola: Achieving Organizational Objectives by Implementing Marketing Plans

China	India	Indonesia
INVESTMENT[a]: $550 MILLION	INVESTMENT[a]: $820 MILLION	INVESTMENT[a]: $630 MILLION
POLITICAL RISK	POLITICAL RISK	POLITICAL RISK
Beijing has said it will curb Coke's expansion in the future.	Some political factions continue to pledge to run foreign goods out of India.	Foreign investors face a tricky transition when President Suharto passes from the scene.
WORKERS	FRICTION	CULTURE
Coke hires over 100 new workers weekly and is having a difficult time finding fresh recruits.	Coke suffered a dispute with its Indian partner, parle.	Mostly a tea-drinking population.
DISTRIBUTION	DISTRIBUTION	DISTRIBUTION
Because Coke relies on independent wholesalers, it can't control coolers, product displays, and pricing.	Coke uses large tricycles to carry tons of its product down winding, narrow streets.	Coke uses a small army of bicycle-riding delivery people to get the soft drink to relatively remote areas.

[a]Investment estimates through 2000.

This chapter and the next provide a foundation for all subsequent chapters by demonstrating the necessity for effective planning and gathering reliable information. These activities provide a structure within which a firm can take advantage of its unique strengths. Marketing planning specifies both the specific target markets that the firm will serve and the most appropriate marketing mix to satisfy those markets. This chapter examines marketing planning. Chapter 6 discusses market research and marketers' applications of decision-oriented information to plan and implement marketing strategies.

WHAT IS MARKETING PLANNING?

Planning is the process of anticipating future events and conditions and determining courses of action for achieving organizational objectives. As the definition indicates, planning is a continuous process that includes specifying objectives and the actions through which a firm can attain them. The planning process creates a blueprint that specifies the means for achieving organizational objectives. It also defines checkpoints at which comparisons of actual performance with expectations indicate whether current activities are moving the organization toward its objectives.

Marketing planning—implementing planning activities devoted to achieving marketing objectives—establishes the basis for any marketing strategy. Product lines, pricing decisions, selection of appropriate distribution channels, and decisions relating to promotional campaigns all depend on plans formulated within the marketing organization.

Top managers at The Coca-Cola Co. develop plans to accomplish their profitability and market share objectives in an environment of intense competition. The company's current plans call for huge investments in the Asian market, notably in China, India, and Indonesia. The major challenges faced by the world's best-known brand and the financial investments necessary to meet those challenges are shown in Table 5.1. One of the most daunting tasks facing

http://www.cocacola.com/

Marketing Dictionary

planning The process of anticipating future events and conditions and determining the courses of action necessary to achieve organizational objectives.

marketing planning The process of anticipating future events and conditions and determining the courses of action necessary to achieve marketing objectives.

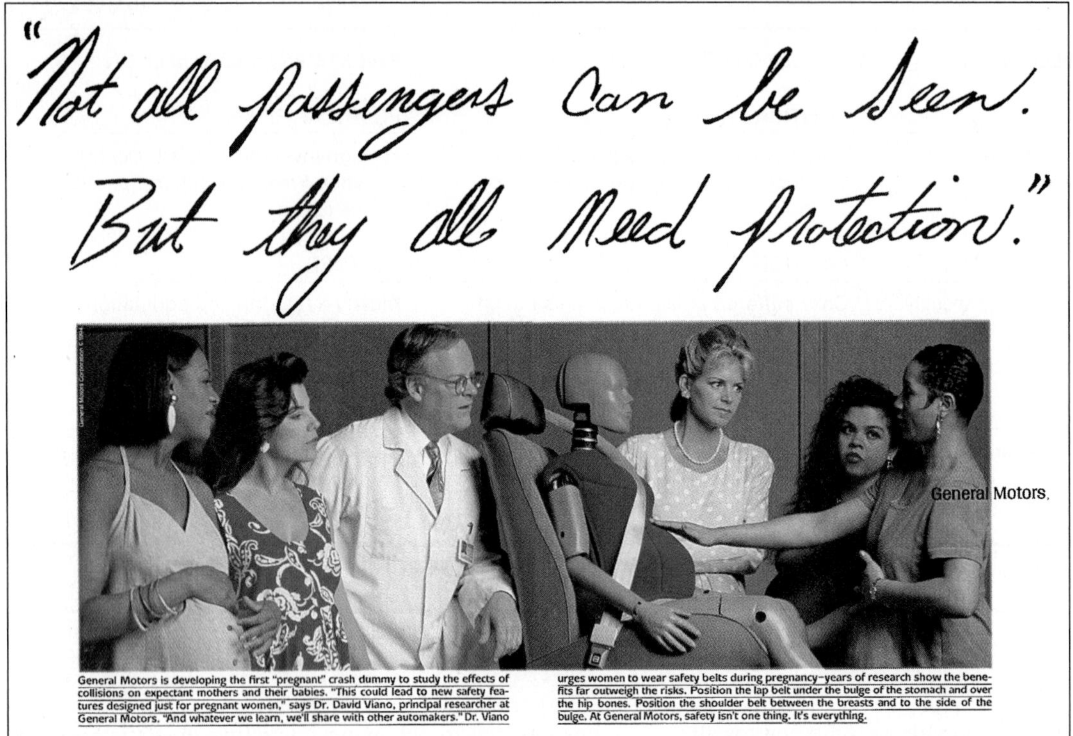
"Not all Passengers Can be Seen.
But they all Need Protection."
General Motors is developing the first "pregnant" crash dummy to study the effects of collisions on expectant mothers and their babies. "This could lead to new safety features designed just for pregnant women," says Dr. David Viano, principal researcher at General Motors. "And whatever we learn, we'll share with other automakers." Dr. Viano urges women to wear safety belts during pregnancy–years of research show the benefits far outweigh the risks. Position the lap belt under the bulge of the stomach and over the hip bones. Position the shoulder belt between the breasts and to the side of the bulge. At General Motors, safety isn't one thing. It's everything.
General Motors.

Figure 5.1 General Motors: Building Relationships with Women Car Buyers

the Atlanta-based multinational is trying to wean Indians from tea and mineral water.

An important trend in marketing planning centers on *relationship marketing.* Recall from Chapter 1 that this term refers to an organization's attempt to develop long-term, cost-effective links with individual customers and suppliers for mutual benefit. Good relationships with customers can arm a firm with vital strategic weapons. Many companies now include relationship-building goals and strategies in their plans. For example, General Motors wants to strengthen its relationships with women, who have increasing clout in vehicle purchases. Chrysler and Ford sell larger percentages of their cars to women than GM does. GM research showed that women expressed neutral attitudes toward the GM brand, while men had stronger positive or negative opinions.

Recognizing strong potential in this market, GM marketers acted proactively to develop relationships with and attract women buyers. GM became a sponsor of "7th on 6th," an annual Manhattan fashion show, and it auctioned five vehicles with designer interiors to raise money for the Concept Cure program to battle breast cancer. Chevrolet sponsored the American Business Women's Association convention, and Cadillac increased its sponsorships of women's events, including the Women's Business Forum. GM targets women through ads featuring women owners like the one in Figure 5.1.[2]

In addition to maintaining databases to track customer preferences, relationship marketers also manipulate spreadsheets, discussed later in this chapter, to answer what-if questions related to prices and marketing performance. Relationship marketing is discussed in greater depth in Chapter 10.

Strategic Planning versus Tactical Planning

Planning is often classified on the basis of its scope or breadth. Some extremely broad plans focus on long-range organizational objectives that will significantly affect the organization for a time period of five or more years. Other, more targeted plans cover the objectives of individual departments or shorter time spans.

Strategic planning can be defined as the process of determining an organization's primary objectives and then adopting courses of action that will eventually achieve them. This process includes, of course, allocation of necessary resources. The word *strategy* is derived from a Greek term meaning "the general's art." Strategic planning has a critical impact on an organization's destiny, because it provides long-term direction for its decision makers.

Big-picture, strategic planning helps companies to create competitive advantages. This process looks for ways to develop new products, expand into unserved areas, and find new markets. Today's strategic planning differs from the "ivory-tower" practices of the 1970s. Now, a more open process works to discover what customers want and how a firm can provide it. No longer limited to upper-level managers, strategic planning now involves many people at different levels of the organization. Many companies assemble diverse teams of both line and staff managers from different functional areas. Some include customers and suppliers as well as first-line employees. These methods bring planning close to market realities.[3]

Strategic planning also helps companies to determine how they will use technology. As UPS Chairman Kent C. Nelson points out, companies are investing large sums in technology. "We can't afford to spend a whole lot of money in one direction and then find out five years later it was the wrong direction," he says.

Mistakes in strategic decisions are costly. In one of the biggest mistakes of its long history, IBM seriously underestimated the potential magnitude of the early PC market and continued to focus its planning on mainframe computers. The company recovered in the 1990s, however, by making changes in its strategic planning.

Recently, IBM announced plans to develop new, affordable products and increase its focus on the consumer market. Big Blue wants to move away from slow-growth products like mainframes and related software and services toward hot segments like PCs for the home market, software, and consulting and network management services. These product lines are growing about 19 percent annually, while mainframe lines are shrinking about 3 percent each year.

IBM's strategy for the home market, a segment in which it has so far built a very low share, is to target repeat PC buyers with household incomes over $50,000 and to add new goods and services. With this relationship-based marketing strategy, IBM hopes to build customer loyalty. Also, to capture a bigger share of the educational market, it acquired Edmark, an educational software developer.

http://www.ibm.com/

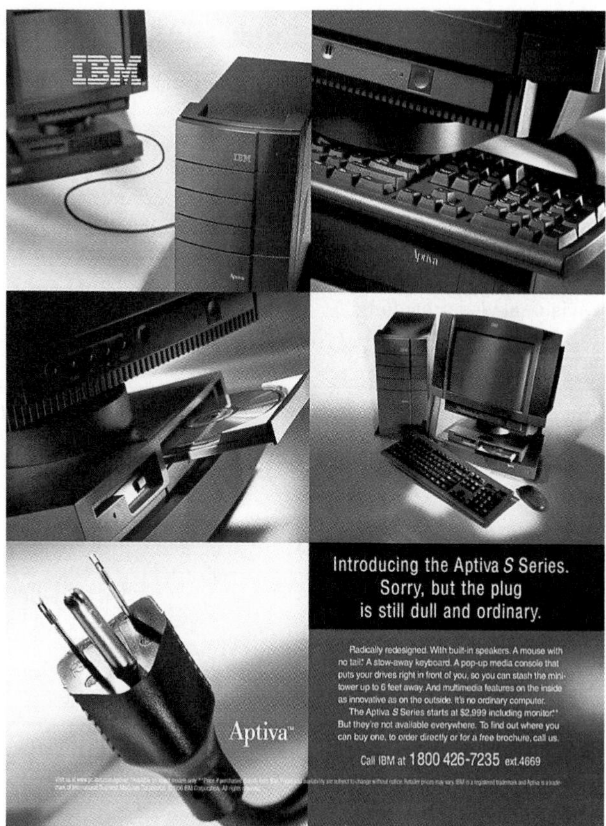
IBM
Introducing the Aptiva *S* Series.
Sorry, but the plug
is still dull and ordinary.
Radically redesigned. With built-in speakers. A mouse with no tail.* A stow-away keyboard. A pop-up media console that puts your drives right in front of you, so you can stash the mini-tower up to 6 feet away. And multimedia features on the inside as innovative as on the outside. It's no ordinary computer.
The Aptiva *S* Series starts at $2,999 including monitor.** But they're not available everywhere. To find out where you can buy one, to order directly or for a free brochure, call us.
Call IBM at 1 800 426-7235 ext.4669
Aptiva™

IBM's tactical plans for its Aptiva PCs include new product features and advertising that informs consumers about the redesigned computers.

Strategic planning is complemented by **tactical planning,** which guides implementation of activities specified in the strategic plan. Tactical plans typically address shorter-term actions than strategic plans, focusing on current and near-future activities that a firm must complete to implement its larger strategies.

For example, IBM defined a variety of tactical plans to implement its strategic plan for the home computer market. It expanded its consumer product lines with new PCs and software, all supported by a $70 million advertising budget. It also redesigned its Aptiva PCs to look better in home settings and to save space. The computers now offer better graphics than earlier models for improved game play, and the monitors have built-in stereo speakers.

To address consumer concerns about the rapidly changing computer industry, IBM introduced new financing options such as a two-year rent-to-own option that includes one free software or hardware upgrade. The company highlights its consumer focus in its online help service and quick links to family-oriented Web pages.[4]

The strategic plans of many of today's leading companies in the fast-food industry focus on capturing greater market share. This overall goal leads the companies to create very visible tactical plans. In 1997, McDonald's dropped prices in an attempt to reverse a troubling decline in sales. The new marketing campaign involved a 55-cent promotion for its Big Mac and other previously higher-priced sandwiches designed to attract price-oriented diners who might otherwise have purchased Burger King's widely advertised 99-cent Whopper. McDonald's limited the price change to its 12,200 U.S. outlets. Still, many franchisees protested that the new price would result in a loss

Marketing Dictionary

strategic planning The process of determining an organization's primary objectives, allocating funds, and then initiating actions designed to achieve those objectives.

tactical planning The process of defining implementation activities that the firm must carry out to achieve its objectives.

Table 5.2 Planning at Different Management Levels

Management Level	Types of Planning Emphasized at This Level	Examples
TOP MANAGEMENT		
Board of directors Chief executive officer (CEO) Chief operating officer (COO) Divisional vice presidents	Strategic planning	Organizationwide objectives; fundamental strategies; long-term plans; total budget
MIDDLE MANAGEMENT		
General sales manager Market research manager Advertising director	Tactical planning	Quarterly and semiannual plans; divisional budgets; divisional policies and procedures
SUPERVISORY MANAGEMENT		
District sales manager Supervisors in staff Marketing departments	Operational planning	Daily and weekly plans; unit budgets; departmental rules and procedures

on every sale, but McDonald's noted that the lower price was available only to customers who also purchased either fries or hash browns and a drink, all high-profit items.[5]

Strategic and tactical planning are not activities limited to large companies. Small firms benefit, as well. Amy Miller, owner of a small chain of superpremium ice cream stores in Houston and Austin, Texas, needed a strategy to keep the outlets from duplicating every other ice cream store. The field was getting crowded, too, with ice cream parlors beginning to rival espresso shops in number. Her differentiation strategy called for selling entertainment with every ice cream cone. Miller's tactics include theme nights, contests, and performing employees. On Sleep-Over Night, employees wear pajamas. The lighting might change from candles on Romance Night to strobe lights for Disco Night. To entertain customers, employees juggle ice cream serving scoops and even balls of ice cream. Contests for free cones keep patrons happy when lines get long.[6]

Planning at Different Organizational Levels

Planning is a major responsibility for every business manager, and managers at all organizational levels devote portions of their work days to planning. However, the relative proportions of time spent planning activities and the types of planning vary. Top management—the board of directors, CEO, COO, and functional vice presidents, such as the chief marketing officer—spend greater proportions of their time engaged in planning than do middle-level and supervisory-level managers. Also, top managers usually focus their planning activities on long-range strategic issues. In contrast, middle-level managers (such as the advertising director, regional sales managers, or the marketing research manager), tend to focus on operational planning—creating and implementing tactical plans for their own departments. Supervisors often engage in developing specific programs to meet goals in their areas of responsibility. Table 5.2 summarizes the types of planning undertaken at various organizational levels.

Gary Hamel, a leading strategy consultant, believes that the planning process needs critical input from a wide range of employees to create the best arrangements for future products and markets. Hewlett-Packard is one firm that encourages broad participation in planning to uncover otherwise unheard views and to find opportunities that fall between the cracks when planning is done only on a department-by-department basis. Strategy sessions bring together general managers, customers, and suppliers to create new marketing opportunities.

These sessions encourage managers to look beyond their own units. For example, a planning session for an auto-industry firm included personnel from units that made diagnostic systems, automotive workstations, and electronic components. The participants—especially customers—generated lots of ideas. "It changes your vision of the business future," comments Thomas E. Vox, general manager of the electronic-instruments group. "You start thinking about how you can get greater value from all the pieces of our company."[7]

Figure 5.2 **The Marketing Planning Process**

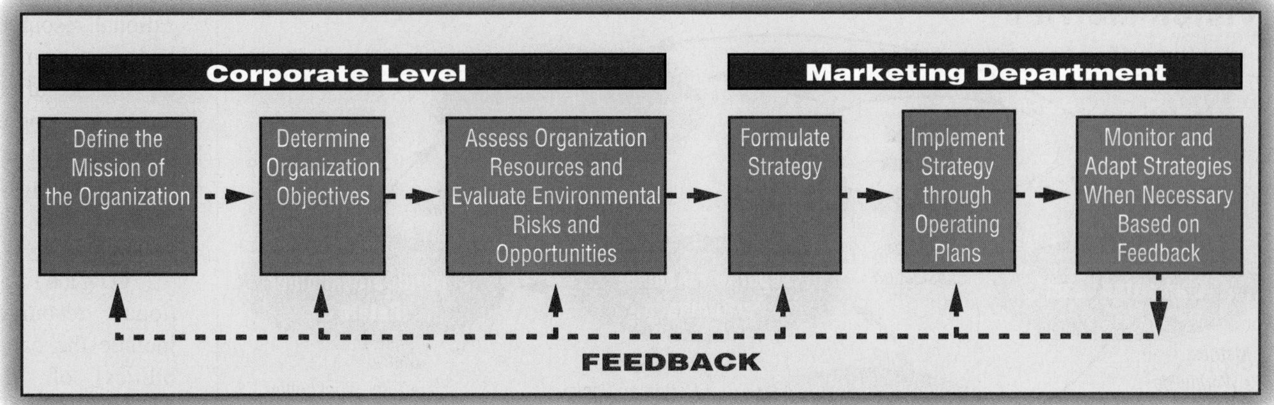
Corporate Level
Marketing Department
Define the Mission of the Organization
Determine Organization Objectives
Assess Organization Resources and Evaluate Environmental Risks and Opportunities
Formulate Strategy
Implement Strategy through Operating Plans
Monitor and Adapt Strategies When Necessary Based on Feedback
FEEDBACK

STEPS IN THE MARKETING PLANNING PROCESS

The marketing planning process begins at the corporate level with the development of objectives. It then moves to develop procedures for accomplishing those objectives. Figure 5.2 shows the basic steps in the process. First, a company must define its mission. It then determines its objectives, assesses its resources, and evaluates environmental risks and opportunities. Guided by this information, the marketing department then formulates a marketing strategy, implements the strategy through marketing plans, and gathers feedback to monitor and adapt strategies when necessary.

Defining the Organization's Mission

The planning process begins with activities to define the firm's **mission,** the essential purpose that differentiates the company from others. The mission statement specifies the organization's overall goals and operational scope and provides general guidelines for future management actions. Adjustments in this statement reflect changing business environments and management philosophies.

The mission and vision statements of Chevron Corp. set out an integrated framework of the energy company's goals, values, strategies, and initiatives. The mission statement is very straightforward:

> We are an international company providing energy and chemical products vital to the growth of the world's economies. Our mission is to create superior value for our stockholders, our customers, and our employees.

Chevron's vision statement supplements its mission statement:

> Our vision is to be Better than the Best, which means:
>
> - Employees are proud of their success as a team.
> - Customers, suppliers, and governments prefer us.
> - Competitors respect us.
> - Communities welcome us.
> - Investors are eager to invest in us.

The vision statement also states Chevron's primary objective: to exceed the financial performance of its strongest competitors and report the highest total stockholder return among comparable firms for the period 1994 to 1998. It then lays out the company's standards for business performance—Committed Team Values, Total Quality Management, and Protecting People and the Environment—and closes with the statement: "We will be guided by the strategic intents in our corporate strategic plan and will measure progress with the vision metrics."

Chevron's vision metrics chart, shown in Figure 5.3, identifies six characteristics that determine the firm's overall success: (1) the commitment of its employee and management team; (2) the satisfaction of its customers; (3) the return to its stockholders; (4) the general public's attitude toward the company; (5) its overall financial performance;

Marketing Dictionary

mission A general, enduring statement of overall organizational purpose.

Figure 5.3 Vision Metrics at Chevron: How the Firm Evaluates Its Success

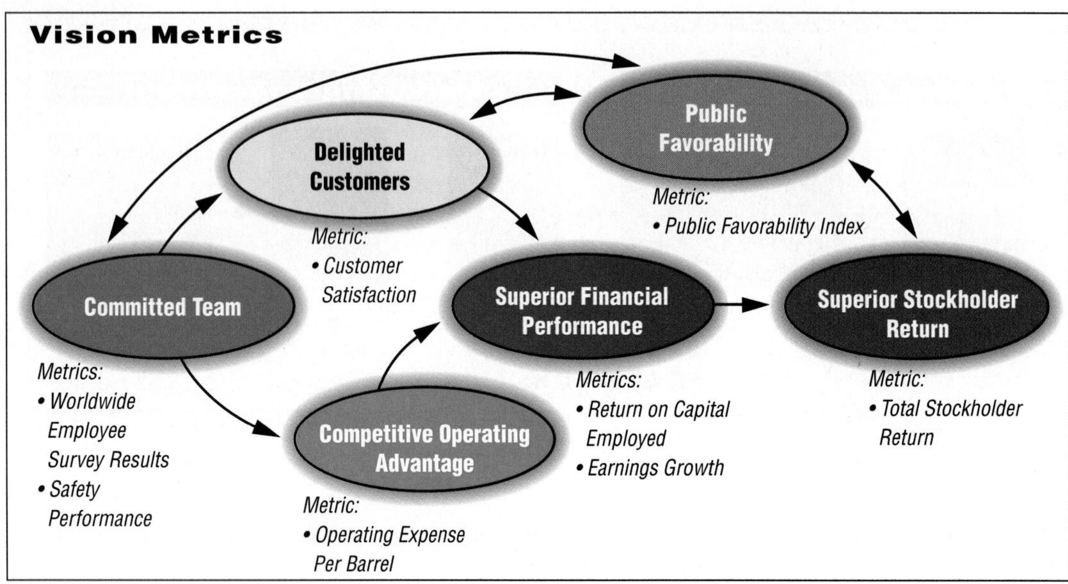
Vision Metrics
Public Favorability
Metric:
• Public Favorability Index
Delighted Customers
Metric:
• Customer Satisfaction
Committed Team
Metrics:
• Worldwide Employee Survey Results
• Safety Performance
Superior Financial Performance
Metrics:
• Return on Capital Employed
• Earnings Growth
Superior Stockholder Return
Metric:
• Total Stockholder Return
Competitive Operating Advantage
Metric:
• Operating Expense Per Barrel

and (6) the competitive advantage it enjoys over other firms in the energy and chemical industries. The connecting arrows illustrate interrelationships between these characteristics. The vision metrics chart also specifies the means by which the firm measures success in each of the six categories.[8]

Determining Organizational Objectives

An organization lays out its basic objectives, or goals, in its mission statement. These objectives in turn guide development of supporting marketing objectives and plans. Soundly conceived objectives should state specific intentions ("generate a 12 percent increase in profits over last year," "attain a 20 percent share of the market by 2001," "increase sales 15 percent over last year"). In addition, they should specify the time periods for their achievement.

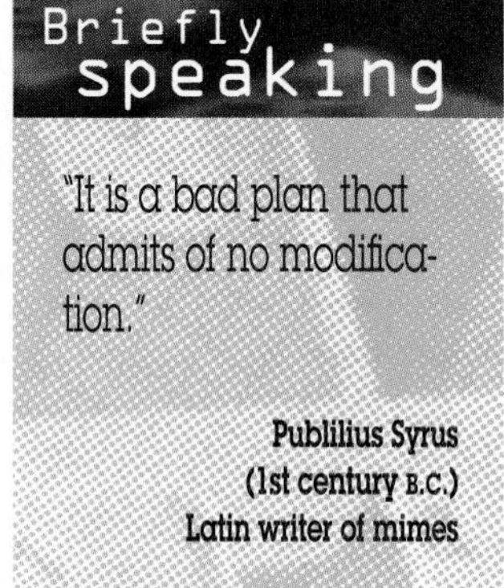
Briefly speaking
"It is a bad plan that admits of no modification."
Publilius Syrus
(1st century B.C.)
Latin writer of mimes

In its continuing attempts to achieve growth and profitability objectives, Visa is focusing on the college market. In this relatively young, potentially affluent market segment, Visa encounters little established brand loyalty. Consequently, it is a lucrative target for dozens of firms. The Visa ad shown in Figure 5.4 appears in such youth-oriented magazines as *Spin* and *Rolling Stone.*

Assessing Organizational Resources and Evaluating Environmental Risks and Opportunities

The third step of the marketing planning process involves a back-and-forth assessment of strengths, risks, and available opportunities. As Figure 5.2 illustrated, organizational resources and environmental factors affect marketing opportunities. Both are important considerations in the planning process.

Organizational resources include the capabilities of the firm's production, marketing, finance, technology, and employees. An organization's planners should pinpoint its strengths and weaknesses. Strengths help them to set objectives, develop plans for meeting those objectives, and take advantage of marketing opportunities. For example, The Coca-Cola Co. identifies several strengths: the world's best-known and most-admired trademark, financial soundness, a global soft-drink production and distribution system, marketing and advertising efficiency, new-product innovations, and a dedicated team of managers and employees.

The environmental components discussed in Chapter 3—the competitive, political-legal, economic, technological, and social-cultural environments—also influence marketing opportunities. Environmental effects can emerge both from within the organization and from the external environment. For example, the fast-changing technology environment requires high-tech companies to react flexibly and change their plans quickly in response to technological breakthroughs. In only a few years, the Internet has transformed the way people communicate and do business. At first, commercial online services like America Online, CompuServe, and Prodigy were the Internet gateways of choice for most consumers, who felt confused by Net protocols and procedures. Once browser technology made the World Wide Web easy to use, these commercial services began losing customers to Internet service providers (ISPs). Many small ISPs experienced phenomenal growth as people rushed to get "wired." The regional Bell companies and AT&T also offered Net access, but companies flocked to ISPs to put their information directly on the Web, and consumers enjoyed direct routes to the Web.

This flow of customers placed tremendous price pressure on the commercial providers. As development costs for their special and unique content areas rose, they felt pressure to lower prices to compete. As ISPs began featuring flat monthly rates for unlimited online access, the commercial online services had to make several changes. AOL and CompuServe added improved Internet access to their services. Prodigy, on the other hand, became an Internet-only provider.[9]

Another result of Internet technology is the increase in new types of businesses such as Web page designers, interactive advertising agencies, and companies that provide secure financial transaction systems. As these technologies mature, growing numbers of companies will factor the Internet into their strategic and tactical plans. At the same time, a shakeout will reorganize Internet-related companies as large companies acquire hot new technologies and smaller ones merge to survive.[10]

The health-care industry is also affected by environmental conditions such as pressure from federal, state, and local governments. Physician Sales & Service (PSS), a Jacksonville, Florida-based distributor of supplies for doctors' offices, attributed its early success to its top-level customer service, for which it charged premium prices. But as cost control became the industry norm, price—once a secondary concern of doctors—became a major concern. To meet his customers' needs yet still provide excellent service, Chief Executive Officer Pat Kelly made some strategic changes to convert PSS into a low-cost supplier. He also started a frequent buyers club to reward his best customers. Through careful planning and cooperation supported by commitment from his employees, who were also stockholders, PSS returned to the growth track. After a difficult transition year, the firm recaptured a leadership role in its industry.[11]

Figure 5.4 **Visa: Pursuing Growth and Profitability Objectives in the College Market**

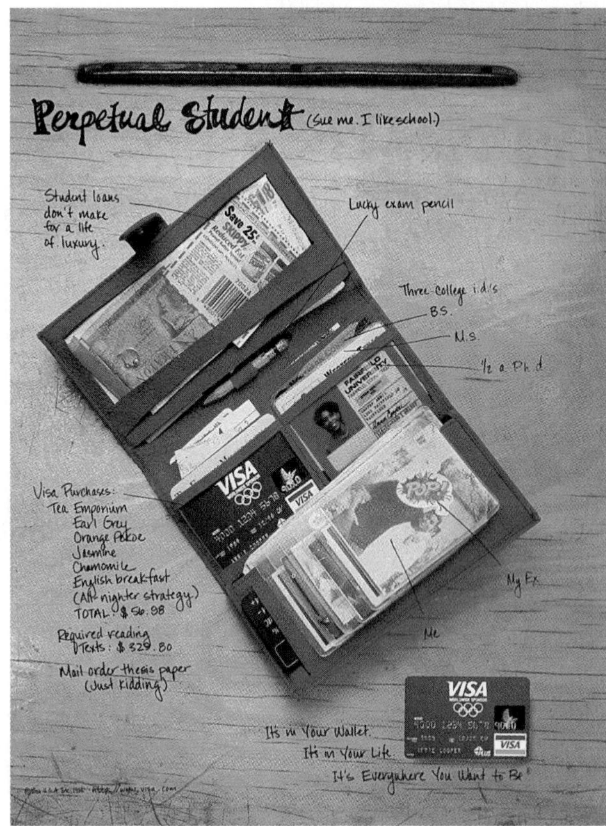
Perpetual Student (Sue me. I like school.)
Student loans don't make for a life of luxury.
Lucky exam pencil
Three college i.d.'s
B.S.
M.S.
1/2 a Ph.d
Visa Purchases:
Tea Emporium
Earl Grey
Orange Pekoe
Jasmine
Chamomile
English breakfast
(All-nighter strategy.)
TOTAL: $ 56.98
Required reading
Texts: $ 329.80
Mail order thesis paper
(Just kidding)
My Ex
Me
VISA
It's in Your Wallet.
It's in Your Life.
It's Everywhere You Want to Be
http://www.visa.com

SWOT Analysis An important strategic planning tool, **SWOT analysis,** helps planners to compare internal organizational strengths and weaknesses with external opportunities and threats. (*SWOT* is an acronym for **s**trengths and **w**eaknesses, **o**pportunities, and **t**hreats.) This form of analysis provides managers with a critical view of the organization's internal and external environments, helping them to evaluate the firm's fulfillment of its basic mission.

As Figure 5.5 shows, matching an internal strength with an external opportunity produces a situation known as *leverage* for the organization. Managers face a *problem* when environmental threats attack their organization's weaknesses.

Sears, Roebuck and Co., once the nation's leading retailer, lost ground to rivals as the competitive environment changed. Its problems increased and its market share fell as customers turned to specialty stores like Circuit City, Home Depot, and CompUSA; discounters such as Wal-Mart, Target, and Kmart; and warehouse clubs like Price/CostCo and Sam's Club. Sears stores operated mostly in major shopping malls, while its competitors placed stores outside malls where they offered low prices, quality merchandise, and wide selections. Another problem arose when Sears management lost sight of what customers wanted. The company tried to be everything to everyone by adding financial services like stock brokerage, real estate, and insurance services to its product mix.

The financial supermarket strategy didn't work, however, and the company sold off its other businesses and

Marketing Dictionary

SWOT analysis A method of studying organizational resources and capabilities to assess the firm's strengths and weaknesses and scanning its external environment to identify opportunities and threats.

Figure 5.5 SWOT Analysis

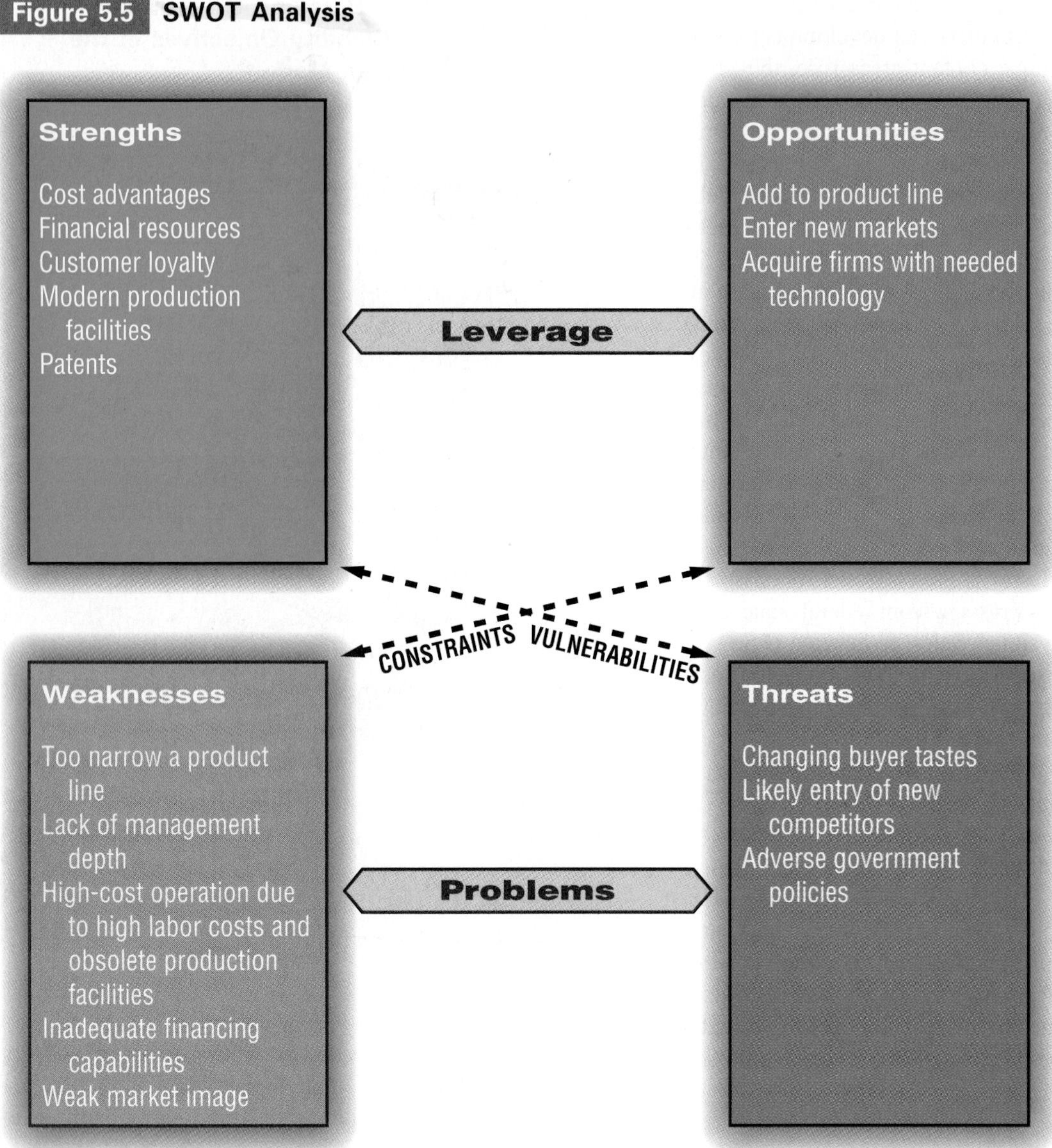
Strengths
Cost advantages
Financial resources
Customer loyalty
Modern production facilities
Patents
Opportunities
Add to product line
Enter new markets
Acquire firms with needed technology
Leverage
CONSTRAINTS
VULNERABILITIES
Weaknesses
Too narrow a product line
Lack of management depth
High-cost operation due to high labor costs and obsolete production facilities
Inadequate financing capabilities
Weak market image
Threats
Changing buyer tastes
Likely entry of new competitors
Adverse government policies
Problems

returned to its retail roots. Sears embarked on a major program to renovate stores and improve merchandise quality. Its "Softer Side of Sears" promotional campaign tried to attract customers for upscale clothing as well as appliances and tools. The strategy succeeded as Sears recovered from its lagging sales and dowdy image. By 1997, apparel led the firm's sales growth, and Sears expanded its market share in consumer electronics—at the expense of superstores like Circuit City and Best Buy.[12]

http://www.sears.com/

To capitalize on one strength—high customer loyalty to its hardware lines like Craftsman tools—Sears opened freestanding hardware stores. Because it learned that customers want convenience more than breadth of assortment, these stores focused on home improvement projects with limited complexity, such as painting, wallpapering, and fixing light switches. This strategy also avoids head-on competition with Home Depot.[13]

Planners anticipate *constraints* when internal weaknesses or limitations prevent their organization from taking advantage of opportunities. As mentioned earlier, online services had to change their strategies to meet competition from Internet service providers. AOL matched the prevailing ISP flat-rate offer of $19.95 per month for unlimited access and immediately encountered a major *constraint.* The soaring demand that resulted from the offer overwhelmed its service facilities. Irate customers filed class action lawsuits, and AOL had to offer refunds because its poor planning had allowed the constraint (inadequate facilities) to turn into a problem.[14]

Both the change in pricing and customer service problems created a *vulnerability* for AOL—an environmental threat to its organizational strength. As the largest online service with the most subscribers, it stood to lose the most from a shift toward ISPs. Industry watchers wondered how the company could make a profit charging the low rate and at the same time spend heavily to develop exclusive content. Meanwhile, competitors rushed to take advantage of AOL's problems. Ameritech and AT&T increased market-

Message for America Online members:

We know you are having problems connecting to America Online when you want to and we are working day and night to get ahead of your demand.

Last year, you told us you wanted an unlimited-use plan—and we delivered. Naturally, we anticipated more usage, and prepared for it, but no one predicted the surge in demand for our unique online services.

Here's what we're doing to fix the problem:

Investing $350 million in the next five months to almost double our capacity to handle more users (more than we spent in our first decade of existence).

Installing 150,000 new modems.

Adding capacity to handle 6,000,000 more connections a day by June.

Cutting back recruitment of new members until we are sure that current members are being served properly.

Offering refunds and credits to our members.

We want to assure you that meeting the surge in demand is our top priority, but it will take some time.

We're focused on one thing: working on serving your needs during this period of unprecedented demand for our service.

Thank you for your patience and support from all of us at America Online.

Steve Case
Founder, Chairman and CEO
America Online, Inc.

Bob Pittman
President and CEO
AOL Networks, Inc.

AMERICA
Online

Busy people can't afford busy signals.

Your time is valuable. You can't afford to squander it.

You need reliable connectivity to read your email, access the Internet, contact clients, and retrieve critical financial news and business information.

At CompuServe, we make sure you get through because we've built our own worldwide network. In fact, millions of business transactions are successfully completed on our network every day. And as an individual online service user, you connect on your first try 97% of the time.

You don't have to settle for busy signals.

Call us at 1-800-554-4080 and request your copy of CSi software.

CSi
COMPUSERVE.
Get on with it.

AOL's attempt to duplicate ISPs' flat-rate pricing structures resulted in a constraint when consumer demand overwhelmed the firm's service facilities. The resulting customer dissatisfaction allowed competitors to take advantage of the firm's marketplace vulnerability.

ing of their Internet access services. Ameritech's ads demonstrated how the company's service would make the Net easy to use, while AT&T launched a major direct-mail campaign promoting its WorldNet service to 10 million of its long-distance customers.[15]

The Strategic Window Professor Derek Abell has suggested the term **strategic window** to define the limited periods during which the key requirements of a market and the particular competencies of a firm best fit together.[16] The view through a strategic window shows planners a way to relate potential opportunities to company capabilities. Such a view requires a thorough analysis of (1) current and projected external environmental conditions, (2) current and projected internal company capabilities, and (3) how, whether, and when the firm can feasibly reconcile the two by implementing one or more marketing strategies.

Microsoft saw a strategic window and made a critical decision. In late 1995, Chairman Bill Gates announced the commitment of the world's largest independent software company to Internet technology. Responding to the growth in Internet usage and users, Gates transformed the large

Marketing Dictionary

strategic window A limited period with an optimal fit between the key requirements of a market and the particular competencies of a firm.

Figure 5.6 **Implementing the Stenz Marketing Strategy**

LEON STENZ, DIVORCE ATTORNEY.

company's strategic direction very quickly, amazing industry experts with a plan to embrace the opportunity and enhance its products through Internet resources. "Every new change forces all the companies in an industry to adapt their strategies to that change," Gates said. Microsoft recognized a threat to its leadership position and moved rapidly to meet it head-on. It figured out how to apply its resources and strengths to the new market opportunity. Within a year, the company had again moved into a leadership role by acquiring small companies with promising Internet technologies, adapting current software products to include Web technology, and developing new products.[17]

Formulating a Marketing Strategy

Opportunity analysis culminates in the formulation of marketing objectives designed to achieve overall organizational objectives and to help planners develop a marketing plan. The marketing plan revolves around a resource efficient, flexible, and adaptable marketing strategy. A **marketing strategy** is an overall, companywide program for selecting a particular target market and then satisfying consumers in that market through a careful balance of the elements of the marketing mix—product, price, distribution, and promotion—each of which represents a subset of the overall marketing strategy.

Implementing a Strategy through Marketing Plans

The sixth step of the marketing planning process consists of implementing the previously developed marketing strategy. The overall strategic marketing plan serves as the basis for a series of operating plans necessary to move the organization toward accomplishment of its objectives. Marketing planning affects activities discussed throughout this text, including analysis and selection of a target market and development of a marketing mix designed to satisfy that market. Advanced marketing texts will add detailed and intensive analysis of operating plans in specific areas of the organization.

Divorce lawyer Leon Stenz implemented his strategic marketing plan through the advertisement shown in Figure 5.6. Located in a small town in northern Wisconsin, Stenz had built a reputation among his clients as a jack-of-all-trades. Despite the high divorce rate in the region (some jokers observe that people find little to do up there except have affairs), Stenz's informal research revealed that people did not think of him as a divorce attorney. As a result, they would drive hours for divorce consultations with attorneys in other cities.

Stenz responded by initiating a low-budget marketing campaign. The poster shown in the figure began appearing in local shops and on billboards with extremely positive results. Not only has Stenz become a local celebrity of sorts, but his business is booming.

TOOLS FOR MARKETING PLANNING

As growing numbers of organizations have discovered the benefits of effective marketing planning, they have developed a number of planning tools to assist in this important function. For example, the marketing audit, discussed in Chapter 2, frequently helps planners to evaluate marketing plans, marketing performance, and customer satisfaction. This section discusses four more tools: the strategic business unit concept, the market share/market growth matrix, the market attractiveness/business strength matrix, and spreadsheet analysis.

Strategic Business Units (SBUs)

Although a relatively small firm may offer only a few goods and services to its customers, a larger organization frequently produces and markets numerous offerings to widely diverse markets. Top managers at major firms need some method for identifying promising product lines that warrant investments of additional resources, as well as those that they should weed out from the firm's product portfolio. The concept of an SBU supports this analysis.

Strategic business units (SBUs) are key business units within diversified firms. Each SBU has its own managers, resources, objectives, and competitors. A division, product line, or single product may define the boundaries of an SBU. Each SBU pursues its own distinct mission, and each develops its own plans independently of other units in the organization.

Figure 5.7 Market Share/Market Growth Matrix

Industry Growth Rate	Relative Market Share: High	Relative Market Share: Low
High	**Stars** Generate considerable income **Strategy:** Invest more funds for future growth	**Question Marks** Have potential to become stars or cash cows **Strategy:** Either invest more funds for growth or consider disinvesting
Low	**Cash Cows** Generate strong cash flow **Strategy:** Milk profits to finance growth of stars and question marks	**Dogs** Generate little profits **Strategy:** Consider withdrawing

Strategic business units focus the attention of company managers so they can respond effectively to changing consumer demand within limited markets. Companies redefine their SBUs as market conditions dictate. Compaq Computer Corp. recently revised its SBU structure into three groups based on the end users of the products. Compaq's Enterprise Computing Group focuses on large business customers that buy sophisticated computers like application servers used in networks, database servers, workstations (a new product for Compaq), and network consulting services. The PC Products Group combines the desktop PC and portable divisions and focuses on small and midsized businesses. The Consumer Products Group produces the company's Presario line of desktop computers for home users. Consolidating servers and workstations into a single SBU improves the effectiveness of marketing these products. This strategic move helps Compaq—a company known for its desktop PCs—to compete in the enterprise customer market against IBM and Hewlett-Packard, companies with worldwide presences in the market for high-end computers.[18]

Market Share/Market Growth Matrix

To evaluate their organization's strategic business units, marketers need some type of portfolio-performance framework. The most widely used framework was developed by the Boston Consulting Group. This **market share/market growth matrix** places SBUs in a four-quadrant chart that plots market share—the percentage of a market that a firm controls—against market growth potential. The position of an SBU along the horizontal axis indicates its market share relative to those of competitors in the industry. Its position along the vertical axis indicates the annual growth rate of the market. After plotting all of a firm's business units, planners divide them according to the matrix's four quadrants, labeled in Figure 5.7 as *cash cows, stars, dogs,* and

Marketing Dictionary

marketing strategy A firm's overall program for selecting and satisfying a target market.

strategic business unit (SBU) A division within a multiproduct firm built around related product groupings or business activities with its own managers, resources, objectives, competitors, and structure for optimal, independent planning.

market share/market growth matrix A marketing planning tool that classifies a firm's products according to industry growth rates and market shares relative to competing products.

Figure 5.8 The Accord: Honda's Star Auto Model

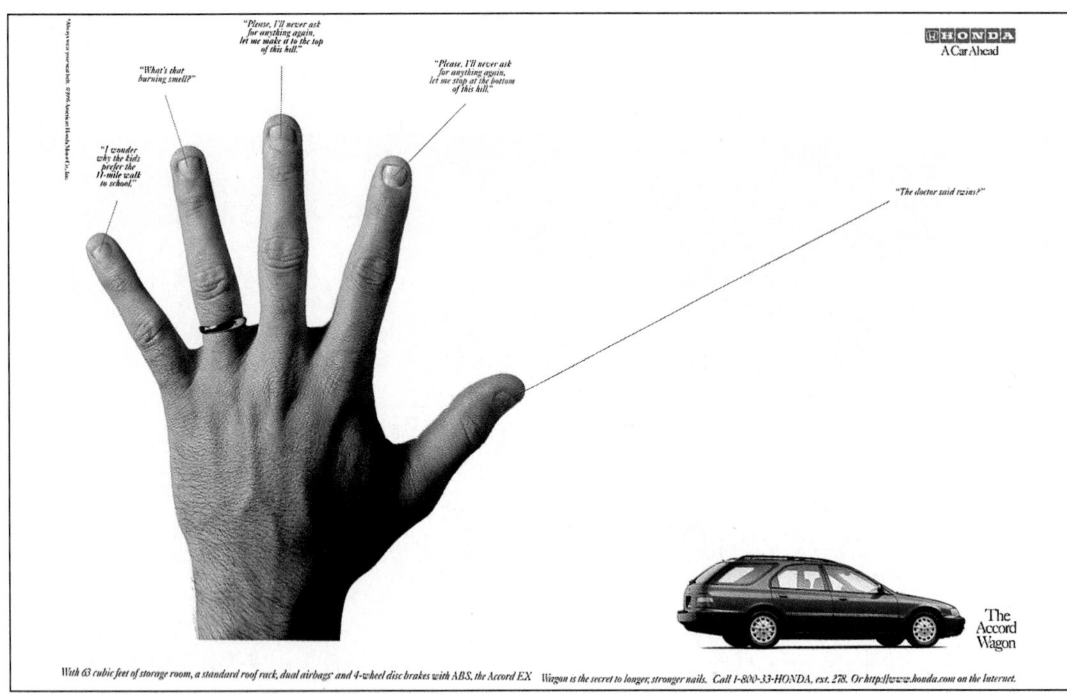
"I wonder why the kids prefer the 11-mile walk to school."
"What's that burning smell?"
"Please, I'll never ask for anything again, let me make it to the top of this hill."
"Please, I'll never ask for anything again, let me stop at the bottom of this hill."
"The doctor said twins?"
HONDA
A Car Ahead
The Accord Wagon
With 63 cubic feet of storage room, a standard roof rack, dual airbags* and 4-wheel disc brakes with ABS, the Accord EX Wagon is the secret to longer, stronger nails. Call 1-800-33-HONDA, ext. 278. Or http://www.honda.com on the Internet.

question marks. Firms in each quadrant require a unique marketing strategy.

Stars represent units with high market shares in high-growth markets. These products or businesses are high-growth market leaders. While they generate considerable income, they need inflows of even more cash to finance further growth. The Honda Accord depicted in Figure 5.8 is such a product. In the ad, Honda reminds owners and potential purchasers that the Accord takes the worry out of driving. The ad cleverly associates the auto model with safety, practicality, and other reasons for consumers to stop biting their nails.

Cash cows command high market shares in low-growth markets. Marketers for such an SBU want to maintain this status for as long as possible. The business produces strong cash flows, but instead of investing heavily in the unit's own promotions and production capacity, the firm can use this cash to finance the growth of other SBUs with higher growth potentials. Gillette Company treats the Sensor razor as a cash cow; the product continues to generate huge profits without the need for large, new investments, so the company can invest instead in developing new generations of razors like the Sensor Excel.

Question marks achieve low market shares in high-growth markets. Marketers must decide whether or not to continue supporting these products or businesses, since questions marks typically require considerably more cash than they generate. If a question mark cannot become a star, the firm should pull out of the market and target other markets with greater potential. Texas Instruments (TI) identified notebook computers as a question mark product. TI's notebook computer sales were growing, and the company ranked fourth in a crowded field. Despite a substantial investment in this product line, TI lost money on its notebooks. It sold the business to Acer Group, a Taiwanese computer manufacturer. This divestiture, along with the sale of its defense operations to Raytheon, intensified the company's focus on the semiconductor business.[19]

http://www.ti.com/

Dogs manage only low market shares in low-growth markets. SBUs in this category promise poor future prospects, and marketers should withdraw from these businesses or product lines as quickly as possible. Products that are dogs for one company may become stars for another Soft-drink maker 7UP performed poorly after Philip Morris acquired it, failing to foresee problems arising from its lack of experience managing a franchise distri-bution network. The beverage unit's performance improved after its sale to Cadbury/Schweppes, which already managed soft-drink product lines.[20]

Market Attractiveness/Business Strength Matrix

Another model that can aid marketing planning is the **market attractiveness/business strength matrix,** a portfolio analysis technique that rates SBUs according to the attractiveness of their markets and their organizational strengths, as illustrated in Figure 5.9. Market attractiveness criteria include market share, growth, size, and stability; potential profitability; extent of government regulation; potential environmental and social impacts; and competitive conditions.[21] Managers must also take into account the organization's specific strengths and areas of competence, including its financial resources, image, relative cost advantages, customer base, and technological capabilities, along with the skills of its personnel.

Figure 5.9 Market Attractiveness/Business Strength Matrix

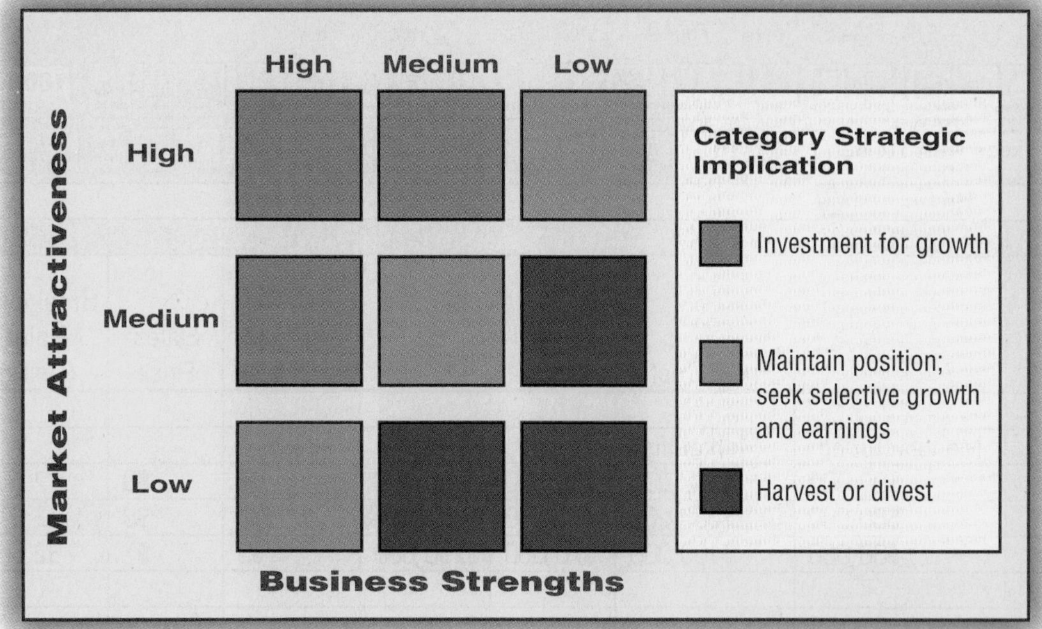
High
Medium
Low
Market Attractiveness
High
Medium
Low
Business Strengths
Category Strategic Implication
Investment for growth
Maintain position; seek selective growth and earnings
Harvest or divest

Based on these criteria, managers create composite evaluations of SBUs. The most promising units in the upper-left area of the matrix offer strong business positions in attractive markets. These initiatives should receive the most company support. Those in the lower-right corner, on the other hand, offer little potential, since they hold weak business positions in unattractive markets. Managers may choose to reduce funding for these operations or discontinue them. In between, other SBUs rank from low to medium on market attractiveness and business strength. Decisions about allocating resources to these borderline SBUs depend on the strengths and weaknesses of the firm's entire portfolio.

Planners apply this matrix in the course of analyzing both their core competencies and their industry environments. This cautious planning prevents wasting investments on resources with low returns. For example, Masco Corp. became an industry leader in metalworking. It decided to capitalize on its expertise and expand into closely related industries, but it entered an industry with poor prospects. Masco encountered a low barrier to entry, but price-sensitive buyers could easily switch to new suppliers. Until the firm identified more attractive industry segments, its growth strategy did not pay off.[22]

Evaluating the Matrix Approach to Planning The market share/market growth matrix emphasizes the importance of creating market offerings that will position the firm to its best advantage. It also acknowledges changes in successful SBUs as they move through their life cycles. A successful product or business typically begins as a question mark, then becomes a star, and eventually drops into the cash-cow category, generating surplus funds that finance its owner's new stars. Ultimately, it becomes a dog at the end of its life cycle and the firm drops it from future plans.

The market attractiveness/business strength matrix is a useful diagnostic tool for identifying SBUs with the greatest and least potential. It can also help managers to identify an organizationwide need for new sources of growth and indicate its most and least attractive markets.

Spreadsheet Analysis

Spreadsheet programs make up a class of computer software that helps planners to answer what-if questions.

Marketing Dictionary

market attractiveness/business strength matrix A portfolio analysis technique that rates SBUs according to the attractiveness of their markets and their organizational strengths.

Figure 5.10 Example of Spreadsheet Analysis

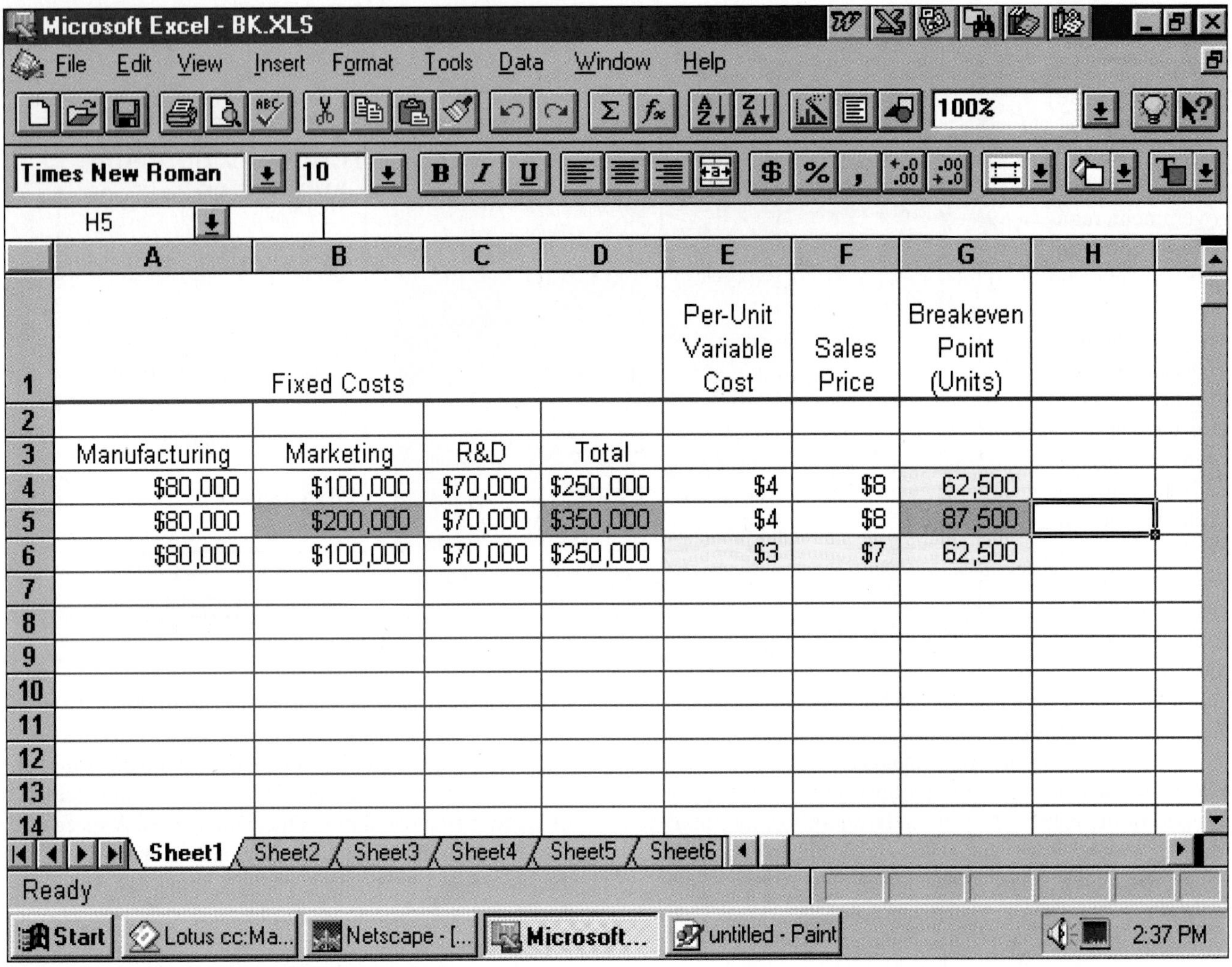

Microsoft Excel - BK.XLS

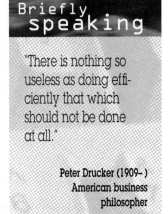

	A	B	C	D	E	F	G	H
1		Fixed Costs			Per-Unit Variable Cost	Sales Price	Breakeven Point (Units)	
3	Manufacturing	Marketing	R&D	Total				
4	$80,000	$100,000	$70,000	$250,000	$4	$8	62,500	
5	$80,000	$200,000	$70,000	$350,000	$4	$8	87,500	
6	$80,000	$100,000	$70,000	$250,000	$3	$7	62,500	

Electronic spreadsheets are the computerized equivalent of an accountant's hand-prepared worksheet. The electronic spreadsheet, like its manual counterpart, lays out a rigid grid of columns and rows that organizes numerical information in a standardized, easily understandable format. The most popular spreadsheet software packages are Lotus 1-2-3 and Excel.

Spreadsheet analysis helps planners to anticipate marketing performance given specified sets of circumstances. For example, a spreadsheet might project the outcomes of different pricing decisions for a new product, as shown in Figure 5.10. In this example, the item will be marketed at $8 per unit and can be produced for $4 in variable costs. The total fixed costs of $250,000 include $80,000 for manufacturing-overhead outlays such as salaries, general office expenses, rent, utilities, and interest charges; $100,000 for marketing expenditures; and $70,000 for research and development to design the product. The spreadsheet calculation, using the basic model on Line 4, reveals that the product would have to achieve sales of 62,500 units in order to break even.

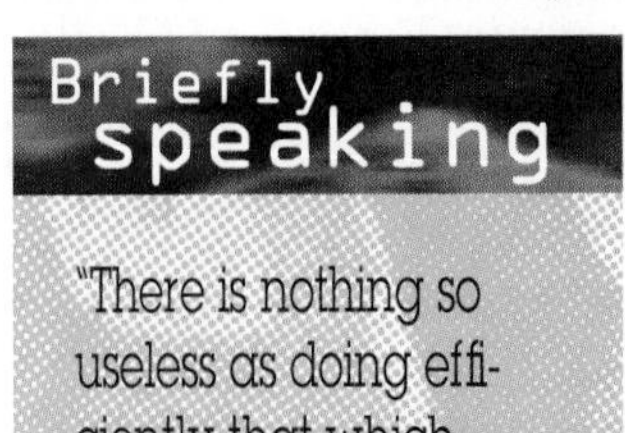
Briefly speaking
"There is nothing so useless as doing efficiently that which should not be done at all."
Peter Drucker (1909–)
American business philosopher

But what if a marketing manager convinces other members of the group to increase marketing expenditures to $200,000? In Line 5 of Figure 5.10, the $100,000 marketing expenditure in Cell 4B changes to $200,000, and the newly calculated breakeven point is 87,500 units. As soon as an amount in one or more cells changes, the software automatically recalculates all affected amounts.

Line 6 of Figure 5.10 demonstrates the impact of a reduction in variable costs to $3 (perhaps the result of switching to lower-cost materials) coupled with a $1 reduction in the product's selling price. The new breakeven point is 62,500 units.

Table 5.3 Benefits and Limitations of Various Forecasting Techniques

Techniques	Benefits	Limitations
QUALITATIVE METHODS		
Jury of executive opinion	Opinions come from executives in many different departments; quick; inexpensive	Managers may lack sufficient knowledge and experience to make meaningful predictions
Delphi technique	Group of experts can accurately predict long-term events such as technological breakthroughs	Time-consuming; expensive
Sales force composite	Salespeople have expert customer, product, and competitor knowledge; quick; inexpensive	Inaccurate forecasts may result from low estimates of salespeople concerned about their influence on quotas
Survey of buyer intentions	Useful in predicting short-term and intermediate sales for firms that serve only a few customers	Intentions to buy may not result in actual purchases; time-consuming; expensive
QUANTITATIVE METHODS		
Market test	Provides realistic information on actual purchases rather than on intent to buy	Alerts competition to new-product plans; time-consuming; expensive
Trend analysis	Quick; inexpensive; effective with stable customer demand and environment	Assumes the future will continue the past; ignores environmental changes
Exponential smoothing	Same benefits as trend analysis, but emphasizes more recent data	Same limitations as trend analysis, but not as severe due to emphasis on recent data

This figure demonstrates the ease with which a marketing manager can use a microcomputer spreadsheet program to determine the potential results of alternative decisions. More complex spreadsheets may include 50 or more columns of data and formulas and yet complete new calculations as quickly as the manager changes the variables.

SALES FORECASTING

A basic building block of a marketing plan is a **sales forecast,** an estimate of a firm's sales or income for a specified future period. In addition to marketing planning, sales forecasts play major roles in new-product decisions, production scheduling, financial planning, inventory planning and procurement, product distribution, and human resource planning. An inaccurate forecast leads to incorrect decisions in each of these areas. A sales forecast is also an important tool for marketing control, because it sets standards against which to measure actual performance. Without such standards, no comparisons can be made. Without a criterion for success, a firm cannot define failure.

Planners rely on short run, intermediate, and long run sales forecasts. A short-run forecast usually covers a period of up to one year, an intermediate forecast covers one to five years, and a long-run forecast extends beyond five years. The time frame of a forecast depends on many factors, including organizational resources, environmental forces, and the intended uses of the forecast.

Although forecasters practice dozens of techniques to divine the future—ranging from computer simulations to studying trends identified by futurists—their methods fall into two broad categories. *Qualitative* forecasting techniques supply rather subjective data, because they report opinions rather than exact historical data. *Quantitative* forecasting methods, by contrast, develop numerical data through statistical computations such as trend extensions based on past data, computer simulations, and econometric models. As Table 5.3 shows, each method has benefits and limitations. Consequently, most organizations combine techniques.

Marketing Dictionary

spreadsheet analysis A marketing planning tool that uses a decision-oriented computer program to answer what-if questions posed by marketing managers.

sales forecast An estimate of company sales for a specified future period.

MARKETING HALL OF FAME

An Evening Out at the Bookstore

At one time, bookstores just sold books, but not anymore. Consider the 40,000-square-foot extravaganza that one book retailer built in Manhattan: Patrons may sip espresso in a 50-seat cafe, check out the latest CDs at a bank of 500 listening stations, and listen to live musical entertainers. Just interested in the books? Sink into one of the comfortable armchairs or sofas scattered throughout the cavernous interior and browse through a best seller or a coffee-table book.

This mega-bookstore belongs to the Borders Group, one of two book-selling giants sweeping the nation with grand new visions of what a bookstore should be. Borders and its chief competitor, New York-based Barnes & Noble Inc., are terrorizing the country's independent book sellers.

Borders' vision is certainly clicking with the book-reading public. Its empire of more than 120 superstores generates over $410 million in sales. The ambitious company is opening 40 superstores a year and expects sales to more than double in just one year. But more than the financial statistics, many people seem impressed by how far the Borders phenomenon has come from its quirky roots.

Borders got its start in an unlikely place for a retailing giant. Two brothers—Tom and Louis Borders—opened their first store in Ann Arbor, Michigan, in 1971. Back then, they sold used books out of a 5,000-square-foot space in the college town. "When I first saw it, Borders was a little, funky, independent bookstore that sold kites," reminisced one original customer. "It had warped floors. It was like no bookstore I'd ever seen. It was what you wanted a bookstore to be."

Borders' runaway success resulted, in part, from its adherence to its original marketing principles. Its owners believed that the Borders stores could never succeed without unparalleled selections. Along with best sellers, they stocked obscure books like those from university presses that only a few customers a year might want. Finding a definitive, multivolume Japanese history, for instance, sends a message to browsers, Borders' visionaries believe, about the section's credibility. "They'll say, 'This store is a great store. I want to come back and browse here again, because there's a good chance I can find what I want,'" says Joe Gable, who has been

Qualitative Forecasting Techniques

Planners apply qualitative forecasting methods when they want judgmental or subjective indicators. Qualitative forecasting techniques include the jury of executive opinion, Delphi technique, sales force composite, and survey of buyer intentions.

Jury of Executive Opinion The technique called the **jury of executive opinion** combines and averages the outlooks of top company executives from such areas as finance, production, marketing, and purchasing. It provides particularly effective input when top managers bring some important capabilities to the process: experience and knowledge about situations that influence sales, open-minded attitudes toward the future, and awareness of the bases for their judgments. This quick and inexpensive method generates effective forecasts for sales and new-product development. It works best for short-run forecasting.

Briefly speaking

"My interest is in the future because I am going to spend the rest of my life there."

Charles F. Kettering
(1876–1950)
American electrical engineer and inventor

Delphi Technique Like the jury of executive opinion, the **Delphi technique** solicits opinions from several people, but it also gathers input from experts outside the firm, such as university researchers and scientists, rather than relying completely on company executives. It is most appropriately used to predict long-run issues, such as technological breakthroughs, that could affect future company sales and the market potential for new products.

The Delphi technique works as follows: A firm selects a panel of experts and sends each a questionnaire relating to a future event. After combining and averaging the answers, the firm develops another questionnaire based on these results and sends it to the experts. The process continues until it identifies a consensus of opinion. Although firms have successfully used Delphi to predict future technological breakthroughs, the method is both expensive and time-consuming.

Sales Force Composite The **sales force composite** technique develops forecasts based on the belief that organization members closest to the marketplace—those with

managing the Ann Arbor bookstore for 21 years.

Also fueling Borders' success is a healthy customer appetite for books. Despite dire warnings about the "dumbing down" of Americans, book sales nationwide are soaring. In 1990, for instance, the U.S. book market totaled $19 billion, and only five years later, sales had jumped 32 percent to $25 billion. During this period, market leaders Borders and Barnes & Noble managed to siphon off growing shares of the industry sales and profits. In 1994, chains accounted for the majority of book sales to adults for the first time. The gap has widened even further since then.

Both Borders and Barnes & Noble have succeeded by creating a true entertainment alternative. Many customers head to one of these superstores as an alternative to a movie or a dinner date. Even nonreaders can have fun in a place like this. "It's a place to browse, to stay for a few hours," says Borders manager Shelly Porter. "A place to go in the community to hang out, to meet people, to bring families to spend an evening."

The latest chapter in planning for these chains is a move into electronic commerce. The Internet has been a good place for booksellers like Amazon.com, which operates only online. Its success prompted Barnes & Noble to affiliate with America Online and also set up a Web site.

http://www.borders.com/

Borders' Web site will feature even more titles than the stores carry along with quick delivery from a distribution center. As Barnes & Noble chairman Len Riggio says, "We have to be a player. Online book selling is going to be a very big thing."

QUESTIONS FOR CRITICAL THINKING

1. **What obstacles might hinder Borders' growth in the future?**
2. **What kind of marketing strategies could independent booksellers use to fend off assaults from the big players?**

Sources: Patrick M. Reilly, "Booksellers Prepare to Do Battle in Cyberspace," *Wall Street Journal,* January 28, 1997, pp. B1, B8; Patrick M. Reilly, "Where Borders Group and Barnes & Noble Compete, It's a War," *Wall Street Journal,* September 3, 1996, pp. A1, A6; and Arthur Salm, "All Booked Up," *San Diego Union-Tribune,* April 8, 1996, pp. E1, E4.

specialized product, customer, and competitor knowledge—offer the best insights concerning short-term future sales. It typically works from the bottom up: Forecasters consolidate salespeople's estimates first at the district level, then at the regional level, and finally nationwide to obtain an aggregate forecast of sales that reflects all three levels.

Few firms rely solely on the sales force composite for their forecasts, however. Since salespeople recognize the role of their sales forecasts in determining sales quotas for their territories, they are likely to make conservative estimates. Moreover, their narrow perspectives from within their limited geographic territories may prevent them from considering the impact on sales of trends developing in other territories, forthcoming technological innovations, or major changes in marketing strategies. Consequently, the sales force composite gives the best forecasts in combination with other techniques.

Survey of Buyer Intentions A **survey of buyer intentions** gathers input through mail-in questionnaires, telephone polls, or personal interviews to determine the purchasing intentions of a representative group of present and

Marketing Dictionary

jury of executive opinion A qualitative sales forecasting method that combines and averages the sales expectations of various executives.

Delphi technique A qualitative sales forecasting method that gathers and redistributes several rounds of anonymous forecasts until the participants reach a consensus.

sales force composite A qualitative sales forecasting method that develops sales estimates based on the combined estimates of the firm's salespeople.

survey of buyer intentions A qualitative sales forecasting method that samples opinions among groups of present and potential customers concerning their purchase intentions.

SOLVING AN ETHICAL CONTROVERSY

Can a Firm Control Too Much Market Share?

A number of studies have confirmed that companies with dominant market shares usually earn above-average profits. Fast-food industry leader McDonald's claims that *per-capita* sales increase in direct relation with the number of outlets operating in a specific market. A few industry observers argue that a company effectively becomes a monopoly when it reaches some threshold market share, justifying close regulation and government restrictions (on pricing changes, acquisitions, and entering new markets, for example). Such regulations have been implemented in Britain through that country's Monopolies Act.

Some instances of marketplace dominance, such as that enjoyed by Intel Corp. in the microprocessor industry, result from patents and investments in research and development. But more varied reasons contribute to Frito-Lay's 55 percent market share in the U.S. snack-food industry.

Stroll down any snack-food aisle in just about any grocery store or convenience outlet in America and you can't fail to notice how many of those packs of potato chips and other salty snacks carry the Frito-Lay name. With such top-selling brands as Lay's potato chips and Rold Gold pretzels, Frito-Lay is America's undisputed monarch of junk food. The PepsiCo subsidiary commands a domestic market share five times as large as that of its nearest competitor. It has achieved this stunning success through a clever combination of a market-saturating distribution strategy, transformation of customer concerns about high-fat content of snack foods into highly profitable new lines of baked products, competitive prices, and restructuring.

But its dominant status now has the federal government joining competitors in scrutinizing Frito-Lay's practices. The Justice Department recently surprised antitrust experts by launching a probe of the salty-snacks industry. Its chief target, insiders confirm, is Frito-Lay. Meanwhile, the smaller snack companies are debating whether to mount legal challenges against their chief nemesis. "The talk of a lawsuit is intensifying," says the owner of one regional pretzel company. "But no one wants to go up against them in court."

Should Government Regulators Aggressively Discourage Food "Monopolies"?

PRO

1. **Limits on competition ultimately restrict choices and raise prices. Consumers always prefer a wide range of selections in grocery stores, for products from snacks to meat. When Frito-Lay out-muscles its competition, shoppers suffer.**
2. **Permitting Frito-Lay to run roughshod over the competition also helps to perpetuate**

potential customers. This method suits firms that serve limited numbers of customers. It often proves impractical for those with millions of customers. Also, buyer surveys gather useful information only when customers willingly reveal their buying intentions. Moreover, customer intentions do not necessarily translate into actual purchases. These surveys may help a firm to predict short-run or intermediate sales, but they employ time-consuming and expensive methods.

Quantitative Forecasting Techniques

Quantitative techniques apply scientific methods to forecast sales. They attempt to eliminate the guesswork of the qualitative methods. Quantitative techniques include such methods as market tests, trend analysis, and exponential smoothing.

Market Tests One quantitative technique, the **market test,** frequently helps planners to assess consumer responses to new-product offerings. The procedure typically begins by establishing a small number of test markets to gauge consumer responses to a new product under actual marketplace conditions. Market tests also permit experimenters to evaluate the effects of different prices, alternative promotional strategies, and other marketing mix variations by comparing results among different test markets. Based on consumer responses in test markets, a firm can predict sales for larger market areas.

http://www.rjrnabisco.com/

R. J. Reynolds Tobacco Co. conducted market testing to develop a new marketing strategy for two popular cigarette brands. Although Winston and Salem make up 56 per-

what some call "retailing's dirty little secret." Food manufacturers pay up to $200,000 to place their products in desirable locations in grocery store aisles. Regional snack companies say they can't match Frito-Lay's deep pockets in competition based on these shelf-space payments. A company might invest $40,000 a year to hold down just one square foot of retail space. Federal investigators want to determine whether Frito-Lay has bought more space than it needs in an effort to squeeze out the competition.

3. Failure to rein in Frito-Lay's practices could lead to the disappearance of food companies. To appreciate Frito-Lay's power, look at what happened to Anheuser-Busch's Eagle Snacks. The country's leading brewer, known for its own marketing genius, conceded that it was no match for Frito-Lay in the snacks business. After losing more than $500 million, the brewer sold its Eagle Snacks business.

CON

1. Frito-Lay earns its identity as a dominant player because it does everything right. It provides consumers with what they demand: fresh, moderately priced, good-tasting snacks. Its success has not resulted from any monopolistic strategies. "They've driven all their competitors out of business by being too successful," says William Leach, who follows the food industry for the investment firm Donaldson Lufkin Jenrette. "There's nothing unethical. They're just better at product development, marketing, and execution. But there is no law against doing well."
2. Punishing a successful company would violate this country's entrepreneurial spirit. It could also damage the interests of millions of shareholders who bought stock in the company because of its demonstrated abilities in the marketplace.

Summary

Unless government regulators step in, Frito-Lay probably will not fall from its pedestal any time soon. The company refuses to become complacent. While expanding its core lines of Fritos, Doritos, potato chip, and pretzel products, Frito-Lay has successfully branched out into the market for reduced-fat products by offering health-conscious snacks. It also keeps track of daily buying trends through its network of 13,000 delivery people. "Frito's a fortress," says Michael Branca, an analyst at NatWest Securities. "And it continues to expand its realm. I'd tell anyone else trying to get into the business, don't try to expand, don't try to impinge on Frito's territory or you'll get crushed."

Sources: "Frito-Lay to Produce Potato Chips at Former Eagle Snacks Plant," March 12, 1997, downloaded from http://www.sosland.com/, May 16, 1997; John Greenwald, "Frito-Lay under Snack Attack," *Time,* June 10, 1996, pp. 62-63; and Robert Frank, "Frito-Lay Devours Snack-Food Business," *Wall Street Journal,* October 27, 1995, pp. B1, B4.

cent of Reynolds' full-price cigarette sales volume and almost half of its U.S. tobacco profits, they have been losing market share in recent years. Management wanted positive test market results before allocating more marketing dollars to the brands. Because these brands tended to attract older smokers and lacked clear identities, Reynolds tested new formulations such as a version of Winston without additives that it marketed in Florida with a "No Bull" ad campaign. The weak response sent marketers back to the drawing board to develop new plans until market testing identified one that would work.[23]

The primary advantage of market tests is the realism that they provide for the marketer. On the other hand, these expensive and time-consuming experiments may also communicate marketing plans to competitors before a firm introduces a product to the total market. Test marketing is discussed in more detail in Chapter 12.

Trend Analysis The technique of **trend analysis** develops forecasts of future sales by analyzing the historical relationship between sales and time. It implicitly assumes that the collective causes of past sales will continue to exert similar influence in the future. When historical data are available, planners can quickly and inexpensively

Marketing Dictionary

market test A quantitative forecasting method that introduces a new product, price, promotional campaign, or other marketing variable in a relatively small test market location in order to assess consumer reactions.

trend analysis A quantitative sales forecasting method that estimates future sales through statistical analyses of historical sales patterns.

MARKETING HALL OF SHAME

Why Swallowing Snapple Made Quaker Oats Gag

Imagine reaching for a star and bringing back a dog. That's just what happened to Quaker Oats when it decided to buy the soft-drink success story of the 1990s. Breakfast cereal and Gatorade marketer Quaker Oats foresaw success in its combination with Snapple, maker of the New Age beverage that comes in such off-beat flavors as kiwi-strawberry and peach-flavored iced tea. Quaker Oats fell in love at first sight, snapping up the quirky beverage company in late 1994 for what proved to be an excessive price of $1.7 billion. But the romance never even enjoyed a honeymoon. Almost immediately, Snapple sales fell as flat as day-old soda and then took a steep dive. Snapple lost $75 million in 1995—a year in which soft-drink sales set an all-time record.

That wasn't even the most embarrassing part. Sales continued to limp along throughout 1996 despite a massive and highly publicized marketing ploy. To add fizz to the brand, Quaker Oats marketers sank $40 million into a huge Snapple summer giveaway. Driving vans stocked with 16-ounce Snapple teas and fruit drinks, employees fanned out across the country. They passed out free samples at beaches, parks, street corners, even the Democratic and Republican political conventions. With so many new Snapple drinkers, Quaker felt sure that it would win over a new group of loyal customers. "We've got a lot to prove," acknowledged CEO William Smithburg on the eve of the big giveaway. "There's no question that Snapple is a major bet for us."

But Quaker lost the bet. Apparently, it might as well have poured all those millions of gallons of Snapple in a river. The anticipated legions of new Snapple customers never materialized. In fact, Snapple sales once again tumbled. Dollar volume sales of the drinks dropped 15 percent during the 12-week giveaway period. "To state

complete trend analysis. For example, if sales last year totaled X and they have increased at Y percent annually for the past several years, a simple equation would give next year's sales forecast:

$$\text{Sales} = X + XY$$

In actual numbers, if last year's sales totaled 520,000 units and the sales growth rate has averaged 5 percent, the sales forecast would be:

$$\text{Sales} = 520{,}000 + (520{,}000 \times 0.05) = 546{,}000$$

Because the sales forecast supplies such a basic building block for marketing planning, trend analysis is a valuable tool. Planners frequently apply it to short-term forecasting problems during periods of steady growth. A more sophisticated version of trend analysis uses a technique called *least squares* to fit a trend equation to past data on sales, market share, or earnings. The following trend analysis equation gives an estimate for a future time period:

$$Y_c = a + bx$$

where:

Y_c = Predicted sales or market share

a = Estimated sales, market share, or earnings at the time period when $x = 0$

b = Slope of the trend line; that is, average change in sales, market share, or earnings for each specified time period

x = Time period (such as one year) over which forecasters project data

To use the trend analysis equation, planners need estimates of a and b. They calculate these estimates from historical data using the least-squares technique. The following two equations give values for a and b:

$$a = \frac{\Sigma Y}{n}$$

$$b = \frac{\Sigma xY}{\Sigma x^2}$$

The mathematical symbol Σ means "the sum of." The variable n refers to the total number of time periods that the forecast covers.

Consider the following example. A small mail-order firm specializing in novelty items wants to forecast sales for next year. The firm's president identifies trend analysis as an appropriate forecasting technique because the company's sales show relatively stable growth and the forecast applies only to the short term. To calculate the needed data for the trend analysis equation, she has created the following table, beginning with a listing of an-

the very obvious, Snapple has been an abject failure," concludes Michael Mouboussin, an analyst at CS First Boston. "It boils down to two things for Quaker to do now: sell the business outright or attempt to run it next year with a vastly altered strategy."

Meanwhile, Snapple posted even more disappointing performance overseas. Quaker pulled out of Japan after sales shriveled there, too. Japanese consumers didn't like the sugary taste of the fruit drinks, the murky appearance of the teas, or the sediment resting at the bottoms of the bottles.

Some industry analysts blame the drink itself and not Quaker's marketing strategies for the poor sales. "(Snapple) appeals much more to the urban yuppies of New York and the West Coast than to middle America," says analyst Nomi Ghez at Goldman Sachs. "It's relatively expensive and the taste doesn't appeal to a large audience. How many people want to drink kiwi-banana-strawberry what-ever?"

In 1997, Quaker decided to bite the bullet and sold the troubled beverage line to Triarc Co. for $300 million—less than one-fifth the $1.7 billion it had paid just two years earlier. One observer calculated that Quaker lost $1.6 million for every day it owned Snapple, based on the purchase price and another $100 million it threw into the business.

The $1.4 billion loss was one of the largest in recent history for a U.S. firm. Triarc, which markets the rival Mistic "New Age" beverage and also owns RC Cola and Arby's fast-food restaurants, is optimistic about turning around the troubled brand.

QUESTIONS FOR CRITICAL THINKING

1. **Can you suggest reasons why the Snapple marketing give-away failed?**
2. **Some people suggest that Snapple was doomed from the start with flavors too exotic for most people. What do you think?**

Sources: Jeanne Dugan, "Will Triarc Make Snapple Crackle?" *Business Week,* April 28, 1997, pp. 64–65; and Bruce Horovitz and Chris Woodyard, "Quaker Oats' $1.4 Billion Wash-out," *USA Today,* March 28, 1997, pp. B1, B2.

nual sales for each year since the firm's establishment nine years ago:

n Time Period	*y* Sales ($ Thousands)	*x*	*xY*	x^2
1	$ 100	−4	−400	16
2	112	−3	−336	9
3	130	−2	−260	4
4	160	−1	−160	1
5	205	0	0	0
6	210	1	210	1
7	240	2	480	4
8	280	3	840	9
9	325	4	1,300	16
	$1,762		1,674	60

Because the firm has been operating for an odd number of years, the method codes the middle year, Year 5, as Time 0. It codes the years prior to Year 5 as −1, −2, and so on. It codes the years following Year 5 as positive 1, 2, and so on. (If the data had involved an even number of observations, the technique would have coded the two middle years as −1 and +1.) The technique then codes the prior years in increments of −2 (−3, −5, −7, and so on); all the years following the middle years are coded in increments of +2 (+3, +5, +7, and so on). The analysis is completed by calculating ΣxY, $\Sigma x,^2$ and n. The first two values are determined by totaling the two columns labeled xY and x^2. Because the number of time periods included in this example is 9, the value of n is 9. These steps lead to calculated values for a and b:

$$a = \frac{1{,}762}{9} = 195.8$$

$$b = \frac{1{,}674}{60} = 27.9$$

Therefore, the trend line for this example is:

$$\begin{aligned} Y &= a + bx \\ &= 195.8 + 27.9x \end{aligned}$$

To forecast next year's sales for the mail-order firm, the planner counts from the Year 5 center value. Since the value for the Year 9 is 4, the value for the next year (Year 10) would be 5. The forecast then substitutes the value 5 for x in the formula:

$$\begin{aligned} \text{Sales} &= 195.8 + 27.9(5) \\ &= 335.3 \\ &= 335{,}300 \end{aligned}$$

Of course, trend analysis cannot be used if historical data are not available, as in new-product forecasting. Also, trend analysis makes the dangerous assumption that future events will continue the patterns of the past. Any variations in the determinants of future sales will cause deviations from the forecast. In other words, this method gives reliable forecasts only during periods of steady growth and stable demand. If conditions change, predictions based on trend analysis may become worthless. For this reason, forecasters have applied increasingly sophisticated techniques and complex, new mathematical models to anticipate the effects of various possible changes in the future.

Exponential Smoothing A more sophisticated method of trend analysis, the **exponential smoothing** technique, weights each year's sales data, giving the greatest weight to results from the most recent years. For example, an exponential smoothing forecast based on sales data for five years might carry weights as follows:

Year	Weight
1993	0.8
1994	0.9
1995	1.0
1996	1.1
1997	1.2

Since causes that have contributed to the most recent sales data are most likely to continue to interact similarly for the next time period, exponential smoothing assigns greater weights to these data than to those for earlier years.

Steps in Sales Forecasting

Although sales forecasting methods vary, the most typical one begins with an environmental forecast of general economic conditions. This background information helps marketers to project industry sales and then to forecast company and product sales. This method is referred to as *top-down forecasting*.

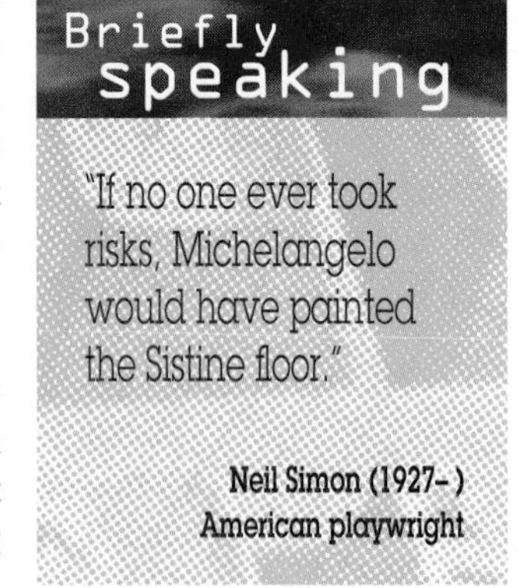
Briefly speaking
"If no one ever took risks, Michelangelo would have painted the Sistine floor."
Neil Simon (1927–)
American playwright

Environmental Forecasting The broad-based **environmental forecast** focuses on events and influences external to the firm that affect its markets, such as consumer spending and saving patterns, balance-of-trade surpluses and deficits, government expenditures, and business investments. By accumulating these projections, planners develop an overall economic forecast.

The most common measure of economic output is the country's gross domestic product (GDP), the sum of all goods and services produced within its borders in a given year. Trend analysis is the most popular method of forecasting increases in the GDP. Since many federal agencies and other organizations develop regular GDP forecasts, a firm may adopt their estimates, which are regularly reported in popular business publications.

Industry Sales Forecasting The general economic forecast combines with other relevant environmental conditions to guide development of an industry sales forecast. Since industry sales often maintain stable relationships with GDP or some other measure of national economic activity, an industry forecast may begin by measuring the degree of this relationship and then applying the trend analysis method. Trade associations and publications for most industries provide short-term, intermediate, and long-term forecasts. These forecasts provide valuable input, because they adjust an overall economic outlook for trends and environmental effects that influence specific industries.

Company and Product Sales Forecasting After completing their industry forecast, marketing planners develop company and product forecasts. This pro-cess begins with a detailed analysis of performance in previous years. Planners review the firm's past and present market share, and invite input from product managers, as well as regional and district sales managers, about expected sales. Since an accelerated promotional budget or introduction of a new product may stimulate additional sales, the forecast should also reflect marketing plans for the coming year.

Product and company forecasts must evaluate such factors as sales of each product; future sales trends; sales by customer, territory, salesperson, and order size; and financial resources. After planners develop the preliminary sales forecast, they ask for reviews of its contents by the sales force and by district, regional, and national sales managers.

Quaker Oats forecasts product sales in future planning for its market-leading Gatorade sports beverage, shown in the ad in Figure 5.11. Worldwide sales of Gatorade exceed $1.2 billion, up from $120 million in 1984. This change represents an average annual growth rate in sales of 20 percent since the company bought the brand in 1983. Several consumer trends drive this impressive sales growth: increased interest in healthy foods and beverages, growing sports participation, expanded sports competition worldwide, and a growing and younger population, especially in Latin America and Asia. Past product sales and consumer trends create enormous growth opportunities for Gatorade.[24]

Grass-Roots Forecasting An alternative approach to top-down forecasting is *grass-roots* or *bottom-up forecasting*. This method begins with sales estimates provided by each salesperson for his or her sales territory. Later analysis by sales and marketing managers combines and refines these

Figure 5.11 **A Bright Future for Gatorade**

There are better things to do than sit around reading magazines.
You live life. you get thirsty.
http://www.gatorade.com
LIFE IS a SPORT DRINK IT UP Gatorade

estimates at the divisional, regional, and national levels. The results reach the national sales manager, who combines them into one sales estimate for the forthcoming time period. Proponents of bottom-up forecasting stress the benefits to employee morale and motivation that result when each member of the sales force participates in developing the forecasts that help to establish sales quotas. In addition, the approach ensures inputs from each individual territory, and personal inputs from the salespeople who maintain direct and continuing contact with the firm's customers.

One shortcoming of grassroots forecasts is that individual salespeople lack perspective on the organization as a whole. Sales estimates for individual territories may not reflect major trends, such as forthcoming market entries of competing products, new products set for introduction by the company, planned price changes, new promotional campaigns, packaging changes, and other variables likely to affect results throughout the marketplace. In addition, since salespeople recognize the relationships between their

Marketing Dictionary

exponential smoothing A quantitative forecasting technique that assigns weights to historical sales data, giving the greatest weight to the most recent data.

environmental forecast A broad-based projection of economic activity that focuses on the impact of external events and influences on the firm's markets.

sales forecasts and sales quotas, they may feel tempted to make relatively low forecasts that they can easily exceed. Consequently, firms that practice bottom-up planning depend heavily upon the compromises and final estimates that result from discussions at the divisional, regional, and national levels.

Since both top-down and grass-roots sales forecasting offer strengths and weaknesses, many marketers combine the two approaches to obtain the most realistic forecasts possible.

New-Product Sales Forecasting Forecasting sales for a new product is an especially hazardous undertaking because it can call on no historical data. Companies typically employ consumer panels to obtain reactions to the products and to gauge probable purchase behavior. Test market data may also guide forecasts.

Since few products introduce totally new features to the market, forecasters can gain insight by carefully analyzing the sales of competing products that the new entry may displace. A new type of fishing reel, for example, will compete in an established market with other kinds of reels. This substitution method provides the forecaster with an estimate of market size and potential demand.

ACHIEVEMENT CHECK SUMMARY

Reread the learning goals that follow, and consider the questions for each goal. Answering these questions will reinforce your grasp of the most important concepts in the chapter and allow you to check how well you have achieved these learning goals. Where a blank appears before a question, answer with *T* or *F;* for multiple-choice questions, circle the letter of the correct answer.

Objective 5.1: Distinguish between strategic planning and tactical planning.

1. ___ When PepsiCo spun off its Taco Bell, Pizza Hut, and KFC fast-food operations into a separate company, it (a) formulated tactical plans; (b) changed its strategic plan; (c) applied relationship marketing concepts; (d) violated the tenets of its mission statement.

2. ___ Tactical planning involves allocating resources to implement actions designed to achieve a firm's strategic objectives.

3. ___ A firm's decision to spend $450,000 on a one-year advertising campaign is an example of strategic planning.

Objective 5.2: Explain how marketing plans differ at various levels in an organization.

1. ___ Top managers devote more time than middle managers to tactical planning.

2. ___ Developing an operational plan such as a departmental budget is typically the responsibility of a supervisory manager.

3. ___ Strategic and tactical planning should reflect input only from employees.

Objective 5.3: Identify the steps in the marketing planning process.

1. ___ A company's first task is to (a) develop a strategic plan; (b) assess its objectives; (c) monitor plans; (d) define its mission.

2. ___ The statement "Introduce three new products over the next two years" is an example of (a) a vision statement; (b) an organizational objective; (c) risk assessment; (d) SWOT analysis.

3. ___ A marketing strategy presents a comprehensive plan that balances the marketing mix and helps the company to reach its marketing goals.

Objective 5.4: Describe the concept of SWOT analysis and its four major elements: leverage, problems, constraints, and vulnerabilities.

1. ___ *SWOT* is an acronym for *strengths, weaknesses, opportunities,* and *timing.*

2. ___ Companies that evaluate their strengths and pursue opportunities that take advantage of those capabilities (a) are vulnerable to environmental threats; (b) focus mainly on external factors; (c) create leverage; (d) pay too much attention to problems.

3. ___ Constraints arise when an organization lacks sufficient internal resources to take advantage of opportunities.

Objective 5.5: Explain how the strategic business unit concept, the market share/market growth matrix, the market attractiveness/business strength matrix, and spreadsheet analysis can be used in marketing planning.

1. ___ By grouping company operating divisions into SBUs, a firm can focus on customer needs and set up distinct strategies for individual SBUs.

2. ___ The Gillette Company's Cricket disposable lighter failed to overtake the rival Bic product, so the company withdrew from the market. According to the market share/market growth matrix, the Cricket would be categorized as a (a) star; (b) question mark; (c) cash cow; (d) dog.

3. ___ The market attractiveness/business strength matrix for analyzing a portfolio of products helps companies to weed out weak products and identify promising candidates for more investments.

Objective 5.6: Identify the major types of forecasting methods.

1. ___ A technique that is not used in quantitative sales forecasting is (a) sales force composite; (b) trend analysis; (c) least-squares analysis; (d) market testing.
2. ___ The Delphi technique solicits forecasts from persons outside the firm.
3. ___ Trend analysis is most useful for new-product sales forecasts.

Objective 5.7: Explain the steps in the forecasting process.

1. ___ Top-down sales forecasting starts by projecting the effects of external market events and industry trends on the firm.
2. ___ Grass-roots forecasting is the last step in top-down forecasting.
3. ___ The sales-force composite method provides a broad view of the company's market situation.

Students: See the solutions section located on page S-1 to check your responses to the Achievement Check Summary.

Key Terms

planning
marketing planning
strategic planning
tactical planning
mission
SWOT analysis
strategic window
marketing strategy
strategic business unit (SBU)
market share/market growth matrix
market attractiveness/business strength matrix
spreadsheet analysis
sales forecast
jury of executive opinion
Delphi technique
sales force composite
survey of buyer intentions
market test
trend analysis
exponential smoothing
environmental forecast

Review Questions

1. List three differences that distinguish strategic planning from tactical planning.
2. What are the basic steps in the marketing planning process? Give an example of a decision that planners might make at each step.
3. Discuss how analysis of an organization's external environment and assessment of internal strengths and weaknesses can identify strategic opportunities and threats. Examine in your answer the concepts of leverage, problems, constraints, and vulnerabilities.
4. Explain the concept of a strategic window. Provide one example for a not-for-profit organization and one for a profit-seeking business.
5. Identify the two major components of a firm's marketing strategy. Why must planners consider them in a specific order?
6. What characteristics differentiate stars, cash cows, question marks, and dogs in the market share/market growth matrix? Give two examples of products in each of the four quadrants of the matrix, and suggest a marketing strategy for each product.
7. What dangers might result from rigid application of SBU portfolio models such as the market share/market growth matrix or the market attractiveness/business strength matrix?
8. Explain how spreadsheet analysis can assist a marketing manager in planning and implementing marketing strategies.
9. Compare the major types of forecasting methods. Explain the steps in the most typical method.
10. Discuss the advantages and risks of basing sales forecasts exclusively on estimates developed by the firm's sales force.

Discussion Questions

1. Prepare a case history of the strategic plans for a company in your area. Leading business magazines often report information of this nature.
2. Describe an application of SWOT analysis to the following marketing situations:
   a. A pharmaceutical company's patent for a market-leading drug is about to expire.
   b. A large construction company is located in a state that just passed a road-construction bond issue.
   c. A large commercial bank is known for its relationships with midsized businesses, supplying loans and mortgages as well as a range of business accounts and services to them. Bank executives begin to worry when two smaller commercial banks in the region merge.
   d. Royal Crown Cola was the first to develop a low-calorie, diet soft drink, but financial, distribution, and size constraints prevented the firm from exploiting its early opportunity to capture and hold the market.
3. *Financial Focus,* a new monthly magazine, was introduced last September. Its sales have continued to grow each month, despite a high cover price at $5 per issue. Monthly unit sales of the product are as follows:

September	14,000	January	28,000
October	16,000	February	29,000
November	23,000	March	33,000
December	24,000	April	12,000

Using the least-squares forecasting method, how many unit sales of *Financial Focus* would you estimate for May? For June?

4. During the first year of operations for Motor City College, enrollment totaled 1,200 students. The following year's enrollment grew to 2,100, and by the third year 2,900 students attended the college. Fourth-year enrollment totaled 4,200 students, and growth continued at a similar rate. A total of 4,400 students attended MCC in Year 5; 4,500 in Year 6; 4,800 in Year 7; 5,400 in Year 8; and 6,000 in Year 9. Apply trend analysis to estimate Motor City College's enrollment for each of the next two years.
5. Which forecasting technique(s) are most appropriate for each product? Defend your answer.
   a. Post Shredded Wheat breakfast cereal
   b. Hootie and the Blowfish rock group
   c. Kinko's copy shops
   d. *Rolling Stone* magazine

'netWork

1. Strategic planning is so important in today's competitive marketplace that a number of companies look for help from specialized consulting firms. A number of these consultants, including the Boston Consulting Group, maintain sites on the Web. Review one or two Web sites such as

http://www.bcg.com/

and then discuss the advantages and disadvantages of contracting with such firms for assistance with strategic planning. If your boss were to recommend this approach, how would you choose an appropriate consulting firm to help with your company's strategic planning?

2. One aspect of strategic marketing planning for a large, multiproduct company involves managing its various strategic business units (SBUs). Managers must analyze the strategic importance, significance, and profitability of each SBU. Dozens of such firms describe their SBUs in their Web site content. Conduct an Internet search and find an example of one such firm. Review the Web description of its SBUs and answer the following questions:
   a. Does the group of SBUs developed by this firm seem appropriate to you?
   b. Which SBUs would you seriously consider adding or deleting? Defend your answer.

3. Web sites give access to a number of software packages designed to assist with sales-forecasting tasks such as time-series analysis, exponential smoothing, and databases for planning. Use your Internet search engine to locate one or two home pages of firms such as

http://www.ecowin.com/

that develop these software packages. If you were a strategic planner, how would you rate this software? Include such performance variables as ease of use, support, thoroughness, modules, and hardware and systems software requirements. Many Web sites provide demonstration versions of featured software; you can study these demos before making your evaluation.

VIDEO CASE 5

GROWING PAINS

Fresh, firm, and juicy. That's what most people want in their apples. Americans have made apples one of their favorite fruits, consuming 10 billion pounds of them each year. Apples come in many varieties, and each person has definite ideas about which is best, whether the personal favorite is a Gala, Red Delicious, or even a Granny Smith.

Thanks to modern technology, fruit-growing and packing companies like Kropf Fruit can supply fresh apples throughout the year. Christian Kropf started this family fruit business in Lowell, Michigan, over a century ago. Through the years, Kropf Fruit has prospered as a supplier to retail grocers throughout the year. Key ingredients in the firm's success were delivering quality apples and building long-term relationships with both area growers and retail customers.

As a medium-sized processor, Kropf entered the decade of the 1990s facing important marketing planning and strategy decisions that would redefine the very nature of the firm by 2000. Kropf executives had identified several important trends, including changes in consumer preferences, consolidation in the retail grocery industry, and increased competition. Supermarket consumers were abandoning such traditional apple favorites as Jonathan, Red Delicious, and Golden Delicious in favor of newly introduced varieties such as Gala and Fuji. In addition, large chain-store operations had continued to increase their domination of the industry, building giant superstores and acquiring independents and smaller chains that had long been Kropf's primary customers. To win over the large chains as customers, a fruit processor had to be capable of filling large-volume orders. Such orders would often supply 2,000 stores rather than 200 or fewer. Because each chain's business was so large, competition among suppliers for this business also intensified.

In addition to traditional favorites like the Red Delicious apples shown above, Kropf meets the needs of an ever changing market by providing new varieties such as Fuji and Gala.

Kropf managers thought they saw a strategic window of opportunity in these trends that might allow them to position the company for the future. First, they had to decide whether Kropf should continue as a medium-sized grower or expand to serve the needs of large customers. They ultimately decided to pursue a growth strategy supported by a new marketing plan. CEO Roger Kropf explained the long-term commitment this way: "From the day you start a tree in the ground, it's going to take four to seven years before you see a money return on your investment."

The Kropf marketing planning process began by defining the firm's mission: To remain a family business while providing customers with high-quality fruit. It set an objective of growing to meet the growing needs of retailers by becoming a major packing and processing company.

In conducting a SWOT analysis, Kropf managers identified several company strengths:

KROPF
Sea Land

Improving Kropf's ability to supply large quantities of fruit to national retailers was one weakness identified in a SWOT analysis.

- Willingness to adapt to changing markets
- An open attitude and a willingness to try new marketing and merchandising ideas
- A welcoming reception for suggestions from customers and input regarding what they liked
- Loyal support from other growers who supplied Kropf with additional fruit

The analysis also identified areas of weakness:

- The firm's current inability to supply the large quantities of fruit demanded by national retailers
- Oversupply of apple varieties that were losing popularity with consumers
- Inadequate equipment to grade, sort, and store new apple varieties

Kropf executives saw opportunities in exporting to international markets, altering the firm's product mix by converting some orchards to grow new apple varieties, and expanding and upgrading its packing facilities. They saw competition from new types of exotic fruit as a major threat.

Based on this assessment, management devised a marketing strategy to achieve their objectives. The plan involved increasing orchard acreage by at least 50 percent to grow new apple varieties. In addition, the plan called for designing new processing facilities with capacity to handle 50 percent more fruit than Kropf currently needed. The installation of high-technology processing and refrigeration equipment would help Kropf to process fruit quickly and efficiently at the lowest possible cost.

Much of Kropf's short-term tactical planning centers around determining apple supply and demand. Apple producers can forecast sales to customers much more easily than they can predict production yields, which vary because of weather conditions. Kropf prepares annual sales forecasts based on past and projected world and U.S. production statistics published by the U.S. Department of Agriculture as a starting point. Kropf marketers adjust these data to the firm's geographic market and to its mix of apple varieties. If the forecast indicates inadequate expected yields from the firm's own orchards and grower-partners, Kropf contracts to purchase additional apples from other growers to meet anticipated customer needs.

Even though Kropf has only partially completed its ten-year growth plan, interim reviews of its execution suggest that the growth strategy was the right choice. The firm had already made significant progress in implementing the new plan by planting some 80,000 new trees and installing new processing equipment. CEO Roger Kropf also acknowledges that the strategic plan is opening marketing doors that the firm's sales representatives were never able to enter before, enabling them to negotiate with some of the largest retailers in the nation. "These retailers today will talk to us in the same way as they might talk to a

Chiquita or a Dole or a very large conglomerate. They give us equal time today that prior to this we wouldn't have gotten."

http://www.kropf-inc.com/

Driven by its new strategic plan, Kropf has grown to become one of the largest regional fruit processors and distributors in the United States. It markets 18 apple varieties ranging from the well-established Golden Delicious to the newer Ginger Gold. It not only markets the yield from its own 1,500 acres, but also another 4,000 acres owned by more than 60 growers. As the grocery industry continues to consolidate, Kropf will continue to adopt appropriate growth strategies.

Questions

1. Relate the Kropf Fruit Co. strategic planning process to the steps in the planning process discussed in this chapter.
2. How important is relationship marketing to Kropf in implementing its growth strategy? Recommend measures by which the firm can strengthen these relationships.
3. Which of the sales forecasting techniques discussed in this chapter appear to give the most valuable information for Kropf marketers in estimating supply and demand conditions for apples?
4. SWOT analysis played an important role in the development of the Kropf strategic plan. Visit the Mind Tools Web site at
   http://www.mindtools.com/swot.html/
   and review the questions suggested there for SWOT analysis. Then find an actual SWOT analysis on the Web. Does the actual analysis of the firm you selected follow the guidelines suggested by Mind Tools? Evaluate the actual analysis. How could it be improved?

Source: "SWOT Analysis—Strengths, Weaknesses, Opportunities, Threats," downloaded from http://www.mindtools.com/swot.html/, April 1997.

APPENDIX 5A

Developing a Marketing Plan

The natural outgrowth of the marketing process is a *marketing plan*—a detailed description of resources and actions a firm needs to achieve its stated marketing objectives. After formulating and implementing this plan, marketers may reevaluate it periodically to gauge its success in moving the organization toward stated objectives.

Although the formats, lengths, and focuses of marketing plans may vary, they typically focus on answering three questions:

- Where are we now?
- Where do we want to go?
- How can we get there?

The following outline illustrates how marketing plans provide answers to each of these questions. The format applies in a manufacturing, wholesaling, retailing, or service setting.

COMPONENTS OF THE MARKETING PLAN

I. Situation Analysis (Where is the firm now?)

A. Historical Background
- Nature of the firm
- Sales and profit history
- Current situation

B. Consumer Analysis
- What customers does the firm serve?
- What market segments can it identify?
- How many consumers want its product?
- How much do they buy and why?

C. Competitive Analysis
- Given the nature of the markets—size, characteristics, competitive activities, and strategies—what marketing opportunities can this firm identify?

II. Marketing Objectives (Where does the firm want to go?)

A. Sales Objectives
- What level of sales volume can the firm achieve during the next year? During the next five years?

B. Profit Objectives
- Given the firm's sales and cost structure, how much profit should it generate?

C. Customer Objectives
- How will the firm serve customers in its target market?
- What does the firm want present and potential customers to think about it?

III. Strategy (How can the firm get where it wants to go?)

A. Product Strategy
- What goods and services should the firm offer to meet consumers' needs?
- What is their exact nature?

B. Pricing Strategy
- At what general level should the firm set prices?
- What specific prices and price concessions are appropriate?

C. Distribution Strategy
- Through what channel(s) will the firm distribute its product offerings?
- What physical distribution facilities does it need?
- Where should it locate those facilities?
- What major characteristics should it define for distribution facilities?

D. Promotional Strategy
- What mix of personal selling, advertising, and sales promotion activities should the firm pursue?
- How much should it spend to communicate what themes through what media?

E. Financial Strategy
- What financial impact will this plan have on a one-year pro forma (projected) income statement?
- How does projected income compare with expected revenue if the firm does not implement the plan?

SAMPLE MARKETING PLAN

The following excerpts from a marketing plan prepared for a motel, the Sleepy Hollow Inn, illustrate the value of such a plan to an organization's pursuit of its objectives.

Figure 5A.1 Sleepy Hollow Lodging Market

	Individuals or Couples	Groups
Business	Salespeople Management personnel People conducting on-premises business	Conventions Seminars, Workshops Union negotiations
Nonbusiness	Vacationers Military personnel People relocating	Tour groups Party groups Sports groups Reunions

Sleepy Hollow Objectives

I. Short Term: 1999

A. Sales Objective

- To increase food sales 100 percent by heightening awareness of the Sleepy Hollow restaurant and by changing consumer attitudes toward motel restaurants—especially the Sleepy Hollow restaurant.

Situation Analysis

I. Consumer Analysis

A. Lodging

The lodging market can be broadly divided into the segments shown in the marketing grid in Figure 5A.1. These distinct groups of potential customers represent the market that the Sleepy Hollow must attract. The basic consumer characteristics most appropriate for analyzing the lodging market include the reason for a guest's stay (business or nonbusiness) and the number of guests staying (individuals, couples, or groups). Businesspeople might include salespeople on regular routes, management personnel on special supervisory trips, or people who wish to do business temporarily from their rooms. Business guests include convention visitors, personnel attending company seminars, and the like. Food sales may come from transactions in the public or private dining facilities. Sleepy Hollow derives revenues from private dining from three basic sources: wedding rehearsal dinners, wedding receptions, and civic luncheons (see Figure 5A.2). The motel may generate potential revenues from these three sources of over $100,000 each year. The Sleepy Hollow appears to have captured a large share of this market. However, further analysis shows that, although total food sales have increased somewhat in recent years, Sleepy Hollow did not generate growth in food sales revenues sufficient to maintain its market share. Management recognizes few competitors for the private dining market, but Sleepy Hollow has directed little marketing effort toward local civic organizations, which are important potential customers.

Figure 5A.2 Sleepy Hollow Food Service Market

	Individuals or Couples	Groups
Guests	Vacationers Salespeople People on family visits People relocating	Tour groups Conventions Sports groups
Nonguests	"Nights out" customers Special occasion customers Regular buffet customers	Tour groups Business meetings Rehearsal dinners Receptions Civic groups

II. Competitive Analysis

A. General Market: Lodging, Food, and Beverage
Sleepy Hollow competes with outlets of two hotel chains for the lodging market and with 24 full-service and fast-food restaurants in the food-service market. The motel contains 20 percent of the available beds in Mount Pleasant, and its restaurant has a seating capacity of 120.

The number of food suppliers and food items available have increased, keeping any rise in prices somewhat lower than the inflation rate. However, laundry service rates have increased due to necessary improvements required of providers by the EPA and OSHA. All channel relationships are strong.

Table 5A.1 shows the total sales for lodging and eating places from 1995 through 1998 in Mount Pleasant along with Sleepy Hollow's share of this market. The figures indicate that total city sales increased 20 percent, but Sleepy Hollow's sales increased only 15 percent.

Table 5A.1 Sleepy Hollow's Share of the Mount Pleasant Market for Lodging and Food (1995–1998)

Year	Mount Pleasant	Sleepy Hollow	Market Share
1995	$24,176,034	$1,214,480	5.0%
1996	23,056,244	1,381,104	6.0
1997	24,942,588	1,423,842	5.7
1998	29,110,886	1,430,086	4.9

B. Lodging
A breakdown of lodging sales for Mount Pleasant and Sleepy Hollow is shown in Table 5A.2. The last column indicates Sleepy Hollow's market share. Although its lodging sales increased substantially during the 1995 to 1998 period, its market share fell. Two new competitors entered the expanding market, cutting into its market share. Sleepy Hollow's market share fell to 13 percent in 1998, while overall sales fell slightly more than 2 percent, and area lodging sales rose more than 17 percent.

C. Food Sales
Sleepy Hollow's current share of the Mount Pleasant and Monroe County market is shown in Table 5A.3. The table also shows how these market shares have changed over the past five years.

D. Beverage
No sales data for alcoholic beverages were available to allow a trend comparison on a state, county, or city level.

Table 5A.2 Sleepy Hollow's Share of the Mount Pleasant Lodging Market (1995–1998)

Year	Mount Pleasant	Sleepy Hollow	Market Share
1995	$5,354,172	$803,112	15.0%
1996	5,209,544	935,658	18.0
1997	6,048,874	978,256	16.2
1998	7,094,854	953,208	13.4

III. Corporate Analysis
Sleepy Hollow was established in 1969, and it remains a family owned business. Operations have yielded a net profit over the years averaging 2.3 percent. The company owns its land and buildings outright, and the facilities are well-maintained. Personnel turnover rates are low. The company can draw on credit for improvements.

IV. Policy Analysis
The local government is raising property and hotel taxes to fund new school buildings and highway improvements. Sleepy Hollow has kept its prices competitive.

BASIC MARKETING STRATEGY STATEMENT

I. Service Strategy

A. Lodging
Maintain high-quality facilities and services. Managers should devote time to producing a marketing plan for long-term improvements such as redecorating and expansion.

B. Food
Develop an identity and image for the restaurant separate and distinct from that of the Sleepy Hollow motel by (1) choosing a new name for the dining facilities, (2) developing a new menu, and (3) making minor changes in decor to create a distinctive dining atmosphere.

C. Beverage
Develop an atmosphere in the lounge that will complement and reinforce the restaurant's new image.

II. Pricing, Distribution, and Promotional Strategies

A. Lodging

- Increase occupancy during seasonal and weekend slack periods by developing and promoting special holiday packages.

Table 5A.3 Sleepy Hollow's Share of the Monroe County and Mount Pleasant Food Market (1995–1998)

Year	Monroe County	Mount Pleasant	Sleepy Hollow	Market Share for Monroe County	Market Share for Mount Pleasant
1995	$20,345,220	$18,821,862	$438,368	2.1%	2.3%
1996	22,546,924	17,846,700	445,446	1.9	2.4
1997	24,430,106	18,893,714	445,586	1.8	2.3
1998	27,989,222	22,016,032	476,878	1.7	2.1

- ▼ Attract participants and spectators to special events through direct-mail promotional literature where names and addresses are available.

B. Food

- ▼ Create awareness of the changes in the restaurant among local residents as well as motel guests by developing a complete promotional campaign and improving in-house promotions. (In-house efforts should include posting lobby signs and placing promotional "tent" cards in rooms.)
- ▼ Attract civic-group luncheons and wedding rehearsal dinners through price dealing and personal selling.

C. Beverage

Improve local residents' awareness of the lounge through a direct-mail campaign.

III. Forecasts and Budgets

A. If the plan is implemented

A $20,000 increase in advertising expenditures should improve both food and lodging revenues. In particular, targeting private dining groups and wedding parties should boost food and beverage revenues. Profits could then fund redecorating and expansion.

B. If the plan is not implemented

Profits should remain in the 4 to 5 percent range unless other competitors enter the market. This profit performance would delay improvement plans and adversely affect long-term profits.

ASSIGNMENT

Follow the format described in this appendix to develop a marketing plan for one of the following businesses:

a. Local retailer
b. Local service provider
c. Local shopping center
d. Not-for-profit organization
e. College or university

CHAPTER 6

MARKETING RESEARCH AND DECISION SUPPORT SYSTEMS

Frito Lay
Home
Back
Forward
Reload
Load Images
Current URL:
http://www.fritolay.com/home.html
Page complete
WOW!
FRITO-LAY SNACKS
Recipes
What's New
Frito Lay
Fun Stuff
Netscape: Mediamark Research
Location: http://www.mediamark.com/
What's New?
What's Cool?
Destinations
Net Search
People
Software
Quick Search
Download Center
The Source
What's New
Applications
Products & Services
Free Data
New Media
Staff Directory
Press Releases
Mediamark Research, Inc.
home
Netscape: Welcome to J.D. Power and Associates: An Inte
Netsite: http://www.jdpower.com/
J.D. POWERguide to Automobiles
J.D. POWER AND ASSOCIATES
International Marketing Information Firm
NEWS
Press
GOODYEAR #1 in Tires
GOODYEAR #1 in TIRES
AT&T
INVESTORS
Newsroom
it's All Within Your Reach
AT&T WorldNet
Inside AT&T Labs
SERVICES
HOME

Chapter Objectives

1. Describe the development of the marketing research function and its major activities.
2. List and explain the steps in the marketing research process.
3. Explain the different sampling techniques used by marketing researchers.
4. Differentiate between the types and sources of primary and secondary data.
5. Identify the methods by which marketing researchers collect primary data.
6. Discuss the challenges of conducting marketing research in global markets.
7. Outline the contributions of marketing decision support systems to the marketing decision process.

The Real Thing--Virtually

Long before the 1996 presidential campaign heated up, business leaders in San Diego were plotting how to lure the Republican convention to their seaside community. The weather certainly increased the appeal. The ocean, the world famous zoo, and even Sea World's killer whale shows were all draws. Yet GOP organizers remained skeptical. They balked at San Diego's convention center, which had a reputation of being too small for major events. But the city's cyber-savvy marketers helped to erase these doubts when they augmented their sales message with computerized virtual reality.

City officials prepared a computer-generated tour of the convention center to convince the skeptics. Computer images of the building's interior and exterior provided a red-carpet electronic tour for the GOP advance team. The Republicans immediately asked to see the view from the worst seat on the convention floor. They wanted to see the view from the skyboxes and what the convention floor would look like from a television network's anchor booth. What they saw eased their fears, and San Diego won the competition.

Special
Nutri-Grain
Crispix
Crispix
Bran Flakes
Bran Flake
Kellogg's
FROSTED FLAKES
CAP'N CRUNCH
CAP'N CRUNCH
Cocoa Puffs
FROSTED FLAKES
Cheerios
Cheerios
Honey Nut Cheerios
Puffed
$2.99

Virtual reality, a technology developed by NASA as a training tool for astronauts, is no longer some futuristic gimmick confined to *Star Trek* episodes and Hollywood movies. Companies are increasingly using its capabilities to design and develop new products like jet engines and even entire buildings. Marketers well beyond San Diego's city limits are using virtual simulations to test products much more cheaply and efficiently than they could in real life.

One of the most attractive selling points for virtual reality marketing is its flexibility. A company can introduce many more variables into a marketing experiment than it could manage while escorting a focus group through a real store. With this technology, marketers can evaluate situations under rapidly changing market conditions. Virtual reality can allow marketers to try out different competitive variables like prices, promotions, and shelf allocations within minutes.

That's exactly what The Goodyear Tire & Rubber Co. did when it conducted a study of 1,000 people who had recently purchased tires or who planned to do so in the near future. Traditionally, Goodyear had sold its tires through its own retail stores, but a lot of unanswered questions clouded the decision to offer the tires in other retail outlets. The company turned to virtual simulations for some of those answers.

A volunteer, sitting in front of a computer, took an imaginary trip through a number of different tire stores stocked with various brands and models of tires. During the trips, the computer program varied the prices and warranty levels of the competing tire brands. Goodyear marketers learned a great deal from these simulations. For instance, the company developed strategies for repricing its product line, identified which of its competitors posed the greatest threat, and pinpointed which of its own brands were vulnerable to attack.

http://www.goodyear.com/

This technology is a valuable tool not only for major corporations. Virtual simulations also provide economical information for small players. Many companies find that prohibitive costs prevent traditional test marketing, which can require producing a sample run of a product and then introducing it into a typical midsize market. Unlike virtual reality marketing, this kind of hands-on consumer testing can take six months to a year, and it costs millions of dollars.

Computer-simulated marketing research could also generate a bonanza of information for overseas marketers. Virtual reality testing can help managers decide whether to enter foreign markets, especially in parts of the world where conventional marketing research is difficult. In Mexico, for instance, researchers can find only sketchy data from UPC scanners and consumer panels.

Some experts warn, however, that virtual reality can never completely solve a marketer's problems. Simply relying upon data culled from virtual reality tests can be a mistake. "Just because it's technically capable, that doesn't mean that when you put the average person behind a computer you're going to get true responses," says Michael Hammer, electronic communications manager with the American Marketing Association in Chicago. "Any time you simulate an experience, you're not getting the experience itself. It's still a simulation."[1]

CHAPTER OVERVIEW

Marketers must not only solve problems as they arise, but also anticipate and prevent those that may occur in the future. To avoid surprises and make the best decisions possible, they require the right information in sufficient quantities to choose effective solutions.

Marketing research is the process of collecting and using information for marketing decision making. This decision-oriented marketing information comes from a variety of sources which provide *data* to the researcher. Some data comes from well-planned studies designed to elicit specific information. Researchers may obtain other valuable intelligence from sales force reports, accounting data, and published reports. Still other data may emerge from controlled experiments and computer simulations. Marketing research aids decision makers by presenting pertinent data in a way that transforms it into useful *information,* analyzing it, and suggesting possible actions.

This chapter deals with the marketing research function, which is closely linked with the other elements of the marketing planning process. Indeed, all marketing research should fit within the framework of the organization's strategic plan.

Information collected through marketing research underlies much of the material on marketing planning and forecasting in Chapter 5 and on market segmentation in Chapter 7. Clearly, the marketing research function is the primary source of the information needed to make effective marketing decisions.

THE MARKETING RESEARCH FUNCTION

Before looking at how marketing research is conducted, let's look at its historical development, the people and organizations it involves, and the activities it entails.

New media technologies such as the World Wide Web and virtual reality are opening up new channels through which researchers can tap into data and information. A key focus of this chapter will be the relationship of technology and marketing research.

Development of the Marketing Research Function

More than 100 years have passed since N. W. Ayer conducted the first organized marketing research project in 1879. A second important milestone in the development of marketing research occurred in 1911, when Charles C. Parlin organized and became manager of the nation's first commercial research department at Curtis Publishing Company.

Parlin got his start as a marketing researcher by counting soup cans in Philadelphia's garbage! Parlin was employed selling advertising space in the *Saturday Evening Post,* but the Campbell Soup Company resisted his offers, believing that the magazine reached primarily working-class readers who preferred to make their own soup rather than spend 10 cents for a can of prepared soup. Campbell was targeting its product at higher-income people who could afford to pay for convenience. In response, Parlin began counting soup cans in the garbage collected from different neighborhoods. To Campbell's surprise, Parlin's research revealed that more canned soup was sold to working-class families than to wealthy ones, who had servants to make soup for them. Campbell's quickly became a *Saturday Evening Post* client. It is interesting to note that garbage remains a good source of information for marketing researchers. Some airlines have studied the leftovers from onboard meals to determine what to serve passengers.

Much early research gathered little more than written testimonials from purchasers of firms' products. Research methods became more sophisticated during the 1930s as the development of statistical techniques led to refinements in sampling procedures and greater accuracy in research findings.

In recent years, advances in computer technology have significantly changed the complexion of marketing research. Besides accelerating the pace and broadening the base of data collection, computers have aided marketers in making informed decisions about problems and opportunities. Computer simulations, for example, allow marketers to evaluate alternatives by posing what-if questions. Marketing researchers at many consumer goods firms simulate product introductions through computer programs to help them decide whether to risk real-world product launches or even to subject products to test marketing.

Who Conducts Marketing Research?

According to the American Marketing Association, 77 percent of the nation's consumer goods manufacturers maintain formal marketing research departments. The comparable number for makers of business products is 51 percent.

The size and organizational form of the marketing research function is usually tied to the structure of the company. Some firms organize research units to support different product lines, brands, or geographic areas. Others organize their research functions according to the types of research they need performed, such as sales analysis, new-product development, or advertising evaluation.[2]

Many firms depend on independent marketing research firms. These independent organizations might handle one part of a larger study, such as conducting consumer interviews. Firms can also contract out entire research studies.

Marketers usually decide whether to conduct a study internally or through an outside organization based on cost. Another major consideration is the reliability and accuracy of the information collected by an outside organization.

A marketing research firm can provide technical assistance and expertise not available within the contracting

Briefly speaking

"Fifty percent of Japanese companies do not have a marketing department, and ninety percent have no special section for marketing research. The reason is that everyone is considered to be a marketing specialist."

Hiroyuki Takeuchi (1934–)
Educator and business writer

Marketing Dictionary

marketing research Collection and use of information for marketing decision making.

firm. Interaction with outside suppliers also helps to ensure that a researcher does not conduct a study only to validate a favorite personal theory or preferred option.

Marketing research companies range in size from sole proprietorships to national and international firms such as A. C. Nielsen, Information Resources Inc. (IRI), and Arbitron. In a recent year, total worldwide revenues from the top 50 marketing research firms equaled $4.6 billion; they earned almost 40 percent of these revenues outside the

http://www.mediamark.com/

United States. In fact, D&B Marketing Information Services, the largest research firm, received 64 percent of its revenues from non-U.S. customers.[3]

Marketing research suppliers can be classified as syndicated services, full-service suppliers, or limited-service suppliers, depending on the primary thrust of their methods. Some full-service organizations are also willing to take on limited-service activities.

Figure 6.1 A Syndicated Marketing Research Service

NOW WHAT?
How do advertisers know that they're communicating with their best prospects? How do media prove they deliver them? ▪ With all the choices out there, there's one choice that's clear to both buyers and sellers of advertising: Mediamark Research. MRI's SURVEY OF THE AMERICAN CONSUMER is the most accurate, best-respected, most widely-used source of data available for marketers and media professionals. It's the source for determining which media deliver which target audiences. ▪ It's one choice that more and more people in our industry agree on. And while Mediamark Research can't guarantee that buyers and sellers will always agree about everything, we do make sure they're equally armed with the best resources.
?
MRI
The Source

Syndicated Services An organization that regularly provides a standardized set of data to all customers is called a *syndicated service.* Mediamark Research Inc. (MRI), for example, operates a syndicated product research service based on personal interviews with adults regarding their exposure to advertising media, as shown in the ad in Figure 6.1. Clients include advertisers, advertising agencies, magazines, newspapers, broadcasters, and cable TV networks.

Full-Service Research Suppliers An organization that contracts with clients to conduct complete marketing research projects is called a *full-service research supplier.* J. D. Power and Associates is a full-service firm that specializes in the domestic and international automobile markets.

http://www.jdpower.com/

A full-service supplier becomes the client's marketing research arm, performing all of the steps in the marketing research process (as discussed later in this chapter).

Limited-Service Research Suppliers A marketing research firm that specializes in a limited number of activities, such as conducting field interviews or performing data processing, is called a *limited-service research supplier.* Working almost exclusively for clients in the movie industry, The National Research Group Inc. specializes in rating entertainment facilities through input from audiences of movie-goers. The firm also prepares studies to help clients develop advertising strategies and track awareness and interest. Syndicated services can be considered a type of limited-service research supplier.

MARKETING RESEARCH ACTIVITIES

Approximately three out of every four new products will eventually fail to attract enough buyers to remain viable. Why? The most important reason given by marketers for new product clunkers is the seller's failure to understand market needs.[4] One important marketing research activity matches new products to potential customers in order to improve those products' chances of success. Marketers also conduct research to analyze sales of their own and competitors' products, to gauge the performance of existing products, and to guide the development of promotional campaigns and product enhancements.

Automakers, for instance, conduct marketing research to pinpoint which paint colors they should offer on new car

Figure 6.2 Types of Questions Marketing Research Can Help Answer

❶ Scanning

- **a.** What kinds of people buy our products? Where do they live? How much do they earn? How many of them can we identify?
- **b.** Are the markets for our products increasing or decreasing? Can research indicate promising markets that we have not yet reached?
- **c.** What economic, social, political, and technological trends are likely to affect our markets? How?

❷ Risk Assessment

- **a.** Which of several product designs is most likely to generate the most success?
- **b.** What price should we charge for our products? How will profits change under various pricing strategies?
- **c.** Where and by whom should our products be sold?
- **d.** How much should we spend on promotion? How should we allocate this amount among products and geographic areas? What type of media will most effectively distribute our message?
- **e.** What costs and benefits can we expect with certain planned marketing strategies?

❸ Monitoring

- **a.** What is our overall market share? What is our share in each geographic area? What is our share for each customer type?
- **b.** Who are our competitors? What are their strengths and weaknesses? How do our strengths and weaknesses compare?
- **c.** Are customers satisfied with our products? How well have we served them?
- **d.** How does the public perceive our company? What is our reputation with the trade?

models.[5] When you buy something from a supermarket, information about what you purchase is automatically recorded through the checkout stand's UPC scanner. The data helps manufacturers and retailers to track sales.[6]

Through exploratory research, 3M Corp. identified a consumer desire for a rustproof, nonfraying soap pad. This finding led to the introduction of two new products thatincreased the firm's scouring pad and sponge sales by 20 percent.[7]

Technology and business-to-business marketers also employ marketing research to develop and refine their goods and services. Netscape, for example, offered free downloads of its Internet software to computer users and then asked for input about the product's performance. AT&T invites small-business owners to participate in roundtable discussions about their communications needs in order to identify how to sell most effectively to the small-business market.

http://www.netscape.com/

Marketing research activities can be divided into three main categories: scanning, risk assessment, and monitoring.[8] Figure 6.2 illustrates the types of questions that each activity can help answer.

Scanning activities search for opportunities and challenges in the firm's environment. As Chapter 3 indicated, a firm's environment can change rapidly. The marketing research function should play a key role in marketers' effort to track and identify any changes in technology, markets, and cultural and economic conditions that will affect the firm. Scanning activities involve primarily future-oriented research.

After identifying potential opportunities and challenges, marketing research helps businesses to develop effective strategies and tactics. These decisions often carry considerable risk: The firm has no guarantee that its chosen programs will succeed. Therefore, marketing researchers direct their *risk assessment* activities toward evaluating the likelihood of commercial success by linking proposed actions to feedback from customers in real or simulated conditions. Risk assessment activities also help the firm to measure the costs and benefits of a particular course of action, such as introducing a new product or implementing a new promotional technique.

Scanning and risk assessment activities focus on the future. Monitoring activities, however, assess current events. This part of marketing research seeks to discover how well past decisions are working out now. *Monitoring* activities include analyzing sales and profit data, customer satisfaction levels, and results from advertising and promotion programs. In a sense, monitoring activities can be defined as diagnostic tools. They aim the marketing research effort at identifying problems and suggesting ways of fixing them.

While marketing research can provide insight into marketers' questions, not every marketing research effort yields valuable results. When marketing research is poorly designed or implemented, companies can face unpleasant surprises. The next section will explain the steps of an effective marketing research process.

THE MARKETING RESEARCH PROCESS

As discussed earlier, businesspeople rely on marketing research to provide the information they need to make effective decisions about their firm's current and future activities. The chances of making a successful decision improve when the right information is provided at the right time in the decision-making process. To achieve this goal, marketing researchers often follow the six-step process shown in Figure 6.3. In the initial stages, researchers define the problem, conduct exploratory research, and formulate a hypothesis to be tested. Next, they create a design for the research study, collect data, and finally, interpret and present the research information in decision making. The following sections take a closer look at each step of the marketing research process.

Briefly speaking

"The art of prophecy is very difficult, especially with respect to the future."

Mark Twain (1835–1910)
American author

Define the Problem

Someone once remarked that well-defined problems are half-solved. A well-defined problem permits the researcher to focus on securing the exact information needed for the solution. Clearly defining the question that research needs to answer increases the speed and accuracy of the research process.

Researchers must carefully avoid confusing symptoms of a problem with the problem itself. A symptom merely alerts marketers that they have a problem. For example, suppose that a maker of frozen pizzas sees its market share drop from 8 percent to 5 percent in six months. The loss of market share is a symptom of the problem the company must solve. To define the problem, the firm must look for the underlying causes of its market share loss.

A logical starting point might be the firm's marketing mix elements and target market. Suppose, for example, that it has recently changed its promotional strategies. Research might then seek to answer the question, "what must we do to improve the effectiveness of our marketing mix?" The firm might also look at possible environmental changes. Perhaps a new competitor entered the firm's market. Decision makers will need information to help answer the question, "what must we do to distinguish our company from the new competitor?"

For an example, consider the experience of Frito-Lay with its Rold Gold Pretzels. While the percentage of households buying pretzels had risen 20 percent between the late 1980s and 1994, the percentage of pretzel lovers choosing Rold Gold had risen from 25 percent to 39 percent. Brand managers believed that they could improve Rold Gold's performance by spending more money promoting the brand. Frito-Lay's top management weren't convinced. They wanted proof that increased promotional spending would translate into better sales. Rold Gold's marketing research team then set out to answer a critical question: Would increased spending on the brand increase sales?[9] The goal in the first stage of the marketing research process was, therefore, to pinpoint the main question that decision makers needed to answer to make successful choices.

Conduct Exploratory Research

Once they have defined the question they want to answer, researchers can begin exploratory research. **Exploratory research** seeks to discover the cause of a specific problem by discussing the problem with informed sources both within and outside the firm, and by examining data from other information sources. The pizza firm, for example, might talk with its wholesalers, retailers, and customers. Executives might also ask for input from the sales force or look for overall market clues.

Rold Gold brand managers looked at several sources in their exploratory investigation of the brand's performance. For example, one generic study of American eating habits showed increasing consumer interest in avoiding fatty foods and looking for low-fat snacks. Another study

http://www.fritolay.com/

showed low consumer awareness for the various pretzel brands available, including Rold Gold. Exploratory interviews with consumers indicated that Rold Gold's package size might affect the brand's performance. Internal data suggested that brand loyalty was also an issue. In 1992, 42 percent of the customers who had bought Rold Gold stopped buying—even as the number of new customers increased. These exploratory findings led Rold Gold researchers to focus on ways to increase consumer loyalty, increase consumption, and determine the most effective outlets for promotional expenditures.[10]

Figure 6.3 The Marketing Research Process

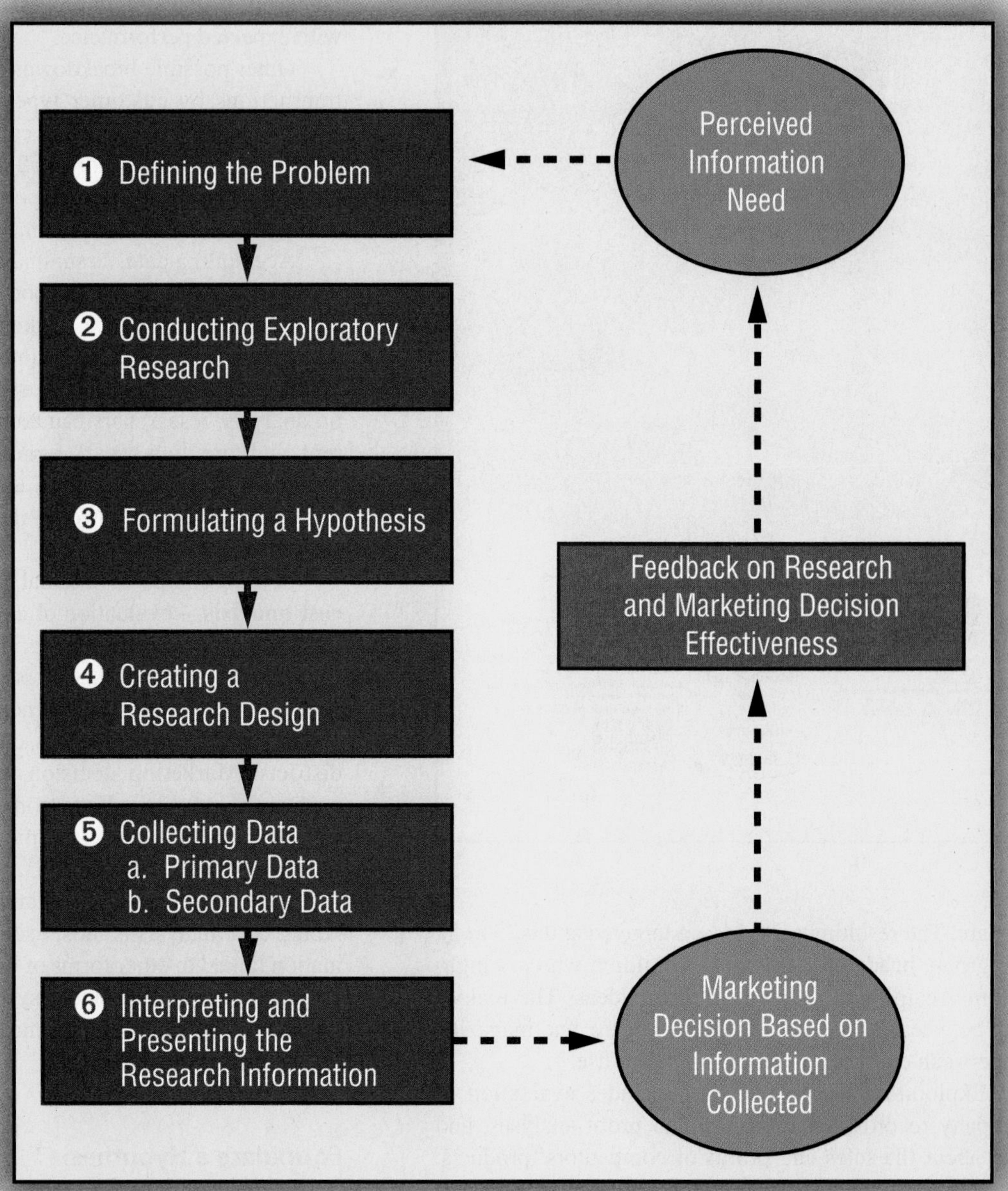
Perceived Information Need
1 Defining the Problem
2 Conducting Exploratory Research
3 Formulating a Hypothesis
4 Creating a Research Design
5 Collecting Data
a. Primary Data
b. Secondary Data
6 Interpreting and Presenting the Research Information
Marketing Decision Based on Information Collected
Feedback on Research and Marketing Decision Effectiveness

The Corning Consumer Products Company, makers of Pyrex and Corning cookware, used exploratory research to come up with an idea for a successful new product. Corning already conducted a semiannual survey of female consumers, the primary market for housewares, to track consumer awareness and usage of Corning products. The firm's marketers reexamined this research for possible new product ideas. They noted that a question about how they used their cookware found that about 50 percent of the respondents used their Pyrex and Corning cookware to bring food to events away from home. After considering this information, Corning decided to pursue the idea of a line of cookware designed specifically for transporting food to social events.[11]

Exploratory research helped Campbell Soup Company to create the recipe advertising campaign illustrated in Figure 6.4. From consumer research, Campbell learned that households with working couples want quick, tasty meals that don't cost much and don't take much time to

Marketing Dictionary

exploratory research Process of discussing a marketing problem with informed sources both within and outside the firm and examining information from secondary sources.

Figure 6.4 **Advertising Guided by Exploratory Research**

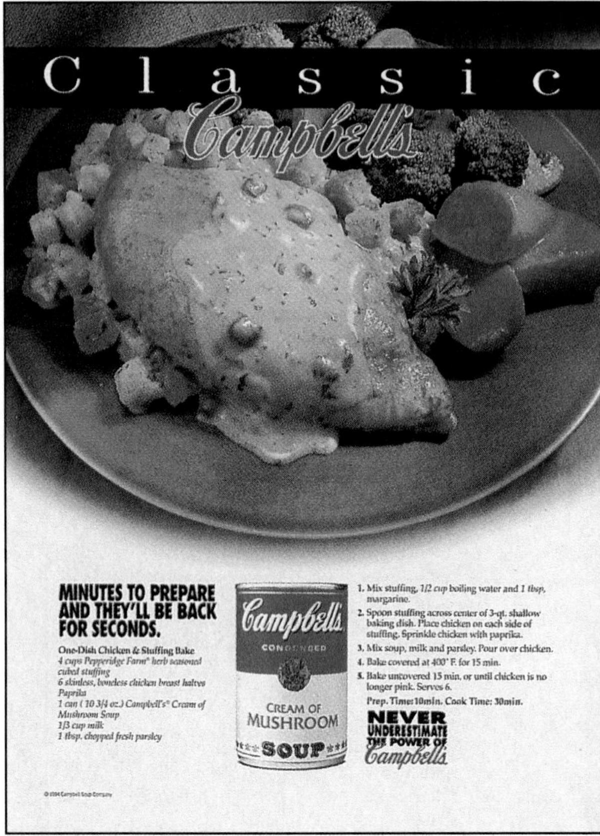
Classic
Campbell's
MINUTES TO PREPARE AND THEY'LL BE BACK FOR SECONDS.
One-Dish Chicken & Stuffing Bake
4 cups Pepperidge Farm® herb seasoned cubed stuffing
6 skinless, boneless chicken breast halves
Paprika
1 can (10 3/4 oz.) Campbell's® Cream of Mushroom Soup
1/3 cup milk
1 tbsp. chopped fresh parsley
Campbell's
CREAM OF MUSHROOM
SOUP
1. Mix stuffing, 1/2 cup boiling water and 1 tbsp. margarine.
2. Spoon stuffing across center of 3-qt. shallow baking dish. Place chicken on each side of stuffing. Sprinkle chicken with paprika.
3. Mix soup, milk and parsley. Pour over chicken.
4. Bake covered at 400° F. for 15 min.
5. Bake uncovered 15 min. or until chicken is no longer pink. Serves 6.
Prep. Time: 10min. Cook Time: 30min.
NEVER UNDERESTIMATE THE POWER OF Campbell's

prepare. The resulting print ads are targeted at the 25 to 54 age group, heads of families with children who are high-volume recipe users looking for new ideas. The recipes take between 10 and 20 minutes to prepare, and magazine readers can clip and save them for future use.

Exploratory research usually includes evaluation of company records, such as sales and profit analyses, and data about the sales and profits of competitors' products. Marketing researchers often refer to internal data collection as *situation analysis.* They may use the term *informal investigation* for exploratory interviews with informed persons outside their firms.

Using Internal Data Marketers can find valuable data in their firm's own internal records. Three commonly available sources of valuable internal data are sales records, financial statements, and marketing cost analyses. Marketers analyze sales performance records to gain an overall view of company efficiency and to find clues to potential problems. Easily prepared from company invoices or a computer database system, this **sales analysis** can give quite revealing results for the marketing executive. The study typically compares actual and expected sales based on a detailed sales forecast by territory, product, customer, and salesperson. Once the *sales quota*—the level of expected sales to which actual results are compared—has been established, it is a simple process to compare actual results with expected performance.

Other possible breakdowns for sales analysis separate transactions by customer type, product, method of sale (mail, telephone, or personal contact), type of order (cash or credit), and size of order. Sales analysis is one of the least expensive and most important sources of marketing information available to a firm.

Accounting data, as summarized in the firm's financial statements, can be another good tool for identifying financial issues that influence marketing. Financial statements, which report nondetailed accounts, contribute mainly by helping analysts to raise more specific questions. Using ratio analysis, researchers can compare performance in current and previous years against industry benchmarks. These exercises may hint at possible problems, but only more detailed analysis would reveal specific causes of indicated variations.

A third source of internal information is **marketing cost analysis**—evaluation of expenses for tasks like selling, warehousing, advertising, and delivery—in order to determine the profitability of particular customers, territories, or product lines. Firms most commonly examine the allocation of costs to products, customers, and territories or districts. Marketing decision makers then evaluate the profitability of particular customers and districts on the basis of the sales produced and the costs incurred in generating those sales.

Like sales performance and financial research, marketing cost analysis is most useful when it provides information linked to other forms of marketing research. A well-designed computer database system can accomplish these linkages as in the course of moving information between the firm's units.[12]

Formulate a Hypothesis

After defining the problem and conducting an exploratory investigation, the marketer should be able to formulate a **hypothesis**—a tentative explanation for some specific event. A hypothesis is a statement about the relationship among variables that carries clear implications for testing this relationship. It sets the stage for more in-depth research by further clarifying what researchers need to test.

As we've already noted, exploratory research uncovered several issues for Rold Gold's brand managers that suggested underlying influences on the product's sales performance. Based on these results, they decided to focus research on ways to increase consumer loyalty and consumption and to target promotional expenditures at the most effective outlets. They tested the hypothesis that, by increasing consumer loyalty and finding the best promotional outlets, they could increase sales of the brand.[13] Similarly, after exploratory research, Corning marketers hypothesized that a line of cookware designed to accommodate cooked food transport would be a successful new product line that would meet consumer needs.[14]

Not all marketing research studies test specific hypotheses. However, a carefully designed study can benefit from the rigor introduced by developing a hypothesis before beginning data collection and analysis.

Create a Research Design

To test hypotheses and find solutions to marketing problems, a marketer creates a **research design,** a series of decisions that, taken together, comprise a master plan or model for conducting marketing research.

In designing a research project, marketers must be sure that the study will measure what they intend to measure. Corning Cookware had only the seed of a new product idea in the concept of transportable cookware. The company developed a prototype product, but marketers recognized the need to conduct further research to make sure that consumers would welcome the product. To truly

http://www.corning.com/

evaluate the new product concept, Corning's research design allowed consumers to interact with and examine samples of the proposed product line. The company also needed to measure consumer reactions to packaging, promotion, and pricing. Simply asking customers whether they liked the idea of transportable cookware would not have provided the intelligence Corning needed to make final product design, promotion, and pricing decisions.

A second important research design consideration is the selection of respondents. Corning decided to conduct its research using women aged 20 and older who purchased cookware and transported food away from home at least occasionally. Interviewing men or women who didn't cook would have provided meaningless research results. Marketing researchers use sampling techniques, discussed later in the chapter, to determine which consumers to include in their studies.

Collect Data

Marketing researchers gather two kinds of data: secondary data and primary data. **Secondary data** is data from previously published or compiled sources. Census data is one example. **Primary data** refers to data collected for the first time specifically for a marketing research study. An example of primary data are statistics collected from a survey asking current customers about their preferences for product improvements.

Secondary data offers two important advantages: (1) It is almost always less expensive to gather than primary data, and (2) researchers usually must spend less time to locate and use secondary data. A research study that requires primary data may take three to four months to complete, while a researcher can often gather secondary data in a matter of days.

Secondary data does have limitations that primary data does not. First, published information can quickly become obsolete. A marketer analyzing population statistics for various areas may discover that the most recent census figures are already out of date because of continued growth and changing demographics. Second, published data collected for an unrelated purpose may not be completely relevant to the marketer's specific needs. For example, census data does not reveal the brand preferences of consumers in a particular region.

Although research to gather primary data can cost more and take longer, the results can provide richer, more detailed information than secondary data offers. The choice between secondary and primary data is tied to cost, validity, and effectiveness. In reality, many marketing

Marketing Dictionary

sales analysis In-depth evaluation of a firm's sales.

marketing cost analysis Evaluation of expenses for tasks like selling, billing, and advertising to determine the profitability of particular customers, territories, or product lines.

hypothesis Tentative explanation for some specific event.

research design Series of decisions that, taken together, comprise a master plan for conducting marketing research.

secondary data Previously published data.

primary data Data collected for the first time.

research projects combine secondary and primary data to fully answer marketing questions. This chapter will examine specific methods for collecting both secondary and primary data in later sections.

Interpreting and Presenting Research Information

The final step in the marketing research process is to interpret the findings and present the research information to decision makers in a format that allows them to make effective judgments. Figure 6.5 illustrates possible differences between marketing researchers and their audiences in interpretations of research results due to differing backgrounds, levels of knowledge, and experience. Marketing researchers should target presentations at the areas of mutual understanding. The cardinal rule of presenting marketing research requires that it assist decision making rather than being an end in itself.

Marketing researchers and research users must cooperate at every stage in the research process. Too many marketing studies go unused because management fears restrictions on the results after hearing lengthy discussions of research limitations or unfamiliar terminology.

Marketing researchers must remember to direct their reports toward management, not other research specialists. They should spell out their conclusions in clear, concise, and actionable terms. Their reports should outline technical details of the research methods in an appendix, if at all. These precautions will increase the likelihood that management will utilize the research findings.

Research User's Knowledge and Experience
Areas of Mutual Understanding
Marketing Researcher's Knowledge and Experience

Figure 6.5

The Research Report and Presentation: Linking the Study and the Research User

MARKETING RESEARCH METHODS

Clearly, data collection is an integral part of the marketing research process. One of the most time-consuming parts of collecting data is determining what method the marketer should use to obtain the data. This section will discuss the most commonly used methods by which marketing researchers find both secondary and primary data.

Secondary Data Collection

Secondary data comes from many sources. The overwhelming quantity of secondary data available at little or no cost challenges researchers to select only what is pertinent.

Secondary data consists of two types: internal and external data. Internal data, as discussed earlier, includes sales records, product performance reviews, sales force activity reports, and marketing cost reports. External data comes from a variety of sources, including government records, syndicated research services, and industry publications. Computerized databases can give access to data from both inside and outside an organization. A *database* is any collection of data retrievable through a computer. A great deal of information is available in this form. The following paragraphs will focus on some databases and other external data sources available to marketing researchers.

Government Data The U.S. government is the nation's most important source of marketing data. Census data provides the most frequently used government statistics. The U.S. government spends more than $2.5 billion to conduct a census of population every ten years, but it makes census information available at no charge in local libraries, on computer disk, and through the Internet. The Bureau of the Census also conducts a periodic census of housing, population, business, manufacturers, agriculture, minerals, and governments.

The census of population breaks down U.S. population characteristics by very small geographic areas. The census determines population traits by city block or census tract in large cities. It divides the populations of nonmetropolitan areas into block-numbering areas (BNAs). The BNAs and census tracts are important for marketing analysis because they highlight populations with similar traits, avoiding diversity within political boundaries such as county lines. This data helps marketers such as local retailers and shopping center developers to gather specific information about customers in an immediate neighborhood without spending time or money to conduct comprehensive surveys.

The U.S. Census is one of the most-used sources of secondary data. To improve its ability to collect demographic data from U.S. residents, the U.S. Census Bureau turned to a $100 million, three-year advertising campaign starting in 1998. These ads for Census 2000 replace the public service announcements the Bureau used in the past. The goal is to reduce the increasing number of recipients who do not return mailed Census questionnaires. In 1980, about 75 percent of the population returned correctly completed questionnaires on time. This figure dropped to 65 percent for the 1990 Census. While expensive, the cost of the campaign is expected to be much lower on a per-household basis than making one or more follow-up visits. For the 1990 Census, these visits accounted for about half of the $2.6 billion cost.[15]

Marketing researchers find even more valuable resources in the government's computerized mapping database called the *TIGER system,* for Topographically Integrated Geographic Encoding and Referencing system. This system combines topographic features such as railroads, highways, and rivers with census data such as household income figures. Marketers can buy digital tapes of TIGER data from the Census Bureau.

Marketers often purchase other information from the federal government, such as:

- *Monthly Catalog of the United States Government Publications*
- *Statistical Abstract of the United States,* published annually
- *Survey of Current Business,* updated monthly
- *County and City Data Book,* typically published every three years, providing data on each county and city of over 25,000 residents

State and city governments serve as additional important sources of information on employment, production, and sales activities. In addition, university bureaus of business and economic research frequently collect and disseminate such information.

Private Data Many private organizations provide information for marketing decision makers. A trade association may be an excellent source of data on activities in a particular industry. Gale Publishing's *Encyclopedia of Associations,* available in most libraries, can help marketers to track down trade associations that may have useful data. Advertising agencies continuously collect data on audiences reached by various media.

Business and trade magazines also publish a wide range of valuable data. Ulrich's *Guide to International Periodicals,* another common library reference, can point researchers in the direction of trade publications that conduct and publish industry-specific research. General business magazines can also be good sources. *Sales & Marketing Management,* for instance, publishes an annual Survey of Media Markets which combines statistics for population, effective buying income (EBI), and retail sales into buying power indexes that indicate each market's ability to buy.

While most general business publications are available at public libraries, few libraries carry specialized trade

Figure 6.6 **A. C. Nielsen: A Major Private Source of Secondary Data**

They're
YOUR customers.
Why
are they
shopping in
someone
else's store?
ONLY
ACNielsen
has the
ANSWER.
With ACNielsen Homescan, you'll know exactly what your customers are buying from your competitors. Because only ACNielsen's Homescan panel of 40,000 shoppers tracks every consumer purchase in all outlets.
We'll tell you who your competitors really are—from grocery to mass merchandisers to pet stores. And what your core shoppers are worth to your business.
The result: you can hold on tighter to all your customers. With the right products in the right place—your place—at the right time.
Get the competitive advantage only ACNielsen Homescan offers. And never ask why again.
For more information, call 1-800-337-1425.
ACNielsen is a copyright of A.C. Nielsen Company. ©1996 ACNielsen. All rights reserved.
ACNielsen

journals. The best way to gather data from these sources may be to contact the publications directly or to use an online periodical database like Dialog's ABI/Inform, available at many libraries and on CompuServe's Knowledge Index. Some trade publications may also maintain World Wide Web home pages that allow archival searches. Larger libraries can often provide directories and other publications that can help researchers find secondary data. For instance, Find/SVP's *FindEx, the Directory of Market Research Reports, Studies, and Surveys* lists a tremendous variety of completed research studies which are available for purchase.

Several national firms offer information to businesses by subscription. Electronic systems that scan UPC bar codes speed purchase transactions, and they also provide data for inventory control, ordering, and delivery. The widespread use of scanning technology to capture sales information has brought this system to 91 percent of chain supermarkets and 75 percent of independent supermarkets.[16] Marketing research companies, such as A. C. Nielsen and Information Resources Inc. (IRI), store this data in commercially available databases. These scanner-based information services track consumer purchases of a wide variety of UPC-coded products. For example, the ad in Figure 6.6 explains how A. C. Nielsen Company's

MARKETING HALL OF FAME

Ford's Most Notorious Marketing Researcher

In the old days, marketing research emphasized testimonials received from ordinary customers. While lacking the sophistication of current methods, these unsolicited testimonials often suggested the strengths and weaknesses of products.

On April 13, 1934, the office of automobile pioneer Henry Ford logged in a unique testimonial. In a message written in Tulsa, Oklahoma, three days earlier, one of the Depression Era's most notorious and elusive criminals congratulated Ford on producing a V-8 engine that was both fast and relatively maintenance free.

The famous outlaw who wrote the letter shown on page 209 was Clyde Barrow, better known as the leader of the Bonnie and Clyde gang. Barrow and Bonnie Parker launched their violent criminal career in 1932. Robbery, kidnapping, and murder were commonplace for Bonnie and Clyde and their associates. The duo terrorized the Southwest and Midwest for more than two years before they were gunned down by police outside Arcadia, Louisiana, on May 23, 1934. They died just over a month after Clyde had penned his gushing letter to Henry Ford. Not surprisingly, the end for Bonnie and Clyde came in a new, four-door Ford powered by a V-8 engine. The sand-colored car had been stolen in Topeka, Kansas.

Barrow drove only stolen Fords. As his letter to Ford indicated, he valued Ford V-8s for their speed. Clyde often escaped police dragnets by driving long distances on back roads at speeds up to 70 mph—an unheard-of pace on the rutted dirt roads. These long-distance escapes required a dependable automobile that didn't need significant maintenance and supplied excellent gas mileage.

Barrow was hardly alone in prizing the V-8 Fords. Ford sold nearly a million of them. This sales volume actually helped Bonnie and Clyde to avoid arrest—they could simply keep switching license plates and blend in with other traffic. When they died, their last Ford sported Arkansas license plates, while more plates from Arkansas, Louisiana, and Texas lay in the backseat.

One reason why Barrow was such a loyal Ford fan was because the car was built like a tank. The V-8 Ford's heavy steel body stopped many police bullets. Lawmen fired high-powered weapons to pierce the car's shell when they ambushed Bonnie and Clyde. The outlaw's last Ford ended up with 160 bullet holes in it. And thanks to Clyde's penchant for penmanship, the Henry Ford Museum in Dearborn, Michigan, possesses one of the most interesting marketing research inputs ever written.

Of course, today Ford or any other major corporation would never dream of capitalizing on research based on the glowing testi-

Homescan panel of 40,000 shoppers tracks consumer purchases in all types of retail outlets. Retailers can use this information to retain customers with the right products at the right time.

Similar services are also offered for markets outside the United States. For instance, IRI's InfoScan service compiles data on products carried in 1,000 grocery stores and drugstores in the United Kingdom. IRI also provides computer data-management software that helps clients track volume sold, changes in market share, and levels of in-store promotion. Many packaged-goods firms subscribe to these databases in efforts to track sales and test the effects of promotions and new products.

However, syndicated services such as IRI and A. C. Nielsen often gather data by different methods. This difference can occasionally cause problems. Recently, for example, Coca-Cola purchased figures from A. C. Nielsen which showed that Coke sales were outpacing Pepsi sales in the U.S. soft drink market. At the same time, Pepsi claimed leadership in the soft drink market, basing its claims on data obtained by IRI. Both research suppliers vehemently defended their own data, which was based on UPC scanning information gathered by each firm from food, drug, and convenience stores. Both manufacturers spent millions of dollars to buy the disputed data.[17]

Online Sources of Secondary Data The tools of cyberspace sometimes simplify the hunt for secondary data. Hundreds of databases and other sources of information are available online, both through the Internet and through commercial online services such as CompuServe. Business expenditures for online information hit $21 billion a year in 1998.[18]

According to a survey of marketing researchers conducted by database supplier Lexis-Nexis, 81 percent of marketing researchers consult online sources in their studies. The marketing researchers reported that they were most likely to search for the following types of information online: competitor intelligence (82 percent), overall market trends (72 percent), production/technology data (46 percent), and intelligence about international markets (36 percent).[19]

Tulsa Okla
10th April

Mr. Henry Ford
Detroit Mich.

Henry Ford
RECEIVED
APR 13 1934
Secretary's Office

Dear Sir:—
While I still have got breath in my lungs I will tell you what a dandy car you make. I have drove Fords exclusivly when I could get away with one. For sustained speed and freedom from trouble the Ford has got ever other car skinned and even if my business hasent been strickly legal it don't hurt enything to tell you what a fine car you got in the V8 -

Yours truly
Clyde Champion Barrow

monials of crooks. But Ford and the other car makers are nonetheless locked in continual marketing skirmishes over research intended to identify superior cars. Take the annual battle over which car model is most popular in America. Since 1992, the Ford Taurus has enjoyed the bragging rights by beating out Honda's Accord. Ford salespeople tout many features, including research studies about the car's safety ratings. But Ford has incurred incredible costs to rack up the sales figures to cement this marketing claim. To win, Ford offers hefty price discounts, and analysts say that the car maker boosts volume by making low-profit sales to rental companies and corporate fleets.

Marketing, it is safe to say, was a lot easier in the old days.

QUESTIONS FOR CRITICAL THINKING

1. **How do you think Henry Ford reacted when he received Clyde Barrow's letter?**
2. **Ford claims that it can sell more cars if it can cite research that shows the Taurus is America's most popular model. Wall Street analysts are skeptical. Who do you think is right?**

Sources: "A Hole Lot of Dough," *The Dallas Morning News,* April 15, 1997, downloaded from Dow Jones News Retrieval, http://nrweblp.djnr.com/, May 13, 1997; Daniel McGinn, Who's on Top? *Newsweek,* October 28, 1996, p. 55; and E. R. Milner, *The Lives and Times of Bonnie and Clyde* (Carbondale, Ill.: Southern Illinois University Press, 1996).

The *Directory of Online Databases,* published quarterly by Cuadra Associates, lists many sources of online information. Figure 6.7 lists some of the most important ones. Government information, private data, and other databases can offer marketers a wide range of data on specific companies, industries, and geographic areas, as well as business-oriented news and reports.

Internet search tools such as Infoseek and Yahoo! can help researchers to track down specific sites that are rich with information. UseNet discussion groups may also provide information and insights that can help answer some marketing questions. Additionally, a post to a UseNet discussion group may draw a response that uncovers previously unknown sources of secondary data.[20]

Researchers must, however, carefully evaluate the validity of information they find on the Internet. People without in-depth knowledge of the subject matter may post information on a UseNet discussion group. Similarly, World Wide Web pages might contain information that has been gathered using questionable research methods. The saying *caveat emptor* (buyer beware) should guide Internet searches for secondary data.

Sampling Techniques

Before undertaking a study to gather primary data, researchers must first identify which participants to include in the study. **Sampling** is the process of selecting survey respondents or research participants. It is one of the most important

Marketing Dictionary

sampling The process of selecting survey respondents or other research participants.

Figure 6.7 Online Sources of Secondary Data

Government Data Sources

U.S. Census Bureau (http://www.census.gov/)—This site provides free access to many census data reports and tables. Also available are international census data from many countries.

U.S. Bureau of Economic Analysis (http://www.bea.gov/)—This site provides national and regional economic information, including gross domestic product by industry.

U.S. Bureau of Labor Statistics (http://stats.bls.gov/)—This site gives access to the BLS survey of consumer expenditures, a report on how U.S. consumers spend their money.

Department of Commerce/STAT-USA (http://www.stat-usa.gov/)—This subscription-based site provides access to hundreds of government-sponsored marketing research studies and other statistical information.

FedWorld (http://www.fedworld.gov/)—This site provides a central access point for locating government information. If you need data from the government but don't know where to find it, start here.

Private Data Sources

Knight-Ridder (http://www.dialog.com/)—This extensive database provides access to thousands of marketing research reports, industry and competitor information, and trade publications. Although it proves itself an excellent source for secondary data of all types, a typical search can be expensive. Knowledge Index, available on CompuServe, provides access to many of the Knight-Ridder databases for an hourly fee.

Lexis-Nexis (http://www.lexis-nexis.com/)—This is another extensive —and expensive—database of directories, trade publications, and legal information.

Search Engines

These search engines can help track down online information on a variety of topics:

Search.com (http://www.search.com/)—This site gives access to over 300 specialized indexes and search engines.

Metacrawler (http://www.metacrawler.com/)—This tool submits your query to nine of the top search engines at once.

Altavista (http://altavista.digital.com/)—This service provides one of the largest search indexes on the Web.

Infoseek Guide (http://www.infoseek.com/)—This search index includes millions of listings.

Yahoo! (http://www.yahoo.com/)—This useful search index divides reference sites into logical groups.

aspects of marketing research design, because if a study fails to involve consumers who accurately reflect the target market, the research will likely yield misleading conclusions.

The total group of people that the researcher wants to study is called the **population** (or **universe**). For a political campaign study, the population would be all eligible voters. For research about a new cosmetics line, it might be all women in a certain age bracket. The *sample* is a representative group from this population. Researchers rarely gather information from a study's total population. If they do, the results are known as a **census.** Unless the total population is small, a census costs so much that only the federal government can afford it (and it uses this method only once every ten years).

Samples can be classified as either probability samples or nonprobability samples. A **probability sample** is one that gives every member of the population a known chance of being selected. Types of probability samples include simple random samples, stratified samples, and cluster samples.

In a **simple random sample,** every member of the relevant universe has an equal opportunity of selection. The draft lottery of the Vietnam era was an example. Each day of the year, draft-age males born on that day had the same chance of joining a conscription list. In a **stratified sample,** randomly selected subsamples of different groups are represented in the total sample. Stratified samples provide efficient, representative groups for such studies as opinion polls, in which groups of individuals share various divergent viewpoints. In a **cluster sample,** researchers select areas (or clusters) from which they draw respondents. This cost-efficient type of probability sample may be the best option where the population cannot be listed or enumerated. A good example is a marketing researcher identifying various U.S. cities and then randomly selecting supermarkets within those cities to study.

In contrast, a **nonprobability sample** is an arbitrary grouping that does not permit the use of standard statistical tests. Types of nonprobability samples are convenience samples and quota samples. A **convenience sample** is a nonprobability sample selected from among readily available respondents. Broadcasters' "on-the-street" interviews are a good example. Marketing researchers sometimes use convenience samples in exploratory research, but not in definitive studies. A **quota sample** is a nonprobability sample that is divided to maintain representation for different segments or groups. It differs from a stratified sample, in which researchers select subsamples by some random process; in a quota sample, they handpick participants. An example would be a survey of owners of imported autos that includes two Hyundai owners, ten Honda owners, four Volvo owners, and so on.

Primary Research Methods

Marketers use a variety of methods for conducting primary research. The three methods for collecting primary data include observation, surveys, and controlled experiments. The choice among them depends on the research questions under study and the marketing decisions that researchers hope to support. In some cases, researchers may decide to combine techniques during the research process.

Observation Method In observational studies, researchers actually view the overt actions of the subjects. Observation is a useful technique when marketers are trying to understand how consumers actually behave in certain situations. Observation tactics may be as simple as counting the number of cars passing by a potential site for a fast-food restaurant or checking the license plates at a shopping center to determine where shoppers live.

Technological advances provide increasingly sophisticated ways to observe consumer behavior. The television industry, for example, relies on data from people meters, electronic remote-control devices that record the TV-viewing habits of individual household members, to measure the popularity of TV shows. Traditional people meters require each viewer to punch a button each time he or she turns on the TV, changes channels, or leaves the room. Marketers have long worried that some viewers don't bother to push buttons each time, which could skew the research findings. In response, Statistical Research Inc. has introduced a simplified remote control that allows even young children to record their TV viewing by choosing familiar onscreen icons.[21]

Arbitron now relies on a passive people meter that uses a computer chip to measure both TV viewing and radio listening. The new people meter has two important advantages for marketers. One is its small size—it can be worn as a pin or beeper—which lets marketers measure media usage in the car, office, or other places away from home. The other plus is the ability to measure both TV watching and radio listening, allowing researchers to combine data for more than one medium. Up to now, re-

Marketing Dictionary

population (universe) Total group that researchers want to study.

census Collection of data on all possible members of a population or universe.

probability sample Sample that gives every member of the population a known chance of being selected.

simple random sample Basic type of probability sample in which every individual in the relevant universe has an equal opportunity of selection.

stratified sample Probability sample constructed to represent randomly selected subsamples of different groups within the total sample.

cluster sample Probability sample in which researchers select geographic areas or clusters, and all of them or chosen individuals within them become respondents.

nonprobability sample Arbitrary grouping that produces data unsuited for most standard statistical tests.

convenience sample Nonprobability sample selected from among readily available respondents.

quota sample Nonprobability sample divided to ensure representation of different segments or groups in the total sample.

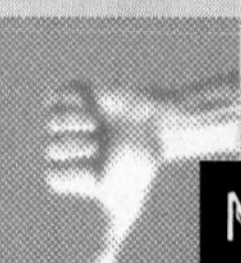

MARKETING HALL OF SHAME

Keebler Misses the Sweet Spot

When the Keebler Co. unveiled its latest taste treat, the company thought it had a winner on its hands. The cookie, aptly named Sweet Spots, was a shortbread cookie with a huge chocolate drop on top. Keebler marketers felt confident that the new cookie would appeal to an enviable target group—upscale women shoppers.

Keebler was so eager to introduce its new dessert morsel, however, that it overlooked some nagging concerns. Looking back on what happened after the cookie's rollout, a Keebler executive summed up the company's experience with this saying: "Listen to the whispers and you won't have to hear the screams." What the nation's second largest cookie company did wrong when introducing the novelty shortbread cookie could provide a valuable lesson for other corporations eager to avoid problems with new products.

In hindsight, Keebler encountered research warning signs all along the way. A big hint of the trouble that lay ahead came from participants in early focus groups. After nibbling on the cookies, the focus group members said they really liked Sweet Spots—but acknowledged that they wouldn't buy them often.

Pricing was another trouble spot, says Linda G. Stewart, Keebler's marketing research director. The company let pricing ambitions dictate the price of a box of Sweet Spots. Originally the company sold the cookie in a 10-ounce box for $2.29. But Keebler quickly repackaged the cookie into a 15-ounce box and put a $3.19 price tag on it. With a stiff price, the cookie became a luxury item, ruling it out as a lunch-box treat.

Pricing out potential customers was not something that Keebler could afford to do. Marketing research had indicated that selling the cookies for more than $3 would result in only a small drop in consumer interest. But Keebler failed to understand that this pricing decision would be disastrous with the small audience who was willing to buy the deluxe item in the first place.

Keebler also waffled on choosing the cookies target market. The original audience was the upscale woman shopper. But then the com-

searchers have been able to measure radio usage only through listeners' handwritten diaries.

Videotaping consumers in action is also gaining acceptance as a viable marketing research technique. French liquor marketer Pernod Ricard used this technique when it sought to introduce a new product, cinnamon schnapps, to U.S. consumers. The company placed video cameras in bars and filmed the Saturday night action. The results gave Pernod Ricard insight into the influences of alcohol consumption on social and party behavior. The findings helped pinpoint the best marketing strategies for the firm.[22]

Clothing chain Urban Outfitters also uses observation to understand its customers. The chain's store managers take videotapes and snapshots of customers in the store and on the street in places where their customers live. The data helps Urban Outfitters to develop "customer profiles" of what people are really wearing. "We're not after people's statements, we're after their actions," explains Richard Hayne, Urban Outfitters president.[23]

Pathfinder Research Group of Acton, Massachusetts, observes shopper behavior through what the firm calls its Talking Shopper program. Pathfinder gives tape recorders to shoppers and asks them to record their thoughts, reactions, and choices while shopping for groceries. The marketing research agency then transcribes the audiotapes to capture customer decision making in action.[24]

Marketers have implemented another new technology to observe consumer behavior—virtual reality. As the chapter's opening story illustrated, virtual reality allows marketers to simulate real-world situations and experiences. They can then observe consumer reactions and behavior to identify priorities for potential marketing strategies and tactics.

Observation is especially useful in high-tech industries. Marketers often encounter difficulty in accurately gauging whether consumers will adopt a new technology without actually showing them the technology and having them interact with it. BellAtlantic Corp., for example, created a mock-up of a living room that contained a prototype interactive TV device. Consumers entered the room and tried the new device much as they would use it in their own homes.[25]

When French electronics maker Thomson developed a new, digital technology for storing, accessing, and playing music, the company hired observational marketing research firm E-Lab to study how, when, and where people listen to music. To get the information, E-Lab researchers followed people as they moved around their homes

pany decided to also go after children's taste buds. Pulling this off proved impossible. The packaging appealed to women, but not to their kids. Keebler also misjudged Sweet Spots' niche. Executives expected Sweet Spots to be a bridge between cookies and candies. However, consumers did not perceive it that way.

Compounding Keebler's problem was its huge gamble in capital equipment. Sweet Spots couldn't be produced with the company's existing machinery, requiring a large investment for a new production line. Unfortunately, the machines experienced problems, and slow sales only aggravated the situation. In hindsight, Stewart says Keebler should have found a way to use its existing manufacturing capabilities.

Keebler can't afford to make too many mistakes when introducing its sugary creations. Success with new products is critical to the company's financial bottom line. More than 20 percent of Keebler's cookie and cracker sales, for instance, originate from products introduced since 1992. "New product success is vitally important," Stewart says. "The balance between established brands and new product is important."

Arguably, Keebler's problems with Sweet Spots were indicative of other troubles the company faced. Keebler's British parent, United Biscuits Holding, put the cookie company up for sale after citing disappointing U.S. sales. "We've been gaining share in the cookie and cracker business, but not fast enough for our parent company," explained a Keebler spokesman. In a transaction valued at $500 million, Inflo Holdings, a joint venture between bread maker Flowers Industries Inc. and a Luxembourg-based investment fund, bought the cookie unit and shortly thereafter, purchased Sunshine Biscuits, Inc. Inflo merged the two companies and scaled back plant operations to try and strengthen Keebler.

QUESTIONS FOR CRITICAL THINKING

1. **What could Keebler have done differently to make Sweet Spots a financial success?**
2. **Do you think it's possible to offer a product that can appeal to affluent women and their children?**

Sources: "The Uncommonly Good History of Keebler Company," downloaded from http://www.keebler.com/keebler/history.html/, April 30, 1997; based on "Keebler Put Up for Sale," *Los Angeles Times,* July 19, 1995, downloaded from http://www.latimes.com/, October 26, 1996; Chad Rubel, "Keebler Learns to Pay Attention to Research Right from the Start," *Market Research,* March 11, 1996, p. 10; and Patrick Lee, "A Red-Letter Day for Corporate Mergers," *Los Angeles Times,* November 7, 1995, pp. D1 and D5.

recording where they listened to music. E-Lab also mailed disposable cameras to consumers and asked them to photograph their home audio equipment. Finally, E-Lab issued beepers to consumers. At certain times of the day, E-Lab researchers beeped the study participants and asked them to describe the reasons they were listening to music.[26]

http://www.elab.com/

Survey Method Observation alone cannot supply some information. The researcher must ask questions to get information on attitudes, motives, and opinions. It's also difficult to get exact demographic information—such as income levels—from observation. To discover this information, researchers can use either interviews or questionaires.

Telephone Interviews A telephone interview provides an inexpensive and quick method of obtaining a small quantity of relatively impersonal information. Telephone surveys have relatively high response rates, especially with repeated calls; calling a number once yields a response rate of 50 to 60 percent, but calling the same number five times raises the response rate to 85 percent.

Telephone interviews do have some limitations. Only simple, clearly worded questions draw appropriate responses, and respondents cannot view pictures to illustrate those questions. Also, it is difficult to obtain information on respondents' personal characteristics by telephone. Finally, the results of the survey may be biased by the omission of households without phones or with unlisted numbers. Certain market segments, such as single women and physicians, are more likely than most people to have unlisted numbers. As a result, some telephone interviewers have tried to reach unlisted numbers by matching digits selected at random to chosen telephone prefixes, perhaps through computerized dialers. However, several states have restricted random dialing, and others propose to do so. The ultimate technological step in telephone interviewing links computerized dialing with a digitally synthesized voice to do the interviewing.

Two obstacles to telephone surveys in the United States and other developed countries are answering

Observational studies are key to the success of Urban Outfitters. By videotaping and taking snapshots of customers in their native habitats, the company gets a feel for what people are really wearing, allowing it to make quick decisions on merchandise.

machines and caller ID systems. Answering machines cause a growing problem for marketing researchers, because many people use them to screen incoming calls. A related obstacle, the caller ID system, displays the telephone numbers from which incoming calls originate, giving receivers the option of ignoring unfamiliar or unwelcome callers. Many consumers favor this option, and caller ID is one of the telephone industry's fastest-growing services. However, some legal experts believe that it violates the caller's right to privacy; in one case, the Pennsylvania state courts ruled it unconstitutional. State laws on caller ID vary. Some require vendors to offer a blocking service to callers who wish to evade the system.

Other obstacles may restrict the usefulness of telephone surveys abroad. In areas where telephone ownership is rare, survey results will be highly biased. Telephone interviewing is also difficult in countries that lack directories or where call volumes congest limited phone line capacity.

Personal Interviews The best means of obtaining detailed information is usually the personal interview, since the interviewer can establish rapport with respondents and explain confusing or vague questions. Although careful wording, and often pretesting, helps to eliminate potential misunderstandings from mail questionnaires, the forms still cannot answer unanticipated questions.

Personal interviews, although slow and expensive to conduct, offer a flexibility and a return of detailed information that often offsets these limitations. Marketing research firms may conduct interviews in rented space in shopping centers, where they gain wide access to potential buyers of the products they are studying. These locations sometimes feature private interviewing compartments, videotape equipment, and food-preparation facilities for taste tests. Interviews conducted in shopping centers are typically called *mall intercepts.* Downtown retail districts and airports provide other valuable locations for marketing researchers.

Focus Groups Marketers also gather research information through the popular technique of focus groups. A **focus group** brings together 8 to 12 individuals in one location to discuss a subject of interest. Unlike other interview techniques that elicit information through a question-and-answer format, focus groups usually encourage a general discussion of a predetermined topic. Focus groups can provide quick and relatively inexpensive insight into consumer attitudes and motivations. Focus groups make a particularly valuable tool for exploratory research, developing new product ideas, and preliminary testing of alternative marketing strategies.[27] They can also aid in development of well-structured questionnaires for larger-scale research. In the past few years, focus groups have gained increasing acceptance as a research technique, and marketing researchers are conducting increasing numbers of these group interviews.[28]

The focus group leader, called a *moderator,* typically explains the purpose of the meeting and suggests an opening topic. The moderator's main purpose, however, is to stimulate interaction among group members in order to encourage their discussion of numerous points. The moderator may occasionally interject questions as catalysts to direct the group's discussion. The moderator's job is a difficult one, requiring preparation and group facilitation skills.

Focus group sessions often last one or two hours. Researchers usually record the discussion on tape, and observers frequently watch through a one-way mirror. Some research firms also allow clients to view focus groups in action through videoconferencing systems.

Marketers use focus groups for a variety of purposes. Corning, for example, consulted focus groups throughout the process of developing its transportable cookware. In the exploratory stages of the research, Corning invited groups of women to discuss how they transported food, and what problems they encountered in doing so. During these focus groups, the company learned that consumers had difficulty transporting food without spilling it, and that they also had trouble keeping food at the correct temperature. In another important issue raised during focus groups, women noted dissatisfaction with the methods they were currently using to transport cooked food.

Corning used this information to refine the product's features. The cookware line was designed with an attractive carrying case that eliminated spills, while the addition of special insulating materials ensured that the product would keep food either hot or cold.

Figure 6.8 **Use of Focus Groups to Gather Research Information**

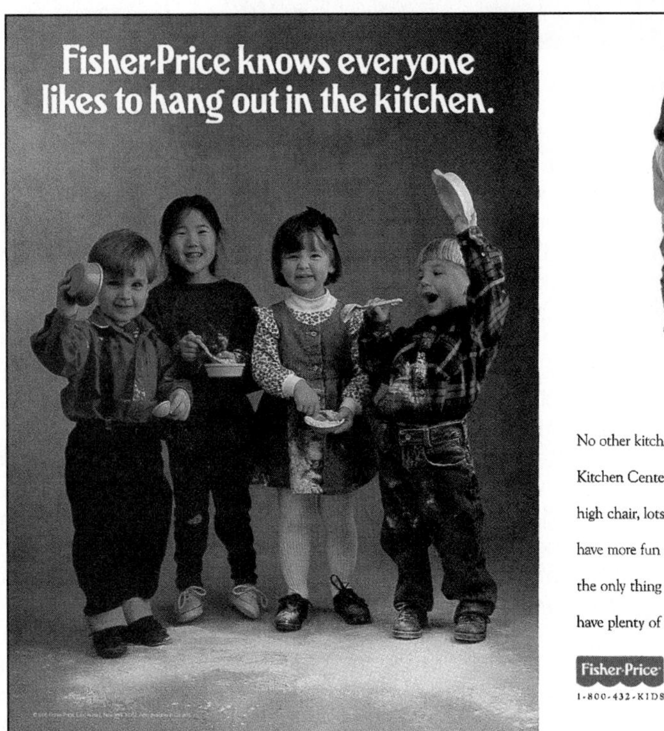
Fisher-Price knows everyone likes to hang out in the kitchen.

The Fisher-Price® Kitchen Center
No other kitchen center is loaded with as much great stuff as our All-In-One Kitchen Center.™ It's got everything, like a microwave with timer bell, built-in high chair, lots of utensils and a unique, multi-side design so more kids can have more fun all around. It's so complete, the only thing to add is something kids have plenty of anyway: imagination.
Fisher-Price
1-800-432-KIDS

After designing the prototype product, Corning conducted a second series of focus groups to test consumer reactions and make further refinements in the sizes, colors, and shapes of the cookware line. Focus groups also provided feedback into the product's name—Pyrex Portables—and packaging.[29]

Fisher-Price Inc. uses focus groups as general indicators of customer appeal for its toys, such as the Kitchen Center shown in the ad in Figure 6.8. The company conducts a few focus groups in one location and then switches to new locations frequently as a way to gauge which groups are attracted to specific products. Focus groups help Fisher-Price to determine whether a product is a strong candidate for marketing support and whether consumers will continue to want it. These interviews also help marketers to confirm that products fit well with the company's image.

Mail Surveys Although personal interviews can sometimes provide very detailed information, cost considerations usually prevent using personal interviews in a national study. A mail survey can be a cost-effective alternative. Mail surveys also provide anonymity that may encourage respondents to give candid answers.

Mail surveys help marketers to track consumer attitudes through ongoing research. Recall that Corning conducts a semiannual survey of consumers to measure customer awareness and satisfaction and provide its marketers with information for new-product development. Mail surveys can also bring back demographic data on customers to support effective market segmentation.

However, mail questionnaires do have several limitations. First, response rates are typically much lower for mail surveys than for personal interviews. Also, because researchers must wait for respondents to complete and return questionnaires, mail surveys usually take a long time to conduct. For a third limitation, questionnaires cannot answer unanticipated questions that occur to respondents as they complete the forms. Complex questions may not be suitable for a mail questionnaire. Finally, unless they gather additional information from nonrespondents, researchers must worry about bias in the results of mail surveys, since

Marketing Dictionary

focus group Information-gathering procedure in marketing research that typically brings together 8 to 12 individuals to discuss a given subject.

SOLVING AN ETHICAL CONTROVERSY

Polls by Corporations and Politicians: Useful Information or Bogus Results?

It's been 50 years since young polling pioneers like George Gallup and Elmo Roper began taking the pulse of American opinion across the country. Gallup, Roper, and others aimed to find out what a true demographic cross-section of Americans felt about the most pressing issues of the day. They asked questions about Americans' preferences in presidential races, World War II, and much more, and the polling phenomenon caught on. Today, Americans feel assaulted daily with poll results that measure our collective whim on just about anything, from the television stations we watch to the number of cups of coffee we drink to the candidates we prefer.

Polls are not just for politicians, though. The business world long ago embraced polling as an essential part of its marketing efforts. Yet the resulting official-sounding percentages may not come from well-designed surveys using representative samples to produce statistically valid results.

Whether a corporation or a political party pays the pollster, polling techniques can be misused. A corporate executive might want poll results that simply reflect his or her own thinking. Arguably, that's what had happened at BMW when the new CEO fought to build an auto plant in the United States. Other BMW executives argued that the company's marketing research indicated a preference by customers for cars built in Germany. "Through the years, we had commissioned all this market research that said people wouldn't buy a BMW made anywhere but Germany," says CEO Bernd Pischetsrieder. "I was convinced that the market research was being done in a way to give us the answer BMW people wanted to hear." Pischetsrieder ultimately prevailed, and the plant, built in South Carolina, was a big success.

Polling by Corporations and Politicians Provides Useful, not Bogus, Results.

PRO

1. **If polls inaccurately measured public sentiments, they would not be such essential tools for marketers today. Studies of consumer attitudes and trends provide important information for marketers. Consumer-products firms, car manufacturers, radio stations, and many other businesses use polling and various other marketing research methods to help plot their next strategic moves.**
2. **Consumer polling often provides critical intelligence for product development, which can cost millions of dollars. Misjudging the attitudes of potential customers can lead to financial disaster. Without consumer surveys, corporations could be less willing to take chances on new products.**
3. **The accuracy of polling has improved dramatically since the early Gallup polls. For instance, critics make much of the pollsters' inaccurate prediction that Harry Truman would lose to Thomas Dewey in a hard-fought presidential election. But no errors of that magnitude have been made since in the presidential political arena.**

important differences may distinguish respondents from nonrespondents.

Researchers try to minimize these limitations by paying careful attention to develop and pretest effective questionnaires before distributing the final version. Researchers can boost response rates by keeping questionnaires short and offering incentives to respondents who complete and return the survey documents.

Fax Surveys The low response rates and long follow-up times associated with mail surveys have spurred interest in the alternative of faxing survey documents. In some cases, faxing provisions may supplement mail surveys; in others, it may be the primary method for contacting respondents and obtaining their answers.

Online Surveys The growing population of Internet users has sparked interest among researchers in going online to conduct surveys and even focus groups. America Online recently conducted a pilot program called "Opinion Rewards" that invited AOL subscribers to participate in small-scale, online focus groups in exchange for free online time. The ten initial users of AOL's program included consumer goods manufacturers, telecommunications companies, and computer manufacturers.[30] Other firms have included questionnaires on their World Wide Web pages to solicit information about consumer demographics, attitudes, and other issues.

Online research can help to speed the survey process and to reduce the costs of other, more traditional survey techniques. Some researchers have also suggested that re-

CON

1. **Polls are no longer as accurate as they once were, for one reason, because people's opinions change quickly. Americans, fed up with unwanted telephone intrusions, are increasingly using their answering machines to screen unwanted calls. Since polls depend upon random samples, the loss of these polling dropouts may skew results.**
2. **Tempting shortcuts in polling procedures can ruin a survey's numbers. Pollsters can use many tricks—for example, asking leading questions or choosing participants who are more likely to give desired responses—to "push" answers in the right direction. "Any journalist with half a pencil knows that only a scientifically chosen survey sample will represent the country's opinions," wrote an essayist in *American Demographics.* "But the temptation to take a biased poll is great if you have a tight deadline and a small budget . . ."**
3. **Academic studies indicate that even seemingly innocuous differences in survey question wording can trigger dramatically different results. "What we're discovering more and more is that very simple little things can have major consequences," says political scientist Herbert Asher of Ohio State University, author of *Polling and the Public: What Every Citizen Should Know.***

In one example of a flawed polling technique, the television networks polled viewers about their feelings on President Bill Clinton's plans to send peacekeeping troops to Bosnia. The CNN poll found that 46 percent favored the plan, but only 33 percent of Americans questioned by CBS pollsters and 39 percent polled by ABC approved of the policy. The answers differed significantly depending upon what questions the surveys posed. CBS described the troops' mission as "enforcing the peace agreement," while ABC and CNN described the troops as part of "an international peacekeeping force."

Summary

Some experts suggest that the best way to sharpen the meaning of polls is to take more time with respondents and ask them open-ended questions. This technique would take longer than current methods and require more money, but the effort could produce more precise surveys. Cynics suggest, however, that corporations don't necessarily want to make their polls scientifically accurate. Many surveys contribute to corporate leadership or promotional studies funded by companies with vested interests in their outcomes. "There sometimes is a close affiliation with the findings and a client's product," concedes David Krane, vice president of Louis Harris and Associates Inc., a national polling outfit.

Sources: Brad Edmondson, "How to Spot a Bogus Poll," *American Demographics,* downloaded from http://www.americandemographics.com/, February 13, 1997; Connie Schulaz, "Results of Many Surveys Suspect Because of Corporate Sponsorship," *San Diego Union-Tribune,* November 3, 1996, p. D5; Jeffrey H. Birnbaum, "Is It Polling or Is It Pushing?" *Time,* February 26, 1996, p. 34; Stephen Budiansky, "Consulting the Oracle," *U.S. News & World Report,* December 4, 1995, pp. 52–58; and Peter Fuhrman, "Never Mind the Market Research," *Forbes,* November 20, 1995, pp. 84–87.

spondents might give more frank and truthful responses to online surveys than to other types of questionnaires. Others point out that the novelty and ease of answering a survey online might encourage high response rates.[31]

However, researchers should remember some drawbacks to online surveys. It may be difficult, if not impossible, to ensure drawing an adequate probability sample.[32] Internet users do not fully represent a cross-section of the real-world population. A company compiling data from a questionnaire on its home page, for example, will receive responses only from people who have visited the site; this bias limits the survey's usefulness as a diagnostic tool for the overall consumer market's reaction. Certain groups—such as females, seniors, and minority groups—are currently underrepresented on the Internet, and this imbalance may limit the effectiveness of Web-based research seeking input from those groups.

Critics have also suggested that the cyberenvironment may affect respondents' behavior.[33] As a result, it may be difficult to determine the authenticity of responses gathered online. For example, one poll on a WWW page found that nearly 20 percent of respondents had posed as a member of the opposite sex on the Internet.[34] As the Internet continues to grow, marketing researchers will undoubtedly begin to answer these and other questions, leading to greater use of online surveys.[35]

The growth of the Internet is also creating a need for new research techniques to measure and capture information about Web-site visitors. At present, no industrywide standards define techniques for measuring Web use. In an

Figure 6.9 **Global Marketing Research Service Provided by Roper Starch**

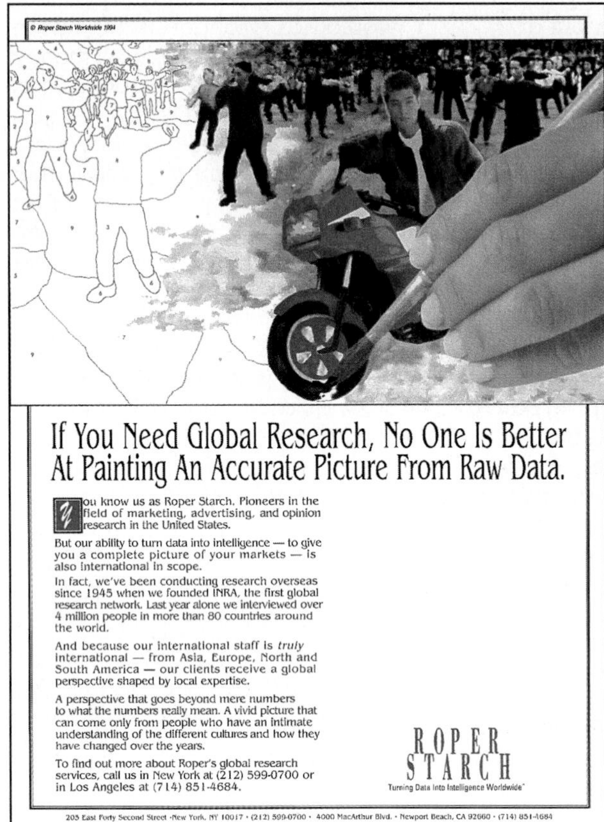
If You Need Global Research, No One Is Better At Painting An Accurate Picture From Raw Data.
You know us as Roper Starch. Pioneers in the field of marketing, advertising, and opinion research in the United States.
But our ability to turn data into intelligence — to give you a complete picture of your markets — is also international in scope.
In fact, we've been conducting research overseas since 1945 when we founded INRA, the first global research network. Last year alone we interviewed over 4 million people in more than 80 countries around the world.
And because our international staff is *truly* international — from Asia, Europe, North and South America — our clients receive a global perspective shaped by local expertise.
A perspective that goes beyond mere numbers to what the numbers really mean. A vivid picture that can come only from people who have an intimate understanding of the different cultures and how they have changed over the years.
To find out more about Roper's global research services, call us in New York at (212) 599-0700 or in Los Angeles at (714) 851-4684.
ROPER STARCH
Turning Data Into Intelligence Worldwide
205 East Forty Second Street · New York, NY 10017 · (212) 599-0700 · 4000 MacArthur Blvd. · Newport Beach, CA 92660 · (714) 851-4684

effort to gather data about visitors to their pages, some business sites ask users to register before accessing the pages. Others merely keep track of the number of "hits" or number of times a visitor downloads a page. Although a number of research firms are attempting to offer Web-tracking services, none has yet emerged as the clear leader.[36]

The Experimental Method The least-used method of collecting primary data is the controlled experiment. A marketing research **experiment** is a scientific investigation in which a researcher controls or manipulates a test group or groups and compares the results with those of a control group that did not receive the experimental controls or manipulations. Although researchers can conduct such experiments in the field or in laboratory settings, most have been performed in the field.

To date, the most common use of this method by marketers has been in test marketing, that is, introducing a new product or marketing strategy in an area and then observing its degree of success. Marketers usually pick geographic areas that reflect the markets they envision for their products. For instance, Seattle and Milwaukee might serve as test markets for a new diet soft drink, because these cities share the lead for the highest per-capita consumption in this product category. Chapter 11 will take a closer look at how marketers test market new products.

The major problem with controlled experiments comes from failure to take into account all the variables in a real-life situation. How can a marketing manager determine the effect of, say, reducing a product's retail price through refundable coupons when competitors simultaneously issues such coupons? Experimentation may become more common as firms develop sophisticated competitive models.

Conducting International Marketing Research

As corporations expand globally, they need to gather correspondingly more knowledge about consumers in other countries. Although marketing researchers follow the same basic steps for international studies as for domestic ones, they do face some different challenges.

U.S. organizations can tap many secondary resources as they research global markets. One major information source is the U.S. government, particularly the Department of Commerce. The Commerce Department regularly publishes two useful reports, *Foreign Economic Trends and Their Implications for the United States* (semiannual) and *Overseas Business Reports* (annual), that discuss marketing activities in more than 100 countries. Other government sources include state trade offices, Small Business Development Centers, and U.S. embassies in various nations.

However, businesses may need to adjust their data collection methods for primary research in other countries, because some methods do not easily transfer across national frontiers. Face-to-face interviewing is the most common method for conducting primary research outside the United States. Focus groups, however, are still a relatively new concept in many countries.[37] While mail surveys are common in the United States, Canada, and Europe, researchers in most of the rest of the world rarely use them.[38] Literacy rates may affect the success of written questionnaires in some areas. Other problems include a lack of standardized address lists and inefficient postal operations.[39] Telephone interviewing is another method that is not always suitable in other countries, especially those where large numbers of people do not have phones.

Researchers also have to accommodate differences in culture. In many countries, social standards prevent discussing personal topics with strangers. In others, certain types of questions may be considered rude or inappropriate.[40] Further, a questionnaire's text may not translate well into another country's language, opening the door to problems with accuracy of data.[41]

Marketers need to consider all of these factors when conducting research abroad. In some cases, businesses may decide to contract with marketing research firms based in the countries they want to study. Also, a number of international research firms offer experienced assistance in conducting global studies. For example, the ad for Roper Starch service in Figure 6.9 explains that the company's international staff interviews some 4 million people in more than 80 countries throughout Asia, Europe, and North and South America, giving clients a global perspective shaped by local expertise.

Figure 6.10 Functions of an MIS

Input Data	Process Data	Produce Information
• Internal • External	• Store • Classify • Analyze • Retrieve	• Focus on Marketplace • Support Marketing Function

COMPUTER TECHNOLOGY IN MARKETING RESEARCH

In a world of rapid change, the ability to quickly gather and analyze business intelligence can create a substantial strategic advantage. A growing number of businesses are attempting to meet this challenge by harnessing the power of computers. As noted earlier, computer databases provide a wealth of data for marketing research, whether they are maintained outside the company or designed specifically to gather important facts about its customers. Chapter 10 will explore how companies use internal databases. This section will address three important uses of computer technology related to marketing research—the marketing information system (MIS), marketing decision support system (MDSS), and data mining.

The Marketing Information System (MIS)

Many marketing managers discover that their information problems result from too much rather than too little information. They may feel pressured to sort through reams of data pertaining to scores of products, hundreds of locations, and thousands of customers. Such data may be difficult to use; even if some of the information is relevant, it may be almost impossible to find.

A marketing information system can help decision makers to obtain relevant information. A **marketing information system (MIS)** is a planned, computer-based system designed to provide managers with a continuous flow of information relevant to their specific decisions and areas of responsibility. The marketing information system is a component of an organization's overall management information system (also often called an MIS) that deals specifically with marketing data and issues.

Properly constructed, a marketing information system can serve as a company's nerve center, continually monitoring the marketplace and providing instantaneous information. As Figure 6.10 shows, an MIS gathers data from both inside and outside the organization; it then processes that data to produce information that is relevant to marketing issues and that supports the marketing function. Processing steps could involve storing data for later use, classifying and analyzing it, and retrieving it easily when needed.

The Coca-Cola Co. uses an MIS to identify potential problems with its customer base. The system routinely collects and stores sales figures from individual bottlers. Every week, the company provides updates to bottlers and Coca-Cola's sales and marketing staff, indicating who is buying the firm's soft drinks, the prices they are paying, and the actions of competitors. This information allows the soft-drink company and its bottlers to explain sales patterns.[42]

An MIS permits a continuous, systematic, comprehensive study of any deviations from marketing goals, and it allows managers to adjust actions as conditions change. Up-to-the-minute information means that they can promptly identify and correct problems.

Marketing Dictionary

experiment Scientific investigation in which a researcher manipulates a test group(s) and compares the results with those of a control group that did not receive the experimental controls or manipulations.

marketing information system (MIS) Planned, computer-based system designed to provide managers with a continuous flow of information relevant to their specific decisions and areas of responsibility.

Figure 6.11 **Components of an MDSS**

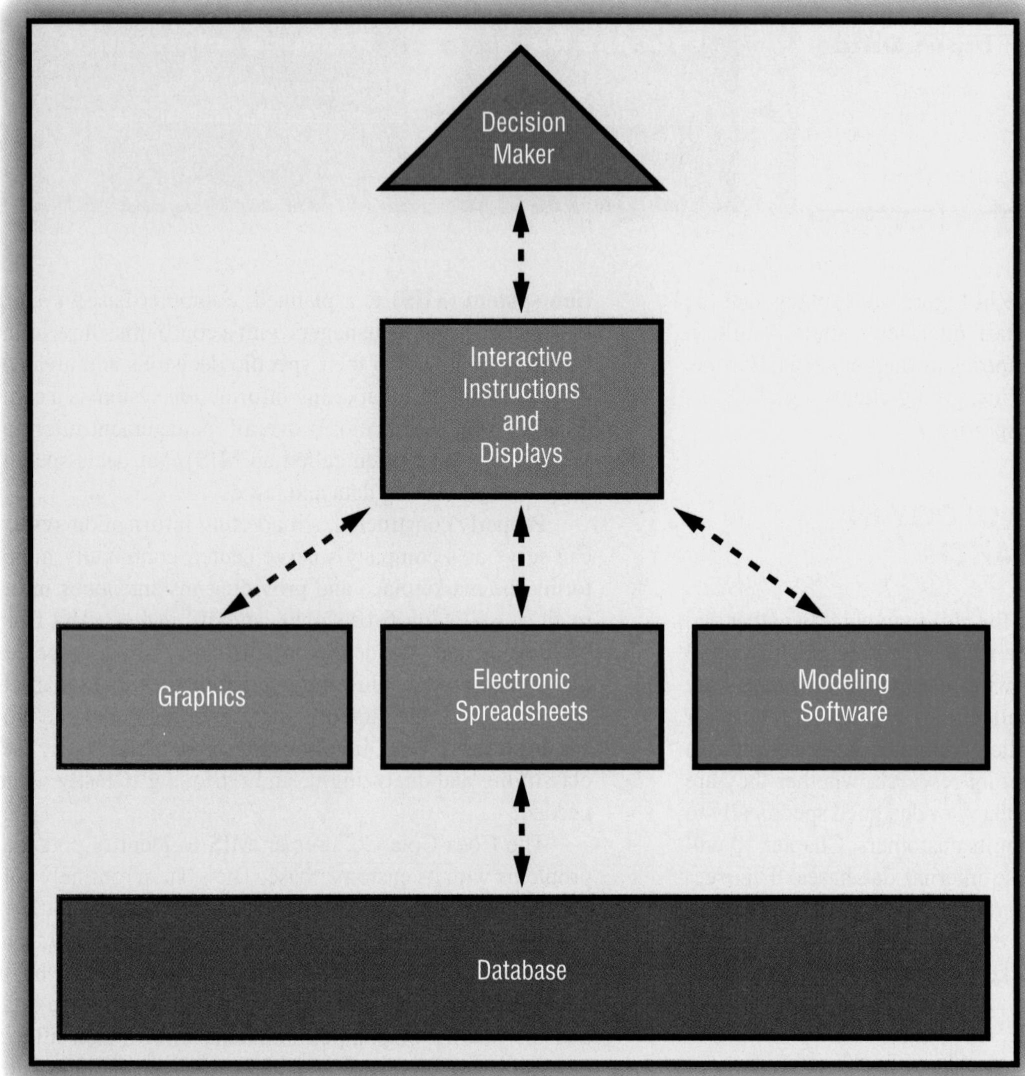
Decision
Maker
Interactive
Instructions
and
Displays
Graphics
Electronic
Spreadsheets
Modeling
Software
Database

The Marketing Decision Support System (MDSS)

A **marketing decision support system (MDSS)** consists of computer software that helps users quickly obtain information and apply it in a way that supports marketing decisions. An MDSS takes the MIS one step further by allowing managers to explore and make connections between such varying information as the state of the market, consumer behavior, sales forecasts, competitors' actions, and environmental changes. An MDSS can create simulations or models to illustrate the likely results of changes in marketing strategies or market conditions. Figure 6.11 shows the components of a typical MDSS, often including databases, graphics functions, electronic spreadsheets, and modeling software. Decision makers access such a system through interactive instructions and on-screen displays.

In general, while an MIS provides raw data, an MDSS develops this data into business intelligence—information useful for decision making. For an example, an MIS might yield a long list of product sales for the previous day. A manager could use an MDSS to transform this raw data into a form that would help him or her make decisions; this activity might include creating graphs that illustrate sales trends or maps that show the areas with the highest sales. The MDSS could also help the manager to estimate the impacts of specific marketing decisions, such as raising prices or expanding into new regions. Possible outputs from an MDSS could include sales analyses, sales forecasts, product line analyses, evaluations of promotional programs, and reports on market share and customer behavior.

Franklin Mint, which sells quality collectibles, uses its MDSS to select promotion tactics. In addition to the names and addresses of customers, the company's database contains demographic, promotional, and purchase data. Franklin Mint marketing managers want to target promotional mailings to customers most likely to buy. The company's MDSS helps them to achieve this goal by analyzing buyer behavior variables using statistical models built into the system. Marketers can then pinpoint the right audience for each promotion and estimate the number of orders it will generate.[43]

Data Mining

Data mining is the process of searching through customer files to detect patterns. The data is stored in a huge database called a *data warehouse.* Software for the marketing decision support system is often associated with the data warehouse. Once marketers identify patterns and connections, they use this intelligence to increase the accuracy of their predictions about the likely effectiveness of strategy options.[44]

Marriott Vacation Club International, for example, fills its database with the names of hotel guests and their motor vehicle records, property records, and warranty cards, along with lists of people who previously had responded to direct-mail appeals. Marriott then mines the database to identify prospects likely to respond to direct-mail messages selling time-shares.

First Commerce Corp., a Louisiana financial institution, uses a similar system. The bank input data on current and recently departed customers into the database. It then tested 70 variables to construct a model of the characteristics of customers most likely to leave. The model allowed the bank to identify customers who seem likely to move high balances to other financial institutions. The bank contacted these customers and offered them new money market accounts as incentives to stay.

As computer technology continues to develop, businesses will likely find new ways of using customer data as a tool for marketing decision making. "The amount of data that we are keeping today is just mind-boggling," notes Charles D. Morgan Jr., CEO of Acxiom Corp., a Conway, Arkansas-based firm specializing in helping businesses build data warehouses. "Our customers today are saying, 'Save everything, because we might find a use for this information a year from now.' "[45]

Marketing Dictionary

marketing decision support system (MDSS) Marketing information system component that links a decision maker with relevant databases and analysis tools.

data mining Process of searching through customer information files to detect patterns that guide marketing decision making.

ACHIEVEMENT CHECK SUMMARY

Reread the learning goals that follow, and consider the questions for each goal. Answering these questions will reinforce your grasp of the most important concepts in the chapter and allow you to check how well you have achieved these learning goals. Where a blank appears before a question, answer with *T* or *F;* for multiple-choice questions, circle the letter of the correct answer.

Objective 6.1: Describe the development of the marketing research function and its major activities.

1. ___ The marketing research function is organized the same way in most firms.

2. ___ If a company wanted to hire an outside firm to conduct all stages of a marketing research study, it would probably contract with (a) a syndicated service; (b) a full-service supplier; (c) a limited-service supplier.

3. ___ Marketing researchers seldom care about financial performance.

Objective 6.2: List and explain the steps in the marketing research process.

1. ___ The goal of exploratory research is to discover possible causes of a specific problem.

2. ___ A hypothesis is (a) a research technique used to identify hypothetical customer needs; (b) a tentative explanation for some specific event; (c) a scientific format for conducting marketing research studies.

3. ___ Research design determines which type of data collection method will be most effective for a particular study.

4. ___ Marketing researchers and their audiences sometimes reach different interpretations of data collected in the course of a study.

Objective 6.3: Explain the different sampling techniques used by marketing researchers.

1. ___ Sampling is the process of choosing the questions to be included in a marketing research survey.
2. ___ The population is (a) the total group to be studied; (b) a representative group; (c) a probability sample.
3. ___ In a simple random sample, all members of the total group have an equal chance of being included in the study.

Objective 6.4: Differentiate between the types and sources of primary and secondary data.

1. ___ Secondary data is often less expensive and time-consuming to gather than primary data.
2. ___ Primary data can provide richer, more detailed information than secondary data.
3. ___ Cost is not an issue in deciding whether to use primary or secondary data sources.

Objective 6.5: Identify the methods by which marketing researchers collect primary data.

1. ___ Observation is a useful method for gathering primary data to help researchers understand customer behavior.
2. ___ Survey methods provide the most effective help for researchers who want to understand consumer attitudes and motives.
3. ___ An example of a commonly used experimental method is (a) conducting a focus group; (b) videotaping customer's shopping behavior; (c) evaluating a marketing strategy's effectiveness in a test market location.

Objective 6.6: Discuss the challenges of conducting marketing research in global markets.

1. ___ Data collection methods transfer easily to other countries.
2. ___ Cultural beliefs may complicate global marketing research.
3. ___ A business may lack the necessary capabilities to conduct its own international marketing research study.

Objective 6.7: Outline the contributions of marketing decision support systems to the marketing decision process.

1. ___ A planned, computer-based system designed to provide a continuous flow of relevant information related to marketing issues is (a) a marketing information system; (b) a marketing decision support system; (c) a data warehouse.
2. ___ A marketing decision support system allows managers to explore and link information from various sources.
3. ___ Data mining is the process of searching through customer files to detect behavior patterns relevant to marketing decisions.

Students: See the solutions section located on pages S-1–S-2 to check your responses to the Achievement Check Summary.

Key Terms

marketing research
exploratory research
sales analysis
marketing cost analysis
hypothesis
research design
secondary data
primary data
sampling
population (universe)
census
probability sample
simple random sample
stratified sample
cluster sample
nonprobability sample
convenience sample
quota sample
focus group
experiment
marketing information system (MIS)
marketing decision support system (MDSS)
data mining

Review Questions

1. Outline the development and current status of the marketing research function. What role did Charles Parlin play in the development of marketing research?
2. List and explain the various steps in the marketing research process. Trace a hypothetical study through the various stages of this process.
3. Distinguish between primary and secondary data. When should researchers collect each type of data?
4. Compare and contrast sales analysis and market cost analysis.
5. What are the major sources of secondary data? What are the advantages and limitations of secondary data?
6. Explain the differences between probability and nonprobability samples. Identify the various types of each.
7. Distinguish among surveys, experiments, and observational methods of primary data collection. Cite examples of each method.
8. Define and give an example of each of the four methods of gathering survey data. Under what circumstances should researchers choose each?
9. How might a company that has never exported its products obtain information about international markets? How does this process compare to domestic marketing research?
10. Distinguish among marketing information systems, marketing decision support systems, and data mining.

Discussion Questions

1. A. C. Nielsen offers data collected by optical scanners from the United Kingdom, France, Germany, Belgium, the Netherlands, Austria, Italy, and Finland. This scanner data tracks sales of UPC-coded products in those nations. If you were a Nielsen client in the United States, what types of marketing questions might this data help you answer?
2. Politicians throughout the country complained

loudly that the most recent census undercounted minorities, illegal aliens, and the homeless. Why did officials express so much concern about the census? In New York, for instance, each person counted is worth $150 in federal funds distributed on the basis of census counts. The Census Bureau tried to minimize the problem by, among other measures, sending enumerators out at night to count the homeless. Suggest other ways in which the Census Bureau could address the undercount problem.

3. A study of Internet users conducted by Yankelovich Partners Inc. indicated that the growth of World Wide Web users has slowed since mid-1995. At the same time, the number of company home pages on the Internet continues to skyrocket. J. Walker Smith, a Yankelovich executive, notes that if the growth of consumer use of the Internet continues to grow, businesses will have to rethink their cyberspace strategies. "Instead of aiming to simply enter a fast-growing industry, where the vast number of new customers virtually assures an audience, companies will have to compete for the attention of a more static consumer base," he says.[46] What types of marketing research activities could help companies to develop strategies that would attract customers to their Internet sites? Would the same types of activities work for different industries? For instance, would a company selling business computer systems use the same research techniques as a small consumer goods manufacturer trying to sell directly through its Web site? Explain.
4. Looking for a new home? Today, one in three of the new homes sold in America is likely to be a manufactured home. Today's manufactured homes are better built using higher-quality materials than those of the past. As a result, the market for manufactured homes has grown to include ever-more-affluent buyers. Alabama-based Southern Energy Homes tries to appeal to upscale buyers by custom-building its homes according to customer specifications. What type of data and information should Southern Energy gather through its ongoing marketing intelligence functions in order to predict demand for its products? Would secondary or primary methods work best? Name some specific secondary sources of data that Southern Energy might study to find useful business intelligence.
5. Discuss some of the challenges McDonald's Corp. might face in conducting marketing research in potential new international markets. What types of research would you recommend the company use in choosing new countries for expansion?

'netWork

1. A. C. Nielsen is one of the largest marketing research firms in the world. Go to their home page located at

http://www.nielsenmedia.com/

and critically evaluate the services provided. Could companies do this research in-house rather than use an outside source? When would it be better to use a company such as A. C. Nielsen? Alternatively, when should a company *not* go outside for research services?

2. Some companies are using the Internet to do focus groups. One rather unusual instance of this is a personal injury lawyer using Web focus groups to obtain ideas on how juries might decide certain cases. The input from the site located at

http://www.cyberjury.com/

is used to structure actual cases. Is this an appropriate use of the Internet? Are there any problems with this? What are they? Is this an example of marketing research? Explain your answer.

3. Critically evaluate how the Internet will change the nature of marketing research. What do you predict the future of research to be on the Internet?

VIDEO CASE 6

TAKING THE PATH OF CUSTOMER FOCUS

In the wake of the Telecommunications Act of 1996, competition in the telecommunications industry is breaking out in full force. The act changed federal law to allow long-distance and local telephone service providers to enter each other's markets. This development brings great news for consumers, who will benefit from exciting offerings at competitive prices. For the phone companies, however, the new era in telecommunications presents difficult challenges. Chuck Lee, chairman and CEO of GTE, says, "In the past, local service providers functioned as monopolies in controlled markets. Now the marketplace is going to set the pace. It will be a free-for-all. Darwinian economics. Survival of the fittest."

According to Jeff Bowden, a consultant who has worked with GTE, "Most telcos [telephone companies] are genetically designed to build things, not serve customer needs. Packaging goods and services cost-effectively redefines the whole nature of the telephone company. It's easier to move organizational boxes around, form a bunch of business units, bring in marketing people, and forget about the customer."

Market research helps GTE find out what customers want, need, and expect from their telephone company. With annual revenues topping $20 billion, GTE is one of the world's largest telecommunications firms, the largest U.S.-based local telephone company, and a leading cellular-service provider. The company began several years to prepare for today's open, competitive environment. It has downsized to cut costs, divested operations, and reorganized its divisions to remove layers of hierarchy. But several surveys have revealed that many GTE customers, given the choice, would switch their phone service. Organizational customers, too, have criticized the company as large, monopolistic, and slow to respond to customer needs.

Walker Information is helping GTE gain a competitive edge in the new marketplace by leading the company along the path of customer focus. Walker is a full-service market research firm with 11 offices worldwide and annual sales of $37 million. The Indianapolis-based firm's six divisions handle different areas of research. Walker's Customer Satisfaction Measurement (CSM) division helps organizations like GTE to identify what their customers want and determine the best ways to meet those needs.

Walker joins several other market research firms in working with GTE to measure its performance and develop new customer satisfaction strategies. This research has led to several new programs that enhance communication with customers and cost effectively meet their needs.

One initiative involves customers directly in development projects for new services. For instance, GTE engineers developed the ACCESSibility Database Service in response to requests from organizational customers that use its ACCESS Settlement and Exchange Service. Customers complained about the number of financial reports generated by the service and asked GTE to create an easy-to-use database that would provide the same information. GTE software engineers visited customer sites, conducted weekly conference calls, and shipped new versions of the database to customers every two to three weeks. This close cooperation gave customers a direct say about how the product would work. "The entire process has been extremely valuable," says Marlene Collman, manager of carrier relations for customer Ameritech Mobile Communications. "When GTE delivered the product, we received exactly what we wanted—not a version that didn't quite fit the bill." The process worked so well, in fact, that GTE plans to incorporate this strategy in all future product-development projects.

Another initiative includes extensive market research into what customers want from personal communication services (PCS). This new generation of wireless technology promises to improve the clarity of voice messages and provide added services such as paging, voice mail, and data transmission. GTE launched what may be the largest PCS trial ever involving 3,000 Tampa residents. Participants chose among several wireless service categories, including the option of totally replacing their residential phone service for more than a year. "We need to answer questions as to how big the market is and what the demand is," explains John Dion, general manager of personal communications networks. "The 'field of dreams' [approach] doesn't work. We need to assess and serve public needs rather than try to get customers to adapt to technology."

A third program involves an extensive study of the company's business procedures by teams of outside consultants together with GTE employees from all levels. The teams conducted more than 1,000 field interviews, made over 10,000 on-the-job observations, and visited 80 top-performing companies to study their methods. One result is the creation of the Customer Call Center, a facility that allows repair service representatives to solve problems while

GTE customers remain on the line. With this "One Touch" concept, almost one-third of all customers who report trouble to repair centers now find their problems solved before they hang up their phones. Just three years ago, the ratio was one out of 200. Responding quickly has helped to convince customers that GTE is a knowledgeable company that values their calls. Also, during one year alone, quick response eliminated the need for 3.5 million service order and repair dispatches.

"GTE," says vice president Mark Feighner, "is trying to establish a continuous response to changing customer and market requirements." The company has made progress in measuring customer satisfaction and developing new products such as Internet access through its GTE.NET service. It's learned that people want to deal with a single provider for all of their telecommunications services, including local, long-distance, and wireless calling and data transmission. Customers also want convenient features that make their lives easier. GTE has responded to these expectations by developing several new services. With Express dialtone, customers who move can obtain full phone service at their new address within two hours by plugging a phone into a wall jack. With SmartCall, customers can choose from an array of optional features, such as caller ID, call waiting, and three-way calling. With GlobalRoam, international travelers can place and receive wireless calls from numerous countries, with the calls automatically billed to their home cellular numbers. InContact allows a customer to connect home, business, and cellular phones; voice mail; and pagers with one number.

Questions

1. What environmental conditions have increased the need for GTE to measure customer satisfaction?

2. Which of the six steps in the market research process does this case illustrate?

3. What types of data has GTE used to explore its customer satisfaction strategies?

4. The work of Walker Information helped GTE to develop GTE.NET, making it the first local telephone company to sign up Internet subscribers. Go to the company's Web site located at

http:www.gte.net/

and review the services it offers. Design a research study that Walker Information might develop to study the satisfaction of customers using GTE's Internet services.

http://www.walker.net

Include Walker Information's CSM (Customer Satisfaction Measurement) function in the design.

Sources: Telephone interview with Kathleen Briody, Public Affairs Coordinator for GTE, May 16, 1997; and "Top 100 Companies by U.S. Research Revenues," *Advertising Age,* May 20, 1996, p. 40.

CHAPTER 7

MARKET SEGMENTATION, TARGETING, AND POSITIONING

What's New?
What's Cool?
Destinations
Net Search
Sprint.
DruPeR's hOusE
"I've earned more than 20,000 college credits in one lifetime
Netscape: Welcome to @Toyota
Back
Forward
Home
Reload
Images
Open
Print
Find
Stop
Netsite: http://www.toyota.com/
People
Software
@Toyota
WEB WORLD WIDE HEADQUARTERS OF TOYOTA USA
CALIFORNIA
US
66
Celebrating Toyota's 40th Anniversary
WHAT'S @TOYOTA/ FEEDBACK
VEHICLES
DEALER SERVICES
INSIDE TOYOTA / NEWSWIRE
BROCHURES & CD-ROMS
Go To: http://www.nj.com/
NJO
NEW JERSEY ONLINE
Get hyped for HS sports. Click here.
May 15, 1997
THE JERSEY JOURNAL
THIS week
See what's HOT!
NJO SECTIONS
News
NewsFlash: News every minute!
AP's The Wire | Weather
Features | Comics New!
News12 | Transit | Lottery
Star-Ledger/Times Archives
WELCOME
AMERICAN EXPRESS VNIVERSITY
A World Wide Web Resource For College Students
Club House
Bright Lights
Wanderlust
Money Pit
The Right Thing
The Cards

Chapter Objectives

1. Identify the essential components of a market.
2. Outline the role of market segmentation in developing a marketing strategy.
3. Describe the criteria necessary for effective segmentation.
4. Explain each of the four bases for segmenting consumer markets.
5. Identify the steps in the market segmentation process.
6. Discuss four alternative strategies for reaching target markets.
7. Summarize the types of positioning strategies and the purposes of positioning and repositioning products.

Targeting the Web

Looking for a college roommate? Ask Druper for some advice. Druper is the host of Sprint Communications' World Wide Web site, Druper's House. Sprint hopes to entice college students to visit Druper for some tongue-in-cheek information about finding roommates, decorating dorm rooms, and living cheaply, along with some serious information about Sprint's long-distance services.

Sprint isn't the only company targeting college students through the Internet. American Express University offers six different sections. Visitors can enjoy virtual tours of far-flung locales like Nepal, get tips on financing their studies and hunting for jobs after graduation, and apply for Amex and Optima cards.

Sprint
DruPeR's hOusE
"STEP into MY place. Sure BEATS the real world."
"I've earned more than 20,000 college credits in one lifetime. So when I say I'm a senior, I mean
If it's not obvious already, you're in my house. And my house is Sprint's house. So poke around and gather a few golden nuggets of information on long distance, while I warm up the left-over pizza."

Sprint also teamed up with Discover Card, Reebok, Hawaiian Tropic, and five other advertisers to sponsor The Spring Break Tour site at Intercollegiate Communications' Student Union Web page. This site gave up-to-the-minute information on where to party and sleep at various spring-break locations. For students who couldn't hit the road, the site offered downloadable video clips of the action, so they could see what they were missing.

Businesses have long searched for ways to target the college market. College students are prime candidates for credit cards, clothing, music and entertainment products, and long-distance phone services. Before online services and the Internet, marketers relied on proven methods such as handing out free samples on campuses and sponsoring concerts. The World Wide Web, however, offers a tantalizing opportunity to reach college students in a new, more direct way.

http://www.sprint.com/college/
http://www.americanexpress.com/student/

No one doubts that college students are already cruising the information superhighway. According to College Trends, a college-focused marketing and media newsletter, 55 percent of college students own computers and between 60 and 98 percent have access to the Web through school facilities. By piggybacking on that access, businesses hope to motivate students to buy their products.

College students aren't the only population segment being targeted by marketers on the Internet. Most research identifies the "average" Web user as a 33-year-old, English-speaking male with an income of $59,000—an ideal target for products like automobiles, electronic equipment, and alcoholic beverages. Toyota's Web site presents an online magazine called *Car Culture* that aims to attract this target group with information about people from around the world who love to drive cars. The Toyota site also features other digizines—*Motor Sports* and *Inside Toyota: Newswire*—each directed at a different target audience.

http://www.studentunion.com/
http://www.toyota.com/

Like the real-world population, however, the residents of cyberspace are becoming increasingly diverse. Baby Boomers in their 40s are nearly as likely as Generation Xers in their 20s to be online. The number of women and minorities with Internet access is also growing. For example, women now account for about 32 percent of Web surfers. However, their use of the Web differs from men's. Women tend to log on for specific, previously determined purposes; they use the Net as a research tool, while men are more likely to surf the Web and stop at anything that catches their interest.

Even senior citizens are surfing the Net. Businesses have launched or sponsored areas on the Web targeting each of these market segments. Intel, for instance, sponsors SeniorNet, a Web community made up of chat groups and information sources for people over 50. Other Web sites target consumers in specific geographic areas. Advance Publications sells advertising space on its news-oriented New Jersey Online Web site to local businesses.

SRI International, a consulting firm, has studied more than the demographic and geographic characteristics of population segments on the Web. The firm recently completed a study designed to measure the traits of Internet users. SRI described 50 percent of current Web surfers as "Actualizers"—upscale, technically oriented professionals who are adventurous and active. These strong consumers travel extensively and earn incomes at or near their occupational peaks. The SRI study adds that wider access to the Internet will attract new population segments with other distinguishing characteristics.

http://www.seniornet.org/
http://www.nj.com/

While the Internet can help marketers to reach specific population segments, some experts warn that it is not yet a mass medium. Some population segments—such as people with limited education and economic resources—may never be part of the cyberworld. However, businesses are finding that they can improve the results of their Internet marketing efforts by focusing their messages toward specific segments of the cybernaut population.[1]

CHAPTER OVERVIEW

Development of a successful marketing strategy begins with an understanding of the market for the good or service. A **market** is composed of people or institutions with sufficient purchasing power, authority, and willingness to buy.

Products seldom succeed by appealing to single, homogeneous markets. Most markets are likely to include consumers with different lifestyles, backgrounds, and income levels. It's unlikely that a single marketing mix strategy will attract all sections of a market. By identifying, evaluating, and selecting a target market to pursue, marketers are able to develop more efficient and effective marketing strategies. The **target market** for a product is the specific segment of consumers most likely to purchase a particular product.

The people on the Internet provide a good example of how diverse a population can be. As the number of people navigating the Internet has grown, so has the diversity of this population. Once the domain of college students and technically oriented professionals, the World Wide Web's audience now includes large numbers of women, minorities, and senior citizens. As a result, the number of World Wide Web sites targeted to specific demographic and special-interest groups has shown a corresponding increase.

This chapter will discuss useful ways for segmenting markets, explain the steps of the market segmentation process, and survey strategies for reaching target markets. Finally, it will look at the role of positioning in developing a marketing strategy.

Briefly speaking

"Segment, concentrate, dominate."

Don Tyson
Senior Chairman, Tyson Foods

TYPES OF MARKETS

Products are often classified as either consumer products or business products. **Consumer products** are those purchased by ultimate consumers for personal use. **Business products** are goods and services purchased for use either directly or indirectly in the production of other goods and services for resale. Most goods and services purchased by individual consumers—books, cleaning services, and clothes, for example—are considered consumer products. Rubber and raw cotton are examples of products generally purchased by manufacturers and, therefore, classified as business products. Goodyear buys rubber to manufacture tires; textile manufacturers such as Burlington Industries convert raw cotton into cloth.

Sometimes a single product can serve different uses. Tires purchased for the family car constitute consumer products; tires purchased by Ford to be mounted during production of its Explorer are business products, because they become part of another product destined for resale. (Some marketers add another term, *commercial products,* for business products like legal services that do not contribute directly to production of other goods.) The key to proper classification of goods and services is determining the purchaser and the reasons for the purchase. The next two chapters focus on segmentation and buying behavior in the consumer markets. Chapter 9 will cover business-to-business markets.

THE ROLE OF MARKET SEGMENTATION

World markets feature a large and diverse population. Any attempt to attract all consumers with a single marketing mix would probably fail. People simply bring too many variables in consumer needs, preferences, and purchasing abilities. Instead, marketers attempt to identify the factors that affect purchase decisions, and then they group consumers according to the presence or absence of these factors. Finally, they adjust marketing strategies to meet the needs of each group.

Take toothpaste. Nearly everyone uses it, yet toothpaste manufacturers have found that consumers have different ideas about what they'd like the product to do. As a result, Crest focuses on preventing tooth decay, Close Up hints at enhanced sex appeal, Gleem emphasizes whiter teeth, Topol promises removal of smoking stains, and Colgate Junior is designed to appeal to kids while satisfying parents' concerns for fluoride protection.

The division of the total market into smaller, relatively

Marketing Dictionary

market People or institutions with sufficient purchasing power, authority, and willingness to buy.

target market Specific segment of consumers most likely to purchase a particular product.

consumer product Good or service purchased by an ultimate consumer for personal use.

business product Good or service purchased for use either directly or indirectly in the production of other goods and services for resale.

homogeneous groups is called **market segmentation.** Both profit-oriented and not-for-profit organizations practice market segmentation to reach both business and consumer markets. Sony Corporation developed its new line of PCs, shown in Figure 7.1, to appeal to repeat computer buyers who focus on technology. The product combines computer capabilities with audio and video technology such as built-in stereo speakers, a microphone, and a CD-ROM drive. Bundled software includes Windows 95, a collection game titles featuring enhanced 3D graphics, CD-ROM magazines, and Internet access.

The popular story of Henry Ford's resistance to market segmentation is worth repeating here. Ford's continued reliance on the Model T cost his firm the leading position in the developing automobile industry. While Ford insisted that his Model T was all that car buyers needed, Alfred P. Sloan Jr. of General Motors developed specific models to suit different groups of customers. Sloan's segmentation strategy worked, and General Motors replaced Ford as the leading U.S. automaker.[2]

Criteria for Effective Segmentation

Segmentation does not promote marketing success in all cases. Effectiveness depends on the following basic requirements:

1. The market segment must present measurable purchasing power and size. Senior citizens are one example. According to Census Data, over 63 million Americans are over 50 years old, and research shows that this consumer group spends more than $900 billion a year.[3]
2. Marketers must find a way to effectively promote to and serve the market segment. Companies targeting the growing Hispanic-American market, for instance, can reach this segment through national TV stations, 375 radio stations, and over 1,000 print publications geared to the Latino market.[4]
3. Marketers must identify segments sufficiently large to give them good profit potential. Exodus Productions, a Pennsylvania clothing company, designs sportswear emblazoned with religious slogans that appeal to born-again Christians. The market for this kind of Christian merchandise totals about $3 billion a year.[5]
4. The firm must target a number of segments that match its marketing capabilities. Targeting a large number of niche markets can produce an expensive, complex, and inefficient strategy. Procter & Gamble Co., the large packaged-goods manufacturer, has decided to target fewer specialized market segments than it served in the past in order to make better use of its marketing resources.[6]

SEGMENTING CONSUMER MARKETS

Market segmentation attempts to isolate the traits that distinguish a certain group of consumers from the overall market. An understanding of the group's characteristics—such as age, sex, geographic location, incomes, and expenditure patterns—plays a vital role in developing a successful marketing strategy. In most cases, marketers seek to pinpoint a number of factors affecting buying behavior in the target segment. For example, toy manufacturers such as Ideal, Hasbro, Mattel, and Kenner look not only at birthrate trends

Figure 7.1 Targeting a Specific Segment of the PC Market

pc by sony
SONY
the future will become vivid
spreadsheets will crumble before creativity
information will marry entertainment
they will have many children
1.800.4SONYPC (1.800.476.6972) www.sony.com/pc

but also at changes in income levels and expenditure patterns. In trying to attract new students, colleges and universities are affected not only by the number of graduating high school seniors but also by changing attitudes toward the value of a college education and trends in enrollment of older adults. Also, few, if any, marketers identify totally homogeneous segments; they always encounter some differences among members of a target group.

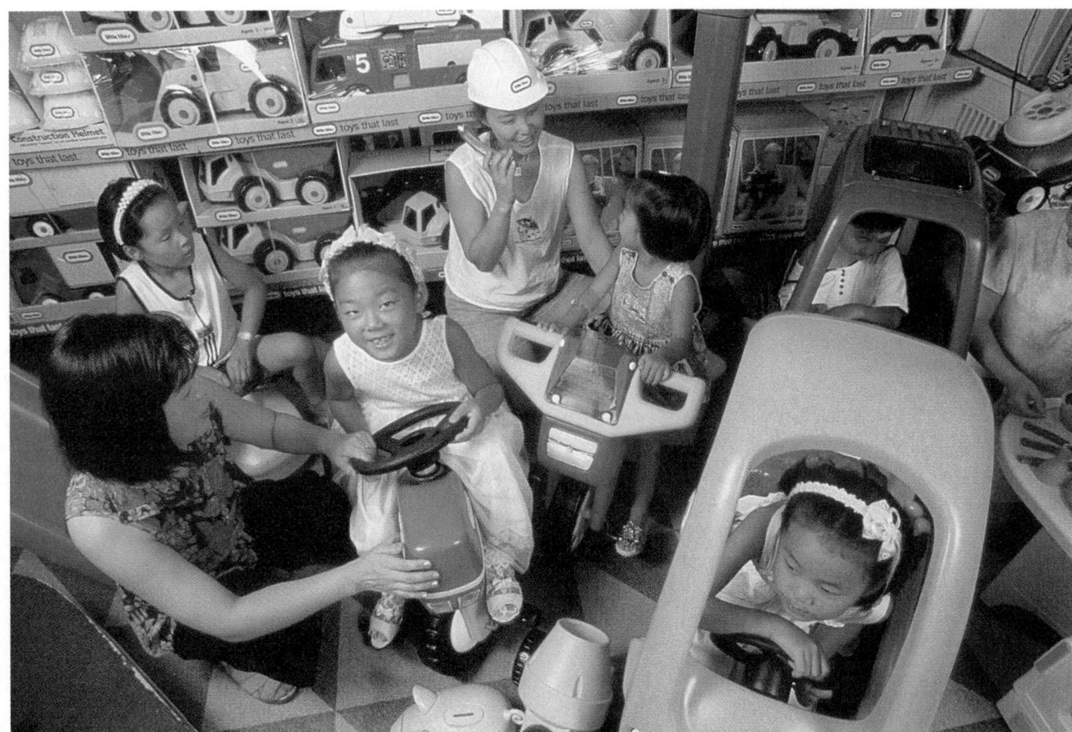

Rubbermaid's Little Tikes toys appeal to tots around the world. Similar product-use patterns and large urban populations make Pacific Rim countries attractive geographic segments for these products. South Korean children can try out toys in more than 95 Korean Little Tike stores.

The four common bases for segmenting consumer markets are geographic segmentation, demographic segmentation, psychographic segmentation, and product-related segmentation. These segmentation techniques can give important guidance for marketing strategies, provided they identify significant differences in buying behavior.

Geographic Segmentation

A logical starting point in market segmentation is an examination of population characteristics. Marketers have practiced **geographic segmentation**—dividing an overall market into homogeneous groups on the basis of their locations—for hundreds of years. While geographic location does not ensure homogeneity of consumer buying decisions, this segmentation approach is useful in spotting product-specific patterns as well as generalized purchase tendencies.

The U.S. population of over 266.5 million is not distributed evenly within the country; rather, people concentrate in states with major metropolitan areas. Projections indicate that Houston and Washington, D.C. will be the top metropolitan areas for population growth and employment growth, respectively, between now and 2005, and both are in the top five for each category. Texas, with five of the top 20 metropolitan areas for population growth, has now moved past New York to rank second in terms of population.[7]

A look at the worldwide population distribution illustrates why so many firms are pursuing customers outside the United States. Many of these people live in urban environments. Over the past 30 years, for instance, South Korea has gone from a mostly rural population to a predominantly urban one. The two metropolitan areas with the world's largest populations, Tokyo and Mexico City, dwarf New York City, the only U.S. city in the top five. Furthermore, the populations of these metro areas are expected to increase still further by the end of the century.[8]

Population size alone, however, may not itself define

Marketing Dictionary

market segmentation Division of the total market into smaller, relatively homogeneous groups.

geographic segmentation Dividing an overall market into homogeneous groups on the basis of population locations.

MARKETING HALL OF FAME

The Best Drinks to "Ensure" and "Boost" Good Nutrition

A decade ago, a major producer of baby formula was grappling with a dismal reality. With the birth rate declining and growing numbers of mothers preferring to breast-feed, the baby-formula business was not exactly a growth industry.

The Ross Products Division of Abbott Laboratories, an infant-formula giant, reacted by aggressively targeting a completely different demographic group—the elderly. In what turned out to be a brilliant example of market segmentation, Ross Products began a full-blown campaign to sell a nutritional supplement for senior citizens.

In the past, Ross Products had peddled its liquid nutritional supplement only to nursing homes and hospitals. But its decision to go after the healthier elderly population has proven to be a blockbuster hit. The drink, sold in 8-ounce cans, generates an estimated $500 million in annual sales. It's not hard to understand the source of these robust sales, considering that Ensure is much pricier than premium beer. A six pack of the beverage sells for up to $10.

Ross Products was a true trailblazer in promoting a product that no customers even knew they wanted. How did the company create a demand for the nutritional supplement where none had existed before? One big clue can be found by examining the advertising blitz, which was directed squarely at older Americans. Ads featuring the slogan "Drink to Your Health" show vibrant, active seniors choosing Ensure for a quick, nutritional meal replacement. The beverage, with flavors such as strawberry, chocolate, eggnog, and butter pecan, appeals to seniors who don't always have the time or inclination to cook for themselves.

The money pouring into Ensure's big push now equals the advertising muscle of some soft drinks. Ross Products' advertising expenditures have now surpassed the amount of money spent to promote Dr. Pepper, and the total equals roughly half of the U.S. ad budget for Coca-Cola. Ensure's promotional war chest has increased dramatically since 1991, when ads began appearing on television and in such magazines as *Good Housekeeping* and *Reader's Digest*.

Ross Products didn't rely exclusively on persuasive national advertising to win fans. It launched a grassroots campaign that brought Ensure right to potential customers' front doors. In conjunction with local aging agencies, elderly shut-ins received bags containing cheery letters from schoolchildren along with Ensure coupons and brochures. In Kansas City alone, nurses distributed 8,600 tote bags through

the decision whether to expand into a specific country. Businesses also need to look at a wide variety of microeconomic variables. Some businesses may decide to cluster together countries that share similar population and product use patterns instead of treating each country as an independent segment.[9]

While population numbers indicate the overall size of a market, other geographic indicators, such as job growth, can also give useful guidance to marketers, depending on the type of products they sell. Food companies might look for geographic segments with large populations, because food is an essential product used by everyone. Car manufacturers, on the other hand, might segment geographic regions by estimated job growth, because employed people are more likely to need new cars.[10]

Geographic areas also vary in population migration patterns. The United States, for example, has traditionally been a mobile society. About one of every six Americans move each year. However, this figure is down from one out of five decades ago. The slowdown has resulted from changes such as economic downturns and increased home ownership due to falling mortgage interest rates.

U.S. census data also indicate two major population shifts over the past decade: toward the Sunbelt states of the Southeast and Southwest, and toward the West. Researchers expect this trend to continue. Of the 20 cities expected to experience the fastest growth in population over the next decade, 14 are in the South and 6 are in the West.[11]

The years after World War II saw a population move away from urban areas toward suburban areas. In recent years, rural areas have seen increases in population as advancements in technology such as e-mail, personal computers, and fax machines have allowed more people to telecommute.[12]

As people migrate from one geographic area to another, regional consumer tastes often change. Catfish, a longtime staple in the diet of the southern United States, is now popular in all parts of the country. By contrast, corn-

the program called "Homebound Remembered."

Ensure's success has not gone unnoticed by competitors. Alternatives are now lining grocery store shelves. Another baby-food maker, Gerber Products Co., a division of Sandoz Ltd., introduced a liquid meal named ReSource. Meanwhile, Mead Johnson, a division of Bristol-Myers Squibb Co., is marketing two beverage choices—Suscatal and Boost. Like Ensure, the firm began marketing Suscatal only in medical facilities. Mead Johnson has positioned Boost as a nutritional energy drink for younger, active adults aged 25 to 54.

Mead Johnson's decision to pursue a younger crowd appears to be part of a growing trend. Ads playing on television now feature graying adults with their grown children praising the health benefits of the quick drinks. Not everyone, however, likes this push to entice Baby Boomers into the fold. In fact, some nutritional experts question the need for Ensure and the other pricey nutritional supplements, because they do not improve on the nutrition from a well-balanced diet. "Clever marketers have decided you can sell a lot of this stuff to yuppies," says Victor Herbert, a professor of medicine and a vitamin researcher at Mount Sinai Medical School in New York. "Nutritional supplements just give you expensive urine."

"We certainly don't want you to stop eating," counters Peter Paradossi, a spokesman for Mead Johnson. "But we offer a realistic food option for people on the go, who can't find time to sit down to a meal."

Regardless of the debate, many senior citizens can't seem to live without the product. When the Salt Lake City meals-on-wheels program announced that it would no longer deliver Ensure because of the cost, elderly customers revolted. As loud protests reached as high as the governor's office, the agency relented. Demand for Ensure is so great in Little Rock, Arkansas, that the local aging agency keeps a priority list to determine who is entitled to the expensive beverage. Those who can produce physicians' prescriptions are guaranteed slots at the top of the list.

QUESTIONS FOR CRITICAL THINKING

1. Can you think of any other product that appeared out of nowhere to capture the imagination and the dollars of a particular age group?

2. Do you think the drive to sell nutritional supplements to younger adults will succeed? Why?

Sources: Michael J. McCarthy, "Abbott Will Settle FTC Charges Linked to Ensure Endorsements," *Wall Street Journal*, January 3, 1997, p. B2; Betsy Spethmann, "Boost Buoys Big Beach Boys Tour," *Brandweek*, June 17, 1996, pp. 1, 6; Laurie Freeman, "Ad Campaigns Pump Up Nutritional Foods," *Discount Store News*, May 6, 1996, p. F40; Michael J. McCarthy, "Formula for Sales: Ensure Spends Millions Pushing Meals in a Can to Aging Population," *Wall Street Journal*, April 25, 1996, pp. A1, A12; Kelly Shermach, "Nutrition Drinks: They're Not Just for Athletes Anymore," *Marketing News*, October 23, 1995, pp. 1, 38, 39.

bread and other popular southern recipes using cornmeal are considered exotic in Great Britain, where cornmeal is available mainly through health-food stores.

The move from urban to suburban areas after World War II created a need to redefine the urban marketplace. This trend radically changed cities' traditional patterns of retailing and led to disintegration in many U.S. cities' downtown shopping areas. It also rendered traditional city boundaries almost meaningless for marketing purposes.

In an effort to respond to these changes, the government now classifies urban data using three categories:

- A **Metropolitan Statistical Area (MSA)** is a freestanding urban area with a population in the urban center of at least 50,000 and a total MSA population of 100,000 or more. Buyers in MSAs exhibit social and economic homogeneity. They usually border on nonurbanized counties. Moorhead, Minnesota; Peoria, Illinois; and Sheboygan, Wisconsin are examples.
- The category of **Consolidated Metropolitan Statistical Area (CMSA)** includes the

Marketing Dictionary

Metropolitan Statistical Area (MSA) Freestanding urban population center.

Consolidated Metropolitan Statistical Area (CMSA) Major population concentration, including the country's 25 or so urban giants.

country's 25 or so urban giants such as New York, Los Angeles, and Chicago. A CMSA must include two or more Primary Metropolitan Statistical Areas.

- A **Primary Metropolitan Statistical Area (PMSA)** is an urbanized county or set of counties with social and economic ties to nearby areas. PSMAs are identified within areas of 1-million-plus populations. Long Island's Nassau and Suffolk counties form part of the New York CMSA, Oxnard-Ventura forms part of the Los Angeles CMSA, and Aurora-Elgin forms part of the Chicago CSMA.

Using Geographic Segmentation Demand for some categories of goods and services varies more in response to regional preferences than that for others. Take pasta sauce. Southerners tend to buy and consume less pasta sauce than the national average. Meanwhile, Boston residents eat 42 percent more pasta than the national average.[13] Adapting to these differences, some national firms develop products and marketing strategies aimed at specific regions while others do not. When researchers at The Coca-Cola Co., for example, discovered that the average southern Californian drank less Coke than the average Hungarian citizen, the company decided to beef up promotional activities in the southern California region.[14] Most major brands get 40 to 80 percent of their sales from what are called *core regions;* elsewhere in the national marketplace, such a good or service is essentially a specialty brand.

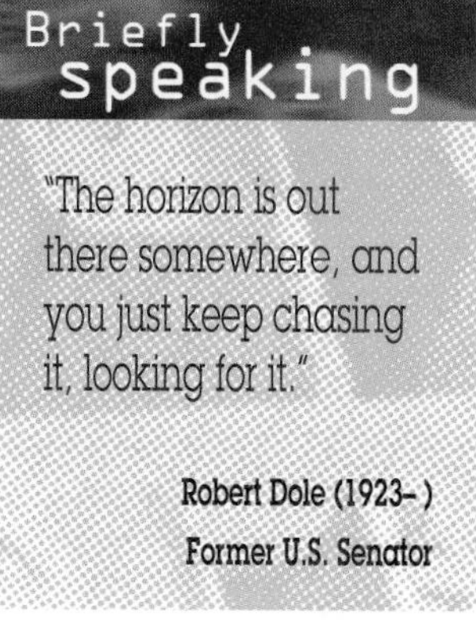
Briefly speaking
"The horizon is out there somewhere, and you just keep chasing it, looking for it."
Robert Dole (1923–)
Former U.S. Senator

Residence location within a geographic area is an important segmentation variable. Urban dwellers may have less pressing needs for automobiles than their suburban and rural counterparts feel, and suburbanites spend proportionately more on lawn and garden care than rural and urban residents. Rural and suburban dwellers may spend more of their household incomes than urban households on gasoline and automobile needs.

Climate is another important factor. Consumers in chilly, northern states, for example, eat more soup than residents in warmer, southern markets.

Geographic segmentation provides useful distinctions only when regional preferences exist. Even then, geographic subdivisions of the overall market tend to be rather large and often too heterogeneous for effective segmentation without the careful consideration of additional factors. In such cases, more than one segmentation variable is used to target a specific market.

Geographic Information System (GIS) Gateway Outdoor Advertising Inc. in Somerset, New Jersey, faced a challenge. The firm sells billboard advertising space, and it wanted to help clients target the best locations for their outdoor ads. A maker of children's athletic shoes, for instance, might want its ads placed near schools or playgrounds or near the homes of large numbers of families. Other clients wanted their billboards placed in locations where people with certain demographic characteristics would most likely see them.

To meet the challenge, Gateway turned to a geographic information system or GIS. Today, when a client asks for a location that meets specific requirements, Gateway can create a three-dimensional map depicting detailed data about the geographical area surrounding each of the company's billboards. Clients can now pinpoint exactly where to place their outdoor ads for the best chances of reaching desired target markets.[15]

Traditionally, marketers obtained much of their geographic data from statistical databases and reports. While these sources provide valuable information, they do not always present it in a format that makes it easy to analyze and use. **Geographic information systems (GISs),** once used mainly by the military, simplify the job of analyzing marketing information by placing data in a spatial format. The result is a geographic map overlaid with digital data about consumers in a particular area.

"With GIS, you don't have to be a specialist at market analysis to see relationships like 'Here are my stores; here are my competitors' stores,'" says Dale Turner, a manager with Supervalu, an Eden Prairie, Minnesota food wholesaler. Supervalu uses its GIS resources to identify favorable sites for new store locations. The GIS also helps to tie advertising and promotional strategies to the demographics of a store's trading area. "GIS can tell you where to run ads for the best return on investment," says Turner. "You won't run ads in areas where you don't have customers or where you have major competitors. You may decide to use direct mail rather than a newspaper."[16]

The earliest geographic information systems were prohibitively expensive for all but the largest companies. Recent technological advances, however, have made GIS software available at much lower cost, increasing usage among even small, entrepreneurial firms.[17] Marketing researchers agree, however, that firms have not yet realized the full potential of GIS technology.

Demographic Segmentation

The most common method of market segmentation—**demographic segmentation**—defines consumer groups according to demographic variables such as sex, age, income, occupation, education, household size, and stage in the family life cycle. This approach is also sometimes called *socioeconomic segmentation.* Marketers review vast quantities of available data to complete a plan for demographic segmentation. One of the primary sources for demographic data in the United States is the Bureau of the Census. Many of the Census Bureau's statistics can be accessed online at http://www.census.gov/. Now let's consider the most commonly used demographic variables.

Segmenting by Gender Gender is an obvious variable that helps to define the markets for certain products. Perfume and cosmetics are mainly purchased by women; men tend to be the main purchasers of electronic equipment.

However, some marketers try to move beyond gender stereotypes. For example, although computer action games appeal primarily to male consumers, software developers are attempting to attract female consumers to the game market by creating less violent titles.[18] Many makers of cosmetics, aware that men are becoming more concerned with their appearance, are developing skin-care and hair-coloring products targeted toward male consumers.

Gender segmentation strategies must also accommodate the growing number of upwardly mobile, female professionals. As the average annual income of U.S. women has increased, so has their purchasing power. Automakers, insurance companies, and financial-services firms are now targeting women directly. For example, Cadillac attempted to woo female consumers by designing a sleek, European-styled car, the Catera. The company decided to pursue female consumers after research showed that they buy almost 40 percent of all luxury cars sold.[19]

Segmenting by Age Many firms identify market segments on the basis of consumers' ages. Indeed, they develop some products specifically to meet the needs of people in certain age groups. Gerber Food focuses on food for infants and toddlers. Del Webb Corp. creates Sun Cities retirement communities. Warner-Lambert developed Halls Juniors cough drops for kids five years and over. As the ad in Figure 7.2 points out, the kid-sized, sugar-free drops come in flavors that appeal to children. Age distributions and projected changes in each age group are important to marketers because consumer needs and wants differ notably among age groups.

Sociologists attribute these differences to the **cohort effect**—the tendency of members of a generation to be influenced and bound together by events occurring during their key formative years, roughly 17 to 22 years of age. These events help to shape the core values of the age group which eventually shape consumer preferences and behavior.[20]

Figure 7.2 **Segmenting Markets by Age**

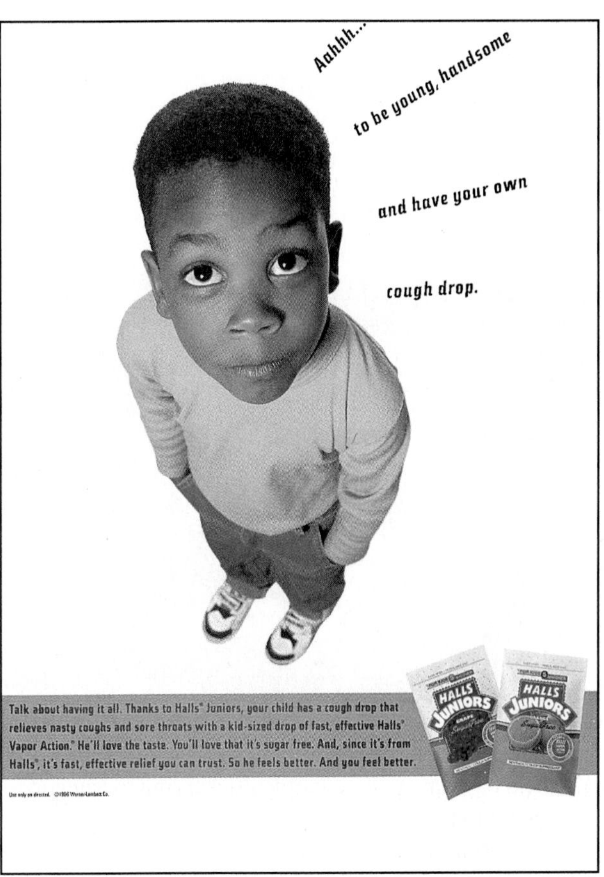
Aahhh...
to be young, handsome
and have your own
cough drop.
Talk about having it all. Thanks to Halls® Juniors, your child has a cough drop that relieves nasty coughs and sore throats with a kid-sized drop of fast, effective Halls® Vapor Action.® He'll love the taste. You'll love that it's sugar free. And, since it's from Halls®, it's fast, effective relief you can trust. So he feels better. And you feel better.
HALLS JUNIORS
HALLS JUNIORS

Generation X People born between 1966 and 1976, dubbed *Generation X* by some marketers, were the first large group to experience day care and the effects of widespread parental divorce. Currently, this age group accounts for 21 percent of the U.S. population. Overall, Xers tend to have more egalitarian views of gender roles than the general population holds, and they react strongly to influences

Marketing Dictionary

Primary Metropolitan Statistical Area (PMSA) Major urban area within a CMSA.

geographic information system (GIS) Computer technology that records several layers of data on a single map.

demographic segmentation Dividing consumer groups according to characteristics such as sex, age, income, occupation, education, household size, and stage in the family life cycle.

cohort effect Tendency for members of a generation to be influenced by the same events.

Figure 7.3 Marketing to Generation X

In the beginning the skier ruled the slopes. Then, slowly, roving bands of snowboarders appeared. Then the great mountain wars began. The clothes. The slang. The music. They agreed on nothing.
Until now. Introducing the limited edition Golf K2. Specially tricked out for frosty weather and complete with a custom roof rack and either a phat K2 snowboard or a sweet pair of K2 skis as standard equipment. And with this introduction, a great light shined upon them, and they realized if they could be brothers on the road, they could be brothers on the mountain.
Thus, with the Golf K2, the cold war endeth.
On the road of life there are passengers and there are drivers.
Drivers wanted.
K2

from their peers. Beyond these basic statements, researchers have encountered difficulties trying to categorize the Generation X age group.

Perhaps because of differences between subgroups within this generation, marketers have had a difficult time devising marketing strategies to attract Xers. Experts suggest that Xers know what they want in a product and are turned off by marketing strategies that seem to talk down to their age group.[21] In fact, many in this age segment don't think of themselves as part of Generation X. A poll by *Mademoiselle* magazine, for example, found that 95 percent of people in this age segment don't think that the term *Generation X* accurately describes them.[22]

Pepsi is one company that tried and failed to develop a product targeted at Xers. The company test marketed a soda called Pepsi XL which contained less sugar than regular Pepsi. Pepsi believed that health concerns of younger soda drinkers would draw them to the product. However, advertising failed to position the product favorably with Xers, some of whom thought of the product as a sort of "grunge Pepsi." Pepsi XL received less than 1 percent of the Florida test market, leading one advertising executive to declare it, "a major miss, both in the youth market and the health market."[23]

The Internet is becoming an important marketing tool for reaching Xers. These computer-literate consumers were among the first exposed to the Internet. One company that uses the Internet to market to Xers, Vans Shoes, has dubbed its Web page at http://www.vansshoes.com/ an "online magazine." At the site, Xers can hear audio interviews with athletes involved in "extreme sports" such as snowboarding, surfing, and skateboarding. Visitors can also download video and audio clips of musical acts sponsored by the company.

Volkswagen is teaming up with other companies whose products appeal to the active lifestyles of Xers. To establish closer ties with this age group, Volkswagen has introduced the limited-edition Golf K2, which comes with a custom roof rack and K2 skis or snowboard, as shown in the ad in Figure 7.3. Volkswagen is also offering a limited-edition Jetta Trek model that includes a bike rack and Trek mountain bike.

Baby Boomers Baby Boomers—people born from 1946 until 1965—are a popular segment to target because of the size of this population: Nearly 42 percent of U.S. adults were born in this period. The values of this age group were influenced both by the counterculture movement of the Woodstock era and the materialistic, career-oriented drive of the 70s and 80s. This contradiction has resulted in some interesting twists in marketing to this group. Mercedes-Benz promotes its C-class and E-class cars to Boomers with Janis Joplin's soundtrack on the ads. The company hopes that Joplin's raspy voice singing, "Oh Lord, won't you buy me a Mercedes-Benz?" will evoke memories and emotions that motivate Boomers to buy."[24]

Like their Xer counterparts, however, different subgroups within this age segment complicate segmentation and targeting strategies. Some Boomers, for example, put off starting families until their 40s, while others have already become grandparents. Also, many members of the group are not behaving as expected. Marketers expected them to follow the pattern of previous generations and buy fewer houses as they aged. However, researchers at the University of Southern California conducted a cohort analysis indicating that housing demand will not decline as Boomers pass age 45. Reasons include higher incomes, more interest in material possessions, and better health—which means longer life spans. Boomers are continuing to own their large homes, and even upgrade their housing, rather than moving to smaller homes.[25]

As Boomers begin to age, marketers are turning their attention toward new opportunities. For example, Baby Boomers are the fastest-growing segment of customers for cosmetics products. As the group looks for ways to maintain youthful appearance, cosmetics manufacturers are introducing products, such as skin creams, moisturizers, and shampoos, geared toward these concerns.[26] For example, Paul Mitchell's Hair Salon Systems shampoo product is designed for thinning hair.

Seniors Marketers are also adapting to a notable trend dubbed *the graying of America.* Currently, only 26 percent of the American population, 63.5 million people, are over age 50. As the Baby Boomers grow older, however, the median age of Americans will dramatically increase. By 2010, 33 percent of the total population will be over 50.[27]

Seniors are already a powerful economic force, since heads of households aged 55-plus control about three-quarters of the country's total financial assets. According to PrimeLife, an Orange, California-based marketing firm specializing in the mature market, over-50 consumers already represent a $900 billion market.[28] Their discretionary incomes and rate of home ownership are higher than those of any other age group. These statistics show why many smart marketers are targeting this group. Some refer to these prosperous consumers as *WOOFS*—Well-Off Older Folks.

The United States is not the only market with an aging population. Most major industrialized nations, including Russia, Japan, and several European countries, are seeing the same demographic trend.

Marketing experts caution about the importance of avoiding stereotypes when targeting older consumers. Although they will respond to promotions and advertising that appeal to the changing interests, needs, and wants of their later years, they often reject appeals that use terms such as *senior citizens, golden years,* and *retirees.*

Segmenting by Ethnic Group According to the U.S. Census Bureau, America's ethnic makeup is changing. Because of comparatively high immigration and birthrates among some minority groups, the Census Bureau projects that by 2050, nearly half of the population will belong to nonwhite minority groups. Currently, the combined buying power of America's minority groups is approximately $750 billion a year.[29]

The three largest and fastest-growing racial/ethnic groups are African-Americans, Hispanics, and Asian-Americans. The following paragraphs take a brief look at the demographic characteristics of each group.

African-Americans are currently the largest racial/ethnic minority group in the United States—some 31 million strong, 13 percent of the U.S. population. A University of Georgia study estimated African-American disposable income to exceed $425 billion for 1996.[30]

Hispanics, the nation's second-largest subculture, account for about 10 percent of the population, or 28 million people. This Hispanic population's growth rate is four times that of the black population, and nine times the growth rate for whites. Census projections predict that by 2010, as many Hispanics as blacks should be living in the United States.[31]

Although Asian-Americans represent a smaller segment than either the African-American or Hispanic populations, they are the fastest-growing segment of the U.S. population. The Census Bureau estimates that the group will grow to 12 million by 2000. Asian-Americans are an attractive target for marketers because they have the fastest rate of growth for median household income of any racial/ethnic segment. The average income per household is $38,960, considerably higher than that of any other ethnic group, including whites.[32] The Asian-American population is concentrated in fewer geographic areas than are other ethnic markets. For instance, a particularly high concentration of Asian-Americans live in California. Companies can lower their costs of reaching Asian-American consumers by advertising in appropriate local markets, rather than on a national scale.

Researchers have identified differences in consumer preferences, motivations, and buying habits among different ethnic and racial segments. Increasingly, businesses are targeting their marketing strategies to more closely match those differences. For example, all three of the major greeting card manufacturers have launched ethnically oriented card lines. Chapter 8 will take a closer look at how ethnic and racial culture affects consumer behavior.

Segmenting by Family Life Cycle Still another form of demographic segmentation employs the stages of the **family life cycle**—the process of family formation and

Marketing Dictionary

family life cycle Process of family formation and dissolution, which affects market segmentation because life stage, not age, is the primary determinant of many consumer purchases.

MARKETING HALL OF SHAME

Mistakes in Mature Marketing

Historically, advertisers have never tried to woo gray-haired consumers with nearly the same enthusiasm they reserve for the younger crowd. Corporate America typically earmarks its biggest advertising dollars to consumers in their 20s, 30s, and 40s.

Conventional wisdom can largely be blamed for the snub. Advertisers typically believe that older Americans are too rigid and stuck in old buying habits to try new products. Marketers evidently believe that their biggest shopping years are over. Also, these reputedly pickier consumers have more time to spend skeptically poking holes in commercial claims.

"Fifty-plus, and most marketers see some doddering 90-year-old," laments Candace Corlett, president of special markets division at Research 100 of Princeton, N.J. But she also notes a few exceptions. Travel, financial services, and breakfast cereals are among the few products that advertisers are making a concerted effort to sell to the mature market.

"In the last five years, companies have taken some initiative to appeal to seniors in some special way," says Richard Reiser, chairman of BAI, a research firm in Tarrytown, N.Y.

But for every exceptional success, marketers have produced many other failures. Business, it would seem, just doesn't get it. Products and advertising appeals geared toward the stereotypical older American do not play well across the country. Yet growing incentives invite companies to properly target this market.

Roughly 56 million Americans are 50 or older—the fastest-growing demographic group in the nation. The number will continue to swell as Baby Boomers turn 50 and become eligible for membership in the American Association of Retired Persons (AARP).

Failures in the mature marketing realm are plentiful. A classic flop was Gerber's attempt to sell prepared foods for seniors. The idea was good, but the packaging—glass jars—wasn't. It made consumers feel like they were buying baby food.

Another notable example comes from the apparel industry. Retailers complain about persnickety customers and lagging sales, but they do not examine why women are not lugging bulging shopping bags home from the malls. As middle-aged women have grown older, their needs and their motivations for buying clothes have dramatically changed. No longer do they purchase outfits for trendy and fashionable styles. They buy comfortable clothes that make them look good.

dissolution. The underlying theme of this segmentation approach is that life stage, not age per se, is the primary determinant of many consumer purchases. As people move from one life stage to another, they become potential consumers for different types of goods and services.

For example, an unmarried person setting up an apartment for the first time is likely to be a good prospect for inexpensive furniture and small home appliances. This consumer probably must budget carefully, ruling out expenditures on luxury items. On the other hand, a young, single person who is still living at home will probably have more money to spend on goods such as sporting and entertainment equipment, personal-care items, and clothing.

As couples marry, their consumer profiles change. Couples without children are frequent buyers of personalized gifts, power tools, furniture, and homes. Eating out and travel may be part of their lifestyles.

The birth of a first child changes any couple's consumer profile considerably. Studies show that a couple having their first child spend an average of $2,000 buying cribs, changing tables, car seats, toys, and baby clothes. Parents usually spend less on the children who follow the first because they've already bought many essential items. *American Baby* magazine estimates that parents spend $13 billion a year on purchases for infants from birth through age one.[33]

The United States has the highest divorce rate in the world.[34] Divorce can dramatically alter an individual's consumer profile. As the household breaks up, the partners may need new household items at the same time that their income levels drop.

"Empty nesters"—married couples whose children have grown up and moved away from home—are an attractive life-cycle segment for marketers. In this stage, people likely own large stocks of household assets. Empty nesters may have the disposable incomes necessary to purchase premium products. Such a household may struggle to maintain a four-bedroom home and a half-acre lawn, making them customers for lawn-care and home-care services, as well as townhouses or condominiums. Later, these peo-

"The fitness industry understands it, so do plastic surgeons, periodontists and those self-improvement gurus," says Alice B. McCord, president of Alice B. McCord & Associates in New York. "Anyone over 40 knows most compliments come in the form of 'You look great,' rather than 'What a wonderfully fashionable something or other you're wearing.'"

"But firms engaged in producing and selling apparel don't seem to get it," McCord adds. "The ad industry and fashion press show the most extreme fashions on models scarcely out of puberty, and then proclaim them winners with their words 'young and sexy.'" This youth orientation does not sit well with most older consumers.

Meanwhile, targeting to seniors is more complicated than deciding to focus on everyone over 50. A 50-something consumer differs dramatically from someone who is 65 or 70 years old. If a company is selling insurance or investment advice, for example, the distinction can be crucial. Shifting into the age of Medicare eligibility eliminates a consumer as a target for primary health insurance. But that same person is now a far more receptive audience for supplementary health coverage.

"It used to be that when you knew someone's age, you knew a lot about him because the population went through life stages, like marriage and having children, at fairly predictable times," says Ross E. Goldstein, a consultant at Torme & Kenney in San Francisco. "Not anymore. My older brother is 52 and has a one-year-old daughter."

Despite the growing number of seniors, many companies remain leery about chasing the elderly markets. Some worry that gearing their message to senior citizens will brand their products as geriatric. "I've watched the process," says Candace Corlett. "They're not sure they can appeal to the mature market without being stigmatized as an old broad, like CBS wound up being, or without losing their young audience. But it can be done."

QUESTIONS FOR CRITICAL THINKING

1. **Do you think marketers face a trickier task targeting teenagers or consumers 50 years of age or older? Why?**
2. **If you were an advertiser, how would you try to target mature consumers? Do you think advertisers will de-emphasize the "standard" appeal of the youth generation as the Baby Boomers become grandparents?**

Sources: Gerry Myers, "Mutual Respect," *American Demographics,* April 1997, downloaded from http://www.marketingtools.com:80/, April 30, 1997; Herschell Gordon Lewis, "Another Look at the Senior Market," *Direct Marketing,* March 1996, pp. 20–23; Roger Rosenblatt, "Come Together," *Modern Maturity,* January/February 1996, pp. 32–39; "Older Consumers Affected by 'Major Life Events'", *Marketing News,* January 15, 1996, p. 6; Chad Rubel, "Mature Market Often Misunderstood," *Marketing News,* August 28, 1995, pp. 28–29; Faye Rice, "Making Generational Marketing Come of Age," *Fortune,* June 26, 1995, pp. 110–113; and Alice B. McCord, "Apparel Retailers Don't 'Get' Older Consumers," *Marketing News,* May 22, 1995, pp. 4, 19.

ple may become customers for retirement centers, supplemental medical insurance, and hearing aids. This is also a prime target market for travel and leisure products. For example, the USAir ad in Figure 7.4 is targeted at seniors whose children have moved away from home. The airline has developed special promotions for customers 62 years or older such as its Senior Saver Fare and Golden Opportunities Coupon Books.

One trend noted by researchers in the past decade is an increase in the number of grown children who have returned home to live with their parents. Some of these grown children bring along families of their own.

Segmenting by Household Type The first U.S. census in 1790 found an average household size of 5.8 persons. By 1960, this number had fallen to 3.4 persons; by the 1990s, it had fallen still further, to 2.7. The U.S. Department of Commerce cites several reasons for the trend toward smaller households: lower fertility rates, young people's tendency to postpone marriage or never marry, the increasing tendency among younger couples to limit the number of children or have no children, the ease and frequency of divorce, and the ability and desire of many young singles and the elderly to live alone.

Population data shows a similar pattern in Pacific Rim countries. The average South Korean household size has decreased from five people in 1975 to less than four today. Taiwan, Hong Kong, and Singapore report similar statistics. Although household size is down, the numbers of households have increased in these countries.

An important U.S. trend over the past 20 years has been the decline of the so-called traditional family, consisting of two parents and their children living in one household. In 1970, this segment comprised 40 percent of all American households; by the 1990s, it had shrunk to just 26 percent. Meanwhile, three other segments—single-parent families, single-person households, and nonfamily group households—have each more than doubled in size during the same time period. These nontraditional households make likely consumers for single-serving and

Figure 7.4 Promoting a Service to Empty Nesters

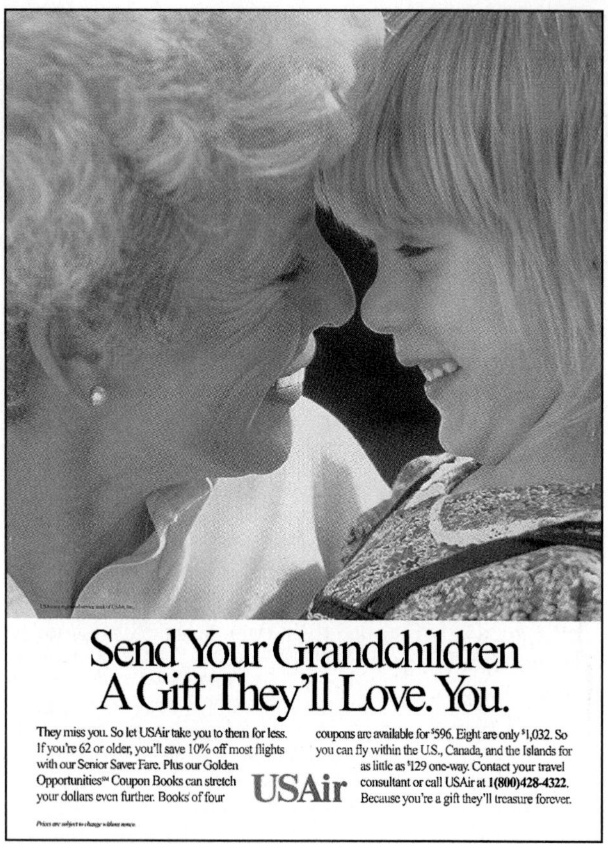
Send Your Grandchildren
A Gift They'll Love. You.
They miss you. So let USAir take you to them for less. If you're 62 or older, you'll save 10% off most flights with our Senior Saver Fare. Plus our Golden Opportunities℠ Coupon Books can stretch your dollars even further. Books of four coupons are available for $596. Eight are only $1,032. So you can fly within the U.S., Canada, and the Islands for as little as $129 one-way. Contact your travel consultant or call USAir at 1(800)428-4322. Because you're a gift they'll treasure forever.
USAir

convenience foods, such as Campbell's Soup for One and Budget Gourmet, Stouffer's, and Weight Watchers' single-serve casseroles.

While the percentage of married-couple families has fallen, the number of unmarried individuals living together has risen. Consequently, the Bureau of the Census has created another category, POSLSQ, which stands for unmarried *people of the opposite sex living in the same quarters.*

Finally, one of the most actively pursued market segments are DINKs—dual-income couples with no kids. With high levels of spendable income, such couples are big buyers of gourmet foods, luxury items, and travel.

Segmenting by Income and Expenditure Patterns The earlier definition of *market* described people (or institutions) with purchasing power. Not surprisingly, then, a common basis for segmenting the consumer market is income. Figure 7.5 shows a wide distribution of income in the United States. Mass-marketers aim their appeals at middle-income groups, while others might target more affluent segments. For example, supermarket company A&P caters to upscale consumers with its 34 Food Emporium stores. Customers browse among a wide variety of gourmet items—everything from Hawaiian blue prawns to caviar—while visiting chefs prepare food samples on-site for customers to try. Advertising for the chain stresses the quality and variety of available products rather than their prices.[35]

Marketers often target geographic areas known for their high incomes. *Sales & Marketing Management* magazine conducts an *Annual Survey of Buying Power,* and the report lists metropolitan markets by income. According to the 1996 survey, Bridgeport-Stamford-Norwalk-Danbury, Connecticut, ranked first, with an average Effective Buying Income (disposable income) of $54,922. Other high-income metropolitan markets among the top ten were Middlesex-Somerset-Hunterdon, New Jersey; Nassau-Suffolk, New York; San Jose, California; Washington, D.C.; and Honolulu, Hawaii.[36]

Engel's Laws How do expenditure patterns vary with income? Over a century ago, Ernst Engel, a German statistician, published what became known as **Engel's laws**—three general statements based on his studies of the impact of household income changes on consumer spending behavior. According to Engel, as family income increases:

1. A smaller percentage of expenditures go for food.
2. The percentage spent on housing and household operations and clothing remains constant.

Figure 7.5 Income Distribution of the U.S. Population

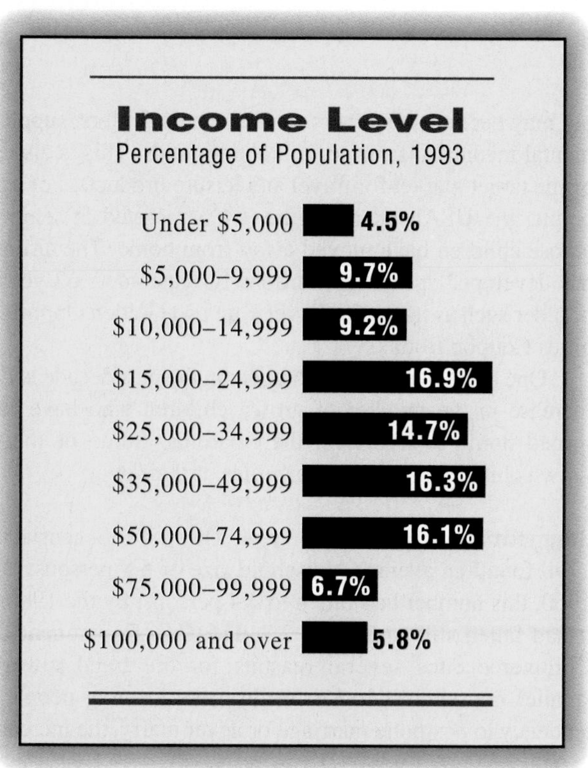
Income Level
Percentage of Population, 1993
Under $5,000 4.5%
$5,000–9,999 9.7%
$10,000–14,999 9.2%
$15,000–24,999 16.9%
$25,000–34,999 14.7%
$35,000–49,999 16.3%
$50,000–74,999 16.1%
$75,000–99,999 6.7%
$100,000 and over 5.8%

3. The percentage spent on other items (such as recreation and education) increases.

Are Engel's laws still valid? Recent studies say essentially *yes,* with a few exceptions. Researchers note a steady decline in the percentage of total income spent on food, beverages, and tobacco as income increases. Although high-income families spend greater absolute amounts on food items, their purchases represent declining percentages of their total expenditures as compared with low-income families. The second law remains partly accurate, since the percentage of expenditures for housing and household operations remains relatively unchanged in all but the very lowest income groups. The percentage spent on clothing, however, rises with increased income. The third law is also true, with the exception of medical and personal care costs, which appear to decline as a percentage of increased income. The ad for Skylondia Retreat in Figure 7.6 is targeted at high-income families, which spend high percentages of their incomes (relative to less affluent families) on such recreational services as luxury fitness retreats and spas.

Engel's laws provide the marketing manager with useful rules about the types of consumer demand that evolve with increased income. They can also give helpful guidance for the marketer evaluating a foreign country as a potential target market.

Figure 7.6 Segmenting by Income and Expenditure Patterns

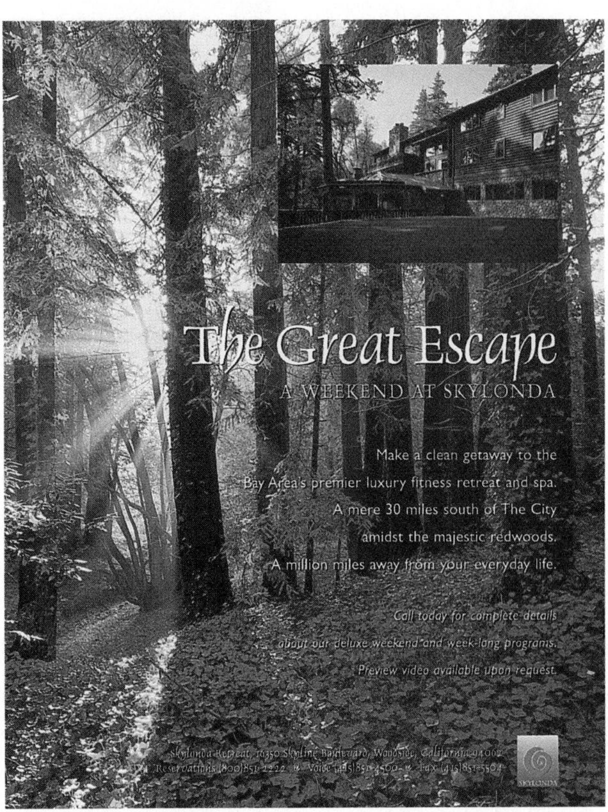
The Great Escape
A WEEKEND AT SKYLONDA
Make a clean getaway to the
Bay Area's premier luxury fitness retreat and spa.
A mere 30 miles south of The City
amidst the majestic redwoods.
A million miles away from your everyday life.
Call today for complete details
about our deluxe weekend and week-long programs.
Preview video available upon request.
SKYLONDA

Demographic Segmentation Abroad Marketers often face a difficult task in obtaining the data necessary for global demographic segmentation. Many countries do not operate regularly scheduled census programs. For instance, the most recent count of the Dutch population is now over two decades old. Germany skipped counting from 1970 to 1987, and France conducts a census about every seven years. By contrast, Japan and Canada conduct censuses every five years; however, the mid-decade assessments are not as complete as the end-of-decade counts.

Also, some foreign data addresses demographic divisions not found in the U.S. census. (Canada collects information on religious affiliation, for instance.) On the other hand, some of the marketer's standard segmentation data for U.S. markets is not available abroad. Many nations do not collect income data. Great Britain, Japan, Spain, France, and Italy are examples. Similarly, family life cycle data is difficult to apply in global demographic segmentation efforts. Ireland acknowledges only three marital statuses—single, married, and widowed—while Latin American nations and Sweden count their cohabitating populations.

One online source of global demographic information is the International Programs Center (IPC) at the U.S. Bureau of the Census. The IPC provides a searchable database of population statistics for many countries on the Census Bureau's World Wide Web page.

http://www.census.gov/

Psychographic Segmentation

Marketers have traditionally referred to geographic and demographic characteristics as the primary bases for dividing consumer and industrial markets into homogeneous market

Marketing Dictionary

Engel's laws Three general statements based on Ernst Engel's studies of the impact of household income changes on consumer spending behavior. As family income increases, (1) a smaller percentage of expenditures go for food, (2) the percentage spent on housing and household operations and clothing remains constant; and (3) the percentage spent on other items (such as recreation and education) increases.

segments. Still, they have long recognized the need for fuller, more lifelike portraits of consumers to develop their marketing programs. As a result, psychographic segmentation can be a useful tool for gaining sharper insight into consumer purchasing behavior.

What Is Psychographic Segmentation? **Psychographic segmentation** divides a population into groups that have similar psychological characteristics, values, and lifestyles. **Lifestyle** refers to a person's mode of living; it describes how an individual operates on a daily basis. Consumers' lifestyles are composites of their individual psychological profiles, including their needs, motives, perceptions, and attitudes. A lifestyle also bears the mark of many other influences, such as family, job, social activities, and culture.

The most common method for developing psychographic profiles of a population is to conduct a large-scale survey that asks consumers to agree or disagree with a collection of several hundred *AIO statements.* **AIO statements** describe various activities, interests and opinions. Data about choices between these statements allows researchers to develop lifestyle profiles. Marketers can then develop a separate marketing strategy that closely fits the psychographic makeup of each lifestyle segment.

Market researchers have conducted psychographic studies on hundreds of goods and services, ranging from beer to air travel. Hospitals and other health-care providers use such studies to assess consumer behavior and attitudes toward health care in general, to learn the needs of consumers in particular marketplaces, and to determine how consumers perceive individual institutions. Many businesses turn to psychographic research in an effort to learn what consumers in various demographic and geographic segments want and need.

Marketers have also used psychographic profiles to identify subgroups within larger demographic groups. For instance, in seeking to understand the differences among Generation X consumers, researchers conducted interviews with people in the target age group. They identified four distinct groups of Xers: "Cynical disdainers" are pessimistic and skeptical about their prospects. "Traditional materialists," on the other hand, are more optimistic; they feel motivated to achieve such symbols of the American dream as careers, homes, and families. "Hippies revisited" are attracted to the lifestyles and values of the 60s; they express themselves through music, fashion, and spirituality. Finally, the "Fifties machos" are conservatives who resist accepting equal gender roles and multiculturalism.[37]

VALS™ 2 In 1978, the research and consulting firm SRI International developed a psychographic segmentation system called *VALS.* The name stands for "values and lifestyles," and the original VALS scheme categorized consumers by their opinions about social issues. A decade later, SRI revised the system to link it more closely with consumer buying behavior. The revised system, VALS 2, is based on two key concepts: resources and self-motivation. **VALS 2** divides consumers into eight psychographic categories. Figure 7.7 details the profiles for these categories and their relationships.

The VALS network chart in the figure displays differences in resources as vertical distances, while its self-orientation is represented horizontally. The resource dimension measures income, education, self-confidence, health, eagerness to buy, and energy level. Self-orientations divide consumers into three groups: principle-oriented consumers have a set of ideas and morals—principles—that they live their lives by; status-oriented consumers are influenced by what others think; action-oriented consumers seek physical activity, variety, and adventure.

According to an analysis of GeoVALS™ data in *American Demographics* magazine, the U.S. city whose population most closely matches the nation's VALS 2 psychographic profile is Baltimore.[38] GeoVALS estimates the percentage of each VALS type in each U.S. residential ZIP code. Curious about which psychographic segment claims you? Visitors to SRI's World Wide Web site can take the questionnaire and get immediate feedback on their VALS 2 types.

http://future.sri.com/

SRI uses the VALS 2 segmentation information with marketers in consulting projects and on a subscriber basis. Product, service, and media data are available by VALS-type from the VALS national database. There are other commercially available psychographic profile systems that offer their own insights to marketers. One is MONITOR, available from Yankelovich, Skelly, and White.[39] A newer syndicated psychographic service, from marketing research firm Odyssey, is the first to focus on the psychographics of users of new technology, such as the Internet. However, SRI also tracks the attitudes, preferences, and behaviors of online services and Internet users through an ongoing study dubbed iVALS.

Psychographic Segmentation of Global Markets Psychographic profiles can cross national boundaries, but the process of segmenting global markets must accommodate cultural differences. SRI, for instance, developed a system for understanding Japanese consumers which took into account traditional aspects of the Japanese culture. The JapanVALS™ study then identified the following consumer segments:

- *Integrators* (4 percent of the population) are active, trend-setting, informed consumers.

Figure 7.7 VALS™ 2 Network

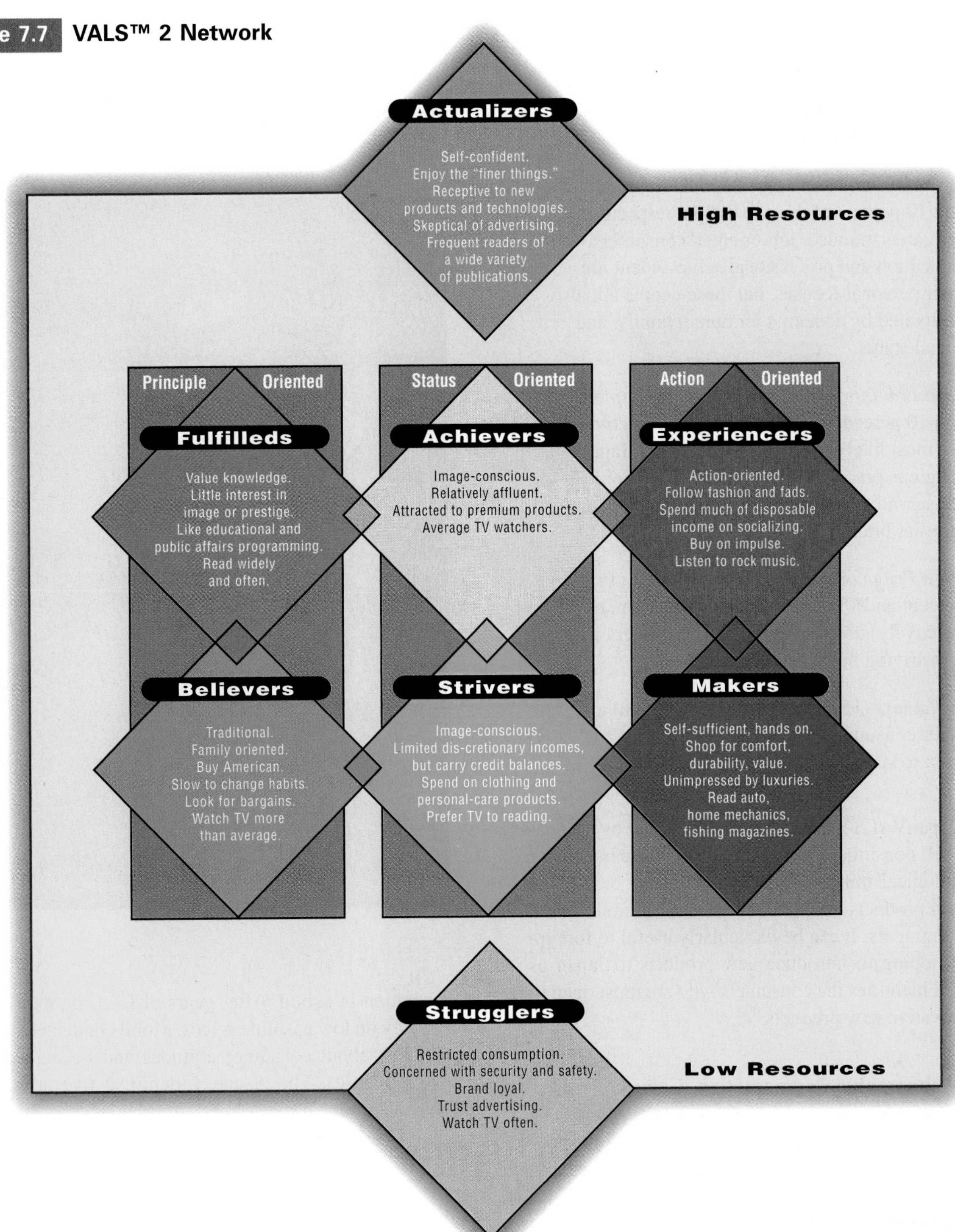
Actualizers
Self-confident. Enjoy the "finer things." Receptive to new products and technologies. Skeptical of advertising. Frequent readers of a wide variety of publications.
High Resources
Principle Oriented
Status Oriented
Action Oriented
Fulfilleds
Value knowledge. Little interest in image or prestige. Like educational and public affairs programming. Read widely and often.
Achievers
Image-conscious. Relatively affluent. Attracted to premium products. Average TV watchers.
Experiencers
Action-oriented. Follow fashion and fads. Spend much of disposable income on socializing. Buy on impulse. Listen to rock music.
Believers
Traditional. Family oriented. Buy American. Slow to change habits. Look for bargains. Watch TV more than average.
Strivers
Image-conscious. Limited dis-cretionary incomes, but carry credit balances. Spend on clothing and personal-care products. Prefer TV to reading.
Makers
Self-sufficient, hands on. Shop for comfort, durability, value. Unimpressed by luxuries. Read auto, home mechanics, fishing magazines.
Strugglers
Restricted consumption. Concerned with security and safety. Brand loyal. Trust advertising. Watch TV often.
Low Resources

They travel frequently and are the most open segment to innovations.

- *Self-Innovators and Self-Adapters* (7 percent and 11 percent of the population, respectively) are motivated by

Marketing Dictionary

psychographic segmentation Dividing a population into homogeneous groups on the basis of psychological and lifestyle profiles.

lifestyle People's decisions about how to live their daily lives, including family, job, social, and consumer activities.

AIO statements Statements in a psychographic survey; choices reflect a respondent's activities, interests, and opinions.

VALS™ 2 Commercially available system for psychographic segmentation of consumers.

fashion trends, social activities, and exciting entertainment possibilities.

- *Ryoshiki Innovators and Ryoshiki Adapters* (6 and 10 percent of the population, respectively) are career-minded, job-oriented consumers. Education and professional achievement are their personal focuses, but these people are also motivated by concerns for home, family, and social status.
- *Tradition Innovators and Tradition Adapters* (6 and 10 percent of the population, respectively) are most likely to adhere to traditional Japanese religious practices and customs. They hold conservative social opinions and look for long-familiar brands.
- *High Pragmatics and Low Pragmatics* (14 percent and 17 percent of the population, respectively) are not very active consumers with few driving interests.
- *Sustainers* (15 percent of the population) are older consumers who dislike innovation and want to sustain the past.

The JapanVALS marketing system is used by companies who sell consumer goods in Japan. By understanding the psychological traits of different segments, businesses can develop products and marketing mixes geared toward the target segments. It can be particularly useful to foreign marketers hoping to introduce new products to Japan as JapanVALS identifies the consumers who are most open to trying innovative new products.[40]

Using Psychographic Segmentation Commercial psychographic profile systems like VALS 2 and MONITOR can paint useful, if broad, pictures of the overall psychological motivations of consumers. However, in the past few years, marketers have started to see limitations in universal labels that describe all of the attitudes and behaviors that a consumer might adopt. Instead, businesses are developing and applying increasingly specific psychographic categories that reflect highly detailed consumer attitudes, actions, and interests related to specific product categories or activities.

The activewear company No Fear conducted intensive research to learn about consumer attitudes related to its clothing. From its research, No Fear developed a lifestyle-advertising program aimed at people who relish the psychological challenge of sports. No Fear places ads, such as the one in Figure 7.8, in magazines for surfing, cycling, and motorcycle racing enthusiasts.

Mobil Corp. offers an example of psychographic segmentation in action. After years of focusing its marketing strategy on low gasoline prices, Mobil conducted extensive research about consumer attitudes and behaviors toward gas purchases. The research identified five primary purchasing groups for gasoline:

Figure 7.8 Using Psychographic Segmentation

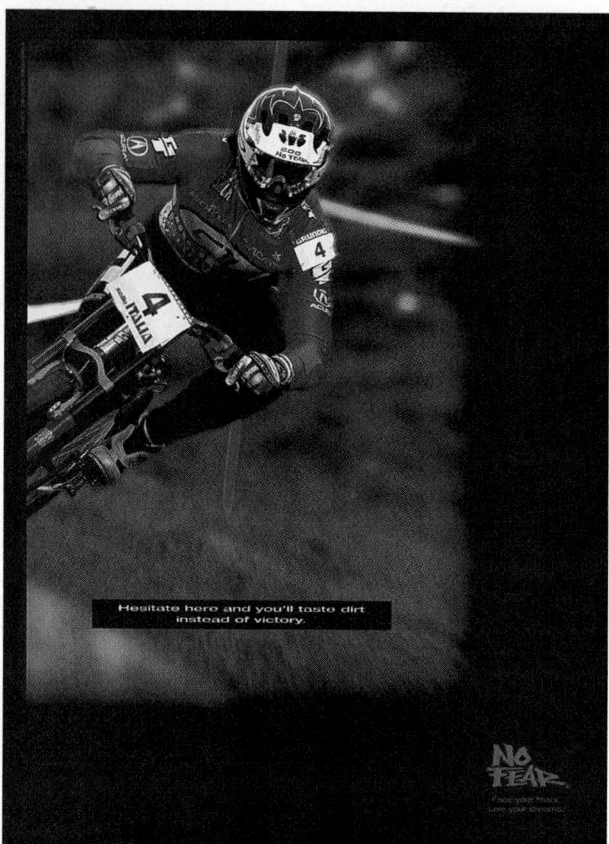
Hesitate here and you'll taste dirt instead of victory.
NO FEAR

- *Road Warriors*—Generally middle-aged, higher-income men who buy premium gas, as well as sandwiches and drinks from station convenience stores. Driving over 25,000 miles a year, this segment also spends the most on gasoline purchases.
- *True Blues*—Men and women with moderate to high incomes. They're brand loyal and sometimes loyal to particular service stations.
- *Generation F3*—*F3* stands for "fuel, food, fast." These consumers are younger, upwardly mobile people constantly on the go. They buy heavily from station convenience stores.
- *Homebodies*—Usually housewives, they spend

time driving their children around during the day. They stop at any convenient gas station.

- *Price Shoppers*—This segment isn't loyal to brands or stations and rarely buys premium gas. They're on tight budgets and spend the least amount they can on gas each year.

Mobil's research convinced the company that its low-price strategy suffered from flaws. The company decided to revise its appeal to focus on three segments: Road Warriors, True Blues, and Generation F3. These three categories, accounting for 59 percent of motorists, spend more money than others to keep their cars on the road. Since Mobil's research also showed that these consumer groups preferred a "quality buying experience," it has embarked on a campaign to spruce up its service. Changes at Mobil stations include cleaner stores, better lighting, friendly and helpful attendants, and even cappuccino stands at some stations. As a result, revenue at some stations is up as much as 25 percent.[41]

As Mobil's experience demonstrates, psychographic segmentation has considerable implications for marketing strategy. Psychographic profiles produce much richer descriptions of potential target markets than other techniques can achieve. The greater detail aids greatly in matching the company's image and product offerings with the types of consumers who use its products.

Psychographic segmentation is a good supplement to segmentation by demographic or geographic variables such as age, income, city, size, education, family life cycle stage, and geographic location. VALS also gives marketers access to each consumer type's media preferences in network television, cable television, radio format, magazine, and newspaper. Psychographic studies may then refine the picture of segment characteristics to give a more elaborate lifestyle profile of the consumers in the firm's target market.

Product-Related Segmentation

Product-related segmentation involves dividing a consumer population into homogeneous groups based on characteristics of their relationships to the product. This segmentation approach can take several forms:

1. Segmenting by the benefits that people seek when they buy a product
2. Segmenting by usage rates for a product
3. Segmenting according to consumers' brand loyalty toward a product

Segmenting by Benefits Sought

This approach focuses on the attributes that people seek in a good or service and the benefits they expect to receive. It groups consumers into segments based on what they want a product to do for them. Compaq Computer Corp., for example, believes that groups of consumers look for different options when they purchase personal computers. As a result, Compaq has introduced five new lines, ranging from laptops to full-sized multimedia machines. One Compaq product line has been dubbed "the sports car of computers," because it offers high-end performance features such as premium speakers and three-dimensional graphics ideal for presenting entertainment CDs. On the other hand, consumers looking for a sleeker computer that fits in more areas of the home might prefer Compaq's flat-screen computer series.[42]

Even if a business offers only one product line, however, marketers must remember to consider product benefits. Two people may buy the same product for very different reasons. A box of Arm & Hammer baking soda may end up serving as a refrigerator freshener, a toothpaste substitute, an antacid, or a deodorizer for a cat's litter box.

Segmenting by Usage Rates Marketers may also segment a total market by grouping people according to the amounts of a product that they buy and use. Markets can be divided into heavy-user, moderate-user, and light-user segments. The **80/20 principle** holds that a big percentage of a product's revenues—roughly 80 percent—comes from a relatively small, loyal percentage of total customers, perhaps 20 percent. While the percentages need not exactly equal these figures, the general principle often holds true: Relatively few heavy users of a product can account for much of its consumption.

The Campbell Soup Company, for example, has found that its core customers—those who buy its soup regularly—make up only 10 percent of total soup purchasers, but they account for 90 percent of products sold.[43] Taco Bell has found that less than 30 percent of its customer base accounts for 70 percent of its sales volume. By developing service and marketing programs aimed at this core customer base, Taco Bell more than doubled its sales in a five-year period.[44]

Marketing Dictionary

product-related segmentation Dividing a consumer population into homogeneous groups based on characteristics of their relationships to a product.

80/20 principle Idea that a big percentage of a product's revenues—roughly 80 percent—comes from a relatively small percentage of total customers—around 20 percent.

Depending on their goals, marketers may target heavy, moderate, or light users, even nonusers. A company may attempt to woo heavy users away from their regular brands to try a new brand. Nonusers and light users may be attractive prospects, because other companies are ignoring them. Usage rates can also be linked to other segmentation methods such as demographic and psychographic segmentation.

Segmenting by Brand Loyalty A third product-related segmentation method groups consumers according to the strength of the brand loyalty they feel toward a product. The classic example of this segmentation technique is airline frequent-flyer programs. Originally targeted at heavy users—business travelers—frequent-flyer programs now help to bind even occasional travelers to specific airlines. The success of these programs has resulted in similar efforts in the hotel industry and elsewhere.

SEGMENTATION OF BUSINESS-TO-BUSINESS MARKETS

Chapter 9 will describe how companies segment business-to-business markets. The overall segmentation process resembles that for consumer markets. However, some specific methods differ. Business-to-business markets can be segmented by demographics, customer type, end-use application, and purchasing situation.[45] Chapter 9 presents examples of each of these approaches.

THE MARKET SEGMENTATION PROCESS

To this point, the chapter has discussed various bases on which companies segment markets. How does a marketer decide which segmentation base to use? As Figure 7.9 shows, marketers follow a five-step decision process.

Stage I: Identify Market Segmentation Process

Segmentation begins when marketers determine the bases on which to identify markets. They follow two methods of achieving this goal. In the first, management-driven method, segments are predefined by managers based on their observation of the behavioral and demographic characteristics of likely users. The other, market-driven method, defines segments by asking customers which attributes are important to them and then clustering responses to identify potential segments.[46] Both methods try to develop segments that group customers who respond similarly to specific marketing-mix alternatives. For example, Procter & Gamble cannot simply target Crest at large families. Management must first confirm that most large families are interested in preventing tooth decay and will be receptive to the Crest marketing offer.

Sometimes marketers have trouble isolating a preferred segment. Many toy and clothing manufacturers would like to target grandparents. These buyers define an important secondary segment for these companies, spending a median of $407 annually buying entertainment, gifts, and clothes for their grandchildren. Yet, marketers have found it hard to identify and reach grandparents. "Grandparents are very hard to find," explains one advertising executive. "You know intellectually that they are somewhere between the ages of 50 and 100. But you can't target them with seniors magazines because a lot of seniors may or may not be grandparents. Also, some marketers may only want to target grandparents with grandchildren who are a certain age."[47]

Stage II: Develop a Relevant Profile for Each Segment

After identifying promising segments, marketers should seek further understanding of the customers in each one. This in-depth analysis of customer characteristics helps managers to accurately match customers' needs with the firm's marketing offers. The process must identify characteristics that both explain the similarities among customers within each segment and account for differences among segments.

The task at this stage is to develop a profile of the typical customer in each segment. Such a profile might include information about lifestyle patterns, attitudes toward product attributes and brands, brand preferences, product-use habits, geographic locations, and demographic characteristics.

Stage III: Forecast Market Potential

In the third stage, market segmentation and market opportunity analysis combine to produce a forecast of market potential within each segment. Market potential sets the upper limit on the demand that competing firms can expect from a segment. Multiplying by market share determines a single firm's maximum sales potential. This step should define a preliminary go or no-go decision for management, since the total sales potential in each segment must justify resources devoted to further analysis.

Peterson Publishing Co., for example, publishes magazines targeted at relatively specialized interests of male consumers. The company's first magazine was *Hot Rod,* a southern California publication covering cars and races. The company then launched other magazines such as *Chevy High Performance, Guns & Ammo,* and *Bow Hunt-*

ing. While *Hot Rod* has a circulation of 800,000, none of the company's 77 spin-offs has a circulation over 150,000. Yet the company grosses over $250 million a year in subscription fees and advertising revenue.[48]

Figure 7.9 Market Segmentation Decision Process

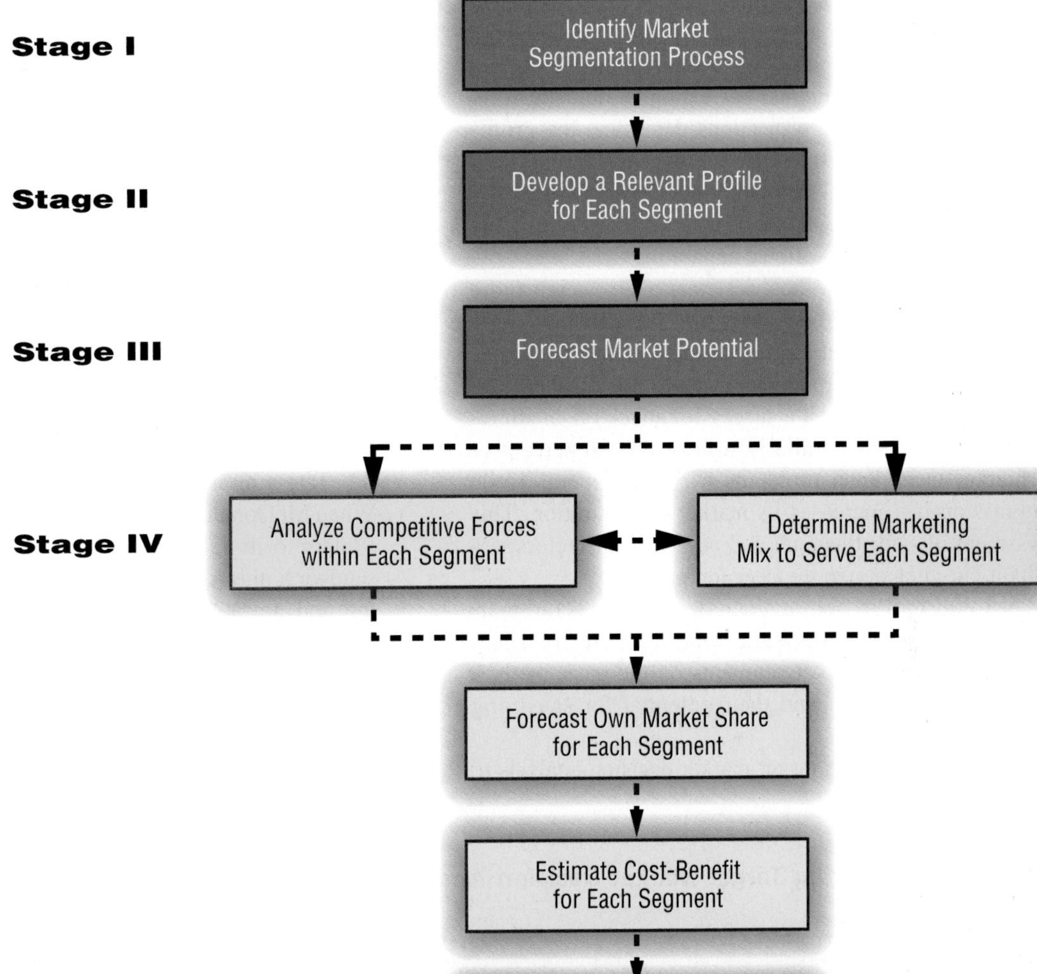
Stage I
Identify Market Segmentation Process
Stage II
Develop a Relevant Profile for Each Segment
Stage III
Forecast Market Potential
Stage IV
Analyze Competitive Forces within Each Segment
Determine Marketing Mix to Serve Each Segment
Forecast Own Market Share for Each Segment
Estimate Cost-Benefit for Each Segment
Stage V
Do Benefits Achieve Company Goals and Justify Development of Each Segment?
Select Specific Market Segments

Stage IV: Forecast Probable Market Share

Once market potential has been estimated, a firm must forecast its probable market share. Competitors' positions in targeted segments must be analyzed and a specific marketing strategy designed to serve these segments. These two activities may be performed simultaneously. Moreover, by settling on a marketing strategy and tactics, a firm determines the expected level of resources it must commit, that is, the costs that it will incur to tap the potential demand in each segment.

David Verzello and Mark Goodwin, owners of the David & Mark Brewing Co. in Atlanta, started their firm to market a microbrew light beer to a very specific target market: patrons at gay bars. Their research showed that gay men and lesbians drink about 30 percent more beer than the average consumption for all drinkers and that Atlanta's gay bars alone sell about 30,000 cases of beer a month. By looking at the number of gays nationwide, the partners estimated the national market for beer in gay bars at $240 million annually. National brands account for about 80 percent of those sales. The partners estimated that their company would earn a profit if they could capture about 5 percent of the remaining 20 percent of total sales. Has it worked? Although the company lost $169,000 in its first year of business, the partners expected to start turning a profit in their second year.[49]

Stage V: Select Specific Market Segments

The information, analysis, and forecasts accumulated through the entire market segmentation decision process allows management to assess the potential for achieving company goals and to justify committing resources to develop one or more segments. For example, demand forecasts together with cost projections determine the profits and the return on investment (ROI) that the company can expect from each segment. Marketing strategy and tactics must be designed to reinforce the firm's image, yet keep within its unique organizational capabilities.

At this point in the analysis, marketers weigh more than monetary costs and benefits; they also consider many difficult-to-measure but critical organizational and environmental factors. For example, the firm may lack experienced personnel to launch a successful attack on an attractive market segment. Similarly, a firm with 60 percent of the market faces legal problems with the Federal Trade Commission if it increases its market concentration. This assessment of both financial and nonfinancial factors is a difficult but vital step in the decision process.

A useful tool to help marketers choose specific markets is **target market decision analysis.** This procedure evaluates potential market segments on the basis of their relevant characteristics and their potential for satisfying business objectives.

Duracell completes target market decision analysis to decide whether to enter new global markets. The company measures market potential by determining the size of a potential market, likely increases in consumer purchasing power, and forecasted growth of battery-powered electronics products. From its analysis, Duracell has decided to market its batteries in emerging markets such as China, India, Poland, Russia, and Vietnam, which represent total battery sales of 10 billion units a year, or about one-half of the world's total battery consumption. Although the enormous potential for sales in these countries seems attractive, Duracell must first persuade consumers to buy its alkaline batteries instead of the less expensive zinc carbon batteries that dominate these markets. Through consistent consumer advertising that emphasizes long life and consumer value, such as the ad in Figure 7.10 directed at Chinese consumers, Duracell attempts to build brand awareness and to inform consumers that its batteries last about six times longer than competing products.

Targeting new segments can be a costly proposition. When McDonald's decided to try to attract more adult consumers to its restaurants, the company launched its new sandwich, the Arch Deluxe, with a $200 million advertising and promotion campaign. Results have been mixed. Some franchises reported a boost in initial dinner business, but analysts suggested that the Arch Deluxe initially added little to McDonald's overall incremental sales.[50] The long-range effect of the company's efforts to attract more adult diners remains to be seen.

Figure 7.10 Applying Target Market Decision Analysis

福
多年年增
禄
厚天天長
寿
長人人歡
DURACELL
喜
得個個强

STRATEGIES FOR REACHING TARGET MARKETS

Much of the marketing effort is dedicated to developing strategies that will best match the firm's product offerings to the needs of particular target markets. An appropriate match is vital to the firm's marketing success. Marketers have identified four basic strategies for achieving consumer satisfaction: undifferentiated marketing, differentiated marketing, concentrated marketing, and micromarketing.

Undifferentiated Marketing

A firm may produce only one product or product line and promote it to all customers with a single marketing mix; such a firm is said to practice **undifferentiated marketing,** sometimes called *mass marketing*. Undifferentiated marketing was much more common in the past than it is today. As noted earlier, Henry Ford built the Model T and sold it for one price to everyone who wanted to buy. He agreed to paint his cars any color that consumers wanted, "as long as it is black." Ford's only concession to more specific customer needs was to add a truck body for Model T purchasers who needed more hauling capacity.

While undifferentiated marketing is efficient from a production viewpoint, the strategy also brings inherent dangers. A firm that attempts to satisfy everyone in the market with one standard product may suffer if competitors offer specialized units to smaller segments of the total market and better satisfy individual segments. Indeed, firms that implement strategies of differentiated marketing, concentrated marketing, or micromarketing may capture enough small segments of the market to defeat another competitor's strategy of undifferentiated marketing.

Differentiated Marketing

Firms that promote numerous products with different marketing mixes designed to satisfy smaller segments are said to practice **differentiated marketing.** Liz Claiborne has branched out from its original target market of selling stylish clothing to career women. The company now makes cosmetics, colognes, and clothing targeted to the male consumer with a taste for style. Claiborne is also targeting Generation X. The company's Curve fragrances, one for men and one for women, follow the preferences of younger consumers.

The differentiated marketing strategy is still aimed at satisfying a large part of the total market. Instead of marketing one product with a single marketing program, however, the organization markets a number of products designed to appeal to individual parts of the total market.[51]

By providing increased satisfaction for each of many target markets, a company can produce more sales by following a differentiated marketing strategy than undifferentiated marketing would generate. In general, however, differentiated marketing also raises costs. Production costs usually rise, because additional products and variations require shorter production runs and increased setup times. Inventory costs rise, because more products require added storage space and more efforts for record keeping. Promotional costs also increase, because each segment demands a unique promotional mix. Despite higher marketing costs, a company may be forced to practice differentiated marketing in order to remain competitive.

Concentrated Marketing

Rather than trying to market its products separately to several segments, a firm may opt for a concentrated marketing strategy. With **concentrated marketing** (also known as *niche marketing*), a firm focuses its efforts on profitably satisfying only one market segment. This approach can appeal to a small firm that lacks the financial resources of its competitors and to a company that offers highly specialized goods and services. ConAgra developed Healthy Choice, a line of prepared foods, for the market segment of busy people concerned about good health. The ad in Figure 7.11 compares the high fat content of an average takeout pizza with the low fat content of the Healthy Choice alternative.

When Susan Yee had trouble finding cosmetics that blended well with Asian skin tones, she recognized a market segment with unmet needs. She founded Zhen Cosmetics, a Minnesota firm that produces hypoallergenic cosmetics designed specifically for Asian-Americans. The company reaches its target market through a catalog and is test marketing its products at upscale retail stores.[52]

Along with its benefits, concentrated marketing has its dangers. Since the strategy ties a firm's growth to a particular segment, changes in the size of that segment or in customer buying patterns may result in severe financial

Marketing Dictionary

target market decision analysis Procedure for evaluating the relevant characteristics and the prospects for satisfying business objectives of potential market segments.

undifferentiated marketing Marketing strategy to produce only one product and market it to all customers using a single marketing mix.

differentiated marketing Marketing strategy to produce numerous products and promote them with different marketing mixes designed to satisfy smaller segments.

concentrated marketing Marketing strategy that commits all of a firm's marketing resources to serve a single market segment.

Figure 7.11 Implementing Concentrated Marketing

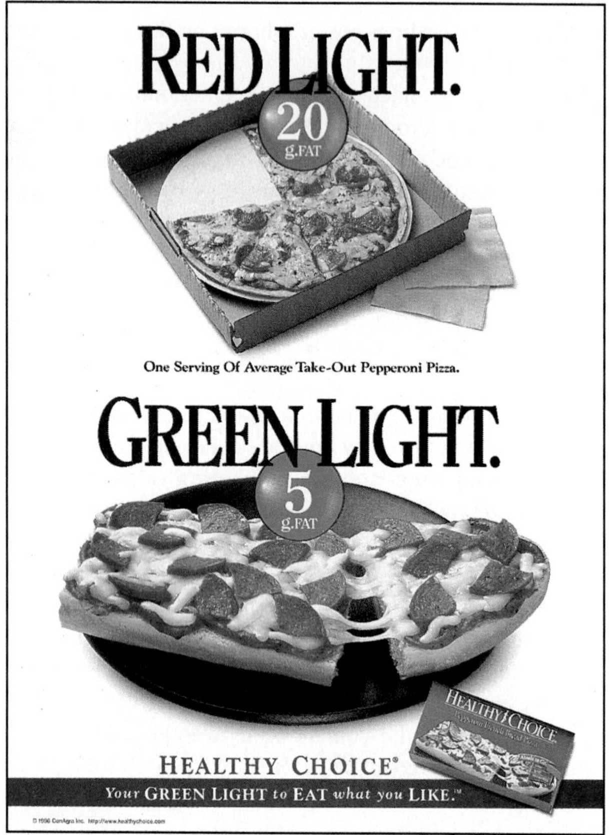
RED LIGHT.
20 g.FAT
One Serving Of Average Take-Out Pepperoni Pizza.
GREEN LIGHT.
5 g.FAT
HEALTHY CHOICE®
Your GREEN LIGHT to EAT what you LIKE.

problems. Sales may also drop if new competitors appeal successfully to the same segment.

Lexus is an example. Toyota broke into the luxury car market by launching a new brand targeted at first-time luxury car buyers. These buyers were younger than traditional luxury car buyers. The strategy worked—but now other luxury car makers like Mercedes-Benz, BMW, and even Cadillac have also targeted the same market with lower-priced cars. As a result, Lexus' growth has slowed.[53]

Micromarketing

The fourth targeting strategy, still more narrowly focused than concentrated marketing, is micromarketing. **Micromarketing** involves targeting potential customers at a very basic level, such as by ZIP code, specific occupation, lifestyle, or individual household. Ultimately, micromarketing may even target individuals themselves.

Fisher-Price Toys, for example, uses micromarketing to target a very specific group: grandparents with grandchildren between birth and age five. As discussed previously, grandparents are an important segment for toy companies because these consumers frequently buy toys as gifts for their grandchildren. To reach this grandparent segment, Fisher-Price sponsored a special newsletter published by Washington, D.C.-based Caring Grandparents of America, a profit-oriented national membership organization. The newsletter sent to CGA members included coupons for Fisher-Price products.[54]

For another example, consider the micromarketing success of Vons Supermarkets. The southern California retail grocery chain enlists customers to join its "VonsClub." Customers in the club can pay for their purchases using special debit cards, and they receive discounts at checkstands on selected items. But Vons' micromarketing efforts really happen after customers leave the store. The company's computer system tracks the purchases of each consumer and then sends out a personalized mailing to each club member with coupons for the items that the individual buys most often.

The Internet may allow marketers to boost the effectiveness of micromarketing. By tracking specific demographic and personal information, marketers can send e-mail directly to individual consumers who are most likely to buy their products.

Selecting and Executing a Strategy

Although most organizations adopt some form of differentiated marketing as their strategies, no single, best choice suits all firms. Any of the alternatives may prove most effective in a particular situation. The basic determinants of a market-specific strategy are (1) company resources, (2) product homogeneity, (3) stage in the product life cycle, and (4) competitors' strategies.

A firm with limited resources may have to choose a concentrated marketing strategy. Small firms, for example, may be forced to select small target markets because limitations in their financing, sales force, and promotional budgets prevent larger efforts.

On the other hand, an undifferentiated marketing strategy suits a firm selling products perceived by consumers as relatively homogeneous. Marketers of grain sell standardized grades of the generic products rather than individual brand names. Some petroleum companies implement undifferentiated marketing to distribute their gasoline to the mass market.

The firm's strategy may also change as its product progresses through the stages of the life cycle. During the early stages, undifferentiated marketing might effectively support the firm's attempt to develop initial demand for the product. In the later stages, however, competitive pressures may force modifications in products and development of marketing strategies aimed at segments of the total market.

The strategies of competitors also affect the choice of a segmentation strategy. A firm may encounter obstacles to undifferentiated marketing if its competitors actively cultivate smaller segments. In such instances, competition usually forces each firm to adopt a differentiated marketing strategy.

Figure 7.12 Competitive Positioning Map for the Pain-Reliever Market

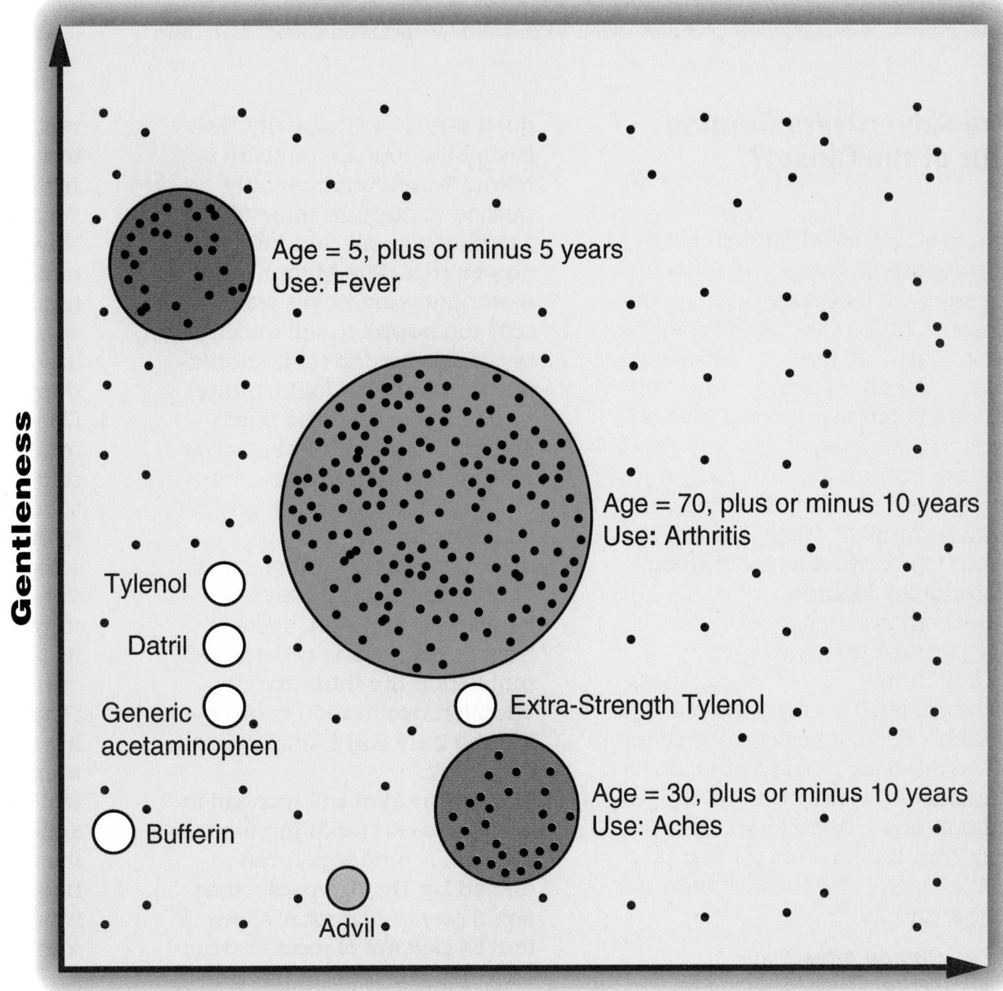
Gentleness
Effectiveness
Age = 5, plus or minus 5 years
Use: Fever
Age = 70, plus or minus 10 years
Use: Arthritis
Tylenol
Datril
Generic acetaminophen
Extra-Strength Tylenol
Age = 30, plus or minus 10 years
Use: Aches
Bufferin
Advil

Having chosen a strategy for reaching their firm's target market, marketers must then decide how best to position the product. The concept of **positioning** seeks to place a product in a certain "position" in the minds of prospective buyers. Marketers use a positioning strategy to distinguish their firm's good or service from those of competitors and to create promotions that communicate the desired position.

To achieve this goal, they follow a number of positioning strategies. Possible approaches include positioning a good or service according to:

1. *Attributes*—Aim toothpaste controls tartar.
2. *Price/quality*—Tiffany's is a quality store.
3. *Competitors*—Avis is number 2, so they try harder.
4. *Application*—Drano opens clogged drains.
5. *Product user*—Miller is for the blue-collar, heavy drinker.
6. *Product class*—Honey Nut Cheerios is a breakfast food.

Whatever the strategy they choose, marketers want to emphasize a product's unique advantages and differentiate it from competitors' options. Companies may even promote similar products by stressing different advantages. Managers at Sprint feel that the long-distance carrier's prices offer a competitive advantage against AT&T, so Sprint ads tend to stress price and value, like the rate of 10 cents a minute. Meanwhile, marketers for AT&T feel that the company has a positive image with customers based on its longevity and experi-ence in telecommunications. AT&T ads often emphasize reliability and the high quality of its overall service.

A **positioning map** provides a valuable tool to help managers position products by graphically illustrating consumers' perceptions of competing products within an industry. For instance, a positioning map might present two

Marketing Dictionary

micromarketing Marketing strategy to target potential customers at basic levels such as by ZIP codes.

positioning Marketing strategy that emphasizes serving a specific market segment by achieving a certain position in buyers' minds.

positioning map Graphic illustration that shows differences in consumers' perceptions of competing products.

SOLVING AN ETHICAL CONTROVERSY

Are Advertisers Coming Out of the Closet?

In a growing trend, though not yet a groundswell, more and more advertisers are stepping out of the closet. Companies as diverse as American Express, Anheuser-Busch, Atlantic Records, and Subaru are beginning to tailor their advertising messages to gay and lesbian consumers. Not long ago, messages that catered to the homosexual market were considered taboo in corporate boardrooms. Companies feared boycotts or other backlash from customers who disapproved of homosexuality.

But in the world of business, sales volume usually wins out. Arguably, companies are reaching out to this once-ignored group for financial, not social, reasons. Corporations have discovered that the gay and lesbian market is a profitable niche that they can no longer snub.

Should Advertisers Target Their Message to Gays and Lesbians?

PRO

1. **Gays and lesbians are often affluent customers who reward good service with loyalty. This is why the tourism industry in Miami Beach unabashedly pushed to capture some of the $17 billion spent annually by gay tourists. The Miami Beach merchants and hotels were only too happy to see the city become a mecca for homosexual vacationers. Unlike many married couples, who bear financial burdens of child-care bills, school tuition and other child-related expenses, gay couples often have more money to spend on themselves. Thanks to the aggressive advertising campaign, some travel experts now consider Miami Beach the third-favorite vacation destination of gays—trailing only San Francisco and New York.**
2. **The gay market will respond favorably to ads featuring their lifestyle. A reader poll conducted by *The Advocate*, a national gay publication, showed that 54 percent of readers wanted to see ads that addressed gay and lesbian themes. Only 13 percent agreed that advertisers should concentrate on the product, not the consumer. "The question Madison Avenue has to ask itself is, 'What is it that the consumer identifies with in advertising?'" says Dave Mulryan, president of a New York ad agency that specializes in the gay and lesbian market. "For gay people, it is to see them-selves, which is still unusual at this stage of the game."**
3. **Concentrating on a narrow market segment, such as gay and lesbian consumers, can succeed better than appealing to the general mainstream. The experience of Subaru, one of the first major advertisers to target the lesbian market with its four-wheel-drive passenger cars, confirms this assertion. "Three years ago we were trying to be a competitor in the mainstream and that . . . wasn't working," acknowledged a Subaru representative. Instead, the company shifted gears and began marketing to narrower but loyal groups, such as gays and lesbians.**

CON

1. **A firm shouldn't risk precious advertising dollars trying to appeal to a homosexual audience. It's hard to make edu-**

different characteristics, price and quality, and show how consumers view a product and its major competitors based on these traits. The positioning map in Figure 7.12 categorizes various brands of pain relievers based on their gentleness, effectiveness, uses, and user age groups.

Marketers can create a competitive positioning map from information solicited from consumers or from their accumulated knowledge about a market. The scattered dots in the figure represent potential customers; the dots clustered in large circles represent target groups, or categories of consumers that demand particular product characteristics. Figure 7.12 helps to explain the success of Extra-Strength Tylenol, which is closely positioned near two market segments. If a product manager sees an opportunity by studying such a positioning map, further research can confirm its depiction of the market.

Sometimes, changes in the competitive environment force marketers to **reposition** a product—changing the position it holds in the minds of prospective buyers relative to the positions of competing products. When they performed a demographic study in 1986, managers of Greenbriar Mall in Atlanta discovered that the community had changed. At that time, 94 percent of its patrons were African-American. They decided to

cated advertising decisions without accurate figures about a basic question like just how big the lesbian and gay market is. Experts often estimate that gay men and lesbians represent anywhere from 1 percent to 10 percent of the total population. In a recent poll conducted by Yankelovich Partners, 6 percent of respondents identified themselves as homosexual.

2. **Since gays and lesbians make up such a small percentage of the population, it doesn't make economic sense to launch an advertising campaign for them. "The gay and lesbian population is where the minority markets were 20 years ago, which is 'We're reaching them in the general market. Do I really need to target them specifically?'" observes Doug Alligood, an advertising executive. "And until there's a clear answer to that, marketers are not going to do a lot."**
3. **Aiming your message at a gay audience can alienate straight customers. The ABC situation comedy *Ellen* may serve as a good example of what can happen. Reports that the star, Ellen DeGeneres, would reveal herself as a lesbian raised threats of a boycott of the show's advertisers by religious conservatives. Advertisers, however, have to worry about more than fundamentalists. In one national poll, 40 percent of respondents said they would prefer not to have a homosexual as a friend.**

Summary

Even though more companies are tailoring their messages to gay audiences, they do not welcome outside publicity about the decision. Take Subaru, for example. In a milestone automotive ad, Subaru features two women sharing a drive in its four-wheel-drive station wagon. The headline read, "It loves camping, dogs, and long-term commitment. Too bad it's only a car." Subaru officials declined to discuss the ad. Marketing experts say that Subaru's unwillingness to talk about the landmark ad illustrates an uneasy, arm's-length relationship between the car maker and this potentially lucrative market. In fact, says Andrew Isen, president of WinMark Concepts Inc., a marketing agency, targeting lesbians remains "the ultimate taboo in the male-driven marketing and advertising world."

QUESTIONS FOR CRITICAL THINKING

1. **Do you believe that marketers will continue to gear more advertising toward gays and lesbians?**
2. **Pick a product. Can you envision a print ad for that product designed to appeal to a gay or lesbian audience?**

Sources: Bill Konigsberg, "Marketing to Gays," *Denver Post,* March 9, 1997, pp. H1, 22H; Tammerlin Drummond, "Not in Kansas Anymore," *Time,* September 25, 1996, pp. 54–55; Skip Wollenberg, "Sponsors Await Gay Milestone on 'Ellen,'" *San Diego Union-Tribune,* September 20, 1996, p. C-2; Cyndee Miller, "The Ultimate Taboo," *Marketing News,* August 14, 1996, pp. 1, 18; Cyndee Miller, "Record Label Puts New Spin on How It Markets to Gays," *Marketing News,* August 12, 1996, pp. 17, 19; Michael Wilke, "Ad Survey Shows Appeal of Gay Themes," *Advertising Age,* May 6, 1996, p. 19; Oscar Suris, "Mum's the Word on Subaru for Gays," *Wall Street Journal,* March 22, 1996, p. B2.

reposition the mall to take advantage of this change. African woodcuts began appearing in mall advertising, and promotional events targeted black shoppers. Managers recruited stores with Afrocentric clothing and accessories to complement chain stores. The mall also concerned itself with giving back to the community. Greenbriar started a college scholarship program in 1988 and donates money to area elementary schools for art programs. These marketing strategies provide a special reason for target customers to shop at Greenbriar, and they help the mall to compete successfully against larger shopping centers.[55]

Marketing Dictionary

repositioning Marketing strategy to change the position of a product in consumers' minds relative to the positions of competing products.

ACHIEVEMENT CHECK SUMMARY

Reread the learning goals that follow, and consider the questions for each goal. Answering these questions will reinforce your grasp of the most important concepts in the chapter and allow you to check how well you have achieved these learning goals. Where a blank appears before a question, answer with *T* or *F;* for multiple-choice questions, circle the letter of the correct answer.

Objective 7.1: Identify the essential components of a market.

1. ___ A market consists of people and organizations with the necessary purchasing power, willingness, and authority to buy.

2. ___ The overall market for a product always includes a homogeneous group of individuals.

3. ___ The target market for a product is the specific segment of prospective customers who are most likely to buy.

4. ___ Products purchased for use directly or indirectly in the production of other goods are classified as (a) consumer products or (b) business products.

Objective 7.2: Outline the role of market segmentation in developing a marketing strategy.

1. ___ *Market segmentation* refers to the process of dividing a total market into several heterogeneous groups.

2. ___ A market segmentation strategy attempts to identify the criteria that affect purchase decisions for various groups.

3. ___ Market segmentation benefits only profit-oriented firms.

Objective 7.3: Describe the criteria necessary for effective segmentation.

1. ___ The firm's ability to effectively promote to and serve a segment is an important consideration in market segmentation.

2. ___ Firms can serve even very small segments if their purchases create potentially profitable opportunities.

3. ___ A firm's marketing capabilities do not limit the number of segments to which it chooses to market.

Objective 7.4: Explain each of the four bases for segmenting consumer markets.

1. ___ Marketers have identified four bases for segmenting consumer markets.

2. ___ The most common form of segmentation is (a) geographic; (b) demographic; (c) psychographic; (d) product-related; (e) none of these; (f) marketers rely equally heavily on all four.

3. ___ Segmenting ethnic groups as markets is an example of (a) geographic segmentation; (b) demographic segmentation; (c) psychographic segmentation.

4. ___ Psychographic segmentation divides a population into groups by looking at consumer lifestyles.

5. ___ Product-related segmentation focuses on consumers' relationships to goods or services.

Objective 7.5: Identify the steps in the market segmentation process.

1. ___ The first step in the market segmentation process is to develop a profile of relevant characteristics for each segment.

2. ___ Target market decision analysis involves identifying the specific characteristics of market segments.

3. ___ Projecting profit and return on investment is not part of the market segmentation decision process.

Objective 7.6: Discuss four alternative strategies for reaching target markets.

1. ___ A marketing strategy should match the firm's products to the needs of particular target markets.

2. ___ Henry Ford's strategy for the Model T is an example of (a) undifferentiated marketing; (b) differentiated marketing; (c) concentrated marketing.

3. ___ Marketing a number of products designed to appeal to individual parts of the total market is called; (a) differentiated marketing; (b) concentrated marketing; (c) micromarketing.

4. ___ Focusing on satisfying the needs of only one market segment is called (a) differentiated marketing; (b) concentrated marketing; (c) micromarketing.

Objective 7.7: Summarize the types of positioning strategies and the purposes of positioning and repositioning products.

1. ___ Developing a marketing strategy aimed at a particular market segment to distinguish a good or service from those of competitors is called (a) marketing mix; (b) positioning; (c) concentrated segmentation.

2. ___ Marketers use a positioning map to (a) determine geographic segments; (b) track changes in sales figures; (c) illustrate how a product compares to its competitors in the minds of consumers.

3. ___ Repositioning is not necessary if the firm's competitive environment changes.

Students: See the solutions section located on page S-2 to check your responses to the Achievement Check Summary.

Key Terms

market
target market
consumer product
business product
market segmentation
geographic segmentation
Metropolitan Statistical Area (MSA)
demographic segmentation
cohort effect
family life cycle
Engel's laws
psychographic segmentation
lifestyle
Consolidated Metropolitan Statistical Area (CMSA)
Primary Metropolitan Statistical Area (PMSA)
geographic information system (GIS)
80/20 principle
target market decision analysis
undifferentiated marketing
differentiated marketing
concentrated marketing

AIO statements
VALS 2
product-related segmentation
micromarketing
positioning
positioning map
repositioning

Review Questions

1. What is a market? Explain the components needed to create a market.
2. Bicycles are consumer goods; iron ore is a business good. Are trucks consumer goods or business goods? Support your answer.
3. Identify and briefly explain the bases for segmenting consumer markets. Which approach is the oldest? Which one is used most frequently?
4. Distinguish among MSAs, PMSAs, and CMSAs. How can marketers use these concepts?
5. How can lifestyles affect market segmentation?
6. Explain the use of benefits sought, usage rates, and brand loyalty as segmentation variables.
7. What market segmentation basis would you recommend for each of the following products, and why?
   a. San Francisco Ballet production
   b. Savin collating photocopier
   c. Healthy Choice fat-free snack foods
8. What is target market decision analysis? Relate this activity to the concept of market segmentation.
9. Outline the basic features of undifferentiated marketing. Contrast differentiated marketing with micromarketing.
10. Name six positioning strategies and give an example of each.

Discussion Questions

1. Frito-Lay markets Cheetos snacks without cheese flavoring in Asia because consumers there prefer steak-flavored and cuttlefish-flavored snacks. What type of segmentation strategy is Frito-Lay employing?
2. Metropolitan Life Insurance Co. (Met) is the nation's leading insurer of middle-class people. By contrast, Equitable and Connecticut General sell to affluent policyholders and have average policy values of over $200,000. Recently, Met has decided to court wealthy clients. The plan is to target people with annual incomes between $150,000 and $200,000. Discuss the segmentation approaches of these companies.
3. Match the following bases for market segmentation with the appropriate examples. Explain your choices.
   a. Geographic segmentation
   b. Demographic segmentation
   c. Psychographic segmentation
   d. Product-related segmentation
   ____ Efforts to promote the Florida Marlins baseball team throughout the Caribbean
   ____ Saab's slogan—"Find your own road"
   ____ Advertisements aimed at Generation X, consumers 17 to 28 years old
   ____ IBM's slogan—"Solutions for a small planet"
4. Use the five-step segmentation decision process shown in Figure 7.9 to help Powerfoods, Inc. determine which segments to target for its Power Bar energy bars, a low-fat, high-carbohydrate nutritional bar that comes in several flavors.
5. The telecommunications market has become increasingly competitive as competitors vie for each other's long-distance telephone customers and add new services, such as Internet access. Discuss possible segmentation and positioning strategies for MCI's general long-distance service and its MCI-World international service.

'netWork

1. Equifax National Decision Systems frequently conducts and updates various surveys. Look at its Financial Forum site

http://www.ends.com/

Who might use this information to position a good or service? Select a sample product and describe how you would apply the information to your positioning decisions.

2. Recall from the chapter text that SRI created VALS to define market segments based on psychographic differences and similarities. Go to SRI's home page

http://future.sri.com/

and link to the VALS 2 service. Complete the survey on this page to place yourself into a VALS segment. Do you agree with the results? What other resources does the SRI home page provide?

3. What is a geographic information system (GIS)? How could such a system contribute to market segmentation? Find a GIS on the Web. Evaluate the service and the information it provides.

VIDEO CASE 7

TARGETING THE BUSINESS TRAVELER

Marriott International offers a broad spectrum of lodging products to meet the varying needs of travelers worldwide. Meeting the changing needs of its guests is Marriott's highest priority. CEO Bill Marriott visits as many as seven hotels a day to make sure that his managers and employees keep satisfying guests so those valued customers will return for another stay. He chats with guests to find out what Marriott can do to improve their visits. Such customer focus helps Marriott to outperform competitors in occupancy and revenue per available room. With sales topping $8.9 billion, Marriott's occupancy rates typically run 10 percentage points above the U.S. industry average.

Marriott entered the hotel business in 1957. During the late 1970s and early 1980s, the constantly changing demands of lodging customers and signs of market saturation by full-service hotels led its managers to consider diversifying their hotel operations. They conducted customer research to identify new market segments and developed products for them: the Courtyard chain for the segment focused on moderate prices; Residence Inn for the long-term-stay market; and Fairfield Inn for the economy segment.

Marriott's success depended on aggressive marketing of its four hotel brands to specific market segments.

Management chose to target the $95 billion company travel market, a huge and fast-growing segment of the overall U.S. market. Each of Marriott's four lodging brands offers services geared to the varying needs of specific groups of business travelers.

Marriott hotels, resorts, and suites attract key organization personnel by offering high-quality service and many amenities. Guests can conduct business in their rooms, assisted by technology such as modems, call waiting, and voice mail. These hotels, with between 250 and 1,000 rooms, provide ideal settings for large meetings and conventions. Recreational facilities include pools and health clubs. Room rates range from $90 to $245.

Each Courtyard property, a moderately-priced hotel chain, has on average 150 guest rooms and a full-service restaurant and lounge. Designed by business travelers for business travelers, the rooms have separate seating and sleeping areas, large desks, reach-anywhere telephones, and cable TV. The Courtyard concept was designed for customer convenience in room designs and quick check-in and check-out functions. Each hotel offers a small gym room, swimming pool, and conference room that accommodates up to 30 people. Rates range from $60 to $90.

Residence Inns are extended-stay hotels. About 115 rooms feature separate living and dining areas and fully equipped kitchens. Many rooms have fireplaces. Several properties have spacious penthouses. Housekeeping services are provided daily, including shopping, laundry, and dry cleaning. A complimentary continental breakfast and evening hospitality hour are provided to all guests. Room rates vary between $75 and $100.

Fairfield Inn is an economy hotel targeted at business travelers who are not interested in amenities such as on-premise restaurants and lounges. Each hotel has about 135 rooms with large, well-lit work desks and reach-anywhere phones. Most hotels have outdoor pools and meeting rooms for up to ten people. Services such as fax, photocopying, and same-day dry cleaning are available. Room rates ranges from $45 to $55.

In developing four different products to satisfy specific groups of business travelers, Marriott applied the principles of market segmentation. Its First Choice program targeted large companies to create customized travel programs that would meet the lodging needs of large firms such as Dow Chemical Company. William Rose, vice president of human resources at Dow, says that his company's annual travel expenses amount to about $100 million in North America. "When you're spending $100 million on something, if you want to manage that, and it's growing pretty rapidly, you've got to break it down into its components. A significant part of that is our lodging."

Marriott wants to build close, long-term relationships with companies like Dow so its hotels become the first choice for these customers' lodging services. Working with these customers, Marriott conducts research to determine its needs and how its products meet them. Marriott marketers conduct focus groups with frequent travelers to learn what they want, when they travel, and what services are important to them. From such a qualitative survey with Dow's business travelers, Marriott discovered a preference for nonsmoking rooms, flexibility of early check-in and late check-out times to accommodate appointment schedules, and complimentary breakfast.

From credit card data supplied by potential customers, Marriott marketers analyze the company's lodging expenses. They also assess the firm's current hotel directory. This study shows divisions between segmented customer needs. Marriott then presents each customer with a research profile of its travel patterns and needs for quality, moderate, economy, and extended-stay lodging, in the process demonstrating how its hotels match the company's needs.

After evaluating Marriott's analysis of its lodging requirements, Dow decided to participate in the First Choice program because it offered significant benefits. In choosing a lodging supplier, Dow considers the following criteria: volume discounting, the ability to provide different lodging segments ranging from economy to quality, the ability to develop a long-term relationship with a reputable supplier, product quality and consistency, safety, and dollar savings.

As a First Choice customer, Dow's William Rose says, "I think that we have a very good match here. Basically, we are buying quality, and Marriott has long been recognized for their total quality management and so has Dow. We're not looking for the lowest price. We're looking for the best total value. And I think that's what they're selling and it's what we're looking for."

Marriott continues to study the market to identify new niches. Now it's turning its focus to international expansion, conducting research to determine how its segmentation strategy can satisfy business travelers in Mexico, Europe, and the Pacific Rim.

Questions

1. Describe how Marriott's segmented approach to lodging meets the four criteria for effective segmentation listed in the chapter.
2. Which bases of segmentation described in the chapter apply to Marriott's four lodging products?
3. Relate Marriott's marketing decisions to the steps in the market segmentation decision process.

4. In February 1997, Marriott introduced a new brand—Marriott Executive Residences. The company has also acquired a 49 percent share of the Ritz-Carlton Hotel Co. Go to Marriott's home page,

   http://www.marriott.com/

   and identify the segment that Marriott is targeting with each of these two products. What is your assessment of these segmentation strategies? Should Marriott develop additional products for other segments?

Sources: Shelly Branch, "So Much Work, So Little Time," *Fortune,* February 3, 1997, p. 116; Allen E. Richardson, "Marriott Eyes Global Growth Options," *USA Today,* March 11, 1996, p. 5B.

Part 2 Microsoft Corp.: Developing a Competitive Strategy

Bill Gates' and Paul Allen's original vision of a computer on every desk and in every home continues to guide Microsoft in everything it does. In pursuit of the vision, Microsoft has grown, adapted, and even reinvented itself in its continuing efforts to remain at the head of an industry characterized by incredible technological change. Although this change continues today and competitors continue to emerge, Microsoft remains committed to the belief that software is the tool that empowers people at work and at home. The company articulates this belief in its customer-oriented mission statement:

> As the world's leading software provider, we strive to continually produce innovative products to meet the evolving needs of our customers. Our extensive commitment to research and development is coupled with dedicated responsiveness to customer feedback. This allows us to explore future technological advancements while assuring that our customers today receive the highest quality software products.

From this mission statement, Microsoft has developed a broad organizational goal:

> Every line of code we write, every interface we design, and every product we release are all working toward the same goal: to create the most exciting new ways to think, work, communicate, and play and to offer these new possibilities to millions and millions of people, in every country in the world.

To achieve its goal, Microsoft continues to follow the marketing strategy of its early years: market innovative products at relatively low prices for mass markets. "We believe in harnessing the sheer volume of the PC market to drive costs lower," says Gates. With its huge sales volume, Microsoft benefits from economies of scale that make lower prices and greater market share possible. Today, the company generates almost half of the world's total personal computer software revenue. Microsoft has shipped 100 million units of Windows; it also dominates the market with an 80 to 85 percent share of operating systems sales for desktop PCs, mostly from equipment manufacturer customers such as Compaq Computer and Dell Computer. The firm's top-selling applications product, Microsoft Office, commands an 85 percent market share.

The first mass market Microsoft entered was computer languages. Then it moved into two other mass markets: operating systems (MS-DOS, followed by Windows); and software applications such as Word and Excel. More recently, Microsoft entered the mass market of network computing for large organizations with the introduction of Windows NT; online network systems with the release of its Internet Explorer Web browser and the introduction of the online Microsoft Network in 1995; and applications software in entertainment and information for the consumer market.

During the 1990s, Microsoft planners began shifting their emphasis from the traditional target of business users to what they saw as a key growth area: the consumer market. Annual sales growth in the business PC market had slowed to 10 percent, while the consumer market was increasing at a 30 percent annual rate. As recently as 1993, Microsoft offered 25 different specific products for the consumer market; today that number has grown to more than 75. Included among these products is the CD-ROM *Encarta,* the world's most popular encyclopedia with sales more than five times as great as the *World Book.*

A $100 million global brand-building promotional campaign was launched recently with the long-term goal of turning Microsoft into a household name. The campaign used the theme "Where do you want to go today?" and targeted consumers in the United States, Canada, Germany, France, the United Kingdom, and Australia. The national markets account for 84 percent of Microsoft's global revenues.

Leveraging Its Financial Strength

From its early years, Microsoft has plowed back earnings from its market-leading products into funding new ventures and investing in research and development to grow the business. These deep financial pockets have given the company an enormous competitive advantage. "It's all about scale economics and market share," says Gates. "When you're shipping a million units of Windows software a month, you can afford to spend $300 million a year improving it and still sell it at a low price."

Betting that the Internet will grow dramatically over the next ten years, Microsoft invested more than $2 billion in R&D in 1997 alone. No software-only company in personal computing can match the firm's research outlays and strong financial position.

Hiring Smart People

"It's so cool to be able to say I work at Microsoft," says Ben Waldman, a software design engineer. "When I tell people I worked on Microsoft Excel, they've literally said, 'I want to shake your hand. I use it every day.'" The company's reputation for an outstanding workforce attracts thousands of job seekers. Microsoft receives some 10,000 résumés each month, and hires about two percent of applicants. It also actively recruits outstanding candidates from competitors and university faculties.

Gates is all too aware of the importance of outstanding employees in his firm's success. These employees are so important to Microsoft because they are responsible for developing new products and creating new markets.

"Take our 20 best people away, and I will tell you that Microsoft would become an unimportant company." says Bill Gates.

Gates' notion of a smart employee goes beyond IQ scores. The ideal Microsoft employee has technical expertise plus the capacity to quickly acquire new skills to keep pace with changing technology. Smart employees are creative and possess market knowledge, an entrepreneurial spirit, problem-solving skills, and the ability to work without needing detailed, constricting rules and procedures. And, because Gates is an incredibly hard worker, he expects his team to work very long hours.

Hands-On Management by the Microsoft CEO

Gates does not manage his firm from some isolated glass-enclosed office. He personally directs Microsoft's planning sessions, during which product division managers announce their three-year product plans. Based on these plans, the marketing staff of each product unit develops a sales forecast and budget plan. Marketers analyze the sales and budget estimates and compare them to the company profit goals. Gates and his top management team review the analysis and determine the number of employees needed for each product unit for the following year.

The Microsoft CEO monitors the progress of all products in the firm's portfolio from a technology and competitive standpoint, especially the market leaders. "The products that comprise 80 percent of our revenue I choose to understand very, very deeply," he says. He monitors the progress of all projects by reviewing monthly status reports and attending quarterly review sessions.

To spot future trends and technologies, Gates frequently meets with the CEOs of all the major hardware and software PC firms. Each year he spends one to two "think weeks" by himself, during which he ponders current problems and future challenges. A voracious reader, Gates closely follows new technologies that help him anticipate future developments.

Researching Consumer Needs

Product development is the heart and soul of Microsoft. As stated in its mission statement, the firm's "dedicated responsiveness to customer feedback" results in the development of products customers want and can easily use. To accomplish this, Microsoft conducts marketing research activities before, during, and after the product-development process.

Microsoft uses an activity-based planning approach, in which products are designed around end-user activities for different types of customers—such as beginners versus advanced users—and different market segments. Observational studies, personal interviews, and telephone surveys are all employed to collect primary research data and supply needed information. Product planners visit customers to observe how they use different software products for activities such as writing documents or preparing budgets. Such observations supply information about how software is used and which features accomplish the tasks most efficiently.

Telephone surveys are also used to supply marketers with demographic data and other general information about typical users of particular products. Users of competitive products are also surveyed. In planning a new version of Microsoft Word, company researchers interviewed 2,400 users of WordPerfect to learn more about the strengths and weaknesses of the word-processing competitor.

Extensive beta tests are conducted prior to the launch of every new product. In beta testing, people try out preliminary versions of new software on their own personal computers for a period of 6 to 12 months. Because Microsoft software is used on so many different types of computers, large-scale beta testing is a highly-effective research tool in detecting technical problems and eliminating them prior to the product's release. Microsoft used about 400,000 beta testers before launching Windows 95 and another 75,000 for Windows NT. Participants include existing customers, other software producers, and distributors of Microsoft products. Beta testers are linked to Microsoft headquarters via e-mail to quickly provide feedback regarding errors and problems encountered with the new software. Participants have also provided a secondary benefit of beta testing: ideas for other new products.

"Microsoft does get an advantage because of the risks we took in developing Windows. Just like any company that took risks and did well, we're entitled to the success that comes out of this," says Microsoft's Bill Gates, in response to the complaints of Apple and Netscape.

Threats to Microsoft's Market Dominance

Despite the firm's remarkable success, Microsoft faces formidable challenges in maintaining its high growth rate and industry leadership position. "A revenue-generating franchise is the most fragile thing in the world," says Nathan Myhrvold, Microsoft's chief technology officer. "No matter how good your product, you are only 18 months away from failure."

One threat Microsoft faces is increasing competition. The competitive environment has changed dramatically from the early days when Microsoft had few rivals. Today, the company faces stiff competition in each of its target markets. In the consumer market, major software competitors include Electronic Arts, Brøderbund, Sega, and Nintendo. In online services, Microsoft competes against such telecommunications giants as AT&T. Other competition comes from startups such as Netscape Communications, whose Navigator software has captured 85 percent of the browser market.

Another serious challenge is the network computer, a new method of desktop computing that threatens Microsoft's operating systems and software. Sun Microsystems and Oracle Corp. are introducing a low-cost network computer that will come equipped with a spreadsheet, word-processing software, and e-mail, and Internet capabilities but will not have a hard drive. Oracle CEO Larry Ellison predicts that people will be buying more network computers and fewer PCs in the future. He estimates that 100 million of the information-access devices, priced at about $500, will be sold in the next few years. "There is no Microsoft software in the network computer," Ellison says. "Today Microsoft gets $400 to $500 per PC for its software, but with the NC they will get zero."

In addition to introducing new products, competitors large and small are filing lawsuits alleging that Microsoft has engaged in activities aimed at reducing competition. After examining one million pages of documents related to an antritrust investigation, the U.S. Department of Justice recently ruled that parts of Microsoft's system contracts were unfair to competitors, and the firm signed a consent decree, agreeing to modify its new contracts. The Justice Department also filed suit to block Microsoft's attempt to acquire Intuit, the maker of the popular Quicken personal finance software program. When Microsoft introduced its Explorer Web browser as part of its Windows 95 operating system, rival Netscape filed a complaint with the Justice Department charging the company with anticompetitive behavior. Another anticompetitive suit was filed by Apple Computer, complaining that Microsoft failed to include Apple in the beta testing of Windows 95.

Questions

1. Outline the elements of the Microsoft competitive strategy. What role does the firm's mission statement play in the creation of this strategy?
2. Describe how Microsoft is leveraging its strengths in shifting its focus from the business market to the consumer market. How does the notion of vulnerablity shown in Figure 5.5 relate to Microsoft's current situation?
3. Evaluate Microsoft's marketing research activities in terms of fulfilling its mission statement.

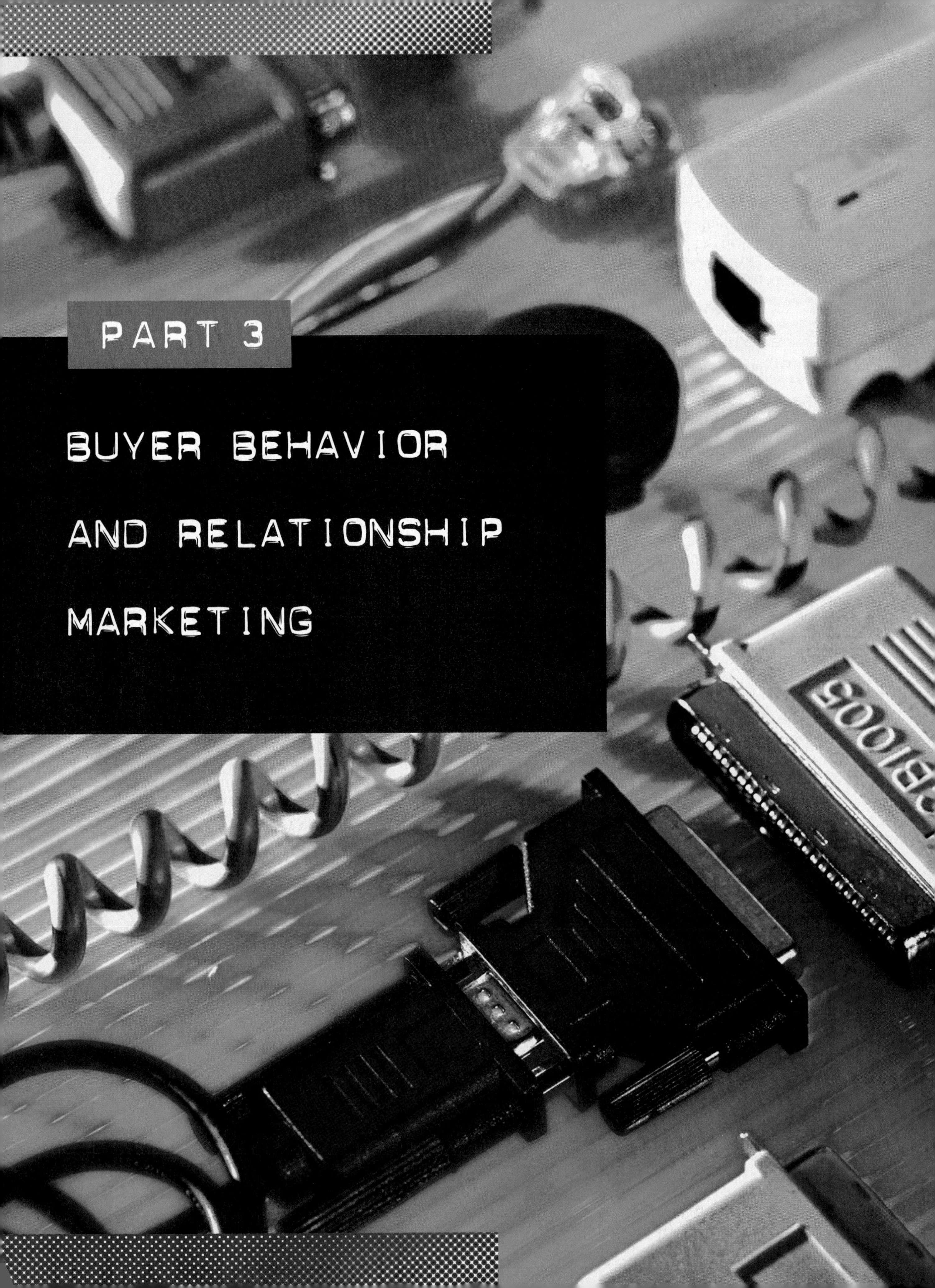

PART 3

BUYER BEHAVIOR AND RELATIONSHIP MARKETING

CHAPTER 8

CONSUMER BEHAVIOR

Chapter Objectives

1. Differentiate between buyer behavior and consumer behavior.
2. Explain how marketers classify behavioral influences on consumer decisions.
3. Identify the interpersonal determinants of consumer behavior.
4. Identify the personal determinants of consumer behavior.
5. Outline the steps in the consumer decision process.
6. Differentiate among routinized response behavior, limited problem solving, and extended problem solving.

http://www.whirlpool.com/
Really Cookin'
Whirlpool
Network
We're Listening
Service Matters
IMPORTANT
Company Stuff
http://www.kelloggs
Kellogg's
Address
http://www.mtv.com/
ONLINE
MUSIC TELEVISION™
http://www.census.gov/
U.S. Census Bureau
News
Search
About the Bure
User Manual
New on the Sit
Access Tools
CenStats CenStore
Your Source for Social, Demographic, and Economic Information
Netscape: BEV Ho
Location: http://www.bev.net/
BLACKSBUR

Life in America's Most Wired City

Some cyberspace advertisers assume that their potential customers are uniformly young, male, and white. No doubt, they also are "techies" with college backgrounds. After all, conventional wisdom holds, it takes some know-how to navigate the Internet. Madison Avenue advertisers have never heard of the folks from Blacksburg, Virginia.

Blacksburg is the most wired city in America, with 40 percent of the town connected to the Internet. In fact, this town tucked away in the Blue Ridge mountains claims the highest per-capita use of e-mail and other Internet tools in the world. Academic researchers are following this municipal experiment in online activity to determine how and why people use networks.

Yet Blacksburg may also provide some valuable lessons to marketers about how new technologies can change consumer behavior. The system plugs in young and old, rich and poor, technical stumblebums and cyberspace wizards. With prodding and a lot of education, the folks in this otherwise typical town are using the Internet in ways that would make some advertisers salivate.

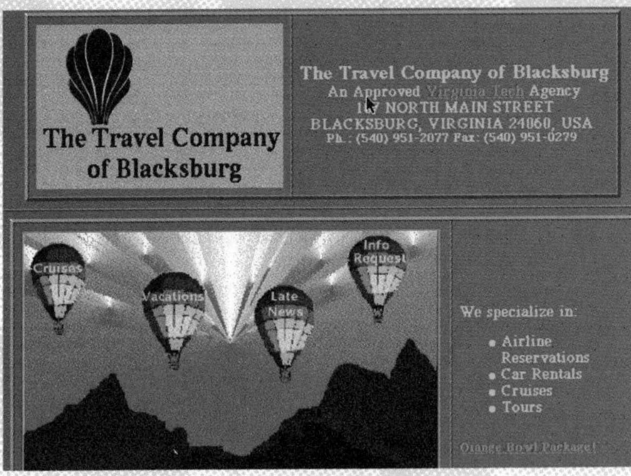
The Travel Company of Blacksburg
The Travel Company of Blacksburg
An Approved Virginia Tech Agency
NORTH MAIN STREET
BLACKSBURG, VIRGINIA 24060, USA
Ph.: (540) 951-2077 Fax: (540) 951-0279
Cruises
Vacations
Late News
Info Request
We specialize in:
Airline Reservations
Car Rentals
Cruises
Tours
Orange Bowl Package!

Blacksburg began its experiment back in 1987, when the Internet was essentially a frontier dominated by academic researchers, corporate scientists, and government agencies. The Virginia Polytechnic Institute located there initiated the project by spending $16 million to build a state-of-the-art digital phone system that placed a high-speed modem on the desk of every student, faculty member, and staffer. By the early 1990s, these Blacksburg residents were clamoring for online connections at home, too. That's when the university brought in Bell Atlantic and the residents of city hall as partners. Bell Atlantic wired the town with high-speed lines, while the town government created community sites on the Internet. To make sure that everyone had access to the technology, computers were placed in public locations and the price for unlimited Internet access in homes was set quite low.

Initially, the residents did not rush for seats on the cyberspace bandwagon, but that hesitation quickly changed. "We started out with 100 members. Now we have 11,000!" says Susanne Huff, an administrator of the Blacksburg Electronic Village, which the folks around here simply call "BEV." "We have doctors, lawyers, restaurants, grocery stores, online. People working at home and sending stuff in to their bosses. It's amazing what's going on! We're trying to enhance our lives. We're just using that line to connect all of us."

This microcosm of Internet activity is a far cry from the cyberbustle of Silicon Valley. The town doesn't look any different physically than it looked before, except for the increased presence of computers. But habits have changed. By surfing from BEV's home page, residents can order groceries online, browse the latest releases at the video store, learn about pizza specials at a local restaurant, and post classified ads. They can even discover what might ail them on a Blacksburg physician's searchable medical database. They can hunt through the university library's catalog without leaving home, learn about trip deals offered by the neighborhood travel agency, e-mail their friends down the street or around the globe, and perform hundreds of other tasks.

http://www.bev.net/

The town's electronic adventure has succeeded, in part, through public education. With unflagging determination, BEV administrators and staffers have visited one community event after another to explain the virtues of the new technology and to share nuts-and-bolts explanations of how it works. At one Lions Club meeting, they ran across some typical skeptics. "I'm interested in Bible study, in business, and in investments," said one white-haired, hard-of-hearing gentleman. "I'm not remotely interested in paying my bills in any way other than the way I do now. I don't want to buy anything I can't touch." He added emphatically, "I can't for the life of me see what I can get out of this."

But the lure of the Internet proved too strong even for this gentleman. Not long after the Lions Club meeting, he was spotted at a Blacksburg restaurant eating a sandwich and reading posts on a Web site devoted to insults from Shakespeare. Now a convert, he predicted, "I figure about mid-November, I'm gonna have my own home page."[1]

CHAPTER OVERVIEW

Why do people buy one product and not another? Answering this question is the basic task of every marketer. The answer directly affects every aspect of marketing strategy, from product development to pricing and promotion. Discovering that answer requires an understanding of buyer behavior, the process by which consumers and business-to-business buyers make purchase decisions. **Buyer behavior** is a broad term that covers both individual consumers who buy goods and services for their own use and organizational buyers who purchase business products.

A variety of influences affect both individuals buying products for themselves and professional buyers purchasing inputs for their firms. This chapter will focus on individual consumer behavior. **Consumer behavior** is the process through which the ultimate buyer makes purchase decisions. Chapter 9 will focus on additional organizational influences affecting business buying decisions.

The study of consumer behavior builds upon an understanding of human behavior in general. In their efforts to understand why and how consumers make buying decisions, marketers borrow extensively from the sciences of psychology and sociology.

The work of psychologist Kurt Lewin, for example, provides a useful classification scheme for influences on buying behavior. (The same concept also sheds light on motivation theory, which is part of the management discipline.) Lewin's proposition is:

$$B = f(P,E)$$

This statement means that behavior (B) is a function (f) of the interactions of personal influences (P) and pressures exerted by outside environmental forces (E).

This statement is usually rewritten to apply to consumer behavior as follows:

$$B = f(I,P)$$

Consumer behavior *(B)* is a function *(f)* of the interactions of interpersonal influences *(I)*—such as culture, friends, and relatives—and personal factors *(P)*, such as attitudes, learning, and perception. In other words, inputs from others and an individual's psychological makeup both affect his or her purchasing behavior. Before looking at how consumers make purchase decisions, the chapter will first consider how both interpersonal and personal factors affect consumers.

INTERPERSONAL DETERMINANTS OF CONSUMER BEHAVIOR

Consumers don't make purchase decisions in a vacuum; rather, they respond to a number of external, interpersonal influences. Consumers often decide to buy goods and services based on what they believe others expect of them. They may want to project positive images to peers or satisfy the unspoken desires of family members. Marketers recognize three broad categories of interpersonal influences on consumer behavior: cultural influences, group influences, and family influences.

Cultural Influences

Culture can be defined as the values, beliefs, preferences, and tastes handed down from one generation to the next. Culture is the broadest environmental determinant of consumer behavior. Therefore, marketers need to understand its role in customer decision making, both in the United States and abroad. They must also monitor trends to spot changes in cultural values.

Marketing strategies and business practices that work in this country may be offensive or ineffective elsewhere. For example, attitudes toward women in business vary around the world. American businesswomen conducting business abroad often encounter cultural differences and must adapt their behavior to customers' and foreign colleagues' expectations. In Iran, for example, a woman must wear a head scarf and trench-coat-type covering called a *manteau* when appearing in public. Makeup is taboo. In Japan, traveling businesswomen must adapt to a culture that still tends to limit women's roles to the family and the home.[2]

Core Values in U.S. Culture While some cultural values change over time, basic core values do not. The work ethic and the desire to accumulate wealth are two such core values in American society. Others are efficiency, practicality, individualism, freedom, youthfulness, activity, and humanitarianism. Even though the typical family structure and family members' roles have changed in recent years, American culture still emphasizes the importance of family and home life. Each of these values influences consumer behavior. Ford Motor Company's advertisement in Figure 8.1 bases its appeal for the Windstar minivan on the core value of the importance of family with its slogan, "We Put Safety Where You Put Your Family. First."

Values that change over time also have their effects. According to Paul Boyer, professor of American cultural history at the University of Wisconsin, the late 1990s have brought a move away from buying luxury cars and high-fashion clothes to show status. Such conspicuous consumption has given way to more subtle signs of wealth and power. Baby boomers are focusing more on family and home. Taking interesting vacations, working out with personal trainers, and even having children are new status symbols. Instead of Mercedes sedans, families are buying expensive sport-utility vehicles like the Toyota Land Cruiser and Chevy Suburban. Dressing down is now the norm.[3]

This trends poses a serious challenge for marketers trying to sell material possessions to consumers who view intangibles like good family lives and personal satisfaction as status symbols. Creative companies are appealing to the '90s desire for simple, comfortable, and environmentally correct products. For example, sportswear maker Patagonia Inc. touts the durability of its premium-priced products made from recycled materials like fleece from old soda bottles.

Other companies are tapping into today's values, as well. Eddie Bauer stores and catalogs feature basic clothes unlikely to go out of style or be eclipsed by new colors every few months. The company's ad campaign, centered around consumers' desire for more free time, has tag lines like, "Take the day off. Call in well."[4]

An International Perspective on Cultural Influences Cultural differences are particularly important for international marketers. Marketing strategies that prove

Marketing Dictionary

buyer behavior Process by which consumers and business buyers make purchase decisions.

consumer behavior Buyer behavior of ultimate consumers.

culture Values, beliefs, preferences, and tastes handed down from one generation to the next.

Figure 8.1 **Core Value: The Importance of Family**

WE PUT SAFETY WHERE YOU PUT YOUR FAMILY. FIRST.
Ford Windstar is the only minivan to earn five stars in government crash tests. The highest possible rating.*
• Engineered with 40 standard safety features, including anti-lock brakes, dual air bags** and a V-6 engine.
• Available 3.8L V-6 engine is the most powerful in its class.
• New tip/slide seat provides easy access to second row from driver's-side entrance.
• www.ford.com
*Driver and passenger front crash test. Govt. MY '98 data useful in comparing vehicles within 500 lbs.
**Always wear your safety belt.
†'97 Windstar Standard MSRP. LX shown w/PEP 477A MSRP $27,175. Tax, title extra.
FORD WINDSTAR
STARTING AT $18,995†
HAVE YOU DRIVEN A FORD LATELY?
Ford

successful in one country often cannot extend to other international markets because of cultural variations. Even though Europe is becoming a single economic market, cultural divisions continue to define multiple markets, with nine different languages and a wide range of lifestyles and product preferences.

Consider, for example, something as basic as selling appliances. Appliance manufacturer Whirlpool discovered

http://www.whirlpool.com/

sharp cultural differences when it attempted to penetrate the European market. The firm's U.S. consumers want to pay the lowest possible price for home appliances, replacing appliances as they wear out. Europeans, on the other hand, regard home appliances as long-term investments and expect more durability and appearance. While Americans often put washers and dryers in the garage, Europeans live in smaller homes and put these appliances in their kitchens, so looks and noise become important considerations. They also equate higher prices with better quality. Whirlpool's European strategy of low-price leadership failed, partially because Europeans considered the low prices to be a sign that the American products were inferior to local brands. The company now markets three different appliance lines priced for affluent, middle-market, and economy-minded consumers.[5]

Cultural influences also affect attitudes toward advertising in other countries. In a study of consumers in 40 countries, researchers discovered that only 9 percent of Russians believe that advertising provides good information, while 23 percent consider it creative and entertaining, compared to global averages of 38 percent and 61 percent, respectively. Until recently, the only advertising most Russians saw was state-sponsored propaganda, which contributed to their cynical attitude. These attitudes present challenges for marketers, who must reeducate Russian consumers.[6]

Subcultures Cultures are not homogenous entities with universal values. Each culture includes numerous **subcultures**—groups with their own distinct modes of behavior. Understanding the differences among subcultures can help marketers to develop more effective marketing strategies.

The culture of the United States, in particular, is composed of significant subcultures that differ by race, nationality, age, rural versus urban location, religion, and geographic distribution. The lifestyle in the southwestern United States emphasizes casual dress, outdoor entertaining, and active recreation. Mormons refrain from buying or using tobacco and liquor. Orthodox Jews purchase and consume only kosher foods. Understanding these and other differences among subcultures contributes to successful marketing of goods and services.

As Chapter 7 indicated, America's racial mix is changing. In the next century, marketers will no longer easily spot the "typical" American. Ethnic and racial minority groups will compose much larger percentages of the population. Marketers will need to be sensitive to these changes and to differences in shopping patterns and buying habits among ethnic segments of the population. Businesses will no longer succeed by selling one-size-fits-all products; they will need to consider consumer needs, interests, and concerns when developing their marketing strategies. Marketing concepts may not always cross cultural boundaries without changes. For example, new immigrants may not be familiar with cents-off coupons and contests. Marketers may need to provide specific instructions when targeting such promotions to these groups.

Efforts to understand both language and culture offer the best way for companies to get their marketing messages to these consumers. Companies that successfully demonstrate this capability are winning customers. For example, McDonald's reaches out to Mexican Americans, who represent about 60 percent of the U.S. Hispanic population, at the Cinco de Mayo (Fifth of May) celebration. It adds fajitas to its menus in selected areas for this holiday, which celebrates the 1862 victory of Mexico over France. Other marketers also run promotions for Cinco de Mayo, Kwanzaa, and other ethnic holidays.[7]

According to the U.S. Census Bureau, the three largest and fastest-growing ethnic subcultures in the United States are African-Americans, Hispanics, and Asians. While no ethnic or racial subculture is entirely heterogeneous, researchers have found that each of these three ethnic segments have identifiable consumer behavior profiles.

Figure 8.2 Promotional Messages Targeted to African-Americans

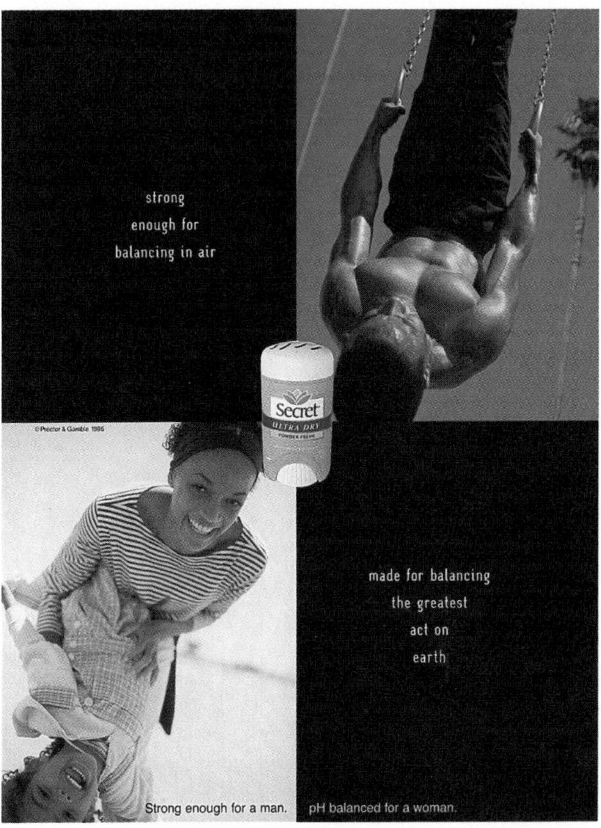
strong
enough for
balancing in air
Secret
ULTRA DRY
made for balancing
the greatest
act on
earth
Strong enough for a man.
pH balanced for a woman.

Profile of African-American Consumers The growing African-American market offers potential success to marketers who understand its buying behavior. On average, African-Americans are less likely to have completed college than other ethnic groups, and they have the highest jobless rate of all minorities.[8] Although as a group they have less disposable income to spend than other ethnic groups, African-Americans are active shoppers. They tend to shop more often—about four times a week—and spend more on clothing than other cultural subgroups. While 70 percent of Caucasians have credit cards, only 30 percent of African-Americans do. These two facts suggest that this group is an excellent target market for marketers of high-fashion clothing and also for credit card companies.[9] Also, 55 percent of African-Americans describe themselves as bargain hunters, compared to 35 percent of nonblacks. African-Americans also use coupons less often than whites and show a preference for promotional messages that appear in media targeted to them.[10] Procter & Gamble targets African-American customers by creating targeted advertising campaigns for its consumer products, such as the ad for Secret deodorant in Figure 8.2, and running the ads in selected media like *Essence* and *Ebony* magazines.

Family structures differ, as well. The median age of the typical African-American family is about five years younger than that of the average white family. This creates differences in preferences for clothing, music, cars, and many other products. African-American households are twice as likely as nonblack households to be headed by women who make major purchase decisions. Further, less than 40 percent of African-American children live in two-parent households. Income differences account for many purchase differences; middle-income African-Americans exhibit purchase behavior similar to that of white, middle-income families. These are important considerations when marketers plan promotional strategies.[11]

http://www.essence.com/

Marketing Dictionary

subculture Subgroup of a culture with its own, distinct modes of behavior.

Figure 8.3 **Spanish-Language Ads in Media Targeted to Hispanics**

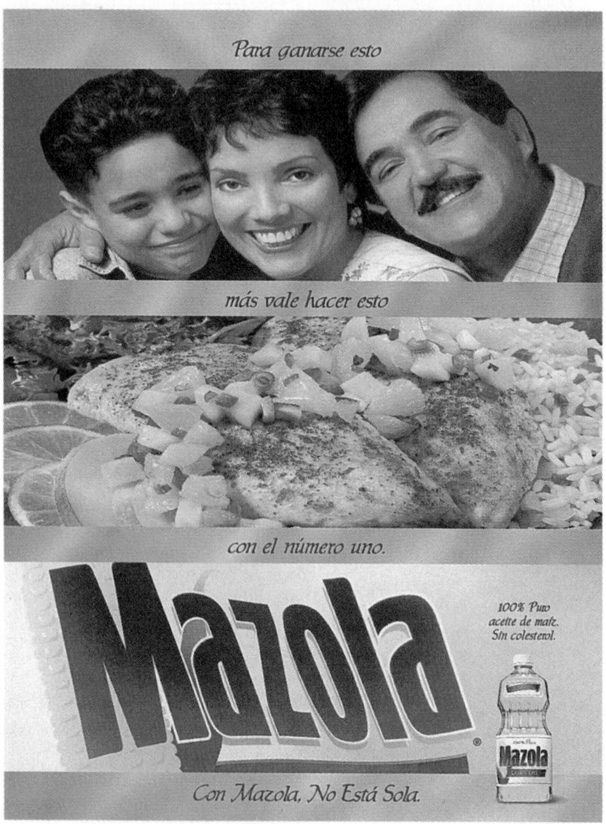
Para ganarse esto
más vale hacer esto
con el número uno.
Mazola
100% Puro aceite de maíz. Sin colesterol.
Mazola
Con Mazola, No Está Sola.

Successful promotions targeted to this ethnic group present marketing messages in credible, culturally sensitive ways.[12] African-American consumers are more likely than others to gather information about prospective purchases by watching advertisements, talking to salespeople, and calling manufacturers' toll-free phone numbers. Direct mail is also an effective medium to reach them.[13]

Another important method for reaching this target group is through community organizations such as church groups. For example, Wachovia Bank in Winston-Salem, North Carolina, conducts financial seminars in black churches in an effort to attract new customers.[14]

While African-Americans like marketers to recognize their cultural heritage in advertisements, they are turned off by promotions that use stereotypes of their culture. Campaigns that rely on humor about African-American culture can backfire. "They might not think it is funny and it could be perceived as tokenism," explains Amy Hilliard-Jones, president of Hilliard-Jones Marketing Group, a Chicago multicultural marketing firm.[15]

Companies try to reach African-American consumers through different approaches than they employ for other groups. Chrysler Corp. sponsors events like the Barry White Icon of Love concert tour and the Jeep and Eagle Health and Fitness Tour, which visited black college campuses. JCPenney introduced a line of African-motif clothing. It was so popular that stores often ran out of that particular merchandise.[16]

Profile of Hispanic Consumers Research shows that Hispanics are highly brand-loyal. One study found that 62 percent of Hispanics regularly bought the same food, beverage, and household brands. Only 35 percent would buy an unfamiliar item based on a sale price.

Hispanics enjoy shopping; in a survey, 83 percent agreed with the statement, "shopping is fun even if no purchase is made."[17] One study found that Hispanics spend more time while at shopping malls than non-Hispanics. They also are more likely to shop with family members or other companions.[18]

Food is an important purchase for many Hispanic households, which are generally larger than those of other population segments. The Hispanic culture also places high value on getting together with friends and relatives to share a meal. As a result, Hispanic households spend more than other consumers at grocery stores each week.[19] They also like to eat out frequently, and many casual and fast-food restaurants actively court this group.

Marketers face several challenges in appealing to Hispanic consumers. First, the 28 million Hispanics in the United States are not a homogeneous group. They come from a wide range of countries, each with its cultural differences. As noted earlier, some 60 percent come from Mexico, about 10 percent each from Central and South America, and 12 percent from Puerto Rico. Cubans represent about 5 percent of the U.S. Hispanic population. Cultural differences between these segments often affect consumer preferences and behavior. Campbell Soup, for example, once tried to market a Puerto Rican brand of canned pinto beans to the general Hispanic population in the United States. The product sold well to Puerto Rican consumers in New York but failed with Cubans in Miami, who prefer black beans.[20]

The degree to which Hispanics have been assimilated into mainstream American culture also plays a role in consumer behavior. One study found more similarities to Anglo consumers among Hispanics with high levels of acculturation, or adaptation to U.S. society, than among Hispanics with low levels of acculturation.[21] Hispanics who are acculturated are also likely to receive messages through general market media, while those who are relatively unassimilated to U.S. society prefer Spanish-language media.

Language is a third challenge that marketers must overcome to reach some Hispanic consumers. Many businesses run Spanish-language advertisements in media targeted to Hispanics. Food marketer CFC International attempted to develop brand loyalty for Mazola corn oil by creating the Spanish-language ad in Figure 8.3, which appeared in *Buenhogar,* the Spanish edition of *Good Housekeeping* magazine. Other firms have established bilingual sales forces.

Marketers need to remember to account for language variations among Hispanic groups who have immigrated from different countries. One confection manufacturer developed a Spanish-language ad to sell its ice-cream sandwiches to Mexican-American consumers in Texas. When the campaign succeeded, the manufacturer then tried to rebroadcast the same ad in Miami, where most Spanish-speaking consumers are Cuban-American. One small problem: The ad's word for ice cream, *nieve,* also means snow. This created no conflict in the vocabulary of Mexican-Americans. To Cubans, however, *nieve* doesn't mean ice cream. It is street slang for cocaine.[22] Needless to say, the campaign caused a stir in Miami.

Marketers also should not assume that all Hispanics understand Spanish; by the third generation after immigration, most Hispanic-Americans speak only English. Furthermore, some recent Mexican immigrants are actually ethnic Indians who have never learned Spanish.

Hispanic shoppers exhibit strong desire for detailed product information. Colgate-Palmolive addresses this need by featuring in-store product demonstrations in locations with large Hispanic customer bases.[23]

Profile of Asian-American Consumers Marketing to Asian-Americans presents many of the same challenges as reaching Hispanics. Like Hispanics, Asian-Americans are spread among culturally diverse groups, many retaining their own languages. The Asian-American subculture actually consists of more than two dozen ethnic groups, including Filipinos, Chinese, Japanese, Indians, Koreans, and Vietnamese. Each group brings its own language, religion, and value system to purchasing decisions.

Take consumer promotions. The Japanese prefer rebates, while the Vietnamese like in-store sampling. Filipinos, on the other hand, are heavy users of cents-off coupons. Knowledge of these differences allows marketers to design promotions targeted to their desired audiences.[24]

Subgroups also differ depending on their levels of consumer acculturation. Recent immigrants from India, for instance, expect high levels of service from businesses. In India, many firms take orders over the phone and deliver products directly to customers' homes. Inexpensive labor allows many households to hire domestic help. As a result, these consumers are attracted to products that promise to make life easier and more convenient.[25]

In Korean-American households, husbands generally make most purchase decisions. Marketers targeting this segment find that ads featuring male spokesmen are usually more successful than those using females. Korean-Americans are also highly brand loyal and place considerable value on product quality.[26]

Chinese-Americans fall into three broad consumer groups. Those from the second, third, and fourth generation after immigration behave similarly to most Americans. Husbands and wives share joint financial and purchase decisions. First-generation Chinese from Hong Kong and Taiwan, many of whom attended U.S. colleges, similarly divide consumer decisions. However, in the households of more recent immigrants from mainland China, the husbands are likely to make the ultimate decisions on larger purchases.[27]

Social Influences

Every consumer belongs to a number of social groups. A child's earliest group experience comes from membership in a family. As children grow older, they join other groups such as friendship groups, neighborhood groups, school groups, Girl Scouts, and Little League. Adults are also members of various groups—at work and in the community.

Group membership influences an individual's purchase decisions and behavior in both overt and subtle ways. Every group establishes certain norms of behavior. **Norms** are the values, attitudes, and behaviors that a group deems appropriate for its members. Group members are expected to comply with these norms. Norms can even affect nonmembers. Individuals who aspire to membership in a group may adopt its standards of behavior and values.

Differences in group status and roles can also affect buying behavior. **Status** is the relative position of any individual member in a group; **roles** define behavior that members of a group expect of individuals who hold specific positions within it. Some groups (such as Rotary Club or Lions) define formal roles, and others (such as friendship groups) impose informal expectations. Both types of groups supply each member with both status and roles; in doing so, they influence that person's activities—including his or her purchase behavior.

The Internet provides an opportunity for individuals to

Marketing Dictionary

norm Value, attitude, or behavior that a group deems appropriate for its members.

status Relative prominence of any individual in a group.

role Behavior that members of a group expect of an individual who holds a specific position within it.

MARKETING HALL OF FAME

Betty Crocker: The New Face of the Nation

When you're out shopping, the first thing you spot when making a selection is probably the label. The label is a product's welcome mat—one that should instantly convey a message about the package contents.

A label can powerfully influence those split-second consumer decisions about which items to carry to the checkout counter. Corporations are well aware of the importance of labels and logos, and they tend to tinker with those features as consumers' tastes and attitudes change. Quaker Oats Co., for instance, slimmed down the once pleasingly plump Aunt Jemima as consumers flocked to low-fat foods.

One of the most famous corporate icons of all time—Betty Crocker—also underwent a makeover recently, just in time for her 75th birthday. Introduced to cooks in 1921, Betty Crocker never existed except in artists' drawings. She got her name from William G. Crocker, who happened to oversee the flour-milling operation for General Mills at the time. But Betty hit a nerve among homemakers.

Perhaps the greatest key to her long-term success has been the ability of her corporate sponsor to recognize and adapt to changes in women's needs. During the Great Depression, for example, Betty Crocker helped women stretch their dollars during a difficult economic time. After World War II erupted, she suggested culinary adaptations to wartime shortages of cooking staples. In 1945, only Eleanor Roosevelt beat Betty Crocker for the title of America's most-admired woman.

Of course, women's lives have changed a great deal in the past 50 years, as well, and Betty Crocker has continued to modify her look and adapt. The Betty Crocker of today is focused on making mealtime as easy and quick as possible for the harried career women. In 1996, General Mills also decided to capitalize on Betty Crocker's popularity and name recognition—the brand is the company's most powerful—by introducing cereals under that name. The line's flavors—Cinnamon Streusel and Dutch Apple, for example—are reminiscent of baked goods.

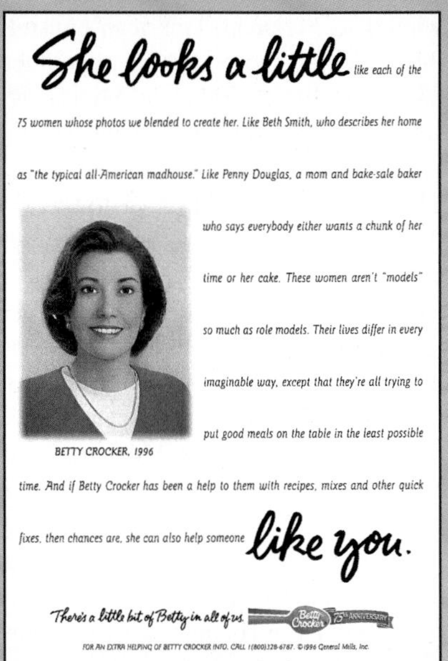
She looks a little like each of the
75 women whose photos we blended to create her. Like Beth Smith, who describes her home
as "the typical all-American madhouse." Like Penny Douglas, a mom and bake-sale baker
who says everybody either wants a chunk of her
time or her cake. These women aren't "models"
so much as role models. Their lives differ in every
imaginable way, except that they're all trying to
put good meals on the table in the least possible
BETTY CROCKER, 1996
time. And if Betty Crocker has been a help to them with recipes, mixes and other quick
fixes, then chances are, she can also help someone like you.
There's a little bit of Betty in all of us.
Betty Crocker
75th ANNIVERSARY
FOR AN EXTRA HELPING OF BETTY CROCKER INFO. CALL 1(800)328-6787. ©1996 General Mills, Inc.

Before the recent change, nine years had passed since General Mills' last makeover of Betty Crocker. (The company has devel-

form and be influenced by new types of groups. Usenet mailing lists and chat rooms allow groups to form around common interests. Some of these online "virtual communities" can develop norms and membership roles similar to those found in real-world groups. For example, members must observe rules for proper protocol in posting messages and participating in chats or face criticism.

The Asch Phenomenon Groups often influence an individual's purchase decisions more than he or she realizes. Most people tend to adhere in varying degrees to the general expectations of any group that they consider important to themselves, often without conscious awareness of this motivation. The surprising impact of groups and group norms on individual behavior has been called the **Asch phenomenon,** because it was first documented in research conducted by psychologist S. E. Asch.

Asch invited research participants to guess which of a set of three unequal vertical lines was closest in length to a fourth line. In control studies, with participants working one at a time, only two of the subjects guessed wrong. Asch then brought participants together in groups of eight; seven members of every group were actually working for Asch, so only the eighth person was a true "naive subject." Again, Asch displayed the set of lines, and his colleagues deliberately gave wrong answers. In a group situation, 37 of the naive subjects guessed wrong, agreeing with the group's incorrect judgment. The Asch phenomenon can be a big factor in many purchase decisions, from major choices such as buying a house or car to deciding whether to buy an item at a Tupperware party.[28]

Reference Groups Discussion of the Asch phenomenon raises the subject of **reference groups**—groups whose

oped eight versions altogether.) For the brand's 75th birthday, the corporation decided to enlist the help of cooks around the country to complete the redesign. General Mills urged its customers to nominate cooks who best embodied the principles that Betty Crocker represents. Of all the entries, 75 were chosen and their pictures contributed elements to a composite drawing to create the new Betty Crocker portrait, as shown in the accompanying ad.

Among those who applauded the change was Caroline Levy, a Lehman Brothers analyst. "I guess they want to put some fire under her tail. I think it's a great idea to revitalize the brand."

The new Betty was unveiled with the logo, "There's a little bit of Betty in all of us." She's younger, darker, and more alluring than past models. Her racial and national origins are deliberately vague. This characteristic certainly reflects the nation's changing demographics.

That move was a smart one, says Akshay Rao, a University of Minnesota marketing professor. "The face of the nation is going to be very different than it was 20 years ago. If they can identify with the person on the brand better because it looks like them, this is a wise thing to do."

In newspaper and magazine ads featuring the new Betty, General Mills explained why it made the switch:

> She looks a little like each of the 75 women whose photos we blended together to create her. Like Beth Smith, who describes her home as "the typical all-American madhouse." Like Penny Douglas, a mom and bake sale baker who says everybody either wants a chunk of her time or her cake. These women aren't "models" so much as role models. Their lives differ in every imaginable way, except that they're all trying to put good meals on the table in the least possible time. And if Betty Crocker has been help to them with recipes, mixes and other quick fixes, then chances are she can also help someone like you.

Of course, some skeptics still believe that tinkering with this cooking icon is silly. "If I am going to buy cake mix, it doesn't matter if she is white," insists Toni Green, director of marketing for the Minneapolis Institute of Arts, who is African-American. "I think sometimes they overthink these things, and I think there are more pressing issues in the world than trying to get a more politically correct woman."

QUESTIONS FOR CRITICAL THINKING

1. **Do you think companies should continually update their marketing icons like the little girl holding the umbrella on the Morton salt boxes? Can an old-fashioned label hold its own allure?**
2. **How can a product's label affect consumer behavior? Name some examples.**

Sources: Gail Seche, "Nutrition: Box Scores," *San Francisco Chronicle*, Wednesday, April 30, 1997, p.1, downloaded from http://www.sfgate.com/; based on Richard Gibson, "Can Betty Crocker Heat Up General Mills' Cereal Sales?" *Wall Street Journal*, July 19, 1996, p. B1; Steven V. Roberts, "Betty, Meet Ashley, a '90s Woman," *U.S. News & World Report*, April 1, 1996, pp. 10–11; and Suzanne Ziegler, "Betty to Go Multi-Ethnic," *Mobile Press Register*, September 1995, pp. 1A, 4A.

value structures and standards influence a person's behavior. Consumers usually try to coordinate their purchase behavior with their perceptions of the values of their reference groups. The extent of reference-group influence varies widely among individuals. Strong influence by a group on a member's purchase requires two conditions:

1. The purchased product must be one that others can see and identify.
2. The purchased product must be conspicuous; it must stand out as something unusual, a brand or product that not everyone owns.

Reference-group influence would significantly affect the decision to buy a Jaguar, for example, but it would have little or no impact on the decision to purchase a loaf of bread.

The status of the individual within a group produces three subcategories of reference groups: a membership group to which the person actually belongs, such as a country club; an aspirational group with which the person desires

Marketing Dictionary

Asch phenomenon Effect of a reference group on individual decision making.

reference group Group with which an individual identifies strongly enough that it dictates a standard of behavior.

Figure 8.4 **Appeal to Individuals in a Dissociative Group**

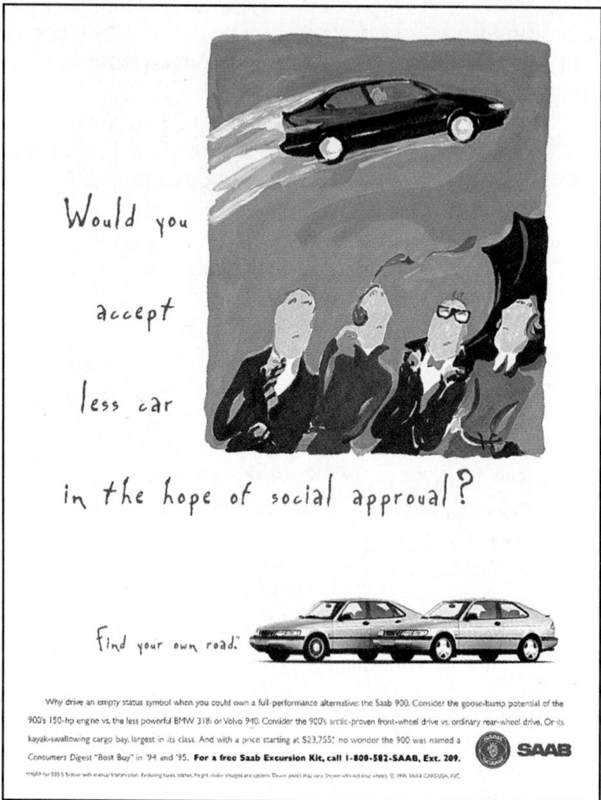
Would you
accept
less car
in the hope of social approval?
Find your own road.
Why drive an empty status symbol when you could own a full-performance alternative: the Saab 900. Consider the goose-bump potential of the 900's 150-hp engine vs. the less powerful BMW 318i or Volvo 940. Consider the 900's arctic-proven front-wheel drive vs. ordinary rear-wheel drive. Or its kayak-swallowing cargo bay, largest in its class. And with a price starting at $23,755,* no wonder the 900 was named a Consumers Digest "Best Buy" in '94 and '95. For a free Saab Excursion Kit, call 1-800-582-SAAB, Ext. 209.
SAAB

to associate; and a dissociative group with which the individual does not want to be identified. The Saab ad in Figure 8.4 encourages buyers to resist the influence of "social approval" and to dissociate from the luxury car buyer group that chooses to "drive an empty status symbol." Saab tells consumers instead to "Find your own road."

Children are especially vulnerable to the influence of reference groups. They often base their buying decisions on outside forces—what they see on television, popular choices among friends, fashionable products among adults. Advertising, especially endorsements by admired people, can have much bigger impacts on children than on adults, in part because children want so badly to belong to aspirational groups.

Reference-group influences appear in other countries, as well. Many young people in Japan aspire to represent American culture and values. Buying products decorated with English words and phrases—no matter how inaccurate they may be—helps them to achieve this feeling.

Social Classes Research conducted a number of years ago by W. Lloyd Warner identified six classes within the social structures of both small and large cities in the United States: the upper-upper, lower-upper, upper-middle, and lower-middle classes, followed by the working class and lower class.

Class rankings are determined by occupation, income, education, family background, and residence location. Note, however, that income is not always a primary determinant; pipe fitters paid at union scale earn more than many college professors, but their purchase behavior may be quite different. Thus, marketers frequently disagree with the adage that, "A rich man is a poor man with money."

Your family characteristics—and your father's occupation in particular—are the primary influences on your social class. This relationship is likely to change as women's careers assume more prominent roles in their families. And social classes are in transition due to other changes, as well. This makes it more difficult to market to their members. People in one social class may aspire to a higher class and therefore exhibit buying behavior common to that class rather than to their own. Middle-class consumers buy products associated with the status of the upper classes. Although the upper classes themselves account for a very small percentage of the population, many more consumers treat themselves to prestigious products at times, including Godiva chocolates, designer accessories, and luxury cars.[29]

Opinion Leaders In nearly every reference group, a few members act as **opinion leaders.** These trendsetters are likely to purchase new products before others in the group and then share their experiences and opinions via word of mouth. As others in the group decide whether to try the same product, they are influenced by the reports of opinion leaders.

Generalized opinion leaders are rare; instead, individuals tend to act as opinion leaders for specific goods or services based on their knowledge of and interest in those products. Their interest motivates them to seek out information from mass media, manufacturers, and other sources and, in turn, transmit this information to associates through interpersonal communications. Opinion leaders are found within all segments of the population.

Information about goods and services sometimes flows from radio, television, and other mass media to opinion leaders and then from opinion leaders to others. In other instances, information flows directly from media sources to all consumers. In still other instances, a multistep flow carries information from mass media to opinion leaders and then on to other opinion leaders before dissemination to the general public. Figure 8.5 illustrates these three types of communication flows.

The Internet brings an interesting new potential to convey information from opinion leaders to other members of online groups. The Internet also allows consumers to directly approach opinion leaders of online groups for information.

Figure 8.5 Alternative Channels for Communication Flows

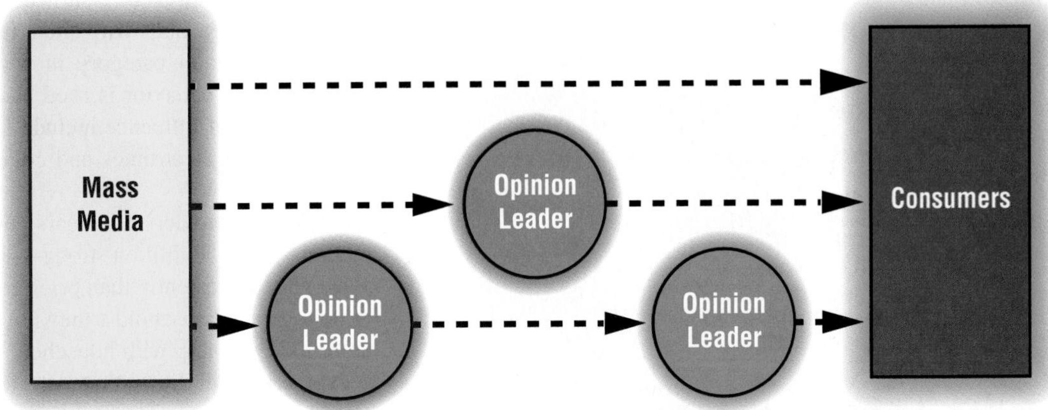
Mass Media
Opinion Leader
Opinion Leader
Opinion Leader
Consumers

In another technology-related development, computer makers have had to change their approach to marketing their products. Consumers no longer rely on computer experts or retail salespeople to influence their purchases of home PCs. The new opinion leaders are fellow computer owners—neighbors, friends, and work associates—who can discuss their actual experiences with specific machines. For instance, Gateway 2000, which sells primarily through mail order, finds that one sale in a neighborhood often leads to others. Apple Computer's Allen Olivo, director of worldwide advertising, agrees that existing Apple users are the primary advocates for the brand. As a result, PC marketing dollars are moving toward mass media, especially television, and away from specialized computer media.[30]

Some opinion leaders influence purchases by others merely through their own actions. Jacqueline Kennedy Onassis was an example. When she was First Lady, the fashions she chose to wear, like her signature pillbox hats, were studied and adopted by many women. After her death, her collection of costume jewelry was auctioned off to the public. Soon afterward, copies of those pieces became best sellers in department stores. Analysts attributed the success of the jewelry to the public perception that Onassis epitomized fashion flair and taste. "Our shoppers think if fake jewelry was good enough for Jackie, it's good enough for them," said jewelry designer Erwin Pearl.[31]

Family Influences

Most people are members of at least two families during their lifetimes—the ones they are born into and those they eventually form as they marry and have children. The family group is perhaps the most important determinant of consumer behavior because of the close, continuing interactions among family members. Like other groups, each family typically has norms of expected behavior and different roles and status relationships for its members.

The traditional family structure consists of a husband and wife. Although these and other members can play an infinite variety of roles in household decision making, marketers have created four categories to describe the role of each spouse:[32]

1. *Autonomic,* in which the partners independently make equal numbers of decisions
2. *Husband-dominant,* in which the husband makes most of the decisions
3. *Wife-dominant,* in which the wife makes most of the decisions
4. *Syncratic,* in which both partners jointly make most decisions

Personal-care items illustrate the autonomic decisions; insurance is typically a husband-dominant purchase; children's clothing is typically a wife-dominant decision; automobile purchases show a syncratic pattern.

The emergence of the two-income family has changed the role of women in family purchasing behavior. In 1950, only one-fourth of married women were employed outside the home; now over 60 percent have paid jobs. In the 1950s and early 1960s, women exercised only limited control of family purchasing decisions. A woman might make buying decisions about household items, but she was likely to defer to her husband on larger expenditures. Today, however, women are likely to have more say in large-ticket family purchases such as automobiles and computers. Studies of

Marketing Dictionary

opinion leader Trendsetter likely to purchase new products before others and then share the resulting experiences and opinions via word of mouth.

Figure 8.6 **Advertising Targeted to Children**

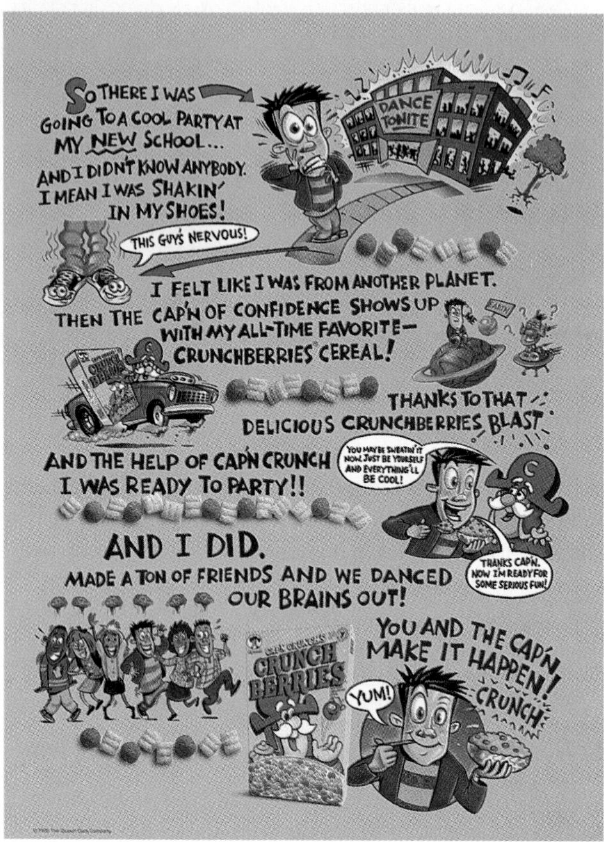
SO THERE I WAS
GOING TO A COOL PARTY AT MY NEW SCHOOL...
AND I DIDN'T KNOW ANYBODY. I MEAN I WAS SHAKIN' IN MY SHOES!
DANCE TONITE
THIS GUY'S NERVOUS!
I FELT LIKE I WAS FROM ANOTHER PLANET.
THEN THE CAP'N OF CONFIDENCE SHOWS UP WITH MY ALL-TIME FAVORITE— CRUNCHBERRIES CEREAL!
EARTH
THANKS TO THAT DELICIOUS CRUNCHBERRIES BLAST
AND THE HELP OF CAP'N CRUNCH I WAS READY TO PARTY!!
YOU MAY BE SWEATIN' IT NOW. JUST BE YOURSELF AND EVERYTHING'LL BE COOL!
AND I DID.
MADE A TON OF FRIENDS AND WE DANCED OUR BRAINS OUT!
THANKS CAP'N. NOW I'M READY FOR SOME SERIOUS FUN!
YOU AND THE CAP'N MAKE IT HAPPEN!
CRUNCH BERRIES
YUM!
CRUNCH

family decision making have also shown that households with two wage earners are more likely than others to make joint purchasing decisions.

While women are becoming more involved in decision making for large family purchases, men's roles are also changing. A recent study shows that 77 percent of all men are now major food purchasers, shopping either alone or with their partners. Members of two-income households often do their shopping at night and on weekends.

As growing numbers of women juggle multiple roles—raising families, building careers, managing households—they develop vital needs for goods and services that save time. One study found that today's time-crunched consumers have little patience for slow-moving cash register lines, ill-fitting merchandise, and returns that waste time.[33]

Children and Teenagers in Family Purchases As women have become busier, they have delegated some family purchase decisions to children, specifically teenagers. This change is especially common in the growing number of single-parent households. Children learn about the latest products and trends because they watch so much television, often becoming the family experts on what to buy. As a result, children have gained sophistication and assumed new roles in family purchasing behavior. For instance, studies have shown that as many as 70 percent of children help with their families' grocery shopping.[34] The major category in which children influence adults' buying behavior is food and beverages. Other important areas of influence include leisure activities, clothing, consumer electronics and computers, and health and beauty aids.

Children under 12 years old represent a huge market—over 50 million strong—in their own right. They also behave differently than prior generations. Growing up in dual-career households, they are more independent and more likely to help with household chores. These children accept responsibilities that were not common until recently.

Children directly influence $158 billion of purchases made by their parents—a number that is growing by 20 percent each year—and they indirectly influence purchases worth about twice that amount. They spend $9 billion of their own money each year, $2 billion on toys and games alone. A recent survey showed that kids ages 5 to 14 spend most of their money on food and beverages (30 percent), playthings (28 percent), and clothes (15 percent). Marketers try to reach children through promotions that engage and reward them. To promote Fruit Roll-Ups, for example, General Mills built a contest around the Spider Man cartoon character that asked youngsters to invent a villain. The grand prize was a $1,000 shopping spree at FAO Schwarz.[35]

Many supermarkets, recognizing children's role in influencing food and beverage purchases, now directly target young customers. Grocery stores sponsor food fairs, sampling, contests, seminars, and cooking classes; some send representatives to local elementary schools in an effort to sell youngsters on the importance of good nutrition. Also, food manufacturers are turning to lively packaging to attract the attention of younger shoppers.

Marketing to children is very challenging, because they tend to behave unpredictably and don't exhibit much brand loyalty. "A lot of the time we still have to rely on gut instinct. And sometimes we're wrong," says Bert Gould, Fox Children's Network senior vice president of marketing. Some companies, like Kellogg and Nickelodeon, are taking advantage of the technological savvy of today's kids and establishing persuasive, interactive sites in cyberspace.[36]

http://www.kelloggs.com/
http://www.mtv.com/

In general, however, children play evolving roles in family purchasing decisions as they grow. Their early influence centers around such choices as toys and cereal brands. Recognizing the influence that children have in cereal purchases, Quaker Oats attempts to reach the youth market by placing colorful ads, such as the one in Figure 8.6 for Cap'n Crunch's Crunch Berries, in children's magazines like *U.S. Kids*. Older children increasingly influence purchases of clothing for them. Teenagers become major consumers of sports equipment, movie tickets, video rentals, computers, and video games. In many families, teens also participate in decisions to purchase more expensive items such as cars and appliances. Because many teens are more technologically savvy than their parents, they play prominent roles in family computer purchases.

The teen market is especially attractive, because these kids spend 84 cents of every dollar they earn. They usually save only to buy more expensive products. Total teen spending should continue to climb as this population reaches 35 million by 2010. Teen buying preferences are important to marketers such as Levi Strauss, which seeks out teen opinions about characteristics such as style and fit on proposed products. General Motors puts its safe-driving magazine, which includes photos of its cars, in high schools. Ads for more mundane products like detergent and grocery items now show up on MTV, as marketers recognize that they can initiate loyal, long-term relationships by targeting teenagers.[37]

Adults can still play roles in larger family consumer behavior. They may continue to recommend products to their parents. Marketers try to influence these relationships by showing adult children in situations with their parents.

Briefly speaking

"Nothing is so powerful as an insight into human nature . . . what compulsions drive a man, what instincts dominate his action . . . if you know these things about a man you can touch him at the core of his being."

William Bernbach (1911–1982)
Founder, Doyle Dane Bernbach advertising agency

PERSONAL DETERMINANTS OF CONSUMER BEHAVIOR

Consumer behavior is affected by many internal, personal factors, as well as interpersonal ones. Each individual brings unique needs, motives, perceptions, attitudes, values, and self-concepts to buying decisions. This section will look at how these factors influence consumer behavior.

Needs and Motives

Individual purchase behavior is driven by the motivation to fill a need. A **need** is an imbalance between the consumer's actual and desired states. Someone who recognizes or feels a significant or urgent need then seeks to correct the imbalance. Marketers attempt to arouse this sense of urgency, that is, making a need "felt," and then influence consumers' motivation to satisfy their needs by purchasing specific products.

Motives are inner states that direct a person toward the goal of satisfying a felt need. The individual takes action to reduce the state of tension and return to a condition of equilibrium.

Maslow's Hierarchy of Needs A. H. Maslow developed a theory that characterized needs and arranged them in a hierarchy to reflect their importance. Maslow identified five levels of needs, beginning with physiological needs and progressing to the need for self-actualization. A person must at least partially satisfy lower-level needs, according to his theory, before higher needs can affect behavior. In developed countries, where relatively large per-capita incomes allow most people to satisfy the basic needs on the hierarchy, higher-order needs may be more important to consumer behavior. Table 8.1 illustrates products and marketing themes designed to satisfy needs at each level.

Physiological Needs Needs at the most basic level concern essential requirements for survival, such as food, water, shelter, and clothing. Ads for Post cereals appeal to physiological needs by stating that, "Breakfast is supposed to be the most important meal of the day."

Safety Needs The second-level needs include security, protection from physical harm, and avoidance of the unexpected. To gratify these needs, consumers may buy mutual fund shares, disability insurance, or security devices. Lysol addresses the safety concerns of mothers with its ad for Basin Tub & Tile Cleaner. The ad shows a baby in a bathtub under the headline, "This is no place for germs." It ends with the tagline, "Deep down you know it's clean."

Social/Belongingness Needs Satisfaction of physiological and safety needs leads a person to attend to third-level

Marketing Dictionary

need Lack of something useful; an imbalance between a desired state and an actual state.

motive Inner state that directs a person toward the goal of satisfying a felt need.

Table 8.1 Marketing Strategies Based on Maslow's Needs Hierarchy

PHYSIOLOGICAL NEEDS	
Products	Vitamins, herbal supplements, medicines, low-fat foods, exercise equipment, fitness clubs
Marketing approaches	Quaker Oatmeal—"Oh, what those oats can do!" Boost nutritional drink—"Your body will thank you." Kaiser-Permanente—"More people turn to us for good health." Ginkoba ginseng—"The thinking person's supplement." Advil—"Advanced medicine for pain."
SAFETY NEEDS	
Products	Car accessories, burglar alarm systems, retirement investments, insurance, smoke and carbon monoxide detectors
Marketing approaches	Allstate Insurance—"You're in good hands with Allstate." Ford Motor Company—"Only your mother is more obsessed with your safety." Lysol Basin Tub & Tile Cleaner—"This is no place for germs." Merrill Lynch—"A tradition of trust."
BELONGINGNESS NEEDS	
Products	Beauty aids, entertainment, clothing
Marketing approaches	Carnival Cruise Lines—"The most popular cruise line in the world." Sears Mainframe Junior Dept.—"Gotta have the clothes." Lady Foot Locker—"One store. Every woman."
ESTEEM NEEDS	
Products	Clothing, cars, jewelry, liquors, hobbies, beauty spa services.
Marketing approaches	Jeep—"There's only one." Movado Museum Watch—"The making of a legendary classic." Bombay Sapphire Dry Gin—"Pour something priceless." BMW—"The ultimate driving machine."
SELF-ACTUALIZATION NEEDS	
Products	Education, cultural events, sports, hobbies
Marketing approaches	Nike—"If you let me play, I will like myself more." Outward Bound Schools—"The adventure lasts a lifetime." Danskin—"Not just for dancing."

needs—the desire to be accepted by people and groups important to that individual. To satisfy this need, individuals may conform to certain standards of behavior and dress in order to feel that they belong. Marketers for Broderbund Software and Nickelodeon target children's social/belongingness needs when they organize "kid's clubs" that promote products with entertainment and group events.

Esteem Needs The desire to feel a sense of accomplishment and achievement, to gain the respect of others, and even to exceed the performance of others, is an apparently universal human trait that emerges after lower-order needs are satisfied. Virgin Atlantic Airlines marketers appeal to this need with the firm's "Upper Class" service that offers chauffeured transportation to and from the airport.

Self-Actualization Needs At the top rung of Maslow's ladder of human needs, people desire to realize their full potential and find fulfillment by fully expressing their talents and capabilities. Self-help and spiritually oriented "New Age" products are aimed at satisfying consumers' needs for self-actualization. For instance, *The Celestine Prophecy,* James Redfield's novel about "spiritual transformation" was on the best-seller list for more than 128 weeks.[38]

Maslow noted that a satisfied need no longer motivates

a person to act. Once the physiological needs are met, the individual moves on to pursue satisfaction of higher-order needs. Consumers are periodically motivated by the need to relieve thirst and hunger, but their interests soon return to focus on satisfaction of safety, social, and other needs in the hierarchy.

Critics have pointed out a variety of flaws in Maslow's reasoning. For example, some needs can be related to more than one level. However, the hierarchy of needs continues to occupy a secure place in the study of consumer behavior.

Perceptions

Perception is the meaning that a person attributes to incoming stimuli gathered through the five senses—sight, hearing, touch, taste, and smell. Certainly a buyer's behavior is influenced by his or her perceptions of a good or service. Only recently have researchers come to recognize that people's perceptions depend as much on what they want to perceive as on the actual stimuli. It is for this reason that Saks Fifth Avenue is perceived so differently from Kmart, Godiva chocolates, or Fannie Mae.

A person's perception of an object or event results from the interaction of two types of factors:

1. *Stimulus factors*—characteristics of the physical object such as size, color, weight, and shape
2. *Individual factors*—unique characteristics of the individual, including not only sensory processes, but also experiences with similar inputs and basic motivations and expectations

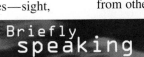

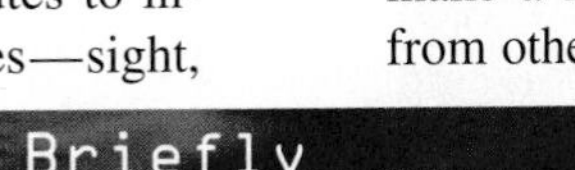
Briefly speaking

"It's the first company to build the mental position that has the upper hand, not the first company to make the product. IBM didn't invent the computer; Sperry Rand did. But IBM was the first to build the computer position in the prospect's mind."

Al Ries (1929–)
Chairman, Trout & Ries, Inc., advertising agency

Perceptual Screens The average American today is constantly bombarded by marketing messages. According to the Food Marketing Institute, for example, a typical supermarket now carries 30,000 different packages, each serving as a miniature billboard vying to attract consumer attention. Over 6,000 commercials a week are aired on network TV. Prime-time TV shows carry more than 15 minutes of advertising every hour. Thousands of businesses have set up World Wide Web sites to tout their goods and services. Marketers have also stamped their messages on everything from popcorn bags in movie theaters to airsickness bags on planes. Lingerie manufacturer Bamboo Inc. even stenciled messages on sidewalks in New York City that read, "From here, it looks like you could use some new underwear."[39]

This unceasing marketing clutter has taught consumers to ignore many promotional messages. In order to function, people respond selectively to attend only to messages that manage to break through their **perceptual screens**—the filtering processes through which all inputs must pass.

All marketers struggle to determine which stimuli do evoke responses from consumers. They must learn how to capture a customer's attention so that he or she will read an advertisement, listen to a sales representative, or react to a point-of-purchase display. In general, marketers seek to make a message stand out, to make it different enough from other messages that it gains the attention of prospective customers.

To break through the perceptual screens of young consumers, Pepsi developed a unique promotion. In exchange for proofs of purchase for Mountain Dew and $35, the company gave teenagers Motorola pagers with six months of free service. Then, once a week for six months, Pepsi beeped the teens with an ad that suggested they dial a toll-free number to hear messages alerting them to promotional offers and prizes from Pepsi, MTV, Sony Music, and other companies.[40]

Advertisers are finding that careful use of humor can be an effective tool for breaking through consumers' perceptual screens. "For years, Madison Avenue was deathly afraid that humor would reflect badly on their product," comedian Marty Ingels told a *USA Today* reporter. "But today, you have automatic product acceptance if you can make people laugh."[41] Budweiser used humor in a TV commercial combining live action and animation to show Clydesdale horses playing football. The commercial aired during the Super Bowl, and both media critics and consumers applauded its wittiness.

To break through clutter in the printed media, marketers can run large ads. Doubling the size of an ad increases its attention value by about 50 percent. Color makes newspaper ads contrast with the usual black-and-white graphics, providing another effective way to

Marketing Dictionary

perception Meaning that an individual creates by interpreting a stimulus.

perceptual screen Consumers' mental filtering processes through which all marketing messages must pass to gain attention.

Figure 8.7 Breaking through Perceptual Screens

Fun

penetrate the reader's perceptual screen. Other methods for enhancing contrast include arranging a large amount of white space around a printed area or placing white type on a dark background. Vivid illustrations and photos can also help to break through clutter in print ads. The Mercedes-Benz of North America ad in Figure 8.7 is different from most car ads that show the product and explain its features. The luxury carmaker uses an attention-getting photo of a rubber ducky with eyes of the car's symbol to project the idea that driving a Mercedes can be fun.

The psychological concept of closure also helps marketers to create a message that stands out. *Closure* refers to the human tendency to perceive a complete picture from an incomplete stimulus. Advertisements that allow consumers to do this often succeed in breaking through perceptual screens. During a Kellogg campaign promoting consumption of fruit with cereal, the company emphasized the point by replacing the letters *ll* in *Kellogg* with bananas. In a campaign featuring a 25-cent coupon offer, Kellogg reinforced the promotional idea by replacing the letter *o* in the brand name with the image of a quarter.

Supermarkets employ a variety of techniques to arouse shoppers' attention. Some of these techniques are more successful than others. A study commissioned by *Promo* magazine found that the most effective attention-grabbing promotional methods were end-of-aisle displays, store circular coupons, and instant, on-pack cents off coupons. Electronic signs with moving words and in-store radio, two other retail marketing methods, were found to have little impact on shoppers.[42]

A new tool that marketers are exploring is the use of virtual reality. Some companies have created presentations based on virtual reality that display marketing messages and information in a three-dimensional format. Eventually, experts predict, consumers will be able to tour resort areas via virtual reality before booking their trips or virtually walk through the inside of computers they are considering buying. Virtual reality technology may allow marketers to penetrate consumer perceptual filters in a way not currently possible with other forms of media.[43]

With selective perception at work screening competing messages, it is easy to see the importance of marketers' efforts to develop brand loyalty. Satisfied customers are less likely to seek information about competing products. Even when advertising by competitors is forced on them, they are less apt than others to look beyond their perceptual filters at those appeals. Loyal customers simply tune out information that does not agree with their existing beliefs and expectations.

Subliminal Perception Some marketers wonder whether they can communicate with consumers without making them aware of the communication. In 1956, a New Jersey movie theater tried to boost concession sales by flashing the words *Eat Popcorn* and *Drink Coca-Cola* between frames of Kim Novak's image in the movie *Picnic*. The messages flashed on the screen every five seconds for a duration of one three-hundredth of a second each time. Researchers reported that these messages, though too short to be recognizable at the conscious level, resulted in a 58 percent increase in popcorn sales and an 18 percent increase in Coca-Cola sales. After the findings were published, advertising agencies and consumer protection groups became intensely interested in **subliminal perception**—the subconscious receipt of incoming information.

Subliminal advertising is aimed at the subconscious level of awareness to circumvent the audience's perceptual screens. The goal of the original research was to induce consumer purchases while keeping consumers unaware of the source of the motivation to buy. All later attempts to duplicate the test findings, however, have been unsuccessful.

Although subliminal advertising has been universally condemned as manipulative, it is exceedingly unlikely that it can induce purchasing except by people already inclined to buy. Three reasons assure that this fact will remain true:

1. Strong stimulus factors are required just to get a prospective customer's attention.

2. Only a very short message can be transmitted.
3. Individuals vary greatly in their thresholds of consciousness. Messages transmitted at the threshold of consciousness for one person will not be perceived at all by some people but will be all too apparent to others. The subliminally exposed message, "Drink Coca-Cola," may go unseen by some viewers, while others may read it as "Drink Pepsi-Cola," "Drink Cocoa," or even "Drive Slowly."

Despite early fears, research has shown that subliminal messages cannot force receivers to purchase goods that they would not consciously want without the messages.

In recent years, subliminal communication has spread to programming for self-help tapes. These tapes play sounds that listeners hear consciously as relaxing music or ocean waves; subconsciously, imperceptibly among the other sounds, they hear thousands of subliminal messages. Americans spend millions of dollars a year on subliminal tapes that are supposed to help them stop smoking, lose weight, or achieve a host of other goals. Unfortunately, the National Research Council recently concluded that the subliminal messages do little to influence behavior.

Attitudes

Perception of incoming stimuli is greatly affected by attitudes. In fact, the decision to purchase a product is strongly based on currently held attitudes about the product, store, or salesperson.

Attitudes are a person's enduring favorable or unfavorable evaluations, emotional feelings, or action tendencies toward some object or data. As they form over time through individual experiences and group contacts, attitudes become highly resistant to change.

Because favorable attitudes likely affect brand preferences, marketers are interested in determining consumer attitudes toward their products. Numerous attitude-scaling devices have been developed for this purpose.

Attitude Components An attitude has cognitive, affective, and behavioral components. The *cognitive* component refers to the individual's information and knowledge about an object or concept. The *affective* component deals with feelings or emotional reactions. The *behavioral* component involves tendencies to act in a certain manner. For example, in deciding whether to shop at a warehouse-type food store, an individual might obtain information about what the store offers from advertising, trial visits, and input from family, friends, and associates (cognitive component). He or she might also receive affective input by listening to others about their experiences shopping at this type of store—whether they liked it or not. Other affective information might lead the person to make a judgment about the type of people who seem to shop there—whether they represent a group with which he or she would like to be associated. The consumer may ultimately decide to buy some canned goods, cereal, and bakery products there, but continue to rely on his or her regular supermarket for major food purchases (behavioral component).

All three components maintain a relatively stable and balanced relationship to one another. Together they form an overall attitude about an object or idea.

Changing Consumer Attitudes Since a favorable consumer attitude provides a vital condition for marketing success, how can a firm lead prospective buyers to adopt such an attitude toward its products? Marketers have two choices: (1) attempt to produce consumer attitudes that will motivate purchase of a particular product or (2) evaluate existing consumer attitudes and then make the product characteristics appeal to them.

If consumers view an existing good or service unfavorably, the seller may choose to redesign it or offer new options. Cruise ships are a good example. After 25 years of continuous growth, passenger bookings began to drop in reaction to media reports of problems such as hurricanes, ship fires, and disease outbreaks. Cruise lines generally focused on attracting experienced passengers rather than new, younger customers who believed that only rich people took cruises and most shipboard activities were geared to senior citizens. Prospective customers feared boredom confined to a ship for a week.

To change these attitudes, the cruise-ship industry opened new markets and developed onboard programs designed to serve the needs of families with children These marketers also added attractions such as adventure excursions ashore and onboard classes. Their advertising conveyed to consumers the message that cruises had changed. Carnival's "Fun Ship" promotion, designed to appeal to the general population, increased its market share to 26 percent. Upscale Holland-America pointed out the value to passengers of its all-inclusive prices; the company also added youth counselors to its staff. Norwegian Cruise Line

Marketing Dictionary

subliminal perception Subconscious receipt of information.

attitude A person's enduring favorable or unfavorable evaluation, emotional feeling, or action tendency toward a product.

MARKETING HALL OF SHAME

It's a Mad, Mad World

Mad cow disease—those three words sent shivers through the beef and restaurant industries in Great Britain after at least ten people contracted a fatal disease that many blamed on sick cattle. The deaths triggered a nationwide public-health crisis and created a marketing nightmare for farmers, small businesses, and corporations whose fortunes were linked to beef.

Business is still trying to recover from the public-relations fiasco, which began with a government announcement that mad cow disease was a likely cause of ten cases of a similar human illness, Creutzfeldt-Jakob disease. Mad cow disease, or bovine spongiform encephalopathy (BSE) to scientists, is a brain malady that has plagued Britain's cattle for more than a decade. But only when a possible link was made with human health did U.K. consumers react swiftly and change their behavior.

Millions of consumers began shunning British beef. Restaurants, such as fast-food chains like McDonald's, Wendy's, and Burger King, removed hamburgers from their menus. What's more, the European Union instituted a global export ban on British beef and its by-products.

http://www.burgerking.com/
http://www.mcdonalds.com/

The widespread panic produced immediate financial fallout. Almost overnight, Britain faced a serious economic crisis. The $6 billion beef industry was confronted with devastating losses as plans were made to destroy up to 800,000 older cattle. Economists predicted that 100,000 workers would lose their jobs if the crisis lasted a year.

Inflation was also a prime worry as grocery bills jumped in price. It was predicted that shoppers could spend $800 million more for imported meat. The price of milk also would skyrocket if just a fraction of dairy cows were destroyed.

The immediate panic that enveloped the country seemed initially to stun government officials, who kicked off a damage-control campaign. In part, they tried to downplay any danger that mad cow disease might pose.

Just five days after the first alarming announcement, Stephen Dorrell, Britain's secretary of state for health and a leader of the government crisis team, exclaimed, "It isn't the cows that are mad, it's the people that are going mad. I eat

began running TV ads that showed close-ups of younger passengers involved in various lively activities. The ads helped to convince younger customers that cruise vacations were not just for seniors. Norwegian's average passenger is now two years younger than those of other cruise lines.[44]

Modifying the Components of Attitude Attitudes frequently change in response to inconsistencies among the three components. The most common inconsistencies result when new information changes the cognitive or affective components of an attitude. Marketers can work to modify attitudes by providing evidence of product benefits and correcting misconceptions. They may also attempt to change attitudes by getting buyers to engage in new behavior. Free samples, for instance, can change attitudes by getting consumers to try a product. Sometimes a product can succeed only if all three components are modified at the same time.

Parmalat, the world's largest producer of milk, needed to modify all three components of consumer attitudes when it introduced Long Life milk. Long Life is a shelf-stable milk in aseptic packaging that keeps the product fresh for six months without refrigeration. In researching consumer attitudes toward the product, the company discovered a belief that fresh milk could come only from refrigerated containers, and that only powdered milk would come in boxes. Consumers were also concerned about the processing methods for Long Life and doubted that it would taste the same as milk sold in the dairy case. "The hurdle we had to face was to convince people that the milk was pure American milk with nothing added," said Mario Messina, executive creative director of the advertising agency that helped Parmalat develop its marketing strategies for the product.

To launch Long Life, Parmalat ran 30-second TV ads explaining its quality and convenience. The company also direct-mailed coupons good for a free quart of the milk to millions of prospective purchasers. Follow-up print ads focused on consumers' questions and concerns about the product. These strategies helped to modify all three attitude components. They changed cognitive perceptions by pro-

beef and I let my children eat beef." Queen Elizabeth and Prime Minister John Major tried to do their part by serving British beef to VIPs. When Germany's Chancellor Helmut Kohl and French President Jacques Chirac—both from countries that had banned British beef—arrived on separate visits, both politely ate the beef served on fancy china. Chatting afterward with reporters, Kohl said that while he ate the meat, he refused to be a marketer for British beef.

Ironically, the government's attempts at calming fears drew attention to the problem. Its pleas were hooted down by some as insincere, creating a credibility problem. "The government has handled this matter with mind-boggling incompetence," insisted Labour Party leader Tony Blair.

In *Business Week*, one commentator suggested that the government's main problem was clumsy explanation of a complex scientific debate. Researchers still cannot say with any certainty that mad cow disease poses any danger to humans at all. Somehow that message got lost. "The only real solution is for government and industry leaders to use scientific information responsibly," the *Business Week* commentator asserted. "No more spectacles like the one last year when Britain's agriculture minister sought to reassure the public by feeding his four-year-old daughter beef in front of television cameras."

The restaurant industry appeared to fare better than the government did. Multinational chains like McDonald's, as well as a string of 2,700 pubs, quickly found safe beef suppliers and publicly announced the switch. In order to keep their customers, many restaurants didn't charge more for meals, even though typical beef bills had risen. These efforts worked, said Laurence Isaacson, director of the London Tourist Board and deputy chairman of Groupe Chez Gerard, which runs ten upscale London eateries. Diners switched to other meats for about two or three weeks, he said, "but now that we've reassured people, there is a trend back to eating prime cuts of beef . . . the worst is over."

QUESTIONS FOR CRITICAL THINKING

1. **Could the British government have averted a crisis by handling the mad cow disease scare differently?**
2. **Do you think corporations, with their marketing and public-relations prowess, are more adept than government at minimizing a crisis in public confidence? Why?**

Sources: "Bracing for a Mad Cow Epidemic," *Business Week*, January 27, 1997, p. 38; "Where's the Beef From?" *USA Today*, April 19, 1996, p. 1D; Paula Dwyer, "Britain, Mad Cows—and Mad Politicians," *Business Week*, April 8, 1996, p. 34; Paul Raeburn, "Commentary: Junk Science and Mass Hysteria," *Business Week*, April 8, 1996, p. 35; Rae Tyson, "Beef Industry Hits Hard Times," *USA Today*, March 5, 1996, p. 4B.

viding information about the product's packaging; they addressed affective concerns by targeting and overcoming consumer doubts about taste and safety; they influenced behavioral responses by inviting consumers to try a quart for free.[45]

Learning

Marketing is concerned as seriously with the process by which consumer decisions change over time as with the current states of those decisions. **Learning,** in a marketing context, refers to immediate or expected changes in consumer behavior as a result of experience. The learning process includes the component of **drive,** which is any strong stimulus that impels action. Examples of drives are fear, pride, desire for money, thirst, pain avoidance, and rivalry. Learning also relies on a **cue,** that is, any object in the environment that determines the nature of the consumer's response to a drive. Examples of cues are a newspaper advertisement for a new French restaurant (a cue for a hungry person) and a Shell sign near an interstate highway (a cue for a motorist who needs gasoline).

Marketing Dictionary

learning Immediate or expected change in behavior as a result of experience.

drive Strong stimulus that impels action.

cue Any object in the environment that determines the nature of a consumer's response to a drive.

Figure 8.8 Evoking the Consumer's Self-Concept in Promoting a Product

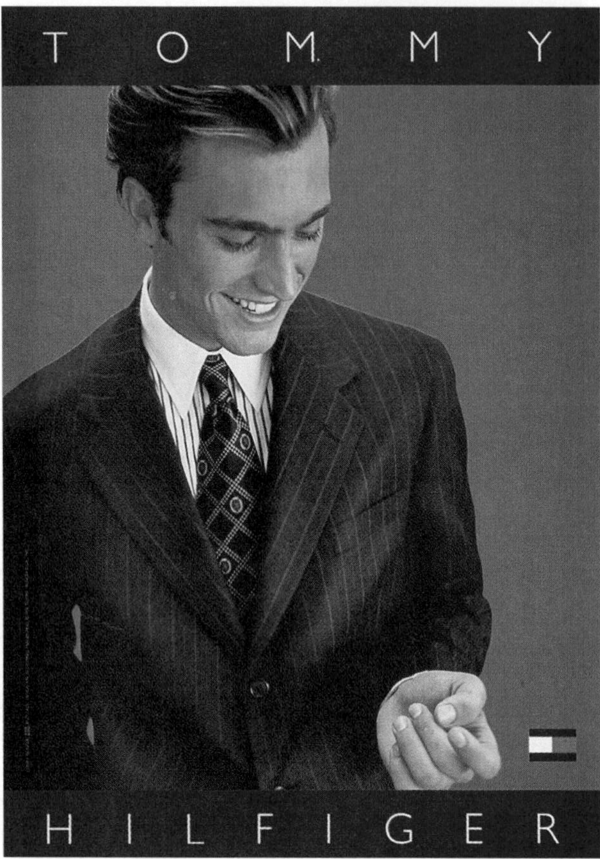
TOMMY
HILFIGER

A *response* is an individual's reaction to a set of cues and drives. Responses might include such reactions as purchasing a package of Gillette Sensor razor blades, dining at Pizza Hut, or deciding to enroll at a particular community college or university.

Reinforcement is the reduction in drive that results from a proper response. As a response becomes more rewarding, it creates a stronger bond between the drive and the purchase of the product. Should the purchase of Sensor razor blades result in better shaves through repeated use, the likelihood that the consumer will make future purchases increases. Reinforcement is the rationale that underlies frequent-buyer programs, which reward repeat purchasers for their loyalty. Such programs, which recall the Green Stamp promotions of an earlier era, give consumers points for buying particular brands; they can redeem these points for premiums like electric can openers or barbecue grills. Another example is an airline's frequent-flyer program, which rewards travelers who use that airline regularly with free airline tickets.

Applying Learning Theory to Marketing Decisions Learning theory has some important implications for marketing strategists, particularly those involved with consumer packaged goods.[46] They must plan to develop a desired outcome such as repeat purchase behavior gradually over time. *Shaping* is the process of applying a series of rewards and reinforcements to permit more complex behavior to evolve over time.

Both promotional strategy and the product itself play a role in the shaping process. Assume that marketers are attempting to motivate customers to become regular buyers of a certain product. Their first step is to induce an initial product trial by offering a free sample package that includes a substantial discount coupon for a subsequent purchase. This example illustrates the use of a cue as a shaping procedure. The purchase response is reinforced by satisfactory product performance and yet another, less substantial inducement (the coupon) for another purchase.

The second step is to entice the consumer to buy the product with little financial risk. The large discount offered by the coupon enclosed with the free sample prompts this action. The package that the consumer purchases has another, smaller discount coupon enclosed. Again, satisfactory product performance and the second coupon provide reinforcement.

The third step is to motivate the person to buy the item again at a moderate cost. A discount coupon accomplishes this objective, but this time the purchased package includes no additional coupon. The only reinforcement comes from satisfactory product performance.

The final test comes when the consumer decides whether to buy the product at its true price without a discount coupon. Satisfaction with product performance provides the only continuing reinforcement. Repeat purchase behavior is literally shaped by effective application of learning theory within a marketing strategy context.

Self-Concept Theory

The consumer's **self-concept**—a person's multifaceted picture of himself or herself—plays an important role in consumer behavior. One young man, for example, may view himself as an intellectual, self-assured, talented, rising young business executive. He will be disposed to buy products that agree with this conception of himself, such as Tommy Hilfiger's dresswear shown in Figure 8.8. A woman who views herself as a fashionable and upwardly mobile leader may purchase designer clothes to reinforce her perceptions.

The concept of self emerges from an interaction of many of the influences—both personal and interpersonal—that affect buying behavior. The individual's needs, motives, perceptions, attitudes, and learning lie at the core of his or her conception of self. In addition, family, social, and cultural influences affect self-concept.

The self-concept has four components: real self, self-image, looking-glass self, and ideal self. The *real self* is an objective view of the total person. The *self-image*—the way an individual views himself or herself—may distort the objective view. The *looking-glass self*—the way an individual thinks others see him or her—may also differ substantially from the self-image, because people often choose to project different images to others than their perceptions of their real selves. The *ideal self* serves as a personal set of objectives, since it is the image to which the individual aspires. In purchasing goods and services, people are likely to choose products that move them closer to their ideal self-images.

THE CONSUMER DECISION PROCESS

Consumers complete a step-by-step process to make purchasing decisions. The length of time and the amount of effort they devote to a particular purchasing decision depends on the importance of the desired good or service to the consumer.

Purchases with high levels of potential social or economic consequences are said to be *high-involvement* purchase decisions. Buying a new car or deciding where to go to college are two examples of high-involvement decisions. Routine purchases that pose little risk to the consumer are *low-involvement* decisions. Purchasing a candy bar from a vending machine is a good example.

Consumers generally invest more time and effort to purchase decisions for high-involvement products than to those for low-involvement products. A car buyer, for example, will probably compare prices, spend time visiting dealer showrooms, and ask for advice from friends before making the final decision. Few buyers invest that much effort in choosing between Nestlé's and Hershey's candy bars. They will still go through the steps of the consumer decision process but on a more compressed scale.

Figure 8.9 shows the six steps in the consumer decision process. First, the consumer recognizes a problem or unmet need. Then he or she searches for goods or services that will fill that need and evaluates the alternatives before making a purchase decision. The next step is the actual purchase act. After completing the purchase, the consumer evaluates whether he or she made the right choice. Much of marketing involves steering consumers through the decision process in the direction of a specific item.

Consumers apply the decision process in solving problems and taking advantage of opportunities. Such decisions permit them to correct differences between their actual and desired states. Feedback from each decision serves as additional experience to help guide subsequent decisions.

Problem or Opportunity Recognition

During the first stage in the decision process, the consumer becomes aware of a significant discrepancy between the existing situation and a desired situation. After recognizing the problem, the consumer must define it as preparation for seeking out methods for its solution. Problem recognition motivates the individual to achieve the desired state of affairs.

Perhaps the most common cause of problem or opportunity recognition is routine depletion of the individual's stock of an item. A large number of purchases simply replenish products ranging from gasoline to groceries. In other instances, the consumer may possess an inadequate assortment of products. The gardening hobbyist may make regular purchases of different fertilizers, seeds, or gardening tools as the season progresses.

A third cause of problem or opportunity recognition is dissatisfaction with a present brand or product type. This situation is common in purchases of new automobiles, furniture, or fall clothing. Consumers often become bored with current products; nothing more than a desire for change may be the underlying rationale for the decision process that leads to a new-product purchase.

Another important effect on problem or opportunity recognition results from changed financial status. Additional financial resources from such sources as salary increases or inheritances may permit some consumers to make purchases that they had previously postponed.

The marketer's main task during this phase of consumer decision making is to help prospective buyers identify and recognize potential problems or needs. For instance, sales personnel in an upscale department store may point out accessories to complete an outfit that a customer has already decided to buy.

Search

During the second step in the decision process, the consumer gathers information related to his or her attainment

Marketing Dictionary

reinforcement Reduction in drive that results from an appropriate consumer response.

self-concept Person's conception of himself or herself, composed of the real self, self-image, looking-glass self, and ideal self.

Figure 8.9 An Integrated Model of the Consumer Decision Process

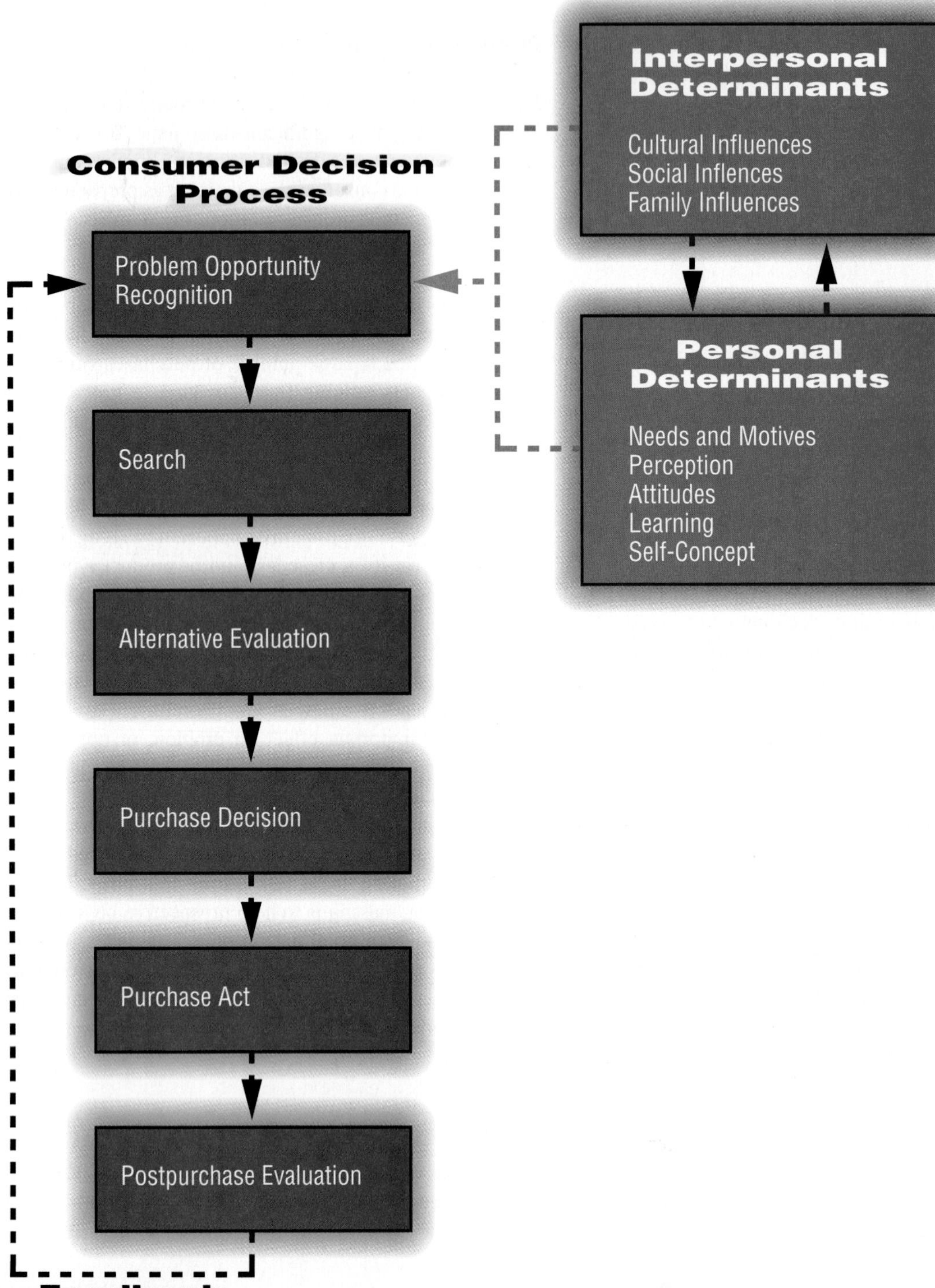
Interpersonal Determinants
Cultural Influences
Social Inflences
Family Influences
Consumer Decision Process
Problem Opportunity Recognition
Search
Alternative Evaluation
Purchase Decision
Purchase Act
Postpurchase Evaluation
Personal Determinants
Needs and Motives
Perception
Attitudes
Learning
Self-Concept
Feedback

of a desired state of affairs. This search identifies alternative means of problem solution. High-involvement purchases may elicit extensive information searches, while low-involvement purchases require little search activity.

The search may cover internal or external sources of information. Internal search is a mental review of stored information relevant to the problem situation. This sequence includes both actual experiences or observations and memories of personal communications or exposures to persuasive marketing messages. An external search gathers information from outside sources, which may include family members, friends and associates, store displays, sales rep-resentatives, brochures, and product-testing publications such as *Consumer Reports.* For some purchases, the Internet may be another source of information. Consumers can search for information directly at corporate World Wide Web sites or ask for recommendations from others through online newsgroups.

Consumers often solve problems through internal search, alone—that is, by relying on mentally stored information to make purchase decisions. Achieving favorable results using a certain car polish may motivate a consumer to repurchase this brand rather than considering other options. Since external search involves both time and effort, consumers will complete it only when memory cannot supply adequate information.

Figure 8.10 **Influencing a Consumer Decision during the Search Process**

When you choose a Mannington
floor for your home, people will notice.
Only Mannington offers you so many
elegant patterns, beautiful textures and
vibrant colors. And with its unrivaled
It must be Mannington.
durability, a Mannington floor assures
you of receiving admiring glances for years
to come. If it looks this good and wears
this well, it must be Mannington. For more
information or the name of the dealer
nearest you, call 1-800-443-5667
IT·MUST·BE
MANNINGTON

The search identifies alternative brands for consideration and possible purchase. The number of brands that a consumer actually considers in making a purchase decision is known in marketing as the **evoked set.** In some searches, consumers already know of the brands that merit further consideration; in others, their external searches develop such information. The actual number of brands included in the evoked set will vary depending on both situational and individual differences.[47] For example, an immediate need might limit the evoked set, as would a lack of knowledge about a product category.

Consumers now choose among more alternative products than ever before. This can confuse and complicate the analysis necessary to narrow the range of choices for consumers. Instead of comparing one or two brands, a consumer often faces a dizzying array of brands and subbrands for everything from toothpaste to tires. "It's getting more complicated," says John Lowe, director of market information for *Consumer Reports.* "It's happening in so many product categories."[48]

Marketers try to influence consumer decisions during the search process by providing persuasive information about their goods or services in a format useful to consumers. As discussed earlier, marketers encounter a difficult challenge in breaking through the clutter that distracts customers. To achieve success and be included in a consumer's evoked set of alternatives, the marketer must find creative ways to meet this challenge. Mannington developed a humorous advertising campaign to influence consumers during their search for floor covering. The funny photo in Figure 8.10 reinforces the ad's message theme: "When you choose a Mannington floor for your home, people will notice."

Alternative Evaluation

The third step in the consumer decision process is to evaluate the evoked set of options identified during the search step. Actually, it is difficult to completely separate the second and third steps, since some evaluation takes place as the search progresses; consumers accept, discount, distort, or reject incoming information as they receive it.

The outcome of the evaluation stage is the choice of a brand or product in the evoked set or possibly a decision to renew the search for additional alternatives, should all those identified during the initial search prove unsatisfactory. To complete this analysis, the consumer must develop a set of evaluative criteria to guide the selection. **Evaluative criteria** may be defined as features that a consumer

Marketing Dictionary

evoked set Number of brands that a consumer considers buying before making a purchasing decision.

evaluative criteria Features considered in a consumer's choice of alternatives.

SOLVING AN ETHICAL CONTROVERSY

Sexually Suggestive Ads: A Positive or Negative Effect on Consumer Behavior?

If Calvin Klein hadn't anticipated the uproar his provocative ads would trigger, perhaps he was the only one who was surprised. The ads included shots by the photographer for Madonna's notorious book, *Sex*. They provoked a firestorm of protests from critics like President Bill Clinton and First Lady Hillary Rodham Clinton, as well as rape crisis counselors and conservative preachers.

Shot in what appeared to be a dreary suburban basement, the ads showed young, very thin models in various stages of undress. One nearly naked male is wearing only an unbuttoned vest and Calvin Klein briefs. Two girls, equally undressed, are shown in sexually suggestive poses.

The controversial campaign prompted the U.S. Justice Department to investigate whether the advertisements violated laws against child pornography. This move only fueled the debate that inevitably arises when marketers appear to step over the line. Was the company going to lose customers because the ads offended them, or would it increase sales by attracting attention to itself, even if that attention had negative overtones?

? *Should Marketers Run Sexually Explicit Ads?*

PRO

1. **Calvin Klein has long created controversial ads that get buyers' attention. In 1980, for instance, 15-year-old model Brooke Shields shared with television viewers the provocative statement that, "Nothing comes between me and my Calvins." In other ads, model Kate Moss posed naked with a large dog, and the well-muscled rapper, Marky Mark, appeared in briefs. Since the ads are not illegal, Calvin Klein's creative process should not be stifled.**
2. **The government treads into a dangerous area when it tries to censor advertisements. One person's pornography is another person's art form. Some people might regard the ads as highly entertaining, while others could consider them trash. Who decides who is right? The only arbiter should be the marketplace. "The government is bowing to political pressure and misusing the child-pornography laws," said Norman Siegel of the New York Civil Liberties Union in defense of the ads. "There is no evidence that the models were sexually abused, and the ads, whatever you think of them, don't descend to obscene."**
3. **Calvin Klein has interpreted the ads very differently from his critics. He sees them as reflecting today's cultural values. In a public statement, Klein made this observation: "We continue to believe in the positive message of these ads. . . . [T]he ad's message about the spirit, independence, and inner worth**

considers in choosing among alternatives. These criteria can either be objective facts (government tests of an automobile's miles-per-gallon rating) or subjective impression (a favorable view of Donna Karan clothing). Common evaluative criteria include price, brand name, and country of origin. Evaluative criteria can also vary with the consumer's age, income level, social class, and culture.

Marketers can attempt to influence the outcome from this stage in three ways. First, they can try to educate consumers about attributes that they view as important in evaluating a particular class of goods. They can also identify which evaluative criteria are important to an individual and attempt to show why a specific brand fulfills those criteria. Finally, they can try to induce a customer to expand his or her evoked set to include the product they are marketing. A travel agent, for example, might ask a client about the family's budget and recreational preferences. The agent might also explain the differences between two destinations, pointing out important considerations, such as weather and activities, that the client had not considered. Finally, the agent might suggest other destinations or resorts, increasing the client's range of choices.

Purchase Decision and Purchase Act

The search and alternative evaluation stages of the decision process result in the eventual purchase decision and the act of making the purchase. At this stage, the consumer has evaluated each alternative in the evoked set based on his or her personal set of evaluative criteria and narrowed the alternatives down to one.

The consumer then decides the purchase location. Consumers tend to choose stores by considering such char-

of today's young people has been misunderstood by some." In an interview with *New York* magazine, Klein insisted, "We're not trying to shock and we're not trying to create controversy."

CON

1. The Calvin Klein ads featured models who appeared underage, contributing to general decadence and overemphasis on sexual messages in today's society. Consumers who dislike these messages will stop buying the company's products to protest the offensive ads. Many will agree with critic Noach Dear, a member of the New York City council, who said, "There is no difference between pedophiles-pornographers . . . and advertisers like Calvin. Both are peddling porn, and both should be subject and held to the same laws."
2. The exploitative ads were even more dangerous because they were so ubiquitous. It wasn't just magazine readers and television viewers who saw the ads. In New York City, for instance, buses and subway cars carried Calvin Klein billboards, exposing youngsters to the ads as they walked down the street. Again, consumers who oppose such flaunting of sexual themes will react negatively to the company.
3. Ads like these may violate a pair of federal child-pornography statutes. A 1978 law makes any "lascivious exhibition" of children a federal crime. A more recent measure requires anyone involved in the production or distribution of sexually explicit material to keep on file the names and ages of actors and models.

SUMMARY

Ultimately, the tempest fizzled when Calvin Klein pulled the television and print ads after they ran for just two months. Prosecutors concluded that the campaign did not violate any federal child-pornography statutes because none of the models were underage. Of course, a question remains about whether consumers who were offended by Calvin Klein's ads will boycott the company's products.

QUESTIONS FOR CRITICAL THINKING

1. Do you think the controversy stirred by the Calvin Klein ads is overblown, or do you think such advertising affects young people in harmful ways? Why?
2. Would you refuse to buy the products of a company that runs offensive ads? Explain the reasons for your decision.

Sources: "Calvin Klein Hires New Creative Director," *Advertising Age-Daily Deadline*, downloaded from http://adage.com/news_and_features, March 19, 1997; "No Prosecution for Klein Ads," *San Diego Union-Tribune,* November 16, 1995, p. A10; "Calvin Klein Ads Probed for Child Porn," *San Diego Union-Tribune,* September 9, 1995, p. A1; Peter Rowe, "Jean Ads Reveal De-Kleining of Our Values," *San Diego Union-Tribune* August 31, 1995, p. E1; Rick Hampton, "Calvin Klein Ads Likened to Child Porn," *San Diego Union-Tribune,* August 20, 1995, p. 15.

acteristics as location, price, assortment, personnel, store image, physical design, and services. In addition, store selection is influenced by the product category. Some consumers choose the convenience of in-home shopping via telephone or mail order rather than traveling to complete transactions in retail stores.

Marketers can smooth the purchase decision and purchase act phases by helping customers to arrange for financing or delivery.

Postpurchase Evaluation

The purchase act produces one of two results. The buyer feels either satisfaction at the removal of the discrepancy between the existing and desired states or dissatisfaction with the purchase. Consumers are generally satisfied if purchases meet their expectations.

Sometimes, however, consumers experience some postpurchase anxieties, called **cognitive dissonance.** This psychologically unpleasant state results from an imbalance among a person's knowledge, beliefs, and attitudes. For example, a consumer may experience dissonance after choosing a particular automobile over several other models when

Marketing Dictionary

cognitive dissonance Postpurchase anxiety that results from an imbalance among an individual's knowledge, beliefs, and attitudes.

some of the rejected models have desired features that the chosen one does not provide.

Dissonance is likely to increase (1) as the dollar values of purchases increase, (2) when the rejected alternatives have desirable features that the chosen alternatives do not provide, and (3) when the purchase decision has a major effect on the buyer. In other words, dissonance is more likely with high-involvement purchases than with those that require low involvement. The consumer may attempt to reduce dissonance by looking for advertisements or other information to support the chosen alternative or by seeking reassurance from acquaintances who are satisfied purchasers of the product. The individual may also avoid information that favors an unchosen alternative. Someone who buys a Toyota is likely to read Toyota advertisements and avoid Nissan and Honda ads.

Marketers can help buyers to reduce cognitive dissonance by providing information that supports the chosen alternative. Automobile dealers recognize the possibility of "buyer's remorse" and often follow up purchases with letters or telephone calls from dealership personnel offering personal attention to any customer problems. Advertisements that stress customer satisfaction also help to reduce cognitive dissonance.

A final method of dealing with cognitive dissonance is to change product options, thereby restoring the cognitive balance. The consumer may ultimately decide that one of the rejected alternatives would have been the best choice and vow to purchase it in the future.

Classifying Consumer Problem-Solving Processes

As mentioned earlier, the consumer decision processes for different products require varying amounts of problem-solving efforts. Marketers recognize three categories of problem-solving behavior: routinized response, limited problem solving, and extended problem solving.[49] The place of a particular purchase within this framework clearly influences the consumer decision process.

Routinized Response Behavior Consumers make many purchases routinely by choosing a preferred brand or one of a limited group of acceptable brands. This type of rapid consumer problem solving is referred to as *routinized response behavior.* A routine purchase of a regular brand of soft drink is an example. The consumer has already set evaluative criteria and identified available options. External search is limited in such cases, which characterize extremely low-involvement products.

Limited Problem Solving Consider the situation in which the consumer has previously set evaluative criteria for a particular kind of purchase but then encounters a new, unknown brand. The introduction of a new shampoo is an example of a limited problem-solving situation. The consumer knows the evaluative criteria for the product, but he or she has not applied them to assess the new brand. Such situations demand moderate amounts of time and effort for external searches. Limited problem solving is affected by the number of evaluative criteria and brands, the extent of external search, and the process for determining preferences. Consumers making purchase decisions in this product category are likely to feel involvement in the middle of the range.

Extended Problem Solving Extended problem solving results when brands are difficult to categorize or evaluate. The first step is to compare one item with similar ones. The consumer needs to understand the product features before evaluating alternatives. Most extended problem-solving efforts involve lengthy external searches. High-involvement purchase decisions usually require extended problem solving.

ACHIEVEMENT CHECK SUMMARY

Reread the learning goals that follow, and consider the questions for each goal. Answering these questions will reinforce your grasp of the most important concepts in the chapter and allow you to check how well you have achieved these learning goals. Where a blank appears before a question, answer with *T* or *F*; for multiple-choice questions, circle the letter of the correct answer.

Objective 8.1: Differentiate between buyer behavior and consumer behavior.

1. ____ Buyer behavior is the process by which consumers and business buyers make purchase decisions.

2. ____ The process by which the ultimate buyers of a product make a purchase decision is called *consumer behavior.*

Objective 8.2: Explain how marketers classify behavioral influences on consumer decisions.

1. ____ Kurt Lewin's model of human behavior states that behavior is influenced by (a) personal influences; (b) social influences; (c) both personal and social influences.

2. ____ Consumer behavior differs substantially from Lewin's model of human behavior.

Objective 8.3: Identify the interpersonal determinants of consumer behavior.

1. ___ The interpersonal determinants of consumer behavior are cultural influences, social influences, and family influences.
2. ___ Cultural values never change.
3. ___ African-Americans, Hispanics, and Asian-Americans are subcultures with similar consumer profiles.
4. ___ The values, attitudes, and behavior that a group deems appropriate for its members are called (a) group roles; (b) group norms; (c) group determinants.

Objective 8.4: Identify the personal determinants of consumer behavior.

1. ___ An individual's needs and motives, perceptions, attitudes, learning, and self-concept all affect his or her consumer behavior.
2. ___ A. H. Maslow theorized that (a) needs can be categorized in a hierarchy of importance; (b) consumer behavior is influenced by a number of factors; (c) consumers are not motivated by external influences.
3. ___ By including humorous messages, advertising can effectively break through consumers' perceptual screens.
4. ___ A customer who is dissatisfied with a product says he'll never use it again. This is an example of (a) perceptual screening; (b) learning; (c) need fulfillment.

Objective 8.5: Outline the steps in the consumer decision process.

1. ___ Buying chewing gum is an example of a high-involvement purchase.
2. ___ Recognizing a need is the first phase of the consumer decision process.
3. ___ Marketers try to influence consumers during the search phase by (a) helping them identify needs; (b) providing persuasive information; (c) helping to arrange financing.
4. ___ Cognitive dissonance is likely to increase (a) when the cost of a purchase rises; (b) when the purchase requires high involvement; (c) when the consumer sees other products with better features; (d) all of the above.

Objective 8.6: Differentiate among routinized response behavior, limited problem solving, and extended problem solving.

1. ___ Buying your regular toothpaste is a routinized response.
2. ___ Deciding to try a new brand of breakfast cereal most likely involves (a) routinized response behavior; (b) limited problem solving; (c) extended problem solving.
3 ___ Buying a new car usually requires extended problem solving.

Students: See the solutions section located on page S-2 to check your responses to the Achievement Check Summary.

Key Terms

buyer behavior
consumer behavior
culture
subculture
norms
status
role
Asch phenomenon
reference group
opinion leader
need
motive
perception
perceptual screen
subliminal perception
attitude
learning
drive
cue
reinforcement
self-concept
evoked set
evaluative criteria
cognitive dissonance

Review Questions

1. What are the primary determinants of consumer behavior? What subclassifications further characterize these determinants?
2. What is culture? How does it affect buying patterns?
3. Identify the subcultures that are most important to marketers in the United States today. Describe the unique consumer behavior characteristics of each subculture.
4. Explain the social influences on consumer behavior. Examine the specific roles of the Asch phenomenon, reference groups, social class, and opinion leaders.
5. For which of the following products is reference-group influence likely to have strong effect on consumer behavior?
   a. Sharp's nonalcoholic brew
   b. Rollerblade in-line skates
   c. Pantene Pro-V shampoo
   d. Trek mountain bikes
   e. Lady Fitness health clubs
   f. Nicotrol stop-smoking patches
6. Outline Maslow's hierarchy of needs. Cite examples of needs at each level.
7. Explain the concept of perception. Detail the effects of perceptual screens, selective perception, and subliminal perception in your explanation.
8. How do attitudes influence consumer behavior? How can marketers change negative attitudes toward a product?
9. Differentiate among the four components of the self-concept: ideal self, looking-glass self, self-image, and real self. Which is the most important to marketers?
10. List the steps in the consumer decision process. Detail your application of this process in a recent purchase.

Discussion Questions

1. U.S. marketers doing business in Spain are sometimes shocked when they are invited to dinner at 10:30 or 11:00 p.m. However, most Spanish restaurants do not open until 9:00 p.m. Furthermore, many businesses are closed for a couple of hours in the afternoon, but they stay open later than comparable U.S. establishments. Relate this situation to the material in Chapter 8.

2. Consider the following advertising line: "New Contadina Light and Cholesterol Free. More to Love. Less to Live With." Does this advertising copy suggest an emerging American core value?
3. Poll your friends about subliminal perception. How many believe that marketers can control consumers at a subconscious level? Report the results of this survey to your marketing class.
4. Many consumers are switching from traditional soft drinks to alternative beverages like Snapple, Arizona Iced Tea, Koala, and Evian Natural Spring Water. What attitude is reflected in this trend? How are soft-drink bottlers trying to counter this trend?
5. Video rentals include previews of movies not yet shown in theaters. How does this information relate to the chapter's discussion of learning theory?

'netWork

1. Has the development of the Internet defined a new subculture of consumers? Who are they? Describe their characteristics.
   a. What values do they share? Do their values vary from site to site and forum to forum?
   b. How do they differ from the larger population?
   c. How should companies market to this new subculture (or set of new subcultures)? Will promotional messages annoy users in noncommerical forums?
2. Assume that you are shopping for a new car. What sources of information can you find on the Net? Find input from both product manufacturers and consumer interest groups. How would you use this information?
3. The World Wide Web offers various sources of information about consumers. Browse around the site at

   http://www.marketingtools.com/

   How can marketers benefit from information like this?

VIDEO CASE 8

BEATING BALDNESS

How do you feel about baldness? Do you emphasize acceptance, based on a belief that a person's character determines what's important, not his outward appearance? Do you perceive bald people as somehow different from full-haired people? Does your attitude about baldness differ between men and women? What if you started losing *your* hair? Would your self-concept change?

Pharmacia and Upjohn Inc., a worldwide pharmaceuticals and health-products company, needed answers to questions like these as it designed a marketing strategy to introduce Rogaine, a prescription drug intended to restore hair growth. Originally developed as a treatment for hypertension, clinical tests revealed that Rogaine encouraged moderate hair growth on some balding male volunteers.

Pharmacia and Upjohn applied to the U.S. Food and Drug Administration (FDA) for approval to market Rogaine as a hair-growth product in the United States. The company also began selling it as Regaine in Europe.

Consumer psychologist Dr. Gar Roper conducted research to uncover men's feelings and reactions about the prospect of hair loss and to learn what would motivate them to contact their doctors to obtain prescriptions for Rogaine. From in-depth personal interviews, Dr. Roper learned that hair loss gave men a general feeling of diminishing confidence and strength. He also learned that men deal with two signals concerning society's acceptance of male baldness.

On one hand, the research found a growing public acceptance of baldness. Bald-Headed Men of America had attracted 20,000 members, and the organization seemed likely to continue to grow. Says founder John Capps III, "Baldness is a matter of mind over matter—if you don't mind, it doesn't matter." On the other hand, society seems to pay close attention to a person's appearance. In a study analyzing consumers' reactions to the balding process, a social psychologist showed pictures of six men in various stages of hair loss to 204 male and female undergraduate students. Study results indicated a tendency among the average undergraduate female, age 21, to shy away from the balding men. The psychologist concluded that people form differing views of balding men.

Some of those men agree. Comments one, "I believe that a person looks better with a full head of hair." He wears a hairpiece that he glues onto his scalp with a special adhesive. Another hair loss sufferer spent $30,000 on eight hair transplant treatments. He says, "It was important for my own sense of well-being, as well as for professional reasons. I feel better about myself."

Rogaine's marketing team used such insights to guide development of advertising that would effectively reach the consumer while staying within the FDA's strict regulatory guidelines. Initial marketing efforts targeted at doctors, nurses, and pharmacists sought to introduce them to Rogaine. Advertising targeted at consumers followed, with the objective of informing consumers that those concerned about hair loss could contact a physician who could prescribe the drug. The ads also included a toll-free phone number. FDA restrictions prohibited Pharmacia and Upjohn from mentioning the name *Rogaine* in the ads. This soft-sell approach established good consumer awareness, but it produced disappointing results, perhaps because most men needed a stronger inducement to get them to a doctor's office.

Rogaine marketers decided to adopt a more aggressive marketing strategy, recognizing the need for a more direct appeal to consumers. With FDA approval, they included the Rogaine name in commercials and urged men to ask their physicians to prescribe it. They developed a video that featured doctors giving technical information; the video also showed men who tried Rogaine with varying degrees of success. Pharmacia and Upjohn created a Dermatology Division to focus on relationship marketing through coordinated ads and public relations messages. The company also became involved in event marketing to build its database, followed by direct marketing and telemarketing.

Pharmacia and Upjohn also experimented with rebates. A patient could choose between a certificate worth $10 toward a first bottle of Rogaine or $20 for sending in the box tops from the first four emptied bottles. Rogaine marketers began targeting hair stylists and barbers by offering "handling fees" to shops that displayed Rogaine. Through these programs, Rogaine's marketing team achieved impressive results in reaching male consumers.

Next, the team turned to a different consumer segment: women. An estimated 20 million American women suffer from hair loss, often due to chemotherapy treatments or to *alopecia areata,* an immune system disorder. In conducting personal interviews with women, Dr. Roper learned that they feel compelling to do something about baldness, because bald women simply cannot manage in society as men can. Women also wanted more information about hair loss than did men. Ads targeting women included a toll-free phone number and the offer of a free information kit. Pharmacia and Upjohn developed a 30-minute infomercial as an effective way to reach women. Jeff Palmer, a Pharmacia and Upjohn public relations specialist, says, "We could give them more information in this format than we could in a 60-second commercial."

Pharmacia & Upjohn has received FDA approval to sell Rogaine over the counter. This change will bring new challenges to Rogaine marketers as they work to apply consumer analysis and promote their innovative product.

Questions

1. What core values might motivate a consumer to try Rogaine?
2. How does the self-concept theory relate to a consumer's decision to purchase Rogaine?
3. How did Rogaine marketers move consumers through the steps in the consumer decision process?
4. A Rogaine Web page **http://www.rogaineonline.com/** offers information on the product's use by men and women. (The page features an interesting and very efficient site map.) Rogaine Online offers a "Users Only Area" as well as testimonials from Rogaine users. Why does Pharmacia and Upjohn offer this service? Who would be likely to use it? How does a consumer access this service? Does it help to attract new Rogaine users?

Sources: Telephone interview with Upjohn Consumer Affairs, May 16, 1997; Michael Wilke, "Pharmacia Prescribes Big Role for OTC Veteran," *Advertising Age,* October 7, 1996, p. 40; and "Rogaine Opens New Category for Infomercials: Pharmaceuticals," *Advertising Age,* March 11, 1996, p. 10A.

CHAPTER 9

BUSINESS-TO-BUSINESS MARKETING

Industry.net
Praxair Home Page
PRAXAIR
AMP
WELLS FARGO
MONDEX
USA

Chapter Objectives

1. List and define the components of the business market.
2. Describe the major approaches to segmenting business-to-business markets.
3. Identify the major characteristics of the business market and its demand.
4. Describe the major influences on business buying behavior.
5. Outline the steps in the organizational buying process.
6. Classify organizational buying situations.
7. Explain the buying center concept.
8. Discuss the challenges of marketing to government, institutional, and international buyers.
9. Summarize key differences between consumer and business-to-business marketing.

Business-to-Business Matchmaking Comes to the Net

Most businesses probably view the Internet as a matchmaking service. After investing thousands of dollars to create a World Wide Web site, a company hopes retail customers will stop by to see what it's selling. But this scenario hardly tells the whole story. Many companies do not yet realize that the Internet can also be a valuable resource to foster business-to-business relationships. This trend is already affecting the jewelry trade.

Through a single home page, Polygon Network Inc. in Dillon, Colorado, has brought together diverse participants in the gem industry. In fact, Polygon serves everyone but the buying public. This electronic intermediary links jewelry manufacturers, independent and chain store jewelers, trade associations, diamond and gem wholesalers, appraising labs, trade publications, and others.

After accessing Polygon's home page with a password, people in the industry can see images of loose diamonds, bangles, and baguettes that others offer for sale. They can read about jewelry store robberies, tap into gem databases, check with labs on stone quality, and monitor industry news. Members also can leave private or public messages for each other.

Where industry does business
Industry.net
I.net News Center
Events & Discussions
Search for Products
Tools & Resources
Societies & Associations
BECOME A MEMBER
Engineering Specialties
Consulting
Control Products
Electronic Components
Electronic Manufacturing
Engineering Software
Industrial Computers
Maintenance, Repair, Operations, & Production
Manufacturing Systems
Mechanical Manufacturing
Motion
Networks
PCs & Workstations
PLCs
March 5, 1997
Boeing upbeat on aircraft orders
The aerospace giant predicts airlines will buy more than 16,000 new jets worth $1.1 trillion over the next two decades. The biggest growth is expected in Asia.
Machine maker shifts into overdrive for Toyota
Vehicle production boosted at Toyota's
381,445
385,657
500,000*
projected
Machine-tool maker Cincinnati Milacron has teamed up with Toyota to develop a plastic injection molding machine that can churn out a bumper in just over a minute.

These changes in gem marketing do not describe an isolated case. An entire industry has materialized to help aspiring cyberplayers link up with other businesses—from marketing consultants to bankers.

The awesome rise of electronic commerce should not obscure its even stronger potential for future growth. Forrester Research, an industry consulting group, has predicted that electronically transacted Internet business would hit $7 billion by 2000.

While it is natural to think that all this revenue will be generated by computer-savvy consumers, it's not the case by a long shot. Business-to-business activity will also play a major role on the Net. With this probability in mind, giants like AT&T, Dun & Bradstreet, and Digital Equipment, as well as nimble computer software start-ups, are working to facilitate electronic commercial transactions. This assistance helps companies without technical know-how to find their own solutions.

For example, Dun & Bradstreet, AT&T, Digital Equipment, and SHL Systemhouse have combined their efforts to sponsor International Business Exchange (IBEX). This clearinghouse gives businesses from all over the world a place to list goods to buy or sell. The negotiation process is anonymous,

and if the participants wish, the system helps with credit checks, financing arrangements, and customs paperwork.

One of the biggest players in this field just got bigger when AT&T's New Media Services unit joined forces with Industry.net, a major matchmaker in business-to-business commerce. Industry.net has always pursued a straightforward strategy: It provides access for members to a wide variety of information they need to make day-to-day buying decisions. Also, it offers its selling clients—primarily manufacturers, distributors, and service providers—the opportunity to market their products to buying members over the Internet through an electronic catalog.

Vendors typically pay $6,000 to $20,000 a year to maintain an electronic storefront through Industry.net. This commercial community encompasses about 200,000 buyers from 36,000 corporations located around the world with $185 billion in annual combined purchasing power. By merging with New Media Services, Industry.net aims to create the World Wide Web's biggest business-to-business marketplace.

http://www.polygon.net/
http://www.industry.net/

"The rules are still being written for business on the Web," notes Jim Manzi, the former Lotus Corp. executive who is Industry.net's chairman and chief executive officer. "In merging with the impressive talent pool of New Media Services, we are forming the foundation for a business that can capture this."

Industry.net's value to customers has increased further with its alliance with PNC Bank Corp. The bank will offer online payment and fund transfer services to Industry.net customers who want to buy and sell through the network. In the past, customers had to go offline to complete business transactions.

The biggest challenge for Industry.net, say analysts such as Barbara Reilly of the Gartner Group Inc. in Stamford, Connecticut, is convincing companies of the "tremendous potential for reinventing the buying and selling process."[1]

CHAPTER OVERVIEW

Although an average person sees more evidence of the consumer market, the business-to-business marketplace is, in fact, significantly larger than sales to ultimate consumers. U.S. companies spend 55 percent of each dollar in revenue buying goods and services.[2] They pay more than $300 billion each year for office and maintenance supplies alone! General Motors spends $70 billion a year through one of the largest purchasing operations in the world. Whether conducted through face-to-face transactions or via telephone, facsimile machines, or electronic communications media like the Internet, organizations must deal with complex purchasing decisions, buying situations that range from local to global exchanges, and differences between multiple decision makers when they purchase products.

Chapter 8 discussed how attitudes, perceptions, family and social influences, and other factors affect consumer buying behavior. This chapter will examine the somewhat different set of determinants affecting sales of goods and services to other organizations.

Some firms focus entirely on business markets. Hoechst sells chemicals to manufacturers, who use them in a variety of products. Advanced Micro Devices, Inc. makes flash memory chips for the cellular phone and Internet-provider markets. Manpower Inc. provides temporary personnel services to firms that need extra workers. Computer Associates, Oracle, and Sybase are software vendors specializing in corporate business applications.

Other firms sell to both consumer and organizational markets. Netscape, best-known for selling its Navigator Web browser to consumers, actually gets about 80 percent of its revenues from corporate customers. It offers a complete line of sophisticated networking software for companies like 3M and Chrysler. Similarly, Eastman Kodak sells film to consumers, and it also sells photofinishing paper, chemicals, and services to wholesale photofinishing companies. The ads in Figure 9.1 illustrate the ways in which Oscar Mayer Foods markets its products both to businesses such as restaurants, through its food-service division, and to consumers.

This chapter will discuss buying behavior in the business market, also known as the *organizational market.* **Business-to-business marketing** deals with organizational purchases of goods and services to support production of other goods and services or daily company operations or for resale.

Figure 9.1 Marketing to Both Business and Consumer Markets

Give
Your
Business
More
SELLING POWER
With
America's #1
Hot Dog Brand.
Oscar Mayer
Oscar Mayer Foodservice
Serving up Solutions
1-800-344-1819
For information circle number 12

INTRODUCING Oscar Mayer FREE
NO FAT
Be The First Kid On Your Block To Have One.
Hey, now you can eat what you love, and still be good. Because Oscar Mayer FREE hot dogs, bologna, turkey breast and chicken have no fat, and the taste that's positively Oscar Mayer.
MANUFACTURER'S COUPON
50¢
SAVE 50¢
on ONE package of any OSCAR MAYER FREE hot dogs, bologna, turkey breast or chicken cold cuts.
50¢
©1995 Oscar Mayer Foods Corporation

MARKETING HALL OF SHAME

Phone Fiasco

Businesspeople seldom think about their telephone area codes. When an area code changes, however, the adjustment can be an irritating experience for businesses and customers alike. Firms must reprint stationery and business cards, and customers must adjust to new telephone numbers. Now, though, thanks to a dramatic difference in new area codes, businesses face even tougher challenges, as well as potential loss of revenues.

Southern Alabama was one of the first regions of the country to receive an area code that did not contain 0 or 1 as the middle number. On the surface, this might not seem like a cause of major headaches, but it quickly became one. "We're being thrown to the wolves," says Ben Hargett, president of DeVan Inspection Co., which inspects cargo in Mobile. So many customers can't reach his new 334 number that Hargett considered moving his firm.

The same is true for businesses in western Washington state, which now has 360 as its area code. Swiss Hike Specialty Travel, an organizer of hiking tours in the Alps, discovered that the network of European hotels and other businesses through which the firm arranged its tours could no longer get through. European computerized phone systems could not handle these new codes, so hotels could not respond to faxes to book or confirm reservations. Potential customers also had difficulty calling the company. "We don't know how many people couldn't reach us, but sales are way down," said owner Larry Garrett.

The new area codes created critical problems for business-to-business transactions because many companies operate their own telephone switching systems, commonly referred to as PBXs or private branch exchanges. PBX systems often do not recognize any area codes without a middle number of 0 or 1. (This problem does not affect residential customers.) Many PBX owners neglected to get their equipment reprogrammed to handle the new codes.

Businesses operating in regions like southern Alabama, eastern Tennessee, western Washington, and northern and western Colorado were the first to receive the new area codes. Businesses in these areas and others complain that both domestic and overseas callers get fast busy signals, a faint static noise followed by disconnects, or recorded messages that the calls could not be completed as dialed. Companies in those areas had to find alternative ways to market themselves and to spread the word that they were still in business. Some turned to direct mail, for example.

"We feel like guinea pigs," complained Lee Schissler, president and chief executive officer of the

NATURE OF THE BUSINESS MARKET

Like final consumers, an organization purchases products to fill needs. However, its primary need—meeting the demands of its own customers—is similar from organization to organization. A manufacturer buys raw materials to create the company's product, while a wholesaler or retailer buys products to resell. Companies also buy services from other businesses. Institutional purchasers like government agencies and nonprofit organizations buy things to meet the needs of their constituents.

Business buying decisions, while handled by individuals, occur in the context of formal organizations. Environmental, organizational, and interpersonal factors are among the many influences in business-to-business markets. Budget, cost, and profit considerations all play parts in business buying decisions. In addition, the organizational buying process typically involves complex interactions among many people and among individual and organizational goals.[3] Later sections of the chapter will return to these topics.

The business-to-business market is a diverse one. Transactions can range from orders as small as a package of paper clips or copier toner for a home-based business to deals as large as thousands of parts for an automobile manufacturer or massive turbine generators for an electric power plant. Businesses are also big purchasers of services, such as telecommunications, computer consulting, and transportation services. Four major categories define the business market: (1) the commercial market, (2) trade industries, (3) government organizations, and (4) institutions.

Components of the Business Market

The **commercial market** is the largest segment of the business market. It includes all individuals and firms that ac-

Mobile Convention and Visitors Corp. He observed that potential customers in other regions were not overhauling their PBX systems. Those who can't get through when they call will call other cities and book their conventions elsewhere. "Businesses aren't motivated to spend money to call south Alabama."

Clint Morgan, a lawyer who represents businesses suing US West Inc., the regional phone company for western Washington, agrees. "We think the impact on the economy of western Washington is going to be horrendous," Morgan said. "We're going to have our own little Cuba here where nobody can get ahold of us."

Businesses can blame their woes on the phenomenal popularity of fax machines, computer modems, pagers, and cellular phones, as well as the normal growth of standard phone service. The demands for new phone numbers eventually exceeded the number available within the 160 possible area codes with the middle number 0 or 1. Using 2 through 9 as middle numbers, however, creates another 640 potential area codes.

For their part, telephone companies say they have been telling businesses for years about the upcoming changes, but many customers have ignored the advice. Despite warnings dating back to 1992, AT&T Global Business Communications Systems, a leading PBX manufacturer, says only half of its customers have upgraded their systems.

To prevent disrupting their businesses, some companies set up toll-free 800 or 888 numbers to avoid new area codes. Still other businesses are urging phone companies to implement "overlaying" phone systems for areas in danger of running out of numbers. For example, rather than dividing the portion of Los Angeles now served by the 310 area code, the phone company could assign the new 562 area code only to new users, leaving existing phone numbers unchanged. But an overlay has its own drawbacks. Many customers will resist dialing 11-digit numbers, traditionally associated with long-distance calls, just to talk to someone in the same city with a new phone number.

QUESTIONS FOR CRITICAL THINKING

1. **Does the overlay system create a fairer solution than dividing area code regions? Explain.**
2. **Describe several marketing solutions by which businesses could overcome this telephone dilemma.**

Sources: Henry Goldblatt, "How Area Codes Got So Confusing," *Fortune*, February 3, 1997, pp. 39, 42; Curt Harler, "It's Time to Reconsider Area Code Overlays," *Communications News*, August 1996, p.4; "How to Deal with the Area Code Crunch," *Telecommunications*, February 1996, p. 49; Chad Rubel, "New Area Codes a Headache for Some Business Marketers," *Marketing News*, May 8, 1995, p. 19; "New Area Codes Spell Business Headaches," *Investor's Business Daily*, April 11, 1995, downloaded from America Online, October 13, 1996; Janine Latus Musick, "Preventing Crossed Wires," *Nation's Business*, December 1995, p. 32.

quire goods and services to support, directly or indirectly, production of other goods and services. When Lufthansa buys aircraft built by the European consortium Airbus Industrie, when Sara Lee purchases wheat to mill into flour for an ingredient in its cakes, when a plant manager orders light bulbs and cleaning supplies for a factory—these transactions all take place in the commercial market. Some products aid in producing another good or service (the new airplane). Others are physically used up in the production of a good or service (the wheat). Still others contribute to the firm's day-to-day operations (the maintenance supplies). The commercial market includes manufacturers, farmers, and other members of resource-producing industries; construction contractors; and providers of such services as transportation, public utilities, financing, insurance, and real estate brokerage.

The second segment of the organizational market, **trade industries,** includes retailers and wholesalers that purchase goods for resale to others. Most of these resale

Marketing Dictionary

business-to-business marketing Organizational purchase of goods and services to support production of other goods and services or daily company operations or for resale.

commercial market Individuals and firms that acquire goods and services to support, directly or indirectly, production of other goods and services.

trade industry Retailers or wholesalers that purchase products for resale to others.

Wells Fargo now earns 10 percent of its profits from small-business loans, a segment virtually ignored by major banks, which remain wary of low margins. Terri Dial (right), executive vice president of Well Fargo's Business Banking Group, reengineered the loan application process for small businesses and equipped loan officers with laptops so they could approve loans immediately for customers like the owners of Dianda's Deli in San Francisco.

products, such as clothing, appliances, sports equipment, and automobile parts, are finished goods that the buyers market to final consumers in their market areas. In other cases, the buyers may complete some processing or repackaging before reselling the products. For example, retail meat markets may carry out bulk purchases of sides of beef and then cut individual pieces for their customers. Lumber dealers and carpet retailers may purchase in bulk and then provide quantities and sizes to meet customers' specifications. In addition to resale products, trade industries buy computers, display shelves, and other products they need to operate their businesses. These goods (as well as maintenance items) and specialized services such as marketing research, accounting, and management consulting all represent organizational purchases. Later chapters provide detailed discussions of the trade industries. Wholesaling is covered in Chapter 14 and retailing in Chapter 15.

Government organizations represent the third category of the business market. These include domestic units of government—federal, state, and local—as well as foreign governments. This important market segment purchases a wide variety of products, ranging from highways to social services. The primary motivation of government purchasing is to provide some form of public benefit, such as national defense or pollution control.

Institutions, both public and private, are the fourth component of the business market. This category includes a wide range of organizations, such as hospitals, churches, nursing homes, colleges and universities, museums, and not-for-profit agencies. Some institutions—state universities, for instance—must rigidly follow standardized purchasing procedures, while others may employ less formal buying practices. Business-to-business marketers often benefit by setting up separate divisions to sell to institutional buyers.

Differences in Foreign Business Markets

Business markets in other countries may differ from those in the United States due to variations in government regulations and cultural practices. Some business products need modifications to succeed in foreign markets. In Australia, Japan, and Great Britain, for instance, motorists drive on the left side of the road. The electrical wiring of a European building differs from that in a building in the United States.

Business marketers must be willing to adapt to local customs and business practices when operating in foreign markets. Something as simple as the time of a meeting, methods of address for associates, or ink colors for documents can make a difference. In France and Germany, most meetings start after 10 A.M., so U.S. businesspeople should not plan breakfast meetings. In Germany, it's considered bad form to call a colleague, even someone you've known for a long time, by his or her first name until specifically invited to do so. Refusing tea is an insult to a Chinese businessperson—but it's important to wait until the host begins eating or drinking. Colors also have special meanings in China, so to avoid sending unintended messages, marketers should limit printed materials to black and white.[4]

SEGMENTING BUSINESS-TO-BUSINESS MARKETS

Like consumer markets, business-to-business markets include wide varieties of customers. By applying market segmentation concepts to groups of business customers, a firm's marketers can develop a strategy that best suits a particular segment's needs. The overall process of segmenting business markets resembles consumer market segmentation, but it divides markets based on different criteria, usually organizational characteristics and product applications. Among the major ways to segment business markets are demographics (size, geographic location), customer type, end-use application, and purchasing situation.[5]

Demographic Segmentation

As with consumer markets, demographic characteristics define useful segmentation criteria for business markets. For example, firms can be grouped by *size,* based on sales revenues or number of employees. Marketers may develop one strategy to reach small firms and another for Fortune 1,000 corporations with complex purchasing procedures. Recently, small businesses—especially companies with under 100 employees—have caught the eye of business-to-business marketers. This fast-growing segment of about 20 million firms offers tremendous potential. Many former corporate executives are starting their own companies. These new entrepreneurs spend money more willingly on technology and equipment than other entrepreneurs. As a result, IBM's fastest-growing market segment is companies of 50 employees or less, who need sophisticated technology to compete against bigger firms.[6]

Service companies, too, may segment their organizational customers by size. Wells Fargo Bank adapted credit scoring, a computerized system to evaluate individual consumer loans, for small-business customers. It then used direct mail to offer lines of credit to small businesses that "prequalified" based on the bank's lending criteria. Customers like Janet Fletcher, owner of B&W Auto Salvage in Dallas, praise the new loan system. Not only does it allow them to avoid filling out lengthy applications—she had to submit only a one-page form to Wells—but approval comes quickly, as well. Fletcher was willing to pay a higher interest rate than she might have found elsewhere for the convenience and flexibility of the loan arrangement. Other small businesses agree; in a recent year, Wells reported a 61 percent increase in earnings from small-business loans.[7]

http://www.wellsfargo.com/

Segmentation by Customer Type

Another useful segmentation approach groups prospects by *type of customer.* Marketers can apply this principle in several ways. They can group customers by broad categories—manufacturer, service provider, government agency, nonprofit organization, wholesaler, or retailer—and also by industry. These groups may be further divided using other segmentation approaches discussed in this section. *SIC codes* provide a useful tool for segmenting business-to-business markets by customer type.

Customer-based segmentation is a related approach often used in the business-to-business marketplace. Organizational buyers tend to detail much more precise product specifications than ultimate consumers do. As a result, business products often fit narrow market segments as compared to consumer products. This fact leads some firms to design business goods and services to meet specific buyer requirements, creating a form of market segmentation.

Standard Industrial Classification (SIC) Codes The federal government's **Standard Industrial Classification (SIC)** system greatly simplifies the process of focusing on a particular type of business customer. This numbering system subdivides the business marketplace into detailed market segments. In this way, it standardizes efforts to collect and report information on U.S. industrial activity.

The SIC codes divide firms into the following broad

Marketing Dictionary

customer-based segmentation Dividing a business-to-business market into homogeneous groups based on buyers' product specifications.

Standard Industrial Classification (SIC) U.S. government classification system that subdivides the business marketplace into detailed market segments.

Figure 9.2 **Standard Industrial Classification (SIC) System**

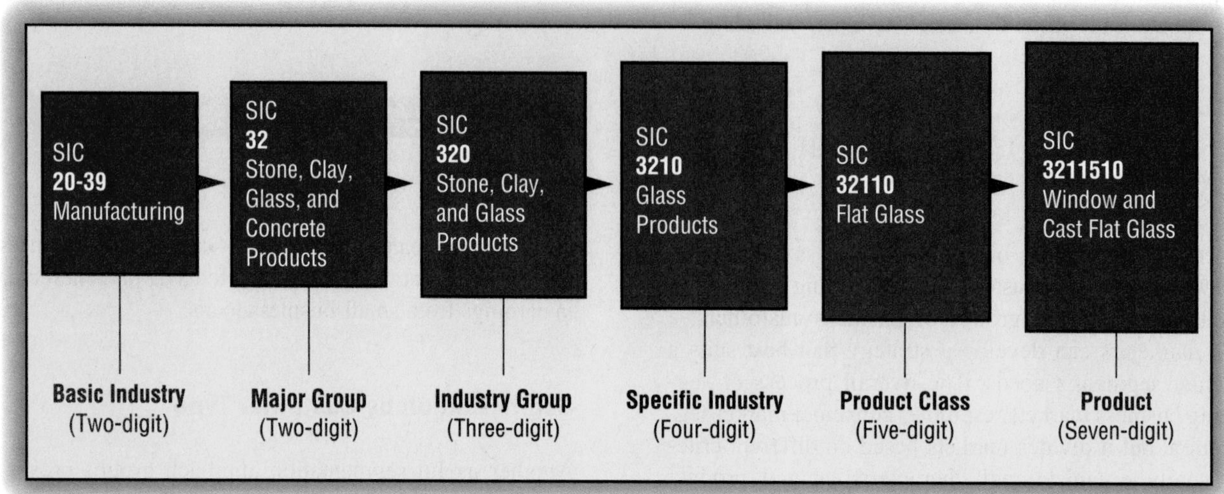
SIC
20-39
Manufacturing
SIC
32
Stone, Clay, Glass, and Concrete Products
SIC
320
Stone, Clay, and Glass Products
SIC
3210
Glass Products
SIC
32110
Flat Glass
SIC
3211510
Window and Cast Flat Glass
Basic Industry
(Two-digit)
Major Group
(Two-digit)
Industry Group
(Three-digit)
Specific Industry
(Four-digit)
Product Class
(Five-digit)
Product
(Seven-digit)

industry divisions: agriculture, forestry, fishing; mining, construction; manufacturing; transportation, communication, electric, gas, and sanitary services; wholesale trade; retail trade; finance, insurance, and real estate services; public administration; and nonclassifiable establishments. The scheme assigns each major category within these classifications its own two-digit number. Three-digit and four-digit numbers subdivide each industry into smaller segments. For example, a major group such as food and kindred goods is assigned SIC 20. A specific industry group such as meats has its own three-digit number, SIC 201. The next category, the specific industry, is indicated by the fourth digit. Poultry slaughtering and processing, for example, is SIC 2015. Government operations and not-for-profit organizations also have SIC numbers. For example, hospitals are SIC 8062.

In its Census of Manufactures report, the Bureau of the Census assembles data at two additional levels: five-digit product classes and seven-digit product or commodity categories. Figure 9.2 gives the seven-digit breakdown for window glass.

Using SIC Codes Most publications on organizational markets label data according to the SIC system. The detailed information for each market segment provides marketers with a comprehensive description of the activities of potential customers broken down by both geographic area and specific industry.

SIC codes provide a useful tool for segmenting markets and identifying new customers. Since each SIC code identifies a relatively homogeneous group of firms, marketers can usually assume that all companies listed within a category share similar business requirements and concerns. For instance, SIC category 3715 includes firms that manufacture truck trailers. Most, if not all, of these firms need to purchase similar raw materials, such as steel wheels, sheet metal, oil, plastic and electric parts, and tires. Suppliers of these components can target potential customers by tracking companies in the 3715 category.

However, marketers must recognize certain limitations of the SIC system. It assigns an individual code to each physical location (a plant or office, for example). A major corporation with many facilities will have multiple SIC codes, depending on the primary products made at specific locations. The four-digit code for the whole organization is based on the product group with the greatest value. Relying solely on SIC codes could give an erroneous picture of a company's operations.

Businesses use SIC code data for more than segmentation. These codes also help them to estimate demand and forecast sales. A supplier of steel wheels, for instance, might analyze present customers and determine that SIC 3715 customers tend to spend about eight cents per dollar of their final shipments on wheels. By obtaining information on the total shipments of SIC 3715 firms, the supplier could develop a market estimate of total wheel sales to companies in this category.[8]

Segmentation by End-Use Application

A third basis for segmentation, **end-use application segmentation,** focuses on the precise way in which a business purchaser will use a product. For example, a printing equipment manufacturer may serve markets ranging from a local utility to a bicycle manufacturer to the U.S. Department of Defense. Each end use of the equipment may dictate unique specifications for performance, design, and price. Praxair, a supplier of industrial gases, might segment its markets according to user: Steel and glass manufacturers might buy hydrogen and oxygen, while food and beverage manufacturers need carbon dioxide. Praxair also sells krypton, a rare gas, to companies that produce lasers, lighting, and thermal windows. Many small and medium-sized companies also segment markets according to end-use application. Instead of competing in markets dominated by large firms, they concentrate on specific end-use market segments.

http://www.praxair.com/

Segmentation by Purchasing Situation

Yet another approach to dividing business markets centers on *purchasing situation.* As a later section of the chapter explains, organizations institute purchasing procedures more complicated than those of consumers. Companies also structure their purchasing functions in specific ways, and for some business marketers, this may be the best way to segment the market. Some companies designate centralized purchasing departments to serve the entire firm, while others allow each unit to handle its own purchasing. A supplier may deal with one purchasing agent or decision makers at several levels. Each of these structures results in different buying behavior. Sellers who understand this fact can separate markets by needs and marketing requirements and respond with appropriate strategies.[9]

Another way to segment customers is by buying situation: Has the company bought the product before, or is this the customer's first order for the good or service? For example, IBM's Integrated Systems Solutions Corp. subsidiary would use a different marketing approach to sell to Lucent Technologies, an existing customer of its computer support services, than to a potential new customer who is unfamiliar with its offering.

CHARACTERISTICS OF THE BUSINESS MARKET

Businesses that serve consumer markets and those that sell to other organizations must understand the needs of their customers. However, several characteristics distinguish the business market from the consumer market: (1) geographic concentration, (2) the sizes and numbers of buyers, (3) purchase decision procedures, and (4) buyer-seller relationships. The next few sections will consider how these traits influence business-to-business marketing.

Geographic Market Concentration

As noted in the previous section, the U.S. business market is more geographically concentrated than the consumer market. Manufacturing firms concentrate in certain regions of the country, making these areas prime targets for business marketers. For example, the Midwestern states that make up the East North Central region—Illinois, Ohio, Wisconsin, Indiana, and Michigan—lead the nation in industrial concentration, followed by the Middle Atlantic and the South Atlantic regions.

Certain industries decide to locate in particular areas to be near customers. Johnson Controls, which makes auto seats and interior trim, has plants in Michigan near major customers Ford and General Motors; plants in other states serve Honda and Toyota. Some types of manufacturing firms establish facilities near power sources. Many chemical plants are located near Niagara Falls. Other industries locate in areas with high concentrations of skilled labor, like the high-technology firms in California's Silicon Valley, or lower-paid labor, like the factories along the U.S.-Mexican border that employ Mexican workers.

By identifying geographical concentrations of customers, business marketers can effectively allocate resources. They may choose to locate sales offices and distribution centers in such areas to provide attentive service.

Sizes and Numbers of Buyers

In addition to geographic concentration, the business market features a limited numbers of buyers. Marketers can draw on a wealth of statistical information to estimate the sizes and characteristics of business markets. Table 9.1 presents a selection of data sources that can support research about domestic and international business markets. The federal government is the largest single source of such statistics. Every five years it conducts both a Census of Manufactures and a Census of Retailing and Wholesaling, which provide detailed information on business establishments, output, and employment. Specific industry studies are summarized in

Marketing Dictionary

end-use application segmentation Segmenting a business-to-business market based on how industrial purchasers will use the product.

Table 9.1 Selection of Data Sources for Business Market Analysis

Title of Publication	Type of Data	Application	Comments
FEDERAL GOVERNMENT			
Census of Manufactures, U.S. Dept. of Commerce (every five years)	General data by 4-, 5-, and 7-digit SIC code on value added, employees, number of establishments, shipments, and materials consumed.	Comprehensive analysis of market potential by area and for specific industries	Broadest array of business data, based on a census, may be dated
County Business Patterns, U.S. Dept. of Commerce (annual)	Statistics on number of establishments and employment by 4-digit SIC code for all U.S. counties	Estimate market potential and evaluate industry concentration by region	Provides effective estimates of potential if number of employees is correlated to industry demand
Standard Industrial Classification Manual, U.S. Bureau of the Budget (every five years)	Complete description of the SIC system, including all 4-digit industries	Evaluate possible industrial users based on products they produce	Lists each 4-digit SIC category and its primary products
U.S. Industrial Outlook, U.S. Dept. of Commerce (annually)	Overall view of over 200 4-digit SIC industries with past and future growth rates in shipments and employment	Projection of future market concentration and potential	Reasonably current data provides useful look at growth prospects in selected industries
Current Industrial Reports, U.S. Dept. of Commerce (monthly to annually)	Series of over 100 reports covering 5,000 products, usually based on 3-digit SIC codes	In-depth analysis of potential by specific industry	Very timely data, published four to eight weeks after collections
A Guide to Federal Data Sources on Manufacturing, U.S. Dept. of Commerce (annually)	Describes nature and sources of all federal government data related to manufacturing	Quick guide to locate appropriate government data	Valuable source document for understanding government statistics
STATE AND LOCAL GOVERNMENT			
State and local industrial directories (usually annually)	Type of data varies, but usually provides individual company data such as SIC code, sales, number of employees, products, and addresses	Defining specific potential customers by state and region	Provides data on firms of all sizes, particularly useful when markets are concentrated in a few states

U.S. Industrial Outlook, an annual government publication providing statistical data and discussing industry trends.

Many buyers in limited-buyer markets are large organizations. The international market for jet engines is dominated by three manufacturers: United Technology's Pratt & Whitney unit, General Electric, and Rolls-Royce. These firms sell engines to the U.S. firm Boeing and the European consortium, Airbus Industrie. These aircraft manufacturers compete for business from passenger airlines like American Airlines, British Airways, KLM, and Singapore Airlines, along with cargo carriers such as Federal Express and United Parcel Service.

Trade associations and business publications provide additional information on the business market. Private firms such as Dun & Bradstreet publish detailed reports on individual firms. This data serves as a useful starting point for analyzing a business market. Finding data in such a source requires an understanding of the SIC system, however, since much of the available statistical information is identified by SIC codes.

Table 9.1 continued

Title of Publication	Type of Data	Application	Comments
TRADE ASSOCIATIONS			
National Machine Tool Builders Assn., Iron and Steel Institute, Rubber Mfrs. Assn.	Sales history of the industry with industrial, financial, and operating data	Evaluation of past and present growth potentials by industry	May provide useful industry data not contained in other sources; e.g., average age of equipment
TRADE PUBLICATIONS			
Sales & Marketing Management: "Special Data Supplement" (updated annually)	Number plants and shipments by SIC (country) code; country percentage of total U.S. shipments by SIC category	Ballpark estimate of market potential by state and country	Very timely source for quickly assessing potential by country and state
Iron Age: "Basic Marketing Data on Metal Working" (annually)	Census of metalworking industry, regional data on plants and employees	Quick estimate of potential for the metalworking industry	Useful for easy estimation of potential for this particular industry
Dun's Market Identifiers, Dun & Bradstreet, New York (continuously updated file)	Data for company SIC, address, locations, sales, and employees	Evaluation for potential sales by individual company	Timely information on specific firms can be obtained quickly
Standard & Poor's Industry Surveys' Basic Analysis, Standard & Poor's Corp., New York (weekly)	Financial and operating data on major industries and companies	In-depth financial analysis of specific companies	Timely, general data on major industries
INTERNATIONAL DATA SOURCES			
The Yearbook of Industrial Statistics, United Nations Statistical Office (annually)	Vol. 1: Basic country data and indicators showing global and regional trends in industrial activity Vol. 2: Statistics for industrial commodities and countries	Look for trends in worldwide industrial activity Review industry activity by area, estimate market potential	Largest compilation of international industrial data covering a ten-year period for each volume
The Yearbook of International Trade Statistics, U.N. Statistical Office (annually)	Quantity and value of exports and imports of various commodities over the previous several years	Estimate market potential for various products by country	Valuable for assessing trends in product and country imports and exports

The Purchase Decision Process

To market effectively to other organizations, businesses must understand the dynamics of the organizational purchase decision process. Suppliers who serve business-to-business markets must work with multiple buyers, especially when selling to larger customers. Decision makers at several levels may influence final orders, and the overall process is more formal and professional than the consumer purchasing process. Purchases typically require a longer time frame, because they involve more complex decisions. Suppliers must evaluate customer needs and develop proposals that meet technical requirements and specifications. Also, customers need time to analyze proposals from competing companies. Often, decisions require more than one round of bidding and negotiation, especially for complicated purchases.

Take the case of Federal Express, when it switched to an active procurement process for its computer hardware and software. In seeking a strategic supplier relationship worth millions of dollars to the chosen vendor, FedEx sent requests for proposals (RFPs) to 47 companies around the world. In return, the company received many unacceptable proposals that failed to properly address the RFP requirements. FedEx representatives spent many months visiting key vendors to find out just what they could, in fact, provide before the company even began negotiating with potential suppliers.[10]

Buyer-Seller Relationships

An especially important characteristic in business-to-business markets is the relationship between buyers and sellers. Such relationships are more intense than consumer relationships, and they require better communication among the organizations' personnel. Before DuPont hired Forum Corp. to manage its corporate training and development activities, the two companies had to discuss the types of training programs DuPont wanted, how Forum Corp. could meet those needs, and how the change would affect DuPont's in-house training employees.[11] This communication didn't stop once Forum Corp. began the assignment. To succeed, Forum Corp. had to interact continually with DuPont to ensure that its efforts satisfied the client.

As Chapter 1 explained, *relationship marketing* involves developing long-term, value-added customer relationships. A primary goal of business-to-business relationships is to provide advantages that no other seller can provide—for instance, lower price, quicker delivery, better quality and reliability, customized product features, more favorable financing terms. For the business marketer, this means expanding the company's external relationships to include suppliers, distributors, and other organizational partners.

Buyer-seller relationships vary for different types of purchases. At most, 10 percent of purchases should involve strategic relationships; another 25 to 30 percent should result from collaborative relationships, and the rest should be arm's-length transactions.[12] For example, a supplier that designs and manufactures a critical component would qualify as a strategic partner, while the company may maintain an arm's-length relationship with its vendor for office supplies.

Close cooperation, whether through informal contacts or under terms specified in contractual partnerships and strategic alliances, enables companies to meet buyers' needs for quality products and customer service, both during and after the purchase process. As the ad in Figure 9.3 explains, The Boeing Company involved employees from the world's top airlines in the design and development of its 777 aircraft. Asian airlines, for example, wanted the plane longer and wider than initially planned. Through close cooperation, Boeing ensured that the new plane met buyers' needs and induced airlines to purchase it. Customers include Japan's All Nippon Airways, Korean Air, Cathay Pacific Airways, Thai Airways International, Singapore Airlines, and Malaysia Airlines. Satisfying the needs of Asian airlines is important to Boeing, because the market is expected to account for 40 percent of world aircraft sales during the next decade.

This chapter includes examples of how buyer-seller relationships enhance business-to-business marketing. Chapter 10 will continue this discussion when it covers

Figure 9.3 The Importance of Establishing Close Buyer-Seller Relationships

No one flies alone.
Aviation is a team sport. For example, people from the world's top airlines worked with us to develop the new 777—some for nearly 10 years. Next, we built a $100 million testing lab, a factory that cost even more, and the world's largest private computer network so our design/production team could work together no matter where each member lived. Teamwork and investment pay off. Before the first 777 was delivered, 144 were on order for some of the world's leading airlines. All of which suggests that, working together, we can do almost anything.
BOEING

such important business-to-business topics as supply chain management, partnership relationships, co-marketing and co-branding, and linkages through the Internet, electronic data interchange (EDI), and vendor-managed inventory.

Evaluating International Business Markets

Business purchasing patterns differ from one country to the next. Researching these markets poses a particular problem for business marketers, since they often lack reliable secondary data for many overseas markets. Still, a variety of information sources cover international business markets. A few, such as Dun & Bradstreet's *Principal International Businesses* and Predicast's *F&S Index,* even classify data according to SIC codes. Table 9.1 lists several other sources of data on international business markets.

In addition to quantitative data such as the size of the potential market, companies must also carefully weigh qualitative features of the foreign market. As explained in Chapters 4 and 8, evaluation must cover cultural values, work styles, and the best ways to enter overseas markets. For example, a company may choose to set up a sales office in a particular location rather than a manufacturing facility if its analysis shows that the local labor supply lacks the right skills for factory work.

Briefly speaking

"Don't overlook the importance of worldwide thinking. A company that keeps its eye on Tom, Dick, and Harry is going to miss Pierre, Hans, and Yoshio."

Al Ries (1929-)
Chairman, Trout & Ries, Inc., advertising agency

In today's international marketplace, companies often practice **global sourcing,** contracting to purchase goods and services from suppliers worldwide. This practice can result in substantial cost savings. Federal Express estimates that it saved over 30 percent on the prices of computer hardware and software by soliciting bids worldwide. Elf Acquitaine, a French producer of oil, natural gas, and chemicals, designed its purchasing process to take advantages of country-to-country differences. If prices in Europe seem too high, the company turns to U.S. vendors.

However, global sourcing requires companies to adopt a new mind set; some must actually reorganize their operations. Customers with multiple multinational locations want an easy purchase process and few price differences due to labor costs, tariffs, taxes, and currency fluctuations. For example, software vendor Oracle Corp. eliminated 27 different price lists in favor of a standardized, worldwide pricing structure. Computer manufacturers like Digital Equipment Company and IBM offer global warranties and consolidated invoices.[13]

BUSINESS MARKET DEMAND

The previous section's discussion of business market characteristics demonstrated considerable differences between marketing techniques for consumer and business products. Demand characteristics also differ in these markets. In business markets, the major categories of demand include derived demand, volatile demand, joint demand, and demand created by inventory adjustments.

Derived Demand

The term **derived demand** refers to the linkage between consumer demand for a company's output and its purchases of business products such as machinery, components, supplies, and raw materials. For example, demand for semiconductor chips within a computer's central processing unit is derived from the demand for personal computers from both business and individual consumers. The early 1996 slowdown in sales of personal computers reduced the demand for chips from producers like Intel, Digital Equipment, and Motorola. When the market picked up, chip production rose, as well.[14] For another example, in 1996, full-service restaurants, cafeterias, delis, and fast-food operations purchased 11.4 billion packets of H. J. Heinz Company's single-serve condiments, jellies, sweeteners, syrups, and salad dressings, promoted in the ad in Figure 9.4. The growing global demand by food-service firms for the packets is driven by consumers' appetite for the convenience and pleasure of dining out.

Organizational buyers purchase two general categories of business products, capital items and expense items. Derived demand ultimately affects both. *Capital items* are long-lived business assets that must be depreciated over

Marketing Dictionary

global sourcing Contracting to purchase goods and services from suppliers worldwide.

derived demand Demand for a business product that results from demand for a consumer product of which it is a component.

Figure 9.4 Derived Demand

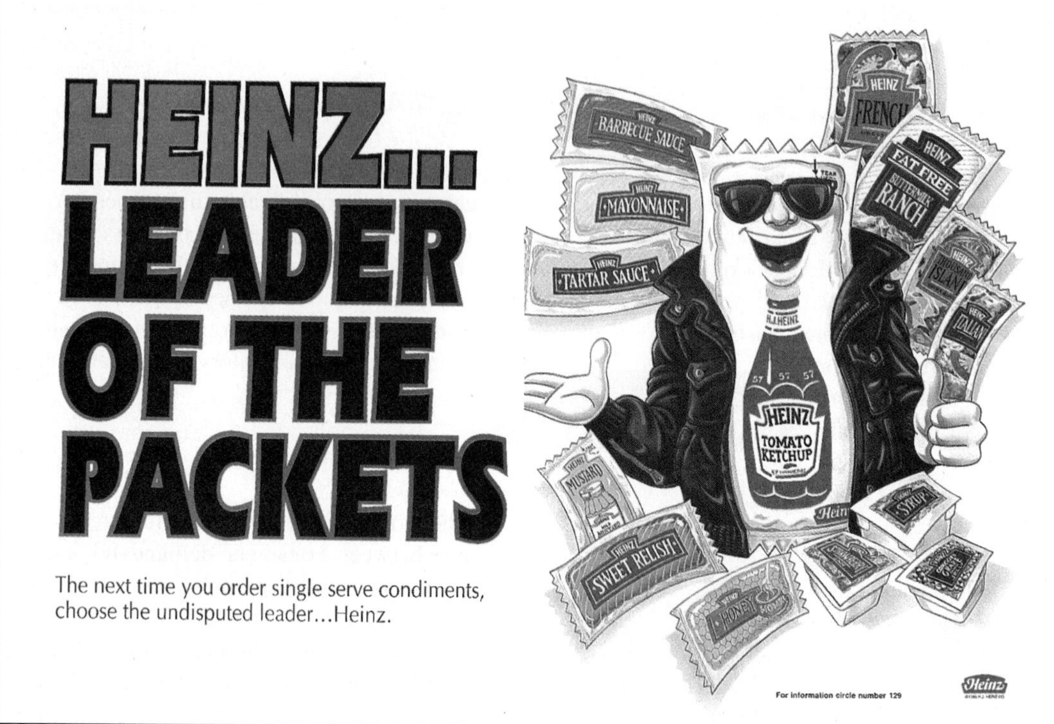
HEINZ...
LEADER
OF THE
PACKETS
The next time you order single serve condiments, choose the undisputed leader...Heinz.
BARBECUE SAUCE
MAYONNAISE
TARTAR SAUCE
FRENCH
FAT FREE
BUTTERMILK RANCH
ITALIAN
HEINZ
TOMATO KETCHUP
MUSTARD
SWEET RELISH
HONEY
SYRUP
For information circle number 129

time. (Depreciation is the accounting function of charging a portion of a capital item's cost as a deduction against the company's annual revenue for purposes ofdetermining its net income.) Examples of capital items include major installations such asnew plants, office buildings, and computer systems.

Expense items, in contrast, are inputs consumed by the production process within short time periods. Accounting procedures usually charge the cost of such products against income in the year of purchase. Examples of expense items include the supplies necessary to operate the business, ranging from paper clips to machine lubricants.

Briefly speaking

"I am like any other man. All I do is supply a demand."

Al Capone (1899–1947)
American gangster

Joint Demand

Another important influence on business market demand is **joint demand,** which results when the demand for one business product is related to the demand for another business product that is necessary for the use of the first item. For example, both coke and iron ore are required to make pig iron. If the coke supply falls, the drop in pig iron production will immediately affect the demand for iron ore.

Another example is the joint demand for electrical power and large turbine engines. If consumers decide to conserve power, demand for new power plants drops, as does the demand for components and replacement parts for turbines.

Volatile Demand

Derived demand creates immense volatility in business market demand. As an example, assume that gas stations derive demand for a certain type of gasoline pump from consumers' demand for a brand whose gallon volume has been growing at an annual rate of 5 percent. Now suppose that the demand for this gasoline brand slows to a 3 percent annual increase. While not a dramatic drop, this slowdown might convince the oil company to keep its current gasoline pumps and replace them only when market conditions improve. In this way, even modest shifts in consumer demand for gasoline would greatly affect the pump manufacturer. This disproportionate impact of changes in consumer demand on business market demand is called the *accelerator principle.*

Inventory Adjustments

Adjustments in inventory and inventory policies can also affect business demand. Assume that manufacturers in a particular industry consider a 60-day supply of raw materials to be the optimal inventory level. Now suppose that economic conditions or other factors induce these firms to increase their inventories to a 90-day supply. The change will bombard the raw-materials supplier with new orders.

Further, innovative *just-in-time (JIT)* inventory policies seek to boost efficiency by cutting inventories to absolute minimum levels and requiring vendors to deliver inputs as the production process needs them. Widespread JIT practices have produced a substantial impact on organizations' purchasing behavior. Firms that practice JIT tend to order from relatively few suppliers. In some cases, JIT may lead to **sole sourcing** for some inputs—that is, the practice of buying a firm's entire stock of a product from just one supplier.

The latest inventory trend, *JIT II,* leads suppliers to place representatives at the customer's facility to work as part of an integrated, on-site customer-supplier team. Suppliers plan and order in consultation with the customer. This streamlining of the inventory process improves control of the goods flow. The team can quickly solve any problems that develop, because all suppliers have personnel on site.[15]

JIT II is popular in the auto industry, where thousands of vendor employees report to work at auto manufacturers' offices and factories. They may even take over some of their customers' internal operations. DuPont and PPG Industries Inc. employees run paint lines at two GM plants.[16]

THE MAKE, BUY, OR LEASE DECISION

Before a company can decide what to buy, it should decide whether to buy at all. The first step in organizational buying requires purchasers to figure out the best way to acquire needed products. In fact, a firm considering the acquisition of a finished good, component part, or service has three basic options:

1. Make the good or provide the service in-house
2. Purchase it from another organization
3. Lease it from another organization

Manufacturing the product itself, if the company has the capability to do so, may be the best route. It may save a great deal of money if its own manufacturing division does not incur costs for overhead and profits that an outside buyer would otherwise charge.

On the other hand, most firms cannot make all of the business goods they need. Often, they would simply have to spend too much to maintain the necessary equipment, staff, and supplies. Therefore, purchasing from an outside vendor is the most common choice. Companies can also look outside their own plants for goods and services that they formerly produced in-house, a practice called *outsourcing* that the next section will describe in more detail.

In some cases, however, a company may choose to lease inputs. This option spreads out costs as compared to lump-sum costs for up-front purchases. The company pays for the use of equipment for a certain time period. For example, a small business may lease a copy machine for several years, making monthly payments. At the end of the lease term, the firm can buy the machine at a prearranged cost or replace it with a different model. This option can provide useful flexibility for a growing business, allowing it to easily upgrade as its needs change. At the other end of the organizational spectrum, companies can lease sophisticated computer systems, heavy equipment, and airplanes. America West Airlines obtains most of its aircraft on short-term leases rather than buying the planes outright or leasing for longer periods. These short leases help the firm to adapt to changing passenger loads and limit its costs.[17]

The Rise of Outsourcing

Imagine a successful company that designs and sells specialized semiconductor chips to enhance a computer's multimedia capabilities—all without owning one production facility! Rather than spend $1 billion to build its own plant, Nevada Corp. designs the chips at its Sunnyvale, California, headquarters and contracts with SGS-Thomson to manufacture them at its factory in France. The firm then sells the chips to Diamond Multimedia Systems, which puts them on multimedia accelerator boards. These arrangements let Nevada concentrate on what it does best—designing chips—and then subcontract the other processes to outside companies with the required expertise.[18]

Welcome to the world of **outsourcing,** the practice of turning to outside vendors for goods and services formerly produced in-house. In their rush to improve efficiency, firms look outside for just about everything—mailroom management, customer service, human resources, accounting, information technology, manufacturing, and distribution. Outsourcing currently generates annual revenues of $100 billion, and it is on the rise among both small and large firms.[19]

Businesspeople once considered outside purchases of component parts or technology services to be signs of weakness—particularly for a major corporation. Now they look favorably on opportunities to deal with cost-effective

Marketing Dictionary

joint demand Demand for a business product that depends on the demand for another business product that is necessary for the use of the first.

sole sourcing Purchasing a firm's entire stock of a product from just one vendor.

outsourcing Acquiring inputs from outside vendors for goods and services formerly produced in-house.

SOLVING AN ETHICAL CONTROVERSY

Is It Fair to Force Company Suppliers to Use Electronic Data Interchange?

In the business-to-business market, electronic commerce is fast becoming a way of life. Corporate giants like Ford Motor Co., Dillard's Department Stores, and Lowe's are now demanding that their suppliers convert their sales and purchasing operations into electronic systems, usually referred to as *electronic data interchange (EDI)*. Major corporations have embraced EDI systems in pursuit of efficiency and cost savings. EDI promises such tantalizing benefits that even the federal Department of Defense is demanding that all its suppliers and contractors convert to such a system.

Not all suppliers share this enthusiasm, however. Many small businesses must struggle to pay for expensive computerized ordering systems, and they resent buyers telling them how to conduct their internal affairs. The experience of Lance Dailey, a merchandising executive at Sears Roebuck, illustrates the reluctance of companies to jump on the electronic commerce bandwagon. Observed Dailey: "I thought if I said, 'Look, here's how important EDI is to us, and here's what we can do to support you,' I'd have people pounding on my door." But it didn't happen.

? ***Can Organizations Legitimately Force Their Suppliers to Use Electronic Commerce?***

PRO

1. **Buyers can also save money through EDI. While small customers often dread the cost of switching to EDI, the investment can be a financial blessing. "It's a good idea to get on board before your vendors and customers start demanding it," says Michael Fidanza, general manger of Ideal Supply Co., an $18-million purveyor of industrial pipes and valves in Jersey City, N.J. His company's move to an electronic system paid off handsomely. One appreciative vendor gave Ideal Supply an extra 5 percent in discounts. Another kicks in $10,000 worth of products for every $50,000 in purchases.**
2. **Switching to EDI can cement stronger relationships between suppliers and customers. Once the purchasing system begins operating, a corporation may hesitate to switch to other suppliers since the change could involve high costs and time-consuming hassles to implement the same system with a competitor.**
3. **EDI is becoming so prevalent in the organizational world that it makes sense for any vendor**

outside suppliers or those with specialized technological expertise. A recent poll showed that 22 of 26 top corporations outsource some operations. About 20 percent of the largest U.S. corporations outsource technology services, and that number is growing.

For example, PepsiCo's employees receive financial planning assistance from KPMG Peat Marwick. TeleTech Holdings, a Denver company, runs call centers for major customers, handling AT&T's customer service and Continental Airlines' reservations. Small organizations like Ballymeade Country Club on Cape Cod are big users of outsourcing. The Club pays $5,000 for payroll and other financial services, compared to a cost of $12,000 to $15,000 for a part-time employee to do the same work.

Outsourcing is not new. In the 1950s, Automated Data Processing (ADP) began to process payroll for other companies. Recently, however, corporate downsizing and cost cutting have accelerated the growth of outsourcing. BellSouth Corp. will spend about $60 million on outsourcing, after it has reduced its workforce by 13,200 employees.

Why Outsource? Why do firms outsource? Surprisingly, the reasons go beyond cost control. The Outsourcing Institute conducted a survey of 30 large and small companies. These respondents ranked "improving company focus" first, followed by "accessing world-class capabilities." Reducing costs came third.

"People want to buy knowledge, not develop it themselves," explains John Halvey, an attorney specializing in outsourcing at Milbank, Tweed, Hadley, and McCoy, a major New York law firm. Mutual Life Insurance Co. of New York chose Computer Sciences Corp. to complete a $205 million, seven-year information technology project primarily to promote quality rather than cut costs. The project did not cost much less than the firm would have spent on in-house development, but it gains more advanced technology and better business capabilities than its own staff might have produced.

In an advertising campaign promoting its outsourcing services, Andersen Consulting differentiates its approach from "tactical" outsourcing, motivated strictly by cost cutting. As the ad in Figure 9.5 indicates, Andersen tries to form strategic alliances with firms to help them improve the quality of their core business processes such as information technology, finance, and administrative operations.

Outsourcing can be a smart strategy if a company

who wants to do business with big retailers. The system also can open up new markets by luring progressive firms that want to conduct business in the most modern ways possible.

CON

1. **Installing one of these systems can be quite expensive, especially for smaller operations. Some companies feel the pressure from purchasers to use one even though they may only fill a couple of orders a month. That's what happened to the owners of Belly Basics, a recently-opened New York City maternity clothing store, after Federated Department Stores—one of its biggest customers—mandated EDI.**
2. **Sellers earn no short-term payoff for installing the expensive EDI systems. Some systems can cost $10,000, a cost with little financial justification. EDI remains relatively new, and smaller companies feel they already have efficient ways of conducting business.**
3. **Large corporations enjoy an unfair advantage in the vendor relationship. If a company pressures a vendor to convert to EDI, there is no guarantee that the company will continue to buy the supplier's products.**

Summary

Despite some resentment, for many vendors the decision about when to move toward electronic purchasing and ordering is only a matter of time. That certainly was the case with Belly Basics, the $1.5-million company that sold 25 percent of its clothing to Federated. The owners of the start-up panicked when the major retailer demanded that they switch to EDI in a matter of months. "We had just started shipping products and weren't ready to change our operations," says Cherie Serota, a Belly Basics owner. But she added, "Whatever it took, we had to do it." To their relief, the entrepreneurs found a range of electronic ordering options available, some with extremely reasonable costs. Instead of purchasing a $10,000 software system and better hardware, Belly Basics hired a third-party outsource firm to process all its Federated orders for about $1,000 a year. Says Jody Kozlow Gardner of Belly Basics, "The whole thing sounded a lot scarier than it is."

Sources: Robert Bellinger, "Electronic Commerce—A Killer Application?" *Engineering Times,* February 3, 1997, p. 22; Phaedra Hise, "Early Adoption Pays Off," *Inc.,* August 1996, downloaded from America Online, October 10, 1996; Karen Schaffner, "Pssst! Want to Sell to Wal-Mart?" *Apparel Industry,* August 1996, pp. 18–19; Phaedra Hise, "How to Survive EDI," *Inc.,* December 1995, p. 131; Godwin J. Udo and Gary C. Pickett, "EDI Conversion Mandate: The Big Problem for Small Businesses," *Industrial Management,* March/April 1994, pp. 6–9; Shawn Tully, "Purchasing's New Muscle," *Fortune,* February 1995, pp. 76–78.

chooses a vendor that can provide high-quality products, perhaps at lower cost than it could achieve on its own. This priority allows the outsourcer to focus on its core competencies. Successful outsourcing requires that companies carefully oversee contracts and manage relationships. Some vendor companies now provide performance guarantees to assure their customers that they will receive high-quality services that meet their needs.

Problems with Outsourcing

Outsourcing is not without its downside, however. Many companies discover that their cost savings average closer to 10 percent than the 20 to 40 percent that vendors promise. Also, companies may sign multiyear contracts that no longer compare well with market conditions after a year or two. Another problem with outsourcing production of proprietary technology concerns internal security.

Suppliers who fail to deliver goods promptly or provide required services can adversely affect a company's reputation with its customers. General Electric had to delay the introduction of a new washing machine because of a contractor's production problems. Southern Pacific Rail had problems with an outsourced computer network.

A major danger of outsourcing is the risk of losing touch with customers. Outsourcing can reduce a company's ability to respond quickly to the marketplace or slow efforts to bring new products to market. Some consultants believe that firms can take outsourcing too far; they advise keeping such important departments as customer service in-house. Another concern is the possible decline in work culture and company pride because outsourcing fragments responsibilities. "A mercenary may shoot a gun the same as a soldier, but he will not create a revolution, build a new society, or die for the homeland," claims a Silicon Valley manager whose company outsources some services.

Outsourcing is a controversial topic with unions, especially in the auto industry, as the percentage of component parts made in-house has steadily dropped. General Motors outsources to acquire about 30 percent of its inputs, compared to 50 percent for Ford and 70 percent for Chrysler. GM had to cut costs aggressively to remain competitive. For example, it required its in-house parts unit, Delphi Automotive Systems, to bid against outside companies for

Figure 9.5 Outsourcing as a Method of Quality Enhancement

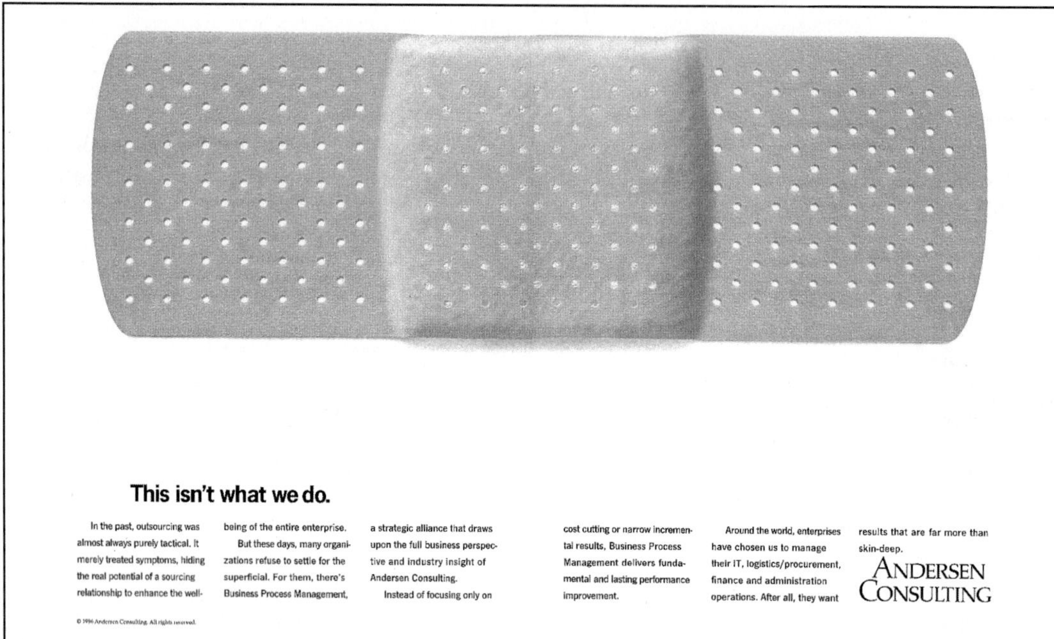
This isn't what we do.
In the past, outsourcing was almost always purely tactical. It merely treated symptoms, hiding the real potential of a sourcing relationship to enhance the well-being of the entire enterprise.
But these days, many organizations refuse to settle for the superficial. For them, there's Business Process Management, a strategic alliance that draws upon the full business perspective and industry insight of Andersen Consulting.
Instead of focusing only on cost cutting or narrow incremental results, Business Process Management delivers fundamental and lasting performance improvement.
Around the world, enterprises have chosen us to manage their IT, logistics/procurement, finance and administration operations. After all, they want results that are far more than skin-deep.
ANDERSEN CONSULTING
© 1996 Andersen Consulting. All rights reserved.

GM's business; it also allowed Delphi to bid for work from Toyota and other companies, however. Because many automotive parts vendors employ nonunion employees, they pay less for labor than their unionized customers. This difference keeps suppliers' prices well below GM's cost to produce the same items internally, inhibiting Delphi's efforts to compete. As a result, outsourcing creates conflicts between GM and the autoworkers' unions, which vigorously fight job loss from outsourcing. In Canada, GM's attempts to outsource brake production led to strikes and plant shutdowns.[20]

Firms are moving more than manufacturing operations outside their plants. Suppliers like Johnson Controls and ITT Automotive also provide design and engineering services. In fact, the Big Three auto makers are reducing their own research and development operations and focusing on their core strengths: engines, transmissions, and styling. They believe that hiring specialized suppliers that only produce brakes and other systems makes more sense than trying to keep up with developments in every area. The Japanese have perfected this type of outsourcing. A Boston Consulting Group study showed that suppliers provide about 80 percent of the engineering on Japanese car models.[21]

THE BUSINESS BUYING PROCESS

Suppose that CableBox Inc., a hypothetical manufacturer of cable television decoder boxes, decides to upgrade its manufacturing facility with $1 million in new automated assembly equipment. Before approaching equipment suppliers, the company must analyze its needs, determine goals that the project should accomplish, develop technical specifications for the equipment, and set a budget. Once it receives vendors' proposals, it must evaluate them and select the best one. But what does *best* mean in this context? The lowest price or the best warranty and service contract? Who in the company is responsible for such decisions?

Clearly, the business buying process is more complex than the consumer decision process described in Chapter 8. Business buying takes place within a formal organization with its budget, cost, and profit considerations. Furthermore, industrial and institutional buying decisions usually involve many people with complex interactions among individuals and organizational goals. To understand organizational buying behavior, business marketers require knowledge of influences on the purchase decision process, the stages in the organizational buying model, types of business buying situations, and techniques for purchase decision analysis.

Influences on Purchase Decisions

Organizational buying decisions react to various influences, some external to the firm and others related to internal structure and personnel. In addition to product-specific factors such as purchase price, installation, operating and maintenance costs, and vendor service, companies must also consider broader environmental, organizational, and interpersonal influences.

Environmental Factors Environmental conditions such as economic, political, regulatory, competitive, and technological considerations influence organizational buying decisions. For example, CableBox may wish to defer purchases of the new equipment in times of slowing economic activity. During a recession, sales to cable companies might drop because households hesitate to spend money on cable service. The company would look at the derived demand for its products, possible changes in its sources of materials, employment trends, and similar factors before committing to such a large capital expenditure.

Political, regulatory, and competitive factors also come into play. For example, passage of a law freezing cable television rates would affect demand, as would introduction of a less expensive decoder box by a competitor. Finally, technology plays a role. For example, cable-ready televisions decreased demand for set-top boxes, and smaller, more powerful satellite dishes may cut into the market for cable TV, reducing derived demand. CableBox can benefit from technological advances, too. As more homes want fast Internet connections, adding cable modems to its product line may present a growth opportunity.

Organizational Factors Successful business-to-business marketers understand their customers' organizational structures, policies, and purchasing systems. A company with a centralized procurement function operates differently than one that delegates purchasing decisions to divisional or geographic units. Trying to sell to the local store when head-office personnel make all the decisions would clearly waste salespeople's time. Buying behavior also differs between firms. For example, centralized buyers tend to emphasize long-term relationships, while decentralized buyers often focus more on short-term results. Personal selling skills and user preferences carry more weight in decentralized purchasing situations than in centralized buying.

Because purchasing operations spend over half of each dollar their companies earn, consolidating vendor relationships can lead to large cost savings. AT&T's program to consolidate vendor contracts is expected to save $1 billion annually. U.S. businesses spend $250 billion a year buying maintenance, repair, and operating supplies.[22] Grainger understands that administrative expenses account for a huge part of the cost of buying these MRO items. In its ad in Figure 9.6, the firm offers help in reducing these costs—"We supply thousands of products . . . enabling you to replace hundreds of suppliers with just one." Grainger can also help companies restructure their entire purchasing processes to improve cost-effectiveness.

Centralized purchasing units work well in companies with multiple divisions that share common purchasing requirements. Cost savings and better terms and service often result from volume purchases and consolidation of purchasing power. Centralized purchasing departments may also benefit by employing specialists to deal with certain types of needs.[23] These representatives may contract nationally with a few suppliers, which supply all units. For example, AT&T needed to control costs of services and routine items, which consumed $12 billion of its $20 billion annual purchasing budget. It now combines orders for travel services, overnight delivery services, and temporary help, instead of allowing individual offices to make their own arrangements. Now 75 firms contract to provide computer programmers instead of 300.[24]

Figure 9.6 **Understanding Customers' Purchasing Systems—Key to Generating Business Sales**

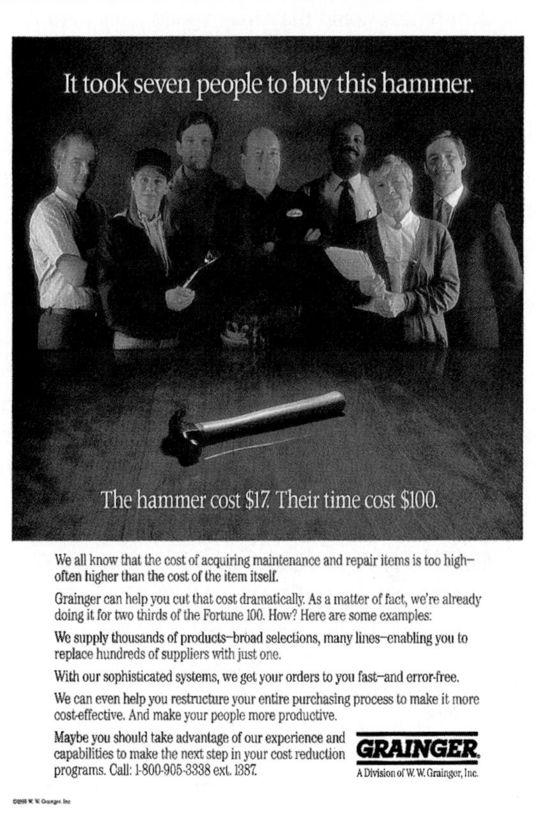
It took seven people to buy this hammer.
The hammer cost $17. Their time cost $100.
We all know that the cost of acquiring maintenance and repair items is too high—often higher than the cost of the item itself.
Grainger can help you cut that cost dramatically. As a matter of fact, we're already doing it for two thirds of the Fortune 100. How? Here are some examples:
We supply thousands of products—broad selections, many lines—enabling you to replace hundreds of suppliers with just one.
With our sophisticated systems, we get your orders to you fast—and error-free.
We can even help you restructure your entire purchasing process to make it more cost-effective. And make your people more productive.
Maybe you should take advantage of our experience and capabilities to make the next step in your cost reduction programs. Call: 1-800-905-3338 ext. 1387.
GRAINGER
A Division of W. W. Grainger, Inc.

Federal Express recently changed back to a centralized purchasing organization for information technology equipment. An employee can no longer order equipment and charge it to his or her cost center. Under the new system, orders go through the purchasing office in Memphis, and they must call for approved products.[25] Companies whose sales representatives continued to visit those local units would lose business until they began to work through the central system.

How many suppliers should a company patronize? A fine line separates maximizing buying power from relying too heavily on a few suppliers. Each company sets its own criteria for this decision. Some organizations engage in **multiple sourcing**—they purchase from several vendors. Spreading orders provides insurance against shortages if one vendor cannot deliver on schedule. However, dealing with many vendors can be counterproductive and take too much administrative time.

Interpersonal Influences Many people may influence business purchases, and they may spend considerable time obtaining the input and approval of various other organization members. Both group and individual forces are at work here. When committees handle organizational buying, they must spend time to gain majority or unanimous approval. Also, each individual buyer brings to the decision process his or her own preferences, experience, and particular needs.

Business marketers should know who will influence buying decisions for their products and each one's priorities. To choose a supplier for an industrial press, for example, a purchasing agent and representatives of the company's production, engineering, and quality control departments may jointly decide. Each of these principals may have a different point of view that the vendor's marketers must understand.

As a result, sales representatives must be well-versed in the technical characteristics of their goods or services, and they must interact effectively with employees of the various departments involved in the purchase decision. In the chemical industry, for example, a salesperson makes an average of seven face-to-face presentations to complete a single sale. When Ameritech decided to consolidate and outsource its data centers, it studied the situation for over a year. Before it chose IBM's Integrated Systems Solutions Corp. subsidiary for a ten-year deal worth many billions of dollars, it worked closely with ISSC's sales representatives and technical support personnel to evaluate how that supplier would provide the computer support services.[26]

The Role of the Professional Buyer Most organizations attempt to make their purchases through systematic procedures employing professional buyers. These technically qualified employees are responsible for securing needed products at the best possible prices. Unlike ultimate consumers, who incorporate periodic buying decisions with other activities, a firm's purchasing department devotes all of its time and effort to determining needs, locating and evaluating alternative sources of supply, and making purchase decisions.

Purchase decisions for capital items vary significantly from those for expense items. Firms often buy expense items routinely with little delay. Capital items, however, involve major fund commitments and usually undergo considerable review.

One way in which a firm may attempt to streamline the buying process is through **systems integration,** centralization of the procurement function. One company may designate a lead division to handle all purchasing. Another firm may choose to designate a major supplier as the systems integrator. This vendor then assumes responsibility for dealing with all of the suppliers for a project and presenting the entire package to the buyer.

A business marketer may set up a sales organization to serve national accounts that deals solely with buyers at geographically concentrated corporate headquarters. A separate field sales organization may serve buyers at regional production facilities.

As the chapter's opening vignette explained, many corporate buyers now use the Internet to identify supplier sources. They view online catalogs to compare vendors' offerings. For example, AMP Inc. put its multilingual catalog of over 40,000 electronics parts on the Web. The company doesn't take orders over the Internet; rather, it still sells through distributors. However, AMP has substantially reduced the $8 million per year it spends for paper catalogs and postage. It also can update the online catalog easily and quickly.[27]

http://www.amp.com/

However, finding the right information on the Web can be a tedious task. To help purchasing professionals sort through the masses of available data, Aspect Development Corp. offers a database of Internet catalogs. Using the database, purchasers can easily cross reference parts from several suppliers.[28]

Model of the Organizational Buying Process

An organizational buying situation requires a sequence of activities similar to the six-step consumer decision model presented in Chapter 8. Figure 9.7 illustrates an eight-stage model for a complex organizational buying process. The additional steps arise because business purchasing introduces new complexities that do not affect consumers. Not every buying situation will follow these precise steps. However, this model presents a useful overview of the general process.[29]

Stage 1: Anticipate or Recognize a Problem/Need/ Opportunity and a General Solution Both consumer and organizational purchase decisions begin when recognition of problems, needs, or opportunities triggers the buying process. Perhaps a firm's computer system has become outdated, or a sales representative demonstrates a new good or service that could improve the company's performance.

Many firms deal regularly with a long-standing problem of streamlining their buying processes for small or routine purchases such as office supplies. At many firms, these transactions can take weeks to process, because the necessary paperwork must go through multiple steps and offices. These steps create time-consuming and expensive delays. At a large company, the internal cost of processing a purchase order can range from $25 for companies that use electronic ordering to as much as $100.[30]

Stage 2: Determine the Characteristics and Quantity of a Needed Good or Service The problem described in Stage 1 translates into a service opportunity for credit card companies. Visa, MasterCard, and American Express have instituted purchasing card programs that allow organizational cardholders to charge MRO—maintenance, repair, and operation—purchases and reduce time-consuming paperwork. Card issuers estimate that their potential market for these items is $240 billion annually.

Because these small orders require about 80 percent of the paperwork and they amount to only 20 percent of a company's purchases, a paperless system can bring substantial benefits. American Express estimates that a card program with only one bill and one payment to process can cut up to 90 percent of the cost of handling multiple requisitions, purchase orders, invoices, and checks. Companies want and need systems that eliminate processing steps, save time, and reduce costs.[31] Allied Signal and National Semiconductor have implemented corporate purchasing card programs. By consolidating lots of tiny purchases, thereby eliminating costly processing steps for purchase orders and checks, National Semiconductor reduced its order processing costs from $30 to pennies.[32]

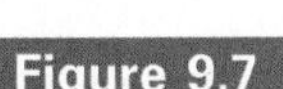
Obtain Feedback and Evaluate Performance
Select Order Routine
Evaluate Proposals and Select Supplier
Acquire and Analyze Proposals
Search for and Qualify Sources
Describe Characteristics and Quantity
Determine Characteristics and Quantity
Recognize Problem and General Solution

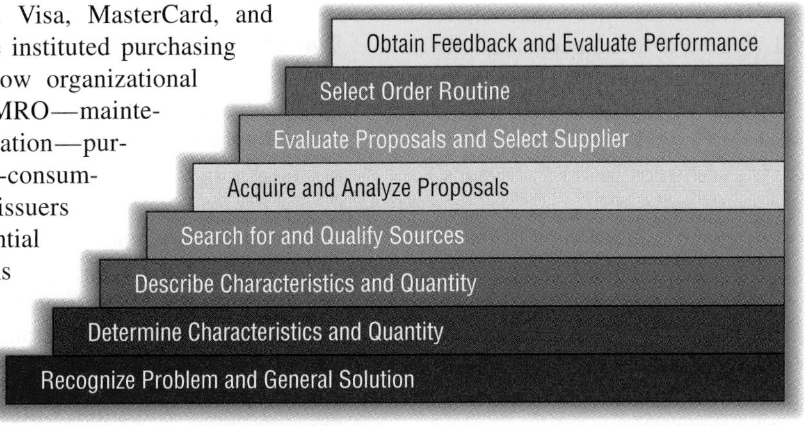

Figure 9.7

Stages in the Organizational Buying Process

Stage 3: Describe Characteristics and Quantity of a Needed Good or Service After determining the characteristics and quantity of needed products, organizational buyers must translate these ideas into detailed specifications. Depending on the type of purchase, a company's technical personnel can play an important role in this early stage of the buying process. For instance, a quality control engineer might establish certain specifications for a product that only a few suppliers could meet. This type of decision could have a big impact on the ultimate evaluation and selection of vendors.

Stages 2 and 3 apply mostly to organizations rather than individual consumers. While consumers may perform these steps, they would complete much more superficial analysis.

Stage 4: Search for and Qualify Potential Sources Both consumers and businesses search for good suppliers of desired products. Customers who are interested in corporate purchasing cards must choose between three vendors: Visa, MasterCard, and American Express. For other goods and services, however, the choice of a supplier may involve more complex decision making. A company that wants to buy a group life and health insurance policy must weigh the varying provisions and programs of many different vendors.

Stage 5: Acquire and Analyze Proposals The next step is to acquire and analyze suppliers' proposals, which they generally submit in writing. A business customer that is considering implementation of a corporate purchasing card system must consider the advantages and disadvantages of this approach. Benefits include reducing the number of invoices that staff must pay and cutting the amount of paperwork and processing time. However, some suppliers may not accept the cards, transaction records may be less detailed, and employees inexperienced in purchasing methods may commit the firm to pay higher prices than it would pay if an experienced purchasing agent were to negotiate with the seller.[33]

If the buyer is a government or public agency, this

Marketing Dictionary

multiple sourcing Spreading purchases among several vendors.

systems integration Centralization of the procurement function within an internal division or as a service of an external supplier.

stage of the purchase process may involve competitive bidding. During this process, each marketer must develop an appropriate bid, including a price, that will satisfy the criteria determined by the customer's problem, need, or opportunity. While competitive bidding is less common in the business sector, a company may follow the practice to purchase nonstandard materials, complex products, or products that are made to its own specifications.

Stage 6: Evaluate Proposals and Select Suppliers Next, buyers must compare vendors' proposals and choose the one that seems best suited to their needs. For example, a company that is evaluating procurement card systems must compare card issuers' fee systems, which can include a purchase-based fee of 1.75 percent to 2.5 percent on the account balance, plus a fixed fee of a few cents for every purchase processed. Proposals for sophisticated equipment, such as a large computer networking system, can include considerable differences between product offerings, and the final choice may involve trade-offs.

Price is not the only criterion for selection of a vendor. Relationship factors like communication and trust may also be important to the buyer. Other factors include reliability, delivery record, time from order to delivery, quality, and order accuracy. Quality was one of the main reasons why insurance company USF&G chose Olsten Staffing Services as a supplier. As the ad in Figure 9.8 explains, USF&G was hiring temporary workers through more than 100 suppliers, and each department or office made its own purchase decisions. The company wanted more quality control and less paperwork. It reviewed 40 firms in its search for a partner that could manage a wide range of temporary workers and streamline the flexible staffing process at headquarters and branch offices throughout the country. USF&G selected Olsten because of its on-time performance, full range of staffing services, and highly trained personnel.

Stage 7: Select an Order Routine Once a supplier has been chosen, buyer and vendor must work out the best way to process future purchases. Ordering routines can vary considerably. Most orders will, however, include product descriptions, quantities, prices, delivery terms, and payment terms. Today companies have many new order options, submitting requests through written documents, phone calls, faxes, or electronic messages.

General Electric operates its own electronic purchasing systems. Its Trading Process Network relies on a World Wide Web-based electronic commerce service created by GE Information Services Division (GEIS). The network matches GE's many buyers with suppliers of everything from appliance parts to copy paper. Purchasing agents can pool orders across several units to enhance their purchasing leverage. The system benefits suppliers, too. They can download proposal information, get diagrams for parts specs, and talk to managers.[34]

Stage 8: Obtain Feedback and Evaluate Performance At the final stage, buyers measure vendors' performance. Sometimes this judgment may involve a formal evaluation of each supplier's product quality, delivery performance, prices, technical knowledge, and overall responsiveness to customer needs. At other times, vendors may be measured according to whether they have lowered the customer's costs or reduced its employees' workloads.

In general, large firms are more likely to use formal evaluation procedures, while smaller companies lean toward informal evaluations. Regardless of the method used, buyers should tell suppliers how they are evaluated.

Classifying Business Buying Situations

As discussed earlier, business buying behavior responds to many purchasing influences such as environmental, organizational, and interpersonal factors. It also involves the degree of effort that the purchase decision demands and the levels within the organization where it is made. Like consumer behavior, marketers can classify organizational buying situations into three general categories, ranging from least to most complex: (1) straight rebuying, (2) modified

Figure 9.8 Supplier Selection Criteria

"Lower costs and higher quality were the goals of our 'Aggressive Sourcing' program. And, after an intensive search, they were the reasons we chose Olsten Staffing."
Laurie Atkinson, Contract Administrator, USF&G
USF+G INSURANCE
When Laurie Atkinson and a team of senior managers set out to reengineer the procurement functions at USF&G's headquarters and branch offices, the first area they tackled was temporary staffing.
"At the time," says Atkinson, "we were using more than 100 staffing vendors. Each department or office made their own decisions. We needed more quality control and less paperwork."
USF&G began searching for a partner with the ability to manage a wide range of temporary staffing needs across the country. They were also looking for systems that could streamline their flexible staffing process. After reviewing 40 firms, they chose Olsten.
"In the year since we began working with Olsten," says Atkinson, with a smile, "we have met or exceeded all our goals. Most important, our internal clients are happy with the service. That's what I call success."
With more than 700 offices, Olsten Staffing Services meets the diverse needs of its global clients with supplemental staff across the spectrum of job skills. As part of Olsten Corporation, one of the largest human resource services providers in the world, we deliver superbly trained personnel, solid on-time performance and a full range of staffing services.
THE ONE CALL THAT WORKS
1-800-WORK NOW
Olsten Staffing Services℠
America is going to work with us℠
Visit us at http://www.worknow.com ©1996 Olsten Corporation. EOE M/F/D/V

rebuying, and (3) new-task buying. Business buying situations may also involve reciprocity. This section looks at each type of purchase by a company like CableBox.

Straight Rebuying The simplest buying situation is a **straight rebuy,** a recurring purchase decision in which an existing customer places a new order for a familiar product that has performed satisfactorily in the past. This organizational buying situation occurs when a purchaser likes the product and the terms of sale. Therefore, the purchase requires no new information. The buyer sees little reason to assess other options and so follows a routine repurchase format. A straight rebuy is the business market equivalent of routinized response behavior in the consumer market.

Purchases of low-cost items such as paper clips and pencils for an office are typical examples. If the products and their prices and terms satisfy the organization, it will treat future purchases as straight rebuys from the current vendor. For instance, CableBox probably has an account with an office supply firm that provides prompt service.

A marketer who wants to ensure continuing straight rebuys should concentrate on maintaining a good relationship with the buyer by providing excellent service and delivery performance. Competitors will then find it difficult to present unique sales proposals that would break this chain of repurchases.

Modified Rebuying In a **modified rebuy,** a purchaser is willing to reevaluate available options. The decision makers see some advantage in looking at alternative offerings using established purchasing guidelines. They might take this step if a marketer allows a straight rebuy situation to deteriorate because of poor service or delivery performance. Perceived quality and cost differences can also provoke modified rebuys. Modified rebuys resemble limited problem solving in consumer markets.

Business marketers want to induce current customers to make straight rebuys by responding to all of their needs. Competitors, on the other hand, try to induce buyers to make modified rebuys by raising issues that will convince them to reconsider their decisions. Suppose that CableBox wants to upgrade its computer equipment. In addition to requesting proposals from its current supplier, IBM, the firm will probably investigate competing proposals from other computer manufacturers like Compaq, Dell, and Hewlett-Packard. Each vendor will promote its computers' technological advantages and other features.

New-Task Buying The most complex category of business buying is **new-task buying**—first-time or unique purchase situations that require considerable effort by the decision makers. The consumer market equivalent of new-task buying is extended problem solving.

A new-task buy often requires a purchaser to carefully consider alternative offerings and vendors. For example, a company entering a new field must seek suppliers of component parts that it has never before purchased. If CableBox were to decide to manufacture cable modems, it would have to buy new equipment and component parts. This new-task buying would require several stages, each yielding a decision of some sort. These would include developing product requirements, searching out potential suppliers, and evaluating proposals. Information requirements and decision makers can complete the entire buying process, or they may change from stage to stage.

Reciprocity **Reciprocity**—a policy to extend purchasing preference to suppliers that are also customers—is a controversial practice in a number of organizational buying situations. For example, an office equipment manufacturer may favor a particular supplier of component parts if the supplier has recently made a major purchase of the manufacturer's products. Reciprocal arrangements traditionally have been common in industries featuring homogeneous products with similar prices, such as the chemical, paint, petroleum, rubber, and steel industries.

Reverse reciprocity is the practice of extending supply privileges to firms that provide needed supplies. In times of shortages, firms occasionally practice reverse reciprocity as they attempt to obtain raw materials and parts to support continuing operations.

The practice of reciprocity suggests close links among participants in the organizational marketplace. It can add to the complexity of organizational buying behavior for new suppliers who are trying to compete with preferred vendors. Although buyers and sellers enter into reciprocal agreements in the United States, both the Justice Department and the Federal Trade Commission view them as attempts to reduce competition.

Marketing Dictionary

straight rebuy Recurring purchase decision in which a customer repurchases a good or service that has performed satisfactorily in the past.

modified rebuy Purchase decision in which a purchaser is willing to reevaluate available options for repurchasing a good or service.

new-task buying First-time or unique purchase situation that requires considerable effort by the decision makers

reciprocity Policy to extend purchasing preference to suppliers that are also customers.

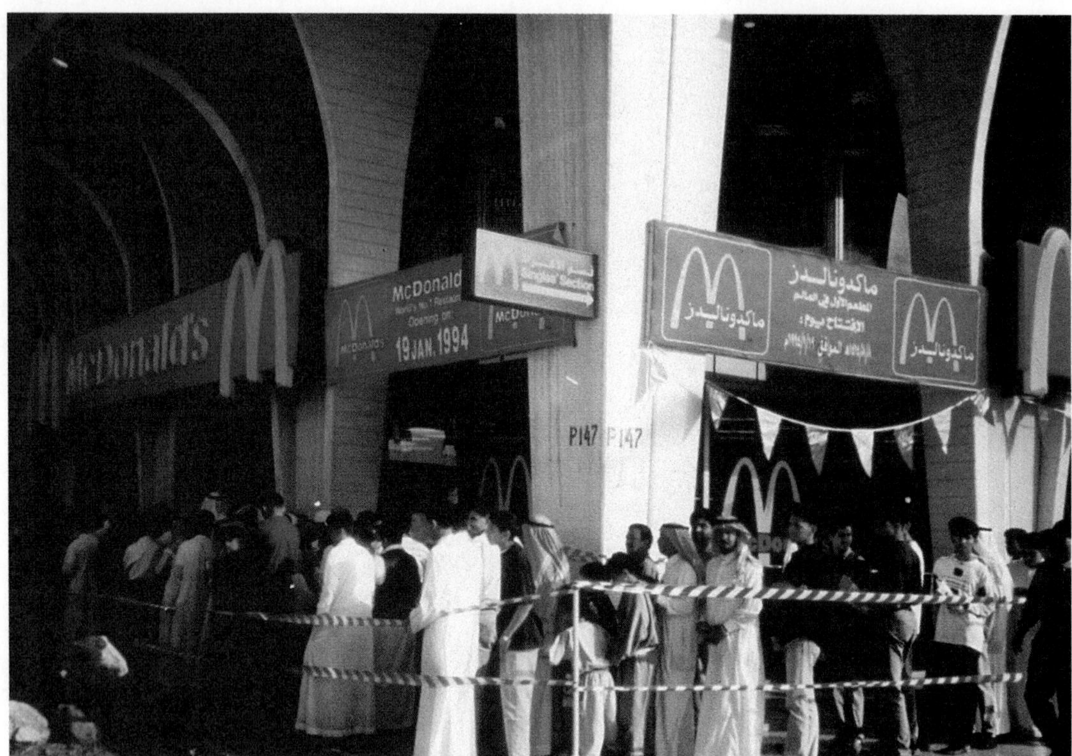
McDonald's
McDonald
19 JAN. 1994
P147

McDonald's Corp. faced a new-task buying situation when it decided to open restaurants in Saudi Arabia. Challenged by the scarcity of local suppliers, R. S. Rekhi, the company's purchasing director for the Middle East, searched around the globe for potential suppliers. As a result, the customers shown here at the grand opening of a restaurant enjoyed burgers that represent a team of global suppliers. The Saudi Big Mac includes sesame seeds and onions from Mexico, buns made of Saudi wheat and Brazilian soy sauce and sugar, beef patties and lettuce from Spain, pickles and special sauce from the United States, cheese from New Zealand, and packaging materials from Germany.

Outside the United States, however, government may take more favorable views of reciprocity. Business-to-business buyers in Canada, for instance, see it as a positive, widespread practice. In Japan, close ties between suppliers and customers are common.

Analysis Tools

Two tools that help professional buyers to make purchase decisions are value analysis and vendor analysis. **Value analysis** examines each component of a purchase in an attempt to either delete the item or replace it with a more cost-effective substitute. For example, airplane designers have long recognized the need to make planes as light as possible. Value analysis supports using DuPont's synthetic material Kevlar in airplane construction, because it weighs less than the metals it replaced. The resulting fuel savings are significant for the buyers in this marketplace.

Vendor analysis carries out an ongoing evaluation of a supplier's performance in categories such as price, back orders, delivery times, and attention to special requests. In some cases vendor analysis is a formal process. Figure 9.9 shows the vendor analysis form that Chrysler uses to measure its suppliers' performance. A checklist set up along these lines helps organizational purchasers to evaluate potential vendors and determine the most effective supply sources for particular inputs.

THE BUYING CENTER CONCEPT

The buying center concept provides a vital model for understanding organizational buying behavior. A company's **buying center** encompasses everyone who is involved in any fashion in its buying action. For example, a buying center may include the architect who designs a new research laboratory, the scientist who works in the facility, the purchasing manager who screens contractor proposals, the chief executive officer who makes the final decision, and the vice president for research who signs the formal contracts for the project. Buying center participants in any purchase seek to satisfy personal needs, such as participation or status, as well as organizational needs.

A buying center is not part of a firm's formal organization structure. It is an informal group whose composition varies among purchase situations and firms. Domestic firms' buying centers typically include anywhere from 4 to 20 participants. Their identities tend to change as the purchasing process moves through its stages.[35]

Buying Center Roles

Buying center participants play different roles in the purchasing decision process. *Users* are the people who will actually use the purchased good or service. Their influence on the purchase decision may range from negligible to ex-

Figure 9.9 **Chrysler's Vendor Analysis Form**

Supplier Rating Chart:
Supplier Name: ____________
Shipping Location: ____________
Commodity: ____________
Annual Sales Dollars: ____________

	5 Ex.	4 Good	3 Sat.	2 Fair	1 Poor	0 N/A
Quality 40%						
Supplier defect rates	___	___	___	___	___	___
SQA program conformance	___	___	___	___	___	___
Sample approval performance	___	___	___	___	___	___
Responsiveness to quality problems	___	___	___	___	___	___
Overall quality rating	___	___	___	___	___	___
Delivery 25%						
Avoidance of late or overshipments	___	___	___	___	___	___
Ability to expand production capacity	___	___	___	___	___	___
Engineering sample delivery performance	___	___	___	___	___	___
Response to fluctuating supply demands	___	___	___	___	___	___
Overall delivery rating	___	___	___	___	___	___
Price 25%						
Price competitiveness	___	___	___	___	___	___
Absorption of economic price increases	___	___	___	___	___	___
Submission of cost savings plans	___	___	___	___	___	___
Payment terms	___	___	___	___	___	___
Overall price rating	___	___	___	___	___	___
Technology 10%						
State-of-the-art component technology	___	___	___	___	___	___
Sharing research development capability	___	___	___	___	___	___
Capable and willing to provide circuit design services	___	___	___	___	___	___
Responsiveness to engineering problems	___	___	___	___	___	___
Overall technology rating	___	___	___	___	___	___

Buyer: ________ Date: ________

Comments: ____

tremely important. Users sometimes initiate purchase actions by requesting products, and they may also help to develop product specifications.

Gatekeepers control the information that all buying center members will review. They may exert this control by distributing printed product data or advertisements or by deciding which salespeople will speak to which individuals in the buying center. For example, a purchasing agent might allow some salespeople to see the engineers responsible for developing specifications but deny others the same privilege.

Influencers affect the buying decision by supplying information to guide evaluation of alternatives or by setting buying specifications. Influencers are typically technical personnel such as engineers, quality control specialists,

Marketing Dictionary

value analysis Systematic study of the components of a purchase to determine the most cost-effective ways to acquire them.

vendor analysis Assessment of supplier performance in areas such as price, back orders, timely delivery, and attention to special requests.

buying center Participants in an organizational buying action

and research and development staff members. Sometimes a buying organization hires outside consultants, such as engineers and architects, who influence its buying decisions.

The *decider* actually chooses a good or service, although another person may have the formal authority to do so. The identity of the decider is the most difficult role for marketers to pinpoint. For example, a firm's buyer may have the formal authority to buy, but the firm's CEO may actually make the buying decision. A decider could be a design engineer who develops specifications that only one vendor can meet.

The *buyer* has the formal authority to select a supplier and implement the procedures for securing the good or service. The buyer often surrenders this power to more influential members of the organization, though. The purchasing agent often fill the buyer's role and executes the administrative functions associated with a purchase order.[36]

Organizational marketers face a critical task of determining the specific role and the relative decision-making influence of each buying-center participant. Salespeople can the tailor their presentations and information to the precise role that an individual plays at each step of the purchase process. Business marketers have found that their initial—and, in many cases, most extensive—contacts with a firm's purchasing department often fail to reach the buying-center participants who have the greatest influence, since these people may not work in that department at all.

Consider the selection of meeting and convention sites for trade or professional associations. A recent study found three general buying-center configurations for this decision. The primary decision maker could be an association board or executive committee, usually with input from the executive director or meeting planner; the meeting planner or association executive might choose meeting locations, sometimes with input from members; finally, the association's annual-meeting committee or program committee might make this selection. Because officers change annually, centers of control may change from year to year. Therefore, destination marketers and hotel operators try to discover how an association makes its decisions on annual conferences, so they can reach the people who actually make the decisions. In many associations, meeting planners act as gatekeepers for information about potential destinations.[37]

Strategies for Marketing to Buying Centers

To develop a marketing strategy for a particular buying center, marketers must identify people who play the various roles. They must also understand how these members interact with each other, other members of their own organizations, and outside vendors. The individual decision participants operate within the constraints of the buying center, their organization, and broader environmental influences. Marketers should not forget, however, to direct their marketing efforts to *individuals,* who are at the center of buying decisions.[38]

Many suppliers find effective support from team selling—introducing other employees in addition to salespeople into selling situations—to reach all of the members of a customer's buying center. Companies may also involve various members of their own supply networks in the sales process. For example, small resellers of specialized computer applications have developed alliances with distributors and major resellers. To sell these technical products to demanding clients, they need to expand the traditional sales and technical support teams. Clients require higher levels of product knowledge and training in the use of the programs. Because many small resellers cannot handle this component, they form alliances with distributors to provide training. In this way, the vendors get the training they need and offer it to their clients.

Florida Supplies and Solutions, based in Jacksonville, discovered the benefits of partnering with TechData Corp., a distributor from Clearwater. It added training services to its existing product lines—computer supplies and some hardware—as a way to tap into new opportunities to sell groupware programs. Sales representatives can now offer customers training and support services when they buy groupware. The ability to sell a complete range of services allowed the company to increase its revenues considerably.[39]

Some companies even become part of the buying center themselves. As noted earlier, that's the idea behind JIT II. At Chrysler Corp., about 600 supplier employees work at the Auburn Hills, Michigan, technical center. They take an active role in purchasing decisions and have a vested interest in their clients' success.[40]

International Buying Centers

Two distinct characteristics differentiate international buying centers from domestic ones. First, marketers may have trouble identifying members of foreign buying centers. In addition to cultural differences in decision-making methods, some foreign companies lack staff personnel. For example, in less developed countries, line managers may make most purchase decisions.

For a second distinction, a buying center in a foreign company may include more participants than U.S. companies involve. International buying centers can range from 1 to 50 people, with 15 to 20 participants being commonplace. Global marketers must recognize and accommodate this greater diversity of decision makers.

International buying centers can change in response to political and economic trends. Many European firms, for instance, once maintained separate facilities in each European nation where they operated in order to avoid tariffs and customs delays. As the European Union lowered trade barriers between member nations, however, many companies closed distant branches and consolidated their buying centers.

Business marketers also must understand the dynamics of a foreign buying center. "Overseas customers make business decisions on a very emotional basis," says Kevin Daley, president of New York-based training company Communispond. Friendship and trust for the vendor's sales representatives play a bigger role in many countries than in the United States. This characteristic is especially prevalent in Latin America. ADD Latin America, a subsidiary of pharmaceutical company Abbott Laboratories, trains its sales force to search for feelings and discover hidden motivators in business buying decisions. Salespeople can impress customers by listening to them, and this attention can make the difference between winning an account and losing it.[41]

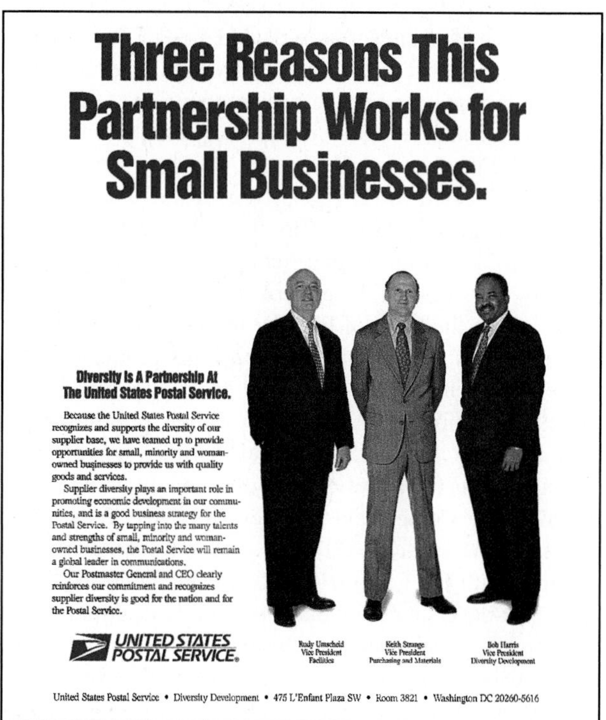
Three Reasons This Partnership Works for Small Businesses.
Diversity Is A Partnership At The United States Postal Service.
Because the United States Postal Service recognizes and supports the diversity of our supplier base, we have teamed up to provide opportunities for small, minority and woman-owned businesses to provide us with quality goods and services.
Supplier diversity plays an important role in promoting economic development in our communities, and is a good business strategy for the Postal Service. By tapping into the many talents and strengths of small, minority and woman-owned businesses, the Postal Service will remain a global leader in communications.
Our Postmaster General and CEO clearly reinforces our commitment and recognizes supplier diversity is good for the nation and for the Postal Service.
UNITED STATES POSTAL SERVICE®
Rudy Umscheid Vice President Facilities
Keith Strange Vice President Purchasing and Materials
Bob Harris Vice President Diversity Development
United States Postal Service • Diversity Development • 475 L'Enfant Plaza SW • Room 3821 • Washington DC 20260-5616

Figure 9.10 Government Purchasing to Promote Supplier Diversity

DEVELOPING EFFECTIVE BUSINESS-TO-BUSINESS STRATEGIES

A business marketer must develop a marketing strategy based on a particular organization's buying behavior and the buying situation. Clearly, many variables affect organizational purchasing decisions. This section will examine three market segments whose decisions present unique challenges to business marketers: units of government, institutions, and international markets. Finally, it will summarize key differences between consumer and business marketing.

Challenges of Government Markets

Government agencies—federal, state, and local—together make up the largest consumer in the United States. Over 80,000 government units purchase a wide variety of products, including office supplies, furniture, concrete, vehicles, grease, ballistic missiles, fuel, and lumber.

To compete effectively for these sales, business marketers must understand the unique challenges of selling to government units. One challenge results because government purchases typically involve dozens of interested parties who specify, evaluate, and/or use the purchased goods and services. These parties may or may not work within the government agency that officially handles a purchase.

For another challenge, government purchases are influenced by social goals such as minority subcontracting programs. The ad in Figure 9.10 announces the U.S. Postal Service's efforts to maintain diversity in its supplier base. The Postal Service's vice presidents of facilities, purchasing and materials, and diversity development work as a team to purchase goods and services from small firms and those owned by minorities and women.

Contractual guidelines create a third important influence in selling to government markets. Government buys products under two basic types of contracts: fixed-price contracts, in which seller and buyer agree to a firm price before finalizing the contract, and cost-reimbursement contracts, in which the government pays the vendor for allowable costs, including profits, incurred during performance of the contract. Each type of contract has advantages and disadvantages. While the fixed-price contract offers more profit potential than the alternative, it also carries greater risks from unforeseen expenses, inflation, and changing political and economic conditions.

Government Purchasing Procedures Many purchases of the U.S. government go through the General Services Administration (GSA), a central management agency that sets federal policy in such areas as procurement, property management, and information resources management. The GSA buys goods and services for its own use and for use by other government agencies. In its role as, essentially, the federal government's business manager, it purchases billions of dollars worth of goods and services. The Defense

Logistics Agency (DLA) serves the same function for the Department of Defense.

The government advertises all purchases over $25,000 in *Consumer Business Daily,* a Department of Commerce publication that appears six days a week. The *Daily* is available by subscription or at many public libraries. For more information on doing business with the GSA, marketers can contact a GSA Business Service Center. In addition to the Washington, D.C. office, Business Service Centers are located in Boston, New York, Philadelphia, Atlanta, Chicago, Kansas City, Fort Worth, Denver, San Francisco, Los Angeles, and Auburn, Washington.

By law, most U.S. government purchases must be awarded on the basis of **bids,** or written sales proposals, from vendors. As part of this process, government buyers develop **specifications**—detailed descriptions of needed items—for prospective bidders. Some purchases demand highly complicated specifications; government specifications for athletic supporters run 22 pages, while the Defense Department imposes 18 pages of specifications for the fruitcakes it buys. Federal purchases must comply with the Federal Acquisition Regulation (FAR), a 30,000-page set of standards originally designed to cut red tape in government purchasing. FAR standards have been further complicated by numerous exceptions issued by various government agencies. Numerous additional restrictions are designed to prevent corruption and favoritism.

State and local government purchasing procedures resemble federal procedures. Most states and many large cities have created buying offices similar to the GSA. Detailed specifications and open bidding are common at this level, as well. Many state purchasing regulations give preference to in-state bidders. For example, the state of Ohio allows a 5 percent preference to businesses based there. The preference reduces the price upon which the in-state bid is evaluated by 5 percent.

Government spending patterns may differ from those in private industry. Because the federal government's fiscal year runs from October 1 through September 30, many agencies spend much of their procurement budgets in the fourth quarter (July 1 to September 30). They hoard their funds to cover unexpected expenditures, and if they encounter no such problems, find themselves with money to spend in late summer. Companies understand this system and keep their eyes on government bulletins, so they can bid on the listed agency purchases, which often involve large amounts. In 1996, PC hardware and software vendors did especially well. Federal government spending for computers rose from $981 million in fiscal 1995 to $1.2 billion in fiscal 1996. Both Dell and Gateway 2000 found that government sales in the fourth quarter of 1996 represented about 40 percent of their annual government totals.[42]

Online with the Federal Government Like their colleagues in the private sector, government procurement professionals are streamlining purchasing procedures with new technology. Rather than paging through piles of paper catalogs and submitting handwritten purchase orders, buyers now prefer online catalogs that help them to compare competing product offerings. In fact, vendors find business with the government almost impossible unless they embrace electronic commerce. As Dendy Young, president of computer products reseller Government Technology Services, comments, "To properly represent your manufacturers, you have to make sure your customers can buy from you any way they want to."

Vendors can sell products to the federal government through three electronic options. Web sites provide a convenient method of exchanging information for both parties. Government buyers locate and order products, paying by credit card, and the vendors deliver the items within about a week. Another route through government-sponsored electronic ordering systems helps to standardize the buying process. GSA Advantage and the National Institutes of Health Computer Store are two of the largest systems. Agencies can search through thousands of products from hundreds of vendors to find the items that meet their needs. The third alternative, value-added networks (VANs), amount to a type of electronic data interchange. However, VANs are losing ground to the Internet as the preferred medium for electronic government commerce.

Many vendors dislike the government's electronic commerce systems. Some feel that they have no choice but to participate in GSA Advantage, for example. They complain about pressures on profits, because the government has created a very competitive environment that cuts margins to the bare minimum.[43]

To help businesses implement electronic purchasing programs, the Department of Commerce established the Electronic Commerce Resource Center (ECRC) program. The ECRC promotes electronic commerce and related technologies to help manufacturers improve their competitive positions in global markets. Through 11 regional centers around the United States, this program provides a variety of consulting, educational, and technical support activities, many of them free or at low cost. For example, companies can take courses like Getting Started in Electronic Commerce, EDI Orientation, EDI Vendor Briefing, and Issues in EDI Implementation.[44]

Challenges of Institutional Markets

Institutions constitute another important market. Institutional buyers include a wide variety of organizations, such as schools, hospitals, libraries, foundations, clinics, churches, and not-for-profit agencies.

This variety is reflected in widely diverse buying practices. Some institutional purchasers behave like government purchasers, because laws and political considerations determine their buying procedures. Many of them, such as schools and prisons, may even be managed by government units. Other, privately managed institutions may, however, implement buying procedures that resemble those of private companies.

Buying practices can differ between institutions of the same type. For instance, in a small hospital, the chief dietitian may approve all food purchases, while in a larger hospital, food purchases may go through a committee consisting of the dietitian plus a business manager, purchasing agent, and cook. Other hospitals may belong to buying groups, perhaps health maintenance organizations or local hospital cooperatives. Still others may contract with outside firms to prepare and serve all meals.

Within a single institution, multiple-buying influences may affect decisions. Many, staffed by professionals such as physicians, nurses, researchers, or professors, may also employ purchasing agents or even entire purchasing departments. Conflicts may arise among these decision makers. Professional employees may prefer to make their own purchase decisions and resent giving up control to purchasing staff. This conflict can force a business marketer to cultivate both professionals and purchasers. For instance, a sales representative for a pharmaceuticals firm must convince physicians and nurses of the value of a certain drug to patients while also convincing the hospital's purchasing department that the vendor offers superior prices, delivery schedules, and service.

Group purchasing is an important factor in institutional markets, since many institutions join cooperative associations to pool purchases for quantity discounts. Universities may join the Education and Institutional Purchasing Cooperative. Hospitals may belong to regional associations. Profit-oriented hospitals may obtain inputs through chains, such as Columbia/HCA Healthcare, with 340 hospitals, 130 surgery centers, and 500 home-health care centers. Central headquarters staff usually handles purchasing for all members of such a chain.

Diverse practices in institutional markets pose special challenges for business marketers. They must maintain flexibility to develop strategies for dealing with a range of customers, from large cooperative associations and chains to medium-sized purchasing departments and institutions to individuals. Buying centers can work with varying members, priorities, and levels of expertise. Discounts and effective distribution functions play important roles in obtaining—and keeping—institutions as customers.

Managers at educational institutions are also discovering the advantages of consolidating their purchasing practices. Massachusetts Institute of Technology once ordered office and laboratory supplies from 20,000 different vendors! To make matters worse, almost 90 percent of the orders totaled under $500. Because the university spent as much to process a $25 order for pens as for a $25,000 package of computer equipment, the situation clearly left room for improvement. By tapping into its internal computer expertise, MIT automated its purchasing system. Using the university's intranet, staff members can order supplies from a Web-based catalog that checks spending limits before authorizing purchases. Contracts with two office suppliers not only give MIT leverage for volume discounts, but they also allow delivery directly to purchasers, not a stockroom. Purchasing cards from American Express further streamline MIT's buying process.[45]

Challenges of International Markets

To sell successfully in international markets, business marketers must consider buyers' attitudes and cultural patterns within areas where they operate. In Asian markets, for example, a firm must maintain a local presence to sell products. Personal relationships are also important to business deals in Asia. Companies that want to expand globally need to establish joint ventures with local partners. United Technologies (UT) invested $500 million in a series of Asian joint ventures, including units that make Carrier air conditioners, Transicold refrigerated trucks, and rail cars. UT believes that its large presence within China will help it to sell U.S.-made products, as well.

Firms that try to tap into the enormous potential of Chinese markets must learn to play by China's rules for business practices. Foreign companies that observe this requirement gain a competitive advantage, such as the right to produce goods for sale in China, as compared to U.S. plants. Insuance companies eager to enter the Chinese market offer special incentives to win operating licenses. Chubb Corp. promised to build an "insurance university" at a cost of $1 million. Similarly, telecommunications firms like Northern Telecom (NORTEL), Alcatel Alsthom, and AT&T are hiring Chinese engineers in product development positions and setting up local laboratories.[46]

Marketing Dictionary

bid Written sales proposal from a vendor.

specifications Written description of a needed good or service.

MARKETING HALL OF FAME

Toshiba and IBM: From Competitors to Partners

Not long ago, Toshiba Corp. unveiled a $1 billion facility for making semiconductor chips in Japan. The project was big news for more than the obvious reasons. First, it represented a technological coup. By ushering in the latest generation of memory chips, Toshiba would manufacture chips with four times the memory of the current ones. But the plant brought more notable developments. Previously, a major Toshiba competitor like IBM would have panicked at such a groundbreaking advancement. Not this time, though.

Toshiba and IBM had called a truce. More than that, these two companies worked together with Siemens of Germany to create the technology for this chip-making breakthrough. In the old days, such corporations wouldn't have dreamed of collaborating on even the smallest projects. Today, business-to-business alliances, particularly between Japanese and American companies, are becoming more and more commonplace. "It's no longer considered a loss of corporate manhood to let others help out," observes Robert C. Timpson, IBM's Asia Pacific president.

This attitude fostered development of an ongoing chip-making partnership. The corporations are now working on developing a 256-megabit chip, and by 2001, a 1-gigabit chip, developed with the help of Motorola Inc., should be on the market.

Many other examples illustrate this new era of global commercial cooperation. Eastman Kodak Co. and its chief rival Fuji Film Co., for instance, jointly created a new advanced photo system. General Motors is now supplying car parts to Toyota Motor Corp., while Canon Inc. and Hewlett-Packard Co. are sharing laser-printer technology. Caterpillar Inc. has joined forces with industrial giant Mitsubishi Heavy Industries Ltd. Caterpillar wants to sell heavy construction equipment in Japan,

International marketers must also respond to economic conditions, geographic characteristics, legal restrictions, and local industries. For instance, many local industries in Spain specialize in food and wine; therefore, Hyster markets smaller forklift trucks to Spanish companies than it sells in Germany, where bigger, heavier trucks serve the needs of that nation's large automobile industry.

Remanufacturing—production to restore worn-out products to like-new condition—can be an important marketing strategy in a nation that cannot afford to buy new products. Developing countries often purchase remanufactured factory machinery, which costs 35 percent to 60 percent less than new equipment.

Foreign governments represent another important business market. In many countries, the government, government agencies, or state-owned companies dominate certain industries, such as construction and other infrastructure sales. Additional examples include airport and highway construction, telephone system equipment, and computer networking equipment. Sales to a foreign government can involve an array of regulations. For example, many governments, like that of the United States, limit foreign participation in their defense programs. Joint ventures and countertrade are common, as are local-content laws, which mandate local production of a certain percentage of a business product's components.

Marketing to Both Business Purchasers and Final Users

Some firms market their goods and services to both consumer and business markets. One example, the J. M. Smucker Company, sells jellies and preserves to consumers, and it also sells filling mixes to companies that manufacture yogurt and dessert products.

http://www.smucker.com/

Table 9.2 shows significant differences between business and consumer-goods marketing. Firms generally market less standardized products to organizational buyers

while Mitsubishi pursues its goal of expanding its exports and competing with Japanese arch rival Komatsu Ltd.

Of course, these strategic alliances have created tricky problems for the federal government's trade officials. For years, America's corporate giants have protested loudly at what they regard as Japanese intransigence at opening its markets. In particular, U.S. companies have complained bitterly about what they consider unfair trade practices by Japan's system of big industrial groups, called *keiretsu*. But Americans are now entering their own agreements with these huge industrial groups. The resulting partnerships have even played havoc with U.S. trade statistics, which track only American products made on U.S. soil and shipped to Japan.

All this corporate togetherness has not dulled competitive instincts. General Motors is trying to undercut Toyota's Corolla sales by manufacturing an Asian car at its newly built $750 million plant in Rayong, Thailand. Hewlett-Packard and Canon are slugging it out in the laser printer field, and even Toshiba and IBM continue to compete fiercely across the globe in the market for laptop computers.

QUESTIONS FOR CRITICAL THINKING

1. **Can you think of any instances where business-to-business collaborations may fail?**
2. **Do you think American protests over Japanese trade practices will diminish because of the new overseas corporate relationships?**

Sources: Stephen H. Wildstrom, "The Laptop Labyrinth," *Business Week,* March 17, 1997, p. 20; Brian Bremner, "Keiretsu Connections, the Bonds between the U.S. and Japan's Industry Groups," *Business Week,* July 22, 1996, pp. 52, 54.; Reinhardt Krause, "Chip Industry Fast Forwards to Next DRAM Generation," *Investor's Business Daily,* July 2, 1996, downloaded from America Online, September 17, 1996; Norm Alster, "IBM Wins in Memory Chips but Strives for Much More," *Investor's Business Daily,* January 23, 1996.

than to ultimate consumers, and customer service is extremely important to buying organizations. Advertising plays a much smaller role in the business market than in the consumer market. Business marketers advertise primarily to enhance their company images and the images of their products and to attract new prospects, who are then contacted directly by salespeople. Personal selling plays a much bigger role in business markets than in consumer markets, distribution channels are shorter, customer relations tend to last longer, and purchase decisions can involve multiple decision makers.

In marketing its jellies to consumers, Smucker uses a varied promotional program that includes TV and print advertising, special offers, grocery store displays, and coupons. The distribution chain includes several intermediaries, leading to infrequent contacts between Smucker employees and retailers.

In contrast, Smucker markets to business customers through personal service and one-on-one selling. Suppose, for example, that a food company is creating a new dessert with a fruit filling. A Smucker salesperson spends a lot of time with the company's research and product development personnel to determine their preferences. From these meetings come detailed specifications for the filling—its taste, color, consistency, and calorie content. The salesperson carries this information to Smucker's research and development department, which prepares samples. Meanwhile, the salesperson negotiates a price with the customer's purchasing department. Since the order would specify large quantities, even a few cents per pound can make a big difference. Once these representatives finalize the transaction, the Smucker facility ships the filling directly to the customer's factory. After delivery of the filling, the salesperson follows up frequently with the customer's purchasing agent and plant manager in an effort to build repeat business.[47]

Marketing Dictionary

remanufacturing Production to restore worn-out products to like-new condition.

Table 9.2 Business-to-Business Marketing versus Consumer Goods Marketing: Some Distinguishing Characteristics

	Business-to-Business Marketing	Consumer-Goods Marketing
Product	Relatively technical in nature, exact form often variable, accompanying services very important	Standardized form, service important but less than for business products
Price	Competitive bidding for unique items, list prices for standard items	List prices
Promotion	Emphasis on personal selling	Emphasis on advertising
Distribution	Relatively short, direct channels to market	Product passes through a number of intermediate links en route to consumer
Customer relations	Relatively enduring and complex	Comparatively infrequent contact, relationship of relatively short duration
Decision-making process	Involvement of diverse group of organization members in decision	Individual or household unit makes decision

ACHIEVEMENT CHECK SUMMARY

Reread the learning goals that follow, and consider the questions for each goal. Answering these questions will reinforce your grasp of the most important concepts in the chapter and allow you to check how well you have achieved these learning goals. Where a blank appears before a question, answer with *T* or *F*; for multiple-choice questions, circle the letter of the correct answer.

Objective 9.1: List and define the components of the business market.

1. ___ Business-to-business transactions involve large purchases by firms.

2. ___ A purchase by Marriott Corp. of linens for its hotels is an example of a trade industry transaction.

3. ___ Government organizations purchase goods and services to use in providing public benefits.

Objective 9.2: Describe the major approaches to segmenting business-to-business markets.

1. ___ Size is a way to segment business-to-business markets.

2. ___ SIC codes help business marketers to target potential customers in a particular geographic area.

3. ___ Companies that assign different sales forces for existing customers and new customers are segmenting their markets by (a) demographics; (b) end-use application; (c) purchasing situation; (d) customer base.

Objective 9.3: Identify the major characteristics of the business market and its demand.

1. ___ Like the consumer market, business markets are geographically spread out with many small buyers.

2. ___ Business purchasing is typically *not* characterized by (a) multiple decision makers; (b) use of several vendors for the same product; (c) greater complexity than consumer buying; (d) short purchase time frames.

3. ___ Derived demand refers to the relationship between the demand for jointly used business products.

Objective 9.4: Describe the major influences on business buying behavior.

1. ___ A change in pollution control laws is an example of an organizational influence on buying behavior.

2. ___ Purchasing strategies have a major impact on a company's financial performance, because purchased goods and services represent 40 cents of every dollar of its revenue.

Objective 9.5: Outline the steps in the organizational buying process.

1. ___ The organizational buying process starts with a description of the characteristics and quantity of the needed product.

2. ___ Competitive bidding occurs only in government markets.

3. ___ Vendor analysis looks at each component of a purchase to see if the item can be deleted or replaced with a more cost-effective substitute.

Objective 9.6: Classify organizational buying situations.

1. ___ Excellent customer service and product quality are keys to maintaining straight rebuy relationships.

2. ___ A modified rebuy is the equivalent of routinized response behavior in consumer markets.

3. ___ A company that wishes to install its first database system faces a modified rebuy situation.

Objective 9.7: Explain the buying center concept.

1. ___ A buying center is a formal group of people that handles purchasing for a particular department or division.

2. ___ An engineer who provides technical requirements for a new automated manufacturing system is an example of (a) a gatekeeper; (b) an influencer; (c) a user; (d) a buyer.

3. ___ The decider is the person in a buying center with the formal authority to make a purchase decision.

Objective 9.8. Discuss the challenges of marketing to government, institutional, and international buyers.

1. ___ Businesses that sell to government agencies can limit their dealings to the particular agencies that needs their products.

2. ___ Group purchasing is not important in institutional markets.

3. ___ Attitudes and cultural patterns influence global consumer marketing, but they are not critical in international business-to-business markets.

Objective 9.9: Summarize key differences between consumer and business-to-business marketing.

1. ___ Business-to-business markets require stronger customer service than consumer markets demand.

2. ___ Business products move through fewer channels than consumer products.

3. ___ Of the following statements, which does not apply to business marketing? (a) Customer relationships last longer in business markets than in consumer markets. (b) Prices of business products are open to negotiation. (c) Business buyers tend to purchase less standardized products that consumers buy. (d) Advertising is more important than personal selling to business marketing.

Students: See the solutions section located on page S-2 to check your responses to the Achievement Check Summary.

Key Terms

business-to-business marketing
commercial market
trade industry
Standard Industrial Classification (SIC)
global sourcing
derived demand
joint demand
sole sourcing
outsourcing
multiple sourcing
systems integration
straight rebuy
modified rebuy
new-task buying
reciprocity
value analysis
vendor analysis
buying center
bid
specifications
remanufacturing

Review Questions

1. Outline the four components of the business market. Cite examples of each.
2. What are the characteristics of the commercial market? Show how each characteristic affects the marketing strategies of firms serving that market.
3. What are SIC codes? How do business marketers use these codes?
4. Contrast organizational buying behavior and consumer purchasing behavior. What are the primary differences and similarities?
5. Give examples of the effect on industrial market demand of derived demand, volatile demand, joint demand, inventory adjustments, and the accelerator principle.
6. What is outsourcing? Explain the advantages and disadvantages of this practice.
7. Discuss the major influences on organizational purchasing with examples of each.
8. Describe the roles in a buying center. Identify the person in an organization who would most likely play each role.
9. In what ways is the government market similar to other organizational markets? How does it differ?
10. Describe major characteristics of institutional and international markets. How might these characteristics affect marketing strategy?

Discussion Questions

1. Comment on the following statement: "There is really no need to separate the study of business-to-business buying behavior from consumer buying behavior."
2. Research the buying process through which your school purchases needed products. Compare this process to the chapter's discussion of institutional markets.
3. Choose a commercial product and analyze its foreign market potential. Report your findings to the class.
4. Investigate the qualifications needed to be a purchasing manager in an industry located in your area. Discuss these qualifications in class. What general statements can you make?
5. How has the federal government market changed in recent years? How should business marketers deal with these developments?

'netWork

1. Technologies such as the Internet could change the way organizations purchase products. What changes would you predict as a result of electronic methods of commerce? What advantages and disadvantages will influence marketing to organizations over the Internet?
2. Organizational purchasers can find many sources of information to help them make purchasing decisions. One of the most widely used is the Thomas Register. Go to the home page of this resource

http://www.thomasregister.com/

If you were a business supplier to another company, how would you use the Thomas Register to gain a competitive edge?
3. Creighton University provides another kind of information that might be useful to purchasing managers

http://econews.creighton.edu/

Evaluate this information, and choose one item you would find useful if you were a purchasing manager. Describe the information and why it would be useful.

VIDEO CASE 9

CREATING KITCHENS TO PLEASE PARTNERS

Business-to-business marketers seldom get the chance to showcase their firm's products in a blockbuster movie. The Delfield Company enjoyed just such an opportunity when the producer of *Jurassic Park* called on it to supply stainless steel equipment for one of the most famous kitchen scenes in movie history. Headquartered in Mount Pleasant, Michigan, Delfield is a leading supplier of commercial kitchen equipment to the food-service industry. The company designs and produces more than 200 products for restaurants, schools, hotels, grocery stores, and military installations. Products include refrigerators, freezers, counters, ventilation systems, cafeteria systems, and display cases.

As a supplier to major chains such as Taco Bell, Arby's, Burger King, Kmart, and KFC, Delfield sees close relationships as the key to success in the business-goods market. Kevin E. McCrone, president and CEO of Delfield, says, "We view the relationships as part of our core business strategy. We have to know what kinds of problems our customers deal with every day. We have to know what space limitations are required and what obstacles our customers meet and face everyday. If we don't, then we won't be able to design and adapt our products to meet their demands."

Delfield has established its strong market position through strategies that emphasize staying close to its customers, giving employees the skills and tools they need to produce quality products, and investing in resources that allow the company to provide excellent customer service. Delfield uses speed and flexibility as competitive weapons in order to quickly respond to changing customer needs.

The company fields 138 representatives who work daily with customers to learn about their needs. Menu changes often drive a kitchen's need for new equipment. Delfield's customers add new products, such as pizza or salads, to compete in new segments and to target different types of consumers. Some customers need help opening food outlets in nontraditional locations such as movie theaters, airports, stadiums, and gas stations; these innovative operations require specially designed equipment.

For example, Delfield formed a strategic alliance with its customer Kentucky Fried Chicken to develop and implement a new concept in fast food. KFC's management had detected two important characteristics in the fast-food market: Customers seemed to like the comfort of buying their food from a familiar restaurant, and competitors had already set up shop in many of the prime, store-front locations traditional for fast-food restaurants. KFC looked for alternative restaurant sites that would ensure convenience and accessibility for customers and decided to place new outlets in high-traffic areas such as stores, airports, and university student centers.

The strategy required a solution to one central problem: Limit space demanded much smaller fast-food restaurants in these settings than regular, stand-alone outlets could accommodate. KFC needed equipment compact enough to fit in a 100-square-foot outlet but capable of meeting all the needs of a regular-sized restaurant.

Delfield took the lead in developing these new compact kitchens, known as SIB ("Small Is Beautiful") units. For seven months, Delfield engineers worked with KFC personnel and other vendors in that firm's supply chain to determine specifications for cooking equipment, fryers, hoods, and ventilation systems. After assembling a prototype SIB unit, Delfield invited representatives from KFC and the other suppliers to a meeting to view the design, evaluate it, and modify it before launching full-scale production.

One participant, who had experience in the operations end of the business, suggested that the high positions of the ovens would cause problems by forcing restaurant employees to lift large pans of hot food over their heads. Because many fast-foot restaurants hire women and senior citizens, who might find this lifting difficult if not dangerous, designers lower the unit by 3 inches. The meeting was a huge success, and KFC ordered eight SIB units from Delfield. Delfield continued to modify the design, based on suggestions from KFC, to make the units more efficient, for instance, by adding components, extra handles, and magnetic latches instead of mechanical ones.

KFC installed one SIB unit in a Wal-Mart store in New York state; it planned others for airports, shopping malls, and food courts. The restaurant chain even negotiated to place one in the staff cafeteria of a major corporation.
Delfield sees a very positive long-term outlook for these small units. According to Richard Zuehlke of Delfield's major account development division, "Building managers want to maximize sales per square foot, and they've found that food is one of the best ways to do this. Consumers like the idea because it's so convenient. They're at the store anyway, so why not pick up something to go from KFC?"
Working closely with customers to meet their needs has made Delfield a market leader, in the process earning the company industrywide recognition. It won an award for food-facilities design by designing versatile equipment to support three different types of restaurant service—servery, full service, and family style—at a Colorado resort.

Delfield buys many component parts and materials from its own team of suppliers. In selecting suppliers, Delfield considers a list of critical questions: Is the company large enough to meet its needs? Do its products and processes meet Delfield's high quality standards? Can the prospective supplier meet strict delivery schedules? Can it offer the technology and service that Delfield needs? Does it reliably maintain its prices?

Delfield builds relationships with its suppliers over long periods of time. For example, it worked with Washington Specialty Metals for many years before choosing the company as its sole source of stainless steel sheets. Delfield also forms strategic alliances with its suppliers. For example, one vendor, a maker of vacuum-formed, plastic trim collars for refrigerated cabinets, announced an 80 percent price hike due to its high scrap rate; in response, Delfield engineers helped to redesign the cabinets. "In vacuum forming, the sharper the radius, the more difficult the process becomes," says Plant Manager Ted Reed. "We'd never given any consideration to that in our designing. It was insignificant to us whether the corner had to be that sharp. So we gave the supplier the opportunity to go to a one-half-inch radius on at least eight parts. It had no effect upon us, but improved their operation significantly." The new design reduced the vendor's scrap rate, allowing the company to cancel the price increase.

Questions

1. Do Delfield's alliances with suppliers and customers give it a competitive edge? Support your answer.
2. How do the three types of demand discussed in the chapter affect the demand for Delfield's SIB units?
3. Which of the three organizational buying situations discussed in the chapter does the purchase of an SIB unit represent? Explain your answer.
4. The Delfield Company's strategic alliances with several companies have directly contributed to the company's success. To form these kinds of relationships, businesspeople must make difficult choices between prospective partners and design complex arrangements to forge the best connections. Numerous companies—some profit-oriented, some not-for-profit—offer services that help clients to build strategic alliances. Find three of these companies on the Web. What services does each one provide? Search the Web and find specific examples of companies and products that have been successful as a result of a strategic alliance. Explain your findings.

Source: Telephone interview with Richard Zuehlke, major account development officer, the Delfield Company, April 18, 1997.

CHAPTER 10

RELATIONSHIP MARKETING

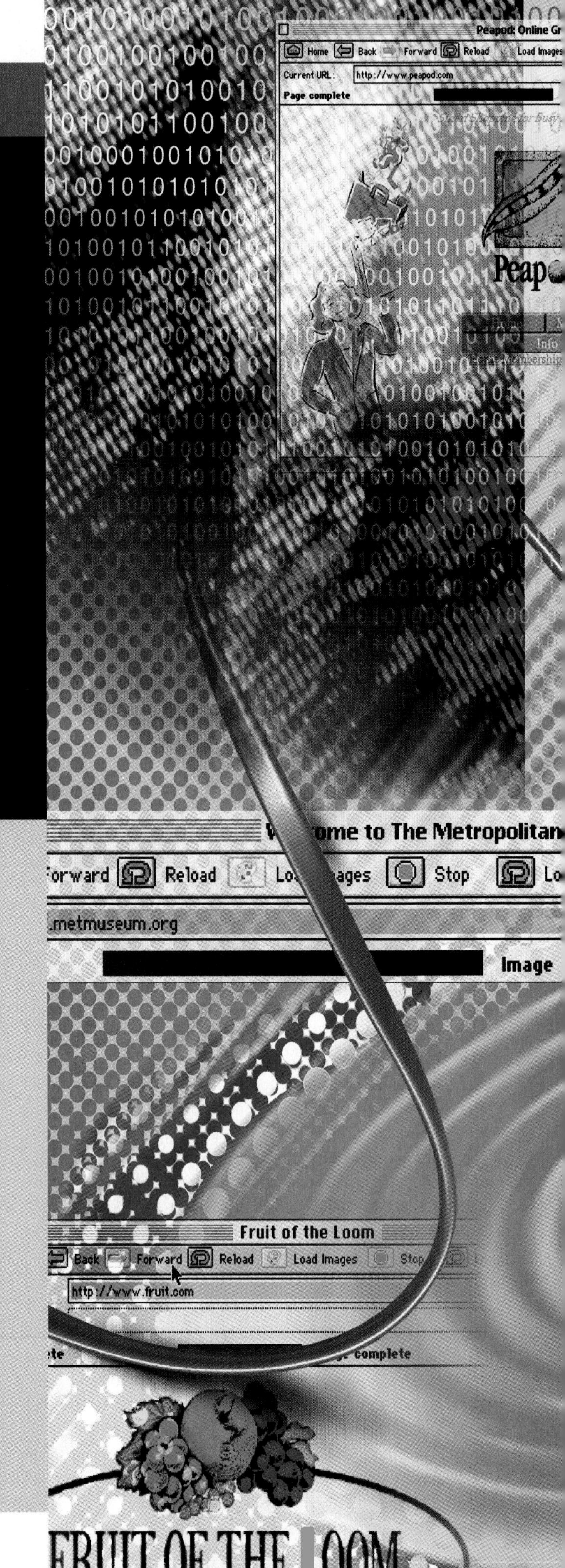

Peapod: Online Gr
Home
Back
Forward
Reload
Load Images
Current URL:
http://www.peapod.com
Page complete
Peap
Welcome to The Metropolitan
Forward
Reload
Stop
.metmuseum.org
Image
Fruit of the Loom
Back
Forward
Reload
Load Images
Stop
http://www.fruit.com
FRUIT OF THE LOOM

Chapter Objectives

1. Contrast relationship marketing with transaction-based marketing.
2. Identify and explain each of the core elements of relationship marketing.
3. Outline the steps in the development of a marketing relationship and the different levels of relationship marketing.
4. Explain the role of databases in relationship marketing.
5. Compare the different types of partnerships and explain how they contribute to relationship marketing.
6. Relate the concepts of co-marketing and co-branding to relationship marketing.
7. Describe how relationship marketing incorporates electronic data interchange, vendor-managed inventories, and national account selling.
8. Discuss the value of strategic alliances to a company's relationship marketing strategy.
9. Identify and evaluate the most common measurement and evaluation techniques within a relationship marketing program.

Online Grocery Shopping with Peapod

Hate going to the grocery store? If you live in Boston, Chicago, Columbus, the San Francisco peninsula, San Jose, or other metropolitan areas, you can cybershop instead on the World Wide Web. "In the next week, thousands of grocery shoppers—most of them women—will sit down at home between 8 P.M. and 1 A.M. in the morning and do their grocery shopping," says Tim Dorgan, president of Peapod Interactive. "Sitting at their personal computers, the kids in bed, maybe sipping a glass of wine, these shoppers will shop for a week's worth of groceries in less than half an hour without having to set foot in a place most of them dread . . . the grocery store."

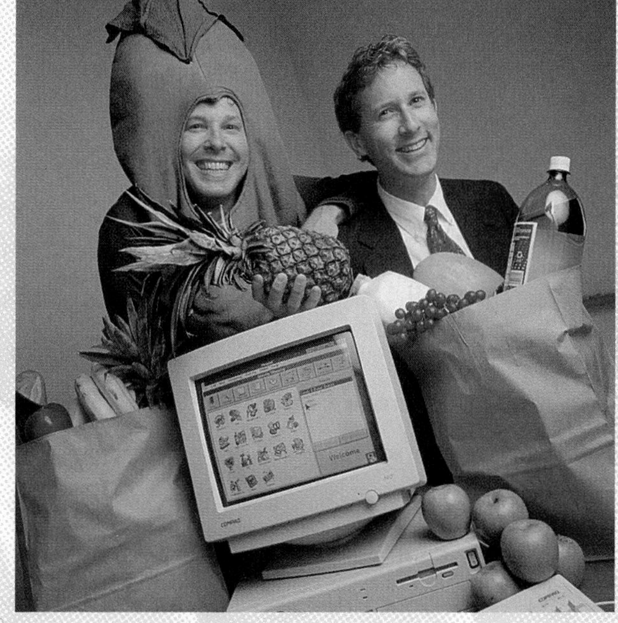

Years ago, people developed close relationships with their neighborhood retailers. The owners of these small, mom-and-pop establishments didn't just sell you goods and services. They were your friends, your neighbors, and your trusted advisors. When you walked into the neighborhood grocery store, the person behind the counter knew what you liked and what you didn't like, and what you were going to buy without your having to ask.

Today, giant supermarket chains have largely supplanted the old mom-and-pops. Close, one-to-one relationships between consumers and providers of goods and services have given way to impersonal mega-malls, cavernous warehouse stores, and faceless bar-code-reading checkout stands. However, some companies have discovered how to use technology to personalize buyer-seller interactions and create long-term relationships in the process. Peapod is one such company.

http://www.peapod.com/

Peapod, based in Evanston, Illinois, is a virtual grocery/drugstore shopping and delivery service. Customers who download free software from its Internet home page can order more than 25,000 different products through their personal computers. For a monthly membership fee of $5 to $7, customers can simply point and click on any item and have the requested products delivered to their chosen locations. Before purchasing an item, Peapod members can display its picture on their computers,

review its nutritional content, and sort a list of items by price, total calories, or other criteria.

According to Cathy Sarkisian, a dedicated Peapod user, the online service saves users time and money. "When you order with a computer, you can do your meal planning the same time that you're ordering," she explains. "You can plan your budget for your groceries because all the prices show and then all the things that are on sale also show. You can go back and forth between different categories instead of walking back and forth between aisles, so you're literally just doing it with buttons rather than your feet."

What makes Peapod's system truly unique, however, is that it "learns" the preferences of its member-customers. If, for example, you like your bananas green, simply put your preference in your customer profile; Peapod's trained staff of shoppers will always ensure that the bananas delivered to you are green. If you have special dietary needs such as vegetarian or kosher foods, your "interaction record," a customer database, will be updated to reflect those requirements. Have a problem with an order? Just pick up the phone and call Peapod's Member Services and Technical Support staff to resolve it quickly and easily.

So, what do Peapod members think about this service? They love it. Says a satisfied, work-at-home mom, "I think Peapod has made a big difference for me—in my ability to get my work done at home—to continue my work, order my groceries, get back to my work, and not have to get the kids all dressed and get to the store, stand in line, and get home. The only thing they don't do for me is put everything away in the cabinets."

Peapod further enhances its customer relationships with a bimonthly newsletter. *Beantalk* includes information on software upgrades and other improvements to the service. The newsletter also carries surveys that provide customer feedback to help the company improve the service. Its relationships extend to its many supplier-partners—retailers like Jewel/Osco, Safeway, and Kroger along with sponsoring manufacturers such as Bristol-Myers Squibb, Frito-Lay, Kraft Foods, and Ore-Ida Foods.

If customer retention rates are any indication of member satisfaction, Peapod's interactive shopping service is a smashing success. With thousands of members and annual revenues of approximately $15 million, Peapod retains more than 80 percent of its customers. Clearly, Peapod delivers on its promise—Friendly People, Superior Service—and lives up to its motto—Smart Shopping for Busy People.[1]

CHAPTER OVERVIEW

As Chapter 1 discussed, marketing revolves around exchange relationships. The shift away from transaction-based marketing, which focuses on short-term, single exchanges, to customer-focused relationship marketing is one of the most important trends in marketing today. Companies like Peapod recognize that they cannot prosper simply by identifying and attracting new customers; to succeed, they must build loyal, mutually beneficial relationships with existing customers, suppliers, distributors, and employees, as well. This strategy also benefits the bottom line, because retaining customers costs much less than acquiring them.

Figure 10.1 Forms of Customer-Marketer Interaction

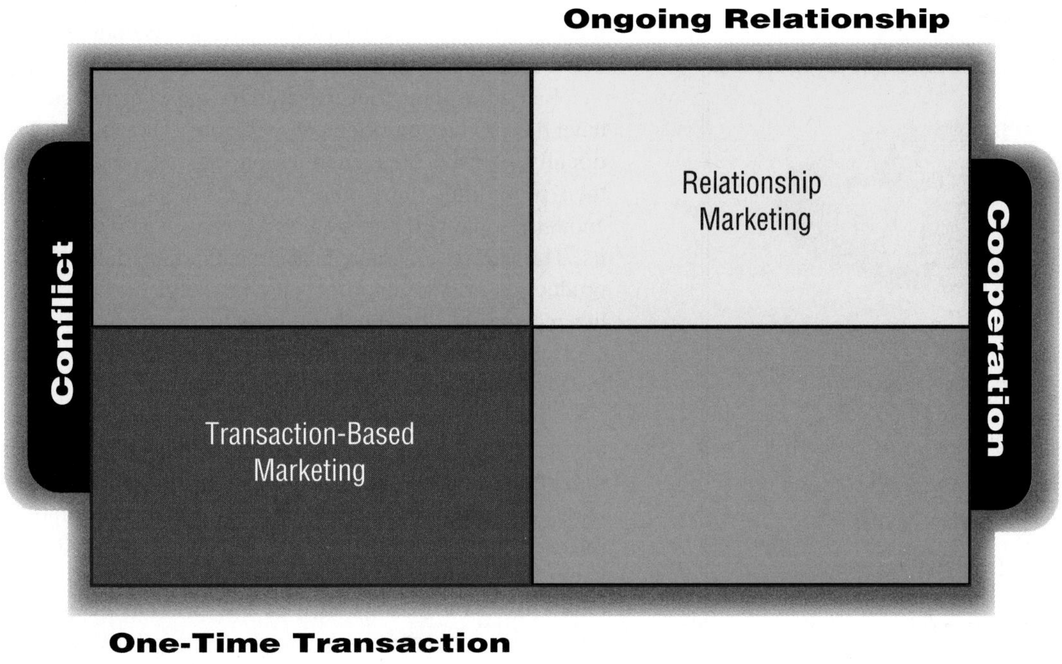

	Ongoing Relationship	
Conflict		Relationship Marketing	Cooperation
	Transaction-Based Marketing	
	One-Time Transaction	

style characteristics. By analyzing this information, the firm can modify its marketing mix to deliver differentiated messages and customized marketing programs to individual consumers. Finally, monitoring each relationship provides a way to measure the success of marketing programs. The company can calculate the cost of attracting a new cus-tomer and how much profit that customer will generate over the relationship.[3]

USAA, an insurance company with a large customer base among members of the U.S. military, also uses technology to enhance its customer relationships. It has developed a sophisticated, automated database for its nearly 3 million policyholders. All policy information and correspondence is consolidated into each member's electronic file. With one phone call, a member can speak to a customer service representative to make changes in or ask questions about any of his or her policies without tolerating transfers from department to department. The USAA representative who accesses this file has all the information necessary to provide personal service, customized for that member.[2]

Building and managing long-term relationships between buyers and sellers is the hallmark of relationship marketing. **Relationship marketing** is the development, growth, and maintenance of long-term, cost-effective relationships with individual customers, suppliers, employees, and other partners for mutual benefit. It expands the scope of a company's relationships to integrate these stakeholders, who also include distributors and retailers, into a company's product design and development, manufacturing, and sales processes.

Building long-term relationships with consumers and other businesses involves three basic steps. First, database technology helps a company to identify current and potential customers with selected demographic, purchase, and life-

As Figure 10.1 illustrates, relationship marketing emphasizes cooperation rather than conflict between these parties. This ongoing, collaborative exchange creates value for both parties.[4] In fact, partnerships, co-marketing, cobranding, and strategic alliances play a major role in relationship marketing programs. The chapter begins by examining the reasons organizations are moving to relationship marketing and the impact of this move on both producers of goods and services and their customers.

RELATIONSHIP MARKETING AND THE CUSTOMER-FOCUSED ENTERPRISE

Over the past several decades, consumers' tastes and demands have undergone significant change. In the days when the Ford Model T was the king of the road, you could buy one from your local dealer in any color you wanted— as long as you wanted black. Henry Ford decided what kind and color of car his factories would build; if you wanted to buy a Ford, that's what you got. Mass production created a

Marketing Dictionary

relationship marketing The development and maintenance of long-term, cost-effective relationships with individual customers, suppliers, employees, and other partners for mutual benefit.

Figure 10.2 Ford Motor Company: Succeeding by Building Long-Term Relationships

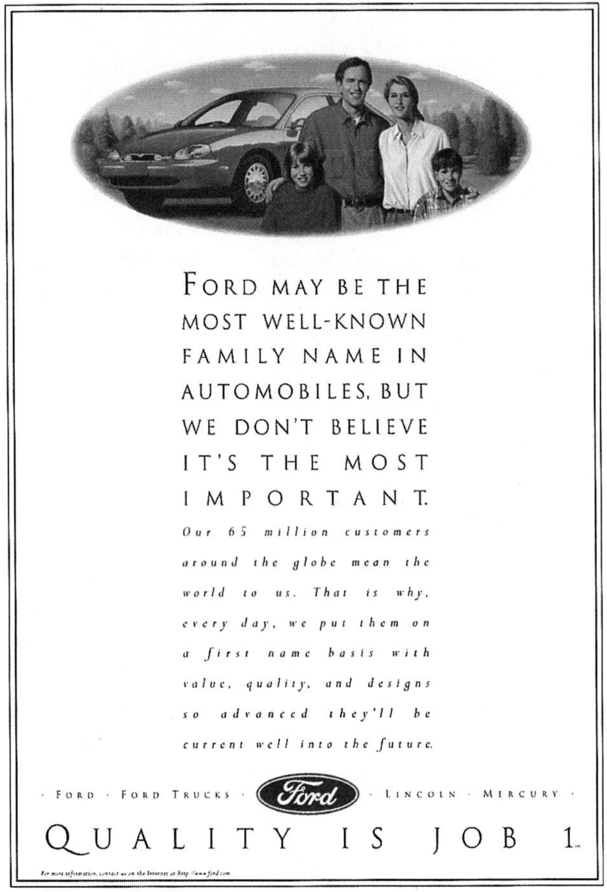
FORD MAY BE THE MOST WELL-KNOWN FAMILY NAME IN AUTOMOBILES, BUT WE DON'T BELIEVE IT'S THE MOST IMPORTANT.
Our 65 million customers around the globe mean the world to us. That is why, every day, we put them on a first name basis with value, quality, and designs so advanced they'll be current well into the future.
· FORD · FORD TRUCKS · Ford · LINCOLN · MERCURY ·
QUALITY IS JOB 1.

flood of affordable products for mass consumption. Mass production worked most efficiently, however, when a company offered few choices to buyers, because it could then standardize parts and procedures to lower production costs and simplify inventory decisions.

Today, not only can customers order a new Ford Mustang GT in most any color they might want, but they can choose from a dizzying array of options. Through Ford's factory ordering program, they can select a powerful optional engine, a convertible top, leather seats, a high-powered stereo system with compact disc player, and many other options. The car will be built to specifications in the Ford factory and delivered to the dealer. Aftermarket companies will further customize any new car with turbochargers, body work, special alloy wheels, and more—for a price, of course.

http://www.ford.com/

Henry Ford might not approve, but today his namesake company emphasizes relationships with its customers, as Figure 10.2 shows. This advertisement prominently features a family rather than the car behind it. Ford's ad sends the message that the company cares about its 65 million customers worldwide, considering them its most important family. It takes a very personal approach: "We put them on a first-name basis with value, quality, and designs."

Since the Industrial Revolution, most manufacturers have run production-oriented operations. They have traditionally focused their energies on making products and then promoting those items to customers, hoping that enough people will buy them to cover costs and earn profits. The shelves of your local grocery store show how a production orientation affects the marketplace. According to a recent study, the number of new products found in grocery stores each year has grown from less than 3,000 a year in 1980 to more than 17,000 a year today.[5]

The emphasis on production led companies to focus on individual sales, or *transactions.* **Transaction-based marketing** involves buyer and seller exchanges characterized by limited communications and little or no ongoing relationship between the parties. In transaction-based marketing, the primary goal is to entice a buyer to make a purchase based on reasons such as low price, convenience, packaging, or similar inducements. This activity serves a short-term goal: create a sale—now. While this style of marketing is still widespread, many organizations are trying a new approach, one that looks at customers in a different light. Indeed, they have found that creating long-term *relationships* with customers pays off in increased sales and decreased marketing costs.

The move from transactions to relationships is reflected in the changing nature of the interactions between customers and sellers themselves. Transaction-based marketing relationships are generally sporadic in nature, often disrupted by conflict. As marketing interactions shift toward a relationship focus, however, conflict changes to cooperation, and infrequent contacts between buyers and sellers become ongoing interactions.

Transaction-based marketing was the norm for decades, but now businesses understand that they must do more than simply creating products and then selling them. With so many goods and services to choose from, customers look for added value from their marketing relationships.

What Is Relationship Marketing?

In rapidly increasing numbers, producers of goods and services have shifted away from transaction-based systems of marketing to longer-term, more customer-focused relationship systems. Table 10.1 summarizes the differences between the narrow focus of transaction marketing and the much broader view that relationship marketing takes.

Table 10.1 Comparing Transaction-Based and Relationship Marketing Strategies

Characteristic	Transaction Marketing	Relationship Marketing
Time orientation	Short-term	Long-term
Organizational goal	Make the sale	Emphasis on retaining customers
Customer service priority	Relatively low	Key component
Customer contact	Low to moderate	Frequent
Degree of customer commitment	Low	High
Basis for seller-customer interactions	Conflict manipulation	Cooperation; trust
Source of quality	Primarily from production	Companywide commitment

Every marketing transaction involves a relationship between buyer and seller. In a transaction-based situation, the relationship may be quite short in duration and narrow in scope. Few if any social relationships may develop between buyer and seller.

For example, a traveler who is running dangerously low on gas in an unfamiliar town will likely stop at the first gas station she encounters, whether or not it carries Shell, her usual brand. She will fill her tank, anyway. When she gets back home, however, she is likely to return to her previous practice of buying her preferred brand from her usual Shell station. The single emergency transaction is unlikely to affect her future gasoline purchase patterns.

The customer-seller bonds developed in a relationship marketing situation, on the other hand, last longer and cover a much broader scope than those developed in transaction marketing. Social interactions (customer contacts) are generally much more frequent and enduring. During these extended dealings, a companywide emphasis on customer service positively influences customer satisfaction and contributes to long-term relationships. In relationship marketing, customer service should extend beyond traditional customers to include excellent service to suppliers and other partners, as well. Chapter 2 emphasized the critical importance of quality in achieving customer satisfaction. Figure 10.3 shows the need to blend quality and customer service with traditional elements of the marketing mix. When a company integrates customer service and quality with marketing, the result is a relationship marketing orientation.[6]

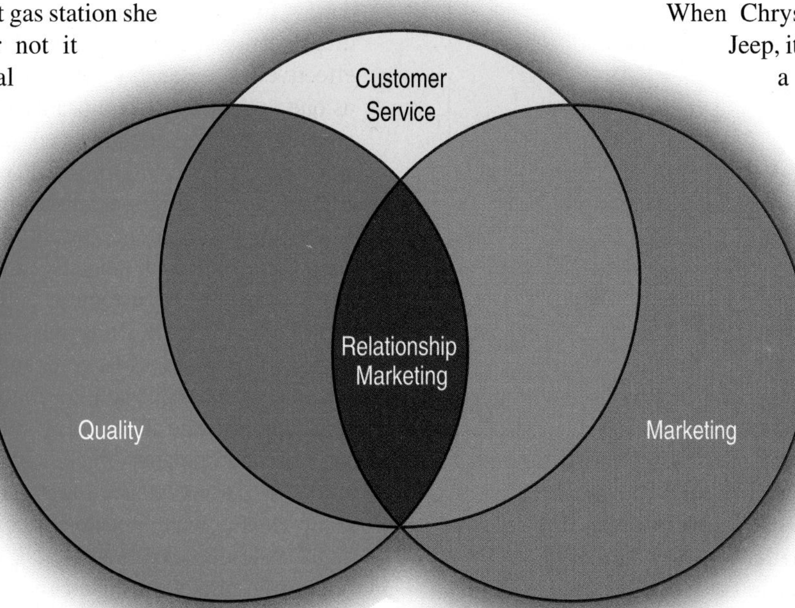
Customer Service
Relationship Marketing
Quality
Marketing

Figure 10.3 Relationship Marketing Orientation

When Chrysler Corp. sells a new Jeep, it is also selling a place in a worldwide network of other Jeep owners and aficionados. The company hopes that the relationships customers develop with other Jeep owners and with the company itself will increase their loyalty to the brand and the likelihood that their next car will be another Jeep.

While the company has long sponsored Jeep Jamborees—weekend off-road training sessions that include camping and back-country treks—it recently took a cue from Saturn Corp. and started Camp Jeep. Through print ads, the company invited Jeep owners to attend the summer gathering and experience a weekend of education and entertainment near Vail,

Marketing Dictionary

transaction-based marketing Buyer and seller exchanges characterized by limited communications and little or no ongoing relationship between the parties.

Figure 10.4 Making Promises to Customers

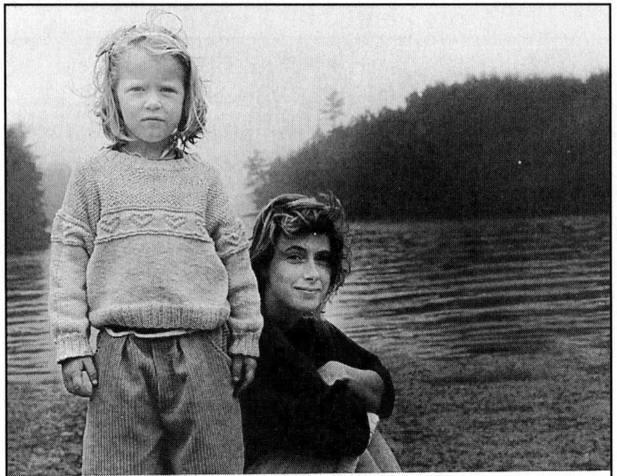

A promise I'll let you color a red rose green.
A promise that a secret whispered is as good as kept.
A promise you can always rely on me.
Nothing binds us one to the other like a promise kept. For more than 140 years, we've been helping people keep their promises by ensuring we have the financial strength to keep ours. That's why families and businesses rely on us to insure their lives and their financial future. We help you keep your promises.
Life & Disability Insurance • Annuities • Pension & Retirement Products • Investment Management

MassMutual
The Blue Chip Company

Colorado. Co-sponsored by Tread Lightly, an environmental group, Camp Jeep was designed to appeal to the Jeep owner's fun-loving, adventurous lifestyle and, through a one-hour TV special about the event, to potential Jeep owners. In addition to "Jeep 101," a special 4×4 off-road driving course, and presentations by Jeep engineers and designers, participants joined in the fun at the camp's Family Activity Center. They also gathered for an outdoor concert featuring nationally recognized recording artists Michael McDonald and Kenny Loggins.[7]

Relationship marketing is creating a new level of social interaction between buyers and sellers. Marketers have discovered that it pays to retain current customers. They can no longer concentrate marketing efforts solely on attracting new customers to their goods and services. For example, Toyota invited German owners of its top-of-the-line Lexus LS 400 automobile to attend an exclusive ballooning excursion, including an overnight stay in a castle in Baden-Baden. Later, the LS 400 owners each received a free bottle of a new vintage of Beaujolais wine before it appeared in German shops and restaurants. Toyota took these actions to make Lexus owners feel that they have an important relationship with their car's manufacturer, one that the company hopes will lead to future sales of Lexus automobiles.[8]

BASIC FOUNDATIONS OF MODERN BUYER-SELLER RELATIONSHIPS

Relationship marketing depends on the development of social ties between buyer and seller whether the buyers are individuals or other companies. This section considers the core elements of the buyer-seller relationship: the three promises that form the basis of relationship marketing and the four dimensions of the relationship marketing model.

Promises in Relationship Marketing

Relationship marketing is based on promises that go beyond obvious assurances that potential customers expect. A whole network of promises—outside the organization, within the organization, and in the interactions between buyer and seller—determine whether a marketing encounter will be positive or negative and either enhance or detract from an ongoing buyer-seller relationship.[9] In Figure 10.4, insurance company Massachusetts Mutual Life effectively stresses the theme of promises: "Nothing binds us one to the other like a promise kept. For more than 140 years, we've been helping people keep their promises by ensuring we have the financial strength to keep ours." In addition to the firm's external promises to policyholders, Mass Mutual implicitly refers to an internal promise to keep the company financially strong, which benefits employees, as well as customers.

Making Promises Most companies make promises to potential customers through *external marketing.* As discussed in Chapters 1 and 2, this term refers to the marketing efforts that a company directs toward customers, suppliers, and other parties outside the organization. These promises communicate what a customer can expect from the firm's good or service. For example, the NBC television network might run an advertisement for its upcoming coverage of the National Basketball Association finals touting the great games, great coverage, and great entertainment that viewers will experience if they tune in the broadcast. In this ad, the network would make a promise to its potential viewers and advertisers about what they could expect and what the network would deliver. In Figure 10.5, Sheraton Hotels promises a traveling executive who stays on its Club Level floor "Everything you have at the office. Except the politics." It also tells potential guests that it is a customer-focused company by including the phrase "Our world revolves around you."

External marketing goes beyond advertising, however. Special sales promotions, the physical design of a business facility, its cleanliness, and the service process provide other ways that companies make promises to potential customers. For example, at Disneyland in California and Walt Disney World in Florida, management makes special

Figure 10.5 Customer-Focused External Marketing Messages

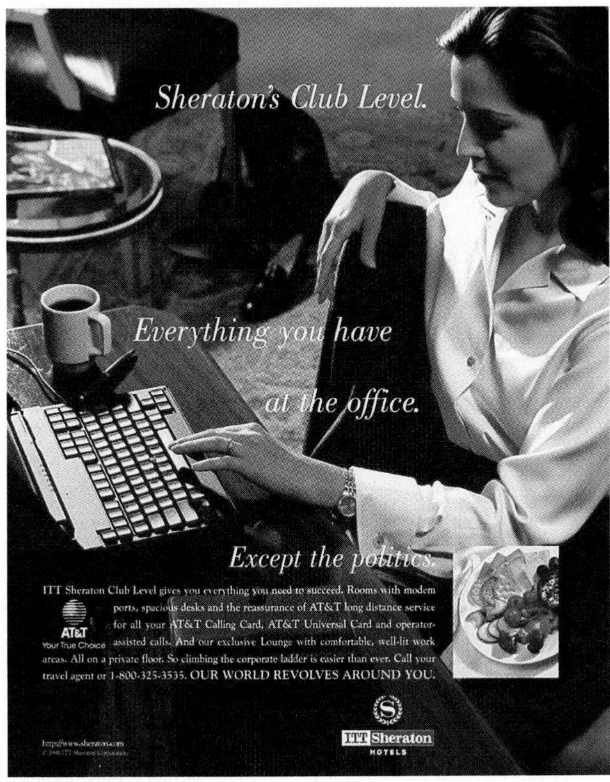
Sheraton's Club Level.
Everything you have at the office.
Except the politics.
ITT Sheraton Club Level gives you everything you need to succeed. Rooms with modem ports, spacious desks and the reassurance of AT&T long distance service for all your AT&T Calling Card, AT&T Universal Card and operator-assisted calls. And our exclusive Lounge with comfortable, well-lit work areas. All on a private floor. So climbing the corporate ladder is easier than ever. Call your travel agent or 1-800-325-3535. OUR WORLD REVOLVES AROUND YOU.
AT&T
Your True Choice
ITT Sheraton
HOTELS

efforts to ensure that the amusement parks remain spotlessly clean at all times. If a visitor drops a box of popcorn or spills soda, a cast member—Disney's term for employees—will soon clean it up. This obsession with cleanliness fulfills Disney's implicit promise to its customers that they can expect a wholesome, family experience when they visit one of its parks.

The promises that companies communicate to potential customers must be both realistic and consistent with one another. A firm that makes unrealistic promises often ends up with a disappointed customer who may not bother to try the good or service again. For example, if an infomercial for a hot new psychic hotline promises to improve your love life, but, after six months and numerous expensive 900 calls your love life is still in the dumps, you are likely to be very disappointed.

Enabling Promises A company can follow through on the promises that it makes to potential customers through external marketing only if it enables these promises through *internal* marketing. Internal marketing includes efforts to recruit talented employees and provide them with the tools, training, and motivation they need to do effective jobs. The company structure itself must facilitate rather than hinder the provision of quality goods and services. Efficient systems and processes, empowered front-line workers, and flat organizational hierarchies all contribute to a company's ability to provide quality goods and services.

Unless a company meets these employee needs, workers can face serious difficulty keeping the promises their employers make through external marketing. American Express Corporate Services promises that its Travel Service Office staff will help its customers' employees, regardless of where they travel. As Figure 10.6 explains, "Our people are just a phone call away, 24 hours a day, 365 days a year" to provide medical, legal, financial, travel, and emergency services. To make this promise, American Express must properly train and motivate its employees.

Finally, if employees aren't properly motivated and rewarded for doing a good job, then they may not bother. Organizations that develop good employee relationship programs will compete more effectively than others that overlook these programs. At the annual Del Mar (California) Fair, management assigns volunteers to check up on fair employees. These "mystery guests" ask staffers for directions to attractions, where to find telephones, and

Figure 10.6 Marketing Based on Internal Promises

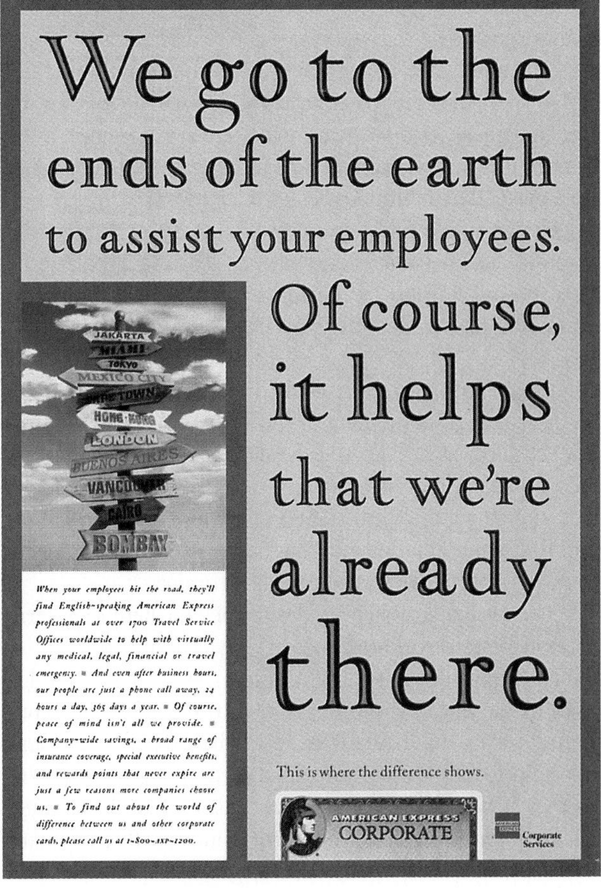
We go to the ends of the earth to assist your employees.
Of course, it helps that we're already there.
JAKARTA
MIAMI
TOKYO
MEXICO CITY
HONG KONG
LONDON
BUENOS AIRES
CAIRO
BOMBAY
When your employees hit the road, they'll find English-speaking American Express professionals at over 1700 Travel Service Offices worldwide to help with virtually any medical, legal, financial or travel emergency. ■ And even after business hours, our people are just a phone call away, 24 hours a day, 365 days a year. ■ Of course, peace of mind isn't all we provide. ■ Company-wide savings, a broad range of insurance coverage, special executive benefits, and rewards points that never expire are just a few reasons more companies choose us. ■ To find out about the world of difference between us and other corporate cards, please call us at 1-800-AXP-1200.
This is where the difference shows.
AMERICAN EXPRESS
CORPORATE
Corporate Services

Figure 10.7 Fulfilling Buyer-Seller Promises

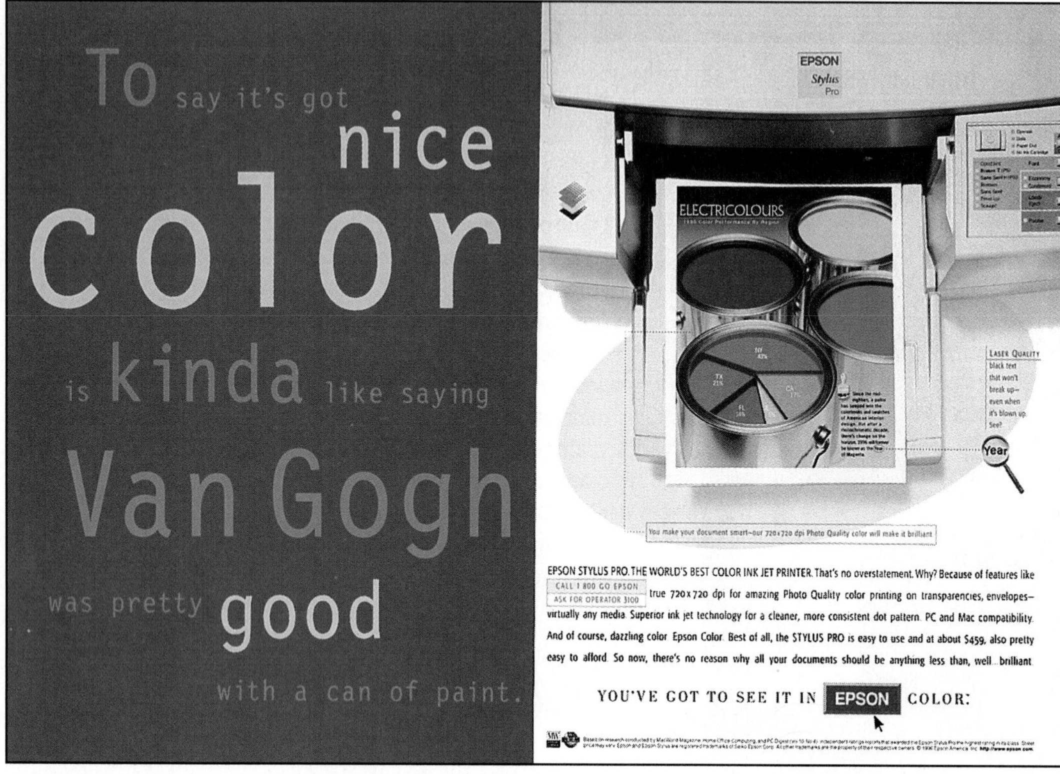
To say it's got nice color is kinda like saying Van Gogh was pretty good with a can of paint.
EPSON
Stylus
Pro
ELECTRICOLOURS
Laser Quality black text that won't break up—even when it's blown up. See?
Year
You make your document smart—our 720x720 dpi Photo Quality color will make it brilliant
EPSON STYLUS PRO. THE WORLD'S BEST COLOR INK JET PRINTER. That's no overstatement. Why? Because of features like true 720x720 dpi for amazing Photo Quality color printing on transparencies, envelopes—virtually any media. Superior ink jet technology for a cleaner, more consistent dot pattern. PC and Mac compatibility. And of course, dazzling color. Epson Color. Best of all, the STYLUS PRO is easy to use and at about $459, also pretty easy to afford. So now, there's no reason why all your documents should be anything less than, well... brilliant.
CALL 1 800 GO EPSON
ASK FOR OPERATOR 3100
YOU'VE GOT TO SEE IT IN EPSON COLOR.

similar questions; they then rate the respondents by courtesy, attitude, and appearance. Employees with perfect scores sport blue ribbons on their uniforms. "We're in the event business, and we want everyone's experience to be wonderful," says exhibits manager Chana Mannen. "And the key to that is employees. A bad run-in with an employee can ruin a fairgoer's day." Fair employees like the program, too, because it provides an extra incentive to be friendly and helpful to the throngs of visitors, many of whom will return year after year if they have a good time.[10]

Keeping Promises Every customer interaction with a business reaches a moment of truth when the business provides a good or service and the customer receives it. This action was defined in Chapter 1 as the exchange process. This exchange, the third stage in the buyer-seller relationship following external and internal marketing, defines the point at which a company keeps its promises.

The exchange also provides the place where long-term relationships develop between buyers and sellers. A company that doesn't keep its promises at the exchange point in the marketing process destroys any hope of continuing buyer-seller relationships. While positive encounters help to build long-term relationships, a negative encounter has a devastating effect. Disney has determined that each guest experiences 74 encounters with cast members in a single visit to one of its amusement parks, yet just one negative experience results in a measurable deterioration in its customer relationships.[11]

Epson America makes many promises in its advertisement for the Stylus Pro color printer shown in Figure 10.7. It calls the Stylus Pro "the world's best color ink jet printer," based on research by major computer magazines. The ad emphasizes high print quality in both color and black and white on a variety of media along with ease of use and affordability. A customer who buys the printer must be able to set it up to print a color page that is "brilliant," as the ad claims. Otherwise, the disappointed customer will likely refuse to buy another Epson product. On the other hand, the consumer who successfully achieves the promised results will not only develop loyalty to the brand but will recommend the product to others.

The Four Dimensions of Relationship Marketing

Clearly, making, enabling, and keeping promises are crucial parts of the relationship marketing process, but developing relationships requires more than promises. All relationships depend on the development of *emotional links* between the parties. Figure 10.8 identifies the four key dimensions of relationship marketing: bonding, empathy, reciprocity, and trust.[12]

Bonding Two parties must *bond* to one another to develop a long-term relationship. In other words, mutual interests or dependencies between the parties must be strong enough to tie them together. If the bonds are weak, then the relationship is in imminent danger of falling apart at any time. Stronger bonds increase the parties' commitment to the relationship.

Federal Express has an interest in minimizing its overhead costs as a way of maximizing its profit. Kinko's, the photocopying and business services store, wants to increase business traffic in its stores. That's why Federal Express locates drop boxes in most Kinko's stores. Federal Express customers drop their shipments in the boxes, limiting the number of individual pickups the company must make. As individual pickups decrease, FedEx needs fewer trucks and truck drivers. Kinko's also gains because business customers who drop packages into the Federal Express boxes may also use Kinko's business services, such as copying documents, printing business cards, or sending faxes.

Federal Express and Kinko's share common interests, and they cooperate with one another to reach their goals. As a result, bonds have developed between the two firms. As time goes on and the relationship matures, both firms hope that the bonds will become progressively stronger.

Empathy *Empathy*—the ability to see situations from the perspective of the other party—is another key emotional link in the development of relationships. Figure 10.9 shows another way that Kinko's promotes its services. Its Corporate Accounts Managers consult with each client and suggest efficient and economical solutions for document needs. This link helps Kinko's to understand what its busy corporate clients need. By showing empathy for customers, Kinko's encourages them to establish relationships: "With Kinko's Corporate on your side, you'll probably make being a hero look easy." At the same time, customers must understand that they can gain increased convenience and time-saving services only by paying Kinko's fees.

Reciprocity Every long-term relationship includes some give-and-take between the parties; one makes allowances and grants favors to the other in exchange for the same treatment when its own need arises. This give-and-take process, termed *reciprocity,* becomes a web of commitments among the parties in the relationship, binding them ever closer together.

For example, when a Xerox sales representative negotiates terms for the purchase of a new photocopier with a client, she might lower the price by 5 percent if the buyer is willing to accelerate payment of the invoice when it is presented. Similarly, the buyer may be willing to accept delivery of the equipment a month early (enabling the salesperson to exceed her sales quota and earn a Caribbean cruise as a bonus) if the seller will extend the warranty for an additional 30 days.

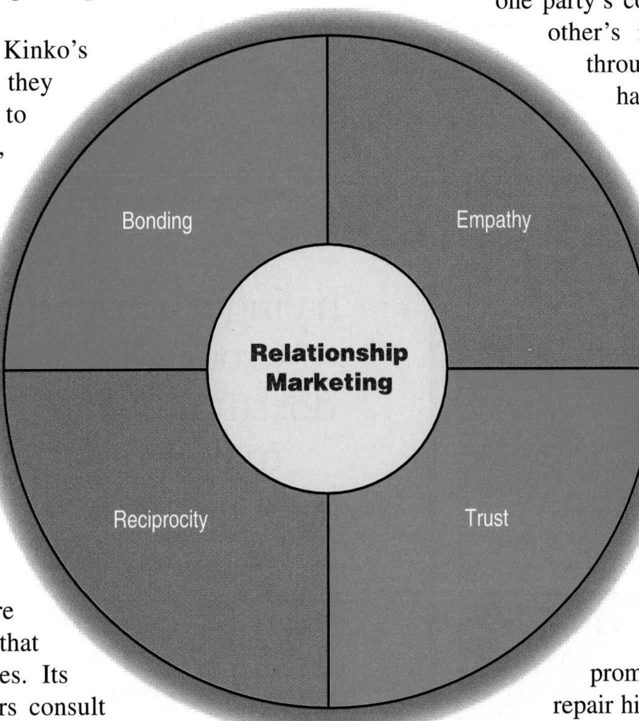
Bonding
Empathy
Relationship Marketing
Reciprocity
Trust

Figure 10.8 Relationship Marketing Dimensions

Trust Trust is ultimately the glue that holds a relationship together over the long haul. *Trust* reflects the extent of one party's confidence that it can rely on another's integrity. When parties follow through on commitments, they enhance trust and strengthen relationships. When they don't fulfill commitments, however, then trust suffers. Stronger trust leads to more cooperation between parties in a relationship. In personal selling situations, studies demonstrate that a customer's level of trust and satisfaction with the salesperson affects the quality of the organizational relationship. Successful salespeople emphasize trust more than their less successful counterparts.[13]

For example, if a customer promises to pay you 30 days after you repair his air conditioning system and the bill remains unpaid 90 days later, any trust that has been built between you and your client will surely be damaged. You will hesitate to offer similar concessions in future sales relationships with this customer.

THE RELATIONSHIP MARKETING CONTINUUM

Like all other interpersonal relationships, buyer-seller relationships function at a variety of levels. As an individual or firm progresses from the lowest level to the highest level on the continuum shown in Table 10.2, the strength of commitment between the parties grows. So, too, does the likelihood of a continuing, long-term relationship. Whenever possible, marketers want to move their customers along this continuum, converting them from Level 1 purchasers, who focus mainly on price, to Level 3 customers, who receive specialized services and value-added benefits that may not be available from another firm.[14]

The First Level of Relationship Marketing

Interactions at the first level are the most superficial and the least likely to lead to a long-term relationship. In the most prevalent examples of this first level, relationship marketing efforts rely on pricing and other financial incentives to motivate customers to enter into buying relationships with a seller. Examples include offers for two Big Macs for the price of one at McDonald's, American Airlines' AAdvantage frequent flyer program, and the General Motors MasterCard that rewards cardholders with credits toward purchases of GM products for every dollar that they charge on their cards.

Although these programs can be very attractive to users, the probability of creating long-term buyer relationships is relatively low. Because the programs are not customized to the needs of individual buyers, they are easily duplicated by competitors. For example, when McDonald's runs its two-for-one special on Big Macs, there's a good chance that Burger King will respond with a similar offer on its Whopper sandwich. Within three years after American Airlines introduced its AAdvantage frequent-flyer program, it had been copied by 23 other airlines. The lesson here is that it takes more than a low price or other financial incentive to create a long-term relationship between buyer and seller.

Figure 10.9 Kinko's Empathy with Corporate Customers

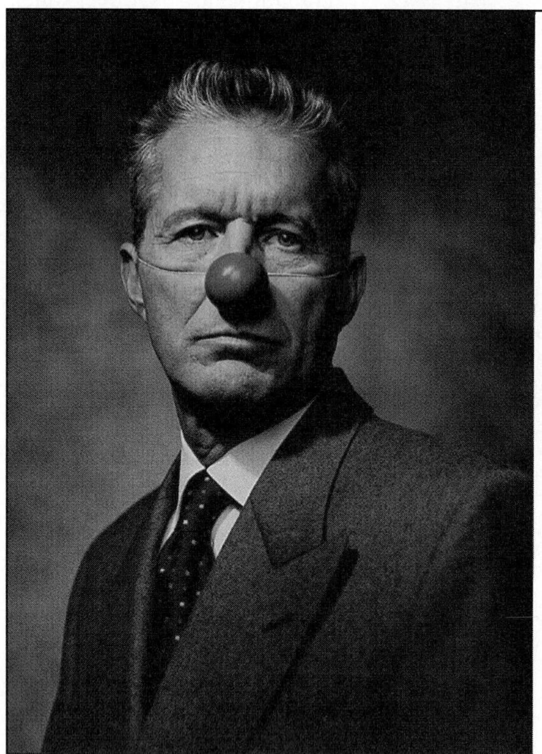

Trying to do it all yourself doesn't *always* make you look like a hero.
In today's business climate, there's a powerful temptation to juggle more work than ever. Now it can be done. With the right kind of help. It's called Kinko's Corporate. An offering of products and services designed to meet the high-caliber needs of corporate customers. What's more, it gives you time to do what you do best while you outsource the rest. Your own Kinko's Corporate Account Manager will work as a consultant to analyze how your company creates and uses printed documents. Then they'll suggest efficient and economical solutions for producing everything from thousands of training manuals to sales reports and color presentations. Your Account Manager can also arrange pick-up and delivery. Even set up a corporate charge account you and your company can use at any of our worldwide locations. With Kinko's Corporate on your side, you'll make being a hero look ordinary. Which is probably why every day more than 200,000 businesses use Kinko's.
The new way to office.™
kinko's corporate
To Learn More, Please Call 1-800-2-KINKOS For Our Brochure.

The Second Level of Relationship Marketing

As buyer and seller reach the second level of relationship marketing, their interactions develop on a *social* level—one that features deeper and less superficial links than the financially motivated first level. Sellers have begun to learn that social relationships with buyers can be very effective marketing tools. Customer service and communication are key factors at this stage.

Like Saturn and Jeep, Harley-Davidson uses social relationships to forge stronger customer bonds. Local dealers sponsor Harley Owners' Groups (HOGs), and the company includes one year of free membership with the purchase of a motorcycle. In addition to member newsletters and magazines, club members can participate in riding rallies, training sessions, and similar activities to increase their motorcycle driving pleasure.[15]

College and university alumni associations are masters of the second level of relationship marketing. They inundate graduates with all sorts of alumni newspapers, magazines, invitations for football game tailgate parties, singles mixers, holiday parties, and any number of other social activities. The institution wants to develop and maintain a long-term social relationship with its graduates—one that goes beyond the few years that they actually spend in school.

The Third Level of Relationship Marketing

At the third level of relationship marketing, social relationships are transformed into structural changes that make buyer and seller true partners in business. As buyer and seller work more closely together, they develop a dependence on one another that continues to grow over time.

Table 10.2 Three Levels of Relationship Marketing

Characteristic	Level 1	Level 2	Level 3
Primary bond	Financial	Social	Structural
Degree of customization	Low	Medium	Medium to high
Potential for sustained competitive advantage	Low	Moderate	High
Examples	American Airlines' AAdvantage program	Harley-Davidson's Harley Owners Group (HOG)	Federal Express' PowerShip program

These partnerships occur between both service companies and industrial marketers. The goal of the Kinko's Corporate program is to develop Level 3 relationships with customers. Kinko's consultants work closely with their clients to solve business problems. Similarly, Ross Controls, a Troy, Michigan manufacturer of pneumatic valves and air-control systems, supplies components for manufacturers like General Motors and Reynolds Aluminum. A decade ago, it implemented its ROSS/FLEX process for customizing products with the objective of improving its ability to meet customers' changing requirements and make them customers for life. Ross personnel begin by learning as much as possible about customers' needs and collaborating with them to develop and manufacture products designed specifically for those needs. To develop "learning relationships," Ross communicates extensively with customers, listening to their concerns and visiting plants to understand how customers use Ross products. The company solicits customer feedback once the system is designed, leading to further improvements and greater customization. ROSS/FLEX has increased the percentage of revenues the company derives from customized rather than standardized products from 5 percent to 20 percent. GM's Metal Fabricating Division uses only Ross valves and insists that its suppliers do the same.[16]

These examples demonstrate applications of relationship marketing in both consumer and business-to-business markets. McDonald's, Burger King, and Harley-Davidson use relationship marketing in consumer markets, and Kinko's Corporate and Ross Controls operate in the business-to-business environment. The next section looks at the nature of buyer-seller relationships in these two markets.

Briefly speaking

"One of our ironclad rules is 'Never do business with anybody you don't like.' If you don't like somebody, there's a reason. Chances are it's because you don't trust him, and you're probably right. I don't care who it is or what guarantees you get—cash in advance or whatever. If you do business with somebody you don't like, sooner or later you'll get screwed."

Harry V. Quadracci
President, Quad/Graphics

BUYER-SELLER RELATIONSHIPS IN CONSUMER GOODS AND SERVICES MARKETS

Marketers of consumer goods and services have discovered that they must do more than simply creating products and then selling them. With a dizzying array of products to choose from, many customers are seeking ways to simplify both their business and personal lives, and relationships provide a way to do this. One reason many consumers form continuing relationships is their desire to reduce choices. Through relationships, they can simplify information gathering and the entire buying process as well as decrease the risk of dissatisfaction. They find comfort in the familiar, the "tried-and-true," developed through ongoing, committed relationships with companies. In fact, studies show that consumers do indeed patronize their habitual stores and malls about 90 percent of the time. Such relationships may lead to more efficient decision making and higher levels of customer satisfaction. Yet consumers also sometimes choose relationships that increase their choices. Direct-mail catalog companies like Lands' End and L.L. Bean and superstores like Office Depot, Circuit City, and CompUSA are popular with customers because they offer more choices than the typical retail store.

Another key benefit to consumers of long-term buyer-seller relationships is the perceived positive value they receive. Relationships add value by giving opportunities to save money through discounts, rebates, and similar offers to frequent buyers, special recognition from the relationship programs, and convenience in shopping.

Marketers should also understand why consumers end

MARKETING HALL OF FAME

The Saturn Homecoming Party

Imagine 44,000 people spending their summer vacations in Spring Hill, Tenn. (pop. 3,500) to pay homage to the Saturn automobile. It really did happen. With General Motors picking up the tab, happy Saturn owners from as far away as Hawaii, Alaska, and even Taiwan swarmed over Spring Hill like ants at a picnic. The guests toured the General Motors assembly plant, danced to top country-western entertainment, gulped down free food and drinks, and sported washable Saturn tattoos. Another 100,000 Saturn owners, who could not experience the Southern hospitality in person, attended parties and picnics sponsored by Saturn dealers across the country.

How did General Motors lure all these people to this flyspeck on the map, and why would it even want to do so? It is all part of Saturn's successful marketing strategy which not only cleverly reaches out to customers but also embraces its employees, retailers, and suppliers. The corporation's effort to generate loyalty among its customers and its workers represents a true textbook case of successful relationship marketing.

Dick from Fort Wayne
Says: "It's nice
to be HOME!
Hi Mom
We love
our Saturn!
Mary & Chuck
SATURN

The special relationship that Saturn nurtures with its customers is "corporately manipulated," said Stuart W. Leslie, a history professor at Johns Hopkins University, who happens to be a Saturn owner. "But it only works because people feel a genuine affection for the company."

With preset car prices, Saturn customers don't have to haggle with car dealers. Consequently, the showroom atmosphere, where salespeople are salaried instead of commissioned, is much more relaxed. The sales staff gives new owners a big, friendly send-off when they pick up the keys to their shiny new vehicle. The unusual bond continues, as Saturn sponsors car clinics and other special events for old customers. Saturn also jealously guards its customers' loyalty. One

relationships. The most common reasons are boredom with their current providers, dissatisfaction with the company's ability to meet consumer expectations, the appearance of a better alternative, or a conflict with the provider. Consumers also dislike the feeling that they are somehow locked into a relationship.[17]

Consumer marketers use relationship marketing techniques like affinity and frequency programs to attract new customers and retain existing ones. Databases also play important roles in developing good relationships with consumers.

The Cost of Gaining and Losing a Customer

One of the major forces driving the push from transaction-based marketing toward relationship marketing is the realization that the expense of gaining a customer is not as high as the cost of losing one. A firm may spend five times as much to attract a new customer as to keep an old one, and customers usually generate more profits for a firm with each additional year of the relationship. A five-year bank customer brings more profitable business than a one-year customer. The typical auto insurance policy doesn't become profitable until the seventh year. Clearly, it makes sense for a firm to spend money developing customer-retention strategies rather than continually looking for new customers.[18]

When a company loses a customer because of poor service or a poor product, it doesn't just lose that person's business; it may lose many potential customers. According to a surprising study conducted for AMR, the parent company of American Airlines, one unhappy passenger tells anywhere from 9 to 13 people about his or her bad experi-

year when Saturn discovered a potential glitch in the cars' cooling systems, it took no chances and replaced them with new ones.

All these efforts have had a measurable effect. In a recent J. D. Power ratings report—the industry benchmarks—Saturn placed first in sales satisfaction and third in customer satisfaction.

Saturn doesn't just try to keep its current customers happy. Through extensive community marketing events, it is always on the prowl for new car buyers. For instance, the company, in conjunction with *Sports Illustrated* magazine, sponsored a nationwide bike recycling project to benefit the Boys & Girls Clubs of America. Saturn also hosts the White House Presidential Scholars Program annually. The automaker picks up the costs for 141 winners, out of a pool of 2,600 outstanding high school students, to attend ceremonies in Washington, D.C. While underwriting a civic good deed, Saturn doesn't pass up the opportunity for positive public relations. The winners, their parents and teachers are escorted to Robert F. Kennedy Stadium to participate in Saturn's demonstration of antilock brakes and other safety features.

But General Motors didn't attain its success solely by focusing on its customers' needs. Unlike the typical assembly plant, where a blue-collar worker may monotonously attach a hubcap or turn certain bolts eight hours a day with little or no opportunity for input, everybody at the Saturn plant is involved in decision making. "We have nothing of greater value than our people," said George Doss III, the firm's western regional manager. "We believe that demonstrating respect for the uniqueness of every individual builds a team of confident, creative members possessing a high degree of initiative, self-respect and self-discipline."

What General Motors has achieved through its Saturn program was not serendipitous. It all began back in the late 1980s when GM formed the "Group of 99" task force. Composed of both blue-collar workers and managers, GM handed the group $3.5 billion to create a new kind of car and a new way of manufacturing the vehicles. The task force ultimately developed the team concept to build its cars. In addition, the company set out to change consumer attitudes by redefining its marketing mix. According to Doss, the marketing mix allocates 25 percent to product; 25 percent to price, promotion, and distribution; and 50 percent to the shopping, buying, and ownership experience. By placing the greatest emphasis on the car-buying experience, Saturn focuses on building relationships.

QUESTIONS FOR CRITICAL THINKING

1. **How did General Motors apply the principles of relationship marketing to its Saturn operations?**
2. **Describe the promises that Saturn made to its stakeholders.**

Sources: J.D. Power and Associates Reports, "Non-Dealer Service More Satisfying to Vehicle Owners, "May 16, 1997, downloaded from http://biz.yahoo.com/prnews/97, on May 19, 1997; "Saturn and General Motors Sponsor Presidential Scholars in Washington," *PRNewswire,* June 20, 1996; "Saturn to Recycle Thousands of Bikes for Boys and Girls Clubs of America Nationwide," *PRNewswire,* June 20, 1996; Chad Rubel, "Partnerships Steer Saturn to New Marketing Mix," *Marketing News,* January 29, 1996, p. 5; and based on information from Kathleen Kerwin and Deidre A. Depke, "Forget Woodstock—These Folks Are Heading to Spring Hill," *Business Week,* June 27, 1994, p. 36.

ence. Also, for every unhappy customer who complains to the airline, 24 unhappy customers don't complain. Of these 24 people who don't bother to complain about bad experiences, some 75 to 90 percent of them will never do business with the company again.[19] This survey underscores the importance of customer satisfaction and quality in relationship marketing programs.

Affinity Programs

Each of us holds certain things near and dear to their hearts. Some may feel strongly about Michigan State University, while others admire the New York Yankees baseball team or singer Mariah Carey. These symbols, along with an almost unending variety of others, are subjects of affinity programs. An **affinity program** is a marketing effort sponsored by an organization that solicits involvement by individuals who share common interests and activities. With affinity programs, organizations create extra value for members and encourage stronger relationships.

Marketing Dictionary

affinity program A marketing effort sponsored by an organization that solicits responses from individuals who share common interests and activities.

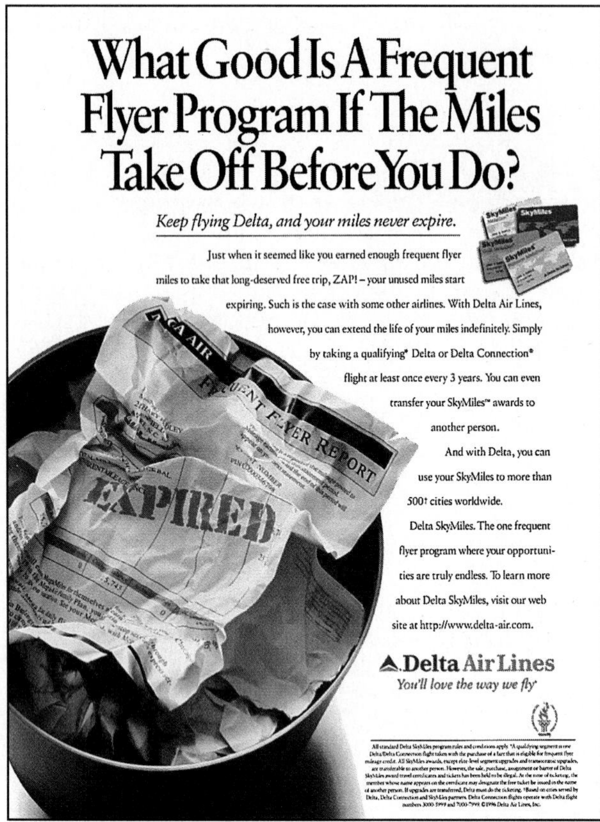
What Good Is A Frequent Flyer Program If The Miles Take Off Before You Do?
Keep flying Delta, and your miles never expire.
Just when it seemed like you earned enough frequent flyer miles to take that long-deserved free trip, ZAP! – your unused miles start expiring. Such is the case with some other airlines. With Delta Air Lines, however, you can extend the life of your miles indefinitely. Simply by taking a qualifying* Delta or Delta Connection® flight at least once every 3 years. You can even transfer your SkyMiles™ awards to another person.
And with Delta, you can use your SkyMiles to more than 500† cities worldwide.
Delta SkyMiles. The one frequent flyer program where your opportunities are truly endless. To learn more about Delta SkyMiles, visit our web site at http://www.delta-air.com.
Delta Air Lines
You'll love the way we fly
FREQUENT FLYER REPORT
EXPIRED

Frequent-user programs ranging from Delta Air Lines' Sky Miles to Subway's "Buy Nine, Get the 10th Free" are common at Level 1 of relationship marketing.

Affinity credit cards are one popular form of this marketing technique. The sponsor's name appears prominently in marketing materials, on the card itself, and on monthly statements. For example, the National Association for Female Executives, a professional networking organization, offers qualified members a Gold Visa or MasterCard with no first-year fee and low interest rates. A not-for-profit organization such as a charity or educational institution may sponsor such a card if the issuer donates a percentage of user purchases to the group.

University credit cards are very popular with many individuals—even those who didn't attend the universities whose names are on the cards. According to MasterCard International Senior Vice President Timothy Malloy, certain universities are more popular than others. "Notre Dame, especially," says Malloy. "We see cards from people who never went there."[20]

Not all affinity programs involve credit cards. KPBS, San Diego's public broadcasting station, sends a diner's card to members who contribute more than $60. The card entitles the members to dining discounts at participating local restaurants.

Frequent Buyer/User Programs

Perhaps the most popular means of practicing relationship marketing are frequent buyer and frequent user programs. Commonly known as **frequency marketing** programs, these marketing initiatives reward customers who purchase a good or service with cash, rebates, merchandise, or other premiums. Buyers who purchase the item more often earn higher rewards. Frequency marketing focuses on a company's best customers with the goal of increasing their motivation to buy even more of the same or other products from the seller. The saying, "All customers are created equal, but some customers are more equal than others," illustrates the 80/20 rule: about 80 percent of a company's profits come from 20 percent of its customers.[21]

Many different types of companies use frequency programs, from fast-food restaurants to retail stores, telecommunications companies, and travel firms. For example, Seattle-based Nordstrom department stores offer customers a 1 percent dividend on purchases after they exceed $1,000 in charges to a company credit card. The dividend increases by 1 percent for each additional $1,000, up to a maximum of 5 percent. The program pays out dividends annually in the form of Nordstrom gift certificates.[22] Other popular frequency marketing programs include airline frequent-flier programs such as United Airlines' Mileage Plus and retail programs like Hallmark Card's Crown Card.

AT&T's primary objective in offering its True Rewards Member Benefit Card is to prompt long-distance callers to use its service rather than those of such rivals as MCI and Sprint. The telecommunications giant has enhanced the card's value, however, through arrangements with other marketers. As the promotional message in Figure 10.10 explains, cardholders also receive discounts and offers from TCBY, Marriott, Harry and David, and Mrs. Fields. The added benefits resulting from these partnerships serve to strengthen the relationship between AT&T and its telephone customers.

Database Marketing

When marketing centers on a one-to-one interaction between an individual salesperson and an individual customer, buyer-seller relationships are fairly easy to track and manage. A few notes jotted in an appointment book often supply enough information. However, when a large, multinational firm such as Shell Oil or Levi Strauss wants to develop lasting relationships with its legions of customers, it needs the help of powerful tools like computer databases.

Database marketing is the use of computers to identify and target specific groups of potential customers. Database marketing provides particularly effective tools for building relationships because it allows sellers to sort through huge quantities of buyer information to fine-tune marketing efforts. This activity helps to create long-term relationships with customers and improve sales.

Today, information technology provides essential support for a first-rate customer relationship. With database systems in place, companies can track buying patterns, develop customer relationship profiles, customize their product offerings and sales promotions, reduce errors, and personalize customer service. Properly used, databases help companies in several ways:

- Selecting their best customers
- Calculating the lifetime values of their business
- Creating a meaningful dialogue that builds genuine loyalty

Effective database marketing improves customer retention and referral rates, boosts sales volume, and reduces direct costs and marketing outlays.

Databases can precisely target potential customers in crowds of less qualified prospects. Des Moines, Iowa-based Meredith Corporation—publisher of *Better Homes and Gardens, Ladies' Home Journal, Traditional Home,* and other popular magazines—has developed a database that contains some 63 million names. When Cadillac asked Meredith to help target specific readers of *Traditional Home,* Meredith easily split the subscriber list between readers under 50 years old and those 50 years and older. The publisher then produced and mailed out two different versions of *Traditional Home,* one to the younger group with an ad for the sporty Cadillac Seville and one to the older group with an ad for the more sedate Cadillac DeVille.[23]

Databases allow sellers to focus their efforts on their best existing customers, measured both by the quantity of product that they purchase and by the profitability of those sales. Each buyer is unique with individual priorities about important features in a relationship—price, service, product quality, and other factors. Databases gather and analyze this information, revealing characteristics and requirements of specific customers. Companies can then use this knowledge to identify potential customers who share a similar profile. Says Alan W. H. Grant, founder of the Boston-based Exchange Partners consulting firm, "Today, using information and technology tools currently available, companies can link their investments in customer relationships directly to the returns those customers generate." Companies can more easily identify the customers who have the highest profit-improvement potential and use databases to understand the specific needs of those subsegments."[24]

Figure 10.10 AT&T's True Rewards Frequency Marketing Program

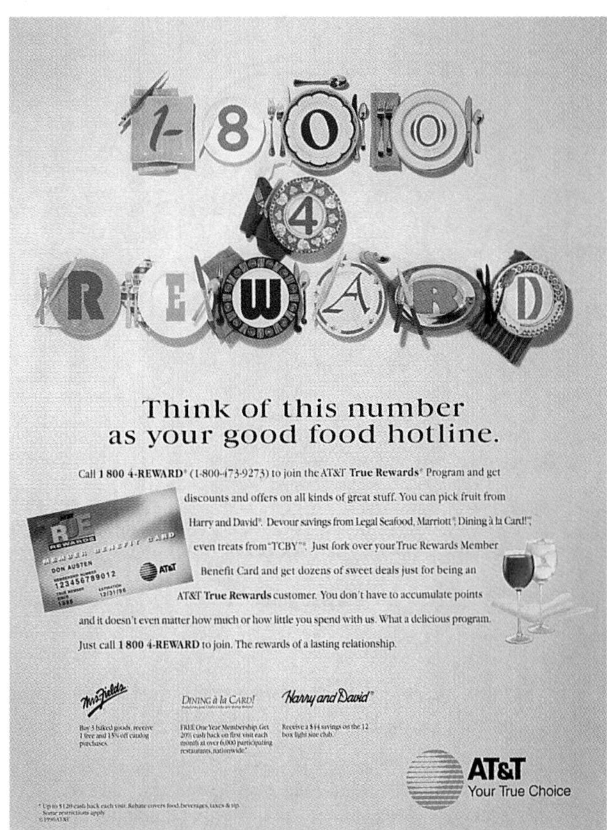
1-800-4-REWARD
Think of this number
as your good food hotline.
Call **1 800 4-REWARD**® (1-800-473-9273) to join the AT&T **True Rewards**® Program and get discounts and offers on all kinds of great stuff. You can pick fruit from Harry and David®. Devour savings from Legal Seafood, Marriott®, Dining à la Card!®, even treats from "TCBY"®. Just fork over your True Rewards Member Benefit Card and get dozens of sweet deals just for being an AT&T **True Rewards** customer. You don't have to accumulate points and it doesn't even matter how much or how little you spend with us. What a delicious program.
Just call **1 800 4-REWARD** to join. The rewards of a lasting relationship.
Mrs. Fields
Dining à la Card!
Harry and David®
AT&T
Your True Choice

Where do organizations find all the data that fill these vast marketing databases? Everywhere! If you have a credit card, you probably filled out a questionnaire as a part of the application process. The information on that questionnaire was entered into a computer system that tracks every purchase you make with the credit card. Likewise, filling out and returning the registration card for a new piece of software also puts your name and other vital statistics into a computer database along with those of the other people who returned their registration cards. Other sources of database information include warranty cards,

Marketing Dictionary

frequency marketing Frequent buyer or user marketing program that rewards customers who purchase a good or service with cash, rebates, merchandise, or other premiums.

database marketing The use of computers to identify and target messages toward specific groups of potential customers.

Figure 10.11 Nike Retail Store Survey Used in Developing Customer Databases

LET'S HEAR FROM YOU . . .

JUST DO IT.

Thank you for visiting our store!

To ensure that we are meeting your expectations, please give us your opinions and comments.

NIKE respects your privacy and will not rent, sell, or trade your name.

TELL US ABOUT YOURSELF (PLEASE PRINT)
NAME: ____
ADDRESS: ____
CITY: ____
STATE: ____ ZIP: ____
PHONE: ( ) ____
STORE VISITED: ____
SALESPERSON'S NAME: ____
TODAY'S DATE: ____

Are you a . . .
□ Male □ Female
□ Resident of Area □ Visitor/tourist of Area
(If Visitor/Tourist) Are you here on . . .
□ Business Trip □ Pleasure Trip □ Both

What is your . . . Date Of Birth: __/__/__ Mo Day Year

My interests include: (Check All That Apply)
□ Aerobics □ Basketball □ Cross-Training
□ Golf □ Hiking □ Running
□ Soccer □ Swimming □ Tennis
□ Volleyball □ Walking
□ Others: ____

Have you been to this store/location before?
□ Yes, been to store before □ No, first visit to store

List other Nike store locations visited: ____

How did you first learn or hear about the NIKE store?
□ Billboard □ Magazine □ Radio
□ Brochure □ Newspaper □ Friend/Relative
□ Other: ____

Did you make a purchase today?
□ YES □ NO
(If Yes) How much money did you spend?
□ Under $50 □ $50 - $100 □ Over $100

How did our CUSTOMER SERVICE meet your expectations:

	Poor 1	2	3	Avg 4	5	6	Excellent 7
Salesperson's Knowledge Of Product	□	□	□	□	□	□	□
Courtesy Of Salesperson	□	□	□	□	□	□	□
Speed Of Service	□	□	□	□	□	□	□

How did our NIKE store and products rate?

	Poor 1	2	3	Avg 4	5	6	Excellent 7
Value For Money	□	□	□	□	□	□	□
Product Selection	□	□	□	□	□	□	□
Visual Presentation	□	□	□	□	□	□	□
Store Layout	□	□	□	□	□	□	□
Ease Of Shopping	□	□	□	□	□	□	□
Cleanliness Of Store	□	□	□	□	□	□	□

How likely are you to return to this store?
□ Very Likely □ Somewhat Likely □ Not Likely At All

I would like to be notified about NIKE's new products or upcoming store events. Please include me on NIKE's mailing list.
□ Yes □ No

Additional comments: ____

cash register scanners in supermarkets and other retail stores, customer opinion surveys like the one for Nike in Figure 10.11, and sweepstakes entry forms.

By combining personal demographic data on individual cardholders with records of buyers' spending habits, a company creates an incredibly valuable source of marketing information. American Express uses its customer database for a "relationship billing" program. Its bills include offers like airfare coupons and sales on special products related to a customer's recent purchases. For example, the company could insert a direct mail offer for gold jewelry only in the bills to women who have purchased jewelry within the previous three months. American Express reported increased spending of more than 15 percent in its first relationship billing programs in Europe, Canada, and Mexico.[25]

Because databases contain such valuable information, database marketers frequently sell their mailing lists to interested parties. Consumers who subscribe to a magazine, such as *Wired,* soon begin receiving unsolicited marketing offers from a variety of related sellers—in this case, computer hardware and software manufacturers and retailers.

In a way, the world of marketing is returning to the old days of one-to-one marketing, where sellers got to know their customers and could tailor each product offer and sales presentation to the specific needs of the individual prospect. Databases have played a major role in the switch from mass marketing to mass customization in companies' marketing programs.

The ability to differentiate customers using databases has made information-driven marketing popular outside the United States, as well. Tesco, Great Britain's second-largest grocery-store chain, uses a frequency marketing card named Clubcard to track cardholder purchases. By analyzing the data derived from Clubcard purchases, Tesco's management can change the mix of products in each store to meet the needs and desires of that outlet's customers. Tesco can act confidently, because Clubcard shoppers account for fully 75 percent of the money spent at its grocery stores. The database information that Tesco collects helps the company to focus on its customers rather than the stores or products. The result is better marketing decisions, enhanced buyer satisfaction, increased loyalty, and the development of long-term relationships.[26]

The Internet can help companies to develop even better customer information databases and also to apply databases in improving customer service. Internet connections bring instant feedback from customers, so firms need not wait for weeks or months to judge responses. This speed helps marketers to respond quickly to market changes. According to John Uppgren of Gage Marketing, consumers tend to give their opinions more willingly via online surveys, promotions, and e-mail messages than through other channels. The Internet may actually provide a better way than traditional methods to reach customers and develop relationships. "The Internet offers companies building a consumer franchise a harvesting ground of opinion and behavior," he says. "Coupled with a home page, a relational database program can record survey results, demographic information, comments on the look and feel of products, and help identify problems in distribution."[27]

Web sites provide real value to visitors and the sponsoring company by allowing information processing and presentations, both based on information likely to be in databases. Gathering such information from the Web is becoming easier thanks to new software that allows companies to link Web sites to their databases while preventing unauthorized access to the databases. At the Metropolitan Museum of Art's Web site, visitors can order items from the museum shop through an online catalog. Clicking on a desired item puts it into the customer's "shopping bag," actually a database on a museum computer. The customer can even save a bag and come back later to finish the order. The completed order goes to the museum's distribution center, reducing the chance for errors and speeding up delivery. This popular service provides a high level of customer satisfaction and convenience, as it helps the museum learn more about customer preferences. To get more information for its databases, the site's home page includes a survey about Web use and museum visiting habits.[28]

http://www.metmuseum.org/

BUYER-SELLER RELATIONSHIPS IN BUSINESS-TO-BUSINESS MARKETS

Relationship marketing is not limited to consumer goods and services. Building strong buyer-seller relationships is a critical component of business-to-business marketing. While businesses enter buyer-seller relationships for some of the same reasons as consumers, the primary reason for a business-to-business relationship is to control uncertainty and reduce risk, thereby increasing profits.[29] The goal is to work with the other party to provide advantages that no other seller can provide. Depending on the particular situation, these advantages could result from lower prices, quicker delivery, better quality and reliability, customized product features, more favorable financing terms, or any number of other factors. Business-to-business marketing involves partnership relationships, along with the development and use of co-marketing and co-branding programs.

Building and Maintaining Business Partnerships

Businesses form partnerships with one another for many reasons. In some cases, choosing a supplier in a nearby town leads to cost savings that flow to the bottom line in the form of increased profits. Partnering can provide a small firm with an added measure of stability in volatile markets. In addition, marketing goods and services through partners offers many advantages to both large and small firms.

A **partnership** is an affiliation of two or more companies to assist each other in the achievement of common goals. Partnerships cover a wide spectrum of relationships, from informal cooperative purchasing arrangements to formal production and marketing agreements. Such a link can involve a single function or activity—for example, product distribution—or all functions, such as the research and development, manufacturing, and marketing of a new product. In business-to-business markets, partnerships form the basis of relationship marketing. To compete effectively in today's global business markets, an organization must be an effective "cooperator."

A variety of common goals motivate organizations to form partnerships. Companies may want to protect or improve their positions in existing markets, gain access to new domestic or international markets, or quickly enter into new markets. Expansion of a product line—to fill in gaps, broaden it, or differentiate it—is another key reason for joining forces. Other motives include sharing resources, reducing costs, warding off threats of future competition, raising or creating barriers to entry, and learning new skills.

More than one goal may apply to a particular partnership. General Mills teamed up with Nestlé S.A. to market its cereals in western Europe, motivated by a desire to access Nestlé's distribution system, including a large sales force, extensive knowledge of the market, and excess manufacturing capacity. This gave General Mills faster entry into western European markets than it could have achieved on its own. To Nestlé, the partnership brought the General Mills brand name and its product development, manufacturing, and marketing expertise.[30]

Choosing Business Partners How does an organization decide what companies to select as partners? The first priority is to locate firms that can add value to the relationship—whether through resources of cash, contacts, extra manufacturing capacity, technical know-how, or distribution capabilities. The greater the value added, the greater the desirability of the partnership. In many cases, the attributes of each partner complement those of the other; each firm brings something to the relationship that the

Marketing Dictionary

partnership Affiliation of two or more marketers to assist each other in the achievement of common goals.

Figure 10.12 Citibank and CIGNA: Mutual Benefits from a Century-Old Business-to-Business Partnership

Relationships
that
ENDURE
You're Interested In
Long-term Partnership,
Not Short-term
Salesmanship.
When You Expand
Around The World, You
Think Your Bank Should
Speak The Language.
CIGNA Found
A Bank Like That.
103 Years Ago.
In 1893, CIGNA retained Citibank—and never looked back. As CIGNA has expanded around the world, it has relied on Citibank's innovative solutions and unrivaled global expertise. Citibank and CIGNA: a century of financial partnership.
CITIBANK

other party needs but cannot provide on its own. Some partnerships join firms with similar skills and resources, perhaps motivated to reduce costs. Firms also want low-risk partners; that is, they prefer limited risk that the other firms will fail to perform as expected.[31]

Organizations must share similar values for a partnership to succeed in the long run. A firm that is a model of ethical behavior probably would not continue a relationship with a partner who suggested compromising product safety to earn extra profits. Similarly, trust is a critical ingredient in the development of partnerships. Each party has to trust that the other has the interests of the partnership at heart and not only its own concerns. Without trust, partnerships crumble and relationships wither. Strength of commitment is another factor in choosing partners, signifying the importance of the relationship to each partner and the desire to continue in the relationship.

Consider the partnership between insurance giant CIGNA and Citibank. As Figure 10.12 points out, the partnership began over 100 years ago in 1893 and the bonds between the two international businesses have strengthened over the decades. Citibank's global solutions to problems in specific foreign markets have helped CIGNA to expand outside the United States. In return, Citibank has benefited from the substantial business it receives from its long-time client.

When two firms form a partnership, the relationship should be designed to achieve a particular purpose. Companies often cooperate in product development, distribution, and marketing partnerships. For example, Microsoft Corp. and Japan's Casio Corp. formed a partnership to develop new consumer electronic devices. Microsoft brings its expertise in operating systems and software applications, while Casio contributes its experience in consumer electronics. The alliance is a way for Microsoft to move beyond the personal computer market. Casio, like many other Japanese companies, wants to develop a relationship with a leading U.S. company in the personal computer field.[32]

Today's successful business-to-business buyer-seller relationships also depend on efficient and effective management capable of delivering superior value to customers. For many firms, this goal requires a shift in thinking away from the old-style, hierarchical management model to a new model that relies on empowering employees by delegating authority to front-line staff members who are in the best position to make decisions. In addition, new partners must focus on building teams, opening channels of communication, and conducting win-win negotiations. Outback Steakhouse, a fast-growing restaurant chain, gives local managers discretion to provide incentives that enhance customer satisfaction. For example, they can give customers free drinks and food samples. Beepers call customers as they continue shopping in adjacent stores until their tables are ready, making long waits easier to accept. "When people feel they're receiving great value with great service, they're going to come back," says Nancy Schneid, marketing vice president.[33]

Types of Partnerships

Companies form four key types of partnerships in business-to-business markets: buyer, seller, internal, and lateral partnerships. This section briefly examines each type.

In a *buyer* partnership, a firm purchases goods and services from one or more providers. For example, a company may contract with a certified public accountant (CPA) to conduct annual audits of its accounting system and to file federal and state income tax returns. Another company might purchase pens, pencils, and other office supplies exclusively from Office Depot.

When a company assumes the buyer position in a relationship, it has a unique set of needs and requirements that the other firm must meet to make the relationship successful over a long period of time. While buyers want sellers to provide fair prices, quick delivery, and high quality, a lasting relationship often requires more effort. To induce a buyer to form a long-term partnership, a seller must also be responsive to the unique needs of the buyer. For example, if the buyer has a rush job that must be done in one hour, a supplier will score highly if it can perform. Similarly, buyers want reliable partners. Suppose that a caterer contracts with a new food supplier to supply ingredients for a major charity fund-raising dinner, but the supplier fails to provide the right quality and type of foods. The caterer is not likely to use the supplier again, and no relationship results.

Disney's
TOY
STORY
Disney's
TOY
STORY

Fast-food marketer Burger King stimulates sales of high-margin products and enhances its image among children as the source of collectible figurines from Disney's *Hunchback* and *Toy Story* films.

Seller partnerships set up long-term exchanges of goods and services in return for cash or other valuable consideration. Sellers, too, have their own unique needs as partners in ongoing relationships. Since sellers depend on steady streams of cash to keep themselves afloat financially, most prefer to develop long-term relationships with their partners. However, from the perspective of a seller, some partners look better than others. For example, sellers prefer to serve buyers that pay their bills on time.

The importance of *internal* partnerships is rapidly becoming recognized in business today. The classic definition of the word *customer* as the buyer of a good or service is now more carefully defined in terms of *external* customers. However, customers within an organization also have their own needs. For example, in a company that manufactures cellular phones, the team that assembles the phones is a customer of the company's purchasing department. In essence, the manufacturing plant "buys" cellular phone parts from the purchasing department, and the purchasing department supplies them. In this partnership, the purchasing department must continue to fulfill the needs of manufacturing by selecting vendors that can provide the parts needed with price, quality, and time frame characteristics specified by manufacturing. Similarly, the payroll department is a customer of all company employees, data processing is a customer of the accounting department, and a supervisor is the customer of his or her employees.

Internal partnerships form the foundation of an organization and its ability to meet its commitments to external entities. For example, if the purchasing department selects a parts vendor that fails to ship inputs on the dates required by manufacturing, production will halt, and phones won't be delivered to customers as promised. As a net result, external customers will likely seek other, more reliable suppliers. Without building and maintaining internal partnerships, it will be very difficult for an organization to meet the needs of its external partnerships.

Lateral partnerships include strategic relationships between firms and their competitors, co-marketing and co-branding alliances, global strategic alliances, alliances with not-for-profit organizations, and research alliances with government organizations. In each of these cases, the relationship reaches external entities, and it involves no buyer or seller interactions.

A later section of this chapter will examine the role of strategic alliances in relationship marketing, but two kinds of lateral partnerships—co-marketing and co-branding—are becoming increasingly important in the marketing efforts of companies today. The next section takes a closer look at these specific forms of relationship marketing.

Co-Marketing and Co-Branding

Co-marketing and co-branding have been around for some time. Today, however, these types of business-to-business relationships have become especially popular as marketers rediscover their benefits.

SOLVING AN ETHICAL CONTROVERSY

Should Relationship Marketers Have Access to Confidential Database Information?

Relationship marketing would not be possible without a great storehouse of knowledge about likes and dislikes of consumers. The burgeoning field of computerized database management permits marketers to take the pulse of current and prospective customers. With the advent of new software and more sophisticated computer technology, consumers' quirks, preferences, and backgrounds can be sliced and diced hundreds of ways. Companies have been collecting purchase data for years from varied sources such as product registration cards with lifestyle survey questions in addition to price scanners, automated teller machines, and mail-order and credit-card purchase records. The increasing popularity of the World Wide Web provides yet another way for companies to learn about consumer preferences. Further, many companies eagerly buy brokered lists of prepackaged data.

With the assistance of reams of computer printouts, companies believe they can improve their rapport with customers based on knowledge of their purchasing patterns and demographic backgrounds. For instance, restaurants are using database marketing techniques to reach customers likely to favor their cuisines and other product characteristics. When Pizza Hut started selling its Stuffed Crust pizza, it rolled out a splashy ad campaign featuring Rush Limbaugh, Ringo Starr, and Donald Trump, but it also quietly mailed discount coupons to millions of Pizza Hut customers it believed would like the Stuffed Crust pizza. Pizza Hut had stuffed its own database with these names after methodically collecting customer information through delivery call-ins. But this wonderful marketing tool comes with a caveat about privacy limits.

Should marketers draw a restrictive line between marketing needs and consumer privacy?

PRO

1. **You can run a successful and highly profitable business without being so snoopy. More companies need to follow American Express and Citibank, which have long been leaders in efforts to protect customers' privacy. For instance, American Express and Citibank offer clients "opt-out" opportunities to purge their names from the companies' mailing lists.**
2. **Some marketing experts suggest marketing benefits for companies that tout their efforts at ensuring consumers' privacy. Making a publicized effort to protect customer privacy could actually become a highly successful way to gener-**

Co-marketing describes formal links between two or more businesses to jointly market each other's products. Most personal computer manufacturers practice co-marketing, putting "Intel Inside" labels on their machines based on the Pentium microprocessor. They also prominently feature the Pentium chip and the "Intel Inside" logo in print advertising. The PC makers gain credibility through their association with the high-quality, cutting-edge reputation of Intel Corp.; Intel benefits because its name appears in more places and more often than it could achieve on its own.

Product tie-ins have long been a popular co-marketing tool for movie producers and consumer goods manufacturers. Remember the movie *E.T.* and its title character's love for Hershey-brand Reese's Pieces candy? This product tie-in led to huge sales for Hershey, while sales of M&M Mars's competing candies suffered.[34] It's no accident that Tom Cruise eats lots of Cocoa Puffs brand cereal in the film *A Few Good Men;* General Mills formed a lucrative co-marketing deal with the film company. BMW's new Z3 sports car was prominently featured in *Goldeneye,* the latest James Bond thriller, as the result of a similar arrangement. Apple Computer's tie-in to *Mission: Impossible* included scenes showing star Tom Cruise toting an Apple PowerBook computer. The company launched an expensive campaign featuring Cruise in its ads and through a Web site for the movie.[35]

Walt Disney Co. is a master at co-marketing. It selected Burger King to help co-market *Toy Story,* the first computer-animated, full-length feature film, by giving away plastic figurines free in its Kid's Meals. The popularity of Disney films led Burger King, Nestlé, Mattel, Payless ShoeSource, and General Mills to happily pay $150 million to join the filmmaker in promoting its blockbuster 1996 animated release, *The Hunchback of Notre Dame.*[36] Such co-marketing programs benefit both parties. Disney gains additional exposure for its film while its co-marketing partners increase their sales activity because

ate more business. "Privacy is going to be the issue for the remainder of this decade," predicts a spokesperson for Associated Credit Bureaus.

3. Marketers' insatiable desire for private information is disheartening to Americans. Alan F. Westin, author of *Privacy & American Business,* recently reported that 82 percent of credit-card holders believe they have lost control over how companies use confidential information about them.

CON

1. While industry awaits the newest generation of privacy-protection technology, the business world should be able to police its own activities. If a company cavalierly passes out confidential tidbits about its customers, those customers might become too alienated to ever return. Companies in the fast-food and full-service restaurant business, for instance, are increasingly appreciating this reality.
2. Plumbing the depths of computer storehouses can ultimately benefit customers because companies can better meet their needs, according to Judd Goldfeder, president of the Customer Connection, a database management firm in Escondido, California, that serves restaurant chains. Understanding the desires of its typical customer means that a company can better serve that person. For example, firms can relate ads and direct-mail campaigns to a customer's interests, cutting down on irrelevant materials; also, supermarkets can supply checkout coupons based on prior purchases. Many consumers seem to appreciate that claim. In one widely quoted industry survey, 55 percent of Americans considered themselves "privacy pragmatists" who were willing to have third parties use their personal information if it would provide them with more choices and opportunities.
3. Clamping down tightly on database gathering could stifle free speech rights. First Amendment advocates fear such a stifling effect if courts force companies to police what happens to data that they pass on to third parties.

Summary

The question of database privacy draws passionate arguments from both sides. While the debate continues, the federal government will no doubt take a keen interest in just how businesses settle the question.

Sources: Leslie Miller, "Firms Push Web Privacy," *USA Today,* March 19, 1997, downloaded from http://www.usatoday.com/, May 19, 1997; Thomas E. Weber, "Browsers Beware: The Web Is Watching," *Wall Street Journal,* June 27, 1996, pp. B10, B12; John N. Frank, "The Brouhaha over Privacy," *Credit Card Management,* May 1996, pp. 32–35; James Morris-Lee, "Privacy: It's Everyone's Business Now!" *Direct Marketing,* April 1996, pp. 40–43; and Sean Mehegan, "The Database Game," *Restaurant Business,* September 1, 1995, pp. 56–63.

the product tie-ins bring children and their parents into the stores.

Sports leagues also like co-marketing. The National Basketball Association (NBA) and Nestlé have a co-marketing arrangement making Nestlé's Crunch the official candy of the NBA. The agreement also renamed a popular annual event the Nestlé Crunch Slam-Dunk competition. Nestlé agreed to develop other NBA-related national product promotions and retail tie-ins with licensed products. "Nestlé has been an excellent partner," said David Schreff, president of NBA Properties Marketing and Media Group. "Their retail strength and promotion capabilities, combined with the relevance of the NBA brand to its consumers, will serve to increase both our businesses."[37]

Co-branding occurs when two or more companies team up to closely link their names together for a single product. Kellogg's Healthy Choice cereal resulted from such a partnership between Kellogg and prepared-food giant ConAgra; other examples include the AT&T Universal Visa credit card and Ben & Jerry's Heath Bar Crunch brand of ice cream. By creating an essentially new product bearing the name of both firms' products, co-branding reflects a much deeper commitment than co-marketing

Marketing Dictionary

co-marketing Formal links between two or more businesses to jointly market each other's products.

co-branding Partnership between two or more companies to closely link their brand names together for a single product.

MARKETING HALL OF SHAME

Rubbermaid's Worst Relationship Decision

Rubbermaid, Inc., the plastic products giant from Wooster, Ohio, has for many years been the darling of both Wall Street and Main Street. Envied by financial analysts for its extraordinary and dependable earnings growth, Rubbermaid has also kept its loyal customers happy with its ever-expanding line of high-quality housewares and durable plastic toys.

But Rubbermaid's story hasn't sounded so cheery lately. It has failed to keep Wal-Mart, its biggest customer, happy. Even worse, Rubbermaid's recent business tactics have genuinely angered Wal-Mart's top executives. The problems that arose between these two corporate giants provide a cautionary tale for any company that fails to heed the lessons of relationship marketing. Marketing to customers makes up only part of the firm's responsibilities; efforts to cultivate solid business-to-business relationships with suppliers and distributors also provide an integral key to success.

So what went wrong for Rubbermaid? The relationship between the two partners began to sour after the price of resin skyrocketed. Rubbermaid uses resin in most of its 5,000 products, from ice cube trays to Little Tyke "Cozy Coupe" toy cars. Rubbermaid was accustomed to buying a rail-car load of resin for less than $50,000, but a succession of price hikes pushed the cost to almost $93,000.

With sticker shock threatening to jeopardize its much-admired earnings record, Rubbermaid executives made the fateful decision to pass along a portion of the increased cost to distributors. Wal-Mart's special relationship with Rubbermaid did not protect it from the price squeeze. Wolfgang R. Schmitt, Rubbermaid's chief executive officer, says the price increases amounted to no more than 6 percent, but distributors balked. Making matters worse, Rubbermaid's sales teams, which weren't used to adversarial relationships, were ill-equipped to convince angry retailers to accept price hikes on familiar products.

Outraged, Wal-Mart fought back, and, in so doing, it helped annihilate Rubbermaid's recent profit performance. It's not hard to see why: With its network of more than 2,200 stores in the United States, Wal-Mart represents more than 15 percent of Rubbermaid's sales of household products. Wal-Mart stopped stocking some Rubbermaid products and ignored the

involves and a potentially longer-term relationship between businesses.

Good Humor-Breyer's resorted to co-branding with other firms when it decided to seek more of the lucrative market for superior-premium ice cream dominated by brands such as Ben & Jerry's Homemade. Breyer's, the leading brand in the premium half-gallon market, knew that competitors offering top-quality ice cream in pint containers commanded far higher retail prices per ounce. However, the firm decided to aim at the one-quart middle ground with Breyer's Blends, containing well-known brands of candies and other treats mixed with the ice cream. Ice cream fanciers can now choose from such Breyer's Blends flavors as Maxwell House cappuccino, Reese's Pieces, Hershey's chocolate, and Sara Lee brownies.[38]

Co-branding is also popular in the credit-card industry. These arrangements resemble affinity programs, except that the card issuers partner with products or brands rather than not-for-profit organizations; those sponsors provide the cards' value-added features. In return, the sponsor gains access to customer and purchase data, which it analyzes for use in marketing programs. The General Motors MasterCard, with about 13 million cardholders, combines two strong brand names with an easy-to-understand program. Consumers earn rebates toward new car purchases equal to 5 percent of all card purchases up to specified annual limits for seven years. GM added marketing co-sponsors to the program like MCI, Marriott, Alamo Car Rental, and Mobil Oil; purchases from these partners earn 10 percent rebates, even in excess of annual limits. The card appears to be successful in building customer relationships. Bill Anderson, GM's director of consumer marketing, reports that cardholders who have used their rebates stay with the card program and in fact increase their charge volumes.[39]

LINKS BETWEEN BUYERS AND SELLERS IN BUSINESS-TO-BUSINESS MARKETS

Partnerships between buyers and sellers are facts of life in today's competitive business environment. Organizations

plastics giant in its promotional handouts. Even worse, Wal-Mart, a stickler for low prices, started offering more shelf space to Rubbermaid's cheaper competitors—Sterilite Corp. and Mobil's Tucker Housewares.

Just how fast the relationship unraveled is clear by listening to Wal-Mart's CEO, David Glass, talk about Rubbermaid. "They've lost their momentum, and I'm not sure why," Glass says. "They don't have any good new products."

Wal-Mart's retaliation has been Rubbermaid's Titanic disaster. Prior to the increase in competition, Rubbermaid had consistently enjoyed 15 percent or larger increases in earnings growth and operating margins of 20 percent. Analysts attribute some of that success to Wal-Mart's past willingness to devote plenty of space to Rubbermaid's extensive line of products. Since then, however, Rubbermaid's earnings have plummeted 30 percent, and the company announced that it would be shuttering nine facilities and laying off 9 percent of its 14,000 employees.

Ironically, Rubbermaid's hard times come at a point when most manufacturers are bending over backward to please powerful retail chains like Wal-Mart, Target, and Kmart. Commenting on the carnage, one securities analyst noted, "Wal-Mart can live without Rubbermaid, but the opposite is not necessarily true."

Wal-Mart wasn't the only retailer that Rubbermaid miffed. Other retailers, assuming that they couldn't pass on higher costs to their shoppers, stopped restocking their shelves with Rubbermaid products. Instead, these retailers turned to Rubbermaid's mortal enemies, who passed along smaller price increases.

"I know resin prices went up dramatically," says an executive at an East Coast retail chain, "but the charge that Rubbermaid passed along was too big an increase with too short notice." In hindsight, Rubbermaid President Chuck Carroll agrees that its tactics were flawed. "We should have been helping customers increase their sales rather than fighting with them so long over prices."

QUESTIONS FOR CRITICAL THINKING

1. **How did Rubbermaid violate the principles of relationship marketing?**
2. **What strategy would you recommend to Rubbermaid to repair its damaged relationship with Wal-Mart?**

Sources: "Rubbermaid Inc. Sees Resin Costs Volatility," Reuters, April 16, 1997, downloaded from http://biz.yahoo.com/finance/97, May 19, 1997; Matthew Schifrin, "The Big Squeeze," *Forbes,* March 11, 1996, pp. 45–46; and Lee Smith, "Rubbermaid Goes Thump," *Fortune,* October 2, 1995, pp. 90–104; and based on information from "The Revolving Door at Rubbermaid," *Business Week,* September 18, 1995, pp. 80–86.

that know how to find and nurture partner relationships, whether through informal deals or contractual co-marketing and co-branding agreements, can enhance revenues and increase profits. Partnering often leads to lower prices, better products, and improved distribution methods, resulting in higher levels of customer satisfaction. Closer relationships also improve communications between partners. This change can be particularly helpful at a time when many firms are dealing with fewer suppliers and requiring adherence to high quality and delivery standards. Partners who know each other's needs and expectations are more likely to satisfy them and forge stronger long-term bonds.

In the past, business relationships were conducted primarily in person, over the phone, or by mail. Today, businesses are using the latest electronic, computer, and communications technology to link up. E-mail, fax machines, the Internet, and other telecommunications services allow businesses to communicate any time, any place. The sections that follow explore the various ways that buyers and sellers are creating links in business-to-business markets.

The Internet

As discussed previously, businesses using the Internet have focused primarily on individual retail consumers. Through Web sites, they provide product information, run sales promotions like coupon offers and contests, solicit customer feedback, and in many cases, set up virtual storefronts where customers can order merchandise. This focus is changing, however, as more companies become familiar with electronic communications. These links will continue to spread with the development of software and security measures necessary for businesses to interact with one another on the Internet. As the ad in Figure 10.13 illustrates, FedEx is ready to conduct business on the Internet. It offers business customers free software so they can ship and track packages and schedule pick-ups on the FedEx interNetShip Web site.

Microsoft, IBM, General Electric Information Services (GEIS), and others are busily developing the systems and software necessary to make business-to-business relationships a reality on the Internet. Says Hellene S. Runtagh, GEIS's president and chief executive officer, "I

Figure 10.13 FedEx: Using the Internet in Business-to-Business Marketing

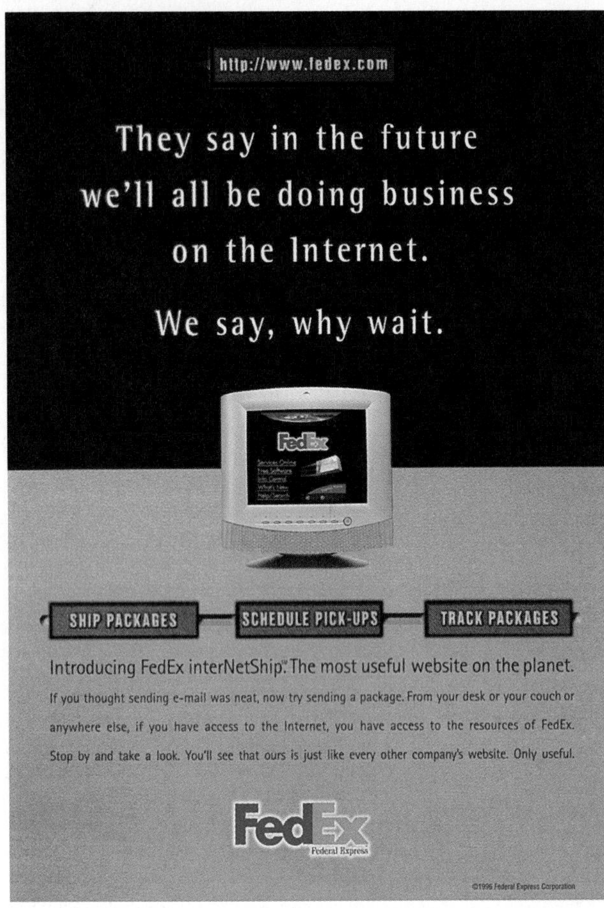
http://www.fedex.com
They say in the future we'll all be doing business on the Internet.
We say, why wait.
SHIP PACKAGES
SCHEDULE PICK-UPS
TRACK PACKAGES
Introducing FedEx interNetShip.℠ The most useful website on the planet.
If you thought sending e-mail was neat, now try sending a package. From your desk or your couch or anywhere else, if you have access to the Internet, you have access to the resources of FedEx. Stop by and take a look. You'll see that ours is just like every other company's website. Only useful.
FedEx
Federal Express
©1996 Federal Express Corporation

really see the Internet as an explosion of electronic commerce. This is the most exciting single change to hit commerce globally in the last 100 years." Entirely new companies are emerging to help firms find business customers and suppliers through the Internet. One example, Industry.net Corp. founded by former Lotus Development Corp. CEO Jim Manzi, has created a virtual industrial mall.[40]

http://www.fruit.com/

Fruit of the Loom, Inc., has bypassed the stage at which many firms develop closed, private networks to link with key customers and instead has placed its ordering system on the Internet. Fruit of the Loom has offered free Web access to each of its 50 key wholesalers. Wholesalers that accept Fruit of the Loom's offer receive a special Activewear Online computer system programmed to display Fruit of the Loom catalogs, process electronic orders, and help manage product inventories, all via the Internet.[41]

The Internet can also help small businesses to develop wider ranges of relationships outside the former limits of their local areas. Using the Internet and the World Wide Web, companies can easily find other organizations to help them grow their businesses, including suppliers, distributors, and complementary companies with whom to partner. For example, a company that wants to sell its products internationally may need to translate its sales materials into different languages. It can search the Web for the home page of a company that offers translation services. Alternatively, a message in a newsgroup may ask for recommendations from other small businesses with the same problem or for information directly from translation firms.[42]

The Use of Databases

As an earlier section noted, databases are indispensable tools in relationship marketing. While that discussion explained the use of databases to target specific kinds of consumers, databases are also used in business-to-business situations.

Using information generated from sales reports, register scanners, and many other sources, sellers can create databases that help to guide their own efforts and those of buyers who resell products to final users. For example, Procter & Gamble marketers poring over sales data from a large warehouse-club store noticed a direct, positive relationship between the sales of Pampers disposable diapers and beer. As sales of disposable diapers increased, so did beer sales; as diaper sales fell, beer sales declined. On closer examination, they found that young fathers sent out to pick up diapers often picked up some beer as well. The Pampers sales representatives convinced their retailing customer to place a beer display near the diaper section of the store. The result: Sales increased 45 percent.[43]

Pennsylvania-based clothing manufacturer VF Corp. has developed an experimental system called *Trendsetter* to sort through its vast sales database and help business customers develop more accurate forecasts of supply levels for emerging fashion trends. The system can track specific kinds, colors, and sizes of clothes—say, brown-dyed Lee jeans sold by the Belk department store chain. The system then forecasts Belk's ideal inventory levels for the product. As a result, VF customers are prepared with the right kinds of merchandise in the right colors and sizes when the latest fashion trends hit their stores.[44]

Electronic Data Interchange

A decade ago, when a store ran a big sale on Nike shoes and ran out of the product, the store's buyer had to phone the company's sales representative to place a rush order. The sales rep, assuming he or she wasn't out visiting other customers, checked the price and availability of the item and then placed an order for more shoes. To officially formalize the transaction, the buyer mailed a copy of a purchase order to the sales rep.

He asked you for the time. He was wearing a watch.
Lee
The Brand That Fits.

Matching Inventory Needs with Sales Expectations: Goal of the VF Corp. Database

While this system worked fine for decades, it just doesn't meet the needs of today's competitive environment. A large retailer such as the Sports Authority or Wal-Mart would scoff at the unbelievable inefficiency and cost of employing a huge staff of buyers to call manufacturers' representatives to check on prices and availability for the thousands of items stocked at each store. They would also object to the tremendous volume of paper-based purchase orders that the old system would generate each day. Fortunately, computers have automated the buying process. At the same time, they have opened new channels for gathering marketing information and creating business-to-business links and long-term relationships.

Electronic data interchange is one such computer-based technology. **Electronic data interchange (EDI)** involves computer-to-computer exchanges of invoices, orders, and other business documents. U.S. businesses currently purchase goods from other businesses through electronic systems to the tune of $500 billion a year.[45] EDI is rapidly gaining popularity, because it allows businesses to reduce their costs and improve their efficiency and competitiveness. Retailers using EDI can implement **quick response** strategies that reduce the time they must hold merchandise in inventory, resulting in substantial cost savings.

Campbell Soup Co. recently spent $30 million to completely revamp its order-processing system and add fully developed EDI capabilities. The firm had discovered that 60 percent of all orders it received by phone or by fax included mistakes. As a result, Campbell's salespeople were spending 40 percent of their time correcting mistakes to get the right products to their customers; this workload interfered with efforts to generate new sales. The old order-processing system took an average of 48 hours from the time an order was received to shipment. The new system reduces this turnaround time to 18 hours. Not only does the new EDI system save time and speed up deliveries, but it also saves the company an estimated $18 million a year. A vice president at Campbell's reported another benefit of EDI: "Even the trees are happy. We're not chopping them down to make paper."[46]

The advantages of electronic data interchange are so compelling that many large firms—including retailers Dillard's, Lowe's, and Eckerd Drug—now require all their vendors to possess and use EDI technology. For firms willing to take the plunge, EDI helps vendors to cement long-term relationships with their customers. Those who are slow making the move may soon find themselves left behind. In a recent letter to potential office supplies vendors,

Marketing Dictionary

electronic data interchange (EDI) Computer-to-computer exchanges of invoices, orders, and other business documents.

quick response Strategies that reduce the time companies must hold merchandise in inventory, resulting in substantial cost savings.

Figure 10.14 Upstream and Downstream Relationships in the Auto Manufacturing Supply Chain

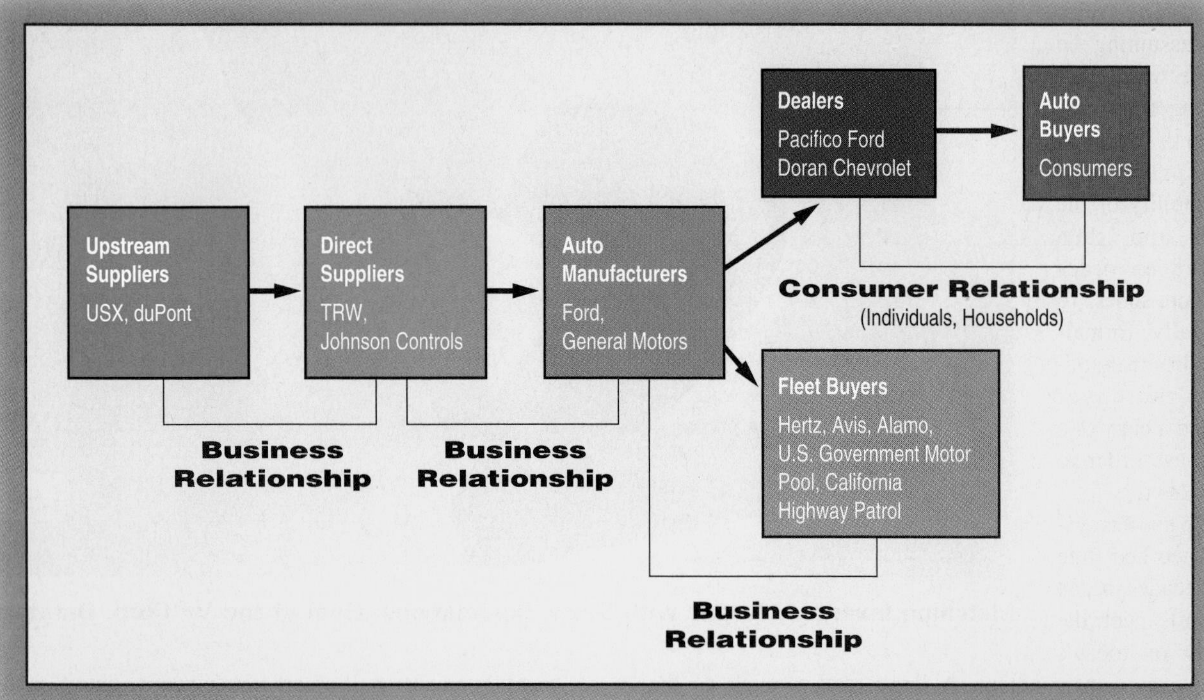
Upstream Suppliers
USX, duPont
Direct Suppliers
TRW, Johnson Controls
Auto Manufacturers
Ford, General Motors
Dealers
Pacifico Ford
Doran Chevrolet
Auto Buyers
Consumers
Fleet Buyers
Hertz, Avis, Alamo, U.S. Government Motor Pool, California Highway Patrol
Consumer Relationship
(Individuals, Households)
Business Relationship
Business Relationship
Business Relationship

Paul E. Konetzny, manager of EDI applications for office supplies giant Staples Inc. wrote, "Our commitment to EDI and to electronic commerce is strong. EDI readiness is necessary to doing business with Staples in the future. We will work with you to implement a partnership which brings benefits to both companies due to increased efficiencies and speed, reduced errors and inventory, and where appropriate through re-engineered processes."[47]

National Account Selling

Some relationships are more important than others. A large manufacturer such as Procter & Gamble pays special attention to the needs of large retailers such as Wal-Mart, Kmart, and others, which sell many millions of dollars of P&G products each year. Manufacturers use a technique called *national account selling* to target their largest, most profitable customers.

The most common approach is to establish cross-functional teams between buyer and seller. To help solidify and nurture a long-term relationship with Wal-Mart, Procter & Gamble has established a multifunctional team to work directly with the Wal-Mart national account. The team functions on organization, systems, and operations levels where approximately 40 employees identify and implement cost-saving measures in the two companies' buyer-seller systems and processes. Procter & Gamble values its relationship with Wal-Mart so much that it houses its team in Bentonville, Arkansas—the retail giant's headquarters.[48]

The advantages of national account selling are many. By assembling a team of individuals to service one account, the seller demonstrates the depth of its commitment to the buyer. This gesture strengthens the buyer-seller relationship. For another advantage, rather than engaging in the kind of adversarial relationship common among many firms, buyer and seller work together, on the same team, to find solutions that benefit *both* parties. Finally, cooperative buyer-seller efforts can bring about dramatic improvements in both efficiency and effectiveness for both firms. These improvements find their way to the bottom line in the form of decreased costs and increased profits.

Vendor-Managed Inventory

The proliferation of electronic data interchange and the constant pressure on suppliers to improve response time has led to a new way for buyers and sellers to do business. **Vendor-managed inventory (VMI)** is an inventory-management system in which the *seller* determines how much product a buyer needs and automatically ships new supplies. Vendor-managed inventory turns the old system of buyer-managed inventory on its head, leading to increased profits for both seller and buyer.

Every day, Del Monte, the California-based producer and distributor of canned fruits and vegetables, receives inventory reports electronically from grocery stores within its network. When the inventory of Del Monte products falls to a predetermined level, a computer instantly issues an order to the shipping department to send that item to the grocery store. The buyers don't have to maintain large amounts of costly, idle inventory in their own warehouses—saving them lots of money. As one Del Monte marketer points out, "One week of inventory in a warehouse costs a retailer some $250,000 a year." Supermarkets using the Del Monte vendor-managed inventory system can reduce their own inventory levels from an average of four weeks down to one and a half weeks.[49]

VF Corp. has developed its own extensive vendor-managed inventory system with several key American retailers including Wal-Mart and JCPenney. For example, Wal-Mart sells millions of pairs of Wrangler and Lee jeans every year through its 2,200-plus stores. Every night, VF's vendor-managed inventory system compiles sales data collected from every one of Wal-Mart's register scanners. The computer notes exactly what items were sold at which stores and checks the company's inventory for replacement items. If the item is in stock, VF ships it to the appropriate Wal-Mart store the next day, where the retailer's staff places it on the shelf one day later. If the item isn't in stock, the computer orders it from the factory, which ships directly to the store within a week. For comparison, VF's old system of inventory replenishment took up to three months to process an order from beginning to end.[50]

Managing the Supply Chain

Good relationships between businesses require careful management of the **supply chain** (also called the *value chain),* the entire sequence of suppliers that contribute to the creation and delivery of a good or service. This process affects both *upstream* relationships between the company and its suppliers and *downstream* relationships with the product's end users. Figure 10.14 illustrates the supply chain for an auto manufacturer such as Ford or General Motors. The first link in the chain, upstream suppliers, consists of companies that produce raw materials such as sheet metal or plastics. The next link includes direct suppliers that use these raw materials to create automobile components and parts. Auto manufacturers purchase these components and assemble them into finished vehicles for purchase by consumers through dealers and by organizations such as fleet buyers. Each business in this chain does more than simply create products. It also markets its products, delivers them, and provides support and service after making a sale.

Effective supply chain management can provide an important competitive advantage for a business marketer, resulting in:

- Increased innovation
- Decreased costs
- Improved conflict resolution within the chain
- Improved communication and involvement among members of the chain

By coordinating operations with the other companies in the chain, boosting quality, and improving efficiency, a firm can improve speed and efficiency. Because companies spend considerable resources on goods and services from outside suppliers—manufacturers can devote over 60 percent of their total budgets to component purchases—cooperative relationships can pay off in many ways. Del Monte and VF Corp. practice supply chain management with their vendor-managed inventory systems.

Strategic Alliances

Strategic alliances are the ultimate expression of relationship marketing. Recall from Chapter 1 that a *strategic alliance* is a partnership formed to create a competitive advantage. These more formal long-term partnership relationships improve each partner's supply chain relationships and enhance flexibility to operate in today's complex and rapidly changing marketplace. The size and location of strategic partners is not important, Strategic alliances include businesses of all sizes, all kinds, and in many locations; it's what each partner can offer the other that is important.

Companies can structure strategic alliances in two ways. The alliance partners can establish a new business

Marketing Dictionary

vendor-managed inventory (VMI) Inventory-management system in which the *seller* determines how much product a buyer needs and automatically ships new supplies.

supply (value) chain Sequence of suppliers that contribute to the creation and delivery of a good or service.

Table 10.3 Resources and Skills That Partners Contribute to Achieve Competitive Advantage in Strategic Alliances

Resources		Skills
Patents Product lines Brand equity Reputation • For product quality • For customer service • For product innovation Image • Companywide • Business unit • Product line/brand Knowledge of product-market	Customer base Marketing resources • Marketing infrastructure • Sales force size Established relationship with: • Suppliers • Marketing intermediaries • End-use customers Manufacturing resources • Location • Size, scale economies, scope economies, excess capacity, newness of plant and equipment Information technology and systems	Marketing skills • Innovation and product development • Positioning and segmentation • Advertising and sales promotion Manufacturing skills • Miniaturization • Low-cost manufacturing • Flexible manufacturing Planning and implementation skills R&D skills Organizational expertise, producer learning, and experience effects

unit in which each takes an ownership position. In such a joint venture, one partner might own 40 percent, while the other owns 60 percent. Alternatively, the partners may decide to form a cooperative relationship that is less formal and does not involve ownership—for example, a joint new-product design team. The cooperative alliance can operate more flexibly and change more easily as market forces or other conditions dictate. In either arrangement, the partners agree in advance on the skills and resources, such as those listed in Table 10.3, that each will bring into the alliance to achieve their mutual objectives and gain a competitive advantage.

Companies form many types of strategic alliances today. Some create *horizontal* alliances between firms at the same level in the supply chain; others define *vertical* links between firms at adjacent stages. The firms may serve the same or different industries. Alliances can involve cooperation among rivals who are market leaders or between a market leader and a follower. Market leaders General Motors and Toyota formed a horizontal strategic alliance for manufacturing. GM wanted to learn Toyota's management

http://www.gm.com/

and manufacturing methods, while Toyota was interested in GM's strategies for labor management and working with U.S. suppliers. GM's manufacturing/marketing alliance with Suzuki and Isuzu is an example of a market leader/follower relationship. The Japanese companies manufacture cars for GM's Geo line, resulting in economies of scale and the opportunity to gain market experience.[51] Home Depot maintains vertical alliances with its major merchandise suppliers, who tailor programs to the chain's needs.

Strategic alliances can be *domestic,* such as the joint venture between MCI, Digital Equipment, and Microsoft. This interindustry alliance among telecommunications, hardware, and software firms sought to develop an integrated package of corporate communications products that would challenge AT&T's alliances with IBM and Netscape. *International alliances* are also on the rise. For example, through shared distribution agreements, Nissan markets Volkswagen cars in Japan and Canadian brewer Molson has the license to produce and sell Japan's Kirin beer in North America. Even research and development has gone global, due in part to the increased cost of developing high-technology products today. Japan's Sony Corp. and Philips, the Dutch electronics firm, partnered to develop videodiscs. Boeing and Japanese firms Mitsubishi, Fuji, and IHI are working together on the new 9U7 aircraft.[52]

In a recent announcement that rocked the foundations of the airline industry, AMR Corp.—parent of American Airlines—formed an alliance with British Airways that stands to create the world's largest airline network. As a result of the partnership, American will funnel passengers onto British Airways flights to Europe, Africa, and Asia; British Airways will funnel passengers onto American Airlines flights to the United States and Latin America. Each partner gains by obtaining access to destinations in parts of the world where its own network is weak.[53]

MANAGING RELATIONSHIPS FOR SUPERIOR PERFORMANCE

Clearly, relationship marketing techniques help companies to create better and more personal ways to communicate with customers and develop long-term relationships. A company's relationship marketing efforts challenge managers to develop strategies that closely integrate customer service, quality, and marketing functions. This goal may require changes in organizational philosophy, structure, and procedures. For example, companies must begin to think of customers as assets and use techniques designed to calculate their value. By analyzing customer databases, marketers can match the costs of acquiring and maintaining customer relationships with the profits received from these customers. This information allows managers to evaluate the return on a proposed relationship marketing program before making the investment.

Assessing the Costs and Benefits

How can organizations determine whether relationship management strategies pay off? Many companies hesitate to commit to large investments in database systems because customized programs cost much more per customer than mass marketing. The first step in evaluating this investment is to identify and compare its costs and benefits, both tangible and intangible. Because customers are assets, a company can analyze its marketing and communication investments in much the same way as it evaluates capital equipment investments.

Look again at VF's vendor-managed inventory system, described on page 357. Before implementing the project, VF had to compare the cost of the computer and other equipment plus associated charges like employee training with the benefits of the inventory system for itself and the retailer. These gains include faster order time, fewer errors, improved manufacturing planning, reduced inventory costs due to lower chance of overstocking, and fewer lost sales from being out of inventory. The program also brings intangible costs and benefits. By simplifying transactions between the parties, it improves their overall relationship. Also, customer satisfaction should rise because the right merchandise will be available on demand.

Without a cost-benefit analysis like this, companies may waste money on programs. If a firm such as Nabisco distributes 50 million cents-off coupons in one year but only about 2 percent are redeemed, it must consider the cost of the mass distribution in relation to the benefits—increased sales to both new and repeat buyers and improved customer relationships. If the actual costs from a prior program or estimated costs for a proposed mailing exceed the benefits, the company should not proceed.

Briefly speaking

"In every instance we found that the best-run companies stay as close to their customers as humanly possible."

Thomas J. Peters (1942–)
American business writer

Structuring Relationships to Achieve Target Performance Levels

Partners can structure relationships in many different ways to improve performance, and these choices will vary for consumer and business markets. First, they should examine existing company systems involved in delivering customer service. By identifying the processes, people, and materials required to deliver the product, potential problem areas can be determined. The places where customer interaction occurs are the risk points. If the customer has a good experience, the relationship is enhanced. Setting standards for these interaction points gives employees guidelines for action and increases the likelihood of achieving the company's goals. Reward programs such as employee-of-the-month recognition or bonuses provide incentives for improved customer service.[54]

In developing consumer relationships, marketers must recognize the inefficiency and high cost of trying to reach all consumers. Instead, they should use databases to identify prospects with the most profit potential. Programs that promote high levels of customer involvement—in design, development, and marketing phases—increase loyalty. As this involvement begins earlier in the process, the company receives more feedback. Through communications from customers—warranty cards, contacts with customer service reps, contests—companies learn about customer priorities. Listening to customer responses can help them eliminate unnecessary activities and focus on ones that customers value by answering a key question: "Would the customer pay for this activity if the firm were to offer it as an option?"

In business-to-business relationships such as vendor/retailer partnerships, it is especially important to structure relationships to build trust. This goal may require suppliers to share detailed financial information on materials and production costs—information some may prefer to remain confidential, fearing that customers could use the data to push for unfair pricing concessions. However, successful partnerships start with the premise that both parties need to make reasonable profits, and cooperation can lead to lower costs and a win-win situation for both parties.[55]

Measurement and Evaluation Techniques

Measuring and evaluating the effectiveness of relationship marketing programs can be very difficult, especially in business-to-business relationships. For example, while managers may see obvious, easily quantifiable benefits from involving suppliers at an early stage in product development, they must also consider equally important qualitative, intangible advantages that may require subjective analysis.

One of the most important measures is the **lifetime value of a customer:** the revenues and intangible benefits (referrals, customer feedback, etc.) that a customer brings to the seller over an average lifetime, less the amount the company must spend to acquire, market to, and service the customer. Long-term customers are usually more valuable assets than new ones, because they buy more, cost less to service, refer other customers, and provide valuable feedback. The "average lifetime" of a customer relationship depends on industry and product characteristics. Customer lifetime for a consumer product like breakfast cereal or laundry detergent may be very short, while that for a computer will last longer.

For a simple example of a lifetime value calculation, assume that a Chinese takeout restaurant determines that its average customer buys dinner twice a month at an average cost of $25 per order over a lifetime of five years. That business translates to revenues of $600 per year and $3,000 for five years. The restaurant can calculate and subtract its average costs for food, labor, and marketing to arrive at the per-customer profit. This figure serves as a baseline against which to measure strategies to increase the restaurant's sales volume, customer retention, or customer referral rate.

Analyzing customer value helps companies to identify their best customers. They cannot do this simply by measuring sales levels. A British consumer electronics company found that while three major customers generated comparable revenue, the costs to service them varied. One required deliveries to over 300 warehouses, while another used a central warehouse. One paid within 30 days; the others took 40 or more. One placed many rush orders; the others made no special demands. As a result, profitability on these accounts varied by over 20 percent. Lifetime value analysis could help this company to determine its costs to service each customer and develop ways to increase profitability and preserve relationships.[56]

Another approach is to calculate the payback from a customer relationship, or how long it takes to break even on customer acquisition costs. For example, assume that America Online spends $40 per new customer on direct mail and enrollment incentives. Based on average revenues per subscriber, the company takes about three months to recover that $40. If an average customer stays with the service 32 months and generates $500 in revenues, the rate of return to AOL is 11.5 times the original investment. Once the customer stays past the payback period, the company should make a profit on that business.[57]

In addition to lifetime value analysis and payback, companies use other techniques to evaluate relationship programs:

- Tracking rebate requests, coupon redemptions, credit-card purchases, and product registrations
- Monitoring complaints and returned products and analyzing why customers leave
- Reviewing reply cards, comment forms, and surveys

These tools give the organization information about customer priorities so that managers can make changes to their systems, if necessary, and set appropriate, measurable goals for relationship programs. A hotel chain may set a goal of improving the rate of repeat visits from 44 percent to 52 percent. A mail-order company may want to reduce time to process and mail orders from 48 to 24 hours. If a customer survey were to reveal late flight arrivals as the number one complaint of an airline's passengers, it might set an objective of increasing the number of on-time arrivals from 87 percent to 95 percent.

Marketing Dictionary

lifetime value of a customer The revenues and intangible benefits (referrals, customer feedback, etc.) that a customer brings to the seller over an average lifetime, less the amount the company must spend to acquire, market to, and service the customer.

ACHIEVEMENT CHECK SUMMARY

Reread the learning goals that follow, and consider the questions for each goal. Answering these questions will reinforce your grasp of the most important concepts in the chapter and allow you to check how well you have achieved these learning goals. Where a blank appears before a question, answer with *T* or *F;* for multiple-choice questions, circle the letter of the correct answer.

Objective 10.1: Contrast relationship marketing with transaction-based marketing.
1. ___ Transaction-based marketing emphasizes long-term customer satisfaction.
2. ___ Which of the following is not part of relationship marketing? (a) high level of communication with customers; (b) quality programs; (c) emphasis on product features; (d) customer service orientation.
3. ___ Relationship marketing strategies make extensive use of mass-market advertising.

Objective 10.2: Identify and explain each of the core elements of relationship marketing.
1. ___ Mothers against Drunk Driving enables promises with its direct-mail campaign for donations.
2. ___ Understanding a situation from the perspective of the other party is called (a) trust; (b) reciprocity; (c) bonding; (d) empathy.
3. ___ A Macintosh computer users group would occupy a position at the high end of the relationship continuum.

Objective 10.3: Outline the steps in the development of a marketing relationship and the different levels of relationship marketing.
1. ___ Of the following benefits, which is not a reason that consumers form relationships? (a) simplify decisions; (b) reduce boredom; (c) decrease risk; (d) save money.
2. ___ It typically costs three times more to keep a customer than to acquire a new one.
3. ___ AT&T's True Rewards program, which gives customers points based on long-distance charges that they can redeem for gifts, is an affinity program.

Objective 10.4: Explain the role of databases in relationship marketing.
1. ___ Database marketing is useful only in marketing programs for existing customers.
2. ___ With the information in databases, companies can design programs tailored to specific customer segments, rather than to their "typical" customers.

Objective 10.5: Compare the different types of partnerships and explain how they contribute to relationship marketing.
1. ___ Companies choose partners based primarily on the financial assets they bring to the relationships.
2. ___ A restaurant supply company and the Olive Garden restaurant chain can form an internal relationship.
3. ___ A partnership between a company and a not-for-profit agency to sponsor a golf tournament is an example of (a) supplier partnership; (b) internal partnership; (c) lateral partnership; (d) buyer partnership.

Objective 10.6: Relate the concepts of co-marketing and co-branding to relationship marketing.
1. ___ Companies in a co-marketing agreement gain additional exposure for their products.
2. ___ Co-marketing programs require stronger commitments and longer-term relationships than co-branding programs.
3. ___ Nike ads featuring Seattle Mariners outfielder Ken Griffey Jr. are part of the shoemaker's co-branding strategy.

Objective 10.7: Describe how relationship marketing incorporates electronic data interchange, vendor-managed inventories, and national account selling.
1. ___ *Electronic data interchange* refers to the use of databases to forecast inventory levels.
2. ___ The customer determines the timing and quantities of product orders in a vendor-managed inventory system.
3. ___ Cooperative buyer-seller teams increase the commitment between companies, thereby strengthening their relationship.

Objective 10.8: Discuss the value of strategic alliances to a company's relationship marketing strategy.
1. ___ Coordinating operations with suppliers tends to improve quality and provide other competitive advantages.
2. ___ Strategic alliances bring together the skills and resources of partners to achieve common goals such as entry into new markets and reducing manufacturing costs.
3. ___ To make a strategic alliance effective, each partner must take an ownership position.

Objective 10.9: Identify and evaluate the most common measurement and evaluation techniques within a relationship marketing program.
1. ___ A company's customers are an asset, and calculating their value provides a way to measure the return on investment of a relationship marketing program.
2. ___ Cost–benefit analysis deals primarily with the financial impact of a relationship marketing program.
3. ___ Customer communication materials are a valuable resource for evaluating relationship marketing programs.

Students: See the solutions section located on page S-2 to check your responses to the Achievement Check Summary.

Key Terms

relationship marketing
transaction-based marketing
affinity program
frequency marketing
database marketing
partnership
co-marketing

co-branding
electronic data interchange (EDI)
quick response
vendor-managed inventory (VMI)
supply (value) chain
lifetime value of a customer

Review Questions

1. Trace the evolution from transaction-based to relationship marketing, and explain why relationship marketing suits today's marketing environment.
2. Briefly describe the three types of promises that form the basis of relationship marketing, and give an example of each.
3. Identify and explain the four dimensions of relationship marketing.
4. Describe the characteristics of relationships at the low, medium, and high points on the relationship marketing continuum.
5. How can companies use affinity programs and frequent-buyer programs to build relationships with consumers?
6. Discuss the benefits of database marketing in both consumer and business-to-business buyer-seller relationships.
7. Summarize the reasons why businesses form partnerships, and identify the four types of business partnerships.
8. Differentiate between co-marketing and co-branding programs.
9. Explain how effective supply chain management and strategic alliances build relationships and provide competitive advantages.
10. What are the major techniques by which companies can measure and evaluate the effectiveness of their relationship marketing programs?

Discussion Questions

1. Select an organization in your area and describe a relationship marketing strategy that could help it to build better customer relationships. How could it use relationship marketing to increase customer retention rates and find new customers?
2. America Online (AOL) and Visa issued a proprietary bank credit card that offers cardholders one free hour of online time for every $200 in card purchases. Explain the types of relationship marketing programs that this partnership represents, and discuss how AOL can use the program to build stronger ties to new and existing customers.
3. A hotel chain's database has information on guests including demographics, number of visits, and lifestyle preferences. Describe how the company can use this information to develop several relationship marketing programs. How can it use a more general database to identify potential customers and personalize its communications with them?
4. Find an example of a strategic alliance in the business press. Analyze the partners' motives for forming the alliance, their level(s) in the supply chain, and the benefits to each one.
5. Why should a company calculate the lifetime value of a customer? How can managers use this information to improve the firm's relationship marketing programs?

'netWork

1. An entire industry has evolved to help marketers develop relationships with their customers. Get onto the Web, use a search engine such as Yahoo!, and conduct a search on the term *relationship marketing.* Locate a company whose sole purpose is to help develop relationships for other companies. After visiting its Web site, briefly describe the specific services provided by this firm. Suggest the types of firms most likely to need these.

2. Can the Internet be used effectively to develop marketing relationships, or is this tool too impersonal? Locate a home page that seems to excel at relationship marketing. Explain why you chose this company.

3. Visit Lucent Technologies' home page

http://www.lucent.com/Internet/

Explain why this can be considered an example of relationship marketing. Is it effective? Why or why not?

VIDEO CASE 10

LAUNCHING TOMMY: THE NEW AMERICAN FRAGRANCE

Designer Tommy Hilfiger is no novice when it comes to relationship marketing. In need of financing to expand his line of designer menswear, Hilfiger formed a partnership with Silas Chou, owner of Hong Kong's oldest textile and apparel firm. The relationship was an unusual one, since most designers simply license their names and designs to manufacturers. But the Chou-Hilfiger alliance made both men partners in design and production. The move turned out to be a brilliant one. Drawing on Chou's long experience in textiles and manufacturing, Hilfiger found that he could produce quality clothing for less than half the cost of competing designer lines such as Ralph Lauren's.

The partnership allowed Hilfiger to differentiate his brand. "I'm positioned in a unique way," he says. "there's a 12-lane highway between The Gap at the low end and Ralph Lauren at the higher end. And that's where I am, affordable, but the same quality as the best."

Chou also benefited from the partnership. His company needed a direct link with an internationally recognized clothing brand. His family business had made its fortune in private-label contracting, but that business was moving from Hong Kong to lower-wage regions in northern China and to India and Vietnam. As Chou points out, "I may be the last generation of the traditional manufacturing family in the Far East. The comparative advantage is gone. Hong Kong is too expensive. That's why I looked to brand names. This is a great business for my children and grandchildren."

In 1989, the first year of their partnership, Hilfiger and Chou generated sales of $25 million. By 1997, Tommy Hilfiger USA was generating over $400 million in sales. During this period, the Hilfiger clothing line expanded into jeans, underwear, athletic wear, golf clothing, women's wear, eyeglasses, wristwatches, and a fragrance.

To market his fragrance, Hilfiger again decided to practice relationship marketing, and once again through an unusual arrangement. He signed a licensing agreement with Aramis Inc., an Estée Lauder subsidiary. For the previous half-century, Estée Lauder had avoided partnerships with outside designers, choosing instead to develop its own fragrance brands. But the Lauder family saw the alliance with Hilfiger as an ideal means of competing in the designer men's fragrance market. "The whole Lauder family is behind this," says Aramis Executive Creative Director Jeanne Chinard. "We were all waiting for him. He is the perfect match for us."

Aramis, which once controlled 50 percent of men's fragrance sales in department stores, had seen its market share drop to about 13 percent. Company executives were counting on Tommy to put Aramis back in the race with Calvin Klein and Ralph Lauren.

The first-year marketing plan for the new fragrance included plans to distribute 750,000 free samples at department stores, supported by magazine advertising, spot TV, and outdoor ads promoting the theme "a new American fragrance." Hilfiger planned to promote Tommy by tying the fragrance imagery into his clothing ads.

Realizing the importance of distribution to the success of a new fragrance, Aramis marketers preceded the launch of the product—dubbed Tommy: The New American Fragrance—by contacting a number of department store chains, including Hudson's Department Stores with which Aramis had enjoyed a long-standing supplier-customer partnership. Hudson's comprises more than 30 midwestern department stores operated, along with Marshall Field's and Dayton's, by Minneapolis-based Dayton Hudson Corp. Aramis saw Tommy as an opportunity to enhance its strategic alliance with Hudson's by co-marketing the new fragrance.

"The person we are appealing to is the person coming to the Hudson stores to purchase new fragrances," says Aramis Regional Marketing Director Daniel Basil. "We know they have a success going in how they marketed Tommy in the ready-to-wear area."

Hudson's marketers also saw benefits from the co-marketing plan with Aramis. "Fragrances are a very important merchandise category for department stores such as Hudson's for two reasons," says company President Dennis Toffolo. "It's very profitable. It generates huge sales. We do close to $200 million in our department store division today with men's and women's fragrances. The men's portion runs about 25 to 30 percent of the $200 million. The Tommy launch could produce about $600,000 to $700,000 for Hudson's."

The co-marketing agreement gave Hudson's exclusive rights to launch and stock the new Tommy fragrance in its geographic area. For its part, Hudson's developed a marketing plan for promoting Tommy in each market through TV ads and visuals within the stores. In-store display designs coordinated with the national Tommy advertising campaign.

Preparing and training Hudson's sales associates for

the product launch was another key component in the marketing plan for Tommy. Aramis account executives worked closely with store salespeople to explain the store visuals and motivate them to sell the new product. Dayton Hudson and Aramis co-sponsored a Tommy launch party for each Hudson's store. Sales training followed, focusing on product knowledge, clientele building, advertising, and individual store selling goals. Each store designated a sales associate as the Tommy team captain to coordinate activities and to provide feedback to Aramis.

An important part of the training centered on teaching the sales associates how to apply database marketing. Because Hudson's customers were heavy purchasers of Tommy Hilfiger clothing, they were likely to be receptive to the new fragrance carrying the Tommy name and marketed using similar imagery. Sales associates learned how to use the Hudson's database to obtain lists of customers who had purchased Tommy Hilfiger clothing. These customers received invitations to receptions introducing the new fragrance along with offers of a free gift and the opportunity to be among the first purchasers of the new product.

The co-marketing alliance between Hudson's and Aramis proved highly successful for both partners, and it strengthened their relationship. The retailer delivered on its promise to enthusiastically promote the new fragrance, and the fragrance maker honored its promise of exclusivity, not allowing any other retailer to carry Tommy during its initial launch period.

Questions

1. Describe the three alliances discussed in this case, and identify the benefits received by each partner.
2. At which level of relationship marketing is the Aramis-Hudson's alliance? Give examples to support your answer.
3. Explain the role of database marketing in Hudson's relationships with its customers.
4. Database marketing played an important role in Hudson's ability to market Tommy. Sharrow Davies Townsend is a San Francisco-based marketing consulting firm that provides database marketing counsel to businesses. Visit the company's Web site at:

   http://www.sharrow.com/

   How does Sharrow define *database marketing?* What benefits does it claim for this type of marketing? What challenges does it identify?

Sources: Telephone interview with Tommy Hilfiger Public Relations Department, May 15, 1997; Jonathan Van Meter, "Hip, Hot Hilfiger," *Vogue,* November 1996, pp. 306-309; Justin Doebele, "A Brand Is Born," *Forbes,* February 26, 1996, pp. 65-66; Matthew Tyrnauer, "It's Tommy's World," *Vanity Fair,* February 1996, pp. 108-113; and Elaine Underwood, "Tommy Hilfiger on Brand Hilfiger," *Brandweek,* February 5, 1996, pp. 23-27.

Part 3 Microsoft Corp. Building Relationships with Businesses and Consumers

Microsoft markets goods and services to both business users and ultimately consumers. Initially, Microsoft targeted only the business market, where it made its fortune by licensing programming languages and operating systems to original equipment manufacturers. As an OEM software supplier, Microsoft adds value to its customers' products by providing the instructions that enable their computers to perform a multitude of tasks. Microsoft's sales force sells software to PC makers that, in turn, sell their equipment to other businesses, governments, institutions, and not-for-profit organizations. Most of Microsoft's OEM revenues come from the licensing of MS-DOS and Windows—revenues that are highly dependent on the number of computers PC makers sell.

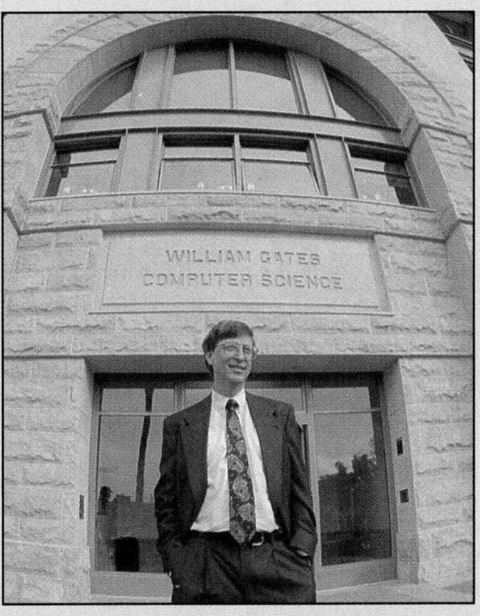
WILLIAM GATES
COMPUTER SCIENCE

As Microsoft expanded its product line with desktop applications software and network systems, it broadened its distribution through corporate licensing agreements. Microsoft salespeople arrange corporate licensing agreements for products such as Microsoft Office, NT Workstation, and SQL Server Client Access. Purchasing and information management teams at Saturn, Pennzoil, AlliedSignal, Charles Schwab, and other corporations buy the software to improve the efficiency of their firm's operations and to boost employee productivity. Microsoft also markets software to wholesalers and retailers. These resellers market Microsoft's business and consumer applications software, computer books, mice, and keyboards.

Partnering with Business Customers

Microsoft formed its first business partnership with Japan's Nippon Electric Company (NEC), a customer introduced to Gates and Allen in 1979 by Microsoft's Far East agent Kuzuhiko Nishi. NEC wanted Microsoft to develop software for its personal computer and also asked Gates and Allen to work with NEC in designing the computer. Five years later, NEC asked Microsoft to develop a Japanese-language version of MS-DOS for a computer that became the best-selling PC in Japan.

Microsoft's partnering alliance with NEC started a pattern of sharing technology and jointly designing products the company repeated with customers like IBM, Apple, and Compaq. Microsoft was instrumental in helping Compaq design language and operating system software for the first IBM-compatible computer. In 1982, Gates assigned a special team to work with Compaq's design engineers. The strategic partnership benefited both companies: Compaq quickly became one of the fastest-growing computer companies, with sales topping $100 million its first year, and Microsoft had new software it could market to new customers plus huge revenues from the software it licensed to Compaq.

Forming strategic alliances is part of Microsoft's current strategy to position the company as the front-runner on the information superhighway. "Industry by industry, we're sitting down with everyone to talk about new things we can do," says Gates. Predicting that the Internet will be a mass market by 2000, Gates is investing heavily in new distribution and content alliances to establish Windows as the Internet platform.

One major move is Microsoft's online and broadcasting ventures with General Electric's NBC television network to create and market multimedia products and television programs for the Microsoft Network. Microsoft and NBC have formed two joint ventures. MSNBC Cable is a 24-hour cable news and information channel, and MSNBC Interactive is an online news service. Interactive is a custom news service that creates a daily Web page for each viewer, including news, weather, and opinion content geared to the viewer's preferences.

The MSNBC joint ventures give Microsoft the opportunity to exploit the converging media and computer market, and NBC benefits by expanding beyond its traditional broadcasting business. "For the future of NBC, this is the most important video service we're involved in," says

NBC President Robert C. Wright. Regarding the ventures as long-term strategic investments in Internet content, Microsoft agreed to pay $220 million over a five-year period for its interest in the cable venture and one-half of the operational funding of both joint ventures for a multiyear period. "It's our biggest outside investment," says Pete Higgins, vice president of Microsoft's Applications and Content Group. "It's the cornerstone of our investment in interactive media."

NBC's Executive Vice President Thomas Rogers, who negotiated the Microsoft and NBC partnership, is optimistic about its future. "We're redefining what our core business is. This is the core business ten years from now."

In another partnership, Microsoft and MCI have formed an alliance to sell each other's goods and services. Microsoft will market MCI services through icons on Windows screens and on Microsoft Network. MCI will use Microsoft's Internet Explorer browser and Internet Information Server as its primary tools and will market both products to its Web hosting service. The alliance covers MCI's network as well as that of Concert, a joint venture between MCI and British Telecommunications, which will offer Microsoft's managed intranet services. Microsoft also formed a joint venture with McCaw Cellular Communications to form Teledesic, a wireless communication network that will deliver phone service worldwide.

Microsoft has joined with American Express to introduce an Internet-based travel service for corporate customers. The service allows business travelers to make airline, car, and hotel reservations within cost and designated airline parameters set by their firms. The service can be accessed on the Internet and on a Windows NT server and will be sold globally through 1,700 American Express offices. In another partnership with VISA International, Microsoft is developing software for electronic shopping and payments with credit cards.

Microsoft is teaming with Hughes Electronics Corp.'s DirecTV in an effort that will allow personal computers to receive video programming. Microsoft has also purchased WebTV Networks, which produces a set-top device that provides Internet access through the television set. The WebTV Internet service is another outlet for Microsoft's MSN and its MSNBC joint venture with NBC. Microsoft is also writing software for TV set-top boxes jointly developed by Intel and General Instrument. In an international alliance formed to develop set-top boxes and software for interactive TV, Microsoft is collaborating with Hewlett-Packard, U.S. West, Telstra (Australia), Deutsche Telekom (Germany), Nippon Telephone and Telegraph (Japan), Olivetti (Italy), and Alcatel (France).

Dreamworks SKG, the new Hollywood studio formed by Steven Spielberg, Jeffrey Katzenberg, and David Geffen, formed a joint venture with Microsoft called Dreamworks Interactive to develop adventure games, interactive stories, and other multimedia software for home consumers.

A Computer in Every Home

Consumers are catching on to computers quickly. "We're going through a sea of change in terms of people's attitudes toward technology—from very unaccepting to quite accepting," says G. Richard Thoman, senior vice president of IBM's Personal Computer Company. Research indicates that in 1985 only 22 percent of the U.S. population felt positive about technology. By 1995, that percentage rose to more than 50 percent. By the end of the century most of U.S. homes will have personal computers.

Bill Gates' vision of a computer in every home is becoming a reality, not only in the United States but also in developed countries around the world. According to Gates, more than one-fourth of PC sales in South Korea are purchased by consumers for home use. "This statistic demonstrates how countries with a strong family structure that put great emphasis on getting ahead by educating children will be fertile ground for products that provide educational advantages," says Gates.

Andreas Barth, senior vice president at Compaq Computer Europe, predicts that by 2000, 50 percent of European homes will have personal computers, up from just 8 percent in the mid-1990s. Although many Japanese homes have video-game machines and word processors, acceptance of personal computers in the home is slow, with only 7 percent of homes having them. According to Gates, the reason is partly because of the difficulty of entering kanji (a Japanese system of writing) characters on a keyboard but also because of Japan's large and entrenched market for dedicated word processing machines. To create greater acceptance, many PC makers are designing computers specifically for Japanese consumers.

Multimedia PCs are taking on a new role as a family's entertainment center and link to the information superhighway. "The three key consumer-electronics categories—audio, video, and communications—are coming together in the PC," say Anindya Bose, director of research at market researcher Link Resources Corp. Computers, not TVs, are becoming the platform for delivering new digital goods and services, from online magazines to interactive games to home shopping and virtual classrooms.

Children and teenagers are driving the growth of multiple-PC families. A Dataquest study revealed that 16 percent of families that own a multimedia PC bought a second computer for their children. One mom says, "I don't want to prioritize who gets to use the computer. I don't want there to be any excuse for Katie not to go the extra mile."

Multimedia PCs are changing consumer behavior. When AST Research Inc. surveyed buyers of its Advantage PCs, it learned that the average household spends 18 hours a week on the computer, almost twice the time it spends watching television. One-third of the families subscribe to online services, many to more than one. A study conducted by market researcher Inteco Corp. revealed that households with multimedia PCs are likely to cancel premium movie channels, preferring to spend their leisure time with online services and CD-ROM titles.

"Computers are fast becoming more important in the home than a television set," says Dennis Cox, AST's marketing director for consumer products.

Software for Every Home

Anticipating these changes in consumer attitudes and behavior, Microsoft is developing a barrage of goods and services for the consumer market and advertising them in print, television, and Web ads around the world. During the early development of its Windows 95 operating system, Microsoft researchers asked consumers what they wanted to do with their computers. Combining consumer wants and needs with new computer technology, Microsoft developers designed the new operating system to make home computing fast and easy. With a simplified graphical interface and capability to handle fast animation, Windows 95, Microsoft hopes, will encourage many people to try computers for the first time. "This is a watershed event, in that the PC becomes a consumer device," says Mark Epley, CEO of Traveling Software Inc.

Envisioning Windows 95 as a foundation for home education and entertainment, Gates formed a new consumer division in 1992 to market CD-ROM games and educational and reference software programs. To make it easy for kids to play its games, the company designed new hardware such as the big EasyBall trackball and SideWinder joystick. And to make sure its games capture kids' attention, Microsoft is hiring creative talent, including outside artists, developers, and writers, to produce exciting titles that focus on the needs of customers.

By incorporating a built-in button inside Windows 95, Microsoft makes it easy for users to subscribe instantly to its online service, Microsoft Network. Serving as a platform to deliver a host of new Microsoft services, MSN "will become a reason to buy a home computer," says Gates. The reason may be tuning in to enjoy one of Microsoft's online content programs, five- to ten-minute "shows" like Retrospect 360, an animated timeline of historical events; 914, a cybersoap; Re-Man, an online comic book; RIFFF, a virtual music studio; Second City Headline News, a news parody updated daily; or Mr. Zodiac, an astrology and horoscope guide. Teams of Microsoft market researchers measure which programs work and which don't work.

The program concept is "brilliant," says Stephen Auditory, president of Zona Research. "They've turned the entire metaphor of an online service upside-down so it's more like broadcast."

Bob Bejan, executive producer of MSN, says that while 30 million people now have access to the Internet, the online programs are intended "to bring the next 10 million online."

To help families learn about computers, Microsoft sponsors Family Technology Nights in cities throughout the United States. Organized by school PTAs and hosted by local technology experts, the free seminars give families tips on buying computer equipment and information about computer technology trends. Seminar leaders show how computers are used and parents and children have the chance to try out equipment. They can also buy Microsoft software at discounted prices. Based on these sales, the participating schools can earn free software.

Questions

1. What aspects of consumer behavior discussed in Chapter 8 bode well for Microsoft's marketing to consumers?
2. In what ways do Microsoft's partnerships with other firms benefit the software company?
3. How is Microsoft helping change consumer attitudes toward personal computers?

Modem

PART 4

PRODUCT STRATEGY

www.p
plantronic
nestle
w.camp
campbel
soup.co
.sony.
www.am
ambranc
levi.c
www.p
pg.con
callawaygo
.com
www.x
xerox
hilton
.citiban
http.co

CHAPTER 11

PRODUCT STRATEGY

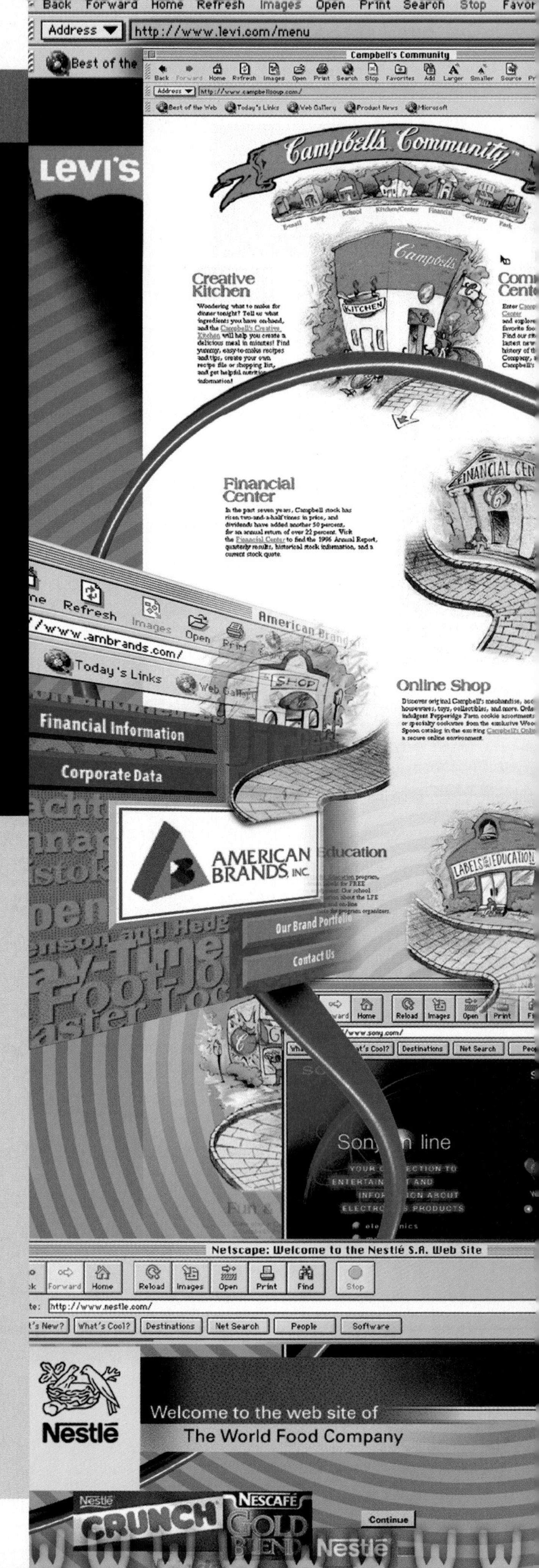

Back Forward Home Refresh Images Open Print Search Stop
Address
http://www.levi.com/menu
Levi's
Campbell's Community
http://www.campbellsoup.com/
Creative Kitchen
Financial Center
Online Shop
Refresh Images Open Print
//www.ambrands.com/
Today's Links
Financial Information
Corporate Data
AMERICAN BRANDS, INC.
Our Brand Portfolio
Contact Us
Education
Netscape: Welcome to the Nestlé S.A. Web Site
Forward Home Reload Images Open Print Find Stop
http://www.nestle.com/
What's Cool? Destinations Net Search People Software
Nestlé
Welcome to the web site of
The World Food Company
CRUNCH
NESCAFÉ
Continue

Chapter Objectives

1. Explain the broader marketing view of products.
2. List the classifications of consumer products, and briefly describe each category.
3. Describe the types of business products.
4. Explain why most firms develop lines of related products rather than marketing individual products.
5. Explain the concept of the product life cycle.
6. Discuss how a firm can extend a product's life cycle.
7. Identify the major product mix decisions that marketers must make.

How Plantronics Headed for Success

Imagine the chief executive officer of The Coca-Cola Co. never drinking Coke or the head of General Motors walking rather than driving one of his cars. The idea sounds far-fetched, but a similar situation developed at Plantronics, Inc., the leading American maker of lightweight telephone headsets.

Robert S. Cecil, Plantronics president and chairman, refused to wear the headset his own company manufactured. The headset, geared primarily to telemarketers, created a hassle for others. The band across the top of the head would mess up a user's hair, and anybody who wore one tended to feel like a telephone operator.

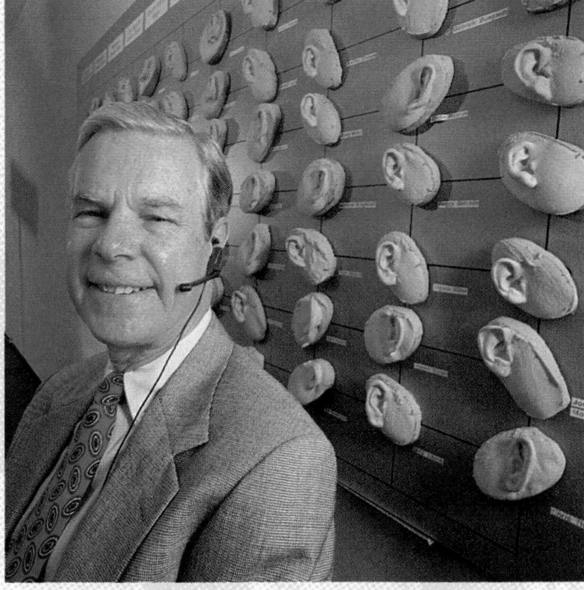

In fact, just about the only people wearing Plantronics headsets were telemarketers who had no choice. The company foresaw modest growth for the product in the telemarketing field at best.

Inevitable financial problems followed, and debt piled up. Marv Tseu, the company's marketing chief, summed up the precarious vision of the company's future: "We saw the cliff out there."

Robert Cecil made a pivotal decision. He reallocated the company's resources to new-product development. He wanted to develop sleek, upscale headsets that professionals who communicate by phone all day—brokers, real estate agents, stock market traders, and executives—would like.

After leaving retirement to take control of the struggling business, Cecil hired industrial designers to develop a better product. He also organized focus groups to learn what people disliked about using the phone. During their research, employees took plaster casts of 700 different ears and scanned hundreds of head shapes into computers in an effort to create the best headset possible.

The company has now regained its financial health. One of the first new products that encouraged the change was a headset called FreeHand. Even Cecil loved wearing one. The lightweight, discreet headset ultimately won an annual *Business Week* award for exceptional product designs. The headset, with its tiny earpiece connected to a small microphone all together no more than 4 inches long, can be worn all day without discomfort.

Plantronics continues to expand its product line with new varieties of headsets. For instance, it has introduced a headset that cancels over 90 percent of the background noise commonly found in large offices.

"People in loud, open offices and call centers tell us they hate to repeat messages because their customers can't hear them over the background noise," says David Huddart, Plantronics vice president of engineering and technology. Reduced background noise enhances the professional image of the user. It also helps customers to focus on their phone conversations.

Plantronics has developed another small headset that hooks over the ear without any headband and weighs a mere one-half ounce. "How a headset fits is just as important as how it sounds," Huddart says. "That's why our development group invests significant research and development resources in both ergonomic and electrical design. Our goal is to make the headset as unobtrusive as possible."

Plantronics sees a vast market for high-quality headsets. Only about 1 percent of 56 million potential office-based customers use headsets today. The company has increased sales by capitalizing upon fears of ergonomic injuries to workers who would otherwise cradle phone receivers between ear and shoulder all day. Plantronics asserts that its headsets could provide significant health benefits. To back up this claim, it cites a study by the Santa Clara Valley Medical Center in San Jose, California, which found that headsets can reduce muscle tension in the back, neck, and shoulders by as much as 41 percent.[1]

http://www.plantronics.com/

CHAPTER OVERVIEW

The first three parts of this book have dealt with preliminary marketing considerations such as marketing research and buyer behavior. Those chapters have covered activities aimed at identifying the firm's target market. Now the attention shifts to the firm's marketing mix.

This part of *Contemporary Marketing* focuses on the first element of the marketing mix—the goods and services the firm offers to its target market. Planning efforts begin with the choice of products to offer. The other variables of the marketing mix—distribution channels, promotional plans, and pricing structures—must accommodate product planning decisions.

This chapter begins with a definition of *product.* It then presents several basic concepts—classifications of products, development of product lines, and the product life cycle—that marketers apply in developing successful products. Finally, the chapter discusses product deletion and product mix decisions.

WHAT IS A PRODUCT?

A narrow definition of the word *product* focuses on the physical or functional characteristics of a good or service. For example, a VCR is a rectangular container of metal and plastic connected via wires to a television set with equipment for recording and replaying video signals on special tapes. But the purchaser has a much broader view of the VCR. Some buyers may want it so they can see soap operas they miss during work hours; others may be interested in warranty and service terms available from the manufacturer; still others may want to rent movies on videotape for home viewing.

Marketing decision makers must acknowledge this broader conception of product; they must realize that people buy *want satisfaction* rather than objects. For example, most buyers know little about the gasoline they buy. In fact, many view it not as a product but as a price they must pay for the privilege of driving their cars.

A broader view of product extends beyond physical or

functional attributes. This total product concept includes package design and labeling, symbols such as trademarks and brand names, and customer-service activities that add value for the customer. Consequently, a **product** is a bundle of physical, service, and symbolic attributes designed to enhance consumer want satisfaction. The advertisement in Figure 11.1 for Europe's aircraft maker, Airbus Industrie, shows the effect of this definition. Airbus promises that delivery of an aircraft to a customer "isn't the tail-end of the relationship; it's the beginning of a partnership." Airbus adds value to its aircraft product through its customer-service activities like spare parts delivery coordinated by a worldwide Customer Service Directorate that can deal with people in 23 languages. It also has developed multimedia training and maintenance resources that it supplies to customers on CD-ROMs.

Some products succeed because they satisfy unique, practical needs. Jason Clute, founder of Dex Products, saw an opportunity when researchers linked sudden infant death syndrome to the sleeping positions of babies. Clute developed a triangular pillow designed to keep infants sleeping on their sides, rather than their stomachs.[2]

Figure 11.1 A Product as a Bundle of Attributes

HELPING KEEP OUR CUSTOMERS ON COURSE.
A340
Airbus Industrie has delivered over 1,300 aircraft to more than 110 customers. But delivery isn't the tail-end of the relationship: it's the beginning of a partnership. Those aircraft will be expected to fly reliably and cost-effectively for many years to come, so Airbus Industrie has created a worldwide Customer Service Directorate, able to deal in 23 languages and with spares back-up in key locations. This ensures that customers get a 24-hour global support and technical service, wherever their aircraft may be.
Airbus Industrie also set standards in the use of CD-ROM and multi-media techniques to help customers be even more effective and thorough in day-to-day operations training and maintenance programs. Building the finest aircraft and keeping them operating with maximum reliability, safety and cost-effectiveness to keep customers profitably on course – that's how Airbus Industrie has become, and will continue to be, a world leader.
AIRBUS INDUSTRIE
SETTING THE STANDARDS

An International Perspective

Consumers in various countries seek different product benefits. A product with a commonplace identity in one country may have a symbolic value in another country, where people willingly pay a premium price for it. Businesses with global reach often must adapt their product strategies to match differences in consumer preferences and behavior in different regions of the world.

Consider the marketing strategies of Nestlé. Although headquartered in Switzerland, Nestlé sells products—everything from wines to chocolates—around the world. The firm's marketing arms span many regions of the world, actively studying consumer tastes and adapting products to satisfy them. For example, people in one country may prefer macaroni and cheese with more sauce, while in another country people want the same product with a different kind of cheese flavoring. The company's bouillon tastes different in China than in Chile. It sells some products under worldwide brand names such as Carnation, Nestlé, Nescafe, Buitoni, and Friskies. In addition, 700 of its local brands are sold only in particular countries.[3]

http://www.nestle.com/

CLASSIFYING CONSUMER AND BUSINESS PRODUCTS

A firm's choices for marketing a product depend largely on the product itself. For example, Wendy's promotes its fast-food service at thousands of locations worldwide through mass-media advertising. Hershey's markets its candy products through candy wholesalers to thousands of supermarkets, convenience stores, discount houses, and vending machine companies. A firm that manufactures and markets

Marketing Dictionary

product A bundle of physical, service, and symbolic attributes designed to enhance buyers' want satisfaction.

forklifts may assign sales representatives to call on industrial and organizational buyers; it may deliver its product either directly from the factory or from a regional warehouse.

Product strategies differ for consumer and business products. As defined earlier, *consumer products* are those destined for use by ultimate consumers, while *business products* (also called *industrial* or *organizational products*) contribute directly or indirectly to production of other products for resale. Marketers further subdivide these two major categories into more specific categories.

Types of Consumer Products

Several classification systems divide up consumer products in different ways. One basic distinction focuses on the buyer's perception of a need for the good or service. So-called *unsought products* are marketed to consumers who do not yet recognize any need for them. Examples of unsought products are life insurance and funeral services. In contrast, most consumers recognize their own needs for various types of consumer products. The most common classification scheme divides consumer products into three groups: convenience, shopping, and specialty products.[4] These categories divide products based on consumers' buying behavior. Figure 11.2 illustrates samples of these three categories, together with the unsought classification.

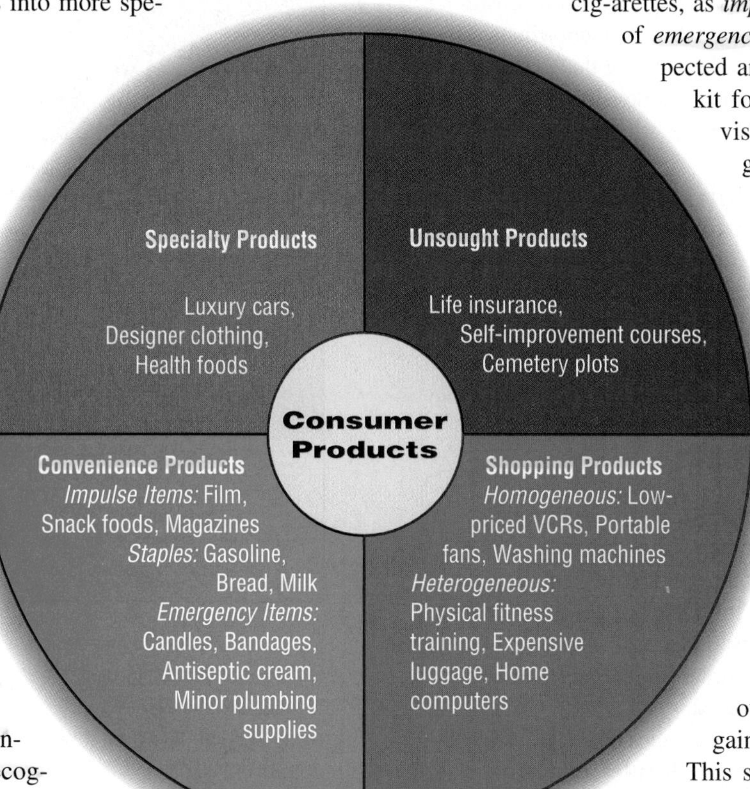
Specialty Products
Luxury cars,
Designer clothing,
Health foods
Unsought Products
Life insurance,
Self-improvement courses,
Cemetery plots
Consumer Products
Convenience Products
Impulse Items: Film,
Snack foods, Magazines
Staples: Gasoline,
Bread, Milk
Emergency Items:
Candles, Bandages,
Antiseptic cream,
Minor plumbing
supplies
Shopping Products
Homogeneous: Low-priced VCRs, Portable
fans, Washing machines
Heterogeneous:
Physical fitness
training, Expensive
luggage, Home
computers

Figure 11.2

Classification of Consumer Products

Convenience Products Goods and services that consumers want to purchase frequently, immediately, and with minimal efforts are called **convenience products.** Milk, bread, and soft drinks—the staples of most 24-hour convenience stores—are all convenience products. So are newspapers, chewing gum, candy, magazines, and most vending machine items. Many service firms such as hair-styling salons, quick-print shops, and dry cleaners also serve convenience buyers.

Sales of convenience products usually hinge on brand names and low prices. Three subcategories further distinguish them from one another: staples, impulse items, and emergency items. Many convenience goods—such as bread, milk, and gasoline—are *staples,* which consumers constantly replenish to maintain steady stock. Most gasoline and candy buyers decide which brands they like and then buy them regularly from certain stores, spending little time deliberating about the purchase decisions.

Marketers label products purchased on the spur of the moment, such as tattoos, or out of habit, such as cig-arettes, as *impulse products.* Purchases of *emergency items* respond to unexpected and urgent needs. A repair kit for a broken water pipe, a visit to a hospital's emergency center for treatment of a sprained ankle, or an ice scraper purchased in the midst of an unexpected storm are all examples of this final subcategory of convenience products.

Consumers rarely visit competing stores or compare price and quality when purchasing convenience products. The costs of acquiring additional information outweigh the potential gains from such comparisons. This statement does not mean, however, that a particular consumer always remains permanently loyal to one brand of gasoline. People continually receive new information from radio and television advertisements, billboards, and word-of-mouth communications. The low prices of most convenience products allow trial purchases of competing brands or products with little financial risk; these trials often lead to new product preferences.

Since consumers devote little effort to purchase decisions for convenience products, manufacturers must strive to make these exchanges as convenient as possible. You can buy candy, cigarettes, and newspapers in almost every supermarket, convenience store, and gas station. Sellers place vending machines in spots that are convenient for customers, such as office building lobbies and factory break rooms.

Retailers of convenience products usually carry several competing brands and devote little promotional effort to any particular one. The promotional burden, therefore, falls on the manufacturer, which must advertise extensively to develop and retain consumer acceptance of the product. Leaf, Inc., for example, runs ads like the one in Figure 11.3 in children's magazines to promote its Jolly Rancher brand of bubble gum. Packaging plays an important role in the marketing strategy for a convenience product. Because most buyers of convenience products make their selections at the points of purchase, a distinctive package can improve a product's visibility on the store shelf.

Store location can also boost a convenience product's visibility. Vendors compete vigorously for prime locations near grocery store checkout lanes, where customers tend to make last-minute, impulse purchases.

Shopping Products In contrast to their purchases of convenience products, consumers buy **shopping products** only after comparing competing offerings in competing stores on such characteristics as price, quality, style, and color. Shopping products typically cost more than convenience products. The category includes clothing, furniture, appliances, jewelry, and shoes. Consumers often shop around for services, as well, such as child care and home and auto repair. The purchaser of a shopping product lacks complete information prior to the shopping trip and gathers information during it.

A college student who will soon graduate may work hard at shopping to make a good impression at her first job interview. She may visit many stores, try on a number of suits, and spend a weekend making the final choice. She may follow a regular route from store to store to survey competing offerings, ultimately selecting those that appeal most strongly to her. When launching a store to carry an assortment of shopping products, marketers must find a location near similar stores so that such shopping expeditions reach their products.

Several important features distinguish shopping products: physical attributes, service attributes (warranties and after-sale service terms), prices, styling, and places of purchase. A store's name and reputation have considerable influence on consumer buying behavior. The brand of a particular product often has less important effects, in spite of the large amounts of money that manufacturers spend promoting these offerings. The personal-selling efforts of salespeople provide important promotional support for shopping products.

Since buyers of shopping products expend some effort in making their purchases, producers focus their resources on relatively few stores as compared with marketers of convenience products. Retailers and manufacturers work closely together in promoting shopping products. Retailers often buy their stocks directly from manufacturers or their representatives rather than from wholesalers. Fashion buyers for department stores and chains of specialty shops make regular buying trips to regional and national markets in New York, Dallas, Los Angeles, and Seattle. Buyers for furniture retailers often go directly to the factories of manufacturers or attend furniture trade shows.

Buyers and marketers treat some shopping products, such as refrigerators and washing machines, as *homogeneous* products. To the consumer, one brand seems largely the same as another. Marketers may try to differentiate homogeneous products from competing products in several

Figure 11.3 **Advertising by the Manufacturer to Promote a Convenience Product**

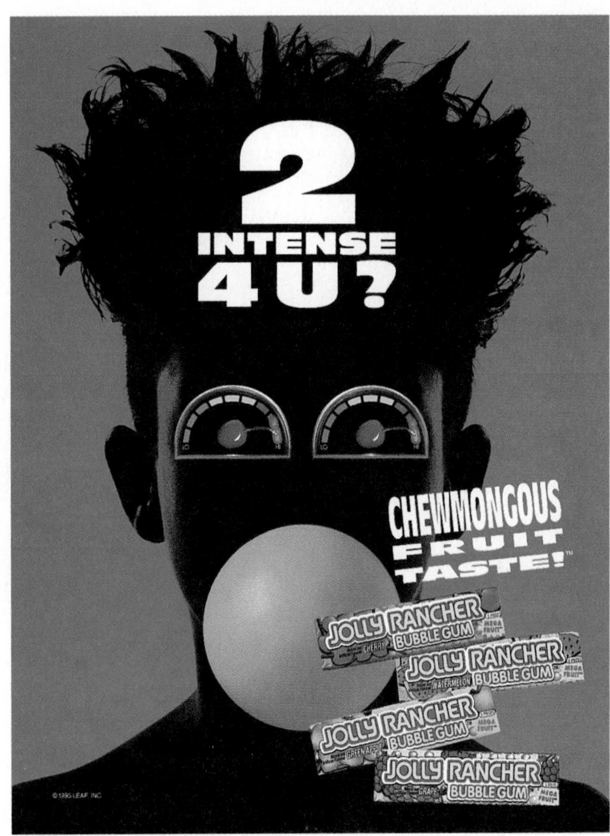
2
INTENSE
4U?
CHEWMONGOUS
FRUIT
TASTE!
JOLLY RANCHER
BUBBLE GUM

Marketing Dictionary

convenience product A good or service that consumers want to purchase frequently, immediately, and with minimal effort.

shopping product A good or service purchased only after the consumer compares competing offerings from competing vendors on such characteristics as price, quality, style, and color.

Figure 11.4 **Promotion for a Heterogeneous Shopping Product**

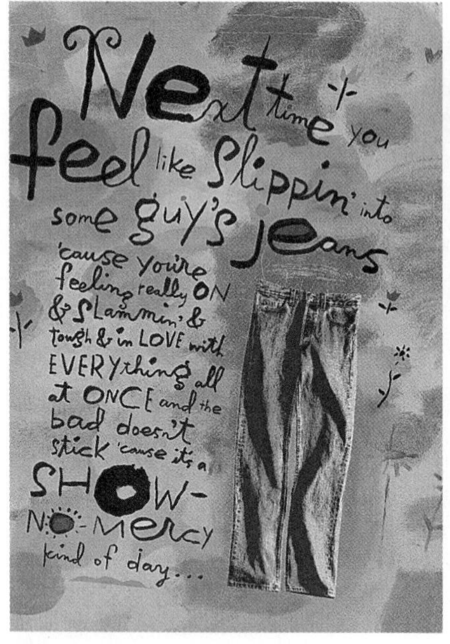
Next time you feel like Slippin' into some guy's jeans
'cause you're feeling really ON & Slammin' & tough & in LOVE with EVERYthing all at ONCE and the bad doesn't stick 'cause it's a SHOW-NO-MERCY kind of day...

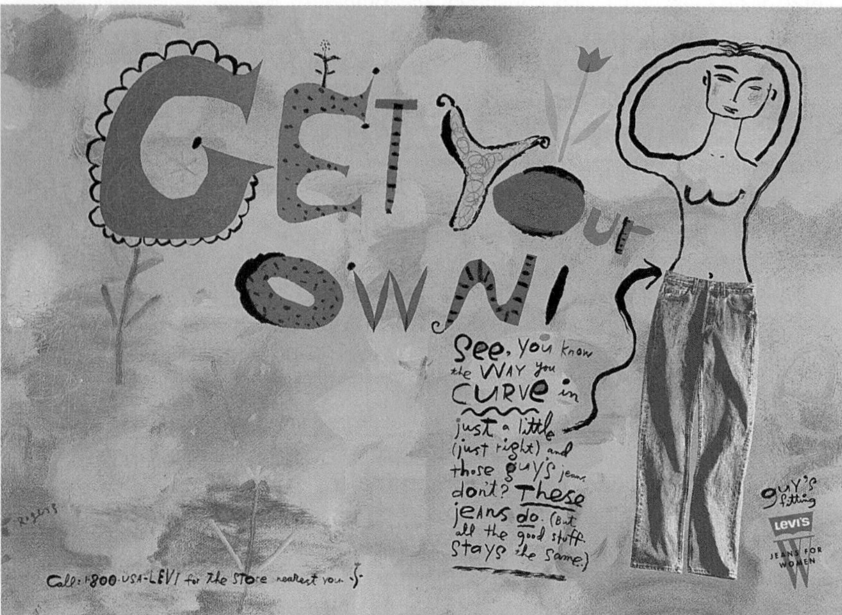
GET YOUR OWN!
See, you know the WAY you CURVE in just a little (just right) and those guy's jeans don't? These jeans do. (But all the good stuff stays the same.)
Call: 1-800-USA-LEVI for the Store nearest you.
guy's fitting
Levi's
JEANS FOR WOMEN

ways. They may emphasize price and value, or they may attempt to educate consumers about less obvious product features that contribute to a product's quality and appeal. An ad campaign by Imperial Windows, for example, pointed out important features to look for in buying a window.

Other shopping products seem *heterogeneous* due to essential differences between them. Examples of heterogeneous shopping products include furniture, clothing, and vacation destinations. Rather obvious differences in features often separate competing heterogeneous shopping products in the minds of consumers. Characteristics such as style, color, and fit affect consumer choices. The ad for Levi's guy's fitting jeans for women in Figure 11.4 illustrates how marketers attempt to influence consumer behavior for heterogeneous shopping products. The ad focuses on the style of the jeans, which give women the comfort of men's jeans as well as a fit designed for women's bodies.

http://www.levi.com/

Specialty Products **Specialty products** offer unique characteristics that cause buyers to prize those particular brands. These products typically carry high prices, and many represent well-known brands. Examples include Gucci handbags, Ritz-Carlton resorts, Tiffany jewelry, and Rolls-Royce automobiles.

German watchmaker A. Lange & Sohne, for example, promotes its goods effectively with a limited ad budget. The firm's watches sell for between $10,600 and $106,400 to buyers looking for supremely crafted timepieces. The company's marketing plays upon its history of craftsmanship. A. Lange & Sohne sold only 700 watches between 1994 and 1995, but these limited sales generated revenue of $14 million.[5]

Purchasers of specialty products know just what they want—and they willingly make special efforts to satisfy those wants. Buyers of such a product begin shopping with complete information, and they refuse to accept substitutes. A Roper Starch study of luxury-goods buyers showed that 65 percent chose products because they believed the items offered high value, while 53 percent said that prestige names influenced their choices. These consumers also tend to be highly loyal. The study also reported that 50 percent of respondents described themselves as brand loyal consumers.[6]

Because consumers are willing to exert considerable effort to obtain specialty products, producers can promote them through relatively few retail outlets. Indeed, some intentionally limit the range of outlets that carry their products to add to their cachet. For example, Louis Vuitton refuses to sell its luxury goods in airport duty-free stores, even though duty-free stores are important distribution outlets for other luxury goods.[7]

Table 11.1 Marketing Impact of the Consumer Products Classification System

Factor	Convenience Products	Shopping Products	Specialty Products
CONSUMER FACTORS			
Planning time involved in purchase	Very little	Considerable	Extensive
Purchase frequency	Frequent	Less frequent	Infrequent
Importance of convenient location	Critical	Important	Unimportant
Comparison of price and quality	Very little	Considerable	Very little
MARKETING MIX FACTORS			
Price	Low	Relatively high	High
Promotion	Advertising and promotion by producer	Personal selling and advertising by both producer and retailer	Personal selling and advertising by both producer and retailer
Distribution channel length	Long	Relatively short	Very short
Number of retail outlets	Many	Few	Very few; often one per market area
Importance of store image	Unimportant	Very important	Important

Both highly personalized service by sales associates and image advertising help marketers to promote specialty products. Because these products are available in so few outlets, advertisements frequently list those locations or give toll-free telephone numbers where customers can find this information.

Applying the Consumer Products Classification System
The three-way classification system of convenience, shopping, and specialty products helps to guide marketers' search for information to use in developing a marketing strategy. Consumer behavior patterns differ for the three types of consumer products. For example, classifying a new food product as a convenience product leadsto insights about marketing needs in branding, promotion, pricing, and distribution methods. Table 11.1 summarizes the impact of the consumer products classification system on the development of an effective marketing mix.

But the classification system also poses problems. The major obstacle to implementing this system results from the suggestion that all products must fit within one of the three categories. Some products fit neatly into one category, but others share characteristics of more than one category. For example, what kind of product is a new automobile? Before classifying the expensive good, which is sold by brand, and handled by a few exclusive dealers in each city, as a specialty product, consider other characteristics. Most new-car buyers shop extensively among competing models and dealers before deciding on the best deal. Effective implementation of the classification system might consider it as a continuum representing degrees of effort expended by consumers. At one end of the continuum, they casually pick up convenience products; at the other end, they search extensively for specialty products. Shopping products fall between these extremes. On this continuum, the new-car purchase might appear between the categories of shopping and specialty products, but closer to specialty products.

A second problem with the classification system emerges because consumers differ in their buying patterns. One person may make an unplanned purchase of new shoes because they are on sale, while another may shop extensively before purchasing a pair that's color-coordinated to a specific outfit. But one buyer's impulse purchase does not make shoes a convenience product. Marketers classify products by considering the purchase patterns of the majority of buyers.

Marketing Dictionary

specialty product A good or service with unique characteristics that cause the buyer to prize it and make a special effort to obtain it.

Types of Business Products

Business products define six categories: installations, accessory equipment, component parts and materials, raw materials, supplies, and business services.[8] Business buyers are professional customers; their job duties require rational, effective purchase decisions. General Mills applies much the same purchase decision process to buy supplies of flour as Pillsbury does. The classification system for business products emphasizes product uses rather than customer buying behavior. Figure 11.5 illustrates the six types of business products.

Installations The specialty products of the industrial market are called **installations.** This classification includes major capital investments for new factories and heavy machinery, telecommunications systems, Boeing 737s for Air New Zealand, and locomotives for Burlington Northern.

Since installations last for relatively long periods of time and their purchases involve large sums of money, they represent major decisions for organizations. Negotiations often extend over several months and involve numerous decision makers. Selling companies often provide technical expertise along with tangible goods. Representatives who sell custom-made equipment work closely with buying firms' engineers and production personnel to design the most satisfactory products possible.

Price typically does not dominate purchase decisions for installations. A purchasing firm buys such a product for its efficiency and performance over its useful life. The firm also wants to minimize breakdowns. Downtime is expensive, because the firm must pay nonproductive employees while they wait for repairs on the machine.

Installations are major investments often designed specifically for the purchasers. Effective operation may also require considerable training of the buyer's workforce along with significant after-sale service. Finally, installations are sold to geographically concentrated buyers. As a result, marketers of these systems typically emphasize highly trained sales representatives, often with technical backgrounds. Advertising, if the firm employs it at all, emphasizes company reputation and directs potential buyers to contact local sales representatives.

Most installations are marketed directly from manufacturers to users. Even a one-time sale may require continuing contracts for regular product servicing. Some manufacturers lease extremely expensive installations to customers rather than selling the products outright and assign personnel directly to the lessees' sites to operate or maintain the equipment.

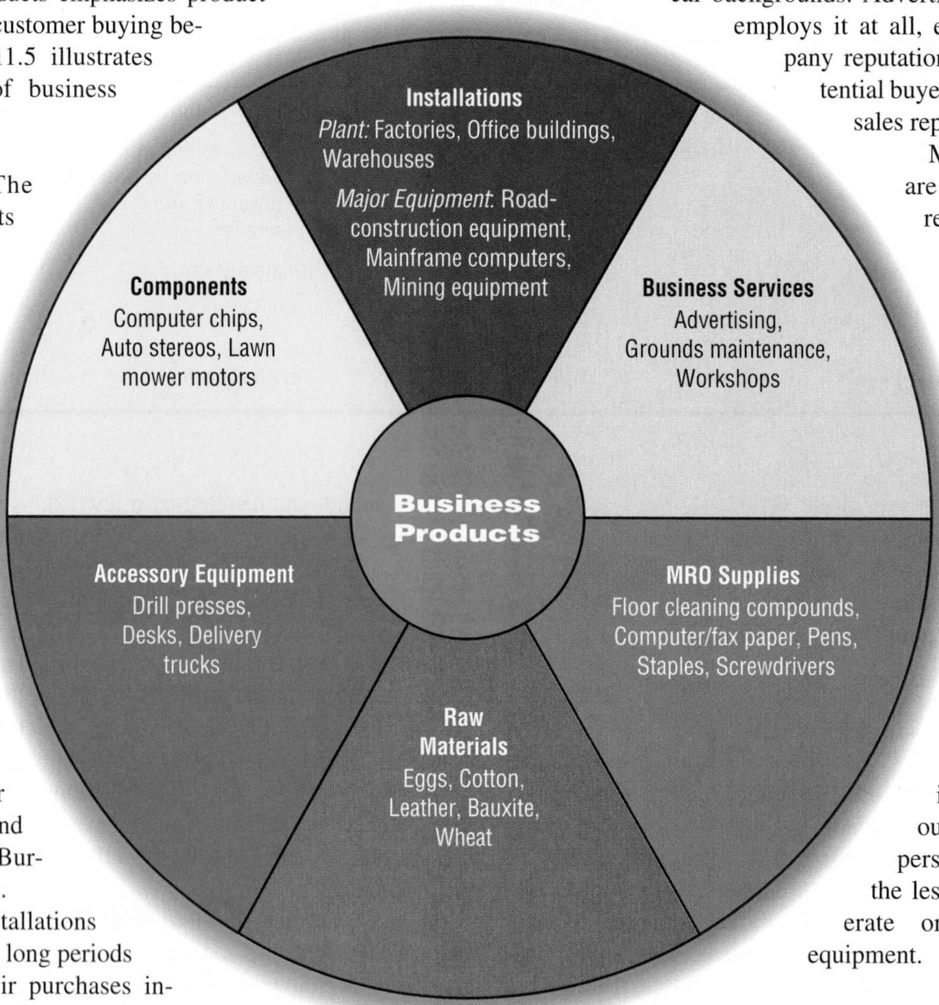

Installations
Plant: Factories, Office buildings, Warehouses
Major Equipment: Road-construction equipment, Mainframe computers, Mining equipment
Components
Computer chips, Auto stereos, Lawn mower motors
Business Services
Advertising, Grounds maintenance, Workshops
Business Products
Accessory Equipment
Drill presses, Desks, Delivery trucks
MRO Supplies
Floor cleaning compounds, Computer/fax paper, Pens, Staples, Screwdrivers
Raw Materials
Eggs, Cotton, Leather, Bauxite, Wheat

Figure 11.5

Classification of Business Products

Accessory Equipment Only a few decision makers may participate in a purchase of **accessory equipment**—capital items that typically cost less and last for shorter periods than installations.

Although quality and service exert important influences on purchases of accessory equipment, price may well significantly affect these decisions. Accessory equipment includes products such as hand tools, portable drills, small lathes, and laptop computers. Although these products are considered capital investments, and buyers depreciate their costs over several years, their useful lives generally are much shorter than those of installations.

Marketing these products requires continuous representation, and it must cope with the widespread geographic dispersion of purchasers. To cope with these market characteristics, a wholesaler—often called an **industrial distributor**—contacts potential customers in its own geographic area. Customers usually do not need technical assistance, and a manufacturer of accessory equipment often can market its products effectively through wholesalers.

Advertising often forms a rather important component in the marketing mix for accessory equipment. Creating such an ad can challenge marketers, who must effectively convey the features and benefits of accessory equipment that often closely resembles competitors' products. The ad in Figure 11.6 shows how Ricoh's advertisements communicate the message that the firm's color copiers provide exceptional color resolution.

Figure 11.6 Conveying the Benefits of Accessory Equipment

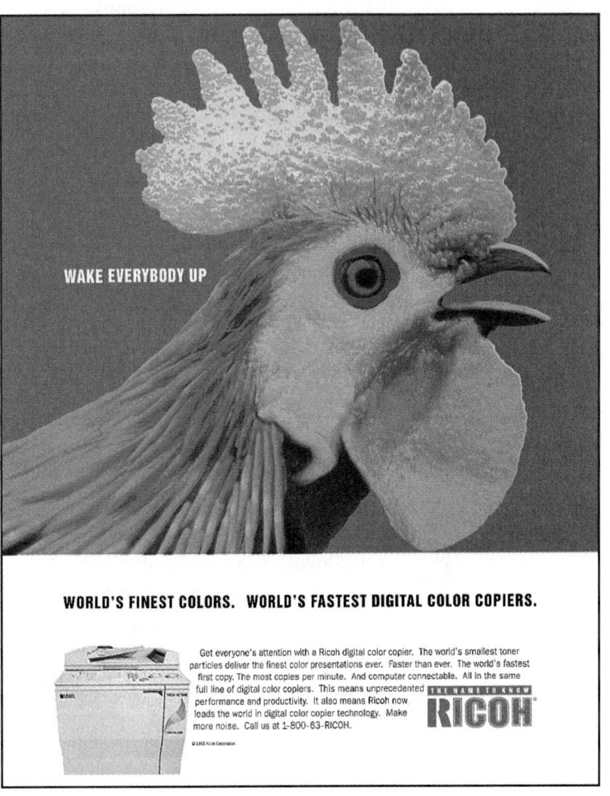
WAKE EVERYBODY UP
WORLD'S FINEST COLORS. WORLD'S FASTEST DIGITAL COLOR COPIERS.
Get everyone's attention with a Ricoh digital color copier. The world's smallest toner particles deliver the finest color presentations ever. Faster than ever. The world's fastest first copy. The most copies per minute. And computer connectable. All in the same full line of digital color copiers. This means unprecedented performance and productivity. It also means Ricoh now leads the world in digital color copier technology. Make more noise. Call us at 1-800-63-RICOH.
THE NAME TO KNOW
RICOH

Component Parts and Materials Whereas business buyers use installations and accessory equipment in the process of producing their own final products, **component parts and materials** represent finished business products of one producer that actually became part of the final products of another producer. Spark plugs complete new Chevrolets; Harley-Davidson motorcycles carry batteries; buyers receive tires with their Dodge pickup trucks. Some fabricated materials, such as flour, undergo further processing before becoming part of finished products. Textiles, paper pulp, and chemicals are also examples of component parts and materials.

C-Cube Microsystems makes computer chips that compress video data. Manufacturers such as Sony and Panasonic install C-Cube's chips in building their own video CD players. C-Cube's computer chips also become components in digital video-editing machines and multimedia computers. As a component manufacturer, C-Cube's success depends on the success of the products that use the firm's microchips.[9]

Purchasers of component parts and materials need regular, continuous supplies of uniform-quality products. They generally contract to purchase these products for periods of one year or more. Marketers commonly emphasize direct sales, and satisfied customers often become permanent buyers. Wholesalers sometimes supply fill-in purchases and handle sales to smaller purchasers.

Raw Materials *Farm products,* such as beef, cotton, eggs, milk, poultry, and soybeans, and *natural products,* such as coal, copper, iron ore, and lumber, constitute **raw materials.** These products resemble component parts and materials in that they actually become part of the buyers' final products.

Most raw materials carry grades determined according to set criteria, assuring purchasers that they will receive

Marketing Dictionary

installation A major capital investment by a business buyer that typically involves expensive and relatively long-lived products, such as a new factory or piece of heavy machinery.

accessory equipment A capital product, usually less expensive and shorter-lived than an installation, such as a laptop computer.

industrial distributor A wholesaling marketing intermediary that handles purchases of small accessory equipment and operating supplies.

component parts and materials Finished business products that become parts of buying firms' final products. Also known as *fabricated parts and materials.*

raw material A business product, such as a farm product (wheat, cotton, soybeans) or natural product (coal, lumber, iron ore) that becomes part of a final product.

Table 11.2 Marketing Impact of the Business Products Classification System

Factor	Installations	Accessory Equipment	Component Parts and Materials	Raw Materials	Supplies	Business Services
ORGANIZATIONAL FACTORS						
Planning time involved in purchase	Extensive	Less extensive	Less extensive	Varies	Very little	Varies
Purchase frequency	Infrequent	More frequent	Frequent	Infrequent	Frequent	Varies
Comparison of price and quality	Quality very important	Quality and price important	Quality important	Quality important	Price important	Varies
MARKETING MIX FACTORS						
Price	High	Relatively high	Low to high	Low to high	Low	Varies
Promotion method	Personal selling by producer	Advertising	Personal selling	Personal selling	Advertising by producer	Varies
Distribution channel length	Very short	Relatively short	Short	Short	Long	Varies

standardized products of uniform quality. As with component parts and materials, sellers commonly market raw materials directly to buying organizations, typically according to contractual terms. Wholesalers are increasingly involved in purchasing raw materials from foreign suppliers.

Price is seldom a deciding factor in a raw materials purchase, since terms are often set at central markets, determining virtually identical exchanges among competing sellers. Purchasers buy raw materials from the firms they consider best able to deliver the required quantities and qualities.

Supplies If installations represent the specialty products of the business market, operating supplies are its convenience products. **Supplies** constitute the regular expenses that a firm incurs in its daily operations. They do not become part of the buyer's final products.

Supplies are sometimes called **MRO items,** because they fall into three categories: (1) *maintenance items,* such as brooms, filters, and light bulbs; (2) *repair items,* such as nuts and bolts used in repairing equipment; and (3) *operating supplies,* such as fax paper, Post-it brand notes, and pencils.

A purchasing agent regularly purchases operating supplies as a routine job duty. Wholesalers often facilitate sales of supplies due to the low unit prices of the products, the small sales totals of orders, and the large numbers of potential buyers. Since supplies are relatively standardized products, heavy price competition frequently keeps costs under control. However, a purchasing agent spends little time making decisions about these products. Exchanges of products frequently demand simple telephone or mail orders or regular purchases from a sales representative of the local wholesaler.

Business Services The **business services** category includes the intangible products that firms buy to facilitate their production and operating processes. Examples of business services are financial services, leasing and renting services that supply equipment and vehicles, insurance, security, legal advice, and consulting.

Price often strongly influences purchase decisions for business services. The buying firm must decide whether to purchase a service or provide it through internal staff. For example, a firm may purchase the services of a public relations agency rather than assume the costs of maintaining an in-house public relations department. This decision may depend on how frequently the firm needs the service and the specialized knowledge required to provide it.

Purchase decision processes vary considerably for different types of business services. For example, a firm may purchase window-cleaning services through a routine and straightforward process similar to that for buying operating supplies. By contrast, a purchase decision for highly specialized environmental engineering services requires complex analysis and perhaps lengthy negotiations similar to those for purchases of installations. This variability of the marketing mix for business services and other business products is outlined in Table 11.2.

DEVELOPMENT OF PRODUCT LINES

Figure 11.7 **Marketing Product Lines in Many Different Industries**

SIEMENS

1908. That was then.

One of the favorites in The Great New York to Paris Race was a motor car named Protos. It was built by a company named Siemens.

1997. This is now.

Today Siemens makes almost everything for an automobile except the automobile itself. We supply 25 of the world's major car makers with over 700 systems and products, from fuel injectors and microprocessors to halogen headlamps. These are only a few of the precision products manufactured and assembled by Siemens at more than 90 U.S. locations. In fact, with 47,000 men and women working nationwide, Siemens is a leader in the kind of thinking that produces innovative technology for everyone. **Siemens. Precision Thinking.**

For more information, write for *Siemens '97*. Box 8003, Trenton, New Jersey 08650

Automation Automotive Electronics Electronic Components Energy Information Systems Lighting Systems Medical Systems Power Generation Telecommunications Transportation

Visit our web site at www.siemens.com on the Internet

© Siemens Corporation 1997

Few firms today market only one product. A typical firm offers its customers a **product line,** that is, a series of related products. Pfizer Pharmaceuticals, for example, markets product lines in three categories. The first, health-care products, includes prescription medicines and hospital-care products. The second, controlled by the consumer health-care products division, sells personal, nonprescription products such as Ben Gay, Visine, and Ban de Soleil. Pfizer sells its third product line, animal health-care products, primarily to veterinarians.[10]

All Pfizer's product lines are loosely centered around a core competence, namely, health-care products. Some firms' product lines span many different types of industries. Siemens AG of Germany, for example, markets products and component parts in industries such as automation, automotive products, electronics, energy, information systems, lighting systems, power generation, telecommunications, and transportation. The Siemens ad in Figure 11.7 describes how the company serves the automotive industry with more than 700 systems and products.

Firms benefit in four ways by developing complete product lines rather than concentrating *solely* on individual products. These motivations for marketing full product lines include the desire to grow, optimal use of company resources, enhancing the company's position in the market, and exploiting the product life cycle. The following paragraphs look at the first three reasons, and the next section of the chapter deals with the product life cycle.

Briefly speaking

"Every accomplishment starts with the decision to try."

Anonymous

Desire to Grow

A company limits its growth potential when it concentrates on a single product. For an example, consider toy maker Trendmasters. The company started life when it introduced Loony Heads, plastic character faces that belched or screamed on command. After selling 3 million Loony Heads, the firm introduced a line of plastic dolls that danced to music played nearby. The latest product in Trendmasters' portfolio is Starcastle, a line of dollhouses that transform into tea sets.[11]

Other firms may introduce new products to offset seasonal variations in sales of their current products. Soup

Marketing Dictionary

supplies Products that represent regular expenses necessary to carry out a firm's daily operations, but not part of the final product.

MRO item Part of business supplies categorized as a maintenance item, a repair item, or an element of operating supplies.

business service An intangible product purchased to facilitate a firm's production and operating processes.

product line A series of related products.

MARKETING HALL OF FAME

How CNS Helped Americans "Breathe Right"

The giants of corporate America love to flash their glitzy commercials during the Super Bowl, the biggest television viewing event of the year. Alongside Anheuser-Busch's talking frogs lusting for Budweiser, an obscure medical-equipment company from Chanhassen, Minnesota, muscled its product front and center on the biggest sporting day of the year. What's more, CNS, Inc., didn't need to pay a cent for its exposure. On the field, many football players in the classic matchup were wearing the company's product.

CNS sells Breathe Right nasal strips, which are worn stretched across the bridge of your nose. Football players like the stiff adhesive strips because they feel relief from congested breathing during games. According to CNS, which has federal Food and Drug Administration approval for its product, the strips gently pull open the sides of the nostrils, potentially improving breathing by 30 percent.

Breathe Right has become an amazing success. In a survey conducted for *Sporting Goods Business,* retailers rated the strips as the hottest new item in the sports-medicine category. "We were one of the first sporting goods retailers to jump on it and the product has been very successful," brags Ron Kohen, team sports buyer for the Herman's sporting goods chain.

Business, however, has not always looked so bright for the 14-year-old company. CNS, which also manufactures brain wave monitors and diagnostic equipment for sleep disorders, had hemorrhaged money throughout its history before introducing Breathe Right. Only after the company broadened its product line to include the strips did sales start booming. Even then, the strips

MAKES BREATHING SO EASY,
YOU CAN DO IT IN YOUR SLEEP.
A stuffed up nose doesn't go away when your head hits the pillow. At best, you might get an uneasy night's rest. But a drug-free Breathe Right® strip lifts and pulls open nasal passages, comfortably and without pinching, so you'll breathe easier all night long. Open up your stuffed nose with a Breathe Right nasal strip. Find them in cough and cold sections everywhere.
Breathe Right

might have sold sluggishly without a smart marketing move. CNS cofounder Daniel Cohen, a neurologist and football fan, sent samples of the strips to trainers for all National Football League teams. One famous player who gave the strips a try was former Philadelphia Ea-

consumption plummets between April and October every year. Campbell Soup Company tries to compensate for this loss of business by advertising heavily during warm

http://www.campbellsoup.com/

months to encourage consumers to think of soup as more than just a cold-weather meal. In addition, the company recently introduced a line of soup products designed for cooking entrées. The product line expansion should help to increase Campbell's year-round sales.

Optimal Use of Company Resources

By spreading the costs of its operations over a series of products, a firm may reduce the average production and marketing costs of each product. Pfizer, for example, applies its expertise in research and development for pharmaceuticals across all three of its product lines. In fact, Pfizer has sometimes successfully sold prescription and over-the-counter versions of similar products.[12]

Hospitals have taken advantage of idle facilities by adding a variety of outreach services. Many now operate health and fitness centers that, besides generating profits themselves, also feed customers into other hospital services. For example, a blood pressure check at the fitness center might result in a referral to a staff physician. A full product line increases the firm's benefit from the full expertise of its personnel as compared to a single product.

Enhancing the Company's Position in the Market

A company with a line of products often makes itself more important to both consumers and marketing intermediaries than a firm with only one product. A shopper who purchases a tent often buys related camping items. Recogniz-

gles running back Herschel Walker. When Jerry Rice, the star wide receiver of the San Francisco 49ers and an allergy sufferer, saw a picture of Walker wearing the product, he wanted to try it.

Rice wore one of the strips during the Super Bowl and ultimately signed an endorsement agreement with CNS to brag about them in print and television ads. Using Breathe Right, Rice observed during one interview, "I can get more air to my muscles. It really opened everything up for me so I could breathe."

Endorsements like these are invaluable, according to Kirk Hodgedon, CNS vice president of consumer marketing. "People see professional players like Jerry Rice or Herschel Walker wearing the product and interest has spread to colleges, high schools, and even youth markets."

The company is capitalizing on this keen interest from professional and amateur athletes by becoming an official sponsor of the NFL and the National Hockey League. It will also run print ads with the theme "Essential Gear" in magazines like *Sports Illustrated, Runner's World,* and *Outside.*

Ironically, CNS didn't start out targeting athletes for its new product. It envisioned the strips as a way for consumers to cut down on nasal congestion and reduce snoring. At first, CNS sold its product in drugstores and supermarkets. After athletes in such sports as tennis, in-line skating, mountain biking, and marathon running expressed an interest, it broadened its focus, eventually shipping packages developed just for athletes to sports outlets.

While the jock market has been a boon, couch potatoes represent an even bigger market, according to Peter Engel, president of Sietsema, Engel & Partners, the Minneapolis-based agency handling the Breathe Right strips account. To attract nonsports users, CNS is advertising on cable television and in general-interest publications. The print ads feature the tagline, "Don't Laugh; It Works," and show Alfred Hitchcock, the Statue of Liberty, and other well-known people and artworks with Breathe Right strips on their noses. "Sports gives you exposure, but the potential for its use is the everyday person," Engel says. "There are a lot more allergy sufferers, sinus and cold sufferers, and medical maladies than professional athletes."

QUESTIONS FOR CRITICAL THINKING

1. Do you think Breathe Right would have succeeded if professional football players had not adopted the product? Why?

2. How should CNS market Breathe Right to nonathletes?

Sources: "Success Doesn't Let Firm Breathe Easy," *Chicago Tribune,* January 30, 1997, downloaded from http://www.chicagotribune.com/, February 6,1997; Ellen Rooney Martin, "Breathe Right Targets a New, Louder Market," *Adweek* (Midwest Ed.), January 15, 1996, p. 5; Chad Rubel, "Creative Marketing a Must to Generate Mass Appeal," *Marketing News,* August 14, 1995, pp. 2, 6; "Breath of Fresh Air," *Sporting Goods Business,* August 1995, p. 92; and Ann Marsh, "Nose Jobs," *Forbes,* March 13, 1995, p. 140.

ing this tendency, Coleman Company has developed a complete line of camping products including canoes, ice chests, sleeping bags, cots, tents, cookers, and trailers. Few would know of the firm if it sold only lanterns. Business buyers often expect a firm that manufactures a particular product to offer related products as well.

THE PRODUCT LIFE CYCLE

Products, like people, pass through stages as they age. Humans progress from infancy to childhood to adulthood to retirement to death, and successful products progress through four basic stages: introduction, growth, maturity, and decline. This progression, known as the **product life cycle,** is depicted in Figure 11.8, along with examples of products that currently fit into each stage. Notice that the product life cycle concept applies to products or product categories within an industry, not to individual brands. Also, some products may move rapidly through the product life cycle, while others pass through those stages over long time periods.

Introductory Stage

During the early stages of the product life cycle, a firm works to stimulate demand for the new market entry. Products in the introductory stage often bring new technical features to a product category. Since the product is unknown to the public, promotional campaigns stress information about its features. Additional promotions directed

Marketing Dictionary

product life cycle The four basic stages through which a successful product progresses—introduction, growth, maturity, and decline.

Figure 11.8 Stages in the Product Life Cycle

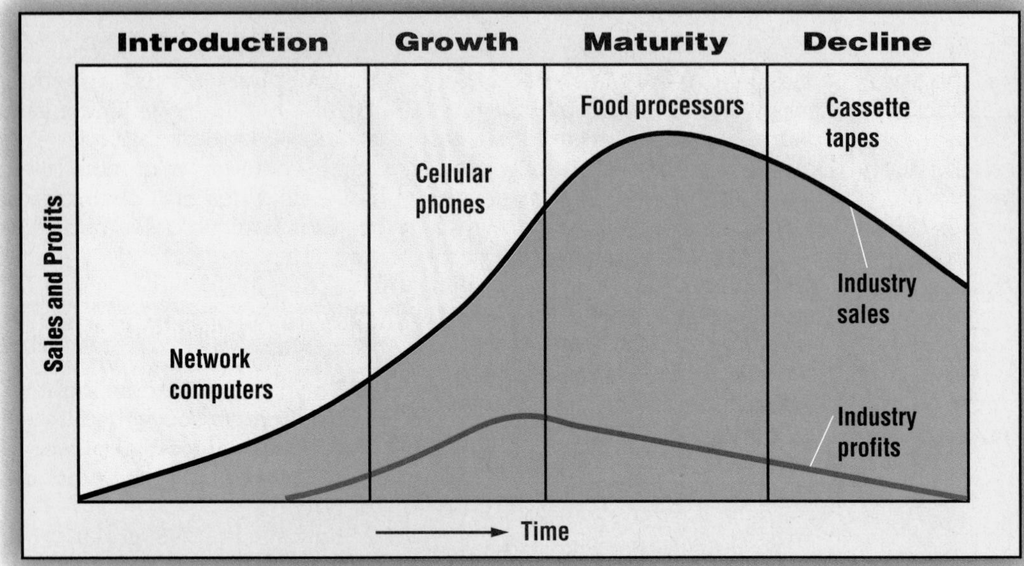
Introduction
Growth
Maturity
Decline
Food processors
Cassette tapes
Cellular phones
Sales and Profits
Industry sales
Network computers
Industry profits
Time

toward distribution channel members try to induce them to carry the product. In this phase, the public becomes acquainted with the product's merits and begins to accept it.

Financial losses are common during the introductory stage as the firm incurs high costs associated with heavy promotion and extensive research and development. Marketers often make mistakes in positioning during the introductory stage. Take Sony's plans to introduce the MiniDisc. Smaller than compact discs, MiniDiscs allow consumers to both play and record on palm-sized players. Sony introduced the MiniDisc in one of the largest promotional music giveaways ever seen. The firm sent over 1 million MiniDiscs to subscribers of *Rolling Stone,* and it sponsored heavy follow-up advertising. At its initial introduction, the new product failed miserably. Some experts pointed to the high cost of the player and the MiniDiscs themselves. Other experts noted that Sony failed to convince consumers that the new product provided an advantage over CDs and cassette tapes.[13]

Briefly speaking

"Competition brings out the best in products and the worst in people."

David Sarnoff (1891–1971)
American communications-industry pioneer,
founder and president of RCA

http://www.sony.com/

Mistakes like Sony's can be costly. In fact, one study found a failure rate as high as 47 percent for market pioneers.[14] However, by finding the correct formula for consumer trial and acceptance during the introductory stage, a business lays the groundwork for future profits. Firms can then focus on recovering their costs and beginning to earn profits as the new product moves into the second phase of its life cycle—the growth stage.

Growth Stage

Sales volume rises rapidly during the growth stage as new customers make initial purchases and early buyers repurchase the product. Word- of-mouth reports and mass advertising encourage hesitant buyers to make trial purchases. The growth stage usually begins when a firm begins to realize substantial profits from its investment. Products currently in the growth stage include cellular phones, specialty coffees, and sport-utility vehicles.

However, the growth stage may also bring new challenges for marketers. Inevitably, success attracts competitors, who rush into the market with similar products. In fact, most firms in a particular industry enter during the product's growth stage. A product that built enviable market share during the introductory stage may suddenly lose sales to competitive products. For example, laptop computers from Apple and IBM now face stiff competition from other computer makers such as Hitachi, NEC, Toshiba, and Acer, which are introducing their own entries at the low and middle ranges of the market.[15] To compete effectively, a firm may need to make improvements and changes to a product. Additional spending on promotion and distribution may also be necessary. Apple Computer has added outdoor advertising to its PowerBook promotional efforts, as shown in Figure 11.9.[16]

Maturity Stage

Industry sales continue to grow during the early part of the maturity stage, but eventually they reach a plateau as the

Figure 11.9 Increasing Advertising during a Product's Growth Stage

PowerBook.
Apple
patrick

backlog of potential customers dwindles. By this time, many competitors have entered the market, and the firm's profits begin to decline as competition intensifies.

In the maturity stage, differences between competing products diminish as competitors discover the product and promotional characteristics most desired by consumers. Heavy promotional outlays emphasize any differences that still separate competing products, and brand competition intensifies. Some firms try to differentiate their products by focusing on attributes such as quality, reliability, and service.

At this stage in the product life cycle, available supplies exceed industry demand for the first time. Companies can increase their sales and market shares only at the expense of competitors. As competition intensifies, competitors tend to cut prices to attract new buyers. Although a price reduction may seem like the easiest method of boosting purchases, it is also one of the simplest moves for competitors to duplicate. Reduced prices decrease revenues for all firms in the industry, unless the price cuts stimulate enough new purchases to offset the loss in revenue on each unit sold.

Disposable diaper manufacturers are currently wrestling with this problem. As the birthrate has declined, the demand for disposable diapers has stagnated. Some manufacturers have responded by slashing prices and increasing promotional spending. Others have introduced product innovations such as Dryper's diapers with baking soda. These maneuvers have not spurred growth in the overall product category. Instead, diaper manufacturers continually struggle to steal market share away from each other. The competition is especially intense among smaller brands, which account for only 28 percent of the total market sales.[17]

Decline Stage

In the final stage of a product's life, innovations or shifts in consumer preferences bring about an absolute decline in industry sales. The safety razor replaced the straight razor years ago, and the electric shaver has taken customers from the safety razor. Later, consumers replaced CB radios with cellular telephones. As Figure 11.10 indicates, the decline stage of an old product often coincides with the growth stage for a new market entry.

As sales fall, industry profits decline, sometimes actually becoming negative. This change forces firms to cut prices further in a bid for the dwindling market. Manufacturers gradually drop the declining products from their product lines and search for alternatives. The emergence of new technologies can help to push mature technologies into decline.

Figure 11.10 Overlapping Life Cycles for Two Products

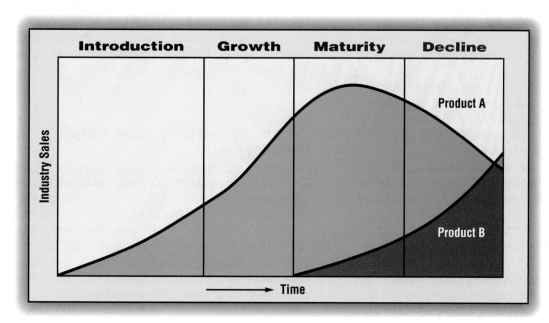

Introduction
Growth
Maturity
Decline
Product A
Product B
Industry Sales
Time

Consider the experience of Smith Corona.

SOLVING AN ETHICAL CONTROVERSY

Should the Liquor Industry Market Spiked Sodas?

In the past, consumers could easily tell the difference between most sodas and alcoholic drinks. In Great Britain, however, this judgment has become harder and harder since marketers began blurring the distinction. Walk into any London liquor store today, and you'll see bottle after bottle of what many people are calling *spiked soda*.

These alcoholic beverages, nicknamed *alcopops*, look and taste a lot like soft drinks. Stores offer alcoholic cola, orange, lemonade, and other fruit flavors that mask the taste of the hard liquor contents. The sweet drinks appeal to teenagers—and so does the packaging. The label of one alcoholic lemonade, for instance, features a zany character who has the drink's name, Lemonhead, plastered across his forehead.

These drinks, with colorful names like Hooper's Hooch and Cola Lips, have brought success to the liquor industry, which had experienced stagnant sales. Some observers suggest that this new product category will bridge the gap between beer and hard liquor. But critics are denouncing the industry for enticing children into developing a taste for alcohol.

Should the Liquor Industry Market Spiked Sodas?

PRO

1. **This new category of alcoholic drinks, which contain 4 percent to 5.5 percent alcohol, is meant strictly for adults. Brewery official Harry Drnec calls them "new-age adult beverages," perfect for grownups who don't like the taste of gin, vodka, bourbon, or other hard liquors. "People generally don't like the taste of alcohol," he says.**
2. **Critics unfairly single out certain alcoholic drinks just because some teenagers are illegally drinking them. Kids also smoke cigarettes and drink beer and wine, but no one suggests banning these legal products.**
3. **It's unfair to blame teenage drinking problems on the new generation of alcoholic beverages. Jane Sabini, a spokeswoman for the makers of Hooper's Hooch, says "false logic" drives the claims that these drinks induce underage drinking. "If brands like Hooper's Hooch had not become available six months ago, most underage drinkers would be drinking other alcoholic drinks just as they did before."**

This leading manufacturer of typewriters saw its market dry up as personal computer technology spread. Smith Corona tried unsuccessfully to replace the dying market for typewriters by branching out into sales of low-priced fax machines and other personal business equipment. Eventually, the company was forced to file for bankruptcy protection.[18]

The traditional product life cycle differs from fad cycles. Fashions and fads profoundly influence marketing strategies. *Fashions* are currently popular products that tend to follow recurring life cycles. Women's apparel and accessories provide the best examples. After more than a decade out of fashion, the miniskirt became stylish again during the early 1990s. Small, wire-rimmed sunglasses, popular during the late 1960s, became fashionable again more than 20 years later. Convertible cars are another example. Popular in the 1950s, they disappeared from the market in the 1970s, but have become stylish again in recent years.

In contrast, *fads* are fashions with abbreviated life cycles. Most fads experience short-lived popularity and then quickly fade, although some maintain residual markets among certain segments. Many marketers rush to introduce products that tie into fads. For example, when the Macarena dance reached the height of its popularity in 1996, Spanish perfume manufacturer Perfumeria Gal launched a new women's fragrance called Macarena. The fragrance was marketed in the United States and Japan.[19]

Using the Product Life Cycle Concept in Marketing Strategy

The product life cycle provides useful guidance for marketing strategy decisions. Marketers can anticipate that sales and profits will assume a predictable pattern throughout the life cycle stages, so they can shift promotional emphasis from product information in the early stages to brand promotion in the later ones. This kind of insight helps marketers to focus on maximizing sales and profits at each stage through appropriate promotional efforts.

CON

1. **The liquor industry is using these beverages to hook youngsters on alcohol at an early age. "These drinks are there to help people who don't have a taste for alcohol develop one," insists Mark Bennett of the British advocacy group Alcohol Concern. Drinks made with colas and fruit drinks that the kids already guzzle tempt them more strongly than wine coolers and other traditionally sweet alcoholic drinks.**
2. **The words of young fans of the drinks reveal the allure and the danger they pose to youngsters. In explaining why she likes spiked sodas, one 13-year-old girl says, "It's sweet and tastes like a normal drink, but it makes you feel a bit more grown up."**
3. **The marketing campaign for spiked soda is just as perilous to the health of children as tobacco industry ads like the cartoonish Joe Camel. Citing controversial advertising geared toward children, Britain's Advertising Standards Authority banned ads for Hooper's Hooch that featured a mischievous cartoon lemon.**

Summary

Not surprisingly, alcopops are traveling far beyond the British Isles. Australian sellers now stock the controversial brews. Bass PLC is test marketing Hooper's Hooch in San Diego and Miami. Meanwhile, another British brewery is negotiating with an unnamed American brewer to carry out U.S. distribution of Mrs. Pucker's, a fruit-flavored alcoholic soda created by a former Anheuser-Busch executive.

"This is a fast-moving market sector which has premium value," says Richard Hall, chairman of Zenith International, a United Kingdom market research group. "I would not be surprised to see a series of launches and expansions into other countries."

So far, the big U.S. breweries aren't divulging whether they plan to develop their own spiked sodas. "We carefully consider all viable opportunities for building our business," says Gregg Billmeyer, director of new products for Anheuser-Busch. "But it would be inappropriate for us to comment on speculation regarding specific new products."

Sources: "Controversy Brews Over Taste, Labels of Soda-Like 'Alcopops,' " *Los Angeles Times,* March 13, 1997, downloaded from http://www.latimes.com, April 2, 1997; adapted from Juliana Koranteng, "Spiked Sodas Concern Advertising Regulators," *Ad Age International,* February 12, 1996, p. 13; and Tara Parker-Pope, "Spiked Sodas, an Illicit Hit with Kids in U.K., Head for U.S.," *Wall Street Journal,* February 12, 1996, p. B1.

At the introductory stage, a firm's marketing efforts should emphasize the goal of stimulating demand. The focus then shifts to cultivating selective demand in the growth period. Extensive market segmentation helps to maintain momentum in the maturity period. During the decline stage, the emphasis returns to increasing primary demand. Chapter 12 will cover new-product strategies in more detail.

Extending the Product Life Cycle Marketing strategists commonly try to extend the life cycles of their products as long as possible. They can often accomplish this goal if they take action early in the maturity stage. Product life cycles can stretch indefinitely as a result of actions designed to increase the frequency of use by current customers, increase the number of users for the product, find new uses, and/or change package sizes, labels, or product quality.

Increasing Frequency of Use During the maturity stage, the industry sales curve for a product reaches a maximum point as the competitors exhaust the supply of potential customers who previously had not made purchases. However, if current purchasers buy more frequently than they formerly did, total industry sales will rise even though no new customers enter the market.

For instance, consumers buy some products in certain seasons of the year. Marketers can boost purchase frequency by persuading these people to try the product year-round. Marketers may try to connect the use of holiday products to additional occasions throughout the year. Kraft Foods has done this for its Jell-O brand by offering free molds with holiday themes.

The Coca-Cola Co. also follows a seasonal marketing calendar to encourage year-round sales of its soft drinks. The company divides the year into five separate schedules of marketplace activities with themed events and advertising reflecting the lifestyle shifts of consumers for each season. For example, in the fall, the company fills promotions with back-to-school themes, while summer promotions focus on outdoor activities.[20]

Increasing the Number of Users A second strategy

Figure 11.11 Extending the Product Life Cycle by Identifying New Uses

USE #345

Off-the-wall solution. *When 3-year-old Lesley Ivy decided to use the living room wall as a canvas, her mother knew exactly what to do. One shot of WD-40® and the rainbow disappeared. It also works great for removing crayon from linoleum and tile floors. Just spray, wait and wipe.*

WD-40. THERE'S ALWAYS ANOTHER USE.

for extending the product life cycle seeks to increase the overall market size by attracting new customers who previously have not used the product. Wolverine World Wide Inc., used this tactic to build a new market for its line of Hush Puppies shoes. In the early 1990s, both consumers and retailers viewed Hush Puppies as out-of-date products suitable only for older wearers. To attract younger buyers, Wolverine added bold colors and fashionable styles to the product line. The firm also ran ads in magazines such as *Wired, Out,* and *Interview.* These efforts opened up a new market for Wolverine with Generation X shoe buyers.[21]

Marketers may find their products in different stages of the life cycle in different countries. This difference can help firms to extend product growth. Items that have reached the mature stage in the United States may still be in the introductory stage somewhere else. Consider America Online. The company experienced dramatic growth in its U.S. subscriber base during the early 1990s. As the U.S. market for online services matured, however, AOL started to bring its service to new subscribers in other countries. It launched a multimillion dollar marketing push in the United Kingdom, where online services were still growth products.[22]

Finding New Uses Still another strategy for extending a product's life cycle is to identify new uses for it. New applications for mature products include oatmeal as a cholesterol-reducer, waxed paper to cover food in microwave cooking, and mouthwash as an aid in treating and preventing plaque and gum disease. The WD-40 company has only one product, yet it excels at finding and promoting new uses for its lubricant. The ad in Figure 11.11 shows one of the company's advertisements promoting WD-40 to help busy mothers to remove children's crayon scribbles from walls.

Changing Package Sizes, Labels, or Product Quality Many firms try to extend their product life cycles by introducing physical changes in their products. Food marketers have brought out small packages designed to appeal to one-person households. Other firms offer their products in convenient packages for use away from home or at the office. Domino's Pizza was the only fast-food pizza chain to experience significant growth in a recent year. The company's introduction of garlic crunch crusts and cheese-filled crusts helped to fuel the success.[23]

Product Deletion Decisions

To avoid wasting resources promoting unpromising products, marketers must occasionally prune product lines and eliminate marginal products. Marketers typically face this decision during the late maturity and early decline stages of the product life cycle. Periodic reviews of weak products should justify either eliminating or retaining them.

A firm may continue to carry an unprofitable product in order to provide a complete line for its customers. For example, while most grocery stores lose money on bulky, low-unit-value items such as salt, they continue to carry them to meet shopper demand.

Shortages of raw materials sometimes prompt companies to discontinue production and marketing of previously profitable items. Due to such a shortage, Alcoa discontinued making its brand of aluminum foil.

A firm may even drop a profitable product that fails to fit into its existing product line. Some of these products return to the market carrying the names of other firms that purchase the brands from the original manufacturers. The introduction of automatic washing machines created a need for low-sudsing detergents. Monsanto produced the world's first detergent of this sort, All, in the 1950s. All succeeded instantly, and Monsanto was swamped with orders from supermarkets throughout the nation. The Monsanto sales force focused primarily on marketing industrial chemicals to large-scale buyers, however, and the company would have needed a completely new sales force to handle the product. Monsanto struggled to keep up, and nine months after the introduction of All, Procter & Gamble introduced the world's second low-sudsing detergent, Dash. Because the Procter & Gamble sales force handled hundreds of consumer products, the company could spread the cost of contacting dealers over all its products. In contrast,

Table 11.3 The Fortune Brands Product Mix

Distilled Spirits	Office Products	Home Improvement and Hardware	Golf and Leisure
PRODUCTS			
Bourbon	Day-Timer calendars	Tool chests	Golf clubs
Cordials	Arts and crafts supplies	Sinks	Golf clothing
	Appointment books		
Whiskey	Time management seminars	Tool boxes	Golf bags
Gin	Binders	Locks	
	Fasteners, paper clips		
Vodka	Computer accessories and supplies	Workbenches	Golf balls
Rum	Office equipment	Hospital carts	Golf shoes
		Kitchen cabinets	
		Faucets	
		Plumbing supplies	
BRANDS			
Jim Beam	Day-Timer	Master Lock	Cobra
Ronrico	AOOO	Moen	
Calvert	Wilson-Jones	Aristokraft	Foot-Joy
Old Holborn			Titleist
Gilbey's			

Monsanto had only All. Rather than attempt to compete, Monsanto sold All to Lever Brothers, a Procter & Gamble competitor with a marketing organization in place capable of effectively promoting the product.

THE PRODUCT MIX

A company's **product mix** is the assortment of product lines and individual product offerings that it sells. The right blend of product lines and products allows a firm to maximize sales opportunities within the limitations of its resources. Marketers typically measure product mixes according to width, length, and depth.

The *width* of a product mix refers to the number of product lines the firm offers. As Table 11.3 shows, Fortune Brands, Inc. markets four major product lines: distilled spirits, office products, hardware and home improvement products, and golf and leisure products. Contrast the width of this product mix with that of PepsiCo. PepsiCo has three main product lines: soft drinks, snack foods, and restaurants. Fortune Brands maintains a wider product mix than PepsiCo offers. However, PepsiCo's product mix shows more consistency, because it strongly emphasizes food products. Product mix *consistency* measures the similarity of a firm's product lines in use, distribution, and target markets. Fortune Brands sells a highly varied mix of products. It does not produce a consistent product mix across product lines.

The *length* of a product mix refers to the number of products a firm sells. Fortune Brands has a product mix 31 products long. (Due to space constraints, Table 11.3 shows only a selection of the company's many products.) Foodbrands America, which specializes in manufacturing food items for restaurant chains, maintains an unusually long product mix: over 1,600 products, including every-

Marketing Dictionary

product mix A company's assortment of product lines and individual offerings.

MARKETING HALL OF SHAME

When Golden Arches Fall

When McDonald's rolled out its Arch Deluxe hamburger, the company made what seemed like an awfully big fuss for ground beef. Ronald McDonald frolicked with the famous Rockettes at Radio City Music Hall in New York City. The company dressed up a prominent dome-shaped theater in Los Angeles like a hamburger. Fireworks exploded over a Toronto stadium, and a giant "sandburger" rose from the beach in San Diego.

Clearly, the new product wasn't just any burger. McDonald's executives hoped that the Arch Deluxe represented the company's ticket to the future. Worried that adults were losing interest in McDonald's menu, the franchise giant introduced a hamburger—complete with potato roll, Dijon-style sauce, tomato, and lettuce—intended to appeal to the older crowd's more sophisticated taste. Several months later, with similar fanfare, it added more menu items to its adult sandwich lineup. The new Deluxe line of burger, chicken, and fish offerings were designed to attract adults while beefing up McDonald's sales revenue.

McDonald's devoted considerable marketing muscle to the Deluxe sandwich line, spending 15 percent of its entire North American marketing budget on the effort. Experts estimate that the company spent $200 million trying to lure adults back to the golden arches. This marketing splash seems only fitting, considering that McDonald's executive chef—yes, the company has one—took two years to create the new hamburger.

Yet for all the energy pumped into the marketing blitz, many signs suggest that the effort failed. *Fortune* magazine has called it a "McFlop" in the making. At the noisy unveiling, McDonald's management predicted that the Arch Deluxe would generate $1 billion in revenues in its first year. But these same officials decline to share actual sales figures.

Some observers say that total sales at McDonald's restaurants have been stagnant at best for the

thing from pepperoni pizza toppings to deli ham and frozen burritos.[24]

http://www.ambrands.com/

Depth refers to variations of each product that the firm includes in its mix. For instance, Fortune Brands sells a wide variety of Day-Timer organizers as part of its office supplies line. The company even makes Day-Timers for children. Time management seminars marketed under the Day-Timer logo add further depth. The company has introduced at least four new premium bourbons under the Jim Beam label.[25] It also promotes a Jim Beam and cola product.

Fortune Brands isn't alone with its deep mix of products. Quaker Oats sells original oatmeal, instant oatmeal, microwave oatmeal, and a number of flavored oatmeals. At one point, Procter & Gamble Co. offered 31 varieties of Head & Shoulders shampoo.[26]

To evaluate a firm's product mix, marketers look at the effectiveness of all three elements—width, length, and depth. Has the firm so far failed to serve a viable consumer segment? It may improve performance by increasing product line depth to offer a product variation that will attract the new segment. Can the firm achieve economies of scale in its sales and distribution efforts by adding complementary product lines to the mix? If so, a wider product mix may seem appropriate. Does the firm gain equal contri butions from all products in its portfolio? If not, it may decide to lengthen or shorten the product mix to increase revenues.

Product Mix Decisions

As products and product lines move through the product life cycle, marketers face some characteristic product mix decisions. In the growth stage, a firm may lengthen or widen its product mix to take advantage of sales opportunities. As a product matures, the company may decide to add variations that will attract new users. A product near the end of its life cycle may be pruned or altered, and new products may extend the product life cycle.

Managing the product mix has become an increasingly important marketing task. In the 1980s, many large firms added depth, length, and width to their product mixes without fully considering the consequences of expansion. By the mid-1990s, many of these same firms contended with unprofitable product lines and products. Retailers couldn't carry the full range of these products, and consumers felt

past decade. According to *Nation's Restaurant News,* the average McDonald's franchise took in $1.4 million in 1986. A decade later, sales had only inched up to $1.5 million—a gain of just 7 percent. In comparison, the consumer price index jumped during that same time more than 40 percent.

Edward Rensi, president and CEO of U.S. operations, responded to some grumbling from the chain's 2,700 franchisees by distributing a memo that stated, "The Arch Deluxe was never intended to be a silver bullet."

Al Ries, a former Burger King consultant, says McDonald's needs to concentrate on its core business: kids and families. Chasing after adults who aren't driving minivans full of kids could backfire and alienate loyal customers. As an example, he cites the television ads that show kids frowning when they see an Arch Deluxe hamburger.

"McDonald's stands for kids, and through kids, family," says Ries, now chairman of the consulting firm Ries & Ries in New York. "By literally saying, 'We don't want you to eat this sandwich,' it undermines their strength." Robert Shulman, who co-authored *The Marketing Revolution,* agrees that hyping burgers that kids won't like is a huge risk with the potential to cannibalize the company's original products.

"McDonald's has to have the courage to realize that people do grow up and move on. You have to abandon some customers who outgrow the concept," Ries insists. "That's the mark of a successful company. Coca-Cola said they could get into the new-age beverages, but for the most part they've kept the focus on colas."

QUESTIONS FOR CRITICAL THINKING

1. **Do you think McDonald's should focus on its core business or continue to reach out for customers with more sophisticated palates? Why?**
2. **Do you think a single firm can simultaneously please all segments of the hamburger market?**
3. **What marketing focus would you implement to attract adult consumers?**

Sources: "Fallon Won't Swallow Integrity, Quits McDonald's Arch Deluxe," *Wall Street Journal,* February 3, 1997, downloaded from http://www.wsj.com/, March 10, 1997; Shelly Branch, "McDonald's Strikes Out with Grownups," *Fortune,* November 11, 1996, pp. 157–162; Greg Burns, "Golden Arch Support," *Business Week,* October 21, 1996, p. 46; and Karen Schwartz, "Amid McHype, Burger Debuts at McDonald's," *San Diego Union-Tribune,* May 10, 1996, p. C-1.

overwhelmed by their choices. Simplification became a common goal of product mix management.[27]

For example, after evaluating its product mix, Procter & Gamble Co. decided that it needed less length and depth.

http://www.pg.com/

The firm cut the number of products it offered by nearly one-third and reduced product mix depth, as well. It cut the number of varieties of Head & Shoulders, for instance, by half. These changes showed up on the firm's bottom line. Procter & Gamble has increased sales while reducing manufacturing and promotional expenses.[28]

Other firms, however, seek to expand their product mixes. This is especially true of newer and smaller firms seeking to grow. Often, firms purchase product lines from other companies that want to narrow their product mixes. Other firms expand their product mixes by acquiring entire companies through merger or acquisition.

Consider the growth of Hain Food Group, Inc. The firm began life with four product lines: a diet drink, a line of nondairy ice creams, a line of frozen organic meals, and a line of soy-based pizzas. The firm's owner, Irwin Simon, knew that growth of his start-up firm demanded expansion of his product mix. He decided to achieve this expansion by increasing the width of the product mix. The firm added a line of kosher frozen foods, rice cakes, and potato chips by purchasing existing product lines from other manufacturers. Hain Food Group then sought to increase length and depth in several of these product lines. For example, the firm now markets regular-sized rice cakes, mini-rice cakes, and flavored rice cakes. As a result of Hain's careful attention to product mix management, today the company offers 250 products and grosses over $69 million a year.[29]

A firm should assess its current product mix for another important reason: to determine the feasibility of a line extension. A **line extension** develops individual offerings that appeal to different market segments while remaining closely related to the existing product line. A line

Marketing Dictionary

line extension Introduction of a new product that is closely related to other products in the firm's existing line.

extension provides a relatively inexpensive way to increase sales with minimal risk. For example, both Hershey's and Mars have introduced low-fat versions of their candy bars. Both companies hope to attract consumers whose concerns with weight and health might otherwise prevent them from buying candy. Procter & Gamble extended its Crisco vegetable oil line by adding varieties seasoned with ingredients such as roasted garlic and lemon butter.[30]

Careful evaluation of a firm's current product mix can also help marketers to make decisions about brand management and new-product introductions. Chapter 12 will examine the importance of branding and brand management, as well as the ways in which a firm builds identity for the products in its product mix. Chapter 12 then focuses on the development and introduction of new products.

ACHIEVEMENT CHECK SUMMARY

Reread the learning goals that follow, and consider the questions for each goal. Answering these questions will reinforce your grasp of the most important concepts in the chapter and allow you to check how well you have achieved these learning goals. Where a blank appears before a question, answer with *T* or *F;* for multiple-choice questions, circle the letter of the correct answer.

Objective 11.1: Explain the broader marketing view of products.

1. ____ Marketers concern themselves only with the physical characteristics of a good.

2. ____ A product is a bundle of physical, service, and symbolic attributes that enhance consumer satisfaction.

Objective 11.2: List the classifications of consumer products, and briefly describe each category.

1. ____ Consumers purchase convenience products after extensive comparisons of price, quality, and style.

2. ____ Soft drinks are an example of a shopping product.

3. ____ Specialty products offer unique features that induce buyers to seek them out.

Objective 11.3: Describe the types of business products.

1. ____ Business products are classified based on their uses rather than on customers' buying behavior.

2. ____ Installations represent major purchase decisions, often requiring months of negotiations.

3. ____ Ink cartridges for a new copy machine are an example of (a) component parts and materials; (b) supplies; (c) accessory equipment; (d) raw materials.

Objective 11.4: Explain why most firms develop lines of related products rather than marketing individual products.

1. ____ A firm usually can achieve consistent growth by marketing only one product.

2. ____ A product line is several unrelated products marketed by the same firm.

3. ____ One reason for producing a line of products rather than a group of individual products is to optimize company resources.

Objective 11.5: Explain the concept of the product life cycle.

1. ____ In the introductory stage of the product life cycle, marketers focus on (a) enticing consumers to try a product; (b) raising prices; or (c) stealing market share from competitors.

2. ____ During the growth stage, marketers often face reduced competition.

3. ____ The decline stage of an old product often coincides with the growth stage for a new market entry.

Objective 11.6: Discuss how a firm can extend a product's life cycle.

1. ____ Marketers cannot extend a product's life cycle indefinitely.

2. ____ By increasing the frequency of purchases by current users, a firm can keep product sales growing.

3. ____ If a product has reached maturity in the U.S. market, a firm might manage to increase market potential by entering other countries.

4. ____ Finding new uses for a product is a good way to encourage consumers to buy more.

Objective 11.7: Identify the major product mix decisions that marketers must make.

1. ____ A product mix is a group of related products.

2. ____ The length of a firm's product mix refers to the number of product lines it offers.

3. ____ The number of variations of each product in a firm's product mix determines the depth of the mix.

4. ____ Line extensions add individual products that appeal to different market segments while remaining closely related to the existing product line.

5. ____ A firm can expand its product mix by buying an established brand.

Students: See the solutions section located on page S-2 to check your responses to the Achievement Check Summary.

Key Terms

product
convenience product
shopping product
specialty product
installation
accessory equipment
industrial distributor
component parts and materials
raw material
supplies
MRO item
business service
product line
product life cycle
product mix
line extension

Review Questions

1. Compare and contrast the narrow and broader views of a *product.* Define the term *total product concept.*
2. Why do consumers buy some unsought products? Cite examples of products that would fall into this category.
3. Why do marketers categorize business products on a different basis from consumer products? Discuss the implication of this difference.
4. Compare a typical marketing mix for a convenience product with one for a specialty product. What are the primary differences in these mixes?
5. Outline the categories of business products. What kind of marketing mix suits each category?
6. What products fall within the business service category? Explain how firms market these intangible products.
7. Explain the product life cycle concept. Include a drawing of the progressive stages in the product life cycle.
8. How can the product life cycle concept influence marketing strategy? Explain how marketers can extend a product's life cycle.
9. What is a product mix? How does the concept help businesspeople to make effective marketing decisions?
10. Explain the concept of line extension. Why do most business firms market lines of related products rather than individual products?

Discussion Questions

1. Classify the following consumer products and discuss how these classification decisions might affect marketing strategy.
   a. In-line skates
   b. Mouthwash
   c. Chanel perfume
   d. Original oil painting
   e. Felt-tip pen
   f. Jantzen swimsuit
   g. Playboy magazine
   h. Ford Taurus car
2. Classify the following business products and explain how these classification decisions could guide development of a marketing strategy.
   a. Land for a factory
   b. Mainframe computer
   c. Cotton
   d. Cooking oil
   e. Light bulbs
   f. Paper clips
   g. Corporate jet
3. Cite a product that serves as an example for each stage of the product life cycle (other than those mentioned in the text). Explain how marketing strategy varies by life cycle stage for each product.
4. Trace the life cycle of a recent fad. What marketing strategy implications can you derive from your study?
5. As discussed in the chapter, Smith Corona based its product mix on typewriters, but the spread of personal computers rapidly reduced the market for those machines. Based on your knowledge of the product life cycle and product mix management, what advice would you give to Smith Corona executives seeking to bring the firm back from bankruptcy? Could Smith Corona extend—or revive—the life cycle for typewriters? What product mix decisions should the firm consider?

'netWork

1. Marketers recognize three general categories of consumer products, one of which is convenience goods. Find a Web site devoted to serving marketers of these goods at the address below.

http://www.c-store.com/

What services does the site provide to convenience store executives and retailers? If you were a producer of convenience goods, how could this site serve you?

2. Many producers of luxury goods promote their products over the Internet. Find two or three sites that feature luxury products. How do these sites differ from comparable sites that advertise nonluxury goods? Should marketers of luxury products advertise on the Net?

3. To study the rapidly evolving technology of product data management, visit the home page of the Product Data Management Information Center at the address below.

http://www.pdmic.com/

What is product data management? Determine how this technology might benefit manufacturers. What type of manufacturers might use this technique?

VIDEO CASE 11

SERVING THE NEEDS OF GOLF PROFESSIONALS

Golf has done a complete flip flop. It used to be the game of the well-to-do. During the 1950s and early 1960s, 70 percent of all golf play took place at posh private country clubs, where members outfitted themselves with merchandise at the adjacent pro shops. By the mid-1970s, however, 70 percent of golfers were teeing off at public courses. "That change in the character of the player also changed the character of the business," says David Branon, president and CEO of Slazenger USA, a privately held manufacturer headquartered in Greenville, South Carolina. "An industry that had been largely dominated by the on-course pro shop was suddenly a multiple outlet industry."

A host of retailers—mass merchandisers, discount retailers, and large sporting goods stores—were stocking their shelves with balls, gloves, bags, and clubs made by Calloway, Wilson, Titleist, Dunlop, and other golf equipment manufacturers to entice the growing number of public-course golfers into their stores. These changes in the golf industry negatively affected golf professionals who operated small, on-course pro shops at private clubs. "He got none of the deals, he got none of the best prices, he could bring no clout or volume to the negotiating table," says Branon.

In 1987, Branon started his company to serve the needs of private-club golf professionals and their customers. Research indicated that the golf pro's customers, private club members, had a high level of discretionary income, played more rounds of golf each year than the average player, and were likely to spend more for apparel and golf equipment than other golfers. In developing the marketing strategy for this segment, Branon made an important product positioning decision by obtaining a U.S. license to use the internationally known Slazenger brand name. "The Slazenger brand has been around since 1881," says Branon. "It has a lot of international panache and a lot of heritage to it and we basically imported the romance of the brand." To enhance the image of its brand, Slazenger has long associated its products with the most prestigious golf and tennis tournaments in the world. It has sponsored events such as the British Open and, since 1972, the Wimbledon lawn tennis championship.

The high visibility of the brand boosted Slazenger USA's early marketing efforts. "In the beginning, we played off of their success around the world," says Don Swarat, senior vice president of sales. "I know some of the earliest accounts I could open were military accounts because they had personnel who had been to Europe and that were familiar with the brand so they were willing to take a chance on that brand over here."

Branon believed the best way to capture the romance of the Slazenger brand would be by developing an upscale line of clothing marketed exclusively through on-course golf professionals so they could protect their prices and profits. Branon offered his menswear at the same price to all pros, whether they ordered 10 items or 10,000. The exclusive distribution of Slazenger USA apparel allowed golf pros to maintain high prices and healthy profit margins, because it freed them from competing with high-volume discount retailers. The exclusive arrangement also enabled the pros to put their private club names and logos on the clothing.

Branon decided to broaden his product offerings to include other golf products such as balls, gloves, and clubs. By offering a complete product mix to the golf pro, Slazenger USA could "increase our meaningfulness to him and increase the validity of our presentation to him as a pro-shop-only company," says Branon. One golf pro says, "They're the first company I've been approached by from a representative standpoint of coming in and making a commitment to the golf pro."

Slazenger USA backs up its commitment to the golf professional with a network of highly trained and skilled sales representatives who work to build strong customer relationships. Visiting customers monthly, sales reps travel in vans equipped as showrooms on wheels, from which they show golf pros their newest products. They also assist the pros in setting up product displays and offer marketing advice to increase product sales. In establishing the company's promotional strategy, "We said we would set out and drive the success of the brand from inside the shop, not outside with massive media campaigns," says Branon. With this approach, "the advocacy of the golf pro would control the marketing power of the brand."

Slazenger also promotes its brand by participating in trade shows. The company's elaborate display at the annual Professional Golf Association trade show in Orlando allows Slazenger marketers to meet with golf pros from around the country who come to see the newest equipment and apparel. The PGA show "gives us an opportunity to project our image . . . as a quality company and a service company," says Swarat. "It gives us an opportunity to listen, because every golf manufacturer is at the show and the buyer goes there to compare."

Developing unique products also helped Slazenger USA to strengthen its relationships with golf pros. The company wanted to enter the golf club market, but realized that mass marketing didn't fit its philosophy of offering exclusive products for pro shops. In response, the company developed the custom-built Crown Limited Club Fitting System. The system relies on the golf pro's expertise to properly fit golf clubs to match each golfer's unique characteristics.

The customized club-design process begins with 3,348 club head variations and incorporates information about the golfer's health, learning styles, playing and practice habits, swing tendencies, and flight patterns. The pro takes kinetic measurements to evaluate the golfer's upper body strength, flexibility, and range of motion, and analyzes the golfer's swing speed. The golf pro uses the results of these tests to specify the design of customized clubs that will help the golfer to perform at his or her best. The clubs are then assembled and sent to customers within 72 hours from the time the order is placed by phone or fax. One golf pro says that the custom-designed clubs "improve my credibility tremendously along with getting my customers a lot more satisfied and happy and enjoying the game."

Slazenger USA has successfully achieved specialty status for its premium-priced product lines. "The best way to protect the special nature of a product is to make the product special," says Branon. "You really have to pay attention to the product. We deal with probably the most discriminating element of both the trade and the consumer. The most dangerous animal in the world is the cynical consumer. We are monomaniacal about the quality of the product."

Questions

1. What type of consumer products does Slazenger USA sell? Describe characteristics of the products that support your classification.
2. Give examples of how Slazenger USA developed a marketing strategy for branding, promoting, pricing, and distributing its products.
3. What benefits did Slazenger USA gain by developing a complete product line?
4. The Internet has provided an additional channel for promoting and distributing a number of products. Considering its current market niche, could Slazenger USA effectively use the Web to enhance its current success? Review other Web sites for golf products, then outline a Web site plan for Slazenger. Include the following criteria in your proposal:
   a. Intended audience
   b. Information content (explain the value of each element and how it will help Slazenger to achieve its objectives)
   c. Objectives of the site
   d. Suggested methods of measuring the success or failure of the Web site

Sources: Telephone interview with Carrie Webb, Slazenger USA Customer Relations Specialist, May 16, 1997; and Kerry Capell, "Tailored Clubs Could Trim Your Score," *Business Week,* February 19, 1996, p. 94.

CHAPTER 12

BRAND MANAGEMENT AND NEW-PRODUCT PLANNING

3M Innovation Network
Market Centers
Product Information
Worldwide Operations
Netscape: Experience the Edm
Back
Forward
Home
Reload
Images
Open
Print
Find
Location: http://www.edmark.com/
What's New?
What's Cool?
Destinations
Net Search
People
Find out about
TECHNOLOGY
Connect Now!
Here Now!
PLAY TO WIN!
EDMA
New site for kids!
FREE Software!
Play Fripple Place Live Online!
Guest Book
Order Online
Callaway GOLF
THE BIGGEST BIG BERTHA TITANIUM DRIVER
Netscape: Callav
Callaway
1997 CATALOG
TOUR STATS & PLAYERS
INVESTOR RELATIONS
DEMO DAYS
ASK A QUESTION
CALLAWAY NEWS
TITANIUM
Welcome to
MONOP
A nice, ruthless, money-
What's New!
About Edmark
Tech Support
Edmark Products
PORTFOLIO

Chapter Objectives

1. Explain the benefits of branding and brand management.
2. Describe the different types of brands.
3. Explain the value of brand equity.
4. Describe how firms develop strong identities for their products and brands.
5. Identify alternative new-product development strategies and the determinants of each strategy's success.
6. Identify the determinants of a new product's rate of adoption and the methods for accelerating the speed of adoption.
7. Explain the various organizational structures for new-product development.
8. List the stages in the new-product development process.
9. Outline the functions of the Consumer Product Safety Commission, and summarize the concept of product liability.

Advance to GO and Collect $200, or Is It £200, or ¥200?

Rich Uncle Pennybags has packed up his stash of money and moved to a new address: cyberspace. The portly gentleman, his balding pate covered with a top hat, is the mascot of the world's top-selling game, Monopoly.

A quick look at Uncle Pennybags' attire confirms that Monopoly has been around for decades. But the old-fashioned game, which drew its inspiration from the Atlantic City boardwalk of yesteryear, is trying to shake off a stodgy image. The quest for a hipper personality has led to a CD-ROM version of Monopoly. The $40 game, complete with three-dimensional graphics and 16-bit digital sound, represents Hasbro Inc.'s attempt to lure kids who were raised on fast-paced Nintendo and Sega games.

The slick new game's animations allow you to watch your opponent thrown into a dark, creepy-looking jail. Before you buy any real estate, you can hop in a classic car and inspect houses on the swank side of town or the other side of the tracks. If you want to play alone, the game will create a virtual competitor for you, and you never have to worry about counting any paper money—the bank automatically keeps track of your assets.

In this age of computerized entertainment, an project to make a digital enhancement of the 60-year-old game might have seemed like an easy decision. But Hasbro executives had to ensure that the glitzy electronic version would not steal customers away from the cardboard game with paper money that Grandma grew up playing. The project required a delicate balancing act. "The last thing you want to do is extend a product such that you cannibalize the parents," says Bob Wann, Hasbro's senior vice president of marketing.

The Hasbro marketing team developed a segmentation strategy to ensure that Monopoly would stay relevant to future customers. That goal actually required the firm to add new choices. Along with the $10 original, Hasbro shipped a $35 limited-edition anniversary game to stores, followed by a $20 gold box edition. While the company declines to disclose figures for individual games, analysts anticipate that the combined brand extensions will boost sales by 50 percent. "You wouldn't expect that from a product that's not in the early stage of its life cycle," Wann observes.

Hasbro also launched a two-tiered marketing program for separate pursuit of users of the interactive and regular versions. Piggybacking on Monopoly's $25 million advertising budget, marketers placed CD-ROM ads in such magazines as *Family Fun* and *Electronic Gaming.* So far, the strategy has

worked for both the cardboard and electronic versions. During its first six weeks on the shelves, for example, the Monopoly CD-ROM sold 150,000 copies. (The breakeven point for an interactive game is between 70,000 and 100,000.) "I really think this will extend the core brand in ways we don't even know yet," says Gary Carlin, director of marketing at Hasbro Interactive Worldwide in Beverly, Massachusetts. The new Monopoly game has succeeded so well that Hasbro has also launched electronic versions of Scrabble and six other popular board games.

According to Tom Dusenberry, president of the Hasbro Interactive unit, the computer games have not damaged the company's classic businesses but actually enhanced them. Today's products offer a new way to play, he explains, but people then want to play the parlor game and enjoy interacting with other people.

Not surprisingly, Hasbro is now exporting its hot new game. Fans in France, Great Britain, Germany, and other countries can now play the electronic version. Amazingly, the game allows players from different countries to compete against each other. When someone in America sells Boardwalk to a player in London, the name changes to Mayfair and the dollars convert into pounds.

http://www.monopoly.com/

The Monopoly Web site helps the game's fans find competitors around the world. "Now you can ruthlessly and globally compete against worthy adversaries," it promises. The Web site also provides snippets of the game's animation to entice those who haven't yet bought it.

Visitors to the site will know immediately that the sweet, old parlor game has changed. On a backdrop of $20 Monopoly bills, they read this greeting: "Welcome to the world of Monopoly, where you can buy it. Rent it. Sell it. Trade it. And if worst comes to worst, mortgage it." The copy fulfills Hasbro's promise: "A nice, ruthless, money-hungry Web site."[1]

CHAPTER OVERVIEW

This chapter reviews the requirements for effective product decisions and their crucial role in determining a firm's success. Developing and marketing a product is a costly proposition. To protect its investment and maximize the return on this investment, a business must carefully nurture both existing and new products. Through careful product planning and promotion, Hasbro successfully protected its original board games while introducing CD-ROM versions to new markets.

This chapter focuses on two critical elements of product planning and strategy. First, it looks at how firms build and maintain identity and competitive advantage for their products through branding. Second, it focuses on the new-product planning and introduction process. Effective new-product planning lays down vital preparation. The needs of consumers change constantly, most firms manage

Figure 12.1 **A Brand Name That Creates an Identity for Children's Clothing**

Emily Dickinson Hath New Clothes,
Too Stylish To Describe With Prose.
How a girl doth bedazzle and beguile, whilst clad in the latest OshKosh® style.
To divine the location of the nearest store, call 1-800-282-4674.
OshKosh
B'gosh®
THE GENUINE ARTICLE
The Biggest Name In Kids' Clothes.™

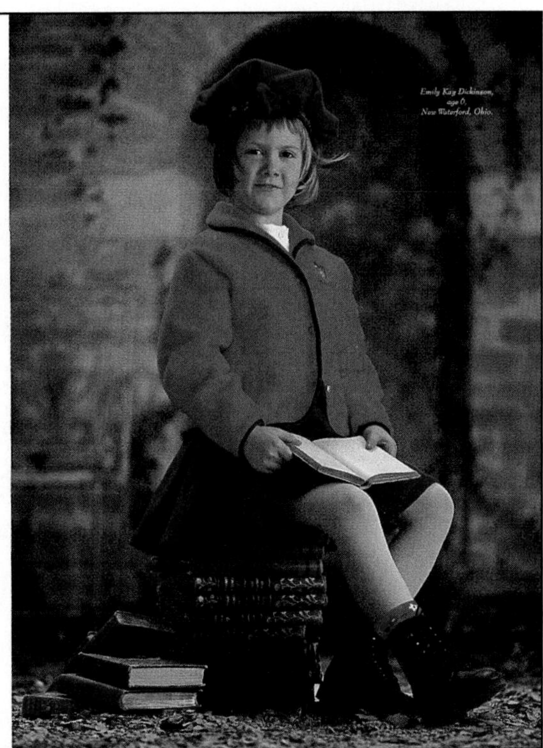
Emily Kay Dickinson,
age 6,
New Waterford, Ohio.

to grow only if they provide innovative and useful products to fill those needs.

MANAGING BRANDS FOR COMPETITIVE ADVANTAGE

Think of the last time you went shopping for groceries. As you moved through the store, chances are, your recognition of various brand names influenced many of your decisions about which products to buy. Perhaps you chose Colgate toothpaste over Crest or loaded Heinz ketchup into your cart instead of the store brand. Walking through the soft-drink aisle, you probably reached for Coke or Pepsi without much thought.

Marketers recognize the potentially powerful influence on consumer behavior of creating and protecting a strong identity for products and product lines. Branding is the process of creating that identity. A **brand** is a name, term, sign, symbol, design, or some combination that identifies the products of one firm and differentiates them from competitors' offerings. For example, the brand name OshKosh B'gosh, the slogan *The Genuine Article,* and the label of blue denim with yellow type identify the lines of children's clothing made by OshKosh B'gosh, Inc. (See Figure 12.1.)

Buyers respond to branding by making repeat purchases of the same product, since they identify the product with the name of its producer. The purchaser can thus associate the satisfaction derived from an ice cream bar, for example, with the brand name Häagen-Dazs. James Lenehan, worldwide chairman of Johnson & Johnson's consumer pharmaceuticals and professional group explains that a recognized brand name helps to simplify consumer choice. "If you have a brand that you know and trust, it helps you make choices faster, more easily," Lenehan says. "Can you imagine going shopping without them?"[2]

Brand Loyalty

Brands achieve widely varying consumer familiarity and acceptance. While a boating enthusiast may insist on a Johnson outboard motor, the same consumer might show little loyalty to particular brands in another product category such as chocolate. Marketers measure brand loyalty in three stages: brand recognition, brand preference, and brand insistence.

Marketing Dictionary

brand A name, term, sign, symbol, design, or some combination that identifies the products of a firm.

Figure 12.2 **Individual Brands Marketed by Nestlé**

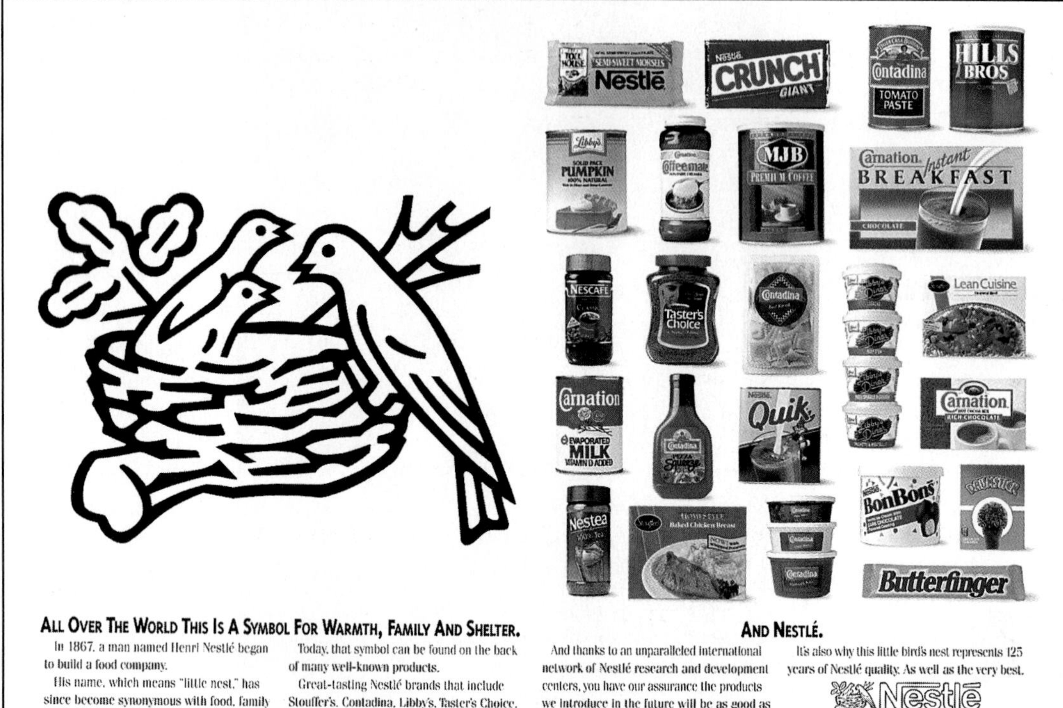
ALL OVER THE WORLD THIS IS A SYMBOL FOR WARMTH, FAMILY AND SHELTER.
In 1867, a man named Henri Nestlé began to build a food company.
His name, which means "little nest," has since become synonymous with food, family and quality throughout the world.
Today, that symbol can be found on the back of many well-known products.
Great-tasting Nestlé brands that include Stouffer's, Contadina, Libby's, Taster's Choice, Hills Bros, Carnation and more.
AND NESTLÉ.
And thanks to an unparalleled international network of Nestlé research and development centers, you have our assurance the products we introduce in the future will be as good as the ones we make today.
It's also why this little bird's nest represents 125 years of Nestlé quality. As well as the very best.
Nestlé
Makes the very best.

Brand insistence, the ultimate stage in brand loyalty, leads consumers to refuse to accept alternatives and to search extensively for the desired product. A product at this stage has achieved a monopoly position with its consumers. Although many firms try to establish brand insistence, few achieve this ambitious goal. Only the most exclusive specialty goods attain this position with large segments of the total market.

Brand recognition is a company's first objective for newly introduced products. Marketers begin promoting new products by trying to make them familiar to the public. Advertising offers one way to increase consumer awareness of a brand. Manufacturers spent over $174 billion on advertising in 1996, the third year in a row that advertising expenditures increased.[3] Other strategies for creating brand recognition include offering free samples or discount coupons for purchases. For Arizona Iced Tea, packaging played a role in attracting consumer attention and brand recognition. The colorful, 24-ounce cans that held the flavored teas clearly differentiated the products from the clear, 16-ounce bottles of the leading competitor, Snapple.[4] Once consumers have used a product, seen it advertised, or noticed it in stores, it moves from the unknown to the known category, which increases the probability that those consumers will purchase it.

Brand preference is the second stage of brand loyalty. At this stage, consumers rely on previous experience with the product when they choose it over competitors' products if it is available. General Motors recognized the importance of brand preference for its Saturn line. After establishing the Saturn brand in the low-priced car market, Saturn introduced a line of mid-sized cars to prevent its primarily younger buyers from shopping elsewhere as they established families. By offering the next step up, General Motors hoped to build brand preference for Saturn.[5]

Types of Brands

Some firms sell their goods without any efforts at branding. These products are called **generic products.** They are characterized by plain labels, little or no advertising, and no brand names.

The most common types of generic products are food and household staples. Some companies market cigarettes and drugs as generic products. These no-name products were first sold in Europe at prices as much as 30 percent below those of brand-name products. The marketing tactic was introduced in the United States in 1977. The market shares of generic products increase during economic recessions, but subside when the economy improves.

Companies that practice branding classify brands in several ways: private, manufacturer's (national), family, and individual brands. In making branding decisions, firms must weigh the benefits and disadvantages of each type of brand.

Manufacturer's Brand versus Private Brand Manufacturers' brands, also called *national brands,* define the image that most people form when they think of a brand. A **manufacturer's brand** refers to a brand name owned by a manufacturer or other producer. Well-known manufacturers' brands include Kodak, Fruit of the Loom, and Heinz.

Many large wholesalers and retailers place their own

brands on the products they market. The brands offered by wholesalers and retailers are usually called **private brands.** For example, Sears sells its own brands Kenmore, Craftsman, DieHard, and Harmony House. Sears also launched a private label line of jeans, Canyon River Blues. Safeway stocks its shelves with such private brands as Bel Air, Canterbury, Cragmont, Party Pride, Manor House, and Scotch Buy. Private brands and generic products expand the number of alternatives available to consumers.

The growth of private brands has paralleled that of chain stores in the United States, most of it occurring since the 1930s. Chains market their own brands after buying the products from manufacturers, which place the chains' private brand names on their own products. Such leading manufacturers as Westinghouse, Armstrong Rubber, and Heinz generate ever-increasing percentages of their total incomes by producing goods for sale under retailers' private labels. In fact, some experts predict that private brands could end up with about 45 percent of the U.S. packaged-goods market. The growth of private brands results largely from the desire of retailers and wholesalers to maintain control over the images, quality levels, and prices of the products they sell. Moreover, private brands usually carry lower prices, sometimes up to 35 percent less, than manufacturers' brands.

Private brands also sell well abroad. Consumers in Germany, the United Kingdom, and France welcome private-label goods, and the practice is gaining strength in other European countries, as well. In fact, one study predicts that private-label sales in Europe will grow 23 percent by the end of the century.[6]

Many manufacturers mount aggressive responses to threats from private brands. For example, The Coca-Cola Co.'s executives went directly to retailers to explain the benefits of branded products. In national presentations, Coca-Cola explained how shoppers who buy branded products tend to spend three to four times more on groceries than shoppers who prefer private-label products. The company increased its advertising and promotional budgets, as well, to protect brand loyalty.[7]

Although some manufacturers refuse to produce private-label goods, most regard such production as a way to reach additional segments of their total markets. Every year, cereal maker Ralston Purina has steadily increased its budget for its 17 private-label cereals such as Corn Flakes and Crispy Rice, its versions of Kellogg's Corn Flakes and Rice Krispies.

Family and Individual Brands A **family brand** is a single brand name that identifies several related products. For example, KitchenAid markets a complete line of appliances under the KitchenAid name, and Johnson & Johnson offers a line of baby powder, lotions, plastic pants, and baby shampoo under one name.

A manufacturer may instead choose to market a product under an **individual brand,** which uniquely identifies a product itself, rather than promoting it under the name of the company or an umbrella name covering similar items. Lever Brothers, for example, markets Aim, Close Up, and Pepsodent toothpastes; All and Wisk laundry detergents; Imperial margarine; Caress, Dove, Lifebuoy, and Lux bath soaps; and Shield and Lever 2000 deodorant soaps. Quaker Oats markets Aunt Jemima breakfast products, Gatorade beverages, and Celeste Pizza. Individual brands cost more than family brands to market, because the firm must develop a new promotional campaign to introduce each new product to its target market. Unique brand names provide extremely effective aids, however, in implementing market segmentation strategies. Nestlé defines individual brand names in marketing its products throughout the world. Individual brands help Nestlé to target products to specific segments. Some of Nestlé's well-known brands targeted at U.S. consumers are shown in the ad in Figure 12.2.

On the other hand, a promotional outlay for a family brand benefits all products in the line. For example, a new addition to the Heinz line gains immediate recognition as part of the well-known family brand. Family brands also

Marketing Dictionary

brand recognition The stage of brand acceptance at which the consumer knows of a brand, but does not prefer it to competing brands.

brand preference The stage of brand acceptance at which the consumer selects one brand over competing offerings based on previous experience with it.

brand insistence The stage of brand acceptance at which the consumer refuses to accept alternatives and searches extensively for the desired good or service.

generic product An item characterized by a plain label, with no advertising and no brand name.

manufacturer's brand A brand name owned by a manufacturer or other producer.

private brand A brand name placed on products marketed by wholesalers and retailers.

family brand A brand name that identifies several related products.

individual brand A unique brand name that identifies a specific offering within a firm's product line to avoid grouping it under a family brand.

Figure 12.3 **Dimensions of Brand Equity: The Young & Rubicam Model**

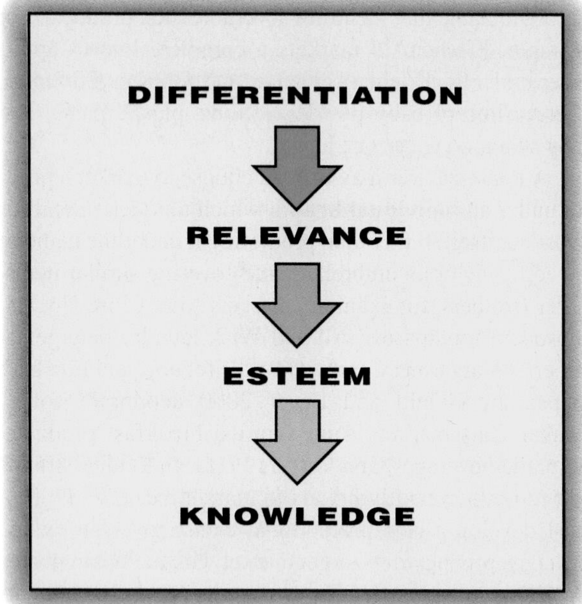
DIFFERENTIATION
RELEVANCE
ESTEEM
KNOWLEDGE

help marketers to introduce new products to both customers and retailers. Since supermarkets stock thousands of items, they hesitate to add new products unless they confidently expect active demand.

Family brands should identify products of similar quality, or the firm risks harming its product image. If Rolls Royce marketers were to place the Rolls name on a less expensive car or a line of discounted clothing, they might severely tarnish the image of the luxury car line. Conversely, Lexus, Infiniti, and Mercedes-Benz put their names on large, luxurious sport-utility vehicles to capitalize on their reputations and enhance the acceptance of the new models in a competitive market.

Individual brand names should distinguish dissimilar products. Quaker Oats markets its dog food line under the Ken-L Ration brand name and its cat food line under the Puss 'n' Boots brand name. Marketers of grocery products, such as Procter & Gamble, General Foods, and Lever Brothers, develop individual brands to appeal to unique market segments. These brands also enable the firms to stimulate competition within their own organizations and to increase total company sales. Consumers who do not want Tide can choose from Cheer, Dash, or Oxydol—all Procter & Gamble products—rather than a competitor's brand.

The Value of Brand Equity

A strong brand identity has important advantages for a firm. First, it increases the chances that consumers will recognize the firm's product or product line when they make purchase decisions. Second, a strong brand identity can contribute to buyers' perceptions of product quality. Branding can also reinforce customer loyalty and repeat purchases. A consumer who tries a brand and likes it will likely look for that brand on a future store visit. All of these benefits contribute to a valuable form of competitive advantage called *brand equity.*

Brand equity refers to the added value that a certain brand name gives to a product in the marketplace. Brands with high equity often confer financial advantages on a firm, because they often command comparatively large market shares, and because consumers may give little attention to differences in price. Studies have also linked brand equity to high profits and stock returns.[8]

In global operations, high brand equity often smooths paths for expansion into new markets. Coca-Cola is a high-equity brand recognized around the world. Similarly, Disney successfully markets products under its brand in Europe, Japan, and even China.

How can a business evaluate brand equity? The global advertising agency Young & Rubicam (Y&R) developed one measurement system called the *Brand Asset Valuator* by examining the brand equity positions of over 8,000 brands around the world. According to Y&R, a firm builds brand equity sequentially on four dimensions of brand personality. As shown in Figure 12.3, they are differentiation, relevance, esteem, and knowledge.

Differentiation refers to a brand's ability to stand apart from competitors. Brands like Disney, Porsche, Rolls Royce, and Victoria's Secret stand out in consumers' minds as symbols of unique product characteristics. According to the Y&R model, marketers who want to develop a strong brand must start with a feature that no competitors match in consumers' minds.

The second dimension in the Y&R model, *relevance,* refers to the real and perceived importance of the brand to a large consumer segment. A large number of consumers must feel a need for the benefits offered by the brand. According to Y&R, brands with high relevance include AT&T, Hallmark, Kodak, and Campbell's.

Esteem is a combination of perceived quality and consumer perceptions about the growing or declining popularity of a brand. A rise in perceived quality increases consumer admiration for the brand. Positive public opinion about a brand also promotes the brand's esteem. On the other hand, negative impressions about a brand's popularity reduce esteem. Brands with high esteem include Microsoft, Hershey's, and Rubbermaid.

The final brand equity dimension is knowledge. *Knowledge* refers to the extent of customers' awareness of the brand and understanding of its identity. Knowledge implies that customers feel an intimate relationship with a brand. Y&R lists Coca-Cola, Jell-O, Kodak, Campbell's, and Crest as brands with high knowledge.[9]

The brand equity concept also extends to nontraditional products such as major league sports teams. The team name, colors, and logos combine to create a strong brand identity that differentiates each team from its rivals. The silver, black, and purple colors of the Colorado Rockies baseball team have proved extremely popular with fans. In 1992, before the team had played any games, sales of licensed merchandise with the team's logo topped those of many major league teams. By 1994, the Rockies ranked first in sales of licensed merchandise, an indication of consumer awareness of the team.[10]

The Role of Brand Managers Because of the value, both tangible and intangible, associated with strong brand equity, marketing organizations invest considerable resources and effort to develop and maintain these dimensions of brand personality. Many large companies assign the task of managing a brand's marketing strategies to a **brand manager.** This marketing professional plans and implements the balance of promotional, pricing, distribution, and product arrangements that lead to strong brand equity.

General Motors recently adopted the brand manager system, long a feature of packaged goods marketing. GM intends the change to strengthen its brands, reduce the number of GM dealers, and end competition between GM brands for customers. The company's brand managers, most of whom it recruited from outside the auto industry, will develop and protect the company's auto brands by meeting consumer needs—not by matching the features of competitors' cars.

In moving to brand management, GM acknowledged the importance of the whole marketing package, rather than the car maker's traditional focus on the product. "The product is nothing more than the representation of the essence of the brand," said GM marketing representative Dean Rotondo. Improving brand identity represents a critical strategic response for GM, which saw its market share drop from 46 percent to 33 percent as different models and divisions competed against each other for customers.[11]

The next section looks at some of the tactics by which marketers try to create strong brand and product identities.

PRODUCT IDENTIFICATION

Organizations identify their products in the marketplace with brand names, symbols, and distinctive packaging. Almost every product that is distinguishable from another gives buyers some means of identifying it. Sunkist Growers stamps its oranges with the name Sunkist. For nearly 100 years, Prudential Insurance Company has used the Rock of Gibraltar as its organizationwide symbol. Choosing how to identify the firm's output represents a major decision for the marketing manager.

Brand Names and Brand Marks

What's in a name? According to researchers, a name plays a central role in establishing brand and product identity. The American Marketing Association has defined a **brand name** as the part of the brand consisting of words or letters that form a name that identifies and distinguishes the firm's offerings from those of its competitors. The brand name is, therefore, the part of the brand that people can vocalize. Firms can also identify their brands by brand marks. A **brand mark** is a symbol or pictorial design that distinguishes a product. It is the part of the brand that people cannot vocalize. The National Federation of Coffee Growers of Colombia created the brand mark shown in the ad in Figure 12.4. Illustrating the origin of the coffee, the brand mark represents a grower with his burro in front of a mountain.

Effective brand names are easy to pronounce, recognize, and remember. Short names, such as Nike, Geo, Crest, and Tide meet these requirements. Marketers try to overcome problems with easily mispronounced brand names by teaching consumers the correct pronunciations. For example, early advertisements for the Korean car maker Hyundai explained that the name rhymes with *Sunday.*

Global marketers face a particularly acute problem in selecting brand names; an excellent brand name in one country may prove disastrous in another. A firm marketing a product in many countries must decide whether to define a single brand name for universal promotions or tailor names to individual countries. Every language has *o* and *k* sounds, so *okay* has become an international word. Every language also has a short *a;* thus, *Coca-Cola, Kodak,* and *Texaco* work as effective brands in any country.

A brand name should also give buyers the correct connotation of the product's image. The *Tru-Test* name for True Value Hardware's line of paints suggests reliable performance. *VISA* suggests a credit card that provides global

Marketing Dictionary

brand equity The added value that a certain brand name gives to a product.

brand manager A marketing professional charged with planning and implementing marketing strategies and tactics for a brand.

brand name The part of a brand consisting of words or letters that form a name to identify and distinguish a firm's offerings.

brand mark A symbol or pictorial design that identifies a product.

Figure 12.4 **An Example of a Brand Mark**

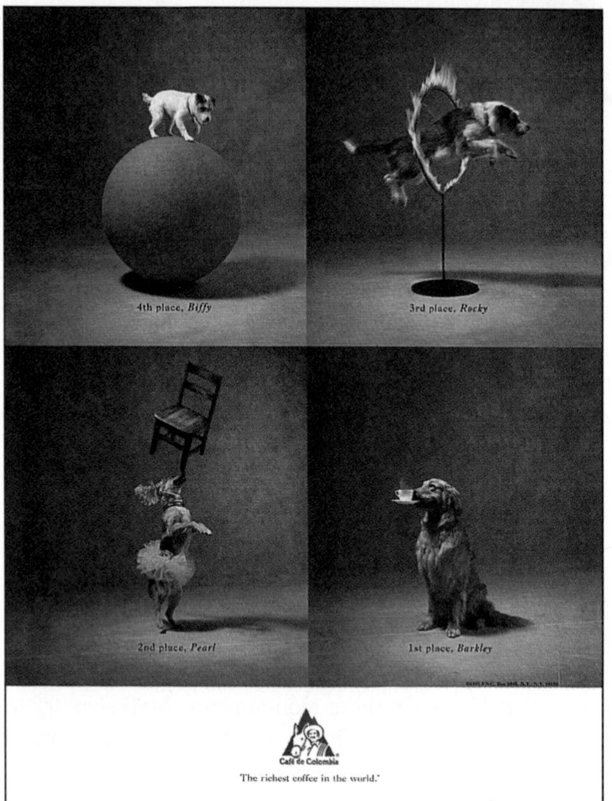
4th place, *Biffy*
3rd place, *Rocky*
2nd place, *Pearl*
1st place, *Barkley*
Café de Colombia
"The richest coffee in the world."

acceptance. Zebco, a manufacturer of fishing equipment, chose *Rhino* as the brand name for a fishing rod to convey the product's strength.

A brand name must also qualify for legal protection. The Lanham Act of 1946 states that registered trademarks must not contain words or phrases in general use, such as *automobile* or *suntan lotion.* These generic words actually describe particular types of products, and no company can claim exclusive rights to them.

Marketers feel increasingly hard-pressed to coin effective brand names, as multitudes of competitors rush to stake out brand names for their own products. Some companies register names before they have products to fit them in order to stop competitors from using them.

When a class of products becomes generally known by the original brand name of a specific offering, then the brand name may become a descriptive **generic name.** If this occurs, the original owner loses exclusive claim to the brand name. The generic names *nylon, aspirin, escalator, kerosene,* and *zipper* originated as brand names. Other generic names that were once brand names include *cola, yo-yo, linoleum,* and *shredded wheat.*

Marketers must distinguish between brand names that have become legally generic terms and those that seem generic only in many consumers' eyes. *Jell-O* is a brand name owned exclusively by General Foods, but many consumers casually apply it as a descriptive name for gelatin desserts. Consumers often adopt legal brand names such as *Jell-O* as descriptive names. Many English and Australian consumers use the brand name *Hoover* as a verb for vacuuming. Similarly, *Xerox* is such a well-known brand name

http://www.xerox.com/

that people frequently—though incorrectly—use it as a verb. To protect its valuable trademark, Xerox Corp. has created advertisements explaining that *Xerox* is a brand name and registered trademark and should not be used as a verb.

Trademarks

Businesses invest considerable resources in developing and promoting brands and brand identities. The high value of brand equity encourages firms to take steps to protect the expenditures they invest in their brands.

A **trademark** is a brand for which the owner claims exclusive legal protection. A trademark should not be confused with a trade name, which identifies a company. *The Coca-Cola Co.* is a trade name, but *Coke* is a trademark of the company. Some trade names duplicate companies' brand names. For example, *Rubbermaid* is the brand name of Rubbermaid, Inc.

Protecting Trademarks Trademark protection confers exclusive legal right to use a brand name, brand mark, and any slogan or product name abbreviation, such as *Bud* for Budweiser or *The Met* for the New York Metropolitan Opera. For example, the ad in Figure 12.5 shows that the DiGiorno Foods Company has trademark protection for the brand name *DiGiorno,* the slogan "Pasta and Sauces for the Eating World," and the artwork that features pasta products. The courts upheld Budweiser's trademark in one case, ruling that an exterminating company's slogan "This Bug's for You" infringed on Bud's rights. Firms can also receive trademark protection for packaging elements and product features such as color, shape, design, and typeface. The U.S. Supreme Court has upheld the legality of protecting a color as a trademark, as long as it meets the ordinary legal requirements for registration. Pink, for example, is a protectable color for Owens-Corning's fiberglass insulation.

To protect a trademark in the United States, a firm must register the brand or brand name with the U.S. Patent and Trademark Office. Under the Lanham Act, the owner must prove that it intends to use the trademark. If the trademark has not appeared on a product within three years, and the owner cannot demonstrate intentions to reuse it, the company will forfeit its rights to the trademark.[12]

http://www.uspto.gov/

U.S. law has fortified trademark protection in recent years. On January 16, 1996, The Federal Trademark Dilution Act of 1995 was added to the Lanham Act to give a trademark holder the right to sue for trademark infringement even if other products using its brand are not particularly similar or easily confused in the minds of consumers. The infringing company does not even have to know that it is diluting another's trademark. The act also gives a trademark holder the right to sue if another party imitates its trademark. Even subliminal confusion between trademarks can lead to a trademark infringement case.

Consider, for example, the case of Philip Morris versus Star Tobacco Corp. Star introduced a new brand of cigarettes with the brand name *Gunsmoke.* The company promoted the brand in ads featuring a cowboy figure with slogans such as "Welcome to Gunsmoke Country." Philip Morris had long promoted its Marlboro cigarettes with a cowboy figure, as well as a similar slogan. Philip Morris sued Star for trademark dilution. The court agreed, stating that Star Tobacco's use of these symbols would give Star "an unfair advantage in the marketplace through consumers' confusion, perhaps subliminal, between the two brands."[13]

When a publisher launched a newsletter for teenage girls called *New Girl Times,* the business faced a trademark infringement suit filed by the *New York Times.* The suit claimed that the newsletter was infringing on a trademark because the masthead of the *New Girl Times* used the same typeface as the trademarked nameplate of the *New York Times.* The lawsuit also asserted that the newsletter's tagline "fit to empower" came too close to the newspaper's trademarked slogan "All the news that's fit to print." The *New Girl Times* publisher was forced to redesign the publication. Attorneys for the *New York Times* defended its right to protect its trademark, no matter how small the publication. As one attorney explained, "It's only strong as long as you enforce it."[14]

The Internet may be the next battlefield for trademark infringement cases. Some companies are attempting to protect their trademarks by filing infringement cases against companies using similar Internet addresses. For example, Avon recently succeeded in stopping a New York woman from using the Internet address *avon.com/* by filing a trademark infringement and dilution suit.[15] Sun Microsystems, Inc. has also asked a number of businesses and individuals to stop using the word *Java* in their domain names. Sun says these names violate the registered trademark for its software program with that name.[16]

In addition, companies need to anticipate implications for trademarks when they modify their products or packaging. For example, when Pepsi recently redesigned its trademark, it replaced a partial circle with a complete circle in the Pepsi design. The company had to reregister for trademark protection, even for such an apparently minor change.[17]

Figure 12.5 Protecting Brands with Trademarks

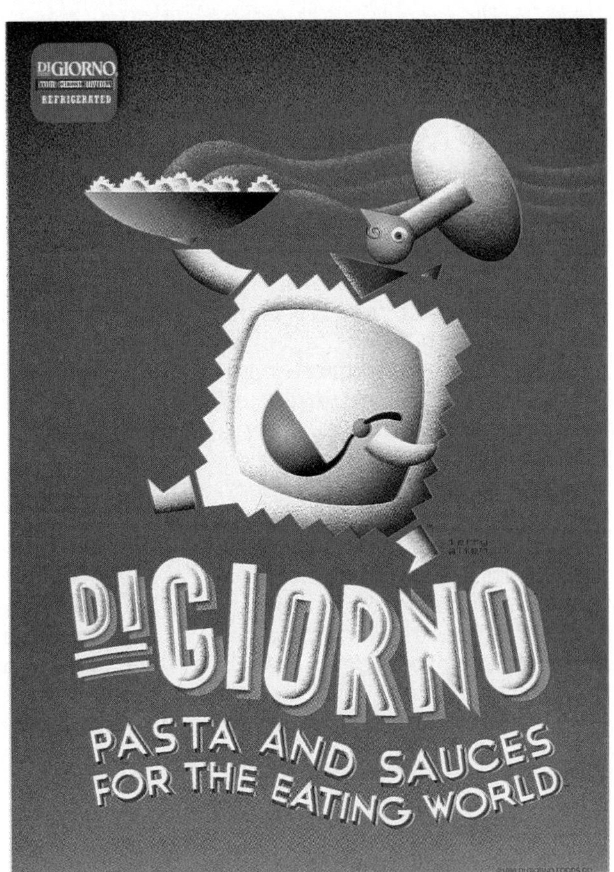
DiGIORNO
REFRIGERATED
DiGIORNO
PASTA AND SAUCES
FOR THE EATING WORLD

Marketing Dictionary

generic name A brand name that has become a generally descriptive term for a class of products.

trademark A brand to which the owner legally claims exclusive access.

SOLVING AN ETHICAL CONTROVERSY

Should the Olympic Games Be Allowed to License Souvenirs?

Gary Baldowski will never forget the day the cops raided his Olympic souvenir hut. His booth was stuffed with T-shirts and other trinkets of the 1996 Atlanta Games, but the officers zeroed in on just one item: a $4 plastic Olympic medal. The unannounced visitors scooped up all 1,000 of the cheap medals and dropped them off at the 96th Precinct, a glass-enclosed room at the Atlanta Olympic headquarters. Without protest, the merchant watched the raid in amazement. "They've got federal marshals with them. What are you going to do, argue?" asked Baldowski, who insists he ordered the offending merchandise from a catalog.

What was the crime? The cheap medals were counterfeit, a serious offense, according to Olympic officials. In fact, organizers considered counterfeiting such a threat to the financial success of the Olympic Games that the U.S. Customs Service launched a two-year effort called "Operation Gold Medal" to weed it out.

Should the Olympic Games Be Allowed to License Souvenirs?

PRO

1. **If the Olympic Games did not license merchandise—from the official Olympic-sponsored salad dressing to the official Olympic watches—the athletes would suffer. Athletic training programs would feel severe cutbacks without the money that comes from legitimate sponsors. "This is a survival issue for the ways the teams and the Games are financed in the U.S.," says Darby Coker, a Olympic committee spokesperson.**
2. **Eliminating licensing agreements would destroy any incentive for companies to contribute money to the Olympics. The Atlanta Games might have lost as much as $75 million in royalties. Without financial backing, America's sports programs would suffer a dramatic setback.**

CON

1. **Requiring vendors to sign costly licensing agreements**

Protecting Trademarks Abroad Companies must protect their trademarks in foreign countries as well as in the United States, as the experience of one U.S. company attempting to expand abroad illustrates. Pressed4Time, a dry-cleaning service that picks up and delivers from customers' homes and offices, decided to open a franchise in Australia. The firm did not register its logo or name in Australia beforehand, however. The oversight ended up as a disaster, when a rival firm applied for and was granted an Australian trademark on Pressed4Time's logo.[18]

Protecting trademarks abroad can cost a great deal of money. PepsiCo registered its new design in more than 200 countries. In some countries, such as Russia and China, the change required the firm to develop the new design using different alphabets. The estimated cost of registering the new design around the world exceeded $20 million.[19]

Packaging

A firm's product strategy must address questions about packaging. Like its brand name, a product's package can powerfully influence buyers' purchase decisions. Many manufacturers have upgraded the packages of their private-label products to convey higher-quality images. For years, Safeway Food Stores sold its own brand of milk, under the Lucerne label, in stodgy-looking red-and-yellow containers with a daisy logo that looked more like an asterisk than a flower. Marketers redesigned the milk carton, adding drawings of a cow and a dairy barn and replacing the old lettering with a crisper typeface. The new packaging revived sales of the private brand to rival those of the national brands Safeway carried.[20]

Firms are applying increasingly scientific methods to their packaging decisions. Rather than experimenting with physical models or drawings, more and more package designers work on special graphics computers that create three-dimensional images of packages in thousands of colors, shapes, and typefaces. Another computer system helps firms to design effective packaging by simulating the displays shoppers see when they walk down supermarket aisles. Companies conduct market research to evaluate current packages and to test alternative package designs. Kellogg, for example, tested its Nutri-Grain cereal's package, as well as the product itself.

A package serves several objectives. All of them can be classified under three general goals:

makes participation prohibitively expensive for small businesses. This requirement effectively shuts the little entrepreneurs out of big events like the Olympics, the Super Bowl, and the World Series.

2. **The licensing agreements can seem meaningless when big-time advertisers skirt the rules. In the trade, this practice is often referred to as "ambush marketing." With tricky wording, advertisers try to imply that they are official sponsors of an event. For instance, in the days leading up to the NCAA basketball championships, Kellogg advertised a promotion to send customers to the tournament, even though General Mills was the official NCAA sponsor.**
3. **The Olympic Games is a worldwide, goodwill event that should belong to all. No one should sell the Olympic trademark.**

Summary

Organizers of the Atlanta Olympics heard stinging criticism for disorganization, particularly early in the games. A tragic bombing killed and maimed tourists and badly disrupted the events. But Olympic officials did succeed in keeping a lot of bogus merchandise out of Atlanta. Halfway through the games, organizers happily expressed their pleasure at how few fraudulent goods were being sold. "I think the word is out that you don't want to mess with the Olympic committee," noted Robert E. Hollander, vice president of the Atlanta Centennial Olympic Properties, the joint merchandising business of the Atlanta and U.S. Olympic committees. Ultimately, Olympic cops seized more than 27,000 counterfeit T-shirts, hats, and other paraphernalia on the streets of Atlanta during the games—less than half of the anticipated amount.

Sources: Melissa Turner, "Battle over Olympic T-Shirt Sales," *Atlanta Journal-Constitution,* May 25, 1997, downloaded from http://stacks.ajc.com/, May 27, 1997; Marc Rice, "Olympic Logo Cops Rounding Up Fake Souvenirs," *Atlanta Journal-Constitution,* July 30, 1996, downloaded from http://www.atlantagames.com/, December 15, 1996; Henry Unger, "Officials Seize 27,000 Bogus T-shirts, Hats," *Atlanta Journal-Constitution,* July 26, 1996, downloaded from http://www.atlantagames.com/, December 15, 1996; "What's Making News Today," *Atlanta Journal-Constitution,* May 30, 1996, downloaded from http://www.atlantagames.com/, December 15, 1996; and "Olympics Crack Down on Counterfeiters," *PROMO,* March 1996, p. 10.

1. Protection against damage, spoilage, and pilferage
2. Assistance in marketing the product
3. Cost effectiveness

Protection against Damage, Spoilage, and Pilferage The original objective of packaging was to offer physical protection for the product. Products typically pass through several stages of handling between manufacturing and consumer purchases, and a package must protect the contents from damage. Furthermore, packages of perishable products must protect the contents against spoilage in transit and storage and while awaiting consumer selection. California-based Fresh International Corp. has developed a unique packaging method that allows premade salad to stay fresh for several weeks. The firm's patented packages release carbon dioxide from lettuce, and nitrogen injected into the bags slows down decomposition and keeps the salad ready to eat.[21]

Fears of product tampering have forced many firms to improve package designs. Over-the-counter medicines are sold in tamper-resistant packages covered with warnings that consumers should not purchase products without protective seals intact. Many groceries and light-sensitive products are packaged in tamper-resistant containers. For example, products in glass jars, like spaghetti sauce and jams, often come with depressed buttons in the lids that pop up the first time anyone opens the containers.

Also, many packages offer important safeguards for retailers against pilferage. Customer shoplifting and employee theft cost retailers several billion dollars each year. To limit this activity, many packages feature oversized cardboard backings too large to fit into a shoplifter's pocket or purse. Efficient packaging that protects against damage, spoilage, and theft is especially important for international marketers, who must contend with varying climatic conditions and the added time and stress involved in overseas shipping.

Assistance in Marketing the Product The proliferation of new products, changes in consumer lifestyles and buying habits, and marketers' emphasis on targeting smaller market segments have increased the importance of packaging as a promotional tool. Many firms are addressing consumer concerns about protecting the environment by designing packages with minimal amounts of biodegradable and recyclable materials. To demonstrate serious concern about environmental protection, Procter & Gamble, Coors,

Figure 12.6 Attention-Getting Packaging Designed to Help Market a Product

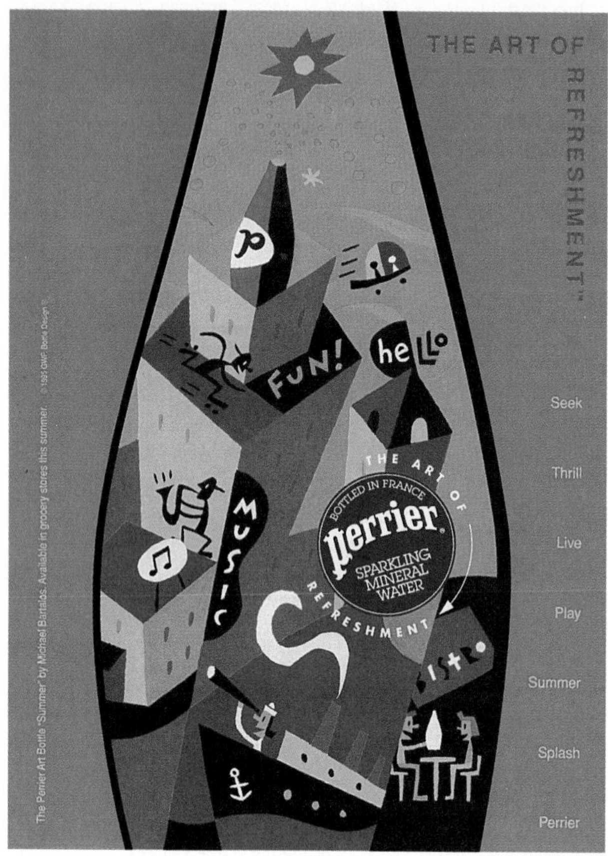
THE ART OF REFRESHMENT™
FUN!
hello
MUSIC
THE ART OF REFRESHMENT
BOTTLED IN FRANCE
Perrier
SPARKLING MINERAL WATER
Seek
Thrill
Live
Play
Summer
Splash
Perrier
The Perrier Art Bottle "Summer" by Michael Bartalos. Available in grocery stores this summer.

McDonald's, Amoco Chemical, and other firms have created ads that describe their efforts to develop environmentally sound packaging.

In a grocery store where thousands of different items compete for notice, a product must capture the shopper's attention. Marketers combine colors, sizes, shapes, graphics, and typefaces to establish distinct identities that set their products apart from those of competitors. Quaker State Corp.'s motor oil was facing increasing competition from Pennzoil and Valvoline as well as private-label motor oils. To help revive sales, Quaker State repackaged its motor oil in bright green bottles intended to catch the eyes of consumers as they walked through stores.[22] Perrier pursued a similar goal to catch the eye and to differentiate its bottled mineral water from competing products through package design. To boost sales during the summer months, Perrier designed a bottle with colorful graphics depicting summer scenes, as shown in Figure 12.6.

Packaging can help to establish a common identity for a group of products sold under a brand name. Luigino's Inc. redesigned the packaging for its Michelina's frozen entrees for this reason. Previously, each entree's package displayed different graphics. A picture of Michelina, the founder's mother, appeared on all packages, but in different locations and varying sizes. Brand managers decided to improve the brand's consistency by creating a uniform look for all of the products. The package design included a new logo and heavy use of the color green to develop brand cohesiveness.[23]

Packages can also enhance convenience for buyers. Pump-dispenser cans facilitate the use of products ranging from mustard to insect repellent. Squeezable bottles of jellies, dessert toppings, and ketchup make the products easier to use and store. Packaging provides a key benefit in convenience foods such as microwaved meals and snacks, juice drinks in aseptic packages, and single-serving portions of frozen entrees and vegetables.

Some firms increase consumer utility with packages designed for reuse. Empty peanut butter jars and jelly jars have long doubled as drinking glasses. Parents can buy bubble bath in animal-shaped plastic bottles suitable for bathtub play. Packaging is a major component in Avon's overall marketing strategy. The firm's decorative, reusable bottles have even become collectibles.

Like the brand name, a package should evoke the product's image and communicate its value. Some companies patent their package designs, which may play crucial roles in consumers' brand insistence. People around the world recognize Coca-Cola's distinctive curved bottle, for example, and the firm plans to make all of its packaging proprietary by 2000. In fact, The Coca-Cola Co. is test-marketing a can design in the shape of the well-recognized glass bottles that it hopes will help its products stand out on retail shelves.[24]

Cost-Effective Packaging Although packaging must perform a number of functions for the producer, marketers, and consumers, it must do so at a reasonable cost. Sometimes changes can make packages both cheaper and better for the environment. Compact-disk manufacturers once packaged CDs in two containers, a disk-sized plastic box inside a long, cardboard box that fit the record bins in stores. Consumers protested against the waste of the long boxes, and finally the recording industry agreed to eliminate the cardboard outer packaging altogether. Now CDs come in just the plastic cases, and stores display them in reusable plastic holders to discourage theft.

Labeling In the past, a label often represented a separate element that was applied to a package; today it is an integral part of a typical package. Labels perform both promotional and informational functions. A **label** carries a product's brand name or symbol, the name and address of the manufacturer or distributor, information about the product's composition and size, and recommended uses for the product. One study showed that consumers finalize 70 percent of their purchase decisions in the store. A label plays an important role in attracting consumer attention and encouraging purchase at this critical point.[25]

Consumer confusion and dissatisfaction over such incomprehensible descriptions as *giant economy size, king size,* and *family size* led to passage of the Fair Packaging and Labeling Act in 1966. The act requires that a label offer adequate information concerning the package contents and that a package design facilitate value comparisons among competing products.

The Nutrition Labeling and Education Act of 1990 imposes a uniform format in which food manufacturers must disclose nutritional information about their products. In addition, the Food and Drug Administration (FDA) has mandated design standards for nutritional labels that provide clear guidelines to consumers about food products. The organization has also tightened definitions for loosely used terms like *light, fat free, lean,* and *extra lean,* and it mandates that labels list the amounts of fat, sodium, dietary fiber, calcium, vitamins, and other components in typical servings.

http://www.fda.gov/

Labeling requirements differ elsewhere in the world. Countries with two common languages may require bilingual labels; in Canada, for example, labels must give information in both French and English. The type and amount of information required on labels also varies among nations. International marketers must carefully design labels to make them conform to the regulations of each country where they sell the products.

Green Labeling Green labeling is a product-related extension of green marketing, as discussed in Chapter 3. Green labeling practices place product seals and environmental claims on packages to designate environmentally safe products. For instance, package labels may describe the packages as recyclable or biodegradable or assert that a product causes less waste than its competitors. One study found that 84 percent of consumers expressed concern about the recyclability, reuse, and overuse of packaging materials.[26]

The U.S. government has noticed the trend and started to regulate these and other environmental claims. The Federal Trade Commission has issued Guides for the Use of Environmental Marketing Claims, a booklet that gives standards for frequently misused terms. Firms that make unsubstantiated or misleading claims on product labels risk fines from the FTC or lawsuits by states whose laws ban deceptive environmental labeling.

Several nations in Europe have developed their own standards for green product labels. The European Union's ecolabel program specifies a standard symbol for products that are manufactured with reduced energy, water, and detergent consumption.

Universal Product Code The **Universal Product Code (UPC)** designation determines another very important aspect of a label or package. Introduced in 1974 as a method for cutting expenses in the supermarket industry, UPCs print numerical bar codes on packages. Optical scanner systems read these codes, and computer systems recognize items and print their prices on cash register receipts. Virtually all packaged grocery items carry the UPC bars. While UPC scanners are costly, they permit both considerable labor savings over manual pricing and improved inventory control. As discussed in Chapter 6, the Universal Product Code is also a major asset for market research.

BRAND EXTENSIONS, BRAND LICENSING, AND CO-BRANDING

Some brands achieve such strong popularity that companies carry them over to unrelated products in pursuit of marketing advantages. The strategy of attaching a popular brand name to a new product in an unrelated product category is known as **brand extension.** Marketers should not confuse this practice with *line extension,* which refers to new sizes, styles, or related products. Brand extension, in contrast, carries over nothing but the brand name. In establishing brand extensions, companies hope to gain access to new customers and markets by building on the equity already established in their brands.

General Mills, for example, introduced a new line of breakfast cereals under the Betty Crocker brand name.

Marketing Dictionary

label The descriptive part of a product's package that lists the brand name or symbol, name and address of manufacturer or distributor, product composition and size, and recommended uses.

Universal Product Code (UPC) A bar code on a product's package that provides information read by optical scanners.

brand extension Application of a popular brand name to a new product in an unrelated product category.

Figure 12.7 Co-Branding by Compaq and Fisher-Price

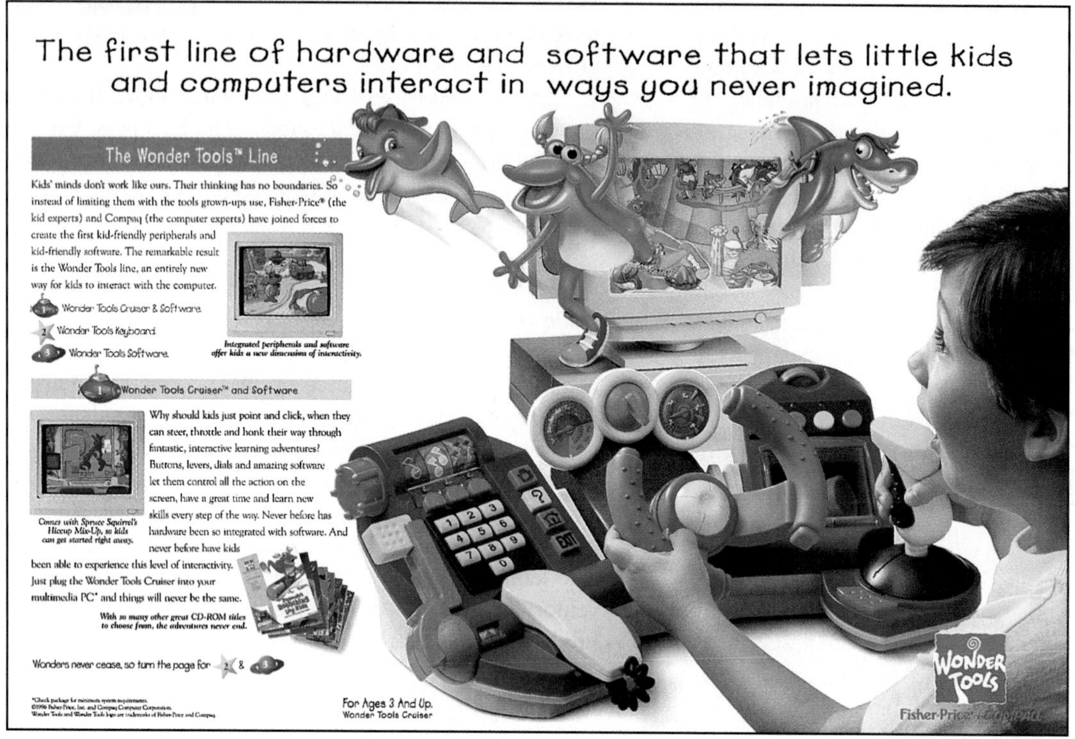
The first line of hardware and software that lets little kids and computers interact in ways you never imagined.
The Wonder Tools™ Line
Kids' minds don't work like ours. Their thinking has no boundaries. So instead of limiting them with the tools grown-ups use, Fisher-Price® (the kid experts) and Compaq (the computer experts) have joined forces to create the first kid-friendly peripherals and kid-friendly software. The remarkable result is the Wonder Tools line, an entirely new way for kids to interact with the computer.
1 Wonder Tools Cruiser & Software
2 Wonder Tools Keyboard
3 Wonder Tools Software
Integrated peripherals and software offer kids a new dimension of interactivity.
1 Wonder Tools Cruiser™ and Software
Why should kids just point and click, when they can steer, throttle and honk their way through fantastic, interactive learning adventures? Buttons, levers, dials and amazing software let them control all the action on the screen, have a great time and learn new skills every step of the way. Never before has hardware been so integrated with software. And never before have kids been able to experience this level of interactivity. Just plug the Wonder Tools Cruiser into your multimedia PC* and things will never be the same.
Comes with Spruce Squirrel's Hiccup Mix-Up, so kids can get started right away.
With so many other great CD-ROM titles to choose from, the adventures never end.
Wonders never cease, so turn the page for 2 & 3
*Check package for minimum system requirements.
©1996 Fisher-Price, Inc. and Compaq Computer Corporation.
Wonder Tools and Wonder Tools logo are trademarks of Fisher-Price and Compaq.
For Ages 3 And Up.
Wonder Tools Cruiser
WONDER TOOLS
Fisher-Price

Although consumers primarily associated the Betty Crocker name with its line of dessert mixes, General Mills has already extended that brand to such diverse products as scalloped potatoes, microwave popcorn, and fruit snacks.[27]

Starbucks Coffee also hopes to grow through brand extensions. Consumers can now buy a line of coffee-flavored ice creams with the Starbucks brand in supermarkets. Starbucks has also teamed up with PepsiCo to launch a bottled cold-coffee drink in the soft-drink sections of supermarkets. Starbucks outlets even offer two jazz CDs under the company's label in its stores.[28]

Brand extensions run considerable risk of brand dilution. **Brand dilution** occurs when a firm introduces too many brand extensions, some of which might not succeed. Scattered marketing programs may erode the firm's brand equity.

Brand Licensing

A growing number of firms are accepting payments from other companies to use the sellers' brand names. This practice, known as **brand licensing,** expands a firm's exposure in the marketplace much as a brand extension does. The brand's owner also receives an extra source of income in the form of royalties from licensees, typically from 4 to 8 percent of wholesale revenues.

Scholastic Books has successfully licensed its *Goosebumps* brand to cover a wide array of products. With 160 children's books in print in the *Goosebumps* series, Scholastic also deals with 44 licensees. Licensed products include a Hasbro Toys board game and Hallmark party goods. The *Goosebumps* logo appears on everything from backpacks and shoes to sheets and flashlights. A popular *Goosebumps* television show adds exposure for all of these products. "*Goosebumps* is a wake-up call for all of us [publishers] to look at all of our books and see how we can expand them into a brand," notes Willa Perlman, the president of Golden Books, a Scholastic competitor.[29]

However, brand experts note several potential problems with licensing. If a licensee produces a poor-quality product or a product ethically incompatible with the original brand, the arrangement could injure the reputation of the brand. For example, if Scholastic were to license the *Goosebumps* name for a cigarette product, the brand's equity would undoubtedly diminish. Moreover, brand names do not transfer well to all products. A *Goosebumps* name plate probably would not help a line of luxury cars to succeed on the market!

Chapter 10 described a practice closely related to brand licensing—co-branding. **Co-branding** joins together two strong brand names, perhaps owned by two different companies, to sell a product. A good example of co-branding is shown in Figure 12.7. Compaq and Fisher-Price have joined together to develop and sell a line of children's computers called *Wonder Tools.* Both brands bring marketing clout to the product. Most parents recognize Fisher-Price as a maker of quality toys. Compaq brings credibility as a computer expert. Combined, the brands create a strong image to attract parents considering buying computers for their children; neither company could match this market strength on its own.

NEW-PRODUCT PLANNING

As its offerings enter the maturity and decline stages of the product life cycle, a firm must add new products to continue to prosper. Regular additions of new products to the firm's line helps to protect it from product obsolescence. For example, Gillette's strategic plan calls for at least 40 percent of sales every five years to come from entirely new products. To meet that goal, Gillette introduces about 20 new products a year.[30]

New products are the lifeblood of any business, and survival depends on a steady flow of new entries. Some new products may implement major technological breakthroughs. Other new products simply extend existing product lines. In other words, a new product is one that either the company or the customer has not handled before. Only about 10 percent of new-product introductions bring truly new capabilities to people who are completely unfamiliar with them.

Figure 12.8 Alternative Product Development Strategies

	Old Product	New Product
Old Market	Market Penetration	Product Development
New Market	Market Development	Product Diversification

Product Development Strategies

A firm's strategy for new-product development varies according to its existing product mix and the match between current offerings and the firm's overall marketing objectives. The current market positions of products also affect product development strategy. Figure 12.8 identifies four alternative development strategies: market penetration, market development, product development, and product diversification.

A *market penetration strategy* seeks to increase sales of existing products in existing markets. Firms can attempt to extend their penetration of markets in several ways. They may modify products, improve product quality, or promote new and different ways to use products. Packaged-goods marketers often pursue this strategy to boost market share for mature products in mature markets. Product positioning often plays a major role in such a strategy.

Product positioning refers to consumers' perceptions of a product's attributes, uses, quality, and advantages and disadvantages relative to competing brands. Marketers conduct market research studies to analyze consumer preferences and construct product positioning maps that plot their products' positions in relation to those of competitors' offerings.

Kraft Foods, Inc. adopted a market penetration strategy for its powdered fruit drink Crystal Light when that product began to move into the maturity stage. The company added water and repackaged the product in plastic bottles, repositioning Crystal Light as a trendy bottled drink. The move propelled Crystal Light sales into a new growth phase. Similarly, Kraft also repositioned its Philadelphia cream

Marketing Dictionary

brand dilution A loss in brand equity that results when a firm introduces too many brand extensions.

brand licensing The practice of allowing other companies to use a brand name in exchange for a payment.

co-branding The practice of combining two strong brands, perhaps owned by different companies, to sell a product.

product positioning Consumers' perceptions of a product's attributes, uses, quality, and advantages and disadvantages in relation to those of competing brands.

MARKETING HALL OF SHAME

Apple: Do the Good Die Young?

Market observers began eulogizing Apple Computer Inc. years ago. Like James Dean, just about everybody claimed, the hippest, most irreverent computer company on earth was going to die young.

Apple Computer sure seemed like a company mangled in a head-on collision. Sales had dropped off dramatically, and the flow of new ideas from some of the smartest technical minds in the business had started drying up. Employees were laid off, and stock value plunged. In perhaps the most alarming whispers for the Silicon Valley legend created by a couple of really smart guys in a garage, people had begun to label Apple "irrelevant."

What went wrong for the makers of what one *Newsweek* writer called the nation's "smoothest, cleverest, and most engaging computer system"? Plenty. For starters, Apple's vaunted, image-making machine failed to successfully convey the company's most critical message: Apple computers were great products!

This ironic lapse contrasts with one of the most vivid images many people recall about Apple: the famous and spectacularly successful television ad it ran just once in 1984. To introduce its new Macintosh line, Apple paid $1.6 million to run a 60-second commercial during the 1984 Super Bowl. In the stunning ad, a marathon runner bursts into an auditorium of drab corporate drones, who are watching their leader—patterned after George Orwell's Big Brother—on a giant screen. The heroine smashes the screen to symbolically save computer users from the dominance of clunky, cumbersome IBM personal computers.

The Macintosh of 1984 offered a different product to the market. It was so ridiculously easy to use that it became the computer of choice in schools. The computer's revolutionary graphics capabilities made it an indispensable tool for such visually oriented jobs as desktop publishing. Also, the Macintosh introduced the now ubiquitous mouse, which even a three-year-old could point and click to control the computer, saving people from typing confusing, coded commands.

Time and time again, however, markets have shown that a company needs more than the best product to win the business wars. In Apple's case, the Silicon Valley legend was blind-sided by Bill Gates and Microsoft. In the late

cheese. The company wanted consumers to think of the product as a spread for more than bagels. Kraft launched an easily spreadable cream cheese called Philly for Toast! and promoted it as a topping for toast in television ads.[31]

A *market development strategy* concentrates on finding new markets for existing products. Market segmentation, discussed in Chapter 7, provides a useful support for such an effort. For example, The Country's Best Yogurt (TCBY) began looking for new markets for its frozen yogurt. It found an attractive one in China. Research showed that the Chinese had a growing appetite for frozen desserts, eating over 1 million tons of ice cream a year. They also preferred American dessert products, but available choices from McDonald's and Baskin Robbins were too expensive for local tastes. TCBY successfully introduced its frozen yogurt as a less expensive alternative, adapting the product somewhat for Chinese taste preferences.[32]

Briefly speaking

"In every instance, we found that the best-run companies stay as close to their customers as humanly possible."

Thomas J. Peters (1942–)
American business writer

The strategy of *product development* refers to the introduction of new products into identifiable or established markets. Seeking new growth in the computer industry beyond its familiar products of operating systems and applications programs, Microsoft launched the Internet access service Microsoft Network (MSN). Microsoft hopes that MSN will outcompete rivals AOL and CompuServe by offering unique entertainment and information content. MSN will also give Microsoft a format for showcasing its Internet browser and other new software products.[33]

In some cases, firms choose to introduce new products into markets in which they have already established positions to try to increase overall market share. These new offerings are called *flanker brands.* Miller Brewing Company has relied on this strategy to increase its share of the beer market. The company has added several new beer brands, including Red Dog, to a product mix that already includes the firm's flagship beer, Miller Genuine Draft.[34]

1980s, Apple Chairman John Sculley resisted steps to increase the company's market share in relation to that of the IBM PC. He refused to lower the prices of the costlier Macintoshes, and he wouldn't license the Mac operating system so other companies could produce low-cost clones. When Apple finally licensed its technology, the gesture seemed a case of too little, too late.

Worst of all, Apple lost its edge with customers. While many people still swear by their Macs, even loyal fans hesitate to buy new ones when the vast majority of software development projects highlight Microsoft Windows-based computers.

Not long ago, industry insiders were predicting that Apple would have to liquidate or become part of a much bigger player. Now these same experts talk more optimistically about the company's chances, but a great deal of skepticism remains. Apple cannot avoid locking horns with Microsoft, which has displayed an amazing ability to market wildly successful products and quickly change directions.

Apple sees its salvation in a new computer operating system—the software that controls interactions between a computer's parts—that would make Microsoft Windows obsolete. Software needs a dramatic redesign to keep up with the demands of ever more powerful computers and rivers of data from the Internet, says Gilbert Amelio, the former National Semiconductor chief hired to engineer an Apple comeback. When in-house development efforts ran into problems, Apple looked elsewhere for operating system technology. It acquired Next Software, a company formed by Apple founder Steve Jobs, whose operating system had the desired features.

"One day everything Bill Gates has sold you up to now, whether it's Windows 95 or Windows 97, will become obsolete," Amelio predicts. "Gates is vulnerable at that point. And we want to make sure we're ready to come forward with a superior answer."

"Apple's survival is no longer in question," Amelio insists. "The issue now is, how exciting is it going to be? How exciting can we make it?"

QUESTIONS FOR CRITICAL THINKING

1. **What do you consider Apple's worst mistake? Why?**
2. **Do you think Gilbert Amelio's optimism is warranted? Can a new Apple operating system save the company?**

Sources: Peter Burrows, "The Soul of a New Machine: Too Little, Too Late," *Business Week*, January 13, 1997, p. 37, Nikhil Hutheesing, "David Amelio versus Goliath Gates," *Forbes*, December 16, 1996, pp. 228–233; Eric J. Savitz, "Apple Lovefest," *Barron's Online*, August 12, 1996, downloaded from http://www.barrons.com/, December 10, 1996; Kathy Rebello, "The Fall of an American Icon," *Business Week*, February 5, 1996, pp. 34–41; and Steven Levy, "How Apple Became Avis," *Newsweek*. August 21, 1995, p. 42.

Finally, a *product diversification* strategy focuses on developing entirely new products for new markets. Some firms look for new target markets that complement their existing markets; others look in completely new directions. Procter & Gamble, for example, established its identity as a maker of such household products as soap, toothpaste, and detergent. Now, P&G is trying to capture a share of the growing prescription drug market. P&G recently received FDA approval on a product called *Helidac Therapy* that eliminates the bacteria that cause stomach ulcers. The project to diversify into prescription drugs exposes P&G to high risk. Industry analysts note that most drug manufacturers spend an average of 12 years and $360 million to get a new product on the market. Plus, P&G's experience lies in selling to and through retailers, not doctors. Why would the packaged-goods giant bother to look for a new market? Pharmaceuticals enticed P&G with a far greater potential payoff than it could expect in any other area where it does business, explains one analyst.[35]

The important consideration of **cannibalization** influences a firm's choice of a new-product strategy. Any firm wants to avoid investing resources in a new-product introduction that will adversely affect sales of existing products. A product that takes sales from another offering in the same product line is said to *cannibalize* that line. While a firm can accept some sacrifice when a promising new product takes some sales from existing, related products, market research should ensure that the new offering will guarantee sufficient additional sales to warrant the firm's investment in its development and market introduction.

Marketing Dictionary

cannibalization A loss of sales of a current product due to competition from a new product in the same line.

Figure 12.9 Stimulating Sales with Samples during the Trial Stage of Adoption

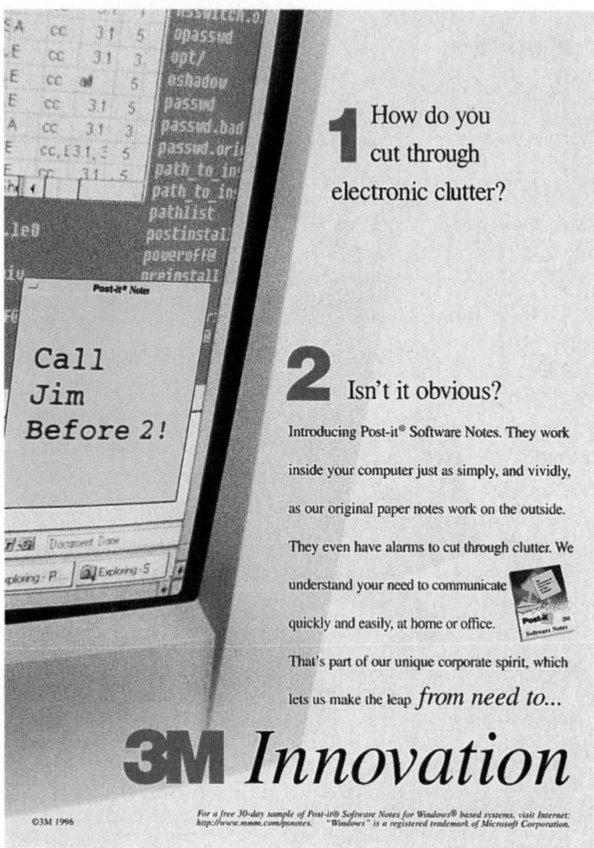
1 How do you cut through electronic clutter?
Call Jim Before 2!
2 Isn't it obvious?
Introducing Post-it® Software Notes. They work inside your computer just as simply, and vividly, as our original paper notes work on the outside. They even have alarms to cut through clutter. We understand your need to communicate quickly and easily, at home or office. That's part of our unique corporate spirit, which lets us make the leap *from need to...*
3M *Innovation*
©3M 1996
For a free 30-day sample of Post-it® Software Notes for Windows® based systems, visit Internet: http://www.mmm.com/psnotes. "Windows" is a registered trademark of Microsoft Corporation.

The Consumer Adoption Process

Consumers' purchases also influence decisions about a new-product offering. In the **adoption process,** potential consumers go through a series of stages from learning of the new product to trying it and finally to deciding whether to purchase it regularly or to reject it. These stages in the consumer adoption process can be classified as:

1. *Awareness.* Individuals first learn of the new product, but they lack full information about it.
2. *Interest.* Potential buyers begin to seek information about it.
3. *Evaluation.* They consider the likely benefits of the product.
4. *Trial.* They make trial purchases to determine its usefulness.
5. *Adoption/Rejection.* If the trial purchase produces satisfactory results, they decide to use the product regularly.[36]

The marketing manager must understand the adoption process in order to move potential consumers to the adoption stage. Once marketers recognize a large number of consumers at the interest stage, they can take steps to stimulate sales by moving these buyers through the evaluation and trial stages. For example, Johnson & Johnson enhanced the evaluation and trial of its disposable contact lenses by offering free trial pairs to consumers. Similarly, when 3M Company first introduced Post-it Notes, it mailed samples to secretaries at Fortune 500 companies.[37] In a later introduction, 3M also offered free 30-day samples of its new high-tech notes program for computers, the Post-it Software Notes shown in Figure 12.9.

http://www.3m.com/

Adopter Categories

Consumer innovators are people who purchase new products almost as soon as they reach the market. Other adopters wait for additional information and rely on the experiences of initial buyers before making trial purchases. Consumer innovators welcome innovations in each product area. Some computer users hurried to install Windows 97 immediately after its introduction. Some physicians pioneered use of new pharmaceutical products for their AIDS patients. Some fans bought the first season tickets to Jacksonville Jaguars games.

A number of studies about the adoption of new products have identified five categories of purchasers based on relative times of adoption. These categories, shown in Figure 12.10, are consumer innovators, early adopters, early majority, late majority, and laggards.

The **diffusion process** brings acceptance of new goods and services by the members of the community or social system. Figure 12.10 shows a normal distribution over the course of this process. A few people adopt at first, then the number of adopters increases rapidly as the value of the innovation becomes apparent. The adoption rate finally diminishes as the number of potential consumers remaining in the nonadopter category diminishes.

Since the categories are based on a normal distribution, marketers can apply standard deviations to quantify them. Innovators make up the first 2.5 percent of buyers to adopt the new product; laggards are the last 16 percent to do so. Figure 12.10 excludes nonadopters—those who never the adopt the innovation.

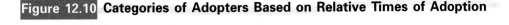

Figure 12.10 Categories of Adopters Based on Relative Times of Adoption

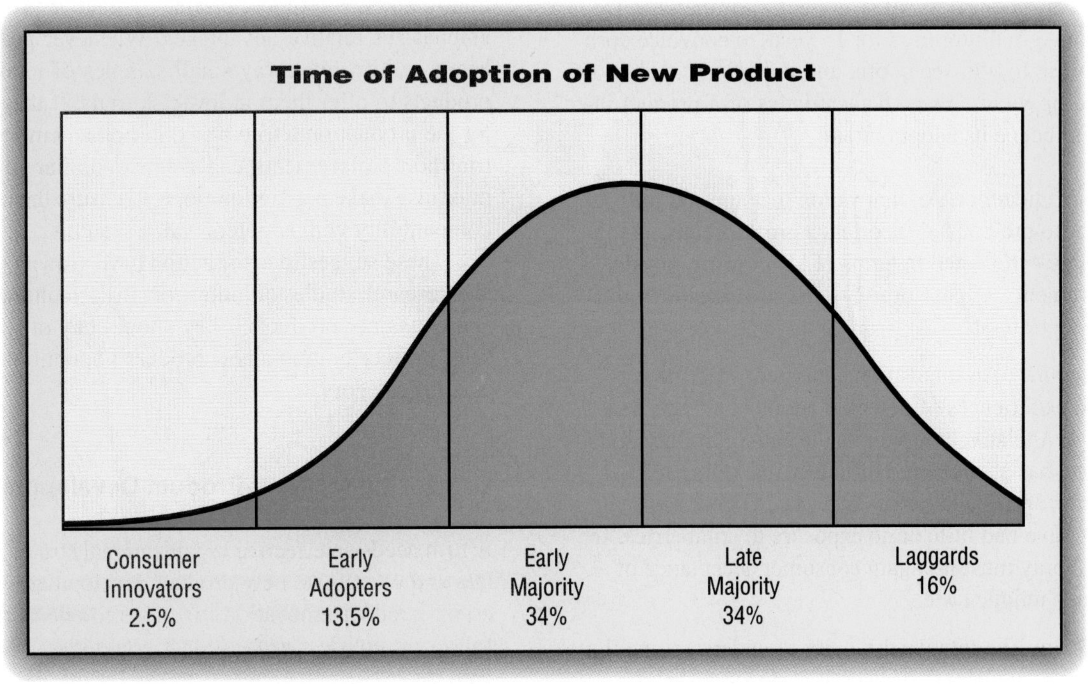

Time of Adoption of New Product
Consumer Innovators 2.5%
Early Adopters 13.5%
Early Majority 34%
Late Majority 34%
Laggards 16%

Identifying Early Adopters Marketers foresee substantial benefits if they can locate the likely first buyers of new products (those in the consumer innovator and early adopter categories). By reaching these buyers early in the product's development or introduction, marketers can treat them as a test market, evaluating the product and discovering suggestions for modifications. Since early purchasers often act as opinion leaders from whom others seek advice, their attitudes toward new products quickly spread to others. Acceptance or rejection of the innovation by these purchasers can help forecast its expected success.

An effort to find and target early adopters in the agricultural industry helped Applied Microbiology to successfully launch a new product, Wipe Out antimicrobial towelettes. Dairy farmers must disinfect cows' teats before milking, but they found it a messy job when they had to dip each cow's teat into a bucket of antimicrobial disinfectant. Wipe Out promised to simplify the process by placing the disinfectant on a towelette similar to a baby wipe that farmers could throw away after each use. Applied Microbiology knew, however, that dairy farmers sometimes resist change. Therefore, the firm set out to identify the dairy farmers most likely to adopt innovations through the use of geodemographics research. Applied Microbiology then mailed samples of Wipe Out to these potential customers that seemed most likely to try the new product.[38]

Unfortunately, first adopters of one new product may follow the pack in adopting other products. A large number of research studies have, however, established some general characteristics of first adopters. These pioneers tend to be younger, have higher social status, be better educated, and enjoy higher incomes than other consumers. They are more mobile than later adopters and change both their jobs and home addresses more often. They also rely more heavily than later adopters on impersonal information sources; more hesitant buyers depend more on company-generated promotional information and word-of-mouth communications.

Marketing Dictionary

adoption process A series of stages through which consumers decide whether or not to become regular users of a new product, including awareness, interest, evaluation, trial, and rejection or adoption.

consumer innovator An initial purchaser of a new product.

diffusion process The sequence of acceptance of new products by the members of a community or social system.

Rate of Adoption Determinants Frisbees progressed from the product introduction stage to the market maturity stage in a period of six months. By contrast, the U.S. Department of Agriculture tried for 13 years to convince corn farmers to use hybrid seed corn, an innovation capable of doubling crop yields. Five characteristics of a product innovation influence its adoption rate:

1. *Relative advantage.* An innovation that appears far superior to previous ideas offers a greater relative advantage—reflected in terms of lower price, physical improvements, or ease of use—and increases the product's adoption rate.
2. *Compatibility.* An innovation consistent with the values and experiences of potential adopters attracts new buyers at a relatively rapid rate. Ocean Spray Inc., for example, has encountered difficulty marketing its cranberry drinks and sauces overseas. Global consumers have had little or no exposure to cranberries, so Ocean Spray must first gain consumer acceptance of the fruit's unique taste.[39]
3. *Complexity.* The relative difficulty of understanding the innovation influences speed of acceptance. In most cases, consumers move slowly in adopting new products that they find difficult to understand or use. Farmers' cautious acceptance of hybrid seed corn illustrates how long adoption can take.
4. *Possibility of trial use.* An innovation that allows limited initial use may meet with early approval. First adopters face two types of risk—financial loss and ridicule from others—if they rush to welcome a new product that provides unsatisfactory service in full. The option of limited sampling reduces these risks and generally accelerates the rate of an innovation's adoption. Donna Karan Beauty Co. recognized the importance of trial usage in promoting acceptance of its Formula line of skin-care products. The company spent close to $5 million on conversion kits, each one containing a month's supply of the products. The company gave away the kits at major department stores in the belief that consumers who tried the products would recognize their benefits.[40]
5. *Observability.* If other consumers can observe the results of initial adopters' use of a product, they may relatively quickly develop interest in it. If early buyers display an innovation's superiority in a tangible form, the adoption rate increases. Applied Microbiology solicited testimonials from early adopters of Wipe Out and incorporated them into promotional activities. The firm even plans to mail new samples to neighbors of the farmers who have already bought Wipe Out.[41]

Marketers who want to accelerate the rate of adoption can manipulate these five characteristics to some extent. Informative promotional messages help to overcome hesitation to adopt a complex product. Effective product design emphasizes relative advantages. Whenever possible, marketers sell or give away small samples of innovative new products to offer them in low-risk trials. If they cannot offer the product on a trial basis, in-home demonstrations or trial home placements can achieve similar results. They must also make positive attempts to ensure the innovation's compatibility with adopters' value systems.

These suggestions for action have grown out of extensive research studies of innovators in agriculture, medicine, and consumer products. They should pay off in increased sales by accelerating a new product's adoption rate in each adopter category.

Organizing for New-Product Development

A firm needs an effective organizational structure to stimulate and coordinate new-product development. Most firms assign product-innovation functions to one or more of the following entities: new-product committees, new-product departments, product managers, and venture teams.

Figure 12.11 Advertising: A Responsibility of Pontiac Sunfire's Product Manager

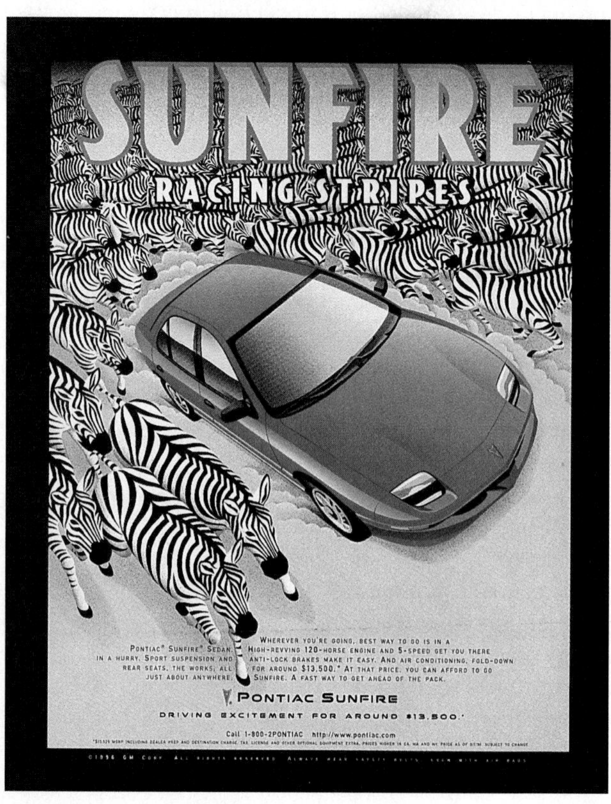
SUNFIRE
RACING STRIPES
WHEREVER YOU'RE GOING, BEST WAY TO GO IS IN A PONTIAC® SUNFIRE® SEDAN. HIGH-REVVING 120-HORSE ENGINE AND 5-SPEED GET YOU THERE IN A HURRY. SPORT SUSPENSION AND ANTI-LOCK BRAKES MAKE IT EASY. AND AIR CONDITIONING, FOLD-DOWN REAR SEATS, THE WORKS, ALL FOR AROUND $13,500.* AT THAT PRICE, YOU CAN AFFORD TO GO JUST ABOUT ANYWHERE. SUNFIRE. A FAST WAY TO GET AHEAD OF THE PACK.
PONTIAC SUNFIRE
DRIVING EXCITEMENT FOR AROUND $13,500.*
Call 1-800-2PONTIAC http://www.pontiac.com

New-Product Committees The most common organizational arrangement for activities to develop a new product centers these functions in a new-product committee. This group typically brings together representatives of top management in such areas as marketing, finance, manufacturing, engineering, research, and accounting. Committee members spend less time conceiving and developing their own new product ideas than reviewing and approving new-product plans that arise elsewhere in the organization. Publishing houses, for instance, often pass ideas for new book projects through editorial review committees that must approve before editors can begin working with authors.

Since members of a new product committee help key posts in the firm's functional areas, their support for any new-product plan likely foreshadows approval for further development. However, new-product committees tend to reach decisions slowly and maintain conservative views. Sometimes members may compromise so they can return to their regular responsibilities.

New-Product Departments Many companies establish separate, formally organized departments to generate and refine new-product ideas. The departmental structure overcomes the limitations of the new-product committee system and encourages innovation as a permanent, full-time activity. The new-product department is responsible for all phases of a development project within the firm, including screening decisions, developing product specifications, and coordinating product testing. The head of the department wields substantial authority and typically reports to the chief executive officer, chief operating officer, or a top marketing officer.

Product Managers **Product manager** is another term for brand manager, a function mentioned earlier in the chapter. This marketing professional determines the objectives and marketing strategies for an individual product or product line. Procter & Gamble assigned its first product manager in 1927, when it made one person responsible for Camay soap. The product manager concept has spread to such marketers as General Foods, Pillsbury, Bristol-Myers, Gillette, and Quaker Oats.

Product managers set prices, develop advertising and sales promotion programs, and work with sales representatives in the field. For example, the product manager for GM's Pontiac Sunfire controlled development and production of the ad shown in Figure 12.11. In a company that markets multiple products, product managers fulfill key functions in the marketing department. They provide individual attention for each product and support and coordinate efforts of the firm's sales force, market research department, and advertising department. Product managers often lead new-product development programs, including creation of new-product ideas and recommendations for improving existing products.

In recent years, advocates of the product management system have modified it to deal with environmental changes. The system was developed to mass market leading brands to large segments of consumers with similar tastes but the increasing fragmentation of the mass market into smaller segments has forced firms to rethink product management. Several firms, including Procter & Gamble, have assigned product managers to work in teams made up of research, manufacturing, and sales managers.

Venture Teams A **venture team** gathers a group of specialists from different areas of an organization to work together developing new products. The venture team must meet criteria for return on investment, uniqueness of product, serving a well-defined need, compatibility of the product with existing technology, and strength of patent protection. Although the organization sets up the venture team as a temporary entity, its flexible life span may extend over a number of years. When purchases confirm the commercial potential of a new product, an existing division may take responsibility for it, or it may serve as the nucleus of a new division within the company or of an entirely new company.

Some marketing organizations differentiate between venture teams and task forces. A new-product **task force** assembles an interdisciplinary group working on temporary assignment through their functional departments. Its basic activities center on coordinating and integrating the work of the firm's functional departments on a specific project.

Unlike a new-product committee, a venture team does not disband after every meeting. Team members accept project assignments as major responsibilities, and the team exercises the authority it needs to both plan and implement a course of action. To stimulate product innovation, the venture team typically communicates directly with top management, but it functions as an entity separate from the

Marketing Dictionary

product manager A marketing professional who determines the objectives and marketing strategies for an individual product or product line.

venture team A new-product development organization that brings together specialists from different functional areas.

task force An interdisciplinary group on temporary assignment to work through functional departments in examining new-product issues.

basic organization. IBM formed a venture team to develop the company's first personal computer. Other firms that have created venture teams include Monsanto, Xerox, Exxon, and Motorola.

THE NEW-PRODUCT DEVELOPMENT PROCESS

Once the firm has defined its organization for new-product development, it can establish procedures for moving new-product ideas to the marketplace. Developing a new product requires a time-consuming, risky, and expensive project. Firms must generate dozens of new-product ideas to produce even one successful product. But most new products do not achieve success in the market. The alarmingly high failure rate of new products averages 80 percent. Firms invest nearly half of the total resources devoted to product innovation on products that become commercial failures. Products fail for a number of reasons, including inadequate market assessments, lack of market orientation, poor screening and project evaluation, product defects, and inadequate launch efforts.

Effective management of the development process increases the likelihood of a new product's success. An essential contribution to new-product success comes from a six-step development process: (1) idea generation, (2) screening, (3) business analysis, (4) development, (5) test marketing, and (6) commercialization. At each step, management faces a continuing choice between abandoning the project, continuing to the next step, or seeking additional information before proceeding further. In most cases, each stage of the process costs more than the previous one and constant evaluation is necessary to avoid investing in what could be a financial disaster for a firm.

Briefly speaking

"Because its purpose is to create a customer, the business has two—and only two—basic functions: marketing and innovation. Marketing and innovation produce results; all the rest are 'costs.'"

Peter Drucker (1909–)
American business writer

Traditionally, most companies have developed new products through **phased development,** a sequential pattern for refining a product concept in an orderly series of steps. Responsibility for each phase passes from product planners to designers and engineers, then to manufacturers, and finally to marketers. The phased development method can work well for firms that dominate mature markets and develop variations on existing products.

However, firms in many markets feel pressured to speed up the development process to keep pace with rapidly changing technologies, shifts in consumer preferences, or competitive pressures. In the electronics industry, for example, a new product that reaches its market just nine months late can sacrifice half of its potential revenue.

This time pressure has encouraged many firms to implement **parallel product development** programs. These innovators assign teams with representatives from design, manufacturing, marketing, sales, and service to carry out development projects from idea generation to commercialization. Venture teams, discussed earlier, follow this parallel development model. This method can reduce the time needed to develop products, because team members work on the six steps concurrently rather than in sequence.

Whether a firm pursues phased development or parallel product development, all phases can benefit from planning tools and scheduling methods such as the program evaluation and review technique (PERT) and the critical path method (CPM). These techniques, originally developed by the U.S. Navy in connection with construction of the Polaris missile and submarine, map out the sequence of each step in a process and show the time allotments for each activity. Detailed PERT and CPM flowcharts help marketers to coordinate all activities entailed in the development and introduction of new products.

Idea Generation

New-product development begins with ideas from many sources: the sales force, customers who write letters asking "Why don't you . . . ," employees, research and development specialists, competing products, suppliers, retailers, and independent inventors. Consumer feedback is an important source of many new-product ideas. In 1987, for example, the Centers for Disease Control advised medical personnel to begin wearing latex gloves during patient procedures as protection against AIDS infection. Large medical-supply firms such as Johnson & Johnson and Baxter Healthcare immediately began stepping up production of their medical latex gloves. A small, upstart San Diego company, Safeskin Corp., took a different path. The company asked health-care workers about the problems they encountered wearing latex gloves ten hours a day. The firm learned that health-care workers were experiencing allergic reactions and dermatitis in reaction to the latex. Based on that information, Safeskin developed a disposable latex glove that prevented the problems that bothered health-care workers. By 1996, Safeskin earned over $150 million from the innovative gloves.[42]

Screening

The critical stage of screening separates ideas with commercial potential from those that cannot meet company objectives. Some organizations maintain checklists of development standards to determine whether a project should abandon an idea or consider it further. These checklists typically include such factors as product uniqueness, availability of raw materials, and the proposed product's compatibility with current product offerings, existing facilities, and present capabilities. The screening stage may also allow for open discussions of new-product ideas among representatives of different functional areas in the organization.

New-product screening can require complex analysis when a firm serves global markets. For example, Nestlé Corp. wanted to add new ice cream products to its product mix. Staff members in each of Nestlé's geographic market areas received assignments to evaluate potential ice cream sales as well as competitors' activities and products in their countries.[43] Based on that information, Nestlé subsequently decided country-by-country whether to add the new ice cream products.

Business Analysis

A product idea that survives the initial screening must then pass a thorough business analysis. The analysis at this stage assesses the new product's potential market, growth rate, and likely competitive strengths. Marketers must evaluate the compatibility of the proposed product with such company resources as financial support for necessary promotion, production capabilities, and distribution facilities.

Concept testing subjects the product idea to additional study prior to its actual development. This important aspect of a new product's business analysis represents a market research project that attempts to measure consumer attitudes and perceptions about the new-product idea. Focus groups and in-store polling can contribute effectively to concept testing.

The screening and business analysis stages generate extremely important information for new-product development, because they (1) define the proposed product's target market and customers' needs and wants and (2) determine the product's financial and technical requirements. Several studies indicate that firms that invest relatively large amounts of time and money in predevelopment activities have enjoyed unusually high rates of product success, low numbers of mistakes, and short product development times.[44]

Edmark, for example, completed a careful business analysis before deciding to develop and introduce a line of mass-market educational software. This relatively obscure firm marketed reading products and workbooks to the school market. Edmark executives realized that the company could grow only if it extended its business beyond selling to teachers and moved into the mass market. In the early 1990s, educational software seemed like an ideal opportunity. Skyrocketing home PC sales combined with few early childhood software titles on the consumer market.

Edmark had to consider several priorities before beginning product development, however. The company would have to hire a team of top-notch programmers capable of producing a winning product. Hiring the team would boost payroll by 20 percent, a difficult decision for a small company already wrestling with cash-flow problems. Once the programmers completed development of the proposed software products, nothing guaranteed that the packages would generate adequate returns on the company's investment. Edmark's executives and board of directors weighed the opportunity and decided that potential rewards justified the risk. The company hired the programmers and entrusted them with the job of developing a top-quality educational software product within six months.[45]

Development

Financial outlays increase substantially as a firm converts a product idea into a physical product. The conversion process is the joint responsibility of the firm's development engineers, who turn the original concept into a product, and its marketers, who provide feedback on consumer reactions to the product design, package, color, and other physical features. Prototypes may go through numerous changes before the original mock-up reaches the stage of a final product.

Many firms implement computer-aided design systems to reduce the number of prototypes that developers must build, thus streamlining the development stage. Interacting with computer-aided design workstations, Rubbermaid developers go from rough sketches to finished products in just a few weeks. The process used to take several

Marketing Dictionary

phased development A sequential pattern for product development through an orderly series of steps.

parallel product development A project-management effort based on teams of design, manufacturing, marketing, sales, and service people who carry out the development process from idea generation to commercialization.

concept testing An initiative to measure consumer attitudes and perceptions of a product idea prior to actual development.

months. This boost in speed provides a crucial competitive advantage for the company, since it can respond more quickly than competitors to new market opportunities.[46]

Consider Palm Computing's experience in developing its new Pilot personal digital assistant. A personal digital assistant, or PDA, is a handheld computer that can store names, addresses, telephone numbers, and other data.

http://www.palm.com/

Guided by focus group research, Palm established a goal of creating a simple PDA with considerably less bulk than current market entries. More importantly, focus groups revealed that potential customers didn't want to pay a lot for a PDA.

Palm knew that it could devote only limited resources to the project. The relatively small company had a budget of only $3 million available for development and introduction. Palm managers also knew that the company didn't have all the technical capabilities it would need to design the product. However, executives saw a viable market for the product that competitors had not yet tapped. They assembled a team of six companies to support product development, including product designers, engineers, programmers, and marketers.

Within eight months, Palm's new PDA started to take shape. Development modified some of the original concepts for the product and kept others. The writing tool alone went through dozens of concepts until the design team settled on one.

Problems then arose with the microprocessor design. Worse, the cost of design and testing had eaten up Palm's financial resources. Palm began looking for financial support, finally selling to US Robotics (recently acquired by 3Com Corp.), which saw promise in the new product.[47] The new owner launched Pilot with an advertising campaign that highlighted its small size, as shown in Figure 12.12.

pilot
U.S.Robotics
Think of it as the most important part of your PC, to go.
Presenting Pilot, the easy way to take the important personal info that's on your PC with you wherever you go.
Enter addresses, phone numbers, and appointments just once — on your Pilot or your PC. Then drop Pilot into its cradle and press the HotSync™ button. That's all it takes to keep your Pilot and PC in sync.
pilot™
Pilot comes complete with its own desktop personal information manager, plus everything you need to be up and running in minutes. It's also compatible with the Windows software you're currently using for personal information management, including Lotus Organizer, Schedule+, Now Up-to-Date, and Sidekick.* And at only 4.5" tall, 5.5 oz, and $299, it fits any pocket *and* pocketbook. To learn where to get one, call 1-800-881-7256. To arrange a demo, go to our web site, http://www.usr.com/palm.
Now available at Circuit City, CompUSA, Computer City, Egghead, Office Depot, OfficeMax and Staples
U.S.Robotics

Figure 12.12 Converting an Idea into a Product

Test Marketing

To gauge consumer reactions to a product under normal conditions, many firms test market their new product offerings. Up to this point, a product development team has obtained consumer information by submitting free products to consumers, who then give their reactions. Other information may come from shoppers' evaluations of competing products. Test marketing is the first stage at which the product must perform in a real-life business environment.

Test marketing introduces a trial version of a new product supported by a complete marketing campaign to a selected city or television coverage area with a population reasonably typical of the total market. A carefully designed and controlled test induces consumers in the test market city to respond naturally to the new offering without knowing about a test. After the test has been under way for a few months and sales and market share in the test market city have been calculated, marketers can estimate the product's likely performance in a full-scale introduction.

In selecting a test market location, marketers look for an area with a manageable size. In addition, its residents should share with the overall population such characteristics as age, education, and income. Finally, self-contained media in the location allow marketers to direct promotional efforts to people who represent the target market of the test-marketed product.

For example, after spending over $20 million on development, Campbell Soup Co. decided to test market its new line of frozen foods designed to meet the specific nutritional needs of medical patients. The firm planned to sell the meals through direct mail, relying heavily on doctor recommendations for promotion. For an initial test market,

Campbell chose Ohio for two reasons. The state accounts for 4 percent of the U.S. population and many residents fit the profile of Campbell's target market: aging baby boomers concerned about their health.[48]

Some firms omit test marketing and move directly from product development to full-scale production. These companies cite four problems with test marketing:

1. Test marketing is expensive. A firm can spend more than $1 million to complete the 12-month to 18-month process, depending on the size of the test market city and the cost of buying media to advertise the product.
2. Competitors who learn about the test marketing project may disrupt its findings. They can skew results by reducing the prices of their own products in the area, distributing cents-off coupons, installing attractive in-store displays, or boosting discounts to retailers to induce them to display more of the competitors' products.
3. Few firms test market long-lived, durable goods due to the major financial investments required for their development, the need to establish networks of dealers to distribute the products, and requirements for parts and servicing.
4. Test marketing a new product communicates company plans to competitors prior to full-scale introduction.

Companies that decide to skip the test marketing process can choose several other options. A firm may simulate a test marketing campaign through computer modeling software. By plugging in data on similar products, it can turn small amounts of information into a sales projection for a new product. Another firm may offer an item in just one region of the United States, adjusting promotions and advertising based on local results before going to other geographical regions. Another option may limit a product's introduction to just one retail chain to help the producing company's marketers carefully control and evaluate promotions and results. In still another method, a firm may try out a new product in another country before marketing it in the United States or worldwide.

Commercialization

The few product ideas that survive all the steps in the development process emerge ready for full-scale marketing. Commercialization of a major new product can expose the firm to substantial expenses. It must establish marketing programs, fund outlays for production facilities, and acquaint the sales force, marketing intermediaries, and potential customers with the new product.

Remember Edmark? The company's team of programmers developed two programs in six months to launch the firm's foray into educational software. The products were Millie's Math House, designed to teach math to children four to eight years old, and KidDesk, which prevented children from accessing their parents' computer files. After the expense of paying for development, Edmark had almost no money left for advertising and promotion. The firm managed to get the two products reviewed positively in publications read by potential buyers. The products won several industry awards for excellence. Parents and children who tried the programs loved them and told their friends.

http://www.edmark.com/

As Edmark soon learned, however, a superior product alone does not ensure market success. Edmark's limited budget didn't allow the firm to promote the product to retailers. Competitors backed their programs with large retail promotion budgets that Edmark couldn't match. As a result, KidDesk and Millie's Math House gained only limited distribution. The products posted dismal initial sales when customers couldn't find them in stores.

Edmark realized that it had missed an important step in commercializing the products. The firm had focused on designing a product that met end-user needs while overlooking customers between it and final users: retailers. Edmark returned to the drawing board and developed a marketing plan that would get the products on the shelves in large stores like CompUSA.[49]

PRODUCT SAFETY AND LIABILITY

A product can fulfill its mission of satisfying consumer needs only if it ensures safe operation. Manufacturers must design their products to protect users from harm. Products

Marketing Dictionary

test marketing A trial introduction of a new product supported by a complete marketing campaign to a selected city or television coverage area typical of the total market.

MARKETING HALL OF FAME

The King of Clubs

To many people, gray-haired Ely Callaway looks like a 77-year-old grandfather. But to weekend duffers everywhere, Callaway is a golf guru—a veritable king of clubs. He's surely a visionary, who built a golfing empire at an age when most men are thinking about retiring.

After spending much of his professional life running a major textiles corporation, Callaway ditched his career for pursuits that certainly promised more fun. He bought a chunk of desert in Southern California to start a winery. After selling the wine business for a tidy profit, he had plenty of time to play golf. One day, he discovered a golf club he loved. When he learned the company was struggling, he bought out its owners.

Renamed Callaway Golf, the re-energized company soon positioned itself as the market's top maker of premium metal clubs. Its Big Bertha drivers made an instant hit with golfers who had spent years trying to shave a stroke or two off their scores. More importantly, the clubs found users among professional golfers seeking a competitive edge. The revolutionary clubs' odd-looking, oversized appearance did not disguise their critical design difference: a "sweet spot" that allows golfers to hit the ball much better than they could with competing clubs.

The new clubs made a hit on Wall Street, too. Since 1992, when the company went public, its revenues have jumped from $132 million to $553 million. During that time, the stock has split three times. With all its success, the company continues to embrace innovation. "Callaway is the leading participant in the golf industry and continues to reinvent itself with new and exciting products," observes Hayley Kissel, an analyst with Merrill Lynch.

Before Callaway became a driving force in its market, the golfing business was a rather sleepy industry. Such names as Hogan, Wilson, and MacGregor dominated the field, but these hallowed companies soon found themselves standing at the first tee as upstarts like Callaway revolutionized the game.

Why did Callaway succeed while the veterans faded? "It's very simple," Callaway explains. "Our product is clearly more satisfying to the user than anybody else's. To do this you've got to stick your neck out and gamble. Fortunately, this is an industry where most of the others won't do it." The company refuses to bring out a new product until its professional staff and experts—including Callaway himself—have thoroughly tested it.

that lead to injuries, either directly or indirectly, can have disastrous consequences for their makers. **Product liability** refers to the responsibility of manufacturers and marketers for injuries and damages caused by their products. As discussed earlier in Chapter 3, there are several major consumer protection laws that affect product safety. These laws include the Flammable Fabrics Act of 1953, the Fair Packaging and Labeling Act of 1966, and the Consumer Product Safety Act of 1972. The Zyrtec ad in Figure 12.13, with its numerous disclaimers inserted by the manufacturer, illustrates the effect the Federal Food and Drug Act of 1906 has on product liability today.

The number of product liability lawsuits filed against manufacturers has skyrocketed in recent years. Although many such claims reach settlements out of court, juries have decided others, sometimes awarding multimillion-dollar settlements. This threat has led most companies to step up efforts to ensure product safety. Safety warnings appear prominently on the labels of such potentially hazardous products as cleaning fluids and drain cleaners to inform users of the dangers of these products and urge their storage out of the reach of children. Changes in product design have reduced the hazards posed by such products as lawn mowers, hedge trimmers, and toys. Product liability insurance has become an essential element of any new or existing product strategy. Premiums for this insurance have risen alarmingly, however, and insurers have almost entirely abandoned some kinds of coverage.

Federal and state legislation plays a major role in regulating product safety. The federal Consumer Product Safety Act of 1972 created a powerful regulatory agency—the Consumer Product Safety Commission (CPSC). The agency has assumed jurisdiction over every consumer product category except food, automobiles, and a few other products already regulated by other agencies. The CPSC has the authority to ban products without court hearings, order recalls or redesigns of products, and inspect production facilities. It can charge managers of neg-

"The product must be demonstrably superior to our competition and pleasingly different in some significant way," he adds.

Callaway certainly maintains thorough research and development efforts. Not long ago, the company opened a $9 million test facility that includes a 260-yard range with three types of grass and four kinds of bunkers. Hundreds of sensors measure the flight of each ball hit from a tee.

http://www.callawaygolf.com/

The company's Great Big Bertha titanium-headed driver costs about $500. The business of making luxury golf clubs might seem vulnerable to an economic downturn, but ironically it offers unusual stability. Callaway products appeal to wealthy golfers who can afford top-of-the-line goods even when others must scrimp to pay greens fees.

Can Callaway continue to leave its competitors in the sand trap? Many experts express doubt. Golfing industry sales have flattened out in the 1990s, after peaking in 1990 with 27.8 million people hitting the links. Today, that number has dipped to between 24 and 25 million. "I think the euphoria has worn off," warns Bud Leedom, publisher of *Golf Insight & Investing,* a San Diego newsletter that focuses on the industry.

Determined to keep its competitive edge, Callaway has lined up its sights on the leading golf ball manufacturers. The company recently announced a project to develop its own line of balls, which would boost its name recognition even higher. Steve Eisenberg, an analyst at Oppenheimer & Co., estimates that capturing just 10 percent of the golf ball market would add $100 million to Callaway's sales.

QUESTIONS FOR CRITICAL THINKING

1. **What qualities support the success of entrepreneurs like Ely Callaway?**
2. **How much do you think Callaway Golf depends upon its creator's energy and vision? Do you think the company will continue to flourish once its founder leaves?**

Sources: "Callaway Golf Reports First Quarter Gains; Net Sales Increase 25% and Net Income Up 26%," *PR Newswire,* April 16, 1997, downloaded from http://fast.quote.com/, April 27, 1997; Mark Veverka, "Callaway Golf May Hit Slowdown as Market Conditions Get Soggier," *Wall Street Journal,* October 9, 1996, p. CA3; Katherine Callan, "Secrets of the Empire Builders," *Success,* September 1996, pp. 29–33; Carolyn T. Geer, "Gold Mine or Sand Trap?" *Forbes,* August 12, 1996, pp. 42–44; and John A. Jones, "Callaway Sets Up to Make Golf Balls as Fine as Its Clubs," *Investor's Business Daily,* May 31, 1996, downloaded from America Online, November 25, 1996.

ligent companies with criminal offenses. In one recent case, for example, the CPSC issued a warning that many brands of miniblinds released lead dust when exposed to heat and sunlight. The agency asked trade associations in the industry to advise manufacturers to change their coatings and to publicize the danger to the public. The CPSC also required manufacturers to put stickers on miniblinds advising consumers that the products met lead-free standards.[50]

The federal government has also enacted a number of other laws designed to protect consumers. For example, The Poison Prevention Packaging Act of 1970 ordered drug manufacturers to place their products in child-resistant packaging. The act was refined somewhat in 1995 by new rules designed to protect children yet allow senior citizens to easily remove caps on drug bottles. To comply with the new rules, manufacturers must show that no more than 20 percent of children under age four should be able to open a medicine container. At the same time, 90 percent of adults must be able to open drug containers within five minutes.[51] In addition, many states have instituted their own product safety statutes.

CPSC activities and the increased number of liability claims have prompted companies to sponsor voluntary improvements in safety standards. Safety planning is now a vital element of product strategy.

Marketing Dictionary

product liability The responsibility of manufacturers and marketers for injuries and damages caused by their products.

Figure 12.13 Disclaimer Required by the FDA for Prescription Drug Advertisements

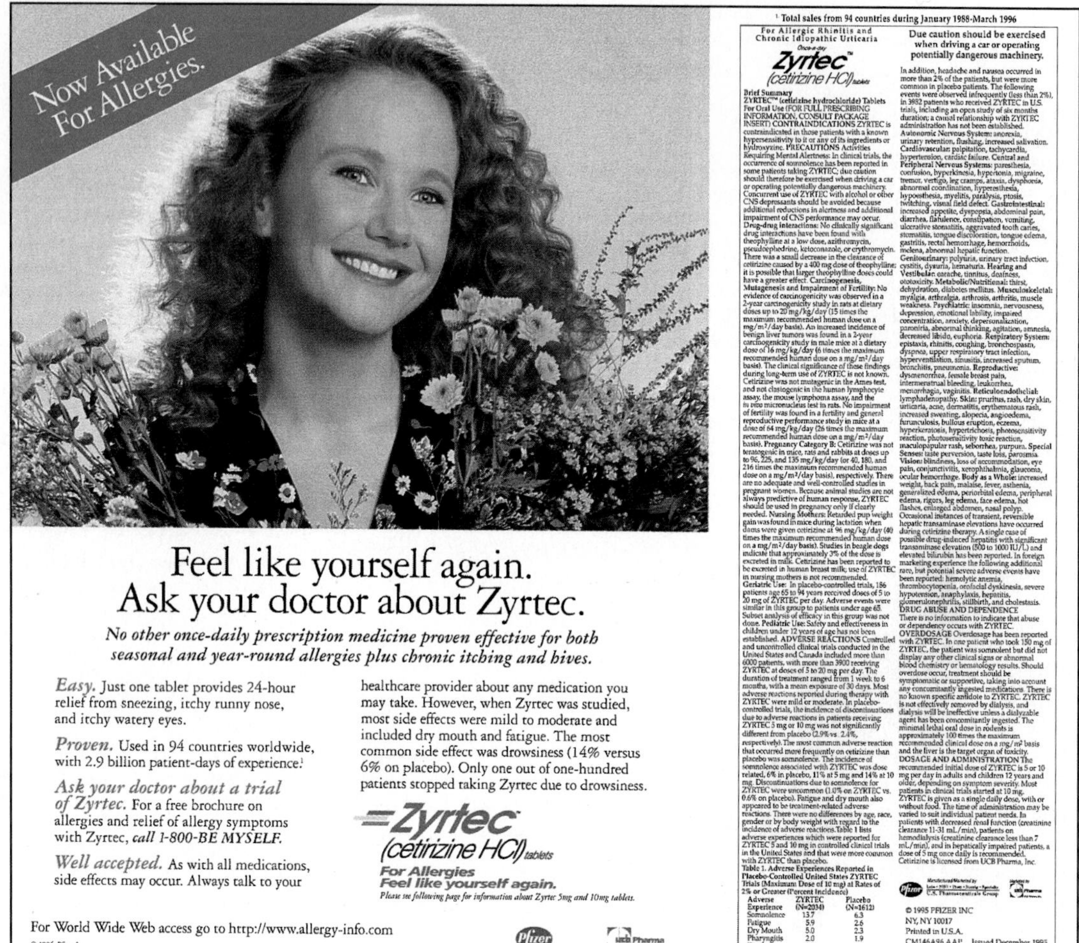
Now Available For Allergies.
Feel like yourself again.
Ask your doctor about Zyrtec.
No other once-daily prescription medicine proven effective for both seasonal and year-round allergies plus chronic itching and hives.
Easy. Just one tablet provides 24-hour relief from sneezing, itchy runny nose, and itchy watery eyes.
Proven. Used in 94 countries worldwide, with 2.9 billion patient-days of experience.
Ask your doctor about a trial of Zyrtec. For a free brochure on allergies and relief of allergy symptoms with Zyrtec, call 1-800-BE MYSELF.
Well accepted. As with all medications, side effects may occur. Always talk to your healthcare provider about any medication you may take. However, when Zyrtec was studied, most side effects were mild to moderate and included dry mouth and fatigue. The most common side effect was drowsiness (14% versus 6% on placebo). Only one out of one-hundred patients stopped taking Zyrtec due to drowsiness.
Zyrtec (cetirizine HCl) tablets
For Allergies
Feel like yourself again.
For World Wide Web access go to http://www.allergy-info.com
Pfizer
Total sales from 94 countries during January 1988-March 1996
For Allergic Rhinitis and Chronic Idiopathic Urticaria
Zyrtec (cetirizine HCl) tablets
Due caution should be exercised when driving a car or operating potentially dangerous machinery.
© 1995 PFIZER INC
NY, NY 10017
Printed in U.S.A.

ACHIEVEMENT CHECK SUMMARY

Reread the learning goals that follow, and consider the questions for each goal. Answering these questions will reinforce your grasp of the most important concepts in the chapter and allow you to check how well you have achieved these learning goals. Where a blank appears before a question, answer with *T* or *F;* for multiple-choice questions, circle the letter of the correct answer.

Objective 12.1: Explain the benefits of branding and brand management.

1. ___ One of the main goals of branding is to create an identity for a product that will differentiate it from competing offerings.
2. ___ Consumers are said to be *brand loyal* when (a) they tell their friends about a brand; (b) they recognize a brand name; (c) they choose a brand over competing products.
3. ___ Most firms achieve brand insistence with their products.

Objective 12.2: Describe the different types of brands.

1. ___ Private brands identify products available only to wealthy consumers.
2. ___ When a single brand name spans several related products, it is called a(n) (a) manufacturer's brand; (b) family brand; (c) individual brand.
3. ___ A firm should market very dissimilar products under a single family brand name.

Objective 12.3: Explain the value of brand equity.

1. ___ *Brand equity* refers to (a) how much a company has invested in a brand; (b) the added value that a brand name confers on a product; (c) the dividend a stockholder receives from a branded product's manufacturer.

2. ___ High brand equity helps a firm to expand into global markets.
3. ___ Brand equity reflects the ability of a product to stand apart from competitors.

Objective 12.4: Describe how firms develop strong identities for their products and brands.

1. ___ An effective brand name should give buyers an idea of the product's image.
2. ___ If a brand name becomes a descriptive, generic name (a) the original owner can sue others for using the name; (b) the original owner has no exclusive claim to the name; (c) the name will help to sell the brand in international markets.
3. ___ Firms can establish trademarks for (a) brand names only; (b) brand names, slogans, and packaging elements; (c) pictorial designs in ads only.
4. ___ Properly designed labels can encourage consumer purchases.
5. ___ A brand extension allows a firm to carry brand equity over to unrelated products.

Objective 12.5: Identify alternative new-product development strategies and the determinants of each strategy's success.

1. ___ A market penetration strategy involves (a) finding a new market for an established product; (b) modifying an existing product in an existing market; (c) introducing a new product into an established market.
2. ___ The strategy of creating a new product for a new market is (a) market development; (b) market penetration; (c) product diversification.
3. ___ Cannibalization occurs when a newly introduced product steals sales from a firm's existing product.
4. ___ A flanker brand is a product that a firm introduces to serve a new market.

Objective 12.6: Identify the determinants of a new product's rate of adoption and the methods for accelerating the speed of adoption.

1. ___ A new-product department is a temporary group set up to develop a specific product or product line.
2. ___ A new-product committee is a review committee with authority over new-product decisions.
3. ___ Marketing professionals with responsibility for developing marketing strategies for products, brands, or product lines are called *product managers.*

Objective 12.7: Explain the various organizational structures for new-product development.

1. ___ First adopters are usually the same people for any product.
2. ___ A product is more likely to achieve consumer adoption if (a) the product is compatible with the values of consumers; (b) it costs a lot of money; (c) it offers more complex features than currently available rivals include.
3. ___ Businesses can seldom influence first adopters.
4. ___ A product design increases the likelihood of adoption if it provides an advantage over existing products.
5. ___ Marketers usually need not supply informative promotional messages to get first adopters to try a new product.

Objective 12.8: List the stages in the new-product development process.

1. ___ In an important part of the screening process, marketers determine how well a product idea fits with the capabilities of the firm.
2. ___ During the business analysis stage, firms evaluate a product's potential acceptance by consumers.
3. ___ Development usually takes less time than other parts of new-product development.

Objective 12.9: Outline the functions of the Consumer Product Safety Commission, and summarize the concept of product liability.

1. ___ The Consumer Product Safety Commission exercises jurisdiction over all consumer products, including food and automobiles.
2. ___ Product safety is an integral feature of a design to satisfy customers.
3. ___ The Consumer Product Safety Commission cannot ban a product without a court hearing.

Students: See the solutions section located on pages S-2–S-3 to check your responses to the Achievement Check Summary.

Key Terms

brand
brand recognition
brand preference
brand insistence
generic product
manufacturer's brand
private brand
family brand
individual brand
brand equity
brand manager
brand name
brand mark
generic name
trademark
label
Universal Product Code (UPC)
brand extension
brand dilution
brand licensing
co-branding
product positioning
cannibalization
adoption process
consumer innovator
diffusion process
product manager
venture team
task force
phased development
parallel product development
concept testing
test marketing
product liability

Review Questions

1. Identify and briefly explain each of the three stages of brand loyalty. How does brand loyalty differ among product categories?
2. Explain the differences among manufacturer's, private, and family brands. Provide examples of each.
3. Describe the advantages of brand equity.

4. Differentiate among the terms *brand, brand name, brand mark, trademark,* and *trade name.* Specify examples of each.
5. List the characteristics of an effective brand name. What differences distinguish brand extensions, brand licensing, and co-branding? Cite examples of each.
6. Outline the different product development strategies. Cite an example of each strategy.
7. What happens during the consumer adoption process? Outline and explain the stages in this process.
8. Outline alternative organizational structures for new-product development. Identify the steps in the new-product development process.
9. What chief purpose does test marketing serve? What potential problems may complicate test marketing?
10. Explain the primary activities of the Consumer Product Safety Commission. What steps can this agency take to protect consumers from defective and hazardous products?

Discussion Questions

1. Using Young & Rubicam's dimensions of brand equity, evaluate the brand equity levels of the following products. Which brands have the greatest brand equity? Explain.
   a. Revlon cosmetics
   b. Cheerios cereal
   c. Citizen watches
   d. Baskin-Robbins ice cream
   e. Marlboro cigarettes
2. Philip Morris Co., which makes Maxwell House coffee, introduced a line of whole-bean coffee products called Maxwell House Private Collection with eight flavors. PM designed the product to capture a share of the growing specialty coffee market. It failed, partially because consumers equated the Maxwell House name with ordinary, canned coffee. If you were a member of the new-product development team at Philip Morris, what would you recommend the company should do to expand its coffee business?
3. Legos, the popular children's building bricks, currently has 85 percent of the construction toy market. However, this share is eroding slightly as new competitors aggressively enter the market. Meanwhile, the company has sold licensing agreements to other firms to manufacture a variety of products under the Lego brand, among them children's clothes and children's books. The Danish toy maker is also building a $100 million amusement park, Legoland, in Carlsbad, California. Discuss the pros and cons of Lego's licensing and expansion plans. What potential dangers do you foresee for Lego's face brand equity? Why?
4. Sunsweet Growers co-op introduced a new product called *Lighter Bake,* a dried plum and apple mix that substitutes for butter and oil in baking. This substitution allows bakers to cut fat and cholesterol from baked goods. The company is placing the product on supermarket shelves near cooking oils at a suggested retail price of $1.99 to $2.29. What problems might Sunsweet encounter in getting consumers to adopt Lighter Bake? What tactics would you recommend to the company to overcome those problems?
5. One of the hottest new consumer electronics products combines a TV and VCR in one unit. According to industry analysts, consumers like the sets because they take up less space than conventional combinations of equipment and are more convenient to use. What other new products might electronics manufacturers combine with a basic TV? Choose one and evaluate its commercial potential. What advantages would it offer consumers? What other products would make up its competition? Would you test market the new product or not? Why?

'netWork

1. A trademark or tradename provides a very important source of a good or service's market identity. NameSearch is an organization that provides an entire portfolio of intellectual property services related to product names. Visit the NameSearch home page at

http://www.tradename.com/

and answer the following questions. What services does the organization provide? Pay particular attention to the NetVigil service. What benefits would a subscriber to this service expect? What kinds of companies would gain the most from the services provided by NameSearch?

2. The World Intellectual Property Organization (WIPO) is an intergovernmental organization created by the United Nations to promote respect for intellectual property rights throughout the world. Visit the organization's home page at

http://www.wipo.int/

and answer the following questions. What objectives does WIPO pursue? How does the organization define the term *intellectual property?* How many states belong to this organization? How does its international focus affect its operations?

3. The Consumer Product Safety Commission is one of many federal government agencies involved in consumer protection. Go to the CPSC home page at

http://www.cpsc.gov/

and report on the agency's statement of its mission. For what products does the agency exert responsibility? Who might need access to the information posted on this Web site?

VIDEO CASE 12

THE BOULEVARD CRUISER

People crowded 12 deep to get a look when General Motors unveiled its new Cadillac Seville STS at the International Automobile Show in Detroit. The highly acclaimed new model generated the first excitement in many years for Cadillac.

For decades, the Cadillac name had symbolized prestige and success. But during the 1980s, the brand suffered as many consumers came to view the cars as gas-guzzling boulevard cruisers. The nameplate remained popular with older consumers who remembered its glory days, but it struck out with younger people, who preferred foreign luxury cars from Lexus, BMW, Infiniti, and Mercedes. Cadillac marketers saw a need for sweeping changes.

Cadillac is the flagship, luxury brand of General Motors, the world's automaker with a 17 percent global market share. GM has positioned Cadillac as the blue-chip component of its product portfolio, which includes Saturn, Pontiac, Chevrolet, GMC trucks, Oldsmobile, and Buick.

Cadillac models successfully maintained the division's status as America's leading luxury car maker until the mid-1980s. To restore the luster, GM management completely revamped Cadillac's product development.

In the past, Cadillac had produced new models through phased development, beginning when designers drafted new plans and passed them on to engineers, who developed the ideas into cars that they hoped consumers would buy and manufacturing engineers could build. Time-consuming changes slowed the process as manufacturing revealed problems with the original designs. In 1955, GM spent less than two years developing a new car model. By the early 1980s, product development took five years or longer.

Cadillac's new-product development process started with consumers, who provided input to guide later design and development. According to Jim Kornas, a GM marketing executive, Cadillac adopted a "simultaneous management approach" to product development. For the first time, Cadillac created a venture team to produce a product. The cross-functional team was responsible for the design, engineering, manufacturing, distribution, and marketing of the Seville STS. Consumers and suppliers participated on the vehicle development team from the very beginning of the project. Even Cadillac's advertising agency, D'Arcy, Masius, Benton, & Bowles Advertising, sat in as a team member.

In an important first step, the STS development team conducted focus groups to determine what the targeted younger car buyers wanted in a luxury car. The STS designers, engineers, and marketers learned that younger buyers thought that Cadillac lacked technology, good engineering, and handling performance. They said Cadillac models lacked any attributes that they wanted. A simple statement seemed to sum up their core belief: "Cadillac doesn't make a car for me." From focus groups, the STS team learned that important attributes for younger buyers included comfort, good handling and performance, and a sporty yet luxurious appearance.

Based on this information, designers prepared a variety of sketches for their new car's interior and exterior. They then returned with these designs to focus group members and asked for reactions. Special computer software helped the team to evaluate the alternative designs for ease of assembly, structural efficiency, and potential production costs. This step revealed the most feasible manufacturing process for the new vehicle before the designs had progressed beyond rough sketches.

Because design costs account for 70 percent to 90 percent of a product's overall cost, using the design for manufacturing (DFM) procedure lowered product costs. This offered the advantage of reducing the number of parts. Older models required 240 components in the bumper system; the new ones needed just 126 parts, saving GM $51 per car. Another benefit was higher quality, because the reduction in parts also reduced the chances for squeaks, rattles, and loose connections. "Problems disappear when parts disappear," said one designer.

During the screening stage, the STS team identified features worth including in the new design. For example, cost-conscious team members wanted to design the car's roof/C-pillar joint as a lap joint, less expensive to produce than a brazed joint but also less attractive. Other team members insisted on the better-looking alternative, despite the higher cost. The team finally decided to go with the brazed joint, believing that it would enhance the car's image as a high-quality vehicle. Team members knew that they had made the right decision when the Lexus LS400 appeared on the market with hand-brazed C-pillars.

During the development stage, STS designers crafted scale models of the car and tested them with consumers. Then they designed a prototype model and introduced it, after testing, as a prelaunch prototype to the media and consumers at the International Automobile Show in Detroit. The new design received rave reviews, and the event generated valuable publicity, as the STS was honored as "car of the year" by three major automobile magazines.

The STS team highlighted press reviews and focus group results in the advertising campaign that launched the new car. A television commercial announced, "The Cadillac Seville STS: The first automobile in history to win not one, not two, but all three major automotive magazine awards in the same year. There's never been a car so acclaimed. It could change the way you think about American cars."

Cadillac intended the advertising to bring young luxury car buyers into its showrooms. The product launch proved so successful that buyers had to wait months for ordered cars as consumer demand far exceeded forecasted sales. Despite this success, the STS team continued to work on innovations. A year later, Cadillac introduced the Northstar system, which set new standards in performance, engineering, and technology. The 4.6-liter Northstar V-8 engine produced more horsepower than the engines of competing luxury models such as the Lexus LS400, Infiniti Q45, and BMW 540i.

Cadillac offered OnStar, a multifaceted customer service system based on another technological innovation, as an option on the 1997 Seville model. OnStar combines the technologies of cellular phones, vehicle on-board computers, and the global positioning system (GPS) satellite navigation system. From voice-activated car phones built into the vehicle's console, drivers can communicate with the OnStar service center to gain access to many services. For example, it can unlock car doors by remote control, notify police and fire departments when a driver has an accident, call a tow truck for roadside service, and provide directions to chosen destinations.

Questions

1. Which of the alternative development strategies discussed in the chapter did Cadillac use in developing the Seville STS?
2. How did Cadillac organize the product development process? What benefits did it gain from this type of organization?
3. Which steps in the product development process described in the chapter does this video case present?
4. As part of the new product's features, Cadillac has introduced the OnStar system. Visit the company's home page located at

   http://www.cadillac.com/

   What information do you find about the OnStar system? What services does OnStar provide beyond emergency assistance? Do buyers receive OnStar services as part of the actual product? Are these services necessary to the success of Seville STS?

Sources: Brian Bremner, Larry Armstrong, Kathleen Kerwin, and Keith Naughton, "Toyota's Crusade," *Business Week,* April 7, 1997, pp. 104–114; and Mike Allen, "Beyond the Car Phone," *Popular Mechanics,* August 1996.

CHAPTER 13

MARKETING OF SERVICES

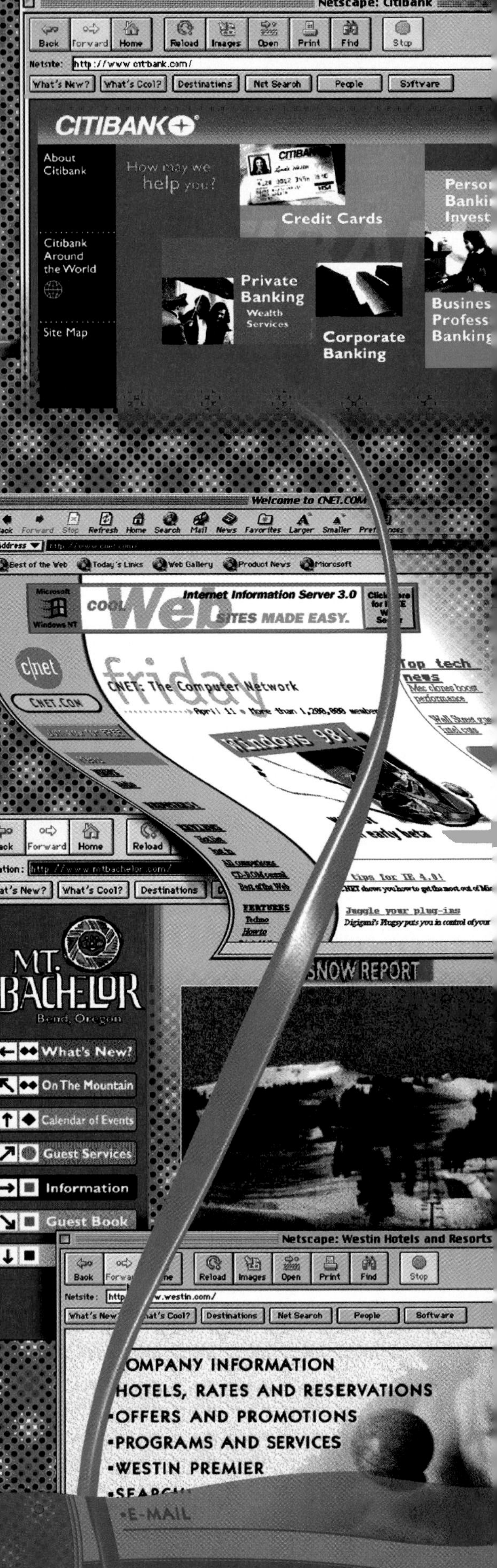

Netscape: Citibank
CITIBANK
About Citibank
How may we help you?
Credit Cards
Citibank Around the World
Private Banking
Wealth Services
Corporate Banking
Site Map
Welcome to CNET.COM
Internet Information Server 3.0
SITES MADE EASY.
CNET: The Computer Network
CNET.COM
friday
MT. BACHELOR
Bend, Oregon
What's New?
On The Mountain
Calendar of Events
Guest Services
Information
Guest Book
SNOW REPORT
Netscape: Westin Hotels and Resorts
HOTELS, RATES AND RESERVATIONS
•OFFERS AND PROMOTIONS
•PROGRAMS AND SERVICES
•WESTIN PREMIER
•E-MAIL
WESTIN

Chapter Objectives

1. Differentiate service offerings from goods.
2. Identify the primary characteristics of services.
3. Explain the concept of service quality.
4. Outline the possible outcomes of a service encounter.
5. Develop a classification system for services.
6. Explain how environmental factors affect services.
7. Discuss market segmentation and the marketing mix for services.

Work-Friendly Hotel Rooms Lure Business Travelers

Mints on the pillow used to impress hotel guests, but not anymore. In the highly competitive market for business travel services, hotels hunt constantly for new ways to lure weary visitors to their lobbies.

Some hotels now rely on technology to gain the allegiance of business "road warriors." Several major hotel chains outfit their rooms with many of the technological tools that businesspeople need to do their work. Business travelers can often send faxes without leaving their rooms. They may find laptop computers waiting on desks roomy enough to accommodate lots of papers. These guests don't have to worry about straining their backs—their room furnishings include ergonomically correct office chairs. Along with complimentary irons and hair dryers, some lucky customers now use in-room photocopying machines or computer printers.

Hotels have marketed these specially equipped rooms under names intended to entice the no-nonsense travelers: "The Room That Works" (Marriott); "The Guest Office" (Westin); "The Business Plan" (Hyatt Regency); "The Business Class Room" (Loew's); and "The Corporate Club Room" (Sheraton). Typically, hotels charge guests a $10 to $20 premium for such a room.

Marriott Hotels started offering its business clientele work-friendly rooms after it solved a mystery that had perplexed the firm's marketers for some time. Why did business travelers reject the spacious accommodations offered in king-size-bed rooms and instead request double beds? A development team assigned to solve the mystery concluded that these guests needed the extra bed to spread out their papers, because hotel rooms offered no place else to put them.

Of course, a firm runs some risks in trying to entice travelers with the latest office necessities. The operations project manager at Westin hotels estimates that the firm spends $2,000 to establish each in-room business center. That significant investment pays for equipment likely to become outdated within three years. That's a steep obsolescence curve—especially considering that hotels typically replace bedding only once every decade.

The operators of the Nob Hill Lambourne Hotel in San Francisco discovered just how quickly new technology turns into a dinosaur. This 20-room hotel and spa became the first in the city to convert

each room into a business center beginning seven years ago. Guests marveled at the 80286 personal computer, fax machine, and two-line phone with voice mail in each room. Realizing woefully inadequacy of the 80286 machines, the hotel sunk $15,000 into cutting-edge technology. Each room is now equipped with a laptop computer that runs Windows 95 and ClarisWorks with an e-mail capability, as well. What's more, each computer provides access to the Internet for no additional charge. If a guest needs a laser printer, hotel staff provide one.

"We really had to rethink our business," says Rob Delamater, the hotel's marketing manager, who notes that the new services are becoming as popular as the spa. "It was important to reinvent our hotel a bit."

Still, some naysayers frown at this drive to provide portable technology to the hotel industry's favored business clientele. "Travelers are self-contained when it comes to the technology," says Bob Dirks, a senior vice president at Hilton. After testing a computer-based office center, Hilton opted for a less ambitious facility with such features as a large console table and a rolling writing desk, as well as an adjustable desk chair and a glare-free desk lamp with a swivel arm. "Our customer is telling us that he doesn't really need a fax machine in the room because he has faxing capacity in his laptop and e-mail is replacing faxing anyway."

Thomas F. O'Toole, Hyatt vice president for marketing, doubts that hotel marketers can so neatly pigeonhole business guests. Different business clients desire different room features. "Some travelers will carry their offices with them," he said. "Others will demand to have it waiting in their rooms, and still others will be content to go the (hotel) business center. There won't be just one room of the future, but several levels of rooms based on a business traveler's particular degree of sophistication."[1]

http://www.westin.com/
http://www.hyatt.com/

CHAPTER OVERVIEW

Marketers develop programs to promote both goods and services in the same manner. Any such program begins with investigation, analysis, and selection of a particular target market, and it continues with creation of a marketing mix designed to satisfy that segment. But while the designs of tangible goods and intangible services both work to satisfy consumer wants and needs, their marketing programs diverge significantly in some ways. This chapter examines both the similarities and the differences in marketing goods and services.

First, however, it defines *services*. Sometimes a product blurs the distinction between services and goods, as when a service provides a good. Consider the retail sector. While all retailers provide services, a further distinction divides them into services retailers and goods retailers. Aaron Rents Furniture offers rentals with options to purchase. It provides both services (rental agreements) and goods (sofas and other furniture), when the buyer eventually takes ownership. Similarly, independent optometrists work in conjunction with Pearle Vision Centers to provide eye examinations (services), while Pearle sells eyeglasses and contact lenses (goods).

WHAT ARE SERVICES?

Figure 13.1 Goods-Services Continuum

Pure Good
Pure Service
Car
Dinner in an Exclusive Restaurant
Movie Theater

The term *service* covers a wide range of products. A general definition identifies **services** as intangible tasks that satisfy consumer and business user needs. Most service providers cannot transport or store their products; customers simultaneously buy and consume these products.

One way to distinguish services employs a product spectrum, or a **goods-services continuum** like that shown in Figure 13.1. This device helps marketers to visualize the differences and similarities between goods and services.[2] A car is a pure good, but the dealer may also sell repair and maintenance services or include the services in the price of a lease. Movie theaters provide pure services, but they also sell goods such as candy, drinks, and popcorn. The car falls at the pure-good extreme of the continuum, because the customer values the repair service less than the car itself, just as movie patrons consider refreshments less important than the entertainment services that the theater provides. In the middle range of the continuum, dinner at an exclusive restaurant has equally important good and service components. Customers derive satisfaction not only from the food and drink, but also from services rendered by the establishment's personnel.

The Importance of the Service Sector

People would probably live very different lives without service firms to fill many needs. No one could place a telephone call, plug into the Internet, or flip a switch for electricity. People would not receive mail, cash a check, take college courses, or even go to the movies if organizations did not provide such services. During an average day, you probably use many services without much thought—but these products probably play an integral role in your life.

Expenditures for services have increased considerably during the past decade. Currently, services represent approximately three-quarters of the U.S. gross domestic product, and nearly 80 percent of all jobs.[3] Furthermore, women have found virtually all of their gains in employment in this sector. Researchers also note that service companies make up almost half of new U.S. businesses.[4]

Observers cite several reasons for the growing economic importance of services, including consumer desire for speed and convenience and technological advances that allow firms to fulfill this demand. For example, swiping a rapid transit system automatic fare card though a turnstile reader reduces lines to buy tokens. Online banking services simplify paying bills and balancing your checkbook. The ad in Figure 13.2 illustrates how technology helps United Airlines to satisfy consumers' desire for speed and convenience. It describes how the company's new software helps people to book their own flights and choose their own seats from their personal computers. These and similar services benefit businesses as well as consumers by reducing firms' need for employees and increasing efficiency.[5]

Services also play an important role in the international competitiveness of U.S. firms. While the United States runs a continuing trade deficit in tangible goods, it has maintained a trade surplus in services for every year since 1970. This trade surplus continues to rise from its current total of roughly $70 billion. Some economists think that precise measurements of service exports would reveal an even larger surplus.

Most service firms emphasize marketing as a significant activity for two reasons. First, the growth potential of service transactions represents a vast marketing opportunity. Second, increased competition is forcing traditional service industries to emphasize marketing in order to compete in the marketplace.

Marketing Dictionary

service An intangible task that satisfies consumer or business user needs.

goods-services continuum A device that helps marketers to visualize the differences and similarities between goods and services.

Figure 13.2 **Technology to Help Satisfy Consumers' Desire for Speed and Convenience**

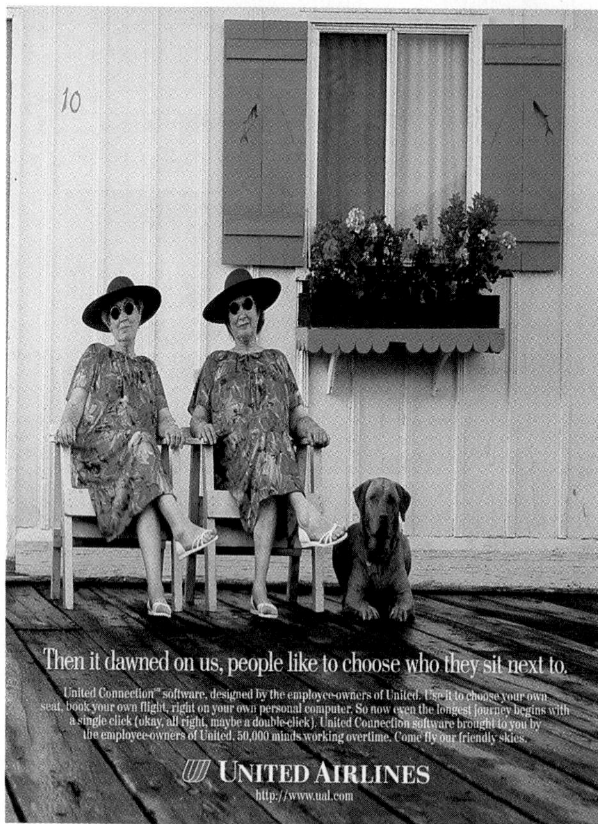
10
Then it dawned on us, people like to choose who they sit next to.
United Connection™ software, designed by the employee-owners of United. Use it to choose your own seat, book your own flight, right on your own personal computer. So now even the longest journey begins with a single click (okay, all right, maybe a double-click). United Connection software brought to you by the employee-owners of United. 50,000 minds working overtime. Come fly our friendly skies.
UNITED AIRLINES
http://www.ual.com

CHARACTERISTICS OF SERVICES

The discussion so far hints at a diverse market for services. This diversity, which exceeds the diversity of the goods market, results from several characteristics that distinguish services from goods:

1. Services are intangible.
2. Services are inseparable from the service providers.
3. Services are perishable.
4. Companies cannot easily standardize services.
5. Buyers often play roles in the development and distribution of services.
6. Service quality shows wide variations.

The following sections discuss these service characteristics in turn. Service marketers must appreciate how each feature uniquely affects a particular service.

Intangibility

Unlike goods, services lack tangible features. A prospective car buyer can pick out a favorite color, take the car for a test drive, feel the upholstery, and examine the engine. Most service buyers cannot, however, see, hear, smell, taste, or touch the products prior to purchasing them. This intangibility often prevents buyers from judging the quality of a service beforehand. Firms essentially ask them to buy a promise.

This fact creates a challenge for service marketers to find ways to communicate the benefits and end results of choosing a particular service provider. Marketers often meet this challenge by emphasizing the service's image in a way that differentiates it from competing products in consumers' minds. Cleveland-based KeyCorp Bank, for example, wanted to portray itself as an accessible resource for consumer financial needs. KeyCorp chose actor Anthony Edwards as a representative because the bank felt that he conveyed a believable and approachable image.[6] BellSouth's ad in Figure 13.3 ties a striking image of the sun to the concept of a powerful source of energy to identify the company as a powerful source of information. BellSouth wants people to think of the company not only as a provider of local and long-distance telephone service but as a single source for every information need, including Internet access and interactive video.

Personal selling provides another important tool for marketers of services. Noncommissioned officers in the military represent a target consumer group for the life insurance policies of Academy Life. Academy sells to this group by hiring retired military personnel or spouses of military personnel as insurance "counselors." The counselors visit service centers run by the Non-Commissioned Officers Association (NCOA) outside military bases, where they explain the benefits of Academy's policies in face-to-face settings. An Academy executive explains that this sales method allows customers to receive personalized assistance from counselors who understand their specific needs. "Because noncommissioned officers tend to be younger and less educated, they usually need more help with financial planning," explains the executive, noting that face-to-face selling allows Academy to provide that help and fully explain the benefits of buying life insurance.[7]

Briefly speaking

"The critical element in selling a service comes in providing support after the sale, because, unlike other types of marketing, the customer can't really try the product until he's already bought it."

Kay Knight Clarke (1938–)
Chairman, Templeton, Inc.

Inseparability

Figure 13.3 **Creating an Image of Strength for a Service Provider**

SOURCE
There's a source of energy. A source of information.
And one simple, powerful source for all of your
words to travel through: BellSouth. Now more than
ever, we're bringing together every kind of technology.
From local and long distance service, to Internet
access, wireless, yellow pages, interactive video and
beyond. So you can pick and choose what you need,
when you need it. All from a single source that connects
you and your words in every way.
Because a word can have many meanings.
But it means nothing until it's shared.
BELLSOUTH®
It's All Here.™
www.bellsouth.com/words

The providers of most services *are* the services in buyers' minds. Consumer perceptions of a service provider become their perceptions of the service itself.

Consider, for example, PacifiCare Health Systems, a large health maintenance organization (HMO). PacifiCare recognizes that consumers view a health plan as the doctors who provide its services. "Doctors are the product," explains Jon Wampler, CEO of PacifiCare's California operations. If PacifiCare's customers feel satisfied with the care they receive from the plan's doctors, they probably will express satisfaction with the HMO. Therefore, PacifiCare works to develop strong connections with its participating doctors, offering information and staff training to help medical offices provide good service. In a recent survey of 85,000 HMO users, PacifiCare received above average ratings for perceived value and overall quality of care.[8]

Perishability

The characteristic of perishability means that service providers cannot maintain inventories of their products. During times of peak demand, those products may fetch high prices that fall drastically over time. For instance, hotels often raise room prices during special events, only to lower them again to normal levels when the events end. Vacant seats on an airplane, unsold symphony tickets, idle aerobics instructors, and unused electric generating capacity all illustrate the perishable nature of services. Organizations like Australia's Quantas Airlines, the Cleveland Symphony, Gold's Gym, and Detroit Edison all must balance high and low demand. Vacation resorts respond to this problem by setting high in-season prices and low off-season prices; long-distance telephone calls cost less during evenings and weekends than during weekdays; and hotels offer low weekend rates.

The perishability of services results from another cause, as well: These products tie up limited resources for limited periods of time. Speedway Motorsports is a good example. The company owns and operates four stock car racetracks. Nascar Stock Car Auto Racing events at Speedway's tracks bring in $76 million in revenues a year. Between racing events, however, the thousands of seats at the racetracks are empty; the firm draws no income when it has no Nascar events scheduled. To compensate for the perishability of its main service offering, Speedway's tracks host car shows, driving schools, concerts, and rallies when Nascar events are not scheduled.[9]

Difficulty of Standardization

Sellers of a single service often cannot standardize the features of their products; a single seller may even encounter difficulties standardizing products for different customers. For example, many luxury hotels now offer concierge services to guests. A concierge helps guests obtain services both inside and outside the hotel during their visits. This member of a hotel's staff may recommend restaurants, arrange for show tickets, or even send out a guest's clothes for dry cleaning. This wide variety of tasks creates many

Figure 13.4 Buyer Involvement in Creating a Service

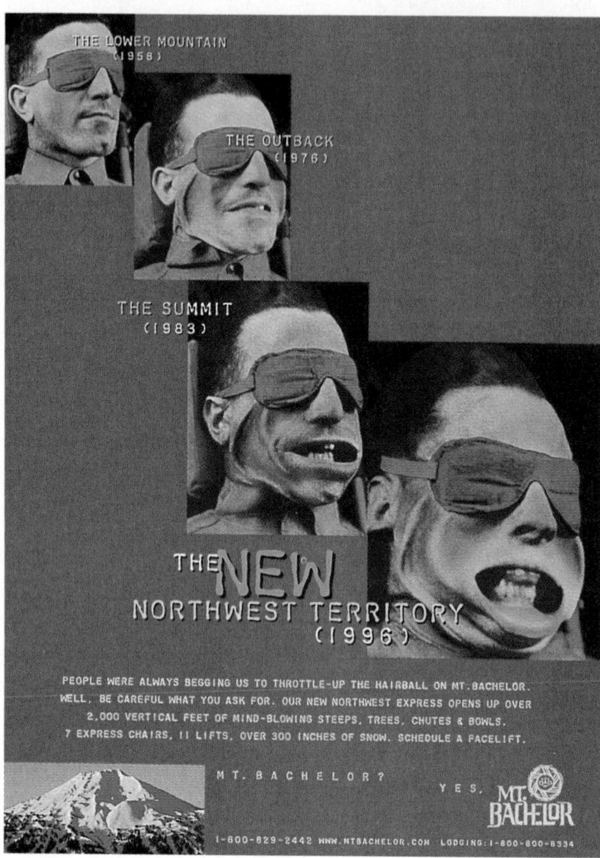
THE LOWER MOUNTAIN
(1958)
THE OUTBACK
(1976)
THE SUMMIT
(1983)
THE NEW
NORTHWEST TERRITORY
(1996)
PEOPLE WERE ALWAYS BEGGING US TO THROTTLE-UP THE HAIRBALL ON MT. BACHELOR. WELL, BE CAREFUL WHAT YOU ASK FOR. OUR NEW NORTHWEST EXPRESS OPENS UP OVER 2,000 VERTICAL FEET OF MIND-BLOWING STEEPS, TREES, CHUTES & BOWLS. 7 EXPRESS CHAIRS, 11 LIFTS, OVER 300 INCHES OF SNOW. SCHEDULE A FACELIFT.
MT. BACHELOR?
YES.
MT. BACHELOR
1-800-829-2442 WWW.MTBACHELOR.COM LODGING: 1-800-800-8334

obstacles for efforts to standardize the concierge service. Each guest presents new needs and desires. Even the best concierge may fail to fill some guest requests—such as tickets to a sold out performance. Some hotels employ concierge staff who have earned the prestigious Les Clefs d'Or designation, certifying ample experience. At other hotels, concierge staff might bring less experience or ability to the job.

In an effort to standardize concierge services, the Hyatt hotel chain plans to automate some of these traditional functions. The chain already has automated check-in terminals similar to ATMs that allow guests to register without assistance from staff. The firm plans to augment the machines so that they can answer guest inquiries about directions, places to eat, or local attractions. Some industry critics doubt that such a "robo-concierge" will replace a human concierge because guests will need help with such diverse, unstandardized problems and questions.[10]

Buyer Involvement

The buyer often plays a major role in the marketing, production, and outcome of a service transaction. A hair stylist's customer may describe the desired look and make suggestions at several stages of the styling process. A client of a tax preparation firm supplies relevant information and frequently works closely with a tax specialist. A new user of an online service such as CompuServe or America Online must learn how to navigate the service's platform to read and send e-mail, participate in chats, and explore the Internet. When people use the services of a ski resort, they must learn how to navigate the slopes. The Mt. Bachelor ad

http://www.mtbachelor.com/

in Figure 13.4 illustrates buyer involvement in experiencing the resort's different ski runs, including the newest and most challenging run designed for people who "were always begging us to throttle-up the hairball on Mt. Bachelor."

Buyers involve themselves in production of tangible goods only when they set customer specifications for major capital items like installations. By contrast, service transactions often require interaction between buyer and seller at the production and distribution stages.

Variable Quality

Variations in quality define another characteristic of services. For example, posh Le Cirque in New York and your local Pizza Hut are both restaurants. Yet their customers experience considerably different cuisines, physical surroundings, service standards, and prices.

Service quality, a topic examined in more detail in the next section, defies easy generalization. Service providers differ substantially from one another, and their products reflect these differences. Consider the difference between Hyatt Legal Services and a prominent Chicago law firm, for example. Similarly, service delivery characteristics can vary greatly. A 20-minute drive to a crowded post office contrasts sharply with a few seconds spent operating a nearby fax machine.

Service marketers need to work toward providing the service quality that customers expect. This important strategic requirement creates potential conflicts between a firm's financial goals and its service goals. For example, in an effort to improve its profits, Delta Air Lines embarked on a two-year program that slashed operating expenses by $1.6 billion. While investors applauded Delta's financial turnaround, however, service suffered. Most of the airline's cuts came from layoffs of experienced flight and ground crews. Soon, customer complaints about the cleanliness of planes increased nearly three-fold. Long waits for tickets and baggage became normal occurrences rather than exceptional events. Flights were increasingly delayed or canceled due to poor maintenance. Customers became disgruntled, and the airline's market share dropped.[11] As Delta's experience shows, the search for the right combination of service quality can pose a difficult challenge. The next section takes a closer look at the priorities for managing service quality.

SERVICE QUALITY

Service quality, the expected and perceived quality of a service offering, defines the primary determinant of consumer satisfaction or dissatisfaction in service-intensive industries. Many firms emphasize the goal of enhancing service quality; those that fail to recognize its importance generally suffer. For example, until recently, a host of government regulations controlled bank services in Japan. As a result, Japanese banks focused their strategies on size more than on serving customers. The poor quality of service

http://www.citibank.com/

gave U.S.-based Citibank a competitive opportunity when it entered the Japanese marketplace. Citibank offered 24-hour ATMs and telephone-banking services, as well as personal attention to consumer needs. As a payoff, Citibank has experienced nearly 50 percent annual growth in Japan over the past three years. Meanwhile, Japanese banks, still struggling to find the right service equation, recently showed the lowest profitability in a survey of banks in 18 countries.[12]

Determinants of Service Quality

Five variables determine service quality: tangibles, reliability, responsiveness, assurance, and empathy.[13] These influences can be described as follows:

- *Tangibles* represent physical evidence of a service. The decor of an attorney's office, a flight attendant's uniform, and a detailed monthly statement from Merrill Lynch are examples.
- *Reliability* refers to the consistency and dependability of the service provider's performance. GM's Mr. Goodwrench advertising campaign emphasizes this determinant of service quality in promoting dealership auto repair services.
- *Responsiveness* involves the willingness and readiness of organization staff to provide service. Responsive services immediately handle an emergency at a medical center, promptly record frequent flyer mileage, and return phone calls before the end of the day.
- *Assurance* refers to the confidence communicated by the service provider. A physician with a friendly bedside manner, H&R Block's guarantee, and the warranty provided by Terminex are examples. As the ad in Figure 13.5 illustrates, PSE&G's commitment to delivering high-quality service to residential and business utility customers is backed by nine written guarantees.

Figure 13.5 Communicating the Assurance Determinant of Service Quality

For PSE&G's Rosemary Jefferson, commitment doesn't end at 5 oclock.
71% of PSE&G employees are community volunteers
Rosemary Jefferson
There are thousands of employees just like Rosemary at PSE&G. People who volunteer their evenings and weekends to helping others in their community. It's that kind of commitment that makes PSE&G feel very confident when we promise our customers the highest standards of service. So confident, we offer nine written guarantees that say we'll perform or we'll pay our residential customers $25 and business customers $100. With employees as committed as Rosemary, we know we'll deliver.
the power of 9
service guarantees
1. We will fix it right the first time.
2. We will turn on existing service by the date promised.
3. We will repair dusk-to-dawn or street lights within 3 working days.
4. We will ensure accurate bills.
5. We will keep all appointments.
6. We will install new dusk-to-dawn or street lights within 10 working days.
7. We will provide new electric service within 5 working days.
8. We will provide new gas service on the date promised.
9. We will respond to a no-heat problem or an individual power outage within the quoted time.
Some restrictions and limitations apply. Call for details.
THE POWER OF COMMITMENT. GUARANTEED.
PSE&G

Marketing Dictionary

service quality The expected and perceived quality of a service offering.

Figure 13.6 Determinants of Perceived Service Quality

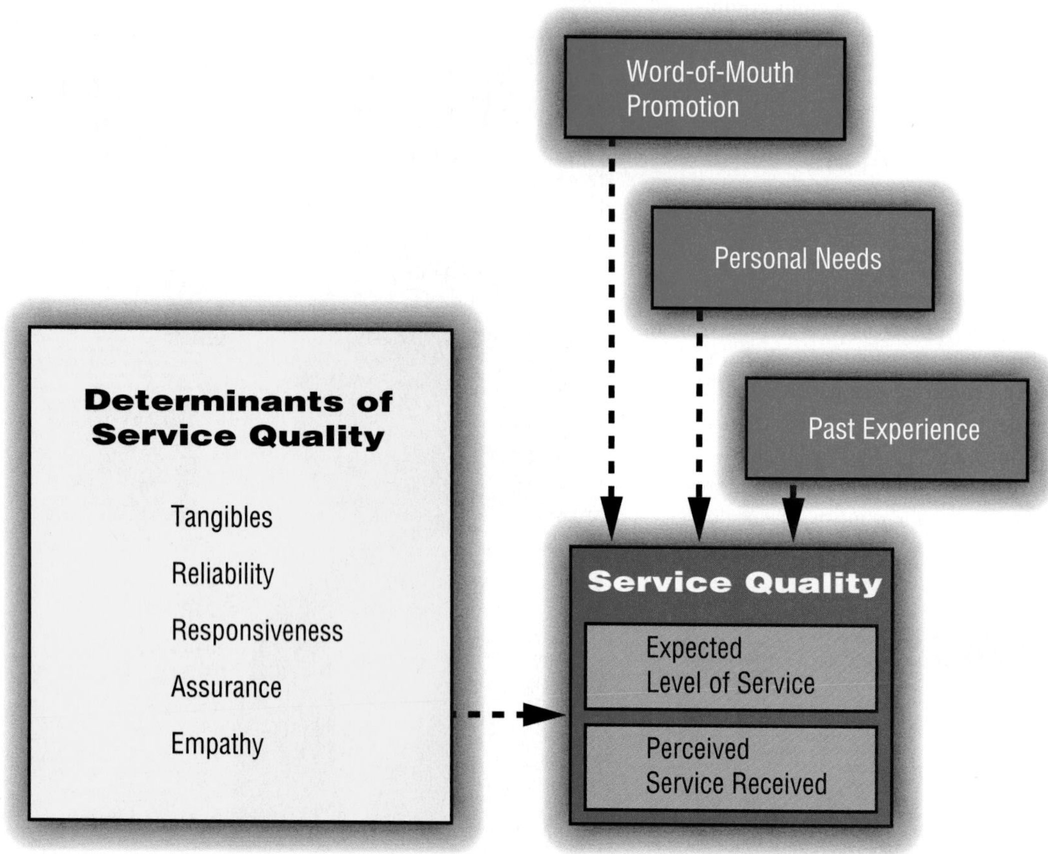
Word-of-Mouth Promotion
Personal Needs
Past Experience
Determinants of Service Quality
Tangibles
Reliability
Responsiveness
Assurance
Empathy
Service Quality
Expected Level of Service
Perceived Service Received

- *Empathy* results from the service provider's efforts to understand customers' needs and then individualize service delivery. Dean Witter's slogan "Serving one investor at a time" illustrates this concept.

Figure 13.6 shows a model of how these influences determine service quality. The five determinants—tangibles, reliability, responsiveness, assurance, and empathy—apply both to the expected service and the perceived service. In addition, word-of-mouth promotion, personal needs, and past experiences influence the expected level of service. For example, you might bring high expectations to a meal at a new Thai restaurant if your neighbors have given it rave reviews. The relationship between expected service and perceived service produces the perceived service quality.

Briefly speaking

"Always give the customer quality, value, selection, and service."

Fred G. Meyer (1917–)
American merchant

Gap Analysis

Service marketers know that **gaps** sometimes separate expected service quality from perceived service quality. Gaps can indicate favorable or unfavorable differences. A bistro with an excellent new chef and staff might provide better service than the after-theater crowd expected, providing a favorable gap. By contrast, if the local newspaper's review had praised the bistro's prompt service, theater patrons might feel disappointed if slow service caused them to miss the opening curtain—an unfavorable gap.

Figure 13.7 illustrates the conflicts that might open gaps. Gap 5—the one just discussed—results from the other four gaps that emerge in the delivery of quality service. For instance, Gap 1 could result if management were to misperceive what buyers wanted. Gap 2 could indicate that the firm sets standards too low to meet customers' expectations. Differences between management intentions and the actual service delivered could produce Gap 3. Finally, Gap 4 could result from management communications to buyers about the service that conflicted with the performance actually delivered.

By analyzing where and how service gaps occur in their operations, managers for a service provider can measure and improve customer satisfaction. However, service firms must carefully measure the variables that indicate quality most accurately in their business and industry. For example, patients undoubtedly have higher expectations about the reliability and assurance of their medical doctors than they may have about other service providers.[14]

The Service Provider

Most buyers form their perceptions of service quality during their **service encounters,** the actual interaction points between the buyers and the service provider. Front-line employees like bank tellers, receptionists, and airline ticket agents determine whether customers emerge satisfied from their service encounters. Some researchers have even suggested that factors like the temperature and colors in waiting areas can influence customer satisfaction with service encounters.[15]

The service encounter can lead to three outcomes: word-of-mouth communication, service switching, and service loyalty. Suppose that you enjoyed a particularly good meal and a pleasant overall experience at the bistro mentioned earlier; you would probably tell your friends about it (word-of-mouth). After a negative experience there, however, you might decide to switch to patronize another restaurant next time (service switching). A record of satisfying service encounters there would build service loyalty among you and your friends; you would become faithful customers.

Figure 13.7 Conceptual Model of Service Quality

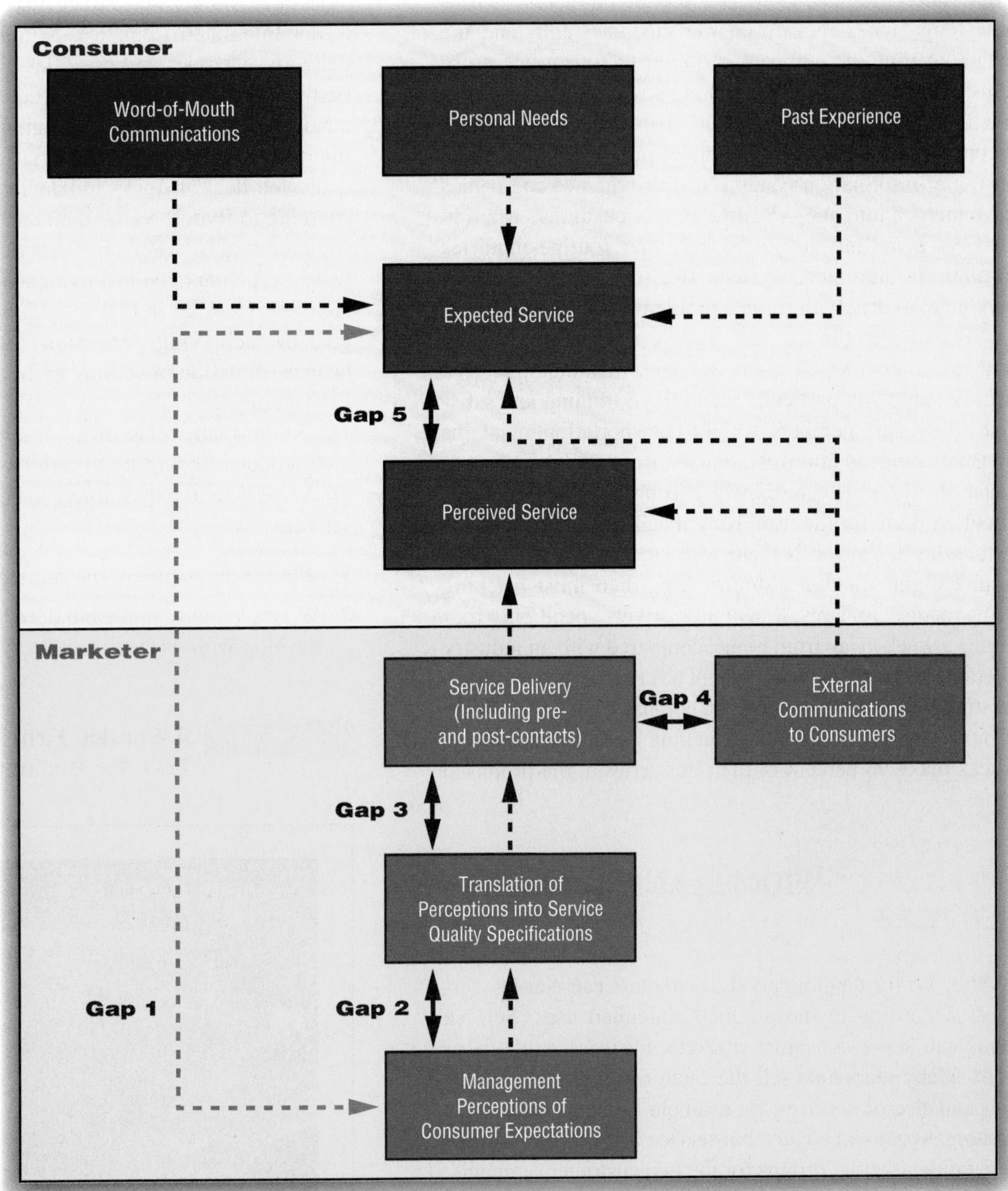
Consumer
Word-of-Mouth Communications
Personal Needs
Past Experience
Expected Service
Gap 5
Perceived Service
Marketer
Service Delivery (Including pre- and post-contacts)
Gap 4
External Communications to Consumers
Gap 3
Translation of Perceptions into Service Quality Specifications
Gap 1
Gap 2
Management Perceptions of Consumer Expectations

Companies must carefully maintain the quality of their service encounters. As discussed in Chapter 2, high customer satisfaction and loyalty often correspond to high profit margins and stock prices. Failure to ensure a quality service encounter can foreshadow disaster for a service firm. Federal regulators considered denying approval for the merger of Nynex Corp. and Bell Atlantic because Nynex had posted an unsatisfactory

Marketing Dictionary

gap A difference between expected service quality and perceived service quality.

service encounter The actual interaction point between a customer and a service provider.

customer service record. The phone company failed to meet a set of performance standards monitored by New York state. The state evaluated service elements such as how long Nynex took to answer customer calls and the length of time the company required to fix service problems. Nynex had compiled a rating so poor that regulators fined the company $19 million. To enhance its service record, Nynex embarked on a major project to improve its customer-information system. Now that the two companies have merged into one—Bell Atlantic—customers can find answers to billing questions and other routine inquiries through an automated system, freeing customer service personnel to deal with service problems.[16]

Because employee performance is intricately linked with the outcomes of many service encounters, service firms need to pay particular attention to training and satisfying their staff members. Knight Transportation maintains unusual company atmosphere in the trucking business, because its truck drivers express strong, positive attitudes about working for the firm. Knight calls its drivers *driving associates* and rewards them with stock options. In addition, Knight schedules shorter trips than most trucking firms require. As a result, Knight's drivers spend only four nights a week away from home, compared with an industry average of more than five. Knight has reaped rewards from treating its drivers this way. The company generates driver turnover half that of other trucking companies, and its trucks make 98 percent of their deliveries at the promised times.[17]

TYPES OF CONSUMER AND BUSINESS SERVICES

As they do for tangible goods, marketers can classify services according to the products' intended uses. Service firms can serve consumer markets, business markets, or both. Many marketers sell the same services—telephone, gas, and electric services, for example—to both consumers and organizational buyers, but service firms often maintain separate marketing groups for the two customer segments.

Consumer services break down into convenience, shopping, and specialty services. Customers for dry cleaning and shoe repair commonly purchase these services as convenience products. Automobile repairs and insurance amount to shopping services, because purchases usually involve some effort by consumers to compare prices and quality. Specialty services include professional services, such as financial, legal, and medical advice.

Business services also define their own categories. Businesses pay for many *adjunct services* that help the buyers by supporting their work toward business goals and objectives. Andersen Consulting, for example, provides consulting services to help businesses improve the effectiveness of their management, finance, and technology programs.

Other service purchases hire outside firms to perform core tasks of the business buyers. For example, Northern Telecom (Nortel) outsourced its distribution activities to Ryder Integrated Logistics. Nortel alerts Ryder about its delivery schedules and priorities. Ryder then identifies the best way of getting Nortel's products to customers. Ryder handles everything from packaging and delivery to disposing of excess packaging materials. Ryder also provides a dedicated fleet of trucks to handle Nortel's needs. By outsourcing to Ryder, Nortel maintains its focus on important strategic issues.[18] Personnel services make up one of the fastest-growing outside providers of business services. The Kelly Services ad in Figure 13.8 promotes the company's goal of "achieving perfection" in carrying out the core business function of staffing to meet the changing needs of its customers.

Several other classification schemes might divide service products according to different criteria. For example, the answers to five questions can help marketers to classify services:

1. What is the nature of the service act?
2. What type of relationship does the service organization develop with its customers?

Figure 13.8 A Service Firm Performing a Core Task for Business Customers

ACHIEVING PERFECTION
We think it's possible. The timeless elegance of a classic car is both proof and inspiration. At Kelly®, we work to achieve perfection one customer at a time. By meeting and exceeding expectations, we have become the quality leader in the design of flexible staffing for business, industry and home health care.

KELLY
SERVICES

3. How much can the service provider customize and adjust the service product?
4. What is the nature of demand for the service?
5. How is the service delivered?

Each of these questions can result in a different classification system. For example, consider just one question about the method of service delivery. This analysis might lead to categories based on whether customers visit the service provider's location, the service provider's staff visits customers, or the parties transact business without physical contact. Services that fall into the first group include a movie theater, beauty salon, fitness club, dentist's office, and fast-food restaurant chain. Carpet cleaning, lawn care, and taxi services all bring staff members to customers' locations. The third category includes firms that complete business transactions via mail or telecommunications contacts, such as a catalog retailer, credit card company, Internet service provider, and long-distance phone company.[19]

ENVIRONMENTS FOR SERVICE FIRMS

Economic, social-cultural, political-legal, technological, and competitive forces vary as much for service firms as for goods producers, and they can affect a service organization's success just as much. Internet and Web technology, for example, have created a host of opportunities for service companies. Online services and Internet service providers like America Online and Netcom connect consumers to the many offerings promoted via the new media. Other companies develop the content for specialty areas on these services, like the Motley Fool investment area or CNET's News.Com technology news area. Systems consultants set up company networks, and site developers

http://www.cnet.com/

and computer graphics specialists design Web pages for businesses. Other consultants train people to use the technology.

Economic Environment

Consumer expenditures for services have grown in parallel with an expansion of business and government services to keep pace with the increasing complexity of the U.S. economy. The resulting sharp increase in spending for services and development of service industries as the major employer of labor rank among the most significant economic trends in the post-World War II economy. Most explanations of these trends highlight changes associated with a maturing economy and by-products of rapid economic growth.

A theory developed by economist Colin Clark describes the growth of service industries. In the first, most primitive stage of economic development, the vast majority of a population work in farming, hunting, fishing, and forestry. As the society becomes more advanced, the economic emphasis shifts from agrarian pursuits to manufacturing activities. The third, most advanced stage of development occurs when most of a society's labor pool works in **tertiary industries**—those involved in production of services. While some people associate service industries with minimal job skills and low pay, many service-sector jobs, such as those in communications and computer software, command high salaries and require complex skills.

As much as consumer expenditures for services have grown, business expenditures for services have shown even more remarkable increases. Servicing the needs of business customers has become a very profitable endeavor that has expanded into many areas. In just one field, for example, companies range from suppliers of temporary help to highly specialized management consulting services. Two causes have driven the rapid growth of business services. First, service firms frequently can perform specialized functions for their customers more cheaply than the customers could do the same jobs themselves. Enterprises that provide maintenance, cleaning, and protection services for office buildings and industrial plants are common examples. Second, many companies lack equipment or expertise they need to perform certain specialized services themselves.

For example, businesses can spend a great deal of money and time handling workers' compensation claims. RTW, Inc. handles workers' compensation programs for over 1,500 companies in four states. RTW sells and services workers' compensation insurance policies but its service doesn't stop there. When a client's employee files a workers' compensation claim, RTW handles all of the paperwork, investigates the claim, and works to get the employee back on the job as quickly as possible. RTW operates counseling and training programs to find and solve the

Marketing Dictionary

tertiary industry An industry that rises to dominance in the third stage of an economy's development; service firms are considered components of tertiary industries.

SOLVING AN ETHICAL CONTROVERSY

Do Funeral Home Chains Depersonalize Death and Exploit Grief for Profit?

These days, when death knocks, you might be surprised who answers the door. Death has become a big business. In ever-increasing numbers, huge funeral home chains are burying loved ones around the globe. One out of ten burials in the United States, for instance, is arranged by Houston-based Service Corp. International.

Consumers have probably never heard of Service Corp. or the other funeral home giants, but they are changing the way companies market death services. This transformation is creating a backlash among consumers who criticize corporate undertakers for turning death into a lucrative business. Rebelling against the chains, some smaller communities are even establishing their own funeral co-ops. Still other consumers are buying the modern equivalent of a pine box at a casket store.

Should Funeral Home Chains Depersonalize Death and Exploit Grief for Profit?

PRO

1. **The rapid consolidation of the death-services industry is unfairly driving up prices. To satisfy the profit demands of shareholders, funeral home chains must continue to hike prices. In the United States, for instance, the average cost of a funeral today is $4,624, according to the National Funeral Directors Association, and that figure doesn't even include the cost of a cemetery plot, flowers, the tombstone, and other expenses.**

   Mergers should allow lower costs for funerals, but instead the chains squeeze even more money from consumers. Chains set prices approximately 17 percent higher than those of independent homes, and they typically charge 16 percent more for a casket.
2. **Some funeral directors are concerned that corporate undertakers can't match the quality of service of a local mortician. That's the main reason why John Desmond, a third-generation funeral director from Troy, Michigan, has decided not to sell his business to SCI. "I'd be concerned because I have no guarantee that the quality of service would be maintained [with SCI]," Desmond says. "I'm not willing to sell my name."**

CON

1. **A major complaint about funeral home chains cites their tendency to boost burial prices**

root causes of workers' compensation claims, a task that many firms are ill-equipped to handle on their own.[20]

Social-Cultural Environment

The social-cultural environment changes over time, causing corresponding changes in consumer preferences for services. For instance, a trend toward reliance on counselors, coaches, and consultants has affected many aspects of modern people's personal, family, and work lives. A few years ago, some of these services were not even available, let alone in demand. Today, some people hire leisure consultants to advise them on what to do in their spare time.

Service marketers often must adjust their offerings and marketing mixes to adapt to social-cultural changes. Maternity services provide a good example. Hospitals and doctors actively recruit pregnant patients, because they recognize that maternity services often lead to lifelong relationships. To attract Baby Boomer parents, hospitals offered such frills as steak and champagne dinners and family birthing rooms. As this group aged, however, hospitals had to adapt their strategies to meet the preferences of Generation X mothers. These new mothers bring more culturally and socially diverse outlooks. They seek even more options when they're pregnant. Midwife services, for example, are increasingly popular. Demanding customers promote a growing emphasis on the perceived value of maternity care.

As a result, hospitals and health-care providers are beginning to adapt their marketing strategies to compete in this changing market. Tampa General Health Care, for instance, welcomes new mothers with no room charges for 48 hours after their medical discharges. Mothers and infants can enjoy inpatient care and assistance even if their insurance companies refuse to cover the cost. Recognizing the growing interest in midwife services, Kaiser Permanente now includes that kind of care as one of its maternity options. The California HMO reports that nearly 90 percent of its maternity patients are choosing to consult midwives with obstetricians as backups.[21]

Political-Legal Environment

Many service businesses operate under closer government regulation than other private companies. Some service industries must comply with regulations of national govern-

when they arrive in a new market. But cost should not be the sole criterion for measuring customers' experiences. "We do not generally try to be the cheapest operator in town," says a representative for Loewen Group Inc., a chain of funeral homes based in Burnaby, British Columbia in Canada. "We believe in providing quality service."

2. Critics should realize that the funeral business must change with the times. Mom-and-pop grocery stores disappeared long ago because they no longer made economic sense. This same phenomenon is now weeding out the weaker funeral parlors. Funeral directors "don't want to think of [death] as big business," says Betty Murray of the National Foundation of Funeral Directors. "But we're in the era of acquisitions and consolidations."
3. Choosing a funeral conglomerate can make the process of saying good-bye to loved ones easier. For instance, Service Corp. has established one-stop shopping by combining the operations of local funeral parlors with those of nearby cemeteries.

Summary

Chains insist that they maintain the sensitivity of a neighborhood undertaker. In most cases, for instance, when SCI gobbles up a funeral parlor, it typically keeps the personnel and the name in place. Most customers never even know of the change in ownership.

But this argument fails to console those who deplore the big chains. One town, Charlottetown on Canada's Prince Edward Island, rebelled against the merger mania in the death business. Some of the residents on this island of fishermen and farmers formed the Hillsborough and Area Funeral Co-op. Operating out of a storefront, the co-op provides funerals that look remarkably similar to traditional ones. But it hires a freelance embalmer and pays a co-op member to oversee the proceedings. Some of the local funeral directors insist that the co-op offers "Flintstone funerals," but customers disagree. "Traditional funeral homes have made quite a business out of death," complains Will MacDonald, who buried his mother and aunt through the co-op. The co-op, he says, offered "a little more warmth."

Sources: "Service Corp. International Reports Record First Quarter Results," PR Newswire, April 22, 1997, downloaded from http://www.prnewswire.com/cnoc/, May 2, 1997; Michael A. Robinson, "Partners' Casket Store Tries to Ease High Cost of Funerals," *San Diego Union-Tribune,* November 26, 1996, p. C2; Robert Tomsho, "Costly Funerals Spur a Co-op Movement to Hold Down Bills," *Wall Street Journal,* November 12, 1996, pp. A1, A6; and Ron Trujillo, "Funeral Giant Moves in on Small Rivals," *USA Today,* October 31, 1995, pp. 1B–2B.

ment agencies such as the Federal Power Commission, the Federal Trade Commission (FTC), the Federal Communications Commission (FCC), and the Securities and Exchange Commission (SEC). The industries subject to federal regulations include banking, electric utilities, television, and telecommunications.

Other service industries answer to state and local regulators. Doctors, attorneys, and dentists must meet state licensing requirements before they can practice. Beauticians, auto mechanics, restaurants, and funeral homes also comply with state and local requirements for fees, taxes, certification, and licensing.

The railroad industry's freight transport business illustrates the potential effect of the political-legal environment on a service business. For many years, a few large companies dominated the rail industry. In 1980, Congress approved legislation that allowed major railroads to divest their unprofitable short routes, leading to the emergence of a new breed of railroad company. Entrepreneurs bought relatively small routes, called *short lines,* from large carriers. One firm that took advantage of the new opportunity was Pioneer Railcorp, which bought up short lines that the major carriers no longer wanted with the hope of turning them into profitable lines.

In the early 1990s, however, the rail industry faced new challenges when the federal government deregulated rates. This move gave small railroads the chance to bid competitively on freight services. However, at the same time, the federal government also instituted tough new safety regulations that caused a rapid increase in the operating costs borne by railroads. Many of the short line railroads that had sprung up during the 1980s felt squeezed by these new regulations. Several sold their lines to competitors like Pioneer. Since 1990, Pioneer has acquired ten new short line routes.[22]

Service firms seeking to expand globally must also consider the political-legal environments in other countries. Several European countries have eliminated government monopolies in telecommunications, allowing U.S. phone companies to compete there. Deregulation of financial services in Latin America opens up new opportunities for accounting firms, insurance companies, and banks. Movie studios anticipate great opportunities in China, the world's most populous country, but they must deal with strict government controls and bureaucratic procedures in the process. The ad for *Forrest Gump* in Figure 13.9 drew large audiences to the Paramount Pictures film, but the success of foreign films in China depends not on consumer

Figure 13.9 **Paramount: Successful Global Expansion in the Political-Legal Environment of China**

荣获1995年 6 项奥斯卡金像奖
美国彩色宽银幕立体声故事片
阿甘正传
阿甘憨憨的
在他眼里，这世界
完全是另外一个模样
汤姆 · 汉克斯
主演
Tom Hanks is
Forrest Gump

demand but on the China Film Ministry. This government agency decides how many foreign films may appear in the country, and it limits both the timing and durations of the engagements. It stocks the country's theaters with 200 Chinese films and only 60 foreign films.

When American Airlines and British Airways sought to merge operations, the two firms faced opposition from the European Commission, the European Union's executive arm. The commission expressed concerns that the alliance would unfairly dominate trans-Atlantic air travel and offered to approve the merger only if the two airlines agreed to cede some of their joint takeoff and landing slots in England. The two airlines initially maintained that the European Commission did not have the authority to block the partnership.[23]

Technological Environment

The technological environment may emerge as the primary determinant of future growth in the service sector. Technological advances can improve the productivity of service workers, open new distribution methods, and even create opportunities for business expansion. **Productivity**—output as measured by the production of each worker—is especially important to service firms. Service marketers hunt constantly for technologically generated opportunities that open new strategic windows for their firms.

Consider, for example, the rise of virtual business schools. Several universities have uncovered a way to reach expanded student markets. Using videoconferencing technology, schools such as Harvard, the University of Michigan, and Dartmouth are beaming class sessions to sites far off campus. Large corporations are often buying these long-distance education services in order to help employees improve their business skills without the time and expense of off-site executive education courses. Instead, students can complete the courses by gathering in a conference room to watch the seminars on television. The universities regard virtual business schools as new sources of revenue and chances to broaden the markets to which they deliver their services.[24]

Major shipping companies, including United Parcel Service and Federal Express, have also applied technology to improve productivity and customer service. Federal Express uses bar-coded labels to track the status of packages as they move through the company's distribution system. Customers can get information about their packages by logging on to FedEx's Web site, which also offers free, downloadable software that customers can use to prepare packages and print bar-coded shipping documents. Federal Express regards the expanded contacts as a win-win situation; it benefits by reducing errors on the customer's end, and customers benefit by speeding up their shipping process.[25]

Although technology can reduce service delivery costs, many service providers have found that they must balance high-tech services with high-touch services or risk alienating customers. In some cases, this combination requires that employees learn new skills. Coastal Federal Credit Union in Raleigh, North Carolina, has implemented service delivery methods such as ATMs and telephone access, reducing the credit union's reliance on human tellers. The technology allows the credit union to retrain tellers to serve as financial counselors instead of merely transaction processors. The combination gives credit union customers greater value than they previously received.[26]

Competitive Environment

Service marketers face several challenges when assessing the competitive environment. In many service industries, especially those regulated by the government, competition may come from government services rather than other service firms. Also, price competition is limited in certain service fields, such as communication, legal, and medical services. In other service industries, not-for-profit organizations such as hospitals, educational institutions, and religious agencies regard competition from a noncommercial point of view. Many service industries feature substantial barriers to entry, requiring a new competitor to make a major financial investment or bring special education or training to the business.

In evaluating its competitive environment, a service firm needs to find ways to differentiate its service from those of direct competitors. The intangibility of many services complicates this basic marketing function. One example is the competitive environment encountered by Internet search companies such as Yahoo!, Infoseek, Lycos, and Excite. These firms help Web surfers locate desired data on the Internet. They also sell advertising space to other firms. The service they provide, however, has become a commodity, as more than 200 information services compete for attention on the Internet. The leading search firms are struggling to make their services stand out. Yahoo! pursues this goal by offering itself as a media company, not just a Web search tool. It has added proprietary content to its Web site in hopes of attracting new and returning users. Infoseek, on the other hand, is attempting to position itself as the search site for businesspeople. The company added software designed to help businesses find what they need more quickly than they could through competitors' services. It also spent more than $5 million on advertising to build its image as the place to find business information on the Net.[27]

Service marketers often need to look beyond obvious direct competitors and evaluate the effects of indirect competitors. For example, a movie theater complex competes not only with other theater complexes, but also with a host of other entertainment and recreation options. Consumers may decide to spend their time and money watching a play, attending a ball game, or even staying home and watching television. Theater owners must find ways to position their service to attract consumers away from these competing activities.

Competition from Government Only government agencies can provide some services, but some official service providers compete with privately produced goods and services. For example, the U.S. Postal Service's Express Mail competes with Federal Express, Airborne, UPS, and other next-day delivery services. Also, the government provides health care for veterans of the armed services through the Veteran's Administration hospital system and for seniors through Medicare and private providers.

Outsourcing in the Service Sector Many goods manufacturers practice outsourcing, or moving company operations and production outside the organization, typically to inexpensive facilities overseas. Outsourcing has also found ready supporters in service industries. AT&T Wireless Services, for example, has an outsourcing agreement with TeleTech to handle all of its customer service calls. TeleTech works closely with AT&T customer service staff to handle customer calls about service and technical support.[28] Several companies also outsource computer programming tasks, sometimes to foreign suppliers. Workers in India, Ireland, the Philippines, Russia, and Singapore handle programming duties for U.S. firms.

THE MARKETING MIX FOR SERVICES

Service marketers can segment markets according to geographic, demographic, psychographic, or product-related criteria to identify target markets for their products. As with goods markets, demographic segmentation is the most common segmentation variable for services marketing. For example, the Lifetime cable TV channel, targeted at women, features programs such as "Our Home," the show promoted in the ad in Figure 13.10.

USAA provides a good example of how a service firm segments its markets. USAA provides a wide range of insurance and financial services to its customers. The company has identified changing needs for insurance services as consumers move through different stages of life, such as getting married, starting families, and retiring. Recall from Chapter 10 that USAA has developed an extensive customer database. In addition to providing customer service representatives with information about customers' policies, it also tracks their successive life stages. As a result, the firm can target the most appropriate services to each customer's needs and maintain long-term customer relationships. In fact, USAA enjoys customer retention rates well above average for the insurance industry.[29]

Along with careful segmentation, satisfying buyers' service needs also requires an effective marketing mix. Service policies, pricing, distribution, and promotion strategies must combine to produce an integrated marketing program. The following sections briefly describe marketing mix considerations for service firms.

Service Strategy

Just as goods manufacturers struggle to find the best product mixes, service firms must also identify the service

Marketing Dictionary

productivity The ratio of output to input of goods and services for a nation, industry, firm, or individual worker.

Figure 13.10 Demographic Segmentation for Services Marketing

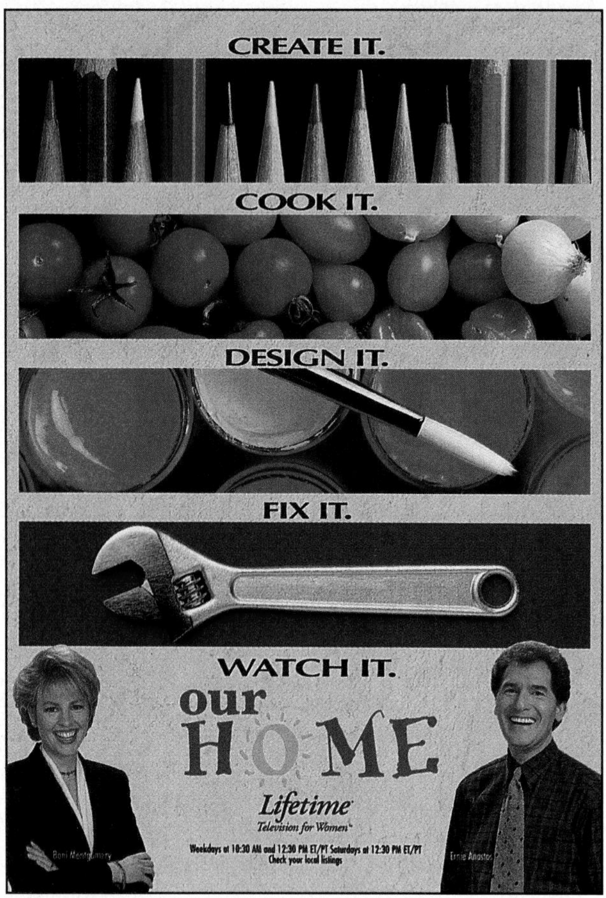
CREATE IT.
COOK IT.
DESIGN IT.
FIX IT.
WATCH IT.
our HOME
Lifetime
Television for Women
Weekdays at 10:30 AM and 12:30 PM ET/PT Saturdays at 12:30 PM ET/PT
Check your local listings
Ernie Anastos

mixes that will successfully attract consumers. The target market chosen for a service often directly influences the elements of the service mix.

Four Seasons-Regent Hotels have targeted buyers of luxury travel. As part of its service strategy, the company has sought to build the Four Seasons-Regent name into a brand recognized worldwide for providing outstanding value-added service. All hotels in the chain emphasize highly personalized service for guests. For example, the hotels offer overnight shoe repair.

Employees make integral contributions to the Four Seasons-Regent service strategy. They receive extensive training so they thoroughly understand not only the tasks involved in their jobs but also the intangible influences on customer satisfaction. Along with its strong personalization, the company has also achieved extensive standardization. Guests can depend on very similar, high-quality experiences at hotels in Hong Kong or the United States.[30]

Service firms often look for ways to extend their service mixes by offering new services. For example, telephone companies have added a variety of new functions to basic telephone access. Customers can identify callers before answering their phones and even block calls from all but previously specified numbers. Phone companies have also added services geared toward the needs of business customers. When a customer calls a single toll-free number for Pizza Hut from anywhere in a five-state area, for example, BellSouth Corp. automatically routes the call to the restaurant closest to the customer's location. Phone companies charge up to $8 a month for each new service added to a customer's basic service, helping the service extensions to expand phone company revenues from existing accounts.[31]

Service businesses must continually adapt their service mixes as environmental conditions change. Travel agents, for instance, have faced a variety of environmental challenges in the past few years. Airlines have reduced the commission fees traditionally paid to travel agents for booking customers. Online travel services, such as Travelocity (described in Figure 13.11), encourage consumers to make their own reservations. In addition, new competitors to traditional travel agencies have entered the market. For example, Docunet is installing automated ticket-printing machines in offices and supermarkets. To adapt to these environmental conditions, some travel agencies have changed their service strategies.

http://www.travelocity.com/
http://www.travelfest.com/

Walk into one of Travelfest's locations in Austin, Texas, and you won't find the typical travel agency. Instead, Travelfest has created "travel stores." Travel destination videos play on 14 monitors. A full-sized replica of an airplane wing hangs over the reservations center. Besides making travel plans, customers can choose from over 20,000 travel-related items, from books and maps to luggage and water purifiers. Customers can apply for travel visas and browse travel and hotel indexes. The stores are open seven days a week from 9 A.M. until 11 P.M.

While Travelfest has adapted its service mix to attract the mass market, Aspen Travel in Jackson Hole, Wyoming, has focused on a narrow niche within the travel market. The agency has moved away from booking vacations to emphasize arranging travel logistics for film production companies. If a film crew needs to get an elephant to Timbuktu, Aspen will find a way to get it there. This change in service strategy required Aspen's staff to develop an entirely new set of skills in a formerly unknown area of expertise, but the change has paid off. Aspen now does 85 percent of its business within this niche market.[32]

The intangible nature of their products prevents service providers from duplicating some tangible goods marketing strategies. For example, these marketers make only very limited packaging and labeling decisions; service marketers rarely use packages as promotional tools. In addition, they cannot usually introduce new services to the market by distributing samples, although some have tried the tactic. Racquetball clubs and cable television channels frequently offer trial periods without charge or at greatly reduced rates to move potential customers through the stages of the adoption process and convert them to regular patrons.

America Online and other online services encourage trial usage by sending out free access software on disks and CDs. Potential users receive free access time when they install the software, a very costly strategy, according to industry analysts. AOL claims it spends $45 to attract each new customer, but some analysts put the cost at closer to $100. It also has a high customer turnover rate: Nearly 60 percent of customers leave the service each year. For AOL at least, trial usage does not guarantee a customer's loyalty.[33]

Figure 13.11 Modifying Service Strategies to Adapt to New Competitors

Take A Power Trip.
Book it with the most powerful, one-stop travel site on the Net.
With Travelocity™, you'll get everything you need to get going: reservations and ticketing on more than 370 airlines; continuously updated information on over 15,000 worldwide destinations; travel events, schedules and activities; chat rooms and travel forums; even a travel merchandise mall.
Travelocity – an exciting new destination, information and reservation source brought to you by SABRE Interactive and Worldview Systems – two of the most powerful names in travel.
http://www.travelocity.com
TRAVELOCITY
Maximum power for the do-it-yourself traveler.

Pricing Strategy

Pricing decisions pose major problems for service firms. In developing a pricing strategy, service marketers must consider the demand for the service; production, marketing, and administrative costs; and the influence of competition. Another key consideration is perceived value: the relationship between a customer's perception of the service's quality and its cost. Customers may happily pay higher prices for unique or extremely high-quality services. However, many service providers face only limited price competition. For instance, the prices charged by most utilities are closely regulated by federal, state, and local government agencies.

Price negotiation is an important part of many professional service transactions. Consumer services that sometimes involve price negotiations include auto repairs, physical-fitness programs, and financial, legal, and medical advice. Direct negotiations sometimes set prices for specialized business services, such as equipment rental, marketing research, insurance, maintenance, and protection services, as well.

Some service marketers group related services together under umbrella prices, a strategy called *bundling.* MCI is attempting to attract mid-sized businesses by bundling network and remote management services. MCI installs network linkages that tie together all of a business's computer systems. Then, it remotely manages the network from a dedicated management center in Dallas. To tempt these targeted mid-sized businesses, MCI offers an average price of $2,700 per desktop per year, compared to the $6,000 to $12,000 annual cost of maintaining each desktop in a separately managed local area network (LAN) system. MCI hopes that the bundling strategy will also attract customers for the company's long-distance voice and data systems.[34]

Distribution Strategy

The distribution channels for services are shown in Figure 13.12. Service providers often distribute their products through simpler and more direct channels than those for goods. This difference results largely from the intangibility of services. Service marketers worry less than goods manufacturers about storage, transportation, and inventory control, and they typically employ shorter channels of distribution. For another consideration, many kinds of service marketers must maintain continuing, personal relationships with their customers. Consumers will remain clients of the same insurance agents, banks, or travel agents if those service providers keep them reasonably satisfied. Similarly, companies often retain public accounting firms and lawyers in relatively permanent arrangements.

Two major exceptions contradict the principle of direct distribution of services: consolidators and franchises. *Consolidators* are commonplace in the air travel business,

MARKETING HALL OF SHAME

Is AOL Online or Offline?

Not long ago, America Online (AOL), the largest commercial online service provider in the country, e-mailed its subscribers to make an irresistible offer. An AOL member could cruise the service's internal features and the Internet 24 hours a day, seven days a week and pay only $19.95 a month for the connection. The new pricing was an instantaneous hit. Subscribers no longer had to worry about their monthly AOL bills—the service would never cost more than a couple of movie tickets and a bucket of popcorn.

Yet AOL overlooked a major flaw in its new, all-you-can-use marketing package. It made the service entirely too popular. The company's daily online sessions jumped by 33 percent to 9 million, which works out to 3.1 million hours of connection time. The flat-rate pricing left subscribers dallying online 20 percent longer than before.

The unprecedented customer demand completely overwhelmed the online provider's system. Irate customers faced monumental cyberspace traffic jams. Instead of cruising the Internet for hours, many unlucky subscribers simply got busy signals when they tried to log on, even late at night. In reaction, AOL employees worked around the clock to add phone lines, computer modems, and network connections.

The flat-rate pricing scheme did not emerge from some hastily conceived marketing come-on. AOL conceived the strategy to stem the hemorrhage in its subscriber base, as current and potential customers flocked to hundreds of cheaper Internet-access services. In fact, the $19.95 price became an industry standard for unlimited use. Along with the mom-and-pop providers, AOL was also locked in battle with such giants as Microsoft Corp. and AT&T, who entered the field with lots of cash.

AOL's problems do not end with its pricing woes. The Federal Trade

particularly for international flights. They purchase seats from airlines at substantial discounts and then resell them to travel agents, to other consolidators, and directly to individual consumers. Franchises provide distribution channels for services that do not allow geographic separation of production from consumption. Mail Boxes Etc., Super Cuts, and Minit-Lube are examples.

Technology can play a major role in the distribution strategy of a service firm. The banking industry is a good example. Before the 1980s, banks provided nearly all of their services through their branch facilities. Customers had to visit branch offices to cash checks, make deposits, apply for loans, and even receive account updates. Banks relied heavily on a "brick-and-mortar" distribution strategy. They invested in adding branch buildings to their networks to serve customer needs.

Starting in the 1980s, however, technological changes led many financial institutions to implement other marketing strategies. Automated teller machines (ATMs) and 24-hour phone service gave customers added options for service delivery. Now many banks have added online banking services that let customers access their accounts from their home computers. As they have expanded these alternate de-

Figure 13.12 Distribution Channels for Services

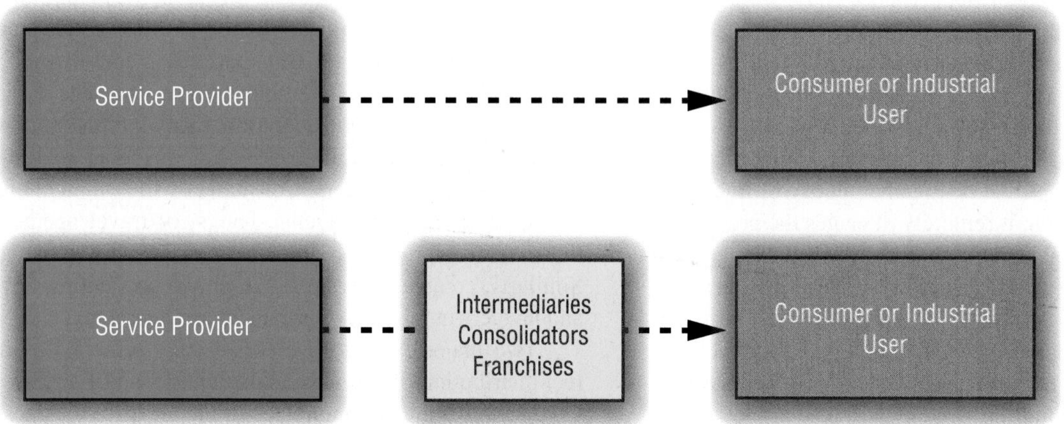
Service Provider
Consumer or Industrial User
Service Provider
Intermediaries
Consolidators
Franchises
Consumer or Industrial User

Commission is examining whether AOL and other online providers follow unfair billing practices. For instance, the FTC is exploring whether online companies create obstacles to canceling their services after free trial periods.

Meanwhile, in the midst of its legal problems, AOL's president, recruited from Federal Express, resigned after just four months. Within a one-and-a-half-month period, AOL's stock price deflated by 40 percent.

But AOL faces an even more ominous threat to its financial health. Some observers predict that the World Wide Web could someday make AOL obsolete, or at least leave it a shell of its former self. People don't need AOL's help to visit the vast expanse of the Internet, threatening its continued success.

But Steve Case, the 38-year-old founder and chief executive officer of America Online, vigorously disagrees with this scenario. Most people, he insists, need AOL because most computer users don't want to cope with the difficulties of going it alone on the Web and subscribing to services à la carte. This kind of service is "probably fine for a technologically astute early adopter, but seems awfully complicated for a consumer market," Case says. "TV would never have gotten to 90 percent market penetration if it had been that hard. If you want to reach a mainstream audience, you have to make it more plug and play. One-stop shopping. One disk to install. One price to pay."

Case says AOL will continue to pursue its current strategy—offering a service that's fun, useful, affordable, and "really, really easy to use."

QUESTIONS FOR CRITICAL THINKING

1. **What strategies would you recommend to AOL to improve its customers' satisfaction with their service encounters?**
2. **Discuss the effect of environmental factors on AOL.**

Sources: "AOL Problems Are Bad News for Businesses," January 28, 1997, downloaded from http://www.usatoday.com/, March 18, 1997; Peter H. Lewis, "An 'All You Can Eat' Price Is Clogging Internet Access," *New York Times,* December 17, 1996, pp. 1A, C5; Gene Koprowski, "AOL CEO Steve Case," *Forbes ASAP Supplement,* October 7, 1996, pp. 94–96; and Amy Barrett, "Online Services Monkey Business in Cyberspace?" *Business Week,* July 1, 1996, p. 96.

livery systems, some banks have chosen to reduce their branch office networks. Wells Fargo, for example, closed many of its branch offices in California.

Some banks, however, are attempting to differentiate themselves from their competitors by adopting personal service strategies that continue to rely on branch networks. City National Bank, a small bank with 23 branches in Los Angeles, sees an opportunity in Wells Fargo's move toward computer delivery. Each branch offers a full range of services delivered by human tellers and customer service personnel. Branch managers and the bank's executive staff also keep themselves readily accessible to customers. City National believes that its distribution strategy will attract account holders who want and need more personalized attention than they can receive through ATMs and computer services.[35]

Cincinnati's Huntington National Bank has developed yet another approach to service delivery. Huntington brings its services to customers through its "branch on wheels." The bank provides a sort of mobile branch through a 38-foot long vehicle dubbed the *BankMobile,* that travels to low-to-middle-income neighborhoods of Cincinnati. Customers can open accounts, apply for loans, and use an ATM mounted on the vehicle. "Accessibility is one of the keys to customer satisfaction," explains Thomas Kelly, Huntington's assistant vice president. "The BankMobile program makes us accessible and visible."[36]

Promotional Strategy

Marketers face several challenges as they develop promotional strategies for services. They must find a way to fill out the intangible images of most services and successfully convey the benefits that consumers receive.

Advertising portrayals of insurance services, for example, must overcome problems of perception, since the end benefit of the service is often, in a sense, a negative event. Insurance also brings extremely intangible benefits. Most people have difficulty even explaining what an insurance company does.

The need to differentiate a service defines a particular goal for promotional strategy. Service marketers must work carefully to identify specific features and benefits that set their company apart from the competition. Since purchase decisions for services often require consumers to buy on trust, service marketers also need to clearly portray a strong company image. Finally, service marketers must avoid overselling the service, since inflated expectations can result in customer dissatisfaction.

Marketers may use symbolic associations or bold graphics to convey the benefits of a particular service. Organizational image advertising also helps service firms to build customer trust. Transamerica insurance accomplishes both goals in advertisements that feature dramatic shots of

MARKETING HALL OF FAME

At Your Service

The relationship started in the usual way. The General Electric Company (GE) sold medical imaging equipment, like CAT scanners and magnetic resonance imaging units, to Columbia/HCA Healthcare. GE also provided service on this equipment. In 1995, GE offered to service all imaging equipment in the more than 300 hospitals that the chain operated, including equipment that GE had not manufactured. Then GE began managing Columbia/HCA's medical supplies—mostly products that GE does not sell. Today, GE also consults with the hospital group's top management to boost productivity through improved operations, better supply-chain management, and employee training. "They've become part of our team," says Sam Greco, Columbia/HCA's chief financial officer.

The expanded relationship pays off for both companies. Columbia/HCA receives high-quality goods, as well as the benefit of GE's management skills. By increasing the number and level of services it provides, GE strengthens its ties to a major customer.

GE hopes to duplicate this scenario many times over with other customers. GE doubts that its world leadership in manufactured products and quality control will continue to propel its upward growth curve in today's competitive business environment. With slowing business product sales, compressing product life cycles, and advanced technology that helps competitors to copy goods, services can provide the competitive edge that GE needs to meet its growth targets.

Since taking over in 1981, Chairman John F. Welch has remade the company several times. No longer a sluggish U.S. industrial conglomerate, GE has transformed itself into an innovative multinational corporation that recently ranked first in profitability among U.S. corporations. Now Welch plans to transform the company yet again by shifting GE's revenue generating activities away from manufacturing and toward services.

Welch has been gradually moving GE in this direction for years. In 1990, services represented 44 percent of revenues, and manufacturing contributed 56 percent. By 1995, the percentages had reversed, and the company now estimates that by 2000, 67 percent of its revenues will come from service products.

The switch enriches the bottom line, too. Hospital cost-cutting programs limit price increases for medical equipment, and competition has sharply reduced prices on the firm's jet engines. Services provide not only another strong revenue source but also significantly higher margins than sales of goods. About 60 percent of GE's profits now come from services—an important advantage at a time when the company faces pricing pressure both at home and abroad.

its pyramid-shaped headquarters building with the tag line "the people in the pyramid are working for you." These ads build the image of a firm dedicated to serving customer needs.

Some service firms try to offer previews of their offerings by using the Internet as a promotional medium. Considering booking a stay at a Hilton Hotel? You can access Hilton's World Wide Web page and visit what the company terms the world's first "cyber-resort." Prospective guests can sign in and get information and descriptions of Hilton properties; they can then make reservations without leaving the site.[37]

http://www.hilton.com/

In addition to advertising, service firms often promote their products through other methods. Banks and investment companies may send regular newsletters to customers highlighting different aspects of their services. Other service providers emphasize direct-mail promotions, setting up elaborate marketing databases to track the preferences and needs of customers.

When service marketers expand globally, their promotional strategies often do not translate easily to new countries. Service firms need to evaluate how customer service needs and preferences differ in each country. For example,

GE's service units cover three main areas: financial services, broadcasting, and aftermarket services. GE Capital Services provides a wide range of financial services, including commercial loans and mortgages, equipment and aircraft leasing, credit card processing, and insurance sales. In its latest venture, a global computer services unit contracts to manage organizational computer networks. A star performer, the rapidly growing GE Capital unit generates about one-third of the parent company's operating profits. In 1986, GE acquired NBC and earned a major place in broadcasting, another services market. Now Welch wants to increase GE's share of business products and aftermarket services.

"Our job is to sell more than the box," explains Welch. The company treats equipment sales as opportunities to get a foot in the door. From there, GE can offer its customers a wide range of services. Some relate directly to the equipment it sells, like servicing airplane engines and medical equipment. GE's management capabilities give it another marketable service. Like Columbia/HCA, many customers acknowledge GE's expertise and want its consultants to help them improve efficiency and cut costs.

Welch's newest strategic initiative is already paying off. Individual business equipment units are developing marketing plans for their own services, and top managers exchange ideas at Service Council meetings. GE Medical Systems has agreed to service contracts with a number of other hospital chains; the unit is also acquiring independent service outlets, and it built an $80 million educational programming training center. In yet another initiative, the unit developed an online diagnostic service for scanning machines to identify and fix problems. The Aircraft Engines unit added new maintenance facilities in Brazil, Britain, and Singapore. It signed a ten-year deal worth $2.3 billion to service 85 percent of British Airways' jet engines—including those made by rivals Pratt & Whitney and Rolls-Royce. Other areas with good growth potential include operating and maintaining utility power plants, locomotive maintenance, and electronic tracking systems for railroads.

Michael Hammer, co-author of *Reengineering the Corporation,* sees the move into services as the next big wave in American industry. "The product you sell is only one component of your business," he says.

QUESTIONS FOR CRITICAL THINKING

1. **Do you agree with Michael Hammer that more companies will be following GE's lead? Give some examples of how other industrial firms can increase their services offerings.**
2. **Relate GE's strategies to the chapter's discussion of the marketing mix for service firms.**

Sources: William M. Carley, "To Keep GE's Profits Rising, Welch Pushes Quality-Control Plan," *Wall Street Journal,* January 13, 1997, pp. A1, A6; Tim Smart, "Jack Welch's Encore," *Business Week,* October 28, 1996, pp. 4–5; and James L. Strodes, "GE Whiz!" *World Trade,* August 1996, pp. 22–24.

when Citibank sought to expand its credit card services to Pacific Rim customers, the bank faced cultural differences. Asian consumers traditionally preferred to pay for purchases with cash. Only 1 percent of Asians carried credit cards. Citibank decided to position MasterCard as a lifestyle product. Television ads showed a young Asian couple traveling to different cities around the world, vacationing in elegant hotels, and dining at upscale restaurants. Other image ads appeared in such eye-catching media as buses.[38]

Personal selling also plays a role in promoting services, because many consumers desire personal relationships with service providers. Future sales opportunities depend upon the quality of the relationship between the salesperson and the prospect. Service salespeople can greatly enhance **relationship quality,** the customer's trust in and satisfaction with the seller. Therefore, these professionals should act as relationship managers.

Marketing Dictionary

relationship quality The customer's trust in and satisfaction with the seller.

ACHIEVEMENT CHECK SUMMARY

Reread the learning goals that follow, and consider the questions for each goal. Answering these questions will reinforce your grasp of the most important concepts in the chapter and allow you to check how well you have achieved these learning goals. Where a blank appears before a question, answer with *T* or *F;* for multiple-choice questions, circle the letter of the correct answer.

Objective 13.1: Differentiate service offerings from goods.

1. ___ Many products have both goods and services components.

2. ___ An example of a pure service is (a) dental care; (b) dinner at McDonald's; (c) a new car dealership.

3. ___ Services are intangible tasks that satisfy consumers' and industrial users' needs.

Objective 13.2: Identify the primary characteristics of services.

1. ___ Services usually have tangible features that customers can consider to evaluate them.

2. ___ In buyers' minds, those who provide a service are the service.

3. ___ Service marketers can differentiate their offerings by striving for service quality.

Objective 13.3: Explain the concept of service quality.

1. ___ Service quality is the major determinant of consumer satisfaction.

2. ___ Gaps sometimes separate expected service quality from perceived service quality.

3. ___ Service firms have little control over the components of service quality.

Objective 13.4: Outline the possible outcomes of a service encounter.

1. ___ A service encounter is the actual interaction point between a customer and a service provider.

2. ___ Service switching usually occurs when a customer feels satisfied with a service encounter.

3. ___ Service loyalty often results from positive management of the service encounter.

Objective 13.5: Develop a classification system for services.

1. ___ Service providers orient their products toward either business customers or consumers.

2. ___ An example of an equipment-based service is (a) a bank; (b) a telephone company; (c) a day-care center.

3. ___ The relationship between a service provider and its customer offers one way to classify services.

Objective 13.6: Explain how environmental factors affect services.

1. ___ Recent conditions in the economic environment have allowed only slow growth for the service sector.

2. ___ Changes in consumer demographics usually don't influence the demand for services.

3. ___ The technological environment produces innovations that lead to increased productivity in the service sector.

4. ___ The competitive environment for services sometimes includes threats from goods producers or the government rather than other service providers.

Objective 13.7: Discuss market segmentation and the marketing mix for services.

1. ___ Most service marketers rely primarily on demographic segmentation.

2. ___ Pricing strategy is usually not an important element of the marketing mix for services.

3. ___ The most important goal of a service provider's promotional strategy is to (a) get the service firm's name in front of customers; (b) diminish the service gap perception; (c) demonstrate tangible benefits.

Students: See the solutions section located on page S-3 to check your responses to the Achievement Check Summary.

Key Terms

service
goods-services continuum
service quality
gap
service encounter
tertiary industry
productivity
relationship quality

Review Questions

1. Explain the difficulties in defining the term *services.* How does the goods-services continuum help marketers to define *services?*
2. What is the current status of the service sector in the U.S. economy? Why is marketing so important to service firms?
3. Identify the key characteristics of services. Explain how each affects the service provider's marketing strategy.
4. What is service quality? What are its determinants?
5. Explain gap analysis. What types of gaps can arise in service quality?
6. Define the term *service encounter.* What are the possible outcomes of a service encounter?
7. How can marketers classify services? Can a service serve both a consumer market and a business market? Explain.
8. Name the environments for service providers. Cite examples of environmental influences likely to affect service providers.
9. Which segmentation method do service marketers most often employ? Identify service-industry examples of each segmentation method.
10. What major differences distinguish the marketing strategies of firms that produce goods from those of service providers? Explain the relative importance of product, pricing, distribution, and promotional strategies for marketers of services.

Discussion Questions

1. Within the U.S. Postal Service, an assistant postmaster general wields authority for marketing. In addition to marketing its services through media advertising and advertorials, the Postal Service has lowered its rates for business mail to compete for business customers. It has also started a Saturday Certain delivery service for retailers that want guaranteed delivery of their ads on specific Saturdays. Why do you think the Postal Service has become such an aggressive service marketer? Discuss.
2. The number of ski resorts in the United States has shown a dramatic drop. In 1980, 845 U.S. ski areas competed; by 1996, only 525 were left. Locations create problems for many resorts. Many are too remote from major cities to attract single-day visitors. For another challenge, as Baby Boomers age, they lose interest in skiing, and younger consumers have not taken to the slopes as actively as Boomers did. Ski resorts also face increased competition for consumer travel and recreation dollars. "The competition for the big resorts isn't other ski areas," notes the editor of the Ski Industry Letter. "It's Disney and Carnival Cruise Lines." Develop a marketing mix for a new ski resort. Who will make up the target market for the resort? What service strategy will it implement? How will pricing, distribution, and promotion contribute to its successful marketing?[39]
3. Pinkerton's, Inc. is a legend in the security and protective services business. Founded in 1850, Pinkerton's provides security services to businesses like General Motors, the Walt Disney Co., NBC, and many others. But slim profit margins characterize the industry. Although sales grew 10 percent in a recent year, Pinkerton's lost $10 million. The company faces competition from hundreds of smaller security firms that currently account for 80 percent of the business market. Many companies hiring security services see little difference between the guards of one service and those of another. In addition, high-tech security methods are reducing the demand for human guards. Which of the service quality characteristics discussed in the chapter should define the most important priorities for Pinkerton's marketers? What steps should Pinkerton's take to differentiate its services from those of competitors?[40]
4. Outline a marketing mix for each of the following service firms:
   a. Local radio station
   b. Residential real estate brokerage firm
   c. Bed and breakfast inn
   d. Law firm specializing in family law
5. Identify at least three services that you have used in the past six months. Apply the gap analysis system discussed in this chapter to evaluate these services based on your expectations prior to the service encounters and your perceptions of the service that you actually received. Did any of the three services leave a gap between these two elements? If so, how? Was it a positive or negative gap? How did you react to the gap? What advice would you give to these service providers to narrow or eliminate the service gaps between customer expectations and customer perceptions of service quality?

'netWork

1. The issue of service quality receives extensive attention in today's environment, in both the service industry and product-related services. Several organizations work specifically to promote quality standards for services. Find one of these organizations on the Web. What purpose does this group pursue? How does it define service quality? Critically evaluate the organization's approach to service quality.

2. Many online services such as America Online and CompuServe compete to take consumers into cyberspace. Visit the home pages of these companies to compare and contrast the services they provide. In your opinion, which service provider offers the best product? Support your conclusion.

3. The health-care industry is undergoing many significant changes. In particular, health maintenance organizations draw wide-ranging attention, and they have attracted many new clients. Each year *U.S. News & World Report* selects its choices for the top HMOs and hospitals. Go to their Web site at

http://www.usnews.com/

Evaluate how the magazine determines its choices. What changes would you make to its criteria?

VIDEO CASE 13

CHANGING TO HELP OTHERS CHANGE

Andersen Worldwide is a $9.5 billion company with two lines of business: accounting/auditing services and consulting services. The consulting business helps its organizational customers to devise strategies that will improve their global competitiveness. Consultants help organizations to improve their strategies, human resources, business processes, and technological systems. Notebook computers serve as virtual offices for consultants on assignment, allowing these experts to use and showcase the same technologies they recommend for their clients.

Customers purchase Andersen's consulting services because "fundamentally they don't have some of the specialist skills that we have internally and they don't have access to the pool of knowledge that we have bought from around the world," says William Stancer, Andersen's marketing director in Europe, the Middle East, Africa, and India. "And if we can take an experience that we've had with a client in Minneapolis and extrapolate that and provide that to a telecommunications company in Belgium, then that is adding real value to that company."

As specialists in managing change for others, staff members of Andersen's consulting unit recognized a need for changes in their own organization. "We weren't getting invited to a lot of very exciting opportunities even though in our view we were the best and biggest in doing this work," says Skip Battle, Andersen's former worldwide managing partner for market development. "We realized we had to develop a separate image for the consulting services marketplace or we wouldn't have the kind of growth we wanted." In 1989, the consulting business took a new name—Andersen Consulting. Continuing to operate as part of Andersen Worldwide, the new unit faced two marketing challenges: (1) it had to establish a new brand identity that would position it for success in the highly competitive global consulting marketplace; (2) it had to transform its decentralized marketing operations into an integrated global marketing effort.

Andersen Consulting lacked both a marketing function and a formal marketing structure. Consulting partners in different geographic areas hired local resources to perform marketing activities, leaving the company's marketing without a national connection and industry and global focus. "That doesn't work in the business we're in," says James Murphy, worldwide managing partner for marketing and communications, who signed on with Andersen Consulting to develop a coordinated marketing program.

Andersen Consulting conducted internal research to test the effectiveness of its marketing activities. The results showed poor focus and weak coordination. Then the company initiated a comprehensive global market research project to learn about customers' perceptions and expectations. The Global Buyer Value Study gathered input from customers in the United States, Canada, and five European countries, revealing performance gaps between customer expectations and Andersen's service delivery in four areas: on-time completion of projects, on-budget completion, industry-specific expertise, and leading-edge solutions.

The findings from this study led development of advertising to promote an image for Andersen Consulting among its target audience. The campaign set a goal of establishing an image of Andersen Consulting as an innovative and farsighted organization that would get things done and deliver results. The campaign targeted organizational "change navigators," representatives among the top four executives in large organizations who wanted to effect change in their companies, recognized the need to take risks to do so, and would look to Andersen Consulting to help guide the change process.

"In this business," says Murphy, "advertising can't close a sale. It can't even help you with the sales discussion. But it can create a personality for you. It can present an aura around your brand. It can connect with the mindset of your buyers. And that's what we decided early on was the role of advertising for Andersen Consulting." In a business that emphasized personal selling targeted at a very narrow audience, Andersen was the first management consulting firm to advertise.

To ensure effectiveness in the campaign, Andersen involved its clients in creating and implementing its image-development program. Senior functional and MIS executives reviewed storyboards for print and broadcast ads and reported whether they found the messages compelling, the visuals stimulating, and the concepts appropriate for production.

Advertising messages focused on positioning the firm to meet the expectations of the marketplace and on making connections on issues confronting large organizations. One ad showed a formally dressed quintet performing classical music when a basketball bounced onto the set and landed in the lap of a musician. The musicians left their instruments and started tossing the ball around as the voiceover explained, "If you'd like your organization to become more adept at handling change, Andersen Consulting can help you integrate all the parts because these days, the organization that performs together, transforms together." Advertising helped Andersen Consulting to establish a brand identity, but the company still needed to coordinate its global marketing efforts. It accomplished this goal by organizing marketing activities based on the industries it served and by supporting the groups through an Integrated Marketing Model. The model's three components included image development, market development, and business development.

Image development relied on advertising, public relations, direct mail, and sponsorship of global special events such as the Andersen Consulting World Championship of Golf tournament. Market development efforts sought to identify market segments, conduct research to determine customer needs, and determine how Andersen Consulting could differentiate its services from those of competitors. For example, the company designed business integration centers for specific industries. At The Retail Place, retail clients encountered new technology that could improve their operating effectiveness. "We bring to life in these integration centers the practical applications of our thinking," says Murphy, "so our clients can come in and see exactly what it could mean to them in their environment."

The business development component of the firm's Integrated Marketing Model focused on building relationships with customers. Andersen Consulting formed business development teams country-by-country to focus on each client's unique business needs. The personalized attention helped to make clients feel special about their relationships with Andersen Consulting.

The company's Integrated Marketing Model helped it to project a consistent image throughout the world. Andersen Consulting has invested heavily in managing its brand, and the effort has paid off. When the company conducted a global awareness study in 1989, results were very low at 26 percent. The percentage today is in the mid-90s. With revenues of over $5 billion, Andersen Consulting has grown to become the world's largest management consulting firm.

Questions

1. What role did advertising play in helping Andersen Consulting establish a global brand identity?
2. Which of the six characteristics that distinguish services from goods affect the marketing program for Andersen Consulting's service?
3. What components can you identify in Andersen Consulting's program for marketing its services to customers?
4. In order to continue to provide clients with leading-edge services that help them to incorporate change and remain competitive, Andersen Consulting has introduced ServiceNet. Go to its Web site at:
   http://www.andersenconsulting.com/
   What is ServiceNet? How will ServiceNet help Andersen Consulting to maintain its image?

Sources: Some of the research material for this video case was downloaded from http://www.andersenconsulting.com/, April 18, 1997; Elizabeth MacDonald, "Andersen Appears to Rule Out Breakup," *Wall Street Journal,* December 23, 1996, p. A2; and "Andersen's Androids," *The Economist,* May 4, 1996, p. 72.

Part 4 Microsoft Corp.: Developing New Products and Expanding into New Markets

Most of the world's personal computers run on Microsoft software. Early on, Gates and Allen realized the importance of finding new markets for their products by first entering the Japanese market and then the European market. Today, Microsoft operates foreign subsidiaries in every region of the world, including in such countries as Brazil, Australia, Greece, South Africa, Norway, the United Arab Emirates, Egypt, Costa Rica, Spain, and Russia. Revenues from international markets account for 58 percent of Microsoft's total revenues.

By expanding into foreign markets and aggressively promoting its name, Microsoft has achieved high brand equity. It's become one of the world's best-known and most highly respected brand names. In a recent survey of business and consumer personal computer users conducted by International Data Group, Microsoft ranked as the number one company among all computer products marketers in "meeting computer needs."

Microsoft's brand-building initiative began in 1983, when the company started marketing to consumers. Understanding the importance of creating consumer demand at retail outlets, Bill Gates hired Rowland Hanson as vice president of corporate communications. Hanson's background was in consumer marketing, most recently as vice president of marketing for Neutrogena. While interviewing Hanson, Gates said, "You know the only difference between a dollar-an-ounce moisturizer and a $40-an-ounce moisturizer is in the consumer's mind. There is no technical difference between the moisturizers." Gates continued, "I know that we will have the physical reality of the software. We will technically be the best software. But if people don't believe it or people don't recognize it, it won't matter. While we're on the leading edge of technology, we also have to be creating the right perception about our products and our company, the right image. And right now I don't think we're doing that."

Hanson began an image-building effort to position Microsoft and its products in the marketplace as a $40-an-ounce brand. He conducted market research studies to learn what influenced software opinion leaders and how Microsoft was perceived by editors of computer magazines. He found that opinion leaders were more influenced by computer magazine articles than by advertising. Hanson began cultivating relationships with magazine editors by preparing news releases and feature articles for them and by designing promotions for opinion leaders, such as enclosing sample disks of Microsoft Word in subscription copies of *PC World.*

Based on focus group interviews with consumers, Hanson redesigned Microsoft's product packaging to present a unified corporate identity. He made Microsoft a brand name by identifying products with the corporate name first followed by the product name. For example, for the company's word processing application Word, Hanson promoted the product as Microsoft Word. Hanson also insisted that product names should communicate to buyers a product feature. When Hanson joined Microsoft, the company was ready to launch a new operating system it planned to market as the Interface Manager. But Hanson convinced Gates that Windows was a much better product name because it conveyed a product feature—the windows that customers would see on their computer screens.

Microsoft continues to spend millions of dollars in promoting its brand. It also spends millions in trying to protect its registered trademarks in the United States and other countries Microsoft has received trademark protection for its products (MSN and Windows NT), its logos (the Internet Explorer logo), and its advertising slogans ("Where do you want to go today?").

In countries throughout the world, Microsoft educates consumers about the benefits of licensing genuine products and educates lawmakers on the advantages of establishing a business climate where intellectual property rights are protected. Despite these efforts, Microsoft is faced with the problem of the unlicensed copying of its software, which results in a significant loss of revenues. Revenue loss is most significant in foreign markets, where laws are less protective of intellectual property rights than they are in the United States. Protecting its trademarks is one of Microsoft's greatest challenges as the company enters the world's biggest emerging software market.

Entering China's Software Market

In China, it's estimated that some 54 million illegal software packages are sold each year. Many of these are knockoffs of Microsoft's products. The illegal copies are priced to sell. For example, new Chinese versions of Windows go for just $5. In this counterfeit market, it's estimated that 80 percent of computers in China run on Microsoft Windows, Windows NT, and MS-DOS operating systems. One industry observer believes the counterfeiting is a boon to Microsoft. Software analyst Darwin Singson of Dataquest Inc. in Hong Kong says, "The pirates are actually helping Microsoft greatly. They are creating a huge installed base of customers."

In the long run Microsoft may benefit from counterfeiting, as it could lead to billions of dollars in sales of new applications software, upgraded product versions, and service contracts. While Microsoft continues trying to protect its trademarks, its primary focus is on developing a legitimate Chinese software market. The company's goal is to establish Windows as the national platform in China. To achieve this goal, Microsoft is sharing its technology, including some proprietary software codes, with China's government ministries and research institutes to co-develop Chinese-language Windows operating systems.

> *"No product stays on top unless it is improved," says Gates.*

Microsoft is also investing $2 million each year in training Chinese technicians and programmers to work on Windows. It has established training programs at Chinese universities and the Chinese Academy of Social Sciences to teach computer architecture, networking, and client-server applications. "Microsoft recognized that Chinese customers need more than products," says Yang Jun, vice president of China National Computer Software and Technology Service Corp. "We need good consulting, good systems integration, and good service."

Through its co-development and training initiatives, Microsoft is positioning itself as the leading supplier of software in China. The Chinese market potential is enormous, and the Chinese government is spending billions of dollars in computerizing its government offices and state-owned industries. In one government project, Microsoft is helping the People's Bank of China install Windows-based personal computers and servers at 10,000 branch locations. In another project, Microsoft is working with the State Administration of Taxation in using Windows and Windows NT connected to Microsoft servers to link the bureau's 3,200 offices and 20,000 personal computers. These government purchases are quickly increasing Microsoft's annual sales in China of $20 million.

> *"We're looking at 100 percent growth every year as far as we can see," says Bryan Nelson, Microsoft's director for Greater China.*

The sales of personal computers to Chinese consumers and small businesses are projected to increase from 1 million units in 1995 to 5 million units by 2000. Microsoft is partnering with Chinese researchers to develop technology in interactive television and Chinese handwriting and speech recognition. Gates believes these technologies are crucial in popularizing personal computers because of the difficulty in entering Chinese characters onto a keyboard.

Developing Product Strategies

The first employee Gates and Allen hired in 1975 was a software developer. Of Microsoft's 21,000 employees today, 8,000 employees—or almost 40 percent of Microsoft's workforce—work in research and product development. Microsoft's success in the marketplace has always depended on its software developers' ability to introduce new products.

Using its core competency of developing software, Microsoft has introduced products to compete in related mass-market segments of the software industry. It has expanded its product line from software languages to operating systems and applications software. Microsoft's newest ventures extend its expertise in PC software to the new mass markets of network operating systems for distributed computing and online services.

The basis of Microsoft's product development strategy is to introduce a new product and continually refine it in later versions until it becomes the industry standard. Microsoft improves its products by keeping pace with advances in hardware technology. As PC technology has advanced with more memory and computing power, Microsoft has added innovative features to its software in updated product versions launched about every two to three years. For example, Microsoft has released six versions of its DOS operating system since 1981, from DOS 2.0 introduced in 1983 to MS-DOS 6.0 released in 1993. Each new version has supported hardware advances with innovations such as multitasking, networking capabilities, and graphical interfaces. This strategy results in increasingly competitive products, as product upgrades help retain Microsoft's loyal existing customer base as well as attract new users.

Microsoft also uses new product versions as launching pads for new generations of products. For example, developers leveraged their graphical programming skills used in MS-DOS upgrades in designing the Windows operating system. With Windows 95, Microsoft has made MS-DOS and the character-based applications software for it obsolete. But Windows has opened new markets for Microsoft. For example, it has created a new market for easy-to-use graphical applications software developed by Microsoft and other software firms. Microsoft released

Microsoft Office the same day it launched Windows 95, allowing customers to buy the new operating system as well as applications software for it.

Windows 95 also allows users to access Microsoft Network directly from within the new operating system. With its NT system, Microsoft has opened a huge market for its BackOffice applications software, a suite of products for networked organizations. "We are a very predictable company," says Gates. "What we did with Windows on the desktop, we're doing with Windows NT on the server. What we did with Office on the desktop, we're doing with BackOffice on the server."

Organizing for New Product Development

As a young company, Microsoft had its software developers write code, test products, market them, negotiate contracts with customers, and provide assistance to customers when they called for help. As Microsoft expanded its product lines, it reorganized its product development process by forming teams of functional specialists. For a large program like Microsoft Word, the project is divided into many small teams that focus on developing one or two product features. These feature teams include a program manager and from three to eight developers and testers.

Program managers describe and document new product features, build product prototypes, help manage the project by keeping it on schedule, and serve as the link between software development and product managers. Developers are the software design engineers who create the individual features of each product and prepare the products for shipping. Microsoft pairs each developer with a software test engineer. Working side-by-side with developers, testers find and fix bugs and provide evaluations of products from different users' perspectives. They test features to make sure they work on different computers—such as Compaq, Apple, IBM, and Dell—and different printers. Microsoft has two foreign test locations: one in Ireland where testers handle products written in European languages; and one in Japan, where testers work on Japanese, Korean, and Chinese products.

Microsoft's marketing specialists are called product managers. Some work in individual product units, but most are part of centralized division marketing groups—for example, one group of product managers works in the Interactive Media Division, another in the Desktop Applications Division, and so on. Product managers are responsible for recognizing and pursuing market opportunities, representing the customer in the product development process, analyzing competitors' products and market trends, positioning products in the marketplace, and developing marketing programs, including product pricing packaging.

The Product Development Process

Microsoft has three primary stages for its product development process: planning, development, and stabilization. Dan Frumin, a program manager for the Microsoft Access database, describes the process:

> Every project has a flow—the beginning is the most fun for program managers, because they get to dream. The middle of the project is the most fun for developers and testers, because that's when they get to go in and do their work: writing a bunch of new code, getting features done, fixing bugs. The last cycle of the project is the most fun for marketers because that's when they figure out what trade shows they're going to attend and when they make their final decisions about how they're going to market it.

During the planning phase, product managers and program managers work together to develop a vision statement for the project. The statement is a marketing vision for the product that includes goals for the project and an analysis of competitors' products. Product and program managers use activity-based planning to analyze product features in terms of how customers will use the product. Program managers use the vision statement to produce a specification document that outlines design features, the project's schedule, and a testing strategy. Using Microsoft's Visual Basic software, program managers create prototypes of the new product that are tested with customers in the company's usability laboratory.

During the development stage, developers write the software code, testers run tests and fix errors in the code, program managers monitor the project's scheduling, and product managers plan the product's pricing, packaging, and promotional strategy. The time it takes to develop a product varies considerably, depending on the product. Consumer application products like Word or Complete Baseball move through development quickly while operating systems products take years to develop. In general, applications products are in development for between 12 and 24 months, and systems products for between three to four years. A team of more than 400 people worked for more than four years to develop the first version of the Windows NT operating system.

During the final stage, stabilization, products are tested outside the company with beta testers. The developers produce a master software diskette for manufacturing, and the product is launched in the marketplace. Working together, project team members prepare a summary document of the entire project, assessing what worked and what didn't work.

Questions

1. Joseph Lung, managing director of Hong Kong-based market research firm ATC Ltd., says this of Microsoft's market development strategy in China: "Microsoft is giving away its family jewels for peanuts." Do you agree or disagree with Mr. Lung's statement? Why or why not?
2. Which product development strategies does Microsoft use in marketing its products?
3. How does Microsoft extend the product life cycle of its products?

PART 5
DISTRIBUTION
STRATEGY

Chapter 14
Distribution

Chapter 15
Retailing

Chapter 16
Logistics and Value Chain Management

www
w.soft
softkey
dell.co
apple.c
www.cate
caterpillar
-body-
-shop.c
amazon.c
www.
home
depot
target.c
w.fedex.c
ebworl
http:w

CHAPTER 14

DISTRIBUTION

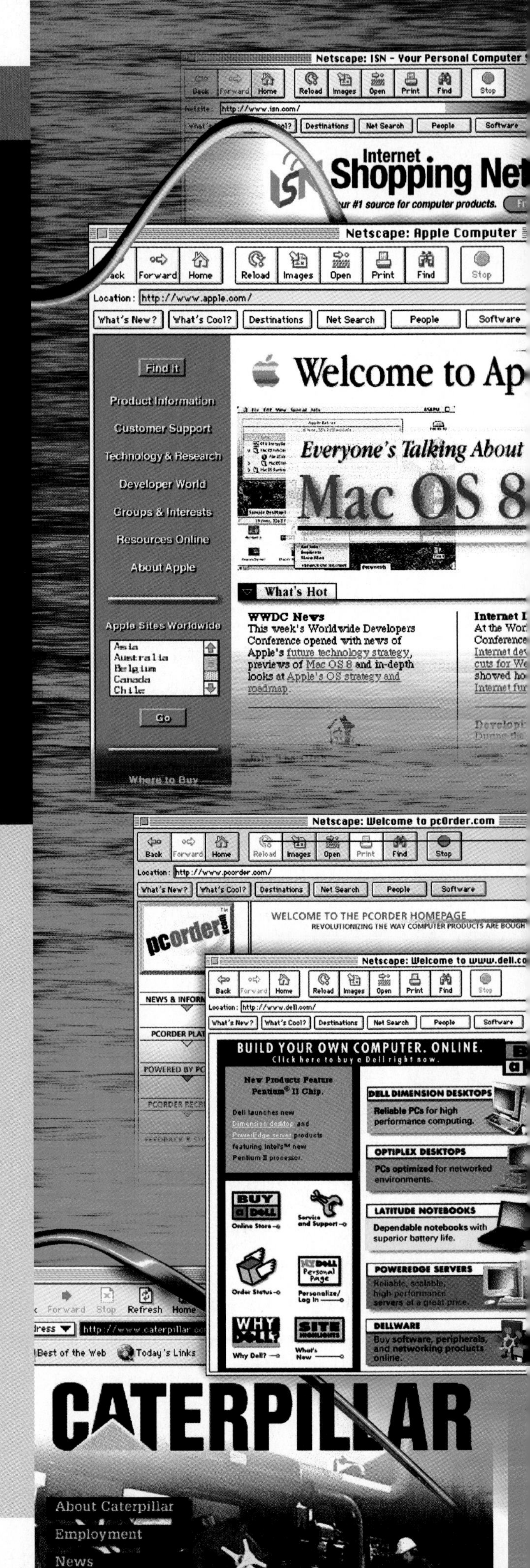

Netscape: ISN - Your Personal Computer
Internet Shopping Net
Netscape: Apple Computer
Location: http://www.apple.com/
What's New? What's Cool? Destinations Net Search People Software
Find It
Product Information
Customer Support
Technology & Research
Developer World
Groups & Interests
Resources Online
About Apple
Apple Sites Worldwide
Asia
Australia
Belgium
Canada
Chile
Go
Where to Buy
Welcome to Ap
Everyone's Talking About
Mac OS 8
What's Hot
WWDC News
This week's Worldwide Developers Conference opened with news of Apple's future technology strategy, previews of Mac OS 8 and in-depth looks at Apple's OS strategy and roadmap.
Netscape: Welcome to pcOrder.com
Location: http://www.pcorder.com/
WELCOME TO THE PCORDER HOMEPAGE
REVOLUTIONIZING THE WAY COMPUTER PRODUCTS ARE BOUGH
Netscape: Welcome to www.dell.co
Location: http://www.dell.com/
BUILD YOUR OWN COMPUTER. ONLINE.
Click here to buy a Dell right now.
New Products Feature Pentium® II Chip.
Dell launches new Dimension desktop and PowerEdge server products featuring Intel's™ new Pentium II processor.
DELL DIMENSION DESKTOPS
Reliable PCs for high performance computing.
OPTIPLEX DESKTOPS
PCs optimized for networked environments.
LATITUDE NOTEBOOKS
Dependable notebooks with superior battery life.
POWEREDGE SERVERS
Reliable, scalable, high-performance servers at a great price.
DELLWARE
Buy software, peripherals, and networking products online.
BUY A DELL
Online Store
Service and Support
Order Status
Personalize/Log In
WHY DELL?
Why Dell?
SITE HIGHLIGHTS
What's New
Best of the Web
Today's Links
CATERPILLAR
About Caterpillar
Employment
News

Chapter Objectives

1. Describe the role that distribution plays in marketing strategy.
2. Describe the various types of distribution channels available to marketers.
3. Identify the functions performed by marketing intermediaries.
4. Summarize the channel options available to a manufacturer that desires to bypass independent wholesaling intermediaries.
5. Identify the major types of independent wholesaling intermediaries and the situations appropriate for each.
6. Outline the major channel strategy decisions.
7. Describe the concepts of channel leadership and management.
8. Discuss conflict and cooperation within the distribution channel.
9. Identify the types of vertical marketing systems.

Software Direct

If you own a computer with a modem, you can buy just about anything you want on the Internet. From out-of-print books to mango chutney, the cybermarket is limitless and open for business 24 hours a day. Until recently, however, all cybershoppers still had to receive their purchases the old-fashioned way—through the mail. After all, you can't download a mountain bike to your computer—at least not yet.

But you can download software purchases, and more and more companies are now moving their products through this new distribution channel. Microsoft Corp. started the ball rolling in late 1995 by permitting a handful of resellers to distribute some of its most popular consumer-market titles over the Internet. Until Microsoft's move, most software delivered over the Internet was aimed at business customers. "This is a very interesting, natural, and obvious evolutionary step" for distributing software, observes Velle Kolde, Microsoft's group manager for emerging channels.

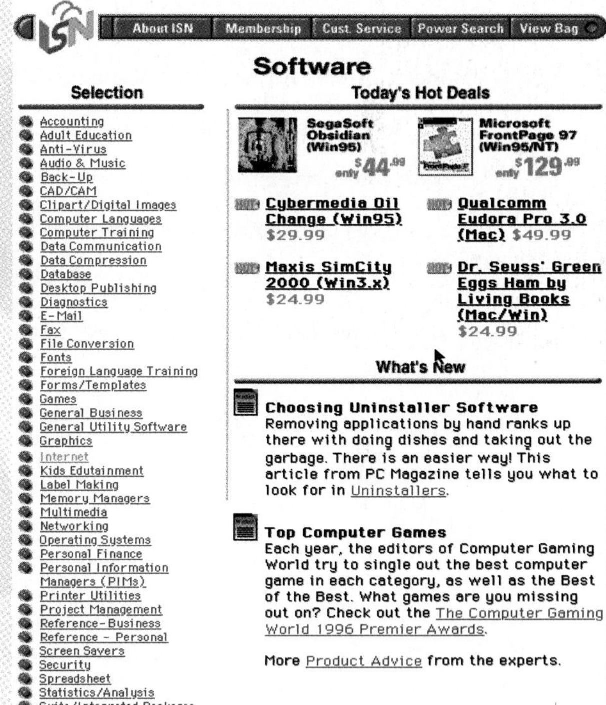

ISN
About ISN
Membership
Cust. Service
Power Search
View Bag
Software
Selection
Accounting
Adult Education
Anti-Virus
Audio & Music
Back-Up
CAD/CAM
Clipart/Digital Images
Computer Languages
Computer Training
Data Communication
Data Compression
Database
Desktop Publishing
Diagnostics
E-Mail
Fax
File Conversion
Fonts
Foreign Language Training
Forms/Templates
Games
General Business
General Utility Software
Graphics
Internet
Kids Edutainment
Label Making
Memory Managers
Multimedia
Networking
Operating Systems
Personal Finance
Personal Information Managers (PIMs)
Printer Utilities
Project Management
Reference-Business
Reference - Personal
Screen Savers
Security
Spreadsheet
Statistics/Analysis
Suite/Integrated Packages
Terminal Emulation
Voice Recognition
Word Processing
Today's Hot Deals
SegaSoft Obsidian (Win95)
only $44.99
Microsoft FrontPage 97 (Win95/NT)
only $129.99
Cybermedia Oil Change (Win95)
$29.99
Qualcomm Eudora Pro 3.0 (Mac) $49.99
Maxis SimCity 2000 (Win3.x)
$24.99
Dr. Seuss' Green Eggs Ham by Living Books (Mac/Win)
$24.99
What's New
Choosing Uninstaller Software
Removing applications by hand ranks up there with doing dishes and taking out the garbage. There is an easier way! This article from PC Magazine tells you what to look for in Uninstallers.
Top Computer Games
Each year, the editors of Computer Gaming World try to single out the best computer game in each category, as well as the Best of the Best. What games are you missing out on? Check out the The Computer Gaming World 1996 Premier Awards.
More Product Advice from the experts.

Microsoft's actions encouraged plenty of imitators. A survey of software publishers by *Soft-letter,* an industry newsletter, suggested that they anticipate generating at least 33 percent of their revenue by electronically distributing their products by 1998. Most of these publishers set up their own Web sites rather than working through resellers to distribute software over electronic channels.

Electronic distribution makes a great deal of sense for many reasons. The cost of doing business can drop dramatically when a firm nearly eliminates shipping, handling, and packaging costs. On a $100 software program, for example, Microsoft saves $10 on the shrink-wrapped boxes, manuals, and diskettes that it would distribute along with software through traditional channels. Further, companies need not invest in a lot of costly warehouse space to keep inventory. Yet another big plus benefits buyers and sellers alike—the inventory can never run out.

Internet Shopping Network, Inc. and Online Interactive, Inc. are two of the many companies now taking advantage of this new distribution channel. In a joint venture, the leading electronic commerce firms have opened a cyberspace shop with more than 900 downloadable software programs.

Why would customers choose to download their own software? Many shop online as the only way they can obtain specialized software titles that regular retail outlets don't carry. Internet shoppers also gain access to new programs before they ever appear on store shelves.

http://www.isn.com/

"We've always catered to individuals and small office/home office users, and the new downloadable software store gives them access to a whole new class of innovative software products," says Bill Rollinson, Internet Shopping Network's vice president of marketing. "We've designed the new store in such a way that it will be extremely easy for our customers to find exactly what they want, to 'test drive' products before purchasing, to read reviews and product information, and ultimately to make intelligent and instantaneous buying decisions."

Executives behind the joint retailing venture also have apparently resolved one of the main flaws with Internet distribution. When Microsoft first announced its plan, skeptics noted that downloading could tie up a customer's computer for hours. Microsoft acknowledged that a system with a 14,400-baud modem would spend four hours downloading its Excel spreadsheet program. In contrast, a shopper at the new virtual store will need only a few minutes to download a purchase onto his or her hard drive.[1]

CHAPTER OVERVIEW

Distribution—moving goods and services from producers to customers—is an important marketing concern. Although good design and creative promotion may motivate consumers to purchase a product, they prove useless if consumers cannot actually buy the product. This and the next two chapters discuss the activities, decisions, and marketing intermediaries involved in the distribution process. This chapter examines basic distribution strategies and the marketing intermediaries that perform the wholesaling function. Chapter 15 looks at another player in the distribution channel, retailers and retailing. Finally, Chapter 16 focuses on logistics, the process of facilitating the movement of information, goods, and services.

DISTRIBUTION STRATEGY

While some computer software manufacturers now reach consumers through electronic distribution channels, most still fight to get their products onto the shelves of computer superstores like CompUSA. SoftKey International, a maker of low-priced software products like CD-ROM calendars, takes a different approach. SoftKey believes that many software purchases are impulse buys. If consumers see a program that looks interesting at an attractive price,

.144http://www.softkey.com/

they'll buy it. Therefore, SoftKey passes up computer stores. Instead, customers can find SoftKey products in Kmart stores, supermarkets, and convenience stores. This distribution strategy helped SoftKey to post sales growth four years in a row, while many other software companies struggle to earn any profits.[2]

SoftKey provides a good example of the importance of distribution strategy to a firm's marketing efforts. Businesses must carefully choose how and where their goods reach consumers by managing their distribution channels. A **distribution channel** can be defined as an organized system of marketing institutions and their interrelationships that promote the physical and title flow of goods and services, along with title that confers ownership, from producer to consumer or business user. Distribution channels provide ultimate users with convenient ways to obtain the goods and services they desire. The choice of distribution channels should support the firm's overall marketing strategy.

Figure 14.1 **Distribution Channels: Bringing Buyers and Sellers Together**

OCLV
TREK
ES!!
Our Y Bikes
inspire the same response
no matter how you ride them.
Call for a free catalog.
1.800.369.TREK USA

THE ROLE OF DISTRIBUTION CHANNELS IN MARKETING STRATEGY

A firm's distribution channels play a key role in its marketing strategy, because they provide the means by which it moves the goods and services it produces to ultimate users. Channels perform four important functions. First, they facilitate the exchange process by cutting the number of marketplace contacts necessary to make a sale. Suppose that you want to buy a new mountain bike. While reading *Rolling Stone* magazine, the ad for Trek USA's Y bike, shown in Figure 14.1, captures your attention. Trek USA does not sell bikes direct, instead, it sells through a network of dealers. So you call the toll-free phone number listed in the ad and find out which bike shops in your area carry Trek products. Local bike retailers form part of the channel that brings you, the buyer, and Trek, the seller, together to complete the exchange process.

In their second important function, distributors adjust for discrepancies in the market's assortment of goods and services via a process known as *sorting*. A single producer tends to maximize the quantity it makes of a limited line of goods, while a single buyer needs a limited quantity of a wide selection of products. Sorting alleviates such discrepancies by channeling products to suit both the buyer's and the producer's needs.

The third function of distribution channels involves standardizing exchange transactions by setting expectations for products and the transfer process itself. Channel members tend to standardize payment terms, delivery schedules, prices, and purchase lots among other conditions.

Finally, distribution channels facilitate searches by both buyers and sellers. Buyers search for specific goods and services to fill their needs, while sellers attempt to find out what buyers want. Channels bring buyers and sellers together to complete the exchange process.

In choosing a channel, marketers try to find and develop the one that best supports the marketing requirements of their product and firm. For example, when Anita Roddick developed a line of all-natural skin-care and hair-care products, she needed to decide how to sell them to customers. Should she try to place them in the display cases of department store cosmetics departments? Would a catalog allow her to sell the products more effectively

Marketing Dictionary

distribution channel An organized system of marketing institutions and their interrelationships that promotes the physical flow of goods and services, along with title that confers ownership, from producer to consumer or business user.

Figure 14.2 Alternative Distribution Channels

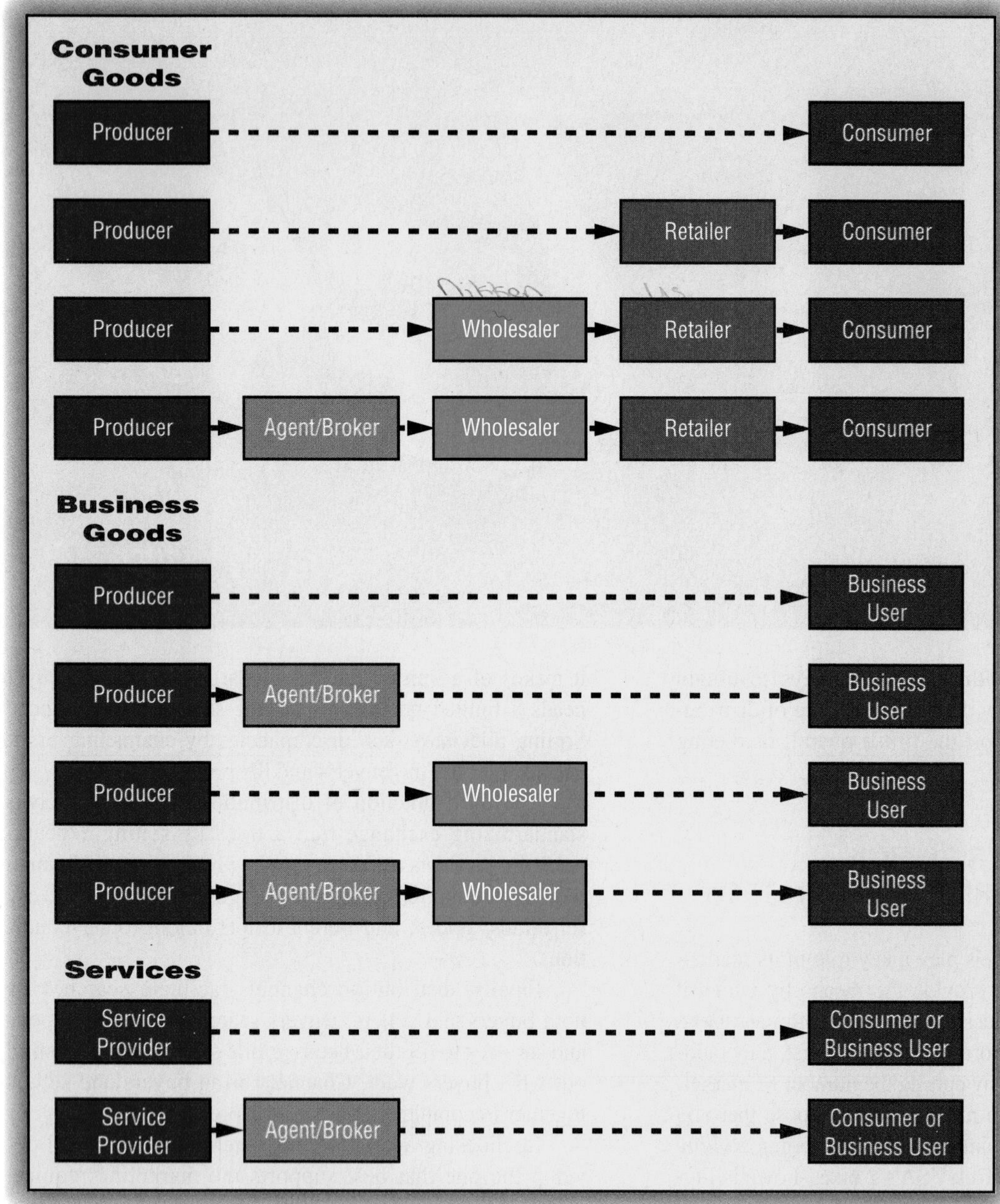
Consumer Goods
Producer
Consumer
Producer
Retailer
Consumer
Producer
Wholesaler
Retailer
Consumer
Producer
Agent/Broker
Wholesaler
Retailer
Consumer
Business Goods
Producer
Business User
Producer
Agent/Broker
Business User
Producer
Wholesaler
Business User
Producer
Agent/Broker
Wholesaler
Business User
Services
Service Provider
Consumer or Business User
Service Provider
Agent/Broker
Consumer or Business User

through direct mail? Should she open her own specialty shop to sell her unique products, bypassing other retail shops?

http://www.the-body-shop.com/

Roddick decided on the last option, because she believed it offered the best opportunity to explain her products' unusual ingredients to potential customers. She rented a tiny retail shop in Brighton, England and displayed her Seaweed and Birch Shampoo, Avocado Moisture Cream, and other products in simple plastic bottles with handwritten labels. Today, her company, The Body Shop International, Inc., has grown to distribute to global markets. The firm operates 1,400 retail stores in 45 countries with sales topping $950 million. Roddick's decision to distribute her products in her own retail stores paid off.[3]

Literally hundreds of distribution channels carry products today, and no single channel best serves the needs of every company. Instead of searching for the best channel for all products, a marketing manager must analyze alternative channels in light of consumer needs to determine the most appropriate channel or channels for the firm's goods and services.

Marketers must remain flexible, however, since channels, like so many marketing variables, may change. Today's ideal channel may prove inappropriate in a few years. For many years, Hallmark Cards sold its greeting cards only in independent specialty card shops licensed to use the Hallmark name. In the past decade, however, consumer shopping habits have changed. Customers started to look for convenience and one-stop shopping. Increasingly, they decided to pick up their greeting cards in supermarkets, drugstores, and other stores they regularly visited rather than stopping specifically at a card store. As its market share began to erode, Hallmark decided to introduce a new line of cards and market them through chain stores such as Wal-Mart, Kmart, and Kroger.[4]

The next section examines the diverse types of channels available to marketers. The chapter then focuses on the decisions marketers must make in order to develop an effective distribution strategy that supports their firm's marketing objectives.

TYPES OF DISTRIBUTION CHANNELS

The first step in selecting a distribution channel determines which type of channel will best meet both the producer's marketing objectives and the distribution needs of customers. Figure 14.2 depicts the major channels available to marketers of consumer and business goods and services.

Clearly, some channel options involve several different **marketing intermediaries.** A marketing intermediary is a business firm that operates between producers and consumers or business users. Another term used for a marketing intermediary is a *middleman.* Retailers and wholesalers are both marketing intermediaries. A retail store owned and operated by someone other than the manufacturer of the products it sells is one type of marketing intermediary. A **wholesaler** is an intermediary that takes title to the goods it handles and then distributes them to retailers, other distributors, or sometimes end consumers. This chapter discusses direct channels and distribution channels involving wholesaling intermediaries. Chapter 15 discusses the role of retailers in channel strategy.

A *short distribution channel* involves few intermediaries; in a *long distribution channel,* many intermediaries work in succession to move goods from producers to consumers. In general, business products tend to move through shorter channels than consumer products due to geographic concentrations and comparatively few business purchasers. Service firms market primarily through short channels, because they sell intangible products, and they need to maintain personal relationships within their channels.

Not-for-profit organizations also tend to work with short, simple, and direct channels. Any marketing intermediaries in such a channel usually act as agents such as independent ticket agencies or fund-raising specialists. In a major distribution decision, both service firms and not-for-profit organizations must designate the specific locations where they will deliver services.

The following sections consider direct selling, the shortest channel, and other channel options involving marketing intermediaries.

Direct Selling

The simplest, most direct distribution channel is a direct channel. A **direct channel** carries goods directly from a producer to an ultimate user. This channel forms part of **direct selling,** a marketing strategy, in which a producer establishes direct sales contact with its product's final user. Direct selling is an important option for goods that require extensive demonstrations to convince customers to buy. As the chapter's opening vignette illustrates, the Internet has initiated a viable, new channel for direct sales.

Direct selling plays an extremely significant role in business-to-business marketing. Most major installations, accessory equipment, and even component parts and raw materials are marketed through direct contacts between producing firms and final buyers. Firms that market products to other businesses often develop and maintain large sales forces to call on potential customers.

Direct selling is also important in consumer goods markets. Direct selling, like Mary Kay and Tupperware, sidestep competition in store aisles by developing networks of sales associates that directly sell their products to consumers. Avon Products, Inc. markets cosmetics, decorative accessories, jewelry, games, and giftware through person-to-person selling. Another well-known practitioner of this method of distribution is Amway. Amway's direct marketing system sells nutritional, personal-care, household cleaning supplies, and health products to consumers. The firm also sells commercial products and services directly to businesses. Amway relies on a network of distributors to identify prospects, demonstrate products, and ultimately convince consumers to buy.

Marketing Dictionary

marketing intermediary A business firm, either wholesaler or retailer, that operates between producers and consumers or business users, also called a *middleman.*

wholesaler A marketing intermediary that takes title to goods and then distributes them further; also called a *jobber* or *distributor.*

direct channel A distribution channel that moves goods directly from a producer to an ultimate user.

direct selling A strategy designed to establish direct sales contact between producer and final user.

Amway
DISH DROPS
NUTRILITE

More than 2.5 million independent Amway distributors market over 6,500 products worldwide. Here, one of Amway Japan's army of more than 1 million independent distributors sells directly to consumers. Amway Japan's remarkably successful operation accounts for more than one-third of the firm's total revenues.

Another direct selling tactic in the consumer goods market is the party plan. The seller recruits someone to invite friends to his or her home, where the seller demonstrates goods and encourages guests to make purchases. Perhaps the best-known company using party-plan selling is Tupperware. However, other firms have used the method to sell everything from lingerie to popcorn. Hand Technologies, a Texas firm, organizes in-home parties to demonstrate and sell personal computers.[5]

Dell Computers and Gateway 2000 both sell computers and computer parts directly to end users they contact through other methods. These highly successful marketers build computers based on customer specifications for performance characteristics such as processor speed, hard drive size, and type of monitor. Gateway shipped 1.3 million computers in a recent year, and its telemarketing center receives over 100,000 calls each day. The firm advertises its products in print ads that feature Gateway's unique packaging.[6]

http://www.dell.com/

John Dell founded Dell Computer Corp. as a 19-year-old college student when he had a hard time tracking down parts for his homemade computer system. "I figured if I bought computer parts from manufacturers, assembled them, and sold them directly, I could bypass overhead costs, save users a lot of money, and also make a profit," explains Dell of his idea for his company. Dell sold his first products by placing small ads in trade magazines, handling orders via mail. Next, he set up a toll-free sales and support telephone number so customers could order over the phone. Within three years, the firm's sales reached $66 million. In the early 1990s, Dell began to target business customers more vigorously than consumers. Today, Dell directly sells computers worth over $2 billion each year.[7]

Dell has also branched out internationally, selling its computers directly to customers in the United Kingdom, Canada, Japan, Australia, and Europe. Dell Computer is not alone. According to the World Federation of Direct Selling Associations, direct selling promotes products in nearly every country of the world. Latin America is a particularly attractive market for direct sales. Consumers there often respond at higher rates than consumers in North America and Europe, because fewer direct sellers compete for consumer attention in Latin America. Nestlé, AT&T, and IBM all sell goods and services directly in that part of the world.[8]

Some consumers share a negative image of direct selling. To combat this image, the World Federation of Direct Selling Associations has developed a Code of Ethics for its members. The code states that direct sellers should avoid misleading, deceptive, and unfair sales practices. Salespeople should also truthfully identify themselves and their companies to potential customers. The code calls for a direct seller to allow a "cooling-off period" after a customer signs a buying agreement during which he or she can revoke the purchase decision without any penalties. It also specifies standards for handling complaints, refunds, and service. Direct Selling Associations in 42 countries, including the United States Direct Selling Association, have adopted the code, and they expect their members to abide by its provisions.[9]

Channels Using Marketing Intermediaries

Although direct channels allow simple and straightforward marketing, they do not always move goods from producers to consumers in the most efficient way. Some products serve geographically dispersed markets or large numbers of potential end users. Other categories of goods rely heavily on repeat purchases. The producers of these goods may find more efficient, less expensive, and less time-consuming alternatives to direct channels by including marketing intermediaries in their distribution channels. This section considers five channels that involve marketing intermediaries.

Briefly speaking

"The farmer is the only man in our economy who buys everything he buys at retail, sells everything he sells at wholesale, and pays the freight both ways."

John F. Kennedy (1917–1963)
35th president of the United States

Producer to Wholesaler to Retailer to Consumer The traditional channel for consumer goods proceeds from producer to wholesaler to retailer to user. This method carries goods between small retailers and literally thousands of small producers with limited lines. Small producers with limited financial resources rely on the services of wholesalers as immediate sources of funds and as conduits to hundreds of retailers that will stock their output. Small retailers draw on wholesalers' specialized buying skills, which help to ensure balanced inventories of goods produced in various regions of the world. The wholesaler's sales force promotes the producer's output to its market. In addition, many manufacturers field their own specialized sales representatives to contact retail accounts. These representatives serve as sources of marketing information, but they do not actually sell products.

Producer to Wholesaler to Business User Similar characteristics in the organizational market often attract marketing intermediaries to operate between producers and business purchasers. The term **industrial distributor** commonly refers to intermediaries in the business market that take title to the goods they handle.

Producer to Agent to Wholesaler to Retailer to Consumer When many small companies serve a market, a unique intermediary—the agent—performs the basic function of bringing buyer and seller together. The agent acts as a wholesaling intermediary, but it does not take title to goods. The agent merely represents a producer by seeking a market for its output or a wholesaler (which does take title to the goods) by locating a source of supply. A later section of this chapter elaborates on the distinction between agents and wholesalers by describing two types of wholesaling intermediaries: merchant wholesalers, which take title to the goods they handle, and agents and brokers, which do not.

Producer to Agent to Wholesaler to Business User Agents and brokers also serve the business market when small producers attempt to market their offerings through large wholesalers. Such an intermediary, often called a *manufacturer's representative,* provides an independent sales force to contact wholesale buyers.

Producer to Agent to Business User For products sold in small units, only merchant wholesalers can economically cover the markets. By maintaining regional inventories, they achieve transportation economies, stockpiling goods and making small shipments over short distances. For a product with large unit sales, however, and for which transportation accounts for a small percentage of the total cost, the producer-agent-business user channel is usually employed. The agent in effect becomes the producer's sales force, but bulk shipments of the product reduce the intermediary's inventory-management function.

DUAL DISTRIBUTION

Dual distribution refers to movement of products through two more distribution channels to reach the same target market. Marketers usually adopt this distribution strategy either to maximize their firm's coverage in the marketplace or to increase the cost effectiveness of its marketing effort. In an example of the first objective, automobile parts manufacturers promote products through both direct sales

Marketing Dictionary

industrial distributor A marketing intermediary in a business channel.

dual distribution A network that moves products to a firm's target market through more than one distribution channel.

In Germany, a reverse channel allows for recycling of some 1.8 million rotary phones, most of them from the former German Democratic Republic (East Germany). Since its reunification with western Germany, this region has updated its telecommunications technology to improve its infrastructure. The phones will be recycled into products ranging from touch-tone phones to park benches.

forces and independent jobbers. The cost-effectiveness goal, on the other hand, might lead a manufacturer to assign its own sales force to sell in high-potential areas while relying on manufacturers' representatives (independent, commissioned salespeople) in lower-volume areas.

REVERSE CHANNELS

While the traditional concept of distribution channels involves movements of goods and services from producer to consumer or business user, marketers should not ignore **reverse channels**—backward movements of goods from users to producers. Reverse channels have gained increased importance with rising prices for raw materials, spreading availability of recycling facilities, and passage of additional conservation laws. For instance, consumers pay refundable deposits for bottled products in states like Maine, Michigan, and Oregon. New Jersey requires businesses and households to separate their trash to aid recycling.

Some reverse channels move through the facilities of traditional marketing intermediaries. In states that require bottle deposits, retailers and local bottlers perform these functions in the soft-drink industry. For other products, manufacturers establish redemption centers, develop systems to rechannel products for recycling, and create specialized organizations to handle disposal and recycling. Other reverse-channel participants include community groups that organize cleanup days and develop recycling and waste disposal systems.

Reverse channels also handle product recalls and repairs. Registration of car owners allow manufacturers to send proper notification in the event of recalls. For example, an automobile recall notice might advise owners to have a problem corrected at their dealerships. Similarly, reverse channels have carried some items to manufacturers' repair centers. The warranty for a small appliance might direct the owner to return a defective unit to the dealer for repairs within 90 days after the sale, and after that period to send it to the factory. Such reverse channels are a vital element of product recall and repair procedures.

WHOLESALING INTERMEDIARIES

As we saw in Figure 14.2, many channels involve marketing intermediaries called *wholesalers.* These firms sell products primarily to retailers or to other wholesalers or business users and only in insignificant amounts to ultimate consumers. **Wholesaling intermediaries,** a broader category, includes not only wholesalers, who assume title to the goods they handle, but also agents and brokers, who perform important wholesaling activities without taking title to goods.

Functions of Wholesaling Intermediaries

Every Friday afternoon, Courtney Young, owner of Gotcha Covered Wholesale in Las Vegas, Nevada, climbs into his

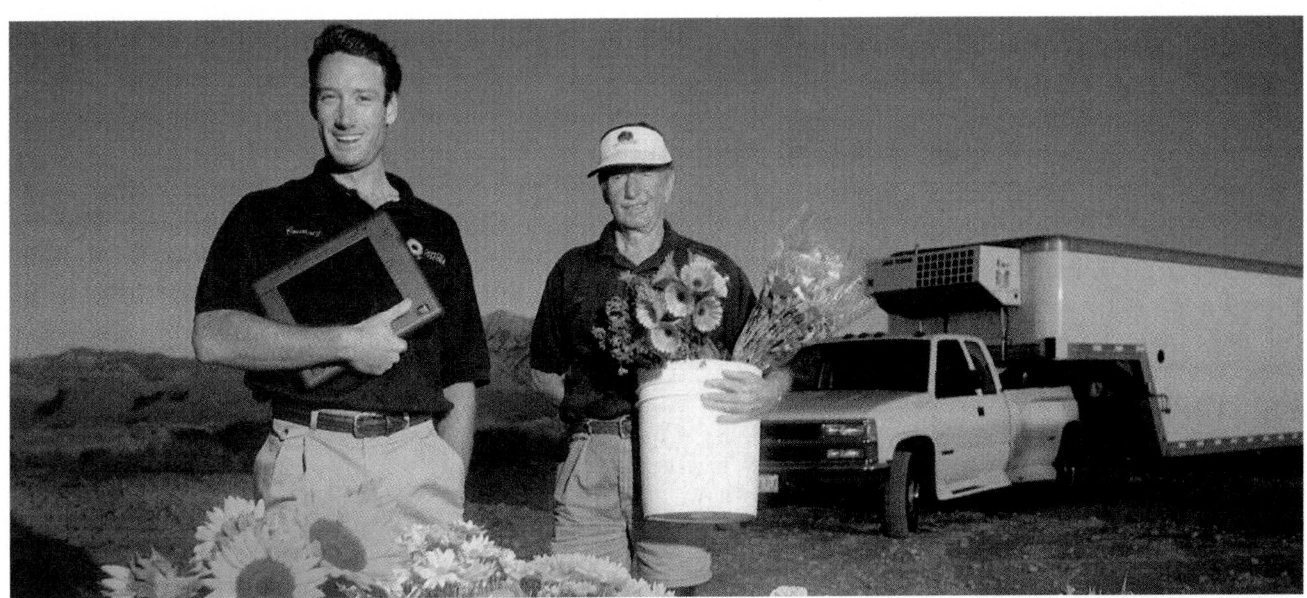

Owner Courtney Young of Gotcha Covered Wholesale and his father use a laptop computer and specially designed software to keep in constant communication with the growers and customers they serve. The computer allows them to prepare on-the-spot invoices for customers and to keep track of growers' inventory, giving the Youngs a competitive advantage over competing flower wholesalers.

refrigerated truck and drives five hours to southern California. Young spends Saturday visiting flower growers in the area, where he purchases a variety of fresh flowers for his customers: retail florists. He keeps a cellular phone in his truck, so a florist who needs a particular type of flower to fill an order can ask him to find it. By Monday morning, Young is back in Las Vegas making deliveries to his florist customers, who use them in floral arrangements for their own retail customers.

Without Young's services, florists would have to contact growers themselves, arrange for transportation, and ensure that vendors correctly filled their orders. Instead, they rely on Young's services as their intermediary, reducing the time and effort they spend to fill their inventory needs. The growers also benefit from the activities of Gotcha Covered in their marketing channels. Without the wholesaler, the flower growers would have to work hard identifying, selling, and servicing florists in Las Vegas. Dealing with Gotcha Covered simplifies the growers' distribution efforts.[10]

Although Gotcha Covered is a relatively small wholesaling operation, the services the firm provides to Las Vegas florists demonstrate the value that wholesalers add in all kinds of distribution channels. As specialists in certain marketing functions, rather than production or manufacturing functions, wholesaling intermediaries can perform these activities more efficiently than producers or consumers can. Their importance results from the utility they create, the services they provide, and the cost reductions their activities allow.

> **Briefly speaking**
>
> "You can do away with the wholesaler but you can't do away with the function s/he performs."
>
> American business saying

Creating Utility Wholesaling intermediaries create three types of utility for consumers. They enhance *time utility* by making products available for sale when consumers want to purchase them. They create *place utility* by helping to deliver goods and services for purchase at convenient locations. They create *ownership* (or *possession*) *utility* when they smooth exchanges of title to products from producers or intermediaries to final purchasers. Possession utility can also result from transactions in which title does not pass to purchasers, as in rental car services.

Marketing Dictionary

reverse channel A path that carries used goods from consumers back to a manufacturer.

wholesaling intermediary A comprehensive term that describes wholesalers as well as agents and brokers.

Table 14.1 Wholesaling Services for Customers and Producer-Suppliers

Service	Beneficiaries of Service: Customers	Beneficiaries of Service: Producer-Suppliers
BUYING	✓	
Anticipates customer demands and applies knowledge of alternative sources of supply; acts as purchasing agent for customers.		
SELLING		✓
Provides a sales force to call on customers, creating a low-cost method of servicing smaller retailers and business users.		
STORING	✓	✓
Maintains warehouse facilities at lower cost than most individual producers or retailers could achieve. Reduces risk and cost of maintaining inventory for producers.		
TRANSPORTING	✓	✓
Customers receive prompt delivery in response to their demands, reducing their inventory investments. Wholesalers also break bulk by purchasing in economical carload or truckload lots, then reselling in smaller quantities, thereby reducing overall transportation costs.		
PROVIDING MARKETING INFORMATION	✓	✓
Offers important market research input for producers through regular contacts with retail and business buyers. Provides customers with information about new products, technical information about product lines, reports on competitors' activities and industry trends, and advisory information concerning pricing changes, legal changes, and so forth.		
FINANCING	✓	✓
Grants credit that might be unavailable for purchases directly from manufacturers. Provides financing assistance to producers by purchasing products in advance of sale and by promptly paying bills.		
RISK TAKING	✓	✓
Evaluates credit risks of numerous, distant retail customers and small business users. Extends credit to customers that qualify. By transporting and stocking products in inventory, the wholesaler assumes risk of spoilage, theft, or obsolescence.		

Providing Services Table 14.1 lists a number of important services provided by wholesaling intermediaries. The list clearly indicates the marketing utilities—time, place, and possession utility—that wholesaling intermediaries create or enhance. These services also reflect the basic marketing functions of buying, selling, storing, transporting, providing market information, financing, and risk taking.

Consider, for example, the services that SYSCO Corp. provides to its customers. SYSCO supplies restaurants, hotels, and other food-service operations with food products. In many cases, this service involves extraordinary efforts to track down raw ingredients on short notice. When one hotel chef discovered he was ten lobsters short for an important meal, he called SYSCO which quickly found a source and assured delivery in time for the dinner. SYSCO provides other services that support smooth operations in food-service operations. Its staff of nutritionists and dietitians work with food-service operators to develop recipes and new menu offerings. Other value-added services include preparation steps like chopping vegetables and tracking the food preferences of consumers to identify new trends important to food-service operators.[11]

Of course, many types of wholesaling intermediaries provide varying services, and not all of them perform every service listed in the table. Producer-suppliers rely on wholesaling intermediaries for distribution, selecting firms that offer the desired combinations of services. In general, however, the critical marketing functions listed in the table form the basis for any evaluation of a marketing intermediary's efficiency. The risk-taking function affects each service of the intermediary.

Figure 14.3 Transaction Economies through Wholesaling Intermediaries

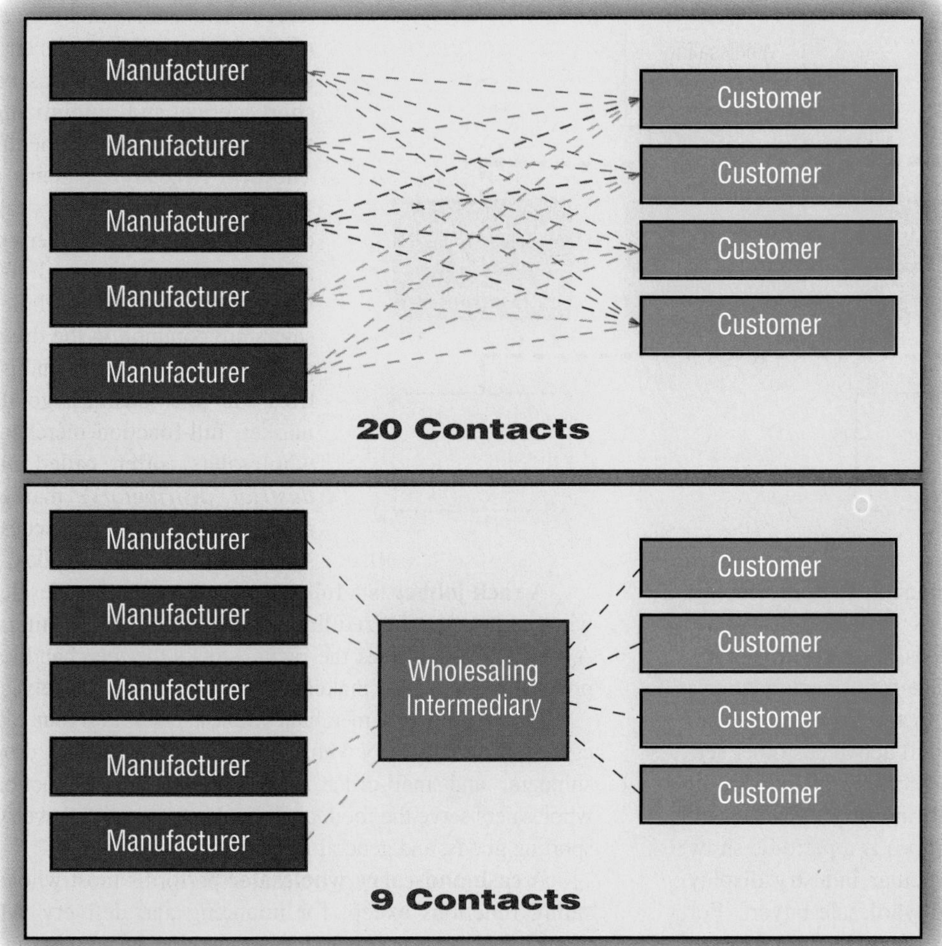
Manufacturer
Manufacturer
Manufacturer
Manufacturer
Manufacturer
Customer
Customer
Customer
Customer
20 Contacts
Manufacturer
Manufacturer
Manufacturer
Manufacturer
Manufacturer
Wholesaling Intermediary
Customer
Customer
Customer
Customer
9 Contacts

Lowering Costs by Limiting Contacts When an intermediary represents numerous producers, it often cuts the costs of buying and selling. The transaction economies are illustrated in Figure 14.3, which shows five manufacturers marketing their outputs to four different retail outlets. Without an intermediary, these exchanges create a total of 20 transactions. Adding a wholesaling intermediary reduces the number of transactions to nine.

Handleman Company is a wholesaler of music recordings, videos, books, and computer software to retailers. Its retail customers avoid the need to order these products individually from large numbers of different manufacturers; instead, they simply call Handleman. The savings in transaction costs is particularly important for these high-volume products that need frequent restocking. Handleman determines that the products reach retailers' shelves and also tracks which titles are selling best.[12]

Types of Wholesaling Intermediaries

Various types of wholesaling intermediaries operate in different distribution channels. Some provide wide ranges of services or handle broad lines of goods, while others specialize in individual services, goods, or industries. Figure 14.4 classifies wholesaling intermediaries by two characteristics: *ownership* and *title flows* (whether title passes from manufacturer to wholesaling intermediary). The three basic ownership structures are as follows: (1) manufacturer-owned facilities, (2) independent wholesaling intermediaries, and (3) retailer-owned cooperatives and buying offices. The two types of independent wholesaling intermediaries are merchant wholesalers, which take title to goods, and agents and brokers, which do not.

Manufacturer-Owned Facilities Several reasons may lead manufacturers to distribute their goods directly through company-owned facilities. Some perishable goods need rigid control of distribution to avoid spoilage; others require complex installation or servicing. Some goods need aggressive promotion. Goods with high unit values allow profitable sales by manufacturers directly to ultimate purchasers. Manufacturer-owned facilities include sales branches, sales offices, trade fairs, and merchandise marts.

A **sales branch** carries inventory and processes orders for customers from available stock. Branches provide a storage function like independent wholesalers and serve as offices for sales representatives in their territories. They are prevalent in marketing arrangements for chemicals,

Marketing Dictionary

sales branch A manufacturer-owned facility that carries inventory and processes orders for customers from available stock.

Figure 14.4 Major Types of Wholesaling Intermediaries

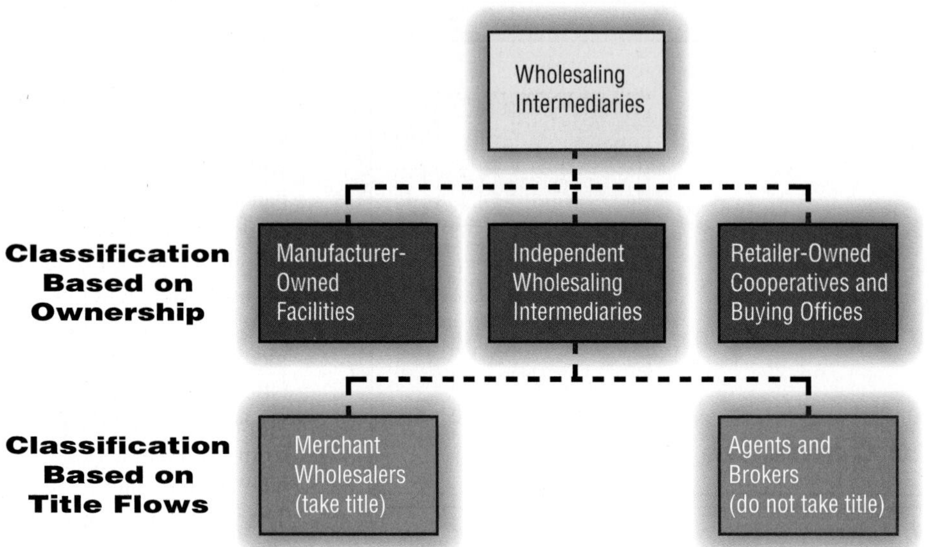
Wholesaling Intermediaries
Classification Based on Ownership
Manufacturer-Owned Facilities
Independent Wholesaling Intermediaries
Retailer-Owned Cooperatives and Buying Offices
Classification Based on Title Flows
Merchant Wholesalers (take title)
Agents and Brokers (do not take title)

commercial machinery and equipment, motor vehicles, and petroleum products.

A **sales office,** in contrast, does not carry inventory, but it does serve as a regional office for a manufacturer's sales personnel. Locations close to the firm's customers help to limit selling costs and support active customer service. For example, numerous sales offices in the Detroit suburbs serve the area's automobile industry.

A **trade fair** (or *trade exhibition*) is a periodic show at which manufacturers in a particular industry display their wares for visiting retail and wholesale buyers. For example, the Internet World Conference sponsors an enormous trade exhibition that brings together over 600 companies to demonstrate their latest Internet technology.

A **merchandise mart** provides space for permanent showrooms and exhibits, which manufacturers rent to market their goods. One of the world's largest merchandise marts is Chicago's Mart Center, a 7-million-square-foot complex that hosts more than 30 seasonal buying markets each year.

Independent Wholesaling Intermediaries Another ownership structure creates independent wholesaling intermediaries. These firms fall into two categories: merchant wholesalers and agents and brokers.

Merchant Wholesalers A **merchant wholesaler** takes title to the goods it handles. Merchant wholesalers account for roughly 60 percent of all sales at the wholesale level. Further classifications divide them into full-function or limited-function wholesalers, as indicated in Figure 14.5. Both SYSCO and Handleman, mentioned in the previous section, are merchant wholesalers.

A full-function merchant wholesaler provides a complete assortment of services for retailers and business purchasers. Such a wholesaler stores merchandise in a convenient location, allowing its customers to make purchases on short notice and minimizing their inventory requirements. The firm typically maintains a sales force whose members call on retailers, make deliveries, and extend credit to qualified buyers. Full-function wholesalers are common in the drug, grocery, and hardware industries. In the business-goods market, full-function merchant wholesalers (often called *industrial distributors*) market machinery, inexpensive accessory equipment, and supplies.

A **rack jobber** is a full-function merchant wholesaler who markets specialized lines of merchandise to retailers. A rack jobber supplies the racks, stocks the merchandise, prices the goods, and makes regular visits to refill shelves.

Limited-function merchant wholesalers fit into four categories: cash-and-carry wholesalers, truck wholesalers, drop shippers, and mail-order wholesalers. Limited-function wholesalers serve the food, coal, lumber, cosmetics, jewelry, sporting goods, and general-merchandise industries.

A **cash-and-carry wholesaler** performs most wholesaling functions except for financing and delivery. Although feasible for small stores, this kind of wholesaling generally is unworkable for large-scale grocery stores. Today, cash-and-carry operations typically function as departments within regular, full-service wholesale operations. However, cash-and-carry wholesalers have succeeded outside the United States, as in the United Kingdom.

A **truck wholesaler,** or *truck jobber,* markets perishable food items such as bread, tobacco, potato chips, candy, and dairy products. Truck wholesalers make regular deliveries to retailers, perform sales and collection functions, and promote product lines.

A **drop shipper** accepts orders from customers and forwards them to producers, which ship directly to the customers. Although drop shippers take title to these goods, they never physically handle or even see the products. These intermediaries operate in industries based on bulky goods that customers buy in carload lots, such as coal and lumber.

A **mail-order wholesaler** is a limited-function merchant wholesaler who distributes catalogs rather than sending sales representatives to contact retail, business, and institutional customers. Customers then make purchases by mail or phone. Such a wholesaler often serves relatively small customers in outlying areas. Mail-order operations operate in the hardware, cosmetics, jewelry, sporting goods, and specialty foods lines as well as in general merchandise.

Table 14.2 compares the various types of merchant wholesalers and the services they provide. Full-function merchant wholesalers and truck wholesalers rank as relatively high-cost intermediaries due to the number of services they perform, while cash-and-carry wholesalers, drop shippers, and mail-order wholesalers provide fewer services and set lower prices, since they incur lower operating costs.

Figure 14.5 Classification of Independent Wholesaling Intermediaries

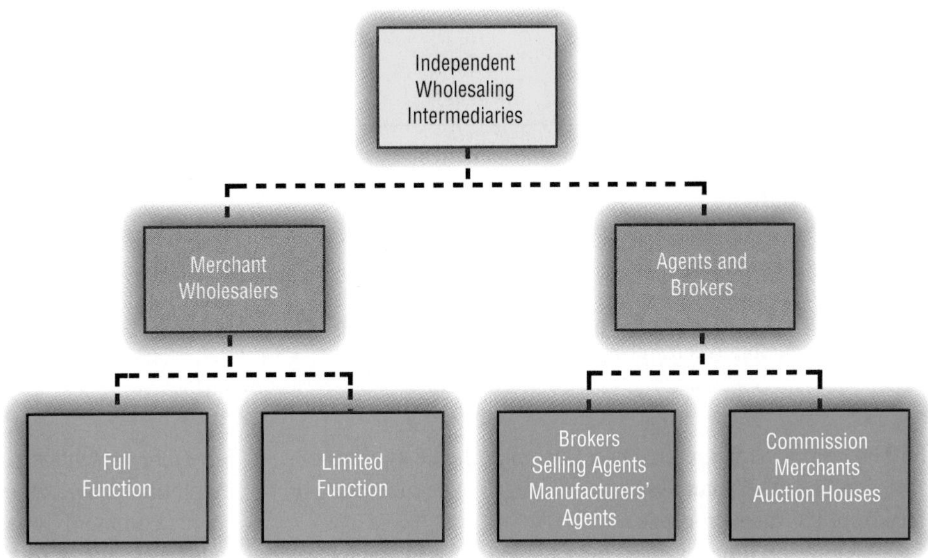
Independent Wholesaling Intermediaries
Merchant Wholesalers
Agents and Brokers
Full Function
Limited Function
Brokers Selling Agents Manufacturers' Agents
Commission Merchants Auction Houses

Agents and Brokers A second group of independent wholesaling intermediaries, **agents and brokers,** may or may not take possession of the goods they handle, but they never take title. They normally perform fewer services than merchant wholesalers, typically working mainly to bring together buyers and sellers. Agents and brokers fall into five categories—commission merchants, auction houses, brokers, selling agents, and manufacturers' agents.

Commission merchants, who predominate in the markets for agricultural products, take possession when producers ship goods such as grain, produce, and livestock to central markets for sale. Commission merchants act as producers' agents and receive agreed-upon fees when they make sales. Since customers inspect the products and prices fluctuate, commission merchants receive considerable latitude in marketing decisions. The owners of the goods may specify minimum prices,

Marketing Dictionary

sales office A manufacturer's facility that serves as a regional office for salespeople, but does not carry inventory.

trade fair A periodic show at which manufacturers in a particular industry display wares for visiting retail and wholesale buyers.

merchandise mart A permanent exhibition facility in which manufacturers display products for visiting retail and wholesale buyers.

merchant wholesaler An independently owned wholesaling intermediary who takes title to the goods that it handles.

rack jobber A full-function merchant wholesaler who markets specialized lines of merchandise to retail stores.

cash-and-carry wholesaler A limited-function merchant wholesaler who performs most wholesaling functions except financing and delivery.

truck wholesaler A limited-function merchant wholesaler who markets perishable food items; also called a *truck jobber.*

drop shipper A limited-function merchant wholesaler who accepts orders from customers and forwards them to producers, which ship directly to the customers who place the orders.

mail-order wholesaler A limited-function merchant wholesaler who distributes catalogs instead of sending sales representatives to contact customers.

agents and brokers Independent wholesaling intermediaries who may or may not take possession of goods, but never take title to them.

commission merchant An agent wholesaling intermediary who takes possession of goods shipped to a central market for sale, acts as the producer's agent, and collects an agreed-upon fee at the time of the sale.

Table 14.2 Comparison of the Types of Merchant Wholesalers and Their Services

Service	Full-Function	Limited-Function Wholesaler			
		Cash-and-Carry	Truck	Drop Shipper	Mail-Order
Anticipates customer needs	✓	✓	✓	—	✓
Carries inventory	✓	✓	✓	—	✓
Delivers	✓	—	✓	—	—
Provides market information	✓	Rarely	✓	✓	—
Provides credit	✓	—	—	✓	Sometimes
Assumes ownership risk by taking title	✓	✓	✓	✓	✓

but the commission merchants sell them at the best prices they can find. The commission merchants then deduct their fees from the sales proceeds.

An **auction house** gathers buyers and sellers in one location and allows potential buyers to inspect merchandise before submitting competing purchase offers. Auction house commissions typically reflect specified percentages of the sales prices of the auctioned items. The auction method of marketing is common in the distribution of tobacco, used cars, artworks, livestock, furs, and fruit.

Brokers work mainly to bring together buyers and sellers. A broker represents either the buyer or the seller, but not both, in a given transaction, and it receives a fee from the client when the transaction is completed. Intermediaries that specialize in arranging buying and selling transactions between domestic producers and foreign buyers are called *export brokers.* Brokers operate in industries characterized by large numbers of small suppliers and purchasers, such as real estate, frozen foods, and used machinery. Since they provide one-time services for sellers or buyers, they cannot serve as effective channels for manufacturers seeking regular, continuing service. A manufacturer that seeks to develop a more permanent channel might choose instead to use a selling agent or manufacturer's agent.

The Internet has created conditions for development of a new type of broker which works to connect customers and sellers in the online world. For example, pcOrder.com Inc., acts as an information clearinghouse for wholesale distributors of computer hardware and software. Customers, primarily organizational buyers and retailers, can visit the pcOrder site to search for information and prices on 150,000 products from more than 800 manufacturers. The participating wholesalers pay pcOrder a commission on each transaction.[13]

A **selling agent** typically exerts full authority over pricing decisions and promotional outlays, and it often provides financial assistance for the manufacturer. Selling agents are often called *independent marketing departments,* because they can assume responsibility for the total marketing programs of client firms' product lines. Selling agents commonly operate in the coal, lumber, and textiles industries; for a small, poorly financed, production-oriented firm, such an intermediary may prove the ideal marketing channel.

http://www.pcorder.com/

While a manufacturer may deal with only one selling agent, a firm that hires **manufacturer's agents,** often known as *manufacturer's reps,* often delegates marketing tasks to many of them. Such an independent salesperson may work for a number of firms that manufacture related, noncompeting products, receiving commissions based on specific percentages of sales. Unlike selling agents, who may contract for exclusive world rights to market a product, manufacturer's agents operate in specific territories. They may develop new sales territories or represent relatively small firms and those with unrelated lines.

The importance of selling agents in many markets has declined, because manufacturers want better control of their marketing programs than these intermediaries allow. In contrast, the volume of sales by manufacturer's agents has more than doubled and now accounts for 37 percent of all sales by agents and brokers. Table 14.3 compares the major types of agents and brokers on the basis of the services they perform.

Retailer-Owned Cooperatives and Buying Offices

Retailers may assume numerous wholesaling functions in an attempt to reduce costs or provide special services. Independent retailers sometimes band together to form buying

Table 14.3 Services Provided by Agents and Brokers

Service	Commission Merchant	Auction House	Broker	Manufacturer's Agent	Selling Agent
Anticipates customer needs	✓	Sometimes	Sometimes	✓	✓
Carries inventory	✓	✓	—	—	—
Delivers	✓	—	—	Sometimes	—
Provides market information	✓	✓	✓	✓	✓
Provides credit	Sometimes	—	—	—	Sometimes
Assumes ownership risk by taking title	—	—	—	—	—

groups that can achieve cost savings through quantity purchases. Other groups of retailers establish retailer-owned wholesale facilities by forming cooperative chains. Large chain retailers often establish centralized buying offices to negotiate large-scale purchases directly with manufacturers.

CHANNEL STRATEGY DECISIONS

Marketers face several strategic decisions in choosing channels and marketing intermediaries for their products. Selecting a specific channel is the most basic of these decisions. Strategy must also resolve questions about the level of distribution intensity, the desirability of vertical marketing systems, and the performance of current intermediaries.

Selection of a Distribution Channel

What characteristics of a franchised dealer network make it the best channel option for Ford Motor Company? Why do operating supplies often go through both agents and merchant wholesalers before reaching businesses' stock rooms? Why would a firm market a single product through multiple channels? Marketers must answer many such questions in choosing distribution channels.

Figure 14.6 presents a checklist of questions that marketers should ask themselves as they determine an appropriate channel strategy. Note that these questions encourage analysis of performance in the marketers' own organization and in its relationships with marketing intermediaries. The final choice follows careful analysis of market, product, producer, and competitive factors. All of these factors have important and often interrelated effects. The overriding consideration, however, is where, when, and how consumers choose to buy the good or service. Consumer orientation dominates channel decisions as much as other areas of marketing strategy.

Market Factors Channel structure reflects a product's intended markets—either for consumers or business users. Business purchasers usually prefer to deal directly with manufacturers (except for routine supplies or small accessory items), but most consumers make their purchases from retail stores. Marketers often sell products that serve both business users and consumers through more than one channel. Apple Computer, for example, sells its products to several different segments: business users, educational

http://www.apple.com/

Marketing Dictionary

auction house An establishment that gathers buyers and sellers in one location where buyers can examine merchandise before submitting competing purchase offers.

broker An agent wholesaling intermediary that does not take title to or possession of goods in the course of its primary function—to bring together buyers and sellers.

selling agent An agent wholesaling intermediary responsible for the entire marketing program of another firm's product line.

manufacturer's agent An agent wholesaling intermediary who represents a number of manufacturers of related but noncompeting products, receiving a commission on each sale.

Figure 14.6 Channel Strategy Checklist

Ask yourself the following questions concerning your own organization:

Yes	No	
☐	☐	**1.** Do I have a clear and factual assessment of how my organization and products are viewed by current and proposed channels?
☐	☐	**2.** Do I know the optimum mix of channels and the intermediaries in each channel?
☐	☐	**3.** Does my incentive and reward system reinforce a common vision and objectives with intermediaries?
☐	☐	**4.** Do my organization and product line have competitive differences that will motivate intermediaries to make selling my products a top priority?
☐	☐	**5.** Does my organization make a conscious effort to avoid competition between channels and/or with my direct sales force?
☐	☐	**6.** Does my organization have a well-researched and effective business generation plan addressing the top priorities of intermediaries?
☐	☐	**7.** Does my sales and marketing staff have the skills necessary to successfully execute that business generation plan?
☐	☐	**8.** Is my organization working in concert with intermediaries to mutually gain and maintain competitive advantage?
☐	☐	**9.** Does my sales and marketing team have a clear understanding of intermediaries' buying priorities and decision-making processes?
☐	☐	**10.** Am I successfully retaining/growing my top producing intermediaries?
☐	☐	**11.** Are current marginal intermediaries costing me too much to support?
☐	☐	**12.** Am I able to attract the new intermediaries with whom I'd like to do business?

Then ask yourself the following questions about marketing intermediaries:

Yes	No	
☐	☐	**1.** Do their sales and marketing teams possess clearly defined profiles of their markets and clear pictures of their customers' decision-making processes?
☐	☐	**2.** Do they have sales and marketing teams trained to effectively address customers' needs?
☐	☐	**3.** Do they have effective business generation plans clearly focused on their clients' high priority needs and wants for my products?

users, and consumers. Apple distributes to the educational segment, which consists of schools, colleges, and universities, through direct selling. Consumers buy Apple computers through a channel that involves both wholesalers and retailers. The firm reaches business users through both direct sales and wholesalers.[14]

Other market factors also affect channel choice, including the market's needs, its geographic location, and its average order size. To serve a concentrated potential market with a small number of buyers, a direct channel offers a feasible alternative. To serve a geographically dispersed potential market in which customers purchase small amounts in individual transactions—the conditions in the consumer goods market—distribution through marketing intermediaries may make sense.

Product Factors Product characteristics also guide the choice of an optimal distribution channel strategy. Perishable goods, such as fresh produce and fashion products with short life cycles, typically move through relatively short channels; complex products, producers of custom-made installations and computer equipment often sell them directly to ultimate buyers. In general, relatively standardized products pass through comparatively long channels. For another generalization, low product unit values call for long channels.

Table 14.4 Factors That Affect Distribution Channel Strategy

	Characteristics of Short Channels	Characteristics of Long Channels
Market factors	Business users	Consumers
	Geographically concentrated	Geographically diverse
	Extensive technical knowledge and regular servicing required	Little technical knowledge and regular servicing not required
	Large orders	Small orders
Product factors	Perishable	Durable
	Complex	Standardized
	Expensive	Inexpensive
Producer factors	Manufacturer has adequate resources to perform channel functions	Manufacturer lacks adequate resources to perform channel functions
	Broad product line	Limited product line
	Channel control important	Channel control not important
Competitive factors	Manufacturer feels satisfied with marketing intermediaries' performance in promoting products	Manufacturer feels dissatisfied with marketing intermediaries' performance in promoting products

Producer Factors Companies with adequate financial, management, and marketing resources feel little need for marketing help from intermediaries. A financially strong manufacturer can hire its own sales force, warehouse its own goods, and grant credit to retailers or consumers. A weaker firm must rely on marketing intermediaries for these services. (In one exception, a large retail chain may purchase all of a manufacturer's output, bypassing independent wholesalers.) A production-oriented firm may need the marketing expertise of intermediaries to offset its own lack of those skills.

A firm with a broad product line can usually market its products directly to retailers or business users, since its own sales force can offer a variety of products. High sales volume spreads selling costs over a large number of products, allowing good returns from direct sales. Single-product firms often regard direct selling as an unaffordable luxury.

The manufacturer's desire for control over marketing of its product also influences channel selection. To ensure aggressive promotion by retailers, producers often choose the shortest available channels. To distribute a new product, the producer may have to implement an introductory advertising campaign before independent wholesalers will agree to handle it. However, businesses in some industries that try to bypass marketing intermediaries may face challenges that limit their distribution.

Gary Stein, owner of the San Diego Soy Dairy, a small manufacturer of tofu products, initially sought to place his product in supermarkets directly, bypassing grocery wholesalers. In addition to special fees for shelf space, he found that the supermarket chains made many demands about product delivery and marketing. For example, the supermarkets insisted on positioning his products next to deli items, while Stein felt that customers would look for them in dairy cases. In addition, since Stein did not sell through a wholesaler, he himself had to meet stringent requirements for delivering and stocking the product each day before 10 A.M., an expensive and time-consuming task. After several months of distributing through supermarket chains, Stein decided to sell his product only through independent health-food stores, where he would have more say in marketing for his products.[15]

Competitive Factors Some firms feel compelled to develop new distribution channels to remedy inadequate promotion of their products by independent marketing intermediaries. In one popular alternative, a manufacturer might add a direct sales force or set up its own retail distribution network (a move discussed later in the chapter). Table 14.4 summarizes the factors that affect the selection of a distribution channel and examines the effect of each one on the channel's overall length.

MARKETING HALL OF FAME

Arrow Shoots to the Top

The effort took many years, but Arrow Electronics, Inc., fought and clawed its way to the pinnacle of its industry. The Melville, New York company can now boast that it is the world's leading distributor of electronic components and computer products.

The most impressive aspect of this success story is the firm's rebound from the most serious threat in its 62-year existence. In 1980, Arrow's senior managers had gathered at a hotel for the company's annual budget meeting. Tragically, fire spread through the conference room, killing 13 top executives. Only John Waddell, one of the company's three top officials, survived. He had stayed behind at headquarters to answer questions about a stock split announced that day.

Hours after the fire, the company's stock dropped 19 percent and it dipped another 14 percent within the first month. Then a two-year slump in the electronics industry jolted Arrow again. But unlike other distributors, which hunkered down to survive the recessionary times, Arrow opted for bold action. That aggressive attitude helps to explain why the gigantic distributor is so successful today.

During this period, Arrow officials decided to gamble by borrowing heavily to finance expansion. Economies of scale, they believed, would fuel growth and outfox timid competitors. Consequently, Arrow began purchasing companies to gain access to their customers, often selling off the physical facilities it acquired.

Arrow's first major acquisition was Cramer Electronics, the industry's second-largest distributor. This deal doubled Arrow's revenues but left it deeply in debt. In the late 1980s and early 1990s, Arrow swallowed the country's third- and fourth-biggest electronics distributors.

Arrow has busily expanded into foreign markets, as well. In its first foray outside the country in 1984, Arrow purchased one of Canada's biggest electronics distributors. After nine more years, Arrow reached the Pacific Rim, where it is now easily the largest multinational electronics distributor, and it continues to buy companies in Asia. Over the past 20 years or so, Arrow's overseas sales have grown from 9 percent to about one-third of its business.

Arrow's acquisition binge has

Determining Distribution Intensity

Another important channel strategy decision is the intensity of distribution. **Distribution intensity** refers to the number of intermediaries through which a manufacturer distributes its goods. The decision about distribution intensity should ensure adequate market coverage for a product. Adequate market coverage varies considerably depending on the goals of the individual firm, the type of product, and the consumer segments in its target market. In general, however, distribution intensity varies along a continuum with three general categories: intensive distribution, selective distribution, and exclusive distribution.

Intensive Distribution An **intensive distribution** strategy seeks to distribute a product through all available channels in a trade area. M&M/Mars, Inc., for example, implements an intensive distribution strategy, placing its products in supermarkets, chain stores, vending machines, and drugstores. Producers of convenience goods try to saturate their markets, enabling purchasers to buy their products with minimum efforts. Usually, an intensive distribution strategy suits products with wide appeal across broad groups of consumers.[16] Examples of goods distributed through this market-coverage strategy include soft drinks, candy, gum, and cigarettes.

Manufacturers often seek continually to expand distribution for these types of products. The Coca-Cola Co., for example, is attempting to boost distribution intensity for its Minute Maid brand of fruit juices. Coke originally sold the juices only in supermarkets, which it served by shipping the refrigerated products directly from its warehouse delivery system. That system was not set up to serve a broader market, though. When Coke sought to sell Minute Maid juices in new outlets such as convenience stores and food-service operations, the company formed a partnership with 80 dairies across the country. The dairies produce and distribute the juices for the soft-drink giant, increasing the product's distribution intensity and market potential.[17]

Selective Distribution In another market coverage strategy, **selective distribution,** a firm chooses only a limited number of retailers in a market area to handle its line. This arrangement helps to control price cutting, since relatively few dealers handle the firm's line. By limiting the number of retailers, marketers can reduce total marketing costs

paid handsome returns. Since 1975, its sales and earnings have soared. Today, the company relies upon more than 500 suppliers, about 14 percent of its inputs coming from semiconductor maker Intel. Arrow's second biggest supplier is Texas Instruments, an electronics components maker.

Arrow invested early and heavily in technology for its facilities and systems. By the mid-1970s, Arrow had implemented a computerized, integrated inventory management system. In the 1980s, its customers placed orders directly through an EDI system. In the mid-1980s, Arrow built the industry's first fully automated distribution center. Its commitment to technology continues today.

Arrow also made a critical decision to split up the distribution networks for its semiconductor sales and the cheaper, less sexy electronic components. Many competitors' sales personnel spend most of their time selling the relatively lucrative semiconductors and ignore the rest of the inventory. Not so at Arrow. Steve Kaufman, the company's president, created a separate division to sell and warehouse other parts such as resistors, connectors, and capacitors. Tom McGinty, an official at Sterling Electronics Corp., says Kaufman made the right move, citing the difficulty of effectively selling both types of products: "As soon as you have semis, your salesmen spend 80 percent of the time selling semis. The biggest orders are in semis."

After digesting its rapid acquisitions, Arrow has shifted its attention to ensuring that its in-house infrastructure can support its growing empire. The company is boosting global coordination, including an effort to integrate its computer systems and its administrative and support functions. But it's still on the lookout for good buys.

QUESTIONS FOR CRITICAL THINKING

1. Do you agree with the decision to split off the sales and distribution functions for semiconductors and other components? Why?

2. What distribution troubles can a company encounter if it rapidly acquires other firms?

Sources: "Arrow Electronics Posts Record Annual Results," February 19, 1997, downloaded from Business Wire, http://www.businesswire.com/, March 13, 1997; adapted from Norm Alster, "Arrow Electronics' Steve Kaufman—Outsider Showed Skeptics How to Rescue an Ailing Firm," *Investor's Business Daily,* February 23, 1996, downloaded from America Online, February 13, 1997; Robert F. Lusch, *Foundations of Wholesaling: A Strategic and Financial Chart Book,* Distribution Research Program, College of Business Administration, University of Oklahoma (1996), pp. B-34–B-35.; and Hoover Business Profiles, downloaded from America Online, January 31, 1997.

while establishing strong working relationships within the channel. Cooperative advertising, in which the manufacturer pays a percentage of the retailer's advertising expenditures and the retailer prominently displays the firm's products, can be utilized for mutual benefit, and marginal retailers can be avoided. Where service is important, the manufacturer usually provides training and assistance to dealers it chooses.

Nike has chosen a selective distribution strategy for some of its product categories. It markets basketball, running, and cross-training shoes in its Air line only to mall-based specialty retailers and high-profile regional and national dealers. To qualify as one of these outlets, dealers must comply with Nike's strict rules for advertising, pricing, and displaying its products.[18]

Exclusive Distribution When a producer grants exclusive rights to a wholesaler or retailer to sell its products in a specific geographic region, it practices **exclusive distribution,** an extreme form of selective distribution. The automobile industry provides the best example of exclusive distribution. A city with a population of 40,000 may have a single Mazda or Pontiac dealer. Exclusive-distribution agreements also govern marketing for some major appliance and apparel brands. When Nautilus decided to start selling its home-fitness equipment through sporting goods

Marketing Dictionary

distribution intensity The number of intermediaries through which a manufacturer distributes its goods.

intensive distribution A channel policy in which a manufacturer of a convenience product attempts to saturate the market.

selective distribution A channel policy in which a firm chooses only a limited number of retailers to handle its product line.

exclusive distribution A channel policy in which a firm grants exclusive rights to a single wholesaler or retailer to sell its products in a particular geographic area.

Figure 14.7 Exclusive Distribution to Maintain a Quality Image

Make
Your Mark
In Life
$2,500 to $3,400
"Available at over 120 exclusive
Michel Perchin dealers worldwide."
Michel Perchin
314-207-0550 ◆ Fax: 314-207-0724 ◆ E-mail: mppen19@mail.idt.net

dealers, the company opted for an exclusive distribution strategy. Nautilus marketers chose only 25 dealers, one in each of the firm's major trading areas, to carry the line of expensive home gyms, recumbent bikes and stair climbers.[19]

Marketers may sacrifice some market coverage by implementing a policy of exclusive distribution. As compensation, however, they often develop and maintain an image of quality and prestige for the product. For example, Michel Perchin uses exclusive distribution to maintain the quality image of its expensive writing instruments, which range in price from $2,500 to $3,400. As the ad in Figure 14.7 indicates, the pens are only "available at over 120 exclusive Michel Perchin dealers worldwide." In addition, exclusive distribution limits marketing costs, since the firm must deal with only a small number of accounts. In exclusive distribution, producers and retailers cooperate closely in decisions concerning advertising and promotion, inventory carried by the retailers, and prices.

Legal Problems of Exclusive Distribution Exclusive distribution presents a number of potential legal problems in three areas: exclusive dealing agreements, closed sales territories, and tying agreements. While none of these practices is illegal per se, all may break the law if they reduce competition or tend to create monopolies.

As part of an exclusive distribution strategy, marketers may try to enforce an **exclusive-dealing agreement** prohibiting a marketing intermediary (a wholesaler or, more typically, a retailer) from handling competing products. Producers of high-priced shopping goods, specialty goods, and accessory equipment often require such agreements to assure total concentration on their own product lines. Such a contract violates the Clayton Act if the producer's or dealer's sales volume represents a substantial percentage of total sales in the market area. The courts have ruled that a seller can use an exclusive-dealing agreement to strengthen its competitive position while initially entering a market. However, the same agreement would violate the Clayton Act if used by a firm with a sizable market share, since it could help the seller to bar competitors from the market.

Producers may also try to set up **closed sales territories** to restrict their distributors to certain geographic regions. Although the distributors gain protection from rival dealers in their exclusive territories, they sacrifice any opportunities to open new facilities or market the manufacturers' products outside their assigned territories. The legality of a system of closed sales territories depends on whether the restriction decreases competition. If it does, the closed sales territories violate the Federal Trade Commission Act and provisions of the Sherman Act and the Clayton Act.

The legality of closed sales territories also depends on whether the system imposes horizontal or vertical restrictions. Horizontal territorial restrictions result from agreements between retailers or wholesalers to avoid competition among sellers of products from the same producer. Such agreements consistently have been declared illegal. However, the U.S. Supreme Court has ruled that vertical territorial restrictions—those between producers and wholesalers or retailers—may meet legal criteria. While the ruling gives no clear-cut rules, such agreements likely satisfy the law in cases where manufacturers occupy relatively small parts of their markets. In such instances, the restrictions may actually increase competition among competing brands; the wholesaler or retailer faces no competition from other dealers carrying the manufacturer's brand, so it can concentrate on effectively competing with other brands.

The third legal question of exclusive dealing involves **tying agreements,** which allow channel members to become exclusive dealers only if they also carry products other than those that they want to sell. In the apparel industry, for example, such an agreement may require a dealer to carry a comparatively unpopular line of clothing in addition to desirable, fast-moving items.

Tying agreements violate the Sherman Act and the Clayton Act when they reduce competition or create monopolies by keeping competitors out of major markets. For this reason, the courts prohibited International Salt Company from selling salt as a tying product with leases of its patented salt-dispensing machines for snow and ice removal. The Supreme Court ruled that such an agreement unreasonably reduced competition among sellers of salt.

Legal problems have also resulted when large retailers have pressured manufacturers to grant them exclusive distribution rights. The FTC brought a suit against Toys 'R' Us, for example, claiming that the toy superstore refused to stock certain toys unless manufacturers agreed not to sell the same products to warehouse and discount stores such as Price/Costco and Wal-Mart. Because Toys 'R' Us sells over 20 percent of the toys sold in the United States, many toy manufacturers complied with the request, granting the retailer exclusive distribution rights. After the FTC launched its investigation, however, some toy makers quickly reconsidered. For example, Rubbermaid, which manufacturers the Little Tykes brand of children's play sets, announced that it would change its policy of granting exclusive distributorships to certain retailers.[20]

Who Should Perform Channel Functions?

A fundamental marketing principle governs channel decisions: *Some member of the channel must perform certain marketing functions; channel members can shift responsibility, but they cannot eliminate central functions.* While wholesaling intermediaries perform many of these functions for manufacturers, retailers, and other wholesaler clients, other channel members could fulfill these roles, instead. Manufacturers may bypass independent wholesaling intermediaries by establishing networks of regional warehouses, maintaining large sales forces to provide market coverage, serving as sources of information for retail customers, and arranging details of financing. Alternatively, manufacturers might push responsibility for some of these functions through the channel to retailers or ultimate purchasers. Large retailers face the same choices, but the principle remains the same: channel members can eliminate an intermediary only when someone else performs its channel functions.

For instance, the *Cincinnati Enquirer* decided to eliminate its practice of selling the newspaper through wholesalers. In the original arrangement, the wholesalers had bought each day's paper in bulk quantities and then sold and delivered it to subscribers, tacking on delivery surcharges. Instead, the newspaper hired a network of delivery agents to bring the paper to subscribers.

The switch proved disastrous. The wholesalers had marketed subscriptions and maintained the paper's subscriber list for many years. When the newspaper brought in its own delivery people, it lost the information on the wholesalers' subscriber lists. The *Cincinnati Enquirer* had to rely instead on its own outdated customer information. In the first weeks after the switch, thousands of customers called to complain that they hadn't received their morning papers, and many canceled their subscriptions. Local television stations aired interviews with disgruntled subscribers. The newspaper spent several months resolving its distribution and subscription problems.[21]

An independent wholesaling intermediary earns a profit in exchange for providing services to manufacturers and retailers. This profit margin is low, however, ranging from 1 percent for food wholesalers to 5 percent for durable goods wholesalers. Manufacturers and retailers could reap these profits, or they could market directly and reduce retail prices—but only if they could perform the channel functions and match the efficiency of the independent intermediaries.

To grow profitably in a competitive environment, a wholesaler must provide better service at lower cost than manufacturers or retailers can provide for themselves. For another competitive tool, wholesalers may perform value-added services, which involve providing extra assistance of some kind.

CHANNEL MANAGEMENT AND LEADERSHIP

Distribution strategy does not end with the choice of a channel. Manufacturers must also focus on channel management, developing and maintaining relationships with the intermediaries in their distribution channels. Positive channel relationships encourage channel members to pay attention to selling and marketing a particular good.

Marketing Dictionary

exclusive-dealing agreement An arrangement between a manufacturer and a marketing intermediary that prohibits the intermediary from handling competing product lines.

closed sales territory An exclusive geographic selling region defined and enforced by a manufacturer for a distributor.

tying agreement An arrangement that requires a marketing intermediary to carry a manufacturer's full product line in exchange for an exclusive dealership.

MARKETING HALL OF SHAME

Marketers Flunk College Distribution

Advertisers love college students. Their return to school each year also brings advertisers to campus showering students with free samples. Kellogg stuffs Pop-Tarts and cereal in free sample bags. Calvin Klein passes out free trial sizes of cK cologne, while those with the munchies can nibble on free M&Ms.

Yet even the savviest advertisers can find humbling failure when they try to crack the college student market. Traditional advertising doesn't always work with this crowd. In fact, arguments about the potential effectiveness of marketing to college students still fuel a raging controversy in the industry.

"College students are a lot smarter, a lot sharper, and a lot more cautious when it comes to advertising," says Mike Hogan, president of Hogan Communications in Burbank, California. "They're turned off by the hard sell of marketers intruding into their territory."

But some industry insiders believe that failures typically result from deficient distribution rather than poor advertising messages. Robert Bugai, president of College Marketing Intelligence, says that marketers waste millions of dollars on materials that never reach the students because of shoddy distribution. Scattered around his headquarters in North Arlington, New Jersey, are thousands of products bound for college campuses that never reached their targets. Walk into one of his rooms and you'll see a mountain of shavers, shaving cream, sample bags, posters, and other goodies.

Bugai says he's seen unopened cartons of U., the national college newspaper, used as doorstops on campuses. Large companies pay big bucks to hawk their wares in this newspaper. He's watched free samples designed to build loyalty snapped up by visiting high school students, and he knows of many college marketing tours that fizzled because no one hung up the posters advertising the events.

All this anecdotal evidence of marketing flops does have real consequences. Bugai says 18 magazines and 15 sampling compa-

Manufacturers also must carefully manage the incentives they offer to induce channel members to promote their products. This effort includes weighing decisions about pricing, promotion, and other support efforts that the manufacturer performs.

Increasingly, marketers are managing channels in partnership with other channel members. Effective cooperation allows all channel members to achieve goals that they could not achieve on their own. Keys to successful management of channel relationships include development of high levels of coordination, commitment, and trust between channel members.[22]

Not all channel members wield equal power in the distribution chain. The dominant and controlling member of a distribution channel is called the **channel captain.** This firm's power to control a channel may result from its control over some type of reward or punishment to other channel members, such as granting an exclusive sales territory or taking away a dealership. Power might also result from contractual arrangements, specialized expert knowledge, or agreement among channel members about their mutual best interests.

The Battle for Shelf Space

Historically, producers or wholesalers have served as channel captains, with power over small, localized retailers. Since producers and service providers typically create offerings and enjoy the benefits of large-scale operations, they still fill the role of channel captain in many distribution networks. However, increasing numbers of retailers are acting as channel captains, as large chains assume traditional wholesaling functions. The widespread use of scanner-based research also means that retailers now provide and share in the information that supports crucial marketing decisions. Some retailers can even dictate product design specifications to manufacturers. The result is a heightening battle for space on store shelves.

Major retailers such as Wal-Mart, Sears, Kmart, and JCPenney often act as channel captains. These retailers often demand generous promotional and pricing concessions from manufacturers as conditions for selling their products. Retailers may also require manufacturers to pay for inventory and distribution support systems such as electronic data interchange (EDI). Manufacturers that cannot

nies have gone out of business since 1988. Many of these outfits fell over the same stumbling block—employees who fail to reliably distribute merchandise and marketing materials.

Bugai says his efforts to alert brand managers, ad agencies, associations, and suppliers to the problems and intricacies of campus marketing have not succeeded. "Very few people paid attention. They acted surprised, but they're very aware of what's going on," he said. "People are in denial. They write it off as part of doing business."

Waste in college marketing programs is "a volatile topic within the college market," agrees David Morrison, president of Collegiate Marketing Co. in Radnor, Pennsylvania. "From the perspective of the service provider, no one wants to talk about it. It raises a vulnerability."

Successful marketers know ways, however, to vastly improve distribution on campuses. For instance, in a study conducted at eight schools, Bugai measured the effectiveness of two college sampling programs—Good Stuff, owned by FX Corp., and Campus Trial Pak/TGIFree, operated by MarketSource Corp. The study reported that 98 percent of students acknowledged receiving the Good Stuff freebies. On the other hand, only 10 percent received the competitor's handouts.

Good Stuff enjoyed a high rate of success because it maintained control of its distribution, Bugai says. It relied upon dorm officials to hand out the kits to students during check-in when the school year started. MarketSource placed its free samples for pickup at the college bookstores, but busy employees didn't make sure that students signed a log sheet and showed their campus IDs.

QUESTIONS FOR CRITICAL THINKING

1. **Is it the advertising itself or the distribution system to blame for the difficulty in marketing to college students? Defend your answer.**
2. **Suggest some distribution strategies to help marketers reach more college students.**

Sources: Adapted from Jennifer Steinhauer, "Generation X Not Elusive to Marketing Guru of 31," *San Diego Union-Tribune*, February 2, 1997, p. I-1; and Cyndee Miller, "College Campaigns Get Low Scores," *Marketing News*, May 8, 1995, pp. 1, 7.

comply with the demands of large retailers may find themselves unable to penetrate the marketplace.

The grocery industry shows another example of power shifting toward retailers. An important cause of this power shift is market share; large grocery chains now control the majority of grocery sales, leaving few channel options for manufacturers. As a result, the grocery retailers gain great bargaining power in their relationships with manufacturers.[23]

Among their demands, many retailers ask producers to pay slotting allowances before they will agree to carry products. **Slotting allowances** are fees that retailers receive to secure shelf space for new products. A manufacturer can pay a retailer from several thousand dollars to $50,000 or more per store per year to get its new products displayed on store shelves. In general, shelf space in highly visible areas costs more. Some retailers may also require manufacturers to pay slotting fees for warehouse storage.[24]

Although grocery retailers most commonly charge slotting allowances, other types of retailers are also beginning to demand them from producers. For example, Egghead Software, a national retailer of computer software, has started to ask for fees to carry new software products on its shelves. According to industry reports, Egghead is charging as much as $16,000 per year per software title. Software makers complain that this fee raises the cost to distribute low-priced software programs through Egghead to prohibitive levels.[25]

Retailers are also imposing a variety of other fees on manufacturers that seek shelf space. The most common, a failure fee, imposes a charge if a new product does not meet sales projections. This fee covers the cost of removing the item from inventory as well as lost revenue. Other

Marketing Dictionary

channel captain A dominant and controlling member of a distribution channel.

slotting allowance A fee paid by a manufacturer to a retailer to assure shelf space for its products.

SOLVING AN ETHICAL CONTROVERSY

Are Retailer Slotting Allowances Fair?

For more than 30 years, National Spices distributed its cooking spices through grocery store chains such as Safeway, Smith's, Smitty's, and Fry's. Now, however, the Arizona-based firm serves only one retail chain in its distribution channel: Fry's.

National Spices' owner Jesse Martinez blames the drastic decline on slotting allowances, the fees that supermarket chains often demand in exchange for stocking particular brands or products. When Mojave Foods Corp., one of National Spices' biggest competitors, offered to pay retailers higher slotting fees if they would drop other spice brands, Smith's and Smitty's both removed National Spices products from their shelves. "They took the money and ran us out," says Martinez.

Are Slotting Allowances Defensible?

PRO

1. **Retailers justify slotting allowances by explaining that they incur costs to stock shelves, price products, and market brands. Slotting allowances help to cover these costs. According to one estimate, slotting allowances generate \$6 billion to \$18 billion a year for retailers, many of which are struggling to maintain slim profit margins.**
2. **Manufacturers introduce nearly 20,000 grocery-related products each year. By some estimates, as many as 90 percent of these products fail. Retailers say they cannot afford to risk carrying new or marginal products without some assurance of compensation from manufacturers.**
3. **Retailers add that manufacturers who dislike slotting allowances still have the choice of distributing their products through alternate channels.**
4. **Slotting fees do not violate the law as long as they do not prohibit fair competition.**

CON

1. **Manufacturers say that refusal or inability to pay a slotting allowance drastically cuts the potential market for a new product. They also point out that retailers depend on new products to draw customers into stores, so they do not assume as much risk as they claim.**
2. **Producers usually pass on the cost of slotting allowances to consumers, resulting in higher prices. For instance, Frookie's**

retailer fees include annual renewal fees to induce them to continue carrying products, trade allowances, discounts on high-volume purchases, survey fees for research done by the retailers, and even fees to allow salespeople to present new items.

Powerful retailers are also asking for price discounts, promotional budgets, and other costly support. For example, many manufacturers offer discounts to retailers that pay their invoices within 15 days. Wal-Mart, however, has let manufacturers know that it expects a greater allowance. The chain pays its bills within 30 days and still takes the discount. Wal-Mart also expects manufacturers to give discounts on freight costs and to provide inventory management and merchandising support to its stores.[26]

Channel Conflict

Channel captains often must work to resolve channel conflicts. Distribution channels work smoothly only when members cooperate in well-organized efforts to achieve maximum operating efficiencies, yet channel members often perform as separate, independent, and even competing forces. Too often marketing institutions see only one step forward or backward along a channel. They think about their own suppliers and customers rather than about vital links throughout the channel. Two types of conflict, horizontal and vertical conflict, may hinder the normal functioning of a distribution channel.

Horizontal Conflict Horizontal conflict sometimes results from disagreements among channel members at the same level, such as two or more wholesalers or two or more retailers, or among marketing intermediaries of the same type, such as two competing discount stores or several retail florists. More often, however, horizontal conflict causes sparks between different types of marketing intermediaries that handle similar products. A retail druggist competes with discount houses, department stores, convenience stores, and mail-order houses, all of which may buy identical branded products from a single producer. Consumer desire for convenient, one-stop shopping has

Cookies estimates that the firm tacks on approximately 50 cents to the price of each box to pay slotting fees.

3. **Slotting allowances provide unfair advantages to large firms. Small manufacturers complain that their inability to afford slotting fees often prevents them from achieving widespread distribution of their products.**
4. **Slotting allowances often exploit a legal gray area. Firms that suffer damage often cannot prove that a manufacturer has manipulated slotting allowances to squeeze competitors out of a market. Recently, slotting allowances have come under scrutiny of the Federal Trade Commission, the government organization that investigates antitrust violations.**

Summary

Some manufacturers have decided not to pay slotting allowances, with mixed results. For example, the makers of Big Head Coffee Cola, a coffee-flavored cola drink, decided they couldn't afford to pay slotting fees. The company has managed only limited distribution in small, independent stores, cutting its chances for growth.

Jay's Foods, which distributes its potato chips in the Chicago area, also refuses to pay slotting fees. The firm does, however, negotiate with supermarkets to provide extra services such as merchandising, shelf stocking, and promotions instead of paying the fees. The tactic appears to be working. Jay's chips maintain their places in supermarket chains and have a 22 percent market share of chip sales in the region.

American Eagle Beverages, the Arizona producer of Athlete's Choice sports drink, has decided to bypass the issue of slotting allowances altogether. The firm has decided not to distribute its products in the United States because of the fees. Instead, American Eagle ships its product south of the border to Mexico, where retailers welcome new products and don't ask for slotting fees.

As for National Spices, the company is struggling to remain profitable within its reduced distribution network. Owner Martinez considered taking Smitty's Supermarkets to court over the issue, but his attorney advised him that a lawsuit promised little or no chance of winning.

Sources: Ken Partch, "Slotting: The Issue That Won't Go Away," *Supermarket Business,* May 1997; Graciela Sevilla, "Tempe Company Drinks Up Success in Mexican Market," *Arizona Republic,* December 26, 1996, p. E1; Frank Green, "Battle for Shelf Control: No Matter Who Wins, Consumers Pay Some Hidden Costs," *San Diego Union-Tribune,* November 4, 1996, p. C1; Chris Kraul, "Justice Probes Salty Snacks' Sales Practices," *Los Angeles Times,* May 25, 1996, p. D1; and Dawn Gilbertson, "Supplier Shelved," *Arizona Republic,* February 4, 1996, p. 1.

drawn products into multiple channels and numerous, rival outlets.

Microsoft Corp. is carefully trying to avoid horizontal conflict as it moves toward distributing its software products via the Internet. The company hopes to increase the amount of software that it distributes to customers over electronic links rather than in packaged boxes on retailer shelves. However, the move could open up conflict with Microsoft's wholesalers and retailers. To avoid this conflict, Microsoft has carefully evaluated the way it rewards its distribution channel partners. The firm is sharing the savings it gains from electronic distribution with its channel partners. Microsoft will continue to rely on these intermediaries to provide financing and customer service to customers.[27]

Vertical Conflict Vertical relationships also cause frequent and often severe conflict. Channel members at different levels find many reasons for disputes, as when retailers develop private brands to compete with producers' brands or when producers establish their own retail stores or create mail-order operations that compete with retailers. Producers may annoy wholesalers when they attempt to bypass these intermediaries and sell directly to retailers or business users. In other instances, wholesalers may anger suppliers by promoting competing products.

Consider the experience of Cadbury Schweppes PLC. This number three manufacturer in the U.S. soft-drink market makes the ingredients for 7Up, Dr Pepper, A&W Root Beer, and Canada Dry beverages. Soft-drink manufacturers rely on bottlers to combine the ingredients, bottle the products, and distribute them. In trying to develop a network of bottlers, Cadbury faces stiff competition from giant rivals Coca-Cola and Pepsi. Some of Cadbury's biggest bottlers also bottle and distribute Coke and Pepsi products, and they have sometimes dropped Cadbury products in favor of carrying the stronger Coke or Pepsi products. In response, Cadbury has had to reinforce relationships with its remaining distributors. To maintain these relationships, the company has set up sales support programs for bottlers, and it also helps with financing so the bottlers can buy vending machines and refrigerated cases for their stores.[28]

The Grey Market Another type of channel conflict results from activities in the grey market. As U.S. manufacturers license their technology and brands abroad, they sometimes find themselves in competition for the U.S. market against versions of their own brands produced by overseas affiliates. These **grey goods,** sometimes called *parallel goods,* enter U.S. channels through the actions of foreign distributors. While licensing agreements usually prohibit foreign licensees from selling in the United States, no such rules inhibit their distributors.

A decade ago, the grey market became a problem for U.S. firms in the electronics field. It then spread to flashlight batteries, photographic film, packaged goods, and the apparel industry. While some manufacturers have protested against this practice, retailers can still legally buy goods through the grey market, since the Supreme Court has ruled that products made under legitimate licenses can legally enter the market regardless of their countries of origin.

Achieving Channel Cooperation

The basic antidote to channel conflict is effective cooperation among channel members. Most channels function harmoniously more often than they erupt in conflict; if they did not, they would cease to function at all. Cooperation is best achieved when all channel members regard themselves as components of the same organization. Achieving this kind of cooperation is the primary responsibility of the dominant member, the channel captain, which must provide the leadership necessary to ensure the channel's efficient functioning.

Caterpillar manufactures heavy equipment like tractors, backhoes, and diesel engines. These expensive machines have long life spans and require ongoing parts and service. Caterpillar treats the 186 independent dealers that sell its equipment as the firm's partners. It believes that independent dealers offer greater insight into local and regional market needs than Caterpillar could achieve by selling through a direct sales force. Caterpillar also believes that dealers effectively provide critical after-sale services like repairs, parts, and training that increase customer satisfaction with Caterpillar's products. Caterpillar strongly emphasizes the priority of developing and maintaining close ties with its dealers. The company actively involves dealers in product design and redesign decisions. Caterpillar jointly conducts customer satisfaction research with each dealer, as well. Additionally, Caterpillar works with dealers to provide customer financing, efficient delivery of repair parts, and training to enhance dealers' selling effectiveness.[29]

http://www.caterpillar.com/

VERTICAL MARKETING SYSTEMS

Efforts to reduce channel conflict and improve the effectiveness of distribution have led to the development of vertical marketing systems. A **vertical marketing system (VMS)** is a planned channel system designed to improve distribution efficiency and cost effectiveness by integrating various functions throughout the distribution chain.

A vertical marketing system can achieve this goal through either forward or backward integration. In *forward integration,* a firm attempts to control downstream distribution. For example, a manufacturer might buy a retail chain that sells its product. *Backward integration* occurs when a manufacturer attempts to gain greater control over inputs to its production process. For example, a manufacturer might buy the supplier of a raw material it uses to make a product. Backward integration can also extend the control of retailers and wholesalers over producers that supply them.

A VMS offers several benefits. First, it improves chances for controlling and coordinating the steps in the distribution or production process. It may lead to development of economies of scale that ultimately save money. A VMS may also let a manufacturer expand into profitable new businesses. However, a VMS also involves some costs. A manufacturer assumes increased risk when it takes over control of an entire distribution chain. Manufacturers may also discover that they lose some flexibility to respond to market changes.[30]

Marketers have developed three categories of VMSs: corporate systems, administered systems, and contractual systems. These categories are outlined in the sections that follow.

Corporate Systems

Where a single owner runs organizations at each stage of the distribution channel, it operates a **corporate marketing system.** Hartmarx Corp. markets its Hart Schaffner & Marx suits through company-owned stores and some independent retailers. At one time, Holiday Corp. owned a furniture manufacturer and a carpet mill that supplied its Holiday Inn motels. Other well-known corporate systems include Firestone, Sherwin-Williams, and Singer. The ad for Sherwin-Williams in Figure 14.8 highlights the firm's corporate marketing system, stating, "And there's only one place to get it—your Sherwin-Williams store."

Administered Systems

An **administered marketing system** achieves channel coordination when a dominant channel member exercises its power. Even though Goodyear sells its tires through independently owned and operated dealerships, Goodyear controls the stock that they carry. Other examples of powerful channel captains leading administered channels include McKesson, Sears, and Montgomery Ward.

Contractual Systems

Instead of common ownership of intermediaries within a corporate VMS or exercising power within an administered system, a **contractual marketing system** coordinates distribution through formal agreements among channel members. In practice, three types of agreements set up these systems: wholesaler-sponsored voluntary chains, retail cooperatives, and franchises.

Wholesaler-Sponsored Voluntary Chain A wholesaler-sponsored voluntary chain represents an attempt by an independent wholesaler to preserve a market by strengthening its retail customers. To enable independent retailers to compete with outlets of rival chains, the wholesaler enters into a formal agreement with retailers to use a common name, maintain standardized facilities, and purchase the wholesaler's products. Often, the wholesaler develops a line of private brands to be stocked by the members of the voluntary chain. The Avis Sports Group is a good example. Formed by Avis Sports, a hunting and fishing equipment wholesaler, the voluntary chain links 500 independent sporting goods stores. In addition to the group's product line, members gain support such as store signage, business-planning help, and cooperative advertising. "If something wasn't done to help these dealers compete, our customer base was going to erode," explains Gary Zurn about why Avis Sports formed the voluntary chain.[31]

A common store name and similar inventories allow the retailers to save on advertising costs, since a single newspaper ad promotes all the retailers in the trading area. IGA (Independent Grocers' Alliance) Food Stores is another good example of a voluntary chain. Other wholesaler-sponsored chains include Associated Druggists, Sentry Hardware, and Western Auto.

Figure 14.8 Sherwin-Williams: Example of a Corporate Vertical Marketing System

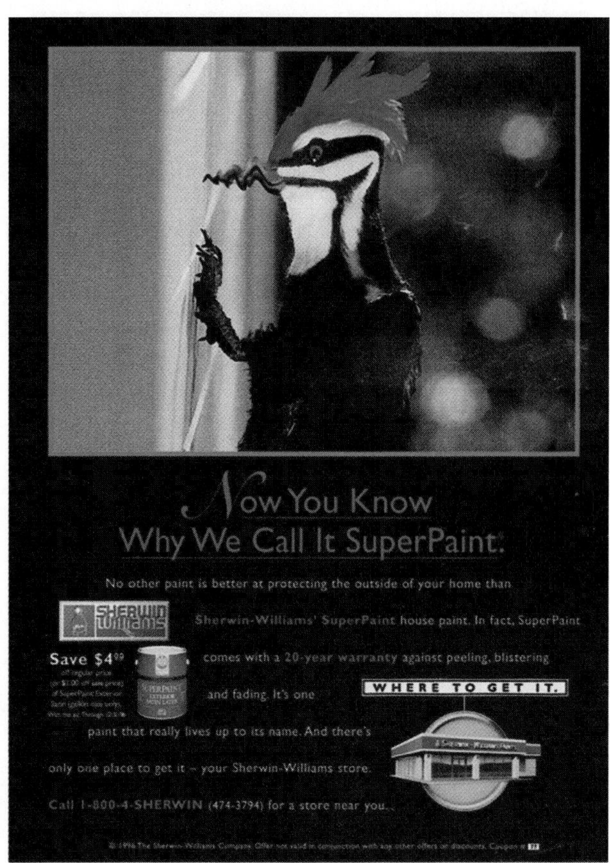
Now You Know
Why We Call It SuperPaint.
No other paint is better at protecting the outside of your home than
Sherwin-Williams' SuperPaint house paint. In fact, SuperPaint
comes with a 20-year warranty against peeling, blistering
and fading. It's one
paint that really lives up to its name. And there's
only one place to get it – your Sherwin-Williams store.
Call 1-800-4-SHERWIN (474-3794) for a store near you.
Sherwin Williams
Save $4.99
WHERE TO GET IT.

Retail Cooperative In a second type of contractual VMS, a retail cooperative, a group of retailers establish a shared wholesaling operation to help them compete with chains. The retailers purchase ownership shares in the wholesaling

Marketing Dictionary

grey good A product manufactured abroad under license from a U.S. firm and then sold in the U.S. market in competition with that firm's own counterpart products.

vertical marketing system (VMS) A planned channel system designed to improve distribution efficiency and cost effectiveness by integrating various functions throughout the distribution chain.

corporate marketing system A VMS in which a single owner runs organizations at each stage in its distribution channel.

administered marketing system A VMS that achieves channel coordination when a dominant channel member exercises its power.

contractual marketing system A VMS that coordinates channel activities through formal agreements among channel members.

Figure 14.9 **Mail Boxes Etc.: A Franchised Service Business**

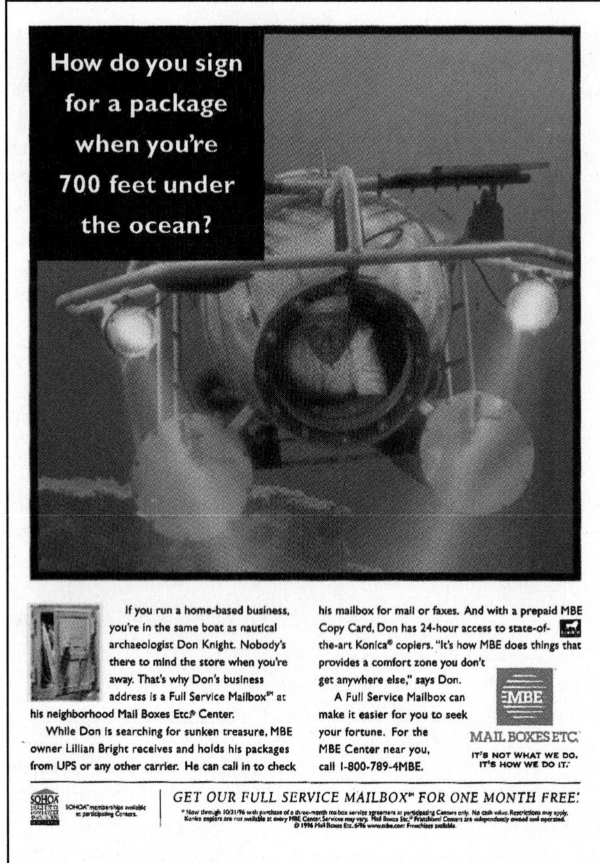
How do you sign for a package when you're 700 feet under the ocean?
If you run a home-based business, you're in the same boat as nautical archaeologist Don Knight. Nobody's there to mind the store when you're away. That's why Don's business address is a Full Service Mailbox℠ at his neighborhood Mail Boxes Etc.® Center.
While Don is searching for sunken treasure, MBE owner Lillian Bright receives and holds his packages from UPS or any other carrier. He can call in to check his mailbox for mail or faxes. And with a prepaid MBE Copy Card, Don has 24-hour access to state-of-the-art Konica® copiers. "It's how MBE does things that provides a comfort zone you don't get anywhere else," says Don.
A Full Service Mailbox can make it easier for you to seek your fortune. For the MBE Center near you, call 1-800-789-4MBE.
MBE
MAIL BOXES ETC.
IT'S NOT WHAT WE DO. IT'S HOW WE DO IT.
SOHOA
SOHOA memberships available at participating Centers.
GET OUR FULL SERVICE MAILBOX℠ FOR ONE MONTH FREE!

operation and agree to buy a minimum percentage of their inventories from it. The members may also choose to adopt a common store name and develop common private brands.

One such retailer cooperative is Pet Team, Inc. The cooperative's 1,200 member retailers do not purchase enough individually to order in bulk directly from manufacturers. The cooperative, however, buys directly from 30 pet food and equipment wholesalers. Members agree to stock at least 75 percent of the cooperative's product lines, and the cooperative negotiates lower prices with the wholesalers than the retailers could achieve on their own. As a result, the independent pet store owners improve their competitiveness against large "pet supermarkets" like PetSmart.[32]

Franchise A third type of contractual vertical marketing system is the franchise, in which a wholesaler or dealer (the franchisee) agrees to meet the operating requirements of a manufacturer or other franchiser.

Franchising has become a huge and growing industry. Over 3,000 U.S. companies distribute goods or services through systems of franchised dealers. Well-known firms offering franchises include McDonald's, Baskin-Robbins, Century 21, H&R Block, and The Body Shop. Franchiser Mail Boxes Etc., shown in Figure 14.9, serves the needs of the growing number of people operating businesses from their homes. The number of franchisee-owned businesses in the United States increased from just over 400,000 to over 560,000 between 1989 and 1995 alone. As mentioned in Chapter 4, numerous firms—at least 400—offer franchises in international markets, including Japan, Canada, the United Kingdom, Australia, and France.

Franchise owners pay from several thousand dollars to hundreds of thousands of dollars to purchase their franchises. While service franchises may cost as little as $5,000, fast-food outlets can cost over $600,000 in franchise fees for each unit. A franchisee also usually pays a royalty on sales to the franchising company. In exchange for these initial and ongoing fees, the franchise owner receives the right to use the company's brand name, as well as services such as training, marketing, advertising, and volume discounts.[33]

The Woman's Health Boutique Franchise System is one example of a franchiser. Company founder Vicki Jones started the firm after she noted that independent medical supply companies were having a difficult time keeping up with the rapid changes in their field. Outlets of the Woman's Health Boutique Franchise System sell products for cancer patients, including wigs, and books on women's health topics. Each franchise owner pays a one-time franchise fee of $25,000 to $35,000.[34]

Franchisers can run into channel conflict if they seek to use other distribution methods that directly compete with their own franchisees. For example, Carvel Ice Cream Bakery built its business selling ice cream desserts through a network of franchised stores. When franchise sales dipped in the late 1980s due to competition from frozen yogurt stores, Carvel decided to create a line of packaged ice cream products for sale in supermarkets. Stunned Carvel franchisees believed that the retail products would further damage their businesses. The Independent Association of Carvel Franchisees filed a lawsuit to keep the parent company from branching into supermarket sales.[35]

ACHIEVEMENT CHECK SUMMARY

Reread the learning goals that follow, and consider the questions for each goal. Answering these questions will reinforce your grasp of the most important concepts in the chapter and allow you to check how well you have achieved these learning goals. Where a blank appears before a question, answer with *T* or *F;* for multiple-choice questions, circle the letter of the correct answer.

Objective 14.1: Describe the role that distribution plays in marketing strategy.

1. ___ Distribution is the process of bringing products to customers for purchase.

2. A distribution channel is (a) a method of allocating products to end users; (b) a system for managing the flow of goods to users; (c) a transportation term.

3. ___ Distribution channels bring buyers and sellers together.

4. ___ Once a distribution channel is established, it probably never will change.

Objective 14.2: Describe the various types of distribution channels available to marketers.

1. ___ The simplest distribution channel is (a) to sell through retail stores; (b) to use wholesalers; (c) to use direct sales or direct marketing; (d) to hire an agent.

2. ___ A Tupperware party is an example of (a) direct selling; (b) wholesaling; (c) retailing; (d) dual distribution.

3. ___ An example of a marketing intermediary is (a) a company's direct sales force; (b) a wholesaler; (c) a sales branch; (d) a merchandise mart; (e) a channel captain.

4. ___ Firms usually practice dual distribution (a) to maximize distribution coverage; (b) to reduce the number of channels; (c) to move goods back from users to producers.

Objective 14.3: Identify the functions performed by wholesaling intermediaries.

1. ___ Wholesaling intermediaries improve channel efficiency.

2. ___ Wholesaling intermediaries can often perform marketing functions more efficiently than manufacturers can.

3. ___ Wholesalers reduce costs by (a) offering wholesale prices to retailers; (b) reducing the number of contacts required between manufacturers and retailers; (c) taking over advertising for manufacturers.

Objective 14.4: Summarize the channel options available to a manufacturer that desires to bypass independent wholesaling intermediaries.

1. ___ Sales branches carry inventory.

2. ___ Sales offices close to customers can help a firm to reduce selling costs and improve customer service.

3. ___ Trade shows and merchandise marts give manufacturers the opportunity to showcase their goods to wholesalers and retailers.

Objective 14.5: Identify the major types of independent wholesaling intermediaries and the situations appropriate for each.

1. ___ A drop shipper (a) receives orders from customers and forwards them to producers; (b) ships directly to retailers who need new inventory; (c) takes goods to a central market for sale; (d) represents buyers to sellers.

2. ___ A merchant wholesaler can perform many marketing functions for manufacturers.

3. ___ A rack jobber (a) represents buyers to sellers; (b) makes sure merchandise is stocked in stores; (c) receives orders from customers and forwards them to producers; (d) takes goods to a central market for sale.

Objective 14.6: Outline the major channel strategy decisions.

1. ___ *Distribution intensity* refers to (a) the amount of inventory on store shelves; (b) the number of intermediaries through which a firm distributes goods; (c) the number of geographic areas covered by a distribution strategy.

2. ___ Intensive distribution is most often used by manufacturers of (a) convenience goods; (b) specialty goods; (c) luxury goods; (d) parts for other manufacturers.

3. ___ One benefit of selective distribution is (a) goods are widely available; (b) improvement in working relationships within the channel; (c) reduction in advertising costs.

4. ___ Exclusive distribution can lead to legal problems if it inhibits competition or creates a monopoly situation.

Objective 14.7: Describe the concepts of channel leadership and management.

1. ___ All channel members are relatively equal in the distribution chain.

2. ___ The term *channel captain* refers to the dominant and controlling member of a distribution channel.

3. ___ Slotting allowances are (a) fees charged by manufacturers to wholesalers that want to carry their goods; (b) fees that retailers charge to manufacturers that want shelf space for new products; (c) the cost of warehousing products before shipment; (d) fees paid by manufacturers to display advertising in stores.

Objective 14.8: Discuss conflict and cooperation within the distribution channel.

1. ___ Which of the following situations is an example of horizontal conflict? (a) Wal-Mart and Kroger Supermarkets both promote and sell Bayer aspirin. (b) Kmart has developed its own brand of aspirin, which it sells on the shelf next to Bayer aspirin. (c) The manufacturer of Bayer aspirin refuses to pay slotting allowances.

2. ___ Which of the following situations is an example of vertical conflict? (a) Wal-Mart and Kroger Supermarkets both promote and sell Bayer aspirin. (b) Kmart has developed its own brand of aspirin, which it sells on the shelf next to Bayer aspirin. (c) The manufacturer of Bayer aspirin refuses to pay slotting allowances.

3. ___ Cooperation between channel members is best achieved by (a) making sure all members are paid adequately; (b) considering all channel members as part of the same organization; (c) focusing on operating efficiencies.

Objective 14.9: Identify the types of vertical marketing systems.

1. ___ A manufacturer decides to open a chain of stores to sell the goods it manufactures. This is an example of (a) forward integration; (b) backward integration; (c) channel cooperation; (d) a reverse channel.

2. ___ The costs of a vertical marketing system include (a) economies of distribution; (b) increased risk;, (c) increased flexibility; (d) increased wholesaling expenses;(e) reduced wholesaling expenses.

3. ___ When a single owner runs organizations at each stage of its distribution channel, it has set up (a) a corporate marketing system; (b) an administered marketing system; (c) a contractual marketing system.

4. ___ An example of a contractual vertical marketing system is (a) McDonald's; (b) Wal-Mart; (c) Sherwin-Williams paint stores.

Students: See the solutions section located on page S-3 to check your responses to the Achievement Check Summary.

Key Terms

distribution channel
marketing intermediary
wholesaler
direct channel
direct selling
industrial distributor
dual distribution
reverse channel
wholesaling intermediary
sales branch
sales office
trade fair
merchandise mart
merchant wholesaler
rack jobber
cash-and-carry wholesaler
truck wholesaler
drop shipper
mail-order wholesaler
agents and brokers
commission merchant
auction house
broker
selling agent
manufacturer's agent
distribution intensity
intensive distribution
selective distribution
exclusive distribution
exclusive-dealing agreement
closed sales territory
tying agreement
channel captain
slotting allowance
grey good
vertical marketing system (VMS)
corporate marketing system
administered marketing system
contractual marketing system

Review Questions

1. Outline the major categories of distribution channels. Cite an example of a firm that uses each type of channel.
2. How do distribution channels create utility? What specific functions do distribution channels perform?
3. What is a wholesaling intermediary? Describe its function(s) in a marketing strategy.
4. Distinguish among the different types of manufacturer-owned wholesaling intermediaries. What conditions might suit each one?
5. Distinguish among the different types of independent wholesaling intermediaries. Why would manufacturers choose to market products through these intermediaries?
6. Outline the major categories of channel decisions. How might the grey market affect a firm's channel decision?
7. Who should perform the various marketing channel functions? How have these arrangements changed over time?
8. Explain the concept of power in the distribution channel. Under what conditions do producers, wholesalers, and retailers act as channel captains?
9. What is channel conflict? Describe the types of channel conflict.
10. Identify the various types of vertical marketing systems. Cite an example of each.

Discussion Questions

1. Outline the distribution channel used by a firm in your area. Why did the company select this particular channel?
2. Match each industry with the most appropriate type of wholesaling intermediary:
   ___ Hardware
   ___ Perishable foods
   ___ Lumber
   ___ Wheat
   ___ Used cars
   a. Drop shipper
   b. Truck wholesaler
   c. Auction house
   e. Commission merchant
   d. Full-function merchant wholesaler
3. Canon's FAXPHONE B540 product is a combination fax and copy machine that sells for $399. The target market for this product is small business owners and people who work in home offices. Suggest distribution channels through which Canon might effectively distribute this product. Should Canon consider dual distribution? If so, what channel conflicts might arise?
4. Find a real-world example of channel conflict. Suggest a resolution to this conflict.
5. Which degree of distribution intensity is appropriate for each of the following products?
   a. *People* magazine
   b. Liz Claiborne sportswear
   c. Dial soap
   d. Apple computers
   e. Waterford crystal

'netWork

1. A significant amount of research centers on slotting allowances, and the FTC frequently reviews cases involving these fees. Search the FTC's Web site at

http://www.ftc.gov/

and other sites for information and current issues involving slotting allowances. Based on the information you find, answer the following questions:

a. What is currently happening with slotting allowances?
b. When are they used?
c. What ethical or legal issues could surface because of slotting allowances?
d. How could marketers avoid these problems?

2. Hundreds of franchisers offer opportunities for individuals to invest in their own businesses. The Internet provides a rich pool of information on franchises, suppliers, and support services. Visit the sites

http://www.entremkt.com/access/
http://www.franchise-conxions.com/

or search for others, and then choose a franchise that seems like a good investment opportunity. Why did you choose this franchise? Support your decision. Do not forget to look at international opportunities.

3. Amway is one of the largest direct-selling, multilevel marketing companies in the world. Visit its home page at

http://www.amway.com/

and then respond to the following questions:

a. What is multilevel marketing?
b. Describe the distribution system of this multilevel, direct-sales organization.
c. Why has Amway enjoyed so much success?

VIDEO CASE 14

CHOOSING CHANNELS

People today hurry a lot. They eat in a hurry. They go to work in a hurry. They want to buy things in a hurry. Convenience stores fill the need for quick and convenient shopping. Next Door Food Stores is a chain of 30 convenience stores in Michigan and Indiana offering rapid service 24 hours a day and stocking some 30,000 grocery and general merchandise items.

Glen Johnson started the company in 1926 as Johnson Oil, a supplier of oil to farmers, and through the years he expanded it into a full-service gasoline business. In the early 1980s, his grandson, David Johnson, took over the business and decided to refocus it by combining the gasoline stations with convenience food stores. This change in focus forced David Johnson to make an important channel strategy decision: Should Next Door perform its own wholesaling or should it form relationships with independent wholesaling intermediaries?

Because Next Door lacked enough sales volume to support its own distribution warehouse, Johnson decided to use several different independent wholesalers. Most products that Next Door sells require intensive distribution. Rack jobbers supply products such as magazines, newspapers, snack foods, and chips. They regularly visit the stores to replenish merchandise from supplies in their trucks. Full-function merchant wholesalers supply the retailer with hundreds of grocery items.

Fabiano Brothers, Inc. is a large beverage distributor that provides a complete assortment of services to Next Door. "Our role is to provide the maximum benefit to the retailer," says Jim Philips, Fabiano's wine division manager. "When we sell a product, we have to be absolutely assured that that product is going to sell for the retailer." Fabiano helps Next Door's managers to determine which products stores should stock based on product movement and the space requirements of each item.

Shelf space is very limited in convenience stores. On average, the square footage of convenience stores is between 3,000 and 3,500 square feet, compared to an average of 30,000 square feet in supermarkets. With space at a premium, Next Door needs to maximize its inventory turnover in order to make a profit. Fabiano supplies sales reports to store managers weekly or monthly, depending on store size, that include information such as inventory turns and product sales and profits. Next Door managers base shelf-space allocation decisions on this information.

Because storage space at convenience food stores is also very limited, Next Door needs products delivered frequently and in small quantities. "In a convenience store, we buy by the box," says James Salisbury, Next Door's vice president of operations. At its warehouses, Fabiano Brothers receives truckload shipments of beverages on large pallets from manufacturers, breaking them down into smaller packages for retailers like Next Door. Fabiano operates its own fleet of trucks to deliver the products just-in-time, helping Next Door to keep its inventory at a minimum and to control its carrying costs. The wholesaler also deploys its own sales force. Sales reps maintain sales history data and track current trends, such as beverage sales by flavor and size, to help merchandise each store based on local market needs.

Tracking current trends helped Fabiano Brothers to recognize the growing popularity of "new-age" beverages such as bottled and flavored water, sports drinks, and flavored tea drinks. Next Door was one of the first retailers in its operating area to allocate refrigerated display space to these new beverages. When Arizona Beverage Company entered the new-age drink category in 1993, it selected Fabiano Brothers as its wholesale distributor because that firm already served the convenience stores "where we want to be," says Sal Demilio, regional manager for Arizona Beverage. The company's flavored tea drinks fit well into Fabiano's product portfolio, and the wholesaler saw great sales potential in the new products introduced in unusually large 24-ounce cans with innovative package graphics.

To ensure effective operation of this channel strategy, Arizona Beverage and Fabiano work together to develop annual plans. With manufacturing plants throughout the country, Arizona Beverage expects Fabiano to provide a extensive distribution and to meet its projected sales targets. "We're there every day where the manufacturer can't be," says Philips, providing service functions such as a sales force calling daily on customers and truck deliveries as often as retailers need them.

Beverages such as Coke and Pepsi are distributed directly to Next Door outlets by local bottling plants. When Coca-Cola representatives offered Next Door a substantial financial incentive for an exclusive distribution relationship, the retailer's management accepted the offer and removed all Pepsi products from its stores. "That was the worst thing we could have done," says Salisbury. "People complained and customers left and said 'we're never coming here because you took our Pepsi out.' We did not convert those Pepsi drinkers to Coke. That was just not going to happen." Next Door returned the financial incentive to Coca-Cola, thanked the company for the offer, and called the local Pepsi bottlers, asking them to bring back their products.

Although the exclusive distribution experiment didn't work out, another experiment—selling branded food within the convenience store setting—is producing much better results. Next Door Food has formed an alliance with fast-food competitor Subway Sandwich Shops, allocating a portion of each store's floor space to operate a franchised Subway outlet. Next Door employees operate the shop, following a standard set of procedures detailed in Subway's operations manual for franchisees. The retailing innovation benefits both Subway and Next Door. Subway and other fast-food brands realize that convenience stores control prime locations, and they want to tap into that strength as part of their expansion programs. The national recognition of fast-food brands draws customers into convenience stores. One Next Door manager said that the Subway shop has increased her in-store sales by 10 percent. On-the-go consumers who want a fast and convenient shopping trip can now visit a Next Door Food Store to fill up their gas tanks, pick up a Subway sandwich, and buy a can of Arizona Iced Tea.

Questions

1. How has Next Door created value for its customers through its channel strategy?
2. Which wholesaling services does Fabiano Brothers provide for Next Door Food Stores?
3. Which type of vertical marketing system does the partnership between Next Door and Subway represent? How does this relationship benefit each alliance partner?
4. The National Association of Convenience Stores, the industry trade association, maintains a Web site as an Internet resource for the convenience store industry. Visit the site at:

   http://www.cstorecentral.com/

   Explain how the Web site could assist Next Door Food Stores in its marketing decisions.

Source: Telephone interview with Barry Chapman, director of human resources, Next Door Food Store, May 1997.

CHAPTER 15

RETAILING

Chapter Objectives

1. Describe the evolution of retailing.
2. Explain the importance of target marketing to retailers.
3. Discuss how the elements of the marketing mix apply to retailing strategy.
4. Identify and explain each of the five bases for categorizing retailers.
5. Compare the basic types of nonstore retailing.
6. Explain the concept of scrambled merchandising.

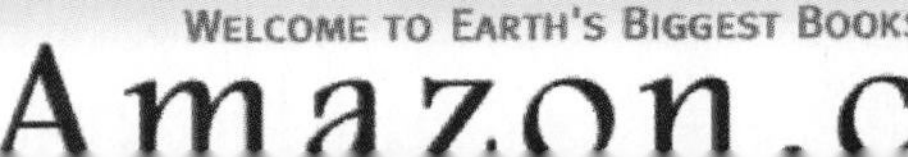

Net Profits: Virtually Attainable?

When talk turns to cyberspace commerce, Virtual Vineyards, a Palo Alto wine retailer, and Amazon.com, a bookstore, are often mentioned as success stories. You can visit each store only one way—you must turn on your computer.

Virtual Vineyards has sold tens of thousands of bottles of wine through the Internet since it opened its online store in 1995. Customers purchase products from the dozens of premium wineries that wine expert and Virtual Vineyards co-founder Peter Granoff finds. The retailer sells products from boutique wineries too small to compete with larger producers and their sizable advertising budgets. Granoff, a professional wine buyer for 20 years, tastes each vintage and ships customers user-friendly notes about it.

http://www.virtualvin.com/

Prices for the company's wines, specialty foods, and gift packs are moderate, delivery is prompt, business is booming, and the creators are happy. Virtual Vineyards avoids inventory and warehouse expenses by filling orders from a central location as it receives them. The Internet allows it to sell to customers around the world from just one virtual storefront, rather than having to set up international branches. In fact, international orders represent 5 percent to 10 percent of Virtual Vineyard's sales.

Virtual Vineyards
WINE SHOP
FOOD SHOP
Welcome!
Sign In or Sign Up
In a Hurry?
Order Wine Now!
Order Food Now!
Order Gifts Now!
Spring Fling Easter Dinner
A Menu from Louise Fiszer
GIFT SHOP
What's New:
Pure nectar for the wine drinker with a sweet tooth: 1992 Dolce!
Gift Certificates!
Wine Shop & Food Shop
Current Specials
Food & Wine Samplers
First Time Visitors
ここでクリックする
Home | Wine Shop | Food Shop | Gift Shop | Site Map
Customer Service | Member Services | Order Form
MasterCard
VISA
CyberCash

"Our plans are to never do paper," says co-founder Robert Olson. He worked for computer manufacturer Silicon Graphics and as an interactive TV marketer before partnering with Granoff to start the store from his home.

But even this widely cited example of Internet marketing has not yet reached breakeven. Virtual Vineyards is not yet profitable—despite an infusion of about $3 million from venture capitalists—though the founders expect to cross that hurdle in 1998. The company invested about $300,000 to set up the site, and it incurs large monthly telecommunications charges, as well. The site has not yet recovered its huge investment in hardware and software. It also uses costly promotions, such as offers of free biscotti (Italian cookies), to lure buyers.

Virtual Vineyards illustrates one of the ironies of online merchandising, which Microsoft's Bill Gates calls the first step toward "friction-free capitalism." Retailers look upon the stampede into cyberspace as a repeat of the prospectors' rush into the California goldfields, but no one is striking it rich yet. While this worries some retailers, many fear letting their competitors corner the cyberspace marketplace.

Statistics show dramatically growing interest in shopping by computer. Computer-literate customers placed orders for $1 billion in merchandise in a recent year, according to New York market researcher Jupiter Communications. Still, that's a far cry from the $50 billion that Americans spent shopping by television and through catalogs.

In addition to individual virtual stores, shoppers can also visit cybermalls that gather many Web shops into single sites. The Internet Mall links visitors to a varied group of boutiques and specialty stores, and Dreamshop provides links to the sites of well-known retailers including Saks Fifth Avenue, Eddie Bauer, Godiva Chocolate, Omaha Steaks, and others. Specialty malls like Classic England, which features shops with English merchandise, provide a way to find unusual merchandise that is not readily available to buyers.

http://www.dreamshop.com/
http://www.classicengland.co.uk/

One of the most highly touted Internet merchants is Jeff P. Bezos, founder of Amazon.com, which is billed as the "Earth's biggest bookstore." Bezos thinks it's premature to worry about profits. "We are not profitable," he says. "We could be. It would be the easiest thing in the world to be profitable. It would also be the dumbest." He explains that Amazon.com prefers reinvesting its earnings in the future of the business.

http://www.amazon.com/

"As a commercial medium, it is maybe 20 months old," says Michael B. Slade, chief executive of Starwave Corp., whose ESPNet Sportszone is one of the most popular World Wide Web sites. "That would be like cable TV in 1977, the magazine industry in 1800, radio at the turn of the century. Yet the pace of what's happened in 18 months is amazing."[1]

CHAPTER OVERVIEW

Retailing may be defined as all activities involved in selling goods and services to ultimate consumers. Although most retail sales occur in retail stores, the definition also encompasses several forms of nonstore retailing, activities such as accepting orders via home computers, telephone and mail-order sales, vending machine sales, and direct selling.

Retail outlets serve as contact points between channel members and ultimate consumers. In a very real sense, retailers represent the distribution channel to most consumers, since a typical shopper has little contact with manufacturers and virtually none with wholesaling intermediaries. Retailers determine locations, store hours, quality of salespeople, store layouts, product selections, and return policies—factors that often influence the image consumers hold of the marketed products more strongly than the products themselves. Both large and small retailers perform the major channel activities: creating time, place, and ownership utilities.

Retailers act as both customers and marketers in their channels. They market products to ultimate consumers and at the same time buy from wholesalers and manufacturers. Because of their critical locations in their channels, retailers often perform an important feedback role. They obtain information from customers and transmit it to manufacturers and other channel members.

EVOLUTION OF RETAILING

Early retailing can be traced to the establishment of trading posts such as the Hudson Bay Company and to pack peddlers who carried their wares to outlying settlements. The first type of retail institution in the United States, the general store, stocked merchandise to meet the needs of a small community or rural area. Here, customers could buy clothing, groceries, feed, seed, farm equipment, drugs, spectacles, and candy. General stores flourished for many years, but the basic needs that had created them also doomed them to a limited existence. Since storekeepers attempted to satisfy customers' needs for all types of goods, they carried small assortments of each item. As communities grew, new stores concentrated on specific product lines, such as drugs, dry goods, groceries, and hardware. The general stores could not compete, and their owners either converted them to limited-line stores or closed them. Most of the few hundred general stores still operating today serve customers in rural areas.

The development of retailing illustrates the marketing concept in operation. Innovations in retailing have emerged to satisfy changing consumer wants and needs. Supermarkets appeared in the early 1930s in response to consumers' desire for lower prices. In the 1950s, innovative discount stores offered consumers convenient parking and low prices in exchange for reduced services. The emergence of convenience food stores in the 1960s satisfied consumer demand for fast service, convenient locations, and expanded hours of operation. The development of off-price retailers in the 1980s reflected consumer demand for brand-name merchandise at prices considerably lower than those of traditional retailers. Similarly, the 1990s have brought a continuation of retailing innovations, as some retailers, like Wal-Mart, have expanded, and others, including once-dominant department stores like Frederick and Nelson in Seattle and Hornes in Pittsburgh, have disappeared. An important concept drives this evolutionary change.

Wheel of Retailing

The **wheel of retailing** attempts to explain the patterns of change in retailing. According to this hypothesis, a new type of retailer gains a competitive foothold by offering customers lower prices than current outlets charge, maintaining profits by reducing or eliminating services. Once established, however, the innovator adds more services, and its prices gradually rise. It then becomes vulnerable to new, low-price retailers that enter with minimum services—and so the wheel turns.

Most major developments in the history of retailing appear to fit the wheel's pattern. Early department stores, chain stores, supermarkets, discount stores, hypermarkets, and catalog retailers all emphasized limited service and low prices. Most of these retailers gradually increased prices as they added services.

Some exceptions disrupt this pattern, however. Suburban shopping centers, convenience food stores, and vending machines never built their appeals around low prices. However, the wheel pattern has held sufficiently consistently in the past to make it a useful general indicator of future retailing developments.

Marketing Dictionary

retailing All activities involved in selling goods and services to ultimate consumers.

wheel of retailing The hypothesis that each new type of retailer gains a competitive foothold by offering lower prices than current suppliers charge, maintaining profits by reducing or eliminating services.

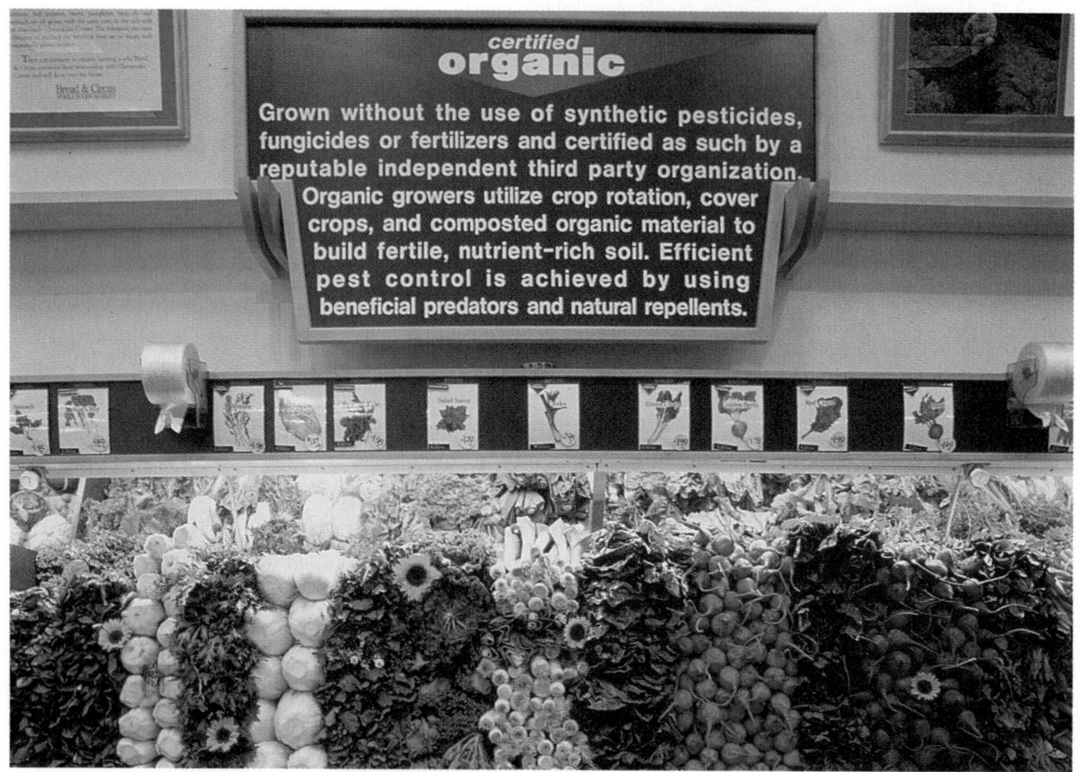
certified
organic
Grown without the use of synthetic pesticides, fungicides or fertilizers and certified as such by a reputable independent third party organization.
Organic growers utilize crop rotation, cover crops, and composted organic material to build fertile, nutrient-rich soil. Efficient pest control is achieved by using beneficial predators and natural repellents.

The Bread & Circus chain of organic supermarkets represents the latest evolution of food retailing. Specializing in organic produce, bulk sales of granola, and environmentally sensitive household products, these "wholesome" supermarkets have emerged to satisfy the needs and desires of today's health-conscious consumers.

RETAILING STRATEGY

Like manufactures and wholesalers, a retailer develops a marketing strategy based on the firm's goals and strategic plans. The organization monitors environmental influences and assesses its own strengths and weaknesses to identify marketing opportunities and constraints. A retailer bases its marketing decisions on two fundamental steps in the marketing strategy process: (1) picking a target market and (2) developing a retailing mix to satisfy the chosen market. The retailing mix specifies merchandise strategy, customer service standards, pricing guidelines, target market analysis, promotion goals, location/distribution decisions, and store atmosphere choices. The combination of these elements projects a desired **retail image**—consumers' perception of the store and the shopping experience it provides. Retail image communicates the store's identity to consumers as, say, an economical, prestigious, or contemporary outlet. All components of retailing strategy must work together to create an image that appeals to the store's target market.

Retail analysts cite compression in the retail cycle in recent years. New retail concepts appear to move through the cycle faster than previous concepts did. For example, warehouse stores have reached maturity only ten years after they first emerged. Stores like Home Depot; Bed, Bath & Beyond; and Circuit City have started to see slowing sales growth after several years of expansion and expensive new store launches.[2]

Target Market

A retailer starts to define its strategy by selecting a target market. The size and profit potential of a target and the level of competition for its business influence this decision. Sometimes this process involves a second look at the retailer's current market and repositioning the company in order to better meet that market's needs.

The importance of identifying and targeting the right market is dramatically illustrated by recent events in the hardware retailing industry. Industry giant Home Depot has dramatically changed the industry by targeting price-conscious, do-it-yourself homeowners with its large warehouse-style stores. The chain's popularity has compelled

http://www.homedepot.com/

other hardware retailers to redefine their target marketing strategies. Grossman's, a regional chain of stores in New England, initially failed to adjust to the increase in competition within the home hardware market. The disastrous results led to Grossman's rapidly losing market share to Home Depot. Now, Grossman's is trying to find a niche selling to contractors and professional builders.

Lowe's, another regional chain, has found a different target market. The chain's research shows that women instigate most home-improvement projects. Lowe's has responded by redesigning stores to enhance their appeal to women shoppers. In addition to large selections of hardware goods, Lowe's stores also stock home appliances such as refrigerators, washing machines, televisions, and computers. The strategy has enabled Lowe's to continue growing in spite of Home Depot's intense competition.[3]

Figure 15.1 Targeting a Select Market Niche

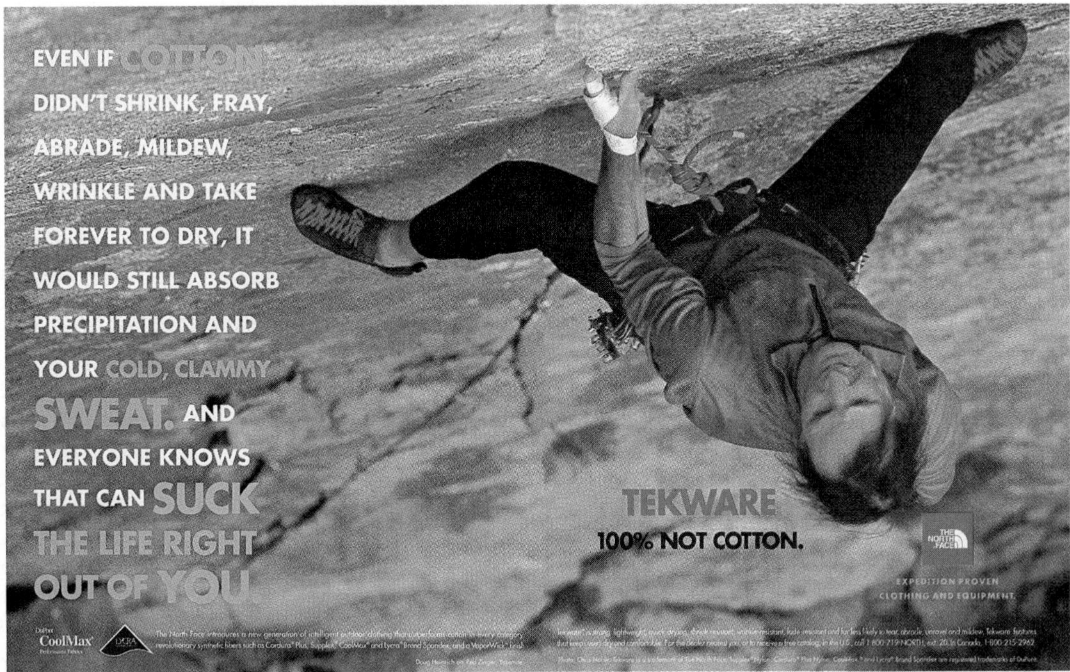
EVEN IF COTTON
DIDN'T SHRINK, FRAY,
ABRADE, MILDEW,
WRINKLE AND TAKE
FOREVER TO DRY, IT
WOULD STILL ABSORB
PRECIPITATION AND
YOUR COLD, CLAMMY
SWEAT. AND
EVERYONE KNOWS
THAT CAN SUCK
THE LIFE RIGHT
OUT OF YOU.
TEKWARE
100% NOT COTTON.
THE NORTH FACE
EXPEDITION PROVEN
CLOTHING AND EQUIPMENT.
CoolMax

While large home-improvement retailers like Home Depot offer broad arrays of products, Orchard concentrates on the needs of what the chain calls *fix-it homeowners.* Visitors to an Orchard store don't find building supplies. Instead they find an assortment of home-repair products such as plumbing and electrical parts, tools, and lawnmowers. "We are not geared to major projects, like adding a room to a house," says an Orchard vice president. "We have our own little niche."[4]

Retailers pore over demographic, geographic, and psychographic profiles to segment markets. E. Diane White targets African-American customers in her Blackberry boutiques. Her stores carry gifts, cards, and other merchandise with African-American themes and designs. White targets locations in retail areas with heavy concentrations of African-American consumers.[5] Learningsmith, a toy retailer, targets educated, high-income parents concerned about their children's education. The chain sells educational toys and activities that these customers usually cannot find at large toy retailers like Toys 'R' Us.[6] By targeting the needs of the growing number of self-employed people, the Staples and Office Depot chains of business supply stores achieved strong growth. The two chains have recently announced plans to merge operations.[7] As the ad in Figure 15.1 illustrates, The North Face targets serious rock climbers and hikers by offering "expedition proven clothing and equipment."

Even retailers that traditionally sought to serve the mass market have shifted their strategies to target more narrowly defined segments. F. W. Woolworth, for example, has shifted emphasis toward its specialty store formats. Specialty stores provide higher sales per square foot and thus higher profit margins and returns on investment than general merchandise stores achieve. Woolworth has opened an array of shoe stores, including Foot Locker, Kids Foot Locker, Lady Foot Locker, and World Foot Locker. It also targeted the female market by starting Northern Reflections, a chain of women's clothing stores, and Northern Traditions, which sells formal apparel for women.

After identifying a target market, a retailer must then develop marketing strategies to attract these chosen customers to its stores. The following sections discuss tactics for implementing different strategies.

Merchandise Strategy

A retailer's merchandise strategy guides decisions about the merchandise that it will offer. In developing a

Marketing Dictionary

retail image Consumers' perception of a store and the shopping experience it provides.

SOLVING AN ETHICAL CONTROVERSY

Should Retailers Pay More Attention to Their Ethical Conduct?

Many voices bemoan the precarious prospects of many retail operations today, but little has been said about how retailers treat customers. Do store employees always promise fair treatment to shoppers? If you can think of instances when you felt slighted or cheated, you are not alone. An academic study of consumer attitudes has revealed little confidence in retailers' ethics, even among the most trusting souls. Poll respondents cited many transgressions, which they suspect happen regularly at stores. Their criticisms include retailers giving preferential treatment to certain customers, failing to tell the complete truth about products, and attempting to sell more expensive models when cheaper ones would better serve customers' needs.

This widespread shopper skepticism only gets worse when people see a high-profile retailer like Sears, Roebuck and Co. entangled in a scandal. Sears' automotive service centers experienced a public relations nightmare a few years ago when customers accused them of systematically overcharging customers for repairs. Sears settled the matter out of court.

Should Retailers Pay More Attention to Their Ethical Conduct?

PRO

1. **Statistics kept by the national Better Business Bureau confirm that retailers need to do some serious soul-searching. According to the BBB, retailing as an industry ranks No. 1 in year-round consumer complaints. Coming in second is the home-improvement and remodeling industry.**
2. **It's never too late to address past wrongs. A retailer can even turn questionable behavior into a marketing triumph. Take, for example, 7-Eleven's response to criticisms for selling food items that had sat on shelves for several days. The company developed commercials that featured Brett Butler and other comics joking about such past problems as stale food, cramped aisles, and high prices.**
3. **Faced with fierce competition for customers, a company that fails to treat each visitor fairly will not keep its doors open for long. "Consumers can't be fooled anymore," says John Grace, a senior vice president at the brand-identity consult-**

merchandise mix, a retailer must decide on general product categories, product lines, specific products within lines, and the depth and width of its assortment.

To develop a successful merchandise mix, a retailer must weigh several priorities. First, it must consider the preferences and needs of its previously defined target market; in addition, the competitive environment influences these choices. The retailer must also consider the overall profitability of each product line and category. Department stores, for example, have suffered from weak sales in recent years as competition from specialty and discount stores has increased. To improve their profitability, some department stores have narrowed their traditionally broad product lines to eliminate high-overhead, low-profit categories such as toys, appliances, and furniture.

Several examples illustrate merchandise strategy choices:

- The PetsMart chain focuses on a relatively narrow product category: pet-care products. However, the chain's stores stock enormous selections within that category. One PetsMart store in San Diego fills over 40,000 square feet of selling space with over 12,000 different pet-care items. From gerbil cages to horse feed, the store strives to fill every conceivable pet-care need. Customers can even purchase freshly baked dog treats from the store's bakery. Pet owners can also purchase veterinary, grooming, and obedience-training services at the store.[8]
- The Laura Ashley company recently changed the merchandise strategy it implements at its 175 U.S. retail locations. Building on market research that showed a growing interest in home furnishings among Baby Boomers, the company reallocated the mix between clothing and furnishings in its stores. Previously, sales of both product categories were divided equally in Laura Ashley stores. The firm hopes to change the mix to about 65 percent from furnishings and 35 percent from clothing. To accomplish this goal, the company has increased store size to make room for larger displays of decorating fabrics, wall coverings, and bath and kitchen accessories. At the same time, the Laura Ashley line of apparel will be updated with more trendy styles.[9]

ing firm Gerstman & Meyers. On the other hand, honesty will very probably appeal strongly to consumers, especially if a company has done something to make consumers wander from their relationship with its brand.

CON

1. **Publicly acknowledging a company's past lapses can backfire, some experts suggest. "People have other things to do than worry about what's wrong with their retailers," says Alan Millstein, editor of the Fashion Network Report and a fashion-industry consultant. "It's foolish to talk about the past and remind people of things that may have not made a difference. Consumers want to know what's in your stores now."**
2. **Businesses, ever mindful of their public relations images, are already concerned about their ethical behavior. Treating customers with respect is a standard part of any successful company's operating procedures.**

Summary

Observers see positive signs that firms are paying close attention to ethics, and many have hired ethics officers. "Ten years ago they were practically nonexistent," observes W. Michael Hoffman, founder and executive director of the Center for Business Ethics at Bentley College in Waltham, Massachusetts. He estimates that 35 percent to 40 percent of major American corporations have established such officers. Since 1991, membership in the Ethics Officer Association at Bentley has jumped from 12 to 300. A key motivation for this sudden interest can be traced to tough, new federal sentencing guidelines. A judge can now punish a corporation with stiff fines for offenses by its employees.

Sears, Roebuck and Co. actually operates one of the best ethics programs, Hoffman says. The new sentencing guidelines, along with the automotive fiasco and discussions about the firm's values and future direction, led to its reforms, says Bill Giffin, Sears vice president of ethics and business policy. Says Giffin, "We measure our success by how many people we help, not how many people we catch."

Sources: Lars Harrison "How to Win a Customer!" *Harrison on Leadership,* February 1997, downloaded from http://www.altika.com/, May 18, 1997; adapted from Kim Campbell, "Ethics Officers Roam Halls in More U.S. Workplaces," *Christian Science Monitor,* June 21, 1996, p. 8; Vivian Marino, "Snow Jobs, Beware of Disaster-Chaser Contractors," *San Diego Union-Tribune,* February 11, 1996, p. H2; Fara Warner, "Some Ads 'Fess Up to Past Problems," *San Diego Union-Tribune,* May 27, 1995, p. A29.

- Nordstrom's department stores are known for carrying larger inventories than many other department stores. The men's shoe department in the Nordstrom's outlet in Skokie, Illinois, for example, carries 28,000 pairs of shoes in sizes from 5 to 17. Although Nordstrom's stores have higher costs than the industry average, the company's executives believe that the merchandise strategy supported by those costs allows Nordstrom's stores to provide better customer service than customers enjoy from competitors.[10]

- The Calla Bay boutique in Seattle practices mass-customization in its merchandise strategy. The store sells personally fitted woman's swimwear. Each customer selects a style from 40 models displayed on mannequins in the store, and an attendant orders the suit based on the woman's individualized measurements and preferences. Aside from the display models, Calla Bay carries no inventory.[11]

Market research can often help retailers to clarify their merchandising strategies. Sears, for example, conducted market research to discover that its primary customers were working mothers, aged 25 to 54, with household incomes of $25,000 to $50,000. When research also showed that these customers bought both appliances and apparel, Sears decided to emphasize women's clothing in its merchandising mix, devoting additional floor space to that product category.[12]

Increasingly, retailers are blending market research with technology in a merchandise planning method called *assortment management.* **Assortment management** refers to a retailer's effort to offer the right product, at the right time and place, to the right customer. To accomplish this,

Marketing Dictionary

assortment management A retailer's effort to offer the right product, at the right time and place, to the right customer.

Barnes & Noble outlets host children's story hours and puppet shows to bring customers into the book superstores. Innovations in customer services have helped fuel the chain's growth. For example, Barnes & Noble was the first major bookseller to open its stores on Sundays.

an innovative company relies on decision support systems that combine data warehouses with sophisticated forecasting tools to accurately predict merchandise demand. By gathering this additional data about its customers, a retailer improves its ability to manage the store's merchandise mix. Assortment management will likely play an expanded role in merchandise strategy in the future. In a study conducted by Ernst & Young's Retail Consulting Group, 42 percent of retailers surveyed identified assortment management as one of the most important technology projects for retailers.[13]

ShopKo Stores, Inc. has built a successful decision support system. The discount retailer's extensive collection of data, called a *data warehouse,* supports inventory and merchandise decisions for its store locations by combining intelligence about customers with information on merchandising trends and marketing opportunities. The system allows individual stores to quickly analyze inventory movement, pinpoint successful product categories and brands, and match them with changes in ShopKo's target markets and promotional strategies. "We're getting much more information much faster," says one ShopKo executive. As a result, ShopKo stores boost the effectiveness of their merchandise mixes.[14]

Briefly speaking

"I solemnly swear and declare that every customer that comes within 10 feet of me, I will smile, look them in the eye, and greet them, so help me Sam."

Wal-Mart discount stores employee pledge

Customer Service Strategy

A retailer may provide a variety of customer services for shoppers. Examples are gift wrapping, alterations, return privileges, bridal registries, consultants, interior designs, delivery and installation, and perhaps even electronic shopping via gift-ordering machines in airports. A retailer's customer service strategy must specify which services the firm will offer and whether it will charge customers for them. Those decisions depend on several conditions: store size, type, and location; merchandise assortment; services offered by competitors; customer expectations; and financial resources.

The basic objective of any customer services focuses on attracting and retaining target customers, thus increasing sales and profits. Some services, such as restrooms, lounges, complimentary coffee, and drinking fountains, enhance shoppers' comfort. Retailers intend other services to attract customers by making shopping easier, faster, or more convenient than it would be without the services. Some retailers, for example, offer child-care services to ease the burden of shopping for customers with children. At Ikea furniture stores, children can romp in supervised playrooms while their parents shop for couches and coffee tables. Several supermarket chains have also designed space for child-care centers in new store locations. At least one chain has found that parents who leave their children at in-store play centers buy more groceries.[15]

A customer service strategy can also support efforts to build demand for a line of merchandise. The Great News cookware store in Pacific Beach, California, needed to find a way to attract customers to its upscale line of gourmet cooking tools. Store owner Ron Eisenberg solved the problem by building a full-scale kitchen at the back of his 5,000-square-foot store. The kitchen offers cooking classes for up to 60 students at a time. These students do not watch standard cooking demonstrations like those in many kitchenware stores; Eisenberg hires top chefs and nationally known experts to teach over 141 different classes that give students hands-on experience in whipping up delicacies. When classes aren't in session, five 31-inch overhead television screens mounted above the kitchen replay the lessons, attracting customer attention to the store's merchandise.[16]

Pricing Strategy

Prices play a major role in consumers' perceptions of a retailer. Consumers realize, for example, that when they enter a Gucci boutique in Milan, New York, or Tokyo, they will find such pricey products as $275 suede pumps and $1,500 boarhide briefcases. Customers of the retail chain Everything's $1.00 expect a totally different line of merchandise; true to the name, every product in the store bears the same low price, including earrings, paperback books, and toiletries.

Prices reflect a retailer's marketing objectives and policies, as described in Chapters 20 and 21. Often price is an important component of an overall competitive strategy. Consider the strategy of Crown Books. Crown's stores contradict the trend toward book superstores like Barnes & Noble and Borders Books outlets. Crown's stores average only 6,000 to 10,000 square feet, compared with the 25,000 to 30,000 square feet of superstores. Crown stores lack coffee shops, and they offer less extensive selections than their larger competitors. The company sets itself apart from rivals by stressing low prices. Crown stores offer discounts up to 40 percent off publisher prices, while competitors never discount more than 30 percent and only on selected titles.[17]

Markups The amount that a retailer adds to a product's cost to set the final selling price is the **markup.** The amount of the markup typically results from two marketing decisions:

1. *The services performed by the retailer.* Other things being equal, stores that offer more services than others charge larger markups to cover their costs.
2. *The inventory turnover rate.* Other things being equal, a store with a higher turnover rate than others can cover its costs and earn a profit while charging a smaller markup.

A retailer's markup exerts an important influence on its image among present and potential customers. In addition, the markup affects the retailer's ability to attract shoppers. An excessive markup may drive away customers; an inadequate markup may not generate sufficient income to cover costs and return a profit.

Retailers typically state markups as percentages of either the selling prices or the costs of products. The formulas for calculating markups are:

$$\text{Markup Percentage on Selling Price} = \frac{\text{Amount Added to Cost (Markup)}}{\text{Selling Price}}$$

$$\text{Markup Percentage on Cost} = \frac{\text{Amount Added to Cost (Markup)}}{\text{Cost}}$$

Consider a product with an invoice cost of $0.60 and a selling price of $1.00. The total markup (selling price less cost) is $0.40. The two markup percentages are calculated as follows:

$$\text{Markup Percentage on Selling Price} = \frac{\$0.40}{\$1.00} = 40\%$$

$$\text{Markup Percentage on Cost} = \frac{\$0.40}{\$0.60} = 66.7\%$$

To determine the selling price knowing only the cost and markup percentage on selling price, a retailer applies the following formula:

$$\text{Price} = \frac{\text{Cost in Dollars}}{100\% - \text{Markup Percentage on Selling Price}}$$

In the previous example, to determine the correct selling price of $1.00, the retailer would calculate:

$$\text{Price} = \frac{\$0.60}{100\% - 40\%} = \frac{\$0.60}{60\%} = \$1.00$$

Similarly, you can convert the markup percentage from one based on selling price to one based on cost and the reverse using the following formulas:

Marketing Dictionary

markup An amount that a retailer adds to the cost of a product to determine its selling price.

$$\text{Markup Percentage on Selling Price} = \frac{\text{Markup Percentage on Cost}}{100\% + \text{Markup Percentage on Cost}}$$

$$\text{Markup Percentage on Cost} = \frac{\text{Markup Percentage on Selling Price}}{100\% - \text{Markup Percentage on Selling Price}}$$

Again, data from the previous example give the following conversions:

$$\text{Markup Percentage on Selling Price} = \frac{66.7\%}{100\% + 66.7\%} = \frac{66.7\%}{166.7\%} = 40\%$$

$$\text{Markup Percentage on Cost} = \frac{40\%}{100\% - 40\%} = \frac{40\%}{60\%} = 66.7\%$$

Marketers determine markups based partly on their judgments of the amounts that consumers will pay for a given product. When buyers refuse to pay a product's stated price, however, or when improvements in other products or fashion changes reduce the appeal of current merchandise, a retailer must take a markdown.

Briefly speaking

"Location, location, location."

William Dillard (1914–)
Founder and chairman, Dillard's department stores

Markdowns The amount by which a retailer reduces the original selling price of a product is the **markdown.** The following formula gives the markdown percentage—the discount amount typically advertised for a product on sale:

$$\text{Markdown Percentage} = \frac{\text{Dollar Amount of Markdown}}{\text{Original Price}}$$

Returning to the previous example, suppose that no one seems willing to pay $1.00 for the product. The retailer has, therefore, decided to reduce the selling price to $0.80. Advertisements for the sale might emphasize the product's 20 percent markdown:

$$\text{Markdown Percentage} = \frac{\$0.20}{\$1.00} = 20 \text{ percent}$$

Markdowns sometimes affect personnel evaluations of retailing workers. For example, a large department store may base its evaluations of buyers partly on the average markdown percentages on the product lines for which they are responsible.

Location-Distribution Strategy

Real-estate professionals often cite location as a potentially determining factor in the success or failure of a retail business. A retailer may choose to locate at an isolated site, in a central business district, or in a planned shopping center. The location decision depends on many conditions, including the type of merchandise, the retailer's financial resources, characteristics of the target market, and site availability.

In recent years, many retail markets have become saturated with stores. As a result, some retailers have reevaluated their location strategies. A chain may close individual stores that do not meet sales and profit goals. In a recent year, national chains closed an average of two store locations for every three they opened. For example, in the mid-1980s, JCPenney had 1,650 locations. Recently, the chain's store count was 1,238. Egghead, a chain of computer software stores, closed 77 of its 156 stores in 1997.[18]

Other retailers have experimented with nontraditional location strategies. McDonald's, for example, now has stores in hospitals, military bases, amusement parks, and gasoline stations. Many U.S. airports have become attractive retailing locations. In fact, U.S. airports are expected to invest about $2 billion annually between 1997 and 2002 in improvements that will include adding and improving retail space. The Walt Disney Company and The Body Shop are two companies that have opened retail stores in airports.[19]

Sunglass Hut has found a successful recipe for its retail location strategy. "Wherever there is a face needing sunglasses, we want there to be a Sunglass Hut located nearby," says Ed Grund, senior vice president. The company has stores in shopping malls and downtown areas of major cities. Additionally, Sunglass Hut places small carts and kiosks in airports, train stations, and resort facilities. The company also operates sunglasses departments in Sears, Dayton's, and Burdine's, leasing space from these department stores. Sunglass Hut is now the world's largest retailer of sunglasses, with 1,751 locations in the United States, Canada, the Caribbean, Mexico, Europe, Australia, and Singapore.[20]

Locations in Planned Shopping Centers A pronounced shift has moved retail trade away from traditional downtown retailing districts and toward suburban shopping centers since 1950. A **planned shopping center** is a group of retail stores planned, coordinated, and marketed as a unit to shoppers in a geographic trade area. Together, the stores provide a single, convenient location for shoppers as well as free parking facilities. They facilitate shopping by maintaining uniform hours of operation, including evening and weekend hours.

Table 15.1 outlines the characteristics of the three main types of planned shopping centers. The smallest, the *neighborhood shopping center,* most often consists of a supermarket and a group of smaller stores such as a drugstore, a dry cleaner, a small-appliance store, and perhaps a beauty shop. This kind of center provides convenient shopping for 5,000 to 50,000 shoppers who live within a few

Table 15.1 Comparing the Types of Shopping Centers

Type	Description	Strengths	Weaknesses
Neighborhood shopping center	Usually contains a supermarket and a group of smaller stores, such as a drugstore, laundry, small-appliance store, and a beauty/barber shop Products: Primarily convenience goods and a few shopping goods Size: Typically 50,000 square feet on 4 acres with a trade area population of 5,000 to 50,000 within a few minutes' driving time	Low rent and operating costs Close proximity to customers	Few tenants Susceptible to competition
Community shopping center	Usually contains a department store or large variety store, plus some professional offices and a bank Products: Primarily shopping goods, with some convenience and possibly specialty stores Size: Typically 150,000 square feet on 10 acres with a trade area population of 20,000 to 100,000 within a few miles	Moderate rent and operating costs Shared promotions Parking availability	Limited shopping variety
Regional shopping center	Usually built around one or more department stores with as many as 200 smaller shops Products: Primarily shopping and specialty goods, possibly supplemented by a convenience store Size: Typically 400,000 square feet on 30 acres with a trade area population of more than 250,000 within 30 minutes' driving time	Large number of stores Drawing power of major retailers Ample parking	High rent and operating costs Strict operating requirements (such as store hours and merchandise sold)

minutes' commute. It typically contains 5 to 15 stores, and the product mix is usually confined to convenience goods and some shopping goods.

A *community shopping center* serves 20,000 to 100,000 people in a trade area extending a few miles from its location. Such a center contains from 10 to 30 retail stores, with a branch of a local department store or a large variety store as the primary tenant. In addition to the stores found in a neighborhood center, a community center probably encompasses more stores featuring shopping goods, some professional offices, and a branch bank.

A *regional shopping center* is a large facility with at least 400,000 square feet of shopping space. Its marketing appeal usually emphasizes one or more major department stores supplemented by as many as 200 smaller stores. A successful regional center needs a location within 30 minutes' driving time of at least 250,000 people. A regional center provides a wide assortment of convenience, shopping, and specialty goods, plus many professional and personal service facilities.

In recent years, the growth of planned shopping centers in the United States has slowed. Many of today's time-pressured consumers prefer the convenience of one-stop shopping at large discount stores like Wal-Mart, which usually operate in self-standing locations.[21] Retail analysts believe that the country is, in effect, "over-malled," and they predict a continuing trend toward closing and consolidating larger shopping centers. While fewer American consumers visit shopping centers, many overseas consumers still eagerly shop in American-style malls.

In reaction to slowing business, shopping centers are

Marketing Dictionary

markdown An amount by which a retailer reduces the original selling price of a product.

planned shopping center A group of retail stores planned, coordinated, and marketed as a unit.

Figure 15.2 Combining Shopping with Entertainment

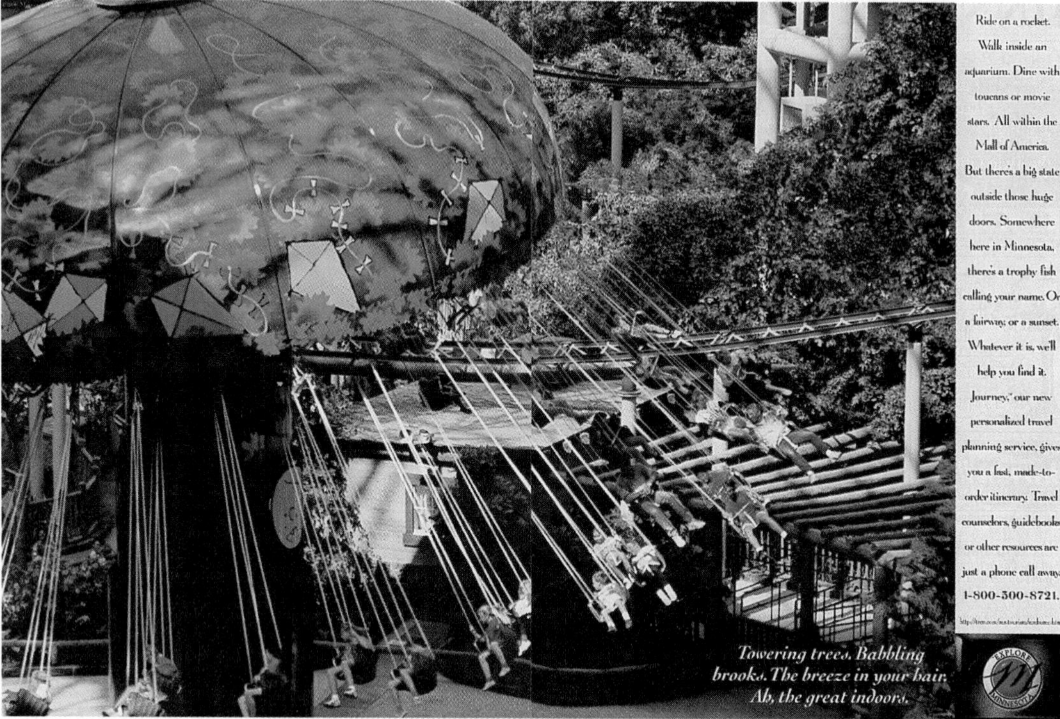
Ride on a rocket. Walk inside an aquarium. Dine with toucans or movie stars. All within the Mall of America. But there's a big state outside those huge doors. Somewhere here in Minnesota, there's a trophy fish calling your name. Or a fairway. or a sunset. Whatever it is, we'll help you find it. Journey," our new personalized travel planning service, gives you a fast, made-to-order itinerary. Travel counselors, guidebooks or other resources are just a phone call away. 1-800-500-8721.
Towering trees. Babbling brooks. The breeze in your hair. Ah, the great indoors.
EXPLORE MINNESOTA

pursuing new retailing strategies. One approach combines shopping with entertainment. A well-known example is the Mall of America in Bloomington, Minnesota. With 4.2 million square feet, the Mall of America is the country's largest regional shopping center. It houses over 30 restaurants, 14 movie theaters, 8 nightclubs, a performing arts center, and a two-tiered, 18-hole miniature golf course with a waterfall. In the center of the $625 million complex is a 7-acre amusement park, Knott's Camp Snoopy, which features 26 thrill rides specially engineered not to annoy shoppers; the log flume ride won't splash them, and the roller coaster runs on quiet rubber wheels. The Mall of America hosts visits by 35 million shoppers each year. The Minnesota Tourism Board promotes the entertainment aspects of the Mall of America in ads such as the one in Figure 15.2, which run in magazines throughout the Midwest.

http://www.mallofamerica.com/

Other shopping centers try to lure customers by targeting new markets. The Modawmin Mall targets Baltimore's large middle-class African-American community. One highlight of the mall, the Kalimba Market, features carts that offer merchandise specifically oriented to the tastes of African-American consumers. The mall also sponsors community events during Kwanzaa and Black History month.[22]

Shopping centers also compete by offering wider ranges of customer services than their competitors. Some hire concierges to help customers locate hard-to-find gifts and order theater tickets; others may offer valet parking, gift-wrap services, parking lot shuttle buses, child care, or diaper-changing rooms.

Another increasingly popular retailing location strategy creates a specialty store shopping center. Unlike a community or regional center, no department store anchors a specialty store center. It sets up a mix of specialty shops and restaurants that target upscale consumers. The Shops at Somerset Square in Glastonbury, Connecticut, is a cluster of small, specialty stores with products and services geared to the needs of working women. Convenience is paramount. Shoppers can call in their sizes and color preferences before visiting stores, and many of the center's retailers set out selections waiting for the shopper when she arrives. The mall's circular shape and the orientation of all store entrances toward the parking lot help busy women to access particular stores. Many of the stores in the mall also offer extended hours.[23]

Promotional Strategy

Retailers practice a variety of promotional techniques to establish store images and motivate consumers to choose their stores over others. Through promotional efforts, retailers communicate information about their stores—locations, merchandise selections, hours of operation, and prices. If a retailer's merchandise selection changes frequently to follow fashion trends, it can effectively promote current styles through advertising. In addition, promotions help retailers to persuade and motivate shoppers and to build customer loyalty.

National retail chains often spend large advertising budgets to purchase advertising space in newspapers, on radio, and on television. Many retail chains promote their stores through advertising circulars inserted into local and regional Sunday newspapers. Relatively small retailers usually cannot match the financial resources of the national chains, forcing them to rely on less costly methods of promoting their businesses. For example, Daffy's, a discount clothing retailer, has placed its ads on city buses and on billboards. Vaughans, a small garden center and flower shop, inserted the paper bag shown in Figure 15.3 in local newspapers to promote a sale of spring bulbs. Customers could bring the bags to the store and fill them with daffodil bulbs for just $4.99.

Many retailers access their customer databases to directly target their promotions. Target Stores, for example, invites expectant parents to register in their Lullaby Club. Target then sends quarterly mailings to these families after their babies are born, and again when the babies reach six months old, nine months old, and at their first birthdays. Target executives point out that young families are usually heavy buyers of the types of products Target stocks: clothes, baby accessories, and toys. Programs like the Lullaby Club help to build a bond with new parents that can last long after their babies grow out of diapers.[24]

http://www.target.com/

The supermarket chain A&P has enrolled over 5 million members in its Bonus Savings Club. When members present their club cards at store checkout stands, they receive discounts on selected products. For A&P, however, the promotional benefits go far beyond the goodwill that the program creates. By combining data from UPC scanners with the names and addresses of club members, A&P has built a profile of each club member that includes how much the person spends, at which locations, and on which brands and products. A&P uses that knowledge to target promotional activities that effectively encourage shoppers to spend more. For example, A&P mails $50 gift certificates to customers for every $500 they spend on groceries, and it rewards them with free cakes on their birthdays.[25]

Other retailers are experimenting with promoting over the Internet. Several supermarket chains, for example, now distribute coupons for special sale items through their Internet sites. The Musicland record chain also uses online promotions. The retail chain has formed a partnership with NetRadio, an Internet-delivered radio station that lets listeners choose the mixes of music and other broadcasts they prefer. As a result, NetRadio has accumulated in-depth knowledge of individual listener preferences. Musicland builds on that knowledge by automatically sending online discount coupons toward purchases of recordings by people's favorite artists. Music lovers download the coupons and redeem them at their nearest Musicland stores.[26]

Figure 15.3 Creative Promotion by a Small Retailer

BAG OF BLOOMS
King Alfred Type Yellow Trumpet
DAFFODILS
Fill this bag full of bulbs for
ONLY $4.99
Bring this bag for fill-up to:
GARDEN CENTER
VAUGHANS
FLOWER SHOP
47th & Willow Springs Rd.
Western Springs, IL • 708/246-3540
Offer good until October 15 or while supplies last. One bag per customer.

Retailers also try to combine advertising with in-store promotional techniques that influence decisions at the point of purchase. Consider, for example, Montgomery Ward's HomeImage stores. The chain perceives HomeImage as "the total home superstore," selling everything from towels and bed linens to appliances under one roof. HomeImage promotes its stores through full-color ad circulars featuring brand-name goods at discount prices. The stores group products and accessories in "solution stations" that offer product information and encourage shoppers to buy. Strategically placed signage makes another contribution to HomeImage's in-store promotion. Eye-catching placards with phrases like "Low Price Guaranteed," and "We Will Not Be Undersold" reinforce HomeImage's value-oriented message. In other areas of the stores, posters show family scenes and inspirational words in an effort to inspire shoppers to create their own warm home environments with HomeImage merchandise.[27]

Many manufacturers have found that retailers expect them to support their products with in-store displays and promotional materials. One relatively new form of in-store promotion places electronic, interactive kiosks at appropriate sites. Lee Apparel, for example, has placed Fit Finder kiosks in several department stores. The machines include tape measures so shoppers can input their measurements and product preferences. The machines then help customers select the best-fitting styles.[28]

A retail salesperson plays an important role in communicating a store image and persuading shoppers to buy. To serve as a source of information, this staff member must bring extensive knowledge about credit policies, discounts, special sales, delivery terms, layaways, and returns to customer encounters. To increase store sales, the salesperson must persuade customers that the store sells what those customers need. To this end, salespeople should receive training in *selling up* and *suggestion selling* techniques.

Selling up tries to convince a customer to buy a higher-priced item than he or she had originally intended. For example, an automobile salesperson might convince a customer to buy a more expensive model than the car that the buyer had originally considered. The practice of selling up must always respect the constraints of a customer's real needs, however. If a salesperson sells someone something that he or she really does not need, the potential for repeat sales dramatically diminishes.

Another technique, **suggestion selling,** seeks to broaden a customer's original purchase to add related items, special promotional products, or holiday or seasonal merchandise. Here, too, the salesperson tries to help a customer to recognize true needs rather than to sell unwanted merchandise. Suggestion selling is one of the best methods of increasing retail sales, and all sales personnel should apply the practice.

The impressions left by sales personnel powerfully influence customers' attitudes toward a retailer. Increasing customer complaints about unfriendly, inattentive, and uninformed salespeople have prompted many retailers to intensify their attention to training and motivating salespeople.

Some retailers have discovered that knowledgeable sales personnel can help to set them apart from competitors. This strength can give an especially valuable edge to smaller retailers competing against large, national chain stores. For instance, No Kidding, a toy store in Brookline, Massachusetts, cannot compete with the steep price discounts of Toys 'R' Us. No Kidding sets itself apart, however, by hiring preschool and elementary school teachers as sales personnel. When parents want to know which toy suits the age and ability characteristics of their child, the sales personnel call on their knowledge of child development and psychology to help customers make well-informed choices.[29]

Store Atmospherics

Brilliantly colored parrots squawk a welcome. A thick tangle of vines and branches forms an overhead canopy. A flash of lightning illuminates a cascading waterfall followed by a roar of thunder. Jungle animals move through the darkness and magical banyan trees talk.

Does this description fit a scene from the latest animated Disney feature? Guess again. The exotic ambience is part of the atmosphere that pulls customers into Rainforest Cafe locations. Part restaurant, part retail store, and part fantasyland, the chain's units capitalize on the latest trend in retailing: using entertainment and education to create environments that lure in customers. "I like to say we have the animation of Disney, the retailing of Warner Brothers, and the live animals of Ringling Brothers Barnum & Bailey Circus," explains Rainforest founder Steve Schussler.[30]

Recent studies show that most people shop for reasons other than just purchasing needed products. As few as 25 percent of mall shoppers come to buy specific items. Common reasons for shopping include dispelling boredom, alleviating loneliness, relieving depression, escaping the routine of daily life, and fulfilling fantasies. As many as 75 percent of shoppers make purchase decisions inside the stores they patronize. Retailers realize that they must find ways to attract customers into their locations before they can motivate these potential buyers to purchase.[31]

While store location, merchandise selection, customer service, pricing, and promotional activities all contribute to a store's consumer awareness, stores also project their personalities through **atmospherics**—physical characteristics and amenities that attract customers and satisfy their shopping needs. Atmospherics include both a store's exterior and interior decor.

A store's exterior appearance, including architectural design, window displays, signs, and entryways, helps to identify the retailer and attract its target market. The Saks Fifth Avenue script logo on a storefront and McDonald's golden arches are exterior elements that readily identify these retailers. Other retailers design eye-catching exterior elements to get customer attention. Life-sized cartoon figures seem poised in mid-flight over the entrance to the Warner Brothers outlet in the Horton Plaza Shopping Center in San Diego, drawing customer interest.

Radio Shack recently decided to improve the atmospheres of its stores to support a marketing goal—achieving recognition as a consumer electronics retail giant. The firm first developed a more contemporary store logo. The new logo displays *RadioShack* as one word in a modern typeface with a red circle containing a capital *R* to the left.[32]

The interior decor of a store should complement the retailer's image, respond to customers' interests, and, most importantly, induce shoppers to buy. Interior atmospheric elements include store layout, merchandise presentation, lighting, color, sounds, scents, and cleanliness. "There are lots of subconscious effects playing on the consumer when he walks into a store," explains one retailing executive. "Things such as lighting, fixtures, staff attitude, and sound are all going to affect the customer's comfort level subconsciously. When you start playing around with these factors, you can generate or prevent sales."[33]

Sportmart is testing a new prototype store that it hopes will set it apart from other sporting goods retailers. The new store concept presents a warmer image than that of a typical sports superstore. The store layout divides floor space into four "worlds" selling merchandise in specific product categories: footgear, outdoors, fitness, and sports. Each of the four worlds occupies its own corner of the store, joined to the others by a wide aisle running down the center. Bright signs and product posters attract customers to the different areas. Sportmart has replaced the industrial-style lighting and ceilings common to warehouse stores with an attractive, finished ceiling and fluorescent lights. Attractive carpeting and simulated wood flooring also soften the atmosphere. Sportmart hopes the new design will attract female shoppers to the store.[34]

Like the Rainforest Cafe, retailers expand beyond interior design to create welcoming and entertaining environments that draw customers. Barnes & Noble bookstores offer comfortable chairs and Starbucks coffee to encourage customers to relax and linger, skimming through books that they may buy. Customers trying on shoes at Larry's Shoes, a small retail chain in Colorado and Texas, enjoy complementary foot massages. Sears brings in Bob Vila, the well-known star of *Home Again with Bob Vila* to speak in its tool sections. Other stores rely on loud music or large-screen video displays to bring the right mix of entertainment to their retailing situations.[35]

TYPES OF RETAILERS

Since new types of retailers continue to evolve in response to changes in consumer demand, no one has devised a universal classification system. Certain differences do, however, define several categories of retailers: (1) shopping effort expended by customers, (2) services provided to customers, (3) product lines, (4) locations of retail transactions, and (5) forms of ownership.

Any retailing operation fits in different categories according to each of the classification schemes. A 7-Eleven outlet may be classified as a convenience store (Category 1) with self-service (Category 2) and a relatively broad product line (Category 3). It is both a store-type retailer (Category 4) and a member of a chain (Category 5).

CLASSIFICATION BY SHOPPING EFFORT

Chapter 10 introduced the idea of classification by shopping effort by dividing consumer goods into convenience goods, shopping goods, and specialty goods based on consumer purchase patterns. Retailers can extend this three-way classification system by considering the reasons why consumers shop at particular retail outlets. The result is a classification scheme that breaks down stores into convenience, shopping, and specialty retailers.[36] This determination influences a retailer's marketing strategies.

Convenience retailers focus their marketing appeals on accessible locations, long store hours, rapid checkout service, and adequate parking facilities. Local food stores, gasoline stations, and some barber shops fit in this category.

Shopping stores typically include furniture stores, appliance retailers, clothing outlets, and sporting goods stores. Consumers usually compare prices, assortments, and quality levels at competing outlets before making purchase decisions. Consequently, managers of shopping stores attempt to differentiate their outlets through advertising, window displays, in-store layouts, well-trained and knowledgeable salespeople, and appropriate merchandise assortments.

Specialty retailers combine carefully defined product lines, services, and reputations in their attempts to convince consumers to expend considerable effort to shop at their stores. Nordstrom, Neiman-Marcus, Lord & Taylor, and Saks Fifth Avenue have accomplished this task sufficiently well to be categorized as specialty retailers.

CLASSIFICATION BY SERVICES PROVIDED

Another category differentiates retailers by the services they provide to customers. Many stores seek to develop unique combinations of service offerings that appeal especially to customers in their target markets. These choices define several retailer types: self-service, self-selection, or full-service retailers.

Since *self-service* and *self-selection retailers* provide few services for their customers, their locations and prices powerfully affect their marketing success. These retailers

Marketing Dictionary

selling up A retail sales technique that tries to convince a customer to buy a higher-priced item than he or she had originally intended.

suggestion selling A retail sales technique that attempts to broaden a customer's original purchase to add related items, special promotional products, or holiday or seasonal merchandise.

atmospherics The combination of physical characteristics and amenities that contribute to a store's image.

MARKETING HALL OF FAME

Old Navy Sets a New Course for the Gap

OLD NAVY
EXIT
OLD NAVY

When Gap, Inc., the trendy retailer known for its classic blue jeans and T-shirts, decided to begin competing with Wal-Mart and other down-scale discounters, it ventured into unknown territory. Wal-Mart intimately knew its legion of penny-pinching customers, but how could the Gap ever hope to relate to these shoppers?

The answer, as it turns out, is yes. Old Navy, the Gap's discount clothing store spinoff, has turned into a textbook study in value-added service. The Old Navy chain succeeds because it provides its customers with amenities new to bargain hunters.

Except for the low prices, an Old Navy outlet doesn't seem to have much in common with a Wal-Mart, Sears, or JCPenney store. Like the upscale Gap, Old Navy exudes its own sense of hipness. Its big stores are decorated with concrete floors, exposed pipes and brick, and whimsical displays. Bushel baskets may overflow with men's boxer

tend to specialize in staple convenience goods that people can purchase frequently with little assistance. The term *limited service* sometimes defines sellers who provide minimal services.

Full-service retailers, on the other hand, focus on fashion-oriented shopping goods and specialty products, offering wide varieties of customer services. As a result, they tend to charge higher prices than self-service retailers charge to cover higher operating costs.

CLASSIFICATION BY PRODUCT LINES

Product lines also define a set of retail categories and the marketing strategies appropriate for firms within those categories. Grouping retailers by product lines produces three major categories: specialty stores, limited-line retailers, and general merchandise retailers. Figure 15.4 compares the number of stores and sales volume for the five largest product lines.

shorts or cotton socks. Near the entrance of each store, you can always find an antique Chevy truck with an Old Navy license plate, displaying colorful merchandise.

Beyond aesthetics, the Gap tried not to duplicate the mistakes of other discounters. For instance, the company learned that shoppers hate the long lines they often must tolerate at competing stores. Old Navy shoppers pay at wide, supermarket-like checkout counters that allow them to leave without delays. Store employees also wear headsets so they can communicate with others and quickly answer customers' questions.

What's more, the Gap placed its Old Navy stores in working-class neighborhoods where its target audience—those with annual incomes between $20,000 and $50,000—live. These shoppers, who collectively spend $75 billion a year, often patronize stores in strip malls. Therefore, Old Navy sets up shop in strip malls, perhaps anchored by a Toys 'R' Us or Target store. Another strategic reason prevented the firm from plunking down Old Navy in regular malls. In such spots, the outlets could very well hurt business at existing Gap, GapKids, and Banana Republic outlets (all owned by Gap, Inc.).

"It doesn't take a brain surgeon to figure out that we're either going into the strip centers to capture a new customer or else we're going to keep putting new businesses into the mall and cannibalize ourselves," says Robert Fisher, Gap's chief operating officer.

Shoppers at Old Navy do not find the same quality as Gap clothes offer, but once again, executives aim at stocking the shelves with the highest-quality merchandise that the low prices allow. Some of the differences between a pair of Gap jeans and an Old Navy pair may even elude some customers. An Old Navy sweater may contain both wool and acrylic, while a Gap sweater would be made only with wool.

Industry experts are once again applauding the Gap's retailing instincts. "It's the most innovative retailing format of the 1990s because it gives consumers low prices and ambiance, rather than goods thrown on tables and blue-light specials," says Alan Millstein, president of Fashion Network Report, a retail consulting firm. Janet Kloppenburg, an analyst with the securities firm Robertson Stephens, agrees: "No other retailer combines low prices, quality merchandise, and an absolutely fun atmosphere to shop in the way Old Navy does."

Old Navy's success comes at a perfect time. In recent years, department stores and mass merchants have threatened the Gap's profits with look-alike jeans and shirts. In reaction, the Gap had to lower prices to move excess inventories out of its stores.

Ironically, the only thing unplanned about Old Navy's emergence on the retail scene is its name. The Gap commissioned an outside firm to develop a name for the new retail endeavor, but executives hated the top suggestions: Forklift and Monorail. Millard "Mickey" Drexler, Gap's chief executive officer, found the perfect name by accident when he and other executives were on a business trip. They spotted the words *Old Navy* on the side of a building. "We just thought that's a great name for a business," Drexler recalls. "And it just stuck."

QUESTIONS FOR CRITICAL THINKING

1. **Does Gap, Inc. still risk steering some of its Gap business to its Old Navy stores—especially among young people? Why?**
2. **Do you think other retailers will begin opening Old Navy clones? If so, what strategy could Gap, Inc. adopt in response?**

Sources: "Gap Inc.'s Fourth-Quarter Earnings Up 11 Percent," February 27, 1997, downloaded from Source News & Reports, http://www.sddt.com/, May 27, 1997; Susan Caminita, "Will Old Navy Fill the Gap?" *Fortune*, March 18, 1996, pp. 59–62; and adapted from Kathleen M. Berry, "The New America: Gap Inc.," *Investor's Business Daily*, March 4, 1996, downloaded from America Online, January 7, 1997.

Specialty Stores

A **specialty store** typically handles only part of a single product line. However, it stocks this portion in considerable depth or variety. Specialty stores include fish markets, men's and women's shoe stores, and bakeries. Although some specialty stores are chain outlets, most are independent, small-scale

Marketing Dictionary

specialty store A retailer that typically handles only part of a single product line.

Figure 15.4 **Retail Establishments—Number and Sales Volume by Kind of Business**

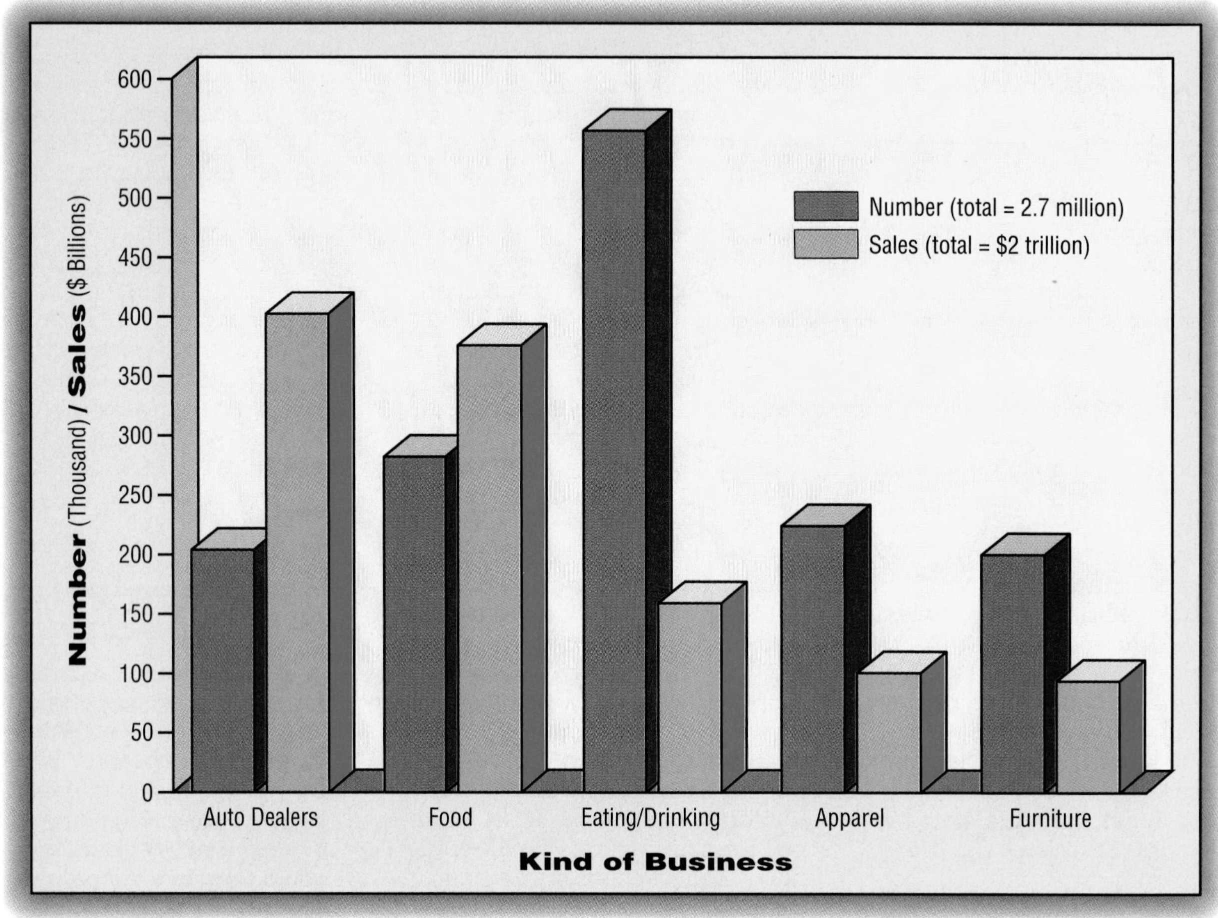

Number (Thousand) / Sales ($ Billions)
600
550
500
450
400
350
300
250
200
150
100
50
0
Number (total = 2.7 million)
Sales (total = $2 trillion)
Auto Dealers
Food
Eating/Drinking
Apparel
Furniture
Kind of Business

operations. They represent perhaps the greatest concentration of independent retailers who develop expertise in providing narrow lines of products for their local markets.

In recent years, large retailers like Montgomery Ward and Woolworth have also become specialty merchants. Recall that the Woolworth umbrella covers a wide range of specialty stores, which it reevaluates constantly to ensure responsiveness to changing market conditions. Woolworth also sets up specialty stores in other countries, which generate 40 percent of the company's total sales.

Specialty stores should not be confused with specialty products. Specialty stores typically carry convenience and shopping goods. The label *specialty* reflects the practice of handling a specific, narrow line of merchandise.

Customers find a large assortment within one product line or a few related lines in a **limited-line store.** This type of retail operation typically develops in areas with population sizes sufficiently large to support it. Examples of limited-line stores are IKEA (home furnishings and housewares), Levitz (furniture), and the Gap (clothing). These retailers cater to the needs of people who want to select from complete lines in purchasing particular products.

In recent years, a new kind of limited-line retailer has emerged. Known as **category killers,** these stores combine huge selections and low prices in single product lines. Stores within this category—like Toys 'R' Us; Bed, Bath, and Beyond; and Home Depot—are among the most successful retailers in the nation. Figure 15.5 shows an ad for a new category-killer chain. The Container Store carries "the world's most extensive and celebrated collection of storage and organization products." Some category killers operate as separate units of larger retailing companies. Kmart, for example, owns several category killer chains, including Sports Authority, Builder's Square, OfficeMax, Borders Book Shops, and Waldenbooks. These and other category killers have taken business away from general merchandise discounters, which cannot compete in selection or price.

On the other hand, some category-killer superstores have had difficulty generating profits. Consider the experience of Tandy Corp.'s Incredible Universe consumer electronics megastores. The stores added a new dimension to the term *category killer,* offering more than 85,000 electronics items in outlets two to three times the sizes of the largest competing consumer electronics superstores. While new Incredible Universe stores attracted a good deal of consumer and media attention, sales did not maintain this brisk initial pace. The cost of operating such huge stores and maintaining enormous inventory levels ran far ahead of revenues. Within a few years, Tandy was forced to close all 17 Incredible Universe stores.[37]

Supermarkets, familiar examples of the specialty store concept, operate in a particularly challenging industry. With profit margins averaging only about 1 percent of sales after taxes, supermarkets compete by carefully planning retail displays in order to sell large amounts of merchandise each week and thereby minimize investments in inventory. Meticulously defined product locations within the store expose each consumer to as much merchandise as possible, thus increasing impulse purchases. In addition to groceries, many supermarkets carry nonfood products, such as magazines, kitchen utensils, toiletries, toys, and plants. They expand their product lines in this way for two reasons: Consumers have shown their willingness to buy such items in supermarkets, and supermarket managers like the profit margins on these items, which are higher than those on food products.

Along with other retailers, supermarkets have faced challenges from superstores. Both Kmart and Wal-Mart have moved into the grocery business, building large stores carrying broad ranges of food and nonfood items along with specialty operations such as deli sections. Some supermarket companies have responded by upgrading their stores to offer gourmet foods and prepared meals for customers. The Eatzi's chain, for example, offers shoppers a choice of 450 prepared entrees as well as a full selection of wines, cheeses, and fresh baked goods. Eatzi's customers can even consult with the store's on-site chefs about menus and recipes.

Other supermarkets are attempting to differentiate themselves by focusing on specific target markets. Whole Foods Markets concentrate on selling organically grown health foods. In Texas, the Fiesta Mart chain targets Hispanic shoppers. The stores carry fresh produce and meats geared to the ethnic group's preferences. On weekends, mariachi bands play in the aisles.[38]

Figure 15.5 **A Category Killer in Container Retailing**

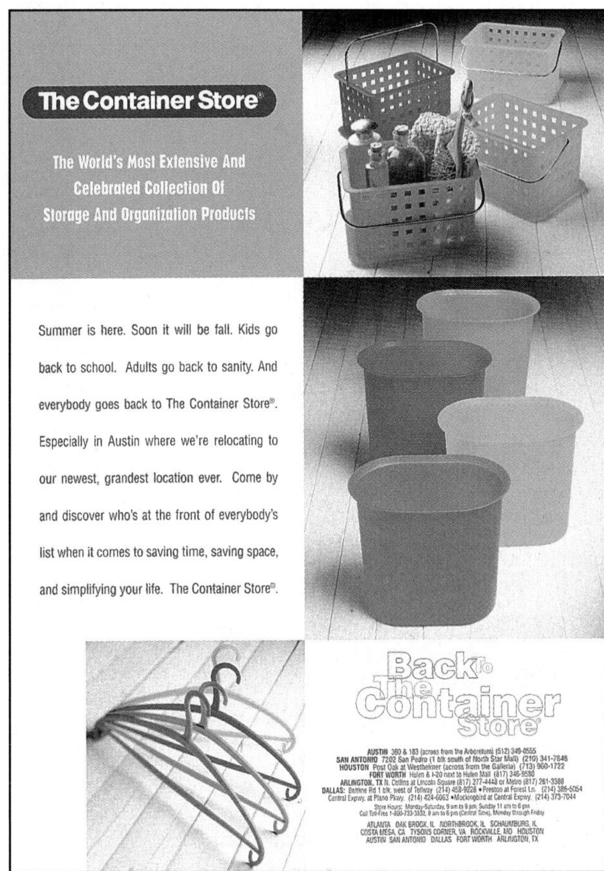
The Container Store®
The World's Most Extensive And Celebrated Collection Of Storage And Organization Products
Summer is here. Soon it will be fall. Kids go back to school. Adults go back to sanity. And everybody goes back to The Container Store®. Especially in Austin where we're relocating to our newest, grandest location ever. Come by and discover who's at the front of everybody's list when it comes to saving time, saving space, and simplifying your life. The Container Store®.
Back To The Container Store®

General Merchandise Retailers

General merchandise retailers distinguish themselves from limited-line and specialty retailers by the large number of product lines they carry. The general store described earlier in this chapter is a primitive form of a **general merchandise retailer**—a store that carries a wide variety of product lines, all stocked in some depth. This category includes variety stores, department stores, and mass merchandisers such as catalog retailers, discount stores, hypermarkets, and off-price retailers.

Variety Stores A retail outlet that offers an extensive range and assortment of low-priced merchandise is called a **variety store.** Less popular today than they once were,

Marketing Dictionary

limited-line store A retailer that offers a large assortment within a single product line or a few related product lines.

category killer A retailer that combines huge selection and low prices within a single product line.

general merchandise retailer A store that carries a wide variety of product lines, stocking all of them in some depth.

variety store A retailer that offers an extensive range and assortment of low-priced merchandise.

Figure 15.6 Sears: Trying to Revitalize Sales of Kids' Clothing

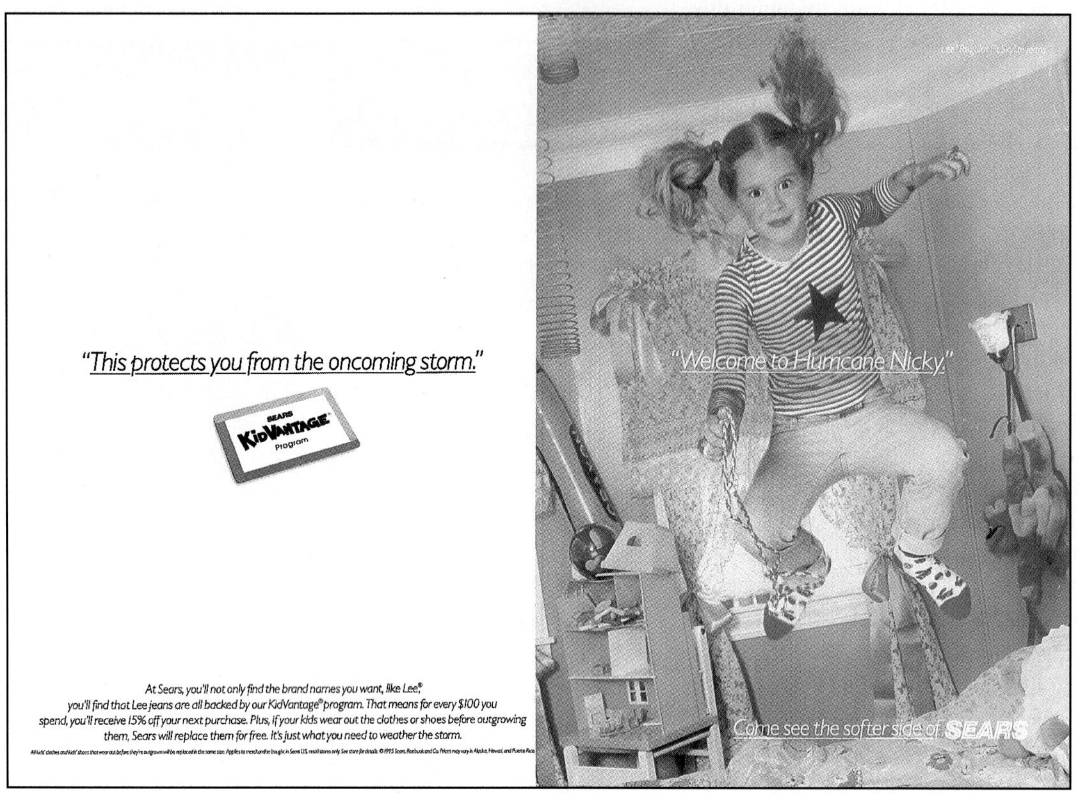
"This protects you from the oncoming storm."
SEARS KidVantage Program
At Sears, you'll not only find the brand names you want, like Lee,® you'll find that Lee jeans are all backed by our KidVantage® program. That means for every $100 you spend, you'll receive 15% off your next purchase. Plus, if your kids wear out the clothes or shoes before outgrowing them, Sears will replace them for free. It's just what you need to weather the storm.
"Welcome to Hurricane Nicky."
Come see the softer side of SEARS

many of these stores have evolved into or given way to other types of retailers such as discount stores. The nation's variety stores now account for less than 1 percent of all retail sales. However, variety stores remain popular in other parts of the world. Many retail outlets in Spain and Mexico are family owned variety stores.

Department Stores A **department store** gathers a series of limited-line and specialty stores under one roof. By definition, this large retailer handles a variety of merchandise, including men's, women's, and children's clothing and accessories; household linens and dry goods; home furnishings; and furniture. It serves as a one-stop shopping destination for almost all personal and household products. Chicago's Marshall Field's is an example.

Department stores built their reputations offering wide varieties of services, such as charge accounts, delivery, gift wrapping, and liberal return privileges. As a result, they incur relatively high operating costs, averaging about 45 to 60 percent of sales.

Department stores have faced intense new competition over the past several years. Relatively high operating costs have left them vulnerable to retailing innovations such as discount stores, catalog merchandisers, and hypermarkets. In addition, department stores' traditional locations in downtown business districts suffered from problems associated with limited parking, traffic congestion, and population migration to the suburbs. Many department stores have closed certain sections, such as electronics, in which high costs kept them from competing with discount houses and category killers.

More recently, department stores have seen their clothing sales revenues slip, as well. Once, these retailers controlled 60 percent of apparel sales; today, their market share has fallen to 50 percent as more clothing shoppers buy at discount houses and off-price retailers.

Department stores have fought back in a variety of ways. They have added bargain outlets and expanded parking facilities in attempts to compete with discount operations and suburban retailers. They have also followed the overall population movement to the suburbs by opening major branches in regional shopping centers. They have attempted to revitalize downtown retailing in many cities by modernizing their stores, expanding store hours, making special efforts to attract the tourist and convention trade, and serving the needs of urban residents. Sears launched its KidVantage program, promoted in the ad in Figure 15.6, to boost its sales of children's apparel. The chain offers free replacements of kids' clothing and shoes that wear out before children outgrow them. In an effort to compete with discount and off-price retailers, the program gives a 15 percent discount on a later purchase for any customer who spends $100 on clothing.

Mass Merchandisers Mass merchandising has made major inroads into department stores' sales by emphasizing lower prices for well-known, brand-name products; high product turnover; and limited services. A **mass merchandiser** often stocks a wider line of products than a department store, but usually without the same depth of assortment within each line. Discount houses, off-price retailers, hypermarkets, and catalog retailers are all examples of mass merchandisers.

Discount Houses The birth of the modern **discount house** came at the end of World War II when New York-based Masters discovered that a large number of customers would shop at a store that charged unusually low prices and did not offer such traditional services as credit, salesperson assistance, and delivery. Retailers throughout the country soon followed the Masters formula, either changing over from traditional operations or opening new stores dedicated to discount retailing. At first, discount stores sold mostly appliances. Today, they offer furniture, soft goods, drugs, and food.

Discount operations had served price-conscious consumers before World War II, but they sold goods chiefly from manufacturers' catalogs; they kept no stock on display and often limited their potential customers. Modern discounters operate large stores, advertise heavily, emphasize low prices for well-known brands, and invite the general public. By eliminating many of the "free" services provided by traditional retailers, these operations learned that they could keep their markups 10 to 25 percent below those of their competitors. After consumers became accustomed to self-service by shopping at supermarkets, they responded in great numbers to this retailing innovation. Conventional retailer Kresge joined the discounting practice by opening its own Kmart stores. Some of the early discounters have since added services, begun to stock increasingly prestigious name brands, and boosted their prices; in fact, many now resemble department stores.

The newest kind of true discounter is the *warehouse club*. These no-frills, cash-and-carry outlets offer consumers access to name-brand products at deeply discounted prices. Their selections include fax machines, peanut butter, luggage, and sunglasses in settings that look like warehouses. Customers must buy club memberships in order to shop at warehouse clubs. The major competitors are Price/Costco and Wal-Mart's Sam's Clubs.

Although discount chains with 50 or more stores account for less than 3 percent of all U.S. retail establishments, they make 11 to 13 percent of all retail sales. Discount store sales are also growing at two to three times the rate of the retail industry as a whole. The three largest discount mass merchandisers in the United States are Wal-Mart, Target, and Kmart. Together they account for almost 80 percent of sales among discount chains.[39]

Off-Price Retailers Another version of a discount house is an **off-price retailer.** This kind of store stocks only designer labels or well-known, brand-name clothing at prices equal to or below regular wholesale and passes the cost savings along to consumers. Its inventory changes frequently as its buyers take advantage of special price offers from manufacturers selling excess merchandise. Off-price retailers such as Loehmann's, Marshall's, and T. J. Maxx also keep their prices below those of traditional retailers by offering fewer services. Dramatic consumer acceptance has pushed off-price retailing into a major industry growth trend.

While many off-price retailers locate outlets in downtown areas or freestanding buildings, a growing number are concentrating in **outlet malls**—shopping centers that house only off-price merchandisers. About 300 outlet centers have opened their doors in the United States, with sales of about $11.4 billion a year. Outlet centers often open in locations near major highways or tourist sites like Disney World or Branson, Missouri, that attract large numbers of potential shoppers.[40]

Like other shopping centers, some outlet malls are facing increased competition for customers, leading them to try new techniques to attract traffic. The San Marcos Factory Shops near Austin, Texas, for example, has added a Sports Court to its facility. The 70,000-square-foot area includes outdoor sports playgrounds like a driving range, a basketball court, and an in-line skating track. Surrounding factory-outlet stores specialize in sporting goods, apparel, and athletic footwear.[41]

Hypermarkets and Supercenters Another innovation in discount retailing created **hypermarkets**—giant, one-stop shopping facilities that offer wide selections of grocery and general merchandise products at discount prices. Store size determines the major difference between hypermarkets and supermarkets. Hypermarkets typically fill up 200,000 or more square feet of selling space, compared to about 44,000 for the average new supermarket. At Meijers, for

Marketing Dictionary

department store A large store that handles a variety of merchandise, including clothing, household goods, appliances, and furniture.

mass merchandiser A store that stocks a wider line of goods than a department store, usually without the same depth of assortment within each line.

discount house A store that charges low prices but may not offer services such as credit.

off-price retailer A store that finds exceptional deals on well-known, brand-name clothing and resells it at unusually low prices.

outlet mall A shopping center that houses only off-price retailers.

hypermarket A giant mass merchandiser of soft goods and groceries that operates on a low-price, self-service strategy.

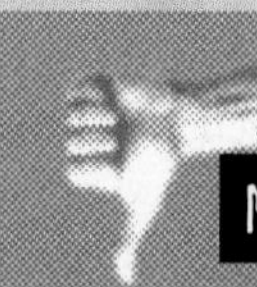

MARKETING HALL OF SHAME

Retail Failures: Who's Next?

Retail failures can produce stunningly spectacular news. If a retailer loses touch with its shoppers, fails to keep pace with competitors, or just makes too many boneheaded decisions, bankruptcy can be the next logical step.

One of the best examples of this possibility occurred back in the 1970s, when W. T. Grant Co. made retailing history by becoming the largest retailer up to that time to collapse. Amazingly, just two years before a bankruptcy judge liquidated the chain, Grant had sales of nearly $1.8 billion and ranked as the 17th largest retailer in the country.

What went wrong? Plenty, and Grant's experiences provide an important lesson to today's retailing market. Grant committed its chief error by trying to evolve into a store that its customers did not want. Shoppers visited Grant's to buy products typically stocked in dime stores during that pre-Wal-Mart era. But Grant executives began clearing floor space for big-ticket items like appliances, furniture, and power tools, which bore the store's own brand.

To enable its customers to buy these items, Grant had to establish a credit program. Soon, it was swamped with bad debt. "If a customer's breath fogged a mirror, the customer was given instant credit," a company executive lamented. Shoppers—who felt comfortable buying stationery, but not a couch, from a Grant clerk—balked at the makeover, and the retailing empire collapsed.

While Grant's demise seemed earth-shattering at the time, retail burnouts are much more common today. The trend shows no signs of slowing down. In 1995, for example, 2,700 stores closed. After just ten days in 1996, the first retailer of the year filed for bankruptcy. All told, retail business failures rose 3.7 percent in 1996, according to Dun & Bradstreet Corp.'s research. The list of losers reveals no particular pattern to those who sought bankruptcy protection. Among the beleaguered retailers are Barney's, the chic, ultra-expensive New York chain; Rickel Home Centers, a Home Depot competitor; Silo Stores, an electronics chain; and Clothestime, a discounter of women's clothes.

example, Michigan and Ohio consumers can buy food, hardware, soft goods, building materials, auto supplies, appliances, and prescription drugs in locations averaging 245,000 square feet. When they finish shopping, a Meijers customer can visit the restaurant, beauty salon, barber shop, bank branch, or bakery within the facility.

The hypermarket concept originated in France with retailer Carrefour. That firm has remained the dominant French hypermarket by acquiring smaller hypermarkets such as Euromarche and Montlaur. Today, it controls a sizable share of France's total food sales, although food products account for only 60 percent of its sales. The retailer has successfully transplanted the hypermarket concept to other countries, too. It has opened stores in Spain, Taiwan, Italy, Argentina, and Brazil.

In the United States, the hypermarket concept has generated mixed results. Carrefour's first U.S. store, located outside Philadelphia, failed to earn a profit. Wal-Mart's experiment with the hypermarket concept also proved less than a success. Customers complained about having to walk too far for limited brand selections, while Wal-Mart found that the stores produced higher operating costs than anticipated.

In response to this record, U.S. retailers have scaled down the true hypermarket concept in favor of **supercenters,** which house many of the same elements as hypermarkets in somewhat smaller facilities. Wal-Mart, for example, has built 260 supercenters in the United States that tie its traditional discount store format with a supermarket. Wal-Mart has found that this combination can more than double sales over its traditional format, and the company is moving to replace many of its conventional stores with supercenters.[42]

According to retail industry analysts, supercenters currently account for about 10 percent to 15 percent of U.S. grocery sales. By 2000, they estimated that between 1,300 and 1,500 supercenters will compete for U.S. consumers' attention. In addition to Wal-Mart, other supercenter operators include Fred Meyer and Kmart.[43]

Showroom and Warehouse Retailers Showroom retailers mail catalogs to their customers and sell the advertised goods from showrooms that display samples. Back-room warehouses fill orders for the displayed products. Price powerfully affects success for catalog store customers. To keep prices low, they offer few services, store most inven-

"The weaker and less fit retailers are falling by the wayside," observes Arthur Martinez, chairman and chief executive of Sears, Roebuck and Co. "There will be continuing industry consolidation and fewer strong players emerging to dominate individual sectors of our industry."

Other experts also predict that more stores will close their doors in what remains of the 1990s. "I think the only way to get the industry back to healthy growth is through consolidation," says Carl Steidtmann, an economist at Management Horizons, a Columbus, Ohio, unit of Price Waterhouse. "There is a need for more mergers and acquisitions, bankruptcies and liquidations."

Retail experts view consolidation as necessary, because the retail market is saturated. Almost every consumer daily passes a mind-boggling selection of shops, and he or she can patronize only so many of them. Stores that fail to offer consumers quality merchandise at competitive prices will become endangered.

Ironically, the failures of weak retailers can ultimately hurt the survivors. A chain operating under Chapter 11 of the bankruptcy code can enjoy some unique competitive advantages. For instance, these retailers don't pay interest on unsecured debt and can wiggle out of long-term leases, which permits them to lower their prices to consumers. "Right now, retail is much the same as airlines a few years ago," says Steidtmann. Cost advantages allowed carriers in Chapter 11 to threaten better-managed companies.

While more casualties are expected, only time will reveal the next victim.

QUESTIONS FOR CRITICAL THINKING

1. **Do you agree about the inevitability of a consolidation of retailers? Why?**
2. **Many believe that in today's competitive retail environment, a company's management skill provides the key to survival. Companies with weak management teams will fail. In what ways can management make a difference?**

Sources: "Clothestime Reorganization," April 9, 1997, downloaded from http://www.businesswire.com/, April 22, 1997; Anne B. Fisher, "The Year the Stores Closed Their Doors," *Fortune,* February 5, 1996, p. 28; adapted from "Barney's in Chapter 11; Sign of Times in Apparel," *Investor's Business Daily,* January 12, 1996, downloaded from America Online, January 8, 1997; and Kathleen M. Berry, "Executive Update Will Find Stores in Chapter 11," *Investor's Business Daily,* November 9, 1995, downloaded from America Online, January 8, 1997.

tory in inexpensive warehouse space, limit shoplifting losses, and handle long-lived products such as luggage, small appliances, gift items, sporting equipment, toys, and jewelry.

CLASSIFICATION OF RETAILERS BY THE LOCATIONS OF TRANSACTIONS

Although most retail transactions occur in stores, nonstore retailing serves as an important marketing outlet for many products. Nonstore retailing includes direct selling, direct-response retailing, and automatic merchandising.

Direct Selling

Chapter 14 mentioned arrangements by some manufacturers who completely bypass retailers and wholesalers. Instead, they set up their own channels to sell their products directly to consumers. Companies that rely on direct selling include Avon, which sells cosmetics; Electrolux Corp., which sells vacuum cleaners; and the Fuller Brush Company, which markets household items. Direct selling also includes the party plan selling methods of companies like Tupperware.

Direct-Response Retailing

Customers of a direct-response retailer can order merchandise by mail or telephone, by visiting a mail-order desk in a retail store, or by computer or fax machine. The retailer then ships the merchandise to the customer's home or to a local retail store. Many department stores and specialty stores issue catalogs to create telephone and mail-order

Marketing Dictionary

supercenter A large store, though still smaller than a hypermarket, that combines groceries with discount store merchandise.

Figure 15.7 **Music Boulevard: An Internet-Based Retailer**

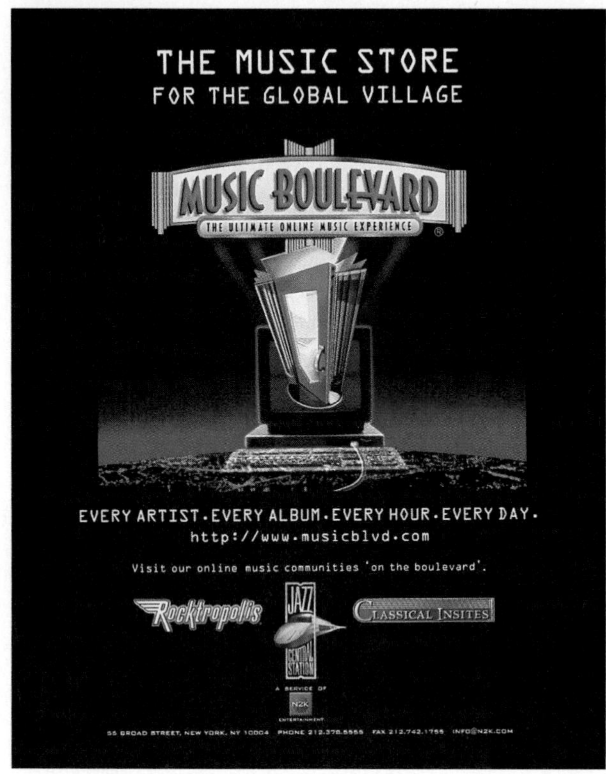
THE MUSIC STORE
FOR THE GLOBAL VILLAGE
MUSIC BOULEVARD
THE ULTIMATE ONLINE MUSIC EXPERIENCE
EVERY ARTIST. EVERY ALBUM. EVERY HOUR. EVERY DAY.
http://www.musicblvd.com
Visit our online music communities 'on the boulevard'.
Rocktropolis
JAZZ CENTRAL STATION
CLASSICAL INSITES
A SERVICE OF
N2K
ENTERTAINMENT

sales and to promote in-store purchases of products featured in the catalogs. Additionally, some firms, such as Lillian Vernon, make almost all of their sales through catalog orders. Mail-order sales have grown about 10 percent a year since 1990, about twice the rate of retail store sales.

Convenience is an important reason why shoppers buy from catalogs. According to a survey conducted by *Catalog Age* magazine, catalog shoppers say they order products by mail to avoid the hassles associated with retail stores. Most of the study's respondents said they shop for gifts through catalogs; books, music, and videos are their most popular purchases.[44]

Mail-order selling began in 1872 when Montgomery Ward issued its first catalog to rural midwestern families, offering only a few choices of clothing and farm supplies. Today, mail-order houses offer a wide range of products, from lingerie (Victoria's Secret) to upscale clothing (J. Crew) and casual apparel and luggage (Lands' End). Many mail-order retailers generate additional sales by enticing consumers to buy from their own stores, as well.

Mail-order sellers try to attract shoppers through exceptional customer service (commonly inviting calls to toll-free phone numbers, and increasingly reaching buyers through computer shopping services like those on CompuServe) and through unique catalogs. Lillian Vernon supplements its general merchandise catalogs with specialty catalogs of children's products and personalized gifts. Jackson and Perkins holiday season catalogs offer a variety of plants for gift giving. Signals advertises merchandise with tie-ins to Public Broadcasting Service programs.

Direct-response retailing also includes **home shopping,** which runs promotions on cable television networks to sell merchandise through telephone orders. One form of home shopping has continued for years. Late-night, 30-second commercials have featured products such as K-Tel Records and Veg-O-Matic vegetable slicers. More recently, TV networks have successfully focused exclusively on providing shopping opportunities. Programming ranges from extended commercials to call-in shows to game-show formats. Shoppers call a toll-free number to buy featured products, and the retailer ships ordered goods directly to their homes. An estimated $4 billion in merchandise is sold this way.[45]

Home Shopping Network, Inc. reaches over 65 million U.S. households. Still, home shopping services have found that, like traditional retailers, they need to carefully manage their merchandise mixes. For example, when the Home Shopping Network tried to move into selling relatively expensive items such as appliances and fine jewelry, the strategy failed.[46]

Internet Retailing

Conventional retailers are anxiously watching the rise of Internet-based retail operators that sell directly to customers via the World Wide Web and online services such as America Online and CompuServe. As described in the opening vignette, these retailers operate from *virtual storefronts,* usually maintaining little or no inventory, ordering directly from vendors to fill customer orders received via e-mail. For example, the N2K Entertainment ad in Figure 15.7 invites customers to shop at its virtual store, Music Boulevard, for online purchases of rock, jazz, and classical music recordings. The growth of Internet-based retail operations has fallen short of some projections, currently accounting for about 2 percent of retail sales.[47] However, analysts predict an explosion in online sales as customer concerns about the security of Internet credit-card transactions abate.

The chapter's opening vignette discussed perhaps the biggest Internet retailing success story to date—Amazon.com. The online retailer allows potential customers to search for books in its database of over 1 million titles. When customers find books that interest them, they complete their purchase transactions via e-mail. Amazon then orders the books directly from the publishers and charges discount prices to customers, who receive their purchases in the mail within five days. A recent estimate evaluated Amazon's sales at well over $10 million.[48]

Conventional retailers and catalog companies are also experimenting with selling through the Internet. Wal-Mart launched two online shopping sites that it hopes will expand its customer base. Shoppers can choose from over 3,000 items, almost none of which are available in the company's traditional stores. Purchased goods arrive via UPS within 48 hours. Wal-Mart believes that the site will allow it to sell products with higher prices than it carries in its regular stores, which cater primarily to price-conscious shoppers. According to Wal-Mart, about 1 million shoppers visited the site on the first day it opened.[49]

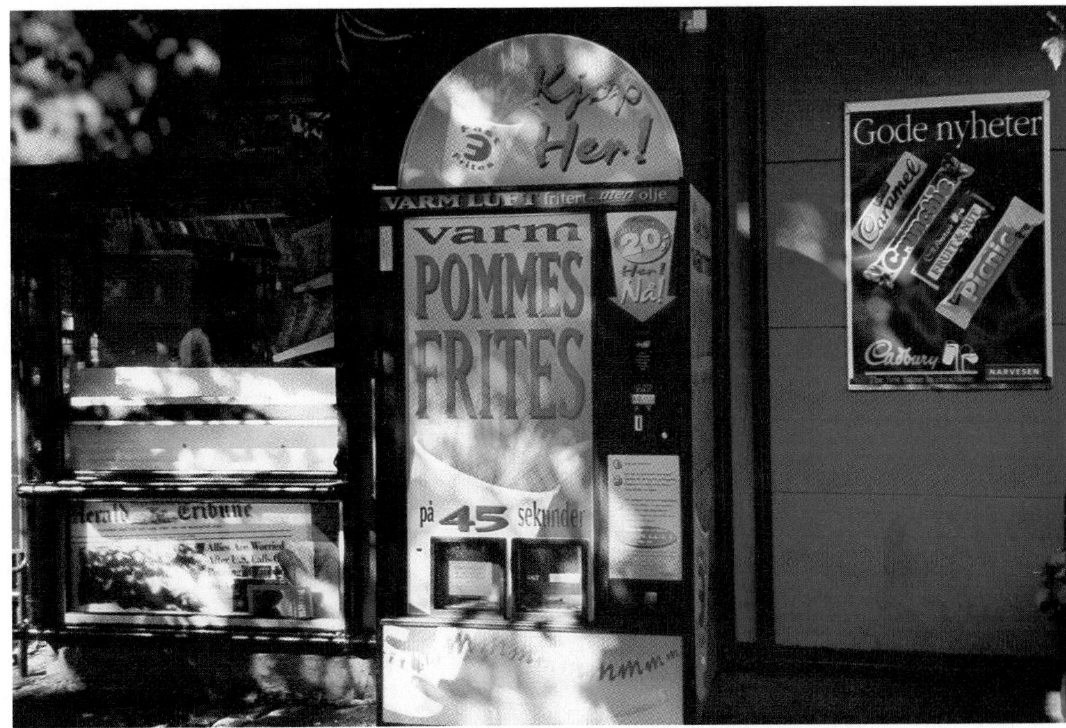
Kjøp Her!
VARM LUFT
varm
POMMES
FRITES
20
Her! Nå!
på 45 sekunder
Gode nyheter
Caramel
Picnic
Cadbury
NARVESEN

The H.J. Heinz Company is stepping up its global investment and leveraging its brand strength through growing foodservice channels. In downtown Oslo, Norway, consumers can buy its Ore-Ida brand french fries *(pommes frites)*, crisp and piping hot, from vending machines.

http://www.wal-mart.com/

Automatic Merchandising

The world's first vending machines dispensed holy water for five-drachma coins in Egyptian temples around 215 B.C. However, the retailing method generated its most rapid growth after World War II, with the introduction of coffee and soft-drink vending machines in the nation's offices and factories. Today, about 4.7 million vending machines sell approximately $25 billion in convenience goods, ranging from soda and snack foods to lottery tickets, to U.S. consumers.

In search of new customers, the industry is experimenting with machines that dispense hot snacks and meals. Specialized vending machines can now cook and serve french fries. Others prepare pizza with a variety of toppings. Consumers are also demanding healthy selections from vending machines. Fat-free and salt-free foods and bottled water are popular choices. Cashing in on the gourmet coffee fad, some vending machines now grind their own beans and offer flavored coffees.[50]

The United States is not the only country where consumers like the convenience of vending machines. Japan, only about the size of Montana, is crowded with as many vending machines as in the entire United States. Japanese consumers can buy a wide variety of goods from vending machines. In addition to food, Japanese consumers pay vending machines for Armani ties, boxer shorts, life insurance, jewelry, and music CDs.[51]

Marketing Dictionary

home shopping A retailing method based on promotions through cable television networks to sell merchandise through telephone orders for home delivery.

CLASSIFICATION OF RETAILERS BY FORM OF OWNERSHIP

A final method of categorizing retailers divides them by ownership structure, distinguishing between chain stores and independent retailers. In addition, independent retailers may join wholesaler-sponsored voluntary chains, band together to form retail cooperatives, or enter into franchise agreements with manufacturers, wholesalers, or service-provider organizations. Each type of ownership has its own unique advantages and strategies.

Chain Stores

Chain stores are groups of retail outlets that operate under central ownership and management to handle the same product lines. Chains have a major advantage over independent retailers in economies of scale. Volume purchases allow chains to pay lower prices than their independent rivals must pay. Since a chain may encompass thousands of retail stores, it can afford advertising layout specialists, sales training, and computerized systems for merchandise ordering, inventory management, forecasting, and accounting to increase efficiency. Also, the large sales volume and wide geographic reach of a chain may enable it to advertise in a variety of media, including television and national magazines.

Wal-Mart, the nation's largest retailing chain, generated sales of over $104 billion from 3,056 stores nationwide in a recent year. The Bentonville, Arkansas-based retail giant is the nation's largest private employer, with 615,000 employees. Another 59,000 people work at Wal-Mart units in Canada, Mexico, China, Argentina, Brazil, and Indonesia.[52]

Independent Retailers

Although most retailers operate small, independent stores, the larger chains dominate a number of fields. The U.S. retailing structure supports a large number of small stores, many medium-sized stores, and a small number of large stores. Even though only 12 percent of the almost 2.7 million retail establishments earn annual sales of $1 million or more, those large operators account for almost three-quarters of all retail sales in the United States. On the other hand, over half of all stores generate yearly sales below $500,000. According to the Department of Commerce, independent retailers account for about 43 percent of all retail sales.

Independents have attempted to compete with chains in a number of ways. Some have failed to do so efficiently and closed their doors. Others have joined retail cooperatives, wholesaler-sponsored voluntary chains, or franchise operations. Still others have concentrated on a traditional advantage of independent stores: friendly, personalized service. Cooperatives like Ace Hardware and Valu-Rite Pharmacies help independents to compete with chains by providing volume buying power as well as nationwide advertising and marketing programs.

SCRAMBLED MERCHANDISING

Many traditional differences no longer distinguish familiar types of retailers, blurring any set of classifications. Anyone who recently has filled a physician's prescription has encountered the concept of **scrambled merchandising,** in which a retailer combines dissimilar product lines in an attempt to boost sales volume. The drugstore you visit after leaving the doctor's office likely carries not only prescription and proprietary drugs, but also garden supplies, gift items, groceries, hardware, housewares, magazines, records, and even small appliances.

Scrambled merchandising developed as retailers hurried to add dissimilar merchandise lines to satisfy consumer demand for one-stop shopping. Some national oil companies, for example, have found that they can increase revenues from their gas station locations by adding convenience stores. These stores stock a growing variety of merchandise such as fresh produce, take-out food, and flowers. At some locations, customers even patronize postal, laundry, and pharmacy services. "We're not trying to be just a gasoline retailer anymore," explains Joseph Bernitt, a Texaco marketing executive.[53]

Scrambled merchandising complicates manufacturers' channel decisions. As they struggle to maintain or increase market share, most have to develop multiple channels in order to reach the diverse array of retailers handling their products.

Marketing Dictionary

chain store A group of stores that operate under central ownership and management to market essentially the same product line.

scrambled merchandising A retailing practice of combining dissimilar product lines to boost sales volume.

ACHIEVEMENT CHECK SUMMARY

Reread the learning goals that follow, and consider the questions for each goal. Answering these questions will reinforce your grasp of the most important concepts in the chapter and allow you to check how well you have achieved these learning goals. Where a blank appears before a question, answer with *T* or *F;* for multiple-choice questions, circle the letter of the correct answer.

Objective 15.1: Describe the evolution of retailing.
1. ___ Innovations in retailing have generally arisen in response to changing consumer needs.
2. ___ The wheel of retailing attempts to explain the merchandise mix decisions made by retail managers.
3. ___ New types of retailers often gain competitive footholds by offering their customers lower prices, which they maintain by reducing or eliminating services.
Objective 15.2: Explain the importance of target marketing to retailers.
1. ___ Retailing today shows a trend toward targeting broad customer segments rather than focusing on narrowly defined segments.
2. ___ Retailers seldom redefine their target markets.
3. ___ Target marketing encourages retailers to develop their marketing strategies before identifying their target market.
Objective 15.3: Discuss how the elements of the marketing mix apply to retailing strategy.
1. ___ Before a retailer can make decisions about pricing, product, or promotion, it must first determine its location strategy.
2. ___ The amount a retailer adds to a product's cost in determining the selling price is called (a) wholesale price; (b) markup; (c) retail price; or (d) markdown.
3. ___ Atmospherics do not influence (a) customer buying behavior; (b) promotion; (c) store image; (d) distribution.
Objective 15.4: Identify and explain each of the five bases for categorizing retailers.
1. ___ Retailers, like consumer goods, may be divided into convenience, shopping, and specialty categories based on the efforts that shoppers are willing to expend in purchasing the products.
2. ___ Full-service retailers often implement discount-pricing strategies.
3. ___ Specialty stores (a) serve niche demographic groups; (b) carry large assortments of one or two product lines; (c) carry large assortments of only part of a single product line.
4. ___ Mass merchandisers are sometimes difficult to distinguish from department stores.
Objective 15.5: Compare the basic types of nonstore retailing.
1. ___ A Tupperware party is an example of (a) direct response selling; (b) direct selling; (c) automatic merchandising.
2. ___ The Lillian Vernon catalog is an example of discount merchandising.
3. ___ When you buy candy from a vending machine, you are using automatic merchandising.
Objective 15.6: Explain the concept of scrambled merchandising.
1. ___ Scrambled merchandising refers to (a) store layout; (b) retailers that carry dissimilar product lines; (c) pricing codes using UPC labels; (d) placing messages in a variety of promotional media.
2. ___ Scrambled merchandising has blurred distinctions between classifications of retailers.
Students: See the solutions section located on page S-3 to check your responses to the Achievement Check Summary.

Key Terms

retailing
wheel of retailing
retail image
assortment management
markup
markdown
planned shopping center
selling up
suggestion selling
atmospherics
specialty store
limited-line store
category killer
general merchandise retailer
variety store
department store
mass merchandiser
discount house
off-price retailer
outlet mall
hypermarket
supercenter
home shopping
chain store
scrambled merchandising

Review Questions

1. Describe the evolution of retailing. What role does the wheel of retailing concept play in this evolution?
2. How do retailers identify target markets? Explain the major strategies by which retailers reach their target markets.
3. A Syracuse, New York, discount store purchases garden hoses for $12 each and sells them for $20 each. What are its markup percentages on selling price and on cost?
4. A Taos, New Mexico, arts and crafts shop purchases decorative wooden carvings for $10 each and sells them for $30 each. What are the shop's markup percentages on selling price and on cost?
5. A carpet store in Flint, Michigan, marks up merchandise 66.67 percent on cost. If the store were to

convert to markup on retail, what would be the equivalent markup percentage?

6. What is the current status of shopping-center development in the United States? Describe the major types of shopping centers.
7. Outline the five bases for categorizing retailers. Cite examples of each subclassification.
8. Identify the major types of general merchandise retailers. Cite examples of each type.
9. Define the term *scrambled merchandising.* Why has this practice become so common in retailing?
10. Differentiate between direct selling and direct-response retailing. Cite examples of both.

Discussion Questions

1. Give several examples of the wheel of retailing in operation. Also, identify situations that do not conform to this hypothesis. What generalizations can you draw from this exercise?
2. Payless ShoeSource is a chain of low-price footwear stores. The chain's 4,265 stores stock an average of 10,000 pairs of shoes in a retail space of 3,000 square feet. The stores are strictly self-service. Store employees make sure the shelves are neat and ring up sales. Payless serves women who buy shoes not only for themselves but for their children as its target customers. Although Payless is the leading retailer in sales of shoes in the $3 to $25 price range, it's facing new competition. Wal-Mart is now the second-biggest seller of low-priced shoes and offers superior products in some categories, such as work boots.[54]

   Suggest promotional, merchandise, location, and service strategies that might help Payless to prevent Wal-Mart from encroaching on its turf. What additional information about the chain's target customers should the firm collect to make these decisions? Should Payless consider expanding into higher-priced shoe lines? Why?
3. Develop a retailing strategy for an Internet retailer. Identify a target market and then suggest mix of merchandise, promotion, service, and pricing strategies that would help a retailer to reach that market via the Internet. What issues must Internet retailers address that do not affect traditional store retailers?
4. Visit a local retail store. Describe the store's pricing, promotion, location, and merchandise strategies. Based on your observations, what customer segment does the store appear to be targeting? How successfully has the store implemented its strategies? What specific changes in strategy would you recommend to the retailer to improve its attractiveness to its target market?
5. Research and then classify each of the following retailers:
   a. Circuit City
   b. Petite Sophisticates
   c. Gap
   d. Rally's
   e. Ethan Allen Galleries
   f. Target

'netWork

1. The Internet hosts many virtual malls. Go to one of them such as http://www.ishopper.com/ and evaluate some of the advantages and disadvantages of online malls. Will these online malls compete directly with traditional malls? How should traditional malls react to this threat?
2. The hypermarket represents a relatively new kind of retailing. Why has this new type of store emerged? Find a hypermarket's site on the Internet. What information does the company offer that might entice consumers into this store? Should these stores advertise differently over the Web than other types of retail stores?
3. Will the Internet affect retailing? If so, how? Will certain segments of consumers likely prefer to purchase over the Internet? Describe them. Will traditional retail stores remain competitive with the new online rivals? How?

VIDEO CASE 15

RENEWING RETAILING

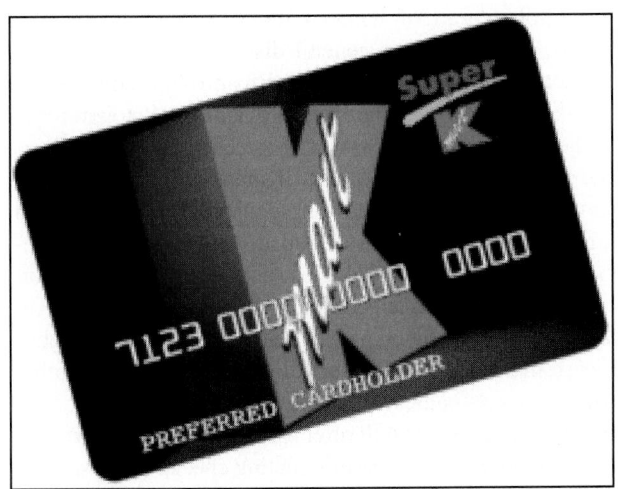
Super K
Kmart
7123 0000 0000 0000
PREFERRED CARDHOLDER

The pioneer of discount retail mass merchandising, Kmart, opened its first store in 1962. The innovative concept succeeded brilliantly from the start because it fit the times. Vast columns of consumers migrating to the suburbs wanted convenient places to shop—places like Kmart stores with their wide assortments of affordably priced merchandise and plenty of parking space. The Troy, Michigan-based company opened hundreds of new stores during the 1960s and 1970s, emerging as the world's top discount retailer by 1980. "Wal-Mart we considered a small country store down in Bentonville, Arkansas," says William Parker, Kmart's vice president of merchandising. "We were doing $18 billion in 1980 and they were doing $7 or $8 billion. Today they do $67 billion, we do $42 billion."

During the 1980s, Kmart continued to add new stores, but not new customers, resulting in steadily declining sales per square foot. New discount retailers such as Toys 'R' Us, Phar-Mor, Target, Best Buy, and Wal-Mart were growing, each taking away a segment of Kmart's business. "Many competitors took what Kmart had done and out-Kmartized Kmart," says J. Patrick Kelly, Professor of Marketing at Wayne State University.

The stream of customers through Kmart's doors dwindled for other reasons, too. The company had lost its focus on servicing customers. "Our stores had become old and tired and outdated," says former Kmart CEO Joseph Antonini. "While customers like our value and our prices and our merchandise, they wanted a better shopping experience." Kmart's research indicated that 49 percent of Wal-Mart shoppers drove past Kmart stores on the way to those rival outlets.

Kmart initiated a companywide renewal strategy to adapt to evolving consumer tastes and competitive challenges. The renewal effort sought to refocus the company on marketing to consumers. To make Kmart a pleasant place to shop, the company started a store modernization program of redesigning and refurbishing existing stores which included widening the aisles and improving the lighting systems. The initiative also replaced older stores with newer, more modern ones. One of the first and most distinct changes the company implemented involved the redesign of the familiar Kmart logo. The new logo—a large red *K* with the word *mart* in white type inside—signaled to consumers the presence of a new or remodeled store.

The renewal strategy also integrated advanced technology and a comprehensive program of marketing, advertising, company communications, and merchandising. "Everything we are doing," says Antonini, "from store modernization to sophisticated technology systems, is being driven by a single idea—that Kmart will only get a larger share of the market by better focusing on and more quickly satisfying the ever-changing needs of the consumer."

At the foundation of Kmart's renewal program,

Today's
K
mart

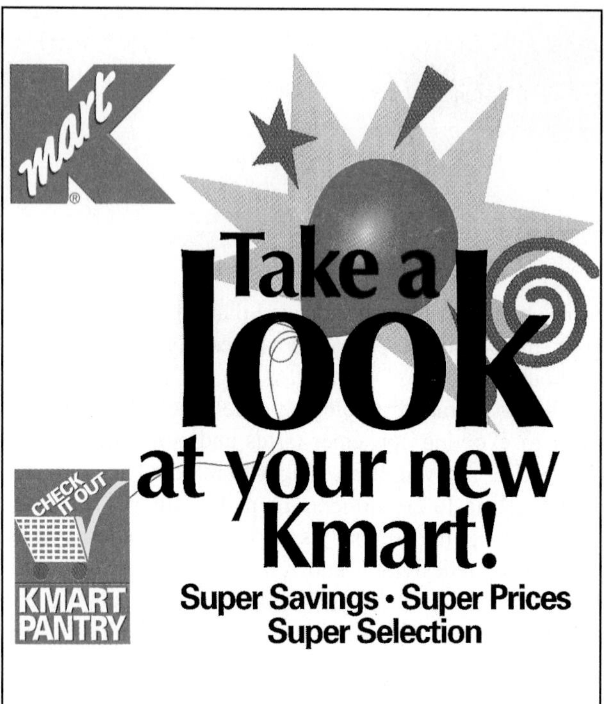
Kmart
Take a look at your new Kmart!
Super Savings • Super Prices
Super Selection
CHECK IT OUT
KMART PANTRY

continuous analysis carefully tracks consumer needs. The company conducted focus groups throughout the country to learn what customers liked and disliked about shopping at Kmart and what the company could do to improve their experiences. For example, many shoppers complained that Kmart's dressing rooms were too small and didn't have enough mirrors. Customers also didn't like the curtained enclosures, preferring instead rooms with doors that would lock and give more privacy. Kmart responded by renovating its dressing rooms, making them larger, adding more mirrors, and replacing the curtains with solid doors.

Consumer research also indicated that today's customers want quality merchandise. Kmart responded by developing quality standards. Merchandise buyers now refer to product quality specifications in negotiations with vendors to ensure that the goods they buy meet Kmart's standards. The company also built a quality assurance and technical design facility to test merchandise and verify that it meets standards before it reaches store shelves.

To remedy shopper complaints about frequent stockouts, Kmart started to update its technology. Management placed a high priority on a program to establish state-of-the-art computer information systems and satellite communications. Kmart invested heavily in automated, supplier-managed inventory systems and electronic data interchange. The company installed point-of-sale scanning at all 50,000 registers and a satellite communication system linking registers to corporate headquarters. These new technologies enable management to track every purchase so they can learn what sells and what doesn't. Kmart buyers use this information in their merchandising decisions, and suppliers use it to manage inventory levels and replenish stock, preventing out-of-stock situations.

Through its own video broadcasting network, Kmart keeps in touch with store personnel three to four times a week. Kmart uses the network as a training tool to update employees about new goods and services and to communicate news about the company.

Another part of Kmart's renewal strategy is Super Kmart, a combination general discount store and supermarket under one roof designed to provide convenient, one-stop shopping. Kmart is also planning a "Dream Store of the Future" concept as a way to eclipse its competitors and increase customer loyalty. Kmart is the only retailer participating in a pilot project sponsored by the National Information Infrastructure Testbed, a consortium examining how emerging technologies such as the Internet, smart cards, and advanced telecommunications will transform retailing. Other project participants include 3M, Hughes Electronics, Hewlett-Packard, IBM, and NCR. Together with these companies, Kmart is using new technologies to develop systems that will offer services for the newest evolution in retailing such as eliminating checkout lines, automatic home delivery for out-of-stock items, and cart scanning rather than scanning individual items.

Kmart's current CEO, Floyd Hall, continues to push forward with the renewal strategy. He wants to increase Kmart's sales per square foot from $195 to $240 in three years. (Wal-Mart tops $300 in sales per square foot and Target tops $250.) To reach his goal, Hall has tied store managers' annual bonuses to customer satisfaction ratings they receive from mystery shoppers. To attract shoppers, Hall has started weekly promotions of high-volume merchandise. He is also allocating space at the front of stores to the Pantry, a redesign concept similar to a convenience store, where shoppers can quickly fill needs like snacks, cereal, and laundry soap. Hall's ideas are increasing store

traffic. "I see a lot of improvement in their stores," says Robert Buchanan, a NatWest Securities Corp. retail analyst, who has issued a buy rating for Kmart stock for the first time in ten years.

Questions

1. What elements of Kmart's renewal strategy are intended to change consumers' perceptions of the company?
2. What role does technology play in Kmart's renewal strategy?
3. Which element of retailing strategy do you think adds the most important contribution to renewing Kmart?
4. Go to Kmart's Web site located at:
   http://www.kmart.com/
   What is Kmart's mission statement? Does the company's renewal effort align well with the mission statement? Support your decision. What modifications would you suggest for the mission statement?

Source: Chris Woodyard, "Shoppers Get Kmart's Attention: Merchant Polishes Its Image with Cleaner Stores, Wider Aisles," *USA Today,* April 9, 1997, Section B.

CHAPTER 16

LOGISTICS AND VALUE CHAIN MANAGEMENT

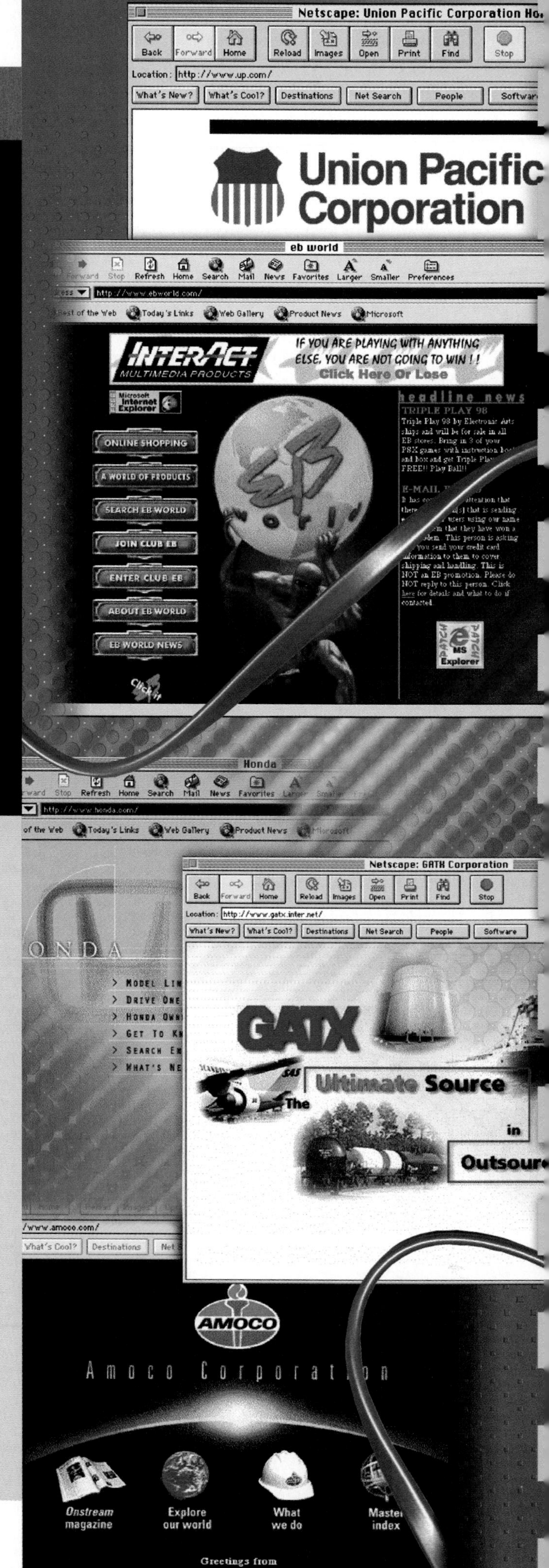

Netscape: Union Pacific Corporation Ho
Location: http://www.up.com/
Union Pacific Corporation
eb world
http://www.ebworld.com/
INTERACT MULTIMEDIA PRODUCTS
IF YOU ARE PLAYING WITH ANYTHING ELSE, YOU ARE NOT GOING TO WIN !!
Click Here Or Lose
headline news
TRIPLE PLAY 98
ONLINE SHOPPING
A WORLD OF PRODUCTS
SEARCH EB WORLD
JOIN CLUB EB
ENTER CLUB EB
ABOUT EB WORLD
EB WORLD NEWS
Honda
http://www.honda.com/
Netscape: GATX Corporation
Location: http://www.gatx.inter.net/
GATX
The Ultimate Source in Outsour
http://www.amoco.com/
AMOCO
Amoco Corporation
Onstream magazine
Explore our world
What we do
Greetings from

Chapter Objectives

1. Explain the role of logistics in an effective marketing strategy.
2. Identify and compare the major components of a physical distribution system.
3. Outline the suboptimization problem in logistics.
4. Explain the impact of transportation deregulation on logistics activities.
5. Compare the major transportation alternatives on the basis of speed, dependability, cost, frequency of shipments, availability in different locations, and flexibility in handling products.
6. Discuss how transportation intermediaries and combined transportation modes can improve physical distribution.

Federal Express: The Logical Choice

"If it absolutely, positively has to be there overnight. . . ." Chances are you've heard these words uttered many times before. The jingle promotes Federal Express, which rapidly delivers packages around the globe thanks to a logistical system that could surely rival that of Santa Claus.

Customers only glimpse the setup through which Federal Express accomplishes its overnight magic. Ask a typical customer about Federal Express, and you will no doubt hear a report about cheerful delivery couriers in crisp uniforms, freestanding drop-off boxes, and reliable delivery of the distinctive orange, white, and purple packages. The outsider's explanation might fail to convey an appreciation of the network that accepts a package in Fairbanks, Alaska, as the sun is setting and sets it down just hours later in the Florida Keys.

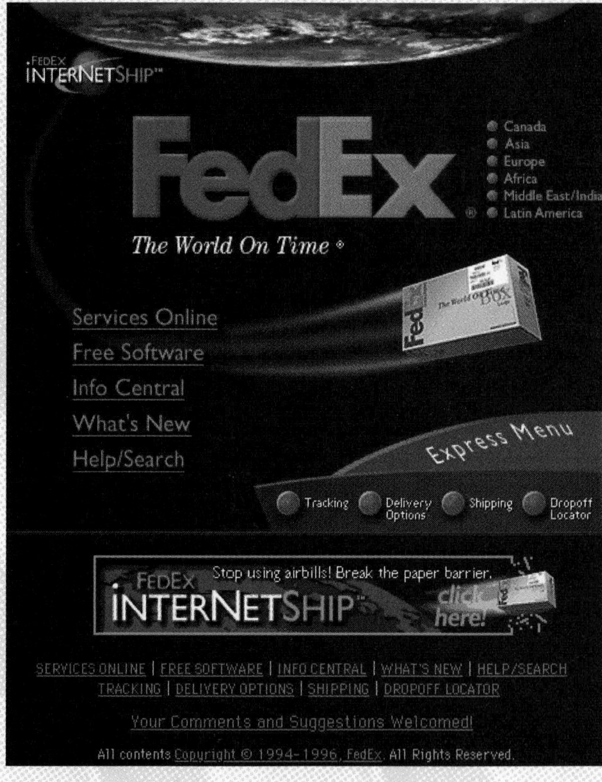

FEDEX INTERNETSHIP™
FedEx
Canada
Asia
Europe
Africa
Middle East/India
Latin America
The World On Time®
Services Online
Free Software
Info Central
What's New
Help/Search
Express Menu
Tracking
Delivery Options
Shipping
Dropoff Locator
FEDEX INTERNETSHIP
Stop using airbills! Break the paper barrier.
click here!
SERVICES ONLINE | FREE SOFTWARE | INFO CENTRAL | WHAT'S NEW | HELP/SEARCH
TRACKING | DELIVERY OPTIONS | SHIPPING | DROPOFF LOCATOR
Your Comments and Suggestions Welcomed!
All contents Copyright © 1994-1996, FedEx. All Rights Reserved.

Relying upon a massive network of jets, vans, trucks, and databases, Federal Express rarely misses a connection. With 99 percent of its packages arriving on time, the Memphis-based firm continues to refine the transportation system it developed long ago to keep it steadily improving. For instance, FedEx not only guarantees next-day delivery, but it can pinpoint the precise location of that package anywhere within its pipeline at any moment. A visitor to the FedEx Web site can locate a particular package simply by typing in its tracking number. This capability does more than satisfy curious customers. By collecting and manipulating the mountains of data generated by its Web site, FedEx improves its understanding of how Internet users conduct transactions in cyberspace.

Taking advantage of its in-house expertise, FedEx now offers services to other companies with weaker logistical, inventory, warehousing, and delivery functions. Its FedEx Logistics Services subsidiary acts as a surrogate for any organization that doesn't want to handle its own logistical needs.

Consider, for example, the partnership between FedEx Logistics and Volvo GM Heavy Duty Truck Corp. In the early 1990s, truck dealers complained about slow deliveries of critical repair parts, causing them to lose business to competitors. To solve the problem, Volvo GM set up a warehouse stocked with a full line of truck parts near FedEx's shipping hub in Memphis. When a dealer needs a part for an emergency repair, someone calls the warehouse on a toll-free hot line. Warehouse staff members immediately ship the part by FedEx, often for arrival that night, helping dealers to provide quick and efficient repair services.

Laura Ashley, the British retailer of apparel, linens, and other items, became one of the early customers of FedEx Logistics. Laura Ashley paid FedEx $250 million to handle all of its telephone ordering and distribution for the next ten years. Someone calls Laura Ashley's toll-free number to order merchandise has no idea that it's really a Federal Express employee taking the information.

But Federal Express pursues ambitions well beyond performing operational grunt work for other companies. It aims to revolutionize the logistics business in time for the twenty-first century, becoming a prime player in moving goods bought through electronic commerce. With sales on the Internet rising dramatically, FedEx's move shows impeccable timing.

http://www.fedex.com/

FedEx hopes to carry the burden for cyberspace retailers with the help of its BusinessLink software package. FedEx executives believe that the software will reduce cost and improve efficiency for Internet retailers while holding down inventory costs despite expanded ranges of products.

If such efficiency sounds impossible, FedEx explains that it can accomplish its goal by relying upon a logistics network that operates with the precision of a drill team. Because FedEx will move goods swiftly, for instance, retailers need to keep little costly inventory collecting dust in warehouses.

"The way to substitute information for mass warehousing is to make a distribution system that's as good as a warehouse," says FedEx founder Fred Smith. "If you think about it, a warehouse is nothing more than a place to put something so you know you've got it. Well, I figured if we could provide the same degree of assurance to people, electronically, that their stuff is 'in the FedEx warehouse'—be it on one of our 500-mile-per-hour planes or a 50-mile-per-hour truck—then they would no longer need to have it in a warehouse."[1]

CHAPTER OVERVIEW

Chapters 14 and 15 concentrated on distribution channel strategy and the marketing activities of wholesaling and retailing. This chapter focuses specifically on **logistics,** the process of coordinating the flow of information, goods, and services among members of the distribution channel. The term *logistics* originally referred to strategic movements of military troops and supplies during battles. Today, however, the term encompasses business-related distribution, as well. Efficient logistical systems support attentive customer service—an important goal of any organization's marketing strategy.

One major subject within logistics, **physical distribution,** covers a broad range of activities aimed at efficient movement of finished goods from the end of the production line to the consumer. Although some marketers use the terms *transportation* and *physical distribution* interchangeably, they do not carry the same meaning. Physical distribution extends beyond transportation to include such important decision areas as customer service, inventory control, materials handling, protective packaging, order

Figure 16.1 **Dubai Ports Authority: An Important Final Link in the Supply Chain for Many International Markets**

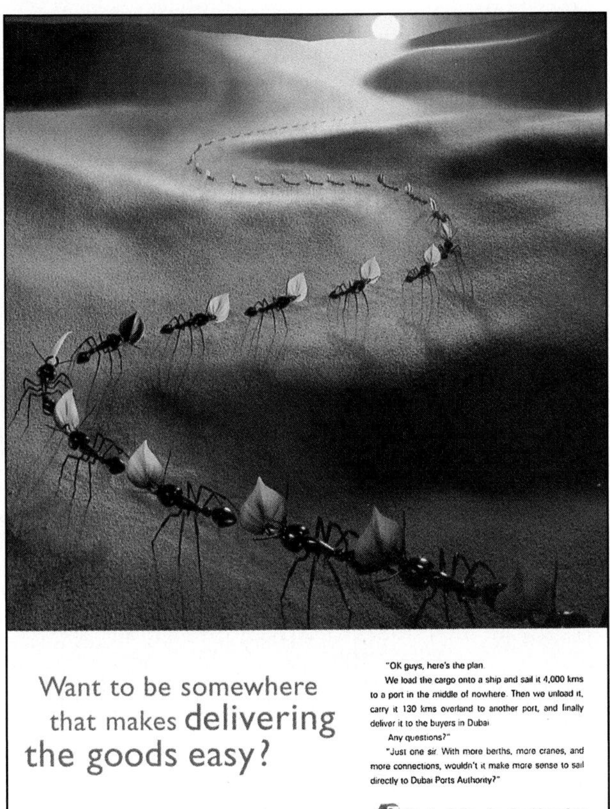
Want to be somewhere that makes delivering the goods easy?
"OK guys, here's the plan.
We load the cargo onto a ship and sail it 4,000 kms to a port in the middle of nowhere. Then we unload it, carry it 130 kms overland to another port, and finally deliver it to the buyers in Dubai.
Any questions?"
"Just one sir. With more berths, more cranes, and more connections, wouldn't it make more sense to sail directly to Dubai Ports Authority?"
Dubai Ports Authority
To find out more, contact The DPA Marketing Department Code 111, PO Box 17000, Dubai, UAE. Telephone (9714) 815000 or fax (9714) 817777

processing, transportation, warehouse site selection, and warehousing. Successful physical distribution systems make careful arrangements for all of these components to ensure effective logistics management.

This chapter adds detail to the discussions of logistics and physical distribution begun in Chapters 14 and 15. First, it focuses on the importance of physical distribution. It then examines several key logistical decisions facing businesses today.

IMPORTANCE OF LOGISTICS

General Motors Corp.'s Suburban is one of the most popular sport-utility vehicles in the country. If you want to buy one, however, prepare yourself for a long wait. This wait highlights the critical role of logistics in overall marketing effectiveness.

GM has set up a computerized system to track the movements of vehicles from factory to dealer and, ultimately, to customers. The system allocates a certain number of Suburbans to each dealer based on that retailer's previous sales figures. Dealers that haven't sold their allotments quickly in the past have to wait for delivery of additional Suburbans. As a result, many customers wait up to several months before their local dealers receive vehicles that fit their specifications. Dealers and buyers both complain loudly and blame the General Motors physical distribution system. GM defends the system for one of its most profitable vehicles as the only fair way to distribute them since a shortage of factory capacity limits production of Suburbans.[2]

The experience of General Motors illustrates the importance of logistics. Effective promotion and a hot product do not ensure marketing success. A firm can satisfy customers only by setting up a logistics system that successfully brings the product from factory to customer. One study of 1,300 companies found that 80 percent valued delivery as highly as product quality for its contribution to satisfying their needs.[3]

Effective distribution requires proper management of the **supply chain.** As discussed in Chapter 10, the supply chain is the complete sequence of suppliers that contribute to creating and delivering a good or service. The supply chain begins with the raw-material inputs to the manufacturing process for a product and then proceeds to the actual production activities. The final link in the supply chain is the movement of finished goods through the distribution channel to end customers. The Dubai Ports Authority's ad in Figure 16.1 uses a humorous graphic to illustrate how the authority's system can facilitate movements of goods to customers throughout the United Arab Emirates.

Marketers can also view the supply chain as a **value chain,** each link of which adds benefits for consumers as goods move from raw materials through manufacturing to distribution. The value chain encompasses all activities that enhance the value of the finished good including design, quality manufacturing, customer service, and delivery. As Chapter 2 explained, customer satisfaction results

Marketing Dictionary

logistics The process of coordinating the flow of information, goods, and services among members of the distribution channel.

physical distribution Activities to achieve efficient movement of finished goods from the end of the production line to the consumer.

supply (value) chain The sequence of suppliers that contribute to the creation and delivery of a good or service.

MARKETING HALL OF FAME

A Salute for Wal-Mart

Drive by a Wal-Mart outlet, whether in a city or a small town, and you'll probably see a parking lot jammed with customers' cars. Wal-Mart seems to offer something for everyone—even the U.S. military.

Faced with monumental logistical problems, Defense Department officials sought help from executives at Wal-Mart, as well as Federal Express, United Parcel Service, and United Services Automobile Association. Wal-Mart impressed the military officials most by cramming acres of merchandise into its stores, despite tight limitations on storage space. Keeping the store shelves stocked without a lot of inventory on hand requires a nimble response system that the military would love to mimic.

Wal-Mart pioneered techniques to apply sales information collected from its cash registers to determine what products each store needed to restock. It has remained on the cutting edge in inventory management methods, recently implementing a data mining system that predicts demand for specific goods at individual stores. This system also analyzes customers' purchases to identify trends.

The military's performance during the Persian Gulf War led the top brass to consult Wal-Mart and other industry leaders to gear up its logistical operations. This decision might surprise casual observers, because the military earned praise for its swift transportation of equipment into the baking Middle Eastern desert. The military managed to transport 7 million tons of war supplies to the 550,000 troops in just a short period of time.

But the mission also revealed plenty of problems. No one, for instance, kept close tabs on just what cargo was loaded onto planes, ships, and trucks. Troops never touched half of the 40,000 containers that arrived in the Middle East—including $2.7 billion worth of spare parts. They didn't even know what supplies a lot of the bulky containers held. "The system broke," conceded the Army's now-retired logistics chief.

Military commanders vowed not to let such mistakes happen

directly from the perceived value of a purchase to its buyer. To manage the value chain, businesses must look for ways to add and maximize customer value in each activity they perform.

Logistical management plays a major role in giving customers what they need when they need it. Therefore, it plays a central role in the value chain. Another important component of this chain, **value-added service,** adds some improved or supplemental service that customers do not normally receive or expect.

Customer satisfaction depends heavily on reliable movements of products to ensure convenient availability. Abbott HealthSystems Division supplies hospitals and other medical facilities with health-care products. One of the company's strategic goals is to position itself as the high-quality and low-cost provider in the industry. To achieve this goal, the firm has set up a network of 46 distribution sites across the country. Abbott placed each site near its customers, usually within 70 miles, to ensure reliable and timely delivery. Abbott has also set up QUICK-LINK, an electronic ordering system that lets hospitals streamline ordering and invoicing procedures. QUICK-LINK also provides an easy way to track the status of any order placed with Abbott.[4]

Logistical Cost Control

In addition to enhancing their products by providing value-added services to customers, many firms are focusing on logistics for another important reason: to cut costs. Distribution functions currently represent almost half of a typical firm's total marketing costs.

Historically, cost cutting efforts have focused on economies in production. These attempts began with the Industrial Revolution, when the emerging science of management emphasized efficient production and a continual drive to decrease production costs and improve the output levels of factories and production workers. But managers now recognize that production efficiency leaves few easy opportunities for further cost savings. Increasingly, managers are looking for possible cost savings in their logistical functions. U.S. businesses spend $700 billion annually on logistics.[5]

To reduce logistics costs, businesses are taking a variety of steps. First, they are reexamining each link in their supply chains to identify activities that do not add value for customers. By eliminating, reducing, or redesigning these activities they can often cut costs and boost efficiency. Amoco Petroleum Products, for instance, has significantly

again. Taking their cues from business, leaders adopted practices such as electronic data interchange to shrink inventories and hasten deliveries. For instance, military purchasers can now order supplies electronically from ships located many miles from a conflict. The supplies reach their destinations by helicopter or transported on pilotless, robot aircraft guided by a satellite navigation system.

High-tech systems are also helping the military to spit-polish logistics operations. Bar codes, radio tags, and laser codes help troops to keep track of supplies, a great improvement over the time-consuming, keypunch systems of the past. Computers also follow truck movements in and out of supply depots, replacing humans filling out pen-and-paper forms. "We'll have piles of information instead of piles of stock," predicts Colonel Merle D. Russ, a senior Army logistics official.

The innovations seem to be working. Pentagon inventories plummeted from $104 billion in 1990 to $76 billion four years later. Inventory is expected to drop to $55 billion by 2001. A state-of-the-art supply depot in Pennsylvania, which functions as a laboratory for many logistics techniques, has cut delivery time from 25.5 days during the Persian Gulf War to just 5.4 days.

But military rules continue to stifle some operational improvements. Logistics officials from the three service branches, for instance, want online access to each other's inventory records. This innovation could further accelerate order fulfillment. "We can save millions and millions," argues Army Colonel Daniel L. Labin. So far, however, his pleas have not changed the policy.

QUESTIONS FOR CRITICAL THINKING

1. **Why did the U.S. Army, with a vast array of technical expertise and resources at its disposal, turn to the private sector to improve its logistics management?**
2. **Suggest some other strategies the military can use to improve its logistics management.**

Sources: Adapted from John W. Verity, "Coaxing Meaning from Raw Data," *Business Week,* February 3, 1997, p. 138; John W. Verity, "Clearing the Cobwebs out of the Stockroom," *Business Week,* October 21, 1996, p. 140; Stan Crock, "The Pentagon Goes to B-School," *Business Week,* December 11, 1995, pp. 98,100; and Art Pine, "Military Borrowing a Page from Wal-Mart Technology," *Morning News of Northwest Arkansas,* May 24, 1995, p. 4A.

reduced its logistics costs this way. The company set up a cross-functional logistics management team that included representatives from both customers and suppliers. The team examined all aspects of Amoco's supply chain and identified areas where the company could gain greater control. The effort led to installation of a computerized scheduling system that connects all internal and external suppliers, distribution centers, and marketing operations. The system alerts all players when inventory levels fall below acceptable levels and supports flexible planning and scheduling of production. This system together with other improvements in Amoco's logistics function allowed the firm to reduce inventory carrying costs by 10 percent and dramatically improve its delivery reliability.[6]

http://www.amoco.com/

Some companies try to cut costs and offer value-added services by outsourcing some or all of their logistics functions to specialist firms. The **third party (contract) logistics firms** specialize in handling logistical activities for their clients. The ad in Figure 16.2 describes the value-added services provided by Caliber Logistics, a worldwide contract logistics firm. Businesses that contract with third-party logistics firms can often reduce costs, because the contract firms apply unique distribution assets, information systems, and expertise to the problems.[7] By current estimates, third-party firms will handle about $25 billion a year in outsourced logistics services by 2000.[8] Through

Marketing Dictionary

value-added service An improved or supplemental service that customers do not normally receive or expect.

third-party (contract) logistics firm A company that specializes in handling logistics activities for other firms.

Figure 16.2 Caliber Logistics: A Third-Party Logistics Service Supplier

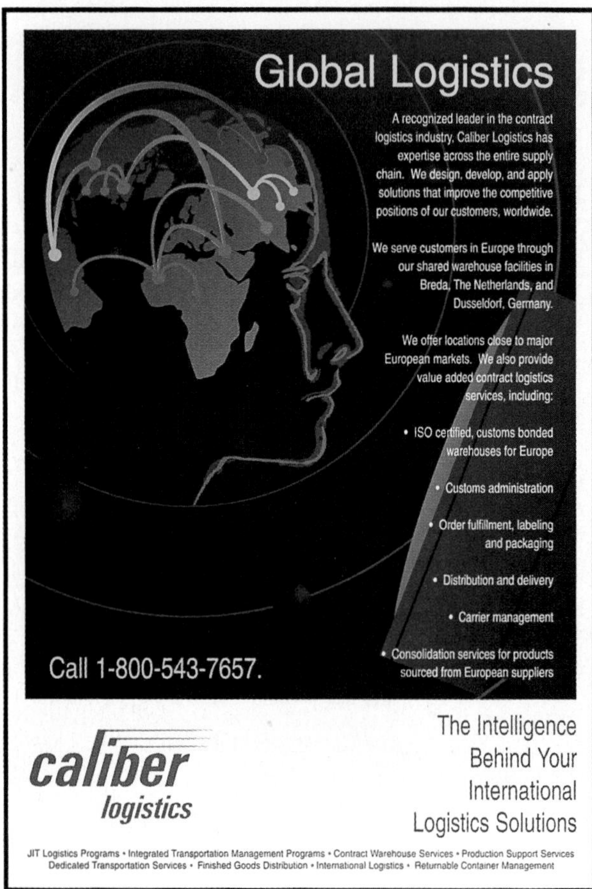
Global Logistics
A recognized leader in the contract logistics industry, Caliber Logistics has expertise across the entire supply chain. We design, develop, and apply solutions that improve the competitive positions of our customers, worldwide.
We serve customers in Europe through our shared warehouse facilities in Breda, The Netherlands, and Dusseldorf, Germany.
We offer locations close to major European markets. We also provide value added contract logistics services, including:
• ISO certified, customs bonded warehouses for Europe
• Customs administration
• Order fulfillment, labeling and packaging
• Distribution and delivery
• Carrier management
• Consolidation services for products sourced from European suppliers
Call 1-800-543-7657.
caliber logistics
The Intelligence Behind Your International Logistics Solutions
JIT Logistics Programs • Integrated Transportation Management Programs • Contract Warehouse Services • Production Support Services
Dedicated Transportation Services • Finished Goods Distribution • International Logistics • Returnable Container Management

such outsourcing alliances, producers and logistics service suppliers cooperate to develop innovative, customized systems that speed goods through carefully constructed manufacturing and distribution pipelines. Although many companies have long outsourced transportation and warehousing functions, today's alliance partners extend familiar methods to intimately combine their operations for mutual benefit.

http://www.gatx.inter.net/

Case Corp., for example, has instituted alliances with third-party logistics specialists Fritz Companies, Inc., and GATX Logistics, Inc. Case sells its agricultural and construction equipment through dealers and distributors in 150 countries. Fritz handles all U.S. and international shipping and freight transportation for these transactions. GATX Logistics handles Case's central warehouse, inspecting, packaging, and shipping repair parts to dealers. By outsourcing these logistics functions, Case reduced its overall physical inventory investment by $30 million and cut staffing by 250 employees. In addition, the company now ships more than 99 percent of orders on or before the deadlines set by customer delivery schedules.[9]

Global marketing has stimulated new growth within the logistics services industry, as full-support companies help firms to plan and execute distribution plans in other countries. For example, when Toro Company, a lawn equipment manufacturer, expanded into Europe, the company needed an efficient way to move repair parts. Initially, Toro shipped needed parts to its European dealers by air freight—a very expensive solution that also caused delivery delays. Toro decided instead to open a parts supply warehouse in Europe and hire a third-party company to manage the operation.[10]

PHYSICAL DISTRIBUTION

The basic notion of a *system* implies a set of interrelated parts. The word is derived from the Greek word *systema,* which refers to an organized relationship among components. The firm's components include such interrelated activities as production, finance, and marketing. Each component must function properly to keep the system working effectively and moving the organization toward its objectives.

A **system,** formally defined, is an organized group of components linked according to a plan for achieving specific objectives. A company's physical distribution system contains the following elements:

1. *Customer service.* What level of customer service should distribution activities support?
2. *Transportation.* How should the firm ship its products?
3. *Inventory control.* How much inventory should the firm maintain at each location?
4. *Protective packaging and materials handling.* How can the firm efficiently handle goods in the factory, warehouse, and transport terminals?
5. *Order processing.* How should the firm handle orders?
6. *Warehousing.* Where will the distribution system locate stocks of goods? How many warehouses should the firm maintain?

All of these components function in interrelated ways. Decisions made in one area affect relative efficiency in others. The physical distribution manager must balance each component so that the system avoids stressing any single aspect to the detriment of overall functioning. For example, a firm might decide to reduce transportation costs by shipping its products by inexpensive—but slow—water transportation. However, slow deliveries would likely force the firm to maintain high inventory levels and raise inventory holding costs, such as warehousing expenses. This kind of mismatch between system elements often leads to increased production costs.

The ad in Figure 16.3 cites components of a total logistics system that led Marriott's vice president of distribution to contract with Penske for transportation services. The change in this element of Marriott's operation helped to reduce its fleet size, reducing both direct distribution costs and capital investment for the necessary equipment while improving customer service.

Figure 16.3 **Marriott: Successful Integration of Penske's Components to Improve Distribution System Performance**

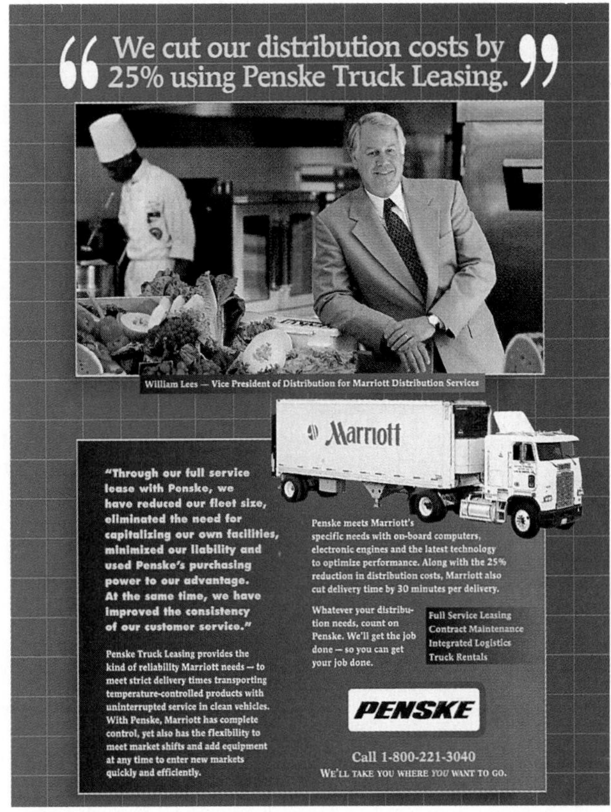
"We cut our distribution costs by 25% using Penske Truck Leasing."
William Lees — Vice President of Distribution for Marriott Distribution Services
Marriott
"Through our full service lease with Penske, we have reduced our fleet size, eliminated the need for capitalizing our own facilities, minimized our liability and used Penske's purchasing power to our advantage. At the same time, we have improved the consistency of our customer service."
Penske Truck Leasing provides the kind of reliability Marriott needs — to meet strict delivery times transporting temperature-controlled products with uninterrupted service in clean vehicles. With Penske, Marriott has complete control, yet also has the flexibility to meet market shifts and add equipment at any time to enter new markets quickly and efficiently.
Penske meets Marriott's specific needs with on-board computers, electronic engines and the latest technology to optimize performance. Along with the 25% reduction in distribution costs, Marriott also cut delivery time by 30 minutes per delivery.
Whatever your distribution needs, count on Penske. We'll get the job done — so you can get your job done.
Full Service Leasing
Contract Maintenance
Integrated Logistics
Truck Rentals
PENSKE
Call 1-800-221-3040
WE'LL TAKE YOU WHERE YOU WANT TO GO.

The Problem of Suboptimization

A logistics manager seeks to establish a specified level of customer service while minimizing the costs of physically moving and storing goods from their production point to their ultimate purchasers. Marketers must first agree on their customer service priorities and then seek to minimize the total costs of moving goods to buyers, while meeting customer service goals. They must mesh all physical distribution elements together rather than setting up independent arrangements, in order to meet customer service levels at minimum cost. Marketers do not always achieve this goal.

Suboptimization results when the managers of individual physical distribution functions attempt to minimize costs, but the impact of one task on the others results in less than optimal results. A frequently used analogy describes a football team composed of numerous talented players who hold league records in pass completions, average yards gained per rush, blocked kicks, and punt return yardage. Unfortunately, however, these individual accomplishments fail to result in winning games if the players do not cooperate in a larger endeavor—scoring more points than their opponents.

Briefly speaking

"The system is the solution."

AT&T advertisement

Suboptimization may cause problems in physical distribution when marketers judge each logistics activity by its ability to achieve its own objectives, some of which may work at cross-purposes with other goals. Suboptimization becomes particularly likely when a firm introduces a new product that may not fit easily into its current physical distribution system. Businesspeople often focus on certain adjustments to their systems without anticipating related problems that eventually arise.

Consider the case of the Mexican assembly plants that have been built just across the U.S. border. U.S. firms originally established these **maquiladoras** to cut their labor and tariff expenses. For example, they send raw materials into Mexico without paying Mexican import duties, and they pay U.S. duties only on the value added to the assembled products that reenter the United States. The border city of Tijuana alone hosts more than 560 *maquiladora* factories. In fact, these operations have

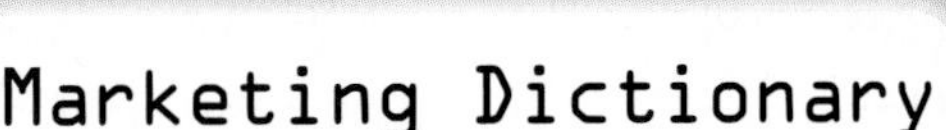
Marketing Dictionary

system An organized group of components linked according to a plan for achieving specific objectives.

suboptimization A condition that results when individual operations achieve their objectives but interfere with progress toward broader organizational goals.

maquiladora A Mexican assembly plant located near the U.S. border.

SOLVING AN ETHICAL CONTROVERSY

In This Era of Downsizing, Should Companies Outsource Their Logistics Operations?

In the business world, success depends critically on manufacturing high-quality products. Businesspeople sometimes pay less attention to just how those products will arrive at their intended destinations.

Logistics management requires close coordination of complex activities, often across distances spanning many time zones. This challenging task imposes an exhaustive drain on manpower. Not surprisingly, some companies would rather pay third parties to handle these tricky operational details.

Nortel, Inc., a producer of telecommunications equipment, is one of many companies that rely upon outside specialists to handle their logistics. Nortel's executives decided to outsource trucking activities for several reasons. For starters, the decision to hire outside help freed Nortel to concentrate on what it does best. The company also felt that a third-party logistics firm could find ways to reduce costs and improve service—tasks that left Nortel struggling. "We looked at our core competency," explains Stephen Bridges, the senior manager of U.S. logistics at Nortel. "We were a manufacturer of telecommunication equipment; we were not a trucking company. We felt that there was a lot more expertise that we could go out and get externally than we could build internally."

Of course, not everyone reacts so enthusiastically to changes that whittle away at employment, replacing the firm's own workers with contract employees. Many observers fear a further loss of already vanishing job security.

Should Companies Outsource Their Logistics Operations?

PRO

1. **Hiring someone else to handle logistics frees a company's time and staff for strategically critical matters. "We're all tired of hearing about core competencies, but this whole idea just isn't going to go away," says Charles Lounsbury, vice president of parts distribution at Toro Company in Minneapolis. "If we can find someone who can do the job better, at a lower cost, why wouldn't you use them?"**
2. **Downsizing has already reduced many companies to just their essential personnel. They may simply lack qualified staff members to run top-flight logis-**

gained a reputation for Tijuana as the TV-set manufacturing capital of the world, since facilities there produce over 10 million sets a year. Firms operating *maquiladora* facilities include Sony, Sanyo, Samsung, and Hyundai.

Although the operators of *maquiladoras* enjoy cost savings by hiring inexpensive labor and paying low customs duties, they must balance these savings against the logistical problems of bringing finished goods across the border. For instance, trucks carrying finished products to the United States frequently wait in traffic jams of up to 5 miles long before they can cross the border. Customs delays often delay goods anywhere from one to three days before they can finally enter the United States. Additionally, these firms must anticipate generally high absentee rates, particularly during holiday weeks like Christmas and Easter. As a result, *maquiladoras* often scale back production schedules during these times.[11]

Briefly speaking

"Businesses planned for service are apt to succeed; businesses planned for profit are apt to fail."

Nicholas M. Butler (1862–1947)
American educator and Nobel laureate

Effective management of the physical distribution function requires some cost trade-offs. By accepting relatively high costs in some functional areas in order to cut costs in others, managers can minimize their firm's total physical distribution costs. Of course, any reduction in logistics cost should support progress toward the goal of maintaining customer service standards.

Customer Service Standards

Customer service standards state goals and define acceptable performance for the quality of service that a firm expects to deliver to its customers. For example, one firm might set a customer service standard that calls for shipping 90 percent of all orders within 48 hours after receiving, and shipping all orders within 72 hours.

Firms may even segment markets based on different levels of customer service that they require. Georgia-Pacific Corp., the nation's largest producer of building materials, uses this strategy. It ships products headed for building contractors via in-house

tics operations. "Today is the era of the lean organization," Lounsbury says. "Turning to a third party may be the appropriate solution to a shortage of resources at your company. Many companies are turning to third parties to leverage their own scarce resources and improve their asset utilization at the same time."

3. Leaving logistics to specialists could ultimately save money. Outsourcing services to an expert in logistics could reduce costs, speed deliveries, encourage innovation, and raise customer satisfaction.

CON

1. If a company chooses to outsource logistics activities, it should retain responsibility for some functions. A parent company needs someone who can scrutinize the actions of third parties. Otherwise, these external suppliers operate with no accountability. "I only know of two firms that outsourced their total logistics," says William Tucker, president of Tucker Company, a transportation intermediary firm. "Neither exists today. In fact, I doubt whether anyone can cite any firm that outsourced its total logistics function to a third party and has survived and prospered for more than two years."
2. Outsourcing inevitably hurts employees. When a company decides to contract with outside suppliers, it often carries out internal layoffs. Eliminating in-house trucking fleets could also unfairly weaken or eliminate unions on the work site. Nortel cited a desire to bypass union influence as one reason for moving business to third-party truckers.

Summary

Any firm contemplating a move toward outsourcing should first conduct an internal audit to explore its present and future logistical demands. Once this exercise is complete, managers must carefully and fairly evaluate their firm's internal logistics branch. They should judge the in-house staff on the same basis as potential third-party suppliers. If a thorough analysis leaves a favorable impression of outsourcing, William Tucker gives this advice: Act conservatively and start slow.

Sources: William J. Holstein, "The New Economy," *U.S. News,* May 26, 1997, downloaded from http://www.usnews.com/, May 27, 1997; adapted from Sana Siwilop, "Outsourcing: Savings Are Just the Start," *Business Week,* May 13, 1996, pp. ENT 24–25; John A. Byrne, "Has Outsourcing Gone Too Far?" *Business Week,* April 1, 1996, pp. 26–28; and Lisa H. Harrington, "Should You Outsource?" *Inbound Logistics,* January 1996, pp. 94–102.

transportation services, including a fleet of 1,000 trucks. These customers demand fast, reliable order fulfillment, so Georgia-Pacific takes no chances with distribution to them. On the other hand, it ships via outside trucking firms and railroads to move raw materials to mills and to more price-sensitive customers like Home Depot. Although it sets different customer service standards for different market segments, Georgia-Pacific still coordinates logistics from a centralized operation. The company estimates it has cut its annual transportation bill from $1.1 billion to $770 million by segmenting customer service needs in this way.[12]

ELEMENTS OF THE PHYSICAL DISTRIBUTION SYSTEM

Designers of a physical distribution system begin by establishing acceptable levels of customer service. They then assemble physical distribution components in a way that will achieve this standard at the lowest possible total cost. This overall cost breaks down into five components: (1) transportation, (2) warehousing, (3) inventory control, (4) order processing, and (5) administrative and other handling costs. The components' relative shares of the total physical distribution cost are shown in Figure 16.4.

Transportation

Transportation costs represent the largest category of logistics-related expenses for most firms. In some companies, transportation accounts for 40 to 60 percent of the distribution costs incurred by businesses.[13] Moreover, for many products—particularly perishable ones—transportation

Marketing Dictionary

customer service standard A statement of goals and acceptable performance for the quality of service that a firm expects to deliver to its customers.

makes a central contribution to satisfactory customer service. South American marketers of orange juice concentrate, for example, need transportation services that provide refrigeration capabilities and reliable, on-time delivery to move their frozen products in a way that satisfies customers in North America and Europe. The ad in Figure 16.5 acknowledges this need and explains the personal commitment of Captain Nilton de Paula of the Brazilian shipping firm Aliança to meet it.

Many logistics managers have found the key to controlling their shipping costs in careful management of relationships with shipping firms. Wilson Sporting Goods sends sports equipment from its U.S. and Asian manufacturing plants to retailers in the United States, Europe, and Latin America. Effective oversight of this extensive distribution operation requires keen attention to costs and reliability. Wilson chooses its transportation methods and suppliers to accomplish this goal. Wilson sends shipments within the United States, for example, via Overnite, a trucking firm. Shipments between countries travel by air freight and cargo ships. By working with a limited number of shipping companies, Wilson can negotiate favorable rates as an important customer. Customer satisfaction is another benefit. In a recent survey, 89 percent of Wilson's retailers rated the company as best or above average for on-time shipments.[14]

Freight carriers set two basic types of rates: class and commodity rates. A **class rate** is a standard rate for a specific commodity moving between any pair of destinations. A carrier may charge a lower **commodity rate,** sometimes called a *special rate,* to a favored shipper as a reward for either regular business or a large-quantity shipment. Railroads and inland water carriers frequently reward customers in this way.

In addition, the railroad and motor carrier industries sometimes supplement this rate structure with *negotiated* or *contract* rates. This method of setting freight rates became popular following the deregulation of these industries in 1980, when shippers and carriers gained authority to negotiate rates for particular services. The two parties finalize terms of rates, services, and other variables and lay them out in a contract.

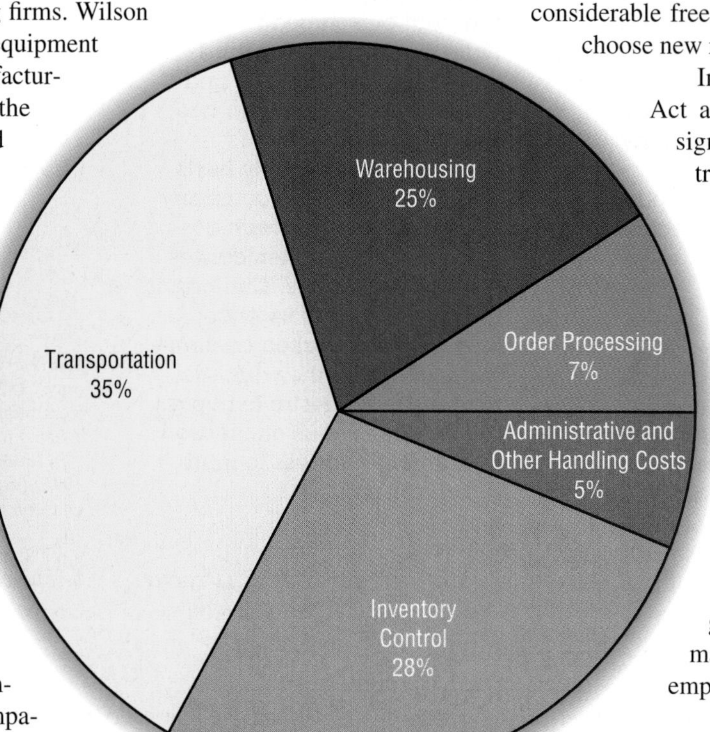
Warehousing
25%
Order Processing
7%
Administrative and
Other Handling Costs
5%
Inventory
Control
28%
Transportation
35%

Figure 16.4

Where the Physical Distribution Dollar Goes

Transportation Deregulation Congress has freed the transportation industry from many of the government restrictions that limited the pricing and customer service practices of transportation carriers. The deregulation of the U.S. transportation industry began in 1977 with the removal of regulations governing cargo air carriers not engaged in passenger transportation. The following year, the Airline Deregulation Act granted passenger airlines considerable freedom to establish fares and choose new routes.

In 1980, the Motor Carrier Act and the Staggers Rail Act significantly deregulated the trucking and railroad industries. These laws enabled transportation carriers to negotiate rates and services with shippers. Before deregulation, no truck carrier served all 48 contiguous U.S. states. Today, more than 4,000 carriers have that authority. In addition, the trucking industry now operates far more efficiently than it did under government regulation; many carriers have reduced empty mileage by two-thirds.

Overall, transportation deregulation has enhanced flexibility for transportation providers, allowing them to design services and rates to match shippers' unique needs. This new flexibility has brought with it real cost savings for U.S. manufacturers, distributors, and, ultimately, consumers. However, the new transportation environment has also increased the importance of physical distribution management for shippers, because the unregulated business now includes a complex and changing range of possibilities.

Classes of Carriers Freight carriers are classified as common, contract, and private carriers. Common carriers, some-times considered the backbone of the transportation industry, provide transportation services for-hire carriers to the general public. The government still regulates their rates and services, and they cannot conduct their operations without permission from the appropriate regulatory authority. Common carriers move freight via all modes of transport.

Contract carriers are for-hire transporters that do not offer their services to the general public. Instead, they establish specific contracts with individual customers and operate exclusively for particular industries (most commonly the motor freight industry). These carriers operate under much looser regulation than common carriers.

Figure 16.5 Aliança: A Shipper Committed to Customer Service

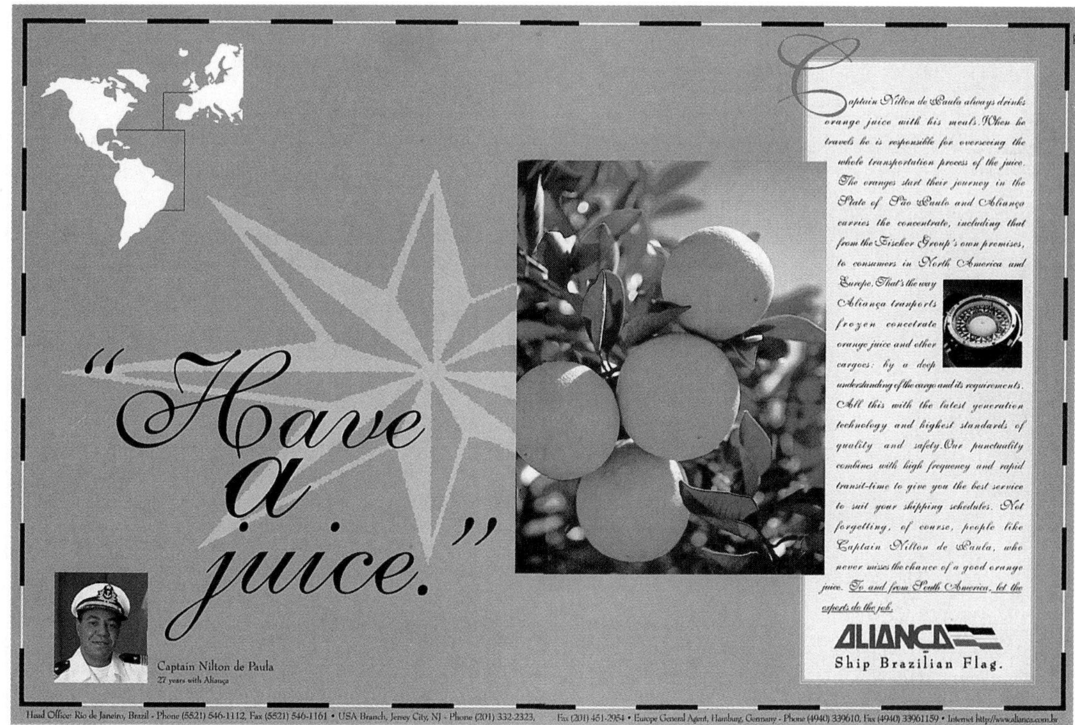
"Have a juice."
Captain Nilton de Paula
27 years with Aliança
Captain Nilton de Paula always drinks orange juice with his meals. When he travels he is responsible for overseeing the whole transportation process of the juice. The oranges start their journey in the State of São Paulo and Aliança carries the concentrate, including that from the Fischer Group's own premises, to consumers in North America and Europe. That's the way Aliança tranports frozen concetrate orange juice and other cargoes: by a deep understanding of the cargo and its requirements. All this with the latest generation technology and highest standards of quality and safety. Our punctuality combines with high frequency and rapid transit-time to give you the best service to suit your shipping schedules. Not forgetting, of course, people like Captain Nilton de Paula, who never misses the chance of a good orange juice. To and from South America, let the experts do the job.
ALIANCA
Ship Brazilian Flag.
Head Office: Rio de Janeiro, Brazil - Phone (5521) 546-1112, Fax (5521) 546-1161 • USA Branch, Jersey City, NJ - Phone (201) 332-2323, Fax (201) 451-2954 • Europe General Agent, Hamburg, Germany - Phone (4940) 339610, Fax (4940) 33961159 • Internet http://www.alianca.com.br

Private carriers do not offer services for hire. Instead, they transport freight only for particular firms, and traditional restrictions have prohibited them from soliciting other transportation business. Since they provide transportation services solely for internally generated freight, they observe no rate or service regulation. The Interstate Commerce Commission (ICC), a federal regulatory agency, permits private carriers to operate as common or contract carriers, as well. Many private carriers have taken advantage of this rule to operate their trucks fully loaded at all times.

Major Transportation Modes Logistics managers choose among five major transportation alternatives: railroads, motor carriers, water carriers, pipelines, and air freight. Each mode has its own unique characteristics. Logistics managers select the best options for their situations by matching these features to their specific transportation needs.

Railroads—The Nation's Leading Transporter Railroads continue to control the largest share of the freight business, as measured by ton-miles. The term *ton-mile* indicates shipping activity required to move 1 ton of freight 1 mile. Thus, a 3-ton shipment moved 8 miles equals 24 ton-miles. Rail shipments quickly rack up ton-miles because this mode provides the most efficient way to move bulky commodities over long distances. For instance, rail carriers transport huge quantities of coal, chemicals, grain, nonmetallic minerals, and lumber and wood products. Rail is also the primary transportation method for automobiles. Approximately 70 percent of the automobiles manufactured in the United States spend at least part of their trips from factories to car dealers' lots on rail cars.[15]

http://www.up.com/

In recent years, the rail industry has consolidated through mergers between large railroad companies. Recent mergers have combined the Burlington Northern with the

Marketing Dictionary

class rate A standard transportation rate established for shipments of a specific commodity between any pair of destinations.

commodity rate A special, favorable transportation rate granted by a carrier to a selected shipper as a reward for either regular business or a large-quantity shipment.

Figure 16.6 **Norfolk Southern: Innovating to Raise Its Service Standards**

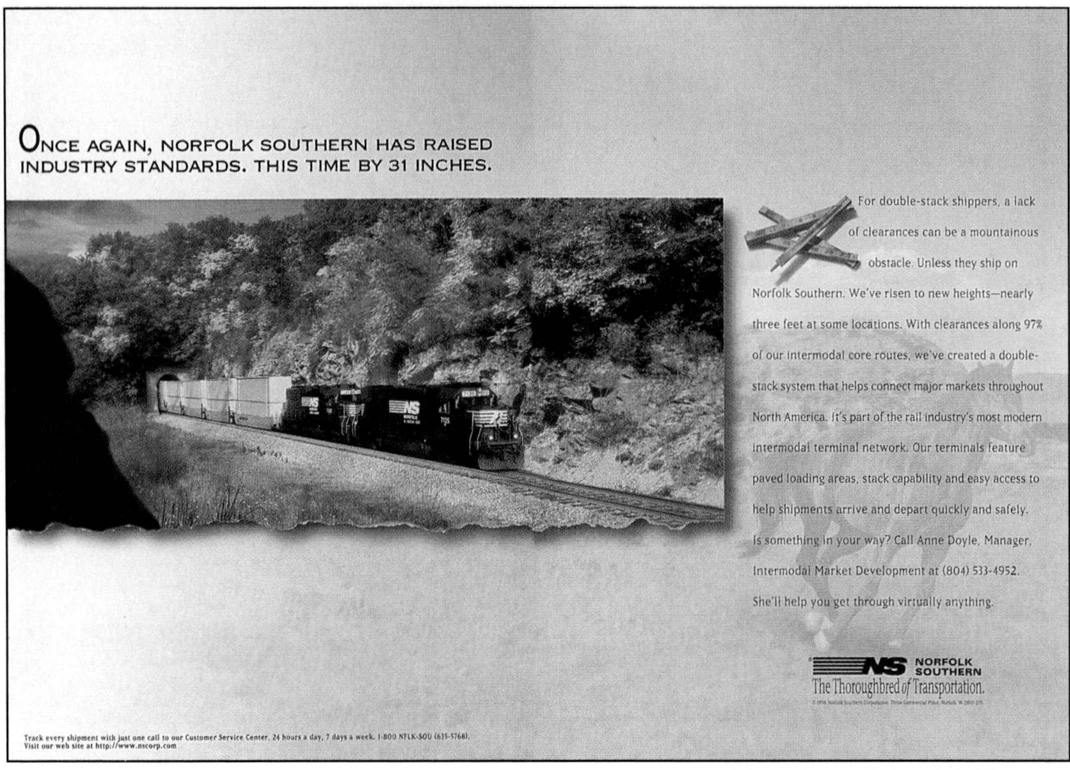
ONCE AGAIN, NORFOLK SOUTHERN HAS RAISED INDUSTRY STANDARDS. THIS TIME BY 31 INCHES.
For double-stack shippers, a lack of clearances can be a mountainous obstacle. Unless they ship on Norfolk Southern. We've risen to new heights—nearly three feet at some locations. With clearances along 97% of our intermodal core routes, we've created a double-stack system that helps connect major markets throughout North America. It's part of the rail industry's most modern intermodal terminal network. Our terminals feature paved loading areas, stack capability and easy access to help shipments arrive and depart quickly and safely. Is something in your way? Call Anne Doyle, Manager, Intermodal Market Development at (804) 533-4952. She'll help you get through virtually anything.
NS NORFOLK SOUTHERN
The Thoroughbred of Transportation.
Track every shipment with just one call to our Customer Service Center, 24 hours a day, 7 days a week. 1-800 NFLK-SOU (635-5768).
Visit our web site at http://www.nscorp.com

Santa Fe and the Union Pacific with the Southern Pacific. While such mergers create nationwide links to simplify shipping decisions, they also reduce shippers' power in rate negotiations.[16] However, over 500 railroads continue to serve limited geographic areas. These railroads, called *short-line railroads,* can offer useful transportation alternatives for regional shipments.[17]

The railroads have improved their service standards through a number of innovative concepts. Unit trains, run-through trains, intermodal (piggyback) operations, and double-stack container trains have substantially improved the efficiency and reduced the cost of rail transport services. The ad for Norfolk Southern Corp. in Figure 16.6 describes how the railroad continues to upgrade its service standards to accommodate intermodal, double-stack shipments throughout North America.

Unit trains carry much of the coal, grain, and other high-volume commodities shipped today, running back and forth between single loading points (such as a mine) and single destinations (such as a power plant) to deliver a single commodity. Run-through trains bypass intermediate terminals to speed up schedules. They work similarly to unit trains, but a run-through train may carry a variety of commodities.

In piggyback operations, highway trailers and containers ride on railroad flatcars, thus combining the long-haul capacity of the train with the door-to-door flexibility of the truck. CSX is developing an "Iron Highway" system that eliminates the need for special equipment and reinforcement for flatcars to carry trailers and containers. CSX's Iron Highway flatcars would allow regular trailers to drive on and off. Through this innovation, CSX hopes to position itself as an alternative to truck travel via road for trips of under 500 miles. The company says the benefits for shippers will include fuel savings and enhanced flexibility.[18] In contrast, a double-stack container train pulls special rail cars equipped with bathtub-shaped wells so they can carry two containers stacked on top of one another. By nearly doubling train capacity and slashing costs, this system offers enormous advantages to rail customers. Double-stack shipments probably will increase in the future.

Railroads have also added new design features to their cargo cars to improve service for customers. For example, the UniversalCar, made by Thrall, is a bilevel automobile carrier. The rail car totally encloses autos so they arrive cleaner than those shipped on open rail cars. The new system also smoothes the ride, reducing the risk of damage to autos en route.[19]

Motor Carriers—Flexible and Growing The trucking industry has grown dramatically over recent decades. It offers some important advantages over the other transportation modes, including relatively fast shipments and consistent service for both large and small shipments. Motor carriers concentrate on shipping manufactured products, while railroads typically haul bulk shipments of raw materials. Motor carriers, therefore, receive greater revenue per ton shipped, since the cost for shipping raw materials is higher than for shipping manufactured products.

Technology has also improved the efficiency of trucking. Many trucking firms now track their fleets via satellite communications systems. Others install sophisticated computer equipment in their trucks, allowing dispatchers to make last-minute changes in pickup and delivery instructions.[20] The Internet is also adding new features to motor carrier service. Shippers who transport products via

http://www.cltl.com/

Chemical Leaman Tank Lines, for example, can track the exact locations of their shipments by visiting the carrier's Web site. The company's satellite tracking system contacts each truck twice every hour and automatically updates the information on the Web site.[21]

Some motor carriers specialize in transporting certain types of goods. In addition, some also provide a variety of logistics services. CSI/Crown, Inc., for example, specializes in meeting the carpeting industry's shipping needs. The firm moves finished carpeting from mills to its own warehouses. As orders come in, the carpet manufacturers alert CSI/Crown, and the company cuts the correct sizes and distributes the carpet via small trucks.[22]

Although many firms have encountered cost barriers trying to maintain and operate private fleets of trucks, others have found competitive advantages in internal transportation capabilities. Some private fleets function as rolling warehouses that efficiently deliver raw materials and finished goods to customers, increasing overall service and customer satisfaction. In fact, businesspeople cite customer service as the primary reason for maintaining private truck fleets. One firm that operates its own motor carrier service, California poultry producer Foster Farms, delivers chickens to supermarkets throughout the region in 130 refrigerated trucks.[23] The firm stresses this capability in its advertising, touting Foster Farms chicken as fresher than competing brands because the firm moves it more quickly to supermarkets.

Figure 16.7 **Water Carriers: Efficient Transportation between International Markets**

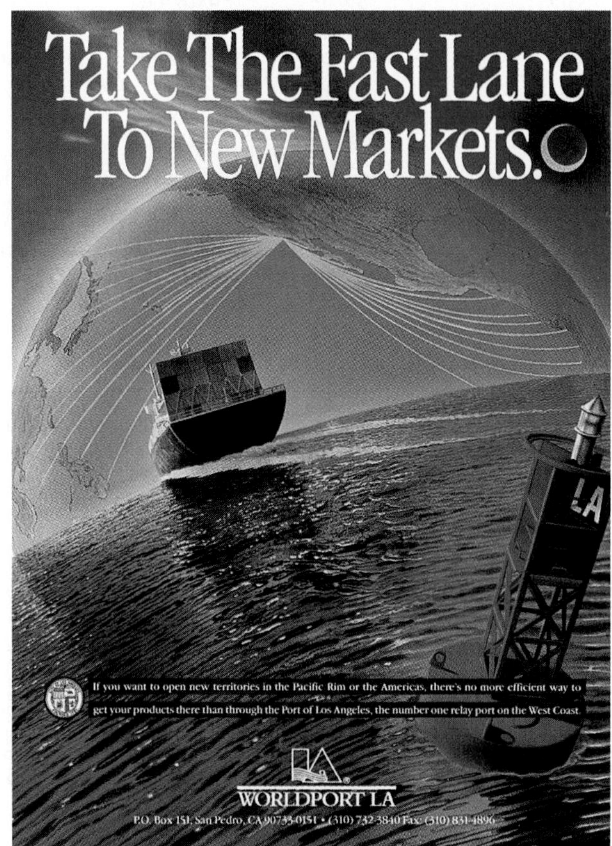
Take The Fast Lane
To New Markets.
LA
If you want to open new territories in the Pacific Rim or the Americas, there's no more efficient way to get your products there than through the Port of Los Angeles, the number one relay port on the West Coast.
WORLDPORT LA
P.O. Box 151, San Pedro, CA 90733-0151 • (310) 732-3840 Fax: (310) 831-4896

Water Carriers—Slow but Inexpensive Two basic types of transport methods move products over water: inland or barge lines and oceangoing, deepwater ships. Barge lines efficiently transport bulky, low-unit-value commodities such as grain, gravel, lumber, sand, and steel. A typical lower Mississippi River barge line may stretch more than a quarter-mile and 200 feet across.

Oceangoing ships operate in the Great Lakes, transporting goods among U.S. port cities, and in international commerce. Oceangoing ships carry a growing stream of containerized freight between West Coast ports such as Worldport LA, promoted in the ad in Figure 16.7, and destinations in China and other Pacific Rim countries.

Shippers that transport goods via water carriers incur very low costs compared to the rates for other transportation modes. Standardized, modular shipping containers maximize savings by limiting loading, unloading, and other handling.

Although ocean carriers have earned a reputation as a slow mode of transportation, technology is speeding service. The new FastShip ocean carrier design facilitates relatively rapid transportation of time-sensitive shipments. The FastShip's special hull lifts the vessel above the surface of the water. Once FastShips become operational, they will be able to move cargo in 5 to 7 days versus the average of 14 to 35 days now required by traditional cargo ships.[24]

Pipelines—Specialized Transporters Although the pipeline industry ranks third after railroads and motor carriers in ton-miles transported, many people scarcely recognize its existence. More than 214,000 miles of pipelines crisscross the United States in an extremely efficient network for transporting natural gas and oil products. Oil pipelines carry two types of commodities: crude (unprocessed) oil and refined products, such as gasoline, jet fuel, and kerosene. So-called *slurry pipelines* carry coal in suspension after it has been ground up into a powder and mixed with water.

Table 16.1 Comparison of Transport Modes

Mode	Speed	Dependability in Meeting Schedules	Frequency of Shipments	Availability in Different Locations	Flexibility in Handling	Cost
Rail	Average	Average	Low	Low	High	Average
Water	Very slow	Average	Very low	Limited	Very high	Very low
Truck	Fast	High	High	Very extensive	Average	High
Pipeline	Slow	High	High	Very limited	Very low	Low
Air	Very fast	High	Average	Average	Low	Very high

Although pipelines offer low-maintenance, dependable methods of transportation, a number of characteristics limit their applications. They even have fewer locations than water carriers, and they can accommodate shipments of only a small number of products. Finally, pipelines represent a relatively slow method of transportation; liquids travel through them at an average speed of only 3 to 4 miles per hour.

Air Freight—Fast but Expensive The significant growth in shipping volume handled by air carriers will probably continue as freight haulers seek to satisfy increased customer demand for fast delivery. In fact, forecasters expect the cargo loads of air carriers to double by 2013. Among the routes likely to see the greatest increase in air cargo traffic are those between Europe and Asia and within Asia itself.[25]

Table 16.1 compares the five transport modes on several operating characteristics. Although all shippers judge reliability, speed, and cost in choosing the most appropriate transportation methods, they assign varying importance to specific criteria when shipping different goods. For example, while motor carriers rank highest in availability in different locations, shippers of petroleum products frequently choose the lowest-ranked alternative, pipelines, for their low cost. Examples of the types of goods most often handled by the various transport modes include the following:

- *Railroads.* Lumber, iron and steel, coal, automobiles, grain, chemicals
- *Motor carriers.* Clothing, furniture and fixtures, lumber and plastic products, food products, leather and leather products, machinery
- *Water carriers.* Fuel, oil, coal, chemicals, minerals, petroleum products
- *Pipelines.* Oil, diesel fuel, jet fuel, kerosene, natural gas
- *Air carriers.* Flowers, technical instruments and machinery, high-priced specialty products

Freight Forwarders and Supplemental Carriers Freight forwarders act as transportation intermediaries, consolidating shipments to gain lower rates for their customers. The transport rates on less-than-truckload (LTL) and less-than-carload (LCL) shipments often double the per-unit rates on truckload (TL) and carload (CL) shipments. Freight forwarders charge less than the higher rates, but more than the lower rates. They profit by consolidating shipments from multiple customers until they can ship at TL and CL rates. The customers gain two advantages from these services: lower costs on small shipments and faster delivery service than they could achieve with their own LTL and LCL shipments.

Freight forwarders offer particularly beneficial help to small companies. Michigan-based Motorkote is a 16-employee company that sells industrial lubricants worldwide. When Motorkote receives an order, it calls ABF, a freight forwarder, which quickly determines the best way to deliver the product. ABF also handles all customs paperwork and solves any problems that arise along the distribution chain. Motorkote President Dave Persell says the service allows his company to compete in the global marketplace by providing efficient and professional transportation of goods.[26]

In addition to the transportation options reviewed so far, a logistics manager can also ship products via a number of auxiliary, or supplemental, carriers that specialize in small shipments. These carriers include bus freight services, United Parcel Service, Federal Express, DHL International, and the U.S. Postal Service.

Intermodal Coordination Transportation companies emphasize specific modes, and therefore serve certain kinds of customers, but they sometimes combine their services to give shippers the service and cost advantages of each. Piggyback service, mentioned in the section on rail transport, is the most widely used form of intermodal coordination. *Birdyback* service, another form of intermodal coordination, sends motor carriers to pick up a shipment from and deliver it to local destinations, while an air carrier

Figure 16.8 Offering Customers Intermodal Coordination

EMERY WORLDWIDE
Contoured to fit your global shipping needs.
At Emery Worldwide, providing logistics solutions tailored to your individual business is our way of helping you answer the competitive challenges of the global marketplace.
We call it *Customer-ization:* shaping our capabilities and schedules to meet your specific global shipping needs, giving you the flexibility to respond to market changes overnight.
To increase efficiencies throughout your global operations, we provide on-line worldwide routing and tracking with our EMCON system, as well as on-line customs clearance by Emery Customs Brokers.
Our advanced EDI capabilities help you minimize paperwork and speed communications. And QuickSource, our fully-integrated logistics and warehousing program, cuts your inventory costs and gets replacement parts to your customers in hours instead of days.
Everything we do is backed by over 50 years of worldwide experience. So, whether you're shipping five-pound packages or heavy freight of any size and shape, call Emery Worldwide for logistics solutions on a global scale. We offer a better fit all the way around. 1-800 HI EMERY (1-800-443-6379).
EMERY WORLDWIDE
A CF Company
WE PUT YOU MILES AHEAD

takes it between airports near those locations. *Fishyback* service sets up a similar intermodal coordination system between motor carriers and water carriers.

Intermodal transportation is growing. In a recent year, more than 9 million rail-truck shipments moved across the United States alone.[27] Consolidated Freightways, Inc., offers customers complete intermodal coordination. The company deploys more than 52,000 tractors and trailers, 14,000 trucks, and 90 jet air freighters. It operates CF MotorFreight, Con-Way Rail Transportation, Menlo Logistics, and Emery Worldwide, promoted in the ad in Figure 16.8. These CF companies have implemented a network of computers and EDI technology to help customers minimize paperwork, reduce inventories, and speed products to market.

Intermodal transportation generally gives shippers faster service and lower rates than either mode could match individually, since each method carries freight in its most efficient way. However, some customers of intermodal shipping have found that the method requires close coordination.

Continental Mills, Inc., a lumber supplier in Seattle, ships nearly 80 percent of its freight via intermodal services. Although the company is satisfied with the transit times it receives, intermodal methods do not always provide satisfactory reliability. Continental Mills' director of distribution works closely with carriers and end customers to control delays in loading and unloading.[28] Many shippers, however, expect intermodal performance to continue to improve. A study conducted by the Intermodal Association of North America and the National Industrial Transportation League showed that 72 percent of shippers expect improvement in the service levels of intermodal firms.[29]

Multimodal Transportation Companies Recognizing the need for coordination of intermodal shipping, multimodal transportation companies have formed to bring combined activities within single operations. Piggyback service generally joins two separate companies—a railroad and a trucking company. A multimodal firm provides intermodal service through its own internal transportation resources. Shippers benefit because the single service assumes responsibility from origin to destination. This unification prevents arguments over which carrier delayed a shipment or who caused loss or damage.

In addition, major U.S. carriers are increasingly looking toward vertical integration to provide coordinated door-to-door service. United Parcel Service (UPS) is a good example. UPS offers global transportation services that move shipments via a variety of transportation options. The firm operates its own fleet of air cargo planes along with an extensive fleet of domestic trucks and trailers. For international deliveries, UPS contracts with local ground carriers. Trucks pick up shipments in the United States, aircraft transport them to airports overseas, and motor carriers deliver them to their local destinations. In addition to transportation, UPS also offers in-house customs and brokerage services to expedite delivery.

MARKETING HALL OF SHAME

Western Digital's Delivery Dilemmas

Employees in Western Digital Corp.'s transportation department once made relatively simple shipping decisions. The company's business led to straightforward freight requirements: Western Digital packed its computer disk drives and other equipment into boxes and then sent them to various manufacturers and distributors, which paid for the shipments upon receipt.

But this routine didn't last. Continuous change in the computer industry forced Western Digital to begin to ship products directly to retailers. Unfortunately, retailers set picky conditions about how their freight must arrive. Western Digital's in-house traffic department failed to keep up with retailers' demands, resulting in serious customer-service problems.

"The transition into the retail market was rough at first," concedes Cindy L. Hogan, director of logistics and trade compliance at Western Digital. "You have to make sure your products are on the shelf for the retailers' sales. If someone goes out to buy your product and it's not there, they're going to buy someone else's."

Recognizing its inadequacies, Western Digital hoped that an outside shipping company would step in and save the situation. But that didn't happen. For three years, Western Digital fielded complaints from customers around the world about mismanagement of their shipments. "The third party never quite filled the role of a traffic department, and we were essentially paying these people the same as we would have for an in-house staff," Hogan observes. "Third parties are the wave of the future, but we didn't go about it the right way," Hogan adds. "We should have been more cautious with whom we chose, instead of accepting them only by their word."

Unpredictable transportation costs complicated Western Digital's distribution woes. After the firm agreed upon certain rates, shippers would tack on extra fees for such adjustments as unforeseen administrative costs and currency fluctuations.

Warehousing

Marketers' products flow through two types of warehouses: storage and distribution warehouses. A **storage warehouse** holds goods for moderate to long periods in an attempt to balance supply and demand for producers and purchasers. They provide most valuable support to logistics managers when their firms sell products with seasonal supply and demand swings. A **distribution warehouse** assembles and redistributes goods, keeping them moving as much as possible. Many distribution warehouses or centers physically store goods for less than 24 hours before shipping them on to customers.

Logistics managers have attempted to save on transportation costs by developing central distribution centers. A manufacturer located in Philadelphia could send direct shipments to customers in the Illinois-Wisconsin-Indiana area, but if each customer placed small orders, the shipper would pay high transportation charges. Instead, it might send a single, large, consolidated shipment to a *break-bulk center*—a central distribution center that breaks down large shipments into several smaller ones and delivers them to individual customers in the area. The Philadelphia firm's logistics manager might set up such a break-bulk center in Chicago to serve customers in surrounding states.

Conversely, a *make-bulk center* consolidates several small shipments into one large shipment and delivers it to a single destination. For example, a large firm may operate several satellite production facilities in the western United States, each one shipping its output to a storage warehouse in Dallas. This arrangement might, however, result in a large number of small, expensive shipments. Instead, the firm could create a make-bulk center in Nevada to receive shipments from suppliers in surrounding areas and consolidate all Dallas-bound deliveries into a single, economical shipment.

Automated Warehouse Technology Logistics managers can cut distribution costs and improve customer service dramatically by automating their warehouse systems. Although automation technology represents an expensive investment, it can provide major savings for high-volume distributors such as grocery chains by minimizing human labor. Instead of a human worker, a computerized system might store orders, choose the correct number of cases, and move them in the desired sequence to loading docks. This kind of warehouse system reduces labor costs, worker injuries, pilferage, fires, and breakage.

Some firms may even gain strategic advantages from their automated warehouse facilities. Electronics Boutique

For its next step, Western Digital hired a consultant, who injected some common sense into the company's shipping operations. The consultant recommended that the company require all freight forwarders to bid competitively on its shipping business. At the time, Western Digital was dealing with about a half-dozen forwarders throughout the world, but none of them had earned the business through competitive bidding. During the new bidding process, Western Digital was amazed to discover that some forwarders offered to include administrative services for which it had paid extra in the past.

Ultimately, the company selected two forwarders—LEP Profit International in Marietta, Georgia, and Air Express International in Darien, Connecticut. The company estimates that it shaved 10 percent to 12 percent from its shipping bill by settling on this pair of forwarders.

"We needed seasoned logistics partners with a global network, superior technology, a grasp of our business, and an ability to develop innovative solutions leveraging those capabilities," Hogan says. "For the first time, we have more visibility for managing our shipping information. We're basically holding to a timely delivery system."

Lastly, to better improve its freight operations, Western Digital scrutinized the packaging for its computer products. Reengineering the packaging triggered dramatic results. With simpler, lighter, and cheaper materials than it had previously used, Western Digital reduced its packaging inventory by 65 percent, cut labor costs, and chopped freight expenses by 52 percent.

QUESTIONS FOR CRITICAL THINKING

1. **What potential dangers does a shipper risk by choosing a third party to handle its transportation needs? How can the shipper avoid these problems?**
2. **What lessons could other companies learn from Western Digital's mistakes?**

Sources: "WDC Comfortable with Range of Wall Street Forecasts for June Quarter," June 3, 1997, downloaded from http://www.wdc.com/, June 4, 1997; Troy Merrell, "Redesigned Package Saves Time and Money," Press Release, Universal Protective Packaging, Inc. downloaded from http://www.uppi.com/, February 9, 1997; Nick Turner, "Drive Maker Western Digital in High Gear for Summertime," *Investor's Business Daily,* August 6, 1996, downloaded from America Online, February 8, 1997; and Chris Gillis, "Western Digital Learned from Mistakes," *American Shipper,* April 1996, pp. 41–46.

sells video games, and computer software through 527 stores in the United States, Canada, and the United Kingdom. The firm knows that video games have extremely short life spans. A new game generates the bulk of its sales in the first two weeks after release. This characteristic creates a need for speedy transportation.

http://www.ebworld.com/

Electronics Boutique automated its 120,000-square-foot warehouse, located in West Chester, Pennsylvania, in an effort to ensure that it quickly receives, processes, and ships games and other merchandise. When a new shipment from a manufacturer arrives in the warehouse, a computerized order management program automatically moves the goods inside in less than 90 minutes. When stores request new stock, an automated system generates the order. A bar-coded label on each shipping carton allows the system to monitor its travels through the warehouse. As the box moves along conveyor belts, workers use bar-code scanners to read the label which tells them the exact contents of the order. Finally, the boxes are sealed and shipped to the stores.

Warehouse automation plays a central role in Electronics Boutique's marketing and merchandising strategy. The company's executives believe that the system helps them to compete by maximizing the product life cycles of new releases.[30]

Warehouse Locations Every company must make a major logistics decision when it determines the number and

Marketing Dictionary

storage warehouse A warehouse that holds goods for moderate to long periods prior to shipment, usually to buffer seasonal demand.

distribution warehouse A facility designed to assemble and then redistribute goods in a way that facilitates rapid movement to purchasers.

Figure 16.9 **Campbell Soup: Controlling Inventory to Spread Cost Effectiveness along the Entire Supply Chain**

BEHIND
EVERY ONE OF
THESE CANS
IS A GREAT
RECIPE.

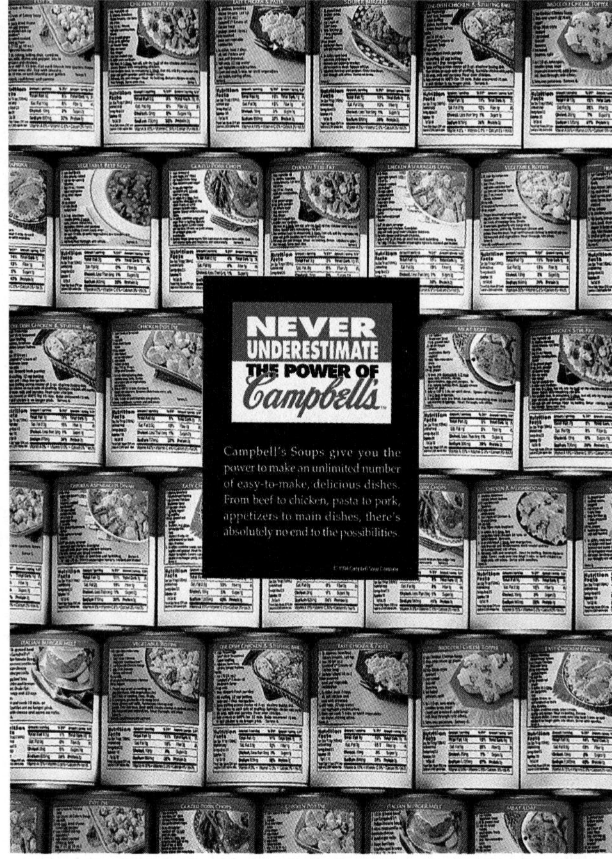
NEVER
UNDERESTIMATE
THE POWER OF
Campbell's
Campbell's Soups give you the power to make an unlimited number of easy-to-make, delicious dishes. From beef to chicken, pasta to pork, appetizers to main dishes, there's absolutely no end to the possibilities.

locations of its storage facilities. The two categories of costs influence this choice: (1) warehousing and materials-handling costs and (2) delivery costs from warehouses to customers. Large facilities offer economies of scale in facilities and materials-handling systems; per-unit costs for these systems decrease as volume increases. Delivery costs, on the other hand, rise as the distance from warehouse to customer increases.

Warehouse location also affects customer service. Businesses must place their storage and distribution facilities in locations from which they can meet customer demands for product availability and delivery times. The location of a warehouse may also influence a firm's ability to provide value-added services to customers.[31]

In locating distribution and storage facilities, firms must also consider population and employment trends. For example, growth in major metropolitan market areas throughout the southern and western United States have caused some firms to reevaluate their location strategies. Although New York, Los Angeles, and Chicago continue to function as the country's main distribution centers, many smaller Sunbelt metropolitan areas now compete for new distribution operations. To attract these companies, state and local governments are offering tax breaks, subsidies for land purchases, and other incentives to businesses.[32]

Inventory Control Systems

Inventory control captures a large share of a logistics manager's attention, because companies need to maintain enough inventory to meet customer demand without incurring unneeded costs to carry excess inventory. In a recent year, for example, U.S. businesses invested $960 billion in manufacturing and retail inventory. They spent over $239 billion to carry this inventory.[33] To avoid unnecessary costs, logistics managers strive to keep inventories at minimum levels. Still, 43 percent of the companies surveyed in a recent study admitted holding the same or greater amounts of inventory than they held five years earlier.[34]

Some firms attempt to keep inventory levels under control by implementing the Japanese concept of just-in-time production. **Just-in-time (JIT)** methods seek to minimize manufacturing and inventory costs by providing essential inputs to production processes in a timely manner. JIT requires manufacturers to form tight partnerships with their suppliers. For example, Setex honors Honda's rigid delivery requirements in order to sell its automobile seats. Setex's deliveries must coincide with Honda's production line requirements. If a white Honda is ready for seat installation, Setex must place the correct seat at Honda's plant shortly before the need arises. Additionally, Honda prefers not to hold any seats in its inventory. As work on a new vehicle begins, Setex alerts its factory to begin building the necessary seats. Within a four-hour window it produces the seats and ships them to the Honda plant 55 miles away. To accomplish this challenging task, the Setex factory has eliminated time-wasting activities and automated most of its manufacturing process. By meeting Honda's production demands, Setex earned an exclusive contract to supply automobile seats to the automaker's Ohio plant.[35]

http://www.honda.com/

JIT principles can also guide control systems for finished-goods inventories. For example, Campbell Soup Company has developed a continuous product replenishment system triggered by consumer purchases of the many soup varieties it produces, as shown in the ad in Figure 16.9. Campbell's electronic ordering system routes shipments from its manufacturing plants to replenish inventory at food retailers' warehouses at the same steady rate as consumers take products off the shelf. The just-in-time delivery system supports efficient control of costs across the supply chain, saving money for retailers and attracting sales for Campbell.

Like other logistics tasks, inventory control can help a firm to build a competitive advantage. Consider how a computerized inventory control system helps Mother's Work, a retailer of maternity clothing. The chain's inventory system tracks every garment in its distribution centers and all 450 stores. Daily updates report which items are selling, where inventory is in transit, and how long it will take to replenish stock. This information gives Mother's Work a jump on trends in fashions, styles, and even color preferences. The data guides the company's systems for reordering stock and designing new products. Acting on the data, the firm can move new ideas from design to store shelves in less than one month. Most other retailers order inventory six months in advance.[36]

Order Processing

Like inventory control, order processing directly affects the firm's ability to meet its customer service standards. A company may have to compensate for inefficiencies in its order processing system by shipping products via costly transportation modes or by maintaining large inventories at many expensive field warehouses.

Order processing typically consists of four major activities: (1) a credit check; (2) recording the sale, which involves recordkeeping tasks such as crediting a sales representative's commission account; (3) making appropriate accounting entries; and (4) locating ordered products, shipping them, and adjusting inventory records. An order for an item that is not available for shipment produces a **stockout.** A firm's order-processing system must advise affected customers of a stockout and offer a choice of alternative actions.

As in other areas of physical distribution, technological innovations improve efficiency in order processing. Master Lock makes built-in locks for school lockers and combination padlocks. For many years, the company struggled with an outdated order system driven by manual entry and verification of orders as they arrived. These laborious activities slowed order fulfillment. Recently, however, Master Lock automated its ordering process. Many customers now interact directly with the Master Lock system via electronic data interchange (EDI). The ordering system tracks each customer's order and includes simple functions for making changes. Additional automation in the firm's warehouse helps workers to find and ship orders using handheld bar-code scanners. Just seven months after installing the new system, Master Lock shipped the largest number of orders in its history without having to hire additional staff.[37]

Protective Packaging and Materials Handling

Logistics managers arrange and control activities for moving products within plants, warehouses, and transportation

Marketing Dictionary

just-in-time (JIT) system A production control system designed to minimize manufacturing and inventory costs by providing essential inputs to production processes in a timely manner.

stockout An order for a product that is unavailable for shipment or sale.

terminals, which together comprise the **materials handling** system. Two important concepts influence many materials handling choices: unitizing and containerization.

Unitizing initiatives seek to combine as many packages as possible into each load that moves within or outside a facility. Logistics managers prefer to handle materials on *pallets* (platforms, generally made of wood, on which goods are transported). Unitizing systems often lash materials in place with steel bands or *shrink packaging*. A shrink package surrounds a batch of materials with a sheet of plastic which shrinks after heating, securely holding individual pieces together. Unitizing promotes efficient materials handling, because each package requires little labor to move, packages rapidly carry large batches of materials, and securing the materials together minimizes damage and pilferage.

Logistics managers extend the same concept through **containerization**—combining several unitized loads. A container is typically a steel box 8 feet wide, and 10, 20, 30, or 40 feet long. Such a container shifts easily between transport modes. A container of oil rig parts, for example, can be loaded in Tulsa and trucked to Kansas City, where rail facilities place it on a high-speed, run-through train to New York City. The port facilities then load it on a ship to Saudi Arabia.

In addition to the benefits outlined for unitizing, containerization also markedly reduces the time required to load and unload ships. Busy ports often unload enormous container ships in less than 24 hours. Containers limit in-transit damage to freight, because individual packages pass through few handling systems en route to purchasers.

Marketing Dictionary

materials handling The set of activities that move production inputs and other goods within plants, warehouses, and transportation terminals.

unitizing The process of combining individual materials into large loads for easy handling.

containerization The process of combining several unitized loads into a single, well-protected load.

ACHIEVEMENT CHECK SUMMARY

Reread the learning goals that follow, and consider the questions for each goal. Answering these questions will reinforce your grasp of the most important concepts in the chapter and allow you to check how well you have achieved these learning goals. Where a blank appears before a question, answer with *T* or *F;* for multiple-choice questions, circle the letter of the correct answer.

Objective 16.1: Explain the role of logistics in an effective marketing strategy.

1. ___ Logistics helps marketers to fulfill their promises by bringing products from factories to customers.

2. ___ The term *value chain* refers to (a) the price a supplier charges; (b) the value added to a good as it moves along the supply chain; (c) the value or benefit that customers perceive in a particular product.

3. ___ Businesses work hard to reduce logistics costs, because these expenses represent nearly half of overall marketing expenses.

Objective 16.2: Identify and compare the major components of a physical distribution system.

1. ___ A physical distribution system seldom influences customer satisfaction.

2. ___ Businesses must carefully manage their relationships with shipping firms.

3. ___ A physical distribution system can function effectively only through an organized relationship among the firm's production, finance, and marketing functions.

4. ___ A business should set the same customer service standards for all customers.

Objective 16.3: Outline the suboptimization problem in logistics.

1. ___ Logistics managers seek to provide a high level of customer service regardless of cost.

2. ___ Suboptimization is a condition in which the manager of each logistics function attempts to maximize customer service regardless of cost.

3. ___ Suboptimization describes a firm's inability to provide good customer service while keeping costs at a minimum.

Objective 16.4: Explain the impact of transportation deregulation on logistics activities.

1. ___ Deregulation has freed transportation companies to provide more flexible services than they could manage under tight regulatory control.

2. ___ Deregulated transportation firms can match their prices to shippers' needs.
3. ___ The new transportation environment has complicated physical distribution management.

Objective 16.5: Compare the major transportation alternatives on the basis of speed, dependability, cost, frequency of shipments, availability in different locations, and flexibility in handling products.

1. ___ Railroads offer the most suitable transportation services for (a) small package shipments; (b) bulk shipments of raw materials; (c) shipments that need to travel only short distances.
2. ___ Motor carriers generally move goods slowly.
3. ___ A cargo ship represents a very expensive option for transporting goods.
4. ___ Air freight carriers can help shippers meet their needs for rapid delivery times.

Objective 16.6: Discuss how transportation intermediaries and combined transportation modes can improve physical distribution.

1. ___ A freight forwarder is (a) a transportation firm that specializes in moving heavy materials; (b) a transportation intermediary that consolidates shipments to earn lower rates than those that individual shippers would pay; (c) a third-party firm that handles logistics management for another firm.
2. ___ Two or more transport modes often combine their capabilities to give shippers the service and cost advantages of each in a process called (a) contract logistics; (b) intermodal coordination; (c) suboptimization.

Students: See the solutions section located on page S-3 to check your responses to the Achievement Check Summary.

Key Terms

logistics	class rate
physical distribution	commodity rate
supply (value) chain	storage warehouse
value-added service	distribution warehouse
third-party (contract) logistics firm	just-in-time (JIT) system
system	stockout
suboptimization	materials handling
maquiladora	unitizing
customer service standard	containerization

Review Questions

1. Why have most companies left logistics as one of the last areas in their operations for careful study and improvement?
2. Outline the basic reasons for the increased attention to logistics management. How has this been influenced by the emergence of a global marketplace?
3. Describe the basic logistics objectives of a firm. Compare and contrast them to the logistics objectives in a military operation like the U.N. peacekeeping efforts in the former Yugoslavia.
4. Explain the contribution of customer service standards to a firm's success. Why are companies today increasing their emphasis on customer service?
5. Who should accept ultimate responsibility for determining customer service standards? Explain. Do you agree or disagree with this statement: An orientation toward customer service should permeate all levels of an organization.
6. Outline the basic strengths and weaknesses of each transportation mode. What types of shipments suit the strengths of each mode?
7. What services do freight forwarders offer to their customers? Under what circumstances would a business want these services?
8. Identify the major forms of intermodal coordination, and give an example of a good for which each offers special advantages. Why have piggyback rail cars become so popular?
9. What considerations should influence the location decision for a new distribution warehouse? What cost trade-offs must a company consider in its location decision?
10. Explain the advantages and potential problems of the just-in-time system of inventory control. Relate your answer to the need to control inventory carrying costs.

Discussion Questions

1. Explain why the study of logistics provides a classic example of the systems approach to business problems.
2. Suggest the most appropriate method for transporting each listed product. Defend your choices.
   a. Iron ore
   b. Cheerios
   c. Heavy earth-moving equipment
   d. Crude oil
   e. Peaches
   f. Lumber
3. Which mode of transportation seems likely to experience the greatest ton-mile percentage growth during the next ten years? Why?
4. Macy's Herald Square flagship store in midtown New York City encountered difficulty getting inventory from its New Jersey distribution center to the store's display floor. "The backlog was terrible," says one Macy's executive. Inventory arrived at the store all day long, and stock people could not keep up with the flow. At any one time, 40 to 50 loaded trucks waited at the distribution center to deliver goods to the store. Another 15 to 20 truckloads sat on the store's reserve floor waiting to reach the sales floor. As a result, salespeople often spent time

stocking new merchandise instead of serving customers. Sometimes, the system's inefficiency prevented advertised sale merchandise from reaching store displays until after the sales had ended.[38] Discuss how Macy's logistics problems affected the store's marketing ability. What recommendations would you make to smooth the flow of inventory from warehouse to sales floor? What benefits would these improvements provide for Macy's? For Macy's customers?

5. Analyze the concept of value-added services as it applies to logistics management. How do improvements in technology like automated warehousing, computerized inventory tracking, order placement, and fulfillment systems relate to the demand for value-added services?

'netWork

1. This chapter discussed *maquiladoras*, assembly plants located in Mexico near the U.S. border. Many companies that provide services to these plants maintain sites on the Web. Locate several of these Web pages. What services do these companies offer? What unique characteristic of these operations requires special services? Why do firms set up *maquiladoras?* How do you think NAFTA has affected these plants?

2. Substantial changes in technology have powerfully influenced logistics management. One of these is the global positioning system (GPS). Find information about GPS technology on the Web and answer the following questions:

- **a.** How does GPS technology work?
- **b.** Why was it developed?
- **c.** How does it contribute to logistics management?
- **d.** What further applications of GPS do you foresee?

3. Just-in-time inventory management is one area that has transformed many supplier-manufacturer relationships. Many companies that provide software for JIT environments maintain Internet sites such as

http://www.syspro.com/
http://www.agamasoft.com/

Visit these Web sites or locate others, and answer the following questions: What processes must a JIT system carefully control? What are the biggest problems that can disrupt a JIT system? How can JIT software help to prevent these problems?

VIDEO CASE 16

LEVERAGING THE LINKS OF LOGISTICS

With revenues of more than $20 billion, Dow Chemical Company is the fifth largest chemical producer in the world. Dow manufactures and supplies more than 2,500 product families, including chemicals, plastics, agricultural products, and environmental services. Most of Dow's products become raw material inputs by business customers.

Dow produces chemicals at 400 processing plants in more than 30 countries. The production process for chemicals involves pumping materials in gas or liquid form out of storage tanks along many pipelines into mixing tanks, where chemical reactions generate the desired products. After later distillation or purification in a tower, pumps move the finished products by pipeline to storage tanks.

Dow's logistics system links the processing plants to business customers worldwide. From its storage tanks, Dow delivers products to buyers via many transportation modes. Oceangoing vessels move products between continents, and barges transport them along rivers and seacoasts. On land, tanker trucks move small shipments short distances, while railroads move large shipments long distances in tanker and hopper cars.

Transporting hazardous chemicals is just one of many challenges Dow faces in continually improving its logistics system. "The real key to logistics is meeting all customers' needs by having the right product at the right place at the right time," says Bill Fillmore, supply chain project leader. In North America, Dow spends over $1 billion a year on logistics activities. Improving logistics provides critical help in maintaining Dow's ability to compete, because improvements enhance customer service, reduce costs, and increase company profits.

In the past, customers bought chemicals on price alone. Today, customers want just-in-time delivery service to reduce their inventory levels and their costs. Logistics efficiency is also a major source of cost reduction at Dow. "We're working to improve the materials management processes at Dow to improve the value of the company and to contribute to shareholder value," says Richard Gerardo, vice president of materials management, North America. A $2-billion-a-year improvement program seeks to increase sales by $1 billion and reduce costs by $1 billion, more than half of the savings coming from materials management improvement. Reducing logistics costs boosts Dow's profits. Gerardo explains, "If you increase sales by a dollar, about 10 percent goes to the bottom line. If you reduce costs by a dollar, a dollar goes to the bottom line."

Dow is using information technology, quality management techniques, and supply chain management to boost the efficiency and effectiveness of its logistics system. Computer systems at processing plants monitor and control movement and storage of products. An electronic data interchange system transmits customer orders from computers at headquarters in Midland, Michigan, to processing plants. Computerized systems track a customer's shipment from the time it leaves the processing plant until it arrives at its destination. Using laptop computers, account managers can instantly communicate shipment status information to customers via e-mail.

Dow and its channel partners practice quality management techniques such as employee empowerment and preventive maintenance to improve chemical logistics safety, quality, and reliability. Employees responsible for transporting hazardous materials in the field are empowered to make necessary decisions on the spot. Through preventive maintenance of logistics equipment, Dow works to ensure safety and reliable deliveries. For example, Dow uses detector cars equipped with ultrasonic devices plus twice weekly visual inspections to monitor rail carriers' tracks.

Dow provides extensive training to its employees as well as customer and supplier employees to keep them up to date on hazardous material transport regulations and safety procedures. In 1996, William Stavropoulos, Dow's president and CEO, announced a $1 billion investment in training, facilities, and research to meet new corporate environmental, safety, and health goals by 2005. One goal targets a global reduction of 90 percent in injury and illness rates, processing safety incidents, and leaks, breaks, and spills. Going beyond mere compliance with local and federal safety and health regulations, the company's proactive environmental strategy seeks to design logistics systems that have no adverse impacts on the natural environment.

Dow conducts phone surveys with customers, asking them to evaluate its product and service performance and compare this performance to that of Dow's best competitors. The program records customer responses to questions such as "How do you rate Dow on a scale of one to five for on-time delivery?" for later playback so employees literally hear the voice of the customer. According to Dick Sosville, vice president of sales and marketing for Dow

North America, the customer satisfaction surveys move Dow toward the goal of becoming a more market-driven company. "Nearly 85 percent of our people never have direct contact with a customer, but all have a hand in serving the customer," says Sosville. "We use the tapes to think about the customer first."

Dow and its channel partners apply supply chain management techniques to improve logistics. For example, one cross-functional team assembled members from Dow, a rail carrier, and a customer to tackle the customer's problem with excess inventory. At any one time, the customer's plant stored 15 rail tank cars of a chemical produced at Dow's processing plant in Freeport, Texas, but it needed only 2 tank cars of the chemical to satisfy its daily production needs.

The team mapped the current logistics process and uncovered three big problems. First, shipping produced inconsistent transit times from Dow's plant to the customer's plant. The average transit time was eight days, but that varied by plus or minus four days. Second, the inconsistent transit time forced the customer to hold excess inventory as protection against running out of stock due to a delayed shipment. Third, the complex transportation routing system required close coordination between four carriers at three interchange points. The team pinpointed one particular interchange that caused the delay and inconsistency in transit time.

After studying the current process and discussing optional routes and interchange points, the team members mapped out a new logistics process and set a goal of keeping 2 tank cars at any one time at the customer's plant, giving the customer just-in-time deliveries to support its daily production needs. Implementation of the new logistics system has resulted in reductions in inventory, tank car usage, and rail interchanges, producing cost savings of more than $200,000 a year.

Questions

1. What role does logistics play in Dow Chemical's marketing strategy?
2. What value-added services does Dow's logistics system provide to customers?
3. What quality improvement initiatives help Dow to enhance the service it provides to customers?
4. Dow has demonstrated a strong commitment to an effective and efficient logistics function. To ensure success in this goal, it offers various career opportunities within logistics. Go to Dow's Web site at:
   http://www.dow.com/
   Evaluate the logistics positions listed there, and identify ones that appeal to you. (*Note:* Exercises similar to this one appear in the "Careers in Marketing" appendix.)

Sources: Some of the research material for this case was downloaded from http://www.dow.com/, April 18, 1997; William Miller, "Making Pollution Prevention Pay," *Industry Week,* May 20, 1996, p. 136-L; William Keenan Jr., "Plugging into Your Customer Needs," *Sales & Marketing Management,* January 1996, pp. 62–66.

Part 5 Microsoft Corp.: Bringing Products to Customers

Microsoft distributes its products primarily through OEM licenses, corporate licenses, and retail packaged products. Most corporate licenses and packaged products are sold through distributors and retailers. In the United States, Microsoft's manufacturing plant and main distribution center is located in Bothell, Washington. The company also operates international manufacturing plants and distribution centers in Dublin, Ireland, and Humacao, Puerto Rico.

Because Microsoft began expanding into international markets soon after the company was founded, building relationships with marketing intermediaries has always been vital to the firm's growth. For example, the contract that Gates signed with Kuzuhiko Nishi in 1977 granting his company, ASCHII Microsoft, exclusive distribution rights for Microsoft BASIC in East Asia resulted in more than $150 million of business. Receiving a 30 percent commission on OEM sales, Nishi set the stage for new revenue sources for Microsoft during its early years. By 1979, almost half of Microsoft's business was coming from Japan.

"I always felt that only young people could develop software for personal computers—people with no tie, working with a Coke and a hamburger—only such people could make a personal computer adequate for other young people," says Kazuya Watanabe

It was Nishi who brought Kazuya "Ted" Watanabe, a manager of Japan's NEC, to Albuquerque in 1978 to meet Gates and Allen. Impressed with the young software developers, Watanabe returned to Japan and persuaded his company to build the first Japanese microcomputer and to hire Microsoft to supply the software for it. And it was Nishi who encouraged Microsoft to become involved in the design of Japanese computers. Years later, Watanabe credited Microsoft in playing a big role in NEC's decision making.

Nishi continued to bring Microsoft together with other Japanese computer makers, convincing them to use Microsoft's software for their new computers. "We were selling BASIC to the Japanese like crazy," said Marc McDonald, Microsoft's first full-time developer. "And that typically would bring us anywhere from $150,000 to $200,000 a pop." Japanese computermakers usually paid Microsoft more than did American OEMs, giving the young company much-needed revenues to hire more developers.

Nishi also helped Microsoft establish an early position in the Japanese operating systems market by convincing Sony, Toshiba, Hitachi, Yamaha, and other Japanese firms to license Microsoft's MSX 8-bit system for their inexpensive home computers used mainly for word processing and playing games. Later, Microsoft developed a Japanese version of BASIC for NEC computers and licensed a Japanese version of MS-DOS. Today Microsoft operates a Japanese subsidiary and continues to build Japanese versions of Windows, Windows NT, and many applications. From the foothold established by Nishi, Microsoft continues to experience high growth rates in Japan. Following the practice of early entry into emerging markets, Microsoft often uses local talent to establish a distribution system.

Developing a Distribution System in India

With its huge population and increasing usage of information technology, India has enormous potential for sizable software sales. When Rajiv Nair, born and raised in India and college-educated in the United States, went to work for Microsoft's first Indian distributor in 1986, he was given the task of building Microsoft's distribution channel from ground up. At that time, the PC software market in India was almost nonexistent because of many problems—software piracy, a poor economy, import restrictions, and 112 percent tariffs.

Nair started a distribution channel by licensing MS-DOS to Indian personal computer makers. In 1989, when India opened the country to imports, Nair began building a network of resellers. A year later Microsoft established a subsidiary in India and named Nair country manager. Although Nair had no U.S. business experience, by this time he had gained a good understanding of the distribution business in India.

As an Indian citizen, Nair appreciated the cultural differences between the United States and India and managed to adapt Microsoft's advertising messages, many of which contained American jargon Indians didn't understand. For example, Nair says, "Microsoft would say that with Windows, you can kiss the C prompt good-bye, but nobody in India would know what that meant."

Nair's biggest challenge was building a network of distributors and resellers. He traveled the country trying to recruit resellers and experimented with different promotions, discounts, and credit arrangements. With money difficult to obtain, Nair had to offer resellers liberal payment terms, often 90 days or more, to help them establish their business. He continues to satisfy resellers by generating consumer demand with advertising and user seminars, offering them cooperative marketing dollars, and giving their salespeople incentives such as rebates or cash for meeting sales quotas.

Nair has built a distribution network of four distributors and 800 resellers in India, making Microsoft the leading supplier of software there with 85 percent of the market for desktop productivity applications. Now Nair is working with resellers to help them expand their client/server business. "The work we did in the early years is paying off now," says Nair. Microsoft's revenues are doubling each year, and Nair expects to sell $100 million of Microsoft software by the end of the century.

Persuading U.S. Retailers to Market Consumer Products

Selling CD-ROMs and multimedia products at retail outlets was a key aspect of Microsoft's consumer products marketing strategy. Large computer retailers such as Egghead and CompUSA were already selling Microsoft's office application products—word processing, spreadsheets, and database software. But Microsoft had to convince these retailers to also carry its CD-ROMs, even though in early 1992 there was little consumer demand for the products. Without consumer demand, major software resellers weren't interested in carrying the software.

Martin Leahy, a former Microsoft sales manager, took on the task of convincing retailers to stock Microsoft's CD-ROMs. He visited retailers across the country, sharing with them Microsoft's anticipation of a large consumer market. He explained to them why they needed to carry consumer products. His reasoning was this: the high prices people paid for the four office products like Word and Excel would gradually fall and so would retailers' revenues. Leahy told the retailers Microsoft believed consumers would purchase up to 20 CD-ROMs, replacing the revenues the retailers would lose on selling productivity software. He also told retailers about the upcoming launch of Microsoft's *Encarta* encyclopedia, which, after years of development, Microsoft believed would be a winning product with a high suggested retail price of $395, giving retailers a generous profit in this new domain of consumer software.

CompUSA, Egghead Software, and other retailers agreed to stock *Encarta*. Microsoft lowered *Encarta's* price to $99 during a pre-holiday promotion from September through December 1993. Sales of Encarta rose from $500,000 in August to $5.4 million in December, and Microsoft's consumer division became the company's fastest-growing unit. As Microsoft and competitors flooded the market with new titles, retailers had to decide which products to carry in their limited shelf space. With its financial resources to secure shelf space and heavily promote products, Microsoft had an advantage when retailers decided which titles they would stock.

Microsoft's multimedia titles were initially sold in computer and consumer electronics stores—Egghead Software, CompUSA, Best Buy, and Elek-Tek. Then the company expanded its distribution to bookstores and mass merchant retailers, including Kmart, Price Costco, Wal-Mart, Target, Sam's Wholesale Club, and Sears, which also sell personal computers.

"We want our consumer products to be where customers are, within arm's length of buyers," says Monica Harrington, Microsoft's group manager, communications.

Microsoft sells consumer software to home PC makers such as Dell Computer, Gateway 2000, and AST, which come preloaded with Microsoft's multimedia titles. The company also markets through direct mail campaigns and catalogs. It targets specific markets through programs like SeniorNet, a group of about 60 centers across the country that teach computer skills to senior citizens. Direct channels like Family Technology Nights for local PTAs are also important for Microsoft. "Educators are major influences on what types of software children and parents use," says Harrington.

Selling Software on the Internet

As described in the opening vignette for Chapter 14, the newest distribution channel for software is the Internet. Forrester Research Inc. predicts that by 1999, half of all software will be distributed electronically. In his book *The Road Ahead,* Gates says,

> More and more, information about goods and services, buyers and sellers, will migrate to the network. Once that happens, then the people who have been profiting as middlemen passing that information along—well, their world becomes very different. Buyers and sellers will go direct. It doesn't take a genius to figure out that the percentage of middlemen will go down quite a bit.

After conducting a six-month trial with three Web-based shopping malls—CyberSource's Software.Net, Online Interactive, and the Internet Shopping Network, Microsoft expanded electronic distribution of its software to its largest resellers, Egghead, CompUSA, and MicroWarehouse. Initially Microsoft offered only Office and Works electronically, but it plans to expand the program to include its Windows operating system and "all of our popular products," says Velle Kolde, group manager of emerging channels. "This will be a good value-added service for corporate customers, but it's not a silver bullet," says David Lokes, director of new media at MicroWarehouse.

The trend of selling software on the Internet is changing software distributors' traditional way of moving packaged products from software makers' factories to businesses and retailers. Stan Dolberg, a Forrester analyst, says, "Resellers are under severe threat." Stream International, a distributor of Microsoft's products and other software makers, plans to survive in the new environment by offering a number of value-added services. "We aim to be the electronic middleman when someone wants to buy software on the Internet," says Mort Rosenthal, Stream's chairman. Stream opened an electronic consumer store on the World Wide Web and offers customers technical support and postsale services. Providing these services for end users are important to software makers. "The channel adds value that will still be important when we distribute electronically," says Johan Leidgren, Microsoft's liaison with resellers. "We do a lot of heavy lifting for them, cheap," says Rosenthal. For example, Stream handles software support phone calls outsourced by many software producers.

Microsoft has formed a partnership with Wal-Mart as its pilot customer to develop new software that will enable retailers to create their own virtual stores on the Internet. "Electronic retailing is a lot more than putting up some Web pages," says Gates. According to Gates, it also requires getting the merchandise up on the site, keeping the site up to date, providing a way to order or cancel a product, and making the entire experience fun for consumers. The new software will help retailers provide consumers with more product choices and information about their goods and services, enable them to close the sale, and help them guide consumers through a logical buying experience.

The electronic retailing software appeals to Wal-Mart. "We've worked very, very hard to be good at in-store retailing," says David Glass, Wal-Mart's CEO and president. "For years we've anticipated being a dominant player in what we call nonstore retailing, which we believe is a concept whose time has arrived."

Microsoft is also using the Internet to strengthen its relationships with OEM customers. It has established the "Microsoft OEM on the Internet," a Web site that makes it easier for system builders who license Microsoft software through distributors to get the information and tools they need in building and marketing their equipment. The site will reduce the time OEMs spend searching for product information, downloadable software, and authorized distributors.

"With OEM on the Internet, the winning strategies they need to maximize the PC systems they build are always within reach," says Debbie Flynn, a Microsoft group product manager. "PC makers who buy through our distribution channel told us they wanted this solution." Microsoft OEM on the Internet provides technical information; marketing, sales and support; summaries of OEM news via e-mail; account management; streamlined product delivery; software downloads; and interactive communications with Microsoft experts.

Providing Technology to Boost Supply Chain Efficiency

To better manage the logistics process, Microsoft has formed the Value Chain Initiative (VCI), an alliance with leading transportation and logistics solution providers, in developing an integrated Windows NT-based Internet product. "The Internet is changing the distribution and supply chain model for doing business," says Mark Walker, Microsoft's worldwide marketing manager for transportation, electronic data interchange, and distribution. "Rather than waiting days or even weeks to track valuable shipping information, retailers and manufacturers can now have immediate access to their supply chain information—from raw materials to consumers' hands."

Calling itself the "Transportation Dream Team," the alliance members are working to create more efficiencies in the current supply chain and enable new supply chain models that facilitate the emerging electronic retailing market, says Graham Clark, Microsoft's group manager of retail and distribution industries. VCI's goal is to create standard tools that collaborate communications and management decision support systems between supply chain members' warehouse, logistics, manufacturing, and distribution systems to minimize delivery times to consumers.

Questions

1. What role does distribution play in Microsoft's marketing strategy?
2. Describe Microsoft's channel strategy for its CD-ROM and multimedia products.
3. Do you agree with Gates's comment about the number of marketing intermediaries declining because of the Internet? Why, or why not?

PART 6

PROMOTIONAL STRATEGY

Chapter 17
Integrated Marketing Communications

Chapter 18
Advertising, Sales Promotion, and Public Relations

Chapter 19
Personal Selling and Sales Management

www.micr
microsoft
.hallmark
w.llbean
planetreebo
covergi
irl.com/
v.hkne
n/ikea
w.athand
pepsi
.ups.c

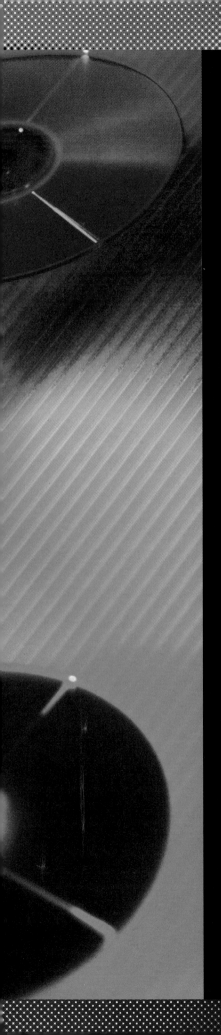

CHAPTER 17

INTEGRATED MARKETING COMMUNICATIONS

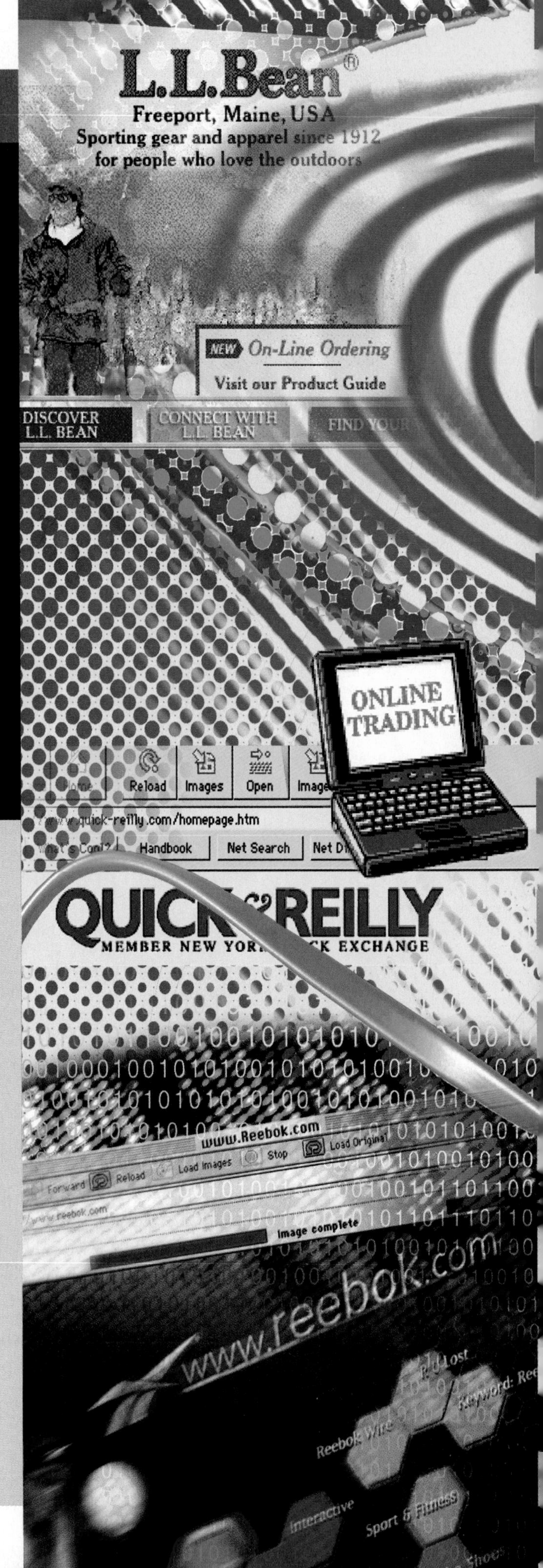

L.L.Bean®
Freeport, Maine, USA
Sporting gear and apparel since 1912
for people who love the outdoors
NEW On-Line Ordering
Visit our Product Guide
DISCOVER L.L. BEAN
CONNECT WITH L.L. BEAN
ONLINE TRADING
Reload
Images
Open
quick-reilly.com/homepage.htm
Handbook
Net Search
QUICK REILLY
MEMBER NEW YOR K EXCHANGE
www.Reebok.com
Reload
Load Images
Stop
Load Original
Image complete
www.reebok.com
Reebok Wire
Interactive
Sport & Fitness

Chapter Objectives

1. Relate the concept of integrated marketing communications to the development of an optimal promotional mix.
2. Explain the relationship of promotional strategy to the process of communication.
3. List the objectives of promotion.
4. Explain the concept of the promotional mix and its relationship to the marketing mix.
5. Discuss the role of sponsorships and direct marketing in integrated marketing communications planning.
6. Identify the primary determinants of a promotional mix.
7. Contrast the two major alternative promotional strategies.
8. Compare the primary methods of developing a promotional budget.
9. Defend promotion against common public criticisms.

Planet Reebok Takes Off

A brief visit to the Planet Reebok Web site clearly shows how busily Reebok International Ltd. promotes itself, its celebrity spokespeople, and its growing array of sports- and fitness-related products. In a video clip, Chinese-American tennis star Michael Chang climbs the Great Wall of China to film a Reebok commercial; Reebok unveils its redesign of men's and women's basketball uniforms for more than 30 of the nation's powerhouse collegiate teams; and the company announces the annual recipients of its Reebok Human Rights Awards. In another announcement, Reebok adds yet another professional soccer team to an impressive roster of worldwide teams it sponsors.

All of this promotional activity is just a sample of the marketing efforts generated by the multibillion dollar corporation headquartered in Stoughton, Massachusetts. In all its advertising and sales promotion activities, from media ads to event marketing, celebrity endorsements, and sponsorships, Reebok's integrated marketing communications project a consistent message in all promotions, including the tag line "This is my planet."

Just how Reebok accomplishes this goal becomes apparent in the company's efforts to convince women to wear its shoes. Starting in the 1970s, Reebok pioneered women's fitness gear at a time when women's athletics were largely ignored. More than two decades later, with those products still representing its core business, Reebok's commitment to women's athletics has continued and burgeoned. "We will make a significant impact in the women's sports business in terms of ad dollars in sports media, sponsorship of women's leagues, and signing key influential athletes," said Kelly Lowell, the company's director of advertising.

http://planetreebok.com/

Reebok has signed endorsement deals with many top female players in basketball, softball, volleyball, soccer, and other sports. For example, the company snagged Rebecca Lobo, who starred on the gold medal-winning U.S. women's basketball team in the 1996 Olympics. Venus Williams, an African-American teenage tennis whiz, also joined the Reebok family. Uniforms of the U.S. Women's Olympic Gymnastics Team sported the Reebok logo. What's more, Reebok is helping to sponsor the Women's Sports Network, which exclusively showcases a variety of women's sports on cable television. Also, it helps underwrite the not-for-profit Women's Sports Foundation.

Reebok scored its biggest endorsement coup by signing Los Angeles Lakers center Shaquille O'Neal. This was a key move as Reebok hungrily eyed the market share of its chief rival, Nike. In fact, one word could describe the motivation behind Reebok's frenetic promotional efforts: Nike. The two competitors account for more than 50 percent of all U.S. athletic footwear sales, but in 1996 Nike appeared to be winning the foot race. While Reebok carved out the women's niche, Nike wooed the men by creating expensive shoes for top male athletes and every male who ever daydreamed of athletic superstardom.

But Reebok was determined to catch up through marketing efforts like its interactive Web site. Reebok executives also hoped that this hip, colorful site, designed by a clever Webmaster fresh out of Boston College, would attract a new generation of savvy customers. The artsy Web site is packed with sporting news, fitness tips, interactive opportunities to chat with big-name athletes, and announcements about the company's philanthropic efforts. "If Reebok's mission is to be the information source for sports and fitness around the world, then we have to address the world through our site with content specific for all consumers around the globe," said Brenda Goodell, Reebok's vice president of new media and programming.

In its event marketing, Reebok tied its Web site to discount coupons during the 1996 summer Olympics in Atlanta. The coupon promotion targeted five Asian markets, including Korea, Taiwan and Hong Kong, with 20 percent discount coupons to customers buying Reebok products in those countries. A variation on this Internet promotion targeted American customers.

Reebok is aggressively pursuing new markets in other ways. Its sponsorship of foreign soccer teams is giving it an international business that rivals Nike's. It's also trying to tap into the fast-growing market for outdoor and hiking gear. The company remains keenly interested in providing shoes for whatever sports teenagers find enchanting at the moment, whether it's in-line skating, wall climbing, or something else. Reebok, for instance, is sponsoring a new in-line skating league called the Professional Hockey Ball Association.[1]

CHAPTER OVERVIEW

Previous chapters have examined product and distribution strategies, two of the four broad variables of the marketing mix. The chapters in Part 6 analyze the third marketing mix variable—promotion. This chapter introduces the concept of integrated marketing communications, briefly describes the elements of a firm's promotional mix—personal and nonpersonal selling—and explains the characteristics that determine the success of the mix. Next, the chapter identifies the objectives of promotion and describes the importance of developing promotional budgets and measuring the effectiveness of promotion. Finally, the chapter discusses the importance of the business, economic, and social aspects of promotion. Chapter 18 covers advertising, sales promotion, and the other nonpersonal selling elements of the promotional mix. Chapter 19 completes this section by focusing on personal selling.

A good place to begin the discussion of promotion is with a definition of the term. **Promotion** is the function of informing, persuading, and influencing the consumer's purchase decision. Consider how this definition applies to Reebok's various marketing techniques discussed at the beginning of the chapter. The company informs one target market—college basketball fans—of the new uniform design; it persuades women, another market segment, to participate in sports through sponsorships that show its commitment to women's sports; through fitness tips, celebrity endorsements, and discount coupons, it influences consumers to equip themselves for sports and leisure activities with Reebok products.

As earlier chapters have discussed, new information technology changes the way marketers approach *communication,* the transmission of a message from a sender to a receiver. Consumers receive **marketing communications**—messages that deal with buyer-seller relationships—from a variety of media, including television, magazines, and the Internet. Marketers can broadcast an ad on network television to mass markets or design a customized direct-mail appeal targeted to a small market segment. Each message the customer receives from any source represents the brand, company, or organization. Unless a company coordinates all these messages, the consumer can become confused and may entirely tune out the message.

To prevent this loss of attention, marketers are turning to **integrated marketing communications (IMC),** which coordinate all promotional activities—media advertising, direct mail, personal selling, sales promotion, and public relations—to produce a unified, customer-focused promotional message. For example, Reebok's tag line, "This is my planet," appears on its print ads and carries through to the Planet Reebok Web page. IMC is a broader concept than marketing communications and promotional strategy. It uses database technology to refine the marketer's understanding of the target audience, segment this audience, and select the best type of media for each segment.

This chapter will show that IMC involves not only the marketer but also any other organizational units that interact with the consumer. Marketing managers set the goals and objectives of the firm's promotional strategy in accordance with overall organizational objectives and marketing goals. Based on these objectives, the various elements of the promotional strategy—personal selling, advertising, sales promotion, direct marketing, publicity, and public relations—are formulated into an integrated communications plan. This becomes a central part of the firm's total marketing strategy to reach its selected market segments. The feedback mechanism, including marketing research and field reports, completes the system by identifying any deviations from the plan and suggesting improvements.

INTEGRATED MARKETING COMMUNICATIONS

As previous chapters have discussed, successful marketers use the marketing concept and relationship marketing to develop customer-oriented marketing programs. The customer is also at the heart of integrated marketing communications. An IMC strategy begins not with the organization's goods and services but with consumer wants or needs and then works backward to the product, brand, or organization. It sends receiver-focused rather than product-focused messages. For example, advertising agency Chiat/Day won the Nissan account because it impressed the client with its understanding of the car *buyer,* while competing agencies focused on the car *business.*

Rather than separating the parts of the promotional mix, IMC looks at these elements from the consumer's viewpoint: as information about the brand, company, or

Marketing Dictionary

promotion Function of informing, persuading, and influencing the consumer's purchase decision.

marketing communication Transmission from a sender to a receiver of a message dealing with the buyer-seller relationship.

integrated marketing communications (IMC) Coordination of *all* promotional activities—media advertising, direct mail, personal selling, sales promotion, and public relations—to produce a unified, customer-focused promotional message.

organization. Even though the messages come from different sources—TV, radio, newspaper, billboards, direct mail, coupons, public relations, the Internet, and online services—consumers may perceive them as "advertising." IMC broadens promotion to include all the ways a customer has contact with the organization, adding to traditional media and direct mail such sources as packaging, store displays, sales literature, and online and interactive media. Unless the organization takes an integrated approach to present a unified, consistent message, it may send conflicting information that confuses consumers.[2]

Figure 17.1 Joint Integrated Marketing Promotion by Kellogg and Nintendo

Kellogg's
'95
Nintendo
$600,000
D.K. GIVEAWAY
A FULLY-INTEGRATED PROMOTION!
MONSTROUS MEDIA
TELEVISION
FSIs
-AND-
ALTERNATIVE
MEDIA
CONSUMER
OFFERS
FEATURED ON MORE
THAN 350,000,000
PACKAGES!
SELL-IN
MATERIALS
BIGGER THAN EVER
TRADE EXTENSIONS

Kellogg and Nintendo used IMC effectively for their $600,000 Donkey Kong Giveaway promotion, a joint campaign to promote eight cereal brands and introduce Nintendo's Donkey Kong Country video game. It was Kellogg's largest promotion ever, with 150 million on-pack promotional offers distributed in about four months. Kellogg and Nintendo took a unified approach to consumer, trade, and sales force promotions. As shown in Figure 17.1, Kellogg's Tony the Tiger joined Donkey Kong characters on promotional displays. On-package promotions included Nintendo-related prize offers—color TVs, Super Nintendo and Game Boy systems, and Donkey Kong Country game cartridges. These messages were accompanied by in-store displays, theme promotions aimed at retail store buyers, special promotional budgets called "Jungle Funds," and sales incentives. Combining the two popular brands leveraged the equity of Nintendo's name, technology, and characters with Kellogg's strong presence in its market. The promotion, which included mass-market advertising targeted to kids, added value to Kellogg's cereals and boosted sales volume while helping Nintendo with its product launch.[3]

Today's marketing environment is characterized by many diverse markets and media, creating both opportunities and challenges. Success of any IMC program depends critically on knowing the members of an audience and what they want. Without good information about existing and potential customers, their purchase histories, needs, and wants, marketers may send the wrong message. But they cannot succeed simply by improving the quality of the messages or sending more of them. IMC must not only deliver messages to intended audiences but also gather responses from them. Databases and interactive marketing are important IMC tools that help marketers collect information from customers and then segment markets according to resulting analysis of demographics and preferences. They can then design specialized communications programs to meet the needs of particular segments.

Customer service telephone lines are a good example of a beneficial application of interactive marketing. Apple Computer's Performa hotline provides the company with valuable information. Service representatives take advantage of the phone interaction to offer news of products that might help users. They also determine the top customer problems for the week and communicate the information to design engineers so they can develop products that address these needs. As a result, Apple can respond to customer needs more quickly than it could when it relied on customer surveys and other forms of market research.[4]

The increase in media options provides more ways to give consumers product information, however, it also can create information overload. Marketers have to spread available dollars across fragmented media markets and a wider range of promotional activities to achieve their communication goals. Mass media such as TV ads, while still useful, are no longer the mainstays of marketing campaigns. In 1960, a company could reach about 90 percent of U.S. consumers by advertising on the three major television networks. Today, these network ads reach less than 60 percent. Audiences are also more fragmented. Therefore, to reach desired groups, organizations are turning to niche marketing through special-interest magazines; buying time on cable television channels for sports, family, science, history, comedy, and women's interests; and reaching out through telecommunications like the Internet.

In addition, marketers frequently encounter problems within their own organizations because separate departments have authority and responsibility for planning and implementing specific promotional mix elements. A company's sales department plans and controls sales presentations; the advertising department works with the firm's advertising agency to create media promotions; sales promotion and direct-marketing activities take place in still other departments. All too often, these disjointed efforts result in an uncoordinated overall promotional effort that fails to achieve the marketers' objectives. Personal selling efforts may not be directly linked with the themes stressed in advertising and sales promotion. Public relations activities may fail to support specific promotional objectives.

These aspects of the business environment, coupled with fragmented promotional efforts in many organizations, have prompted the move toward integrated marketing communications to coordinate all promotional activities. Such coordination frequently produces a competitive advantage based on synergy and interdependence among the various elements of the promotional mix. With an IMC strategy, marketers can create a unified personality for the product or brand, choosing the right elements from the promotional mix to send the message. At the same time, they can develop more narrowly focused plans to reach specific market segments and choose the best form of communication to send a particular message to a specific target audience. IMC provides a more effective way to reach and serve target markets than less well-coordinated strategies.

http://www.microsoft.com/

Yet, despite the interest in IMC, actual implementation is low. A recent survey indicated that less than one-third of respondents have annual marketing communications plans, and only 15 percent use database marketing for more than mailing lists. "IMC requires more intensive planning, intensive customer analysis, and careful measurement of results," says Bob Tucker of Tucker Chicago, the marketing communications agency that conducted the survey. Many marketers find it difficult to move from the idea of IMC to implementation. For example, many organizations arrange authority in vertical structures, while IMC requires horizontal communication between departments.[5]

Importance of Teamwork

IMC requires a big-picture view of promotion planning, a total strategy including all marketing activities, not just promotion. Successful implementation of IMC requires that everyone involved in every aspect of promotion—public relations, advertising, personal selling, and sales promotion—function as a team. They must present a consistent, coordinated promotional effort at every point of customer contact with the organization. In this way, they avoid duplication of efforts, increase marketing effectiveness, and reduce costs.

Teamwork involves both in-house resources and outside vendors. It involves marketing personnel; members of the sales force who deal with wholesalers, retailers, and organizational buyers; and customer service representatives. A firm gains nothing from a terrific advertisement featuring a toll-free 800 number to call for more information if callers reach a surly operator! The company must train its representatives to send a single, positive message to consumers and also to solicit information for the customer database.

IMC also challenges the traditional role of the advertising agency. A single agency may no longer fulfill all of a client's communications requirements, including traditional advertising and sales promotions, interactive marketing, database development, direct marketing, and public relations. To best serve client needs, an agency must often assemble a team with members from other companies.

Microsoft's worldwide launch of Windows 95 incorporated many layers of promotion—public relations, celebrity endorsements, events, advertising, and retailer incentives—unfolded through a team effort. This promotion for the first simultaneous, global product rollout spanned 24 hours and cost over $200 million. The festivities started in Wellington, New Zealand, with the sale of the first copy of the software. The events moved west to Australia, where a huge Windows 95 box sailed into Sydney harbor on a barge. Other highlights included a submarine trip for journalists in Poland (to show what it's like "to live in a world without Windows") and a live question-and-answer session with Microsoft Chairman Bill Gates in Spain. The company hosted a Windows 95 carnival at its headquarters, covered live on the Internet. Sponsored by about 120 companies involved in the creation and marketing of Windows 95 software, the event included an appearance that evening by Gates with Jay Leno on *The Tonight Show.*

A team of thousands participated in the product launch, from top Microsoft executives to outside vendors to local retailers. A 60-member corporate marketing team coordinated the overall promotion. Each Microsoft field office developed and implemented its own promotions. Local retailers opened for 95 minutes of "Midnight Madness" to sell the program, attracting media coverage. Product manager Lora Shiner says, "The marketing world for high-tech products has changed dramatically. . . . We used to just buy ads in computer magazines and try to influence technologically savvy users."[6]

Role of Databases in Effective IMC Programs

Databases, discussed earlier in the chapters on marketing research and market segmentation, are key elements of any successful IMC program. The move from mass marketing to a customer-specific marketing strategy requires not only a means of identifying and communicating with the firm's target market, but also information regarding important characteristics of each prospective customer. Organizations can compile different kinds of data into complete databases with customer information, including names and addresses, demographic data, lifestyle considerations, brand preferences, and buying behavior. This information provides critical guidance in designing an effective IMC strategy that achieves organizational goals and finds new opportunities for increased sales and profits.

The kind of data collected—about wholesalers/distributors, retailers, and consumers—and the level of detail depend on the organization's needs, the type of product, and its distribution channels. Too many companies focus exclusively on consumers and ignore their wholesaler and retailer channel partners. A company that makes a component sold to computer manufacturers may not need data on the retailers that sell the computers to final users; information about its own wholesalers and distributors may suffice. On the other hand, a computer manufacturer that sells through a variety of channels, including distributors and several types of retailers that serve different end users, will want the most complex database possible with information on all three groups.[7]

Gerland's Food Fair, a Houston supermarket, uses database technology to compete with national chains like Albertson's and Kroger. It was the first grocer in Houston to create a frequent shopper program that analyzed data from existing databases to spot trends. "If you want to go toe-to-toe with the big guys, you have to be uniquely different in your marketplace," said Kevin Doris, chief operating officer for the 20-store chain. A bar-coded key ring scanned at checkout allows the system to identify loyal customers and tell how often they visit, what they buy, and how much they spend. Participants then receive benefits like special coupons for items they purchase or discounts on their next orders.

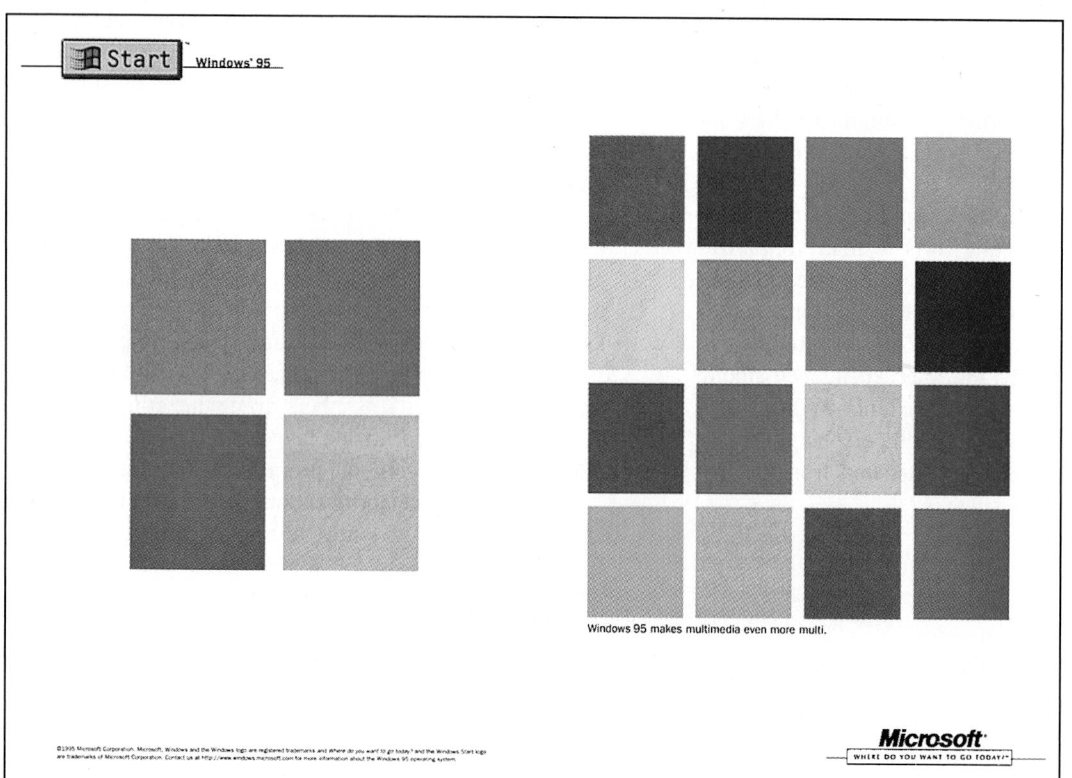
Start
Windows 95
Windows 95 makes multimedia even more multi.
Microsoft
WHERE DO YOU WANT TO GO TODAY?

Advertising agency Wieden & Kennedy was part of the team that launched Microsoft's Windows 95. The agency's global print campaign, which ran in more than 20 countries and in a dozen languages, supported Microsoft's other promotional activities.

With this detailed knowledge, Gerland's recast its marketing program to include more types of communications—interactive marketing through in-store kiosks, targeted direct mail, and television ads; it reduced its reliance on mass advertising like general newspaper ads. The program increased sales and profits and raised the rate of customer retention, despite increased competition, in an industry where stores see 25 to 50 percent of their customers defect each year. This loyalty pays off, since the top 30 percent of a retailer's customers account for about 75 percent of its sales, while the bottom 30 percent contribute just 3 percent.[8]

THE COMMUNICATIONS PROCESS

Figure 17.2 shows a general model of the communications process and its application to promotional strategy. The *sender* acts as the source in the communications system as he or she seeks to convey a *message* (a communication of information, advice, or a request) to a *receiver.* An effective message accomplishes three tasks:

1. It gains the receiver's attention.
2. It achieves understanding by both receiver and sender.
3. It stimulates the receiver's needs and suggests an appropriate method of satisfying them.

Figure 17.2 Relating Promotion to the Communications Process

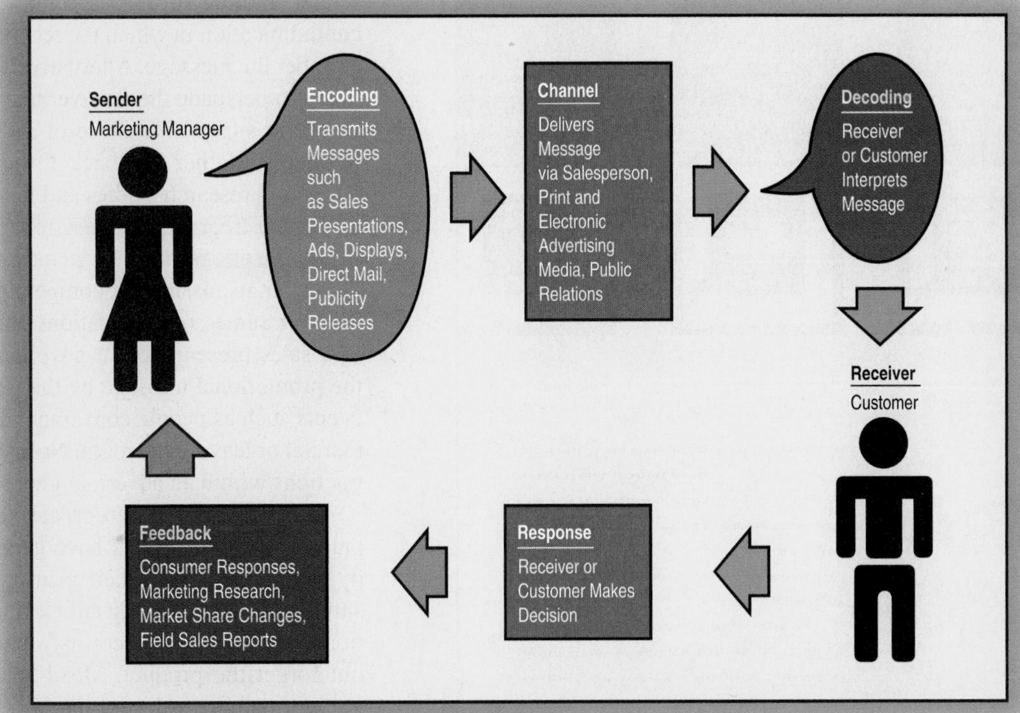
Sender
Marketing Manager
Encoding
Transmits Messages such as Sales Presentations, Ads, Displays, Direct Mail, Publicity Releases
Channel
Delivers Message via Salesperson, Print and Electronic Advertising Media, Public Relations
Decoding
Receiver or Customer Interprets Message
Receiver
Customer
Response
Receiver or Customer Makes Decision
Feedback
Consumer Responses, Marketing Research, Market Share Changes, Field Sales Reports

These three tasks are related to the **AIDA concept** (attention-interest-desire-action) proposed by E. K. Strong over 60 years ago as an explanation of the steps through which an individual reaches a purchase decision. First, the promotional message must gain the potential consumer's attention. It then seeks to arouse interest in the good or service. At the next stage, it stimulates desire by convincing the would-be buyer of the product's ability to satisfy his or her needs. Finally, the sales presentation, advertisement, or sales promotion technique attempts to produce action in the form of a purchase or a more favorable attitude that may lead to future purchases.

The message must be *encoded,* or translated into understandable terms, and transmitted through a communications channel. *Decoding* is the receiver's interpretation of the message. The receiver's response, known as *feedback,* completes the system. Throughout the process, *noise* can interfere with the transmission of the message and reduce its effectiveness.

The marketing manager is the sender in Figure 17.2. He or she encodes the message in the form of sales presentations, advertising, displays, or publicity releases. The *channel* for delivering the message may be a salesperson, a public relations outlet, or an advertising medium. Decoding is often the most troublesome step in marketing communications, because consumers do not always interpret promotional messages in the same way that senders do. Since receivers usually decode messages according to their own frames of reference or experiences, a sender must carefully encode a message in a way that matches the frame of reference of the target audience.

Consumers today receive many sales messages through many media channels. This communications traffic can create confusion as noise in the channel increases. Consumers choose to process only a few messages each, and ignored messages waste communications budgets.

Feedback, the receiver's response to the message, provides a way for marketers to evaluate the effectiveness of the message and tailor their responses. The New Jersey

Marketing Dictionary

AIDA concept Acronym for attention-interest-desire-action, the traditional explanation of the steps an individual must take to complete the purchase decision.

Figure 17.3 Promotion Designed to Produce Feedback from Prudential Clients

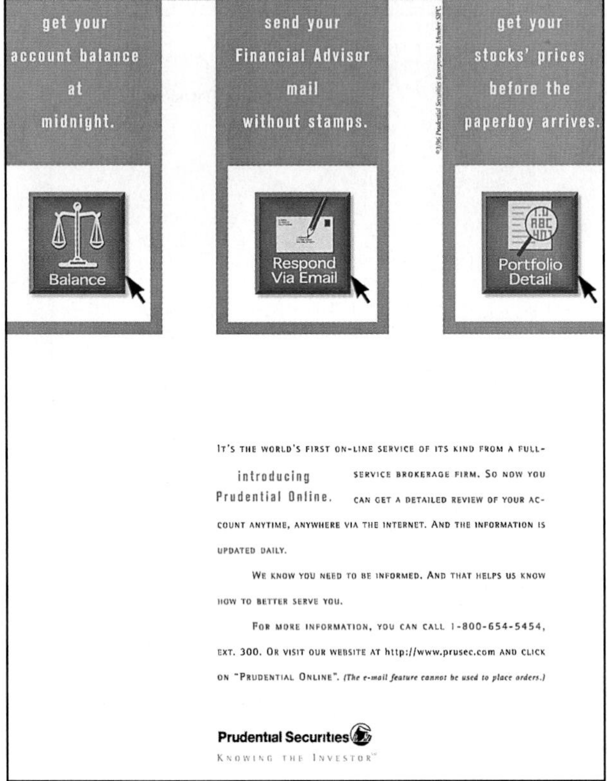
get your account balance at midnight.
Balance
send your Financial Advisor mail without stamps.
Respond Via Email
get your stocks' prices before the paperboy arrives.
Portfolio Detail
introducing Prudential Online.
It's the world's first on-line service of its kind from a full-service brokerage firm. So now you can get a detailed review of your account anytime, anywhere via the Internet. And the information is updated daily.
We know you need to be informed. And that helps us know how to better serve you.
For more information, you can call 1-800-654-5454, ext. 300. Or visit our website at http://www.prusec.com and click on "Prudential Online". (The e-mail feature cannot be used to place orders.)
Prudential Securities
Knowing the Investor

real-estate agency Murphy Realty Better Homes and Gardens sent questionnaires to 75,000 households identified as future home buyers. The response was good—a 4 percent return in three weeks—and half of the respondents included names and addresses with their answers to questions like how long they planned to stay in their present homes and what kind of homes they would look for if they planned to move. Based on this feedback about what customers wanted, Murphy's agents could call potential clients when homes that matched their needs came on the market, placing them a step ahead of rival agencies.[9]

Feedback may take the form of attitude change, purchase, or nonpurchase. In some instances, organizations use promotion to create favorable attitudes toward their goods or services in the hope of future purchases. Other promotional communications have the objective of directly stimulating consumer purchases. When Prudential Securities wanted to improve customer service to encourage more positive client attitudes, it turned to the interactive capabilities of the Internet's World Wide Web. As described in Figure 17.3, Prudential Online not only keeps clients informed, but it also helps Prudential to know how to serve them. The proprietary online service enhances its customers' ability to communicate via e-mail with their personal financial advisors, obtain securities quotes, and review their accounts any time.

Even nonpurchases may serve as feedback to the sender. Failure to purchase may result from ineffective communication in which the receivers do not believe or remember the message. Alternatively, the message may have failed to persuade the receiver that the firm's goods or services are superior to those of its competitors. Marketers frequently gather feedback through such techniques as marketing research studies and field sales reports.

Noise represents interference at some stage in the communications process. It may result from disruptions such as transmissions of competing promotional messages over the same communications channel, misinterpretation of a sales presentation or advertising message, receipt of the promotional message by the wrong person, or random events such as people conversing during a television commercial or leaving the room. Noise can also result from distractions within an advertising message itself.

In their attempts to create novel promotional campaigns, many marketers have generated noise themselves by failing to convey their primary selling points to consumers. Such ads may seem clever but generate low emotional appeal. Consumers may remember the advertising but forget the product. Mead Johnson ran an ad for its Pablum baby cereal with the headline, "The First Supper for a good start." It featured 12 babies instead of the 12 disciples, in a parody of Leonardo Da Vinci's *Last Supper.* The ad included no information about the product, so it did not attract the attention of new parents by promoting the cereal. Even worse, it offended art lovers and religious people.[10]

A major promotional failure was ABC's short-lived weekly comedy, *The Dana Carvey Show.* Its novel approach featured the sponsoring company or its product in the show title and spoofed the promotion during the show itself. The sponsor had no control over the show's content. PepsiCo units Taco Bell, Pepsi, and Pizza Hut bought most of the advertising time for the first nine episodes, considering the experiment an exciting, different idea, a way to make advertising stand out.

However, Taco Bell pulled its support after the first episode, "The Taco Bell Dana Carvey Show." Even though the firm got plenty of exposure—a dancing taco and the company's signature bell flanked Carvey in the opening scene and in other skits—the advertiser complained about too many risqué references. Managers decided that the show didn't offer the type of promotion Taco Bell wanted. Another concern was the blurring of lines between programming and commercials. The other sponsors later withdrew and the show was canceled.[11]

Noise can be especially problematic in international communications. Disruption often results from too many competing messages. Italian television channels, for instance, broadcast all advertisements during a single half-

Table 17.1 Examples of Marketing Communications

Type of Promotion	Sender	Encoding by Sender	Channel	Decoding by Receiver	Feedback
Personal selling	Sun business products	Sales presentation on new model of workstation	Sun sales representative	Office manager and employees dicusss Sun sales presentation and those of competing suppliers.	Order placed for Sun workstation.
Dollar-off coupon (sales promotion)	Kraft salad dressing	Coupons prepared by Kraft marketing department and advertising agency	Coupon insert in Sunday newspaper	Newspaper reader sees coupon for salad dressing and saves it.	Salad dressing purchased by consumer using coupon.
Television advertising	Universal Studios theme park	Advertisement developed by Universal's advertising agency featuring the new Jurassic Park	Network television ads during programs with high percentages of viewers under 20 years old	Teens and young adults see ad and decide to try out the new park.	Theme park tickets are purchased.

hour slot each night. Noise might stem from differences in technology, such as a bad telephone connection, or from poor translation into another language. Nonverbal cues, such as body language and tone of voice, are important parts of the communication process, and cultural differences may lead to noise and misunderstandings. For example, in the United States, the round *o* sign made with the thumb and first finger means "okay." However, in Mediterranean countries, it means "zero" or "the worst." A Tunisian interprets this sign as "I'll kill you," and to a Japanese it means "money."

U.S. companies have created some well-meant failures in their international communications. Software giant Microsoft had a major public-relations problem in Mexico and other Latin American countries. The Spanish thesaurus included in its popular Word for Windows program contained a number of offensive synonyms for ethnic groups. The program listed *man-eater* and *savage* as synonyms for *Indian*—an extremely offensive mistake in a country where most of the population's ancestors were Aztec and Mayan Indians. The same was not true for the English thesaurus, which gave *cave dweller, ancient tribe,* and *aborigine* as alternatives to *Indian.* Other slurs included *man-eater, cannibal,* and *barbarian* as synonyms for the Spanish term for black people. "I see this as profoundly dangerous because it is a lack of respect for our dignity as Mexicans and for our indigenous roots," commented one congresswoman. Microsoft quickly revised the dictionary and distributed it free over the Internet.[12]

Faulty communications can be especially risky on a global level, where noise can lead to some interesting misinterpretations. Here are four recent international examples:

- *On a sign in a Bucharest hotel lobby:* The lift is being fixed for the next day. During that time, we regret that you will be unbearable.
- *From a Japanese information booklet about using a hotel air conditioner:* Cooles and Heates: If you want just condition of warm in your room, please control yourself.
- *In an Acapulco hotel:* The manager has personally passed all the water served here.

Table 17.1 illustrates the steps in the communications process for several examples of promotional messages. Although the types of promotion may vary from a highly personalized sales presentation to such nonpersonal promotions as television advertising and dollar-off coupons, each goes through every stage in the communications model.

OBJECTIVES OF PROMOTION

What specific tasks should promotion accomplish? The answers to this question seem to vary as much as the sources

MARKETING HALL OF SHAME

The Decade's Two Worst Promotions

Promotional ideas that look great on paper can sometimes be just too good. When a promotion exceeds all expectations, it can ironically create aggravating financial distress for the sponsor and trigger an embarrassing public-relations nightmare.

That is what happened recently to two corporate veterans with heavy-duty advertising budgets: PepsiCo and Sprint Corp. The experiences of these two companies provide a warning to any marketers who expect to generate new business by offering free products.

PepsiCo's troubles began not long after it launched its "Pepsi Stuff" promotion in the spring of 1996. The rules were simple. Customers who guzzled enough soda and saved the peel-off strips from Pepsi or Diet Pepsi containers were entitled to free clothing emblazoned with the soft drink logo.

PEPSI
CONTAINS: FILA MOUNTAIN BIKES, PEPSI BLUE SHADES, PEPSI BLACK LEATHER JACKETS, PEPSI BALL CAPS, PEPSI SPORT WATCHES, PEPSI BEACH CHAIRS, PEPSI BEACH TOWELS, PEPSI BEACH SHORTS, PEPSI TEES, PEPSI CANVAS DUFFEL BAGS, PEPSI MINI SPORT BALLS AND BAGS, PEPSI FLEECE CREW AND HOODED SWEATSHIRTS, PEPSI BIG TRAVEL BAGS, TEVA® SPORT SANDALS, PEPSI DENIM JACKETS, PEPSI KICK SACKS, PEPSI PHONE CARDS, AND PEPSI SOFT CD CASES.
DRINK PEPSI GET STUFF
Whoa! Now there's even more great stuff inside every Pepsi. And the best part is, the more Pepsi you drink, the more cool Pepsi Stuff you'll get. It's that simple. All you do is collect Pepsi Points on specially marked packages of Pepsi and Diet Pepsi, send 'em in and score Pepsi Stuff free*. For even more details, get a close-up of the Pepsi Stuff catalog, available at participating stores, or call 1-800-341-2424.
*Plus shipping and handling
BEACH HOUSE
PEPSI STUFF IS IN THE HOUSE! TUNE IN AND CHECK IT OUT.
Offer ends October 31, 1996. Not available in all areas. PEPSI, PEPSI-COLA, DRINK PEPSI GET STUFF, the PEPSI STUFF logo, and the PEPSI BALL design are trademarks of PepsiCo, Inc. Fila cycles licensed by Fila Sport S.P.A., Biella, Italy
FILA CYCLES

At the outset, the industry praised PepsiCo's latest ad campaign as a clever way to reenergize the company's core cola business. With The Coca-Cola Co. flexing its muscles as a highly visible corporate sponsor of the Atlanta Summer Olympics, Pepsi would have a million fans wearing its logos on clothing—in Coke's hometown, no less.

Initially, Pepsi executives were worried that the contest rules were too hard. To win, soda drinkers would have to buy 200 2-liter bottles of Pepsi or Diet Pepsi. As it turned out, Pepsi executives were fretting for the wrong reason. Bottlers say redemptions ran about 50 percent higher than expected, and Pepsi decided to cancel the last phase of its $125 million dollar campaign.

Pepsi didn't run out of prizes—it gave away about 4.5 million items—and company reps said

one consults. Generally, however, marketers identify the following objectives for promotion:

1. Provide information to consumers and others
2. Increase demand
3. Differentiate a product
4. Accentuate a product's value
5. Stabilize sales

Provide Information

The traditional function of promotion was to inform the market about the availability of a particular good or service. Indeed, marketers still direct large portions of current promotional efforts at providing product information for potential customers. For example, the typical newspaper advertisement for a university or college extension program emphasizes information such as the availability, times, and locations of different courses. Industrial salespeople inform buyers of new products and how they work. Retail advertisements provide information about merchandise, prices, and store locations and hours.

In addition to traditional print and broadcast advertising, companies now distribute videocassettes as low-cost tools to give consumers product information. A ten-minute video costs about $1.50 to duplicate and send (not including production costs), compared to $8 or more for a full-color brochure. The consumer regards the video as a nov-

the jump in sales volume more than paid for the extra costs. But some insiders suggested that its beefed up sales volume might be attributed to soda prices that were 10 percent lower than the previous year.

While Pepsi has managed to please most of its customers, Sprint didn't fare as well when it modified its "Free Friday" plan. The promotion was an attempt to gain advantage in the fierce competition among the nation's long-distance telephone carriers. According to the rules of its marketing promotion, Sprint agreed not to charge business customers for long-distance calls made on Friday for a year.

Startled by the huge volume of calls generated by business customers, Sprint executives quickly concluded that the "Free Friday" offer was becoming far too popular. Then the telecommunications giant's problems were compounded when some residential telephone customers managed to sign up for the promotion, even though it was designed exclusively for businesses.

Realizing its mistake, Sprint tried to limit the financial damage. First, it barred free overseas calls for the newest business customers and eliminated free calls to nine countries with unusually high call patterns. In addition, the company demanded that residential customers prove their business status. But the move embittered many residential customers, who complained that their long-distance service was eliminated entirely. "They've been selling so much Sprint Sense that they've forgotten to keep some for themselves," complained Keith Jarrett, a systems engineer in Oakland, California, whose residential service was cut. Even Sprint's small-business marketing chief, Robin Loyd, acknowledged the company's mistake, stating, "It was our fault."

Snafus such as these are nothing new in the world of marketing, but there are ways to avoid them. "Programs of this type must be carefully and properly designed," warns James Powell, a spokesman for Maytag Corp. in Newton, Iowa. He should know since Maytag provides a notorious example of free promotions going horribly awry. In 1993, the appliance manufacturer made an incredible offer: Any British customer who bought a Hoover appliance was entitled to a free round-trip airline ticket. Maytag had to cough up $36 million to honor its expensive obligation to British consumers, who spent as little as $150 to earn their tickets.

QUESTIONS FOR CRITICAL THINKING

1. **How could PepsiCo have improved the design of its giveaway program?**
2. **How can companies ensure that they avoid duplicating mistakes like these in other giveaway promotions?**
3. **Could Sprint have softened its financial blow without alienating customers?**

Sources: "Pepsi Giveaway Promotion Perhaps Too Successful," downloaded from http://sddt.com/files/, April 25, 1997; Robert Frank, "Pepsi Cancels an Ad Campaign as Customers Clamor for Stuff," *Wall Street Journal*, June 27, 1996, p. B1; Gautam Naik, "Sprint Backs Off 'Fridays Free' as Calls Climb," *Wall Street Journal*, April 11, 1996, p. B2; and Gautam Naik, "Sprint Long-distance Promotion Disconnects, Disaffects Customers," *Wall Street Journal*, April 8, 1996, p. B1.

elty that stands out from other promotions, so he or she is less likely to throw out the cassette. In fact, about 70 percent of recipients view them.

A video can effectively tell a long story that requires action or is ill-suited to print ads or 30-second television ads. World Wildlife Fund, a not-for-profit environmental conservation organization, included videos in its membership renewal packages to show some of the projects accomplished with membership funds. Lexus used videos to demonstrate model changes in the LS400. DuPont Agricultural Products used a two-cassette series to explain a herbicide product that required information too complex for a print ad. The videos showed the product development, product benefits, and testimonials from farmers. After three months, half of the recipients remembered the tapes, far more than expected.[13]

Increase Demand

Most promotions pursue the objective of increasing demand for a good or service. Some promotions are aimed at increasing *primary demand*, the desire for a general product category. When P&G first introduced Pampers disposable diapers in Hungary, most Hungarian parents used overpants with paper inserts to diaper their babies. Early P&G television commercials there focused on generating interest in the novel product and demonstrating its superiority.

More promotions, however, are aimed at increasing *selective demand*, the desire for a specific brand. Guinness Import Co. found that its typical St. Patrick's Day promotions boosted sales for about a month. It wanted a unique promotion with longer-lasting benefits that also gained new accounts, increased loyalty of existing accounts, and increased brand awareness. A promotional contest to give away a genuine Irish pub turned out to be a winner for Guinness, and it also reinforced the pub-quality image of the brand. The campaign received good media coverage, and Aer Lingus, the Irish airline, provided 100 round-trip airfares in exchange for placement of its logo on entry forms and displays. In the contest's first year, 30,000 entrants wrote essays about "A Perfect Pint of Guinness." An Irish American from Boston won and ran his pub in Cobb, Ireland for a year, becoming a goodwill ambassador for Guinness when he returned. Sales of the beer, which had been stagnant, increased substantially, due in part to the attention focused by the promotion. Guinness repeated the contest the following year and 36,000 wrote about their most memorable pints of Guinness.[14]

WWF
Saving Life On Earth

To give its members information about projects accomplished with their financial contributions, World Wildlife Fund included videos in its membership renewal kits.

Differentiate the Product

A frequent objective of the firm's promotional efforts is *product differentiation.* Homogeneous demand for many products results when consumers regard the firm's output as virtually identical to its competitors' products. In these cases, the individual firm has almost no control over marketing variables such as price. A differentiated demand schedule, in contrast, permits more flexibility in marketing strategy, such as price changes.

In the very competitive category of economy hotels, most budget chain ads emphasize price as the reason to stay at their hotels. The Travelodge chain wanted a way to differentiate itself from its peers. "We asked our customers what they liked and hated [about budget hotels]—and what did they like about Travelodge specifically," says Dwight Gould, senior vice president of Marketing and Sales. Travelodge had a stodgy image, so it used focus groups to find out which promotions other than price appealed to consumers. Because their target customers—vacationing families—liked family entertainment, the chain created package deals with tickets to local attractions like zoos, theme parks, and movies. This very popular value-added feature differentiated the product and also encouraged longer stays.

Business travelers, who account for 35 percent of Travelodge room sales, wanted the personal touch, so the company gave them free phone cards to call home. Its biggest hit was the "Everything's Coming Up Roses" campaign. A business traveler who stayed six nights over a four-month period could have a dozen roses delivered anywhere in the United States, plus a frequent guest program for any who exceeded that requirement. This group increased their average stay from about seven to ten nights, and the chain's overall room bookings rose 15 percent as a result of its promotional strategy.[15]

Accentuate the Product's Value

Promotion can explain the greater ownership utility of a product to buyers, thereby accentuating its value and justifying a higher price in the marketplace. This objective benefits both consumer and business products. Two decades ago, Amoco Chemical Co. launched a campaign called "The Chemistry's Right at Amoco" featuring its chemical products. Promotions showed sports and adventure activities to illustrate the roles that chemicals play in consumers' daily lives and how chemicals solve customer needs. Amoco makes the same basic products as its competitors, so the ads emphasized not the liquids or powders it sells but the value of the company's resources. They featured stories about customers who used the products, creating a broader human interest. The ad in Figure 17.4 showcased a giant waterslide made by Whitewater Specialties from durable resins manufactured by Amoco; another showed a race car with plastic engine parts provided by Amoco. Amoco's ad campaign, ranked by *Business Week* as the best read and remembered, not only increased the company's profile with product developers, but also helped the firm to triple revenues in 15 years.[16]

Stabilize Sales

For the typical firm, sales are not uniform throughout the year. Sales fluctuations may result from cyclical, seasonal, or irregular demand. Stabilizing these variations is often an objective of promotional strategy. Coffee sales, for example, follow a seasonal pattern, with purchases and consumption increasing during the winter months. To stimulate summer sales of Sanka brand decaffeinated coffee, General

Foods created advertisements that included a recipe for instant iced coffee, promoting it as a refreshing, caffeine-free summer beverage. Hotels and motels often seek to supplement high occupancy during the week from business travelers by promoting special weekend packages at lower room rates. Some firms sponsor sales contests during slack periods that offer prizes to sales personnel who meet goals.

Figure 17.4 Advertisement Accentuating a Product's Value

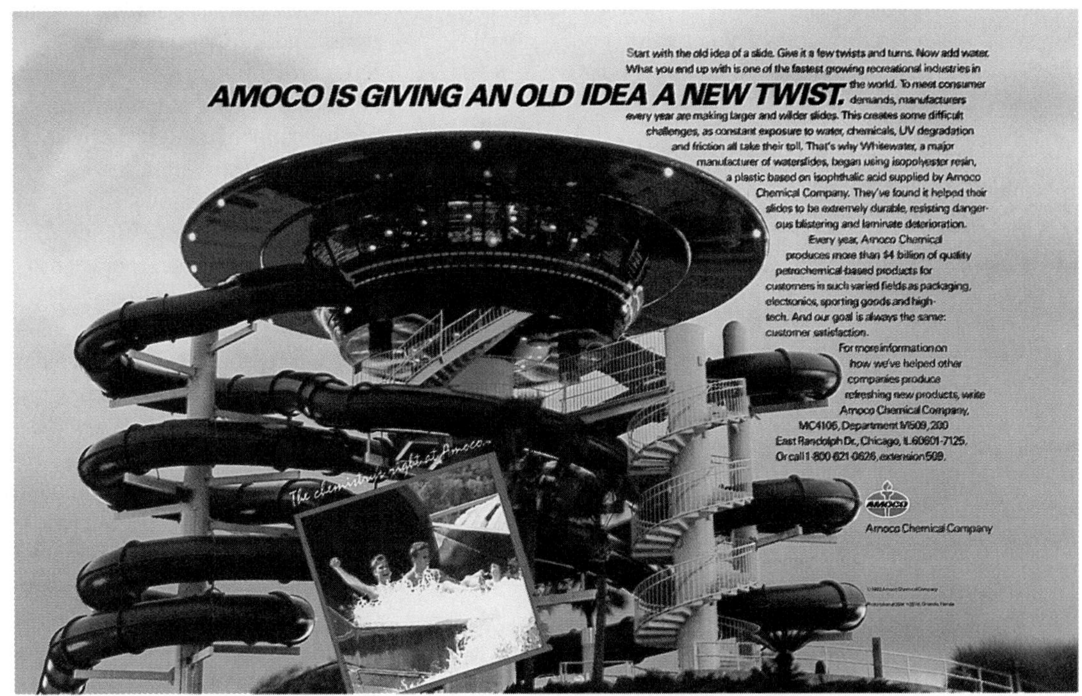
AMOCO IS GIVING AN OLD IDEA A NEW TWIST.
Start with the old idea of a slide. Give it a few twists and turns. Now add water. What you end up with is one of the fastest growing recreational industries in the world. To meet consumer demands, manufacturers every year are making larger and wilder slides. This creates some difficult challenges, as constant exposure to water, chemicals, UV degradation and friction all take their toll. That's why Whitewater, a major manufacturer of waterslides, began using isopolyester resin, a plastic based on isophthalic acid supplied by Amoco Chemical Company. They've found it helped their slides to be extremely durable, resisting dangerous blistering and laminate deterioration.
Every year, Amoco Chemical produces more than $4 billion of quality petrochemical-based products for customers in such varied fields as packaging, electronics, sporting goods and high-tech. And our goal is always the same: customer satisfaction.
For more information on how we've helped other companies produce refreshing new products, write Amoco Chemical Company, MC4106, Department M509, 200 East Randolph Dr., Chicago, IL 60601-7125. Or call 1-800-621-0626, extension 509.
The chemistry's right at Amoco.
AMOCO
Amoco Chemical Company

THE PROMOTIONAL MIX

Like the marketing mix, the **promotional mix** requires a proper blend of numerous variables to satisfy the needs of the firm's target market and achieve organizational objectives. In fact, the promotional mix is a subset of the marketing mix, with its product, pricing, promotion, and distribution elements. With the promotional mix, the marketing manager attempts to achieve the optimal blending of various elements to attain promotional objectives. The components of the promotional mix are personal selling and nonpersonal selling, including advertising, sales promotion, direct marketing, and public relations.

Personal selling, advertising, and sales promotion, the most significant elements, usually account for the bulk of a firm's promotional expenditures. However, direct marketing and public relations also contribute to efficient marketing communications. Later sections of this chapter examine direct marketing, and Chapters 18 and 19 present a detailed discussion of the other elements. This section will simply define the elements and discuss their advantages and disadvantages.

Personal Selling

Personal selling, the original form of all promotion, may be defined as a seller's promotional presentation conducted on a person-to-person basis with the buyer. This direct form of promotion may be conducted face-to-face, over the telephone, through videoconferencing, or through interactive computer links between the buyer and seller. Today, about 14 million people in the United States are employed in personal selling, and the average sales call costs about $300.

Nonpersonal Selling

Nonpersonal selling includes advertising, sales promotion, direct marketing, and public relations. Advertising and

Marketing Dictionary

promotional mix Blend of personal selling and nonpersonal selling (including advertising, sales promotion, direct marketing, and public relations) designed to achieve promotional objectives.

personal selling Interpersonal promotional process involving a seller's person-to-person presentation to a prospective buyer.

Figure 17.5 A Joint Promotion Using Licensing

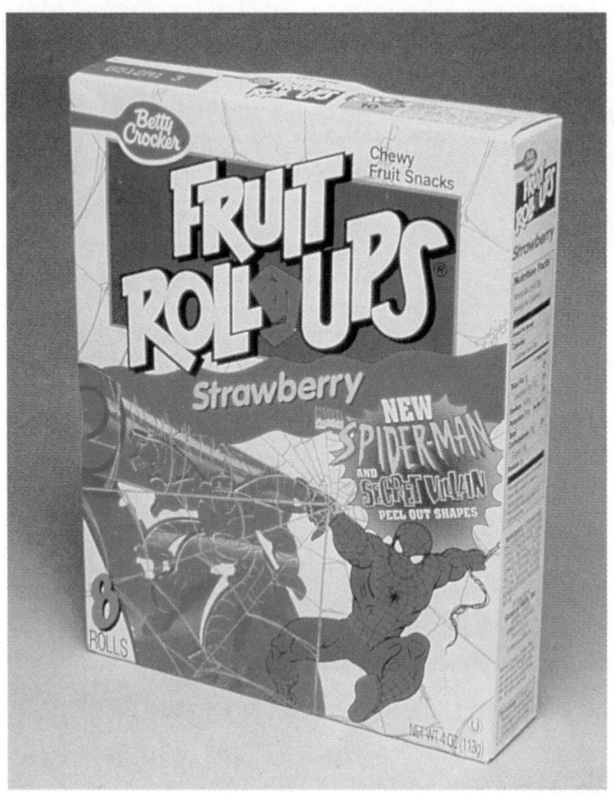
Betty Crocker
Chewy
Fruit Snacks
FRUIT ROLL UPS
Strawberry
NEW
SPIDER-MAN
AND
SECRET VILLAIN
PEEL OUT SHAPES
8
ROLLS

sales promotion are usually regarded as the most important forms of nonpersonal selling. About one-third of marketing dollars pay for media advertising and two-thirds fund trade and consumer sales promotions.

Advertising is any paid, nonpersonal communication through various media about a business firm, not-for-profit organization, product, or idea by a sponsor identified in a message that is intended to inform or persuade members of a particular audience. Advertising primarily involves the mass media, such as newspapers, television, radio, magazines, and billboards. Advertising also includes less traditional forms of promotion such as commercials on videotapes, electronic media, videoscreens in supermarkets, and messages on signs pulled by airplanes. Businesses have come to realize the tremendous potential of advertising and advertising is a major promotional mix component for thousands of organizations. Mass consumption and geographically dispersed markets make advertising particularly appropriate for goods and services marketed by sending the same promotional messages to large audiences.

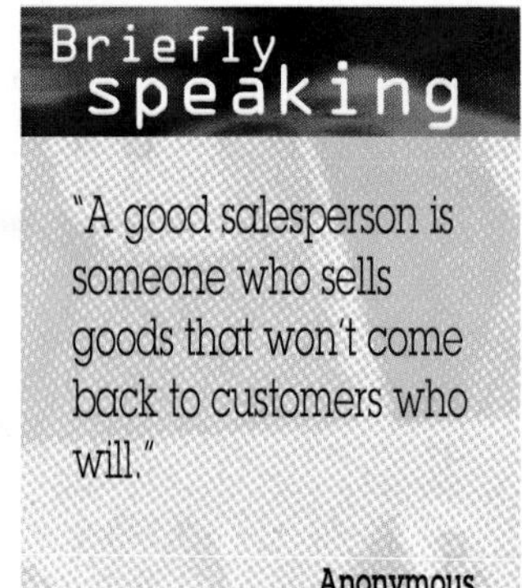
Briefly speaking
"A good salesperson is someone who sells goods that won't come back to customers who will."
Anonymous

Sales promotion consists of marketing activities other than personal selling, advertising, and public relations that stimulate consumer purchasing and dealer effectiveness. This broad category includes displays, trade shows, coupons, contests, samples, premiums, product demonstrations, and various nonrecurrent, irregular selling efforts. Sales promotion provides a short-term incentive, usually in combination with other forms of promotion, to emphasize, assist, supplement, or otherwise support the objectives of the promotional program.

Figure 17.5 shows how marketers use comic book characters to promote their products. Betty Crocker licensed the Spiderman character to promote its fruit snacks, including stickers and on-pack comics with packages of Fruit Roll-Ups. DC Comics created stories combining Kellogg's Tony the Tiger with popular athletes in a *Sports Illustrated* tie-in. Personal appearances supported the comic book campaigns.[17]

Sales promotion geared to marketing intermediaries is called **trade promotion.** Companies actually spend about as much on trade promotion as on advertising and consumer-oriented sales promotion combined. Trade promotion strategies include offering free merchandise, buyback allowances, mechandise allowances along with sponsorship of sales contests to encourage wholesalers or retailers to sell more of certain products or product lines.

Another element in a firm's integrated promotional mix is **direct marketing,** defined by the Direct Marketing Association as "the use of direct communication to a consumer or business recipient designed to generate a response in the form of an order (direct order); a request for further information (lead generation); or a visit to a place of business to purchase specific goods or services (traffic generation)."[18] While many people equate direct marketing with direct mail, this promotional category also includes telephone marketing (telemarketing), direct-response advertising and infomercials on television and radio, direct-response print advertising, and electronic media.

Public relations refers to a firm's communications and relationships with its various publics. These publics include customers, suppliers, stockholders, employees, the government, the general public, and the society in which the organization operates. Public relations programs can conduct either formal or informal contacts. The critical point is that every organization, whether or not it has a formally organized program, must be concerned about its public relations.

Publicity is an important part of an effective public relations effort. It can be defined as nonpersonal stimulation of demand for a good, service, person, cause, or organization through unpaid placement of significant news about it in a published medium or favorable presentation of it through radio, television, or the stage. Compared to personal selling, advertising, and even sales promotion, expenditures for public relations are usually low in most firms. Since they don't pay for it, companies have less control over the publication by the press or electronic media of good or bad company news. For this reason, a consumer may find this type of news source more believable than if the information were disseminated directly by the company.

As Table 17.2 indicates, each type of promotion has both advantages and shortcomings. Although personal selling entails a relatively high per-contact cost, it wastes less effort than do nonpersonal forms of promotion such as advertising. Personal selling often provides more flexible promotion than the other forms because the salesperson can tailor the sales message to meet the unique needs—or objections—of each potential customer.

The major advantages of advertising come from its ability to create instant awareness of a good, service, or idea; build brand equity; and deliver the marketer's message to mass audiences for a relatively low cost per contact. Major disadvantages of advertising include the difficulty in measuring its effectiveness and high media costs. Sales promotions, by contrast, can be more accurately monitored and measured than advertising, produce immediate consumer responses, and provide short-term sales increases. Direct marketing gives an action-oriented choice, permits narrow audience segmentation and customization of communications, and produces measurable results. Public relations efforts such as publicity frequently offer substantially higher credibility than other promotional techniques. The marketer must determine the appropriate blend of these promotional mix elements to effectively market the firm's goods and services.

SPONSORSHIPS

An increasingly common marketing activity integrates several elements of the promotional mix: commercial sponsorship of an event or activity. **Sponsorship** occurs when an organization provides cash or in-kind resources to an event or activity in exchange for a direct association with that event or activity. Essentially, the sponsor purchases two things: (1) the exposure potential with the activity's audience, and (2) the image associated with the activity by its audience. The sponsorship arrangement typically involves advertising including direct mail, sales promotion, and personal selling at the event itself. It also introduces another form of relationship marketing, bringing together the event, its participants, and the sponsoring firms.

Sponsorship Spending

Two-thirds of the $5.9 billion spent annually by commercial sponsors goes to sporting events, ranging from the Olympics and national sports leagues to auto racing and local sports events. Anheuser-Busch, Philip Morris, The Coca-Cola Co., General Motors, and PepsiCo are the top spenders for U.S. sports sponsorships. General Motors' Buick and Cadillac divisions sponsor PGA golf tours as a way to form a bond with the sport's affluent, well-educated players and fans. Sponsorship is also an international promotional activity; among the sponsors of the annual Tour de France bicycle race are the U.S. Postal Service, Italian car manufacturer Fiat, and Credit Lyonnais, a major French bank.

Sports sponsorships are such powerful marketing tools that the Arizona Diamondbacks Major League Baseball team had already arranged several major sponsorships two years prior to playing its first game. Fans will buy soft drinks from PepsiCo and beer from Miller Brewing in a Phoenix stadium named for Bank One. PepsiCo, whose deal is worth at least $40 million for 15 years, also has marketing rights for a TV show and the Diamondback-themed soda cans.[19]

A recent trend emphasizes local, grass-roots sponsorships as a way to increase the value of national and

Marketing Dictionary

advertising Paid, nonpersonal communication through various media by a business firm, not-for-profit organization, or individual identified in the message with the hope of informing or persuading members of a particular audience.

sales promotion Marketing activities other than personal selling, advertising, and publicity that stimulate consumer purchasing and dealer effectiveness (includes displays, trade shows, coupons, premiums, contests, product demonstrations, and various nonrecurrent selling efforts).

trade promotion Sales promotions aimed at marketing intermediaries rather than ultimate consumers.

direct marketing Direct communications other than personal sales contacts between buyer and seller.

public relations Firm's communications and relationships with its various publics.

publicity Stimulation of demand for a good, service, place, idea, person, or organization by unpaid placement of commercially significant news or favorable media presentations.

sponsorship Provision of funds for a sporting or cultural event in exchange for a direct association with the event.

Table 17.2 Comparison of the Five Promotional Mix Elements

	Personal Selling	Advertising	Sales Promotion	Direct Marketing	Public Relations
ADVANTAGES	Permits measurement of effectiveness	Reaches a large group of potential consumers for a relatively low price per exposure	Produces an immediate consumer response	Generates an immediate response	Creates a positive attitude toward a product or company
	Elicits an immediate response	Allows strict control over the final message	Attracts attention and creates product awareness	Covers a wide audience with targeted advertising	Enhances credibility of a product or company
	Tailors the message to fit the customer	Can be adapted to either mass audiences or specific audience segments	Allows easy measurement of results	Allows complete, customized, personal message	
			Provides short-term sales increases	Produces measurable results	
DISADVANTAGES	Relies almost exclusively upon the ability of the salesperson	Does not permit totally accurate measurement of results	Is nonpersonal in nature	Suffers from image problem	May not permit accurate measurement of effect on sales
	Involves high cost per contact	Usually cannot close sales	Is difficult to differentiate from competitors' efforts	Involves a high cost per reader	Involves much effort directed toward nonmarketing-oriented goals
				Depends on quality and accuracy of mailing lists	
				May annoy consumers	

international sponsorships. "A consumer at home watching TV sees Coca-Cola as an official sponsor and it's not that big of a deal," comments Jim Andrews of International Entertainment Group, an industry organization. "But if a company is sponsoring a hockey clinic in someone's local area, then it has [added] meaning to the consumer." McDonald's sponsors World Cup Soccer and the Mayor's Cup soccer tournament in Chicago. John Hancock sponsors not only the Olympic hockey team and New York and Boston marathons but also local hockey and running clinics.

The remaining 35 percent of sponsorship spending (after sporting events) is divided among four categories. Marketers spend 11 percent of every sponsorship dollar on pop music and entertainment tours, while cause marketing and sponsorship of festivals, fairs, and annual events each account for 9 percent. The final 6 percent is allocated to the arts.[20]

Arts sponsorships offer companies unique ways to promote themselves and reach specific target markets. Ford Motor Co. sponsored a traveling show of Latin-American folk art and hosted parties for local Latin community leaders throughout the tour. Goya Foods sponsored the Francisco Goya exhibit at the Metropolitan Museum of Art in New York. The company's name appeared in large gold letters at the exhibit entrance and on posters and catalogs, and its ethnic food products were served in the museum restaurant. The $245,000 cost was money well spent. "It got us to a new and more sophisticated audience. I think that will up our sales in the long run," said Goya President Joseph Unanue.[21]

Marketers underwrite varying levels of sponsorships depending on the amount their companies wish to spend and the types of events. For example, a marketer might choose to be a *title sponsor* of an event. The title sponsor's name would be included in the event title and displayed in other places such as the hospitality tent, on-site signs, merchandise, and tickets. Examples of title sponsorships include the FedEx Orange Bowl football game and the Cadillac Seniors Professional Golf Association Tour. Total costs for a title sponsorship typically amount to $750,000 plus a commitment to purchase $1 million in TV advertising during the event's telecast.

Corporate sports sponsorships have moved into new arenas—literally. Recently corporations have begun sponsoring major league sports stadiums. San Francisco's Candlestick Park became 3Com Park at a cost of $4 million for 4 years. The cost will be considerably higher for Denver's Pepsi Center—about $50 million for a 20-year term—and St. Louis' TransWorld Dome cost TWA Airlines $26 million for 20 years. Such sponsorships appeal to companies because they can reach many thousands of consumers every time the stadium hosts a game or concert, making them a cost-effective form of promotion compared to a 30-second television commercial.[22]

Figure 17.6 Sponsorships Race Ahead

PRODIGY
BREATH SAVERS
SUGAR FREE MINTS
BUSCH
STP
CHAMPION
Gatorade
Prestone
FRAM
PERFECT CIRCLE
GOODYEAR

Some marketers choose less expensive forms of sponsorship. A *presenting sponsor* receives the same benefits as the title sponsor (other than use of the company name in the event title) for perhaps a $300,000 fee plus $500,000 in television advertising. As many as seven firms can be *associate sponsors,* which entitles them to on-site signs for $30,000 to $35,000. Many events also include official product sponsors. Infiniti was title sponsor for the U.S. Men's Amateur Tennis Tournament, and Evian bottled water and Adidas sports apparel were product sponsors. Banners with the sponsors' names and logos were displayed in local tennis clubs around the country.

Growth of Sponsorships

Commercial sponsorship of sporting and cultural events is not a new phenomenon. Aristocrats in ancient Rome sponsored gladiator competitions and chariot races featuring teams that were often supported financially by competing businesses. Over 2,000 years ago, wealthy Athenians underwrote drama, musical, and sporting festivals. Craft guilds in fourteenth-century England sponsored plays (occasionally insisting that the playwrights insert "plugs" for their lines of work in the scripts). In the United States during the 1880s, streetcar companies commonly sponsored local baseball teams.[23]

Sponsorship as a promotional alternative has grown rapidly over the past three decades. During this period, corporate sponsorship spending has increased faster than promotional outlays for advertising and sales promotion. In recent years, sponsorship spending has grown at annual rates of 10 to 15 percent, as compared with single-digit average annual increases in marketing outlays for advertising and sales promotion.

Sponsorships are showing up in a variety of new formats and places. Planters LifeSavers Co. expanded its NASCAR sponsorship by teaming up with Olive Garden Restaurants, as shown in Figure 17.6. In a creative campaign, the company increased brand recognition of its BreathSavers mints in the South. Samples of BreathSavers were given away at race tracks, and with every check at Olive Garden restaurants.

In a new twist, major sports leagues are now recruiting firms to sponsor events on the World Wide Web. IBM sponsored Web-site activities for the National Hockey League All-Star Game, and the National Football League, NBC, and Microsoft co-sponsored the Super Bowl site. Microsoft was title sponsor, for a cost of $225,000. Other companies such as Visa bought advertising spots at much lower rates based on the number of viewers.[24]

Several factors have influenced the growth of commercial sponsorships:

- *Government restrictions on tobacco and alcohol advertising.* Prohibition of tobacco advertising on radio and television and the growing reluctance of newspaper and magazine publishers to accept print ads for alcoholic beverages and tobacco products has led marketers to seek out alternative promotional media.

- *Escalating cost of traditional advertising media.* Commercial sponsorships are increasingly viewed as highly cost-effective marketing tools when compared with traditional advertising.

- *Additional opportunities resulting from diverse leisure activities.* Members of the leisure-conscious U.S. society feel strong attractions to sporting activities, and their interests have become more diverse. This trend is evident from the recent growth in activities such as beach volleyball, in-line skating, and parasailing, as well as the increasing array of sporting events featured on television and in newspapers and magazines. Media coverage of these events, in turn, permits marketers to use sponsorships as a means of reaching specific target markets.

- *Greater media coverage of sponsored events.* Media coverage, of sports and cultural activities, particularly on radio and television, has become more intensive in recent years. In addition to coverage on sports radio stations and television super channels, exclusive coverage by ESPN, ESPN2, and ESPNEWS, the Golf Channel, Fox Sports, and regional sports networks have increased the demand for sports programming. As a consequence, sponsors gain even greater exposure for their money.

- *An increasingly global media.* Anyone who watches the televised Wimbledon tennis championships or Formula One auto racing knows that sponsorship is not limited to the United States. The world's largest television audience for a sporting event does not watch the Super Bowl; its viewers tune in to the World Cup soccer championships. Global marketers recognize sponsorship as an effective way to reach an international audience in a manner that is universally understood.

- *The proven effectiveness of sponsorship.* More and more marketers are realizing that sponsorship works. Sponsorship spending that is properly planned, linked to predetermined objectives, and aimed at specified target markets can buy highly effective marketing contacts. Moreover, sponsorships represent alternatives to the increased clutter associated with advertising and direct mail.

How Sponsorship Differs from Advertising

Even though sponsorship spending and traditional advertising spending both represent forms of nonpersonal selling, they are more different from than similar to one another. Chief among these differences are the sponsor's degree of control versus that of the advertising, the nature of the message, audience reaction, and measurements of effectiveness.

Marketers have considerable control over the quantity and quality of market coverage when they advertise. Sponsors, on the other hand, must rely on signs to present their messages. Also, they have little control of sponsored events beyond matching the audiences to profiles of their own target markets. In addition, sponsorship is a mute, nonverbal medium, since the message is delivered in association with an activity possessing its own personality in the eyes of its audience. By contrast, a traditional advertisement allows the marketer to create an individual message containing an introduction, a theme, and a conclusion.

Audiences react differently to sponsorship as a communications medium than to other media. The sponsor's investment provides a recognizable benefit to the sponsored activity that the audience can appreciate. As a result, sponsorship is often viewed more positively than traditional advertising.

Assessing Sponsorship Results

To assess the results of sponsorships, marketers utilize some of the same techniques by which they measure advertising effectiveness. However, the differences between the two promotional alternatives often necessitate some unique research techniques, as well. A few corporate sponsors attempt to link expenditures to sales. Kraft General Foods, for example, evaluates the effectiveness of its NASCAR sponsorship by comparing Country Time lemonade sales in the races' primary southeastern U.S. markets with sales in other markets. Other sponsors measure improved brand awareness and image as effectiveness indicators; they conduct traditional surveys before and after the events to secure this information. Still other sponsors measure the impact of their event marketing in public relations terms. Typically, a researcher will count press clippings featuring a sponsor's name or logo, and then translate this number into equivalent advertising costs.

Despite the impressive visibility of special events like soccer's World Cup and football's Super Bowl, these events do not necessarily lead directly to increased sales. Performance Research, a Newport, Rhode Island marketing research firm, conducted a sponsor loyalty survey to see how often sponsorships motivate consumers to purchase the sponsors' products "almost always" or "frequently." Car racing was by far the best performer in terms of influencing purchases; the top three sponsorships were NASCAR racing at 72 percent; World of Outlaws sprint-car racing, 71 percent; and Indy-car events, at 68 percent. Other sports events ranked as follows: tennis, 52 percent; professional cycling, Major League Baseball, and the National Basketball Association, each with 38 percent; the National Football League, 36 percent; the America's Cup (sailing), 34 percent; and the Olympics, 30 percent. Due to increased attendance at NASCAR events, nontraditional sponsors like the Cartoon Network, Prodigy, QVC, and Heilig-Meyers Furniture are joining Miller Brewing, Camel cigarettes, and STP auto products as NASCAR sponsors. As marketing consultant Joyce Julius explains, "Those aren't just cars—they're moving billboards." In addition to having their logos on cars, sponsors also appear on T-shirts, mugs, and other merchandise tie-ins.[25]

Using Sponsorship in a Promotional Strategy

Despite its limitations with regard to message control and delivery along with problems in measuring effectiveness, the number of firms using sponsorship as a component of the promotional mix continues to grow each year. Figure 17.7 illustrates the step-by-step approach to finalizing a sponsorship deal.

Figure 17.7 Steps in the Sponsorship Process

1

The Product
El Capitan parkas and cold-resistant outerwear, high-priced, lightweight, waterproof winter sportswear in fashion colors that provide maximum protection against low temperatures and bitter winds.

The Market
Most sales are during late fall and winter months. Consumers are typically teens and Generation Xers and active snow skiers. Performance, quality, and styling justify the premium price.

The Problem
El Capitan has low brand awareness due in part to the strong preference for well-established brands such as Gore-Tex.

The Solution
El Capitan marketers contact SportSearch, an international research firm that advises the firm to consider sponsoring a sporting event, snowboarding, which would appeal to the target market and coincides with the peak selling season.

The Decision
El Capitan decides to sponsor the "Snowboarding 2000" series of events at 11 eastern and western U.S. ski resorts since it is the nation's fastest growing sport, it appeals to participants and spectators who match the firm's target market, and it is quickly becoming an international sport. SportSearch is hired to conduct research to determine the right consumer psychographics. Fans will be interviewed to determine their levels of brand loyalty, their roles as opinion leaders, and how they feel about the event's sponsor.

6

The Cost
SportSearch estimates $400,000 would pay for sampling, an official sponsorship, on-site entertainment, and various promotional campaigns such as discounted event tickets, contests, and product coupons.

The Results
After the winter season, SportSearch conducts a general marketing study to determine the results of the sponsorship. Findings are compared to consumers with similar demographic and psychographic profiles.

8

The Commitment
SportSearch reports are positive. El Capitan marketers renew their sponsorship, add new events, and increase sport marketing spending, but decide to monitor the returns from its sponsorship program on a semiannual basis.

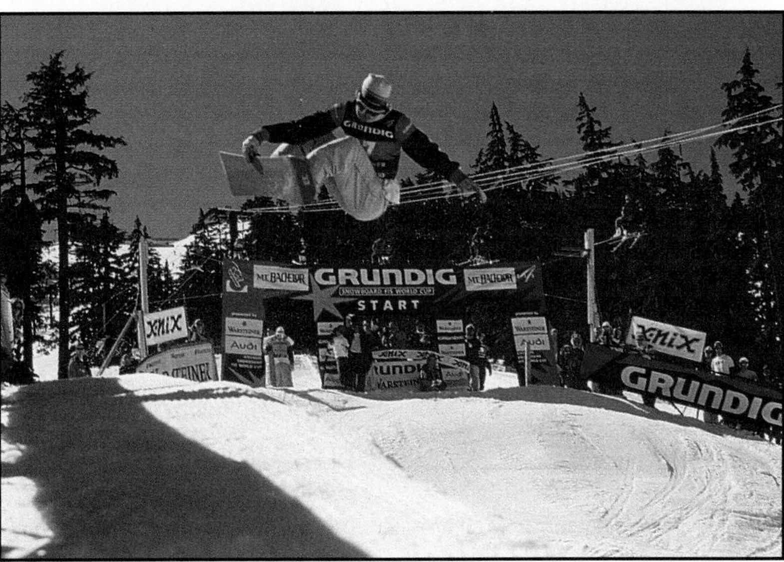
GRUNDIG
START
GRUNDIG

DIRECT MARKETING

Few promotional mix elements are growing as fast as direct marketing. By 2000, sales revenues from such direct marketing activities as interactive electronic media, direct mail, telemarketing, infomercials, and direct-response advertising are expected to exceed $1.6 billion. Both consumer and business-to-business marketers rely on this promotional mix element to generate orders or sales leads (requests for more information) that may result in future orders. Direct marketing also helps simply to increase store traffic (visits to the store or office to evaluate and perhaps purchase the advertised goods or services). In fact, 56 percent of all direct marketing expenditures are targeted at lead generation. Marketers intend another 32 percent to entice customers to make direct orders, and they focus the final 12 percent on increasing store traffic. As Figure 17.8 shows, two-thirds of total direct marketing revenues are generated through telephone marketing and direct mail.[26]

Direct marketing communications pursue goals beyond creating product awareness; marketers intend them to generate action—placing an order, getting more information, visiting a store—by calling a toll-free number, sending back a form or coupon, sending an e-mail message, or making some other type of response. This action orientation is a major reason for direct marketing's popularity. Other advantages include its interactive nature and the ability to narrowly target market segments and customize communications to them. Because direct marketing communications involve some type of response, marketers can measure results more easily than the outcomes of other forms of advertising and promotion. Also, companies can try different direct marketing packages and media combinations to see which gets the best response. Direct marketing is, therefore, a very powerful tool that helps organizations win new customers and also enhance relationships with existing ones.

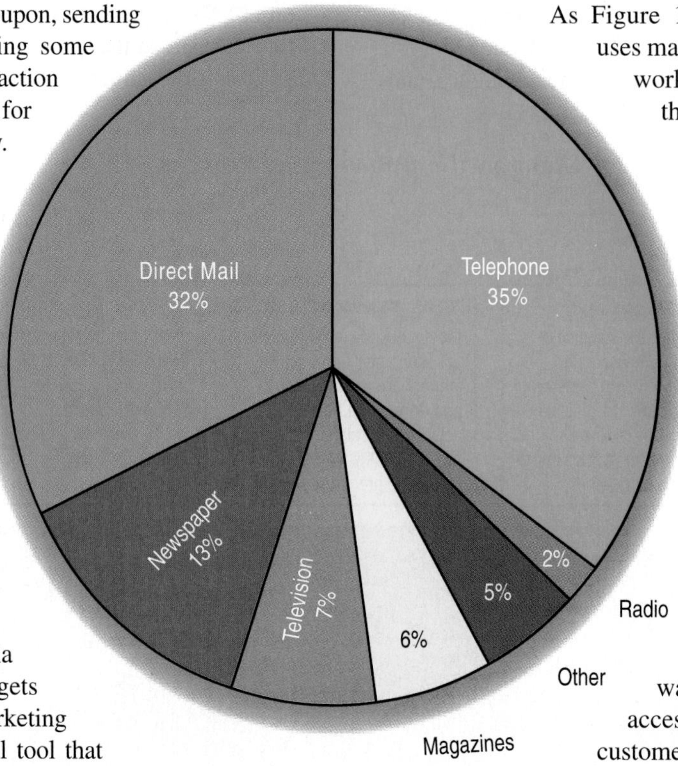

The growth of direct marketing parallels the move toward integrated marketing communications (IMC) in many ways. For example, both respond to fragmented media markets and audiences, growth of customized products, shrinking network broadcast audiences, and use of databases to target specific markets. Lifestyles also play a role, because today's busy consumers want convenience and time savings.

Databases are an important part of direct marketing. Using the latest technology to create sophisticated databases, a company can select a narrow market segment and find good prospects within that segment based on desired characteristics. Capitol One Financial Corp., the second largest direct-mail credit-card issuer, sees itself not as a credit-card company but as a database marketer. Its database includes information based on mailings to over 200 million potential customers and provides the ability to test offers with different interest rates and fees on different customer groups. It then evaluates the response and retention rates to see which offer has the strongest appeal for each group. Clearly, marketers can cut costs and improve returns on dollars spent by identifying those customers who are most likely to respond to a message and eliminating others from their lists.[27]

Direct Mail
32%
Telephone
35%
Newspaper
13%
Television
7%
6%
5%
2%
Radio
Other
Magazines

Figure 17.8 Direct Marketing Sales by Media Category

Direct Marketing Communications Channels

As Figure 17.8 shows, direct marketing uses many different media forms. Each works best for certain purposes, although marketers often combine two or more media on one direct marketing program. For example, a company can start with telemarketing to screen potential customers and follow up by sending more material to interested consumers by direct mail. Quick & Reilly (Q&R) Discount Brokers used two media for an interactive direct marketing program. A visitor to Q&R's Web page who sends an electronic inquiry receives a package with software on a CD-ROM and online access for more information and customer support.[28]

Direct Mail

Direct mail is a major component of direct marketing. It comes in many forms, ranging from sales letters, postcards, brochures, booklets, catalogs, and house organs (periodicals issued by organizations) to video and audio cassettes. Direct mail offers advantages like the ability to select a narrow target market, achieve intensive coverage, send messages quickly, choose from various formats, provide complete information, and personalize each mailing piece.

http://www.quick-reilly.com/

Figure 17.9 Targeted Direct Mail: John Michael Kohler Arts Center

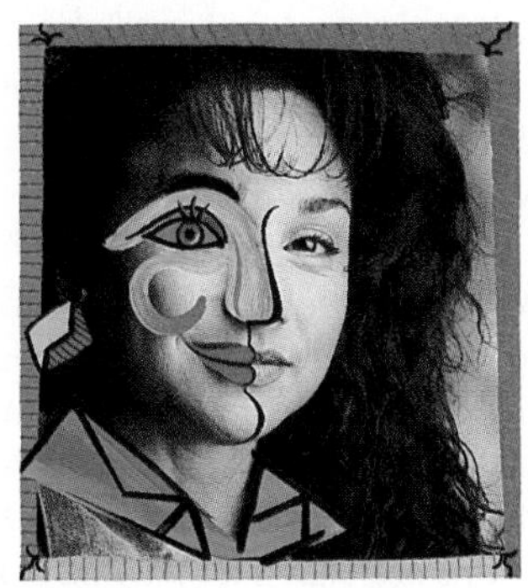

AN EXPERIENCE THAT WILL CHANGE YOU INSIDE AND OUT.

Response rates are measurable and higher than other types of advertising. In addition, direct mailings stand alone and do not compete for attention with magazine articles and television programs. On the other hand, the per-reader cost of direct mail is high, effectiveness depends on the quality of the mailing list, and some consumers object strongly to what they consider "junk mail."

Direct mail marketing relies heavily on database technology to develop lists of names and segment them according to the objectives of the campaign. Recipients get targeted materials, often personalized with their names within the ad's content. Both not-for-profit and profit-seeking organizations make extensive use of direct mail. The John Michael Kohler Arts Center in Sheboygan, Wisconsin, targets direct mail such as the brochure in Figure 17.9 to community members in a six-county area. Affected by cuts to the National Endowment for the Arts, the not-for-profit JMKAC uses direct mail to increase local financial support for its museum and theatre, music, and dance programs, promising contributors the benefits of "An experience that will change you inside and out."

Levi's for Girls, recognizing that kids love mail but don't get much, targeted girls ages 7 to 11 with a direct mail campaign to promote brand awareness and increase store traffic. The company sent a "Back to School Fun Book" with activities and a contest as well as pictures of models in Levi's for Girls clothing. To enter the contest, girls had to drop off their completed forms at participating stores, which required an adult's help. Despite this obstacle, the campaign generated high response rates and doubled brand awareness among the target group.[29]

Catalogs are a popular form of direct mail, with more than 10,000 different consumer specialty mail-order catalogs—and thousands more for business-to-business sales—finding their way to almost every mailbox in the United States. In a typical year, they generate almost $40 billion in consumer sales and $24 billion in business-to-business sales. The selection includes general-merchandise catalogs, like JCPenney, and specialty catalogs like PC/Mac Connection and The Chef's Catalog. Companies often develop several versions of their catalogs for different audiences. In addition to its general catalog, Lillian Vernon sends Lilly's Kids to families and those who order children's merchandise as gifts. Catalogs are an ideal format for customized marketing. Marketers can divide their products into narrow categories—desserts, cheese, fishing equipment, cookware—for specific segments.

After its catalog business declined, Sears eliminated its all-inclusive catalog in 1993. Based on market research showing that about 20 percent of U.S. households like to shop at home and that customers preferred the more focused catalogs, it switched to more than 20 Sears specialty catalogs, including the Craftsman tool book. Sears vice president John H. Costello explained the rationale behind the move:

> We have a heritage of satisfaction guaranteed, a reputation for quality, and a strong database of desirable customers. Launching specialty catalogs enabled us to preserve a relationship with these customers and leverage the value of our database. . . . We mail only to customers with a proven purchase history. For example, we mail our Workwear catalog to customers who have bought workwear from us. Our database is unusually fertile. It combines our catalog sales, retail sales and credit information.[30]

Catalogs can be a company's only or primary sales method—Spiegel, L. L. Bean, Lands' End, Eddie Bauer, and Patagonia are some well-known examples—and they may also supplement the store-based offerings of retailers like Nordstrom, Saks Fifth Avenue, and Neiman Marcus. New technologies are changing catalog marketing. Today's catalogs can be updated quickly, providing consumers with

Figure 17.10 Combining Two Media: L. L. Bean's Direct-Response Print Ad

L.L.Outfitted
4551 AG
Great fall weekends start with your new L.L.Bean Catalog.
Whether you're outfitting a journey to the mountains, or an overnight in the backyard, you can count on L.L.Bean for all your clothes and gear. We offer over 400 items for fall, from paddles to pullovers, tents to turtlenecks, all 100% guaranteed, honestly priced, and delivered faster than ever by Federal Express.® That's why for over 80 years, most folks have started their fall adventures by opening their L.L.Bean Catalog.
So before you head out this weekend, why not open yours and give us a call?
Can't find your catalog? We'd be happy to send you another.
Just call or write us.
1-800-985-2326
LL#4430830
© 1994 L.L.Bean, Inc.
L.L.Bean®
Casco Street, Freeport, ME 04032-9984

the latest information and prices. CD-ROM catalogs allow marketers to display products in three-dimensional views and include video sequences of product demonstrations. The CD-ROM catalog of White Flower Farms, a Litchfield, Connecticut, mail-order nursery, takes on a different dimension. It allows customers to select from the firm's more than 2,000 plant offerings, simulate planting them, and see how they will grow under local conditions, thereby eliminating some uncertainty.[31]

Although many consumers like to receive direct mail, others object to unsolicited communications. In response, the Direct Mail/Marketing Association established its Mail Preference Service. This consumer service sends name-removal forms to people who do not wish to receive direct-mail advertising. It also provides add-on forms for those who like to receive a lot of mail.

Telemarketing

Any person whose dinner is interrupted by a sales call can attest that telemarketing is the most frequently used form of direct marketing. It provides marketers with a high return on their expenditures, an immediate response, and the opportunity for personalized, two-way conversations. **Telemarketing** refers to direct marketing conducted entirely by telephone. It can be classified as either outbound or inbound contacts. *Outbound telemarketing* involves a sales force that uses only the telephone to contact customers, reducing the cost of making personal visits. The customer initiates *inbound telemarketing,* which typically involves calling a toll-free number to obtain information and make purchases at their convenience. Like direct mail, telemarketing taps into databases to target calls based on customer characteristics like family income, number of children, and home ownership. For example, income is an important criterion for banks who use telemarketing to solicit new credit-card customers.

Telemarketing is gaining importance in the marketing strategies of many firms; revenues from phone sales are expected to grow about 9 percent per year to $600 billion by 2000. New *predictive dialer* devices improve telemarketing's efficiency and reduce costs by automating the dialing process to skip busy signals and answering machines. When the dialer reaches a human voice, it instantaneously puts the call through to a salesperson. This technology is often combined with a print advertising campaign that features a toll-free number for inbound telemarketing. In Figure 17.10, direct marketer L. L. Bean's print ad displays its products and gives consumers a way to get the latest catalog by calling a toll-free number. Electronic shoppers can also use the company's Web address.

http://www.llbean.com/

Business-to-business telemarketing is on the rise, as well. Marketers at Xerox and the long-distance phone companies use telemarketing to develop sales leads. "It's more cost-effective than having salespeople out here cold-calling," explains Ellen Ryan, director of telemarketing at Wunderman Cato Johnson, a major direct marketing agency.[32]

Because recipients of both consumer and business-to-business telemarketing calls often find them annoying, the Federal Trade Commission passed a Telemarketing Sales Rule in 1996. The rule cracks down on abusive telemarketing practices by establishing allowed calling hours and regulating call content. Companies must clearly disclose details of any exchange policies, maintain lists of people who do not want to receive calls, and keep records of telemarketing scripts, prize winners, customers, and employees for two years. While designed to protect customers against fraud—with losses estimated in excess of $40 billion, almost 10 percent of telemarketing-generated revenues—the rule also helps telemarketers by improving the practice's image.[33] Consumers can cut down on undesirable sales calls by requesting that the DMA Telephone Preference Service put them on the "do not call" list.

Direct Marketing via Broadcast Channels

Broadcast direct marketing can take three basic forms: brief direct-response ads on television or radio, home shopping channels, and infomercials. Direct-response spots typically run 30, 60, or 90 seconds and include product descriptions and toll-free numbers for ordering. Often shown on cable television and independent stations and tied to special-interest programs, they encourage viewers to respond immediately. Radio direct-response ads also provide product descriptions and addresses or phone numbers to contact the sellers. Radio proves expensive compared to other direct marketing media, and listeners may not pay close enough attention to catch the number or write it down while in the car, which accounts for a major portion of radio listening time.

Home shopping channels like Quality Value Channel (QVC) and Home Shopping Network (HSN) represent another type of television direct marketing. Broadcasting around the clock, these and similar channels offer consumers a variety of products, from jewelry and kitchen equipment to insurance. Customers place orders via toll-free numbers and pay for their purchases by credit card. They work best for products in the $20 to $50 range. Louis Knickerbocker, whose company L. L. Knickerbocker develops and sells products through these networks, believes that both home shopping and infomercials are good brand-building tools. "It's not brain surgery to sell on TV," he says. "You have to put out a good product; tie a celebrity, designer, or inventor to the product; and make an event out of it."[34]

Infomercials are 30-minute or longer product commercials that resemble regular television programs. Because of their length, infomercials don't get lost like 30-second commercials do, and they permit marketers to present their products in more detail. Infomercials also provide toll-free phone numbers so viewers can order products or request more information. Although infomercials incur higher production costs than prime-time, 30-second ads on national network TV, they generally air on less expensive cable channels and in late-night time slots on broadcast stations. However, these timing limitations may prevent a company from reaching desired audiences. Another disadvantage of infomercials is their poor image.

For many years, companies used this type of advertising to sell "miracle products" like beauty aids promising a more youthful appearance, the Thighmaster, the ECT Ionizer air purifier, Ginsu knives, and expensive fitness equipment like the Abflex and Power Rider. Today, however, infomercials generate about $1 billion in revenue, and they contribute not only to direct sales but as part of integrated marketing communications programs by Fortune 500 companies. They can help companies build brand equity and increase retail sales by providing lots of information, including demonstrations and testimonials. Infomercials provide cost-effective selling tools, and responses via toll-free numbers help companies to build databases.

As Figure 17.11 points out, production for the average infomercial is $300,000, and the marketer spends from $600,000 to several million dollars to air it for a year. Still, this total is low compared to most companies' total promotional budgets. Sears, for example, spends $500 million per year just for retail ads. Infomercials showcasing some of its Craftsman tools resulted in significant increases in retail sales. The cost often proves reasonable compared to the sales generated by successful infomercials. Among those producing over $100 million in sales are "Fitness Breakthroughs," with Jane Fonda demonstrating her treadmill; "Hidden Keys to Loving Relationships," with couples Kathie Lee and Frank Gifford and Connie Selleca and John Tesh; Richard Simmons' Deal-a-Meal program; and "Will Your Kids Make the Grade?" with John Ritter promoting the "Where there's a will, there's an A" program.

Companies like Volvo, Philips Electronics North America, Lexus, Microsoft, and Apple Computer recognize the value of the infomercial's long time frame to inform and educate consumers about product benefits. Nissan targeted female buyers with its infomercial on how to buy a car. Steve Dworman, publisher of *Infomercial Market Report,* credits Microsoft's special Windows 95

Marketing Dictionary

telemarketing Promotional presentation involving the use of the telephone for outbound contacts by salespeople or inbound contacts initiated by customers who want to obtain information and place orders.

infomercial Commercial for a single product running 30 minutes or longer in a format that resembles a regular television program.

Figure 17.11 What's in a 30-Minute Infomercial?

ADVERTISING

ADVERTISING ON HOME-SHOPPING CHANNELS OR THROUGH two-minute infomercials is great if your product has mass appeal, costs $20 to $50, enjoys a four-to-one markup, and is easily explained. If—and only if. Perhaps those caveats explain the growing interest in half-hour infomercials. It's a format that lets you strut your stuff . . . if you do it right.

No matter how you do it, those 30 minutes don't come cheap. As you might suspect, there's more to making an infomercial than meets the eye. And be forewarned: the industry hit rate is a dismal 10%. We asked Tim Hawthorne, cofounder of the National Infomercial Marketing Association (NIMA) and chairman of Hawthorne Communications, in Fairfield, Iowa, to help us itemize the costs.

—*S.G. and Robina A. Gangemi*

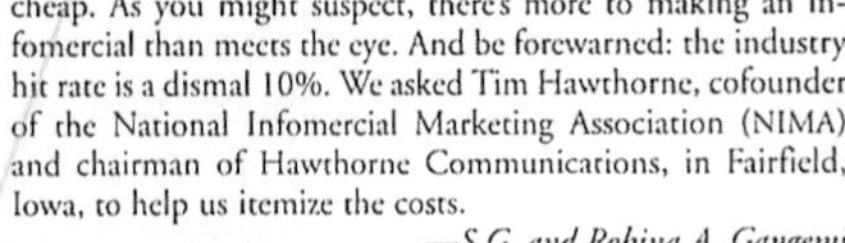
1-800-321-4100
ZENITH

Production: $100,000 minimum, $200,000 average. That is what successful infomercial ad agencies charge to write the script, hire talent, and tape your show.

Testing: $10,000 minimum, $25,000 average. You'll need to test lots of time slots and markets to confirm sales projections, the effectiveness of your message, price points, and premiums. Allot two weeks. That will give you enough time to gauge direct sales and gather sales leads.

Inbound telemarketing: $2,000 to $5,000. That's how much it costs to retain a telemarketing agency and to prepare its operators to handle your calls. What you're selling had better be worth the $2.50 to $30 you'll pay for each qualified lead or order.

Media: $50,000/month minimum, $500,000/month average. If your infomercial tests well, the most profitable times to run it are late nights, mornings, and Saturday and Sunday daytimes.

VIEWER DISCRETION ADVISED:

You can slash up-front costs by hiring an infomercial direct-marketing service. Such services either take a cut of revenues or buy your product wholesale. But you give up control. NIMA (202-962-8342) can refer you to both ad agencies and direct marketers.

program with "legitimizing" infomercials as a marketing tool for major companies.[35]

Other Direct Marketing Channels

Print media like newspapers and magazines do not support direct marketing as effectively as telemarketing and direct mail do. However, magazine ads with toll-free numbers can promote success in inbound telemarketing campaigns. Companies can place ads within the magazines or newspapers themselves, include reader-response cards, or place special inserts targeted for certain market segments within the publications.

Electronic media are the newest avenue for direct marketing. The Internet and online service providers like America Online, CompuServe, and Prodigy offer many online shopping services through their customers' personal computers. Members can buy everything from flower arrangements and gourmet foods to airline tickets. Individual companies like Hot Hot Hot and Peapod (described in Chapters 1 and 10, respectively) sell products through their Web sites. Web surfers can also find product information for items not sold online, like cars.

Electronic media deliver data instantly to direct marketers and help them to track customer buying cycles quickly. As a result, they can place customer-acquisition programs online for about 50 to 80 percent less than traditional programs cost. Ogilvy & Mather Direct's Mike Troiano has cited another advantage of online communications: "The medium lets marketers and consumers talk the way people are used to talking—one-on-one, in real time. . . . Interactive marketing is available like direct mail: not intrusive, like television commercials." The Web is an especially effective direct marketing medium to reach consumers in their 20s.

Products that adapt well to direct marketing via the Web include books, music CDs, wine, and gourmet foods. Security First Network Bank offered a six-month "cyber-CD" (certificate of deposit) with an interest rate about 1.5 percent above the market rate. The savings from the Internet's lower marketing and servicing costs allowed the firm to give consumers the higher interest rates and at the same time attract customers from around the world.[37]

Kiosks provide another outlet for electronic sales. Price Costco's Quest buying service allows consumers to purchase a wide range of product offerings using computer terminals with touch-screen technology.

DEVELOPING AN OPTIMAL PROMOTIONAL MIX

By blending advertising, personal selling, sales promotion, and public relations to achieve marketing objectives, marketers create a promotional mix. Since they can refer to no quantitative measures to determine the effectiveness of each mix component in a given market segment, the choice of a proper mix of promotional elements presents one of their most difficult tasks. Several factors influence the effectiveness of a promotional mix: (1) the nature of the market, (2) the nature of the product, (3) the stage in the product life cycle, (4) the price, and (5) the funds available for promotion.

Nature of the Market

The marketer's target audience has a major impact on the choice of a promotion method. When a market includes a limited number of buyers, personal selling may prove a highly effective technique. However, markets characterized by large numbers of potential customers scattered over sizable geographic areas may make the cost of contact by personal salespeople prohibitive. In such instances, extensive use advertising may make sense. The type of customer also affects the promotional mix. Personal selling works better in a target market made up of industrial purchasers or retail and wholesale buyers than in a target market consisting of ultimate consumers. Similarly, pharmaceutical firms use large sales forces to sell prescription drugs directly to physicians and hospitals, but they advertise to promote over-the-counter drugs for the consumer market. When a prescription drug receives FDA approval to be sold over the counter, the drug firm must switch its promotional strategy from personal selling to consumer advertising.

As spending rises by specific ethnic groups such as Hispanics, African-Americans, and Asian-Americans, more marketers are designing appropriate communications to reach them. Impact Media's door-to-door sampling programs—attractively designed door-hanger bags full of samples—are particularly effective with Hispanic consumers, who often view samples as gifts. The company distributes the packets twice a year to about 25 million households. This strategy works better than direct mail, newspaper sampling, or in-store sampling. It also costs less, results in better household penetration, and yields a higher response rate. General Mills, Lipton, Kellogg, Pepsi, and Procter & Gamble are among the companies using Impact Media's program.[38]

Briefly speaking

"Advertising is what you do when you can't go to see somebody. That's all it is."

Fairfax Cone (1903–1977)
Founder of Foote, Cone & Belding advertising agency

Nature of the Product

A second important factor in determining an effective promotional mix is the product itself. Highly standardized products with minimal servicing requirements usually depend less on personal selling than do custom products with technically complex features and/or requirements for frequent service. Consumer products are more likely to rely heavily on advertising than are industrial products.

Promotional mixes vary within each product category. For example, installations typically rely more heavily on personal selling than the marketing of operating supplies does. In contrast, the promotional mix for a convenience product is likely to involve more emphasis on manufacturer advertising and less on personal selling. On the other hand, personal selling plays an important role in promotion of shopping products, and both personal and nonpersonal selling are important in promotion of specialty goods. A personal-selling emphasis is also likely to prove more effective than other alternatives in promotions for products involving trade-ins.

Stage in the Product Life Cycle

The promotional mix must be tailored to the product's stage in the product life cycle. In the introductory stage, heavy emphasis on personal selling helps to inform the marketplace of the merits of the new good or service. Salespeople contact marketing intermediaries to secure interest in and commitment to handling the offering. Trade shows frequently inform and educate prospective dealers and ultimate consumers. Advertising and sales promotion at this stage create awareness and stimulate initial purchases.

Marketers of new products may need to work closely with customers to answer questions and adjust their promotional mixes as needed. As the good or service moves into the growth and maturity stages, advertising gains relative importance in persuading consumers to make purchases. Marketers continue to direct personal-selling efforts at marketing intermediaries in an attempt to expand distribution. As more competitors enter the marketplace, advertising begins to stress product differences to persuade consumers to purchase the firm's brand. In the maturity and early decline stages, firms frequently reduce advertising and sales promotion expenditures.

Mature products often require creative promotions, as with Polaroid's "See What Develops" campaign. While its core product—the instant camera—wasn't obsolete, sales had stagnated due to such factors as 1-hour photo processing, advanced photo systems, and digital imaging. The advertising campaign used charming and humorous ads to position Polaroid as the product for the times when you really need it. To revive the product, the ads created a sense of fun by presenting amusing possibilities like the one in Figure 17.12, where the parents of a college student are talking about their daughter's new boyfriend—without having seen the Polaroid snapshot.[39]

Price

The price of the good or service is the fourth factor that affects the choice of a promotional mix. Advertising dominates the promotional mixes for low-unit-value products due to the high per-contact costs in personal selling. These costs make the sales call an unprofitable tool to promote lower-value goods and services. Advertising, in contrast, permits a low promotional expenditure per sales unit because it reaches mass audiences. For low-value consumer goods, such as chewing gum, soft drinks, and snack foods, advertising is the most feasible means of promotion. On the other hand, consumers of high-priced items like luxury

Figure 17.12 Polaroid's Creative Promotion for a Mature Product

Tom, I spoke to Laurie today. Yeah? How is she?
She sounds good. She says it's no harder than high school. That's our girl.
Sounds like she's in love again, too. Not another football player?
I don't think so. She's sending a Polaroid shot of him. Maybe we should invite him for Thanksgiving.
Steven
Polaroid *See what develops.*

cars expect lots of well-presented information. High-tech, direct marketing promotions like videocassettes, CD-ROMs, fancy brochures, and personal selling appeal to these potential customers.

Funds Available for Promotion

A real barrier to implementing any promotional strategy is the size of the promotional budget. A single, 30-second television commercial during the Super Bowl telecast costs an advertiser $1.2 million. While millions of viewers may see the commercial, making the cost-per-contact relatively low, such an expenditure exceeds the entire promotional budgets of thousands of firms.

For the Dustbuster Dirt-Minotaur promotion, Black & Decker was able to work with a limited budget by using publicity as part of its IMC program. It sent promotional kits, complete with an 800-number that kids could call to receive a free comic book, to parenting magazines, columnists, and TV stations as material for their articles and shows.[40] Table 17.3 summarizes the factors that influence the determination of an appropriate promotional mix: nature of the market, nature of the product, stage in the product life cycle, and price.

PULLING AND PUSHING PROMOTIONAL STRATEGIES

Marketers may implement essentially two promotional alternatives: a pulling strategy and a pushing strategy. A **pulling strategy** is a promotional effort by the seller to stimulate final-user demand, which then exerts pressure on the distribution channel. When marketing intermediaries stock a large number of competing products and exhibit little interest in any one of them, a firm may have to implement a pulling strategy to motivate them to handle the product. In such instances, this strategy is implemented with the objective of building consumer demand so that consumers will request the product from retail stores.

Advertising and sales promotion often contribute to a company's pulling strategy. Sears, Roebuck and Co.'s IMC strategy used a combination of these promotional mix elements for its National Collegiate Athletic Association (NCAA) women's and men's basketball promotion. The retailer sponsored a "Legends of the Final Four" sweepstakes with tickets to the next year's Final Four tournament, accompanied by stars Kareem Abdul-Jabbar and Sheryl Swoopes, as the grand prize. Broadcast and print ads supported the contest. Sears even included a cause marketing component in the promotion. It sold limited-edition trading cards with pictures of former Final Four players, donating proceeds to Coaches vs. Cancer.

This campaign brought event marketing into Sears' "softer side" marketing effort. "We believe that the recognition of women's equality in . . . sports is important to the female head of household that Sears is targeting," said Softlines Marketing Director Brian Kelly. The "softer side" campaign, illustrated in Figure 17.13, was part of Sears' successful marketing strategy that increased store sales by changing its image from a hardware and appliance retailer to a general merchandiser.[41]

In contrast, a **pushing strategy** relies more heavily than a pulling strategy on personal selling. Here the objective is promoting the product to the members of the marketing channel rather than to final users. To achieve this goal, marketers employ cooperative advertising allowances, trade discounts, personal-selling efforts by salespeople, and other dealer supports. Such a strategy is designed to gain marketing success for the firm's products by motivating representatives of wholesalers and/or retailers to spend extra time and effort promoting the products to customers.

While pulling and pushing strategies are presented here as alternative methods, few companies depend entirely on either one. Most firms combine the two methods. For example, firms in the pharmaceutical industry have

Table 17.3 Factors Influencing Choice of Promotional Mix

	Factor	Emphasis: Personal Selling	Emphasis: Advertising
Nature of the market	Number of buyers	Limited number	Large number
	Geographic concentration	Concentrated	Dispersed
	Type of customer	Business purchaser	Ultimate consumer
Nature of the product	Complexity	Custom-made, complex	Standardized
	Service requirements	Considerable	Minimal
	Type of good or service	Business	Consumer
	Use of trade-ins	Trade-ins common	Trade-ins uncommon
Stage in the product life cycle		Often emphasized at every stage; heavy emphasis in the introductory and early growth stages in acquainting marketing intermediaries and potential consumers with the new good or service	Often emphasized at every stage; heavy emphasis in the latter part of the growth stage, as well as the maturity and early decline stages, to persuade consumers to select specific brands
Price		High unit value	Low unit value

long pursued pushing strategies to promote prescription drugs to doctors and other health-care professionals. These strategies have included activities like advertising in trade journals, sponsoring professional meetings, funding research on the effects of various drugs, and providing free samples to health-care practitioners. Recently, drug manufacturers have adopted pulling strategies by advertising directly to consumers. For example, Glaxo Wellcome advertises its Flonase, a prescription allergy medication, in consumer magazines.

Consumer goods marketers also use both strategies extensively. "Half of consumer decisions are owned by retailers, because of their ability to impact how consumers see brands in stores," says Jeffrey Hill, Meridian Consulting. To compete for the best advertising time slots and shelf space, manufacturers must figure out which strategies work best for their major retailers. About half of their promotional budgets—$30 million a year—pay for cash incentives to get retailers to stock their products.

However, a move toward consumer-oriented programs has directed more promotional dollars toward ads that build brand image and pull in customers than to trade promotions. Manufacturers seem to prefer this switch to advertising that pulls customers into stores to buy their products. These include general advertisements along with custom ads for specific retailers. Procter & Gamble, for example, pays for ads that feature its major retailers like Wal-Mart, Kmart, Target, and grocery chains. It also sends general direct-mail pieces like coupon promotions and places ads in newspapers and national magazines and on television.[42]

Timing also affects the choice of promotional strategies. The relative importance of advertising and selling changes during the various phases of the purchase process. Prior to the actual sale, advertising usually is more important than personal selling. Marketers often argue that one of the primary advantages of a successful advertising program is its support for the salesperson who approaches the prospect for the first time. Selling then becomes more important than advertising at the time of purchase. Personal selling provides the actual mechanism for closing most sales. In the post-purchase period, advertising regains primacy in the promotional effort. It affirms the customer's decision to buy a particular good or service and reminds him or her of the product's favorable qualities in an attempt

Marketing Dictionary

pulling strategy Promotional effort by a seller to stimulate demand among final users, who will then exert pressure on the distribution channel to carry the good or service, pulling it through the marketing channel.

pushing strategy Promotional effort by a seller to members of the marketing channel intended to stimulate personal selling of the good or service, pushing it through the marketing channel.

to reduce any cognitive dissonance (discussed earlier) that might occur.

The promotional strategies used by car marketers illustrate this timing factor. Car makers spend heavily on consumer advertising to create awareness before consumers begin the purchase process. At the time of their purchase decisions, however, the personal-selling skills of dealer salespeople provide the most important tools for closing the sales. Finally, advertising frequently maintains post-purchase satisfaction by citing awards such as *Motor Trend*'s Car of the Year or results of J. D. Power's customer-satisfaction surveys to affirm buyers' decisions.

Figure 17.13 Use of a Pulling Strategy by Sears

"He went in for tires."
Corded jacket, $50
Satin blouse, $36 Skirt, $36
All by Apostrophe
"But this is what stopped me in my tracks."
Come see the softer side of SEARS

BUDGETING FOR PROMOTIONAL STRATEGY

Promotional budgets may differ not only in amount but also in composition. Industrial firms generally invest larger proportions of their budgets in personal selling than in advertising, while the reverse is usually true of most producers of consumer goods. Figure 17.14 shows how different types of manufacturers typically allocate their promotional budgets.

Evidence suggests that sales initially lag behind promotional expenses for structural reasons—funds spent filling up retail shelves, boosting low initial production, and supplying buyer knowledge. This fact produces a threshold effect in which few sales may result from substantial initial investments in promotion. A second phase might produce sales proportionate to promotional expenditures, the most predictable range. Finally, promotion reaches the area of diminishing returns where an increase in promotional spending fails to produce a corresponding increase in sales.

For example, an initial expenditure of $40,000 may result in sales of 100,000 product units for a consumer goods manufacturer. An additional $10,000 expenditure may generate sales of 30,000 more units and another $10,000 in an additional 35,000 units. The cumulative effect of the expenditures and repeat sales will have generated increasing returns from the promotional outlays. However, as the advertising budget moves from $60,000 to $70,000, the marginal productivity of the additional expenditure may fall to 28,000 units. At some later point, the return may actually become zero or negative as competition intensifies, markets become saturated, and marketers employ less effective advertising media.

To test the thesis that promotion encounters a saturation point, Anheuser-Busch marketers once quadrupled their advertising budgets in several markets. After three months, the company's distributors demanded an advertising cut. Many claimed that beer consumers were coming into their stores demanding, "Give me anything *but* Bud."

The ideal method of allocating promotional funds would increase the budget until the cost of each additional increment equals the additional incremental revenue received. In other words, the most effective allocation procedure increases promotional expenditures until each dollar of promotional expense is matched by an additional dollar of profit. This procedure—referred to as *marginal analysis*—maximizes the input's productivity. The difficulty arises in identifying the optimal point, which requires a precise balance between marginal expenses for promotion and the resulting marginal receipts.

Traditional methods for creating a promotional budget include the percentage-of-sales and fixed-sum-per-unit methods, along with meeting the competition and task-objective techniques. Each method is briefly examined in Table 17.4.

Figure 17.14 Allocation of Promotional Budgets

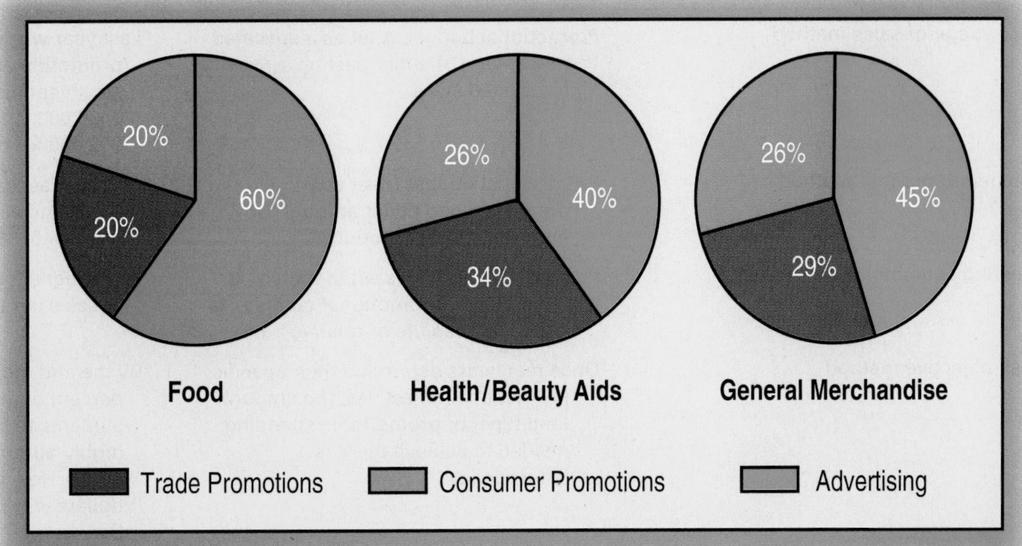
20%
20%
60%
26%
40%
34%
26%
45%
29%
Food
Health/Beauty Aids
General Merchandise
Trade Promotions
Consumer Promotions
Advertising

The **percentage-of-sales method** is perhaps the most common way of establishing promotional budgets. The percentage can be based on sales either for some past period (such as the previous year) or forecasted for a future period (the current year). While this plan is appealing in its simplicity, it does not effectively support achievement of basic promotional objectives. Arbitrary percentage allocations based on either historical or future sales figures fail to provide required flexibility. Further, the method employs circular reasoning in which the promotional allocation depends on sales rather than vice versa, as it should. For example, a decline in sales would force the marketer to further curtail the firm's promotional outlays, probably contributing to additional revenue losses.

The **fixed-sum-per-unit method** differs from budgeting based on a percentage of sales in only one respect: It allocates a predetermined amount to each sales or production unit. This amount can also reflect either historical or forecasted figures. Producers of high-value, consumer durable goods, such as automobiles, often use this budgeting method.

Another traditional budgeting approach, **meeting competition,** simply matches competitors' outlays, either in absolute amounts or relative to the firms' market shares. However, this approach usually only preserves the status quo in which each company retains its percentage of total sales. Expenditures that meet a competitor's budget do not necessarily pertain to a firm's own promotional objectives. Therefore, this method seems inappropriate for most contemporary marketing programs.

The **task-objective method** develops a promotional budget based on a sound evaluation of the firm's promotional objectives. As a result, it attunes its allocation of funds to modern marketing practices. The method involves two sequential steps:

Marketing Dictionary

percentage-of-sales method Allocating funds for promotion during a given time period based on a specified percentage of either past or forecasted sales.

fixed-sum-per-unit method Allocating promotional expenditures as a predetermined dollar amount for each sales or production unit.

meeting competition method Allocating promotional spending to match that of a competitor, either as an absolute amount or relative to the firms' market shares.

task-objective method Allocating promotional spending by defining goals and then determining the amount of promotional spending needed to achieve them.

Table 17.4 Promotional Budget Determination

Method	Description	Example
Percentage-of-sales method	Promotional budget is set as a specified percentage of either past or forecasted sales.	"Last year we spent $10,500 on promotion and had sales of $420,000. Next year we expect sales to grow to $480,000, and we are allocating $12,000 for promotion."
Fixed-sum-per-unit method	Promotional budget is set as a predetermined dollar amount for each unit sold or produced.	"Our forecast calls for sales of 14,000 units, and we allocate promotion at the rate of $65 per unit."
Meeting competition method	Promotional budget is set to match competitors' promotional outlays on either an absolute or relative basis.	"Promotional outlays average 4 percent of sales in our industry."
Task-objective method	Once marketers determine their specific, promotional objectives, the amount (and type) of promotional spending needed to achieve them is determined.	"By the end of next year, we want 75 percent of the area high-school students to be aware of our new, highly automated fast-food prototype outlet. How many promotional dollars will it take, and how should they be spent?"

1. The firm's marketers must *define realistic communication goals* that they want the promotional mix to achieve. For example, a firm might specify a goal of a 25 percent increase in brand awareness or a 10 percent rise in the number of consumers who recognize certain specific, differentiating features in a product. This key step specifies in quantitative terms the objectives that promotion should attain. These objectives in turn become integral parts of the promotional plan.

2. Marketers must *determine the amount* (as well as the *type) of promotional activity required for each objective* they have set. Combined, these units become the firm's promotional budget.

A crucial assumption underlies the task-objective approach: Marketers can measure the productivity of each promotional dollar. That assumption explains why the objectives must be carefully chosen, quantified, and accomplished through promotional efforts. Generally, budgeters should avoid general marketing objectives such as "We want to achieve a 5 percent increase in sales." A sale is a culmination of the effects of *all* elements of the marketing mix. A more appropriate promotional objective might be "to achieve an 8 percent response rate from a targeted direct-mail advertisement."

Promotional budgeting always requires difficult decisions. Still, recent research studies and the spread of computer-based models have made it a more manageable problem than it used to be.

MEASURING THE EFFECTIVENESS OF PROMOTION

It is widely recognized that part of a firm's promotional effort is ineffective. John Wanamaker, a successful nineteenth-century retailer, observed: "I know half the money I spend on advertising is wasted, but I can never find out which half."

Measuring the effectiveness of promotional expenditures has become an extremely important research issue, particularly among advertisers. Studies aimed at this measurement dilemma face several major obstacles, including the difficulty of isolating the effect of the promotional variable.

Most marketers would prefer to use a *direct-sales-results* test to measure the effectiveness of promotion. Such an approach would reveal the specific impact on sales revenues for each dollar of promotional spending. This type of technique has always eluded marketers, however, due to their inability to control for other variables operating in the marketplace. A firm may receive $20 million in additional sales orders following a new, $1.5 million advertising campaign, but the market success may really have resulted from price increases for competing products rather than from the advertising outlays.

Because they encounter difficulty isolating the effects of promotion from those of other market elements and outside environmental variables, many marketers have simply abandoned all attempts at measurement. Others, however, turn to indirect evaluation. These researchers concentrate on quantifiable indicators of effectiveness, such as *recall* (how much members of the target market remember about specific products or advertisements) and *readership* (size and composition of a message's audience). The basic problem with indirect measurement is the difficulty of relating these variables to sales. For example, does extensive ad readership lead to increased sales?

Marketers need to ask the right questions and understand what they are measuring. Professor Don Schultz, an expert in IMC, advises them to focus on the returns their promotional investments will generate and ask: "We spent $X; how many dollars will we get back?" Promotion to build sales volume produces measurable results in the form of short-term returns; brand-building programs, however, and efforts to generate or enhance consumers' perceptions of value in a product, brand, or organization cannot be measured over the short term.[43]

Technology helps marketers to track results of promotional spending. In their trade promotions, companies can negotiate pay-for-performance deals—retailer incentives based on what consumers actually buy, not what the stores order. Retailers have discretion to use their trade promotion dollars where they work best, such as targeted programs, loyalty builders, and database marketing.[44]

One way companies measure performance is by incorporating some form of direct response into their promotions. This technique also helps them to compare different promotions for effectiveness and rely on facts rather than opinions. Consumers may say they will try a product in response to a survey question yet not actually buy it. Targeting promotions like these improves their response rates. Pharmaceutical manufacturer Menly and James used a database to find people with arthritis who didn't use Ecotrin, the firm's coated aspirin product. They sent one of three direct-mail offers to these people: a free sample with a 50-cents-off coupon, a $1 rebate coupon, and an invitation to send for a free sample. Surprisingly, the firm received the highest response—75 percent—to the offer to send for a sample; the other promotions produced good responses, as well, with over 50 percent of the coupons redeemed. The normal redemption rate for nontargeted coupon offers averages only 1 to 2 percent.

The latest challenge facing marketers is how to measure the effectiveness of electronic media. As companies rush onto the World Wide Web, they are also moving quickly to develop techniques to measure the success of their Web advertising. But traditional numbers that work for other media forms are not necessarily relevant indicators of effectiveness for a Web site. For one thing, the Web combines both advertising and direct marketing. Web pages effectively integrate advertising and other content, such as product information, that may be the page's main feature. For another consideration, consumers generally choose the advertisements they want to see on the Net, whereas traditional broadcast or print media automatically expose consumers to ads.

Like the Web itself, measurement tools are still in their infancy. The most quoted statistic is the number of *hits,* or user requests for a file. This information is not very meaningful, however, as it does not indicate whether the visitor reads the file. One click could translate into many hits, depending on how many files a particular page requires. *Visits* represent the pages downloaded or read in one session. Regardless of how many pages users view, the characteristics of the visitors, where they live, and what interests them most define more important information than hits or visits.[45]

Scott Young, president of Perception Research Services, which specializes in evaluating communications effectiveness, says, "I'd advise buyers against going strictly by the numbers in assessing new media opportunities. By resisting temptation to place Internet buying neatly into existing frameworks, media buyers can capitalize on the subtleties of the Web as an advertising medium and leverage their dollars."

The typical Internet ad has two parts, a (1) *banner* placed on a Web site with a short advertising message and

Figure 17.15 Measuring 7UP's Internet Advertising Effectiveness

SO MANY USERS. SURPRISINGLY LITTLE BACKWASH.
http://www.7UP.com
There's no better way to carbonate your brain. Tap into the freshest sounds in alternative music while exploring the first site to let you download the Universal Voter Registration form. If you hurry, you might even land a one-of-a-kind summer job in the music industry that you won't be able to find anywhere else (record companies, recording studios, talent agencies...). And how about winning a free t-shirt with just one lucky click*: 100% cotton and guaranteed to fend off doing laundry for three or four more days.
7UP.com
It's an UP thing.™

MARKETING HALL OF FAME

The IMC Program that Cares Enough to Send the Very Best

Searching for the perfect sentiment, Americans buy well over 7 billion greeting cards each year. That breaks down to more than 31 cards for every man, woman, and child.

Hallmark Cards, Inc. sells the largest chunk of those sappy, funny, and heart-felt cards. With 40,000 retail outlets and an inexhaustible supply of cards, ornaments, mugs, gift wrap, party supplies, and more, Hallmark is the undisputed leader in the industry. The Kansas City-based greeting-card giant boasts nearly $4 billion in annual sales and enjoys 42 percent of the U.S. greeting card market. American Greetings trails in second place with 35 percent.

To maintain its first-place status, Hallmark does more than just write lovely captions on clever cards. The company focuses like a laser on its customers and has doggedly followed its commitment to integrated marketing communications. Almost everyone is familiar with the slogan, "When you care enough to send the very best." The company emphasizes this theme in its print and television advertising. Ads also focus on brand recognition, showing card recipients turning the card over to see if it is a Hallmark card. Sales promotions also help the company to reach consumers, such as free sample packets with purchases of three cards and sponsorship of the popular Hallmark Hall of Fame series of television specials.

Hallmark has followed this approach since the early 1990s after realizing that its marketing message wasn't effectively reaching working women—its target audience. (Women purchase more than 85 percent of all greeting cards.) But Hallmark encountered mounting difficulty trying to communicate with women preoccupied by work, children, and household obligations.

To reinvigorate its relationship with women despite their hectic lifestyles, Hallmark decided to learn everything it could about them. It developed an ambitious database system to keep in close touch with its most valued customers through its "Very Best" program. When they present a plastic card, the information system keeps track of all their Hallmark purchases; program members are rewarded with discounts, free samples, and a newsletter. "It's called relationship marketing," says Brad Moore, Hallmark advertising vice president. "These are people you want to talk to directly; they are very heavy users."

Hallmark tapped into the Internet boom by establishing strategic alliances to offer cards through cyberspace. Leading the greeting-card industry in consumer technology-based initiatives, Hallmark now sells cards through America Online, as well as CompuServe's Electronic Mall and Interactive Television Network's shopping channel. Hallmark also plans to reach customers through Microsoft

(2) a *link* to more information elsewhere, perhaps on the advertiser's home page. The two major techniques for setting Internet advertising rates are cost per impression (CPM) and cost per response (click-throughs). *Cost per impression (CPM)* is an advertising approach that relates the cost of an ad to every thousand people who view it. In other words, anyone who sees the page containing the banner or other form of ad creates one impression. This measure assumes that the site's principal purpose is to display the advertising pitch. *Cost per response* is a direct marketing technique that relates the cost of an ad to the number of people who click on it. Measurement based on click-throughs assumes that those who actually click on an ad want more information and therefore consider the ad valuable.

Both rating techniques have merit. Site publishers point out that click-through rates are influenced by the creativity of the ad's message, which they do not control. Advertisers, on the other hand, point out that the Web ad has value to those who click on it additional information.

Young suggests that both are useful measurements. Even though viewers may not click on an ad, it may influence them, just as print and broadcast ads without any response mechanisms help to build brand awareness. Therefore, marketers must look beyond input measures and evaluate what visitors take from the site, such as attitudes and ideas.[46]

If 7UP marketers decide to measure the effectiveness of promotional messages in their Web site, such as that shown in Figure 17.15, they can benefit from the specialized services of Nielsen and Internet Profiles (I/Pro). These companies' I/Count service monitors total visits and the users' geographical and organizational origins. I/Audit

Network and AT&T PersonalLink Market Square. In addition, Hallmark has teamed up with Micrografx Inc. to develop software so customers can make cards on their personal computers.

"Our goal is to offer compelling solutions that make it easy and fun for people to express themselves to one another," said Doranne Hudson, Hallmark vice president of emerging brands and channels. "We're creating a dynamic, flexible portfolio of opportunities and running each idea out for the consumer to try, to see what resonates with shoppers," she added. "Hallmark has lined up with the best strategic partners in the new marketplaces. We're really having great fun."

http://www.hallmark.com/

Of course, not every marketing approach that Hallmark tries turns to gold. Although the firm was a major player in the push to scatter computerized greeting-card kiosks throughout the country, it had to rethink this strategy. The company discovered that kiosks weren't as popular as originally hoped. The heaviest card consumers—women 40 years of age and older—preferred to buy cards off the rack. Younger adults liked the concept but became impatient with the eight to ten minutes they had to spend creating cards. Consequently, Hallmark reduced the number of its touch-screen kiosks from 2,700 to 1,500, slashed the cost of computerized cards from $3.50 to $2.95, and is experimenting with even lower prices. This episode illustrates how the No. 1 card maker can follow trends closely and make changes when necessary.

The price cut, as well as a move toward easily identifiable graphics including Warner Brothers characters, is paying off. As Hallmark spokeswoman Adrienne Lallo put it, "Lo and behold, the average performance started to improve. Now we are very happy. But the technology is changing so rapidly, and it's a little difficult to anticipate what's going to become a hit with consumers."

QUESTIONS FOR CRITICAL THINKING

1. **Is Hallmark's move into cyberspace marketing a smart idea? Explain.**
2. **How has Hallmark practiced relationship marketing in its integrated marketing communications program?**

Sources: "Resurgence in Letter, Card Sending at Home, in Office," January 23, 1997, downloaded from http://www.prnewswire.com/, May 19, 1997; M. R. Kropko, "Card Makers Struggling with Computer Kiosks," *Marketing News,* June 3, 1996, p. 6.; Gerri Hirshey, "Happy Day to You," *New York Times Magazine,* July 2, 1995, pp. 20–45; and "Hallmark Cards Launches Greeting Cards on America Online," *Business Wire,* June 20, 1995.

measures in more detail, including site visits, the paths by which users reach the site, what pages they visit once there, and the length of time they spend at the site. In respect for users' privacy, Nielsen/I/Pro services currently measure only corporate usage, not home usage.[47]

Another technological innovation has revolutionized evaluation of consumer advertising and sales promotion: the *single-source* research system. It combines scanner-generated buying information from supermarkets with data about consumer demographics and the television advertising and in-store promotions to which those consumers are exposed. From this data, marketers can measure the effectiveness of their advertising and sales promotions, determine why sales increase or decrease, discover which consumers respond to which promotions, and test the short-term and long-term profitability of advertising and sales promotion. Single-source data helps marketers to avoid wasting money on ineffective communications.

THE VALUE OF MARKETING COMMUNICATIONS

The nature of marketing communications is changing as new formats transform the traditional idea of an advertisement or sales promotion. Sales messages are now placed subtly, or not so subtly, in movies and television shows, blurring the lines between promotion and entertainment and changing the traditional definition of *advertising.* Elizabeth Taylor made cameo performances in four CBS comedies over a two-hour period, looking for her missing black

SOLVING AN ETHICAL CONTROVERSY

Should Product Promotion Target Children?

In homes across the country, thousands of children spend hours glued to computer screens, playing games that feature cartoon characters hawking the latest toys. Others exchange messages online with Tony the Tiger and other mascots of sugary sweets. Today, some children scramble into school buses plastered with ads for Burger King and 7UP. At a grade school in Kentucky, kids who read books win goodies from Pizza Hut, while posters hanging in a Washington, D.C. school bear the Miller High Life logo.

The overwhelming number of advertisers who take advantage of television and the Internet to promote their products has made it difficult for children to avoid the allure of advertising. Since its first broadcasts, television has bombarded kids with carefully tailored marketing messages. In fact, right now advertisers are spending about $1 billion a year on television spots just to reach kids 11 years of age and under. But today's children are also absorbing advertising jingles and pitches at school and on kid-friendly Internet sites.

Just what commercial messages are appropriate for children—and who should decide—is a topic of hot debate as children face this ever increasing barrage of advertising.

Should Government Regulate the Proliferation of Children's Advertising?

PRO

1. **As children's contacts with cyberspace grow at a tremendous rate, they encounter a logical frontier for advertising restrictions. The need for limitations results from the intrusive nature of this advertising form. Consumer groups, for instance, lament that Web sites are requiring children to provide extensive information about themselves before allowing them to explore.**

   "Many children's Web sites cannot be accessed unless children fill out a probing survey first," complains Shelley Pasnik of The Center for Media Education in Washington, D.C. "Children are getting unsolicited e-mail from spokescharacters asking them to play with them online, and of course the characters themselves are also the products."
2. **Children don't have the ability to differentiate hype from truth. Adults must protect them from the onslaught of marketing messages.**
3. **Advertising on elementary and secondary school campuses could be especially harmful, because children will assume it has the backing of the principals and teachers. Promotional material from Lifetime Learning Systems, which produces advertising-related materials for schools, backs up this claim. "Coming from school, all these materials carry an extra measure of credibility that gives your message added weight." Unlike a television commercial, students sitting in a school bus plastered with**

pearls—just before the launch of her Black Pearls perfume. The star was part of the story, but the scripts made no direct mention of the perfume. Another type of promotion makes advertisements into mini-shows. The cast of the popular television show *Friends* reproduced their roles from the show in a commercial promoting Diet Coke. Products also appear in the shows themselves; Junior Mints and Price Club wholesale club stores were featured on *Seinfeld,* and author and celebrity Martha Stewart guest starred on *Ellen,* signing her actual cookbook at the sitcom's fictional bookstore. Product tie-ins abound, from Pepsi in the movie *Flipper* to the Dodge Ram truck in *Twister.* Messages show up on shopping carts, buses, and even police cars.[48]

Despite new tactics by advertisers, promotion has often been the target of criticism. People complain that it offers nothing of value to society and simply wastes resources. Others criticize that promotion encourages consumers to buy unnecessary products that they can't afford. Many ads seem to insult people's intelligence, and they criticize the ethics—or lack thereof—displayed by advertisers and salespeople. New forms of promotion are considered even more insidious because marketers make pitches that don't look like paid advertisements. Many of these complaints cite true problems. Some salespeople use unethical sales tactics. Some product advertising hides its promotional nature or targets consumer groups that can least afford the advertised items. Many television commercials do contribute to the growing problem of cultural pollution.

While promotion can certainly be criticized on many

Burger King logos can't turn off the images.

CON

1. The Federal Trade Commission is reviewing a petition that would create restrictions and offer guidelines for cyberspace advertising aimed at children, but industry executives grumble that the proposed restrictions are draconian. "Some of the guidelines are unrealistic, such as avoiding interaction with spokescharacters," says Bryan Waters, vice president of technology and production at McGraw-Hill Home Interactive. "Can you imaging going into the Disney site and not seeing Pocahontas and Mickey Mouse? It's just not going to happen."
2. Advertisers who design marketing campaigns for liquor and cigarettes have taken the most heat, but those industries vigorously deny any attempt to lure children with ads. They say they are simply developing marketing messages for adult customers. Hoping to head off possible action by the Food and Drug Administration affecting its advertising toward children, Philip Morris Co. has suggested its own more modest guidelines. By making this proposal, Philip Morris is following the popular and preferred trend in advertising of self-policing.
3. Advertising at schools is a worthwhile pursuit because chronic underfunding often prevents school districts from providing even basic books, materials, and equipment. Advertisers can help to underwrite some of these expenses.

Summary

The proliferation of children's advertising has hardly gone unnoticed in Washington, D.C. Congressional representatives regularly pose on Capitol Hill railing against amoral advertisers who convince kids to eat more sugar-laden cereal, or worse, con them into thinking that drinking alcohol makes them cool.

Meanwhile, the trend toward reaching across the Internet toward school-age children is expected to explode as more and more children become computer savvy. *Digital Kids Report*, a trade publication, estimates that 15 million consumers under the age of 18 will be using online services regularly by 2000. Clearly, the jury is still out as to whether companies should gather marketing data from kids on the Internet and whether the children require special protection from advertising aimed at them.

Sources: William S. Galkin, "Cyber Privacy for Children Still Thorny Issue," *Baltimore Business Journal,* March 31, 1997, downloaded from http://www.amcity.com/, April 25, 1997; Suein L. Swang, Timothy Noah, and Laurie McGinley, "Philip Morris Proposes Curbs on Sales to Kids," *Wall Street Journal,* May 16, 1996, p. B1; Nora Fitzgerald, "Watching the Kids, the Internet Opens a New Front in the Battle over Children's Ads," *Adweek,* May 6, 1996, p. 26; and Betsy Wagner, "Our Class Is Brought to You Today By . . . , Advertisers Target a Captive Market: School Kids," *U.S. News & World Report,* April 24, 1995, p. 63.

counts, it also plays a crucial role in modern society. This point is best understood by examining the social, business, and economic importance of promotion.

Social Importance

Criticisms of promotional messages as tasteless and without contributions to society sometimes ignore the fact that our social framework provides no commonly accepted set of standards or priorities for these judgments. We live in a varied economy characterized by consumer segments with differing needs, wants, and aspirations. What one group finds tasteless may be quite appealing to another. Promotional strategy faces an averaging problem that escapes many of its critics. The one generally accepted standard in a market society is freedom of choice for the consumer. Consumer buying decisions eventually determine acceptable practices in the marketplace.

Promotion has also become an important factor in campaigns aimed at achieving socially oriented objectives, such as stopping smoking, family planning, physical fitness, and elimination of drug abuse. The 17 days of the quadrennial Olympic Games highlight human victories in dozens of sports and at least one universal desire: to end the suffering that accompanies war. The International Olympic Committee works diligently with the United Nations to enact a global truce during the games. Advertising agencies donate their expertise to creating public service announcements (PSAs) informing the general public of this truce. The PSA created by HMS/McFarland & Drier of Miami shown in Figure 17.16 makes a poignant statement about the effects of war on a country's future.

Promotion performs an informative and education task crucial to the functioning of modern society. As with everything else in life, what is important is *how* promotion is used rather than *whether* it is used. Chapter 18 will return to the subject of ethics in advertising.

Figure 17.16 Promotional Message Addressing a Universal Social Concern

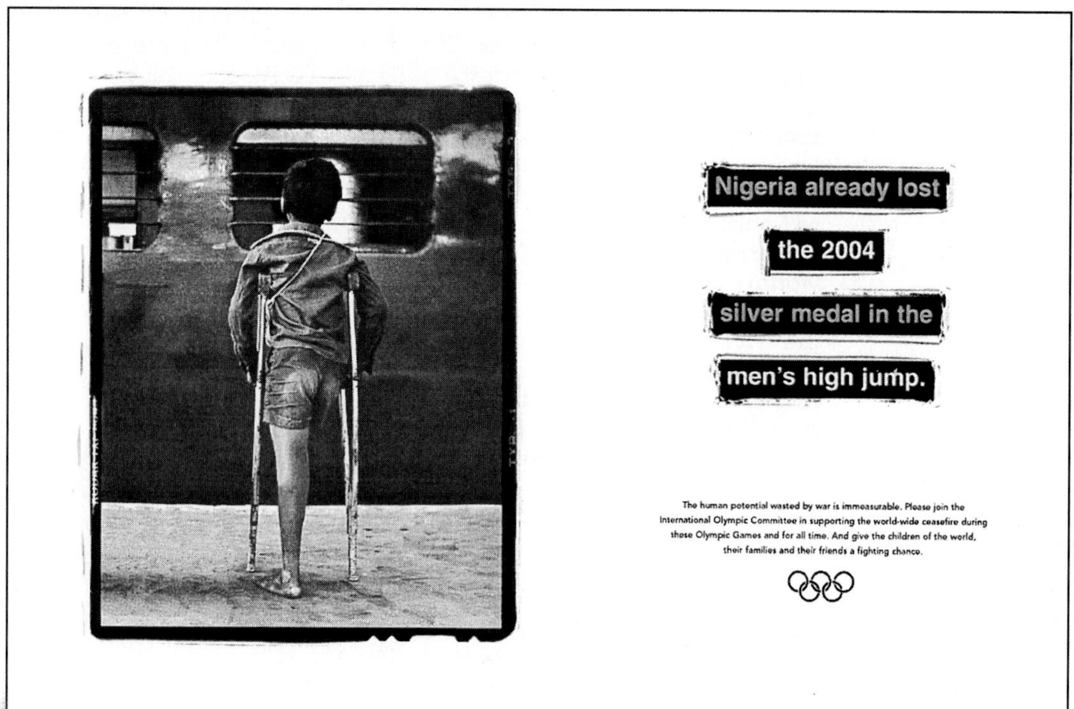
Nigeria already lost
the 2004
silver medal in the
men's high jump.
The human potential wasted by war is immeasurable. Please join the International Olympic Committee in supporting the world-wide ceasefire during these Olympic Games and for all time. And give the children of the world, their families and their friends a fighting chance.

Business Importance

Promotional strategy has become increasingly important to both large and small business enterprises. The well-documented long-term increase in funds spent on promotion certainly attests to management's faith in the ability of promotional efforts to encourage attitude changes, brand loyalty, and additional sales. It is difficult to conceive of an enterprise that would not attempt to promote its good or service in some manner. Most modern institutions simply cannot survive in the long run without promotion. Business must communicate with its publics.

Nonbusiness enterprises also recognize the importance of promotional efforts. The U.S. government spends about $300 million a year on advertising and ranks 36th among all U.S. advertisers. The Canadian government is the leading advertiser in Canada, promoting many concepts and programs. Religious organizations have acknowledged the importance of promotional channels to make their viewpoints known to the public at large.

Economic Importance

Promotion has assumed a degree of economic importance, if for no other reason, because it provides employment for thousands of people. More importantly, however, effective promotion has allowed society to derive benefits not otherwise available. For example, the criticism that promotion costs too much isolates an individual expense item and fails to consider its possible beneficial effects on other categories of expenditures.

Promotional strategies increase the number of units sold and permit economies of scale in the production process, thereby lowering the production costs for each unit of output. Lower unit costs allow lower consumer prices, which, in turn, make products available to more people. Similarly, researchers have found that advertising subsidizes the information contents of newspapers and the broadcast media. In short, promotion pays for many of the enjoyable entertainment and educational opportunities in contemporary life as it lowers product costs.

ACHIEVEMENT CHECK SUMMARY

Reread the learning goals that follow, and consider the questions for each goal. Answering these questions will reinforce your grasp of the most important concepts in the chapter and allow you to check how well you have achieved these learning goals. Where a blank appears before a question, answer with *T* or *F;* for multiple-choice questions, circle the letter of the correct answer.

Objective 17.1: Relate the concept of integrated marketing communications to the development of an optimal promotional mix.

1. ____ In a company that practices integrated marketing communications, different departments often wield authority and responsibility for individual promotional elements.

2. ____ An IMC strategy begins with the product and works forward toward the consumer.

3. ____ Databases and interactive marketing are important IMC tools that help marketers to design mass-communications programs.

Objective 17.2: Explain the relationship of promotional strategy to the process of communication.

1. ____ The term *marketing communications* refers to advertisements appearing in print and broadcast media.

2. ____ The process by which promotional messages reach the consumer involves all of the following except:

a. decoding
b. feedback
c. noise
d. differentiation

3. ____ The newspaper that runs a press release about a new product represents the encoding of the message.

Objective 17.3: List the objectives of promotion.

1. ____ Reebok uses promotions focused on primary demand to increase consumer demand for its aerobic shoes.

2. ____ Royal Caribbean's ads explain that consumers should pay more for its cruises than for competing products because they offer better service, more activities, and other unique benefits. These ads are an example of promotion designed to:

a. stabilize sales
b. increase demand
c. accentuate the product's value

3. ____ Suppose that a toy manufacturer runs summer trade promotions to encourage retailers to stock up on its products. This promotion is intended to differentiate its products.

Objective 17.4: Explain the concept of the promotional mix and its relationship to the marketing mix.

1. ____ Public relations is a component of the personal selling element in the promotional mix.

2. ____ The promotional mix is a subset of the overall marketing mix.

3. ____ Promotional techniques geared toward distributors, retailers, and wholesalers are called:

a. direct marketing
b. trade promotion
c. joint advertising
d. public relations

Objective 17.5: Discuss the role of sponsorships and direct marketing in integrated marketing communications planning.

1. ____ Organizations sponsor events in order to gain media exposure for their products and benefit from the images associated with the events.

2. ____ Commercial sponsorships cost more than traditional advertising media.

3. ____ Which of the following statements about direct marketing is not true?

a. The Internet can be used for direct marketing.
b. Marketers can measure the results of direct marketing more easily than those of other forms of advertising and promotion.
c. Major companies are now using infomercials to describe the benefits of their products.
d. Direct mail represents the largest category of consumer direct marketing spending.

Objective 17.6: Identify the primary determinants of a promotional mix.

1. ____ A company that sells industrial products will typically spend most of its promotional budget on mass-market advertising.

2. ____ The stage in a product's life cycle is an important determinant of a firm's integrated marketing strategy.

3. ____ Promotion cost per sales unit is one reason for choosing advertising to promote low-priced items.

Objective 17.7: Contrast the two major alternative promotional strategies.

1. ____ A pulling strategy relies heavily on personal selling to the members of the marketing channel.

2. ____ An advertisement for Burger King that includes a two-for-one coupon would form part of a pulling strategy.

3. ____ Companies select either pulling or pushing strategies when promoting their products.

Objective 17.8: Compare the primary methods of developing a promotional budget.

1. ____ A gourmet caterer with sales of $150,000 spent $5,000 for promotion last year. Projected sales are expected to reach $180,000 next year, so it has budgeted $6,000. Which method does the firm use to set its promotional budget?

a. task-objective
b. meeting the competition
c. percentage-of-sales
d. fixed-sum-per-unit

2. ____ The task-objective approach allocates a predetermined amount for each sales or production unit; this amount can be based on either historical or forecasted costs.

3. ____ Marketers using the fixed-sum-per-unit method of promotional budgeting begin by setting reasonable promotional objectives, such as achieving 60 percent consumer awareness by the sixth month after introducing a new product.

Objective 17.9: Defend promotion against common public criticisms.

1. ____ Using product tie-ins in television shows and movies is an unethical promotional practice.

2. ____ Promotion helps to create demand for products and generates employment, an economic benefit to society.

3. ____ An ad describing how gasoline additives reduce air pollution makes a social contribution to society.

Students: See the solutions section located on pages S-3–S-4 to check your responses to the Achievement Check Summary.

Key Terms

promotion
marketing communication
integrated marketing communications (IMC)
AIDA concept
promotional mix
personal selling
advertising
sales promotion
trade promotion
direct marketing
public relations
publicity
sponsorship
telemarketing
infomercial
pulling strategy
pushing strategy
percentage-of-sales method
fixed-sum-per-unit method
meeting competition method
task-objective method

Review Questions

1. Contrast integrated marketing communications (IMC) with the promotional mix concept. Explain the current emphasis on IMC by marketers.
2. Relate the steps in the communications process to promotional strategy and the AIDA concept. Explain the concept and causes of noise in marketing communications. How can marketers deal with noise?
3. Compare the five basic objectives of promotion. Cite specific examples.
4. Explain the concept of the promotional mix. What is its relationship to the marketing mix?
5. Discuss the reasons for the growth of direct marketing and briefly describe the key media that carry its messages.
6. Identify the major determinants of a promotional mix. Describe how they affect the selection of an appropriate blend of promotional techniques.
7. Under what circumstances should marketers adopt a pushing strategy for their promotions? When would a pulling strategy be effective?
8. Identify and briefly explain the alternative methods of developing a promotional budget. Which is the best approach?
9. How can a firm attempt to measure the effectiveness of its promotional efforts? Which techniques most effectively evaluate promotional success?
10. Identify the major public criticisms of promotion. Prepare a defense for each criticism.

Discussion Questions

1. "Perhaps the most critical promotional question facing the marketing manager concerns when to use each component of promotion." Comment on this statement. Relate your response to the product's classification, product value, marketing channels, price, and timing of the promotional effort.
2. What mix of promotional variables would you use for each of the following products? Why?
   a. Valvoline motor oil
   b. Toro snow blower
   c. Independent marketing research firm
   d. Road construction equipment
   e. Customized business forms
   f. Children's shoes
3. Develop a hypothetical promotional budget for the following firms. State percentage allocations instead of dollar amounts for the various promotional variables (such as 30 percent for personal selling, 60 percent for advertising, and 10 percent for public relations).
   a. Acura cars
   b. Marriott Courtyard Hotels
   c. Amoco Chemical Co.
   d. Fidelity Investments
4. Trace the history of advertising by physicians, dentists, and lawyers. How do these professionals currently promote their services? What restrictions apply to their promotional efforts?
5. Identify one or more firms and/or products associated with the following events or activities. Suggest methods for measuring the effectiveness of sponsorship spending on these events.
   a. Women's professional tennis tour
   b. Concert tour by a pop music star
   c. World Cup Soccer
   d. Arts exhibition
   e. PGA golf tournament

'netWork

1. Mecklermedia is well-known for using numerous forms of promotion. Visit their home page, then evaluate their effectiveness in practicing the concept of integrated marketing communications.

2. CyberGold

http://www.cybergold.net/

is one marketer that puts its money where its Web site is. It pays Internet users from 50 cents to a few dollars to look at advertising. Visit the firm's Web site, then briefly explain how it works and the types of marketers who advertise there. Evaluate the wisdom of paying viewers to click through these ads.

3. Visit the Web sites of three or four companies with substantial sales outside the United States. Identify the potential problems involved in using cyberspace marketing to expand beyond the domestic market. How have these firms avoided these problems on their Web sites?

VIDEO CASE 17

FLYING HIGH—FROM NEARBY SKIES

Traverse City offers visitors a variety of attractions. Some visitors are lured to the northwestern Michigan city by such attractions as the National Cherry Festival, nearby ski slopes, or opportunities for leisurely vacations along the shores of Lake Michigan. Folks from big cities like Chicago and Detroit are relocating to Traverse City, lured by the twin benefits of its rapidly growing, diverse economy and a simpler lifestyle.

In fact, only one part of Traverse City's infrastructure seemed left out of the area's growth—the local air terminal, Cherry Capital Airport. Most people traveling into and out of the city chose to travel by car rather than to fly. In fact, one research study revealed that 70 percent of people

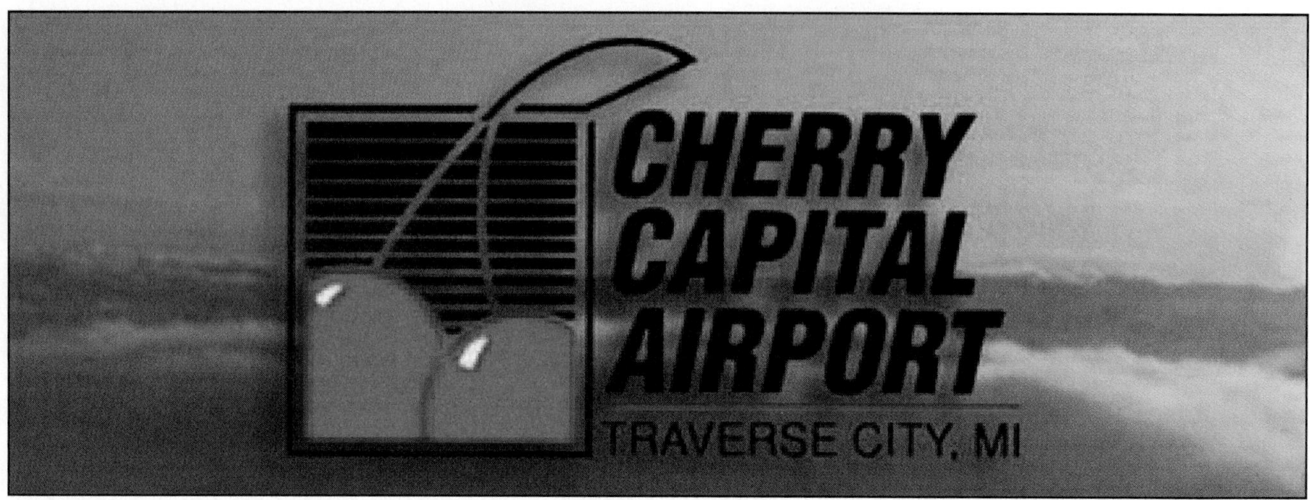
CHERRY
CAPITAL
AIRPORT
TRAVERSE CITY, MI

traveling by air chose to drive two hours to Grand Rapids or, even worse, four hours to Detroit to catch planes there. Unless airport management could do something to convince people to use Cherry Capital Airport, they saw a bleak future for local air service.

They traced Cherry Capital's problems directly to the 1978 deregulation of the airline industry. Deregulation ushered in a new era in which airports had to compete for air service. "With deregulation, we suddenly had no jet flights to Detroit or Chicago," says Hal VanSumeren, executive director of the Traverse City Area Chamber of Commerce. "Service deteriorated to a point that our manufacturers were telling us that they were no longer going to expand in our area until air service was improved."

Cherry Capital's marketers decided to devise an integrated marketing communications strategy aimed at increasing passenger traffic and improving airline service. As Airport Director Steve Cassens put it, "Not only do we have to sell the customer who's coming to the airport, but we have to convince the airlines that they should be in this market."

Business travelers are important to the success of any airport since they book many flights on short notice and at relatively high fares. These revenues allow the airlines to offer discounted fares to other passengers. "You can't discount seats unless you have that core group that's using the airlines on a regular basis," says Cassens. The number of airlines serving an airport has a major impact on the level of service it offers to the flying public. Realizing this fact, Cherry Capital marketers knew they had to persuade airline decision makers that their airport could command a sufficiently large market to support profitable flights to and from Traverse City.

Cassens and his staff identified four target audiences: passengers, businesses, airlines, and travel agents. They began by conducting a market research study to learn about the travel patterns, preferences, and priorities of current and potential air travelers. At the top of the list of factors influencing customer satisfaction was frequency of flights. Second on the list was competitive fares, followed by the types of aircraft that service an airport's flights. These findings became the basis for Capital City's new integrated marketing communications strategy.

One component of the new strategy was personal selling. Airport personnel made personal sales calls to area travel agents, informing them of the services provided by the local airport and the increased frequency of outbound and inbound flights. Salespeople also supplied prospects with data showing the competitiveness of air fares for flights from the airport and encouraged them to recommend Cherry Capital to their clients.

Special events such as air shows added another promotional element to boost exposure for the airport among potential passengers and to promote good will in the community. These events permitted Cherry Capital to showcase its modern facilities to potential air travelers, and they encouraged visitors to become familiar with the roads leading to the airport. To generate publicity for the airport, Cherry Capital marketers nurtured relationships with media outlets and assisted them in preparing radio and TV stories and public-interest articles to appear in area newspapers.

Advertising was a major element in Cherry Capital's IMC strategy. The ad campaign theme was inspired by Cassens' experience while driving on a Michigan road. Narrowly avoiding a duck that was crossing the road on foot, Cassens wondered why a duck would walk when it could fly. Then the inspiration for the campaign hit him: Ads could ask the same question of Traverse City travelers who made long auto drives when they could have flown. Thus, the "Fly from Nearby" campaign was born. Television ads featured a goose choosing Cherry Capital's convenient service. The ads gave the goose a personality and put him in humanlike situations.

One ad, "Goose on Foot," showed the feathered star landing, crossing the road, and waddling into Cherry Capital's attractive terminal. Narration announced, "Starting your trip from Cherry Capital Airport is convenient and saves you time and money. So why take to the road when you can fly?" Another ad featured the goose making a dramatic U-turn in a car after getting a call on his cell phone with the urgent message to get to Chicago immediately because "your sister's having an egg!" An "Office Goose" ad targeted at business travelers portrayed the bird behind an executive-sized desk signing a contract with his floppy foot. When told to go to Boston right away, the business bird again took advantage of Cherry Capital Airport, described by the narrator as "your connection to the world."

The award-winning campaign captured public attention, and the "Fly from Nearby" theme was expanded from TV ads to radio, magazine, and newspaper messages. It also filled sales presentation materials and airport communications. To promote the airport on the Internet, Brauer designed an entertaining and informative Web site. Traverse City travelers can access the site to learn about flight schedules, local events, and weather conditions.

Cherry Capital's promotions have changed travelers' attitudes about the airport and its services, resulting in growth in passenger traffic from 180,000 in 1989 to over 300,000 today. The airport expects to double that number over the next ten years. The promotions have also succeeded in bringing in travelers from a larger geographic area. Increased traffic has resulted in increased jet service and more daily flights. Airlines now servicing Traverse City include major carriers such as Northwest and American, as well as regional carriers such as United Express and Great Lakes Airlines. Daily nonstop flights take travelers to and from Chicago and Detroit. Cherry Capital is now profitable and undergoing a major expansion program to accommodate expected future growth.

Questions

1. Which of the promotional objectives discussed in this chapter are illustrated in Cherry Capital's IMC strategy?
2. Explain how Cherry Capital applied integrated marketing communications in achieving its promotional objectives.
3. Does Cherry Capital's promotional strategy represent a pulling strategy, a pushing strategy, or both? Support your answer with examples.
4. Visit the Cherry Capital Web site at
   http://www.tvcairport.com/
   Do you feel that this Web site is an effective component of the airport's integrated marketing communications package? Suggest methods for improving the site as a component of the airport's overall promotional campaign.

Sources: Personal interviews with Steve Cassens, director, Cherry Capital Airport, March 1997, and Hal VanSumeren, executive director, Traverse City Area Chamber of Commerce.

CHAPTER 18

ADVERTISING, SALES PROMOTION, AND PUBLIC RELATIONS

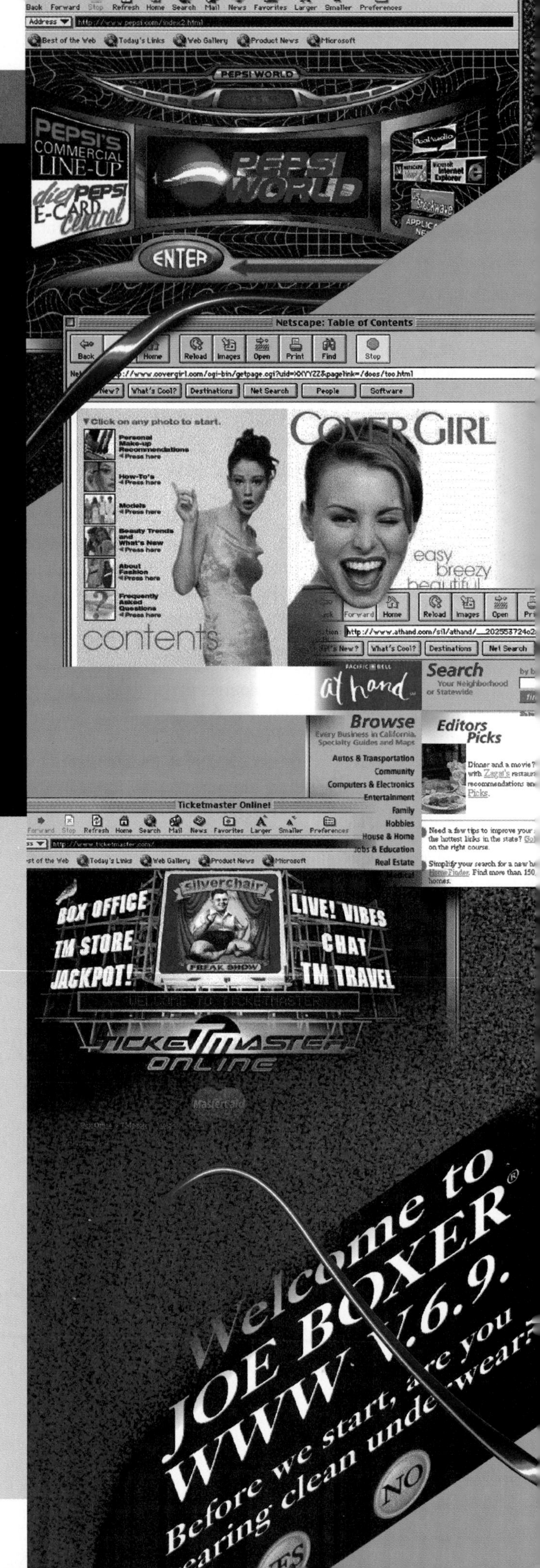

PEPSI WORLD
PEPSI'S COMMERCIAL LINE-UP
diet PEPSI E-CARD central
ENTER
Netscape: Table of Contents
Click on any photo to start.
COVERGIRL
easy breezy beautiful
contents
at hand
Search
Browse
Editors Picks
Ticketmaster Online!
BOX OFFICE
TM STORE
JACKPOT!
LIVE! VIBES
CHAT
TM TRAVEL
TICKETMASTER ONLINE
Welcome to JOE BOXER® WWW V.6.9.
Before we start, are you wearing clean underwear?
NO

Chapter Objectives

1. Explain the current status of advertising, sales promotion, and public relations in today's promotional strategies, and identify two recent trends in advertising.
2. Identify the major types of advertising.
3. Describe the process of creating an advertisement.
4. List and compare the major advertising media.
5. Outline the organization of the advertising function and the role of an advertising agency.
6. Identify the principal methods of sales promotion.
7. Explain the roles of public relations, publicity, and cross promotions in an organization's promotional strategy.
8. Explain how marketers assess promotional effectiveness.
9. Discuss the importance of ethics in a firm's promotional activities.

Advertising Goes Interactive

How do you provide a personalized makeup consultation service online? Or create an online business directory that combines consumer information with business listings? Harnessing the resources of the Internet to meet these challenges—and at the same time to build customer relationships—is the specialty of Ikonic Interactive, Inc., a pioneer in creative use of interactive media.

Formed in 1985, this San Francisco-based company is one of the new breed of specialized multimedia agencies. A leading developer of Web sites and other interactive media such as electronic kiosks, CD-ROMs, and interactive television, the company also partners with traditional advertising agencies, which rely on its technical expertise to meet their clients' needs.

contents
askcovergirl
Click on any photo to start.
Personal Make-up Recommendations
Press here
How-To's
Press here
Beauty Trends and What's New
Press here
Models
Press here
About Fashion
Press here
Frequently Asked Questions
Press here
About Navigator
Buttons like these will always be here to help you find your way.
MAP
[Makeup Tips] [Beauty Trends] [About Fashion] [How-to's] [Models] [FAQ] [Map]
[Guarantee Limitations] [Legal Terms]

Ikonic currently focuses on using interactive technology to build intimacy between big brands and individual consumers through one-to-one interactions. "The Internet today is probably the most powerful medium for communicating the essence of brand in a personalized fashion," says Ikonic CEO Robert May. Ikonic and its peers provide ways for advertisers and consumers to conduct online conversations. Advertisers can offer messages on demand that address specific consumer requests, while consumers gain new ways to interact with site sponsors.

Take, for instance, the site Ikonic developed for Procter & Gamble's Cover Girl brand. The visitor to the Cover Girl Web site meets a virtual makeup consultant who guides the user through a series of questions about lifestyle along with skin, hair, and eye color. The online advisor then determines the best products for that individual, including the actual shades and packaging options.

http://www.covergirl.com/
http://athand.com/

This personalized advice takes the guesswork out of choosing the right makeup. A user with a fair complexion, blonde hair, and green eyes who wants to spend minimal time on makeup receives different recommendations than one with olive skin, dark brown hair, and brown eyes who loves to experiment with a variety of shades.

The easy-to-use interface masks the Web site's technical complexity. At its heart, a database stores information about matches between products and user characteristics; it also stores information about specific users in personal profiles for future reference. Customers can ask questions and try different options at their convenience, 24 hours a day, without leaving home or dealing with potentially untrained clerks. Cover Girl regards the site as a double blessing, since this unique promotion costs just a fraction of the amount spent by brands that deploy in-store consultants.

Each visitor to the Cover Girl site has a unique, customized experience. The interactive component of the promotion produces a relationship between the brand and the consumer, building trust and interest.

Pacific Bell's At Hand megasite provides the same benefits through a comprehensive directory created by Ikonic. At Hand offers Internet users a unique way to find information. It combines directory listings for California merchants—organized around theme areas like House & Home, Entertainment & Leisure, and Sports & Outdoors—with editorial content and detailed local maps. "Instead of cluttering up the page with lots of banner ads, we will integrate topically related advertising into the viewer's environment—advertising when you ask for it is information," explains Pacific Bell Spokesperson Jeff Killeen.

It is the editorial content—designed and produced by Ikonic—that sets At Hand apart from other online directories. It combines a rich mix of resources, including news, event calendars travel guides, restaurant and movie reviews, and articles from such well-known specialty magazines as *Travel & Leisure, Food & Wine,* and *Billboard.* All of these features supplement a searchable database of listings for over 1 million California businesses.

"At Hand makes the most of the Internet's customizing capabilities," says Ikonic CEO May. When users explore a specific topic in the directory, they see not only the names of local merchants, but also lists of relevant articles, current advertiser promotions, coupons, and discount offers.

The Cover Girl and At Hand sites show advertising's new, more subtle direction. With interactive advertising, marketers provide users with customized experiences that add value, building a bond of trust between consumers and brands over time. According to May, this innovation takes relationship marketing to a new level. As consumers communicate with a company at Web sites connected to online databases, they establish personalized dialogues and create deeper levels of interaction. The result of this feedback is increased customer loyalty, lower marketing costs, and less inefficiency.[1]

CHAPTER OVERVIEW

As Chapter 17 explained, promotion has both personal and nonpersonal elements. This chapter examines the nonpersonal elements of promotion: advertising, sales promotion, and public relations. Thousands of organizations rely on these components to play critical roles in their integrated marketing communications strategies and promotional mixes. While advertising is the most visible form of nonpersonal promotion, marketers spend three times as much on sales promotion. The two often work more effectively together than either works separately, and ads often drive promotional campaigns. For example, McDonald's used TV spots to support tie-in promotions with the *Batman, 101 Dalmations,* and *Mighty Morphin' Power Rangers* movies.

This chapter begins with a discussion of the importance of promotional planning, and then it examines each major category of nonpersonal promotion. First, it considers *advertising,* focusing on the global reach of the industry and the rise of interactive advertising, the different types of advertisements, and media choices. Next, it turns to sales promotion, discussing *consumer promotion* methods such as samples, coupons, and specialty advertising and *trade promotions* like dealer incentives and trade shows. Public relations and publicity are also important components of a firm's IMC programs, providing effective support for its other promotional activities. Another important trend—the rise in cross promotions—is also analyzed. The chapter then examines alternative methods of assessing promotional effectiveness. Finally, it explores the issue of promotional ethics.

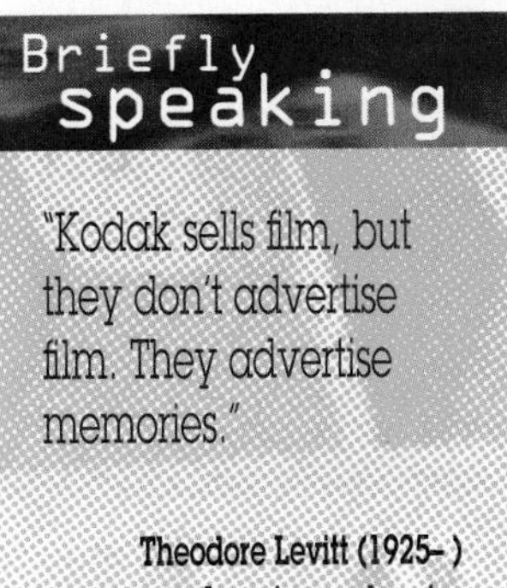
Briefly speaking
"Kodak sells film, but they don't advertise film. They advertise memories."
Theodore Levitt (1925–)
American educator

ADVERTISING

If you wanted to become a member of the U.S. Senate, you would have to communicate with every potential voter in your state. If you were to develop new computer software and start a company to market it, you would face slim chances of success without an effort to inform and persuade students, businesspeople, and other potential customers of the usefulness of your offering. In these situations, you would discover, as have countless others, the need to advertise as a way to communicate with buyers. As defined in Chapter 17, **advertising** is paid, nonpersonal communication through various media by a business firm, not-for-profit organization, or individual identified in the message with the hope of informing or persuading members of a particular audience.

Today's wide-ranging markets make advertising an important part of business. Since the end of World War II, U.S. expenditures on advertising and related costs have risen faster than the gross domestic product and most other economic indicators. Furthermore, the advertising industry employs about 212,000 Americans.

Each year, the nation's two leading advertisers, Procter & Gamble and Philip Morris Companies, spend over $2.5 billion each, while General Motors spends about $2 billion, and eight more firms—including Ford, Disney, and Sears, Roebuck and Co.—each spend over $1 billion. Total annual expenditures for advertising in the United States exceed $160 billion, or approximately $615 for every man, woman, and child.[2]

Advertising expenditures vary among industries and companies. Cosmetics producers often are cited as examples of firms that spend high percentages of their revenues on advertising and promotion. Marketers of fragrances like Chantilly spend, on average, 10 percent of total sales revenues on advertising and promotion like that illustrated in Figure 18.1. Advertising spending ranges from 0.5 percent of sales in the carpet and rugs industry to more than 16 percent in the special cleaning preparations category.

As previous chapters have discussed, the emergence of the marketing concept, with its emphasis on a companywide consumer orientation, boosted the importance of marketing communications. This change, in turn, expanded the role of advertising. Today, a typical consumer is exposed to hundreds of advertising messages each day. Advertising provides an efficient, inexpensive, and fast method of reaching the ever-elusive consumer. Its current role rivals those of sales promotion and personal selling. Indeed, advertising has become a key ingredient in the effective implementation of the marketing concept.

Advertising Goes Global

Advertising is an important element of promotion in other countries, too. As Chapters 1 and 4 discussed, companies operate in a worldwide economy, marketing their products across national borders. Major reasons for the growth of

Marketing Dictionary

advertising Paid, nonpersonal communication through various media by a business firm, not-for-profit organization, or individual identified in the message with the hope of informing or persuading members of a particular audience.

Figure 18.1 Cosmetics: An Industry That Allocates Ten Percent of Sales to Advertising and Promotion

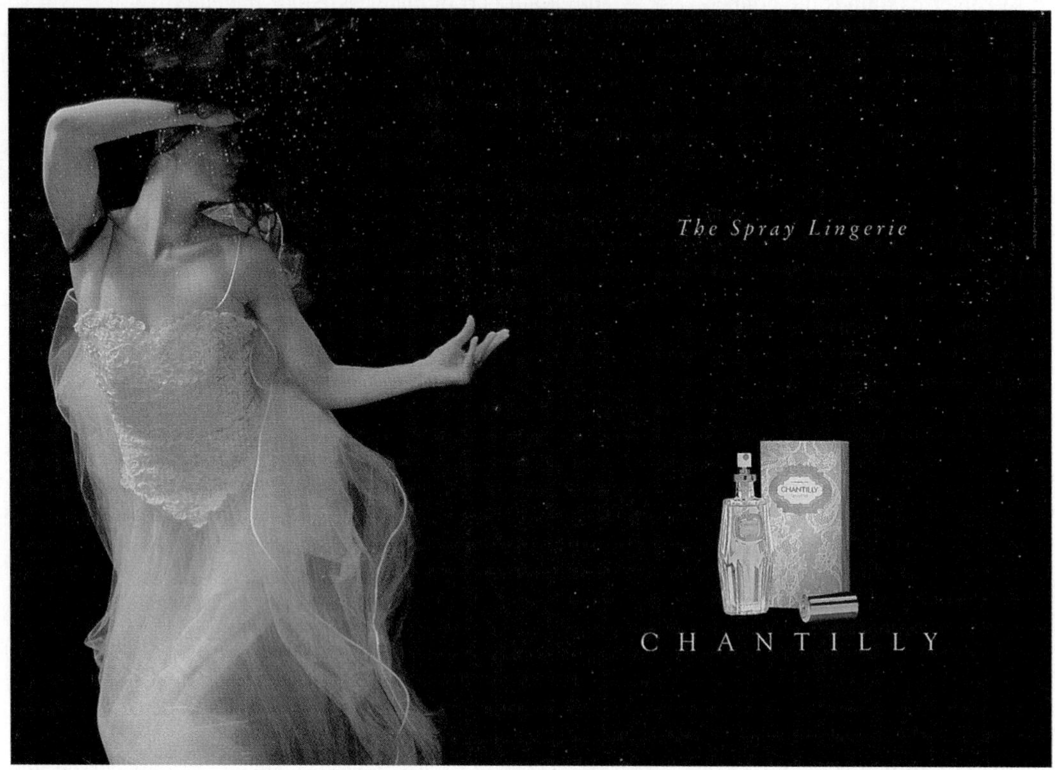
The Spray Lingerie
CHANTILLY

advertising worldwide include growth in the number of multinational corporations and global brands, increased trade among nations, worldwide improvement in living standards, and innovations in communications and transportation. As companies begin to saturate the markets in their own countries, they search out new opportunities overseas. They find that advertising offers the most effective way to reach the most consumers and deliver information about their products.

Before running advertising campaigns in other countries, marketers must study the social, political, economic, and legal environments in those nations. The ads they create must recognize and accommodate these factors. Slogans, images, or symbols that work well in one language or country, for example, may fail dismally in another. Ads considered too risqué in the United States, for example, may be acceptable in Europe.

Recently, Anheuser-Busch ran into a problem with its use of Native American actors in British ads for Budweiser beer. The Indians were included to symbolize the beer's American origin. Native American advocacy groups in the United States were outraged, calling the company insensitive to the higher-than-average incidence of alcoholism among this group and the negative stereotype it presents. British consumers were unaware of the connection between Indians and alcohol, though; the campaign became Budweiser's most popular in the United Kingdom, and sales rose about 20 percent. Brian Fraser, who created the ad, acknowledges that it would not work in the U.S. market—and it wasn't meant to do so. The campaign raises the issue whether advertisers can ever create ads that are acceptable worldwide. Some marketers believe that any attempt could result in bland ads with little appeal.[3]

Some products lend themselves to global campaigns, however, using the same basic message in all countries. For an international brand like Nike, a universal campaign like the ad in Figure 18.2 is likely to get the message across in any language by featuring an international celebrity like tennis star Andre Agassi and the famous Nike swoosh.

Other companies such as Nabisco and Nestlé give their products different names suited to different countries and cultures. Yet the advertising may still use a consistent theme. Nestlé used a similar ad campaign with a serial romance for its premium instant coffee, called Taster's Choice in the United States and Gold Blend in Britain.

Advertising for packaged goods requires marketers to be especially sensitive to nuances and cultural interpretations. What works in one country may offend in another. In Japan, ads appealing to the consumer's individuality or promoting a product on the basis of low price would not be effective, while those emphasizing company longevity and product reliability would create favorable impressions. The amount of advertising is important, too. When Snapple drinks were launched in Japan, it cost just under $2 million—most of which went for a television commercial that aired late at night. This commitment was woefully inadequate to promote a new product in Japan's intensely competitive soft-drink market.[4]

PepsiCo's Frito-Lay snack-food unit was more successful in introducing potato chips to the Thai market. Although it is not customary in Thailand to advertise snack foods on television, Frito-Lay coupled a major television campaign with in-store free samples to familiarize consumers with the product. One ad showed a Thai child star eating the chips, effectively using the company's "bet you can't eat just one" slogan.[5]

Figure 18.2 **Nike Apparel: Global Advertising of a Global Brand**

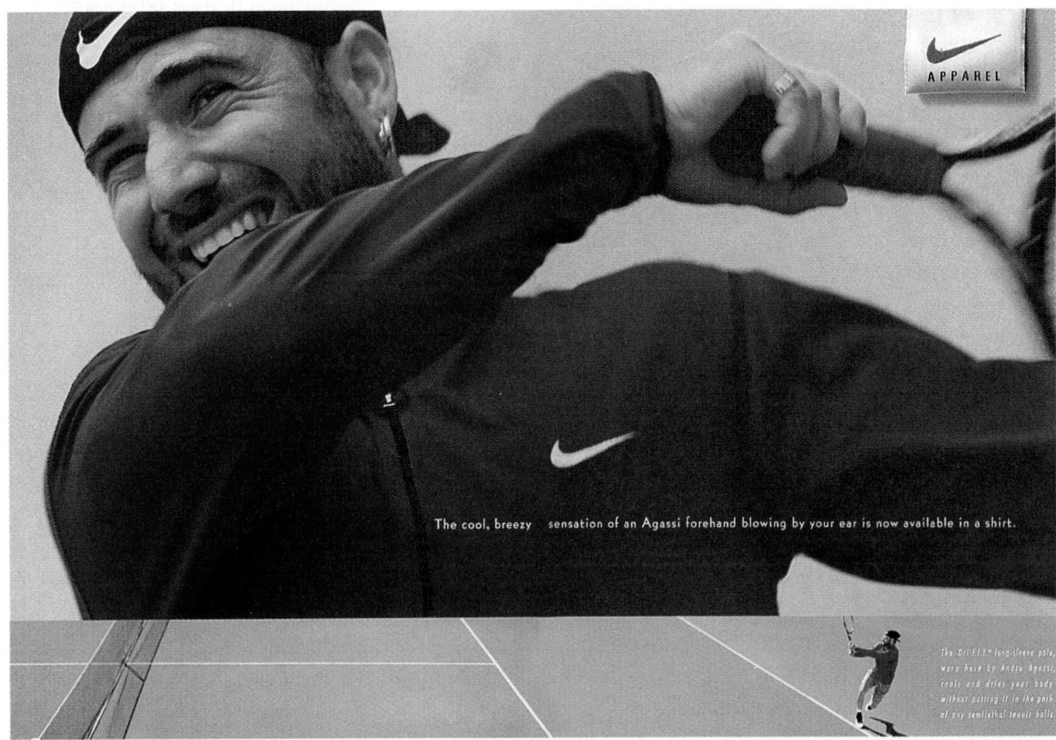
APPAREL
The cool, breezy sensation of an Agassi forehand blowing by your ear is now available in a shirt.

Interactive Advertising

Advertising messages also float across idle computer screens in offices around the country. Net surfers play games with embedded ads from the site sponsors. Companies offer free e-mail service to people willing to receive ads with their personal messages. Video screens on shopping carts display ads for products shoppers see as they wheel down grocery store aisles.

Welcome to the world of interactive advertising. As discussed in Chapter 1, interactive advertising directly involves the consumer through mutual or reciprocal communication. It takes many forms, from Web sites to mall kiosks. Multimedia technology, the Internet, and commercial online services are changing the nature of advertising from a one-way, passive communication technique to a more effective way to facilitate two-way marketing communications. The advertising creates a dialogue, providing more materials when the user asks. The advertiser's challenge is to gain and hold consumers' interest in an environment where they control what they want to see.

Interactive advertising changes the balance between marketers and consumers. Unlike the traditional role of advertising—providing brief, entertaining, attention-catching messages—interactive media provide information to help consumers throughout the purchase and consumption processes. As consumers choose among growing numbers of products in the course of their fast-paced lives, they want more information in less time to help them make necessary comparisons between available products. Today, online resources fill the gap between ads and personal selling, especially for higher-priced products like appliances and cars and for specialty goods such as consumer electronics and computer products. Advertising is moving from an emphasis on brief, one-way spots or single-page print ads to layered, interactive advertisements, where consumers choose to learn more about products and also provide information about themselves to the advertiser.

Successful interactive advertising adds value by offering the viewer more than just product-related information. An ad on the World Wide Web can do more than promote a brand; it can also create a company store, customer service line, and other content. For example, the colorful Baskin Robbins Birthday Center Web site portrayed in Figure 18.3 allows the visitor to send a personalized birthday greeting via e-mail. The e-mail message includes fun facts about the day the recipient was born, along with information about how to get an animated "e-cake." The site also includes party planning ideas with innovative themes for adult and kid parties, links to other birthday-oriented sites offering party supplies, reminder services, and astrological readings. Product information that whets cyber-appetites, birthday fun facts, and lists of Baskin Robbins' stores near the visitor round out the site.[6] This site provides a good example of how advertising can support editorial content in a way that is helpful rather than intrusive. In addition, when site visitors need real birthday cakes, they will think favorably of Baskin Robbins products. The result is improved brand loyalty and a solid relationship with the consumer.

Most companies deliver their interactive advertising messages through proprietary online services and the

Figure 18.3 Interactive Advertising on the World Wide Web

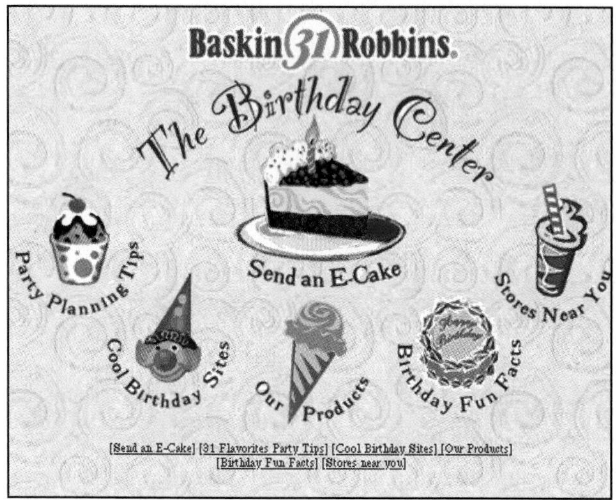
Baskin 31 Robbins.
The Birthday Center
Party Planning Tips
Send an E-Cake
Stores Near You
Cool Birthday Sites
Our Products
Birthday Fun Facts
[Send an E-Cake] [31 Flavorites Party Tips] [Cool Birthday Sites] [Our Products]
[Birthday Fun Facts] [Stores near you]

Internet's World Wide Web. Online advertising revenues, about $200 million in 1996, are expected to reach $2 billion in 2000. Web resources earned about 55 percent of total online advertising revenue in 1996, but it will represent 90 percent by 2000.

However, Web advertising is still only a small part of companies' overall promotional expenditures. Even though it places ads on over 25 different sites, Intel Corp. spends less than 5 percent of its ad budget on the Web. CNN's Web site generates about $10 million in ad revenues compared to $338 million for time on CNN's cable channels.[7]

The novelty of Internet advertising leads the list of numerous problems for advertisers, such as lack of standards to measure effectiveness and limited creative and scheduling options. Despite these difficulties, many companies have successfully embraced the Internet and used it to their advantage. Interactive ads are discussed in more detail in subsequent sections of this chapter.

Figure 18.4 Advertising Intended to Assist Personal Selling

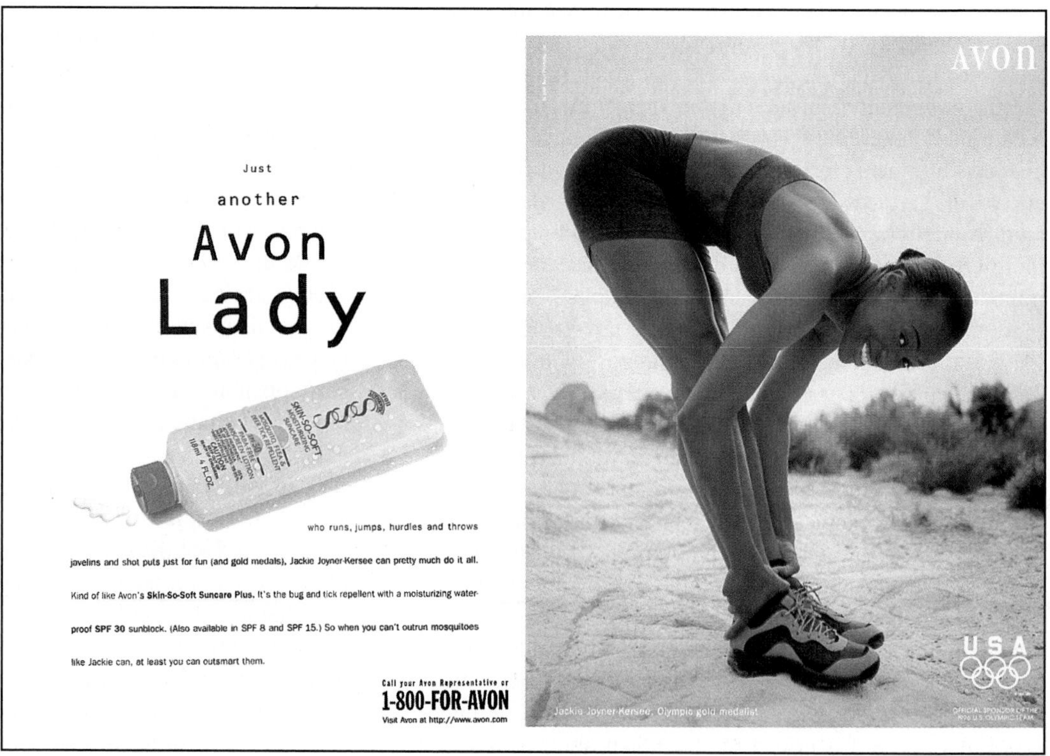
AVON
Just
another
Avon
Lady
SKIN-SO-SOFT
who runs, jumps, hurdles and throws
javelins and shot puts just for fun (and gold medals), Jackie Joyner-Kersee can pretty much do it all.
Kind of like Avon's **Skin-So-Soft Suncare Plus.** It's the bug and tick repellent with a moisturizing water-
proof **SPF 30** sunblock. (Also available in SPF 8 and SPF 15.) So when you can't outrun mosquitoes
like Jackie can, at least you can outsmart them.
Call your Avon Representative or
1-800-FOR-AVON
Visit Avon at http://www.avon.com
Jackie Joyner-Kersee, Olympic gold medalist
USA

Advertising Objectives

Traditionally, advertisers stated their objectives as direct sales goals. A more realistic standard, however, views advertising as a way to achieve communications objectives, including informing, persuading, and reminding potential customers of the product. Advertising attempts to condition consumers to adopt favorable viewpoints toward a promotional message. The goal of an ad is to improve the likelihood that a customer will buy a particular good or service. In this sense, advertising illustrates the close relationship between marketing communications and promotional strategy.

Effective advertising can enhance consumer perceptions of quality in a good or service, leading to gains in customer loyalty, repeat purchases, and protection against price wars. In addition, perceptions of superiority pay off in the firm's ability to raise prices without losing market share.

Where personal selling is the primary component of a firm's marketing mix, ads like the one for Avon in Figure 18.4

Figure 18.5 Elements of Advertising Planning

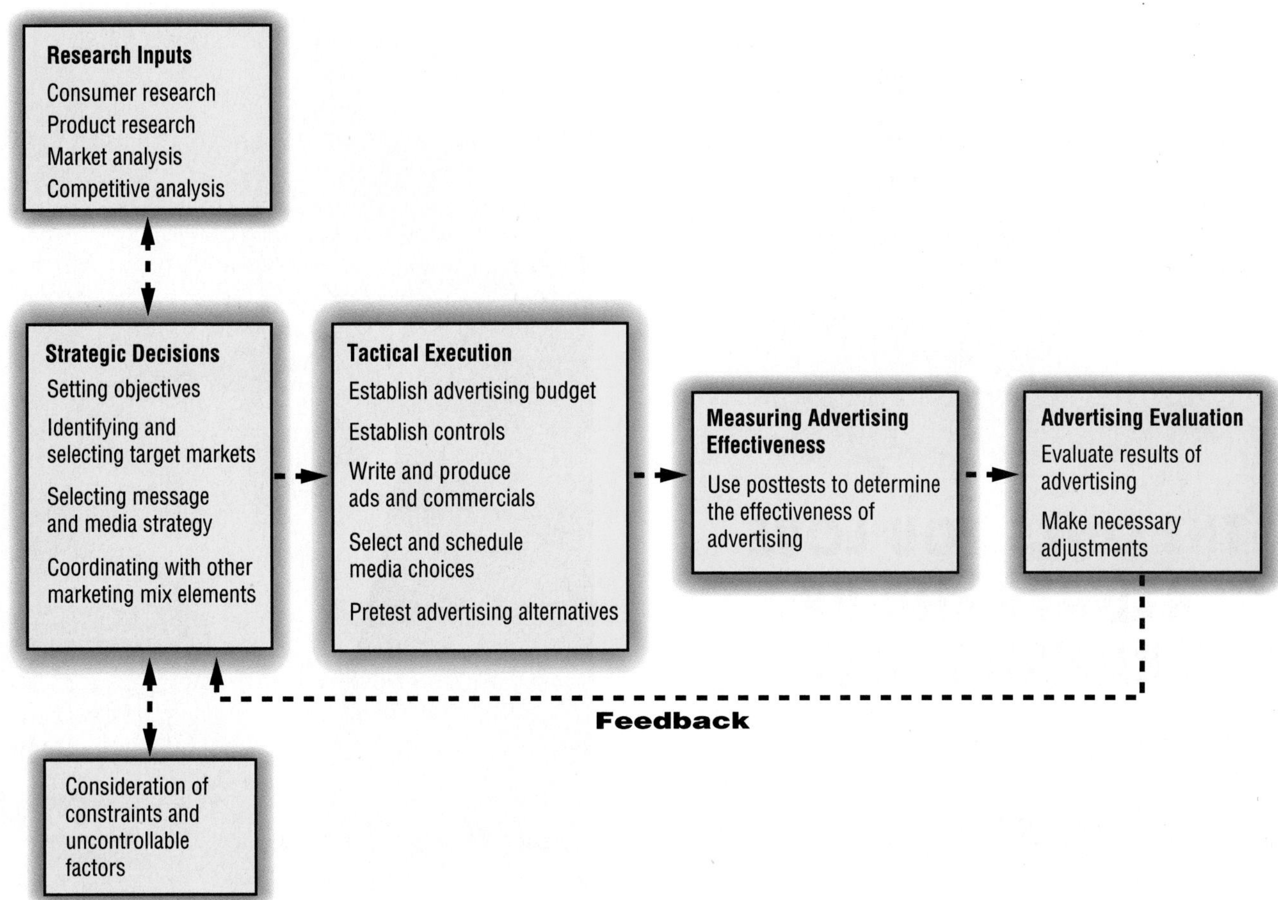
Research Inputs
Consumer research
Product research
Market analysis
Competitive analysis
Strategic Decisions
Setting objectives
Identifying and selecting target markets
Selecting message and media strategy
Coordinating with other marketing mix elements
Tactical Execution
Establish advertising budget
Establish controls
Write and produce ads and commercials
Select and schedule media choices
Pretest advertising alternatives
Measuring Advertising Effectiveness
Use posttests to determine the effectiveness of advertising
Advertising Evaluation
Evaluate results of advertising
Make necessary adjustments
Feedback
Consideration of constraints and uncontrollable factors

may perform support roles assisting salespeople. Avon aims much of its advertising at assisting the neighborhood salesperson by strengthening customers' images of Avon, its products, and its salespeople. State Farm Insurance intends its slogan, "Like a good neighbor, State Farm is there," to change consumers' perception of insurance salespeople as annoying policy pushers. Because the insurance firm can sell policies only through agents, the slogan's objective is to persuade consumers to respond favorably to those agents. The ads emphasize that policyholders can count on State Farm's representatives even after the sale.

Translating Advertising Objectives into Advertising Plans

Once a company defines its objectives for an advertising campaign, it can develop its advertising plan. Market research guides managers in making strategic decisions that guide choices in technical areas such as budgeting, copywriting, scheduling, and media selection. Posttests measure the effectiveness of advertising and form the basis for feedback concerning possible adjustments. The elements of advertising planning are shown in Figure 18.5.

Marketers should carefully follow a sequential process in any advertising decision. Novice advertisers often focus too closely on the technical aspects of creating advertisements and ignore more basic steps, such as market analysis. The type of advertisement suited to a particular situation depends largely on the results of the planning phase of this process.

As Chapter 7 explained, positioning involves developing a marketing strategy that aims to achieve a desired position in a prospective buyer's mind. Marketers use a positioning strategy that distinguishes their good or service from those of competitors. Effective advertising then communicates the desired position by emphasizing certain product characteristics such as performance attributes, price/quality, competitors' shortcomings, applications, user needs, and/or product classes.

Figure 18.6 Product and Institutional Advertising

THE ONES YOU LOVE
ALWAYS END UP
HURTING YOU.
Maalox

Here's the direction.
You thought milk was just
a kid thing. But the plot
thickens and you discover
your bones are still
growing until you're 35.
You're on a mad quest for
calcium. AND... ACTION.
You open the fridge,
you grab the lowfat milk,
you drink it. CUT.
Not from the carton.
TAKE 2. Let's use a glass.
MILK
Where's *your* mustache?™

TYPES OF ADVERTISING

Advertisements fall into two broad categories: product and institutional ads. **Product advertising** is nonpersonal selling of a particular good or service. The average person usually thinks of this kind of promotion when talking about advertisements. **Institutional advertising,** in contrast, promotes a concept, an idea, a philosophy, or the goodwill of an industry, company, organization, person, geographic location, or government agency. This term has a broader meaning than *corporate advertising,* which is typically limited to nonproduct advertising sponsored by a specific profit-seeking firm.

Institutional advertising is often closely related to the public-relations function of the enterprise. The Maalox ad in Figure 18.6 featuring a burger large enough to need a construction permit is an eye-catching example of product advertising. The second ad, showing mustachioed filmmaker Spike Lee in the award-winning "Got Milk?" campaign, is an institutional ad designed to increase public awareness. The ultimate objective is to increase overall milk consumption rather than increase market share for a specific brand.

The primary objective of an advertising message defines three additional categories: informative, persuasive, and reminder ads. **Informative advertising** seeks to develop initial demand for a good, service, organization, person, place, idea, or cause. The promotion of any new market entry tends to pursue this objective, because marketing success at this stage often depends simply on announcing availability. Therefore, informative advertising is common in the introductory stage of the product life cycle.

Persuasive advertising attempts to increase demand for an existing good, service, organization, person, place, idea, or cause. It is a competitive type of promotion suited to the growth stage and the early part of the maturity stage of the product life cycle.

Reminder advertising strives to reinforce previous promotional activity by keeping the name of a good, service, organization, person, place, idea, or cause before the public. It is common in the latter part of the maturity stage and throughout the decline stage of the product life cycle.

Comparative Advertising

Figure 18.7 **Comparative Advertising: Sustacal versus Ensure**

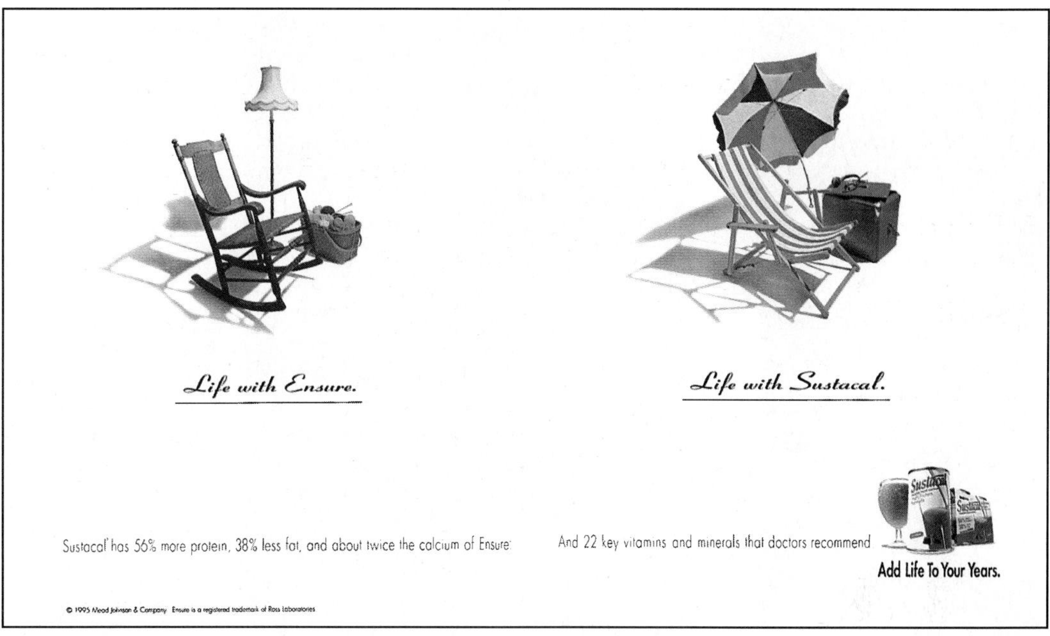
Life with Ensure.
Life with Sustacal.
Sustacal has 56% more protein, 38% less fat, and about twice the calcium of Ensure.
And 22 key vitamins and minerals that doctors recommend
Add Life To Your Years.
© 1995 Mead Johnson & Company Ensure is a registered trademark of Ross Laboratories

Comparative advertising is an advertising strategy that emphasizes messages with direct or indirect promotional comparisons between competing brands. Firms whose goods and services do not lead their markets often favor comparative advertising strategies. Most market leaders do not acknowledge in their advertising that competing products even exist. Procter & Gamble and General Foods, for example, traditionally have devoted little of their huge promotional budgets to comparative advertising. Many less dominant firms use the technique extensively, however.

When Mead Johnson marketers decided to take on market leader Ensure in the market for high-protein liquid dietary supplements, they relied on comparative advertising for their Sustacal brand. As Figure 18.7 illustrates, the Sustacal ads make specific superiority claims for their product as compared to the competitor.

Marketers of over-the-counter medications rely heavily on comparative advertising. Makers of Tylenol, Advil, and other pain relievers frequently compare their own products with those of their competitors. Ads for Aleve tout dosage differences, claiming that only one Aleve tablet substitutes for multiple doses of Advil. Some Tylenol ads mention concerns about combining medications for high blood pressure with ibuprofen (a key Advil ingredient).[8]

The Federal Trade Commission (FTC) actually encourages comparative advertising. Regulators believe that such ads keep markets competitive and inform consumers about their choices. "Where there is competition through advertising, prices tend to go down because people can shop around," said FTC official Joel Winston.[9]

Comparative advertising has become commonplace in the automobile and truck markets. Many commercials compare products specifically to their competitors. Marketers must remember, however, that comparative advertising is less easily accepted in some countries than in the United States. Even in the United States, marketers who

Marketing Dictionary

product advertising Nonpersonal selling of a good or service.

institutional advertising Promoting a concept, an idea, a philosophy, or the goodwill of an industry, company, organization, place, person, or government agency.

informative advertising Nonpersonal promotion that seeks to announce the availability of and develop initial demand for a new good, service, organization, person, place, idea, or cause.

persuasive advertising Competitive, nonpersonal promotion that seeks to increase demand for an existing good, service, organization, person, place, idea, or cause.

reminder advertising Nonpersonal promotion that seeks to reinforce previous promotional activity by keeping the name of a good, service, organization, person, place, idea, or cause in front of the public.

comparative advertising Nonpersonal selling efforts that emphasize direct or indirect promotional comparisons between competing brands.

Figure 18.8 Effective Use of Celebrity Testimonials

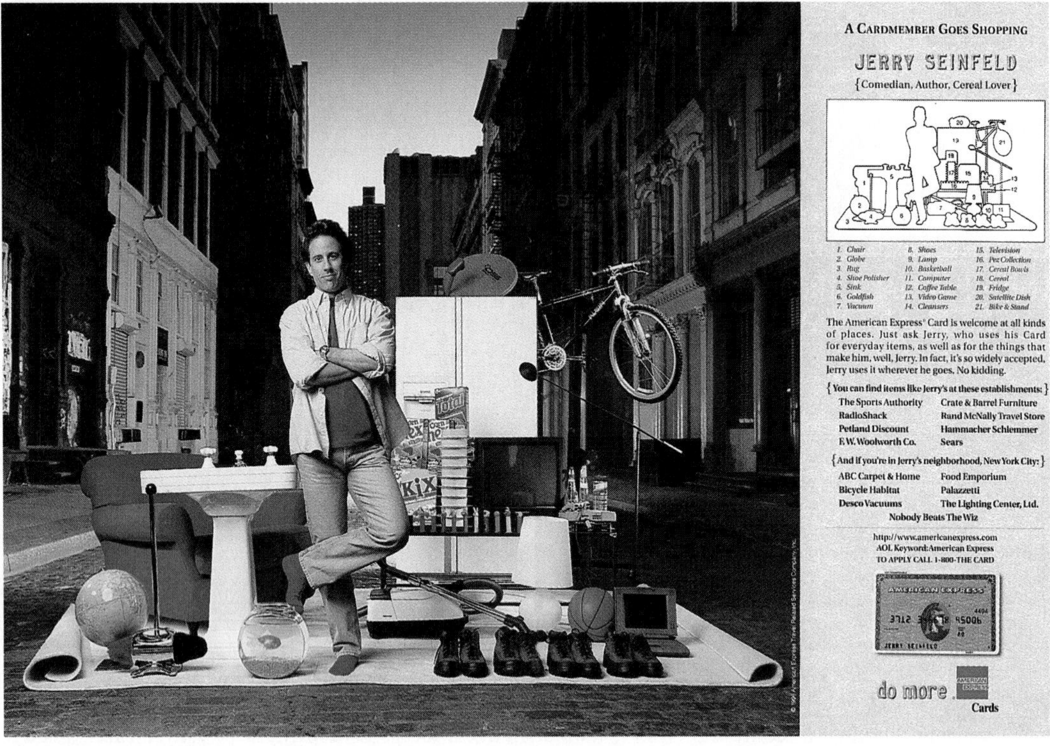
A CARDMEMBER GOES SHOPPING
JERRY SEINFELD
{Comedian, Author, Cereal Lover}
1. Chair
2. Globe
3. Rug
4. Shoe Polisher
5. Sink
6. Goldfish
7. Vacuum
8. Shoes
9. Lamp
10. Basketball
11. Computer
12. Coffee Table
13. Video Game
14. Cleansers
15. Television
16. Pez Collection
17. Cereal Bowls
18. Cereal
19. Fridge
20. Satellite Dish
21. Bike & Stand
The American Express Card is welcome at all kinds of places. Just ask Jerry, who uses his Card for everyday items, as well as for the things that make him, well, Jerry. In fact, it's so widely accepted, Jerry uses it wherever he goes. No kidding.
{You can find items like Jerry's at these establishments:}
The Sports Authority
Crate & Barrel Furniture
RadioShack
Rand McNally Travel Store
Petland Discount
Hammacher Schlemmer
F.W. Woolworth Co.
Sears
{And if you're in Jerry's neighborhood, New York City:}
ABC Carpet & Home
Food Emporium
Bicycle Habitat
Palazzetti
Desco Vacuums
The Lighting Center, Ltd.
Nobody Beats The Wiz
http://www.americanexpress.com
AOL Keyword: American Express
TO APPLY CALL 1-800-THE CARD
AMERICAN EXPRESS
JERRY SEINFELD
do more.
AMERICAN EXPRESS
Cards

contemplate making comparative claims should ensure that they can substantiate their information. Inaccurate comparative advertising may produce lawsuits. Also, advertising experts disagree on the long-term effects of comparative advertising. It may be a useful strategy only in limited circumstances.

Celebrity Testimonials

Many marketers hire celebrity spokespeople to try to boost the effectiveness of their advertising messages. About 20 percent of all U.S. ads include celebrities. Celebrity advertising is also popular in foreign countries. In Japan, 80 percent of all ads use celebrities, both local and U.S. stars. U.S. celebrities featured in Japanese ads include actors Harrison Ford for Kirin Beer, Brad Pitt for Honda, Jodie Foster for Keri Cosmetics and Latte Coffee, and Paul Newman for Evance watch stores. While Japanese celebrities appear more frequently, Japanese consumers view foreign stars differently, as images more than people, which helps marketers to sell products. They also associate American stars with quality.[10]

The number of celebrity ads and the dollars spent on those ads have both increased in recent years. Professional athletes are among the highest-paid product endorsers. In a recent year, basketball players Michael Jordan and Shaquille O'Neal earned $40 million and $17 million, respectively, in endorsements; golfers Jack Nicklaus and Arnold Palmer each earned $14 million, and tennis star Andre Agassi added $13 million in endorsement income to his tennis winnings.

The primary advantage of associations with big-name personalities is improved product recognition in a promotional environment filled with hundreds of competing 15-second and 30-second commercials. (Advertisers use the term *clutter* to describe this situation.)

Do celebrity endorsements work? Several studies of consumer responses show that they do indeed improve believability, recall, and brand recognition. Celebrity endorsements also create positive attitudes, leading to greater brand equity. Because investors view celebrity advertising positively, it is generally seen as a marketing strategy likely to produce an upward effect on future profits.[11]

A celebrity testimonial generally succeeds when the celebrity is a credible source of information for the promoted product. The most effective ads of this type establish relevant links between the celebrities and the advertised goods or services. Figure 18.8 pairs comedian Jerry Seinfeld, who is extremely popular with TV viewers 25 to 40 years old, with the American Express card. By featuring Seinfeld, American Express hopes to attract his many fans to apply for the card and to broaden its acceptance among this age group, who may not realize that they can use the card to pay for both special and everyday items. Marketers also use sports figures to bring credibility to ads. Michael Jordan's endorsement of Gatorade is also believable, because athletes drink similar beverages.

Celebrity advertising can prove disastrous, however, if the celebrity becomes involved in a scandal or controversy. In addition, a celebrity who endorses numerous products may create marketplace confusion when customers remember the cele-brity but relate the ad to a competing brand. Only 31 percent of those surveyed said that Jerry

Seinfeld appeared in American Express ads; another 14 percent thought he was a spokesperson for either Visa or MasterCard. Sprint spokeswoman Candace Bergan fared better with a 63 percent correct match. However, one respondent in five misidentified her as an MCI spokesperson.[12]

Some advertisers try to avoid such problems by using cartoon characters as endorsers. Met Life ads have included characters from the *Peanuts* cartoon strip for years, Bugs Bunny joined Michael Jordan in Nike ads, and Pepsi put Wile E. Coyote together with football star Deion Sanders. Advertisers like cartoon characters because they never say anything negative about the product, do exactly what the marketers want them to do, and can't get involved in scandals. The only drawback is high licensing fees; popular characters can cost more than live celebrities.[13]

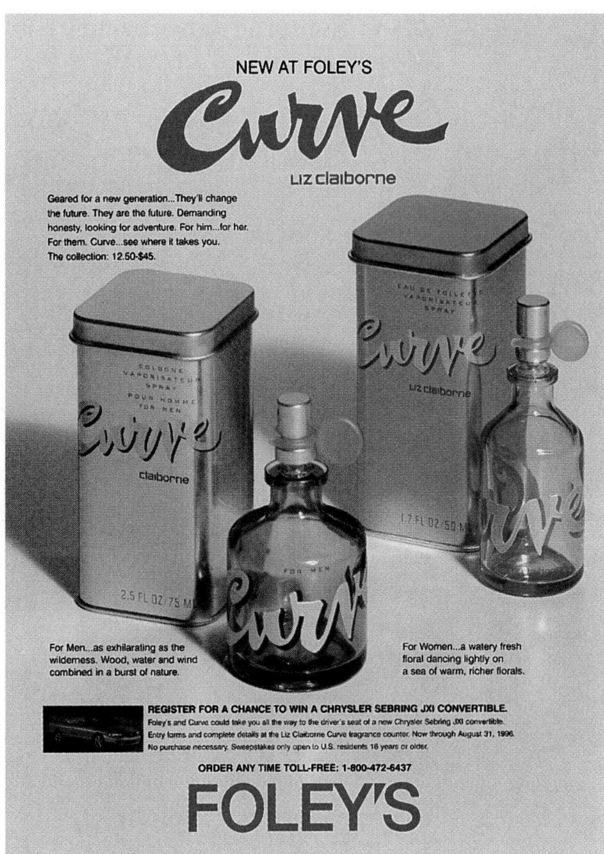
NEW AT FOLEY'S
Curve
LIZ claiborne
Geared for a new generation...They'll change the future. They are the future. Demanding honesty, looking for adventure. For him...for her. For them. Curve...see where it takes you.
The collection: 12.50-$45.
For Men...as exhilarating as the wilderness. Wood, water and wind combined in a burst of nature.
For Women...a watery fresh floral dancing lightly on a sea of warm, richer florals.
REGISTER FOR A CHANCE TO WIN A CHRYSLER SEBRING JXI CONVERTIBLE.
Foley's and Curve could take you all the way to the driver's seat of a new Chrysler Sebring JXI convertible.
Entry forms and complete details at the Liz Claiborne Curve fragrance counter. Now through August 31, 1996.
No purchase necessary. Sweepstakes only open to U.S. residents 18 years or older.
ORDER ANY TIME TOLL-FREE: 1-800-472-6437
FOLEY'S

Foley's department stores and Curve perfume pooled their resources by developing this cooperative advertising.

Retail Advertising

Retail advertising encompasses all advertising by stores that sell goods or services directly to the consuming public. While this activity accounts for a sizable portion of total annual advertising expenditures, retail advertising varies widely in its effectiveness. One study showed that consumers often respond with suspicion to retail price advertisements. Source, message, and shopping experience seem to affect consumer attitudes toward these advertisements.[14]

The problem results from retail stores often treating advertising as a secondary activity. Except for some retail giants, they rarely hire advertising agencies. Instead, store managers usually accept responsibility for advertising along with their other duties. To correct this deficiency, management should assign one individual both the responsibility and the authority to develop an effective retail advertising program.

Cooperative Advertising

A retailer often shares advertising costs with a manufacturer or wholesaler in a technique called **cooperative advertising.** For example, an apparel marketer may pay a percentage of the cost of a retail store's newspaper advertisement featuring its product lines.

Cooperative advertising campaigns originated to take advantage of the media's practice of offering lower rates to local advertisers than to national ones. Later cooperative advertising became part of programs to improve dealer relations. The retailer likes the chance to secure advertising that it could not run otherwise. Cooperative advertising can create vertical links, as when a manufacturer and retailer coordinate their resources. It can also involve firms at the same level of the supply chain. In a horizontal arrangement, a group of retailers—for example, all the Lexus dealers in a metropolitan area—might get together.

Intel Corp. spends more than $500 million a year on its extensive cooperative ad program. Intel gives PC manufacturers 6 percent of their total chip purchases as rebates in exchange for placement of the "Intel Inside" logo on packaging and advertisements. The PC companies spend that money on advertising, and Intel also pays half of the cost of print ads and two-thirds of the cost of broadcast ads. Intel

Marketing Dictionary

retail advertising Nonpersonal selling by stores that offer goods or services directly to the consuming public.

cooperative advertising Sharing advertising costs between a retailer and a manufacturer of the advertised good or service.

Figure 18.9 Using Humor in Advertising Messages

Jeremy
"It's moments LIKE THESE
YOU NEED MINTIES"

and its ad agencies negotiate discounts and incentives with print and broadcast outlets worldwide for PC marketers who are Intel customers.[15]

CREATING AN ADVERTISEMENT

Marketers spend over $160 billion a year on advertising campaigns in the United States alone. With so much money at stake, marketers must ensure that they create good ads that increase sales and enhance their organizations' images. They cannot afford to waste resources on a bad ad that may lead to consumer disdain for a product, boycotts, and even federal investigations. For example, Kathie Lee Gifford's Wal-Mart ads, mentioned in the Marketing Hall of Shame feature, prompted government agencies to investigate claims that the garments were produced in sweatshops.

As an earlier section discussed, research helps marketers to create better ads. Research can pinpoint goals that the ad needs to accomplish, such as educating consumers about product features, enhancing brand loyalty, or improving consumer perception of the brand. These objectives should guide the design of the ad. Marketers can also discover what appeals to consumers and test ads with potential buyers before committing funds for a campaign.

Advertising Messages

The strategy for creating a message starts with a product's customer benefits and moves to the creative concept phase, in which marketers strive to bring an appropriate message to consumers using both visual and verbal components. They work to create an ad with meaningful, believable, and distinctive appeals—one that stands out from the clutter and escapes "zapping" by the television remote control.

Usually, ads are not created in an isolated fashion, but as part of specific compaigns. An *advertising campaign* is a series of different but related ads appearing in different media within a specified time period and using a single theme. The "Pepsi for Generation Next" ad campaign theme is a current example.

In developing a creative strategy, advertisers must decide how to communicate their marketing message. They must balance message characteristics like the tone of the appeal, the extent of information provided and the conclusion to which it leads the consumer, the side of the story the ad tells, and its emphasis on verbal or visual primary elements.

Should the tone of the advertisement focus on a practical appeal such as price, or should it evoke an emotional response of, say, fear, humor, or fantasy? In recent years, the use of fear appeals in advertising has escalated. Ads for insurance, cars, and automotive products like tires all carry messages that incorrect buying decisions endanger the well-being of consumers and, in many cases, their children. Public service campaigns against smoking and substance abuse evoke fears of damage to health and social rejection with slogans like "This is your brain. This is your brain on drugs" and "Friends don't let friends drink and drive." Fear appeals pursue a goal of encouraging consumers to do what is necessary to remove the identified threats, usually to avoid undesirable behavior or purchase the advertised products. Fear appeals don't work for all products. Viewers practice selective perception and tune out statements they perceive as too strong. These messages work best for products that solve problems and remove the indicated fears.

Humorous ads seek to create positive moods and catch viewer attention. Humor can improve audience awareness and recall and enhance the consumer's favorable image of the ad and the brand. But advertising professionals differ in their opinions of the effectiveness of humorous ads. Some believe that humor distracts attention from brand and product features; consumers remember the humor but not the product. Humorous ads, because they are so memorable, may lose their effectiveness sooner than ads with other kinds of appeals. However, to date, no one has offered conclusive proof that they help to persuade. In general, they don't generate desired actions.

Although radio and television are considered the best media for humorous ads, Figure 18.9 shows that print ads can also use humor effectively. This Australian ad for

Nestlé's Minties candy combines the brand's 75-year-old slogan with a humorous visual, leaving the reader to conclude that Minties can soften life's little setbacks.

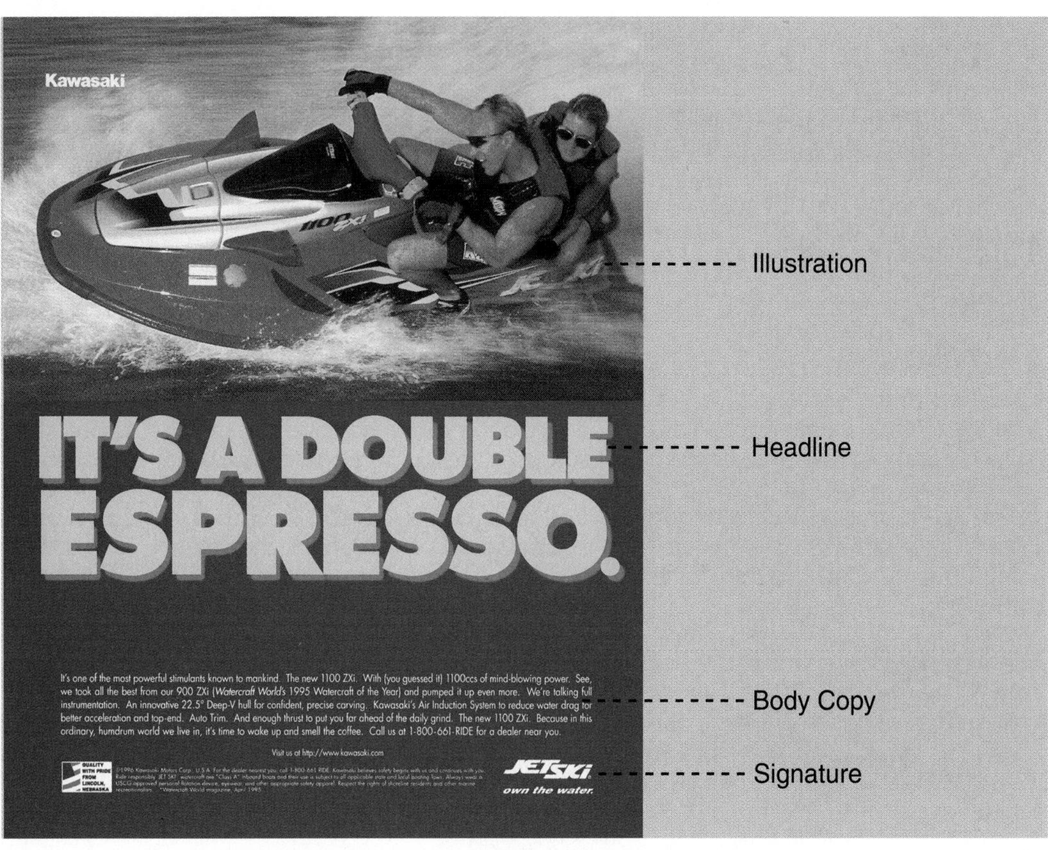
Kawasaki
IT'S A DOUBLE ESPRESSO.
It's one of the most powerful stimulants known to mankind. The new 1100 ZXi. With (you guessed it) 1100ccs of mind-blowing power. See, we took all the best from our 900 ZXi (*Watercraft World's* 1995 Watercraft of the Year) and pumped it up even more. We're talking full instrumentation. An innovative 22.5° Deep-V hull for confident, precise carving. Kawasaki's Air Induction System to reduce water drag for better acceleration and top-end. Auto Trim. And enough thrust to put you far ahead of the daily grind. The new 1100 ZXi. Because in this ordinary, humdrum world we live in, it's time to wake up and smell the coffee. Call us at 1-800-661-RIDE for a dealer near you.
Visit us at http://www.kawasaki.com
QUALITY WITH PRIDE FROM LINCOLN, NEBRASKA
JETSKI
own the water.
Illustration
Headline
Body Copy
Signature

Figure 18.10 **Elements of a Typical Advertisement**

Developing and Preparing Ads

The final step in the advertising process—the development and preparation of an advertisement—should flow logically from the promotional theme selected. This process should create an ad that becomes a complementary part of the marketing mix with a carefully determined role in the total marketing strategy. Preparation of an advertisement should emphasize features like its creativity, its continuity with past advertisements, and possibly its association with other company products.

What immediate tasks should an advertisement accomplish? Regardless of the chosen target, an advertisement should (1) gain attention and interest, (2) inform and/or persuade, and (3) eventually lead to a purchase or other desired action.

It should gain attention in a productive way; that is, it should instill some recall of the good or service. Otherwise, it will not lead to buying action. Gillette Company found this objective difficult to achieve with a commercial that showed a chimpanzee shaving a man's face. After testing the commercial in two cities, one Gillette spokesperson noted that lots of people remembered the chimp, but hardly anyone remembered the product. The ad stimulated fantastic interest in the ape but no payoff for Gillette.

An advertisement should also inform and/or persuade. For example, many insurance advertisements provide informative details about policy features. Many also include persuasive testimonials designed to appeal to prospective purchasers.

Stimulating buying action is often difficult because an advertisement cannot actually close a sale. Nevertheless, if an ad gains attention and informs or persuades, it probably represents a worthwhile investment of marketing resources. Too many advertisers fail to suggest how audience members can purchase their products if they desire to do so. Creative design should eliminate this shortcoming.

The ad for Jet Ski in Figure 18.10 is a slick, sophisticated promotion that celebrates one of the most powerful stimulants known to mankind—the ability to accelerate. The figure also identifies the four major elements of a print advertisement: headline, illustration, body copy, and signature. *Headlines* and *illustrations* (photographs, drawings, or other art work) should work together to generate interest and attention. *Body copy* serves to inform, persuade, and stimulate buying action. The *signature,* which may include the company name, address, phone number, slogan, trademark, or product photo, names the sponsoring organization. An ad may also have one or more *subheads*—headings subordinate to the main headline that either link the main headline to the body copy or subdivide sections of the body copy.

After advertisers conceive an idea for an ad that gains attention, informs and/or persuades, and stimulates purchases, their next step involves refining the thought sketch into a rough layout. Continued refinements of the rough layout eventually produce the final version of the advertisement design ready to execute, print, or record.

MARKETING HALL OF SHAME

Celebrity Testimonials from Hell

It was an advertiser's worst nightmare. For many years, people had watched O. J. Simpson sprinting through airports as he endorsed his favorite rental car company, Hertz. The former football star and sports commentator had become synonymous with the rental-car agency.

That all changed when Simpson's ex-wife Nicole was found brutally murdered outside her Los Angeles condominium. Charged and later acquitted of her murder, Simpson's career as Hertz's spokesperson abruptly ended.

While many corporations love to link celebrities to their products, they tread a minefield of hidden dangers. An expensive promotional effort might backfire and result in undesirable negative publicity and harm to a product's image if a personality becomes controversial. A celebrity doesn't have to stand trial in a gory murder case to make advertisers flee. A recent example of a damaged celebrity is Nike endorser, Dallas Cowboy star Michael Irvin, who became entangled with several drug-related charges. Heavyweight boxing champion Mike Tyson lost his credibility as an endorser after he was imprisoned on sexual assault charges, and Pepsi's glittery association with Michael Jackson disintegrated after rumors surfaced about the reclusive singer's personal life.

A celebrity endorsement also can bomb if the star is not a suitable match to endorse a product. Studies on celebrity endorsements show that the star must be considered both trustworthy and credible before he or she can click with consumers.

Despite the hazards, marketers can reap a huge payoff if they find

The creation of each advertisement in a campaign requires an evolutionary process that begins with an idea and ultimately results in a finished ad for distribution through print or electronic media. The idea itself must first be converted into a thought sketch, a tangible summary of the intended message.

Advances in technology allow advertisers to create increasingly interesting and eye-catching advertisements. Sophisticated computer software lets artists merge multiple images to create a single one or to pull together a variety of diverse elements to create a natural, seamless look. Computer-generated images appeal to younger, computer-literate consumers. For example, a Reebok ad produced by computer incorporated memorable special effects such as Shaquille O'Neal playing basketball against eight images of himself; a Chevron ad includes car characters that giggle and squeal; and a little boy finds himself sucked into a Pepsi bottle as he desperately tries to get the last drop of his soda.[16]

Creating Interactive Ads

Production of interactive advertising requires different creative methods than traditional advertising. Advertisers probably cannot achieve their goals simply by transferring print or television ads to the World Wide Web or placing *banner ads*—strip ads placed on the edges of larger photos or ads—on popular advertising-supported Web sites. Web surfers want engaging, lively content that takes advantage of the medium's capabilities and goes beyond what they find elsewhere. Polaroid Corp. maintains a site devoted to parenting; it offers activities that use instant photos for parents and kids to do together. The site's interactive features integrate the company's commercial message with useful content; in the process, they also build brand identity.[17]

Advertisers and specialists who create Internet ads are still learning how to use the Web and other interactive media effectively. The Web doesn't yet match television's ability to provide high-quality moving pictures, sound, passive entertainment, and commercial breaks distinct from programming. Yet Web ads tend to compete with television ads and pack their content with video and audio clips. This orientation overlooks the Web's major advantages: providing information, exchanging input through two-way communications, offering self-directed entertainment, and allowing personal choice.[18]

Web advertisers are now moving beyond banner ads, the earliest type of Web advertising, and devoting their marketing dollars to creating their own sites rather than placing ads on other sites. Ads that remain on other sites offer limited flexibility and require frequent changes. They serve primarily as links to the sponsors' main content sites. The Pepsi World banner shown on the left in Figure 18.11 takes viewers from the popular search engine Yahoo! to the company's hot spot (shown on the right of Figure 18.11) on the Web. Says a DDB Interactive spokesman of the site,

the perfect spokesperson for the right audience. Kmart and Jaclyn Smith, an actress who appeared in the 1970s television series *Charlie's Angels,* provides one example of a financially successful partnership. More than a decade ago, Kmart launched a women's clothing line with Smith. Today, Kmart sells over $150 million a year in Smith-labeled clothing, and the brand is considered one of the five most popular women's wear brands.

Celebrity endorsements, however, aren't always positive for the stars. For instance, Kathie Lee Gifford, the morning talk-show hostess, found herself buffeted by a storm of controversy when reports surfaced that products in her line of clothing sold at Wal-Mart were manufactured in sweatshops. Workers in New York were working 60-hour weeks to make blouses for Gifford's clothing line, and seamstresses in Honduras were earning a mere 31 cents an hour to sew Gifford-label pants. Since the embarrassing revelations, Gifford has become a crusader against sweatshops.

QUESTIONS FOR CRITICAL THINKING

1. **Should companies use endorsements by politicians to sell products?**
2. **Would you use a product that was endorsed by someone charged with a crime? Do you think others would?**

Sources: Annie Groer and Ann Gerhart, "The Reliable Source," *Washington Post,* May 12, 1997, p. B3; adapted from Beth J. Harpaz, "Celebrity Labels Hide a Problem Retailers Say They Can't Control," *San Diego Union-Tribune,* June 18, 1996, p. C4; Dana Milbank, "Gap Ad Shows Perils of Using Polls in Pitches," *Wall Street Journal,* April 9, 1996, pp. B1, B9; Cyndee Miller, "Celebrities Hot Despite Scandals," *Discount Store News,* May 15, 1995, pp. A32, A33; and Alan R. Miciak and William L. Shanklin, "Choosing Celebrity Endorsers," *Marketing Management,* winter 1994, pp. 50–59;

"The challenge was to push the technology envelope and also come up with something entertaining and hip."[19]

Web-site developers can now add 3-D effects to their sites, a capability that provides new opportunities for advertisers. For example, graphics can show products in life-like representations. Retailers can create 3-D stores where visitors simulate walking through the virtual aisles viewing merchandise on display; Web sites need no longer provide their information in catalog-like formats.

MEDIA SELECTION FOR ADVERTISING

One of the most important decisions in developing an advertising strategy is the selection of appropriate media to carry the firm's message to its audience. A mistake at this point can waste literally millions of dollars on ineffective advertising. The media selected must be capable of accomplishing the communications objectives of informing, persuading, and reminding

Figure 18.11 Creating Internet Ads

PEPSI WORLD
WWW.PEPSI.COM

PTV
WASTELAND

potential customers of the good, service, person, or idea advertised.

Research should identify the ad's target market to determine its size and characteristics. Advertisers then match the target characteristics with the media best able to reach that particular audience. The objective of media selection is to achieve adequate media coverage without advertising beyond the identifiable limits of the potential market. Finally, cost comparisons between alternatives should determine the best possible media purchase.

Table 18.1 compares the major advertising media by noting their shares of overall advertising expenditures as well as their major strengths and weaknesses. *Broadcast media* include television and radio. Newspapers, magazines, outdoor advertising, and direct mail represent the major types of *print media.*

The table reveals that newspapers and television are the leading advertising media, followed closely by direct mail. Radio, magazines, and outdoor advertising rank at the bottom. Since 1950, newspaper, radio, and magazines have all lost market share to television. While interactive advertising still accounts for well under 1 percent of total advertising expenditures, this category is expected to grow considerably over the next five years.

Television

Even though the broadcast media of television and radio account for only 30 cents of every advertising dollar spent, television offers so many characteristics favorable to effective advertising that it has grown to rival newspapers as the dominant advertising medium. Although television ad spending equals that for newspaper ads with a 23 percent share of overall advertising revenues, the relative attractiveness of the two media differs for marketers who want to reach local and national markets. Most newspaper advertising revenues come from local advertisers. In contrast, television is the dominant medium for national advertising.

Television advertising can be divided into four categories: network, national, local, and cable ads. Columbia Broadcasting System (CBS), National Broadcasting Company (NBC), American Broadcasting Company (ABC), Fox, Warner Bros. (The WB), and United Paramount Network (UPN) are the six major, national networks. Their programs accounted for about one-third ($11 billion) of total television advertising expenditures in a recent year. About 6,000 ads per week air on network television—over ten minutes of advertising per prime-time hour. The most expensive ads run during the Super Bowl—for the 1997 game, 30-second spots sold for $1.2 million each. A national spot ad is a nonnetwork broadcast ad by a general advertiser. Local spots consist of commercials developed and sponsored by area firms, primarily retailers. The leading categories of products promoted by network television advertising are automotive goods, food and food products, toiletries, consumer services, and over-the-counter drugs.

An important trend affecting television advertising is the rapid growth of cable television. Cable's share of the national viewing market is now 30 percent, up from 22 percent in 1992, while the networks' share has fallen from 74 percent to 66 percent. In the critical prime-time viewing period, cable's share has climbed steadily from 7.5 percent in 1985 to 24 percent today, compared to a slide from 70 percent to 49 percent for major network affiliates. Satellite television has also contributed to increased cable penetration, which now reaches about 72 percent of U.S. homes.

As cable audiences grow, programming improves, and ratings rise, advertisers are committing more dollars to cable television. Cable advertising offers companies access to more narrowly defined target audiences than other broadcast media can provide. The great variety of special-interest channels devoted to subjects such as food, history, home and garden, health, ethnic issues, and others attract specialized audiences and permit niche marketing.

Cable offers a number of options for marketers attempting to reach the nearly 30 million Hispanic Americans. As Figure 18.12 points out, Galavision is the nation's largest Spanish-language network with 5 million subscribers. Its viewers have average household incomes of more than $31,000; 34 percent are college educated.

Television advertising offers the advantages of powerful impact, mass coverage, repetition of messages, flexibility, and prestige. Its disadvantages include loss of control of the promotional message to the telecaster (which can influence its impact), high costs, high mortality rates for commercials, and some public distrust. Compared to other media, television can suffer from lack of selectivity, since specific TV programs may not reach consumers in a precisely defined target market without a significant degree of wasted coverage. However, the growing specialization of cable TV channels should help to resolve that problem.

Radio

Radio campaigns can also be classified as network, national, and local ads. Radio accounts for about 7 percent of total advertising revenue and 13 percent of local expenditures. It competes with other media by offering several advantages, beginning with immediacy; studies show that most people regard radio as the best source for up-to-date news. Other benefits include low cost, flexibility, mobility, and practical and low-cost access to carefully selected audiences. Disadvantages include fragmentation, the temporary nature of messages, and a lack of research information as compared with television.

Table 18.1 Comparison of Advertising Media Alternatives

Medium		Advantages	Disadvantages
BROADCAST MEDIA			
	Television 23%[a]	Great impact; mass coverage; repetition; flexibility; prestige	Temporary nature of message; high cost; high mortality rate for commercials; distrust; lack of selectivity
	Radio 7%	Immediacy; low cost; flexibility; practical audience selection; mobility	Fragmentation; temporary nature of message; little research information available
PRINT MEDIA			
	Newspapers 23%	Flexibility; community prestige; intensive coverage; reader control of exposure; coordination with national advertising; merchandising service; special techniques	Short life span; hasty reading; relatively poor reproduction
	Direct mail 15%	Selectivity; intense coverage; speed; flexibility of format; complete information; personalization	High per-person cost; dependency on quality of mailing list; consumer resistance
	Magazines 5%	Selectivity; quality of reproduction; long life; prestige associated with some magazines; extra services offered by some publications	Lack of flexibility
	Outdoor advertising 1%	Quick communication of simple ideas; repetition; ability to promote products available for sale locally	Brevity of message; public concern over aesthetics
ELECTRONIC/PRINT COMBINATION			
	Interactive <1%	Ultimate in flexibility; two-way communication; self-directed entertainment; personal choice	Lack of standards to measure effectiveness; limited scheduling options; relatively poor reproduction compared with traditional media

[a]An additional 25 percent is spent on a variety of miscellaneous media, including Yellow Pages advertising, business papers, transit advertising, point-of-purchase displays, cinema advertising, and regional farm papers.

Figure 18.12 Targeting Hispanic Americans through Spanish-Language Cable Channels

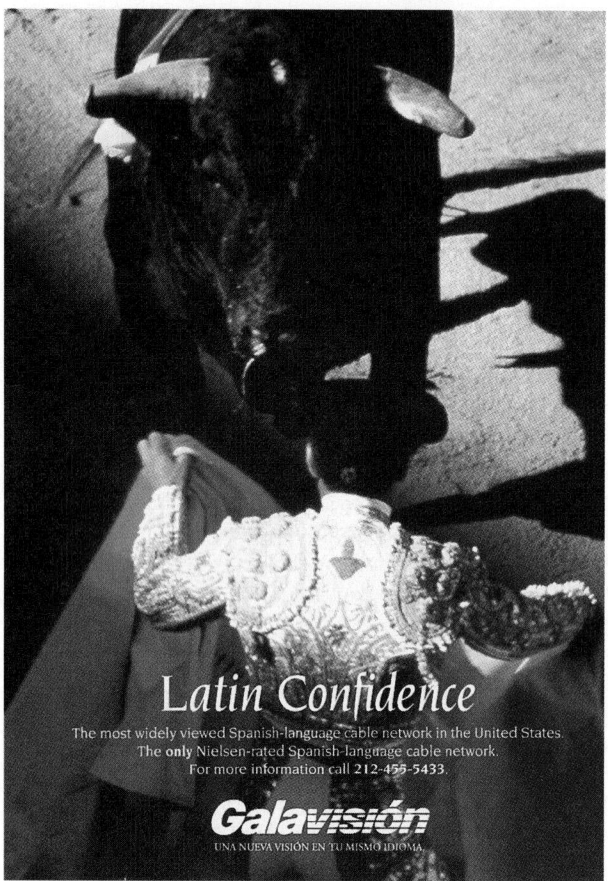
Latin Confidence
The most widely viewed Spanish-language cable network in the United States.
The only Nielsen-rated Spanish-language cable network.
For more information call 212-455-5433.
Galavisión
UNA NUEVA VISIÓN EN TU MISMO IDIOMA.

Due to the medium's advantages, U.S. radio ad revenues are growing faster than revenues for all other media except cable television. Advertisers like the chance to reach people while they drive. With an increase in commuters, this market is growing. Stations can adapt to local preferences by changing format—for example, from country and western to all-news or rock to talk radio. The variety of stations allows advertisers to easily target audiences and to tailor their messages to those listeners. For example, marketers of agricultural products like Sandoz Agro Inc., Ciba Crop Protection, and DuPont Agricultural Products develop strong customer awareness by consistently advertising on farm broadcasts.

Radio is also useful in overseas markets. Avis Rent-a-Car has attempted to bolster its 15 percent market share in Great Britain by launching its first national radio advertising campaign there. The ads seek to inform consumers that the company serves the leisure rental market as well as the corporate market and to position Avis as an alternative to local companies.[20]

Newspapers

Newspaper advertising continues to dominate local markets. It accounts for 23 percent of total advertising revenues. Newspapers' primary advantages start with flexibility, since advertising can vary from one locality to the next. Newspapers offer community prestige, since readers recognize that they have deep impacts on their communities. They allow intensive coverage for ads; in a typical location, a single newspaper reaches 90 percent of the homes. Readers control their exposure to the advertising message, so they can refer back to newspaper ads, unlike those in electronic media. Newspapers facilitate coordination between local and national advertising, they offer powerful merchandising services (such as promotional and research support), and they give access to some special techniques such as single-sheet or multipage insert ads. They also suffer from disadvantages: short life span, hasty reading (the typical reader spends about 40 minutes reading the newspaper), and relatively poor reproduction quality.

Magazines

Magazines are divided into three basic categories—consumer, farm, and business publications. Together, they account for about 5 percent of total advertising expenditures, 40 percent of which appears in weekly magazines. The primary advantages of magazine advertising come from selectivity in reaching precise target markets, quality reproduction, long life, the prestige associated with some magazines, and the extra services that many publications offer. The primary disadvantage is that magazines lack the flexibility of newspapers, radio, and television.

Modern Maturity is the nation's leading magazine measured by annual paid subscriptions with 23 million. Other leading magazines include *Reader's Digest, TV Guide, National Geographic,* and women's magazines such as *Better Homes & Gardens, Family Circle, Good Housekeeping,* and *McCall's.*

Media buyers study circulation numbers and demographics information for various publications to choose placement opportunities and negotiate rates. These figures are independently certified. As with television ads, the automotive industry leads in magazine advertising expenditures, followed by marketers of toiletries, mail order/direct response, business and consumer services, and apparel. The magazines shown in Figure 18.13 are examples of the many publications targeting women at different stages in their lives. Editors of the different G+J magazines intend them specifically for such age and life-cycle categories as teens, active women, pregnant women and new moms, home enthusiasts, and household decision makers.

Figure 18.13 Targeting Different Female Life-Cycle Segments through Magazine Advertising

G+J Magazines for every stage of a woman's life.
Senior year in high school is definitely bittersweet. I can't wait to go to college – I'll be living on my own, taking only courses that interest me, meeting new guys. I just can't imagine doing it all without my friends. I mean, I've known some of them more than half my life!
G+J helps guide women from one stage of their life to the next, with magazines edited specifically for teens, active women, expecting and new moms, home enthusiasts and household decision makers. Women going through transitions have new needs and a need for new products. These are optimal times for advertisers to capture an untapped market or to reinforce brand loyalty.
G+J magazines are the one constant in the lives of one in two American women. Call John Heins, President, at (212) 463-1103, to learn more.
G+J USA Publishing

Direct Mail

As discussed in Chapter 17, forms of direct-mail advertising include sales letters, postcards, leaflets, folders, broadsides (which are larger than folders), booklets, catalogs, and house organs (periodicals published by organizations to cover internal issues). The advantages of direct mail come from selectivity, intensive coverage, speed, formal flexibility, completeness of information, and the chance to personalize each mailing piece. Disadvantages of direct mail are its high cost per reader, its dependence on the quality of mailing lists, and some consumers' resistance to it.

Despite the advances in computer-generation of personalized direct-mail ads, some companies prefer to get personal the old-fashioned way. Irresistible Ink, a Minnesota company, employs about 150 people to prepare handwritten messages for clients. The Fort Worth Symphony Orchestra used these letters in a fund-raising campaign and found them significantly more effective than standard, printed direct-mail pleas.[21]

Outdoor Advertising

Outdoor advertising takes the form of posters (commonly called *billboards),* painted bulletins or displays (such as those that appear on the walls of buildings), and electric spectaculars (large, illuminated, and sometimes animated signs and displays). This form of advertising has the advantages of ready communication of quick and simple ideas, repeated exposure to a message, and strong promotion for locally available products. Outdoor advertising is particularly effective along metropolitan streets and in other high-traffic areas. Its disadvantages are the brevity of exposure to its messages and public concern over aesthetics. The Highway Beautification Act of 1965, for example, regulates the placement of outdoor advertising near interstate highways. This medium accounts for approximately one percent of all advertising expenditures.

New technologies are helping to revive outdoor advertising, offsetting the huge drop that resulted from limitations on ads for tobacco and alcohol products. Technology livens up the billboards themselves with animation, large sculptures, and laser images. Digital message signboards can display winning lottery numbers or other timely messages like weather and traffic reports.

Chick-fil-A, a regional fast-food chain that sells chicken sandwiches, had a limited advertising budget and used billboards because they offered a cost-effective way to reach consumers. The billboards, illustrated in Figure 18.14, had three-dimensional cows appearing to paint their own message, complete with misspellings. The unusual billboards caused a sensation, bringing the company considerable publicity from magazine and newspaper stories. The company expanded the campaign into additional markets, and the cows became a part of in-store displays and other promotions.

Other Advertising Media

As consumers filter out appeals from traditional ads, marketers need new ways to catch their attention. In addition to the major media, firms use many other vehicles to communicate their messages. Transit advertising includes ads

Figure 18.14 Use of Outdoor Advertising to Attract Fast-Food Customers

EAT MOR CHICKIN
Chick-fil-A

placed both inside and outside buses, subway trains and stations, and commuter trains. Some firms place ads on taxi tops, bus shelters and benches, telephone booths, and parking meters. A growing but controversial form of advertising in the United States, cinema advertising, has been popular in European countries for many years. About half of the 23,000 U.S. movie theaters accept commercials. Major companies like Nike, Mercedes, MCI, and Discover Card spend about $30 million a year on commercials that run before feature films. Movie-theater ads have proved especially effective for targeting young people aged 12 to 24 years old, although the Disney Company will not allow ads to run before its movies. BMW, however, targets an older audience by showing its ads with R-rated movies.

Ads appear in printed programs of live-theater productions, and firms such as PepsiCo and Chrysler advertise on movie videocassettes. Directory advertising includes the familiar Yellow Pages in telephone books along with thousands of other types of directories, most of them business related. Some firms display messages on hot-air balloons, blimps, banners behind airplanes, and scoreboards at sporting events. Others turn to ads on garbage trucks, school buses, and even police cars.

Creativity pays off in foreign markets, too. Intel Corp. distributed 1 million bike reflectors in China with the words "Intel Inside Pentium Processor." By putting its name on China's many bicycles, Intel hopes to build brand awareness with consumers, not just businesses. The company also uses billboards and television ads to position itself in what it expects to become the next large market for home computers.[22]

Interactive Media

As noted earlier, all traditional advertising media share a major disadvantage in their reliance on one-way communications. Targets of advertising messages have low levels of involvement; they are passive recipients of marketing communications. Since marketers realize that two-way communications provide more effective methods for achieving promotional objectives, they are interested in **interactive media,** communication channels that induce message recipients to participate actively in the promotional effort. Achieving this involvement is the big task facing contemporary marketers.

Companies use interactive advertising media like the World Wide Web to supplement their messages over traditional media. Interactive marketing agency Modem Media recommends that a company spend about 3 to 5 percent of its television budget for Web-related advertising. As the earlier discussion of the Cover Girl, Pacific Bell's At Hand, and Baskin Robbins sites indicated, the Web provides a way to build strong brand loyalty by getting viewers involved with products. Companies do not have to actually sell the products over the Web to get results.

Development costs for a Web ad depend on its complexity and implementation of techniques like animation, sound, and other special effects. The cost of placing an ad on the Web varies greatly for different sites. Web advertising costs depend on the popularity of the host site and the audience it delivers. Most publishers set charges by formulas for cost per thousand impressions (CPM), generally calculated monthly. An impression occurs each time a user downloads a page with the ad banner. Site publishers guarantee the number of impressions and typically offer selections of rate packages. More targeted sites charge higher fees. Stated rates for a banner ad on a general site may cost $15 to $20 per thousand viewers, while a specialized site may cost up to $100 per thousand.[23]

Sites that Web surfers frequently target, like Newspage ($275 CPM) and the *Wall Street Journal* ($80 CPM), are among the most expensive. Netscape, Yahoo!, and Pathfinder have rates similar to those of print publications; their basic CPM figures range from $20 to $30. Directories and search engines also sell ads on pages showing the results of keyword searches. For example, Infoseek charges $1,000 per keyword, based on an average of 20,000 impressions ($50 CPM); the higher rate gives more targeted viewing. A viewer who searches for the keyword *cruise* might show special interest in an ad for a travel agency that appears on the results page.[24]

Figure 18.15 **Hypothetical Media Schedule for a New Car Introduction**

Medium	Jan	Feb	Mar	Apr	May	June	July	Aug	Sept	Oct	Nov	Dec
Direct mail											■	
Outdoor and transit advertising										■	■	■
Newspaper												
Cooperative advertising	■	■	■	■	■	■	■	■	■	■	■	■
Television												
Holiday special												■
Selected network shows	■	■	■	■	■	■	■	■	■	■	■	■
Football	■								■	■	■	■
Baseball			■	■	■	■	■	■	■	■		
Magazine												
Magazine 1	■	■	■	■	■	■	■	■	■	■	■	■
Magazine 2	■	■	■	■	■	■	■	■	■	■	■	■
Magazine 3	■	■	■	■	■	■	■	■	■	■	■	■

MEDIA SCHEDULING

Once advertisers have selected the media that best match their advertising objectives and promotional budget, attention shifts to **media scheduling**—setting the timing and sequence for a series of advertisements. A variety of factors influence this decision, as well. Sales patterns, repurchase cycles, and competitors' activities are the most important variables.

Seasonal sales patterns are common in many industries. For example, an airline might reduce advertising during peak travel periods and boost its media schedule during low travel months. (See the discussion of promotion as a variable for stabilizing sales in Chapter 17.) Repurchase cycles may also play a role in media scheduling—products with shorter repurchase cycles will more likely require consistent media schedules throughout the year. Competitors' activity is still another influence on media scheduling. For instance, a small firm may elect to avoid advertising during periods of heavy advertising by its rivals.

Advertisers use the concepts of reach, frequency, and gross rating points to measure the effectiveness of media scheduling plans. *Reach* refers to the number of different people or households exposed to an advertisement at least once during a certain time period, typically four weeks. *Frequency* refers to the number of times an individual person is exposed to an advertisement during a certain time period. By multiplying reach times frequency, advertisers quantitatively describe the total weight of a media effort, which is called the campaign's *gross rating point.*

Hypothetical Media Schedule

Figure 18.15 shows a hypothetical media schedule for advertising devoted to the introduction of a new automobile designed to appeal primarily to male buyers. The model is introduced in November with a direct-mail piece offering test drives to recipients. Extensive outdoor and transit advertising support the direct-mail blitz during a three-month introductory period, and the firm airs commercials during a Christmas television special early in December.

The car's manufacturer also advertises during selected network shows throughout the year, as well as on football

Marketing Dictionary

interactive media Communication channels that induce message recipients to participate actively in the promotional effort.

media scheduling Setting the timing and sequence of a series of advertisements.

MARKETING HALL OF FAME

The Best Print Ad Featuring a Mustache

Milk: it's boring and bland. It's hard to imagine how a product associated with a cud-chewing cow could create a highly praised advertising splash. But one of the most memorable advertising campaigns of the 1990s celebrates milk. The ads—on television, in magazines, and on billboards—seem to be everywhere, always portraying milk with a whimsical spin. In the print spots, celebrities from fashion models to sports heroes to movie stars are smiling with little, white milk mustaches.

The campaign's hilarious television commercials feature people in desperate need of a glass of milk. A priest who has just eaten a piece of cake bangs frantically on an empty vending machine in a quest for milk. An Aaron Burr expert can't answer a radio trivia question about his favorite historical figure because his mouth is cemented shut with gooey peanut butter.

The "Got Milk" television ads were so successful that they spawned a $100 million nationwide campaign. The quirky spots won awards and are considered one of the most successful campaigns of all time.

When dairy industry marketers first approached Madison Avenue about an ad campaign, things looked grim. Milk sales had been slumping for three decades. Further, in a new threat to an already bleak situation, consumers had become so infatuated with low-fat and no-fat foods that they were banishing milk from their refrigerators. Apparently, only the pint-sized peanut-butter crowd still loved milk.

In explaining the ads' appeal, Jay Schulberg, a marketing veteran who dreamed up the print campaign at Goodby, Silverstein & Partners, said the milk mustache was a real winner. "It's a universal symbol of people who drink milk," he said. "It's something that every single person on earth can identify with. It conjures up memories of youth."

He decided to center the ad campaign around celebrities to at-

and baseball telecasts. The manufacturer advertises extensively in magazines, as well. Since women are expected to purchase 40 percent of the total number of cars sold, one women's publication carries ads for the model every month, and two national magazines carry ads in alternating issues: one for the first two weekly issues and the second for the last two weeks each month. Finally, newspapers run cooperative advertising for which the manufacturer and dealer share the costs.

ORGANIZATION OF THE ADVERTISING FUNCTION

Although the ultimate responsibility for advertising decision making often rests with top marketing management, organizational arrangements for the advertising function vary among companies. A producer of a technical industrial product may interact with one person within the company, who works primarily to write copy for submission to trade publications. A consumer goods company, on the other hand, may staff a large department with advertising specialists.

The advertising function is usually organized as a staff department reporting to the vice president (or director) of marketing. The director of advertising is an executive position with responsibility for the functional activity of advertising. This position requires not only a skilled and experienced advertiser but also an individual who communicates effectively within the organization. The success of a firm's promotional strategy depends on the advertising director's willingness and ability to communicate both vertically and horizontally. The major tasks typically organized under advertising include advertising research, design, copywriting, media analysis, and, in some cases, sales and trade promotion.

Advertising Agencies

Many major advertisers hire independent **advertising agencies,** firms of marketing specialists who assist advertisers in planning and preparing advertisements. Most large advertisers cite several reasons for relying on agencies for at least some portion of their advertising. Agencies typically employ highly qualified specialists who provide a degree of creativity and objectivity that is difficult to sustain in a corporate advertising department. Some also manage to reduce the cost of advertising by allowing the advertiser to avoid many of the fixed expenses associated with maintaining an internal advertising department.

tract and sustain consumers' attention. Despite the white mustaches, it was important that these VIPs still retain their sex appeal. The print ads were intentionally designed to pose the celebrities as though for a poster or portrait. The world-renowned photojournalist Annie Liebovitz was hired to take the shots.

The advertisers set about wooing celebrities who would appeal to their target audience—women aged 25 to 44. Among those who agreed to pose were supermodels like Iman, Kate Moss, and Christie Brinkley. The advertisers hoped that these glamorous women could make drinking milk look hip. To reach older women, some ads featured comedian Joan Rivers and actress Lauren Bacall. Some ads also featured attractive male celebrities like tennis player Pete Sampras and quarterback Steve Young. The campaign appeared in more than 50 magazines.

The award-winning ads ranked at the top of the Video Storyboard Tests survey of the most popular print ads. They are credited with halting declining milk consumption and even triggering an increase in milk buying in some parts of the nation.

QUESTIONS FOR CRITICAL THINKING

1. **Categorize the "Got Milk" and "Milk Mustache" campaigns by the types of ads, and describe the message and appeal strategies.**
2. **What made the milk advertisements a success?**
3. **Do you think this type of campaign could work for other food products? Why?**

Sources: Carol Emert, "'Got Milk' Ad Agency Wins Top Spot at Clios," *San Francisco Chronicle,* May 15, 1997, p. D2; Sally Goll Beatty, "Milk-Mustache Ads: Cream of the Crop," *Wall Street Journal,* May 20, 1996, p. B6; Philip Lempert, "With Zippy Food Ads, Old Ideas Go by the Boards," *San Diego Union-Tribune,* March 28, 1996, p. F23; and Dottie Enrico and Melanie Wells, "Creativity: Milk's Formula for Ad Success," *USA Today,* December 18, 1995, pp. 1B, 2B.

Effective use of an advertising agency requires a close relationship between the advertiser and the agency. The agency must have thorough knowledge of the advertiser's good or service and channels of distribution, competitors' strategies, and available media that can deliver the ads to the appropriate consumer and trade markets.

Traditionally, agencies have received compensation in the form of 15 percent commissions based on media and production billings. Today, agencies derive only about 13 percent of their revenues from the standard 15 percent commission; about 43 percent reflects commissions—but at rates below 15 percent. About one-third of advertisers have adopted guaranteed-profit systems in which the advertiser negotiates a fee with the agency based on the cost of producing the ads and the agency's profits. Other advertisers have adopted performance-based compensation plans. For the "Softer Side" campaign, Sears and its ad agency, Young and Rubicam, chose evaluation measures based on growth in customer awareness as indicated by surveys, growth in apparel business, and total profits.[25] Since 1992, the proportion of companies using some form of incentive pay for advertising suppliers rose from 13 percent to 20 percent as more companies have sought to relate their advertising costs to performance. In this age of downsizing and cost-cutting, companies want proof of results for their ad dollars.

While many people consider New York's Madison Avenue the center of the advertising world, Tokyo-based agencies lead the world with total advertising billings of $40 billion. London-based WPP Group is the world's largest agency, but such giants as Omnicom Group and Grey Advertising account for New York's second-place standing among the world's largest advertising centers.

Figure 18.16 shows a hypothetical organization chart for a large advertising agency. Although job titles may vary among agencies, the major functions may be classified as creative services; account services; marketing services, including media services, marketing research, and sales promotion; and finance and management.

Marketing Dictionary

advertising agency Marketing specialist firm that assists advertisers in planning and implementing advertising programs.

Figure 18.16 Advertising Agency Organization Chart

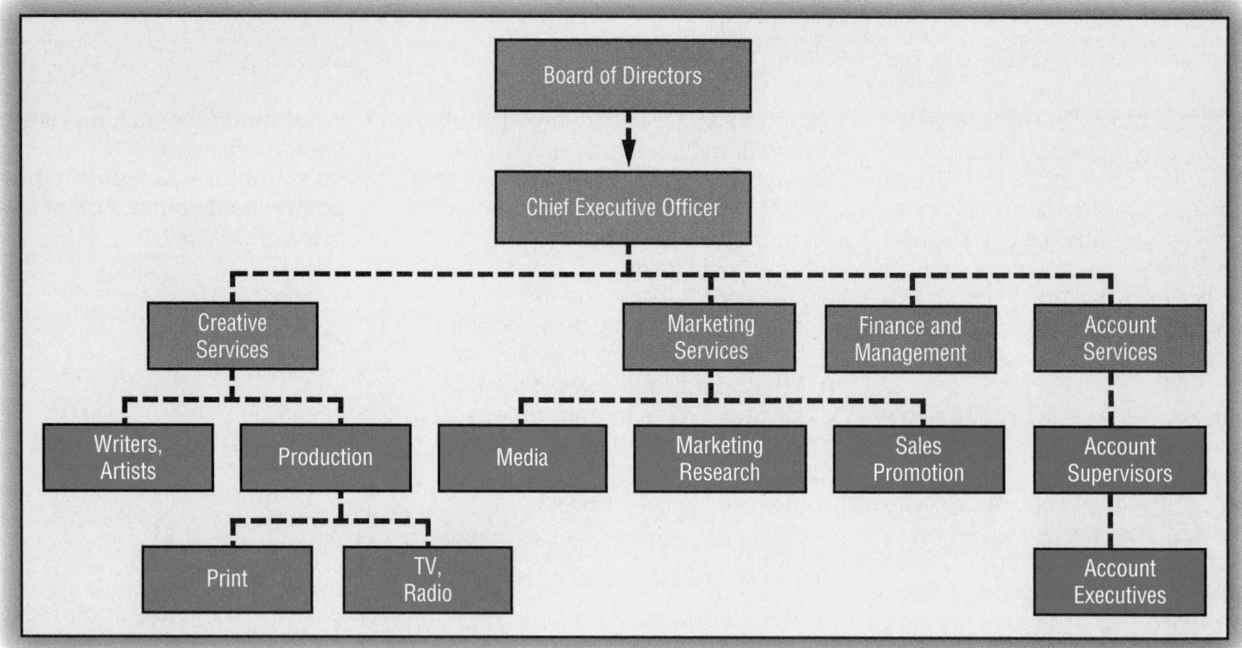
Board of Directors
Chief Executive Officer
Creative Services
Marketing Services
Finance and Management
Account Services
Writers, Artists
Production
Media
Marketing Research
Sales Promotion
Account Supervisors
Print
TV, Radio
Account Executives

The Evolving Advertising Agency

Specialty firms like media services companies are taking over certain functions previously handled by advertising agencies. Boutique agencies serve special needs for specific market segments such as sales promotion, direct marketing, and, as discussed in the opening vignette, interactive advertising.

Spending on interactive ads plays an increasingly important role in overall media plans. For this reason, advertisers choose agencies carefully based on their interactive capabilities and effectiveness at blending content and advertising. Steve Wilkie, senior advertising manager for the Levi's brand, advises, "Any agency that wants to be the sole agency for a client needs to embrace the interactive world and lead their clients." To compete, major full-service advertising agencies are setting up special divisions—Ogilvy & Mather Interactive, for example—acquiring smaller boutique agencies, or forming alliances with smaller multimedia specialists.[26]

SALES PROMOTION

Although marketers sometimes mistakenly relegate it to a secondary role in their firm's overall promotional strategy, another type of nonpersonal selling actually commands double the promotional dollar outlays of advertising. **Sales promotion** may be defined as marketing activities other than personal selling, advertising, and publicity that enhance consumer purchasing and dealer effectiveness. Companies spend approximately $250 billion each year on such consumer and trade sales promotion activities as coupons, sampling, displays, trade shows and exhibitions, demonstrations, and various nonrecurrent promotional efforts.

Sales promotion techniques were originally intended as short-term incentives aimed at producing immediate consumer buying responses. Traditionally, these techniques were viewed as supplements to other elements of the firm's promotional mix. Today, however, marketers recognize them as integral parts of many marketing plans, and the focus of sales promotion has shifted from short-term to long-term goals of building brand equity and maintaining continuing purchases. For example, a frequent-flyer program enables an airline to build a base of loyal customers where it had none before.

Both retailers and manufacturers use sales promotions to offer consumers extra incentives to buy. Rather than emphasizing product features to make them feel good about their purchases, these promotions are likely to stress price advantages. The general objectives of sales promotion are to speed up the sales process and increase sales volume. Through a consumer promotion, a marketer encourages consumers to try the product, use more of it, and buy it again. The firm also hopes to foster sales of complementary products and increase impulse purchases.

Figure 18.17 **Eight Most Popular Consumer Promotion Techniques**

Technique	Percentage of Marketers Who Use It
Coupons in retailer ads	90
Cents-off	90
In-store coupons	88
Refunds	85
Electronic, in-store displays	83
Samples of established products	78
Premiums	75
Sweepstakes	70

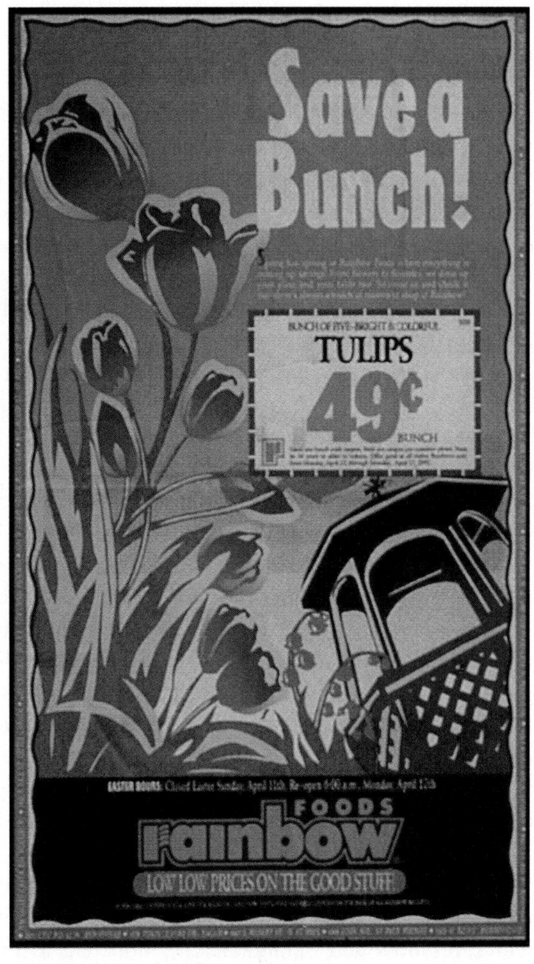
Save a Bunch!
BUNCH OF FIVE BRIGHT & COLORFUL
TULIPS
49¢
BUNCH
FOODS
rainbow
LOW LOW PRICES ON THE GOOD STUFF

Sales promotion complements advertising, and marketers often produce their best results when they combine the two. Ads create awareness, while sales promotions lead to trial or purchase. Promotions encourage immediate action because they impose limited time frames. For example, cents-off coupons and rebates have expiration dates. In addition, sales promotions produce measurable results, making it relatively easy for marketers to evaluate their effectiveness.

It is important to understand what sales promotions can and cannot do. They can encourage interest from salespeople and consumers in both new and mature products; help introduce new products; encourage trial and repeat purchases; increase usage; neutralize competition; and reinforce advertising. On the other hand, sales promotions cannot overcome poor brand images, product deficiencies, or poor training for salespeople. They provide only a quick fix for some problems and may lead to competitive retaliation. While they increase volume in the short term, they often lead to lower profits.

Sales promotion techniques may serve all members of a marketing channel. In addition, manufacturers may use trade promotion methods to promote their products to resellers. A single promotional strategy may well combine more than one option, but probably no promotional strategy has ever used all of them in a single program. While the different types are not mutually exclusive, promotions generally are employed selectively. Sales promotion techniques include the following consumer-oriented promotions: samples, bonus packs, premiums, coupons, price-off deals, rebates, contests, sweepstakes, and specialty advertising. Trade-oriented promotions include trade allowances, point-of-purchase advertising, trade shows, dealer incentives, and training programs.

Consumer-Oriented Sales Promotions

Consumer-oriented sales promotions implement pulling strategies to get new and existing customers to try or buy products. Other objectives include encouraging repurchases by rewarding current users, boosting sales of complementary products, and increasing impulse purchases. These promotions also attract consumer attention in the midst of advertising clutter. If overused, however, they can damage brand equity, because consumers begin to expect price discounts. Figure 18.17 lists the most popular consumer promotion techniques for firms using this element of

Marketing Dictionary

sales promotion Marketing activities other than personal selling, advertising, direct marketing, and publicity that stimulate consumer purchasing and dealer effectiveness. Sales promotion includes displays, trade shows, coupons, premiums, product demonstrations, and various nonrecurrent selling efforts.

the promotional mix and includes an example of a coupon, the most commonly used form of sales promotion.

Coupons, Price-Off Deals, and Refunds *Coupons,* the most widely used form of sales promotion, offer discounts, usually in the form of specified price reductions, on the buyer's next purchase of a good or service. The consumer can redeem a coupon at a retail outlet, which receives a handling fee from the manufacturer. Mail, magazine, newspaper, and package insertions are the standard methods of distributing coupons. Free-standing inserts (FSIs) in Sunday newspapers account for about 75 percent of all coupons distributed. The average household receives about 3,000 coupons a year at an overall cost of about $8 billion per year to marketers.

Despite the popularity of coupons as a method of sales promotion, marketers recognize their inefficiency. Of almost 300 billion coupons issued in a typical year, only 2 percent—less than 6 billion—are actually redeemed.

Convinced that coupons erode brand loyalty and cost too much to print, distribute, and process, packaged-goods giant Procter & Gamble has cut their use by 50 percent. P&G has eliminated them entirely in such markets as Buffalo, Rochester, and Syracuse, New York. Early tests of reaction to the move produced no major consumer resistance, and retailers reported satisfaction in not having to handle coupon redemptions.

Marketers often redirect promotional dollars saved by reducing coupon use toward *co-marketing* activities in which retailers and manufacturers cooperate to promote specific brands at certain stores. Kool-Aid commercials in the Midwest invite viewers to "come on in to Kroger" for 10 packs of their favorite flavors at $1.29; Post cereal ads in California point out that recently reduced prices on cereals are even lower at Albertson's. By switching from coupons and other short-term promotions to co-marketing, both parties benefit from the same ad: The manufacturer generates awareness and loyalty for the brand and the retailer improves productivity by building store traffic.

In a typical co-marketing campaign, a marketer will offer each retailer in a city a week of exclusive advertising. In return, the retailer agrees to order a certain amount of a product and display it prominently. The retailer also provides input about the ad's content in order to coordinate its appeal with those of other ads it currently runs.[27]

Price-off deals (sometimes referred to as *cents-off deals)* are just what the name implies: reductions in price of about 10 percent to 25 percent off the regular prices of products. Package copy informs consumers about this type of promotion, which guarantees that the manufacturer's promotional dollars do reach the consumer. Price-offs reward current users and encourage repeat purchases, but retailers do not like them because they create inventory problems.

Refunds offer cash back to consumers who send in proof of purchasing one or more products. For example, the maker of the hair regrowth product Rogaine offered customers a $5 refund for purchasing one package. Refunds help packaged-goods companies to increase purchase rates, promote multiple purchases, and reward product users. They can reinforce brand loyalty, but many consumers find the refund forms too bothersome to complete.

Samples, Bonus Packs, and Premiums Distribution of samples and premiums is one of the best-known consumer sales promotion techniques. *Sampling* refers to the free distribution of a product in an attempt to obtain future sales. Samples may be distributed door-to-door, by mail, via instore demonstrations, or by including them in packages with other products.

Sampling is a very popular technique that produces a higher response rate than most others. About three-quarters of the consumers who receive samples try them. In fact, a recent survey showed that 92 percent of consumers preferred receiving free samples rather than coupons.[28] With sampling, marketers can target potential customers and be sure that the product reaches them. Sampling provides an especially useful way to promote new or unusual products, because it gives the consumer a direct product experience. For example, Ocean Spray used sampling to introduce Europeans to the cranberry's unusual taste.

Sampling is an expensive form of sales promotion. Not only must the marketer give away small quantities of a product that might otherwise have generated revenues through regular sales, but also the market is, in effect, closed for the time it takes consumers to use up the samples. In addition, the marketer may encounter problems in distributing the samples. Hellman's marketers annoyed consumers instead of pleasing them when the firm distributed sample packets of Italian and French salad dressing in home-delivered copies of the *New York Times.* Many of the packets burst when the papers hit the driveways.[29]

Many companies are going mobile to promote their products. Trucks or trailers decorated with company logos tour from town to town, demonstrating products and giving out samples and coupons at retail locations, college campuses, beaches, and local events. These traveling promotions become events themselves, drawing large crowds. By attracting consumer attention, they generate product trials, help local retailers, and offer good public relations opportunities. Another advantage is the chance to interact with customers and gather feedback.

These mobile sales promotions cover a variety of products, and they also serve as traveling billboards on highways. Johnsonville Foods has a truck with a convertible barbecue grill capable of cooking 300 of the firm's sausages at a time. Clairol has a mobile beauty salon, and Kodak's Image Magic vehicle develops photos at events it visits. Miller Brewing promoted its sponsorship of the reunion of two Led Zeppelin band members with a 67-foot truck outfitted as a traveling museum and multimedia show with videos. Miller also uses vehicles with concert stages to reach ethnic markets: the Machina Musica for Hispanics, Sound Express for African Americans, and Miller Music Live for the general market.[30]

A *bonus pack* is a specially packaged item that gives the purchaser a larger quantity at the regular price. For instance, Irish Spring soap offered four bars for the price of three, and L'Oreal offered 25 percent more of its Perma-Vive shampoo for the same price as the smaller package.

Premiums are items given free or at reduced cost with purchases of other products. They have proven effective in motivating consumers to try new products or different brands. A premium should have some relationship with the product or brand it accompanies, though. For example, the service department of an auto dealership might offer ice scrapers to its customers.

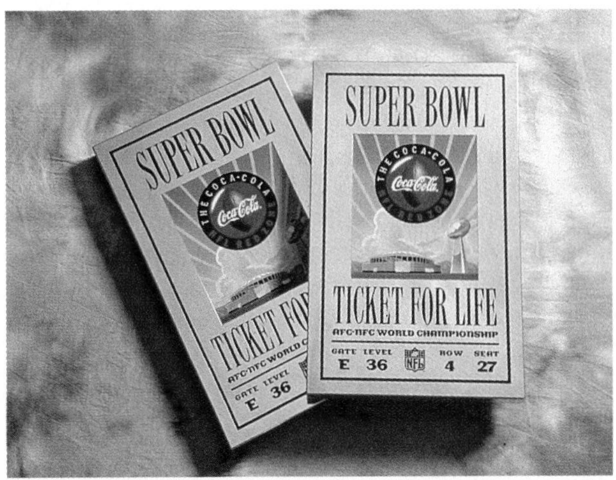
SUPER BOWL
THE COCA-COLA
Coca-Cola
TICKET FOR LIFE
AFC-NFC WORLD CHAMPIONSHIP
GATE LEVEL
E 36
NFL
ROW SEAT
4 27

The lucky winner of the Coca-Cola NFL Red Zone contest received lifetime tickets to the Super Bowl. The promotion asked Coke drinkers to match their Coke NFL Red Zone number, found under the cap or tab on Coke Classic bottles and cans, with the total number of points scored from the Red Zone (the area between the goal line and 20-yard line) during certain Monday Night Football games. Runner-up winners received trips to Super Bowl XXXI, NFL Starter jackets, or coupons for Coke products. National TV, print, and local radio ads supported the promotion.

Contests and Sweepstakes Firms often sponsor contests and sweepstakes to introduce new goods and services and to attract additional customers. *Contests* require entrants to solve problems or write essays, and they may also require proofs of purchase. A recent contest by Irish brewer Guinness gave a pub in Ireland to the author of a winning essay. *Sweepstakes* choose winners by chance, so no product purchase is necessary. They are more popular than contests with consumers because they don't take as much effort to enter. Marketers like them, too, because they are inexpensive to run and the number of winners is predetermined. With some contests, the sponsors cannot predict the number of people who will correctly complete the puzzles or gather the right number of symbols from scratch-off cards.

Contests, sweepstakes, and games offer substantial prizes in the form of cash or merchandise as inducements to potential customers. While contests can reinforce a company's image and advertising message, they don't contribute much to building brand loyalty. Participants focus on the contest, not the product.

Contests and sweepstakes also provide popular ways to attract visitors to many Web sites. GTE, for example, featured its "Win the World" sweepstakes in a banner ad on Yahoo!. Companies like WebStakes and NetStakes specialize in Web-based sweepstakes, designing and implementing customized sweepstakes for companies that want to deliver their brand messages to targeted audiences; these sophisticated services use elaborate databases, and they also track entrant activity. During the 1996 Summer Olympic Games in Atlanta, NetStakes and Infoseek co-sponsored a 20-site cooperative sweepstakes called "'i' on Atlanta" designed to draw attention to the participating sites.

In recent years, a number of court rulings and legal restrictions have limited the use of contests. As a result, any firm contemplating using this promotional technique should engage the services of a specialist.

Specialty Advertising Specialty advertising is a sales promotion technique that places the advertiser's name, address, and advertising message on useful articles that are distributed to target consumers. The origin of specialty advertising has been traced to the Middle Ages, when artisans gave wooden pegs bearing their names to prospects, who drove them into the walls at home to serve as convenient hangers for armor. In modern times, corporations began putting their names on a variety of products in the late 1800s, as newspapers and print shops looked for ways to make more money from their presses.

Marketers give out more than $8 billion worth of specialty advertising items each year. Wearable products,

Marketing Dictionary

specialty advertising Sales promotion technique in which marketers distribute articles such as key rings, calendars, and ballpoint pens bearing their firm's name or other advertising message.

including T-shirts, baseball caps, and jackets, are the most popular products, followed by writing instruments. Other popular forms of contemporary specialty advertising include desk and business accessories, mouse pads, calendars, and glassware/ceramics.

Advertising specialties help to reinforce previous or future advertising and sales messages. Consumers like these giveaways, which generate stronger responses to direct mail, resulting in three times the dollar volume of sales as compared to direct mail alone. Companies use this form of promotion to highlight store openings and new products, motivate salespeople, increase visits to trade-show booths, and improve customer relationships.

Trade-Oriented Promotions

Sales promotion techniques can also contribute effectively to campaigns aimed at such channel members as retailers and wholesalers. **Trade promotion** is sales promotion that appeals to marketing intermediaries rather than to consumers. Marketers use trade promotion in push strategies by encouraging resellers to stock new products, continue to carry existing ones, and promote both effectively to consumers. As discussed earlier, the typical firm actually spends half of its promotional budget on trade promotion—as much money as it spends on advertising and consumer-oriented sales promotions combined. Successful trade promotions offer financial incentives. They require careful timing, attention to costs, and easy implementation by retailers. These promotions should bring quick results and improve retail sales.

Trade Allowances Among the most common trade promotion methods are **trade allowances,** deals offered to wholesalers and retailers that purchase or promote specific products. These offers take various forms. A *buying allowance* gives retailers a discount on goods. These include *off-invoice allowances,* through which retailers deduct specified amounts from their invoices or receive free goods, such as one free case for every ten ordered, when they order certain quantities. When a manufacturer offers a *promotional allowance,* it agrees to pay the reseller a certain amount to cover the costs of special promotional displays or extensive advertising featuring the manufacturer's product. The goal is to increase sales to consumers by encouraging resellers to promote effectively.

Some retailers require vendors to pay special *slotting allowance* before they agree to take on new products. These fees guarantee so-called *slots,* or shelf space, in the stores for the new items. Retailers defend these fees as essential to cover the added costs of carrying the products, such as redesigning display space and shelves, setting up and administering control systems, managing inventory, and taking the risks inherent in stocking new products.

Figure 18.18 POP Display Offering Free T-shirts

CHAMPION
"I USE CHAMPION SPARK PLUGS IN ALL MY ENGINES!"
CORY McCLENATHAN
FREE
T-SHIRTS!
CHAMPION
MADE IN U.S

These fees can be sizable, from several hundred dollars per store to many thousands for a retail chain and millions for nationally distributed products. The ability of stores to demand slotting allowances indicates how much power retailers hold today. Many marketers consider these fees as a form of blackmail or bribery that only increases retailer profits.

The objective of any trade allowance assumes that retailers will pass savings on to consumers, but many manufacturers are concerned about potential abuses. Some retailers take advantage of promotions to stock up when wholesale prices are low, then resell the goods at regular prices once the promotions end. Procter & Gamble marketers estimate that only about 30 percent of its expenditures for trade promotions reach consumers, while 35 percent is lost through retailer inefficiency and another 35 percent goes to store profits. As a result, P&G and other consumer-goods manufacturers are turning to "everyday low price" policies, in which they lower product prices instead of offering trade allowances. The products cost retailers about the same as regular prices reduced for trade allowances, and the manufacturers ensure that consumers benefit by receiving lower prices.[31]

Point-of-Purchase Advertising A display or other promotion located near the site of the actual buying decision is known as **point-of-purchase (POP) advertising.** This method of sales promotion capitalizes on the fact that buyers make many purchase decisions within the store, so it encourages retailers to improve on-site merchandising. They directly benefit the retailer by creating special displays designed to stimulate sales of the item being promoted. These free-standing promotions often appear at the ends of aisles, such as the Champion spark plugs display pictured in Figure 18.18.

In-store promotions of consumer goods are common. Such displays may provide useful supplements for themes developed in other areas of promotional strategy. A life-sized, in-store display of a celebrity who appears in television advertising can very effectively reinforce the broad-

Trade Shows To influence resellers and other members of the distribution channel, many marketers participate in trade shows. These shows are often organized by industry trade associations, perhaps as part of the associations' annual meetings or conventions. Vendors who serve the industries are invited to appear at the shows to display and demonstrate their products for members. Every year, over 4,300 different shows in the United States and Canada draw over 1.3 million exhibitors and 85 million attendees. The National Restaurant Association, for example, holds the annual National Restaurant/Hotel/Motel Show in Chicago each May. More than 100,000 members attend, gathering from all 50 U.S. states and 70 countries, along with almost 2,000 exhibitors.

Trade shows rank second to advertising in marketing communications budgets. Because of the expense involved, a company must evaluate the value of such a show on several criteria, such as direct sales, any increase in product awareness, image building, and any contribution to the firm's marketing communications efforts. Trade shows give especially effective opportunities to introduce new products and to generate sales leads. Some types of shows reach ultimate consumers as well as channel members. Home, recreation, and automobile shows, for instance, allow businesses to display and demonstrate home-care, recreation, and other consumer products to entire communities.

Dealer Incentives, Contests, and Training Programs

Manufacturers run dealer incentive programs and contests to induce retailers and their salespeople to increase sales and promote products. These channel members receive incentives for performing promotion-related tasks and win contests by reaching sales goals. Manufacturers may offer major prizes like trips to resellers. *Push money* is another incentive that gives retail salespeople cash rewards for every unit of a product they sell. This benefit increases the likelihood that the salesperson will try to convince a customer to buy the product rather than a competing brand.

For more expensive and highly complex products, manufacturers often provide specialized training for retail salespeople. This background helps salespeople to explain features, competitive advantages, and other information to consumers. Training can be provided in several ways: a manufacturer's sales representatives can conduct training sessions during regular sales calls, or the firm can distribute sales literature and videocassettes.

PUBLIC RELATIONS

Chapter 17 defined **public relations** as the firm's communications and relationships with its various publics, including customers, employees, stockholders, suppliers, government agencies, and the society in which it operates. Organizational public relations efforts date back to 1889, when George Westinghouse hired two people to publicize the advantages of alternating-current electricity and to refute arguments for direct-current systems.

Public relations is an efficient, indirect communications channel through which a firm can promote products, although it serves broader objectives than those of the other components of promotional strategy. It is concerned with the prestige and image of all parts of the organization.

Marketing Dictionary

trade promotion Sales promotion aimed at marketing intermediaries rather than ultimate consumers.

trade allowance Deal offered to wholesalers and retailers for purchasing or promoting a specific product.

point-of-purchase (POP) advertising Display or other promotion located near the site of an actual buying decision.

public relations Firm's communications and relationships with its various publics.

Today, public relations plays a larger role than ever within the promotional mix, and it may emphasize more marketing-oriented information. In addition to its traditional activities, such as surveying public attitudes and creating a good corporate image, PR also supports advertising in promoting the organization's goods and services.

Approximately 160,000 people work in public relations in both the not-for-profit and profit-oriented sectors. Some 1,800 public-relations firms currently operate in the United States. The largest are Hill & Knowlton, Burson-Marsteller, Ogilvy Public Relations Group, and Fleishman-Hillard. In addition, thousands of smaller firms and one-person operations compete to offer these services.

Public relations is in a period of major growth as a result of increased public pressure on industry regarding issues of corporate ethical conduct, environmentalism, and internationalism. International expenditures on public relations are growing more rapidly than those for advertising and sales promotion. Many top executives are becoming more involved in public relations. The public expects top managers to take greater responsibility for company actions than they have accepted in the past. Those who refuse are widely criticized.

The PR department is the link between the firm and the media. It provides press releases and holds news conferences to announce new products, formation of strategic alliances, management changes, financial results, or similar developments. The PR department may issue its own publications, as well, including newsletters, brochures, and reports.

A PR plan begins much like an advertising plan with research to define the role and scope of the firm's overall public relations and particular public-relations challenges. Next come strategic decisions on short-term and long-term goals and markets, analysis of product features, and choices of messages and media channels—or other PR strategies such as speaking engagements or contests—for each market. Plan execution involves developing messages highlighting the benefits that the firm brings to each market. The final step is to measure results.

Randy Jones, publisher of *Worth,* calls himself the P. T. Barnum of publishing. He travels the globe to promote his new magazine for investors with median household incomes of $120,000. Jones uses proactive marketing public relations to promote his magazine to advertisers, media planners, and readers. He hosted a beach party for fashion advertisers on Italy's Tuscan coast, sponsored a cruise for readers on the QE2, cosponsors investment seminars with advertisers, and plans lavish dinner parties for influential people such as CEOs, political and media figures, artists, and academics. Jones believes proactive MPR gives *Worth* exposure the magazine couldn't get in any other way.

Marketing and Nonmarketing Public Relations

Nonmarketing-oriented public relations activities communicate about general management issues. When a company makes a decision that affects any of its publics, input from public-relations specialists can help to smooth its dealings with those publics. A company that decides to close a plant would need advice on how to deal with the local community. Other examples include a company's attempts to gain favorable public opinion during a long strike or an open letter to Congress published in a newspaper during congressional debate on a bill that would affect a particular industry. Although some companies organize their public-relations departments separately from their marketing divisions, PR activities invariably affect promotional strategies.

Marketing public relations describes a more narrowly focused type of public-relations activities that directly support marketing goals. They involve an organization's relationships with consumers or other groups about marketing concerns. MPR can be either proactive or reactive. With *proactive* MPR, the marketer takes the initiative and seeks out opportunities for promoting the firm's products, often including distribution of press releases and feature articles. For example, companies send press releases about new products to newspapers, television stations, and relevant consumer, business, and trade publications.

MPR can be a very powerful tool, because it adds news coverage to reinforce direct promotion. IKEA Home Furnishings' Houston store raised public awareness by sponsoring a children's health and safety fair with free immunizations and vision and hearing tests. Kids also received T-shirts and free haircuts. Several local charities received food, toys, and money from IKEA.[32] To increase Saturday travel, Northwest Airlines used PR to publicize a price promotion involving a December shopping trip to the Mall of America near Minneapolis. It spent no money on advertising or other promotions but sent press releases to travel publications and major newspapers in target markets. CNN, the *New York Times,* and regional papers carried the story, and television cameras followed visitors around the mall as they shopped. The campaign was so successful that Northwest's sales were three times greater than expected.

http://www.netvigator.com/ikea/

Reactive MPR responds to an external situation that has potential negative consequences for the organization. In 1996, *Consumer Reports* magazine rated the Isuzu Trooper and Acura SLX as "not acceptable" after reporting that the two sport-utility vehicles were likely to roll over in quick turns. Trooper sales dropped 40 percent the following month. The two automakers immediately used reactive MPR to respond to these allegations.[33]

Other examples of reactive MPR are responses to product tamperings, such as the deaths caused by cyanide in Tylenol (1982) and Sudafed (1991) capsules. Prompt corrective action and strong PR campaigns from the makers of these products—Johnson & Johnson and Burroughs Wellcome, respectively—prevented these situations from becoming disasters.[34]

Publicity

The aspect of public relations that is most directly related to promoting a firm's products is **publicity,** nonpersonal stimulation of demand for a good, service, place, idea, person, or organization by unpaid placement of significant news about it in a print or broadcast medium. Firms generate publicity by creating special events, holding press conferences, and preparing news releases and media kits.

In one of the most successful recent promotions blending advertising and publicity in a single event, Taco Bell chose April Fools' Day to announce its purchase of the Liberty Bell. Full-page ads noted that the company would rename the monument as the Taco Liberty Bell, and it urged other marketers to sponsor national monuments in an effort to reduce the national debt. Thousands of angry protest calls clogged radio talk shows and Taco Bell's customer service hotline before the fast-food marketer issued a news release confessing to the hoax and announcing a $50,000 donation for restoration of the Liberty Bell. The story produced over 400 TV mentions and thousands of radio reports and newspaper stories worth millions of dollars in media exposure.[35]

While publicity generates minimal costs compared to other forms of promotion, it does not deliver its message entirely free of cost. Publicity-related expenses include the costs of employing marketing personnel assigned to create and submit publicity releases, printing and mailing costs, and related expenses.

Firms often pursue some publicity to promote their images or viewpoints. Other publicity efforts involve organizational activities such as plant expansions, mergers and acquisitions, management changes, and research and development programs. A significant amount of publicity, however, provides information about goods and services, particularly new ones.

Because many consumers consider news stories to be more credible than advertisements as sources of information, publicity releases are often sent to media editors for possible inclusion in news stories. The media audiences perceive the news as coming from the communications media, not the sponsors. The information in a publicity release about a new good or service can provide valuable assistance for a television, newspaper, or magazine writer, leading to eventual broadcast or publication. Publicity releases sometimes fill voids in publications, and at other times they become part of regular features. In either case, they offer firms valuable supplements to paid advertising messages.

New Trends in Public Relations

Public relations, like other forms of promotion, is moving into cyberspace. For example, underwear marketer Joe Boxer was among the first to request customer feedback over the Internet. It also publicized its Web site by including the address on its products. The goal of this effort is better customer relations and immediate feedback rather than selling Joe Boxer products online. Other firms are

Marketing Dictionary

publicity Stimulation of demand for a good, service, place, idea, person, or organization by unpaid placement of commercially significant news or favorable media presentations.

recognizing the value of using interactive media to get their messages directly to consumers. "Anyone doing PR today who ignores the Internet is as shortsighted as the PR person in the late 1940s who ignored TV," says an AT&T advertising spokesperson.

http://www.joeboxer.com/

The latest twist on public relations is *experiential marketing,* a combination of IMC, PR, and relationship marketing. For example, McDonald's introduced its Arch Deluxe burger with an extensive PR campaign. Its agency secured spots for Ronald McDonald, the company's clown spokesman, on the Academy Awards broadcast and the Today show, at the Kentucky Derby, and with Dennis Rodman at a Chicago Bulls basketball game. The PR events drove the advertising; ads that showed Ronald dancing and playing golf grew out of the PR campaign.

Nabisco and other food companies use PR to get closer to the consumer. Nabisco polled callers to a toll-free 800 phone number on their favorite color for a spring pastel version of Oreo cookies. It also sponsored a contest and national talent search, asking consumers to describe their favorite cracker toppings. In just two weeks, 25,000 people called requesting auditions. Accompanying this promotion, an ad campaign featured recipes. The mobile sales promotions described earlier in this chapter are also forms of experiential marketing.[36]

CROSS PROMOTION

In a recent trend, marketers have begun to combine their promotional efforts for related products using a technique called **cross promotion,** in which marketing partners share the cost of a promotional campaign that meets their mutual needs—an important benefit in an environment of rising media costs. Relationship marketing strategies like co-marketing and co-branding are forms of cross promotion. Marketers realize that these joint efforts between established brands provide greater benefits in return for both companies' investments of time and money, and such promotions will become increasingly important to many partners' growth prospects.

The movie industry is one of the most prominent users of cross promotion. Movie studios frequently partner with fast-food chains, as Chapter 10 discussed. The movie studios, which spend an average of $54 million to produce and promote a film, find cross promotions bring effective ways to create public awareness of their films. Kids who open their meals and see movie characters are likely to ask their parents to see the movies.

Burger King's promotions for Disney's *Toy Story, The Lion King, Pocahontas,* and *The Hunchback of Notre Dame* were very valuable to both parties. During the *Toy Story* tie-in, sales of Burger King's Kids Club meals doubled. In addition, each kid's meal is generally part of a larger family check, so overall sales rise. The cost for these major promotions can reach $100 million, which includes not only the 50 to 60 cents paid for premium toys, but also coordinated placemats, bags, store decorations, and point-of-purchase displays. Media placement costs can add another $50 million.

McDonald's scored a marketing coup in 1996 when Disney announced a ten-year global promotional alliance with the company after five years with rival Burger King. The Disney-McDonald's partnership includes 14 to 17 promotions a year, sponsorship of Disney's new theme park Animal Kingdom, and $100 million in royalty payments. It also involves all Disney units—film, television, cable, the ABC TV network, and theme parks—and precludes Disney tie-ins with any other fast-food companies. In a related partnership, Disney and Mattel have signed a three-year deal giving the toy maker global rights to produce toys based on Disney movies and television programs.

FREEEEE!
with required UPC symbols
Goosebumps
THRILLOGY
3 Mini-Books by R.L. STINE
Here's how to collect all three books ONLY from HERSHEY'S, PEPSI-COLA, and FRITO-LAY.
• "DON'T MAKE ME LAUGH" is FREE inside specially marked packages of DORITOS brand Tortilla Chips, RUFFLES brand Potato Chips, CHEE.TOS brand Cheese Flavored Snacks and Frito-Lay VARIETY PACKS.
• For "HALLOWEEN GAME" from Hershey's and "BAD DOG" from Pepsi, see mail-in certificate below.
READING is a SCREAM!
Reese's
HERSHEY'S MILK CHOCOLATE SNACK SIZE
Almond Joy SNACK SIZE
KitKat SNACK SIZE
Doritos
Ruffles
PEPSI
• Pepsi Points good for "Pepsi Stuff" through October 31, 1996 are found on specially marked packages of Pepsi and Diet Pepsi while supplies last. See Pepsi Stuff Catalog in store for details.
• With each request for "HALLOWEEN GAME" you will receive a "Haunted Library" to store the 3 Mini-Book Collection.
MAIL IN CERTIFICATE/NOT REDEEMABLE IN STORES
Please send me the following FREE Goosebumps Mini-Books
Mini-Books are 3"x3½" & 20 pages.
For the Book: "HALLOWEEN GAME" I've enclosed TWO UPC symbols from any 8 oz. or larger bags of HERSHEY'S, REESE'S, KIT KAT, PETER PAUL, YORK, TWIZZLERS or AMAZIN' FRUIT candies. I will also receive a "Goosebumps Haunted Library" to store the 3 Mini-Book Collection.
For the Book: "BAD DOG" I've enclosed ONE UPC symbol from a 24-pack/Cube or 12-pack, OR TWO UPCs from 2-liter bottles of PEPSI-COLA (Diet, Regular, Caffeine Free, Caffeine Free Diet or Wild Cherry), MOUNTAIN DEW (Regular or Diet), or LIPTON BRISK Iced tea (all flavors).
Send this original, completed certificate with required UPCs to:
Goosebumps "THRILLOGY" Offer
P.O. Box 1288, Grand Rapids, MN 55745-1288
Name:
St. Address:
City:
State:
Zip:
Phone: ( )
MANUFACTURER COUPON | EXPIRES 11/1/96
SAVE 40¢
on any two 8 oz. or larger bags of candy
HERSHEY'S Reese's York Peter Paul
Twizzlers AMAZIN' FRUIT KitKat
LIMIT ONE COUPON PER PURCHASE.

Fans of author R. L. Stine's best-selling *Goosebumps* books were offered three new titles not available in bookstores during a cross promotion with the author, the publisher (Scholastic, Inc.), PepsiCo, and Hershey Foods.

In a different type of cross promotion, PepsiCo and Hershey Foods teamed up with Scholastic Books and R. L. Stine, author of the popular *Goosebumps* series of children's books. Stine wrote three special minibooks just for the promotion. Kids acquired the books by sending in coupons from Pepsi-Cola packages or Hershey newspaper insert ads or by buying special packages of Doritos chips containing the mini-books. (Chip maker Frito-Lay is a PepsiCo unit.) Sponsor logos and instructions about how to get the other books appear on the back covers of the books. A Halloween-themed book was promoted with Hershey's candy.[37]

http://www.ticketmaster.com/

Cross promotions are also taking place on the Internet. Pepsi and Ticketmaster are sponsoring online chat sessions twice a month through Ticketmaster's Web site. Called Pepsi Live! @ Ticketmaster Online, the chats feature leading popular music performers like singer Tori Amos. Participants qualify to win free concert tickets, backstage passes, and other prizes. The sponsors promote the chats on their respective Web sites with ongoing activities like prizes and giveaways. By teaming up with TM Online, Pepsi expanded the concept of its Pepsi World site and provided consumers the chance to connect with favorite music and sports stars.[38]

http://www.pepsi.com/

MEASURING PROMOTIONAL EFFECTIVENESS

Because promotion represents such a major expenditure for many firms, they need to determine whether their campaigns accomplish appropriate promotional objectives. Companies want their advertising agencies and in-house marketing personnel to demonstrate how promotional programs contribute to increased sales and profits. Marketers are well-aware of the number of advertising messages and sales promotions that consumers encounter daily—and they know that these people practice selective perception and simply screen out the messages.

Novel forms of advertising and sales promotion, such as inserting ads in videocassettes, cinema advertising, animated billboards, and new types of sales promotions, are aimed at increasing the likelihood that the messages will draw the attention of their target audiences. The Internet and other interactive media also provide different ways to reach the right people. All of these efforts pursue a common objective: to enhance the likelihood that the company's promotional messages will be received and remembered.

By measuring promotional effectiveness, organizations can evaluate different strategies, prevent mistakes before spending money on specific programs, and improve their promotional programs. As the earlier discussion of promotional planning explained, any evaluation program starts with objectives and goals; otherwise, marketers have no yardstick against which to measure effectiveness. However, determining whether an advertising message has achieved its intended objective is one of the most difficult undertakings in marketing. Sales promotions and direct marketing are somewhat easier to evaluate because they evoke measurable consumer responses. Like advertising, public relations is also difficult to assess on purely objective terms.

Measuring Advertising Effectiveness

Measures to evaluate the effectiveness of advertising, while difficult and costly, are essential parts of any marketing plan. Without an assessment strategy, marketers will not know whether their advertising achieves the objectives of the marketing plan or if the dollars in the advertising budget are well spent. To answer these questions, they conduct two types of research. *Message research* tests consumer reactions to an advertisement's creative message. Pretesting and posttesting, the two methods for performing message research, are discussed below. The other major category, *media research,* assesses how well a particular medium delivers the advertiser's message, where and when to place the advertisement, and the size of the audience. Buyers of broadcast time base their purchases on estimated Nielsen rating points, and the networks have to make good if ratings don't reach promised levels. Buyers of print advertising space pay fees based on circulation. These claims are independently certified by specialized research firms.

Marketing Dictionary

cross promotion A technique in which marketing partners share the cost of a promotional campaign that meets their mutual needs.

Figure 18.19 **Magazine Advertisement with Starch Scores**

STARCH AD-AS-A-WHOLE
Noted % Associated % Read Most %
M 48 44 19
STARCH Seen %
M 48
Loves bloody elbows.
Digs chain-grease
Craves road-rash hip
STARCH Read Some %
M 38
Detests a sweaty midriff.
Polartec® fabric pulls sweat away from your skin and disperses it evenly so it evaporates quickly. Keeping your skin drier than with any other fabric available. With over 100 other Climate Control Fabrics™, Polartec keeps you cool when it's hot, warm when it's cold, dry when you sweat. So you can perform at your peak. Look for the label.
MALDEN MILLS
POLARTEC
STARCH Signature %
M 44

The "Ad-As-A-Whole" label indicates the percentage of readers interviewed who "Noted" the ad in the issue. "Associated" it with a specific advertiser or product, and "Read Most" (more than 50%) of the ad copy. This label summarizes the ad's total readership.

The "Seen %" label indicates the percentage of readers interviewed who saw the illustration.

This "Read %" label indicates the percentage of readers interviewed who read the headline.

The "Signature %" label indicates the percentage of readers who saw the logo or signature.

Pretesting **Pretesting** assesses an advertisement's likely effectiveness before it actually appears in the chosen medium. The obvious advantage of this technique is the opportunity to evaluate ads during the development stage. Marketers can conduct a number of different pretests, beginning during the concept phase in the campaign's earliest stages when they have only rough copy of the ad, and continuing until the ad layout and design are almost completed.

Pretesting employs a variety of evaluation methods. Focus groups can discuss their reactions to mockups of ads using different themes, headlines, or illustrations. To test magazine advertisements, the Batten, Barton, Durstine & Osborn ad agency cuts ads out of advance copies of magazines and then inserts the ads it wants to test. Interviewers later check the impact of the advertisements on readers who receive free copies of the revised magazines.

Another ad agency, McCann-Erickson, uses a *sales conviction test* to evaluate magazine advertisements. Interviewers ask heavy users of a particular item to pick one of two alternative advertisements that would convince them to purchase it.

To screen potential radio and television advertisements, marketers often recruit consumers to sit in a studio and indicate their preferences by pressing two buttons, one for a positive reaction to the commercial and the other for a negative reaction. Sometimes, proposed ad copy is printed on a postcard that also offers a free product; the number of cards returned represents an indication of the copy's effectiveness. *Blind product tests* are also frequently used. In these tests, people are asked to select unidentified products on the basis of available advertising copy.

Mechanical devices offer yet another method of assessing how people read advertising copy. One mechanical test uses a hidden camera to photograph how people's eye movements read ads. The results help advertisers to determine headline placement and copy length. Another mechanical approach measures the galvanic skin response, changes in the electrical resistance of the skin produced by emotional reactions.

Posttesting **Posttesting** assesses advertising copy after it has appeared in the appropriate medium. Pretesting generally is a more desirable measurement method than posttesting because it can save the cost of placing ineffective ads. However, posttesting can be helpful in planning future advertisements and in adjusting current advertising programs. For example, a posttest conducted by the Partnership for a Drug-Free America revealed that one ad showing a drug addict playing Russian roulette had sent a dangerously incorrect message—that suicide is the only escape for heavy drug users. The test helped the partnership avoid making the same mistake in creating new ads.[39]

In one of the most popular posttests, the *Starch Readership Report,* interviewers ask people who have read selected magazines whether they observed various ads in them. A copy of the magazine is used as an interviewing aid, and each interviewer starts at a different point in the magazine. For larger ads, respondents are also asked about specifics, such as headlines and copy. Figure 18.19 shows an advertisement with the actual Starch scores. All such *readership,* or *recognition,* tests assume that future sales are related to advertising readership.

Unaided recall tests are another method of posttesting the effectiveness of advertisements. Respondents do not see copies of the magazine after their initial reading but must recall the ads from memory. Interviewers for the Gallup and Robinson marketing research firms require people to prove they have read a magazine by recalling one or more of its feature articles. The people who remember particular articles receive cards with the names of products advertised in the issue. They then list the ads they remember and explain what they recall about those ads. Finally, the respondents answer questions about their potential purchases of the advertised products. Readership tests conclude Gallup and Robinson interviews. Burke Research Corp. conducts telephone interviews the day after a commercial has aired on television to test brand recognition and the advertisement's effectiveness. Another unaided recall test is adWatch, a joint project of *Advertising Age* magazine and the Gallup Organization. It measures ad awareness by telephone polling that asks each consumer to name the advertisement that first comes to mind of all the ads he or she has seen, heard, or read in the previous 30 days.

Inquiry tests are another popular form of posttest. Advertisements sometimes offer gifts—generally product samples—to people who respond to them. The number of inquiries relative to the advertisement's cost forms a measure of its effectiveness.

Split runs allow advertisers to test two or more ads at the same time. Although they traditionally place different versions in newspapers and magazines, split runs on cable television systems frequently test the effectiveness of TV ads. With this method, advertisers divide the cable TV audience or a publication's subscribers in two: Half view Advertisement A and the other half view Advertisement B. The relative effectiveness of the alternatives is then determined through inquiries or recall and recognition tests.

Regardless of the exact method they choose, marketers must realize that pretesting and posttesting are expensive efforts. As a result, they must plan to use these techniques as effectively as possible.

Measuring Sales Promotion Effectiveness

Because many sales promotions, especially consumer-oriented techniques, result in direct consumer responses, marketers can relatively easily track their effectiveness. As with other elements in the promotional mix, they must weigh the cost of the promotion against the benefits. They can measure the redemption rate of cents-off coupons, for example, and coupons often carry printed codes indicating their sources to let manufacturers and retailers know which media provide the highest redemption rates. To evaluate sampling, one of the most popular types of consumer promotions, marketers want to know how effectively it induces consumers to actually buy the product once they try the sample. Sweepstakes and contest entries can also be tracked.

Studies have shown that sampling does promote trial purchases. As yet, however, marketers have found no definitive answers about whether sampling helps the rate of repurchase.

Some trade promotions—allowances, contests, and dealer incentives, for example—give easily measurable results like sales increases or heavier customer traffic. Others, however, like trade shows and training programs, may require more subjective judgments of the first results, such as greater product awareness and knowledge, while sales gains will take longer to show up.

Measuring Public Relations Effectiveness

As with other forms of marketing communications, organizations must measure PR results based on their objectives both for the PR program as a whole and for specific activities. In the next step, marketers must decide what they want to measure. This choice includes determining whether the message was heard by the target audience and whether it had the desired influence on public opinions.

Marketing Dictionary

pretesting Assessment of an advertisement's effectiveness before it actually appears in the chosen medium.

posttesting Assessment of an advertisement's effectiveness after it has appeared in the appropriate medium.

SOLVING AN ETHICAL CONTROVERSY

Should the Federal Government Place More Restrictions on Tobacco Advertising?

Tobacco advertising has long been on the hot seat. Decades ago, U.S. government regulators chased tobacco ads off television and radio, and now the powerful industry is under increasing pressure as it tries to protect its advertising turf in other arenas.

Not long ago, for instance, Philip Morris sent its Marlboro man to athletic events. Threatened with a federal lawsuit, the tobacco giant agreed to remove cigarette signs in stadiums and other sporting venues where they appeared in the background of pictures beamed to millions of television viewers. The Food and Drug Administration contended that the signs violated the ban on television advertising of cigarettes. To retain an advertising presence at sporting venues, the tobacco giant must now put its signs in more discreet places.

In its most hotly debated move, the FDA is seeking to restrict tobacco advertising that it deems accessible to children. As part of a sweeping regulatory proposal, the FDA would restrict cigarette ads to black-and-white text in magazines for which teens and children represent at least 15 percent of the readers. The agency also would forbid tobacco companies from promoting their products on billboards within 1,000 feet of schools. What's more, the regulation would ban brand-name sponsorships of sporting events and concerts.

?

Should these additional restrictions be implemented?

PRO

1. **Cigarette companies glamorize smoking by featuring healthy, beautiful people who are enjoying themselves in gorgeous settings. Regulators should curb cigarette advertising, because it acts so effectively to hook new smokers. According to researchers, young people are three times more responsive than adults to cigarette advertising. The ads are tailor-made for impressionable children, not adults, insists American Cancer Society Chairman George Dessart. Cigarette companies are also displaying a real talent for attracting Generation Xers. RJR Nabisco, for instance, is wooing hip Xers with new brands like Red Kamel and Moonlight Tobacco.**
2. **Smoking exacts a terrible toll on Americans' health. Cigarette smoking remains the largest avoidable cause of premature death and disability in the United States. Smokers are two times more likely to**

The simplest and least costly level of assessment involves outputs of the PR program: whether the target audience received, paid attention to, understood, and retained the messages directed to them. To make this judgment, the staff would count the number of media placements and gauge the extent of media coverage. They would count attendees at any press conference, evaluate the quality of brochures and other materials, and pursue similar activities. Formal techniques include tracking publicity placements, analyzing how favorably their contents portrayed the company, and conducting public opinion polls.

To analyze PR effectiveness more deeply, a firm could conduct focus groups, interviews with opinion leaders, and more detailed and extensive opinion polls. The highest level of effectiveness measurement looks at *outcomes:* Did the PR program change people's opinions, attitudes, and behavior? PR professionals measure these outcomes through before-and-after polls (similar to pretesting and posttesting) and more advanced techniques like psychographic analysis, cluster analysis, and communicants audits.[40]

Evaluating Interactive Media

Chapter 17 discussed several ways to measure how many users view Web advertisements: hits (user requests for a file), impressions (the number of times a viewer sees an ad), and click-throughs (when the user clicks on the ad to get more information). However, some of these measures can be misleading. Because each page, graphic, or multimedia file equals one hit, simple interactions can easily inflate the hit count. For example, a page design increases hits when it includes a lot of small graphics which the viewer clicks to move to other pages. The same effect occurs when the design places small amounts of information on each page, so that a viewer has to link to other pages to get the whole story. Software downloads at a site also count as hits. In these cases, tracking hits or impressions doesn't tell an advertiser anything about the effectiveness of an ad. "Impressions are a vague, unsatisfactory measurement," said Ann Lewnes, director of worldwide advertising for Intel. "If you don't click on a banner, you aren't taking advantage of the medium."

suffer heart attacks and strokes and have a 70 percent greater death rate from heart disease than do nonsmokers.

3. The cigarette industry's offer to regulate itself is a cynical attempt to avoid even tougher laws. For instance, Philip Morris has proposed restricting the advertising children see, but it wants a big favor in return: a guarantee that the FDA will be blocked from ever regulating tobacco products.

CON

1. The industry's advertising is aimed at encouraging adult smokers to switch brands. Luring customers from another cigarette company is virtually the only way for tobacco conglomerates to increase market share. Adults have the ability to decide whether to look at the advertising or buy cigarettes because of it.

   The companies are not interested in attracting kids to the habit. To support this assertion, Philip Morris has unveiled its own set of antismoking initiatives aimed at young people. The tobacco industry's proposal would impose a more limited set of restrictions on cigarette sales and advertising than those of regulators with the goal of reducing youth smoking.

2. The tobacco industry is not convinced that cigarettes cause cancer or heart disease. It disputes the scientific studies that establish these links and calls many of them flawed or biased.

3. Limiting a company's ability to market its legal product violates its First Amendment right to free speech. Such a restriction will not hold up in the courts.

Summary

Just as in the past, when regulators came gunning for the cigarette industry, it responded by proposing its own restrictions. Whether the strategy will work this time remains to be seen. Meanwhile, the tobacco industry has to fight opponents not only here but also overseas. To the delight of European antismoking groups, Philip Morris is under legal siege in France, Belgium, Italy, and Holland for running controversial ads claiming that second-hand smoke poses no greater health risk than eating cookies and drinking milk.

Sources: "Tobacco Ads a Local Call," *San Francisco Chronicle,* April 30, 1997, p. A20; Matthew Rose, "French Court Blocks Philip Morris Ads that Liken Passive Smoke to Cookies," *Wall Street Journal,* June 27, 1996, p. B14; Suein L. Hwang, "Philip Morris Proposes Curbs on Sales to Kids," *Wall Street Journal,* May 16, 1996, pp. B1, B5; "Journal of Marketing Probes Teens and Cigarette Ads," *Marketing News,* April 22, 1996, p. 18; and "RJR's New Ad Campaign: It's Hip to Smoke," *Wall Street Journal,* April 16, 1996, pp. B1, B14.

Click-through rates remain rather low with current designs—2 to 3 percent on average, with 7 percent considered outstanding. To increase effectiveness, advertisers must give viewers who do click through something good to see. Successful Web campaigns use demonstrations, promotions, coupons, and interactive features.

Marketers need to look beyond such traditional measures of advertising effectiveness as cost per thousand (CPM) to choose sites for their Web ads. In addition to the cost of the banner, key factors to evaluate include the content the site offers, where on the screen the banner will appear, how much control the advertiser has over the ad, and how well the site tracks usage/visitor information. For maximum effectiveness, advertisers should place ads carefully, where they will reach users interested in their particular site or product. Fidelity Investments marketers would gain by paying a higher CPM for an ad on the stock quotes page at CNN's Web site rather than buying a cheaper slot on its more general front page.[41]

Unlike Nielsen ratings for broadcast media and print media's audited circulation numbers, the Web does not yet have a standard measurement system. A number of companies like I/Pro, NetCount, and Interse offer different Web tracking and counting systems. At least two auditing services, Audit Bureau of Verification Services and BPA International, are currently in operation.[42]

ETHICS IN PROMOTION

Chapter 3 introduced the topic of marketing ethics and noted that promotion is the element in the marketing mix that raises the most ethical questions. People actively debate the question whether or not marketing communications contribute to better lives. Many view advertising negatively as a kind of propaganda rather than a source of information. They criticize it for exerting too much influence on consumers, creating unnecessary needs and wants, overemphasizing sex and beauty, and sending inappropriate messages to children. Ads with racist, sexual, sexist, or ageist themes are also under attack for content labeled *offensive.* Let's now take a closer look at ethical concerns in promotional activities.

Advertising Ethics

Even though laws allow certain types of advertising, many promotions still may involve ethical issues. For example, many people believe in curtailing advertising to children, as discussed in the Solving an Ethical Controversy box from Chapter 17. To woo younger consumers, especially teens and those in their 20s, advertisers make messages as unlike advertisements as possible; they design ads that seem more like entertainment.

Liquor advertising on television is another gray area. Beer marketers advertise heavily on television and spend far more on advertising in print and outdoor media than do marketers of hard-liquor brands. Some members of Congress want much stricter regulation of all forms of liquor advertising on television and other media. This change would restrict ads in magazines with 15 percent or more youth readership to black-and-white text only. Critics decry advertisements with messages implying that drinking the right beer will improve one's personal life or help to win a sports contest. Many state and local authorities are considering more restrictive proposals on both alcohol and tobacco advertising.[43]

Marketers must also carefully draw the line between advertising and entertainment. The History Channel, a part of some cable TV selections, had to withdraw a planned series of company profiles in the face of harsh criticism because the series featured documentaries about the channel's sponsors, and those firms had some control over the final products.

In cyberspace ads, it's often even more difficult to separate advertising from editorial content. Many sites resemble magazine and newspaper "advertorials" (special advertising sections with articles on a topic) or television infomercials. For example, one site, Smarter Eating and Living based on a *CBS This Morning* series, provides nutrition tips and recipes, all of which include Kraft products. The site's content does state that it is sponsored by *CBS This Morning* and Kraft Foods, but unlike printed advertorials, the word *advertisement* does not appear on each page. Many such sites display the sponsors' names only on the home pages, so that users linking to other pages may not be aware of the sponsor's name or stake in the content.[44]

Puffery and Deception **Puffery** refers to exaggerated claims of a product's superiority or the use of subjective or vague statements that may not be literally true. The following statements are examples of puffery:

"The most advanced system ever developed"

"The ultimate one-cup coffee machine" (referring to Folger's instant coffee)

"If it tastes too good to be fat free, it's Kraft Free."

Exaggeration in ads is not new. Consumers seem to accept a tendency for advertisers to stretch the truth in their efforts to distinguish their products and get customers to buy. This inclination may provide one reason that advertising does not encourage purchase behavior as successfully as sales promotions do. A tendency toward puffery does raise some ethical questions, though: Where is the line between claims that attract attention and those that provide implied guarantees? To what degree do advertisers deliberately make misleading statements?

The Uniform Commercial Code standardizes sales and business practices throughout the United States. It makes a distinction between puffery and any specific or quantifiable statement about product quality or performance that constitutes an "express warranty," which obligates the company to stand behind its claim. General boasts of product superiority and vague claims are puffery, not warranties. They are considered so self-praising or exaggerated that the average consumer would not rely on them to make a buying decision.

Over the years, consumers have filed many lawsuits because they believed that ads made false claims. Some have pursued obviously frivolous claims. In one case, a customer tried to sue Honda because, contrary to its ad's promise, he didn't meet the "nicest people" while in his Honda Civic! Clearly, that statement was never meant to be taken literally.

A quantifiable statement, on the other hand, implies a certain level of performance. Tests can establish the validity of a claim that a brand of long-life light bulbs outlast three regular light bulbs. A company that told a potential customer it had installed thousands of its irrigation systems was sued when the buyer discovered that only 25 or 30 had actually been sold. The courts upheld the customer's suit, because the statement could have been considered as an indication of quality and reliability.[45]

Ethics in Sales Promotion and Public Relations

Both consumer and trade promotions can also raise ethical issues. Sales promotions provide opportunities for unscrupulous companies to take advantage of consumers. For example, companies may not fulfill rebate and premium offers or mislead consumers by inaccurately stating the odds of winning sweepstakes or contests. Trade allowances, particularly slotting allowances, have been criticized for years as a form of bribery.

Several public relations issues open organizations to criticism. Various PR firms perform services for the tobacco industry; publicity campaigns defend unsafe products. Also, marketers must weigh ethics before they respond to negative publicity. For example, do they admit to problems or product deficiencies or try to cover them up? It should be noted that PR practitioners violate the Public Relations Society of America's Code of Professional Standards if they promote products or causes widely known to be harmful to others.

Marketing Dictionary

puffery Exaggerated claims of a product's superiority or the use of subjective or vague statements that may not be literally true.

ACHIEVEMENT CHECK SUMMARY

Reread the learning goals that follow, and consider the questions for each goal. Answering these questions will reinforce your grasp of the most important concepts in the chapter and allow you to check how well you have achieved these learning goals. Where a blank appears before a question, answer with *T* or *F;* for multiple-choice questions, circle the letter of the correct answer.

Objective 18.1: Explain the current status of advertising, sales promotion, and public relations in today's promotional strategies, and identify two recent trends in advertising.

1. ___ The average U.S. business spends more on advertising than on sales promotion.

2. ___ Most U.S. advertisements can effectively promote the same products in other countries after simply translating them into those countries' native languages.

3. ___ Interactive advertising allows consumers rather than advertisers to control how much information the consumers receive.

Objective 18.2: Identify the major types of advertising.

1. ___ An advertisement for the Fidelity Magellan mutual fund is an example of product advertising.

2. ___ Informative advertising is well-suited to the maturity stage of a product's life cycle.

3. ___ Consumers generally have positive attitudes toward products endorsed by celebrities.

Objective 18.3: Describe the process of creating an advertisement.

1. ___ Fear appeals influence consumers to take action to remove perceived threats.

2. ___ A successful advertisement for a financial planning company would be likely to provide a firm conclusion for the consumer.

3. ___ Which of the following choices is not a major objective when creating an advertisement? (a) gain attention; (b) implement interactive technology; (c) inform and persuade consumers; (d) encourage purchase behavior.

Objective 18.4: List and compare the major advertising media.

1. ___ Magazines are the most popular advertising medium.

2. ___ Cable television's popularity is increasing because it allows advertisers to target audiences more precisely than they can with ads on network stations.

3. ___ The apparel industry spends the most of any industry on both television and magazine advertising.

Objective 18.5: Outline the organization of the advertising function and the role of an advertising agency.

1. ___ Today, advertising agencies earn most of their revenue by billing 15 percent commissions on media placements.

2. ___ Tokyo ranks first among the world's cities in advertising billings.

3. ___ Knowledge of interactive media is an important criterion when choosing an advertising agency.

Objective 18.6: Identify the principal methods of sales promotion.

1. ___ Consumer promotions account for the biggest percentage of a firm's communications budget.

2. ___ Sales promotions are good tools for raising interest in mature products.

3. ___ Slotting allowances allow retailers to take discounts on the invoice prices of goods.

Objective 18.7: Explain the roles of public relations, publicity, and cross promotions in an organization's promotional strategy.

1. ___ Public relations efforts usually target customers rather than investors, employees, or news media.

2. ___ Publicity involves paying a fee to obtain placement of company-supplied information in various news media.
3. ___ The appearance of Reese's Pieces candy in the film *E.T.* is an example of cross promotion.

Objective 18.8: Explain how marketers assess promotional effectiveness.

1. ___ Marketers evaluate how well consumers react to advertising through message research.
2. ___ Cents-off coupons represent the most popular consumer sales promotion technique.
3. ___ "Hits" are the best measure of effectiveness for interactive advertisements.

Objective 18.9: Discuss the importance of ethics in a firm's promotional activities.

1. ___ The blurring of lines between advertising and entertainment has become a major ethical concern.
2. ___ The slogan "BMW: the ultimate driving machine" is an example of puffery.
3. ___ Puffery is illegal.

Students: See the solutions section located on page S-4 to check your responses to the Achievement Check Summary.

Key Terms

advertising	sales promotion
product advertising	specialty advertising
institutional advertising	trade promotion
informative advertising	trade allowance
persuasive advertising	point-of-purchase (POP) advertising
reminder advertising	public relations
comparative advertising	publicity
retail advertising	cross promotion
cooperative advertising	pretesting
interactive media	posttesting
media scheduling	puffery
advertising agency	

Review Questions

1. Explain the wide variation in advertising expenditures as percentages of sales among the different industries mentioned in the chapter text.
2. Describe the primary objectives of advertising. Offer an example of a local advertising campaign, and explain how the campaign seeks to accomplish specific objectives.
3. Identify the six basic types of advertising. Give a specific example of each.
4. Discuss the relationship between advertising and the product life cycle. What types of advertising match up with specific product life cycle stages?
5. What major advantages and disadvantages characterize each of the advertising media? Give examples of types of advertisers most likely to use different media.
6. Discuss the organization of the advertising function. Consider all the major activities associated with advertising.
7. Under what circumstances are celebrity spokespersons likely to effectively enhance advertising? Give recent examples of effective and ineffective use of spokespersons in advertisements.
8. Why is retail advertising so important today? Relate cooperative advertising to the discussion of alternative promotional strategies in Chapter 17.
9. Distinguish between advertising and sales promotion. Explain the principal methods of sales promotion, and give an example of each.
10. Describe the public relations component of a firm's promotional mix. Do you agree with the assertion that publicity is free advertising?

Discussion Questions

1. Many state governments operate lotteries. Suggest a promotional plan for marketing lottery tickets with particular emphasis on the nonpersonal-selling aspects of the promotional mix.
2. Choose a candidate who ran for political office during the most recent election. Assume that you were in charge of advertising for this person's campaign, and develop an advertising strategy for your candidate. Select a campaign theme and choose media outlets for your message. Finally, design an advertisement for the candidate.
3. Review the changes in the relative importance of the various advertising media during the past 40 years that are mentioned in the chapter. Suggest likely explanations for these changes.
4. Present an argument favoring the use of comparative advertising by a marketer who is currently preparing an advertising plan. Make any necessary assumptions.
5. Develop a sales promotion program for each of the following marketers. Justify your choice of each sales promotion method employed in the program.
   a. Independent real estate agent
   b. Retail paint store
   c. Local tailor
   d. Local UHF television station

'netWork

1. London-based public relations firm Shandwick bills itself as the "largest and best independent public relations consultancy in the world." Although most of its PR activities are done in the United Kingdom, its work frequently extends to continental Europe and beyond. A subsidiary office currently operates in the United States.

Review their home page at

http://www.shandwickuk.co.uk/

Explain how their home page description of their offerings would justify their claims as the "largest and best" PR company. Is the Shandwick home page an effective public relations tool? Defend your answer. Give a brief scenario of how you might use them in a public relations capacity. Can you find differences between this British public relations firm and PR firms in the United States?

2. How do you think the Internet will change mass advertising as we currently know it? How should the advertising industry adjust (or should it?) to accommodate this change? Will the Internet cause any other changes in the promotional mix? Explain your answer.

3. AMIN Worldwide, the Advertising & Marketing International Network, is an alliance of over 50 independently-owned communication agencies. Go to its home page at

http://www.commercepark.com/amin/

Explain the purpose of this network. Why did this group come into existence? Can you locate any similar alliance of marketers or advertisers on the Internet?

VIDEO CASE 18

CREATING ADVERTISING THAT CHARMS, DISARMS, AND DELIVERS

What's a zoo to do when government funding dries up at about the same time that the community loses interest? Faced with the loss of state funding and an alarming decline in attendance, the Detroit Zoo turned to W. B. Doner for help. Doner is a full-service advertising agency co-headquartered in the Detroit suburb of Southfield, Michigan and Baltimore, Maryland. The 60-year-old agency's annual billings of $550 million rank it as the 45th largest ad agency in the world. Its status as a full-service agency permits Doner to help clients meet their marketing objectives through such services as strategic planning and research, media, public relations, and creative.

"Great creative can change the destiny of a company," was a favorite saying of agency founder W. B. "Brod" Doner. He spent decades instilling in his team a passion for creative efforts that would persuade and motivate buyers to act, thus producing results for the client. His philosophy emphasized creating advertising that would "charm, disarm, and deliver." The agency's success in these efforts clearly shone in Doner's creative work for the Detroit Zoo, work that would deliver results that exceeded zoo management's expectations.

Doner's creative team began their analysis of the zoo's problems by focusing on its ability to compete for entertainment dollars. Doner CEO Alan Kalter phrased the question this way: "What are we going to do to stimulate visits to the zoo?" The agency's creative staff decided to focus on ways to offer added value to zoo visitors. Their

DETROIT ZOOLOGICAL INSTITUTE

brainstorming sessions led to a new exhibit featuring giant models of dinosaurs moving around a natural setting. The zoo named the exhibit *Dinosauria* and the specially-designed logo appeared on company letterheads and internal documents as well as on media kits assembled to publicize the new attraction.

The Dinosauria exhibit targeted several objectives. One was to increase zoo attendance by 20 percent. Another was to tighten the zoo's relationship with the community. As Zoo Director Ron Kagan put it, "The idea is not to have a blockbuster in order to bring people here one time. We really wanted to relate the community to the zoo and how wonderful it is."

Doner used the Dinosauria logo as the centerpiece of its advertising campaign for the new exhibit. Highlighting the Detroit Zoo's status as a not-for-profit organization, Doner's media staff solicited offers of free advertising and space from the media, eventually lining up radio, TV, and magazine partners to deliver the zoo's message to the public. Their efforts produced overwhelming success: Zoo attendance jumped 33 percent over the previous year. The increase in visitors stimulated an $800,000 spurt in revenue from admissions and sales of food and beverages and gift-shop goods. The added cash inflows replaced most of the loss in state funding.

Doner's work with the Detroit Zoo does not produce revenues for the firm: it is done on a *pro bono* (free) basis as part of the agency's contributions to the community. However, it is rewarded financially for its successful effort for profit-seeking. Doner's work in helping British Petroleum establish a worldwide brand identity is one example of a commercial project. BP had managed its global operations country by country, and the firm had also mounted different promotional campaigns in different countries. Increased competition from other global brands, however, forced BP marketers to realize the need to project a unified worldwide image. Advertising Director Roy Croft summed up the marketing problems caused by the company's individual country campaigns: "It gave us a very fragmented image, certainly among those of our customers who traveled between markets."

Market research uncovered a sturdy, old-fashioned image for BP among consumers, who regarded it as a second-level brand below such competitors as Exxon, Texaco, and Fina. Most travelers recognized the BP brand and associated it with BP gas stations, but they did not acknowledge the company's status as an international supplier of fuel for railroads, airplanes, ocean liners, trucks, and helicopters. This research led to the creation of Doner's mission campaign, with ads showing swarms of helicopters, trains, trucks, and a jet converging on a BP gas station. The campaign was translated into 19 languages and ran in 30 markets. Posttests conducted in these markets showed improvement in both brand awareness and brand image, moving BP from third or fourth place in every market to either first place or tied for first place.

For the past ten years, Doner has also created advertising and special promotions for the 2,800-outlet Arby's restaurant chain. "The agency is unique in its ability to create ad campaigns that build equity for the Arby's brand while also driving next-door sales," says Arby's Franchise Association CEO Lloyd Fritzmeier. Doner has helped to position Arby's as the quality and taste leader in fast-food restaurants. Fritzmeier views Doner "as one of our most important partners—not as a supplier or vendor. We are fortunate to have an agency that understands our customers, our industry, our brand, and our franchise system."

Another retailer that appreciates Doner's understanding of its industry and customers is Lowe's, the giant home improvement and building materials retail chain. Doner created the "Lowe's Knows" campaign to differentiate Lowe's from such competitors as Home Depot and Builder's Square. "The ultimate battleground and the end point of differentiation for companies like ours—big-box retailers—is service," says Lowe's Senior Vice President of Marketing Dale Pond. "And customers typically define service as salespeople who are knowledgeable about the retailer's products and about using them." Doner addressed that customer perception in creating the "Lowe's Knows" theme and such variations as "Lowe's Knows Plumbing" and "Lowe's Knows Landscaping." The campaign has worked so well that the theme has become part of all Lowe's communications, from recruitment brochures to store signage.

Questions

1. Based on the comments in this case made by clients, what characteristics differentiate W. B. Doner from other advertising agencies?
2. Do you agree with the statement made by Doner's founder that "Great creative can change the destiny of a company"? Support your answer with examples from this case.
3. Give examples of how Doner helps clients to achieve the advertising objectives discussed in the chapter.
4. Successful marketing plans frequently rely on thorough customer research. Visit the Detroit Zoo Web site at

   http://www.detroitzoo.org/

   Does the zoo's home page solicit customer information? Write a brief proposal suggesting changes to this home page to improve its effectiveness as a research tool.

Sources: The following articles appeared in the March 3, 1997 issue of *Advertising Age:* John McDonough, "Shop's 'Vest Picket' Origins Lead to Billings of a Half-Billion Dollars," pp. C1–C2; John DeCerchio, "Ososis, Fiat Passed Doner Philosophy," p. C6; Dale Pond, "Service-Oriented Ads Succeed for Lowe's," p. C8; Lloyd Fritzmeir, "Building Equity While Driving Sales for Arby's," p. C8; and Bob Purvis, "BP Goes for TV Creative," p. C10.

CHAPTER 19

PERSONAL SELLING AND SALES MANAGEMENT

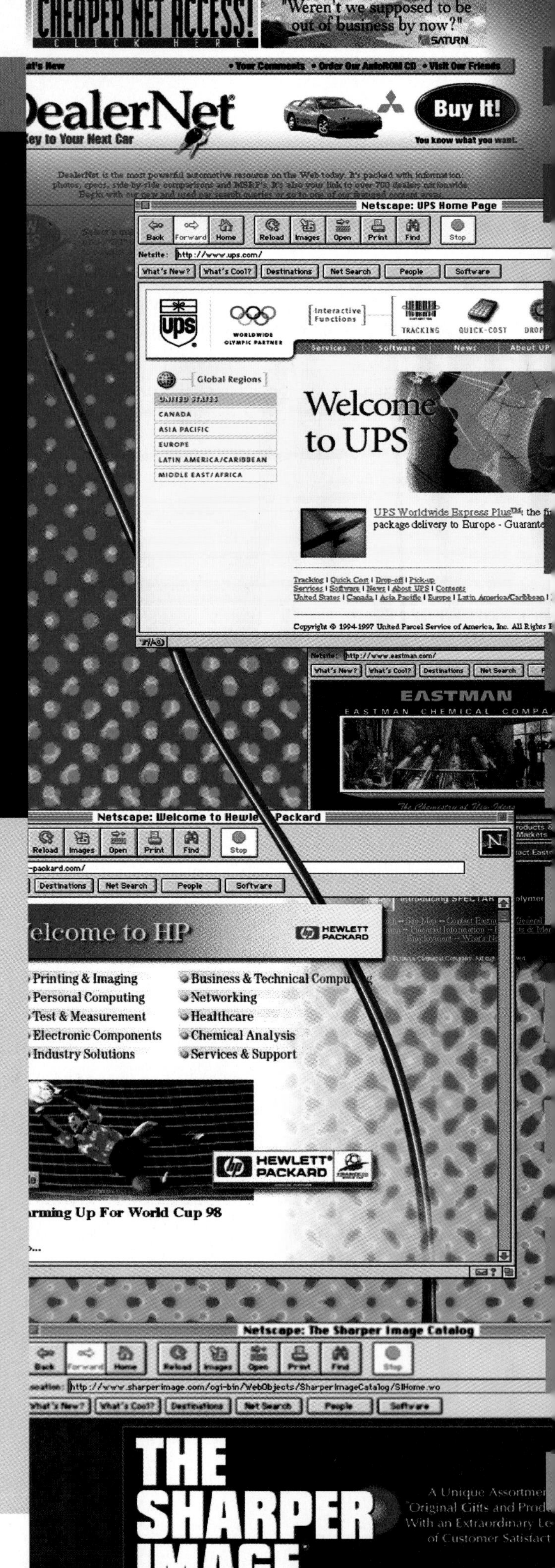

CHEAPER NET ACCESS!
CLICK HERE
"Weren't we supposed to be out of business by now?"
SATURN
• Your Comments • Order Our AutoROM CD • Visit Our Friends
Buy It!
You know what you want.
Netscape: UPS Home Page
http://www.ups.com/
Global Regions
UNITED STATES
CANADA
ASIA PACIFIC
EUROPE
LATIN AMERICA/CARIBBEAN
MIDDLE EAST/AFRICA
Welcome to UPS
TRACKING
QUICK-COST
http://www.eastman.com/
EASTMAN
Netscape: Welcome to Hewlett-Packard
HEWLETT PACKARD
Printing & Imaging
Personal Computing
Test & Measurement
Electronic Components
Industry Solutions
Networking
Healthcare
Chemical Analysis
Services & Support
Netscape: The Sharper Image Catalog
http://www.sharperimage.com/cgi-bin/WebObjects/SharperImageCatalog/SIHome.wo
THE SHARPER IMAGE

Chapter Objectives

1. Explain the conditions that determine the relative importance of personal selling in the promotional mix.
2. Contrast field selling, over-the-counter selling, and telemarketing.
3. Describe each of the four major trends in personal selling.
4. Identify the three basic sales tasks.
5. Outline the steps in the sales process.
6. Describe the sales manager's boundary-spanning role.
7. List and discuss the functions of sales management.
8. Discuss the role of ethics in personal selling and sales management.

Cyber-Kicking the Car Tires

Since long before the days of tail fins, automobiles have been bought and sold in essentially the same way. Each customer visited a dealership, met with a salesperson, listened to a presentation about the various models and features, took a test drive, and negotiated the price. All this is changing as consumers turn to new methods of buying cars. Now they can reach out via their personal computers to get specifications on all make and models, comparison shop, apply for loans, and get instant approval over the Internet.

Automakers, retail car dealers, and auto shoppers use technology to their advantage. By embracing Web sites and commercial online services, automakers and dealers help customers do their homework about brands, models, colors, and prices before contacting dealers. Chrysler Corp. has provided a good example of how car makers use technology to link dealers to interactive showrooms. Chrysler dealers use special software to create customized, high-quality Web pages targeted to specific car buyers' demographics and purchase considerations. The corporate Web site helps customers to locate dealers, complete with maps and information about hours, product lines, and phone numbers. Shoppers can browse through all sorts of buying information and compare several local dealers before they step into the showroom.

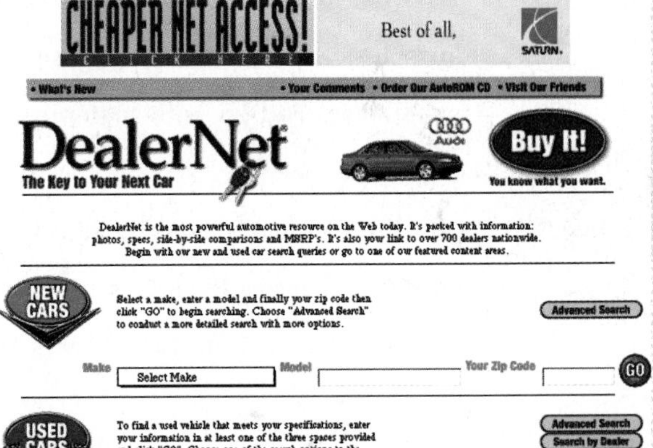
CHEAPER NET ACCESS!
Best of all,
SATURN.
• What's New
• Your Comments • Order Our AutoROM CD • Visit Our Friends
DealerNet
The Key to Your Next Car
Audi
Buy It!
You know what you want.
DealerNet is the most powerful automotive resource on the Web today. It's packed with information: photos, specs, side-by-side comparisons and MSRP's. It's also your link to over 700 dealers nationwide. Begin with our new and used car search queries or go to one of our featured content areas.
NEW CARS
Select a make, enter a model and finally your zip code then click "GO" to begin searching. Choose "Advanced Search" to conduct a more detailed search with more options.
Advanced Search
Make
Select Make
Model
Your Zip Code
GO
USED CARS
To find a used vehicle that meets your specifications, enter your information in at least one of the three spaces provided and click "GO". Choose one of the search options to the right to conduct a more specific search.
Advanced Search
Search by Dealer
List Dealers by State

An estimated 4,000 auto dealers have their own Web pages. In addition, a number of cybermarketing specialists have packaged offerings from a number of dealers. The DealerNet Virtual Showroom, shown here, provides Web page links to the virtual car lots of 44 different new and used auto retailers. Through DealerNet, shoppers can directly compare different cars by tapping into 8,000 pages of information on 1,600 different models.

http://www.chryslercorp.com/
http://dealernet.com/

Until recently, auto buyers who needed financing had to wait for hours or even days as loan applications were prepared, reviewed, and finally processed. ADP Dealer Services has responded to this opportunity by creating its AutoConnect system linked to Web pages of financing sources such as NationsBank and many auto dealers. When you access the system, special software analyzes your

application, pulls your credit report from a database, and tells you if you're approved. If everything works well, you simply go to the dealership to sign the loan papers and pick up the vehicle.

The big question, though, is whether cyberselling works. After all, buying an automobile ranks second only to buying a home among most people's major purchase decisions. Marketers at AutoByTel, a computerized auto-selling service, report huge successes. In its first nine months on the Internet, AutoByTel generated more than 50,000 requests for information. All this interest translated into more than $300 million in new-car purchases.

Not everyone reacts with enthusiasm to this new way of selling cars through virtual showrooms and arm-chair shopping. Some dealers worry that cybermarketing will hurt their profits by destroying traditional geographic boundaries between markets. "Every dealer has an exclusive territory where they expect to sell," says Hal Swartz, co-owner of a New Jersey Chrysler-Plymouth dealership. If online selling takes off, what will prevent other Chrysler dealers from trying to sell cars in Swartz's territory?

Still, many shoppers see substantial advantages over the traditional approach to auto purchases. In fact, consumers rate purchasing a car as their most anxiety-provoking and least satisfying retail experience. Fed up with high-pressure tactics at the retail showroom, they welcome these changes to the old system.

Some industry experts believe that dealers cannot escape the Internet if they hope to remain competitive. "Dealers have to participate in the future of automotive retailing," says Mark Thimming, a dealership consultant for Coopers & Lybrand. "It's the only way they will survive."[1]

CHAPTER OVERVIEW

Chapters 17 and 18 focused on the concept of promotion, the promotional mix, and the use of advertising and other nonpersonal promotional activities in achieving marketing objectives. This chapter will discuss the challenges involved in personal selling and outline the professional qualities that managers look for in hiring effective salespeople. Perhaps the most important attribute of a salesperson is the ability to communicate effectively with people.

Personal selling, as defined in Chapter 17, is an interpersonal influence process. Specifically, it involves a seller's promotional presentations conducted through a person-to-person contact with a buyer. This activity is an inherent function of any enterprise. Accounting, engineering, personnel, production, and other organizational activities produce no benefits unless a seller matches the firm's good or service to the need of a client or customer. The 15 million people employed in sales occupations in the United States testify to selling's importance. While the average firm's advertising expenses may represent from 1 to 3 percent of total sales, selling expenses likely equal 10 to 15 percent. In many firms, personal selling represents the single largest marketing expense.

Personal selling is likely to be the primary component of a firm's promotional mix in certain, well-defined conditions:

1. When consumers are geographically concentrated
2. When individual orders account for large amounts
3. When the firm markets expensive, technically complex goods or services, or when products require special handling
4. When transactions involve trade-ins
5. When products move through short channels
6. When the firm markets to relatively few potential customers

Table 19.1 summarizes the factors that influence the importance of personal selling in the overall promotional mix according to the type of variable involved: consumer, product, price, or distribution channels.

Table 19.1 Personal Selling versus Advertising in the Promotional Mix

Variable	Conditions That Favor Personal Selling	Conditions That Favor Advertising
Consumer	Geographically concentrated Relatively low numbers	Geographically dispersed Relatively high numbers
Product	Expensive Technically complex Custom made Special handling requirements Transactions frequently involve trade-ins	Inexpensive Simple to understand Standardized No special handling requirements Transactions seldom involve trade-ins
Price	Relatively high	Relatively low
Channels	Relatively short	Relatively long

THE EVOLUTION OF PERSONAL SELLING

Selling has been a standard business activity for thousands of years. The earliest peddlers sold goods in which they had some type of ownership interest after manufacturing or importing them. These people often viewed selling as a secondary activity.

Selling later became a separate business function. The peddlers of the eighteenth century sold to the farmers and settlers of the vast North American continent. In the nineteenth century, salespeople called *drummers* sold to both consumers and marketing intermediaries. These early sellers sometimes used questionable sales practices and techniques and earned undesirable reputations for themselves and their firms. Negative stereotypes persist today. To some people, the term *salesperson* conjures up unpleasant visions of Arthur Miller's antihero Willy Loman in *Death of a Salesman*:

> Willy is a salesman. . . . He don't put a bolt to a nut. He don't tell you the law or give you medicine. He's a man way out there in the blue, riding on a smile and a shoe shine. And when they start not smiling back—that's an earthquake.

But selling is far different from what it was in its early years. Far from the fast-talking, joke-telling, back-slapping caricatures in some novels and comic strips, today's salesperson is usually a professional. Professors Thomas Ingram and Raymond LaForge define *sales professionalism* as "a customer-oriented approach that employs truthful, nonmanipulative tactics to satisfy the long-term needs of both the customer and the selling firm."[2] Professional salespeople are problem solvers who focus on satisfying the needs of customers before, during, and after the sales. Armed with knowledge about their own firm's goods or services, those of competitors, and their customer's business needs, salespeople pursue a common goal of creating long-term relationships with customers.

Personal selling today is a vital, vibrant, dynamic process. As domestic and foreign competition increase the emphasis on productivity, personal selling is taking on a more prominent role in the corporate marketing mix. Salespeople must communicate the subtle advantages of their firms' goods and services over those of competitors. Their role has changed from persuader to consultant and problem solver. In addition, mergers and acquisitions along with a host of new products and promotions have expanded the scope and complexity of many selling jobs.

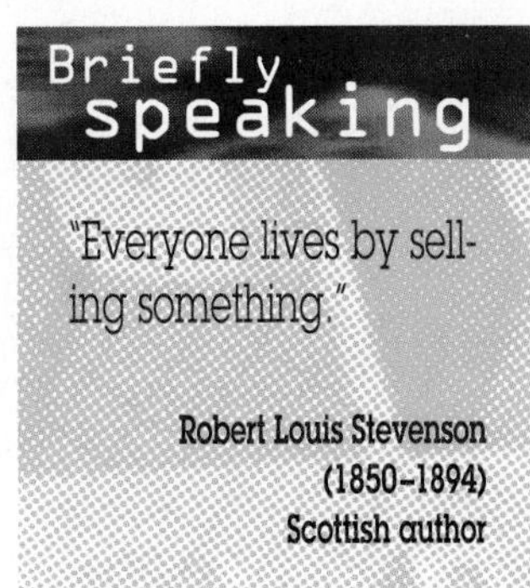
Briefly speaking
"Everyone lives by selling something."
Robert Louis Stevenson
(1850–1894)
Scottish author

As discussed in Chapter 10, the move toward relationship marketing affects all aspects of an organization's marketing function, including personal selling and sales management. This change involves marketers in both internal and external relationships and forces them to develop different sales skills. Instead of working alone, many salespeople now join their efforts in sales teams. The customer-focused firm wants its salespeople to form long-lasting relationships with buyers by providing high levels of customer service, rather than going for quick sales. Even the way salespeople perform their jobs is changing. Growing numbers of companies are

Marketing Dictionary

personal selling Interpersonal promotional process involving a seller's person-to-person presentation.

integrating communications and computer technologies into their sales routines. We will cover these trends in more detail later in the chapter.

Personal selling is an attractive career choice for today's college and university students. Approximately 60 percent of all marketing graduates choose sales jobs as their first marketing positions, in part because they see attractive job prospects. The Bureau of Labor Statistics projects that jobs in selling and marketing occupations requiring college degrees will show faster than average rates of growth as compared with all occupations during the next ten years. A sales background provides visibility for an individual and serves as an excellent route to the top of the corporate hierarchy. Many corporations are headed by executives who began their careers in sales.

THE THREE SELLING ENVIRONMENTS

When they think of personal selling, most people imagine end users buying products directly from salespeople, such as when people buy cars or clothes for their personal use. These are called *direct-to-customer sales.* However, many salespeople work at *business-to-business sales,* calling on wholesalers and retailers and selling to purchasing agents and committees in businesses, units of government, and institutions, such as schools and hospitals.

Personal selling occurs in several environments: field selling, inside selling, over-the-counter selling, and telemarketing. Each of these environments includes both business-to-business and direct-to-consumer selling.

Field Selling

Field selling involves making sales calls on prospective and existing customers at their businesses or homes. Some situations involve considerable creative effort, such as in-home sales of encyclopedias or insurance and industrial sales of major computer installations. Often the salesperson must convince customers first that they need the good or service and then that they need the particular product the salesperson is selling. Field sales of large industrial installations also often require considerable technical expertise.

Field selling is an essential ingredient in the Timken Company's marketing strategy. The firm's business-to-business sales force calls on industrial buyers in hundreds of industries around the world. Its sales professionals work to provide precision products wherever wheels or shafts turn, from disk drives to drilling rigs, from dental drills to rolling mills.

In fairly routine field selling situations, such as calling on established customers in industries like food, textiles, or wholesaling, salespeople may act basically as order takers who process regular customers' orders. Field selling may involve regular visits to local stores or businesses, or it may involve many days and nights of travel, by car or plane, every month. Salespeople who travel a great deal are frequently labeled *road warriors.* A recent study found that over half of the

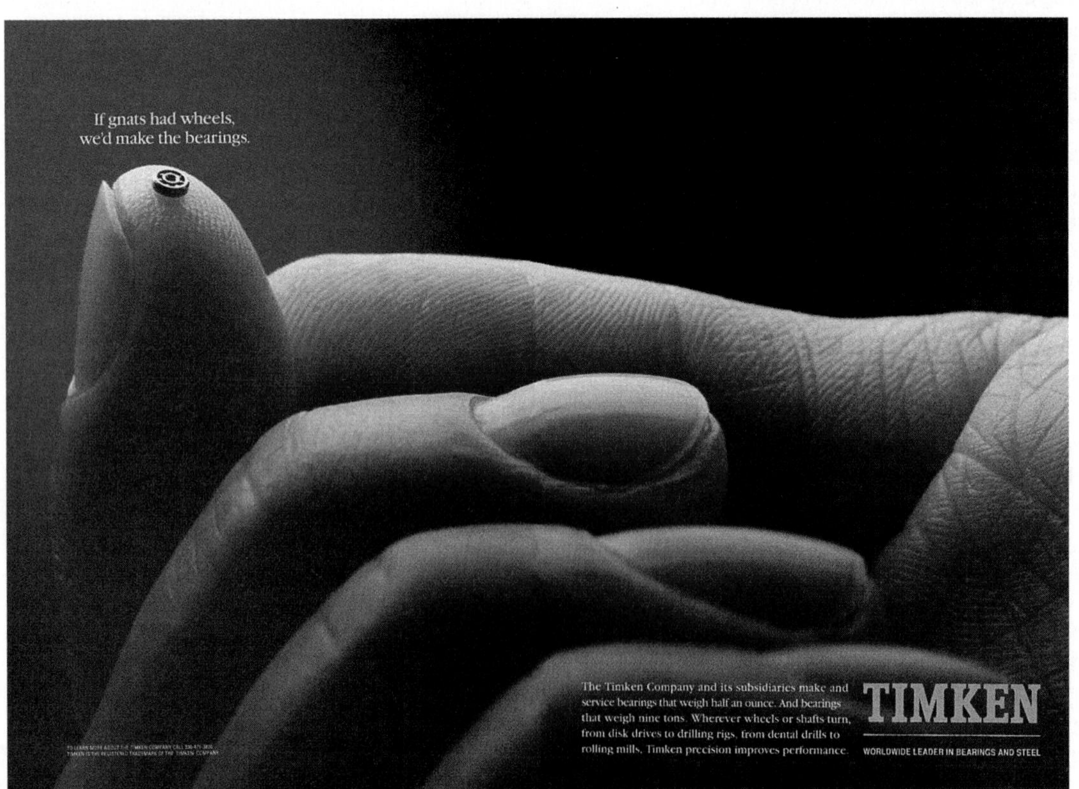
If gnats had wheels,
we'd make the bearings.
The Timken Company and its subsidiaries make and service bearings that weigh half an ounce. And bearings that weigh nine tons. Wherever wheels or shafts turn, from disk drives to drilling rigs, from dental drills to rolling mills. Timken precision improves performance.
TIMKEN
WORLDWIDE LEADER IN BEARINGS AND STEEL

Although advertising aids the Timken sales efforts by increasing buyer awareness of the firm and its line of high quality bearings and steel products, the firm's promotional emphasis is on one-to-one continuing relationships between its highly-trained professional sales force and industrial buyers around the world.

salespeople surveyed spent more than $500 per month on travel with an average cost of $2,045 a month.

American companies that practice direct-to-consumer field selling, like Avon and Amway, have moved into global markets. For example, over 15,000 Russian Avon ladies sell cosmetics. However, unlike in the United States, where salespeople go to customers' homes and offices, in Russia they sell in factories, airports, and other public places. "Russians are afraid to open their doors to strangers," explained Maria Geraysova, Avon's Russian sales director. Also, those customers don't want people coming into their homes and passing judgment on their housekeeping. Despite these differences, Russian sales of Avon products are soaring from the increased desire for Western goods. Russian women like the products, whose prices are below those of European brands sold in department stores. Avon has no shortage of sales force recruits, either, because the firm pays salaries considerably higher than what the women could earn in other professions.[3]

http://www.avon.com/

Over-the-Counter Selling

The second sales environment, **over-the-counter selling,** typically describes selling in retail and some wholesale locations. Most over-the-counter sales involve direct-to-customer transactions, although wholesalers serve business customers. Customers visit the seller's location on their own initiative to purchase desired items. Some visit their favorite stores because they enjoy shopping and consider it a type of leisure activity. Others come in response to many kinds of invitations, including direct-mail appeals, personal letters of invitation from store personnel, and advertisements for sales, special events, and new-product introductions. From the salesperson at Egghead Software to the diamond purveyor at Tiffany's, this type of selling typically involves providing product information and arranging for completion of sales transactions.

Telemarketing

The telephone provides a third environment for personal selling, **telemarketing,** in which salespeople make their presentations through telephone calls. Telemarketing serves two general purposes—sales and service—and two general markets—business-to-business and direct-to-customer markets. (Marketing research surveys are not usually considered as part of telemarketing.) As Chapter 17 noted, telemarketing is a form of direct marketing that can be classified by outbound and inbound messages.

Outbound telemarketing involves a sales force that relies on the telephone to contact customers. This selling approach is designed to reduce the substantial costs of personal visits to customers' homes or businesses. Most consumers have had the experience of being interrupted—and perhaps annoyed—by outbound telemarketers. Surveys indicate that up to 60 percent of consumers are so bothered by telemarketing that they will not listen to a telephone sales presentation.

Why, then, is outbound telemarketing such a popular sales technique? Companies like it because it is cost-effective and it works. An average telemarketing call costs less than $10, while an average field sales call costs almost $500. Despite some people's annoyance at receiving unsolicited calls, others do respond. Outbound calling has a 6 to 8 percent positive response rate, compared to only 2 percent for a standard direct-mail appeal. Telemarketers can evaluate their success in various ways: total calls made per work shift, calls per hour, revenue per sale or per hour, and profitability, among others.[4] In general, outbound telemarketing calls geared to men get the best responses between 7 P.M. and 9 P.M., whereas women tend to respond more favorably to telemarketers between 10 A.M. and 4 P.M.

The effectiveness of telemarketing as a sales technique is demonstrated by the size of the industry. Over 900 telemarketing agencies currently employ almost 5 million people in the United States. The industry is a major employer of workers with special career needs: college students, people with disabilities, senior citizens, full-time homemakers, and people with second jobs.

At the same time, the technique has produced enough consumer complaints about unwanted calls to prompt action by regulatory agencies. Since 1996, the Federal Trade Commission's Telemarketing Sales Rules (outlined in

Marketing Dictionary

field selling Face-to-face sales presentations made at prospective customers' homes or businesses.

over-the-counter selling Personal selling conducted in retail and some wholesale locations in which customers visit the seller's place of business on their own initiative.

telemarketing Promotional presentation involving outbound telephone contacts by salespeople or inbound contacts by customers who want to obtain information and place orders.

Figure 19.1 **What Telemarketers Must—and Must Not—Do**

- Identify the caller.
- Restrict calls to daytime and early evening hours (not after 9 P.M.).
- Maintain a do-not-call list. Consumers who ask not to be contacted again should not receive calls for one year. Violators are subject to legal action by the consumer, Federal Communications Commission, and state attorney general.
- Disclose the total cost of all goods or services along with refund policies.
- Release the phone line within five seconds after an autodialer recognizes that the other party has hung up the phone.
- Never send unsolicited advertisements by fax.
- Disclose the odds of winning prizes and any restrictions on winning prizes or receiving merchandise. Also, specify that the customer does not have to make a purchase to win a prize.

Figure 19.1) have granted certain protections to consumers. The requirements do not, however, apply to calls placed by charities and political organizations.

Inbound telemarketing typically involves a toll-free phone number that customers can call to obtain information, make reservations, and purchase goods and services. This form of selling provides maximum convenience for customers who initiate the sales process. Many large catalog merchants like The Sharper Image, Lillian Vernon, and Lands' End, maintain open inbound telemarketing lines 24 hours a day, seven days a week. Indeed, one can call L. L. Bean even on Christmas Day to place an order! Inbound telemarketing has become so widespread that the supply of 800 numbers recently ran out. The Federal Communications Commission has recently set up a new 888 phone exchange to accommodate the daily requests for new toll-free numbers.

http://www.sharperimage.com/

Most firms use telemarketing to support other types of selling. Telemarketing supports the internal sales effort at Household Bank, a savings bank with 180 branches around the United States. Recently, the bank implemented a major telemarketing campaign to tell checking and savings account customers about other services that it offered. This relationship-oriented bank trains its marketing representatives to use relationship selling techniques to learn customers' needs before launching into sales presentations.[5]

Some firms sell only through telemarketing. CDW Computer Centers of Buffalo Grove, Illinois, is a major, catalog-based direct seller of computer products. Its catalog features over 20,000 hardware, software, and peripheral products. The fast-growing company attributes its 75 percent average annual earnings growth to its training program for telemarketing salespeople. After four weeks of training, new sales representatives spend additional time in the company's showroom familiarizing themselves with products. When they join the sales team, they bring not only strong sales and service skills but solid product knowledge as well.

CDW places a premium on customer service. Both business and individual customers need to feel comfortable with the salespeople who are advising them on purchases of technical products. The salesperson who makes initial contact with a customer retains that account. "Our account executives are trained to develop one-to-one relationships with our customers so that we become the supplier of choice," explains Harry Harczak, chief financial officer. The program is working; CDW's customer database is the source of 80 percent of its sales.[6]

RECENT TRENDS IN PERSONAL SELLING

Personal selling today requires different strategies than salespeople practiced in the past. Rather than selling one-on-one, salespeople may sell to teams of corporate repre-

Table 19.2 Buyer's Expectations from Salespeople

Buyers prefer to do business with salespeople who:

- Orchestrate events and bring to bear whatever resources are necessary to satisfy the customer
- Provide counseling to the customer based on in-depth knowledge of the product, the market, and the customer's needs
- Solve problems extremely proficiently to ensure satisfactory customer service over extended time periods
- Demonstrate high ethical standards and communicate honestly at all times
- Willingly advocate the customer's cause within the selling organization
- Create imaginative arrangements to meet buyers' needs
- Arrive well-prepared for sales calls

sentatives called *decision-making units.* Especially in business-to-business sales situations involving technical products, customers expect salespeople to answer technical questions—or to bring along someone who can. They also want representatives to understand technical jargon and communicate using sophisticated technological tools. Patience is also required, because the sales cycle for a single transaction, from initial contact to closing, may take years. The average industrial sale takes at least four sales calls to close, and the parties spend even more time as purchases involve larger and more expensive products.[7]

To address these concerns, companies are turning to relationship selling, consultative selling, team selling, and sales-force automation—major personal selling trends affecting the sales forces of companies of all sizes. This section will briefly explain these trends, which have taken root in recent years. The balance of the chapter will then examine their effects on personal selling activities.

Relationship Selling

As competitive pressures mount, more firms are emphasizing **relationship selling,** a technique in which a salesperson builds a mutually beneficial relationship with a customer through regular contacts over an extended period. Such buyer-seller bonds become increasingly important as companies buy more inputs from fewer suppliers and look for companies that provide strong customer service and satisfaction. Salespeople must also find ways to distinguish themselves from others selling similar products. To create strong, long-lasting relationships with customers, salespeople must meet buyers' expectations. Table 19.2 summarizes the results of several surveys that indicate what buyers expect of professional salespeople.

Customer relationships have become so important in personal selling that many companies now encourage buyers to shop for sales representatives before buying from their firms. Prudential Securities, for example, ran an advertising campaign that emphasized the importance of finding an account executive who understands the client's needs and exhibits the right investment style.

Relationship selling is especially important in business-to-business sales. Veteran salesperson Larry Maunder, who rose through the ranks to become vice president of sales at Cascade Corp. in Portland, Oregon, believes that this strategy is the only one that works in industrial selling—and the key to repeat business. It has brought success at Cascade, the leading manufacturer of lift-truck attachments in the world. Not only does the company have the lion's share of the competitive U.S. market, but it also has about 70 percent of the world market. Maunder attributes this market domination to the loyal relationships that the company has forged with independent dealers and extensive repeat business. He encourages his sales managers and representatives to learn all they can about customers and their problems as a way to win their trust. High-pressure sales techniques may bring short-term orders, but these methods do not lead to long-term relationships. "Relationship selling is not about getting an order; it is about convincing customers that you will be there after the order, no matter what," he explains.[8]

Marketing Dictionary

relationship selling Regular contacts over an extended period to establish a sustained seller-buyer relationship.

A more formalized version of relationship selling is *partnering,* in which two or more companies agree to pursue multiple business solutions together. Chapter 10 described how partnerships can take many forms and involve different stages of the supply chain. Companies that establish sales-oriented partnerships with their suppliers discover benefits beyond cost savings and operational efficiencies. Such relationships improve cooperation, customer service, and trust.[9]

Unlike transaction selling, in which the sales presentation focuses on product features, functions, price, and performance, partnering is a complex sales process that often involves reciprocal commitments and the sharing of internal company data between buyer and seller. Through its 24 diversified businesses, GE Capital engages in strategic partnerships with thousands of other firms. In addition to providing creative financing for its clients, GE Capital can handle such functions as domestic and international transportation. As Figure 19.2 points out, the firm follows a customer-oriented motto: "Our business is helping yours."

Consultative Selling

The once-popular "good-old boy" sales style—getting chummy with customers, buying meals or drinks, giving the standard sales presentation, applying pressure, and expecting to get the sale on that basis—is rapidly going the way of the dinosaur. Today's salespeople need a different model to satisfy cost-conscious, knowledgeable buyers. They are moving toward **consultative selling,** which involves meeting customer needs by listening to customers, understanding—and caring about—their problems, paying attention to details, and following through after the sale. It works hand-in-hand with relationship selling to build customer loyalty.

Customers respond to committed consultative sellers. Carrie Thomas is a leading sales representative for Duplex Products, a Detroit producer of business forms and systems. Her success is best explained by customer Linda Zitka of GMAC, the General Motors financing unit: "She picks up on things I never realized I told her," says Zitka. "I get the feeling that it's her project as well as mine." Thomas' softer selling technique also wins points—and more business—as she looks for long-term solutions and ways to help GMAC become more efficient rather than making blatant sales presentations.

Women tend to excel in consultative selling. John Pickens, a sales manager for New Orleans-based Entergy Corp., a major electric utility, points out that men who are good consultative sellers display the same strengths as the successful women sales representatives. But it's the women who set the standards, he acknowledges.[10]

Figure 19.2 GE Capital: Building Long-Term Relationships through Problem Solving and Strategic Partnering

Our Business Is Helping Yours®
Do What You Do Best...Even Better.

Your business has a good foundation. Now it's time to build on it. But you could be serving your clients in ways you haven't yet dreamed of. And we can help. We go beyond creative financing by providing innovative solutions to all kinds of business needs. Like helping a circus move across the country by supplying the needed vans and flatbeds through a flexible one-way rental program. Or helping a company solve technological problems with its computer network, and tap into global markets by creating administrative software to allow the service of global customers.
At GE Capital, we're 24 diversified businesses. Each one devoted to helping you build your business–so you can do what you do best...even better. To find out more, call 1-800-243-2222.

GE Capital
Our Business Is Helping Yours®

Team Selling

One of the latest developments in the evolution of personal selling is **team selling,** in which the salesperson joins with specialists from other functional areas of the firm to complete the selling process. Teams can maintain formal, continuing positions within the firm or join forces for a specific, temporary selling situation. Some salespeople have hesitated to embrace the idea of team selling. Many still view personal selling as a "Lone Ranger" kind of profession, with a salesperson working pretty much alone, except for long-distance supervision and regular monitoring of sales results. However, in sales situations that call for detailed knowledge of new, complex, and ever-changing technologies, team selling can give a company a competitive edge in meeting customers' needs. Many customers prefer to interact with teams, which make them feel well-served. For another advantage, team selling helps to form relationships between companies rather than individuals.[11]

Recall from Chapter 10 that Saturn builds in the concepts of teams and relationships throughout the organization, including selling. The customer pays the listed sticker price—without the age-old haggling that set salesperson against customer. When you pick up your car, you are surrounded by a team of representatives from sales, service, parts, and reception, all trained in customer relations. They let out a cheer, snap your picture, and hand you the keys, in a ritual that indicates the Saturn's devotion to the idea of a long-term customer relationship.

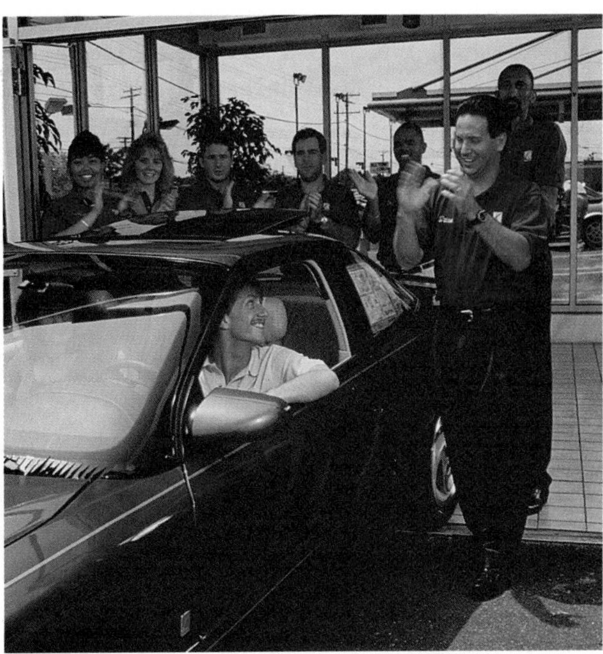

The Saturn team—from sales, customer service, and parts—join with the customer to make the auto purchase experience both memorable and rewarding, and to celebrate the beginning of a long-term relationship.

Sales Force Automation

A major trend in personal selling is **sales force automation (SFA)**—the application of new technologies to the sales process. Broadly, the term encompasses tools from pagers and cellular phones, to voice and electronic mail, to laptop and notebook computers. More narrowly, it refers to the use of computers by salespeople for activities beyond the basic functions of word processors, spreadsheets, and connections to order-entry systems.

The benefits of SFA include improvements in the quality and effectiveness of sales calls due to improved access to information; low selling, printing, and training costs; improved product launches; and attentive customer service. For example, Executone Systems, a vendor of voice communication systems, discovered that its pilot SFA program reduced the cost of a sale to one-third the original cost. Beverage Distributors Corp.'s $250,000 investment in notebook computers saved the company a minimum of $800 per month in phone charges and $150,000 a year in postage.[12]

SFA usage differs sharply by industry: food, beverage, and pharmaceutical industries are using sophisticated, third-generation systems, whereas many apparel companies have not yet moved to SFA. A recent survey showed that for about half the top salespeople, a cellular phone was the extent of the new technology they used.

Software for sales force automation falls into several categories. Most salespeople use basic productivity and general purpose programs like word processors, e-mail, and spreadsheets. Contact managers help salespeople organize their prospect lists and remember when to make follow-up calls. More expensive systems may integrate order processing and other types of information.[13]

Some traditional salespeople argue that selling requires a process of telephone calls and face-to-face interactions,—which, they say, can't be replaced by technology. However, automation can increase productivity and free up time for more and better-focused sales calls. Andy Miller, sales manager for Kids Stop, a reseller of closeout children's clothing, uses a sales management computer program to send faxes to major accounts. Instead of

Marketing Dictionary

consultative selling Meeting customer needs by listening to them, understanding—and caring about—their problems, paying attention to details, and following through after the sale.

team selling Combination of salespeople with specialists from other functional areas to promote a product.

sales force automation (SFA) Applications of computers and other technologies to improve the efficiency and competitiveness of the sales function.

Five essential functions. One machine.
Combine a Xerox Document WorkCenter™ 250 with your brilliant ideas, and you've got everything you need to do your best work ever. Right at home.
It's a fax, a printer, a copier, a scanner and a PC fax. Everything about the Document WorkCenter was designed to make you more productive, more professional than ever.
It handles multiple jobs simultaneously, so you'll never miss a fax or wait to print. And super-high resolution means clear text and crisp images. Everything looks smart and professional. Including you.
We've even included award-winning TextBridge Professional Edition® software. This easy-to-use package lets you scan in any document from the Document WorkCenter straight into your own word processing program. Imagine bringing paper to life. No re-typing. No wasted time.
The Document WorkCenter's easy to install, easy to use. And at $699, it's also easy to afford. That price even includes our *Service While You Sleep* program, a big part of the Xerox commitment to customer service. It means if you should ever have a problem, we'll bring a free replacement to your door the next business day.
$699
Visit Office Depot, OfficeMax or Staples to learn more and take one home. You can also visit us at http://www.xerox.com/soho.html or just phone 1-800-TEAMXRX, extension 804.
You'll discover the Document WorkCenter 250 truly is a simpler way to do good work.
You're on your own, but you're not alone.
Fax
Scan
Copy
PC Fax
Print
DOCUMENT WorkCenter 250
The all-in-one office partner.
THE DOCUMENT COMPANY
XEROX

Sales force automation tools such as the Xerox WorkCenter 250, which combines printing, photocopying, faxing, and scanning capabilities in a single machine, allow salespeople to complete multiple tasks simultaneously and to work from their homes.

calling only 25 people a day by phone, he can automatically send a promotional offer by fax to hundreds of accounts at night—and have orders waiting for him in the morning. He can also consult his account database to target certain groups, such as buyers for toddlers' clothing. In just one year, his active accounts grew from 100 to 600.[14]

With SFA tools, both large and small companies can increase their efficiency and spend more time on client acquisition and retention. Indeed, 31 percent of companies surveyed about the rewards of SFA cited improvements in customer service and satisfaction as the top benefit, while 24 percent emphasized productivity gains.[15] SFA helps both large and small companies to improve sales force productivity. Qiagen, a California biotechnology company, outfitted its 40 salespeople with modem-equipped laptop computers. Instead of communicating with headquarters via the phone and overnight courier services, the salespeople received weekly updates and information about new sales prospects via modem. Not only have sales increased, but the company has spent less on computers than on its ongoing courier charges.[16]

Perhaps the ultimate outcome of SFA is the *virtual office,* a work-place that exists in only electronic space. *Voice mail,* a computer-based, call-processing system that can handle both incoming and outgoing calls, is a key fixture of the virtual office. It enables sales representatives to communicate with customers through a sort of electronic bulletin board. Information such as price changes, sales-incentive programs, and meeting times can be transmitted by giving customers a digital code, eliminating the need to play "telephone tag" when salespeople are away from the phone.

IBM has created an entire sales region made up of virtual offices. IBM salespeople and sales managers in its midwestern region—a total of 15,000 employees—no longer have assigned offices. Instead, they work from their homes. The company provides extra phone lines, computers, faxes, and other equipment at its own expense. Anyone who needs an office for the day goes to one of IBM's eight regional "office hotels." The company has saved $12 million a year in costs for physical space and, equally important, has pushed salespeople into the field near their customers.[17]

SALES TASKS

Today's salesperson is more concerned with establishing long-term buyer-seller relationships and helping customers select products that will meet their needs than with simply selling any available goods or services. Where repeat purchases are common, the salesperson must help buyers settle on purchases in their own best interests; otherwise, dissatisfaction will prevent future sales. The salesperson must remember that the seller's interests are tied to the buyer's in a symbiotic relationship.

Not all selling situations require the same activities. While all sales activities assist customers in some manner, the exact tasks that salespeople perform vary from one position to another. Still, three fundamental sales tasks form the basis of a sales classification system: (1) order processing, (2) creative selling, and (3) missionary sales.

However, most sales personnel do not fall into a single category; they often perform all three tasks to some extent. A sales engineer for a computer firm may spend 50 percent of his or her work time on missionary sales, 45 percent on creative selling, and 5 percent on order processing. Most selling jobs are classified on the basis of these primary selling tasks.

Most businesses focus sharply on improving productivity throughout their operations, and sales force productivity does not escape attention. With the climbing cost of travel and compensation for experienced salespeople, each sales rep must spend time efficiently and effectively in order to raise productivity.

Order Processing

Order processing can involve both field selling and telemarketing, but it is most often typified by selling at the wholesale and retail levels. For instance, a Pepsi-Cola route salesperson who performs this task must take the following steps:

1. *Identify customer needs.* The route salesperson determines that a store has only 7 cases left in stock when it normally carries an inventory of 40 cases.
2. *Point out the need to the customer.* The route salesperson informs the store manager of the inventory situation.
3. *Complete (write up) the order.* The store manager acknowledges the need for more product. The driver unloads 33 cases, and the manager signs the delivery slip.

Order processing is part of most selling positions. It becomes the primary sales task in situations with readily identified needs acknowledged by the customer. Even in such instances, however, salespeople who work primarily processing orders will seek to convince their wholesale or retail customers to carry more complete inventories of their firms' products or to handle additional product lines. They also try to motivate purchasers to feature some of their firms' products in special displays, increase the amount of shelf space devoted to their products, and improve products' locations in the stores.

Sales force automation is easing order processing tasks. In the past, salespeople would write up order documents on customers' premises but spent much time after the sales visit completing the orders and transmitting them to headquarters. Today, many companies have automated order processing. With portable computers and state-of-the-art software, a salesperson can place an order, on the spot, directly to headquarters, thus freeing up valuable time and energy. Computers have even eliminated the need for some of the traditional face-to-face contacts for routine reorders.

Wal-Mart was an early adopter of SFA. In the 1980s, the retail giant installed an information system that electronically transmits inventory replacement orders from retail stores directly to the company's distribution centers and even its suppliers. The information system triggers orders based on reorder guidelines established at Wal-Mart headquarters. Suppliers' salespeople can now concentrate on providing new-product information and enhancing merchandising support.[18] As SFA takes over order processing tasks, it frees salespeople for more creative selling.

Creative Selling

When a purchase requires considerable analytical decision making, the salesperson must use **creative selling** techniques to solicit an order. While the order processing task deals primarily with maintaining existing business, creative selling generally seeks to develop new business by either adding new customers or introducing new goods and services. New products often require energetic creative selling. The salesperson must first identify the customer's problems and needs and then propose a solution based on the new good or service. Creative selling may occur in telemarketing, over-the-counter selling, and field selling. It may be the most demanding of the three sales tasks.

Creative selling may demand that a firm reorganize its entire approach to sales. James River Corp. sells a variety of paper products such as paper plates, napkins, toilet tissue, and Dixie cups to retailers. James River used to send three or more salespeople to grocery chains, each selling one product line. If all three sales representatives secured orders, the store had to buy a full truckload of each product from each salesperson to get the lowest price. Today, a team of product experts calls on the store to sell the retailer truckloads with mixed products at the lowest price. This change reduced inventory costs for James River's customers, and sales teams have benefited by sharing marketing information about how shoppers buy paper products.

Marketing Dictionary

order processing Selling, mostly at the wholesale and retail levels, that involves identifying customer needs, pointing them out to customers, and completing orders.

creative selling Personal selling situations in which buyers must complete considerable analytical decision making, creating a need for skillful proposals of solutions for customer needs.

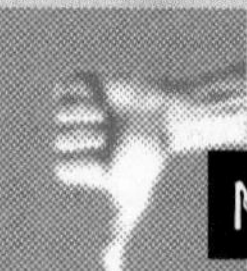

MARKETING HALL OF SHAME

The Worst Sale Ever Made

A title like this is bound to set you thinking about the subject of this feature. Some of the world's best purchases are also the worst sales. With this in mind, lots of candidates fall into this category: the $24 price tag to buy Manhattan Island, Jack trading the family cow for those magical beans, Bill Gates paying a few thousand dollars for the rights to MS-DOS. This story, however, is about Sears, the store that personified retailing for most of the twentieth century. In fact, it wasn't until the early 1990s that Wal-Mart was able to knock Sears off its perch as the nation's largest retailer.

The company's formal name is Sears, Roebuck & Company. And, as you might have guessed, the company was actually founded by two partners, Richard W. Sears and Alvah C. Roebuck. The story of their partnership and Roebuck's eventual decision to sell his half of the company is certainly a candidate for the worst sale ever made.

The retailing legacy began in 1886 when Richard W. Sears, a Minnesota railway agent, bought a shipment of watches being returned to its maker. With his timepieces, he launched R. W. Sears Watch Co. and six months later moved to Chicago.

Needing a watch repairman with his own tools, Sears placed a classified ad in a newspaper. The man he hired was none other than Roebuck who had traveled from Hammond, Indiana, to apply for the job. In 1889, Sears sold the watch business, but he remained wedded to the world of retail. Sears and Roebuck, both ambitious young men in their twenties, formed a mail-order business that in 1893 was christened Sears, Roebuck & Company. In 1896, the partners produced their first mail-order catalog, full of merchandise and some amazing inducements. The company offered its customers—who were primarily farmers—low prices and money-back guarantees.

Starting a small business at the turn of the century—or any other period for that matter—wasn't easy. The two partners experienced tough financial times. At one point, Sears left the company, only to return a short time later. Then Roebuck decided to quit, making the fateful decision to sell his part of the business for $25,000.

In hindsight, it was a huge mistake. Scrambling to enlarge its mail-order inventory, the company was about to become a retailing giant. Just how bad the de-

By rearranging their displays based on this information, retailers won market share from competing stores.[19]

Robert Talbott Inc., a California maker of bow ties, used SFA to expand its creative selling effort. With the constant change in men's fashions and new competition from big retailers like J. Crew and the Gap, Talbott management realized the importance of sales flexibility. A recently adopted pen-based information system allows its sales force to access proprietary software, developed especially for the firm, along with up-to-the-minute information on product availability. The salesperson can, with the touch of the unit's special pen, enter orders for anywhere from a few ties to thousands of them, in any available color and pattern combination the customer wants. Information on pattern and color outages can be obtained on the same day the order is placed, helping salespeople to maintain customer service and improve goodwill for Talbott.[20]

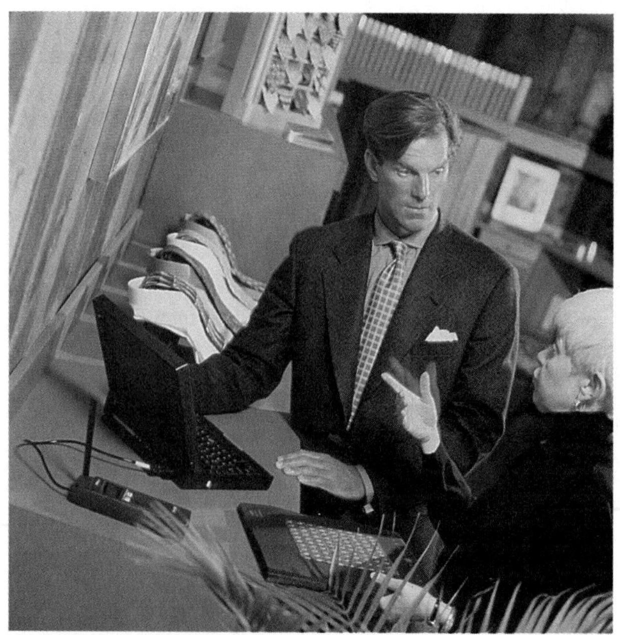

With Talbott's sales force automation system, sales reps use real-time information on color and pattern availability to complete complex customer orders.

Missionary Sales

In **missionary sales,** an indirect type of selling, salespeople sell the firm's goodwill and provide information and

cision was would only be apparent much later. The retailer's humble start as a catalog company exploded in a dizzying series of expansions. In 1924, it opened its first retail store to let farmers actually handle the merchandise before they bought it. A year later, Sears rolled out a line of tires called Allstate, which eventually expanded into an insurance powerhouse. The Illinois company eventually became so big that it went on a buying binge, gobbling up other companies. It bought a shopping center development company in the late 1950s and acquired several savings and loans. Meanwhile in the 1970s and 1980s, the retailer diversified into financial services by acquiring Coldwell Banker, the real estate outfit, and Dean Witter Reynolds, the stock brokerage firm. The creator of the Discover Card also bankrolled the Sears Tower, which at the time was the world's tallest building. With partners, it even launched Prodigy, the online service, long before most people knew what the Internet was.

All that diversification eventually bedeviled the retailing legend. Wall Street abandoned the stock as investors questioned whether Sears could pull out of its financial funk. But in the 1990s Sears bounded back. After shedding its ancillary businesses, Sears was once again just a retailer—the first time since 1931. Thanks to its restructuring, sales are once again healthy.

The company's longevity would have surprised Roebuck, who never completely severed his ties with Sears. During its boom years, his old partner offered Roebuck his former stake in the company. Roebuck declined, but he did become a salaried employee of the company. Eventually Roebuck left to start a business that made motion picture projectors. Later he became a real estate agent in Florida, but that venture failed. Some time after his friend and partner Richard Sears had died, Roebuck returned once more to Chicago and finally retired from Sears as a clerk. When he died in 1948, his only financial claim to Sears was the stock from his profit-sharing plan.

QUESTIONS FOR CRITICAL THINKING

1. **Do you think bad business decisions, such as the one Alvah Roebuck made, happen every day?**
2. **Can you think of other sales that were as poorly timed as Roebuck's?**

Sources: "Sears Roebuck Earnings Up 20 Percent," Reuters, April 17, 1997, downloaded from http://pathfinder.com/business/, May 21, 1997; "Sears, Roebuck and Co.," *Hoover Business Profiles,* downloaded from America Online, December 3, 1996.; and Cyndee Miller, "Sears Comeback an Event Most Marketers Would Kill For," *Marketing News,* July 15, 1996, pp. 1, 14.

technical or operational assistance. For example, a toiletries company's salesperson may call on retailers to check on special promotions and overall stock movement, even though a wholesaler actually takes orders and delivers merchandise. A pharmaceuticals salesperson seeks to persuade doctors (the indirect customers) to specify the company's product brand in prescriptions. However, the company actually completes ultimate sales through a wholesaler or directly to the pharmacists who fill prescriptions.

Missionary sales may involve both field selling and telemarketing. Many aspects of team selling can also be seen as missionary sales, as when technical support salespeople help to design, install, and maintain equipment, when they train customers' employees, and when they provide information or operational assistance. For example, Hallmark fields teams of sales and marketing personnel who concentrate on pleasing the retailers who buy its greeting cards. Hallmark used to sell pretty much the same mix of cards to every store, but sales teams now can customize a retailer's selection. Missionary salespeople use information gathered by bar-code systems for items sold at individual stores, along with merchandising information sent from headquarters to their laptop computers, to develop specific displays and promotions tailored to a retail market's demographics.[21]

THE SALES PROCESS

After describing various selling environments and sales tasks, the chapter now considers how salespeople actually sell. If you have worked in a retail store or simply sold candy or wrapping paper to raise money for your band, swim team, or other organization, you will recognize some

Marketing Dictionary

missionary sales Indirect type of selling in which specialized salespeople promote the firm's goodwill among indirect customers, often by assisting in product use.

of these activities, although perhaps you didn't know how they were formally classified.

What are the steps involved in selling? While the terminology may vary, most authorities agree on the following sequence: (1) prospecting and qualifying, (2) approach, (3) presentation, (4) demonstration, (5) handling objections, (6) closing, and (7) follow-up.

As Figure 19.3 indicates, the steps in the personal selling process follow the attention-interest-desire-action (AIDA) concept discussed in Chapter 17. Once a salesperson has qualified a prospect, he or she attempts to secure that buyer's attention. The presentation and demonstration steps are designed to generate interest and desire. Successful handling of buyer objections should arouse further desire. Action occurs at the close of the sale.

Salespeople modify the steps in this process to match their customers' buying processes. The Girl Scout whose Aunt Ada buys boxes and boxes of Thin Mint cookies every year probably needs no presentation and could just call to say she's taking cookie orders. She might also remind her aunt about how much she appreciates each year's order and highlight the new cookies in the hope of adding some to the standard order. If every other house has a girl also selling the cookies, the scout may need to join with other members of her troop to find new customers in different locations, such as the lobbies of local grocery stores.

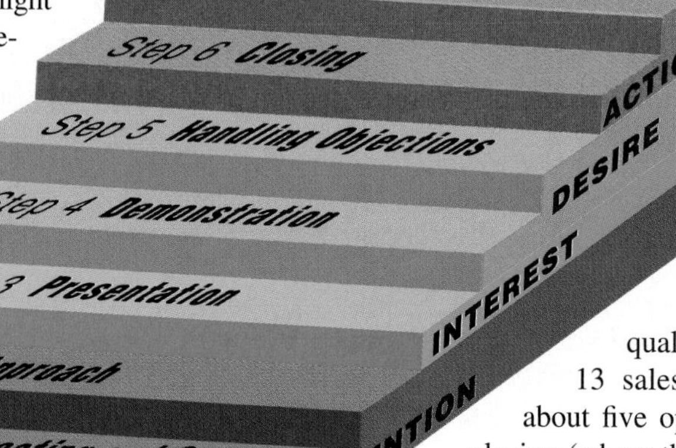
Step 7 Follow-Up
Step 6 Closing
Step 5 Handling Objections
Step 4 Demonstration
Step 3 Presentation
Step 2 Approach
Step 1 Prospecting and Qualify
ACTION
DESIRE
INTEREST
ATTENTION

Figure 19.3 The AIDA Concept and the Personal Selling Process

Prospecting and Qualifying

Prospecting, efforts to identify potential customers, is difficult work involving many hours of diligent effort. Leads about prospects may come from many sources: computerized databases, trade show exhibits, previous customers, friends and neighbors, other vendors, nonsales employees in the firm, suppliers, and social and professional contacts. While a firm may emphasize personal selling as the primary component of its overall promotional strategy, direct mail and advertising campaigns also help to identify prospective customers.

The advertisement shown in Figure 19.4 is designed to inform art-supplies purchasers of the creative and colorful assortments available from Plaza Artist Materials. The goal of the message is to encourage visits by artists to the firm's retail outlets in New York, Nashville, Richmond, and Silver Spring, Maryland, where knowledgeable salespeople will assist them.

New sales personnel may feel frustrated by prospecting, because they usually receive no immediate payback. Without prospecting, however, they will make no future sales. Firms must seek out potential users of new and existing goods and services. Prospecting is a continuous process, because the firm will inevitably lose some customers over time, and new potential customers or first-time prospects will emerge.

Qualifying—determining that the prospect really is a potential customer—is another important sales task. Not all prospects are qualified to make purchase decisions. A person with an annual income of $25,000 may wish to own a $200,000 house, but he or she brings a questionable ability to actually become a real-estate customer.

Qualifying can work two ways. The sales representative determines that the prospect has the authority and resources to make a purchase decision. Likewise, prospects must agree that they are candidates for the goods or services that the salesperson offers. Without both of those conditions, further contact is not likely to lead to a sale and will waste the time of both salesperson and prospect. By one estimate, for every 36 sales prospects identified, 13 turn out to be qualified sales leads. These 13 sales leads may generate about five opportunities that reach closing (where the salesperson asks for the order) and, eventually, a second order.[22]

Sales force automation software is a valuable tool for systematically qualifying leads. At Telepress, an Issaquah, Washington, specialty printer, salespeople may spend years cultivating a prospect before receiving an invitation to bid on a project. The sales representative starts with a large database of potential customers and offers an inexpensive premium—a memo pad with the prospect's name on it—during a phone call to introduce the company. During the same call, customers provide information the sales representative needs to decide whether they qualify as pros-pects. Customized mailings follow the initial contact. The software helps the company's marketing director and customer service staff to focus on the best prospects and also to coordinate subsequent mailings and phone calls—an important task because several contact people often reach each customer.[23]

The Internet provides another tool for generating and qualifying leads. With demographic data available from and about Web site visitors, companies can identify the types of sites the members of their target markets visit.

Placing ads and links at those sites can provide valuable sales leads as potential customers request product information. Targeted incentives like contests and free offers can help to attract the desired audience and encourage them to self-qualify by filling out a form with personal information. These leads must then be integrated into existing company sales channels.[24]

Figure 19.4 **Use of Advertising to Generate Sales Prospects**

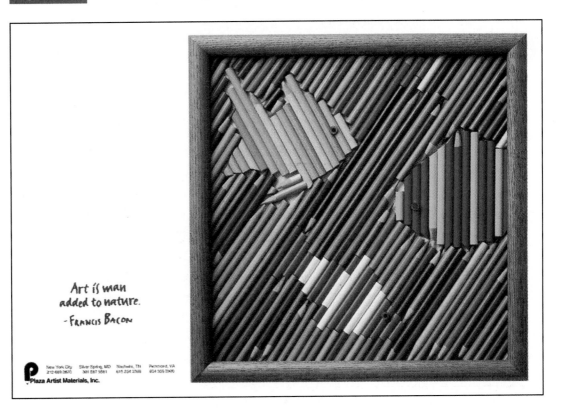

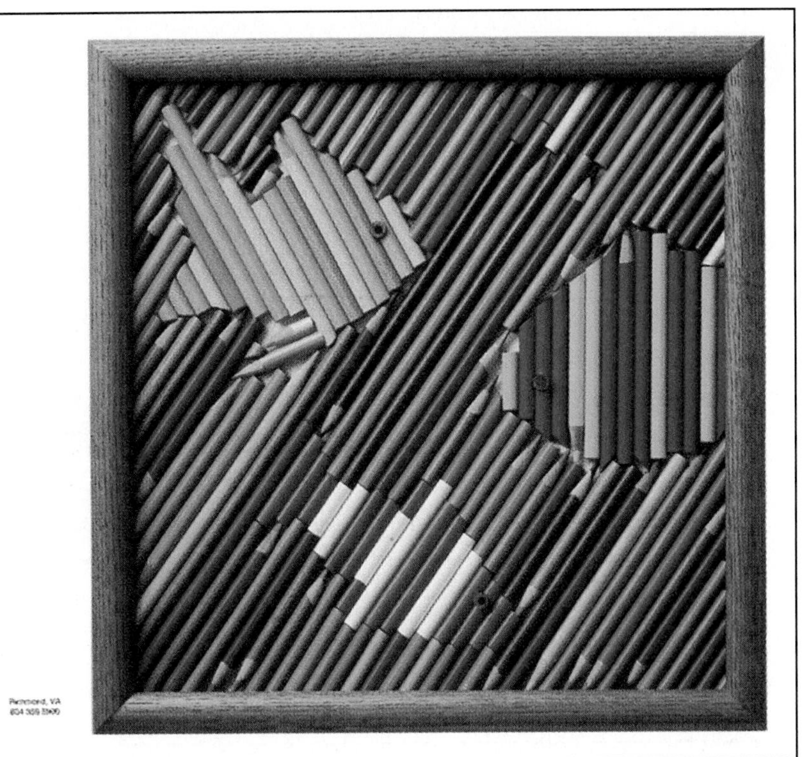
Art is man
added to nature.
-Francis Bacon
Plaza Artist Materials, Inc.

Many firms engage in telemarketing as a cost-effective way of prospecting and qualifying. Telemarketers pass on qualified leads to field salespeople, who can concentrate on prospects most likely to buy.

On a larger scale, companies that are considering exporting their products must identify countries where they might find interested buyers and whether they must observe any business methods or procedures unique to those nations. In addition, exporters must be aware of any cultural expectations of salespeople. For example, Mexico is a lucrative export market for U.S. goods and services. Mexican customers spend seven of every ten pesos of their import purchases to buy U.S.-made products. Popular imports include high technology goods, environmental services, construction services, medical products, and household products. Mexican businesspeople prefer to deal with small firms that demonstrate interest in long-term business relationships. Experts advise U.S. exporters to invest in local services and training and to avoid talking about illegal immigration to the United States.

Asia represents the fastest growing market in the world, one that presents a major new sales opportunity for many companies. China's purchases of goods and services exceed \$100 billion; Taiwan's \$91 billion in exports place it 13th among trading nations. According to John Naisbitt, author of *Megatrends Asia,* many Western corporations don't understand how to enter these markets. Setting up branch offices and bringing in brand names may not provide a sufficient sales effort. Successful companies typically form joint ventures with well-connected local partners to establish local companies and may introduce new brands for each market. French telecommunications giant Alcatel has done just that in China, an especially difficult market because of its many regions and dialects. Likewise, Taiwan's Acer Group sets up companies throughout Asia.[25]

Approach

Once the salesperson has identified a qualified prospect, he or she collects all available, relevant information and plans

Marketing Dictionary

prospecting Personal-selling function of identifying potential customers.

qualifying Determining that a prospect has the needs, income, and purchase authority necessary to become a potential customer.

Figure 19.5 **Basing the Sales Approach on Market Research Findings**

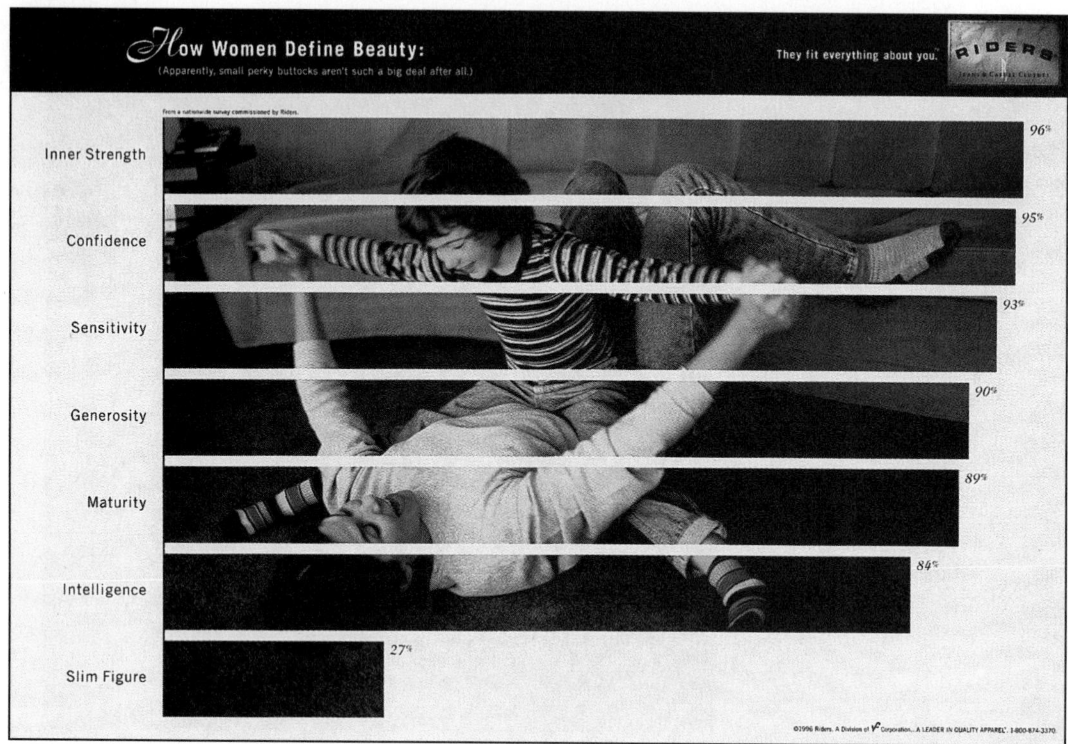
How Women Define Beauty:
(Apparently, small perky buttocks aren't such a big deal after all.)
They fit everything about you.
RIDERS
From a nationwide survey commissioned by Riders.
Inner Strength
96%
Confidence
95%
Sensitivity
93%
Generosity
90%
Maturity
89%
Intelligence
84%
Slim Figure
27%

an **approach**—the salesperson's initial contact with the prospective customer. Information about the prospect can provide invaluable help to ease the initial contact for telemarketers and field salespeople. They can gather information from secondary sources (magazine or newspaper articles) or from the prospect's own published literature (annual reports, press releases, Internet sites). In collecting information, the salesperson must avoid invading the prospect's privacy. A sales professional does not use unethical tactics to obtain personal information about a prospect.

Information-gathering makes **precall planning** possible. A salesperson who has gathered relevant information about a prospect can make an initial contact armed with knowledge about the prospect's purchasing habits; his or her attitudes, activities, and opinions; and common interests between the salesperson and the prospect. This kind of preparation often provides key help for winning an account.

Retail salespeople usually cannot complete precall planning, but they can compensate by asking leading questions to learn more about the purchase preferences of buyers. Business marketers have access to far more data than retail sellers, and they should review it before scheduling the first sales contact. Market research studies often provide invaluable information that serves as the basis of a sales approach. VF Corp. sales representatives used the results of a national survey of female self-perceptions, shown in Figure 19.5, to convince retail buyers to stock the firm's looser-fitting Riders jeans and casual clothing.

Presentation

The salesperson gives the sales message to a prospective customer in a **presentation.** The seller describes the product's major features, points out its strengths, and concludes by citing illustrative successes. In one popular form of presentation, a features-benefits framework, the seller talks about the good or service in terms that are meaningful to the buyer. The salesperson relates product features to customer needs and explains the benefits of those features, rather than listing technical specifications.

The presentation should deliver a well-organized, clear, and concise message emphasizing positive information. Printed sales-support materials (charts, product literature, marketing research reports, product reviews), charts displayed on a laptop computer, and audiovisual aids such as videotapes enhance the clarity and effectiveness of a sales presentation. The level of preparation depends on the type of sales call. For a routine call, a salesperson may need only up-to-date product knowledge and information about the prospect. When the salesperson is competing with several other companies for an account, a major presentation requires in-depth preparation and rehearsals to ensure perfect delivery.

The traditional method of sales presentations, the canned presentation, originally was developed by John H. Patterson of National Cash Register Company during the late 1800s. The **canned presentation** is a memorized, standard sales talk that ensures uniform coverage of the points that management deems important. The dinnertime telemarketing call is an example of a canned presentation that follows the same script, although it may provide the salesperson with different options depending on answers to specific questions. While canned presentations are still used in such areas as door-to-door *cold canvassing*—making unsolicited sales calls on random groups of people—and telemarketing, most salespeople have long since abandoned them. Many customers resent standardized appeals, because many salespeople seem compelled to complete the presentations before asking for the sale. Over half of the potential buyers in such a situation feel that the appeal wastes their time; they react angrily and decide not to buy. Flexible presentations are nearly always needed to match the unique circumstances of each purchase decision. Proper planning and sensitivity to the customer's reactions are important parts of presentations tailored to each prospective customer.

Figure 19.6 **Demonstration—A Critical Step in Consumer Decision Making**

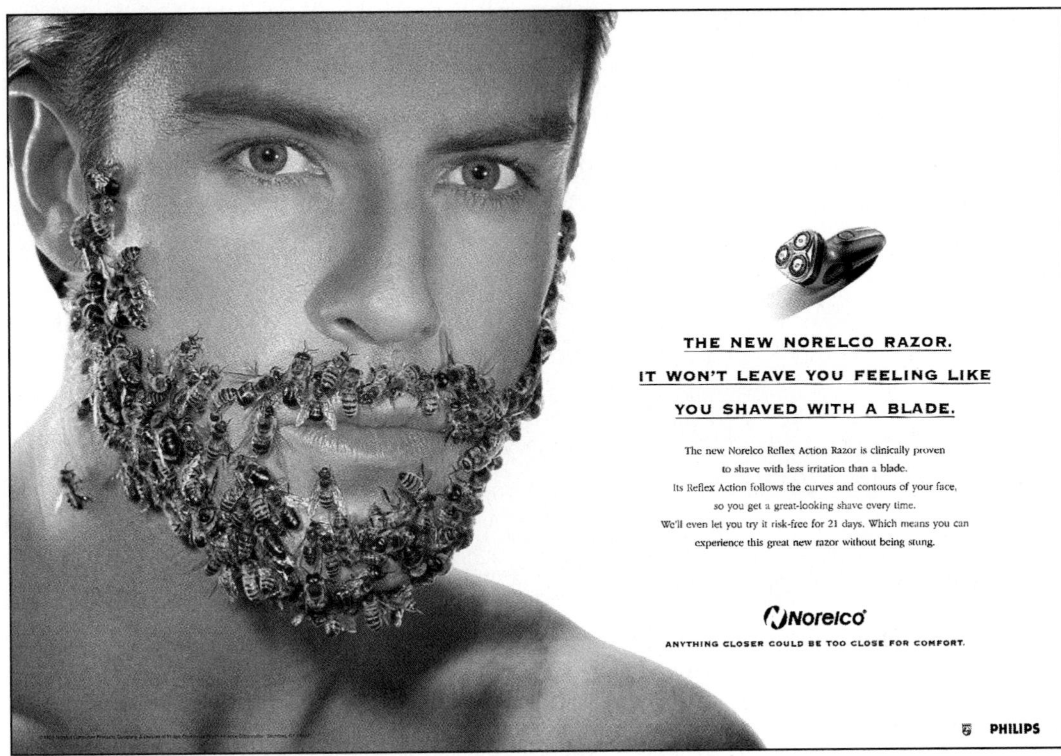
THE NEW NORELCO RAZOR.
IT WON'T LEAVE YOU FEELING LIKE
YOU SHAVED WITH A BLADE.
The new Norelco Reflex Action Razor is clinically proven
to shave with less irritation than a blade.
Its Reflex Action follows the curves and contours of your face,
so you get a great-looking shave every time.
We'll even let you try it risk-free for 21 days. Which means you can
experience this great new razor without being stung.
Norelco
ANYTHING CLOSER COULD BE TOO CLOSE FOR COMFORT.
PHILIPS

Increasingly, presentations are employing high-tech tools. For years, companies from auto manufacturers to vacation resorts, summer camps, and colleges have sent videotaped presentations to interest consumers. These days, many companies send presentations recorded on CD-ROMs. Some companies promote or explain new goods and services on Internet Web sites.

Computer-based multimedia presentations are considered the next wave in sales force automation. With a multimedia-equipped laptop or a larger PC or LCD projection computer, salespeople can enhance their presentations with color, animation, video, audio, and interactivity—as well as the latest product and pricing information. Ingersoll-Rand salespeople, for example, sell air compressors with the help of laptops and powerful presentation software. With these tools, a salesperson can view engineering drawings or animations of compressor operations; they can also compute energy or cost figures on the spot.

Demonstration

One important advantage of personal selling over most advertising is its ability to actually demonstrate a good or service to the potential buyer. As the advertisement in Figure 19.6 illustrates, creative print illustrations and television commercials sometimes simulate product demonstrations. This striking photograph for the Norelco Reflex Action Razor dismisses the old argument about whether an electric razor can shave with less irritation than a blade. The ad focuses on comfort, and few readers can look at its image without believing that anything closer would be too close for comfort.

Still, a static magazine advertisement or even a quasi-demonstration of a product in action on a television screen fails to convey the message of the real product in operation. A demonstration ride in a new automobile, for

Marketing Dictionary

approach Salesperson's initial contact with a prospective customer.

precall planning Use of information collected during the prospecting and qualifying stages of the sales process and during previous contacts with the prospect to tailor the approach and presentation in a way that matches the customer's needs.

presentation Describing a product's major features and relating them to a customer's problems or needs.

canned presentation Memorized sales talk that ensures uniform coverage of the points that management deems important.

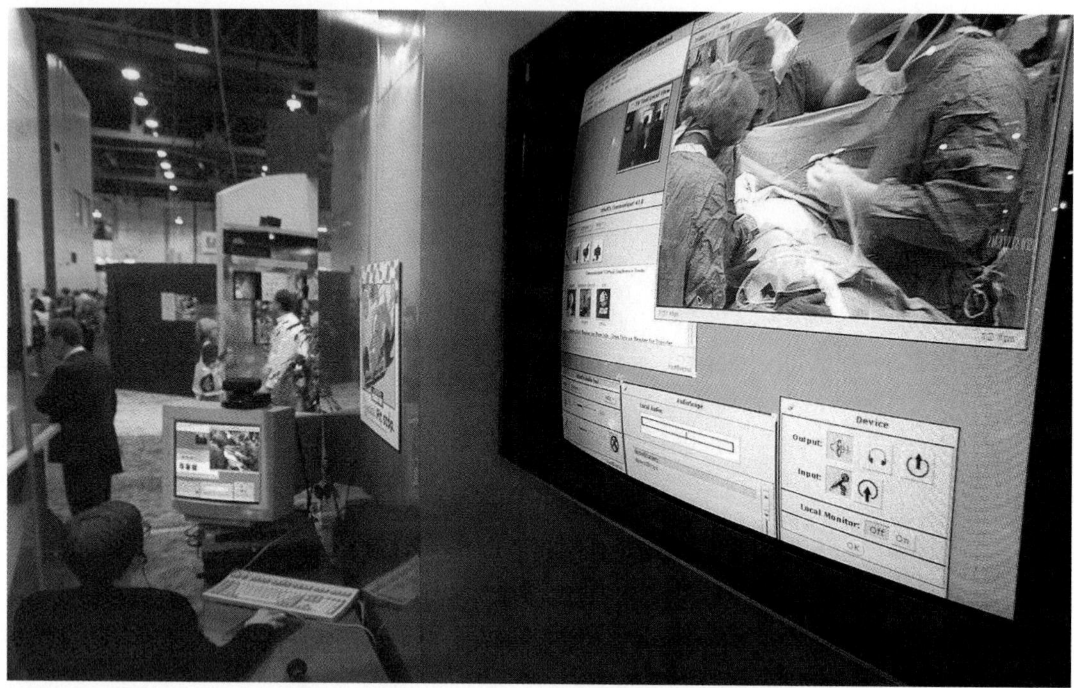
Device
Output:
Input:
Local Monitor:

AT&T used an attention-getting demonstration—a live broadcast of neurosurgery—to attract attendees at a telecommunications trade show. The continuous live broadcast of neurosurgery being performed at a Pittsburgh hospital demonstrated the use of AT&T's high-speed voice, data, and image transfer technology in a medical application. The dramatic demonstration drew attendees to AT&T's exhibit and resulted in hundreds of sales leads.

example, involves the prospect in the presentation. It awakens customer interest in a way that no amount of verbal presentation can achieve.

Firms are now using new technologies to increase the effectiveness of their demonstrations. Multimedia interactive demonstrations are now common. Sales representatives for magazines such as *Forbes* and *Newsweek,* for instance, use data stored on CD-ROMs or interactive laser disks to demonstrate the demographic and circulation patterns for their magazines. These presentations use full-color video and sound, along with animation, statistics, and text to sell advertising space.

The key to a good demonstration—one that gains the customer's attention, keeps his or her interest, convinces, and stays in the customer's memory—is planning. The salesperson should check and recheck all aspects of the demonstration prior to its delivery.

Handling Objections

A vital part of selling involves handling objections. *Objections* are expressions of sales resistance by the prospect, and reasonable salespeople expect them: "Well, I really should check with my spouse." "Perhaps I'll stop by next week." "I like everything except the color." Objections typically involve the product's features, its price, and services to be provided by the selling firm.

A sales professional uses each objection as a cue to provide additional information for the prospect. In most cases, an objection such as "I don't like the color of the interior" is a way of asking about other available choices or product features. A customer's question reveals an interest in the product and gives the seller an opportunity to expand a presentation by supplying additional information. For instance, testimonials from satisfied customers may effectively respond to product objections. Also, providing a copy of the warranty and the dealer's service contract may resolve a buyer's doubts about product service.

During this stage of the selling process, salespeople often receive objections concerning competitors' products. Professional salespeople avoid criticizing the competition. Instead, they view objections as opportunities to provide more information about their own goods or services. Often, this activity requires them to conduct extra, behind-the-scenes research.

Sales force automation can help sales representatives to handle certain objections by making information immediately available. Right in the customer's office, the salesperson can confirm available inventory and shipping date of the desired amount and type of a certain product, for example. A salesperson for Curtin Matheson Scientific, a distributor of clinical and scientific laboratory supplies, was greeted by a new buyer with complaints about the company's service and delivery. The sales representative used a laptop to review the company's purchase records to show that all but one order was shipped for same-day or next-day delivery. "Because I had that information right at my fingertips," he said, "I was able to dispel her bad image of us and keep her as a customer."[26]

Closing

Figure 19.7 Number of Sales Calls Required to Make a Sale

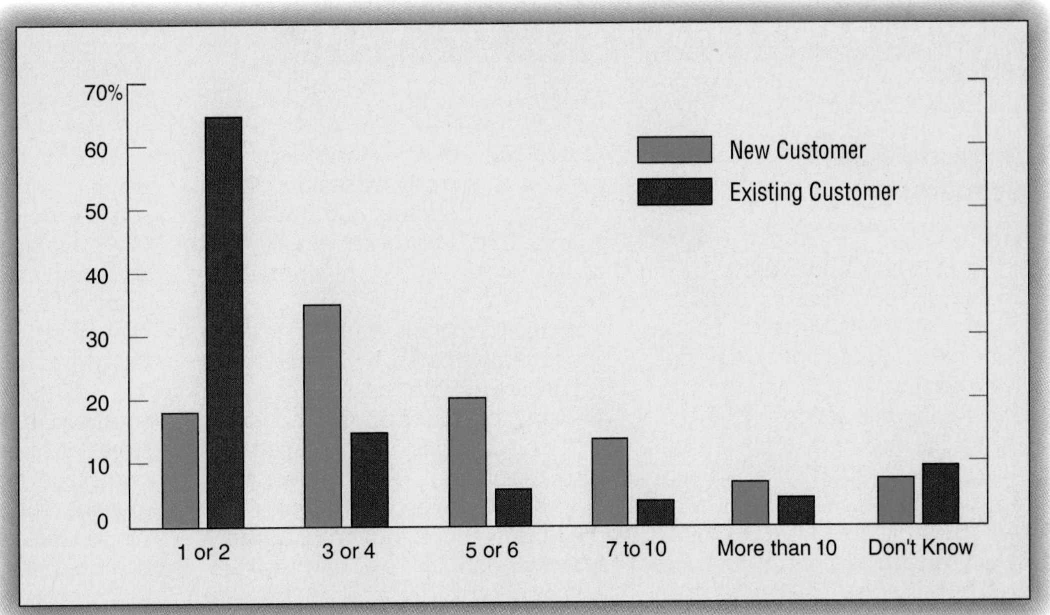
70%
60
50
40
30
20
10
0
New Customer
Existing Customer
1 or 2
3 or 4
5 or 6
7 to 10
More than 10
Don't Know

The moment of truth in selling is the **closing**—the point at which the salesperson asks the prospect for an order. If the sales representative's presentation effectively applies the product features to the customer's needs, the closing should be the natural conclusion. However, a surprising number of sales personnel find it difficult to actually ask for an order. A survey of over 3,000 salespeople revealed that 80 percent fail to close when the buyer is ready, and many customers are ready to close much earlier than the salespeople are.[27]

Effective salespeople learn when and how to close a sale. They practice several common methods of closing a sale:

1. The *"If I can show you . . ."* technique first identifies the prospect's major concern in purchasing the good or service and then offers convincing evidence of the product's ability to resolve it. ("If I can show you how the new heating system will reduce your energy costs by 25 percent, would you be willing to let us install it?")
2. The *alternative-decision* technique poses choices for the prospect, in which either alternative suits the salesperson. ("Will you take this sweater or that one?")
3. The *SRO (standing room only)* technique warns the prospect to conclude a sales agreement, because the product may not be available later or an important feature, such as price, will soon change.
4. *Silence* can be a closing technique, since a discontinued sales presentation forces the prospect to take some type of action (either positive or negative).
5. An *extra-inducement close* offers special incentives designed to motivate a favorable buyer response. Extra inducements may include quantity discounts, special servicing arrangements, or layaway options.

Getting to a closing point may require selling efforts over a span of time. Figure 19.7 shows the typical number of sales calls needed to complete sales with new and existing customers.

Follow-Up

The word *close* can be misleading, since the prospect's acceptance of the seller's offer begins much of the real work of selling. In the competitive sales environment of the 1990s, a successful salesperson seeks to ensure that today's customers will make future purchases. One cannot succeed by simply closing each sale and moving on to the next prospect. Relationship selling requires the salesperson to reinforce the customer's purchase decision and make sure that the company delivers high-quality goods or services on schedule. Salespeople must also ensure that customer service needs are met and that satisfaction results from all

Marketing Dictionary

closing Stage of the personal selling process at which the salesperson asks the customer to make a purchase decision.

MARKETING HALL OF FAME

The World's Best Salesperson

Don't want to buy a car? Then you'd better avoid Bob Tasca's Lincoln-Mercury showroom. Tasca's ability to close deals and keep finicky customers coming back has turned him into a legend at Ford Motor Co.

Tasca started his East Providence, Rhode Island, dealership more than 20 years ago at a time when Ford's Lincoln-Mercury division was ailing nationally. It was faring even worse in Providence, where it represented less than 1 percent of the local market. But Tasca made a profit from the very first month, and today he grosses more than $60 million a year from a single showroom. He's cocky—who wouldn't be if they were declared No. 1 in their business? But his key to success is sticking to a winning sales formula. He demands that he and his employees make sure every customer is happy with his or her car. And unlike a lot of people in the industry, Tasca really means it. If a customer isn't satisfied with the new car, the dealership will return the money.

"Satisfying customers means fixing problems," Tasca declares. "Satisfy the customer first and she'll buy from you again and again." His attention to customer service has resulted in an amazing level of loyalty. The dealership's customer loyalty rating, defined by repeat purchases, registers year after year at roughly 65 percent. By comparison, the average dealership nationwide has a loyalty rating of under 20 percent.

What's amazing is that Tasca treats non-customers with the same care as paying ones. Here's just one example: A woman who bought a Lincoln Continental from another New England dealer experienced car problems during a lengthy road trip down South. With the car still under warranty, the Southern dealer and the one up North argued over which had to reimburse the woman. Totally disgusted, the woman visited the Tasca dealership one day to see if he could help. She had been lured to Tasca's by his advertising slogan, "You Will Be Satisfied." Even though Tasca had no connection with the dispute, he immediately reimbursed the woman. He then endured the hassle of getting a refund from Ford.

"A service request from a non-

of a customer's dealings with the company. Otherwise, another company will get the next order.

These postsales activities, which often determine whether a person will become a repeat customer, constitute the sales **follow-up.** Whenever possible, the sales representative should contact a customer to gauge satisfaction with a purchase. This step allows the salesperson to provide psychological reinforcement for the customer's original decision to buy. It also gives the seller opportunities to correct any sources of discontent with the purchase and to secure important market information and additional sales.

Follow-up helps to strengthen the bond that salespeople try to build with customers in relationship selling. Automobile dealers often keep elaborate records of their previous customers so that they can promote new models to individuals who already have shown a willingness to buy from them. Some auto dealers assign representatives from their service departments to call several days after customers' appointments and make sure that the work has satisfied them. One successful travel agency never fails to telephone customers when they return from their trips. Proper follow-up is a logical part of the selling sequence.

As part of their follow-up, salespeople should also conduct a critical review of every call they make. They should ask, "What allowed me to close that sale?" or "What caused me to lose that sale?" Such continuous review results in significant sales dividends.

Krissann Torok knows the importance of follow-up and credits it with her rise from industrial sales representative to become the first female regional manager in Goodyear Tire & Rubber's automotive division. For example, she acted as troubleshooter for one customer who needed Goodyear to make a new type of hose. She took care of any glitch that came up, maintained frequent communication between Goodyear and the customer, and visited the plants twice each week. Torok acted as the customer's advocate within Goodyear, sending a strong message that she cared about solving any problems.[28]

MANAGING THE SALES EFFORT

The overall direction and control of the personal-selling effort is in the hands of hierarchically organized **sales management.** For example, in a typical geographical sales structure, a district or divisional sales manager might report to a regional or zone manager, and these people, in turn, may report to a national sales manager or vice president of sales.

customer really amounts to a golden opportunity, not an unfair imposition or a pain in the neck," Tasca says. The woman was treated like a queen at Tasca's dealership and returned when it was time to buy a new car.

Tasca, however, is hardly running a charity. In fact, one thing he won't do to increase foot traffic is slash prices. While he splurges on customer service and makes sure his cars are equipped with the most popular features, he will not dicker. If there are 100 identically equipped GS Mercury Sables on the lot, for instance, each of them will be sold for the same price.

"We don't compete on price, there's just one price and we don't come down on price to beat another dealer," Tasca says. While this might seem like a turnoff for customers, he insists it isn't necessarily so. Unlike other dealers, his sales force doesn't have to gouge some customers to compensate financially for the great deals more savvy shoppers obtained. "Because we don't compete on price, we don't try to maximize profit on each deal either. We don't have to because we don't do losing deals that we then have to try to make up for."

Tasca also excels in motivating his sales team. Once during the mid-seventies, when sales were in a funk, Tasca woke up his troops in dramatic fashion. He walked into his sales meeting at the start of the week and handed out a blank check to each of his 20 salespeople. He told his puzzled employees that they could fill in the amount for their paycheck that week. "What do you think you could sell if you really applied yourself?" he asked his audience. At first everybody was overjoyed—a real blank check. But then they began to think realistically about how many sales they could make in the next few days. The check ploy worked. Sales jumped that week.

QUESTIONS FOR CRITICAL THINKING

1. **Discuss how Tasca meets the buyer expectations listed in Table 19.2.**
2. **Evaluate Tasca's success in terms of his marketing and management strategies.**

Sources: "Customer Service Super Secrets," January 1997, downloaded from http://www.papertrade.com/, May 15, 1997; Bob Tasca, "You Will Be Satisfied," *Selling Success,* May 1996, pp. 59–66; and Bob Tasca, *You Will Be Satisfied* (New York: HarperCollins, 1995).

Sales managers perform a **boundary-spanning role** in that they link the sales force to other elements of the internal and external environments. The internal organizational environment consists of top management, other functional areas in the firm, and other internal information sources. The external environment includes trade groups, competitors, customers, suppliers, and regulatory agencies.

The sales manager's job requires a unique blend of administrative and sales skills, depending on the specific level of this position in the sales hierarchy. First-level sales managers need very strong sales skills to train and directly lead members of the sales force. Higher in the sales management structure, however, positions require more managerial skills and fewer sales skills. A typical salesperson devotes nearly 75 percent of his or her time to face-to-face selling, telephone selling, and travel. By contrast, sales managers devote 55 percent of their time to administration, internal meetings, and coordinating account services. The time allocations are shown in Figure 19.8.

Like other promotional activities, personal selling requires effective planning and strategic objectives. These strategies include selling existing products to new customers, selling new products, servicing customer accounts to enhance retention and satisfaction, and expanding customer relationships by selling more products to existing customers.

Goal setting is also important. Sales managers cannot simply set revenue and profit goals. Bill Delmont, vice president and director of worldwide sales at United Parcel

Marketing Dictionary

follow-up Postsale activities that often determine whether a one-time purchase will lead a buyer to become a repeat customer.

sales management Activities of planning, organizing, staffing, motivating, compensating, evaluating, and controlling salespeople to ensure their effectiveness.

boundary-spanning role Sales manager's activities to link the sales force to other elements of the organization's internal and external environments.

Figure 19.8 **How Salespeople and Sales Managers Spend Their Time**

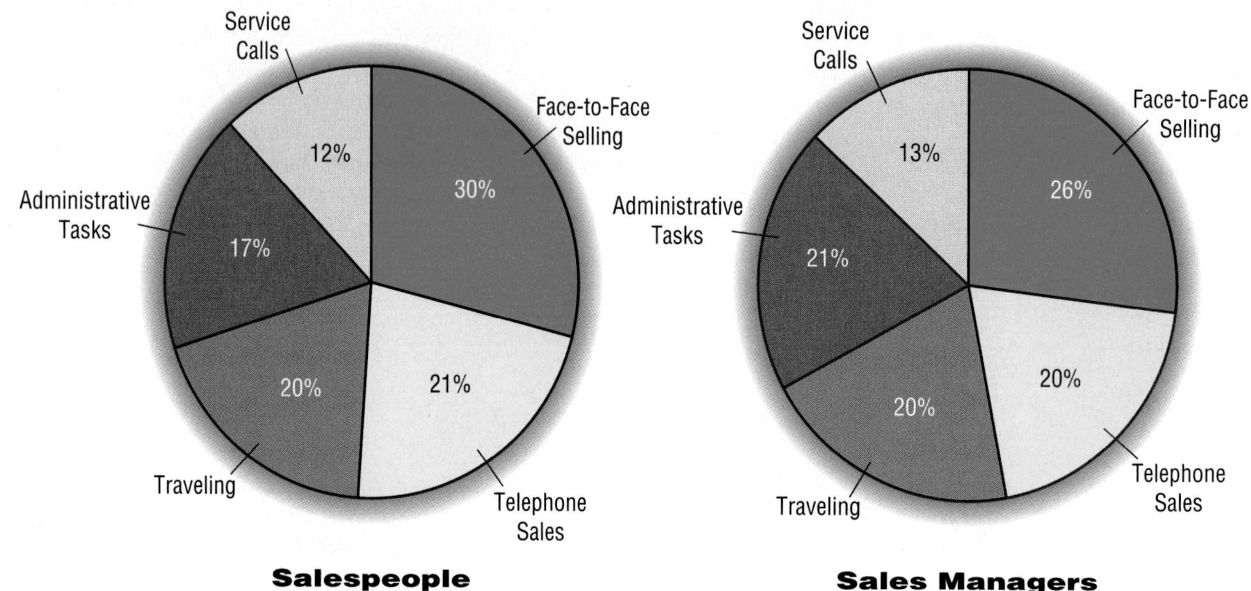
Service Calls
12%
Face-to-Face Selling
30%
Administrative Tasks
17%
20%
21%
Traveling
Telephone Sales
Salespeople
Service Calls
13%
Face-to-Face Selling
26%
Administrative Tasks
21%
20%
20%
Traveling
Telephone Sales
Sales Managers

Service, points out that customer satisfaction is the most important criterion of sales success. He recommends developing a formal customer satisfaction index. Any decrease in the index level provides a good indication of trouble ahead. "Sales and service are one," he says. At American Express Financial Advisors, client and sales representation rank ahead of sales growth as performance objectives for sales teams.[29]

http://www.ups.com/

Sales management is the administrative channel for sales personnel; it links individual salespeople to general management. The sales manager performs seven basic managerial functions: (1) recruitment and selection, (2) training, (3) organization, (4) supervision, (5) motivation, (6) compensation, and (7) evaluation and control.

Sales managers perform these tasks in the late 1990s in a demanding and complex environment. They must manage increasingly diverse sales personnel that include growing numbers of women and minorities. Women account for almost half of the nation's professional salespeople, and their number is growing at a faster rate than that for men. The fastest growth rates reflect new salespeople of Hispanic and Asian descent. However, only 26 percent of business-to-business salespeople are women. As the workforce composition continues to change, companies will need more people to fill growing numbers of selling positions such as product specialists, sales consultants, telemarketers, and customer service and sales support representatives.

A firm's expansion into global markets challenges the sales manager to develop sales personnel in other countries. Sometimes this change may require new ways of organizing sales units, as in the earlier examples of Acer and Alcatel, or training salespeople. Roger Liston, director of sales training at Seagate Technology, a computer disk drive manufacturer, adapts his training programs to the cultural, social, and business norms of the countries where Seagate sells its products. Liston spends time learning about the country's culture, its sales process, the nature of customer relationships, and other cultural influences on sales. In Australia, for example, Liston noticed that the laid-back and relaxed culture led to very low-key sales calls. While these representatives effectively developed relationships, they were not so good at closing sales. In his sales training, therefore, he described how to find suitable prospects, explained the differences between competing products, and showed when to close. Another weakness of many non-American salespeople is selling mostly on price, not value. Liston shows his staff how to emphasize value.[30]

Recruitment and Selection

Recruiting and selecting successful salespeople is one of the sales manager's greatest challenges. The turnover rate for salespeople is the highest of all white-collar professions. Sources of new candidates for sales jobs include colleges and universities, trade and business schools, sales and nonsales personnel in other firms, and the firm's current nonsales employees.

Not all of these sources provide equally productive personnel. One problem area involves the reluctance of some high school guidance counselors and college instructors to promote the advantages of selling careers to students. In fact, however, a successful sales career offers satisfaction in all five areas that a person generally considers when deciding on a profession:

1. *Opportunity for advancement.* Studies have shown that successful sales representatives advance rapidly in most companies. These people can advance either within the sales organization or through lateral moves to more responsible positions in other functional areas of their firms.
2. *High earnings.* The earnings of successful salespeople compare favorably with those of successful people in other professions. The average, top-level, consumer goods salesperson can earn more than $75,000 per year.
3. *Personal satisfaction.* A salesperson derives satisfaction from achieving success in a competitive environment and helping customers satisfy their wants and needs.
4. *Security.* Contrary to what many students believe, selling provides substantial job security. Experience has shown that economic downturns affect personnel in sales less than people in most other employment areas. In addition, companies have continuing needs for good sales personnel.
5. *Independence and variety.* Sales representatives most often operate as rather independent businesspeople or as managers of sales territories. Their varied work provides opportunities for involvement in numerous business functions.

Briefly speaking

"An outstanding salesperson is someone who sells goods that won't come back to customers who will."

Anonymous

Careful selection of salespeople is important for two reasons. First, the selection process involves substantial amounts of money and management time. Second, selection mistakes damage customer relations and sales force performance, and they are costly to correct.

Sales managers typically follow a seven-step process in selecting sales personnel: application, screening interview, in-depth interview, testing, reference checks, physical examination, analysis, and hiring decision. After screening applications, the manager conducts initial interviews. Promising applicants return for in-depth interviews. During these interviews, the sales manager looks for personal characteristics like enthusiasm, good organizing skills, ambition, persuasiveness, ability to follow instructions, and sociability.

Next, the company may use testing in its selection procedure, including aptitude, intelligence, interest, knowledge, and/or personality tests. One testing approach is gaining in popularity: the *assessment center.* This technique presents candidates with situational exercises, group discussions, and various job simulations to allow the sales manager to measure a candidate's skills, knowledge, and ability. Assessment centers enable managers to see what potential salespeople can do rather than what they say they can do. After testing, the manager checks references to ensure that job candidates have represented themselves accurately. A physical examination is usually included before the final analysis and hiring decision.

Training

To shape new sales recruits into an efficient sales organization, management must conduct an effective training program. The principal methods of sales training include on-the-job training, individual instruction, in-house classes, and external seminars. Popular training tools include videotapes, lectures, role-playing exercises, slides, films, and interactive computer programs.

Simulations can help salespeople to improve their selling techniques. Another key tool for training is sales force automation. Knowing that salespeople who are not very computer literate can balk when presented with SFA tools, Minneapolis-based Carlson Wagonlit Travel carefully trained its salespeople when it implemented its SFA system. Employees met in small groups to learn how to use their laptop computers. They learned basic computer skills in the first day-long session. A second session was held a month later, after salespeople had spent some time gaining experience with their equipment.[31]

Ongoing sales training is also important for veteran salespeople. Sales managers conduct much of this type of training in an informal manner. In one standard format, the sales manager travels with a field sales representative periodically and then composes a critique of the person's work. Sales meetings, training tapes, classes, and seminars are other important forms of training for experienced personnel.

Organization

A sales manager is responsible for the organization of the field sales force. General organizational alignments, usually determined by top marketing management, may be based on geography, products, types of customers, or some combination of these factors. Figure 19.9 presents simplified organizational charts illustrating each of these alignments.

Figure 19.9 **Basic Approaches to Organizing the Sales Force**

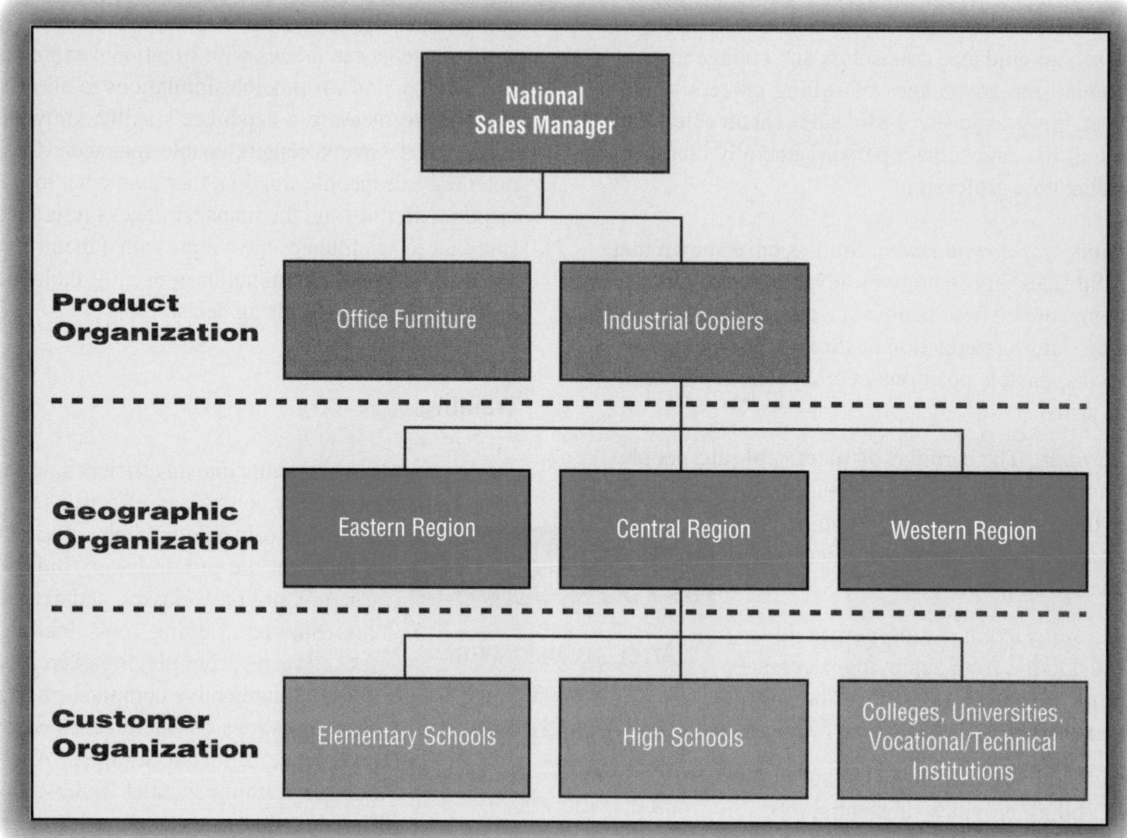
National Sales Manager
Product Organization
Office Furniture
Industrial Copiers
Geographic Organization
Eastern Region
Central Region
Western Region
Customer Organization
Elementary Schools
High Schools
Colleges, Universities, Vocational/Technical Institutions

A product sales organization would designate specialized sales forces for each major category of the firm's products. This approach is common among industrial product companies such as Alcoa that market large numbers of similar but separate products, usually very technical or complex in nature, through different marketing channels.

Firms that market similar products throughout large territories often use *geographic specialization.* For example, multinational corporations may define different sales divisions for different continents. Geographic organization may be combined with one of the other organizational methods. However, companies are moving away from traditional territorial sales representatives as they adopt customer-focused sales forces. Jerome A. Coletti, president of Stamford, Connecticut-based consulting firm The Alexander Group, believes that organizing the sales force by customers makes more sense. He also recommends that small to mid-sized firms should dedicate their direct sales forces to the largest, most profitable customers or prospects, or those with the best growth potential. The rest of the customer base can be handled with alternative channels: telemarketing for low-end customers, business partnerships for mid-range customers.[32]

A customer-oriented organization would use different sales forces for each major type of customer the firm serves. Some firms use separate sales forces to sell to consumer and organizational customers. Others have sales forces for specific industries, such as financial services, educational, and automotive buyers. Sales forces can also be organized by customer size, with separate sales forces assigned to large, medium, and small accounts.

Hewlett-Packard (HP) recently realigned its sales and marketing activities, revising a geographical organization to create one based on three customer segments: retail consumers, commercial resellers, and enterprise (business)

http://www.hewlett-packard.com/

accounts. The Consumer Sales and Marketing division focuses on individuals and small businesses. The Commercial Channel Sales Force has responsibility for major resellers who sell to business customers, regardless of size, around the world. Finally, HP's largest business customers work with members of the Enterprise Sales Force, who can help these major customers develop the sophisticated, integrated systems they require. This new sales alignment fits well with the company's emphasis on building close customer relationships. As its director points out, "It is vital that we understand how end users want to buy, how they use HP products, and how they want to be supported."[33]

A growing trend among firms using the customer-oriented organizational structure is the **national accounts organization.** This structure, designed to strengthen a firm's relationship with large and important customers, involves assigning senior sales managers or sales teams to large accounts in each market. The classic example of a national account selling situation is the relationship between Wal-Mart and its major vendors. Many companies, including Procter & Gamble, set up sales offices near Wal-Mart's Bentonville, Arkansas headquarters. This arrangement places dedicated sales resources close to this key account.

Professionals who sell to national accounts need strong relationship selling skills, attention to pricing issues, and high commitments to customer service and support. Organizing by national accounts helps sales representatives to arrange cooperation between departments to meet customer needs, because they know the large buyers will place regular orders. According to Sally Silberman, director of international sales for consumer durable goods manufacturer Kimball International, national account customers consider consistent pricing more important than the lowest pricing. Customers who develop solid relationships with their national account representatives often get outstanding service, too.[34]

Global account teams are a variation on the national account selling theme as companies extend their global marketing techniques to the personal selling area, as well. These global leaders are replacing country managers with global account teams composed of local sales representatives for their largest industrial customers. For example, electronics component manufacturer AMP Inc. of Harrisburg, Pennsylvania, set up global account teams in the United States, Europe, and Japan. "We had great pressure from customers to support them on a world basis," said Ted Dalrymple, vice president of global marketing. The company locates managers with responsibility for global accounts close to the buyers' headquarters. They manage the overall relationship, coordinating the efforts of a worldwide sales team and local sales representatives.

Despite the advantages of this system for AMP, local sales staff did not welcome the change. Managers and sales representatives found their best customers reassigned to the global team, leaving them with smaller, less profitable accounts. They also had to learn to share relationship management with the global team.[35]

The individual sales manager must also organize the sales territories within his or her area of responsibility. Factors such as sales potential, strengths and weaknesses of available personnel, and workloads are considered in territory allocation decisions.

Supervision

A source of constant debate among sales managers concerns the supervision of the sales force. It is impossible to pinpoint the exact amount of supervision that is correct in each situation, since this arrangement varies with the individuals involved and the environments in which they operate. However, the concept of *span of control* helps to reach some generalizations. The span of control refers to the number of sales representatives who report to the first level of sales management. The optimal span of control depends on such factors as complexity of work activities, ability of the individual sales manager, degree of interdependence among individual salespeople, and the extent of training each salesperson receives. Johnson, Kurtz, and Scheuing suggest a 6-to-1 ratio as the optimal span of control for first-level sales managers supervising technical or industrial salespeople. In contrast, they suggest a 12-to-1 ratio if the sales representatives are calling on wholesale and retail accounts.[36]

Sales managers may also accompany subordinates on sales calls. Executives at Eastman Chemical accompany representatives on sales calls several times a year. The visits are carefully orchestrated in advance with the local salespeople. These calls may open new doors higher up in the customers' organizations, lend prestige to the sales situations, and also help Eastman's managers to build customer relationships and understand the influences on buying decisions. As one representative described his sales calls with Eastman's CEO, "He made it clear that he

http://www.eastman.com/

Marketing Dictionary

national accounts organization Organization scheme that assigns sales teams to a firm's largest accounts.

Figure 19.10 Electronic Entertainment Products Used as Sales Incentive

SONY
WHOEVER SAID
"HARD WORK IS ITS OWN REWARD"
NEVER WON A SONY.
For desired results, offer desired rewards.
Sony gives you both by designing customized incentive
programs, and fulfilling them with the world's
most acclaimed entertainment products.
For rewarding information about an incentive program
for your company, call the Sony Special Markets Group
at 800-833-6302 or FAX 609-655-0897.
Circle No. 146 on Reader Service Card

wanted to talk to contacts the sales representative would call on—people responsible for day-to-day activities."[37]

Motivation

The sales manager should not take lightly this responsibility for motivating the sales force. The problem-solving emphasis of the sales process often leads to considerable mental pressures and frustrations. Sales often result only after repeated calls on customers, and the transactions may, especially with new customers and complex technical products, involve long completion periods. Efforts to motivate salespeople usually take the form of debriefings, information sharing, and both psychological and financial encouragement. Appeals to emotional needs, such as ego needs, personal recognition, and peer acceptance, are examples of psychological encouragement. Monetary rewards and fringe benefits, such as club memberships and sales contest awards, are types of financial incentives.

However, incentive programs that offer prizes may not effectively motivate employees. Poorly planned programs—for example, those that set targets too high, fail to publicize their terms, allow only top performers to participate, or exclude spouses from trips—can actually have adverse effects. Companies should not expect these programs to solve all of their sales problems.[38] A popular incentive for salespeople is electronics merchandise, such as the Sony entertainment products shown in Figure 19.10.

Sales managers can improve sales force productivity by understanding what motivates individual salespeople. They can gain insight into the subject of motivation by studying the various theories of motivation developed over the years. One theory that has been applied effectively to sales force motivation is the **expectancy theory** proposed by Victor Vroom. According to this theory, motivation depends on an individual's expectations of his or her own ability to perform the job and the relationship between performance and attaining rewards that the individual values.

Sales managers can apply the expectancy theory of motivation by following a five-step process:

1. Let each salesperson know in detail what management expects in terms of selling goals, service standards, and other areas of performance. A Coopers & Lybrand study found benefits in setting goals more frequently than just once a year. Companies that set only annual goals (about seven out of every ten companies) met or exceeded their sales goals at the lowest rates among the firms studied, whereas those that set goals more frequently (monthly, quarterly, or semiannually) reported greater success in meeting sales goals.[39]

2. Make work valuable by assessing the needs, values, and abilities, of each salesperson and then assigning appropriate tasks.

3. Make work achievable. Leaders must inspire self-confidence in their salespeople and offer training and coaching to reassure them.

4. Provide immediate and specific feedback, guiding those who need improvement and giving positive feedback to those doing well.

5. Offer rewards that reinforce the values of each salesperson. Managers at Cable & Wireless, a Virginia-based long-distance provider for businesses, used a reward system to encourage use of their new SFA program. When sales representatives turned on their computers, they immediately viewed the amounts of their year-to-date sales commissions. Explained a Cable & Wireless salesperson, "The thing I'm concerned most with is making money. You can bet I'll use the system when I can immediately find out what my paycheck is going to say."[40]

Compensation

Because monetary rewards provide an important source of motivation, methods of compensating sales personnel requires critical attention from managers. Basically, sales compensation can be based on a commission plan, a straight salary plan, or some combination. Bonuses based on end-of-year results are another popular form of compensation.

A **commission** is a payment tied directly to the amount of sales or profits created by a salesperson's orders. For example, a sales representative might receive a 5 percent commission on all sales up to a specified quota and 7 percent on sales beyond that point. While commissions reinforce selling incentives, they may cause some sales force members to shortchange nonselling activities, such as completing sales reports, delivering sales promotion materials, and performing normal account servicing.

A **salary** is a fixed payment made periodically to an employee. A firm that bases compensation on salaries rather than commissions might pay a salesperson a set amount every week. A company must balance benefits and disadvantages in paying predetermined salaries to compensate management and sales personnel. A straight salary plan gives management more control over how sales personnel allocate their efforts, but it reduces the incentive to expand sales. As a result, many firms develop compensation programs that combine features of both salary and commission plans.

Because good salespeople are both hard to find and expensive to train, sales managers want to encourage productive workers to stay with their firms. Incentive plans that favor experienced sales representatives tend to provide fewer benefits for new representatives, who are not yet fully productive. Some companies, therefore, have developed interim compensation plans for new recruits, such as a straight salary for a given period of time or a commitment that the salesperson will not earn less than a certain amount, but can earn more, during the training period.[41]

The typical U.S. salesperson earns $50,000 in total annual compensation. Figure 19.11 shows total sales compensation figures for various levels of sales personnel. Salary plus bonus is the most common sales pay plan: 44 percent of respondents in a recent compensation survey worked under such a plan, while fewer than 1 percent of all salespeople were paid by straight commissions.[42]

Well-managed incentive programs can motivate salespeople and improve customer service. For example, ITT Sheraton adopted a sales incentive plan that paid commissions for telemarketing sales. Instead of basing commissions for domestic reservations agents on just the number of nights they booked, commissions now reflect the number of nights and the average rates of the rooms. The new plan encourages agents to suggest that customers upgrade to nicer accommodations. With more earnings levels, the plan gives employees more incentives to reach higher levels, especially at the end of a month. In addition to commissions, salespeople can earn team rewards, and annual performance bonuses help to reduce turnover. After just one pay period under the new system, room revenues rose 3 percent.[43]

However, commission programs can also backfire. Some retailers, like Sears and electronics chain Highland Superstores, modified their compensation systems after discovering that salespeople were treating customers too aggressively or recommending unnecessary services.

A number of large companies including Electronic Data Systems Corp., Digital Equipment Corp., and Hewlett-Packard have recently instituted pay-for-profits plans. These compensation schemes reward sales representatives for profits they bring in rather than just for achieving certain revenue targets. IBM's program ties 60 percent of sales commissions to profits. Since 1991, salespeople have had some latitude on pricing. An information system gives sales representatives the profit margins on various products, so that when they close deals, they know how much profit they have given away. To keep salespeople from pushing fast-turnover, high-profit-margin products that don't meet customers' needs, the remaining 40 percent of the sales commission is tied to customer satisfaction measures.[44]

Marketing Dictionary

expectancy theory Theory that motivation depends on an individual's expectations of his or her ability to perform a job and how that performance relates to attaining a desired reward.

commission Incentive compensation directly related to the sales or profits created by a salesperson's orders.

salary Fixed compensation payments made periodically to an employee.

Figure 19.11 Annual Pay for Sales Representatives and Sales Managers

Sales Positions	Compensation
Outbound Telemarketing Representative	$$$$$$$ $33,000
Sales Representative	$$$$$$$$$ $43,100
Technical Product Consultant	$$$$$$$$$$$$ $51,800
Senior Sales Representative	$$$$$$$$$$$$$$ $63,250
Key Account Executive	$$$$$$$$$$$$$$$ $68,300
National Account Executive	$$$$$$$$$$$$$$$$$$$ $88,100
Sales Management Positions	
First-Level Field Sales Supervisor	$$$$$$$$$$$$$$$$ $72,200
Second-Level Field Sales Supervisor	$$$$$$$$$$$$$$$$$$$ $84,400
Third-Level Field Sales Supervisor	$$$$$$$$$$$$$$$$$$$$$$$$$ $113,100
National Sales Executive	$$$$$$$$$$$$$$$$$$$$$$$$$$$$ $127,300

Because of the increasing popularity of team selling, companies are setting up reward programs to recognize performance of business units and teams. Today, about one in four companies rewards business unit performance. About 13 percent of companies provide team performance rewards, compared to 5 percent in 1991.

Evaluation and Control

Perhaps the sales manager's most difficult tasks involve evaluation and control. This manager must resolve basic problems like setting standards and choosing instruments with which to measure sales performance. Sales volume, profitability, and investment return are the usual indicators for evaluating sales effectiveness. They typically involve the use of **sales quotas**—specified sales or profit targets that the firm expects salespeople to achieve. For example, a manager might expect a particular sales representative to sell $300,000 in Territory 414 during a given year. In many cases, quotas form part of compensation systems. SFA tools have greatly improved the ability of sales managers to monitor the effectiveness of their sales professionals. Database programs enable sales managers to break out revenue by salesperson, by account, and by geographic area.

As implied earlier, scorekeeping in the sales organization is beginning to change from simple systems based on sales quotas. Other measures, such as customer satisfaction, profit contribution, share of product-category sales, and customer retention are also coming into play. These changes have resulted from three factors:

- ▼ An increasingly long-term orientation, which results from wider involvement with total quality management and relationship-building efforts
- ▼ The realization that evaluations centered on sales volume alone can lead to overselling and excessive inventory problems, which work against customer relationship building
- ▼ The need to encourage sales representatives to develop new accounts, provide customer service, and emphasize new products. A concentration on sales quotas tends to focus salespeople's attention on short-term selling from which they can generate the most sales today.[45]

Regardless of the key indicators in the evaluation program, the sales manager must follow a formal system of decision rules. Such a system supplies information to the sales manager for action. This input helps the sales manager to answer three general questions.

First, where does each salesperson's performance rank relative to the predetermined standards? This comparison should fully consider the effect of uncontrollable variables on sales performance. Preferably, each adjusted rank should be stated as a percentage of the standard. This system simplifies evaluation and facilitates converting various ranks into a single, composite index of performance.

The second evaluation question asks, what are the salesperson's strong points? As one way to answer this question, the sales manager might list areas of the salesperson's performance in which he or she has surpassed the respective standard. As another way, the manager might categorize a salesperson's strong points in three areas of the work environment:

1. *Task, or technical ability.* This strength appears in knowledge of the products (end uses), customers, and company, as well as selling skills.

2. *Process, or sequence of work flow.* This strength pertains to actual sales transactions—the salesperson's application of technical ability and interaction with customers. Managers frequently measure process performance based on personal observation. Other measures are sales calls and expense reports.

3. *Goal, or end results (output) of sales performance.* Sales managers usually state this aspect of the salesperson's work environment in terms of sales volume and profits.

The third evaluation question asks, what weaknesses or negatives appear in the salesperson's performance? The manager should categorize these faults as carefully as the salesperson's strong points. The sales manager should explain candidly but kindly the employee's weak areas. Because few people like to hear this part of an evaluation and consequently tend to listen with only "half-an-ear," the manager should make sure the employee understands any performance problems that he or she needs to correct and how the manager will measure progress. The manager and employee should then establish specific objectives for improvement and set a timetable for judging the employee's improvement.

In completing the evaluation summary, the sales manager should follow a set procedure:

1. Separately measure each aspect of sales performance for which a standard exists. This precaution helps to prevent the *halo effect,* in which the rating on one factor influences those on other performance variables.

2. Judge each salesperson on the basis of actual sales performance rather than potential ability. This principle emphasizes the importance of rankings in the evaluation.

3. Judge each salesperson on the basis of sales performance for the entire period under consideration rather than for particular incidents. As an evaluator, the sales manager should avoid reliance on isolated examples of the salesperson's success or failure.

4. Review each salesperson's evaluation for completeness and evidence of possible bias. Ideally this review would be made by the sales manager's immediate superior.

While evaluation includes both revision and correction, the sales manager must focus attention on correction. This priority translates into a drive to adjust actual performance to conform with predetermined standards. Corrective action, with its obviously negative connotations, typically poses a substantial challenge for the sales manager.

ETHICAL ISSUES IN SALES

As the previous chapter discussed, promotional activities raise many ethical questions, and personal selling is no exception. The pervasive presence of personal selling in people's daily lives and the vast differences in the training, experience, and professionalism of different types of salespeople combine to produce a negative image of the profession for many. Plays like *Death of a Salesman,* television shows, and movies reinforce the poor image.

Today's highly paid, highly professional salesperson knows that long-term success comes from building and maintaining mutually satisfying relationships with clients. Still, the stereotype lingers. A recent Gallup poll offered still more evidence of how much people dislike certain types of salespeople. Auto sales was considered the least ethical among 26 careers, and insurance sales fared only slightly better, ranked at 23.

Some people feel that ethical problems are inevitable due to the very nature of the sales function. They simply don't trust someone who will personally benefit by completing a sales transaction.

Thousands of companies are working to overcome the stigma associated with sales careers and to educate the general public about the contributions of today's sales professionals. They promote their own advantage in this image-building, because salespeople generate revenue, link their companies to customers, and provide valuable product information to customers and members of the marketing channel, as well as supply feedback for the producer. By recruiting highly ethical, educated individuals and training them in relationship-selling techniques, companies develop sales forces able to win customers' respect and trust. By stressing consultative-selling techniques, sales professionals meet customer needs without resorting to unethical behavior. In addition, sales managers create ethical sales environments in several ways:

- Promoting ethical awareness during training programs, sales meetings, and sales calls
- Making sure that all employees—salespeople and other company personnel—know that the firm opposes unethical conduct

Marketing Dictionary

sales quota Level of expected sales for a territory, product, customer, or salesperson against which evaluations compare actual results.

SOLVING AN ETHICAL CONTROVERSY

Building a Sales Force by Raiding Competition

In the business world, it happens all the time. A competitor swoops in with a dazzling compensation and benefits package, an outstanding territory, and (perhaps) a promise of rapid promotion to sales management—and lures away a firm's best salesperson. The raider gets to welcome into its ranks a new employee who knows the ropes and won't require a lot of time to learn the sales routine. Meanwhile, the abandoned company must scramble to fill a gaping hole in its sales force.

The consequences of this age-old industrial practice is more than just inconvenience. Salespeople are privy to trade secrets, pricing and delivery schedules, marketing plans and other sensitive information. In the wrong hands, these secrets can bolster a competitor's revenue figures, while harming the salesperson's previous employer. Luring away a rival's salespeople, however, isn't always a guaranteed way to improve a sales force's performance. The strategy can backfire.

Should companies raid competitors for new salespersons?

PRO

1. **Hiring somebody who's already in the field can be a quick and easy way to fill a vacancy in your sales force. "A rep who's hired from the competition can start selling immediately," says John Swain. "Other than getting used to a new culture, there isn't much of a training period."**
2. **Hiring away talent can provide better opportunities for salespeople. Ex-Xerox manager Frank Pacetta, the new marketing vice president at Danka Business Systems, hired dozens of sales managers, marketing executives and sales reps from Xerox during the first few months on his new job. Job dissatisfaction was a major reason that this Florida-based copier distributor was able to lure away so many Xerox veterans. These Xerox employees had been demoralized by massive downsizing, and they were troubled that the company seemed fixated on bolstering its stock price by cutting any costs it could.**
3. **Filling a sales staff with the competitor's workforce can be a logical way to launch a new business endeavor or product line. For example, Marriott Ho-**

- Establishing control systems to monitor ethical conduct.

Ethical Dilemmas

Despite management efforts to foster ethical behavior, from time to time, salespeople may find themselves in ethical dilemmas involving their employers, fellow employees, and customers. Common ethical breaches between salespeople and their employers include improper use of company assets and cheating. Use of a company car for personal purposes is one such possibility; padding expense reports is another. A salesperson might resort to deception in an attempt to win a sales contest, such as hold orders to place them after a contest begins or shipping unordered merchandise that customers will not return until after the contest ends.

Sexual harassment is another problem faced by many sales representatives. An Ohio State University study reported that about 30 percent of business-to-business saleswomen—and 20 percent of men in sales—have experienced unwanted sexual advances from customers. The pharmaceutical firm Astra USA recently fired its president and established a formal sexual harassment policy after female sales representatives complained about such harassment from company executives.[46]

For another type of unethical conduct, sellers sometimes offer bribes to secure sales. While offers of gifts such as pens and tickets to sporting events are accepted business practices, salespeople can misuse them. Since expensive gifts may be considered a form of bribery, many firms prohibit their employees from accepting any gift from a sales representative.

Customer demands for cash kickbacks present another type of ethical dilemma. Suppose, for example, that a salesperson calls on an important business customer who is planning to order new copiers for most departments. The purchasing manager offers the account if the sales representative will share half of the commission on the sale. Although the representative knows this deal is illegal and has signed the company's strong code of ethical conduct, a strong desire to make the sale causes a conflict.

In cases like this, possible options include going along with the unethical request, ignoring the request, confronting the person, or reporting the behavior. Michael Hoffman, director of the Center for Business Ethics at

tel Corp. marketers wanted to create a business travel division in 1990, but they had no in-house experience in that field. Marriott hired a former Holiday Inn executive who had the necessary background.

CON

1. **Luring away sales reps is not a good way to seek a competitive advantage. The new employee will not necessarily fit into the corporate culture of the new company. "Salespeople from one organization are very often not compatible with a competitor," says Roy Chitwood, president of Max Sacks International, a sales management consulting firm. "Raiding a competitor's sales for nothing more than competitive reasons can hurt a company."**
2. **Hiring the "enemy" can cause morale problems. "These people used to be the bad guys," says Jon Hawes, director of the Fisher Institute for Professional Selling at the University of Akron. "Team spirit can be shot down by bringing in somebody from a competitor." Damaging employee cohesiveness, Professor Hawes adds, is the greatest worry a company should have when it targets its recruiting efforts at a competitor.**
3. **Salespeople eager to jump to another company could be damaged goods. These workers may be experiencing job burn-out or they could be finding it difficult to do well in a changing marketplace.**

Summary

Hiring away workers from bitter rivals is a routine part of the industrial landscape. It happens whether it is Microsoft and IBM, Nike and Reebok, or Coke and Pepsi. While the business world may debate whether the practice of stealing talent is ethical, it's quite unlikely to change. Not when there are superb workers just waiting for a better opportunity. Just listen to Frank Pacetta, who is hardly contrite about his raiding activities at his former employer: "Xerox may not be a great company anymore, but many of the people who work there are," he says. "And I love taking those people from Xerox."

Sources: Pete Barlas, "Netcom Claims Former Exec Took Employees, Company Secrets, " *The Business Journal of San Jose*, May 5, 1997; Geoffrey Brewer, "I'm Going to Be Their Worst Nightmare," *Sales & Marketing Management*, August 1996, pp. 42–48; and Andy Cohen, "Should you Steal Your Rival's Reps?" *Sales & Marketing Management*, December 1995, pp. 60–63.

Bentley College, recommends telling the purchasing manager that the representative wants to gain the buyer's business without resorting to such tactics. If the purchasing agent refuses to move forward on these terms, Hoffman recommends that the salesperson report the incident to a manager, who should speak to the customer representative's supervisor. He encourages firms to develop companywide codes of ethics to assist salespeople with such situations and to protect all parties.[47]

ACHIEVEMENT CHECK SUMMARY

Reread the learning goals that follow, and consider the questions for each goal. Answering these questions will reinforce your grasp of the most important concepts in the chapter and allow you to check how well you have achieved these learning goals. Where a blank appears before a question, answer with *T* or *F;* for multiple-choice questions, circle the letter of the correct answer.

Objective 19.1: Explain the conditions that determine the relative importance of personal selling in the promotional mix.

1. ____ Personal selling expenses represent a smaller outlay for most companies than advertising.

2. ____ Personal selling is likely to be relatively important to a firm when its consumers are geographically concentrated and relatively few in number.

3. ____ Companies are likely to rely on personal selling when many intermediaries help to move products between the manufacturer and the final consumer.

Objective 19.2: Contrast field selling, over-the-counter selling, and telemarketing.

1. ____ A salesperson who visits Farmer Brown and shows him a new insect-resistant seed is engaged in field selling.

2. ____ When Farmer Brown buys insect-resistant seed on the Internet, the transaction involves telemarketing.

3. ____ The Brown family receives repeated phone calls from a seed company after 10 P.M., but other than hanging up or disconnecting the phone when they go to bed, they cannot do much about it.

Objective 19.3: Describe each of the four major trends in personal selling.

1. ___ Relationship selling involves establishing a sustained relationship, sometimes formalized and sometimes not, between buyer and seller.

2. ___ Relationship selling works because the buyer wants to improve the relationship by focusing on the seller's short-term sales goals.

3. ___ Team selling programs often achieve immediate popularity with salespeople, because these naturally gregarious people don't mind sharing sales responsibility.

4. ___ Though expensive, SFA pays off in all selling situations.

Objective 19.4: Identify the three basic sales tasks.

1. ___ The three basic sales tasks are order processing, creative selling, and closing the sale.

2. ___ Selling a brand-new health insurance program to a business customer is a good example of order processing.

3. ___ The most demanding of the three sales tasks is (a) order processing; (b) creative selling; (c) missionary selling.

4. ___ An example of missionary selling is (a) a detail salesperson who visits a store's lingerie department to help organize the company's product displays; (b) the annual Butterball Turkey hotline that consumers can call at Thanksgiving with questions about cooking turkeys; (c) both of the above.

Objective 19.5: Outline the steps in the sales process.

1. ___ The first step in the sales process is (a) approach; (b) prospecting and qualifying; (c) presentation.

2. ___ Information gathered from secondary sources provides no help in preparing a sales approach, because every other competing salesperson has access to the same information.

3. ___ A customer's objections often reveal an underlying interest in the product and gives the salesperson an opportunity to provide additional information.

4. ___ Most salespeople find closing a sale the easiest part of the sales process.

5. ___ Follow-up activities after a sale strengthen the bond between seller and buyer and allow the salesperson to reinforce the customer's decision to buy.

Objective 19.6: Describe the sales manager's boundary-spanning role.

1. ___ The sales manager's boundary-spanning role results from his or her responsibility for overseeing salespeople in several geographic areas.

2. ___ The sales manager links the sales force to elements of the company's internal and external environments.

3. The external environment to which the sales manager helps link the sales staff includes all of the following except: (a) trade groups; (b) competitors; (c) customers; (d) the department that approves travel and entertainment vouchers; (e) suppliers; (f) regulatory agencies.

Objective 19.7: List and discuss the functions of sales management.

1. ___ One of the greatest challenges for sales managers is (a) the general organizational alignment of the sales force; (b) recruiting and selecting successful salespeople; (c) keeping travel costs down.

2. According to the expectancy theory, motivation depends on (a) individuals' expectations of their ability to perform their jobs and be rewarded for that performance or (b) individuals' perceptions of how fairly their firms compensate them.

3. ___ Commission plans provide strong selling incentives, but they sometimes backfire by causing salespeople to shortchange nonselling activities or focus on their own paychecks rather than customers' needs.

Objective 19.8: Discuss the role of ethics in personal selling and sales management.

1. ___ Sales managers can reduce the occurrences of unethical behavior through training, supporting the company code of ethics, and monitoring ethical conduct.

2. ___ Sexual harassment is a problem faced only by female sales representatives.

3. ___ Giving gifts to customers is an example of unethical behavior.

Students: See the solutions section located on page S-4 to check your responses to the Achievement Check Summary.

Key Terms

personal selling
field selling
over-the-counter selling
telemarketing
relationship selling
consultative selling
team selling
sales force automation (SFA)
order processing
creative selling
missionary sales
prospecting
qualifying
approach
precall planning
presentation
canned presentation
closing
follow-up
sales management
boundary-spanning role
national accounts organization
expectancy theory
commission
salary
sales quota

Review Questions

1. How does personal selling differ within the three major selling environments? Give examples of local firms that operate in each environment.
2. What is meant by *relationship selling?* Why is this trend becoming so important in personal selling?
3. What is meant by *team selling?* Why is it considered important?
4. Explain how sales force automation (SFA) can improve the sales function in a company.
5. Cite two local examples of each of the three basic sales tasks.

6. Under what conditions will salespeople likely employ canned presentations? What major problems does this method create?
7. Give an example of each function performed by sales managers in an organization.
8. Compare the types of sales compensation plans. Point out the advantages and disadvantages of each.
9. Explain how a sales manager's problems and areas of emphasis might change in dealing with each of the following types of employees:
   a. Telephone salespeople
   b. Over-the-counter, retail salespeople
   c. Field sales representatives
   d. Missionary salespeople
10. Give three examples of ethical dilemmas that salespeople encounter.

Discussion Questions

1. As marketing vice president of a large paper company, you are asked to address a group of university students about selling as a career. List the five most important points you would make in your speech.
2. Explain and offer examples of the effects of the following conditions on the marketer's decision to emphasize personal selling or advertising:
   a. Geographic market concentration
   b. Length of marketing channels
   c. Degree of product technical complexity
   d. Price
   e. Number of customers
   f. Prevalence of trade-ins
3. What sales tasks are involved in selling the following products?
   a. Hewlett-Packard laser printers
   b. American Cancer Society contribution plans (to an employee group)
   c. 1995 Jeep Cherokee
   d. Fast food from Pizza Hut
   e. Janitorial supplies for use in plant maintenance
4. Describe the job of each of the following salespeople in terms of basic sales tasks and sales environments.
   a. Salesperson in a Blockbuster Video store
   b. ERA real estate sales representative
   c. Route driver for Pepperidge Farm snack foods (sells and delivers to local food retailers)
   d. Sales engineer for Apple computers
5. Suppose that you are the local sales manager for the telephone company's Yellow Pages division supervising six representatives who call on local firms to sell advertising space. What type of compensation system would you use? What types of sales force automation tools would help your employees to present the benefits of advertising in the Yellow Pages? How would you evaluate your sales personnel?

'netWork

1. The Internet has become an increasingly popular means of finding sales positions. Go to one of the many career Web sites such as

http://careermosaic.com/ OR http://www.jobweb.org/

and identify a sales job that could be just right for you. Draft a cover letter that you could use to arrange an interview for that job. Attach a printout of the information you find on the job.

2. *Sales & Marketing Management* is a magazine devoted to sales and marketing. Go to its home page located at

http://www.smmmag.com/

and examine their review of sales force automation (the smt link). Choose one of the technological innovations discussed that you feel would be most beneficial to business-to-business salespeople. Explain why this was your choice.

3. Automaker Saturn Corp. has been highly effective in the use of team selling. Go to its home page

http://www.saturncars.com/

Does the Saturn home page promote the team-selling environment? Explain. Identify two or three advantages and disadvantages of the firm's decision to use team selling. How might the salespeople at Saturn benefit from the home page?

VIDEO CASE 19

SELLING THE FREE-STANDING INSERT

"We have always believed that our sales organization should have tremendous visibility, power, authority, and input in everything we do," asserts Valassis Communications CEO David Brandon. "We adopt the philosophy that everything starts with the sale and satisfying the customer. Virtually all the rest of the employees and the rest of the functions of the company are there to support the sales effort."

In 1971, Valassis introduced an innovative product in the coupon industry, the free-standing insert, or FSI. FSIs are glossy, multipage, color-coupon supplements placed in the middle of Sunday newspapers and often in daily papers. About 90 percent of all coupons in the United States are distributed through this method, including discount offers and promotional messages from America's top packaged-goods marketers. Each week more than 56 million coupon supplements, each averaging 28 pages, are distributed to some 400 newspapers nationwide.

FSIs are extremely popular with both consumers and marketers. Newspaper readership surveys consistently report that the Valassis coupon supplements rank second only to the front-page news in popularity. Consumer-goods marketers frequently incorporate FSIs in their marketing programs, lured by the advantages of high-quality color reproduction, targeted reach to specific regions and cities, and cost efficiency compared to other methods of coupon distribution.

The complex process of producing an FSI begins when a Valassis salesperson convinces a client to place a coupon promotion in a future edition of a newspaper. The salesperson communicates the order to the category management department, which records the physical size of the promotional purchase and the product category, such as cereal or baby food. A computerized layout program supports design of the complete booklet. Customer orders are then processed and forwarded to the printing area where the ad layouts are finalized and the booklet is printed. The FSIs are then distributed to newspapers throughout North America.

Every Valassis employee who comes into contact with a customer is considered to be a member of the sales team. The company commits itself to teamwork among its employees and with customers with the goal of exceeding customer expectations. According to Executive Vice President Al Schultz, "If there's a problem with a printed product that we've produced, the head pressman can meet with the customer and feel a part of the process. I believe that teamwork goes well beyond just the people who are dealing with the customers every day to virtually everyone in our organization—from top executives to people who are pulling inserts off the back of a press."

The Valassis sales and service philosophy is based on individualized customer service. But the company didn't start out with that approach. "There was a time," Brandon recalls, "that I felt that if you just regimented everything and got very process oriented and very uniform and consistent that you would be rewarded. What we started finding was that as our customers started to move in their own directions, we were impeding their ability to get where they wanted to go because we were asking them to adapt to our system. And they're the customer!"

Valassis learned the hard way that "customers don't want to be lumped together with a bunch of other customers and be retrofitted into some kind of packaged, homogenized program that a company offers for service quality," says Brandon. Therefore, Valassis management developed a new sales and service approach that substantially increased the number of employees in customer service, sales assistance, and backup support roles. At one point, Valassis had three times the number of service-related employees as did its major competitors. Although many competitors viewed this as an advantage due to the added overhead costs incurred by Valassis, Brandon saw it quite differently. "What we really did was amass this very powerful weapon that allowed us to outperform them in the marketplace in a way that our customers see the most."

The Valassis sales force plays a major role in ensuring customer satisfaction. Salespeople are expected to work in the field building relationships with customers rather than in the office. As Brandon points out, "We pay them extremely well. We incent the living daylights out of them. We reward them for extraordinary performance. And we really put them out front to lead our organization."

Valassis sales managers take a flexible approach in evaluating their salespeople, measuring performance by sales volume, market share, and ability to generate sales at profitable prices. Since the firm believes in empowering its employees, salespeople exercise considerable discretion in how they perform sales tasks. However, every Valassis salesperson must maintain high ethical standards. "There's nothing so important in a salesperson as their ethics," says Schultz. "In this market today, if you don't have credibility and a high degree of ethics, you're not going to be successful long term."

Because Valassis uses a consultative selling approach, creativity and problem-solving skills are vital to each salesperson's success. Research and creative pre-call planning are keys to helping salespeople convince potential clients of the value of investing a significant portion of their advertising budget in FSIs. Valassis subscribes to the Lexis/Nexis online news service to assist its sales force in preparing sales presentations. Sales representatives review recent articles about their clients looking for information on market share, sales revenues, advertising expenditures, and current issues and problems. This knowledge helps a salesperson to understand a particular customer's needs and develop ways in which Valassis can help to satisfy them.

Many long-term customers depend on Valassis sales representatives to play major roles in planning their FSI promotions. When baby food maker Gerber, a frequent Valassis client, wanted a special coupon insert for a Baby Week promotion, the Valassis team developed a unique promotion. Gerber Consumer Service Director Mack Jenks was extremely impressed with the result. "Valassis showed that they were thinking progressively. They weren't taking the vehicle that had been the same thing the past 15 years. I was impressed that they were willing to think beyond that."

Creating new and different promotions keeps Valassis a leader in the industry. "I don't think you could find two customers that we do business with where we do anything the same," says Brandon. "We adapt to them. We give them what they want. They like it that way."

Questions

1. Review the determinants of the relative importance of personal selling and advertising in a firm's promotional mix from Table 19.1. Which determinants powerfully influence the Valassis sales promotional mix?
2. Describe how Valassis implements the principles of relationship selling and team selling.
3. Which of the three sales tasks described in this chapter is most important to a Valassis salesperson? Defend your answer.
4. Over 25 years ago, Valassis introduced the innovation of the free-standing insert. Today, the Internet has created another channel for coupon distribution. Conduct an Internet search for online coupons before answering the following questions:
   a. What kinds of online coupons did you find?
   b. In your opinion, does the system you encountered offer an effective way to distribute coupons? Explain your answer.
   c. Compare online coupons with FSIs from a recent issue of your local newspaper. What are the pros and cons of each? Consider both the interests of both businesses and shoppers in your answer.

Sources: Personal interviews with David Brandon and Al Schultz of Valassis Communications, Inc. and Mack Jenks of Gerber, March 1997.

Part 6 Microsoft Corp.: Promoting the Company and Its Products

In 1994, *Advertising Age* selected Bill Gates as Marketer of the Year for "his acumen as chief executive and marketer" of Microsoft. "What marketing is about is communicating, and Bill is a great communicator," says Gordon Eubanks, CEO of software marketer Symantec Corp. Communicating is a large part of Gates' job. He devotes about one-third of his time to promoting Microsoft's products to customers and prospective customers.

During Microsoft's early years, selling the company's languages directly to computermakers was one of Gates' tasks. "For the first three years, most of the other professionals at Microsoft focused solely on technical work, and I did most of the sales, finance, and marketing, as well as writing code," says Gates. "I was barely out of my teens, and selling intimidated me."

Driven by his vision and Microsoft's desire to grow, Gates traveled around the country calling on potential customers and trying to negotiate deals with computermakers. Personal selling was the key promotional element in implementing Microsoft's marketing strategy, which was to earn a royalty by convincing computermakers to buy licenses for its software.

Another reason personal selling was so important to Gates was the need to establish a legitimate market for Microsoft's software. "In the early years of selling Altair BASIC, our sales had been far lower than the widespread usage of our software suggested they should be," says Gates. That's because many early software users were computer hobbyists, and many hobbyists copied software rather than buying it and then resold it or made copies for other people.

Gates became the new software industry's spokesperson against piracy. He publicized his viewpoint in an "Open Letter to Hobbyists," asking them to stop copying Microsoft's software and to buy it so the company could earn a profit. The letter appeared in a 1976 issue of *Computer Notes,* a newsletter published by MITS for its Altair customers. Part of the letter said:

> The feedback we have gotten from the hundreds of people who say they are using BASIC has all been positive. Two surprising things are apparent, however. (1) Most of these users never bought BASIC (less than 10 percent of all Altair owners have bought BASIC), and (2) The amount of royalties we have received from sales to hobbyists makes the time spent on Altair BASIC worth less than $2 an hour.

Gates ended his letter by asking the people who he claimed stole Microsoft's software to pay up. Gates didn't receive many checks, but his letter generated lots of publicity for Microsoft in the emerging microcomputer industry. David Bunnell, editor of the MITS newsletter, sent copies of Gates' letter to computer magazines as well as to hobbyists' publications like the *Homebrew Club Newsletter,* where the letter was reprinted along with Gates' signature. Gates was also gaining recognition from the "Software Notes" column he and Allen wrote for the MITS newsletter. Later, when Bunnell started his own magazine, *PC World,* he continued to give Gates and Microsoft enormous press coverage.

When MITS sponsored the First Annual World Altair Computer Convention in 1976, everyone interested in the new industry came—computer society presidents; Altair dealers, owners, and programmers; and editors and publishers of *Popular Electronics, Byte, Interface, Creative Computing,* and other major computer magazines. To this influential group, Gates delivered the opening talk for the convention's software session and demonstrated his software. Later that year, at the National Computer Conference in New York, Gates handed out a flyer about Microsoft that became the basis for the company's first print ad. The ad's slogan was "Microsoft: What's a Microprocessor Without It?" Placed in the journal *Digital Design,* the ad introduced Microsoft as "the company that will efficiently produce and implement quality software for any microprocessor, in any amount, at any level of complexity. Why not contact them about your microsoftware needs?"

Gates attended every computer fair and trade show, setting up a booth to demonstrate Microsoft's software and taking the opportunity to promote it, to meet new people face-to-face, to learn what was happening in the industry, and to find new customers. At the 1977 National Computer Convention, for the first time a special area was designated for personal computers and their software developers. Microsoft's booth drew a large crowd. And everyone listened to Gates as he presented his vision about PCs as a member of the convention's panel on personal computing and software.

"I sure do more press stuff than other CEOs," said Gates. "But, you know, we have a message. We try to sell millions of copies of stuff that you don't drink or smoke. I guess you've got to do a lot of press interviews."

To strengthen his relationships with computermakers, Gates began publishing *Microsoft Quarterly.* He hired several salespeople to service the growing number of OEM accounts. Gates and his sales team were very successful in selling to computermakers. By the early 1980s, however, Microsoft was growing rapidly and beginning to distribute its software at computer stores, a new channel that required a different promotional approach.

Assembling a Marketing Team

Beginning in 1980, Gates started hiring a team of marketers to broaden the company's appeal to a wider audience. Steven Ballmer joined Microsoft as assistant to the president and was put in charge of marketing. Pam Edstrom was hired as public relations manager. Jon Shirley, a 24-year veteran of Radio Shack, was named Microsoft's president. Jim Harris, a marketing manager at Intel, joined Microsoft as head of its OEM sales force. And, as discussed in the Part IV case, Rowland Hanson became the company's vice president of corporate communications.

Promoting to Business Customers

To generate interest about Microsoft and to showcase Bill Gates as the company's communicator, Edstrom launched a massive public relations campaign that resulted in reams of media coverage. In November 1982 Gates appeared on the cover of *Money* magazine. *People* magazine profiled Gates as one of 1983's "25 Most Intriguing People." In early 1984, *Fortune* included a full-page photo of Gates in its article, "Microsoft's Drive to Dominate Software." Later in that same year, Jane Pauley interviewed Gates on the *Today* show, and, on the same day he appeared on the cover of *Time*. *Esquire* chose Gates as one of the "Best of the New Generation" of 1984.

Thanks to Edstrom's PR work, Gates was becoming one of the most visible and sought after CEOs in the world, delivering keynote speeches at trade shows industry conferences and sharing his expertise at user group meetings and product launches.

Edstrom left Microsoft to form her own PR agency, Waggener Edstrom. Today the agency handles Microsoft's business-related PR work. For its consumer PR, Microsoft recently hired a new agency, Shandwick Seattle. Together, the agencies generate the thousands of articles about Microsoft and Bill Gates that seem to appear daily in newspapers and computer, business, and general interest magazines.

During the early 1980s, the number and size of computer magazines began to grow along with the PC industry. Microsoft placed print ads in these computer publications to reach the key corporate decision makers. The informative ads were technically oriented and targeted at managers of information systems. As the business market broadened, Microsoft began advertising in general business magazines like *Fortune* and *Business Week.* "Word-of-mouth is the primary thing in our business," says Gates. "And advertising is there to spur word-of-mouth, to get people really talking about 'the latest thing.'"

Microsoft's marketing team also began devising new promotions for corporate customers. They chose the 1983 Comdex show in Las Vegas, where Gates gave the keynote address, to get people excited about Microsoft's new Windows 1 operating system. The marketers decorated the Las Vegas airport with Windows banners, put Windows advertising plates on taxicabs, and gave away Windows key chains to people who rented cars at Budget and Avis. At hotels, they slid plastic bags with Windows information under the doors of guests' rooms. They printed cocktail napkins that said "Look Through the Microsoft Windows" and that contained $1 discounts at local restaurants.

As its sales grew, Microsoft allocated more money for product launch promotions. The company budgeted more than a million dollars for the spectacular eight-city launch of Windows 3 in 1990. Topped off with a show at City Center in New York, the promotion included demonstration stations where people could try out the software, press release kits, "Witness the Transformation!" buttons, and free copies of Windows 3. Gates promoted the product by appearing in a series of satellite TV interviews in cities across the country. Microsoft was learning that backing products with splashy promotions paid big dividends. Within weeks of the launch, Microsoft reported that sales of Windows 3 hit 400,000 copies.

A few months later Gates gave the keynote address at the 1990 Comdex show at the Las Vegas Hilton to an overflow crowd where he delivered his "Information at Your Fingertips" message. With Microsoft software, Gates promised that desktop PCs would be hooked up to networked computer databases, giving employees instant information. Gates packed the place "just the way Elvis used to," said a trade show organizer.

In 1992, Microsoft added television advertising to its promotional mix. It used network and cable TV ads in launching its much-improved Windows 3.1 operating system. The TV ads were scheduled to run ten days before IBM planned to launch the new version of its OS/2 operating system. "This is an intense period in software marketing. There is a big battle looming out there," said Gerald McGee, managing director of Microsoft's agency at the time, Ogilvy & Mather. "This is not a time to be silent, reticent, and shrink back." Microsoft's $8 million promotion included print ads and a direct mail effort that offered the new Windows version to current customers for $49.99 rather than the full price of $79.99. Both print and TV ads carried the theme "Making It Easier," showing business buyers how Windows made their employees' work easier.

Promoting Microsoft to Consumers

Microsoft had to reorient its promotional approach when it began marketing software to consumers. The company's goal was to establish Microsoft as a technology leader while informing consumers of the benefits of software for the home. "What we wanted people to think is how exciting software is, how it's advancing, and how there's one company leading the way with a lot of great products," says Gates.

Because retail stores are the main distribution outlets for consumer software, Microsoft's promotional plan for consumer products included TV ads and print ads in magazines like *Home PC* and *Computer Life* that would bring buyers into the stores, and packaging and merchandising within the stores to encourage people to buy. Microsoft offers a cooperative advertising program for retailers and provides them with point-of-purchase revolving displays that hold up to 96 Microsoft titles.

To promote its CD-ROM titles, Microsoft took its Explorasaurus Bus on a ten-city tour. Decorated with dinosaurs and astronauts, the 45-foot tractor-trailer stopped at retailers to let kids try out the interactive product demonstrations. The promotion also included an "Imagine the Magic" contest targeted at kids age 6 to 11. The contest asked kids to describe "What could the coolest computer do?" Winners received a trip to Kids' Technology Summit at Microsoft headquarters and a meeting with Bill Gates.

From focus group interviews conducted for its *Encarta* multimedia encyclopedia, Microsoft marketers learned that sampling increased consumers' intent to buy. When *Encarta* was described to focus group members, about 15 percent said they would consider buying the product, but 80 percent said they would consider buying if they had a chance to try it out. Based on this and other similar studies, Microsoft added sampling to its consumer promotions. For example, the company offers consumers a CD sampler that allows them to view 36 software titles for $4.95 and includes a $10 coupon toward a purchase.

Sampling is also part of Microsoft's direct-response TV ads. During a pre-Christmas promotion, Microsoft ran 60-second spots that generated 60,000 calls to an 800 number. Callers received a free video that showed how four families used 12 of Microsoft's different multimedia products.

Promoting the Brand

In 1994 Microsoft made a radical change in its promotional strategy, shifting from a long focus on promoting individual products to creating a corporate campaign that would project a unified global image. "The product line is expanding dramatically, and the audiences we have to talk to is expanding," said Greg Perlot, Microsoft's director of advertising and market research. "Our need to integrate our programs is significant." Microsoft hired the Wieden & Kennedy ad agency, which created Microsoft's global $100 million campaign asking customers "Where do you want to go today?" Microsoft used the same advertising slogan for the $200 million product launch of Windows 95 described in Chapter 17.

Wieden & Kennedy also handles the promotion of Microsoft Network. In 1996, it launched Microsoft's first TV campaign focused on the Internet, with global TV ads supported by print emphasizing the Microsoft brand rather than individual products.

Advertising on the Web

For Microsoft, advertising on the Web is a worthy investment. Microsoft is the Web's biggest advertiser. The company opened a Web site as part of its $4 million print campaign promoting Windows NT to corporate buyers. To promote Office 97, Microsoft spent $14 million in print and Web ads. People who buy Office 97 become part of Microsoft's new direct e-mail promotion. Over the Internet, Microsoft monitors how customers use the Office 97 suite and then e-mail them information of product upgrades and promotional messages.

Microsoft intends to become the biggest Internet advertising seller. According to Pete Higgins, Microsoft's group vice president of applications and content, advertising and transaction fees could account for 20 to 30 percent of Microsoft's online revenues by the end of the century.

While ad revenues mostly come from selling banners linking advertisers' Web sites, Microsoft plans to generate sales from ads companies place to sponsor Microsoft's

Web content shows and *Slate,* its online magazine. MSN Web advertisers include CNET: The Computer Network, Internet Shopping Network, Bell Atlantic, Chrysler, Kellogg, and Gatorade. About 50 companies, including AT&T, Ford Motor Company, and Fidelity Investments, are MSN advertisers.

In 1996, Microsoft spent $2.6 billion for sales and promotional expenditures. The company plans to increase its spending on product-specific promotions, brand advertising, and product support activities.

"The Internet as a source of information has gone from irrelevant to right up there with word-of-mouth," says Rob Shoeben, Microsoft's group manager who oversees Windows advertising.

Selling and Support Services

Steven Ballmer, who heads Microsoft's worldwide Sales and Support Group, manages the 10,000 people who sell and service Microsoft's products and who comprise 46 percent of the company's workforce. Salespeople call on OEM accounts, corporate accounts, wholesalers, and retailers. In 1996, Microsoft hired a national sales manager to build a separate MSN sales force.

Since the release of Windows 3.0 in 1990, Microsoft has experienced an enormous increase in demand for user support services, especially from the growing number of home software buyers. Thousands of customers call the company each day with questions about the new operating system and applications for it. From marketing research studies and customer satisfaction surveys, Microsoft has learned that PC users consider follow-up product support as important as the product itself. According to Bob Johnson, director of software services for Dataquest, excellent support produces 35 percent more purchases of a firm's products and a 40 percent increase in upgrade purchases.

Until 1990, Microsoft paid little attention to customer support services. That changed after one of Gates' "think weeks." From less than a few dozen customer support people, Microsoft organized a Product Support Services (PSS) division and staffed it with more than 2,000 customer support engineers in the United States and another 1,000 working abroad. To ensure that the quality of its service is high, Microsoft spends about $550 million each year in customer support services, which are organized according to product groups. Customer support engineers answer questions from callers and provide solutions to their problems.

Because telephone calls from customers are expensive, Microsoft is turning to automated services, electronic deliver—from CD-ROMS to the World Wide Web—and outsourcing to third parties. One of its automated support services is FastTips, a 24-hour service that provides technical information about Microsoft's products and answers to the most commonly asked questions. Software developers are working on a new technology that uses language queries and artificial intelligence to detect problems and deliver solutions to customers. Microsoft is also testing a pilot program with corporate customers that uses videoconferencing technology so support engineers can jointly work with customers instead on making site visits to diagnose and solve problems.

Questions

1. Describe Microsoft's promotional mix for corporate customers and for the consumer market.
2. What types of advertising does Microsoft use? Give an example of each type.
3. Many industry experts say that Bill Gates is Microsoft's best salesperson. Do you agree? Why or why not?

PART 7

PRICING STRATEGY

INC. © 1988

CHAPTER 20

PRICE DETERMINATION

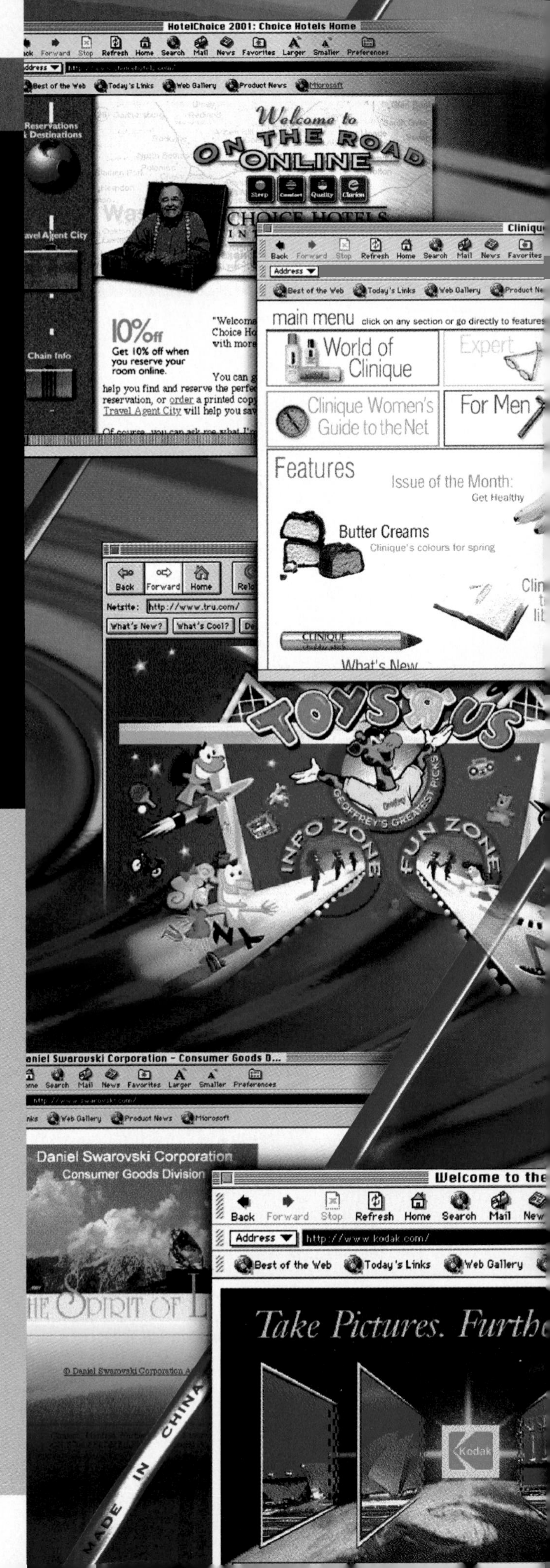

HotelChoice 2001: Choice Hotels Home
Welcome to
ON THE ROAD ONLINE
10% off
Get 10% off when you reserve your room online.
main menu click on any section or go directly to features
World of Clinique
Clinique Women's Guide to the Net
For Men
Features
Issue of the Month: Get Healthy
Butter Creams
Clinique's colours for spring
http://www.tru.com/
What's New?
What's Cool?
GEOFFREY'S GREATEST PICKS
INFO ZONE
FUN ZONE
Daniel Swarovski Corporation
Consumer Goods Division
MADE IN CHINA
http://www.kodak.com/
Take Pictures. Furth
Kodak

Chapter Objectives

1. Outline the legal constraints on pricing.
2. Identify the major categories of pricing objectives.
3. Explain the concept of price elasticity and its determinants.
4. List the practical problems involved in applying price theory concepts to actual pricing decisions.
5. Explain the major cost-plus approaches to price setting.
6. List the major advantages and shortcomings of using breakeven analysis in pricing decisions.
7. Explain the superiority of modified breakeven analysis over the basic breakeven model.
8. Identify the major issues related to price determination in international marketing.

Long-Distance Phone Wars Go Local

Everyone with a telephone has become a target in the long-distance telephone wars of the 1990s. Telecommunications giants AT&T, MCI, and Sprint have struggled among themselves and with dozens of other lesser-known competitors for phone customers' long-distance business. Now the battles are about to move into the local markets.

The Telecommunications Act of 1996 promises to turn the phone industry upside down. The landmark legislation invited the long-distance heavyweights to compete in the $100-billion local phone market. Also, the regional Bell operating companies (the so-called *Baby Bells*) gained access to the $70-billion long-distance market.

No one can yet predict the precise effect of this change on consumers' wallets, but prices will surely react. In recent years, long-distance rates charged by the three biggest providers have differed by only a penny or two per minute. That price stability will likely disappear once the Baby Bells charge into the fray.

Industry analysts caution consumers that even an all-out price war would lead to savings barely sufficient to pay for a dinner out. The typical monthly telephone bill for Americans reaches only $50, including both local and long-distance charges, so even a large-percentage reduction would not amount to much cash.

The Baby Bells have long held a formidable weapon in the market for local phone service. After all, these regional phone companies actually own the wires that stretch into businesses and homes. But changing regulations will muzzle the strength of this once-dominant advantage. A provision of the Telecommunications Act requires the Baby Bells to sell access to their networks, so long-distance carriers can reach local customers. Availability of this link to local telephone customers removes a major obstacle to market entry, and it may also drive down rates as the long-distance price war moves onto a new battle front.

Despite this major legal victory, the telecommunications giants would prefer not to depend on local telephone carriers for their communications infrastructure. Huge sums are being poured into technology in an effort to find methods of offering local service without using Ameritech, Pacific Bell, and the other local telephone carriers as intermediaries.

AT&T
AT&T SERVICES
Wednesday, 02-Apr-97 10:00:13 EST
AT&T SERVICES
FOR YOUR HOME
FOR YOUR BUSINESS
ON THE NET
HELP
WRITE TO US
HOME
AT&T Services
For Your Home
On the Net
For Your Business
FOR YOUR BUSINESS
Look in For Your Business for time- and money-saving solutions. From at-home businesses to global corporations, we can help make your company more productive.
FOR YOUR HOME
AT&T has services For Your Home to keep you and your family in touch. Toll-free numbers, follow-me numbers, collect calling, wireless, ISDN and lots more.
ON THE NET
Are you doing business On The Net or surfing for fun? Look here for everything from Internet access to Net savvy AT&T PocketNet™ phones.
WORLD OF SERVICES
Consumers are discovering a World of Services: wireless, long distance, home entertainment, online and all-in-one credit cards. AT&T brings all your connections together.

With digital, wireless networks similar to cellular phone networks, the long-distance carriers could bypass these intermediaries and potential competitors. AT&T has created an electronic box for the home market that plugs local customers into its wireless system. The box is expected to cost about $300, but it would enable users to purchase local phone service for as little as $10 a month—about half the current typical monthly charge for local phone service in U.S. markets.

http://www.att.com/

The project forms part of AT&T's lightning offensive against the Baby Bells that began just after the new federal deregulation law took effect. In an effort to block the Baby Bells from marching into the long-distance business, it launched a preemptive discount pricing scheme for local phone markets in various U.S. cities. In an attack against Ameritech in Illinois, for instance, AT&T offered rock-bottom prices for local-toll calling, that is, calls to numbers outside the callers' local markets but that did not cross into long-distance markets. AT&T may launch another price offensive in Connecticut to foil Southern New England Telecommunications Corp., which has already grabbed 15 percent of the state's long-distance market.

"In competitive markets you can only be aggressive, giving the customers value, or you will lose," says Joseph Nacchio, AT&T's president of consumer services. "We will be the market leader when the dust settles—and will be as aggressive as necessary to get there."

Ultimately, many big and small telephone companies will pursue the same objective: capture customers by offering complete bundles of phone services. Under this scenario, customers will receive their local and long-distance service—along with paging, cellular, and Internet access—from one company. Each consumer will tailor a communications package to personal needs and pay one price for it.

"All market research indicates that one-stop shopping is popular with consumers," says Eric Rabe, assistant vice president with Bell Atlantic. "If you're a company that can only offer some of these, you're at a disadvantage."[1]

CHAPTER OVERVIEW

As a starting point for examining pricing strategy, consider the meaning of the term *price.* A **price** is the exchange value of a good or service—in other words, what it can be exchanged for in the marketplace. Price does not necessarily involve money. In earlier times, the price of an acre of land might have been 20 bushels of wheat, three head of cattle, or one boat. This barter practice continues in some areas of the world. However, in a modern monetary system, *price* refers to the amount of funds required to purchase a product.

As AT&T marketers recognize, the method of setting prices on its phone service can be a major component of a successful marketing strategy. At the same time, prices are both difficult to set and dynamic; they shift in response to a number of variables. A higher-than-average price can convey an image of prestige, while a lower-than-average price may connote good value. Price can also powerfully affect a company's overall profitability and market share.

This chapter discusses the process of determining a profitable but justifiable (fair) price. The chapter focuses on management of the pricing function and discusses pricing strategies, price-quality relationships, and pricing in both the industrial and public sectors. It also looks at the effects of various conditions on price determination, including legal constraints, competitive pressures, and changes in global markets.

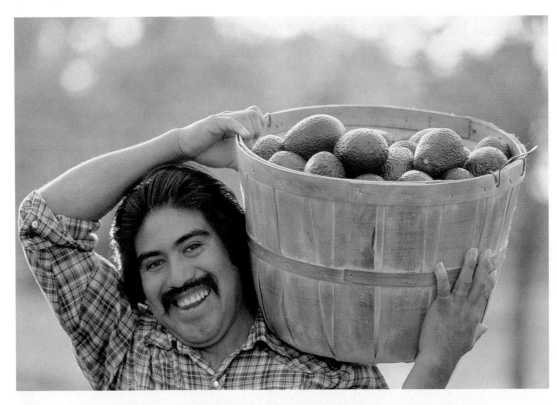

Although Mexican farmers can produce a Hass avocado for about 25 percent of what California growers must spend, federal restrictions keep them out of many U.S. markets. As a result, Americans find higher prices at the supermarket.

LEGAL CONSTRAINTS ON PRICING

Pricing decisions must recognize a variety of legal constraints imposed by both federal and state governments. Tariffs sometimes permit firms to set prices on domestically produced goods well above world market levels. For example, Los Angeles supermarket shoppers recently paid $1.79 for California-grown Hass avocados, while Toronto purchasers were buying Mexican-grown produce for 79 cents each. The U.S. Department of Agriculture, alleging that Mexican avocados may carry seed weevils and other pests, severely restricts their importation into the western United States. Although the Mexican-grown variety holds a commanding 73 percent share of the Canadian market and dominates the markets in both Japan and Europe, the USDA restrictions allow U.S. growers to set prices higher than world market levels.[2]

Briefly speaking

"A thing is worth whatever the buyer will pay for it."

Publilius Syrus
(1st century B.C.)
Latin writer of mimes

Pricing is also regulated by the general constraints of U.S. antitrust legislation, as outlined in Chapter 3. The following sections discuss some of the most important pricing laws.

Robinson-Patman Act

The **Robinson-Patman Act** (1936) typifies Depression-era legislation. Known in some circles as the *Anti-A&P Act,* it was inspired by price competition from the developing grocery store chains—in fact, the original draft was prepared by the United States Wholesale Grocers Association. Legislators saw the country in the midst of the Great Depression, and they intended the law

Marketing Dictionary

price The exchange value of a good or service.

Robinson-Patman Act A federal law prohibiting price discrimination that is not based on a cost differential as well as selling at unreasonably low prices to eliminate competitors.

Figure 20.1 Protecting Brand Image by Avoiding Price Discounting

AROMATICS ELIXIR
CLINIQUE
Aromatics Elixir photographed for Clinique by Irving Penn.

primarily to save jobs. They perceived the developing chain stores as threats to traditional retailing and employment, and established the act to counteract the trend.

The Robinson-Patman Act, which technically was an amendment to the Clayton Act, prohibits price discrimination in sales to wholesalers, retailers, and other producers; basically, differences in price must reflect cost differentials. The act also disallows selling at unreasonably low prices in order to drive competitors out of business. The Clayton Act had applied only to price discrimination between geographic areas, which injured local sellers. Supporters justified the Robinson-Patman legislation by arguing that the chain stores might secure volume discounts from suppliers, while small, independent stores would continue to pay undiscounted prices.

The willingness of book publishers to cut special deals for big customers recently led the American Booksellers Association to file suit. The ABA, acting on behalf of small, independent booksellers, charged that five publishers were giving unjustly lower prices and promotional allowances to big chains such as B. Dalton and Barnes & Noble.[3]

Firms accused of price discrimination often argue that they set price differentials to meet competitors' prices and that cost differences justify variations in prices. When a firm asserts that it maintains price differentials as good-faith methods of competing with rivals, a logical question arises: What constitutes good-faith pricing behavior? The answer depends on the particular situation.

A defense based on cost differentials works only if the price differences do not exceed the cost differences resulting from selling to various classes of buyers. Marketers must then justify the cost differences; indeed, many authorities consider this provision one of the most confusing areas in the Robinson-Patman Act.

The varying interpretations of the act certainly qualify it as one of the vaguest laws that affect marketing. Courts handle most charges brought under the act as individual cases. Therefore, domestic marketers must continually evaluate their pricing actions to avoid potential Robinson-Patman violations.

The Robinson-Patman Act does not cover export markets, though. U.S. law does not prohibit a domestic firm from selling a product to a foreign customer at a price significantly lower than the domestic wholesale price.

Unfair-Trade Laws

States supplement federal legislation with their own **unfair-trade laws,** which require sellers to maintain minimum prices for comparable merchandise. Enacted in the 1930s, these laws were intended to protect small, specialty shops, such as dairy stores, from *loss-leader pricing* tactics, in which chain stores might sell certain products below cost to attract customers. Typical state laws set retail price floors at cost plus some modest markup.

Although most unfair-trade laws have remained on the books for the past 60 years, marketers had all but forgotten them until recent years. Then in 1993, Wal-Mart, the nation's largest retailer, was found guilty of violating Arkansas' unfair-trade law for selling drugs and health and beauty aids below cost. The lawsuit filed by three independent drugstore owners accused the mass merchandiser of attempting to drive them out of business through predatory pricing practices. Wal-Mart appealed the decision, but similar lawsuits have been filed in several other states, all seeking to end the chain's low-price marketing strategy.[4]

Fair-Trade Laws

The concept of fair trade has affected pricing decisions for decades. **Fair-trade laws** allow manufacturers to stipulate minimum retail prices for their products and to require retail dealers to sign contracts agreeing to abide by these prices.

The basic argument behind this legislation asserts that a product's image, determined in part by its price, is a property right of the manufacturer. Therefore, the producer should have the authority to protect its asset by requiring retailers to maintain a minimum price. The image of Clinique skin-care products, shown in Figure 20.1, is affected

http://www.clinique.com/

by the images of the retail stores that feature the Clinique lines and the prices that these stores charge. Although Clinique marketers do not set final retail prices, they distribute selectively through carefully chosen retail stores. This way, they can coordinate the prices charged by their retail partners and discourage price discounting, which might adversely affect the Clinique image.

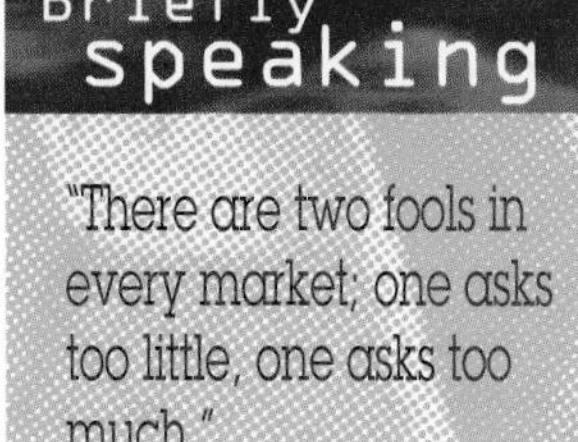
Briefly speaking

"There are two fools in every market; one asks too little, one asks too much."

Russian proverb

The origins of fair-trade legislation trace back to lobbying efforts by organizations of independent retailers fearful of chain store growth. The economic mania of the Depression years was clearly reflected in these statutes. In 1931, California became the first state to enact fair-trade legislation. Most other states soon followed; only Missouri, the District of Columbia, Vermont, and Texas failed to adopt such laws.

A U.S. Supreme Court decision invalidated fair-trade contracts in interstate commerce, and Congress responded by passing the *Miller Tydings Resale Price Maintenance Act* (1937). This law exempted interstate fair-trade contracts from compliance with antitrust requirements, thus freeing states to keep these laws on their books if they so desired.

Over the years, fair-trade laws declined in importance as discounters emerged and price competition gained strength in marketing strategy. These laws became invalid with the passage of the *Consumer Goods Pricing Act* (1975), which halted all interstate enforcement of resale price maintenance provisions, an objective long sought by consumer groups.

THE ROLE OF PRICE IN THE MARKETING MIX

Ancient philosophers recognized the importance of price in an economic system. Some early written accounts refer to attempts to determine fair or just prices. Price continues to serve as a means of regulating economic activity. Employment of any or all of the four factors of production—natural resources, capital, human resources, and entrepreneurship—depends on the prices that those factors receive. An individual firm's prices and the resulting purchases by its customers determine how much revenue the company receives. Prices, therefore, influence a firm's profits as well as its employment of the factors of production.

PRICING OBJECTIVES

Just as price is a component of the total marketing mix, pricing objectives also represent components of the organization's overall objectives. As Chapter 5 explained, marketing objectives state the outcomes that executives hope to attain. They derive from and support the overall objectives of the organization. The objectives of the firm and its marketing organization guide development of pricing objectives, which in turn lead to development and implementation of more specific pricing policies and procedures.

A firm might set a major overall objective of becoming the dominant producer in its domestic market. It might then develop a marketing objective of achieving maximum sales penetration in each region, followed by a related pricing objective to set prices at levels that maximize sales. These objectives might lead to adoption of a low-price policy

Marketing Dictionary

unfair-trade law A state law requiring sellers to maintain minimum prices for comparable merchandise.

fair-trade law A statute (enacted in most states) that permits manufacturers to stipulate minimum retail prices for their products.

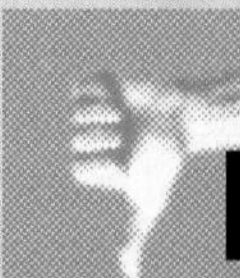
MARKETING HALL OF SHAME

The Price of Price Fixing

Not many people know what lysine is, but the Federal Bureau of Investigation learned plenty during its undercover investigation of methods for setting prices on the livestock feed additive in the global marketplace. The investigation stirred a flurry of media attention when the Archer-Daniels-Midland Co. (ADM) agreed to pay a $100 million fine—the largest criminal antitrust settlement in American history. ADM, which runs television ads calling itself the "supermarket to the world," admitted it fixed prices of lysine and citric acid, used for food flavoring.

But that agreement did not end the agribusiness giant's legal woes. Months later, a federal grand jury indicted three of ADM's former top executives on criminal antitrust charges. One of the trio, Michael Andreas, is the son of ADM's chairman and chief executive officer, Dwayne Andreas. Before taking a leave of absence from the firm, Michael Andreas was widely considered the heir apparent to succeed his 78-year-old father, an ADM legend. Also indicted was Terrance S. Wilson, who oversaw the company's corn-processing operations. Wilson retired two days after ADM pleaded guilty to price rigging.

The FBI faces a potentially monumental task proving that a corporation has engaged in price fixing. In the ADM case, however, an undercover insider helped to shed light on ADM's disregard for antitrust laws. Mark Whitacre, a former ADM executive, approached the FBI with his concerns regarding the Decatur, Illinois, company's attempts to artificially hike prices. Eager for an insider's help, the FBI equipped Whitacre with a hidden tape recorder.

By Whitacre's estimate, he taped 1,500 conversations—many of them incriminating—with ADM managers over two and a half years. He also recorded, and sometimes videotaped, ADM officials conspiring with foreign competitors to set prices. In addition, he says he captured on tape both Michael and Dwayne Andreas repeating the company's unofficial mantra—"The competitor is our friend and the customer is our enemy."

The U.S. Justice Department's continuing prosecution in the ADM case, however, doesn't promise the cut-and-dried result that the tapes might suggest. Investigators worry that Whitacre, their star witness, is no choir boy. He has acknowledged diverting millions of dollars from ADM into his personal accounts.

implemented by offering substantial price discounts to channel members.

Price also affects, and is affected by, the other elements of the marketing mix. Product decisions, promotional plans, and distribution choices all impact the price of a good or service. For example, products distributed through complex channels involving several intermediaries must be priced high enough to cover the markups needed to compensate wholesalers and retailers for services they provide. Basic so-called "fighting brands" intended to capture market share from higher-priced, options-laden competitors must carry relatively low prices to entice customers to give up some options in return for a cost savings.

While pricing objectives vary from firm to firm, they can be classified into four major groups: (1) profitability objectives, (2) volume objectives, (3) meeting competition objectives, and (4) prestige objectives. Profitability objectives include profit maximization and target-return goals. Volume objectives pursue either sales maximization or market-share goals.

Profitability Objectives

Classical economic theory bases its conclusions on certain assumptions. For one, it presumes that firms will behave rationally. Also, theorists expect that rational behavior will result in an effort to maximize gains and minimize losses.

At first glance, auto insurer Progressive Corp. might seem irrational in its pursuit of profit maximization. It targets customers whom other insurers avoid. However, the company's marketing plan actually lays out an effective way to achieve profitability objectives.

Progressive markets its insurance to what is known in the industry as a *nonstandard group.* Its customers include people whose policies have been canceled or rejected by other insurers for various reasons, including numerous accidents and difficulty reading English. Despite its unusual customer base, however, Progressive is one of the most profitable insurance firms in the country. In the past ten years, its revenues have grown more than 20 percent each year, over twice the industry average. During the same period, the company's return on shareholders' equity has av-

Furthermore, he has failed to pay taxes on the money. Whitacre defends the arrangement as a typical procedure for compensating ADM executives. In a surprising move, the Justice Department indicted Whitacre along with the two ADM officials he helped to bring down.

http://www.admworld.com/

Observers continue to wonder whether ADM has learned any lessons from this messy stain on its corporate reputation. After agreeing to pay the $100 million fine, it released a statement saying that the plea bargain "brings to a close all Department of Justice investigations of alleged misconduct by ADM." The statement assured stock market investors that ADM had resolved the criminal matter, and it would "focus exclusively on growing its business and maximizing shareholder value."

The Justice Department's opinion differs, however; investigators describe the case as far from closed. "ADM is trying to give the agreement a spin," suggests Gary Spratling, a deputy assistant attorney general. "The investigations will continue." The company's agreement protects it only from further prosecution for a specific list of antitrust violations if it cooperates with the Justice Department.

Meanwhile, if ADM insiders feel shame at their company's conduct, they don't act like it. Before the younger Andreas began his leave of absence, the board gave him a 15 percent raise. It also fattened Dwayne Andreas' $3 million salary. Clucking disapproval, a *Fortune* magazine article insisted that the supermarket to the world is acting more like an "international den of thieves."

QUESTIONS FOR CRITICAL THINKING

1. **Do you think that the pricing scandal will hurt ADM's public image, or does the corporation gain some insulation from popular criticism, since it markets its products to producers and intermediaries rather than directly to the public?**
2. **What obstacles would the federal government have to overcome to investigate and prove that a company has engaged in price fixing?**

Sources: Ronald Henkoff, "Betrayal: The ADM Scandal," *Fortune*, February 3, 1997, pp. 82–91; Scott Kilman and Thomas M. Burton, "Two Ex-ADM Aides May Be Indicted in Criminal Price-Fixing Case Today," *Wall Street Journal*, December 3, 1996, pp. A3, A6; and Ronald Henkoff, "ADM Still Doesn't Get It," *Fortune*, November 11, 1996; and Ronald Henkoff, "The ADM Tale Gets Even Stranger," *Fortune*, May 12, 1996, pp. 113–120.

eraged 20 percent, compared to 8 percent for the industry. In an era when most insurance companies lose 10 percent underwriting auto insurance, Progressive earns almost 1 percent profit a year.

The insurer's secret for success lies in careful research and smart pricing. Progressive invests far more than its competitors do in researching and analyzing accident data. This insight allows it to predict the likelihood of each policyholder having an accident; the firm then sets its premiums according to this probability. Important characteristics in calculating a premium include a policyholder's gender, age, ticket history, and type of car. The company would charge a 35-year-old woman with one speeding ticket $605 to insure a Ford Taurus, $666 for a BMW 325i, and $728 for a Mazda Miata.

Careful attention to details can also lead to profit maximization. CEO Peter Lewis keeps a close eye on Progressive's policies and business ventures, and the firm quickly pulls out of any that could sap overall profits. He says, "We just don't allow unprofitable businesses to continue."[5]

Profits are a function of revenue and expenses:

$$\text{Profits} = \text{Revenue} - \text{Expenses}$$

Revenue is determined by the product's selling price and number of units sold:

$$\text{Total Revenue} = \text{Price} \times \text{Quantity Sold}$$

A profit maximizing price, therefore, rises to the point at which further increases will cause disproportionate decreases in the number of units sold. A 10 percent price increase that results in only an 8 percent cut in volume will add to the firm's revenue. However, a 10 percent price hike that results in an 11 percent sales decline will reduce revenue.

Economists refer to this approach as *marginal analysis*. They identify **profit maximization** as the point at which the addition to total revenue is just balanced by the increase in total cost. Marketers must resolve a basic problem of how to achieve this delicate balance when they set prices. Relatively few firms actually hit this elusive target. A significantly larger number prefer to direct their efforts toward more achievable goals.

Figure 20.2 Price as a Tool to Achieve Volume Objectives

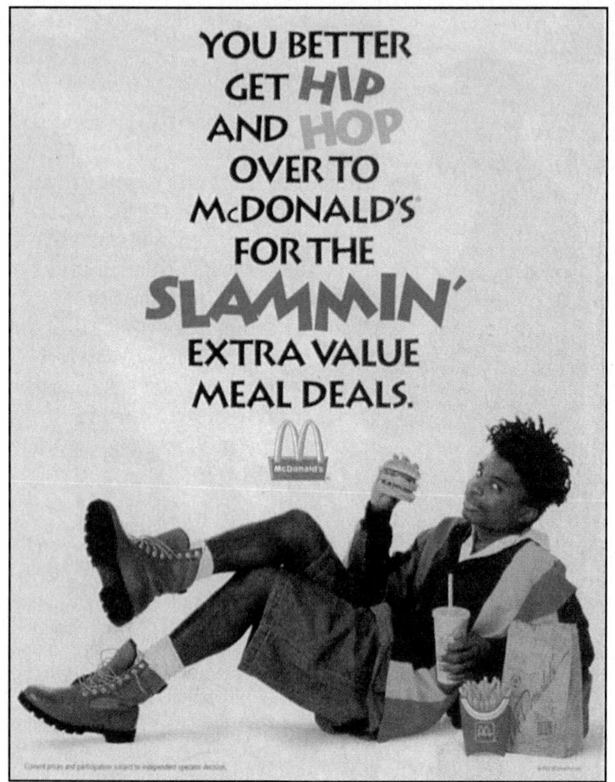
YOU BETTER
GET HIP
AND HOP
OVER TO
McDONALD'S
FOR THE
SLAMMIN'
EXTRA VALUE
MEAL DEALS.

Consequently, they commonly set **target return objectives**—short-run or long-run goals usually stated as percentages of sales or investment. The practice has become particularly popular among large firms in which other pressures interfere with profit maximization objectives. Target return objectives offer several benefits for marketers in addition to resolving pricing questions. For example, they serve as tools for evaluating performance. They also satisfy desires to generate "fair" profits as judged by management, stockholders, and the public.

Volume Objectives

Many business executives argue that pricing behavior actually seeks to maximize *sales* within a given profit constraint. In other words, they set a minimum acceptable profit level and then seek to maximize sales (subject to this profit constraint) in the belief that the increased sales are more important than immediate high profits to the long-run competitive picture. Such a company continues to expand sales as long as its total profits do not drop below the minimum return acceptable to management.

Fast-food restaurants compete fiercely to maximize sales. One effective tool in this effort is price. To encourage additional sales to each customer, McDonald's pioneered the concept of extra-value meals. The company bundled burgers with more profitable french fries and drinks, as illustrated in Figure 20.2. The strategy proved particularly effective with fast-food's heavy users, young males searching for a lot of food at low cost.

Sales maximization can also result from nonprice variables such as service and quality. McDonald's, for instance, guarantees a free meal to any consumer who doesn't like the service or the food. Burger King has started offering table service for customers who don't feel like waiting in line.[6]

Another volume-related pricing objective—the *market share objective*—sets a goal to control a portion of the market for a firm's good or service. The company's specific goal may target maintaining its present share of a particular market or increasing its share, say, from 10 percent to 20 percent.

Volume-related goals such as sales maximization and market share objectives play important roles in most firms' pricing decisions.

The PIMS Studies Market share objectives may provide critical support for achievement of other organizational objectives. High sales, for example, often mean high profits. The extensive **Profit Impact of Market Strategies (PIMS) project,** conducted by the Marketing Science Institute, analyzed more than 2,000 firms to measure the characteristics that determine success. This research identified two of the most important determinants of profitability as product quality and market share. Ads like the one in Figure 20.3 help to enhance Kodak's profitability and position as the global market leader in its class. "Imagine if it's my first time in Acapulco or my first grandchild and I use another film—my wife is gonna kill me," said one consumer when asked whether he would switch from Kodak to a lesser-known film brand with a smaller market share. A recent analysis of 48 studies confirmed the link between market share and profitability.[7]

http://www.kodak.com/

The relationship between market share and profitability is evident in PIMS data that reveal an average 32 percent return on investment for firms with market shares over 40 percent. In contrast, average ROI decreases to 24 percent for firms with market shares between 20 percent and 40 percent. Firms with minor market shares (less than 10 percent) generate average pretax investment returns of approximately 13 percent.[8]

The relationship also applies to a firm's individual

brands. The PIMS researchers compared the top four brands in each market segment they studied. Their data revealed that the leading brand typically generates after-tax returns on investment of 18 percent, considerably higher than the second-ranked brand. Weaker brands, on average, fail to earn adequate returns.

Figure 20.3 **Enhancing Brand Strength by Linking Market Share to Profitability**

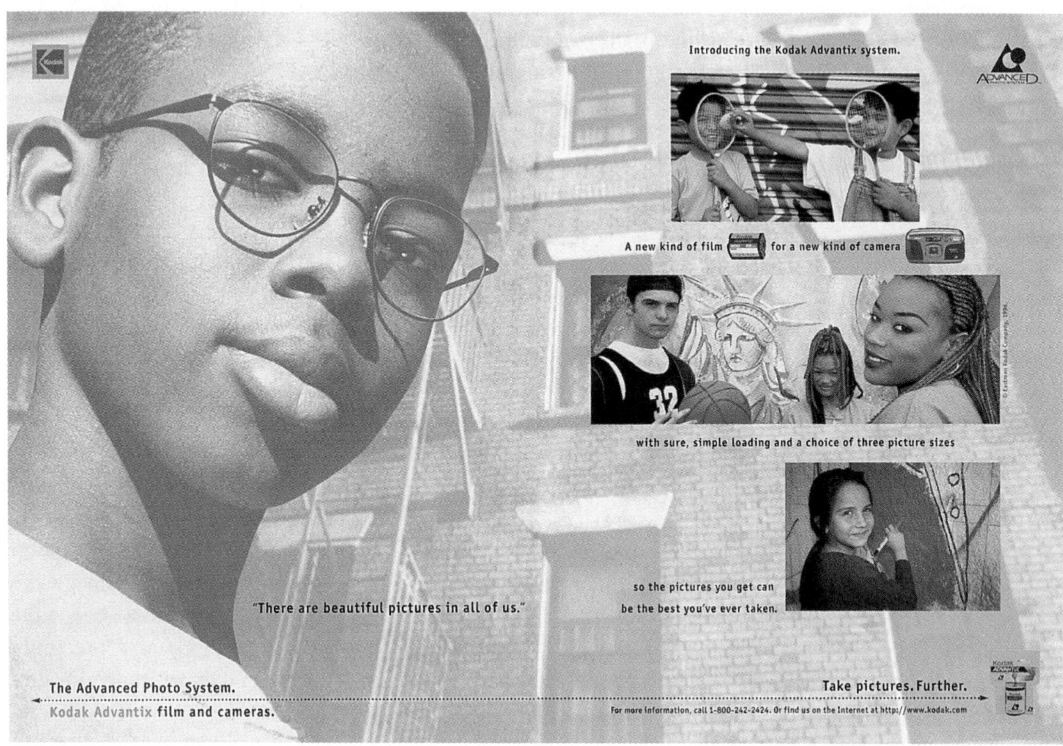
Introducing the Kodak Advantix system.
ADVANCED
A new kind of film
for a new kind of camera
with sure, simple loading and a choice of three picture sizes
so the pictures you get can be the best you've ever taken.
"There are beautiful pictures in all of us."
The Advanced Photo System.
Kodak Advantix film and cameras.
Take pictures. Further.
For more information, call 1-800-242-2424. Or find us on the Internet at http://www.kodak.com

Marketers have developed an underlying explanation of the positive relationship between profitability and market share. Firms with large shares accumulate greater operating experience and lower overall costs relative to competitors with smaller market shares. Accordingly, segmentation strategies might focus on obtaining larger shares of smaller markets and avoiding smaller shares of larger ones. A firm might achieve higher financial returns by becoming a major competitor in several smaller market segments than by remaining a relatively minor competitor in a larger market.

In any industry, most companies fight constantly for greater control of their markets as a survival strategy. Snack-maker Frito-Lay, with approximately 55 percent of the U.S. market, dominates its industry so completely that competitor Anheuser-Busch was unable to find a buyer for its Eagle-brand line of snack foods. A-B discontinued the line, even though it controlled 10 percent of the U.S. market.

The breakfast cereal industry offers another example of the relationship between price and market share. In addition to giving shoppers 20 percent lower prices for their favorite cereals, the recent rounds of price cuts also succeeded in driving firms with low market shares out of the marketplace. Fourth-place Ralcorp decided to give up the branded cereal game, selling its Chex line to General Mills. The firm continued to compete in this market only as a producer of private-label cereals.[9]

Meeting Competition Objectives

A third set of pricing objectives seeks simply to meet competitor's prices. In many lines of business, firms set their own prices to match those of established industry price leaders.

These kinds of objectives de-emphasize the price element of the marketing mix and focus competitive rivalries more strongly on nonprice variables. Pricing is a highly

Marketing Dictionary

profit maximization The point at which the additional revenue gained by increasing the price of a product equals the increase in total costs.

target return objective A short-run or long-run pricing practice intended to achieve a specified return on either sales or investment.

Profit Impact of Market Strategies (PIMS) project A research program that discovered a strong positive relationship between a firm's market share and its return on investment.

visible component of a firm's marketing mix and an easy and effective tool for obtaining a differential advantage over competitors; still, other firms can easily duplicate a price reduction themselves. The airline price competition of recent years exemplifies the actions and reactions of competitors in this marketplace. Because such price changes directly affect overall profitability in an industry, many firms attempt to promote stable prices by meeting competitors' prices and competing for market share by focusing on product strategies, promotional decisions, and distribution—the nonprice elements of the marketing mix. Choice Hotels International, whose franchises include Rodeway, Comfort Inn, Quality Inn, and four other motel chains, has long competed for the loyalty of older travelers. Its pricing strategy emphasizes big discounts to attract this price-sensitive segment. As a result, more than 30 percent of Choice customers are 60 years or older, and the company regards this group as its largest and fastest-growing market segment. Now, the hotel chain is also testing the appeal of nonprice elements, such as room design, to these customers. It has equipped 25 percent of Rodeway's rooms with telephones and TV remote controls with large buttons and numbers. Softly lighted wall switches help guests to navigate at night, and, instead of doorknobs, lever handles make doors more accessible to arthritic hands. Says a Choice manager, "The test is that you should be able to open every door and every drawer with your fist."[10]

http://www.choicehotels.com/

Value Pricing When price discounts become normal elements of a competitive marketplace, other marketing mix elements gain importance in purchase decisions. In such instances, overall product value, not just price, determines product choice. In recent years, a new strategy—**value pricing**—has emerged to emphasize benefits a product provides in comparison to the price and quality levels of competing offerings. This strategy typically works best for relatively low-priced goods and services. Notes one consultant, "Value is the hot message in the marketplace."[11]

Laundry detergents are a good example. The label on Dash detergent proclaims *Value Price,* while Arm & Hammer's label assures customers that it *Cleans Great! Value Price, too!* Yes detergent announces *Great Value!* while Ultra Rinso claims *Super Value* and the back label on Ultra Trend brags that it offers *hard-working performance at a reasonable price.* The label on another detergent, All, simply advises customers to *Compare & Save.*

Value-priced products generally cost less than premium brands, but marketers point out that *value* doesn't necessarily mean *cheap.* Says a Procter & Gamble manager, "Value is not just price but also is linked to the performance and meeting expectations and needs of consumers." The challenge for those who compete on value is to convince customers that low-priced brands offer quality comparable to that of a higher-priced product.

Many marketers anticipate growing importance for the value pricing strategy. "Value pricing is like chicken pox—it tends to be catching," notes one consultant. "Ultimately every manufacturer goes to value pricing. Value positioning is going to break out in other categories, and they will all get 'value positioning' disease. No one wants to let any competitor get any sort of edge."[12]

Prestige Objectives

The final category of pricing objectives, unrelated to either profitability or sales volume, encompasses prestige objectives. Prestige pricing establishes a relatively high price to develop and maintain an image of quality and exclusiveness that appeals to status-conscious consumers. Such objectives reflect marketers' recognition of the role of price in creating an overall image for the firm and its goods and services.

Prestige objectives affect the price tags of such products as Baccarat crystal, Louis Vuitton luggage, Rolls Royce automobiles, Rolex watches, and Tiffany jewelry. When a perfume marketer sets a price of $135 or more an ounce, this choice reflects an emphasis on image far more than the cost of ingredients. Analyses have shown that ingredients account for less than 5 percent of a perfume's cost. Thus, advertisements for Joy that promote the fragrance as the "costliest perfume in the world" use price to promote product prestige.

In contrast to low-price strategies used by marketers of economical auto models such as Kia, Chrysler's Neon, and Ford's Escort, ads for the exotic Lamborghini sports car emphasize the brand's special image. The ad in Figure 20.4 targets upscale clientele interested in the vehicle's exotic design and how it fits into their lifestyle; it also seeks to attract a buyer financially able to write out a $239,000 check for a new Diablo VT (or $255,000 for the even more upscale Diablo SE). To increase prestige, the ads appear only in upscale magazines like *The Robb Report;* they focus on speed and sensual beauty instead of price.[13]

While ads for luxury products may hint at high prices, few have openly mentioned price in the past. Cosmetics companies, for instance, seldom talk price in their advertisements. In the value-sensitive 1990s, however, some marketers of prestigious products have experimented with their own version of value pricing.

Cosmetics manufacturer Estée Lauder now includes product samples and retail prices in its advertisements. Marketing campaigns for Swarovski, which makes high-quality Austrian crystal jewelry, have always focused on the handmade, unique nature of each piece without citing any statistics. Recent ads, however, inform readers that Swarovski creates "fine fashion jewelry from $75 to

http://www.swarovski.com/

$1,000"; these ads also list the prices of pictured pieces. The firm made this change because, says President Sherry Baker, "People assume our jewelry is much more expensive" than it actually is.

Value pricing for prestige products stirs controversy, however. Some marketers feel that the strategy lures customers who otherwise would be scared away. Explains one consultant, "They need to tell consumers their products are within their reach." Others prefer the old-fashioned approach. Says one cosmetics marketer, "We absolutely would never talk price. We deal in an image-driven category, and we don't believe you should put a price on image."[14]

Figure 20.4 Advertisement Emphasizing Prestige

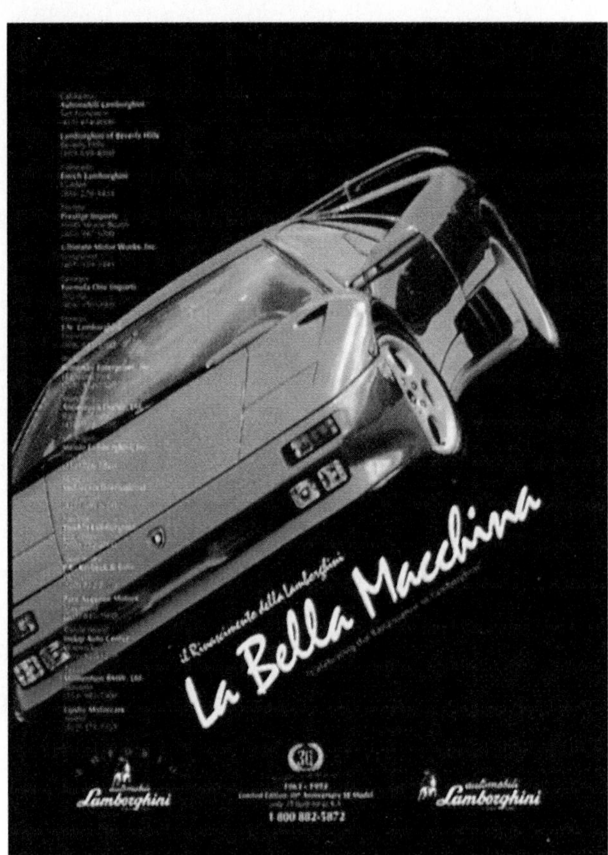
La Bella Macchina
Lamborghini
Lamborghini

Pricing Objectives of Not-for-Profit Organizations

Pricing typically is a very important element of the marketing mix for a not-for-profit organization. Pricing strategy can help these groups to achieve a variety of organizational goals:

1. *Profit maximization.* While not-for-profit organizations by definition do not cite profitability as a primary goal, they often try to maximize their financial returns on single events or series of events. A $1,000-a-plate political fund raiser is a classic example.
2. *Cost recovery.* Some not-for-profit organizations attempt to recover only the actual costs of their activities. Mass transit, publicly supported colleges, and toll bridges are common examples. The amount of costs that prices recover is often dictated by tradition, competition, and/or public opinion.
3. *Providing market incentives.* Not-for-profit groups may set lower-than-average prices or offer goods or services free of charge to encourage usage. Seattle's bus system offers free service in the downtown area in an attempt to reduce traffic congestion, encourage retail sales, and minimize the effort required to access downtown public services.
4. *Market suppression.* Prices can also discourage consumption. High prices help to accomplish social objectives independent of the costs of providing goods or services. Illustrations include tobacco and alcohol taxes, parking fines, tolls, and gasoline excise taxes.

METHODS FOR DETERMINING PRICES

Marketers determine prices in two basic ways—by applying the theoretical concepts of supply and demand and by completing cost-oriented analyses. During the first part of this century, most discussions of price determination emphasized the classical economic concepts of supply and demand. Since World War II, however, the emphasis has

Marketing Dictionary

value pricing A pricing strategy that emphasizes benefits a product provides in comparison to the price and quality levels of competing offerings.

Figure 20.5 Enhancing Value through Customary Pricing

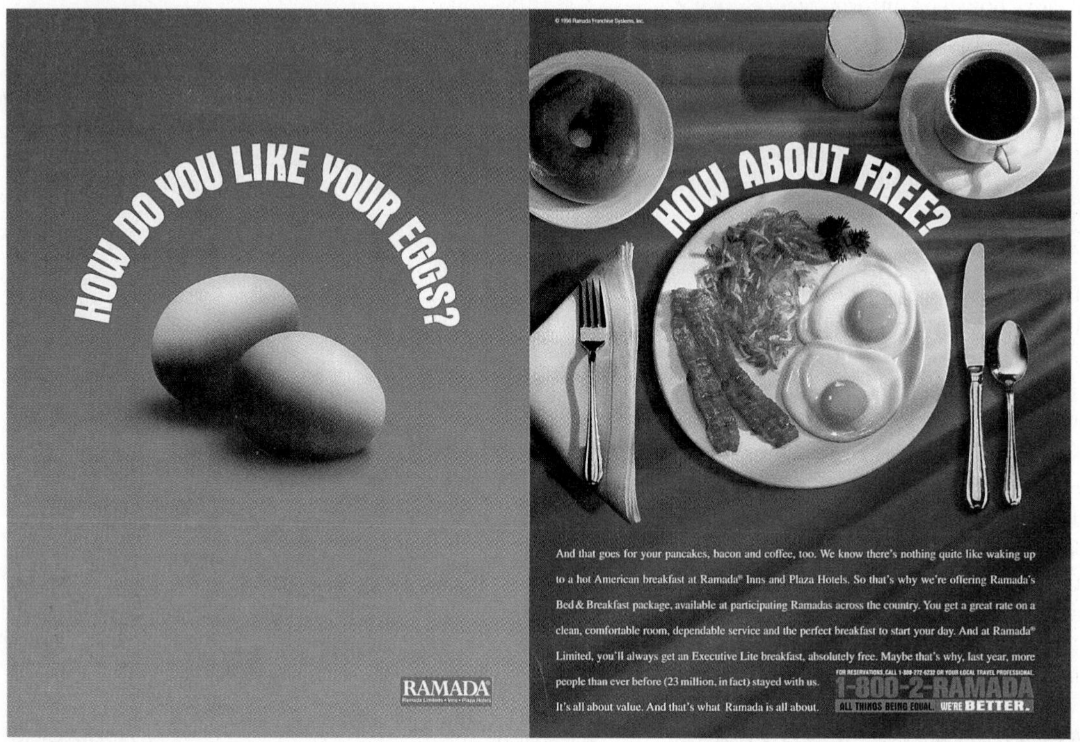
HOW DO YOU LIKE YOUR EGGS?
RAMADA
HOW ABOUT FREE?
And that goes for your pancakes, bacon and coffee, too. We know there's nothing quite like waking up to a hot American breakfast at Ramada® Inns and Plaza Hotels. So that's why we're offering Ramada's Bed & Breakfast package, available at participating Ramadas across the country. You get a great rate on a clean, comfortable room, dependable service and the perfect breakfast to start your day. And at Ramada® Limited, you'll always get an Executive Lite breakfast, absolutely free. Maybe that's why, last year, more people than ever before (23 million, in fact) stayed with us.
It's all about value. And that's what Ramada is all about.
1-800-2-RAMADA
ALL THINGS BEING EQUAL. WE'RE BETTER.

shifted toward cost-oriented pricing. Hindsight reveals certain flaws in both concepts.

Treatments of this subject often overlook another concept of price determination—one based on the impact of custom and tradition. **Customary prices** are retail prices that consumers expect as a result of tradition and social habit. Candy makers have attempted to maintain traditional price levels by considerably reducing product size. Similar practices have prevailed in the marketing of soft drinks as bottlers attempt to balance consumer expectations of customary prices with the realities of rising costs.

Wm. Wrigley Jr. Co., manufacturer of such chewing gum standards as Juicy Fruit, Doublemint, and Big Red, took advantage of the weakness in the industry's customary pricing strategy by introducing a smaller-quantity pack at a lower price. While its competitors continued to offer only seven-stick packs for 35 cents, Wrigley priced its five-stick packs at 25 cents. To spur impulse buying, the company prominently displayed the price on the package. The strategy was so successful that within two years of its inception, Wrigley discontinued selling seven-stick gum packs.

Ramada Inns have grown rapidly during the last ten years by maintaining moderate prices and emphasizing value. Hundreds of print ads similar to the one shown in Figure 20.5 have promoted themes like "a great rate for a clean, comfortable room, dependable service, and the perfect breakfast to start your day." By adding features such as a free, hot breakfast while maintaining its room rates, Ramada has enhanced the value of its offering. The firm did not attempt to change room rates competitive with Holiday Inn, Best Western, and Courtyard by Marriott at $50 to $75, since this level had become a well-established customary price. Ramada guests expect to pay this price when they book rooms, so the firm distinguishes itself in other ways.

At some point, however, someone has to set initial prices for products. In addition, competitive moves and cost changes necessitate periodic reviews of price structures. The remaining sections of this chapter discuss traditional and current concepts of price determination. They also consider how marketers can most effectively integrate the concepts to develop realistic pricing systems.

PRICE DETERMINATION IN ECONOMIC THEORY

Microeconomics suggests a way of determining prices that assumes a profit-maximization objective. This technique attempts to derive correct equilibrium prices in the marketplace by comparing supply and demand. It also requires more complete analysis than actual business firms typically conduct.

Demand refers to a schedule of the amounts of a firm's good or service that consumers will purchase at different prices during a specified period. **Supply** refers to a schedule of the amounts of a good or service that producers will offer for sale at different prices during a specified time period. These schedules vary for different types of market structures. Businesses operate and set prices in four types of market structures: pure competition, monopolistic competition, oligopoly, and monopoly.

Pure competition is a market structure composed of so many buyers and sellers that no single participant can significantly influence price. Pure competition presupposes other market conditions, as well: homogeneous products and ease of entry for sellers due to low start-up costs. While most of today's businesspeople encounter this market structure only in theory, the agricultural sector exhibits many characteristics of a purely competitive market, making it the closest actual example.

Monopolistic competition, the market structure that typifies most retailing, features large numbers of buyers and sellers. These diverse parties exchange heterogeneous, relatively well-differentiated products, giving marketers some control over prices.

Relatively few sellers compete in an **oligopoly.** Each seller may affect the market, but no single seller controls it. High start-up costs form significant barriers to entry for new competitors. Each firm's demand curve in an oligopolistic market displays a unique kink at the current market price. Because of the impact of a single competitor on total industry sales, competitors usually quickly match any attempt by one firm to generate additional sales by reducing prices. Price cutting throughout such an industry reduces total industry revenues. Oligopolies operate in the petroleum refining, automobile, and tobacco industries.

The availability of alternative air transportation from such discount carriers as Southwest Air and ValuJet forces established air carriers to maintain competitive air fares—or risk losing business to the upstarts. When these alternatives disappear (such as when ValuJet was temporarily grounded following a 1996 crash), prices often rise. For example, business travelers saw average fares jump 47 percent in a single month for flights between Atlanta and Charlotte when ValuJet's flights were halted, leaving only Delta and USAir to serve the route.[15]

Figure 20.6 How One Regulated Monopoly Reduces Prices

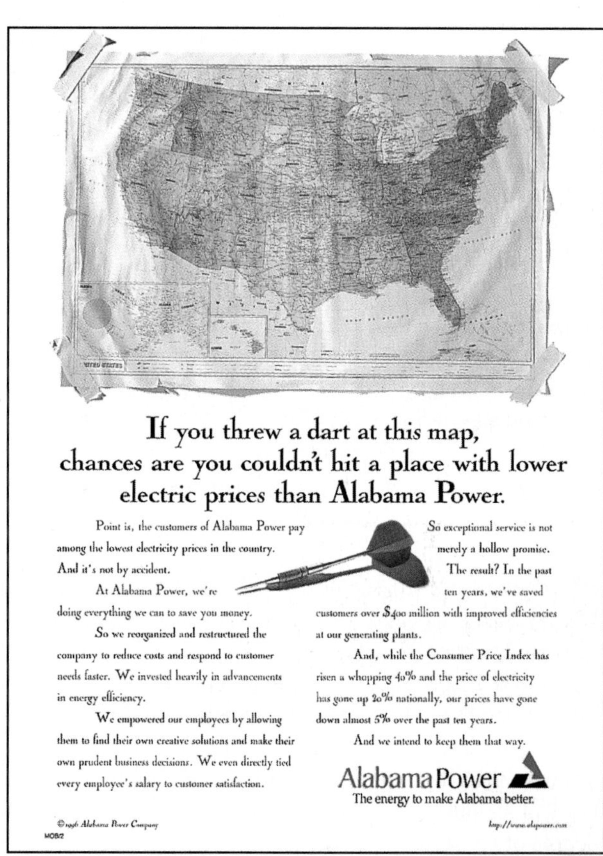
If you threw a dart at this map, chances are you couldn't hit a place with lower electric prices than Alabama Power.
Point is, the customers of Alabama Power pay among the lowest electricity prices in the country. And it's not by accident.
At Alabama Power, we're doing everything we can to save you money.
So we reorganized and restructured the company to reduce costs and respond to customer needs faster. We invested heavily in advancements in energy efficiency.
We empowered our employees by allowing them to find their own creative solutions and make their own prudent business decisions. We even directly tied every employee's salary to customer satisfaction.
So exceptional service is not merely a hollow promise.
The result? In the past ten years, we've saved customers over $400 million with improved efficiencies at our generating plants.
And, while the Consumer Price Index has risen a whopping 40% and the price of electricity has gone up 20% nationally, our prices have gone down almost 5% over the past ten years.
And we intend to keep them that way.
Alabama Power
The energy to make Alabama better.
MOB/2

A **monopoly** market structure features dominance by only one seller of a product for which buyers can find no close substitutes. Antitrust legislation has nearly eliminated monopolies; only temporary monopolies, such as those created through patent protection, and regulated monopolies, such as utility companies, continue to operate without competitors. The government allows regulated monopolies in markets where competition would lead to uneconomical duplication of services. In return for such a license, government agencies reserve the right to regulate the monopoly's rate of return.

Even though public commissions set prices charged by regulated monopolies in their states, these monopolies still affect rates through productivity improvements. As the Alabama Power Co. ad shown in Figure 20.6 states, the electrical utility has reduced prices almost 5 percent over the past ten years to offer its

Marketing Dictionary

customary price The traditional amount that customers expect to pay for a certain good or service.

demand A schedule of the amounts of a firm's product that consumers will purchase at different prices during a specified time period.

supply A schedule of the amounts of a good or service that a firm will offer for sale at different prices during a specified time period.

pure competition A market structure in which many buyers and sellers exchange homogeneous products, so no single participant has a significant influence on price.

monopolistic competition A market structure in which large numbers of buyers and sellers exchange heterogeneous relatively well-differentiated products, so marketers exert some control over prices.

oligopoly A market structure in which relatively few sellers compete, while high start-up costs form barriers to keep out new competitors.

Table 20.1 Distinguishing Features of the Four Market Structures

	Type of Market Structure			
Characteristics	**Pure Competition**	**Monopolistic Competition**	**Oligopoly**	**Monopoly**
Number of competitors	Many	Few to many	Few	No direct competitors
Ease of entry into industry by new firms	Easy	Somewhat difficult	Difficult	Regulated by government
Similarity of goods or services offered by competing firms	Similar	Different	Can be either similar or different	No directly competing goods or services
Control over prices by individual firms	None	Some	Some	Considerable
Demand curves facing individual firms	Totally elastic	Can be either elastic or inelastic	Kinked; inelastic below kink; more elastic above	Can be either elastic or inelastic
Examples	200-acre farm	Old Navy stores	Mobil	Commonwealth Edison

customers some of the lowest electricity prices in the United States through technology advancements and exceptional service.

Table 20.1 compares the four types of market structures on the basis of number of competitors, ease of market entry by new firms, similarity of competing products, control over price by individual firms, and elasticity or inelasticity of an individual firm's demand curve. Elasticity—the degree of consumer responsiveness to changes in price—is discussed in more detail in a later section.

Cost and Revenue Curves

Marketers must set a price for a product that generates sufficient revenue to cover the costs of producing and marketing it. A product's total cost is composed of total variable costs and total fixed costs. *Variable costs* change with the level of production (such as labor and raw materials costs), while *fixed costs* remain stable at any production level within a certain range (such as lease payments or insurance costs). *Average total costs* are calculated by dividing the sum of variable and fixed costs by the number of units produced. Finally, *marginal cost* is the change in total cost that results from producing an additional unit of output.

The demand side of the pricing equation focuses on revenue curves. *Average revenue* is calculated by dividing total revenue by the quantity associated with that amount of revenue. Average revenue actually corresponds to the firm's demand curve. *Marginal revenue* is the change in total revenue that results from selling an additional unit of output. Figure 20.7 shows the relationships of various cost and revenue measures; the firm maximizes its profits when marginal costs equal marginal revenues.

Table 20.2 illustrates why the intersection of the marginal cost and marginal revenue curves defines the logical point at which to maximize revenue. Although the firm can earn a profit at several different prices, the price at which it earns maximum profits is $22. At a price of $24, it earns $66 in profits—$4 less than the $70 profit at the $22 price. If marketers set a price of $20 to attract additional sales, the marginal costs of producing the extra units ($7) exceed the marginal revenues from selling them ($6), and total profits decline.

The Concept of Elasticity in Pricing Strategy

Although the intersection of the marginal cost and marginal revenue curves determines the profit-maximizing level of output, the table shows widely varying impacts on sales revenue for price changes at different levels. In order to understand why revenue fluctuates so dramatically, it is necessary to understand the concept of elasticity.

Elasticity measures the responsiveness of purchasers and suppliers to price changes. Elasticity of demand is the percentage change in the quantity of a good or service demanded divided by the percentage change in its price. Suppose that a 10 percent increase in the price of eggs results in a 5 percent decrease in the quantity of eggs demanded; these figures yield a price elasticity of demand for eggs of 0.5. Similarly, a product's price elasticity of supply is the percentage change in the quantity firms choose to supply divided by the percentage change in price. If a 10 percent increase in the price of shampoo results in a 25 percent increase in the quantity supplied, then the price elasticity of supply for shampoo equals 2.5.

Consider a case in which a 1 percent change in price causes more than a 1 percent change in the quantity supplied or demanded. Numerically, the elasticity measure would then exceed 1.0. When the elasticity of demand or supply is greater than 1.0, business people say that the product has *elastic* demand or supply. If a 1 percent change in price results in less than a 1 percent change in quantity sold, then the product's elasticity of demand or supply is less than 1.0, a condition called *inelastic* demand or supply. For example, researchers have found relatively inelastic demand for cigarettes; a 10 percent increase in cigarette prices results in only a 4 percent sales decline.

Figure 20.7 Determining Price by Relating Marginal Revenue to Marginal Cost

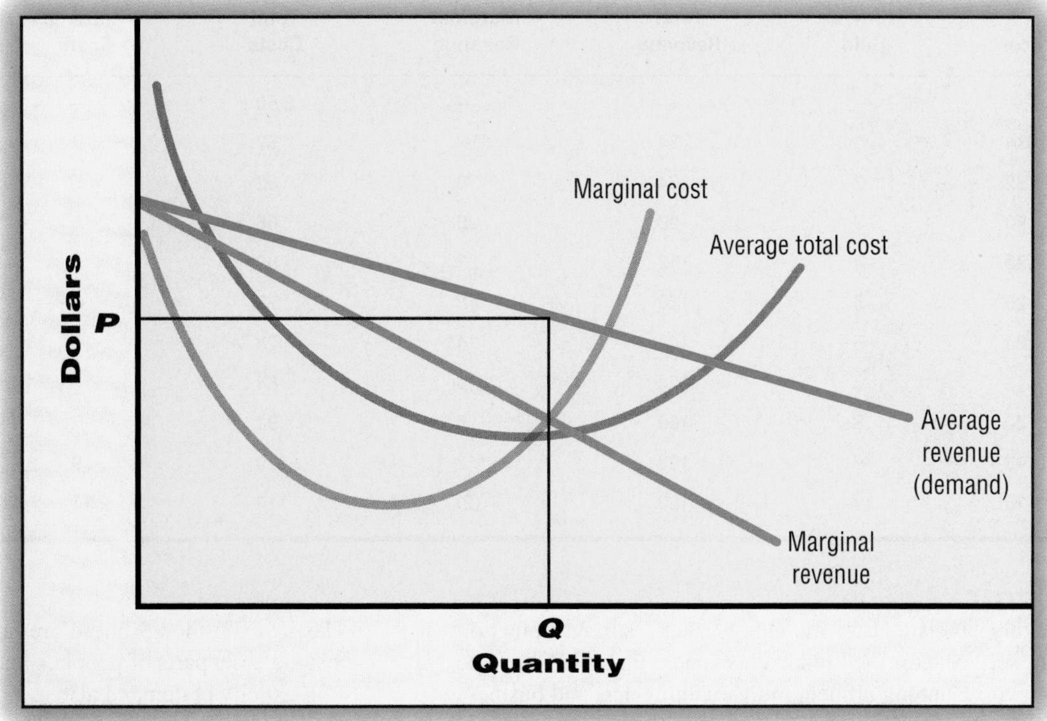
Marginal cost
Average total cost
Dollars
P
Average revenue (demand)
Marginal revenue
Q
Quantity

In countries such as Argentina and Brazil, annual inflation rates have sometimes topped 100 percent, reflecting dramatic increases in prices on almost all products. These higher prices have led to elastic demand for some products, such as houses and cars; many of the cars on Argentina's roads are over ten years old, and the nation's housing market is severely depressed. For other products, demand has been inelastic; families continue to pay the rising price of food because, after all, they need to eat. However, even if inflationary prices do not affect demand for some products, they can alter consumers' buying patterns. One Brazilian woman, for instance, buys all the food she can afford as soon as she gets each paycheck. As she puts it, "Things only get more expensive if I buy later. To survive, I must make provisions for the month."[16]

Determinants of Elasticity Why are elasticities of supply or demand high for some products and low for others? What determines demand elasticity? One major influence on a product's elasticity of demand is the availability of substitutes or complements. If consumers can easily turn to close substitutes for a good or service, they tend to show elastic demand for it. Growing use of e-mail by businesses and individual households thwarted attempts by the U.S. Postal Service to increase revenues through a price increase. When the cost of sending a first-class letter increased 10 percent a few years ago, total revenue generated by the price increase actually declined.[17] The relatively inelastic demand for motor oil reflects its role as a complement to a more important product, gasoline.

Compaq Computer Corp. changed its marketing strategy for desktop computers from an emphasis on technological prowess to a focus on prices consistently among the lowest in the industry. This change in strategy powerfully boosted demand for Compaq's products. In one year, the company's income rose 63 percent.[18]

Elasticity of demand also differs for necessary and luxury products. For example, the Shangri-La chain of

Marketing Dictionary

monopoly A market structure in which only one seller dominates trade in a good or service for which buyers can find no close substitutes.

elasticity A measure of the responsiveness of purchasers and suppliers to changes in price.

Table 20.2 Price Determination Using Marginal Analysis

Price	Number Sold	Total Revenue	Marginal Revenue	Total Costs	Marginal Costs	Profits (Total Revenue −Total Costs)
—	—	—	—	$ 50	—	($50)
$34	1	$ 34	$34	57	$ 7	(23)
32	2	64	30	62	5	2
30	3	90	26	66	4	24
28	4	112	22	69	3	43
26	5	130	18	73	4	57
24	6	144	14	78	5	66
22	7	154	10	84	6	70
20	8	160	6	91	7	69
18	9	162	2	100	9	62
16	10	160	(2)	110	11	50

luxury hotels and resorts enjoys such a strong reputation for service, comfort, and exclusiveness that it has become a favorite among affluent individual travelers and business professionals. The combination of privacy and exclusiveness depicted in Figure 20.8 attracts a select group of upscale travelers, who consider reservations at Shangri-La hotels essential components of their trips to China or other Asian and Pacific Island destinations. Because such a customer views Shangri-La accommodations as a necessity, not a luxury, sales remain strong despite the high room rates.

Most people regard high-fashion clothes such as $2,000 Armani suits as luxuries. If prices for designer outfits increase, people can respond by purchasing lower-priced substitutes instead. In contrast, medical and dental care are considered necessities, so price changes have little effect on the frequency of medical or dental visits.

However, under the continuing influence of higher prices, some products once regarded as necessities may be dismissed as luxuries, leading to decreasing demand. For instance, German consumers have traditionally been eager buyers of brand-name consumer electronics goods. As prices and unemployment in Germany have risen, however, demand for these products has become highly elastic. As a result, retail outlets have encountered dramatically declining electronics sales.

Elasticity also depends on the portion of a person's budget that he or she spends on a good or service. People no longer really need matches, for example; they can easily find good substitutes. Nonetheless, the demand for matches remains very inelastic because people spend so little on them that they hardly notice a price change. In contrast, the demand for housing or transportation is not totally inelastic, even though these are necessities, because both consume large parts of people's budgets.

Elasticity of demand also responds to consumers' time perspectives. Demand often shows less elasticity in the short run than in the long run. Consider the demand for home heating fuel. In the short run, people pay rising prices because they find it difficult to cut back on the quantities they use. Accustomed to living with specific temperature settings, dressing in certain ways, and so forth, they prefer to pay more rather than to explore other possibilities. Over time, though, they may find ways to economize. They can better insulate their homes, dress more warmly, or even move to warmer climates.

Sometimes the usual patterns do not hold true. Alcohol and tobacco, which are not necessities but do occupy large shares of some personal budgets, also are subject to inelastic demand.

Elasticity and Revenue The elasticity of demand exerts an important influence on variations in total revenue as a result of changes in the price of a good or service. Assume, for example, that New York City officials are considering alternative methods of raising more money for the city budget. One possible fund-raising method would change the subway fare. But should the city raise or lower the price of a ride?

The correct answer depends on the elasticity of demand for subway rides. A 10 percent decrease in fares should attract more riders, but unless it stimulates more than a 10 percent increase in riders, total revenue will fall. A 10 percent increase in fares will bring in more money per rider, but if more than 10 percent of the riders stop using the subway, total revenue will fall. A price cut will increase revenue only for a product with elastic demand, and a price increase will raise revenue only for a product with inelastic demand. New York City officials seem to believe that the demand for subway rides is inelastic; they raise fares when they need more money for the city budget.

Figure 20.8 **Shangri-La Hotels: Inelastic Demand for a Service Viewed as a Necessity by Upscale Travelers**

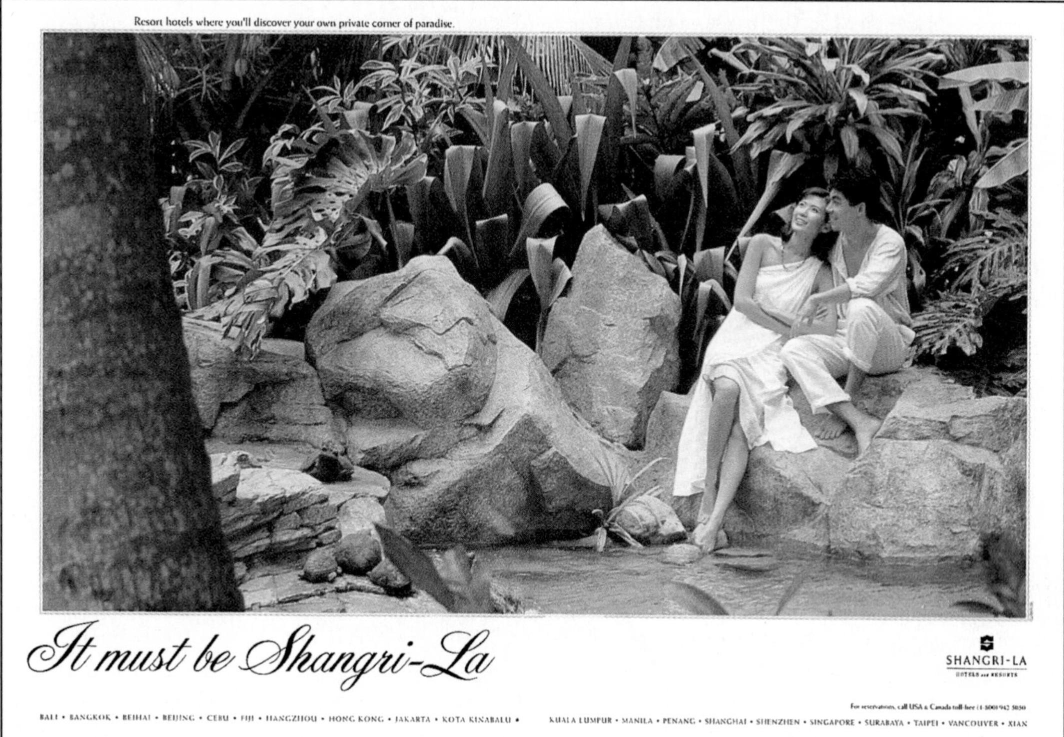
Resort hotels where you'll discover your own private corner of paradise.
It must be Shangri-La
SHANGRI-LA
HOTELS and RESORTS
BALI • BANGKOK • BEIHAI • BEIJING • CEBU • FIJI • HANGZHOU • HONG KONG • JAKARTA • KOTA KINABALU • KUALA LUMPUR • MANILA • PENANG • SHANGHAI • SHENZHEN • SINGAPORE • SURABAYA • TAIPEI • VANCOUVER • XIAN

Practical Problems of Price Theory

Marketers may thoroughly understand price theory concepts but still encounter difficulty applying them in practice. What practical limitations interfere with price setting?

First, many firms do not attempt to maximize profits. Economic analysis can give results no more exact than the assumptions on which it is based. For example, actual situations sometimes produce exceptions to the presupposition that all firms attempt to maximize profits. Second, it is difficult to estimate demand curves. Modern accounting procedures provide managers with clear insight into their firms' cost structures, so managers can readily comprehend the supply sides of their pricing equations. But they can only approximately estimate demand at various price levels. Demand curves reflect marketing research estimates that often give less exact statements than cost figures. Although marketers can identify sources of demand, they often have trouble measuring customer response in real-world settings.

PRICE DETERMINATION IN PRACTICE

The practical limitations inherent in economic pricing theory have forced practitioners to turn to other techniques. **Cost-plus pricing,** the most popular method, calculates a base-cost figure per unit and then adds a markup to cover unassigned costs and to provide a profit. The only real difference among the multitude of cost-plus techniques is the relative sophistication of their costing procedures. For example, a local apparel shop may set retail prices by adding a 45 percent markup to the invoice price charged by its supplier. The retailer expects this markup to cover all other expenses and give the owner a reasonable return on clothing sales.

In contrast to this rather simple pricing mechanism, a large manufacturer may employ a complex pricing formula calculated by computer. However, this method adds only a sophisticated procedure for calculating costs to the retailer's simple technique. In the end, someone still must make a decision about the markup. The apparel shop and the large manufacturer may figure costs differently, but they are remarkably similar in completing the markup side of the equation.

Marketing Dictionary

cost-plus pricing The practice of adding a percentage or specified dollar amount (markup) to the base cost of a product to cover unassigned costs and provide a profit.

MARKETING HALL OF FAME

Beanie Babies—Creating Markets by Creating Shortages

MAIN MENU

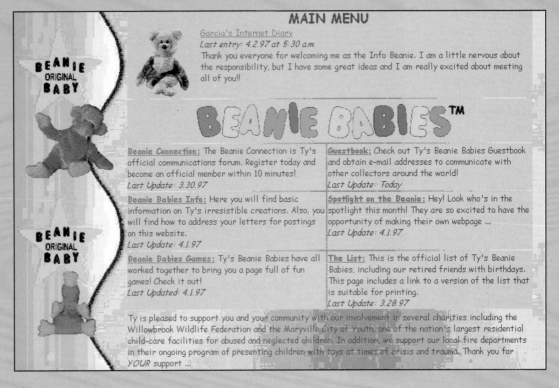

Garcia's Internet Diary
Last entry: 4.2.97 at 5:30 a.m.
Thank you everyone for welcoming me as the Info Beanie. I am a little nervous about the responsibility, but I have some great ideas and I am really excited about meeting all of you!!

BEANIE ORIGINAL BABY

BEANIE BABIES™

Beanie Connection: The Beanie Connection is Ty's official communications forum. Register today and become an official member within 10 minutes!
Last Update: 3.30.97

Guestbook: Check out Ty's Beanie Babies Guestbook and obtain e-mail addresses to communicate with other collectors around the world!
Last Update: Today

Beanie Babies Info: Here you will find basic information on Ty's irresistible creations. Also, you will find how to address your letters for postings on this website.
Last Update: 4.1.97

Spotlight on the Beanie: Hey! Look who's in the spotlight this month! They are so excited to have the opportunity of making their own webpage ...
Last Update: 4.1.97

Beanie Babies Games: Ty's Beanie Babies have all worked together to bring you a page full of fun games! Check it out!
Last Updated: 4.1.97

The List: This is the official list of Ty's Beanie Babies, including our retired friends with birthdays. This page includes a link to a version of the list that is suitable for printing.
Last Update: 3.28.97

Ty is pleased to support you and your community with our involvement in several charities including the Willowbrook Wildlife Federation and the Maryville City of Youth, one of the nation's largest residential child-care facilities for abused and neglected children. In addition, we support our local fire departments in their ongoing program of presenting children with toys at times of crisis and trauma. Thank you for *YOUR* support ...

Go figure. One of the most popular new toys to hit store shelves since the Ninja Turtles craze is an unassuming gaggle of stuffed animals that can each fit inside a kid's hand.

Children, as well as some adults, can't get enough of these Beanie Babies, though the demure characters hardly look exciting enough to cause a stampede. The colorful animals are distinctly low-tech. Understuffed with beans, they are perfect for cuddling or perhaps throwing at a pesky little brother. Each Beanie Baby carries a ready-made name—Legs the Frog, Squealer the Pig, Cubbie the Bear, and other cutesy monikers.

An even smaller version called Teenie Beanie Babies created a stampede when McDonald's made it the prize in what proved to be its most successful Happy Meals promotion in company history. The fast-food chain ordered 100 million babies for the planned five-week promotion, but franchises were overwhelmed by demand for the pint-sized collectibles.

Continuing a long tradition of fads—Rubik's Cubes, Cabbage Patch Dolls, Tickle Me Elmos, and others—Beanie Babies in both sizes have struck a nerve with consumers. Richard Gernady, whose Illinois store sold 5,000 Beanie Babies in one week, gushes about the plush animals. They are as big, he insists, as "Elvis, Sinatra, and the Beatles combined." Another amazed observer is Jim Weaver, a

An International Comparison

Cost-plus pricing often works well for a business that keeps its costs low, allowing it to set its prices lower than those of competitors and still make a profit. American toy retailer Toys 'R' Us keeps costs low by buying directly from manufacturers rather than going through wholesalers and other intermediaries. This strategy has helped the company take 25 percent of the U.S. market. Now Toys 'R' Us has entered the Japanese toy market, the largest outside the United States. The company has already opened more than 30 stores in Japan.

The retailer spent two years in negotiations, often compromising, before it opened its first Japanese store. The Japanese distribution system imposes far more structure on a retailer's business than America's system, and

http://www.tru.com/

Japanese toy manufacturers refused to bypass wholesalers. Some, such as Bandai Company, agreed to supply Toys 'R' Us through affiliated wholesalers. Others, such as Nin-

United Parcel Service driver who encounters Beanie Baby fans whenever he tries to unload a hot shipment at a store. "How many times can you buy something for 5 bucks that's going to drive a kid bananas?" he asks.

The $5 price of a Beanie Baby puts the toy within reach of a kid on an allowance. But the price isn't necessarily the sole cause of the frenzy. Some experts suggest that clever manipulation of supply is fueling the Beanie Baby demand. Fans cannot find the toys, developed in 1993 by industry veteran Ty Warner, in many toy stores. None of the big discount chains like Toys 'R' Us or Wal-Mart figure in product distribution plans. Instead, Warner's privately held company, Ty Inc., distributes the animals only through specialty stores such as card and novelty shops, candy stores, hospital and hotel gift shops, and museums. But Warner's manipulation of the supply pipeline goes even further. Ty Inc. will sell no more than 36 of each animal in the line per store every month.

If Warner permitted the big stores to sell huge quantities of his animals, their mystique would disappear. "This thing could grow and be around for many years just as long as I don't take the easy road and sell it to a mass merchant who's going to put it in bins," Warner says.

Selling the toys at stores off the beaten path has only made them more desirable for fans bent on finding one of everything. So far, Ty Inc. has introduced 73 brightly colored animals. In addition, the company retires animals after they've been in circulation for a while. This policy prompts collectors to search for the new Beanies as soon as they are released from the factory, which happens only twice a year.

Toy industry insiders wonder how long the phenomenon can last. One skeptic is Russ Berrie, a veteran seller of plush toys who also avoids the big stores. Sales of his company's troll dolls jumped from $44 million to $250 million in just one year. After that, sales froze. "On April 12, 1993, at 1:42 P.M., every person in the U.S. stopped buying trolls," Berrie recalls. "Ty is doing a terrific job, but he's got a blip up and at some point that blip is going to have to come down."

Berrie isn't the only one wondering what all the fuss is about. A columnist writing for *Entertainment Weekly*, made this observation: "Stores can't keep the cute, $5 dolls in stock. If they were called 'A Sock Full of Beans,' you could get them for 50 cents."

Yet Warner, who expects to sell 100 million Beanie Babies a year in addition to 100 million of the smaller McDonald's version, remains an optimist. "People are saying this Christmas will be the last, but every time we make a shipment, they want twice as many as we can possibly get to them," Warner says. "As long as kids keep fighting over the products and retailers are angry at us because they cannot get enough, I think those are good signs."

QUESTIONS FOR CRITICAL THINKING

1. What do you think would happen to Beanie Babies if Ty Inc. did begin distributing the toys through the major chains? Do you think that marketing Teenie Beanie Babies as a Happy Meals prize will cause the regular-sized toy to lose its allure?

2. Before introducing Beanie Babies, Ty Inc. sold larger stuffed animals at $10 to $20. Do you think setting a price that children could afford on their own helped to trigger the success of the smaller plush toys?

Sources: Katy Kelly, "A Teenie Bit of Hysteria," *USA Today,* April 17, 1997, p. D1; Beanie Baby Web site, http://www.ty. com/, downloaded February 1997; Gary Samuels, "Mystique Marketing," *Forbes,* October 21, 1996, pp. 276–277; and "Beanie-Mania," *People,* July 1, 1996.

tendo, agreed to deal directly with Toys 'R' Us, but insisted on maintaining prices that were "acceptable to other wholesalers," according to a Nintendo spokesperson.

Larry Bouts, president of the Toys 'R' Us Japanese unit, admits that this insistence complicates the company's pricing strategies. While it will probably sell products in Japan for 10 percent to 15 percent below regular retail prices, higher costs will stop it from selling at discounts like those it offers to U.S. consumers. But Bouts recognizes that flexibility and compromise are a necessary part of doing business in a different culture. "We must earn our way into Japan," he says. "We must take time."[19]

Alternative Pricing Procedures

The two most common cost-oriented pricing procedures are the full-cost method and the incremental-cost method. *Full-cost pricing* sums all relevant variable costs in setting a product's price. In addition, it allocates shares of fixed costs that do not relate directly to the production of any specific product. Under full-cost pricing, if Order 515 in a printing plant amounts to 0.000127 percent of the plant's total output, then its price reflects 0.000127 percent of the firm's overhead expenses. In this way, the firm recovers all costs plus an amount added as a profit margin.

Full-cost pricing suffers from two basic deficiencies.

SOLVING AN ETHICAL CONTROVERSY

Does Cost-Plus Pricing Injure the Terminally Ill?

For years, an AIDS diagnosis amounted to a death sentence. Anyone carrying the human immunodeficiency virus could look forward only to a descending spiral of illness that ultimately ended in a painful death. But the prognosis has miraculously changed for thousands of patients as new medications have dramatically extended their lives. New protease inhibitor drugs combined with older antiviral medications are now allowing otherwise terminally ill patients to lead fairly normal lives.

But a harsh reality has tempered jubilation over this medical breakthrough. The prices of these medical cocktails can easily reach $10,000 to $15,000 a year. Many AIDS patients simply cannot spend several hundred dollars or more each month at their neighborhood drugstores. This reality has produced considerable turmoil within the pharmaceuticals and insurance industries, as well as federal and state government agencies. Executives responsible for pricing decisions, consumer representatives, and politicians all grapple with the same dilemma—how can terminally ill patients obtain expensive, life-saving drugs at prices they can afford? So far, the needs of patients have clashed with the interests of drug companies, which typically set prices through cost-plus methods that ensure they will recover their huge research and development expenses.

Does Cost-Plus Pricing Harm the Terminally Ill?

PRO

1. **A drugmaker's policy of adding a certain markup to its full cost unfairly hurts needy patients in the United States. Customers here pay a higher price for drugs than patients in other countries pay. In effect, they subsidize patients in other countries, where prescription drug prices may not reflect the millions of dollars that their producers invested in R&D. In a tiny Mexican border town, for instance, a bottle of 90 Valium tablets sells for $8.75 versus $138.00 in the United States. A customer can buy a vial of Prozac in Mexico for $31.60, which is $38.35 cheaper than prices across the border. Drugs also cost less in European countries and Canada than in the United States, since those nations' governments control prices.**
2. **Prescription drug prices have historically risen at a rate far outpacing inflation. In fact, drug prices have jumped as high as 50 percent for the most popular prescription drugs during the past five years. Yet customers need these drugs in order to live; they cannot choose to do without their med-**

First, it fails to consider competition or demand for the product. (Perhaps no one wants to pay a price that covers the firm's costs plus a profit! Perhaps someone would pay much more.) Second, any method of allocating overhead (fixed expenses) makes arbitrary and possibly unrealistic judgments. Manufacturers often allocate overhead in proportion to direct labor hours. Retailers sometimes assign fixed costs based on the square footage areas of individual profit centers. Regardless of the technique employed, it is difficult to show a cause-effect relationship between the allocated costs and selling expenses for most products.

One way to overcome the arbitrary allocation of fixed expenses is with *incremental-cost pricing,* which attempts to use only those costs directly attributable to a specific output in setting prices. Consider a small-scale manufacturer with the following income statement:

Sales (10,000 units at $10.00)		$100,000
Expenses:		
Variable	$50,000	
Fixed	40,000	90,000
Net profit		$ 10,000

Suppose that a big customer offers a contract to buy an additional 5,000 units. Since the firm's peak season is over, it can produce these products at the same average variable cost as its normal output. Assume that the labor force would be idle otherwise. How low should the firm price its product in order to win the contract?

Under the full-cost method, the lowest price would be $9 per unit, obtained by dividing the $90,000 expense total by an output of 10,000 units. Incremental-cost pricing, on the other hand, would permit any price above $5.10, which would significantly increase the possibility of securing the additional contract and keeping the facility busy. This price would be composed of the $5.00 variable cost to produce each unit plus a $0.10-per-unit contribution to fixed expenses and overhead. With the new order at a $5.10 price, the income statement would change to:

Sales (10,000 at $10.00; 5,000 at $5.10)		$125,500
Expenses:		
Variable	$75,000	
Fixed	40,000	
		115,000
Net profit		$ 10,500

ications, as they can for an extravagance like Häagen-Dazs ice cream. A seriously ill patient without money or adequate insurance coverage could die for lack of medicine. Access to drugs is an especially critical need for the elderly (who tend to depend more than other population groups on medicines), because Medicare does not cover medication costs.

3. Cost-plus pricing even hurts patients whose prescription costs are covered by managed-care programs. Many HMOs limit the amounts they will pay for costly drugs. A cap of $3,000 a year is typical.

CON

1. Drug companies need to set fair prices on their products—just as any other industry must—in order to remain financially viable. The pharmaceuticals world, already rocked by fundamental changes that have resulted in sharply reduced profit margins, cannot give up any more revenue. In the 1980s, drug companies enjoyed 15 percent to 20 percent increases in profits each year, but now the industry is retrenching. This trend has led to massive layoffs and numerous mergers.
2. Drug costs already have declined as health maintenance organizations and pharmacy benefit managers, who buy drugs in bulk for their members, are demanding cheaper prices from pharmaceutical companies. In fact, 55 percent of Americans now receive discounted medicines through managed-care programs.
3. If drug prices do not reflect costs for research and other activities, drug companies will no longer be able to fund the development projects that lead to breakthroughs like protease inhibitor drugs.

Summary

Much depends on a mutually tolerable solution to the affordability problem, because the demand for revolutionary new AIDS drugs is only expected to increase. With many AIDS patients on public assistance, state health departments are scrambling to locate funding for the life-saving treatments. Colorado's experience is typical—the money ran out three and a half months before the end of the fiscal year. "Because the medicines were so new, we had no idea what the demand would be," says Pamela R. Snyder, the director of Colorado's AIDS drug program. "The drugs are effective. People want them. The demand just grew and grew."

Sources: Adapted from Christine Gorman, "Border Bargains," *Time*, February 19, 1997, p. 54; Robert Pear, "Expense Means Many Can't Get Drugs for AIDS," *New York Times*, February 16, 1997, pp. 1, 14; and George Tabere, "Drugmakers Have an Urge to Merge as They Try to Get Their Profits Back Up," *Time*, September 4, 1995.

Thus incremental pricing boosts overall profits.

Admittedly, the illustration makes two essential assumptions: (1) The firm can isolate markets to prevent sales at the lower price from affecting the prices it receives in other markets. (2) No legal restrictions affect the firm's price. The example does illustrate, however, that incremental pricing can sometimes enhance profits.

Breakeven Analysis

Breakeven analysis is a technique for determining the quantity of goods or services that a firm must sell at a given price in order to generate sufficient revenue to cover its total costs. Figure 20.9 graphically depicts the process. The total cost curve includes both fixed and variable elements, and the horizontal line represents total fixed costs. The figure assumes that average variable cost remains constant per unit, as in the example for incremental pricing.

The breakeven point is the point at which total revenue just equals total cost. In Figure 20.9, a selling price of $10 and an average variable cost of $5 result in a per-unit contribution to fixed cost of $5. A formula gives the breakeven point in units sold, that is the number of units the firm must sell to cover its costs:

$$\text{Breakeven Point (in Units)} = \frac{\text{Total Fixed Cost}}{\text{Per-Unit Contribution to Fixed Cost}}$$

$$\text{Breakeven Point (in Units)} = \frac{\$40{,}000}{\$5} = 8{,}000 \text{ Units}$$

where the per-unit contribution equals the product's price less the variable cost per unit. The following formula gives the breakeven point as a dollar-sales figure:

Marketing Dictionary

breakeven analysis A pricing technique that determines the number of products that a firm must sell at a specified price in order to generate enough revenue to cover total cost.

Figure 20.9 Breakeven Chart

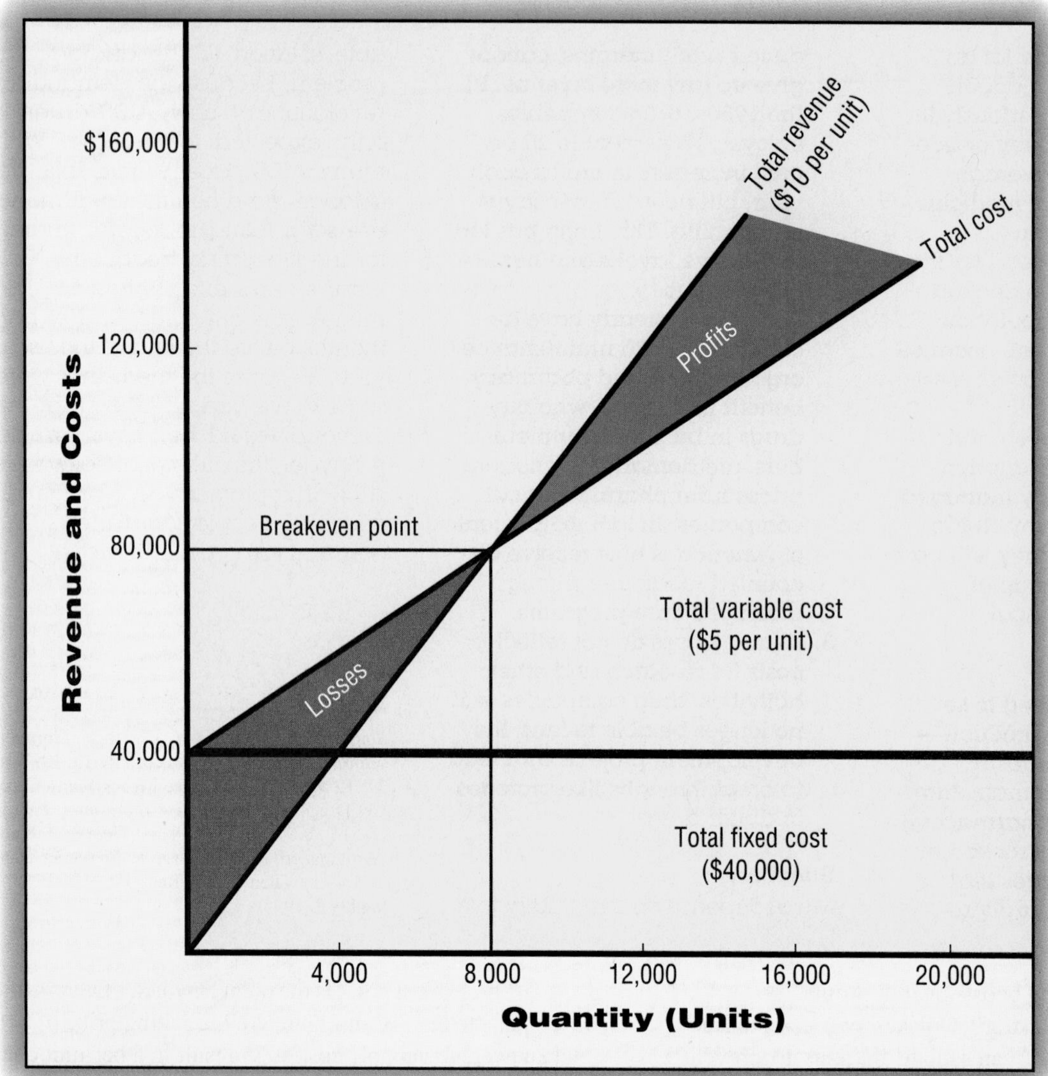
$160,000
120,000
80,000
40,000
Revenue and Costs
Total revenue
($10 per unit)
Total cost
Profits
Breakeven point
Total variable cost
($5 per unit)
Losses
Total fixed cost
($40,000)
4,000
8,000
12,000
16,000
20,000
Quantity (Units)

Target Returns Although breakeven analysis indicates the sales level at which the firm will incur neither profits or losses, most firms' managers include some target profit figures in their analyses. Some managers set desired dollar return amounts when considering proposals to introduce new products or take other marketing actions. A retailer may set a profit goal of $250,000 as a hurdle for a decision to expand to a second location. Other analysts express target returns in percentages, such as a 15 percent return on sales. These target returns can be modified as follows:

$$\text{Breakeven Point (in Dollars)} = \frac{\text{Total Fixed Cost}}{1 - \text{Variable Cost per Unit Price}}$$

$$\text{Breakeven Point (in Dollars)} = \frac{\$40{,}000}{1 - \$5/\$10} = \frac{\$40{,}000}{0.5} = \$80{,}000$$

Once sales reach the breakeven point, the firm gains sufficient revenues to cover all fixed costs. Any additional sales will generate per-unit profits equal to the difference between the product's selling price and the variable cost of each unit. As Figure 20.9 reveals, sales of 8,001 units (1 unit above the breakeven point) will produce net profits of $5 ($10 sales price less per-unit variable cost of $5). Once sales have covered all fixed costs, the per-unit contribution becomes the per-unit profit.

$$\text{Breakeven Point (including specified dollar target return)} = \frac{\text{Total Fixed Cost} + \text{Profit Objective}}{\text{Per-Unit Contribution}}$$

$$= \frac{\$40{,}000 + \$15{,}000}{\$5} = 11{,}000 \text{ Units}$$

If the price analyst wants to express target return as a percentage of sales, the breakeven formula can include it as a variable cost. Suppose that the marketing manager in the earlier example seeks a 10 percent return on sales. This goal translates into a desired return of $1 for each product sold (the $10 per-unit selling price plus the 10 percent return on sales). The basic breakeven formula remains unchanged, although the variable cost per unit increases to reflect the target return; also, the per-unit contribution to

Table 20.3 Revenue and Cost Data for Modified Breakeven Analysis

	Revenues		Costs			Breakeven Point (Number of Sales	
Price	Quantity Demanded	Total Revenue	Total Fixed Cost	Total Variable Cost	Total Cost	Required to Break Even)	Total Profit (or Loss)
$15	2,500	$ 37,500	$40,000	$12,500	$ 52,500	4,000	$(15,000)
10	10,000	100,000	40,000	50,000	90,000	8,000	10,000
9	13,000	117,000	40,000	65,000	105,000	10,000	12,000
8	14,000	112,000	40,000	70,000	110,000	13,334	2,000
7	15,000	105,000	40,000	75,000	115,000	20,000	(10,000)

fixed cost falls to $4. As a result, the breakeven point increases from 8,000 to 10,000 units:

$$\text{Breakeven Point} = \frac{\$40{,}000}{\$4} = 10{,}000 \text{ units}$$

Evaluation of Breakeven Analysis Breakeven analysis offers an effective tool for marketers who need to assess the sales required to cover costs and achieve specified profit levels. Both marketing and nonmarketing executives easily understand this information, and it may help them to decide whether a proposed price would yield a suitable return at realistic sales levels. However, it has its shortcomings.

First, the model assumes that costs fit definitely into fixed and variable categories. Some costs, such as salaries and advertising outlays, may be either fixed or variable depending on the particular situation. In addition, the model assumes that per-unit variable costs do not change at different levels of operation. However, variations may result from quantity discounts, improvements in workforce efficiency, or other economies resulting from increases in production and sales. Finally, the basic breakeven model does not consider demand. It focuses on cost without directly addressing the crucial question of whether consumers will actually purchase the product at the specified price and in the quantities that the firm needs to break even or generate profits.

Marketers must modify breakeven analysis and the other cost-oriented pricing techniques to incorporate demand analysis. They must examine pricing decisions from the buyer's perspective. Such decisions cannot be made in a management vacuum limited to cost information.

TOWARD REALISTIC PRICING

Traditional economic theory considers both costs and demand in determining an equilibrium price. The dual forces of supply and demand balance one another at the point of equilibrium. In actual practice, however, most pricing decisions relate largely to cost. Since purely cost-oriented pricing methods violate the marketing concept, these tools need modifications that will add demand analysis to the pricing decision.

Marketers must conduct consumer research on such issues as price elasticity, consumer price expectations, sizes of specific market segments, and buyer perceptions of strengths and weaknesses of substitute products. Only with this information can they develop sales estimates at different prices. Because much of this data involves perceptions, attitudes, and future expectations about present and potential customers, it often gives less precise estimates than cost estimating procedures supply.

The Modified Breakeven Concept

The breakeven analysis method illustrated in Figure 20.9 assumes a constant $10 retail price regardless of quantity. But what happens at different retail prices? **Modified breakeven analysis** combines the traditional model with an evaluation of consumer demand.

Table 20.3 summarizes the cost and revenue effects of a number of alternative retail prices. The $5 unit variable cost and the $40,000 total fixed cost reflect accounting estimates, as in the basic breakeven model. Market research provides the expected unit sales for each retail price. The table provides enough information to calculate the

Marketing Dictionary

modified breakeven analysis A pricing technique that evaluates consumer demand by comparing the quantities that a firm must sell at a variety of prices in order to cover total costs together with estimates of expected sales at those prices.

Figure 20.10 Modified Breakeven Chart

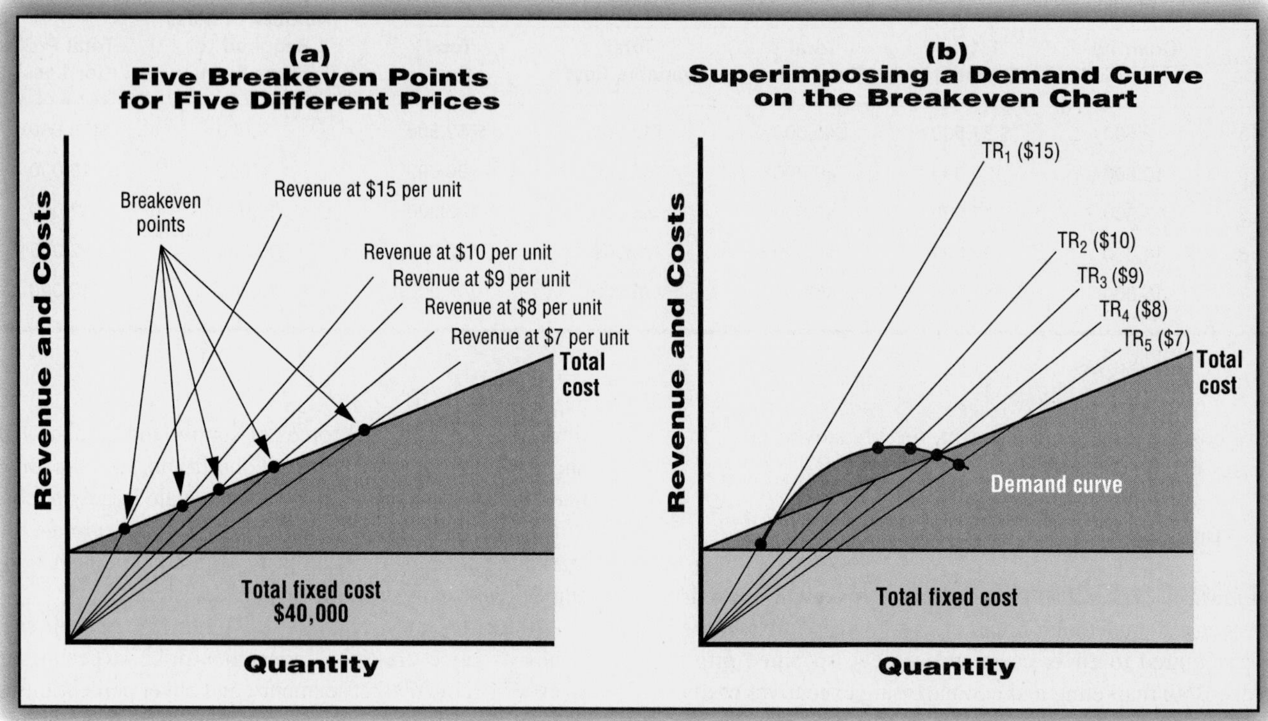
(a)
Five Breakeven Points for Five Different Prices
Breakeven points
Revenue at $15 per unit
Revenue at $10 per unit
Revenue at $9 per unit
Revenue at $8 per unit
Revenue at $7 per unit
Total cost
Total fixed cost $40,000
Revenue and Costs
Quantity
(b)
Superimposing a Demand Curve on the Breakeven Chart
TR1 ($15)
TR2 ($10)
TR3 ($9)
TR4 ($8)
TR5 ($7)
Total cost
Demand curve
Total fixed cost
Revenue and Costs
Quantity

breakeven point for each of the five retail price alternatives. These points are shown in Panel A of Figure 20.10.

The data in the first two columns of Table 20.3 represent a demand schedule; they indicate the number of units consumers are expected to purchase at each of a series of retail prices. Panel B of Figure 20.10 superimposes these data onto a breakeven chart to identify the range of feasible prices for the marketer to consider.

The range of profitable prices stretches from a low of approximately \$8 (TR_4) to a high of \$10 (TR_2), with a price of \$9 (TR_3) generating the greatest projected profits. Changing the retail price produces a new breakeven point. At a relatively high \$15 (TR_1) retail price, the breakeven point is 4,000 units; at a \$10 retail price, it is 8,000 units; at the lowest price considered, \$7 (TR_5), the firm must sell 20,000 units to cover its costs.

Modified breakeven analysis contributes to price analysis by forcing marketers to consider whether consumers will likely purchase the quantity of a good or service their firm must sell to break even at a given price. It demonstrates that selling a large number of units does not necessarily produce added profits, since—other things remaining equal—lower prices stimulate additional sales. Consequently, pricing decisions must consider both costs and consumer demand.

GLOBAL ISSUES IN PRICE DETERMINATION

A firm must adopt a pricing strategy that reflects its overall marketing strategy whether it serves only domestic markets or reaches out to serve global customers, as well. Prices must support the company's broader marketing decisions, including product development, advertising and sales, customer support, competitive plans, and financial objectives.

In general, five pricing objectives guide efforts to set prices in global marketing. Four of these repeat the pricing objectives discussed earlier in the chapter: profitability, volume, meeting competitors' prices, and prestige. In addition, some international marketers work to achieve a fifth objective: price stability.

In the global arena, marketers may choose profitability objectives if their company acts as a price leader in its markets, that is, it tends to establish international prices. Profitability objectives also make sense for a low-cost supplier that can make a good profit on sales.

Volume objectives become especially important when nations lower trade barriers, exposing domestic markets to foreign competition. As the European Community lowered economic barriers between countries, for instance, competition for customers soared. In a recent trend, many European firms have merged to form larger companies that can achieve volume objectives. As one economist notes, "Merger activity [is] a way to get economies of scale." French supermarket chain Casino, for example, recently acquired a competing chain, Rallye, to strengthen its market share in its home country.

6 U.S.G.A. Championships
38 U.S.G.A. Match Play Wins
2 Professional Victories
In Just 7 Starts
ONE PLAYER
ONE DREAM
ONE BALL
Titleist
#1 ball in golf.

The combined $60 million multiyear endorsement fees Titleist and Nike paid to golfing phenomenon Tiger Woods seemed much more reasonable after the 21-year-old's blowout win at the Masters. The fees are expected to be recouped through increased sales as Tiger takes them to new heights—both in the United States and in the vast golf markets of Asia. Woods, with a Thai mother and a Buddhist heritage, is expected to make a much bigger impact in the Pacific Rim than he has in the U.S. He is the main attraction at a major Nike golf event in Japan.

Increased competition in Europe has also spurred firms to work toward the third pricing objective, meeting competitors' prices. Dutch corporation Philips Electronics offers U.S.-style coupons that give buyers 10 percent to 15 percent discounts off the prices of kitchen appliances. Aldi and Lidl, two German-owned food retailers, have opened discount outlets in France, forcing native French stores such as Carrefour to reduce prices. Automaker Fiat once boasted a 54 percent share of the Italian car market; its share has dropped to 44 percent thanks to inroads by competitively priced models from Ford of Europe, Inc. Fiat is fighting back by offering $1,600 rebates and zero-interest financing on certain models.

Prestige is a valid pricing objective for internationally marketed products promoted through associations with intangible benefits, such as high quality, exclusiveness, or attractive design. A product that offers strong perceived benefits can carry a high price. Marketers must recognize, however, that cultural perceptions of quality can differ from one country to the next. Some products that command prestige prices in the U.S. market seem like run-of-the-mill offerings to consumers in other nations; some products with far from prestigious images in America seem exotic to overseas consumers. American patrons, for instance, view McDonald's restaurants as affordable fast-food eateries, but Chinese customers see them as fashionable places for relatively expensive meals.

Marketers often struggle to achieve the fifth, highly desirable pricing objective, price stability, in international markets. Wars, terrorism, economic trends, changing governments and political parties, and shifting trade policies can alter prices. Consider an example from the computer industry. A few years ago, U.S. computer manufacturers sold their products in Europe for prices 30 percent to 50 percent above those in the U.S. market. Today, the spread of competition within the European Community has forced computer prices down until they average only 10 percent higher than U.S. prices, a differential barely large enough to cover manufacturers' costs to retool machines to make products for the European market. Falling prices have slashed profits for both American and European manufacturers, including IBM, Compaq, and Olivetti.

Price stability can be especially important for producers of commodities—goods and services that compete with easily accessible substitutes from other nations. Countries that export international commodities, such as wood, chemicals, and agricultural crops, suffer economically when the prices of those goods fluctuate. Nicaragua, which exports sugarcane, may have to cope with drastic changes in its balance of payments when the international price for sugar shifts. This threat makes it vulnerable to stiff price competition from sugarcane producers in other countries.

In contrast, countries that export value-oriented products, rather than commodities, tend to enjoy more stable prices. Prices of electronic equipment and automobiles tend to fluctuate far less than prices of sugarcane and bananas.

ACHIEVEMENT CHECK SUMMARY

Reread the learning goals that follow, and consider the questions for each goal. Answering these questions will reinforce your grasp of the most important concepts in the chapter and allow you to check how well you have achieved these learning goals. Where a blank appears before a question, answer with *T* or *F;* for multiple-choice questions, circle the letter of the correct answer.

Objective 20.1: Outline the legal constraints on pricing.

1. ___ Unfair-trade laws require sellers to maintain minimum retail prices for comparable products.

2. ___ Price discrimination is prohibited under the Consumer Goods Pricing Act.

3. ___ Interstate enforcement of fair-trade laws was banned under the Robinson-Patman Act.

Objective 20.2: Identify the major categories of pricing objectives.

1. ___ Pricing objectives include all of the following except: (a) profit maximization objectives; (b) meeting competitors' prices; (c) market-share objectives; (d) quality performance objectives; (e) prestige objectives.

2. ___ Profits are: (a) the most important objective for a firm; (b) the result of supply and demand; (c) a function of revenue and expenses; (d) depend primarily on the quantity of product sold.

Objective 20.3: Explain the concept of price elasticity and its determinants.

1. ___ Elasticity measures the responsiveness of manufacturers and distributors to inventory levels.

2. ___ If customers can easily find close substitutes for a good or service, producers tend to encounter elastic demand for it.

3. ___ When a product's elasticity of demand or supply measure exceeds 1.0, marketers describe demand or supply as *elastic.*

Objective 20.4: List the practical problems involved in applying price theory concepts to actual pricing decisions.

1. ___ All firms try to maximize profits.

2. ___ Analysts sometimes struggle to estimate demand at various price levels.

3. ___ Using computer software, managers can accurately forecast demand for a product and thereby determine a good price.

Objective 20.5: Explain the major cost-plus approaches to price setting.

1. ___ Cost-plus pricing methods include incremental-cost pricing and full-cost pricing.

2. ___ Full-cost pricing bases decisions on competition and demand for the product.

3. ___ Incremental-cost pricing helps to overcome problems with arbitrary allocation of fixed expenses by limiting its analysis to costs directly attributable to a specific output.

Objective 20.6: List the major advantages and shortcomings of using breakeven analysis in pricing decisions.

1. ___ Breakeven analysis: (a) is a means of setting prices to determine rates of production; (b) determines the quantity that a firm must sell to cover its total costs; (c) assumes that per-unit variable costs change at different levels of operation; (d) indicates how much profit a firm will make by producing a specified quantity of a good or service.

2. ___ Breakeven analysis: (a) cannot reflect target return objectives; (b) considers how much of a product consumers will likely purchase; (c) helps marketers to set profitability objectives; (d) frequently supports price determination.

Objective 20.7: Explain the superiority of modified breakeven analysis over the basic breakeven model.

1. ___ Modified breakeven analysis helps marketers to determine prices regardless of demand.

2. ___ An increase in quantity sold does not necessarily boost profits.

3. ___ Costs and consumer demand are equally important in determining the best price for a product.

Objective 20.8: Identify the major issues related to price determination in international marketing.

1. ___ Global pricing strategies almost always depend on demand in the domestic market.

2. ___ A firm's global pricing strategy reflects its global marketing strategy.

3. ___ In addition to the four major categories of pricing objectives, marketers must consider price stability in their international pricing strategies.

Students: See the solutions section located on page S-4 to check your responses to the Achievement Check Summary.

Key Terms

price
Robinson-Patman Act
unfair-trade law
fair-trade law
profit maximization
target return objective
Profit Impact of Market Strategies (PIMS) project
value pricing
customary price
demand
supply
pure competition
monopolistic competition
oligopoly
monopoly
elasticity
cost-plus pricing
breakeven analysis
modified breakeven analysis

Review Questions

1. Distinguish between fair-trade laws and unfair-trade laws. As a consumer, do you support such laws? Would your answer change if you owned a small retail store?
2. Identify the major categories of pricing objectives. Give an example of each.
3. How do the pricing objectives of not-for-profit organizations differ from those of profit-seeking firms?
4. What major implications did the PIMS studies produce for pricing decisions? Suggest possible explanations for the relationships those studies revealed.
5. Explain the concept of elasticity. Identify each force that influences elasticity, and give a specific example of how it affects the elasticity of demand and supply for a good or service.
6. Explain the advantages of incremental-cost pricing rather than full-cost pricing. What potential drawbacks limit applications of incremental-cost pricing?
7. Why do many firms choose to de-emphasize price as a marketing tool and instead concentrate on the other marketing mix variables in seeking to achieve competitive advantages?
8. What help do marketers gain when they locate the breakeven point for a product in the course of price determination? What primary dangers do they encounter by relying solely on breakeven analysis in pricing decisions?
9. What is the breakeven point for a product with a selling price of $20, average variable costs of $12, and related fixed costs of $18,500? What impact would a $2-per-unit profit requirement have on the breakeven point?
10. Identify the conditions that affect prices in international marketing.

Discussion Questions

1. Categorize each of the following pricing objectives according to the system discussed in the chapter text. Suggest a company or product likely to utilize each pricing objective.
   a. Prices to produce a 5 percent increase in profits over the previous year
   b. Prices no more than 6 percent higher than those quoted by independent dealers
   c. Prices to produce a 5 percent increase in market share
   d. Prices to produce a 25 percent return on investment (before taxes)
   e. Prices that follow those set by the firm's most important competitors in its market segments
   f. The highest prices in the product category to maintain a favorable brand image
2. Describe the market situations for the following products. Defend your answers.
   a. Local telephone service
   b. Cellular phones
   c. Soccer balls
   d. Copper
   e. Rice
   f. Home carbon monoxide detectors
   g. Toothbrushes
   h. Snowboards
3. How do marketers determine prices for the following products, and what do these procedures have in common?
   a. Ticket to a movie theater
   b. Your college tuition
   c. Local property tax rate
   d. Printing services for graduation announcements
4. EuroTech Development of Lubbock, Texas, is considering a proposal to introduce a new product advocated by its research and development staff. The firm's marketing director estimates that the product can be marketed at a price of $35. Total fixed cost is $139,000, and average variable cost is calculated at $24 per unit.
   a. What is the firm's breakeven point in units for the proposed product?
   b. The company president has suggested a target profit return of $107,000 for the proposed product. How many units must it sell in order to both break even and achieve this target return?
5. The marketing research staff at Milwaukee-based Consolidated Novelties has developed the following sales estimates for a proposed new item designed to be marketed through direct-mail promotion: The new product has a total fixed cost of $60,000 and a $7 variable cost per unit.

Proposed Selling Price	Sales Estimate (Units)
$ 8	55,000
10	22,000
15	14,000
20	5,000
24	2,800

a. Which of the proposed selling prices would generate a profit for Consolidated Novelties?
b. The company's director of marketing estimates that an additional $0.50 per unit allocation for extra promotion will produce the following increases in sales estimates: 60,000 units at an $8 unit selling price, 28,000 units at $10, 17,000 units at $15, 6,000 units at $20, and 3,500 units at $24. Indicate the feasible range of prices if this proposal is implemented and the predicted sales increases actually occur.
c. Indicate the feasible price or prices if the firm decides not to implement the $0.50 per unit additional promotional expense and management insists on a $25,000 target return.

'netWork

1. Saturn follows some very nontraditional marketing practices, especially in its pricing strategy. Go to the company's home page at

http://www.saturncars.com/

and calculate the price for a new Saturn SC1. Evaluate Saturn's pricing strategy versus that of a typical competitor.
2. Several times over the past three decades, food-industry firms have attracted the attention of antitrust regulators, particularly in connection with mergers, pricing fixing, price discrimination, and monopolies. Find information on the Web about one of these cases. Explain the situation that triggered antitrust enforcement and the outcome. What could or should the targeted firms have done to avoid these problems?
3. Marketers began placing banner ads on the Internet in order to create product awareness and increase revenue. Apparently, however, banners seldom generate enough revenue to justify their cost. Use concepts discussed in this chapter to suggest methods by which providers of Internet advertising space can generate additional revenue.

VIDEO CASE 20

PRICING A LIFESAVER

How do you set the price for a product that could mean the difference between life and death for its customer? Richard Davis had to make that decision in determining the price for a bulletproof vest he designed. Davis is CEO of Second Chance Corp., a major supplier of body armor to police departments and law enforcement agencies throughout the world.

Most people don't realize the importance of body armor in the daily routine of today's law enforcement officers. Several trends threaten the safety of police officers and heighten the demand for protective armor, including the dramatic increase in violent crime, the proliferation of firearms, and the growing number of high-caliber semiautomatic and automatic weapons in the hands of criminals.

Davis started his company after falling victim to a violent crime while on duty as a police officer. As a reaction, he developed a new type of comfortable and concealable bullet-resistant vest designed to protect the vital organs of the torso. The new body armor was introduced with an unforgettable video demonstration of Davis wearing his Second Chance vest and shooting himself to demonstrate his confidence in the product's effectiveness.

Second Chance offers three lines of comfortable, custom fit vests. The basic vest, The ComfortLite brand, starts at around $200. The middle-of-the-line product, the SuperfeatherLite, is priced between $500 and $600. The Monarch, Second Chance's high-end line, carries a price tag of $800 to $1,000.

Low entry barriers attract many competitors to the body armor industry. Newcomers can begin operating with minimal capital investments, but weak experience, poor distribution networks, and inability to offer custom-designed, uniform-quality products doom most of them to go out of business in a few years. New entries soon follow and struggle with the same production and marketing handicaps. Second Chance executives consider three to four large, reputable firms as their major competitors, and they carefully monitor the marketing activities of these rivals to assess potential threats in their market.

A number of factors affect prices of Second Chance products: production costs, trade discounts for channel members, prices charged by competitors, and customer perceptions of product value. This pricing strategy differs from those of most competitors, who tend to set minimum profit margin goals and then pursue volume pricing strategies. Group vice president Thomas Bachner explains why Second Chance pursues a different strategy: "Our philosophy is to peg the value of the product and get as much high-volume business with that high value so we can maximize our profit margins."

The pricing of the Monarch brand is an excellent example of this strategy. This vest is thin, light, soft, flexible, and the only waterproof product in the marketplace. Although its production cost is only slightly higher than those of other Second Chance vests, company marketers deliberately set the price higher than that of any other vest in the market to support its perceived value.

The largest current target market for Second Chance products is the law enforcement community of North America. Department buyers consider a number of evaluative criteria to determine which vest to purchase for their officers. At the top of the list of criteria is the range of bullets the body armor needs to stop. Second, buyers check for certification by the National Institute of Justice. Then they consider price and comfort. Some buyers are highly price sensitive; others are not. Price-sensitive buyers typically include part-time officers or those who patrol economically depressed areas. Other buyers rank comfort as the main concern. When comfort-oriented buyers see Second Chance's Monarch ad showing two hands crushing the vest into a ball, they frequently call the company to ask where they can buy it without asking about price.

Most of Second Chance's sales volume is generated through police equipment distributors and dealers. The company publishes a recommended retail price list and offers trade discounts to channel members along a graduated scale that depends on purchase volume. Discounts range from 3 percent up to 57 percent for dealers that purchase at least $150,000 annually. To encourage quick payments, Second Chance pays all freight charges for prepaid shipments.

For very large orders, Second Chance participates in competitive bidding. Bachner has developed a breakeven analysis system to help him in preparing bids. The company recently won a lucrative bid to supply the City of Chicago with 12,000 vests. Even though Second Chance's price was fourth lowest of 15 bidders, it received the contract after the Chicago Police Department evaluated lowest bidders on three factors: ability to custom fit, company reputation, and ability to produce in volume and deliver at least 400 vests per week.

Second Chance currently exports body armor to the United Kingdom, Sweden, Italy, Venezuela, Mexico, and Canada. Exports account for 10 to 25 percent of total sales. In pricing exports, Second Chance marketers take into account a number of additional factors, including competition in local markets, rates of exchange, special tariffs, and value-added taxes. Distributors in each international market purchase the vests at specified prices that vary according to annual sales volume. Since these representatives bring knowledge about their own markets, Second Chance relies on them to set the retail prices for the different product lines.

In a little more than two decades, Second Chance has become the leader for the body armor industry in units sold and in the numbers of lives saved annually. It also enjoys strong brand preference in the law enforcement industry. Always paying primary attention to satisfying the needs of the end user, Second Chance is successful in marketing the right products at the right prices.

Questions

1. Which of the pricing objectives discussed in the chapter apply to Second Chance?
2. Which type of market structure described in the chapter best describes the body armor industry? Defend your answer.
3. Is demand for body armor price elastic or price inelastic? Explain.
4. In addition to its lines of concealable body armor, Second Chance has used its expertise to develop a number of other products. Visit the firm's Web site at
   http://www.secondchance.com/
   Identify the product extensions that Second Chance has added to its offerings. Should the firm apply the same pricing strategy for the new products that it uses for lines of concealable body armor? Explain.

Sources: Personal interview with Thomas Bachner, group vice president of Second Chance Corp., March 1997.

CHAPTER 21

MANAGING THE PRICING FUNCTION

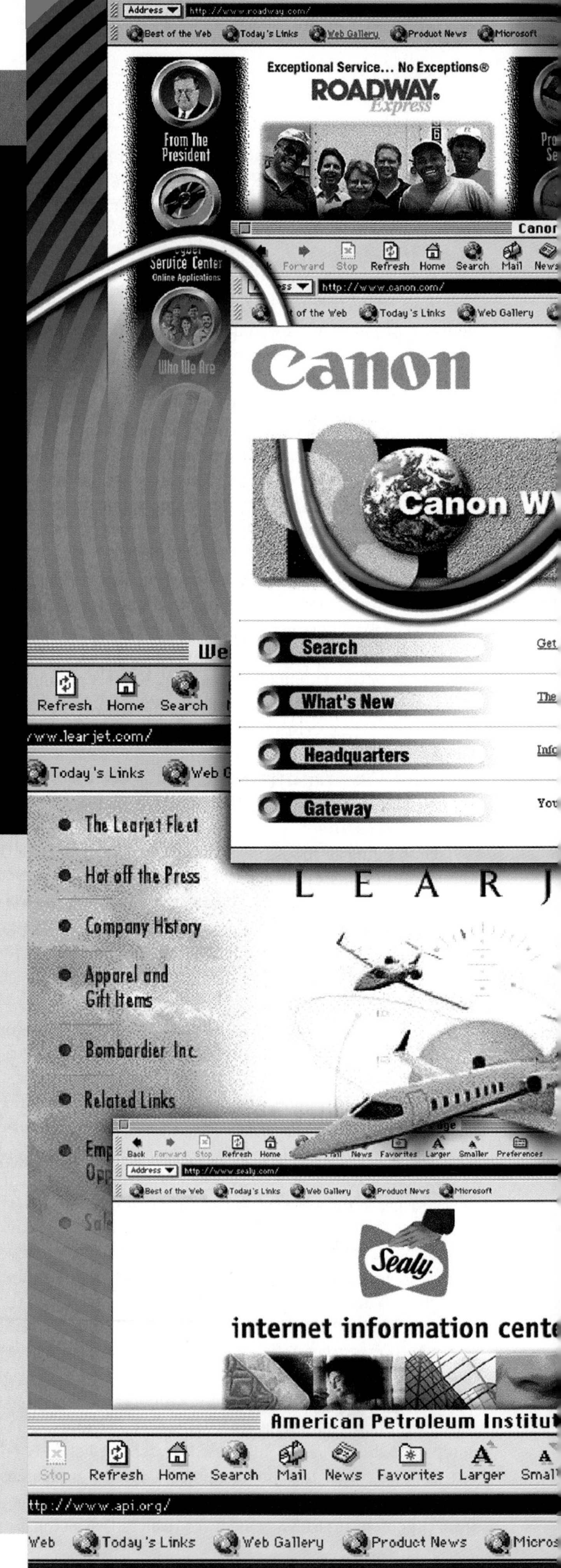

Exceptional Service... No Exceptions®
ROADWAY
Express
From The President
Service Center
Online Applications
Who We Are
http://www.canon.com/
Canon
Canon WW
Search
What's New
Headquarters
Gateway
www.learjet.com/
The Learjet Fleet
Hot off the Press
Company History
Apparel and Gift Items
Bombardier Inc.
Related Links
LEARJ
http://www.sealy.com/
Sealy
internet information cent
American Petroleum Institut
ttp://www.api.org/

Chapter Objectives

1. Compare the alternative pricing strategies and explain when each strategy is most appropriate.
2. Describe how prices are quoted.
3. Identify the various pricing policy decisions that marketers must make.
4. Relate price to consumer perceptions of quality.
5. Contrast competitive bidding and negotiated prices.
6. Explain the importance of transfer pricing.
7. Compare the three alternative strategies for pricing exports.

Why Gasoline Prices Just Keep Going Up

Grumbling about high gasoline prices is as futile as complaining about taxes. You can't really do anything about either one.

In the United States, consumer perceptions of costly trips to the pump often lead to cyclical volleys of complaints. Seemingly overnight, motorists will notice that a $10 bill buys a lot less gas than it once bought. If prices remain high for a time, self-styled experts begin pontificating about greedy oil companies.

But greed alone does not completely explain why gas prices spike up and then settle back down to a level comfortable for most drivers. The most recent episode of skyrocketing prices illustrates the influences of some key variables in gasoline pricing.

http://www.api.org/

During the last big jump in gas prices, low product inventories carried by the nation's oil refiners played a central role. To reduce costs, refiners decided to limit the amounts of oil they kept on hand, in effect switching to a just-in-time inventory system. By postponing crude oil purchases until they were needed, refiners reduced their storage and handling expenses. But Kenneth Haley, chief economist for Chevron Corp., notes that, "It also leaves us susceptible to greater price volatility."

AMERICAN PETROLEUM INSTITUTE
Representing the Nation's Oil and Gas Industries.
Programs & Services
API in Brief
Info Mart
ONLINE SERVICES
Industry Data
Publications
EnCompass
PROTECTING OUR PLANET
FACTS ABOUT PETROLEUM
News & Views
WHAT'S NEW
Links to Other Sites

Drivers must also share some of the blame for rising prices. When Americans forsake economy cars for sport-utility vehicles, minivans, and other gas guzzlers, their own purchase decisions trigger growing demand for fuel. In addition, Congress relaxed national speed limit requirements, and faster driving also sent cars speeding to the pumps. People also boost demand for limited petroleum supplies when they burn oil to heat their homes, especially during harsh winters in the East and Midwest.

Meanwhile, America's ongoing dispute with Iraq has also influenced pump prices. As punishment for its aggression leading up to the Persian Gulf war, United Nations sanctions prohibited Iraq from selling its oil on the world market. Promising negotiations raised the possibility, however, that Iraq might resume oil exports. Refiners postponed buying large amounts of crude, waiting for Iraqi

supplies to hit the market, reducing the price for everybody. The negotiations failed, however, and Iraqis did not escape the embargo, leaving refiners scrambling for scarce supplies.

Of course, some skeptics insist that oil companies deliberately manipulate prices to bilk their customers, a criticism that the oil companies vigorously deny. Surely one of the industry's fiercest critics is Tim Cohelan, an attorney and veteran public interest advocate, who has filed a lawsuit in California against Texaco, Chevron, Shell, and other major oil companies. In his suit, Cohelan alleges that the companies sell excess gas between themselves to limit the state's supply and that they exploited the introduction of relatively costly, clean-burning fuel in California as a cover for dramatic increases in prices. He further alleges that refiners restrict production of petroleum in an artificial attempt to raise prices. "Money has been siphoned by these companies out of the pockets of the average Joe," Cohelan says. "It's unconscionable."

For Americans' bitter complaints about gas prices, they pay quite reasonable fuel bills. U.S. motorists enjoy some of the lowest gas prices in the world—about half as much as drivers pay in many European countries, where governments commonly add $2 to $3 per gallon in taxes. "When you look at the real price of gasoline," says Kevin Lindemer of Cambridge Energy Research, "it's about what you paid in 1947."[1]

CHAPTER OVERVIEW

Companies translate pricing objectives into pricing decisions in two major steps. First, someone must accept responsibility for making pricing decisions and administering the resulting pricing structure. Second, someone must set the overall pricing structure—that is, basic prices and appropriate discounts for channel members, quantity purchases, and geographic and promotional considerations.

Princeton economist Alan Blinder, a former member of President Clinton's Council of Economic Advisers, conducted research to determine how frequently companies change prices on major products. He found that most businesses change the amounts they charge customers only slowly, even when they clearly recognize strong demand. While half of the companies Blinder questioned reported changing prices once a year or less often, only one out of ten makes a price change more than once a month.

Businesses may hesitate to shift prices for a number of reasons. When demand is strong, instead of raising prices they may choose to scale down customer service and incentives. They may also wait to raise prices until they see what their competitors will do. (Few businesses want the distinction of being the first to charge higher prices.) Since many businesses base their prices on manufacturing costs rather than consumer demand, they may wait for increases in their own costs before responding with price changes. These increases generally emerge more slowly than changes in consumer demand. Finally, since many business executives believe that steady prices will help to preserve long-term relationships with customers, they are reluctant to raise prices even when strong demand probably justifies the change.[2]

Chapter 20 introduced the concept of price and its role in the economic system and marketing strategy. This chapter extends that topic to consider who in an organization should accept responsibility for pricing decisions and how to develop a sequential method for making such decisions. It examines various pricing strategies, criteria for administration of pricing structures, and pricing practices such as negotiated prices, competitive bidding, and pricing in the public sector. Finally, it looks at pricing strategies appropriate for companies that export products outside their own countries' borders.

PRICING STRATEGIES

The specific strategies that firms use to price their goods and services grow out of the marketing strategies they formulate to accomplish overall organizational objectives. One firm's marketers may price products to attract customers across a wide range; another group of marketers may set prices to appeal to a small segment of a larger market; still another group may simply try to match competitors' price tags.

In general, firms can choose from three pricing strategies: skimming, penetration, and competitive pricing. The following sections look at these choices in more detail.

Figure 21.1 Learjet Corporate Jets: Distinctive Products Marketed through a Skimming Pricing Strategy

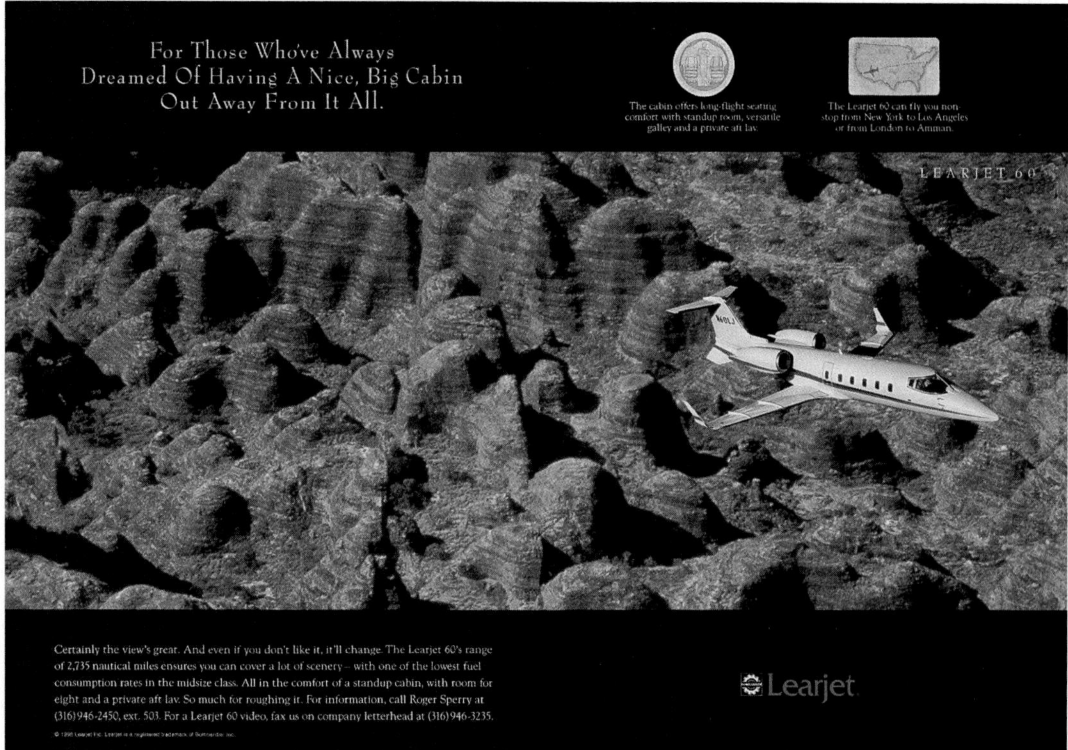
For Those Who've Always
Dreamed Of Having A Nice, Big Cabin
Out Away From It All.
The cabin offers long-flight seating comfort with standup room, versatile galley and a private aft lav.
The Learjet 60 can fly you nonstop from New York to Los Angeles or from London to Amman.
LEARJET 60
Certainly the view's great. And even if you don't like it, it'll change. The Learjet 60's range of 2,735 nautical miles ensures you can cover a lot of scenery – with one of the lowest fuel consumption rates in the midsize class. All in the comfort of a standup cabin, with room for eight and a private aft lav. So much for roughing it. For information, call Roger Sperry at (316)946-2450, ext. 503. For a Learjet 60 video, fax us on company letterhead at (316)946-3235.
Learjet

Skimming Pricing Strategy

A **skimming pricing strategy** is sometimes called *market-plus pricing,* because it intentionally sets a relatively high price compared to the prices of competing products. The name comes from the expression *skimming the cream.*

A company may practice a skimming strategy in setting a market-entry price when it introduces a distinctive good or service with little or no competition. Searle Pharmaceutical charges $700 for a year's supply of its new ulcer-preventive drug Cytotec. To justify the high price, Searle management points out that the drug often keeps patients from undergoing ulcer surgery, which carries an even higher price tag of $25,000 or more.[3]

http://www.learjet.com/

The Learjet brand name is a widely known indicator of the ultimate in corporate jets. The distinctive shapes of the planes attract customers among businesses, executive travelers, and celebrities. As Figure 21.1 shows, the firm's advertisements ignore price and instead focus on product benefits such as cabin comfort and ability to fly nonstop from New York to Los Angeles.

Some companies use skimming strategies to distinguish high-end products from those of competitors. Black Shield, Inc., sells its Crown Jewel Connoisseur's Popcorn Collection in upscale stores such as Neiman-Marcus for an upscale price—$16 for a 3-pound box. Black Shield marketers expect consumers to willingly pay extra for the gourmet popcorn, which includes six varieties of hybrid corn grown especially for flavor.[4]

Improvements in existing products may allow firms to change from other pricing structures to skimming strategies. Consider the lowly toothbrush, which until recently sold mainly on the basis of price—the cheaper, the better. Then several manufacturers introduced new features designed to improve the effectiveness of their toothbrushes. Procter & Gamble now sells the Crest Complete

Marketing Dictionary

skimming pricing strategy A pricing strategy involving the use of a high price relative to competitive offerings.

Figure 21.2 **Price Reductions to Expand a Product's Total Market**

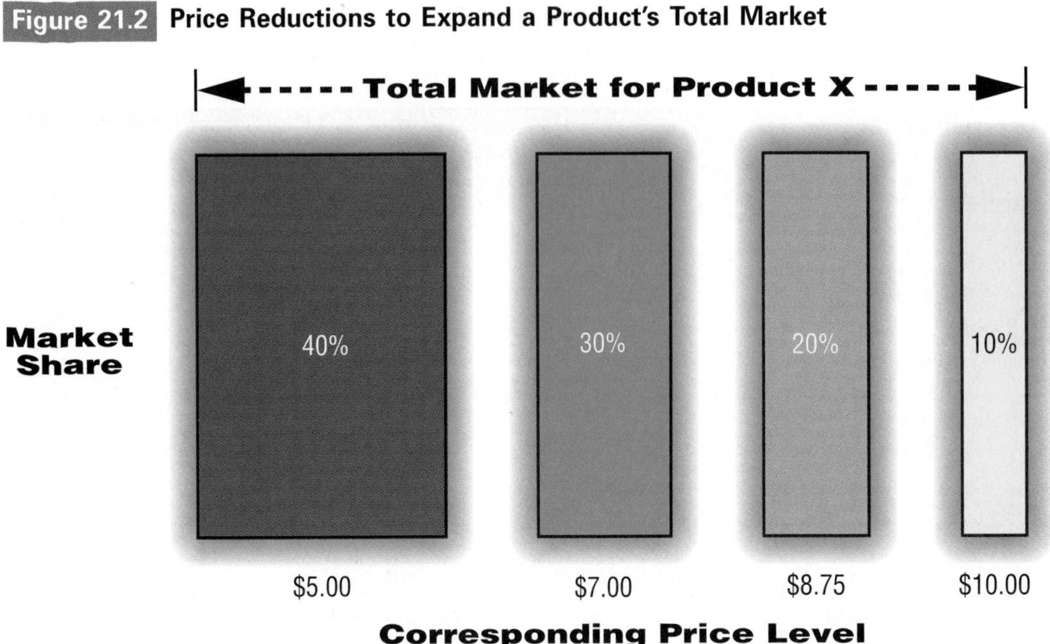
Total Market for Product X
Market Share
40%
30%
20%
10%
$5.00
$7.00
$8.75
$10.00
Corresponding Price Level

Toothbrush with rippled bristles designed to reach 37 percent deeper between teeth. Colgate-Palmolive has introduced the Colgate Precision model, which is equipped with three different lengths of bristles. SmithKline Beecham markets the Flex brush with a tiny spring in the handle intended to stop overly enthusiastic consumers from brushing too hard and hurting their gums. Oral-B's brushes carry blue bristles that fade to white after four months' use to remind customers to buy new ones. In a single year, these improvements raised the average toothbrush price from $1.71 to $1.90 and turned the brush business into one of the fastest-growing health and beauty care segments in supermarkets and drugstores.[5]

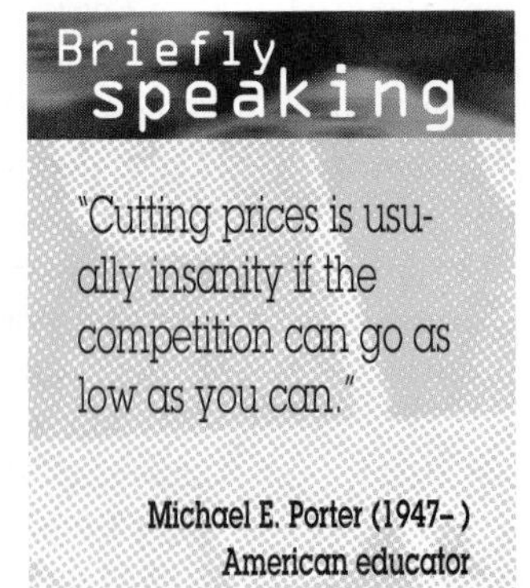
Briefly speaking
"Cutting prices is usually insanity if the competition can go as low as you can."
Michael E. Porter (1947–)
American educator

A firm may maintain a skimming strategy throughout most stages of a product's life cycle. Sometimes this tactic works and sometimes it does not. Searle and other pharmaceutical manufacturers can keep prices for some drugs relatively high due to continued demand. On the other hand, U.S. sales of the Jaguar XJS have plunged 64 percent in the last five years. In response, Jaguar has cut the price by 18 percent, from $60,500 to $49,750.

A skimming strategy offers several benefits. For one, it allows a manufacturer to quickly recover its research and development (R&D) costs. Drugmakers cite this argument as one reason why new drugs cost so much, pointing out that no other industry invests as much in research and development. Pharmaceutical manufacturers invest an average of 16 percent of sales income in R&D, compared to 8 percent for computermakers and 4 percent in the aerospace industry.[6] A skimming strategy also allows a firm to maximize revenue from a new product before competitors enter the field. In many industries, increasing competition eventually drives down initially high prices, as occurred with VCRs and personal computers.

A skimming strategy offers a useful tool for segmenting a product's overall market on a price basis. For a new product that represents a significant innovation, a relatively high price conveys an image of distinction, helping the product to appeal to buyers with low sensitivity to price. Laser printers were introduced in the last decade carrying prices of several thousand dollars, but today the best-selling laser printer models cost only $1,000. Other examples of products introduced under skimming strategies include television sets, Polaroid cameras, digital watches, and pocket calculators. Subsequent price reductions have allowed these products to appeal to new, more price-sensitive market segments.

A third advantage of a skimming strategy is that it permits marketers to control demand in the introductory stages of a product's life cycle and then adjust productive capacity to match demand. A low initial price for a new product risks problems if demand outstrips the firm's production capacity, resulting in consumer and retailer complaints and possibly permanent damage to the product's image. Excess demand occasionally leads to poor-quality products, as the firm strives to satisfy consumer desires for the product with inadequate production facilities.

During the late growth and early maturity stages of its life cycle, a product's price typically falls for two reasons: (1) the pressure of competition and (2) the desire to expand its market. Figure 21.2 shows that 10 percent of the market would buy Product X at $10.00, and another 20 percent would buy at a price of $8.75. Successive price declines expand the firm's market and meet challenges posed by new competitors.

A skimming strategy brings one chief disadvantage: It attracts competition. Potential competitors see innovative firms reaping large financial returns and decide to enter the market. This new supply forces the price even lower than its eventual level under a sequential skimming procedure. However, if patent protection or some other unique, proprietary ability allows a firm to exclude competitors from its market, it may continue a skimming strategy for a relatively long period.

Penetration Pricing Strategy

A **penetration pricing strategy** sets a low price as a major marketing weapon. Marketers often price products noticeably lower than competing offerings when they enter new industries characterized by dozens of competing brands. Once the product achieves some market recognition through consumer trial purchases stimulated by a product's low price, marketers may increase the price to the level of competing products. Marketers of consumer products such as detergents often use this strategy. A penetration pricing strategy may also extend over several stages of the product life cycle as the firm seeks to maintain a reputation as a low-price competitor.

A penetration pricing strategy is sometimes called *market-minus pricing* because it implements the premise that a lower-than-market price will attract buyers and move a brand from an unknown newcomer at least to the brand-recognition stage or even the brand-preference stage. Since many firms begin penetration pricing with the intention of increasing prices in the future, success depends on generating many consumer trial purchases.

Pearl Drops uses a penetration pricing strategy to compete with Rembrandt, its better-known, market-leading competitor in the whitening toothpaste category. Pearl Drops marketers originally implemented the strategy to build quick success in entering this market niche and carving out a profitable market share. As the ad in Figure 21.3 shows, Pearl Drops combines its product superiority claim with a price 50 percent below its competitor's to generate reader attention and stimulate trial purchases.

General Motors used a penetration pricing strategy when it introduced its new Saturn car at a relatively low but nonnegotiable price. The earliest models of the Saturn SL sports sedan sold for $2,000 less than comparable Toyota and Honda automobiles. More recently, Ford has tried to capture market share from the successful Saturn by posting nonnegotiable prices on Escorts that average about $2,000 less than the Saturn SL2's price.[7]

Retailers may use penetration pricing to lure shoppers to new stores. These may take such forms as zero-interest charges for credit purchases at a new furniture store, two-for-one offers for golfers at a new driving range, or offering first-day customers a 12-inch, black-and-white television set for $29.

Figure 21.3 Pearl Drops: Succeeding with a Penetration Pricing Strategy

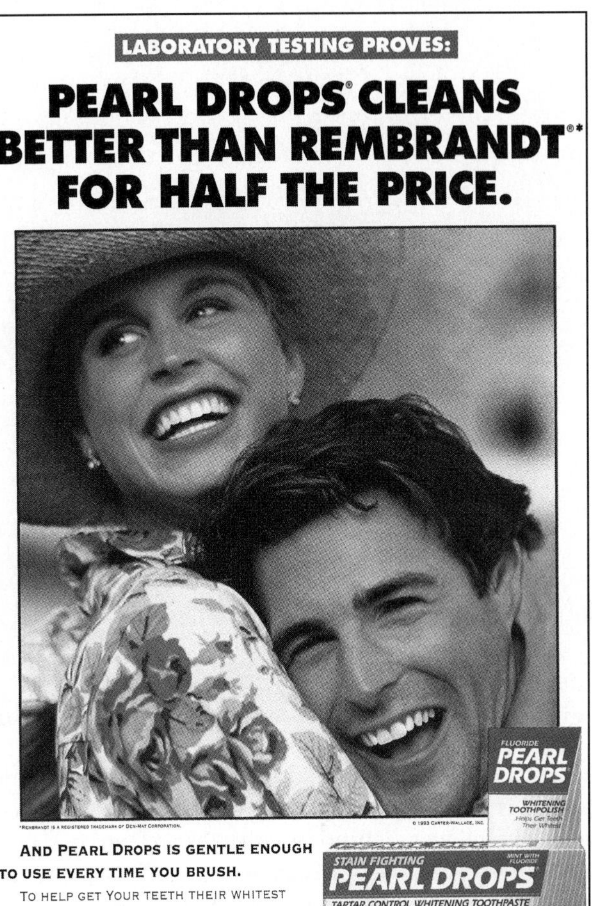
LABORATORY TESTING PROVES:
PEARL DROPS® CLEANS BETTER THAN REMBRANDT®* FOR HALF THE PRICE.
FLUORIDE
PEARL DROPS
WHITENING TOOTHPOLISH
*REMBRANDT IS A REGISTERED TRADEMARK OF DEN-MAT CORPORATION.
© 1993 CARTER-WALLACE, INC.
AND PEARL DROPS IS GENTLE ENOUGH TO USE EVERY TIME YOU BRUSH.
TO HELP GET YOUR TEETH THEIR WHITEST USE PEARL DROPS WHITENING TOOTHPASTE.
STAIN FIGHTING
PEARL DROPS
TARTAR CONTROL WHITENING TOOTHPASTE
Helps Get Teeth Their Whitest

Penetration pricing works best when a good or service experiences highly elastic demand. Large numbers of highly price-sensitive consumers pay close attention to this kind of appeal.[8] The strategy also suits situations in which large-scale operations and long production runs result in low production and marketing costs. Finally, penetration pricing may be appropriate in market situations in which introduction of a new product will likely attract strong competitors. Such a strategy may allow a new product to reach the mass market quickly and capture a large share prior to entry by competitors. Research shows that about 25 percent of companies frequently use penetration pricing strategies.

Marketing Dictionary

penetration pricing strategy A pricing strategy involving the use of a relatively low entry price as compared with competing offerings to help secure initial market acceptance.

Figure 21.4 **Canon: Succeeding with a Competitive Pricing Strategy**

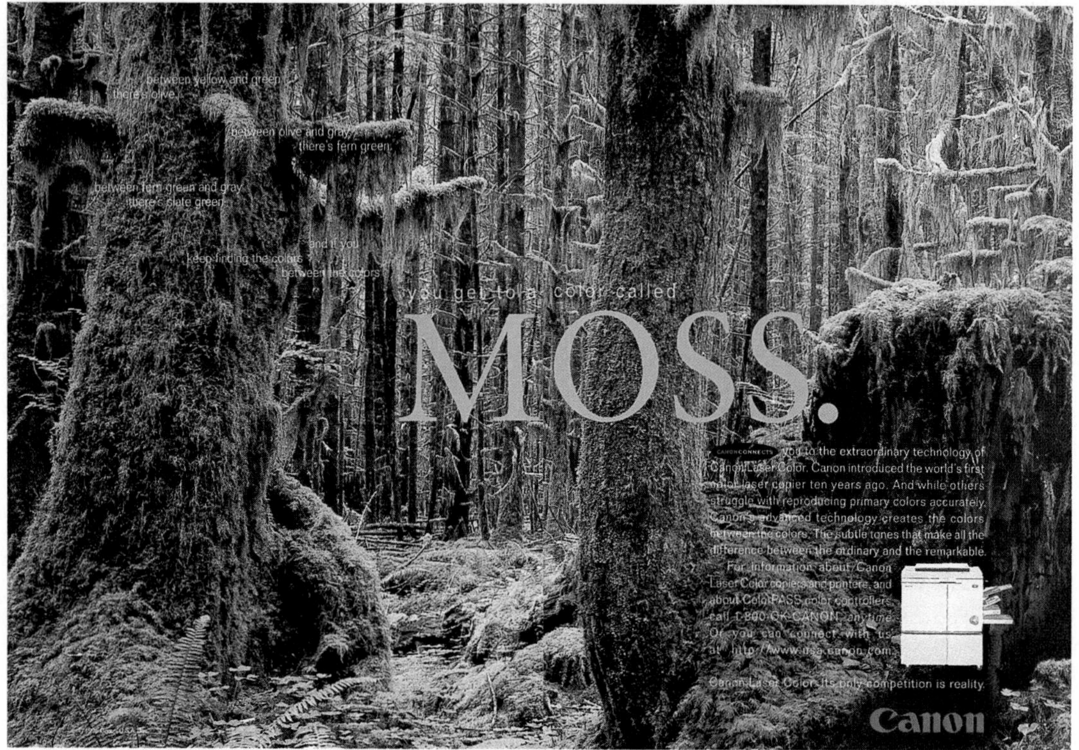
between yellow and green
there's olive.
between olive and gray
there's fern green.
between fern green and gray
there's slate green.
and if you
keep finding the colors
between the colors
you get to a color called
MOSS.
CANONCONNECTS you to the extraordinary technology of Canon Laser Color. Canon introduced the world's first color laser copier ten years ago. And while others struggle with reproducing primary colors accurately, Canon's advanced technology creates the colors between the colors. The subtle tones that make all the difference between the ordinary and the remarkable.
For information about Canon Laser Color copiers and printers, and about ColorPASS color controllers, call 1-800-OK-CANON anytime. Or you can connect with us at http://www.usa.canon.com.
Canon Laser Color. Its only competition is reality.
Canon

Everyday Low Pricing Closely related to penetration pricing is **everyday low pricing (EDLP),** a strategy devoted to continuous low prices rather than relying on short-term price-cutting tactics such as cents-off coupons, rebates, and special sales. EDLP can take two forms. In one, retailers like Kmart compete by offering low retail prices to consumers; in the other, manufacturers seek to set stable wholesale prices undercutting those that competitors offer to retailers, which often rise and fall due to trade promotion deals.

Chapter 18 described Procter & Gamble's decision to lower its list prices on many products while simultaneously reducing promotion allowances to retailers. Retailers have traditionally relied on these allowances to fund in-store promotions such as shelf merchandising and end-aisle displays. The program led to many dramatic price cuts:

- Cheer, Era, Gain, and Tide detergents sold at prices averaging 6.5 percent below those of the previous year.
- Average prices for Bounty paper towels declined by 4.8 percent.
- P&G intensified the disposable diaper price war through price cuts averaging 20 percent for Pampers Trainers and Luvs training pants.

This move to everyday low pricing quickly spread to other product categories:

- Kleenex facial tissue prices fell an average of 8 percent.
- Sprint's off-peak, long-distance telephone calls, which had averaged 15.4 cents per minute two years earlier, cost only 10 cents per minute.[9]

Some retailers reacted negatively to P&G's move to EDLP. Many grocery store managers operate on "high-low" strategies that set profitable regular prices offset by frequent specials and promotions. "It takes away our flexibility as a retailer," claims Claire D'Amour, vice president for corporate affairs at Big Y Foods. "Basically, P&G is saying we have one option—take it or leave it. . . . P&G is trying to wrestle control of the marketplace from the retailer."

Other retailers feel that EDLP will ultimately benefit both sellers and buyers. "What we want is the lowest possible prices for our customers—we're their purchasing agent," says Mickey Clerc, vice president for advertising for Winn-Dixie stores. "Our customers can't eat trade promotions." Supporters of EDLP in the grocery industry point out that it already succeeds at two of the biggest competitors, Wal-Mart and warehouse clubs. One manager notes that supermarkets "can scream and yell all they want that they don't like P&G's strategy, but it's consumers and Wal-Mart putting them out of business."

Marketing theorists express differing opinions about the prospects of EDLP emerging as a dominant pricing strategy. Ronald Curhan, a professor at Boston University's Graduate School of Management, thinks not: "Everyday low pricing will not win. It serves best when compared with high-low pricing." Instead, Curhan predicts a range of pricing formats in the late 1990s. But Kevin Price of Marketing Corp. of America describes EDLP as, "a good thing for the industry. . . . This is the single largest change in business practices with the greatest financial implications that has ever hit the grocery business. Those that figure it out and get on the bandwagon are going to be in great shape."[10]

Competitive Pricing Strategy

Although many organizations rely heavily on price as a competitive weapon, even more implement **competitive pricing strategies.** They try to reduce the emphasis on price competition by matching other firms' prices and concentrating their own marketing efforts on the product, distribution, and promotion elements of the marketing mix. As pointed out earlier, while price offers a dramatic means of achieving competitive advantage, it is also the easiest marketing variable for competitors to match. In fact, in industries with relatively homogeneous products, competitors must match one anothers' price reductions in order to maintain market share and remain competitive.

Retailers like Wal-Mart and Target share the same strategy. Both stores advertise price-matching pledges, assuring consumers that they will meet—and beat—competitors' prices. For example, grocery store managers regularly raise and lower the prices on hundreds of key items to stay within boundaries set by local competition.

Even when they sell relatively heterogeneous products, marketers analyze the prices of major competing offerings and ensure that their own prices do not markedly differ. When IBM entered the personal computer market, its marketing efforts emphasized the versatility and power of its machines. However, the firm's marketers also quickly pointed out that each PC in the line carried a competitive price.

Under competitive pricing, a price reduction spreads financial effects throughout an industry as other firms match the drop. Unless the lower prices can attract new customers and expand the overall market enough to offset the loss of per-unit revenue, the price cut will leave all competitors with less revenue. Research shows that nearly two-thirds of all firms set prices at standard levels for comparable products as their primary pricing strategies.

By pricing their products at the general levels of competitive offerings, marketers largely negate the price variable in their marketing strategies. They must then emphasize nonprice variables to develop areas of distinctive competence and attract customers. More than a dozen firms compete with one another in the color copier market. While many of them emphasize price as a primary component of their marketing mixes, market leader Canon is moving toward a new strategy by running ads that position its laser color copier as a technologically superior product. The Canon ad shown in Figure 21.4 points out the benefits to customers of its commitment to advanced technology by powerfully illustrating the copier's color reproduction capabilities. The ad does not mention price, since Canon sets prices comparable to those of competing firms. As one industry analyst says, "If your only position is, 'We're the cheapest,' then you're going to get killed every time."

http://www.canon.com/

PRICE QUOTATIONS

Firms' methods for quoting prices depend on many industry conditions, including competitive trends, cost structures, and traditional practices, along with the policies of individual firms. This section examines the reasoning and methodology behind price quotation practices.

Consider the competitive environment facing Boeing Aircraft. After many prosperous years, the aircraft manufacturer is encountering mounting competition from around the world, including America's McDonnell Douglas, Europe's Airbus Industrie, Russia's Aviastar, and Asia's Taiwan Aerospace. CEO Frank Shrontz plans to strike back by cutting costs 25 percent on Boeing's internal operations. Among the first targets: Boeing's bloated inventory and extended manufacturing process. The company currently maintains parts in stock worth about $8 billion, and it takes over a year to manufacture a plane. By cutting inventories and manufacturing time in half, Boeing could save $400 million a year in financing costs and $600 million in storage, handling, and transportation costs. Lowering these costs would allow Boeing to keep its prices at competitive levels.[11]

Most price structures are built around **list prices**—the rates normally quoted to potential buyers. Marketers usually determine list prices by one or a combination of the methods discussed in Chapter 20. The sticker price on a

Marketing Dictionary

everyday low pricing (EDLP) A pricing strategy of continuously offering low prices rather than relying on short-term price-cutting tactics such as cents-off coupons, rebates, and special sales.

competitive pricing strategy A pricing strategy designed to de-emphasize price as a competitive variable by pricing a good or service at the general level of comparable offerings.

list price An established price normally quoted to potential buyers.

Figure 21.5 **The Take on a $25 T-Shirt**

Production Costs
54%
Cost of T-Shirt $3.50
Silk-Screening, Processing, and Transportation $2.50
Licensing Fee Paid to Recording Artist $7.50
Marketing Costs
46%
Payment to Concert Vendor $4.00
Payment to Concert Arena $7.50
$25
WORLD TOUR '98
DALLAS JAN 12
HOUSTON JAN 13
DENVER JAN 19
LAS VEGAS JAN 22
SAN DIEGO JAN 24
TIJUANA JAN 27
SEATTLE JAN 29
CHICAGO JAN 30

new automobile is a good example: It shows the list price for the basic model and then adds the prices of options.

T-shirts offer another familiar example of list prices. About 1 billion of them were bought in the United States last year, generating sales revenues of $10 billion. Many of the most lucrative sales involved T-shirts sporting images of sports stars or musical groups printed on them. But where does the money go when you purchase a concert T-shirt at a list price of $25? Figure 21.5 supplies the answers.

Although 54 percent of the $25 list price goes for production costs, the $7.50 licensing fee paid to the recording artist accounts for nearly half of the total. The remaining 46 percent is paid to the retailer (the concert arena) and to concert vendors.

Reductions from List Price

The amount that a consumer pays for a product—its **market price**—may or may not equal the list price. Discounts and allowances sometimes reduce list prices. A list price often defines a starting point from which discounts set a lower market price. Marketers offer discounts in several classifications: cash, trade, and quantity discounts.

Cash Discounts Consumers, industrial purchasers, or channel members sometimes receive reductions in price in exchange for prompt payment of bills; these price cuts are known as **cash discounts.** Discount terms usually specify exact time periods, such as 2/10, net 30. This notation means that the customer must pay within 30 days, but payment within 10 days entitles the customer to subtract 2 percent from the amount due.

Cash discounts represent a traditional pricing practice in many industries. They fulfill legal requirements provided that all customers can take the same reductions on the same terms. Sellers originally instituted such discount practices to improve their own liquidity positions, reduce their bad-debt losses, and cut collection expenses. Whether these advantages outweigh the relatively high cost of capital that sellers incur by offering cash discounts depends on the need for liquidity as well as alternative sources (and costs) of funds.

Trade Discounts Payments to channel members for performing marketing functions are known as **trade discounts** or *functional discounts.* Earlier chapters discussed the services performed by various channel members and the related costs. A manufacturer's list price must incorporate the costs incurred by channel members in performing required marketing functions and expected profit margins for each member.

Trade discounts initially reflected the operating expenses of each category, but they have become more or less customary practices in some industries. The Robinson-Patman Act allows trade discounts as long as all buyers in the same category, such as all wholesalers and all retailers, receive the same discount privileges.

Figure 21.6 shows how a chain of trade discounts works. In the first instance, the trade discount is "40 percent, 10 percent off list price" for wholesalers. In other words, the 40 percent discount on the $40 product is the trade discount the retailer receives to cover operating expenses and earn a profit. The wholesaler receives 10 percent of the $24 price to retailers to cover expenses and earn a profit. The manufacturer receives $21.60 from the wholesaler for each order.

In the second example, the manufacturer and retailer decide to bypass the wholesaler. The producer offers a trade discount of 45 percent to the retailer. In this instance, the retailer receives $18 for each product sold at its list price and the manufacturer receives the remaining $22. Either the retailer or the manufacturer must assume responsibility for the services previously performed by the wholesaler, or they can share these duties between them.

Figure 21.6 Chain of Trade Discounts

"40 PERCENT, 10 PERCENT OFF" TRADE DISCOUNT

List Price	–	Retail Trade Discount	–	Wholesale Trade Discount	=	Manufacturer Proceeds
$40	–	$16 ($40 × 40%)	–	$2.40 ($24 × 10%)	=	$21.60 ($40 – $16 – $2.40)

"45 PERCENT" TRADE DISCOUNT

List Price	–	Retail Trade Discount	=	Manufacturer Proceeds
$40	–	$18 ($40 × 45%)	=	$22 ($40 – $18)

Quantity Discounts Price reductions granted for large-volume purchases are known as **quantity discounts.** Sellers justify these discounts on the grounds that large orders reduce selling expenses and may shift some costs for storage, transportation, and financing to buyers. The law allows quantity discounts provided they apply on the same basis to all customers.

Quantity discounts may specify either cumulative or noncumulative terms. *Cumulative quantity discounts* reduce prices in amounts determined by purchases over stated time periods. Annual purchases of at least $25,000 might entitle a buyer to a 3 percent rebate, while purchases exceeding $50,000 would increase the refund to 5 percent. These reductions are really patronage discounts, since they tend to bind customers to a single source of supply.

Noncumulative quantity discounts provide one-time reductions in list price. For example, a firm might offer the following discount schedule for a product priced at $1,000 per unit:

1 unit	List: $1,000
2–5 units	List less 10%
6–10 units	List less 20%
Over 10 units	List less 25%

Many businesses have come to expect quantity discounts from suppliers. Resisting these expectations can create competitive trouble for a firm. When United Parcel Service balked at providing quantity discounts for large clients such as DuPont, it created an opportunity for

Marketing Dictionary

market price A price that a consumer or marketing intermediary actually pays for a product after subtracting any discounts, allowances, or rebates from the list price.

cash discount A price reduction offered to a consumer, industrial user, or marketing intermediary in return for prompt payment.

trade discount A payment to a channel member or buyer as compensation for performing marketing functions; also known as a *functional discount.*

quantity discount A price reduction on a large-volume purchase.

Figure 21.7 **Advertising Rebates to Stimulate Sales**

1996 LeSabre Limited Sedan
1996 Century Custom Sedan
Two of Buick's best values are now even better, with this available feature.
A $1000 certificate. It is one feature we are sure you will enjoy using. So from Oct. 15 until Dec. 31, 1995, when you purchase a '95 or '96 Buick LeSabre or Century, you will get $1000 off.
What's more, now through Nov. 30, 1995, you can combine it with our national offer for a total savings of $2500 off a '95 LeSabre or '95 Century.
To take advantage of this offer, all you have to do is simply fill out the certificate. Then after determining your best deal, present the certificate along with a valid driver's license to prove you are 50 years old or older.
The LeSabre, America's best-selling family car, and the affordable Century have both won numerous awards over the years. In fact, both cars have been voted Best Overall Value in their respective classes by IntelliChoice,® Inc. in 1994 and 1995.*
Tear out the certificate and bring it to your Buick dealer today. After all, this feature is available for a limited time only. *To locate your nearest Buick dealer call 1-800-4A-BUICK.*
BUICK®
The New Symbol For Quality In America.
SAVE $1000 OFF A LESABRE OR CENTURY.
$1000
CUSTOMER NAME
ADDRESS
CITY
STATE
ZIP
DEALER CODE
VIN OF VEHICLE
PURCHASE DATE
CUSTOMER SIGNATURE
DATE
DEALER SIGNATURE
DATE
BUICK®
The New Symbol For Quality In America.
USA
Official Sponsor of the 1996 U.S. Olympic Team

competitors. One rival, Roadway Package System, lured several UPS customers by offering discounts to a wide range of organizational clients.

http://www.roadway.com/

Marketers typically favor combinations of cash, trade, and volume discounts. For example, American Lock & Supply Inc., an Anaheim, California, wholesale distributor of locks and other door hardware, offers hundreds of pricing alternatives to its industrial and retail customers. It seeks to maximize customer satisfaction by offering not only volume discounts, but also price discounts tailored to the amounts of customized service buyers require and how promptly they pay their bills.[12]

> **Briefly speaking**
>
> "I found the greater the volume, the cheaper I could buy and the better value I could give customers."
>
> **Frank W. Woolworth (1852–1919)**
> **American merchant**

Allowances Allowances resemble discounts by specifying deductions from list price. The major categories of allowances are trade-ins and promotional allowances. **Trade-ins** often figure in sales of durable goods such as automobiles. The new product's basic list price remains unchanged, but the seller accepts less money from the customer along with a used product—usually the same kind of product as the buyer purchases.

Promotional allowances reduce prices as part of attempts to integrate promotional strategies within distribution channels. Manufacturers often return part of the prices that buyers pay in the form of advertising and sales-support allowances for channel members. Automobile manufacturers frequently offer allowances to retail dealers to induce those retailers to reduce prices and stimulate sales.

Rebates In still another way to reduce a consumer's cost, marketers may offer a **rebate**—a refund of a portion of the purchase price. Rebates have appeared most pro-minently in promotions by automobile manufacturers eager to move models during periods of slow sales. However, firms have also offered rebates for sales in product categories ranging from appliances and sports equipment to grocery products and toiletries.

Automobile marketers sometimes offer eye-catching rebates. The ad shown in Figure 21.7 presents a $1,000 rebate certificate to customers 50 years old or older if they buy either of two Buick models. The ad promises an additional $1,500 discount from the so-called *sticker prices* of the cars. Along with combined savings of $2,500 off of list price, the ad emphasizes product quality. The copy describes the LeSabre as America's best-selling family car and mentions recent awards for best overall value.

Bed manufacturer Sealy recently introduced its first rebate program to consumers. The promotion seeks to persuade buyers to "put more focus on the upper end of the category," according to David McIlguham, Sealy's vice president of marketing. Rebate amounts range between $10 and $50 on super premium beds, and between $15 and $75 on ultra premium beds. Notes McIlguham, "The retailer has a real tool to move the consumer up, and there's a real incentive for the consumer to consider $699, $799, and $899 beds," thereby reversing "an alarming trend" toward less expensive products. Television advertisements for the promotion featured an animated frog that croaked "rebate, rebate."[13]

http://www.sealy.com/

Geographic Considerations

Geographic considerations strongly influence prices when costs must cover shipping heavy, bulky, low-unit-cost materials. Buyers and sellers can distribute transportation expenses in several ways: (1) The buyer pays all transportation charges; (2) the seller pays all transportation charges; or (3) the buyer and the seller share the charges. This choice has particularly important effects for a firm seeking to expand its geographic coverage to distant markets. How can a firm compete when local suppliers in the distant markets are able to avoid the considerable shipping costs that it must pay? The seller's pricing can implement several alternatives for handling transportation costs.

FOB plant, or *FOB origin,* prices include no shipping charges. The buyer must pay all freight charges to transport the product from the manufacturer's dock. The seller pays only to load the merchandise aboard the carrier selected by the buyer. The abbreviation *FOB* means "free on board." Legal title and responsibility pass to the buyer after the seller's employees load the purchase and accept a receipt from the representative of the common carrier.

Many marketing intermediaries, such as Virginia-based General Medical Corp., sell only on FOB plant terms to downstream channel members. These distributors feel that their customers have more clout than they do in dealing with long-distance carriers. They prefer to assign transportation costs to the channel members in the best positions to negotiate the most cost-effective shipping terms.

Sellers may also quote prices as *FOB origin-freight allowed.* These terms permit buyers to subtract transportation expenses from their bills. The amount such a seller receives for its product varies with the freight charged against the invoice. This alternative, also called **freight absorption,** is popular among firms with high fixed costs, because it helps them to considerably expand their markets by quoting the same prices regardless of shipping expenses.

When a firm quotes the same price, including transportation expenses, to all buyers, it adopts a **uniform delivered price** policy. Such a pricing structure is the exact opposite of FOB origin pricing. This system resembles the pricing structure for mail service, so it is sometimes called *postage-stamp pricing.* The price quote includes a transportation charge averaged over all of the firm's customers, meaning that distant customers actually pay a smaller share of shipping costs while nearby customers pay what is known as *phantom freight* (the amount by which the average transportation charge exceeds the actual cost of shipping).

Zone pricing modifies a uniform delivered pricing system by dividing an overall market into different zones and establishing a single price within each zone. This pricing structure incorporates average transportation costs for shipments within each zone as part of the delivered price of goods sold there; by narrowing distances, it reduces but does not eliminate phantom freight. The primary advantage of zone pricing comes from easy administration methods that still help a seller to compete in distant markets. The U.S. Postal Service's parcel rates depend on zone pricing.

In a **basing point system,** the price of a product to a customer includes the list price at the factory plus freight charges from the basing point city nearest the buyer. The basing point specifies a location from which to calculate freight charges—not necessarily the point from which

Marketing Dictionary

trade-in A credit toward the selling price of a new product offered in exchange for a used product, usually of the same kind.

promotional allowance Part of a buyer's purchase price returned by a manufacturer as a cash payment to fund advertising or sales promotion by other channel members in an attempt to integrate promotional strategy within the channel.

rebate A refund of a portion of a product's purchase price, usually granted by its manufacturer.

FOB plant A "free on board" price that does not include shipping charges; also called *FOB origin.*

freight absorption A pricing system that incorporates transportation costs by allowing a buyer to deduct shipping expenses from the price paid for the goods.

uniform delivered price A price-setting system that incorporates transportation costs by quoting all buyers the same price, including average transportation expenses for all shipments.

zone pricing A price-setting system that incorporates transportation costs by dividing an overall market into geographic regions and setting a single price, including average freight charges, for purchases in each region.

basing point system A pricing system common in some industries during the early twentieth century that incorporated transportation costs by quoting factory prices plus freight charges from the basing point cities nearest the buyers.

SOLVING AN ETHICAL CONTROVERSY

Rock 'n' Roll's Holy War

Pearl Jam, the popular alternative rock band from Seattle, created quite an uproar when it decided to launch a Wal-Mart-style rock tour. The musicians envisioned staging economy concerts where no ticket cost more than $18—a modest sum by today's music-industry standards. "All the band wants to do is to be able to tour with a cheap ticket price," insisted Kelly Curtis, Pearl Jam's manager.

But Ticketmaster, the country's largest ticket distributor, immediately attacked the idea. Ticketmaster has contracted for exclusive rights to ticket distribution at most big American venues, giving it considerable clout in the industry. The company complained that such cheap tickets would not permit it to make enough money handling sales. "If Pearl Jam wants to play for free, we'll be happy to distribute their tickets for free," cracked Fred Rosen, Ticketmaster's chief executive officer.

Negotiations between the musicians and the ticketing agency eventually disintegrated. Pearl Jam publicly derided Ticketmaster as a greedy monopoly strangling the industry. Urged by the band's attorney, the U.S. Justice Department investigated the ticket seller for possible antitrust violations. Pearl Jam members Jeff Ament and Stone Gossard took the opportunity to appear at a hearing (as pictured here), but federal prosecutors eventually closed their investigation without charges or much fanfare.

Was Pearl Jam Right to Fight Ticketmaster?

PRO

1. **After buying out competitors such as Ticketron, Ticketmaster has established a virtual monopoly capable of wielding far too much power over the concert industry. Musicians fear criticizing the agency publicly, but whispered reports accuse Ticketmaster of delaying payments of ticket receipts for months, blocking concert bookings, and manufacturing computer problems to disrupt ticket sales for troublesome groups.**
2. **The world's largest ticket distributor, which sells 52 million tickets a year, also tacks on bloated fees that create a financial burden for some people who want to attend concerts or sporting events. Ticketmaster pockets between $4 and $18 for every ticket it processes, charging high prices for the most popular acts.**

CON

1. **As the intermediary in the channel for concert entertainment, Ticketmaster actually collects reasonable handling charges. Pearl Jam asked the company to assess no more than $1.80 in service charges per ticket, and it agreed to lower its service fee to $2.50, plus $2.30 more for orders handled by phone. Management felt, however, that the price**

the goods are shipped. In either case, the actual shipping point does not affect the price quotation. Such a system seeks to equalize competition between distant marketers, since all competitors quote identical transportation rates. Few buyers would accept a basing point system today, however.

The best-known basing point system was the Pittsburgh-plus pricing structure common in the steel industry for many years. Steel buyers paid freight charges from Pittsburgh regardless of where the steel was produced. As the industry matured, manufacturing centers emerged in Chicago, Gary, Cleveland, and Birmingham. Still, Pittsburgh remained the basing point for steel pricing, forcing a buyer in Atlanta that purchased steel from a Birmingham mill to pay phantom freight from Pittsburgh.

PRICING POLICIES

Pricing policies contribute important information to buyers as they assess the firm's total image. A coherent policy provides an overall framework and consistency that guides day-to-day pricing decisions. Formally, a **pricing policy** is a general guideline that reflects marketing objectives and influences specific pricing decisions.

Decisions concerning price structure generally tend to focus on technical, detailed questions, while decisions concerning pricing policies cover broader issues. Price structure decisions take the firm's pricing policy as a given, from which they specify applicable discounts. Pricing policies have important strategic effects, particularly in guiding competitive efforts. They form the basis for more practical price structure decisions.

could not go any lower. Otherwise, said CEO Fred Rosen, the company would "have to change our name to Targetmaster."

2. While many rock fans applauded Pearl Jam's rebellion against high ticket prices, music-industry insiders blame scalpers for the worst excesses in today's pricey entertainment market. These opportunists often gobble up tickets for the best seats and then add hundreds of dollars to the prices of the highly desirable tickets. For instance, scalpers hawked Rolling Stones tickets with face values of $55 for $350 each.
3. Ticketmaster deserves its cut of concert revenue, because it provides a valuable service to the bands and their fans. The ticketing Goliath developed a sophisticated computer system that helps entertainers to sell large numbers of tickets. It also only earns a tiny percentage of every ticket price. Out of a $55 ticket, $25 to $30 goes into the entertainers' pockets for salaries, travel, and living expenses; the rest covers ticketing costs, sound system and lights, insurance, advertising, unions, catering, facility rent, and promoter's costs.

Summary

Ultimately, Pearl Jam's war with Ticketmaster hindered its ability to tour for many months. When the musicians did resume concerts, they played at many smaller venues not controlled by Ticketmaster. The itinerary for one concert swing featured stops in Augusta, Maine; Buffalo, New York; and Charleston, South Carolina. The band connected with a startup ticket agency—Fans, Tours & Tickets—that agreed to price the tickets at $15.00 to $22.50, tacking on an extra $2.50 fee.

Sources: A.J. Jacobs and Chris Nashawaty, "The Price Ain't Right," *Entertainment Weekly,* June 13, 1997; "Ticket Jam Solved, Pearl Jam Set to Tour," *San Diego Union-Tribune,* July 27, 1996, p. E8. Robert Hawkins, "Pearl Jam's Fight Not Flagging in Ticket War," *San Diego Union-Tribune,* June 22, 1995, p. 5; and adapted from Janice Castro, "Rock 'n' Roll's Holy War," *Time,* June 20, 1994, pp. 46–50.

Firms implement variations of four basic types of pricing policies: psychological pricing, price flexibility, product line pricing, and promotional pricing. Specific policies deal effectively with various competitive situations; the final choice depends on the environment within which marketers must make their pricing decisions.

Psychological Pricing

Psychological pricing applies the belief that certain prices or price ranges make products more appealing to buyers than others. No research offers a consistent foundation for such thinking, however, and studies often report mixed findings.

Nevertheless, marketers practice several forms of psychological pricing. Chapter 20 discussed one—prestige pricing. Two more psychological pricing techniques include odd pricing and unit pricing.

Marketing Dictionary

pricing policy A set of general guidelines that reflect marketing objectives and influence specific pricing decisions.

psychological pricing A pricing policy based on the belief that certain prices or price ranges make a good or service more appealing than others to buyers.

Figure 21.8 **Odd Pricing in a Personal Computer Advertisement**

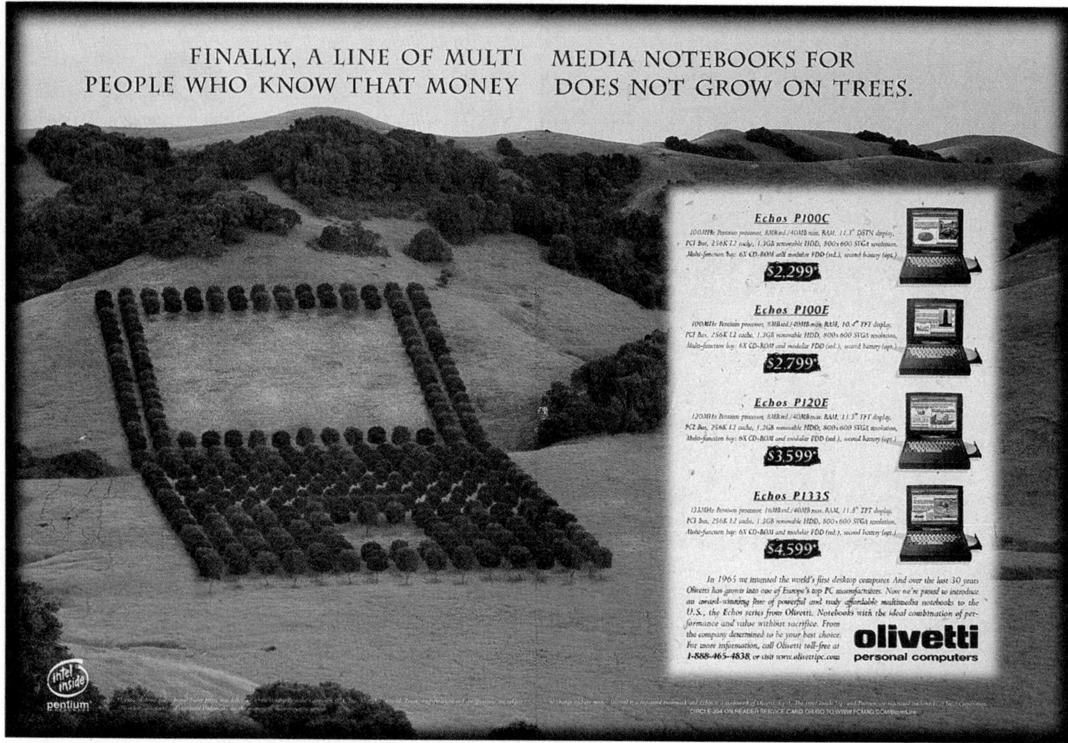
FINALLY, A LINE OF MULTI MEDIA NOTEBOOKS FOR
PEOPLE WHO KNOW THAT MONEY DOES NOT GROW ON TREES.
Echos P100C
$2,299*
Echos P100E
$2,799*
Echos P120E
$3,599*
Echos P133S
$4,599*
In 1965 we invented the world's first desktop computer. And over the last 30 years Olivetti has grown into one of Europe's top PC manufacturers. Now we're proud to introduce an award-winning line of powerful and truly affordable multimedia notebooks to the U.S., the Echos series from Olivetti. Notebooks with the ideal combination of performance and value without sacrifice. From the company determined to be your best choice. For more information, call Olivetti toll-free at 1-888-465-4838, or visit www.olivettipc.com
olivetti
personal computers
intel inside
pentium

In **odd pricing,** marketers set prices at odd numbers just under round numbers. Many retailers assume that a price of $4.99 appeals more strongly to consumers than $5.00, supposedly because buyers interpret it as $4.00 plus change. Odd pricing originated as a way to force clerks to make change, thus serving as a cash control device. Odd pricing remains a common feature of contemporary price quotations. The prices of all five Olivetti multimedia notebook computers featured in Figure 21.8 reflect this policy.

Some producers and retailers practice odd pricing but avoid prices ending in 5, 9, or 0. These marketers believe that customers view price tags of $5.95, $5.99, or $6.00 as regular retail prices, but they think of an amount like $5.97 as a discount price.

Unit pricing states prices in terms of some recognized unit of measurement (such as grams and liters) or a standard numerical count. Unit pricing arose to improve convenience when consumer advocates complained about the difficulty of comparing the true prices of products packaged in different sizes. These advocates felt that posting prices in terms of standard units would help shoppers to make better-informed purchases. Some supermarket chains have come to regard unit pricing as a competitive tool, and they feature it extensively in advertising. However, unit pricing has not improved consumers' shopping habits as much as supporters originally envisioned that it would. Instead, research shows that standard price quotes most often affect purchases only by relatively well-educated consumers with high earnings.

Price Flexibility

Marketing executives must also set company policies for **price flexibility**—that is, the choice between just one price or variable prices. Generally, one-price policies suit mass selling marketing programs, whereas variable pricing suits marketing programs based on individual bargaining. In a large department store, customers do not expect to haggle over prices with retail salespeople; instead, they expect to pay the amounts shown on the price tags. Generally, customers pay less only when the retailer replaces regular prices with sale prices.

By contrast, customers expect variable pricing policies in car dealerships; few expect to pay sticker prices. Many buyers decide on price offers only after conducting research to determine dealers' actual costs and then adding amounts that seem like fair profits. Studies of car purchases reveal a typical "haggle range" between dealer cost and sticker price. On an expensive car, the haggle range can cover $2,000 or more. In fact, the industry's variable pricing practices contribute to a feeling of dread among some people when they must shop for cars. Says one dealer, "The customer's worst fear is that he will buy a car, and his neighbor will then get a better deal." This concern accounts for the growing popularity of "one-price" policies at car dealerships, pioneered by Saturn.[14]

While variable pricing adds some flexibility to selling situations, it may conflict with provisions of the Robinson-Patman Act. It may also lead to retaliatory pricing by competitors, and it may stir complaints among customers who find that they paid higher prices than necessary.

Product Line Pricing

Since most firms market multiple product lines, an effective pricing strategy must consider the relationships among all of these products instead of viewing each in isolation. **Product line pricing** is the practice of setting a limited number of prices for a selection of merchandise. For example, a clothier might offer three lines of men's suits—one priced at $375, a second at $525, and the most expensive at $695. These price points define important product characteristics that differentiate the product lines and contribute to customer choices to trade up and trade down.

Retailers practice extensive product line pricing. In earlier days, five-and-dime variety stores exemplified this technique. It remains popular, however, because it offers advantages to both retailers and customers. Shoppers can choose desired price ranges and then concentrate on other product variables such as colors, styles, and materials. Retailers can purchase and offer specific lines in limited price categories instead of more general assortments with dozens of different prices.

Airlines have long divided their seating areas according to product line pricing. Each flight offers a certain percentage of discount, business-class, first-class, and regular-price seats on each flight. On an overseas flight, for instance, the industry averages about 18 percent business-class seats. A round-trip business-class ticket from Houston to Paris on Continental Airlines costs $3,538—46 percent more than the regular coach fare and several times more than the discount fare.[15]

Marketers must resolve one problem with product line pricing, though. Once they decide how to distribute prices among their products, both retailers and manufacturers may have difficulty making adjustments. Rising costs, therefore, force sellers to either change the price lines, which results in confusion, or reduce costs through production adjustments. The second option opens the firm to the complaints that its merchandise isn't what it used to be.

Dealers' Secret Profit

Ever wonder how a car dealer can stay in business and still offer those "$99 Above Cost" specials? The answer lies in a little-known item called *holdback* that is built into most invoice prices. For example, the Ford Taurus LX with a sticker price of $20,980 costs the dealer $19,137, according to the *Hearst Black Book* price guide. Included in the dealer's invoice price is a holdback of 3 percent of the sticker price, or $629. These holdbacks will be refunded by the manufacturer—typically once a quarter—following the car's sale regardless of what the dealer got for the car. So selling a Taurus at "cost" still gives the dealer a gross profit of $629.

Audi says it has no holdback. Most others do. Here's a list compiled from automakers and from information provided by James Bragg, author of *New Car Buyer's and Leaser's Negotiating Bible.*

3% of Sticker Price

Chrysler (Chrysler, Dodge, Eagle, Jeep, Plymouth)
Ford Motor (Ford, Lincoln, Mercury)
General Motors (Buick, Cadillac, Chevrolet, Geo, GMC,Oldsmobile, Pontiac, Saturn)
Isuzu, Mercedes-Benz, Porsche, Rolls-Royce, Saab

2% of Sticker Price

BMW, Jaguar, Nissan, Subaru, Toyota, Volkswagen

Flat Amounts

Volvo

Promotional Pricing

In **promotional pricing,** a lower-than-normal price is used as a temporary ingredient in a firm's selling strategy. Some promotional pricing arrangements form part of recurrent marketing initiatives, such as a shoe store's annual "buy one pair, get the second pair for one cent" sale. For another example, a new pizza restaurant might run an opening special with artificially low prices to attract customers. Another firm may introduce a promotional model or brand with special pricing to begin competing in a new market.

Retailers rely most heavily on promotional pricing. In one type of technique, stores offer **loss leaders**—goods priced below cost to attract customers who, the retailer hopes, will also buy other, regularly priced merchandise. Loss leaders can form part of an effective marketing program, but states with unfair-trade laws prohibit the practice, as discussed in Chapter 20.

Marketing Dictionary

odd pricing A pricing policy that ends prices with odd numbers just under round numbers to make them seem low—for instance, $9.99 rather than $10.00.

unit pricing A pricing policy that states prices in terms of recognized units of measurement or standard numerical counts.

price flexibility A pricing policy that permits variable prices for different customers.

product line pricing The practice of setting a limited number of prices for a selection of merchandise.

promotional pricing A technique that temporarily lowers prices below normal levels in a temporary marketing campaign.

loss leader A product offered at a price below cost to attract customers to a store in the hope that they will also buy other merchandise at regular prices.

MARKETING HALL OF FAME

Trendmasters: Succeeding by Delivering Full Markups

Walk down the aisles of any Toys 'R' Us store, and you'll see familiar brand names of toys that have been entertaining children for decades. Mattel continues to dress its incredibly popular Barbie doll in a limitless collection of outfits. Parker Brothers' Monopoly shares display space with other classic board games. Still more shelves carry Hasbro's Play-Doh and G.I. Joe.

Toys 'R' Us virtually defines the big league of toy retailing, so what novice toymaker would hope to reach its shelves? Of course, most would-be toy sellers who contact Toys 'R' Us never make it past the front door. But Jill Hill, a toy buyer for the giant chain, says she takes about 40 calls a day from people insisting they have created great toys, and a significant number of these callers ultimately see their creations in the stores' aisles.

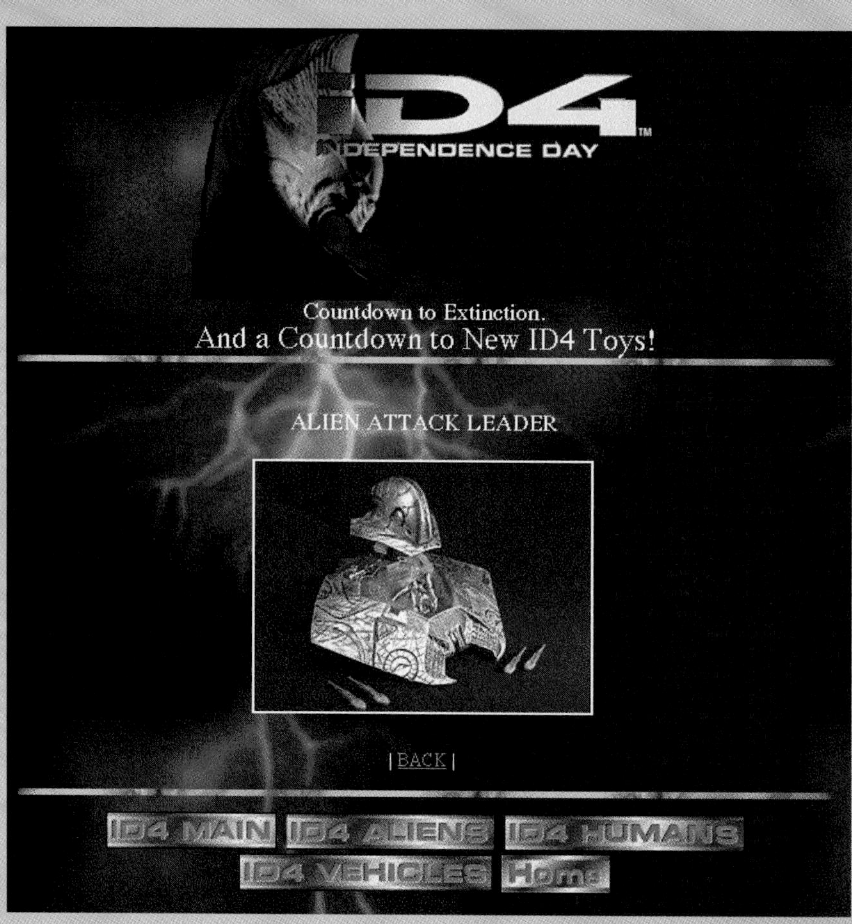
ID4
INDEPENDENCE DAY
Countdown to Extinction.
And a Countdown to New ID4 Toys!
ALIEN ATTACK LEADER
| BACK |
ID4 MAIN
ID4 ALIENS
ID4 HUMANS
ID4 VEHICLES
Home

One reason for the toy giant's interest in newcomers results from its pricing policies. Toys 'R' Us sets prices that allow it to make little money on the well-known merchandise of Hasbro and Mattel, which represent 30 percent of American toy sales. Sometimes the chain even prices these blockbuster toys at a loss just to entice parents and grandparents to enter the door. For instance, the big retailer often loses money on each Monopoly set it sells. The com-

Retailers frequently use a variant of loss-leader pricing called *leader pricing*. To avoid violating minimum-markup regulations and to earn some return on promotional sales, they offer so-called *leader merchandise* at prices slightly above cost. Among the most frequent practitioners of this combination pricing/promotion strategy are supermarkets and mass merchandisers such as Wal-Mart, Kmart, and Target. Retailers sometimes treat private-label products (like Sam's Choice colas at Wal-Mart stores) as leader merchandise, since prices of the store brands average 5 percent to 60 percent less than those of comparable national brands. While store brand goods generate lower per-unit revenues than national brands would produce, higher sales volume will probably offset some of the difference, as will related sales of high-margin products like toiletries and cosmetics.

http://www.kmart.com/

Marketers should anticipate two potential pitfalls when making a promotional pricing decision:

pany feels pressured to price the sought-after toys with no profit margins or just tiny ones in the highly competitive retail toy field. "When a toy from one of the big players is blowing off the shelves, we make nothing," laments Roger Goddu, a Toys 'R' Us executive.

The big retailer earns a healthy profit from sales of new toys from upstart companies, though. "We like the margins with the little guys," Goddu acknowledges. Not surprisingly then, Toys 'R' Us generates 15 percent of volume selling products of companies with less than $30 million in annual sales revenue. More than 60 percent comes from companies that generate less than $100 million in sales each year.

Knowledge of this pricing pattern prompted two toy entrepreneurs to court Toys 'R' Us. Russell Hornsby, a former designer for Mattel, and Leo Hauser, a former sales executive in the novelty gift business, launched their own toy company called Trendmasters seven years earlier in St. Louis. The company's first toys all featured sound-activated responses. Loony Heads, for instance, were plastic characters that screamed or burped at a child's urging. The company sank the $2 million or so generated from the obnoxious Loony Heads into a project to create plastic dolls that danced to music.

Both Trendmasters toys stirred fads and then eventually disappeared from the shelves, but they generated enough cash to help the entrepreneurs develop even more successful toys, including a line of doll houses that turn into tea sets. Trendmasters' early successes helped it to snag the rights to produce all the toys linked to the movie *Independence Day*. Twentieth Century Fox picked Trendmasters for the line of 11 products after Hasbro supplied disappointing quality in the toys it designed for an earlier Arnold Schwarzenegger movie.

Visibility and credibility aren't the only perks that new toymakers gain by reaching the shelves of Toys 'R' Us. That's the experience of a father-and-son duo from Orange County, California, who developed a finger-flick football game. After selling their game directly to the toy giant, the pair gained access to plenty of expert advice about producing, packaging, and marketing their products.

http://www.trendmaster.com/

QUESTIONS FOR CRITICAL THINKING

1. **If Toys 'R' Us were to start putting higher prices on its big sellers, would it leave as much room on the shelves for the products of other toymakers? Why?**
2. **Before a new toy company places its product in stores, how important should marketers regard correct pricing? What considerations affect this type of decision?**

Sources: "Toys 'R' Us Posts 57 Percent Profit Jump," Reuters, May 19, 1997; Robert La Franco, "Wanted: Newcomers with Bright Ideas," *Forbes,* October 21, 1996, pp. 272–274; and adapted from Kenneth M. Chanko, "The Toy Store Independence Play," *Entertainment Weekly,* July 28, 1995.

1. Some consumers do not react strongly to promotional pricing.

2. By maintaining an artificially low price for a period of time, marketers may lead customers to expect it as a customary feature of the product. For example, grocers treated poultry as a loss leader during the 1930s and 1940s, and it has long suffered price pressure as a result. Airlines may suffer a similar fate. Pervasive ticket discounting has taught consumers to expect to pay prices below full fare. As a result, airlines are losing money, because many travelers will fly only if they can get discounted fares. On average, only about 6 percent of the passengers on Continental Airlines' overseas flights buy nondiscounted, business-class seats.[16]

Price-Quality Relationships

One of the most thoroughly researched aspects of pricing is its relationship to consumer perceptions of product quality. In the absence of other cues, price serves as an important indicator of a product's quality to prospective purchasers. Many buyers interpret high prices as signals of high-quality products.

Figure 21.9 Emphasizing Competitive Prices for Quality Products

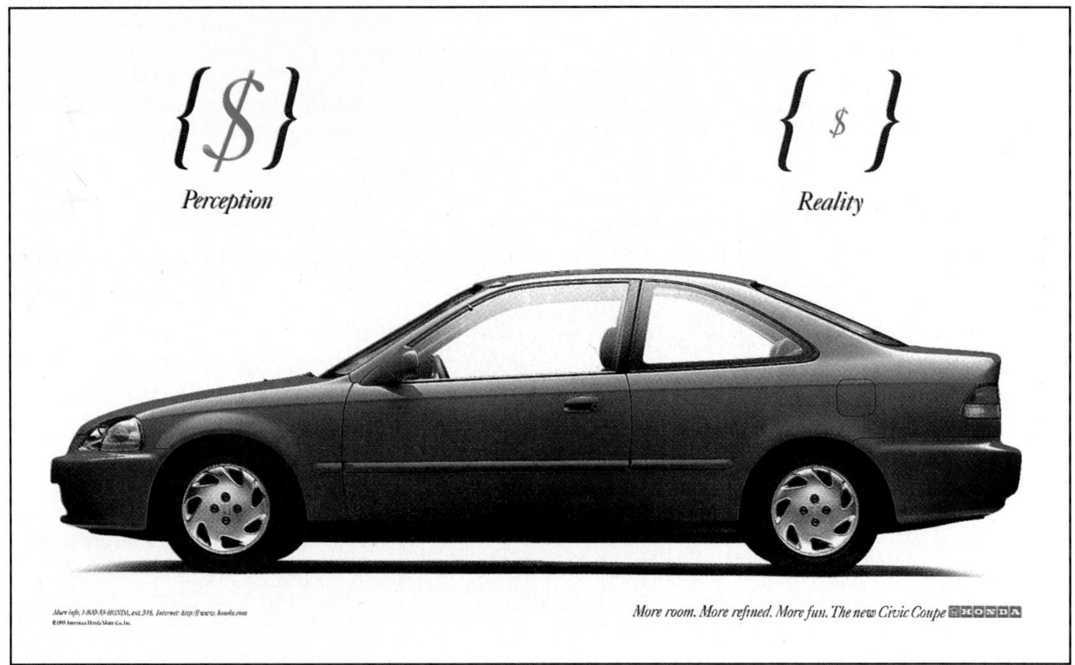
{$}
Perception
{$}
Reality
More room. More refined. More fun. The new Civic Coupe HONDA

The relationship between price and perceived quality provides a widely used tool for contemporary marketers. Ads for Trotter's expensive 450ST treadmill equate its above-average price with above-average taste: "Call it exclusive, call it privilege—but some people just don't like to sweat with the masses." The ads describe the exercise machine as "the treadmill of choice for the educated buyer who values health above price."[17]

Honda's reputation for quality pays a big role in its frequent ranking as the most popular line of automobiles in America. Concerned that customers for the company's Accord and Civic models might worry about high cost associated with so many advantages over competitors, Honda marketers decided to address the issue directly in the ad shown in Figure 21.9. They intended the ad's "perception-reality" message to dispel this potential misconception by inviting auto buyers to compare Honda's prices with those of competitors.

Probably the best statement of the price-quality connection is the idea of *price limits.*[18] Supporters of this idea argue that consumers define certain limits within which their product-quality perceptions vary directly with price. A potential buyer regards a price below the lower limit as too cheap, whereas a price above the higher limit seems too expensive. This perception holds true for both national brands and private-label products. A University of Iowa professor studied scanner data on grocery purchases and discovered an ironic fact: if a store offers too good a deal, people aren't interested. If the price of a private-label product differs from that of a name brand by less than 10 percent, "people won't buy," says the professor. On the other hand if the price gap exceeds 20 percent, consumers won't buy because "they will impute inferior quality."[19]

In Brazil, hyperinflation has left little relationship in consumers' minds between price and quality. In the early 1990s, a consumer could buy a deluxe ice-cream sundae or two kitchen blenders for 950 cruzados ($15). Moreover, prices for a single product also vary tremendously from store to store. For example, consumers could end up paying anywhere from 2 cruzados (3 cents) to 21 cruzados for a pencil eraser.

COMPETITIVE BIDDING AND NEGOTIATED PRICES

Many government and organizational procurement departments do not pay set prices for their purchases, particularly for large, nonrecurring purchases such as a weapons system for the Department of Defense. Instead, they determine prices through competitive bidding, a process in which they invite potential suppliers to quote prices on proposed purchases or contracts. Detailed specifications describe the good or service that the government or organization wishes to acquire. One of the most important tasks in purchasing management is to develop accurate descriptions of products that the organization seeks to buy. This process generally requires the assistance of the firm's technical personnel, such as engineers, designers, and chemists.

In some cases, industrial and government purchasers negotiate contracts with favored suppliers instead of inviting competitive bids from all interested parties. The terms of such a contract emerge through offers and counteroffers between the buyer and the seller.

Where only one supplier offers a desired product or where projects require extensive research and development work, buyers and sellers often set purchase terms through negotiated contracts. In addition, some state and local governments permit their agencies to negotiate purchases under certain limits—say, $500 or $1,000. This policy seeks to eliminate economic waste that would result from obtaining and processing bids for relatively minor purchases.

Figure 21.10 Transfer Pricing to Escape Taxation

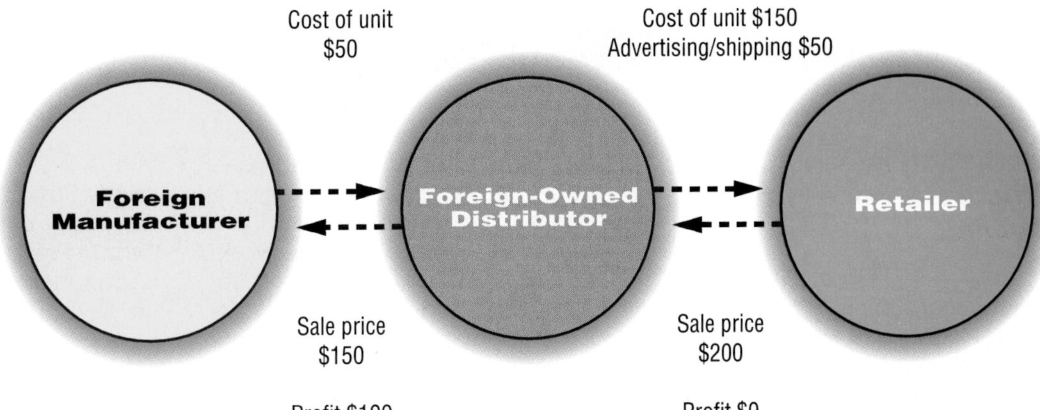
Cost of unit
$50
Cost of unit $150
Advertising/shipping $50
Foreign Manufacturer
Foreign-Owned Distributor
Retailer
Sale price
$150
Sale price
$200
Profit $100
Profit $0

THE TRANSFER PRICING DILEMMA

A pricing problem peculiar to large-scale enterprises is the determination of an internal **transfer price**—the price for moving goods between **profit centers,** which are any part of the organization to which revenue and controllable costs can be assigned, such as a department. As companies expand, they tend to decentralize management and set up profit centers as a control device in the newly decentralized operation.

In a large company, profit centers might secure many needed resources from sellers within their own organization. The pricing problem becomes, what rate should profit center A (maintenance department) charge profit center B (sales department) for the cleansing compound used on B's floors? Should the price be the same as it would be if A did the work for an outside party? Should B receive a discount? The answers to these questions depend on the philosophy of the firm involved.

Transfer pricing can be a complicated process, especially for multinational organizations. The government closely monitors transfer pricing practices, because these exchanges offer easy ways for companies to avoid paying taxes on profits. Figure 21.10 shows how this type of pricing manipulation might work. Suppose that a South Korean VCR manufacturer sells its machines to its U.S. subsidiary for distribution to dealers. Although each unit costs $50 to build, the manufacturer charges the distributor $150. In turn, the distributor sells the VCRs to retailers for $200 each. This arrangement gives the South Korean manufacturer a $100 profit on each machine, on which it pays taxes only in South Korea. Meanwhile, the American distributor writes off $50 for advertising and shipping costs, leaving it with no profits—and no tax liability.

Companies may run into legal trouble over transfer pricing, even if they intended no wrongdoing. A few years ago, the Internal Revenue Service (IRS) disputed Apple Computer's tax returns. The argument arose over transfer pricing on products that Apple bought from its Singapore manufacturing plant. The IRS slapped Apple with a bill for back taxes on $100 million that it claimed constituted extra income.[20]

SETTING AND MANAGING PRICES IN GLOBAL MARKETS

A wide variety of internal and external conditions can affect a marketer's global pricing strategies. Internal influences include the firm's goals and marketing strategies; the costs of developing, producing, and marketing its products; the nature of the products; and the firm's competitive strengths. External influences include general conditions in international markets, especially those in the firm's target markets; regulatory limitations; trade restrictions; competitors' actions; economic events; customer characteristics; and the global status of the industry.

In general, a company can implement one of three export pricing strategies: a standard worldwide price, dual pricing, or market-differentiated pricing. Exporters often

Marketing Dictionary

transfer price A cost assessed for a product exchanged between profit centers within a single firm.

profit center Any part of an organization with responsibility for revenue and controllable costs.

MARKETING HALL OF SHAME

Marketing in Japan, Where the Prices Are Insane!

International shoppers have long spread legends of stratospheric retail prices in Japan. Without grumbling, a Tokyo commuter will hand over $6 for a cup of coffee. In the evening, this same person may dine on a $50 steak. Prices like these explain why Japanese consumers spend roughly twice as much as a typical American shopper for the same products. Although this difference sounds outrageous, Japanese consumers have tolerated bloated price tags for years.

Why would they put up with such excessive prices? For one reason, they lacked a frame of reference for judging the fairness of retailers' demands. A nation of purchasers didn't realize that consumers elsewhere in the world paid far less for new CD players, refrigerators, and other goods. Today's Japanese consumers have become much more aware of these price variations now that 12 million of them vacation overseas each year.

Further, they didn't worry especially about rising merchandise costs as long as their salaries continued to climb. Since 1949, the average worker's salary had grown each year—often at a healthy 3 percent—until the trend lost momentum. In fact, in the mid-1990s, salaries actually dipped slightly.

The steady climb in wages ended in a brutal Japanese recession that has endured throughout the 1990s. These events have made Japanese shoppers resistant to price inflation. "People don't want to spend money," says Kikuo Yamaguchi, head of the Institution for Consumer Behavior, a Tokyo research group. "Their income has stagnated because of the bad economy and they have started to wonder why they have to spend so much money on consumption."

Japanese have lived without the price discounting that Americans take for granted for many reasons. First, government regulatory policies and manufacturers' cartels have inhibited price-based competition. For decades, manufacturers have balked at selling to discount chains. When stores tried to slash prices, manufacturers typically fought back in court. Shiseido, the cosmetics giant, won a

set standard worldwide prices, regardless of their target markets. This strategy can succeed if foreign marketing costs remain low enough that they do not impact overall costs, or if their prices reflect average unit costs. A company that implements a standard pricing program must monitor the international marketplace carefully, however, to make sure that domestic competitors do not undercut its prices.

The dual pricing strategy distinguishes prices for domestic and export sales. Some exporters practice cost-plus pricing to establish dual prices that fully allocate their true domestic and foreign costs to product sales in those markets. While these prices ensure that an exporter makes a profit on any product that it sells, final prices may exceed those of competitors. Other companies opt for flexible cost-plus pricing schemes that allow marketers to grant discounts or change prices according to shifts in the competitive environment or fluctuations in the international exchange rate.

The third strategy, market-differentiated pricing, makes even more flexible arrangements to set prices according to local marketplace conditions. The dynamic global marketplace often requires frequent price changes by exporters who choose this approach. Effective market-differentiated pricing depends on access to quick, accurate market information.[21]

ACHIEVEMENT CHECK SUMMARY

Reread the learning goals that follow, and consider the questions for each goal. Answering these questions will reinforce your grasp of the most important concepts in the chapter and allow you to check how well you have achieved these learning goals. Where a blank appears before a question, answer with *T* or *F;* for multiple-choice questions, circle the letter of the correct answer.

Objective 21.1: Compare the alternative pricing strategies and explain when each strategy is most appropriate.

1. ____ Marketers often practice penetration pricing in industries with few products and little competition.
2. ____ Most firms follow variations of the competitive pricing strategy.

suit against the Kawachiya retail chain after the discounter sold makeup at greatly reduced prices. Government regulations forbidding discounting have long protected the country's legion of mom-and-pop stores.

But change is stirring in Japan. Despite regulations, discounters are muscling into markets and gaining market share. In reaction, even the much protected mom-and-pop stores are beginning to give buyers a break.

While price wars have occasionally disrupted the steady growth in prices, recent ones seem more serious, because the big retailers and manufacturers are taking part. Toyota, for instance, has unveiled a sport-utility vehicle with a downright reasonable price—compared with typical Japanese car prices—of $16,000. "We've manufactured a car that meets the current customer need," says Mie Aoyama, a Toyota spokeswoman. "In a bad economy, they want simple and practical cars." The arrival of cheaper American cars in Japan has also forced carmakers to lower prices.

Critics of Japanese firms' old pricing policies welcome a seemingly irreversible trend toward discounting. They predict that the cost-of-living gap between Japan and the other industrialized nations will soon begin to narrow. "To think that the existing order and institutions can be maintained is impossible," says Isao Nakauchi, a pricing rebel who heads a retail empire of 360 department stores. "People have changed their way of buying things."

QUESTIONS FOR CRITICAL THINKING

1. **American exporters to Japan are following retailers there and beginning to lower prices. For instance, J. Crew once charged $130 for a wool sweater in Japan, but the retailer now sells the same garment for $72. (In U.S. outlets, this sweater retails for $48.) Do you think these price reductions, which were triggered by the Japanese recession, will persist after the economy improves? Why?**
2. **Why do you think that high Japanese consumer prices have lasted this long?**

Sources: Edward J. Lincoln, "Japan Hasn't Really Failed," *New York Times,* February 22, 1997; Andrew Pollack, "The Questions Facing Japan: Can Its Vibrant Engine Ever Be Restarted?" *New York Times,* January 2, 1997; Edward W. Desmond, "The Failed Miracle," *Time,* April 22, 1996, p. 61; Norihiko Shirouzu, "Luxury Prices for U.S. Goods No Longer Pass Muster in Japan," *Wall Street Journal,* February 8, 1996, pp. B1, B10; and Junko Fujita, "Amid Japan's Worst Recession in Decades, Stores Are Slashing Prices," *Christian Science Monitor,* November 16, 1994, p. 9.

3. ___ A skimming pricing strategy sets a high market-entry price for a product with little or no initial competition.

Objective 21.2: Describe how prices are quoted.

1. ___ Methods for quoting prices depend on all of the following variables, except: (a) cost structures; (b) traditional industry practices; (c) the quantity produced; (d) policies of individual firms.

2. ___ FOB plant pricing: (a) sets price objectives; (b) allows a buyer to deduct transportation expenses from a bill; (c) includes no shipping charges; (d) sets a single price within each region.

3. ___ Price quotes involve all of the following elements except: (a) list prices; (b) customer demand; (c) market prices; (d) trade discounts.

Objective 21.3: Identify the various pricing policy decisions that marketers must make.

1. ___ A pricing policy is a general guideline based on a firm's pricing objectives.

2. ___ Marketers follow pricing policies in making long-term competitive pricing decisions.

3. ___ Pricing policy choices include psychological pricing, unit pricing, price flexibility, product line pricing, and promotional pricing.

Objective 21.4: Relate price to consumer perceptions of quality.

1. ___ In general, consumers perceive a high price as a symbol of high quality.

2. ___ Price limits are directly associated with supply and demand.

3. ___ The concept of price limits suggests that unusually low prices may indicate poor quality.

Objective 21.5: Contrast competitive bidding and negotiated prices.

1. ___ Buyers and sellers negotiate prices most often when: (a) multiple suppliers compete for an order; (b) only one available supplier can fill an order; (c) contracts cover unchanging and routine purchases; (d) prices are set once and remain unchanged.

2. ___ Competitive bidding involves all of the following situations, except: (a) price quotations from various suppliers on a proposed contract; (b) input from engineers, designers, and other technical personnel; (c) specifications that describe the project; (d) limits on the contract price.

Objective 21.6: Explain the importance of transfer pricing.

1. ___ A transfer price determines the cost of goods or services exchanged between departments or divisions within a larger organization.

2. ___ Transfer pricing assigns simple, clear-cut costs for exchanges between profit centers.

3. ____ Profit centers function as control devices in large, decentralized organizations.

Objective 21.7: Compare the three alternative strategies for pricing exports.

1. ____ Firms almost always implement the same pricing strategies for domestic and export sales.
2. ____ Firms can implement three alternative export pricing strategies: a standard worldwide price, dual pricing, or market-differentiated pricing.
3. ____ Market-differentiated pricing allows a firm to price its products according to local marketplace conditions.

Students: See the solutions section located on page S-4 to check your responses to the Achievement Check Summary.

Key Terms

skimming pricing strategy
penetration pricing strategy
everyday low pricing (EDLP)
competitive pricing strategy
list price
market price
cash discount
trade discount
quantity discount
trade-in
promotional allowance
rebate
FOB plant
freight absorption
uniform delivered price
zone pricing
basing point system
pricing policy
psychological pricing
odd pricing
unit pricing
price flexibility
product line pricing
promotional pricing
loss leader
transfer price
profit center

Review Questions

1. What is a skimming price strategy? What benefits does it offer for a firm?
2. What is penetration pricing? Under what circumstances do marketers prefer penetration pricing?
3. What is everyday low pricing? Explain why it stirs controversy among marketers and retailers.
4. Contrast the freight absorption and uniform delivery pricing systems. Cite examples of each.
5. How does a basing point system incorporate transportation costs? Discuss Pittsburgh-plus pricing in the steel industry.
6. Define the term *pricing policy.* List and discuss the reasons for establishing pricing policies.
7. When does a price become a promotional price? What pitfalls does a firm risk in promotional pricing?
8. How does price relate to consumer perceptions of quality? Give examples of your perception of an acceptable price range for a common consumer good or service, such as toothpaste, a haircut, or mouthwash. How might a price outside this range affect your image of the product's quality?
9. What is a transfer price? How does it affect management of a large organization?
10. Describe three possible strategies that a company might follow to price exports.

Discussion Questions

1. Skimming pricing, penetration pricing, and competitive pricing are the three alternative pricing strategies. Which of the three appears most appropriate for the following products? Defend your answers.
   a. Sega video game
   b. Laser-disk player
   c. Fuel additive that substantially increases automobile mileage
   d. Ultrasensitive burglar, smoke, and fire alarm
   e. New brand of hairspray
2. Frequent-flyer programs are discount schemes designed by airlines to secure and reward consumer loyalty. In what category of discount plans do these programs fit? Explain. What potential dangers may limit the effectiveness of such programs?
3. How do sellers quote prices for each of the following products?
   a. Quantas Airlines ticket to Sydney
   b. Installation of a neon sign by a local contractor
   c. Warm-up suit from a sportswear retailer
   d. New Mitsubishi Eclipse automobile
4. Assume that a product sells for $100 per ton and that Pittsburgh is the basing point city for calculating transportation charges. Shipping from Pittsburgh to a potential customer in Cincinnati costs $10 per ton. The actual shipping costs of suppliers in three other cities are $8 per ton for Supplier A, $11 per ton for Supplier B, and $10 per ton for Supplier C. Using this information, answer the following questions:
   a. What delivered price would a salesperson for Supplier A quote to the Cincinnati customer?
   b. What delivered price would a salesperson for Supplier B quote to the Cincinnati customer?
   c. What delivered price would a salesperson for Supplier C quote to the Cincinnati customer?
   d. How much would each supplier net (after subtracting actual shipping costs) per ton on the sale?
5. Interview one or more administrators at your school. Can you find any examples of transfer prices? Discuss.

'netWork

1. From the information available at Southwest Airlines' Web site,
http://www.iflyswa.com/
which of the pricing strategies discussed in the chapter body does the airline use? Should the airline continue to use this strategy? What forces might require a change in pricing strategy?
2. Should a system of delivering products over the Internet affect those products' prices? Explain. How should companies integrate the Internet into their pricing strategy decisions?
3. In order to allow customers to pay for goods and services over the Web with some sense of security, vendors have created cyberbucks or e-cash systems. Go to
http://www.digicash.com/
and evaluate this new form of exchange. Will it work effectively? If so, under what circumstances will it work? Would you recommend alternative forms of payment for transactions over the Web?

VIDEO CASE 21

COMBATING COMPETITION IN THE COOKIE MARKET

Ah, the cookie aisle. Who can pass it without slipping a package or two into the grocery cart? People involved in the cookie industry view this aisle less benignly. The trade, from producers to wholesalers to retailers, refers to the cookie aisle as a combat zone. Cookie marketing competition is intense, with all participants fighting for more market share. That's because the cookie industry is mature, and the rate of growth averages a very slow 1 percent to 2 percent per year. In this industry, firms gain additional sales only by taking market share away from competitors.

The cookie industry displays an oligopolistic market structure. Nabisco is the market leader with about a 33 percent market share, followed by Keebler with 13 percent. Combined sales of dozens of private-label store brands account for another 13 percent of the market. The remaining 40 percent is divided among a number of brands, including Pepperidge Farm, Sunshine, and Archway.

The Archway Cookie Co. controls about 4 percent of the U.S. cookie market. Headquartered in Battle Creek, Michigan, Archway bakes and distributes about $400 million worth of cookies each year. Harold and Bruce Swanson founded Archway in 1936 as a small bake shop specializing in donuts, cakes, and cookies. When they decided to expand operations and begin selling their cookies in grocery stores, both the Swansons and their retailer partners were amazed at the positive customer response.

"What makes Archway particularly strong from a competitive standpoint is that we make a product that holds to the traditional values of Americans," says Senior Vice President Thomas Olin. Archway cookies are large, soft, have no preservative, and generally contain no artificial ingredients. Their unique home-baked taste comes from slow baking and cooling processes. Over 100 different varieties of Archway Home Style cookies are currently marketed in several different cookie categories. For example, Archway offers 15 varieties in the oatmeal category, such as apple-filled and date-filled flavors. Customers can see what they're buying because Archway presents its cookies in see-through packages.

A strict policy ensures the freshness of Archway cookies. Distributors who deliver Archway cookies to grocery stores also rotate the packages on the retailers' shelves. Moreover, they remove packages a month *before* the freshness date stamped on the labels, while competitors pull their products from retail shelves on the date marked on the package. Distributors carry handheld computers to provide retailers with timely billing data and to give Archway marketers accurate, up-to-date sales and inventory information.

Archway's product strategy, packaging, and distribution enable the company to pursue a value-oriented pricing strategy. "Essentially what we're trying to capture is a value relationship with the consumer," says Olin, "and [that value] is based on the freshness of the products, the varieties we offer, the taste, and the quality of raw materials, as well as the shape of the package."

Archway marketers practice value pricing to carve out a distinctive niche in the competitive cookie environment. The company pursues two major pricing objectives. "First, we try to establish ourselves in the middle of the road in the consumer marketplace," says company representative Eugene McKay III. "We don't want to be perceived as being a high-priced product. Our second pricing objective is to make sure that we have a fair rate of return internally, meaning that not only must the company make a reasonable profit, but our distributors and the retailers also have to make their fair share." Attractive profit margins within the distribution system provide important incentives for channel members to promote Archway cookies to their customers.

Archway sells its products to wholesale distributors, which resell them to grocery stores. Consider, for example, a package of cookies carrying a suggested retail price of $2.00. The Archway distributor typically purchases the cookies for $1.33 and resells them to the retail grocer for $1.60. Each marketing intermediary covers operating expenses and generates profits based on the margin between the purchase price and the price it receives upon selling the product.

Archway marketers consider a number of factors in setting suggested retail prices as well as the prices they charge their wholesale customers. Pricing variables include production and marketing costs, the prices of competing products, and typical markups in the industry. In addition, price lining differentiates product lines. For example, the Super Pak cookie line is a value-priced line. Each package contains 18 cookies and carries a higher price than the smaller packages, but it offers a better per-unit value to customers.

The fastest-growing segment of the cookie market is the fat-free cookie. With a 175 percent annual growth rate, fat-free cookies are a profitable venture to both manufacturers and retailers. Archway generally prices its fat-free products higher than conventional alternatives due to the high consumer demand. As McKay points out, "Consumers may be willing to spend more for certain types of products if there's a higher perceived value, or a need for that product. . . . If we establish it as a fat-free product, the consumer is willing to pay much more for it."

Archway runs price-off promotions periodically to increase sales volume and attract new customers. Its Cookies for Kids program combines a price-off promotion with cause marketing. For the promotion, Archway asks retailers to set up a special in-store display and reduce the prices of the cookies. Each package sold results in a donation to the Children's Miracle Network hospital in the local community. The promotion has proven highly successful, inducing shoppers to boost their cookie purchases at reduced prices for a worthy cause; at the same time, the promotion increases Archway's volume three to four times the sales that it would have generated without the promotion.

Questions

1. Which pricing strategy described in this chapter best describes Archway's methods? How would the firm's pricing decision differ if it had selected the opposite strategy?

2. Describe Archway's pricing policy for its fat-free line of cookies. How does the firm use promotional pricing in marketing its cookies?

3. Using the example shown in Figure 21.6, draw the chain of discounts received by each channel member for the $2.00 package described in the case.

4. Visit the Archway Web site at
   http://www.archwaycookies.com/
   Does the online information available to customers support the firm's value-pricing strategy? Give examples to support your answer. Compare Archway's home page to those of such competitors as Nabisco, Keebler, and Pepperidge Farm. How do the sites reveal the companies' pricing strategies?

Sources: Interviews with Thomas Olin and Eugene McKay III, senior vice presidents, Archway Cookie Co., May 1997.

Part 7 Microsoft Corp.: Pricing Software

Seat-of-the-pants pricing is probably the best way to describe Microsoft's pricing policy during its early years. Gates says, "One of the bigger early contracts was Texas Instruments, where we bid $99,000 to provide programming languages for a home computer they were planning. We picked that price because we were too shy to make a bid in the six figures. Afterward we realized they would have paid a lot more, and we thought, 'I guess this is what the big shots do: They bid big numbers.'"

Now Microsoft is one of the big shots. The risks Bill Gates has taken through the years have paid off handsomely. On revenues of $8.7 billion in 1996, Microsoft's earned net income totaled $2.2 billion. Since the company went public in 1986, its stock has appreciated 10,000 percent.

Microsoft has been successful in the marketplace by achieving high volume sales to earn profits on products that involve high development costs. Steven Ballmer explains, "Software businesses are all fixed-cost businesses. And so volume is absolutely everything . . . because you've got to amortize that fixed cost very broadly." Software license volume increases, rather than increased per-unit prices, have been the principal factor in Microsoft's revenue growth.

Gates says of his company today, "Just to keep the thing running at breakeven, we have to sell $15 million a day."

Early on Gates recognized the connection between sales volume and the need to establish Microsoft's products as industry standards. Microsoft got to the top by defining software standards for operating systems. Gates says,

> We gave IBM a fabulous deal—a low, one-time fee that granted the company the right to use Microsoft's operating system on as many computers as it could sell. This offered IBM an incentive to push MS-DOS, and to sell it inexpensively. Our strategy worked. . . . Our goal was not to make money directly from IBM, but to profit from licensing MS-DOS to computer companies that wanted to offer machines more or less compatible with the IBM PC. IBM could use our software for free, but it did not have an exclusive license or control of future enhancements. This put Microsoft in the business of licensing a software platform to the personal-computer industry.

Microsoft's software prices change depending on competitive market pricing and cost factors. European and Far Eastern software prices are generally higher than in the United States due to higher localization costs and higher costs of distribution.

Introducing Per-Processor Licensing Fees

In 1988 Microsoft introduced a pricing practice that offered OEM customers a low royalty fee for MS-DOS if they agreed to pay a per-processor licensing fee. The fee applied to each computer the OEM shipped, even though the computer didn't include the MS-DOS operating system. Because Microsoft gives OEMs only one master copy of its software, per-processor licensing fees gives the company an easy way to track how many computers each OEM ships. The practice also makes it difficult for competitors to convince the OEMs to purchase their software. Usually licensing contracts are negotiated for two years.

Microsoft promotes volume sales by offering generous volume discounts to both OEM and corporate customers. For example, the Microsoft Open License Pak for medium-size corporate customers has three plans. Level A offers discounts to businesses with purchases of between 50 and 100 units within a two-year period. Level B applies to purchases of between 101 and 500 units, and Level C between 501 and 1,000 purchases. The program also gives discounts for upgrades to other Microsoft products. Microsoft gives its salespeople latitude in negotiating contracts with customers.

Bundling Software at Lower Prices

Microsoft has increased the market share of its applications software by bundling several products together and selling the bundle at a lower price than the sum of individual products when they are purchased separately. For example, retail customers may pay $300 each for Microsoft Word, Excel, and PowerPoint. Microsoft has integrated these individual products into a suite—Microsoft Office—that costs about $250, a huge discount compared to buying the individual applications separately.

Gates told the audience at a software industry forum in 1981, "It's only through volume that you can offer reasonable software at a low price."

Microsoft also offers its applications software at different price points depending on the products included in a suite. The Microsoft Office Standard product includes the Excel spreadsheet program, Word, a word processing program, and PowerPoint presentation graphics program. The Microsoft Office for Windows 95 also includes the Microsoft Schedule+ calendar and scheduling program. The Microsoft Office Professional version includes all of the above plus the Microsoft Access database management system.

As part of its marketing strategy to increase the market share for the Office suites beyond 80 percent, Microsoft developed a program whereby independent software developers can purchase a license for $1,000 for an unlimited number of applications and are required to use some core suite features. For the fee, developers can use Microsoft's graphical user interface and join Microsoft in several co-marketing plans.

Pricing New Products

To promote sales of new products, Microsoft often offers them at special introductory prices. For example, Microsoft promoted its new database program Access with a low introductory price of only $99. Aggressive pricing played a large role in marketing its revised Windows 3.1 operating system. Through a direct mail campaign, Microsoft offered current customers the new version for $49.99 instead of $79.99.

For the Windows 95 version of its Office suite, Microsoft offered introductory discounts for resellers and retailers as well as a 20 percent discount for corporate users who would migrate early to the new operating system, marking the first time the company offered the same discounts directly to its corporate customers that it extends to distribution channel members. The discount was intended to speed up the anticipated slow corporate migration to Windows 95.

Retail Pricing Policy

For many years Microsoft provided a suggested retail price for its products. In 1994 it established a new policy that relies on distribution channel members to set prices for its software packages. Microsoft made the policy change believing that suggested retail prices are no longer in line with actual selling prices. For example, Microsoft provided a suggested retail price of $495 for its Excel 5.0. but, because of volume discounts and promotional tie-ins, the product was offered by different resellers at prices ranging from $299 to $329. Microsoft believed the difference between suggested retail and actual prices was confusing to inexperienced software buyers. In announcing the new policy, Geoff Saunders, Microsoft's marketing manager for channel policies, said that the high list price might scare off some customers.

Questions

1. Describe Microsoft's pricing objectives in terms of its marketing goals.
2. Why does Microsoft offer special low prices on new products? What pricing strategy is reflected by this practice?
3. What role does price discounting play in Microsoft's pricing strategy?

APPENDIX

Careers in Marketing

Like most college students, Howard University marketing major Anthony Mason began pursuing career opportunities at the start of his senior year. The 22-year-old New Yorker had been keeping abreast of news in the business world and, since he was particularly interested in working for Ford Motor Company, he had paid special attention to news affecting the automobile industry.

On the day of his campus interview with Ford recruiters, Mason chose to wear a plain-cut gray suit and white shirt with a conservative tie. He carried several extra résumés with him because, he says, "You really can never be too prepared." About ten minutes before the actual interview began, Mason wondered nervously whether he had forgotten anything and had sufficiently prepared himself. He gained consolation from the knowledge that, regardless of how the interview turned out, he already had job offers in hand from International Paper and Citibank.

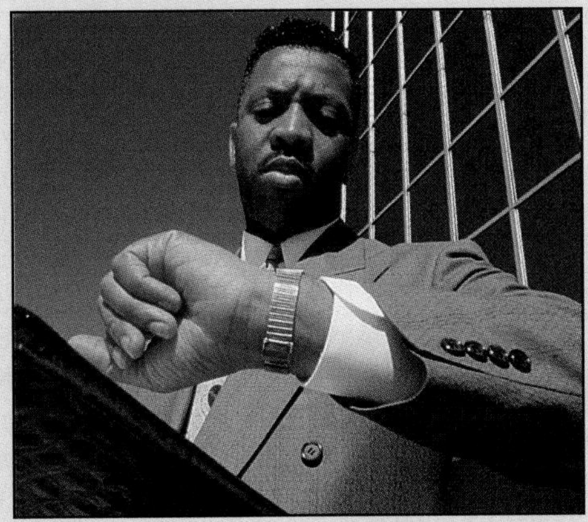

Anthony Mason double-checks the time before beginning an on-campus interview with Ford Motor Co. recruiters.

The interview with the two Ford recruiters lasted only 15 minutes, but was a grueling session of questions and answers for Mason. "Give me a situation in which you had to persuade someone to agree with you. How did you overcome that conflict? What was the result?" Mason took his time answering questions and carefully worded his responses. He recalls, "The questions took me a while to think about, but I felt really good coming out. They were up-front and told me what the deal was, the positive and the negative. That's what I look for in an interview—a taste for what the job will be like." Ford was obviously impressed—Mason was invited to Detroit for a final interview.[1]

INTRODUCTION

Each June, thousands of college graduates like Anthony Mason enter the job market, flooding prospective employers with résumés and cover letters requesting interviews. Of the many career paths chosen by business graduates, marketing is the single largest employment category in the U.S. labor force, and job growth in the field is expected to accelerate. The U.S. Bureau of Labor Statistics estimates that the number of jobs in marketing, advertising, and public relations management will grow much faster than the average for all occupations through 2005.

The dawning of the twenty-first century is witnessing an expansion of marketing activities far beyond the narrow boundaries of packaged goods and business products. Every successful organization—profit-seeking or not-for-profit—recognizes the necessity of effective marketing to accomplish its goals of providing customer satisfaction by offering high-quality goods or services to specific markets. Art institutes, museums, religious and human-services organizations, festivals, college and professional sports teams, and charitable, cultural, and entertainment events employ most of the same marketing techniques typically associated with producers and retailers of consumer and business goods. All of these organizations seek out highly motivated, professionally educated marketing specialists to design and implement these customer-driven programs.

This appendix, along with the videos and computer software that supplement the text, provides information to help you make educational and career decisions.

- Video Career Profiles are designed to give you insights into how marketers see themselves and their jobs. They are included in most of the end-of-chapter videos.
- Special career design software, *Discovering Your Marketing Career,* will help you to focus your goals more narrowly by identifying careers related to your interests and aptitudes.

These tools will help you to create an educational and employment plan to guide your marketing career in the right direction.

This appendix briefly describes many of the marketing

positions you have read about throughout the text. Specifically, the descriptions focus on the following aspects of marketing careers:

- Electronic résumés
- Specialized programs at various universities
- Use of an internship to create a competitive advantage in the workplace
- Types of positions available, job descriptions, career paths, and salaries
- Marketing employment trends and opportunities
- Employment prospects for women and minorities in marketing
- Sources of additional information

As you begin a career in marketing, you will have to apply many of the principles and concepts you have studied in this course, including how to target a market, capitalize on brand equity, position a product, and use market research techniques. Even in jobs that seem remote from the marketing discipline, this knowledge will help you to stay focused on the most important aspect of business: the customer. Looking for a job that will fulfill your career goals is much the same as marketing a product (your skills) to a customer (the company).

YOUR RÉSUMÉ

The résumé is probably the most important document that a job seeker can provide to a potential employer. The résumé's written record of credentials often provides the only information available to employers on which to base their evaluation and selection of a job candidate. For this reason, the résumé becomes a critical tool for obtaining an entry level position.

A résumé is a comprehensive summary of academic, professional, and personal accomplishments that makes focused statements about a job candidate. There is no one best way to write a résumé; however, it should provide accurate information that is related to the type of job desired in a direct, concise manner. Many computer software packages are available that require little more than filling in the blanks. Your Career Services Center can assist you in résumé writing, as well.

Three basic formats are used in preparing a résumé:

1. *Chronological:* Arranged in reverse chronological order; emphasizes job titles and organizations with descriptions of responsibilities held and duties performed. This format highlights continuity and career growth.
2. *Functional:* Accents accomplishments and strengths, placing less emphasis on job titles and work history. This format reduces repetitive language in job descriptions.
3. *Combined:* Emphasizes skills first, followed by employment history. This format suits students who need to show their responsibility and potential, but have employment histories not directly related to their desired jobs.

Most résumés include full names, mail and e-mail addresses, and telephone and fax numbers. Statements of career objectives typically follow. Academic information is provided next, followed by experience and work history. Applicants with limited work histories and no internship experience typically focus on relevant personal activities and interests. Most résumés close with lists of references.

Applicants are stronger candidates for employment when they can cite academic, work, and internship experiences related to their career objectives. For this reason, it is critical that you include any and all pre-professional and extracurricular activities in your résumé.

The important thing to remember in writing an effective résumé is to present the most relevant information in a clear, concise manner that emphasizes your best attributes.

Résumé Proofreader Wanted

Over the years, human resources recruiter Robert Half & Associates has collected a number of nuggets from résumés submitted by jobseekers, of which a select few follow:

"I operate computers like my father drove tractors—by the seat of his pants."

"It's best for employers that I not work with people"

"Enclosed is a ruff draft of my résumé."

"Size of employer: Very tall, probably over 6'5"."

"P.S.: If you hire me away from this nightmare, you'll also save me thousands in therapy."

"Left job to rum the family business."

"Am a perfectionist and rarely if if ever forget details."

Cover Letter

Letters of transmission, or cover letters, serve several purposes. Primarily, however, they seek to motivate employers to read the enclosed résumé.

The cover letter must provide specifically targeted information, from addressing the letter to the appropriate person in the organization to mentioning when to expect a follow-up call. The following list offers several tips mentioned by career-services counselors:

- ▼ Always address the letter to a specific person.
- ▼ Follow the salutation with a colon, not a comma.
- ▼ State which position you are applying for, where you learned about it, and why you are interested in that position.
- ▼ List specific examples of skills and contributions you offer; set a confident but not arrogant tone.
- ▼ Avoid overuse of *I* and *me* in the cover letter. Do not use slang or cliché phrases.
- ▼ Make certain your cover letter is neat and attractive; print it on high-quality paper, and limit it to one page.
- ▼ Mention any follow-up action that you plan to take, such as a call, and state when you will call.
- ▼ Express appreciation for being considered for the position.
- ▼ Sign the letter in black or blue ink.

Again, the Career Services Center on campus is likely to offer assistance in preparing cover letters as part of its job search support services for students and alumni. Correct form and accuracy are important in a cover letter, since employers often use the cover letter to evaluate written communication skills.

After a reasonable time has passed—one to three weeks—it is appropriate to call to verify that the résumé arrived, and to inquire about any additional questions and/or possible dates for interviews.

Letters of Recommendation

Letters of recommendation serve as testimonials to your performance in academic and work settings. The best references provide information relative to the desired industry or marketing specialty, as well as opinions of your skills, abilities, and character. References may be obtained from former or current employers, supervisors from volunteer experiences, professors, and others who can attest to your academic and professional competencies.

An effective letter of recommendation typically contains the following elements:

1. Statement of the length and nature of the relationship between the writer and the job candidate.
2. Description of the candidate's academic and career growth and potential.
3. Review of important achievements.
4. Evaluation of personal character (what kind of colleague the candidate will make).
5. Summary of the candidate's outstanding strengths and abilities.

Because letters of recommendation take time and effort, allow ample time for your references to compose them—as long as a month is not unusual. When you ask someone to write a letter of recommendation, you should always provide a résumé and any other information relative to the recommendation, along with a stamped, preaddressed (typed) envelope.

Career Facts

▶ Almost half of the major firms in North America look for employees through online recruiting sources. The most popular sources: the Internet (47 percent), electronic résumé banks (21 percent), and automated telephone listings (19 percent).

▶ While 20 million Japanese are currently enrolled in English-language classes, less than 50,000 U.S. students are learning to speak Japanese.

▶ Women comprise one-third of the world's workforce. More than half of all women between the ages of 18 and 64 work outside the home—59 percent in developed nations and 49 percent in developing regions.

Don't let failure get to you. Some of today's top business leaders who didn't give up include:

▶ **Jack Welch**, CEO of General Electric, who managed a plastics plant that blew up.

▶ **Ed Artzt**, CEO of Procter & Gamble, who had to deal with a warehouse full of a new detergent that crystallized just before he was to bring it to market.

▶ **Bernard Marcus**, who founded Home Depot after being fired from a regional hardware chain.

▶ Need additional examples? How about **Sam Walton**, whose first store failed, or **Walt Disney**, who was fired from an ad agency because he couldn't draw.

Supporting Documents

In addition to a cover letter, résumé, and letters of recommendation, candidates should include photocopies of transcripts, writing samples, or graphics products in their credentials packages. For example, if you are applying for a position in public relations, advertising, or sport marketing, you may want to include examples of professional writing, graphics, or audio/visual tapes to support written evidence of your credentials. Research and service projects that resulted in published or unpublished articles may also fill out the package.

Electronic Résumés

The electronic age has affected every aspect of the business world, including finding a job. Today, most of the *Fortune* 1,000 companies and many other large corporations use special computer software to receive, sort, store, and retrieve résumés from hopeful job applicants.

A computer system can scan data from thousands of résumés in a few seconds to find a dozen promising candidates for a job opening. For example, a company seeking an international marketing specialist may need a person with fluency in multiple languages and experience with international trade laws and practices. By searching for specific key words, the software retrieves the résumés that contain the desired information.

Gone are the days when a flashy résumé printed on expensive, colored paper was sufficient to catch the attention of most recruiters. Now a computer is likely to review these documents. That means your résumé must contain the key words associated with your skills, experience, achievements, interests, and personality. In fact, printing your résumé in a fancy font can often confuse the computer's scanning process, causing it to discard your unreadable résumé!

Dow Chemical keeps 20,000 résumés in its computer system and relies solely on its customized software to select the most suitable candidates for a position. Previously, the total cost involved in hiring a single Dow employee averaged $10,000. After installing the $100,000 computerized personnel-search system, the cost per hire fell to $7,500, and the firm recouped the money it spent for the installation after only 40 hires. Massachusetts-based Stratus Computers receives 15,000 résumés a year.

Job seekers also benefit from electronic recruiting. These systems have extended the life span of a résumé from less than a year to two or more. Traditionally, job candidates submitted résumés in response to advertisements for particular job openings. Recruiters reviewed the résumés at that time for that job. Now, however, they can review a stored résumé for any job that becomes available during a much longer time span, giving applicants more chances at all the jobs that become available.

An estimated 3,500 Web sites currently carry job postings. The three most comprehensive job banks list openings around the globe. The largest, Online Career Center

http://www.occ.com/

contains 55,000 job listings. In second place with 20,000 listings is Monster Board

http://www.monster.com/

E-Span's job bank currently contains 10,000 listings. Its Web address is:

http://www.espan.com/

All three of these online employment exchanges update their job rosters daily.

Each of these sites is designed to make it easy for you to identify job opportunities that best match your interests. If, for example, you decide to limit your job search to a single city such as Boston, you would simply type BOSTON into Online Career Center's QuickSearch screening system and almost immediately get over 2,600 listings. You could then narrow your scope to, say, sales positions and the list would shrink to 203 Boston listings.

Experts predict rapid development of a nationwide or even a worldwide database of résumés, allowing companies to search among everyone in the world looking for work. Both Monster Board and E-Span maintain online résumé banks that many employers and employment recruiters often peruse.[2]

SPECIALIZED GRADUATE EDUCATION

Not everyone will graduate with a bachelor's degree and enter the job market. Many marketing graduates choose to continue their studies by pursuing MBA degrees or entering master's programs specially suited to their career goals. A student who wishes to extend formal education in a specialized degree program should seek advice on specific programs from instructors who teach in these areas. For example, a market research professor is likely to have information on master's programs in that field at such institutions as the University of Georgia and Southern Illinois University at Edwardsville.

INTERNSHIPS CREATE COMPETITIVE ADVANTAGE

Internships have been described as a critical link in bridging the theory-practice educational gap. They serve as learning experiences for interns, providing a practical application of classroom theory as well as a means of gaining hands-on experience. Internships are becoming even more critical to networking and job hunting as students strive to reach ambitious career goals. They help to carry students between the academic present and the professional future.

An internship is a partnership between the student, the

university, and the agency or internship site. All of these parties assume definite responsibilities, perform specific functions, and achieve benefits as a result of their involvement. Internships offer valuable culminating experiences for marketing students. They provide opportunities to apply the ideas and theories presented in the classroom to the experience in a work environment.

Through an internship, an individual makes the transition from student to professional and establishes a link between theory and practice. Interns gain valuable, practical work experiences under the supervision of both university faculty and on-site marketing practitioners.

The internship fills out a student's professional credentials and allows for exploration of career options while observing and interacting with professionals at work. In some instances, internships are precursors for specific employment opportunities, allowing students to demonstrate technical proficiency while providing cost-effective personnel training for the industry as a whole.

The effectiveness of an internship experience depends on the quality of involvement by the student, the agency or site, and the university coordinator. Students interested in completing internships should discuss the matter with their instructors. Instructors can explain university requirements and identify any on-campus specialists who recommend potential interns, help them complete applications, and arrange interviews with potential internship providers. An excellent source of information about the nation's outstanding internships can be found at your local bookstore: Mark Oldman and Samer Hamadeh, *America's Top 100 Internships* (New York: Villard Books, published annually).

Briefly speaking

"I hear and I forget.
I see and I remember.
I do and I understand."

Confucius (551–479 B.C.)
Chinese philosopher and teacher

MARKETING POSITIONS

The basic objective of any firm is to market its goods or services.[3] Marketing responsibilities vary among organizations and industries. In a small firm, the owner or president may assume marketing responsibilities. A large firm needs a staff of experienced marketing, advertising, and public-relations managers to coordinate these activities. Some typical marketing-management positions are described in the following sections. (Please remember, however, that specific titles of positions may vary among firms.)

Marketing, Advertising, and Public-Relations Managers

Marketing management spans a range of positions, including vice president of marketing, marketing manager, sales manager, advertising manager, promotion manager, and public-relations manager. The vice president directs the firm's overall marketing policy, and all other marketers report through channels to this person. Marketing managers work with product development and market-research managers to develop the firm's detailed marketing strategies. Sales managers direct the efforts of sales professionals by assigning territories, establishing goals, developing training programs, and supervising local sales managers and their personnel. Advertising managers oversee account services, creative services, and media services departments. Promotion managers direct promotional programs that combine advertising with purchase incentives in order to increase the sales of the firm's goods or services. Public-relations managers conduct publicity programs and supervise the specialists who implement them.

Job Description Top marketing-management positions often involve long hours and extensive travel. Work under pressure is also commonplace. For sales managers, job transfers between headquarters and regional offices may disrupt family life. Approximately 460,000 marketing, advertising, and public-relations managers are currently employed in the United States in virtually every industry.

Career Path For most marketing, sales, and promotion-management positions, employers prefer degrees in business administration, preferably with concentrations in marketing. In highly technical industries, such as chemicals and electronics, employers prefer bachelor's degrees in science or engineering combined with master's degrees in business administration. Liberal arts students can also find many opportunities, especially if they have business minors. Most managers are promoted from positions such as sales representatives, product or brand specialists, and advertising specialists within their organizations. Skills or traits that are most desirable for these jobs include maturity, creativity, high motivation, resistance to stress, flexibility, and the ability to communicate persuasively.

Salary The median annual salary for marketing, advertising, and public-relations specialists ranges from $24,000 for a marketing assistant to $146,050 for a marketing vice president. The median incomes for specific positions in each field are shown in Table 1.

Sales Representatives

Millions of items are bought and sold every day. The people a firm hires to carry out this activity work under a variety of titles such as sales representative, account manager, manufacturer's representative, sales engineer, sales agent,

Table 1 Median Salaries for Marketing-Management Positions

Marketing assistant	$ 24,000
Advertising manager	44,000
Sales promotion manager	45,000
Brand manager	61,000
Direct-marketing manager	66,000
Regional sales manager	69,000
VP for marketing	146,050

Sources: Justin Martin, "How Does Your Pay Really Stack Up?" *Fortune,* June 26, 1995, pp. 79–86; and U.S. Department of Labor, Bureau of Labor Statistics, *Occupational Outlook Handbook,* (Washington, D.C.: U.S. Government Printing Office, 1996), p. 60.

Table 2 Median Compensation in Sales Professions

Senior sales representative	$ 68,300
Major account representative	71,200
National account representative	76,100
District sales manager	83,700
National account sales manager	85,600
Regional sales manager	92,300
Top sales executive	122,700

Source: Data reported in "What Sales Jobs Pay," *U.S. News & World Report,* October 28, 1996, p. 97.

retail salesperson, wholesale sales representative, and service sales representative. Most companies require that all marketing professionals spend some time in the field to experience the market firsthand and understand the challenges faced by front-line marketing personnel.

Job Description All salespeople must fully understand and competently discuss the products offered by the company. Salespeople usually develop prospective client lists, meet with current and prospective clients to describe the firm's products, and then follow up. In most cases, the salesperson must learn about each customer's business needs in order to identify products that best satisfy them. These professionals answer questions about the characteristics and costs of their offerings and try to persuade potential customers to purchase them. After the sale, many representatives revisit their customers to see that the products met their needs and to explore further business opportunities or referrals with them. Some sales of technical goods and services involve lengthy interactions. In these cases, a salesperson may work with several clients simultaneously over a large geographical area. Those responsible for large territories may spend most of their time traveling to make sales presentations. Retail or telephone salespeople may spend most of their work days on the phone or on the sales floor.

Briefly speaking

"I learned something early in life. If you sell, you'll never starve. In any other profession, you can find yourself out on the street saying, 'They don't want me anymore.' But if you can sell, you will never go hungry."

George Foreman (1949–)
American boxing champion

Work as a sales representative can be rewarding for those who enjoy interacting with people, like competition, and feel energized by the challenge of expanding sales in their territories. Successful sales professionals should be goal-oriented, persuasive, self-motivated, and independent people. In addition, patience and perseverance are important qualities for a sales representative.

Career Path The background needed for a sales position varies according to the product line and market. A college degree is desirable, and many companies run their own formal training programs for sales representatives that can last up to two years. This training may take place in a classroom, in the field with a mentor, or—most often—a combination of both methods. Similarly, the career ladder in retail sales typically involves moving to positions of greater responsibility and higher earnings potential over a period of time.

Salary Salary ranges for sales positions vary widely. In a recent year, annual earnings for middle-level sales representatives in service industries averaged $48,400; those selling technical services typically earn more than those selling nontechnical services. Annual earnings for manufacturer's and wholesale representatives averaged about $46,500. Sales trainees can expect to earn between $19,800 and $35,400, depending on the industry they join; producers of industrial goods pay the most and service providers pay the least for trainees. As Table 2 indicates, salaries increase substantially at higher levels of management.

Advertising Specialists

Advertising is one of the ten hottest career fields in the United States today. In fact, for the second year in a row, the position of interactive advertising executive has made the list of high-demand career specialties with a starting salary of $25,000, a five-year median salary of $65,000, and a potential salary of more than $250,000. The position also carries a high "coolness" factor of 8 on a scale of 10

Table 3 Average Salaries for Positions in Advertising

Advertising copywriter	$ 50,000
Art director	47,500
Account executive	62,500
Creative director	300,000

Source: Justin Martin, "How Does Your Pay Really Stack Up?" *Fortune,* June 26, 1995, pp. 79–86.

and a low burnout factor of 3. Within the next ten years, employment in this category is expected to grow by 400 percent.[4]

Many firms maintain small groups of advertising specialists who serve as liaisons between those companies and outside advertising agencies. The leader of this liaison function is sometimes called a *marketing communications manager.* Positions in an advertising agency include the categories of account services, creative services, and media services. Account services functions are performed by account executives, who work directly with clients. An agency's creative services department develops the themes and presentations of the advertisements. This department is supervised by the creative director, who oversees the copy chief, art director, and their staff members. The media services department is managed by the media director, who oversees the planning group that selects media outlets for ads.

Job Description Advertising can be one of the most glamorous and creative fields in marketing. Because the field combines the best of both worlds, that is, the tangible and scientific aspects of marketing along with creative artistry, advertising attracts people with a broad array of abilities.

Career Path Most new hires begin as assistants or associates for the positions they hope to acquire, such as copywriters, art directors, and media buyers. Often, a newly hired employee must receive two to four promotions before becoming manager of these functions. College degrees in liberal arts, graphic arts, journalism, psychology, or sociology, in addition to marketing training, are preferred for entry-level positions in advertising.

Salary In recent years, professionals in the advertising industry have enjoyed a considerable increase in average annual earnings. Table 3 lists the average base salaries for various positions in advertising agencies in the United States.

Public-Relations Specialists

Specialists in public relations serve as advocates for businesses and other organizations. They strive to build and maintain positive relationships with various publics. They may assist company executives in drafting speeches, arranging interviews, overseeing company archives, responding to information requests, and handling special events, such as sponsorships and trade shows, that provide promotional value to the firm.

Job Description Public-relations specialists normally work a standard 40-hour week, but sometimes they need to rearrange their normal schedules to meet deadlines or prepare for major events. Occasionally they are required to be on the job or on call around the clock to respond to an emergency or crisis. Over 109,000 public-relations specialists are employed in the United States, two-thirds of them in service industries. Public-relations positions tend to be concentrated in large cities near press services and communications facilities. However, that centralization is changing with the increased popularity of new communications technologies such as the Internet and World Wide Web, which allow more freedom of movement. Many public-relations consulting firms are located in New York, Los Angeles, Chicago, and Washington, D.C.

Essential characteristics include creativity, initiative, good judgment, and the ability to express thoughts clearly and simply—both in writing and in spoken statements. An outgoing personality, self-confidence, and enthusiasm are also recommended traits of public-relations specialists.

Career Path A college degree combined with public relations experience, usually gained through an internship, is considered excellent preparation for public relations. Many entry-level public relations specialists hold degrees with a major in advertising, marketing, public relations, or communications. New employees in larger organizations are likely to participate in formal training programs; those who begin their careers at smaller firms typically work under the guidance of experienced staff members. Entry-level positions carry such titles as research assistant or account assistant. Potential career paths include promotion to account executive, account supervisor, vice president, and eventually senior vice president.

Salary According to a recent salary survey, the median salary for all public-relations job titles was $46,204. Entry-level PR specialists in corporate settings typically earn higher salaries than their counterparts in not-for-profit organizations receive. By contrast, senior public-relations executives of not-for-profit organizations receive higher salaries, on average, than those in the business sector. The highest pay in PR goes to those involved in investor relations and international and environmental affairs.

Entry-level salaries average $49,800 for a publicity agent and $55,400 for an in-house publicist.

Purchasing Agents and Managers

The two key marketing functions of buying and selling are performed by trained specialists. Just as every organization is involved in selling its output to meet the needs of customers, so too must all companies make purchases of goods and services required to operate their businesses and turn out items for sale.

Modern technology has transformed the role of the purchasing agent. The transfer of routine tasks to the computer now allows contract specialists, or procurement officers, to focus on products, suppliers, and contract negotiations. The main function of this position is to purchase the goods, materials, supplies, and services required by the organization. These agents ensure that suppliers deliver quality and quantity levels that suit the firm's needs; they also secure these inputs at reasonable prices and make them available when needed.

Purchasing agents must develop good working relationships both with colleagues in their own organizations and with suppliers. As the popularity of outsourcing has increased, the selection and management of suppliers have become critical functions of the purchasing department. In the government sector, this role is dominated by strict laws, statutes, and regulations that constantly change.

Job Description Purchasing agents can expect a standard work week with some travel to suppliers' sites, seminars, and trade shows. Over 600,000 people work in purchasing jobs in the United States, most of them in manufacturing and government.

Career Path Organizations prefer college-educated candidates for entry-level jobs in purchasing. Strong analytical and communication skills are required for any purchasing position. Often, new hires into the field enroll in extensive company training programs to learn procedures and operations; training may include a production planning assignment. In private and public industries, professional certification is becoming an essential criterion for advancement. A variety of associations serving the different categories of purchasing confer certifications on agents, including Certified Purchasing Manager, Professional Public Buyer, Certified Public Purchasing Officer, Certified Associate Contract Manager, and Certified Professional Contract Manager.

Salary An entry-level purchasing agent can expect to earn $42,240 annually. The industry average is $52,800 and the typical salary for a firm's chief purchasing agent should approximate $63,360.

Wholesale and Retail Buyers and Merchandise Managers

Buyers working for wholesalers and retail businesses purchase goods for resale. Their goal is to find the best possible merchandise at the lowest price. They also influence the distribution and marketing of this merchandise. Successful buyers must understand what appeals to consumers and what their establishments can sell. Bar codes on products and point-of-purchase terminals have allowed organizations to accurately track goods that are selling and those that are not; buyers frequently analyze this data to improve their understanding of consumer demand. Buyers also check competitors' prices and sales activities and watch general economic conditions to anticipate consumer buying patterns.

Job Description Approximately 361,000 people are currently employed in the United States as wholesale and retail buyers and merchandise managers. These jobs often require substantial travel, as many orders are placed on buying trips to shows and exhibitions. Effective planning and decision-making skills are strong assets in this career. In addition, the job involves anticipating consumer preferences and ensuring that the firm keeps needed goods in stock, so it requires resourcefulness, good judgment, and self-confidence.

Career Path Most wholesale and retail buyers begin their careers as assistant buyers or trainees. Larger stores seek college-educated candidates, and extensive training includes job experience in a variety of positions. Advancement often comes when buyers move to departments with larger volumes or become merchandise managers to coordinate or oversee the work of several buyers.

Salary Median annual earnings of wholesale and retail buyers average $25,100. However, income depends on the amount and type of product purchased as well as seniority. Buyers often receive cash bonuses based on their performance.

Market Research Analysts

Market research analysts provide information that helps marketers to identify and define opportunities; they generate, refine, and evaluate marketing actions and monitor marketing performance. Market research analysts devise methods and procedures for obtaining needed data. Once they compile data, analysts evaluate it and then make recommendations to management.

Job Description Firms that specialize in market research and management consulting employ the majority of the

Table 4 Mean Compensation for Market Research Positions

Director	$80,860
Assistant director	67,560
Statistician	50,380
Senior analyst	45,770
Analyst	36,740

Source: Cyndee Miller, "Marketing Research Salaries Up a Bit, But Layoffs Take Toll," *Marketing News,* June 19, 1995, pp. 1, 3.

nation's market research analysts. Positions are often concentrated in larger cities, such as New York, Washington, D.C., and Chicago. Those who pursue careers in market research need to work accurately with detail, display patience and persistence, work effectively both independently and with others, operate objectively and systematically, and be effective oral and written communicators in presenting their results. Creativity and intellectual curiosity are essential for success in this field.

Career Path A bachelor's degree with emphasis in marketing provides sufficient qualifications for many beginning jobs in market research. Because of the importance of quantitative skills, this education should include courses in calculus, linear algebra, statistics, sampling theory and survey design, and computer science. Students should try to develop experience in conducting interviews or surveys while still in college. A master's degree in business administration or a related discipline is advised to improve opportunities for advancement.

Salary As Table 4 indicates, compensation in this field ranges from $36,740 for market research analysts to over $80,000 for a typical director of market research. Compensation levels throughout the industry have shown large percentage increases over the past ten years, and this trend will likely continue.

Logistics: Material Receiving, Scheduling, Dispatching, and Distributing Occupations

Often overlooked by marketing students, the area of logistics offers a myriad of career positions. Titles under the heading of logistics include material receiving, scheduling, dispatching, materials management executive, distribution operations coordinator, distribution center manager, and transportation manager. The logistics function includes responsibility for production and inventory planning and control, distribution, and transportation.

Table 5 Mean Compensation for Logistics Positions

Top logistics management executive	$135,100
Top supply-chain manager	176,000
Transportation manager	71,400
Top quality control executive	118,700
Outbound operations manager	47,100
Inbound operations manager	42,200
Inventory planning and control manager	76,700
Freight rate specialist	44,000
Dispatcher (transportation)	39,900

Source: Data reported in Jim Thomas, "Completing the Compensation Puzzle," *Distribution,* September 1996, pp. 35–36.

Job Description Approximately 3.8 million people are employed in logistics positions in the United States today, including material receiving, scheduling, dispatching, and distribution. These positions demand good communication skills and ability to work well under pressure.

Career Path Computer skills are highly valued in these jobs. Employers look for candidates with degrees in logistics and transportation. However, graduates in other business disciplines often succeed in the field.

Salary Annual earnings for logistics management positions are reported in Table 5.

TRENDS AND OPPORTUNITIES

Table 6 reports projections from the Bureau of Labor Statistics of employment for selected marketing occupations through 2005. Some sales positions, such as those in the financial and services sectors, are forecasted to do particularly well over this time period.

DIVERSITY IN THE MARKETING PROFESSION

The job market has changed dramatically in the past 30 years. Ethnic minorities and women of all races have increased their presence, and they will continue to do so. While Table 7 indicates that the battle for equality is not yet over, it does show considerable progress for women, African-Americans, and Hispanic-Americans.

According to the Small Business Administration, women are starting small firms at twice the rate of males.

Table 6 Employment Projections for Selected Marketing Positions through 2005

Occupation	Recent Employment	Projected Growth through 2005
Insurance sales workers	418,000	14–24%
Manufacturer's and wholesale sales representatives	1,503,000	14–24
Marketing, advertising, and public-relations managers	461,000	over 35
Purchasing agents and managers	621,000	14–24
Real estate agents, brokers, and appraisers	374,000	14–24
Retail sales workers	4,261,000	25–34
Securities and financial services sales representatives	246,000	over 35
Service sales representatives	612,000	over 35
Wholesale and retail buyers	621,000	14–24

Source: U.S. Department of Labor, *Occupational Outlook Handbook,* Bureau of Labor Statistics (Washington, D.C.: U.S. Government Printing Office, 1996), pp. 61, 69–71, 236–239.

Women-owned businesses in the United States employ more people than all of the Fortune 500 companies. However, employment of African-Americans and Hispanics in marketing is not proportionate with their shares of the total population.

The wage gap between genders continues to generate serious concern. In 1979, women holding bachelor's degrees earned average annual wages of $30,161, while men brought in $54,391. Almost 20 years later, women had increased their earnings some $9,000 to $39,271, while men's salaries grew by about $7,000 to $61,008. Although the disparity seems to be narrowing, the problem remains an important one.[5] Table 8 compares the salaries of men and women working in various advertising positions.

ADDITIONAL INFORMATION SOURCES

General information about careers in marketing is available from the sources listed below. Information sources are grouped by the job categories described in the discussion of marketing positions.

General Marketing

American Marketing Association, 250 South Wacker Dr. Suite 200, Chicago, IL 60606
http://www.ama.org/

Table 7 Female and Minority Employment in Selected Marketing Occupations

Occupation	Percentage of Total Employees: Female	African-American	Hispanic
Purchasing managers	41.5%	6.6%	3.1%
Marketing, advertising, public relations managers	35.7	2.2	3.3
Sales occupations	49.5	7.8	6.9
Supervisors/proprietors	38.9	5.6	5.6
Sales representatives:			
Advertising sales	52.9	4.2	4.7
Insurance sales	37.1	5.8	4.6
Real estate sales	50.7	3.4	4.5
Retail/personal services	65.6	11.4	8.9
Securities/financial services	31.3	5.7	5.0

Source: U.S. Bureau of the Census, *Statistical Abstract of the United States* 116th edition (Washington, D.C.: U.S. Government Printing Office, 1996), pp. 405–406.

Table 8 Median Base Salary by Gender and Advertising Position

Position	Male	Female
CEO	$130,000	$123,000
Creative director	95,000	74,000
Art director	55,000	48,000
Chief copywriter	58,000	53,000
Media director	72,000	52,000
Senior account executive	78,000	64,000
Account executive	47,000	42,000

Source: Data from R. Craig Endicott, "Cracks Emerge in Gender Gap, Starting with the VP-Marketing," *Advertising Age,* December 11, 1995, pp. 25–27.

Sales

Sales and Marketing Executives International, 458 Statler Office Tower, Cleveland, OH 44115

Manufacturers' Agents National Association, 23016 Mill Creek Road, P.O. Box 3467, Laguna Hills, CA 92654

National Retail Federation, 100 West 31st Street, New York, NY 10001
http://www.nrf.com/

Securities Industry Association, 120 Broadway, New York, NY 10271
http://www.sia.com/

Advertising and Promotion

American Association of Advertising Agencies, 666 Third Ave., 13th Floor, New York, NY 10017

American Advertising Federation, Education Services Department, 1400 K St. NW, Suite 1000, Washington, DC 20005

Council of Sales Promotion Agencies, 750 Summer St., Stamford, CT 06901

Promotion Marketing Association of America, Inc., 322 Eighth Ave., Suite 1201, New York, NY 10001

Public Relations

Public Relations Society of America, Inc., 33 Irving Place, New York, NY 10003–2376
http://www.prsa.org/

PR Reporter, P.O. Box 600, Exeter, NH 03833

Public Relations News, Service Department, 127 East 80th St., New York, NY 10021

Purchasing

National Association of Purchasing Management, Inc., P.O. Box 22160, Tempe, AZ 85285
http://www.napm.org/

National Institute of Governmental Purchasing, Inc., 115 Hillwood Ave., Falls Church, VA 22046

National Contract Management Association, 1912 Woodford Rd., Vienna, VA 22182

Federal Acquisition Institute, General Services Administration, 18th and F Streets NW, Washington, DC 20405

Wholesale and Retail Buyers and Merchandise Managers

National Retail Federation, 100 West 31st St., New York, NY 10001
http://www.nrf.com/

Market Research

Marketing Research Association, 2189 Silas Deane Hwy., Suite 5, Rocky Hill, CT 06067

DISCOVERING YOUR MARKETING CAREER—A SOFTWARE APPLICATION

If you purchased a new copy of *Contemporary Marketing,* Ninth Edition, you should have received a CD-ROM with software to help you plan your career along with your copy of the text. If your book contains a CD-ROM disk titled *Discovering Your Marketing Career,* please continue reading.

Selecting a career ladder to climb is no easy task. In today's competitive job market, the most desirable and highest-paying jobs will go to the most qualified candidates. A degree in marketing will prepare you for a number of entry-level positions. However, job-hopping in order to determine the career that best suits you is likely to create a detrimental image for you. Successful applicants understand well their own interests and abilities, the general characteristics of the jobs they seek, and how their interests and abilities might fit an employer's needs. You should have noticed that these three criteria resemble closely the elements leading to customer satisfaction in all business transactions.

Discovering Your Marketing Career is a computer application that will help you to determine which marketing careers most closely match your skills, experience, and interests. The software invites your input to questionnaires for each major career track in marketing to help you determine how well each one suits you. After you complete the questionnaire, the software generates an in-depth report assessing your compatibility with that track. The report also prints out a detailed profile of the career itself, its long-term opportunities, and compensation levels. Once you have narrowed down your interests, you can begin engaging in the software's job search activities. The activities include guidelines for field research on careers, résumé preparation, letter writing, and preparation of telephone scripts. By matching your interests to the demands of a particular marketing career, you can decide which elective courses will strengthen your marketability as a job candidate.

Notes

CHAPTER 1

1. Melanie Berger, "Making the Web Work," *Executive's Guide to Sales & Marketing Technology,* March 1997, pp. 30–33; Chad Rubel, "It's OK to Think Cheap in Starting a Net Plan," *Marketing News,* January 29, 1996, p. 12; and Michelle V. Rafter, "Ad Gurus Still Exploring Secrets to Selling on Web," *San Diego Union-Tribune's Computer-Link,* January 2, 1996, p. 8.
2. David Fischer, "Global Hopscotch," *U.S. News & World Report,* June 5, 1995, pp. 43–45.
3. Kerry A. Dolan, "The Wide, Wide World of Wal-Mart," *Forbes,* March 25, 1996, p. 38.
4. Peter F. Drucker, *The Practice of Management* (New York: Harper & Row, 1954), p. 37.
5. Joseph P. Guiltinan and Gordon W. Paul, *Marketing Management,* 6th ed. (New York: McGraw-Hill, 1996), pp. 3–4.
6. Tom Dollocano Jr., "Watching Windows," *Sales & Marketing Management,* August 1996, p. 23.
7. Jerry Flint and Paul Klebnikov, "Would You Want to Drive a Lada?" *Forbes,* August 26, 1996, pp. 66–69; and Brandon Mitchener, "Ford, Belarus Form Venture for Cars, Vans," *Wall Street Journal,* April 11, 1996, p. B5.
8. Zachary Schiller, "Make It Simple," *Business Week,* September 9, 1996, p. 102.
9. Cacilie Rohwedder, "Global Products Require Name-Finders," *Wall Street Journal,* April 11, 1996, p. B6.
10. Wroe Alderson, *Marketing Behavior and Executive Action* (Homewood, Ill.: Richard D. Irwin, 1957), p. 292.
11. Robert J. Keith, "The Marketing Revolution," *Journal of Marketing,* January 1960, p. 36.
12. Franklin Crawford, "Trend Setting at Its Best," *Ithaca Journal,* January 15, 1996, p. 4A.
13. Keith, "Marketing Revolution," p. 38.
14. Theodore Levitt, *Innovations in Marketing* (New York: McGraw-Hill, 1962), p. 7.
15. General Electric Company, *Annual Report,* 1952, p. 21.
16. Kwaku Atuahene-Gima, "Market Orientation and Innovation," *Journal of Business Research,* February 1996, pp. 93–103.
17. "Partnering for Products," *Inc.,* February 1996, p. 94.
18. Nancy Shullins, "Not Peanuts Anymore," *San Diego Union-Tribune,* May 28, 1996, pp. C1, C6.
19. James T. Bennett and Thomas J. DiLorenzo, *Unfair Competition: The Profits of Nonprofits* (Lanham, MD: Hamilton Press, 1989), pp. 11–16.
20. David Crary, "Mounties Start Cashing in on Disney Deal," *Marketing News,* August 12, 1996, p. 7.
21. John Bizzell, "Cause Marketing Takes on a New Look," *Brandweek,* August 19, 1996, p. 14; and "Cancer Society to Sell Its Name to Nicotine Patch, Juice Companies," *San Diego Union-Tribune,* August 17, 1996, p. A10.
22. Marla Matzer, "Rapper, Actor, Dunker, Brand," *Brandweek,* July 15, 1996, p. 24. See also Darryl Howerton, "There's No Business Like Shaq Business," *Sport,* February 1997, pp. 52–57.
23. Louis E. Boone, "Using Sport to Segment the Tourism Market: The Robert Trent Jones Golf Trail," *Proceedings of the Seventh Bi-Annual World Marketing Congress* (Melbourne, Australia: Academy of Marketing Science, 1995).
24. Alison DaRosa, "Traveler's Checks," *San Diego Union-Tribune,* May 5, 1996, p. F3.
25. Boone, "Using Sport to Segment."
26. "Waiting for the Smoke to Clear," *Reputation Management,* May/June 1995, pp. 49–51.
27. Cyndee Miller, "Broadway Increases Marketing to Reach Younger Theater Crowd," *Marketing News,* September 9, 1996, pp. 1–2.
28. Peter Lucas, "Card Marketers Go for the Gold," *Credit Card Management,* May 1996, pp. 22–23.
29. Nevin J. "Dusty" Rodes, "Marketing a Community Symphony Orchestra," *Marketing News,* January 29, 1996, p. 2.
30. Solange De Santis, "Marketing Muses Sell the Bard with Slogans, Stunts," *Wall Street Journal,* February 8, 1996, p. B1.
31. Bruce Horovitz, " 'Attitude Wear' Maker Seeks Broader Appeal," *USA Today,* July 10, 1995, pp. B1, B2.
32. Luc Hatlestad, "Compaq Reduces System Prices for Second Time in 10 Weeks," *InfoWorld,* May 13, 1996, p. 32; and Gary McWilliams, "Compaq Starts a PC Brawl," *Business Week,* March 18, 1996, p. 40.
33. Glenn J. Lakinowski, "Reggie Winners—Tie-Ins Formed the Winning Strategies in 1995," *PROMO,* March 1996, pp. R8–R10.
34. Catherine Arnst, "Hold the Phone—It's a Marketing Free-for-All," *Business Week,* February 19, 1996, p. 32.
35. Robert L. Rose, "For Whirlpool, Asia Is the New Frontier," *Wall Street Journal,* April 25, 1996, pp. B1, B4.
36. Ibid.
37. Edward Forrest and Richard Mizerski, eds., *Interactive Marketing* (Lincolnwood, Ill.: NTC Business Books, 1996, p. xi.
38. John Deighton et al., "The Future of Interactive Marketing," *Harvard Business Review,* November/December 1996, pp. 151–162.
39. Hilary Rosner, "Redefining Interactivity," *Brandweek,* November 27, 1995, pp. 18–19.
40. T. L. Stanley, "iStation Music Merchandising Kiosks Extend onto the I-Way," *Brandweek,* December 4, 1995, p. 9; and visit to Web site http://www.worldwidemusic.com/, June 6, 1996.
41. Hillary Rosner, "Growing Pains," *Adweek,* July 8, 1996, p. 18; and "Online Users: The Latest Figures," *Advertising Age,* July 22, 1996, p. 30.
42. R. Craig McClaren, "The Web Means Business," *PROMO,* December 1995, p. 31; and David Sussman, "Goldrush in Cyberspace," *U.S. News & World Report,* November 13, 1995, p. 73.
43. Thomas L. Ainscough and Michael G. Luckett, "The Internet for the Rest of Us: Marketing on the World Wide Web," *Journal of Consumer Marketing* 13, no. 2 (1996), p. 37.
44. "Pillsbury Bake-Off Cooks Online," *PROMO,* February 1996, p. 128.
45. This typology is explained in Ainscough and Luckett, "Internet for the Rest," pp. 41–44, from which several of the section's examples are drawn.

46. "CyberCritique of the Week," *Advertising Age,* February 12, 1996, p. 24.
47. Rusty Weston, "Five Ways to Do Business on the Internet," *Inc. Technology* 3 (1995), p. 76.
48. Patrick Henry Bass, "Riding the Information Superhighway," *Black Enterprise,* March 1996, p. 92.
49. R. Lee Sullivan, "Toll Booths on the Info Superhighway," *Forbes,* March 25, 1996, p. 118.
50. Raju Narisetti, "P&G to Gamble More on Cyber Surfing," *Wall Street Journal,* April 18, 1996, p. B10; and Jack Egan, "Cashing In on the Internet," *U.S. News & World Report,* November 13, 1995, p. 83.
51. Martin Christopher, Adrian Payne, and David Ballantyne, *Relationship Marketing* (Oxford: Butterworth-Heinemann, 1993), pp. viii, 22–25.
52. Leonard L. Berry, "Relationship Marketing of Services—Growing Interest, Emerging Perspectives," *Journal of the Academy of Marketing Science,* fall 1995, pp. 236–237.
53. Mike Pearce, "Loyalty in a Foreign Climate," *Marketing—Choosing and Using Customer Loyalty Supplement,* April 4, 1996, p. iii.
54. "Preparing for a Point to Point World," *Marketing Management,* spring 1995, p. 33.
55. B. Joseph Pine II, Don Peppers, and Martha Rogers, "Do You Want to Keep Your Customers Forever?" *Harvard Business Review,* March/April 1995, p. 111.
56. Yumiko Ono, "Draft Seeking Joint Marketing Arrangements," *Wall Street Journal,* March 11, 1996, p. B7.
57. Don L. Boroughs, "The Bottom Line on Ethics," *U.S. News & World Report,* March 20, 1995, pp. 62–63.
58. "News from the Warehouse," *The Price/Costco Connection,* April 1996, p. 3.
59. Valerie Lynn Gray, "Marketing: The Route to the Top," *Black Enterprise,* February 1997, p. 61.

CHAPTER 2

1. Patricia Lamiell, "The Internet, You Can Bank on It," *San Diego Union-Tribune's ComputerLink,* October 29, 1996, pp. 1, 16; Seth Lubove, "Cyberbanking," *Forbes,* October 21, 1996, pp. 108–116; Jeff Pelline, "Banks Invest in Courtesy," *CNET News,* October 4, 1996, downloaded from http://www.news.com/, November 4, 1996; Jill Andresky Fraser, "Will Banking Go Virtual?" *Inc. Technology,* September 17, 1996, pp. 49–52; and Kate Fitzgerald, "Banks Hoping to Cash in on Virtual Service," *Advertising Age,* April 1, 1996, p. 34.
2. Joseph P. O'Leary, "The CEO and Customer Satisfaction," *Management Review,* September 1996, p. 62.
3. Frederick F. Reichheld, "Learning from Customer Defections," *Harvard Business Review,* March/April 1996, p. 56.
4. Douglas MacDonald, "A Conversation with Dr. Val Feigenbaum," *Tenneco Symposium,* summer 1992, pp. 20–24.
5. Wilton Woods, "After All You've Done for Your Customers, Why Are They Still Not Happy?" *Fortune,* December 11, 1995, pp. 178–180.
6. Reichheld, "Learning from Customer Defections."
7. "Wining and Dining the Whiners," *Sales & Marketing Management,* February 1993, pp. 73–75.
8. Robert C. Blattberg and John Deighton, "Managing Marketing by the Customer Equity Test," *Harvard Business Review,* July/August 1996, p. 136.
9. "Americans Are More Finicky Than Ever," *Fortune,* February 3, 1997, pp. 108–109.
10. Ian P. Murphy, "Aided by Research, Harley Goes Whole Hog," *Marketing News,* December 2, 1996, pp. 16–17.
11. Suzanne Kapner, "Delivering Great Service—Not Lip Service," *Nation's Restaurant News,* August 5, 1996, pp. 62–64.
12. Keith L. Bond, "Survey Customers to Enhance Retention," *Rough Notes,* September 1996, pp. 18–20.
13. Andrew Rogers, "Inside Knowledge," *Marketing,* May 16, 1996, pp. 35–36.
14. Robert F. Lusch, Thomas Boyt, and Drue Schuler, "Employees as Customers: the Role of Social Controls and Employee Socialization in Developing Patronage," *Journal of Business Research* 35 (1996), pp. 179–187. See also Randall Lane, "Pampering the Customers, Pampering the Employees," *Forbes,* October 14, 1996, pp. 74–80.
15. Amy Zuber, "Treat Employees Like You Want Guests Treated, Expert Says," *Nation's Restaurant News,* June 10, 1996, p. 92.
16. Jeffrey H. Dyer, "How Chrysler Created an American Keiretsu," *Harvard Business Review,* July/August 1996, p. 42.
17. David L. Epstein, "Taco Bell Keeps Its Guests from Going South of the Border," *Telemarketing & Call Center Solutions,* July 1996, pp. 164–169.
18. Reichheld, "Learning from Customer Defections."
19. Ibid.
20. Mary Walton, *The Deming Management Method* (New York: G. P. Putnam, 1986), p. 26.
21. Rahud Jacob, "More than a Dying Fad?" *Fortune,* October 18, 1993, pp. 66–67.
22. Baldrige Award home page, http://www.quality.nist.gov/, downloaded October 23, 1996.
23. Ibid.
24. Peter Szekely, "Study Finds Profit in Employee Empowerment," *USA Today,* June 6, 1996, p. 4B.
25. "Employee Involvement Helps Bottom Line," *Employee Benefit Plan Review,* July 1996, p. 50.
26. Ellen Neuborne, "Fashioning a Revolution in Service," *USA Today,* March 29, 1996, p. B1.
27. Szekely, "Profit in Empowerment."
28. Neuborne, "Revolution in Service."
29. M. Dale Beckman, David L. Kurtz, and Louis E. Boone, *Foundations of Marketing,* 5th ed. (Toronto: The Dryden Press, 1992), pp. 582–584.
30. Louis E. Boone and Dianne Wilkins, "Benchmarking at Xerox: A Case Study," *Proceedings of the Academy of Business Administration London International Conference,* June 1994, pp. 569–574.
31. "Best Practices," downloaded from The Benchmarking Exchange Web site, http://www.benchnet.com/, October 28, 1996.
32. Harry K. Brelin, "Benchmarking: The Change Agent," *Marketing Management* 2, no. 3 (1993), pp. 33–37.
33. John A. Byrne, "Management Meccas," *Business Week,* September 18, 1995, p. 132.

34. Ibid., p. 125.
35. Neuborne, "Revolution in Service."
36. Rita Koselka, "The New Mantra: MVT," *Forbes,* March 11, 1996, p. 114.
37. Ibid.
38. Clive Jeanes, "Achieving and Exceeding Customer Satisfaction at Milliken," *Managing Service Quality* (1995), pp. 6–11.
39. Kevin Burden, "3Com Does Things Right," *Computerworld,* September 16, 1996, p. 100.
40. Stephen F. Wiggins, "New Ways to Create Lifetime Bonds with Your Customers," *Fortune,* August 21, 1995, p. 115.
41. Kim McLain, "Swinging into the Future," *EDI World,* September 1996, pp. 20–22.
42. Joshua Macht, "Are You Ready for Electronic Partnering?" *Inc. Technology,* November 4, 1995, downloaded from America Online. October 30, 1996.
43. Keith Naughton, "Revolution in the Showroom," *Business Week,* February 19, 1996, pp. 70–71.
44. Neil Gross, "New Tricks for Help Lines," *Business Week,* April 29, 1996, p. 97.
45. Thomas Anderson, "Millipore: Marketing Products to the Global Desktop," in *The Internet Strategy Handbook: Lessons from the New Frontier of Business,* ed. by Mary J. Cronin (Boston: Harvard Business School Press, 1996), pp. 115–137.
46. Jackie Freiberg and Kevin Freiberg, "Is This Company Completely Nuts?" *Executive Excellence,* September 1996, p. 20; and Del Jones, "Low-Cost Carrier Still Challenges Industry," *USA Today,* July 10, 1995, p. 5B.

CHAPTER 3

1. Lisa Sanders, "Going Green with Less Red Tape," *Business Week,* September 23, 1996, pp. 75–76; Stephen Budiansky, "Being Green Isn't Always What It Seems," *U.S. News & World Report,* August 26, 1996, p. 42; "Stalking the Green Consumer on the Internet," *Marketing News,* February 26, 1996, p. 7; Jacquelyn Ottman and Joel Makower, "Post-Mortem for Green Consumerism," *Business Ethics,* July/August 1995, p. 52; and Weld Royal, "It's Not Easy Being Green," *Sales & Marketing Management,* July 1995, pp. 84–90.
2. Matthew Rose and Martha Brannigan, "Dominion Resources Mulls Bid for East Midlands," *Wall Street Journal,* November 7, 1996, pp. A3, A8; and Steven Lipin, "British Telecommunications and MCI Unveil $20.88 Billion Merger Agreement," *Wall Street Journal,* November 4, 1996, p. A3.
3. David E. Kalish, "Technology Bringing Photo Labs to Homes," *Mobile Register,* November 30, 1996, p. 7B.
4. Jeff Cole and Evan Ramstad, "Texas Instruments Auctions Defense Unit," *Wall Street Journal,* November 6, 1996, p. A3.
5. "March of the Superstores," *Time,* September 16, 1996, p. 68.
6. Peter H. Lewis, "Stressed Net on the Verge of Collapse?" *San Diego Union-Tribune's ComputerLink,* September 24, 1996, p. 16.
7. Theresa Humphrey, "DuPont to Cut 2,800 Jobs, Shift to Machinery," *San Diego Union-Tribune,* November 15, 1996, p. C2.
8. Hilary Rosner, "FTD, 800-FLOWERS Face New Reality with Web," *Brandweek,* January 6, 1996, p. 9.
9. Nick Wingfield, "IE 4.0 Beta in Time for Xmas," *CNET News,* November 8, 1996, downloaded from http://www.news.com/, November 21, 1996; and Neal Goldsmith and Ed Rosenfeld, "Browser Battles," *BusinessTech,* September 1996, downloaded from http://businesstech.com/, October 3, 1996
10. Catherine Yang, "How Do You Police Cyberspace?" *Business Week,* February 5, 1996, pp. 97–99.
11. Catherine Yang, "The Cops Are Coming," *Business Week,* June 10, 1996, pp. 32–33.
12. Kate Fitzgerald, "Antitrust Cast Threatens the Image of Toys 'R' Us," *Advertising Age,* May 27, 1996, p. 6.
13. Yang, "Cops Are Coming."
14. Peter Frisch, "Tired of Phone Wars? Get Ready for a Fight to Sell Natural Gas," *Wall Street Journal,* April 16, 1996, pp. A1, A6.
15. Peter Coy and Gary McWilliams, "Electricity: The Power Shift Ahead," *Business Week,* December 2, 1996, pp. 78–82.
16. Yumiko Ono, "FCC Head Queries Liquor Group on Ads," *Wall Street Journal,* November 18, 1996, p. B8.
17. Skip Wollenberg, "Voluntary Liquor Ban Ends," *San Diego Union-Tribune,* November 8, 1996, pp. A1, A26; Michael Krantz, "Seagram's on the Box," *Time,* June 24, 1996, p. 49; and "Seagram Sets off a Spot of Controversy," *U.S. News & World Report,* June 24, 1996, p. 17.
18. Amy Barrett, "Baby Bells Are Bawling," *Business Week,* November 4, 1996, pp. 94–95.
19. David Whitford, "The Marketeer," *Inc. 500 1995,* pp. 86–95.
20. James C. Cooper and Kathleen Madigan, "The Economy's Heat Is Setting off Alarm Bells," *Business Week,* September 16, 1996, pp. 39–40.
21. Ann Perry, "Credit Card Firms Getting Selective, Trying New Tricks," *San Diego Union-Tribune,* September 1, 1996, p. I1; and Peter G. Gosselin, "Credit Mania: Borrowing Trouble?" *San Diego Union-Tribune,* May 12, 1996, p. I-3.
22. James C. Cooper and Kathleen Madigan, "Will the Economy Look This Good on Inauguration Day?" *Business Week,* November 18, 1996, p. 35.
23. "A Glimpse of Disruption," *Brandweek,* December 16, 1996, p. 30.
24. I. Jean Dugan, "Suddenly a Scramble for Good Help," *Business Week,* September 16, 1996, pp. ENT4–6.
25. Nick Anderson, "Mexico's Economy Is Slowly on the Mend," *San Diego Union-Tribune,* May 18, 1996, p. C1; and Elisabeth Malkin, "Pitching to Peso-Pinchers," *Business Week,* May 15, 1995, pp. 82–83.
26. Keith Naughton, "An Electric Car Propelled by Star Power?" *Business Week,* December 9, 1996, p. 40; and Jean Halliday, "GM Energizes EV1 Launch with $8 Mil Ad Blitz," *Advertising Age,* December 2, 1996, p. 12.
27. Brooke Crothers, "Grove's Graphics Chip Due in '97," *CNET News,* November 18, 1996, downloaded from http://www.news.com/, November 21, 1996.
28. Stephen V. Brull, "The Wave of Gizmos Coming Soon from Japan," *Business Week,* November 25, 1996, pp. 62–68.

29. Suzanne Galante, "Will Online Banking Pay Off?" *CNET News,* November 7, 1996, downloaded from http://www.news.com/, November 7, 1996; and Mike Ricciuti, "Banking Rivals Take Battle Online," *CNET News,* July 23, 1996, downloaded from http://www.news.com/, November 7, 1996.
30. Aaron Lucchetti, "Getting in Gear," *Wall Street Journal,* November 18, 1996, pp. R18–R20.
31. Daniel Shannon, "Dunkin' Donuts, Taco Bell Add Low-Fat Fare," *PROMO,* March 1995, pp. 1, 65.
32. Yumiko Ono, "Fat Fear No Bar to Candy, Just Chocolate," *San Diego Union-Tribune,* November 14, 1996, p. D2.
33. Mike Yamamoto, "Web Finds the Niche," *CNET News,* September 23, 1996, downloaded from http://www.news.com/, November 24, 1996.
34. Stephanie Bentley, "Ben & Jerry's Gets a Chilly Reception," *Marketing Week,* April 12, 1996, pp. 21–22.
35. David W. Cravens and Gerald G. Hills, "Consumerism: A Perspective for Business," *Business Horizons,* August 1970, p. 21.
36. "Texaco to Pay $176 Million in Bias Suit," *Wall Street Journal,* November 18, 1996, p. A3; and Shelley Donald Coolidge, "Boycotts of Companies Grow as a Protest Tool," *Christian Science Monitor,* November 15, 1996, pp. 1, 9.
37. "Ethics Training Prevalent," *San Diego Union-Tribune,* September 30, 1996, p. C1; and "Firms Making Ethics a Part of Corporate Life," *Mobile Register,* April 16, 1995, p. 6F.
38. Lisa Brownlee, "Ad Executives Break Ranks over Tobacco," *Wall Street Journal,* November 13, 1996, pp. B1, B8.
39. Hazel Kahan, "A Professional Opinion," *Marketing Tools,* October 1996, downloaded from http://www.marketing tools.com/, November 24, 1996.
40. Barbara Carton, "Gillette Faces Wrath of Children in Testing on Rats and Rabbits," *Wall Street Journal,* September 5, 1995, pp. A1, A6.
41. "Four Retailers Agree to Settle Complaints on Zero-Interest Ads," *Wall Street Journal,* September 17, 1996, p. B6.
42. James F. Engel and Roger D. Blackwell, *Consumer Behavior,* 6th ed. (Hinsdale, Ill.: The Dryden Press, 1990), p. 783.
43. Lands' End Catalog, December 1996, p. 74; and Michael Ryan, "They Call Their Boss a Hero," *Parade,* September 8, 1996, pp. 4–5.
44. Elisabeth Malkin, "Cleanup at the *Maquiladora,*" *Business Week,* July 29, 1996, p. 48.
45. Paul N. Bloom, Pattie Yu Hussein, and Lisa R. Szykman, "Benefiting Society and the Bottom Line," *Marketing Management,* winter 1995, pp. 8–13.
46. Bob Ortega, "Wal-Mart Store Comes in Colors, But Is All Green," *Wall Street Journal,* June 11, 1993, pp. B1, B10.
47. Ibid.
48. Frank Allen, "U.S. Companies Plan Alliance on Recycling," *Wall Street Journal,* September 14, 1992, p. A3.

CHAPTER 4

1. Geoff House, "Global Couch Potatoes," *World Trade,* October 1996, pp. 50–54; Wayne Walley, "Programming Globally—with Care," *Advertising Age International,* September 18, 1995, p. 114; and Jeffrey D. Zbar, "Niche Audiences Are Growing," *Advertising Age International,* July 1996, p. 118.
2. Robert L. Rose and Carl Quintanilla, "How Some Small Companies Land Sales Far beyond the U.S.," *Wall Street Journal,* December 20, 1996, pp. A1, A6.
3. "The New Economy Needs Free Trade," *Business Week,* December 30, 1996, p. 194.
4. Amy Borrus, "How Exports Create Jobs," *Business Week,* August 12, 1996, p. 22; and John Merline, "Do Trade Walls Shield Workers? Protectionist Claims Are Misleading, Data Show," *Investor's Business Daily,* March 1, 1996, downloaded from America Online, December 22, 1996.
5. Michael Czinkota and Ilkka A. Ronkainen, *International Marketing,* 5th ed. (Fort Worth, Tex.: The Dryden Press, 1998), p. 5.
6. Rebecca Piirto Heath, "Think Globally," *Marketing Tools,* October 1996, downloaded from http://www.marketingtools.com/, November 30, 1996; and Andrew Tanzer, "The Pacific Century," *Forbes,* July 15, 1996, pp. 109–113.
7. Claudia Penteado, "Coke Taps Maternal Instinct with New Latin American Ads," *Advertising Age,* January 13, 1997, p. 113; and Mark L. Clifford and Nicole Harris, "Coke Pours into Asia," *Business Week,* October 28, 1996, pp. 72–78.
8. Kim Clark, "A Bigger, Richer World," *Fortune,* August 5, 1996, p. 102; and Michael H. Martin, "When InfoWorlds Collide," *Fortune,* October 28, 1996, p. 130.
9. Jeffrey A. Tannenbaum, "Among Fast-Growing Small Concerns, Exporters Expand the Most, Study Says," *Wall Street Journal,* June 19, 1996, p. B2.
10. Robert L. Rose and Carl Quintanilla, "How Some Small Companies Land Sales Far beyond the U.S."
11. Alice Z. Cuneo, "New Markets Lure Retailers Wanting Growth," *Advertising Age International,* October 1996, p. 118.
12. T. L. Stanley, "Hollywood Heads East," *Brandweek,* January 29, 1996, p. 37.
13. David Lieberman, "Hollywood Studios Woo Asian Market," *USA Today,* January 22, 1996, p. 37.
14. "Mickey Mao," *The Economist,* August 3, 1996, pp. 32–33.
15. Tara Parker-Pope, "Custom-Made," *Wall Street Journal,* September 26, 1996, p. R22.
16. Raju Marisetti, "Can Rubbermaid Crack Foreign Markets?" *Wall Street Journal,* June 20, 1996, pp. B1, B4.
17. Linda Grant, "Stirring It Up at Campbell," *Fortune,* May 13, 1996, p. 82; and Heath, "Think Globally."
18. Information from the Population Reference Bureau Web site, downloaded from http://www.prb.org/prb/, December 21, 1996.
19. Examples based on Pope, "Custom-Made."
20. G. Pascal Zachary, "Major U.S. Companies Expand Efforts to Sell to Consumers Abroad," *Wall Street Journal,* June 17, 1996, p. A6.
21. Pope, "Custom-Made."
22. Norihiko Shirouzu, "Snapple in Japan: How a Splash Dried Up," *Wall Street Journal,* April 15, 1996, pp. B1, B3.
23. Miriam Jordan, "Marketing Gurus Say: In India, Think Cheap, Lose the Cold Cereal," *Wall Street Journal,* October 11, 1996, p. A7.
24. James Cox, "Great Wal-Mart of China: Red Letter Day as East Meets West in the Aisles," *USA Today,* September 11, 1996, pp. 1B, 2B.

25. *Statistical Abstract of the United States, 1996,* 116th edition (Washington, D.C.: U.S. Bureau of the Census, 1996), p. 830.
26. Michael Laris, "The Price of the Deal," *Newsweek,* December 9, 1996, p. 44.
27. Brian Bremner, "Is Japan Headed for Another Recession?" *Business Week,* December 16, 1996, pp. 48–49.
28. Edward W. Desmond, "The Failed Miracle," *Time,* April 22, 1996, p. 61; and Bremner, "Is Japan Headed for Another Recession?"
29. Gale Eisenstodt, "Toyotas for Asparagus," *Forbes,* July 3, 1995, pp. 76–77.
30. Joan Delaney, "Vive la Difference," *International Business,* May 1996, pp. 42–43.
31. John Pearson and Gail DeGeorge, " 'Cuba Trade' This Hornet's Nest Is Really Buzzing," *Business Week,* November 25, 1996, p. 58; and Adam Zagorin, 'Punishing Cuba's Partners," *Time,* June 24, 1996, p. 54.
32. Mark L. Clifford, "Modern India on Hold," *Business Week,* International edition, April 19, 1996, downloaded from America Online, January 4, 1997.
33. Bob Davis, Peter Gumbel, and David P. Hamilton, "To All U.S. Managers Upset by Regulations: Try Germany or Japan," *Wall Street Journal,* December 14, 1995, pp. A1, A9.
34. Fara Warner, "Tobacco Brands Outmaneuver Asian Ad Bans," *Wall Street Journal,* August 6, 1996, pp. B1, B3.
35. "Tariffs and 'Buy Local' Policies Cited as Hi Tech Companies' Top Barriers to Global Trade in Coopers & Lybrand Study," *Business Wire,* August 12, 1996, downloaded from http://www.businesswire.com/, August 28, 1996; and Linda Radosevich, "Third Wave, Third World," *Forbes ASAP,* December 4, 1995, pp. 64–65.
36. Amy Borrus and Joyce Barnathan, "It's Time to Get China into the WTO," *Business Week,* July 1, 1996, p. 46; and Teri Agins, "Silk Importers Fear Tariff Would Spell Ruin," *Wall Street Journal,* June 5, 1996, p. B1.
37. Helene Cooper and Bhushan Bahree, "Nations Agree to Drop Computer Tariffs," *Wall Street Journal,* December 13, 1996, p. A2.
38. Czinkota and Ronkainen, *International Marketing,* pp. 38–40.
39. Gail DeGeorge and John Pearson, "U.S. Business Isn't Afraid to Shout *Cuba Si!*" *Business Week,* November 5, 1995, p. 39.
40. Bruce Einhorn, "Why the WTO Is Stuck in the Muck," *Business Week,* December 16, 1996, p. 50; and Helene Cooper and Bhushan Bahree, "World's Best Hope for Global Trade Topples Few Barriers," *Wall Street Journal,* December 3, 1996, pp. A1, A14.
41. William C. W. Weinberger, "Mexico Is Having a Substantial Recovery," *Forbes,* December 30, 1996, p. 35; Amy Borrus, "Singing the NAFTA Blues," *Business Week,* December 6, 1966, pp. 54–55; and Bill Cormier, "NAFTA a Good Deal for Many—But Not All," *Mobile Register,* February 25, 1996, p. 18A.
42. Sara Silver, "Driving Jobs North," *San Diego Union-Tribune,* December 3, 1996, pp. C1, C6; Sara Silver, "NAFTA's Impact on Jobs? Nobody Really Knows," *San Diego Union-Tribune,* December 3, 1996, pp. C1, C6; Borrus, "NAFTA Blues;" and Cormier, "NAFTA Good Deal."
43. John Merline, "Protecting Our Way to Growth?" *Investor's Business Daily,* February 29, 1996, downloaded from America Online, December 22, 1996.
44. Merline, "Trade Walls?"
45. Maxine Lans Retsky, "Who Needs the New Community Trademark?" *Marketing News,* June 3, 1996, p. 11.
46. "Marketers Push for a Modernization of European Postal Systems," *Advertising Age International Daily,* November 27, 1996, downloaded from http://adage.com/, January 1, 1997; and Heath, "Think Globally."
47. Heath, "Think Globally."
48. Jeff Jensen, "Nike Deals in U.S., Abroad to Aid Apparel Business," *Advertising Age,* October 14, 1996, p. 8.
49. Evelyn Tan Powers, "New Delhi McDonald's Skips the Beef," *USA Today,* October 14, 1996, p. 2B.
50. Vijai Maheshwari, "All Set to Muscle in on Moscow," *Business Week,* December 16, 1996, pp. 24–25.
51. "Italian Fila Sports Signs Up Nike Manufacturer," *Advertising Age International Daily,* December 31, 1996, downloaded from http://www.adage.com/, January 1, 1997.
52. Kris Oser, "Japan Call Center Promotes U.S. Catalogs," *DM News/Global Direct Marketing,* August 21, 1995, p. 4; and Heath, "Think Globally."
53 Zachary, "Major U.S. Companies Expand Efforts."
54. Andrew Tanzer, "Stepping-Stones to a New China?" *Forbes,* January 27, 1997, pp. 78–82.
55. Greg Steinmetz and Leslie Scism, "Allstate Tries a New Number in Germany," *Wall Street Journal,* November 1, 1996, p. A10.
56. "SyQuest and Legend to Form Joint Venture Company in China," *Business Wire,* September 10, 1996, downloaded from http://businesswire.com/, September 13, 1996.
57. Pete Engardio, "Time for a Reality Check in Asia," *Business Week,* December 2, 1996, pp. 58–66.
58. Karen Lowry Miller, "Piling into Central Europe," *Business Week,* July 1, 1996, pp. 43–44.
59. James Srodes, "U.S. Tops Investment Charts, Coming and Going," *World Trade,* November 1996, p. 10.
60. *Annual Report, 1996,* Procter & Gamble Company, Cincinnati, Ohio; and "The 100 Largest U.S. Multinationals," *Forbes,* July 15, 1996, p. 289.
61. *Annual Report, 1996,* Procter & Gamble, pp. 10–11.
62. Paul R. La Monica, "Battling Batteries," *Financial World,* January 30, 1996, pp. 58–62.
63. Dexter Roberts, "Winding Up for the Big Pitch," *Business Week,* October 23, 1995, p. 52.
64. Douglas Lavin, "Coke in Venture with France's Danone to Distribute Orange Juice Overseas," *Wall Street Journal,* September 25, 1996, downloaded from http://www.wsj.com/, October 3, 1996.
65. Norihiko Shirouzu, "Luxury Prices for U.S. Goods No Longer Pass Muster in Japan," *Wall Street Journal,* February 8, 1996, pp. B1, B10.
66. Janet Aschkenasy, "Give and Take," *International Business,* September 1996, pp. 10–12; and Nigel M. Healey, "What Is Corporate Barter?" *Business Economics,* April 1996, pp. 36–41.
67. "Foreign Investors' Spending to Acquire or Establish U.S. Businesses Continued to Increase in 1995," Press Release, Bureau of Economic Analysis, July 9, 1996; and James

Srodes, "U.S. Tops Investment Charts, Coming and Going," *World Trade,* November 1996, p. 10.

68. Gustavo Lombo, "The Land of Opportunity," *Forbes,* July 15, 1996, p. 292; and "The 100 Largest Foreign Investments in the U.S.," *Forbes,* July 15, 1996, pp. 293–300.
69. "Shiseido Is Seeking to Acquire Its Fourth Factory in the U.S.," *Wall Street Journal,* December 3, 1996, p. B11.
70. Kim Clark, "A Bigger, Richer World," *Fortune,* August 5, 1996, pp. 104, 108.

CHAPTER 5

1. Steve Lohr, "Competition Intensifies for Athletic Sites on Internet," *New York Times,* June 26, 1996; Steven Henry Madoff, "Art in Cyberspace: Can It Live without a Body?" *New York Times,* January 21, 1996; John Markoff, "Nintendo's New Video Game Faces Internet Challenge," *New York Times,* May 16, 1996; and Mathew S. Scott, "Entertainment in Cyberspace," *Black Enterprise,* December 1995, pp. 66–72.
2. Jean Halliday, "GM Looking to Woo Developing Clout of Females," *Advertising Age,* June 17, 1996, p. 39.
3. John A. Byrne, "Strategic Planning," *Business Week,* August 26, 1996, pp. 46–52.
4. Ira Sager, "It's Hot! It's Sexy! It's . . . Big Blue?" *Business Week,* March 4, 1996, p. 39; Ira Sager, "Serious Fun from IBM," *Business Week,* June 17, 1996, pp. 34–35; and Bradley Johnson, "IBM Taps $45 Mil for ThinkPad," *Advertising Age,* March 16, 1996, pp. 1, 42.
5. Richard Gibson, "McDonald's Franchisees Approve Cuts in Some Sandwich Prices to 55 Cents," *Wall Street Journal,* March 3, 1997, p. B4.
6. John Case, "Corporate Culture," *Inc.,* November 1996, downloaded from America Online, January 20, 1997.
7. Byrne, "Strategic Planning," p. 50.
8. *Annual Report, 1995,* Chevron Corporation, p. 6.
9. Jared Sandberg and Bart Ziegler, "Internet's Popularity Threatens to Swamp the On-Line Services," *Wall Street Journal,* January 18, 1996, pp. A1, A6.
10. Paul M. Eng, "War of the Web," *Business Week,* March 4, 1996, pp. 71–72.
11. Case, "Corporate Culture."
12. Robert Berner, "Sears Bucks Trend with 25% Gain in Profit and 11% Increase in Sales," *Wall Street Journal,* January 24, 1997, p. B4; and Byrne, "Strategic Planning," p. 49.
13. Byrne, "Strategic Planning," p. 49.
14. Amy Barrett, Paul Eng, and Kathy Rebello, "For $19.95 a Month, Unlimited Headaches for AOL," *Business Week,* January 27, 1997, p. 35; and Stewart Alsop, "A Few Kind Words for America Online," *Fortune,* March 17, 1997, p. 159.
15. "Ameritech, AT&T Call Up Ads for Net Access Services; AOL Problems Create Window of Opportunity," *Advertising Age,* January 20, 1997, p. 32; and Janet Kornblum, "AOL Cries Uncle to Attorney General," *CNET* News.Com, January 29, 1997, downloaded from http://www.news.com/, January 29, 1997.
16. Derek F. Abell, "Strategic Windows," *Journal of Marketing,* July 1978, pp. 21–26; see also John K. Ryans Jr. and William L. Shanklin, *Strategic Planning: Concepts and Implementation* (New York: Random House, 1985), p. 11.
17. *Annual Report, 1996,* Microsoft Corporation, p. 3; and Kathy Rebello, "Bill's Quiet Shopping Spree," *Business Week,* January 13, 1997, pp. 34–35.
18. Bob Francis and Justin Hibbard, "Compaq Shuffles Divisions to Shift Focus beyond PCs," *Computerworld,* July 8, 1996, p. 8.
19. Evan Ramstad, "TI Agrees to Sell Notebook Line to Acer Group," *Wall Street Journal,* January 24, 1997, p. B14.
20. David J. Collis and Cynthia A. Montgomery, "Competing on Resources: Strategy in the 1990s," *Harvard Business Review,* July/August 1995, p. 125.
21. A meta-analysis of 48 studies revealed a positive relationship between market share and profitability. See David M. Szymanski, Sundar G. Bharadqaj, and P. Rajan Varadarajan, "An Analysis of the Market Share-Profitability Relationship," *Journal of Marketing,* July 1993, pp. 1–18.
22. Collis and Montgomery, "Competing on Resources," p. 126.
23. Lori Bongiorno, "These Brands Aren't Smoking," *Business Week,* January 20, 1997, p. 34.
24. *Annual Report, 1994,* and *Annual Report, 1995,* Quaker Oats Company.

CHAPTER 6

1. Cynthia L. Webb, "When Republicans Arrive He'll Squeeze 'Em In," *San Diego Union-Tribune,* July 15, 1996, p. B1; James Curtis, "Virtual Virtues," *Marketing,* July 11, 1996, p. 28; Tom Dellecave Jr., "Curing Market Research Headaches," *Sales & Marketing Management,* July 1996, pp. 84–85; Raymond R. Burke, "Virtual Shopping: Breakthrough in Marketing Research," *Harvard Business Review,* March/April 1996, pp. 120–131; and Bruce V. Bigelow, "Show & Tell, Virtual Reality Gave GOP Panel Quite a View," *San Diego Union-Tribune,* January 15, 1995, p. 11.
2. Gilbert A. Churchill Jr., *Basic Marketing Research,* 3rd ed. (Fort Worth, Tex.: The Dryden Press, 1996), p. 16.
3. "Top 50 U.S. Research Organizations," *Marketing News 1996 Business Report on the Marketing Research Industry,* June 3, 1996, p. H4.
4. Jeffrey D. Swaddling and Mark W. Zobel, "Beating the Odds," *Marketing Management,* winter/spring 1996, p. 21.
5. Tim Triplett, "Carmakers Driven by Quest to Find Tomorrow's Color," *Marketing News,* August 28, 1995, p. 38.
6. "Two Decades On, Scanners Are Still Under-Used," *PROMO/Progressive Grocer Special Report,* July 1994, p. S4.
7. Swaddling and Zobel, "Beating the Odds."
8. Eli Seggev, "A Role in Flux," *Marketing Management,* winter 1995, p. 35.
9. Chad Rubel, "Research Results Must Justify Brand Spending," *Marketing News,* February 26, 1996, p. 12.
10. Ibid.
11. Marcia Mogelonsky, "Out to Launch," *Marketing Tools,* September 1996, downloaded from http://www.marketingtools.com/ on October 8, 1996.
12. Terrance V. O'Brien, Denise D. Schoenbachler, and Geoffrey L. Gordon, "Marketing Information Systems for Consumer Products Companies: A Management Overview," *Journal of Consumer Marketing* 12, no. 5 (1995), pp. 16–36.
13. Rubel, "Research Results."
14. Mogelonsky, "Out to Launch."

15. Haya El Nasser, "Census Will Count on Pricey, Slick Advertising," *USA Today,* January 3, 1997, p. 3A.
16. "Scanners Still Under-Used."
17. Robert Frank, "Conflicting Market Data on Coca-Cola and PepsiCo Roil Beverage Industry," *Wall Street Journal,* January 4, 1996, p. B5.
18. Joe Mullich, "Streamlining Online Info," *Advertising Age,* December 11, 1995, p. 12.
19. Claudia Montague, "Researching Researchers," *Marketing Tools,* September 1996, downloaded from http://www.marketingtools.com/, October 8, 1996.
20. Phaedra Hise, "Getting Smart On-Line," *Inc. Technology,* March 19, 1996, pp. 59–65.
21. Elizabeth Jensen, "Networks Blast Nielsen, Blame Faulty Ratings for Drop in Viewership," *Wall Street Journal,* November 22, 1996, p. A1.
22. Leah Ricard, "Helping Put Data in Focus," *Advertising Age,* July 11, 1994, p. 18.
23. Justin Martin, "Ignore Your Customer," *Fortune,* May 1, 1995, p. 126.
24. Chad Rubel, "Two Research Techniques Probe Shoppers' Minds," *Marketing News,* July 29, 1996, p. 16.
25. Bart Ziegler, "Old Market Research Tricks No Match for Technology," *Wall Street Journal,* November 1, 1994, p. B1.
26. Bruce G. Posner, "The Future of Marketing Is Looking at You," *Fast Company,* October/November, 1996, p. 105.
27. Norton Paley, "Getting in Focus," *Sales & Marketing Management,* March 1995, pp. 92–95.
28. Leslie M. Harris, "Expanding Horizons," *Marketing Research,* summer 1996, p. 12.
29. Mogelonsky, "Out to Launch."
30. Betsy Spethmann, "AOL, M/A/R/C, 10 Marketers Test Research via Internet," *Brandweek,* March 4, 1996, p. 9.
31. Judy Strauss, "Early Survey Research on the Internet: Review, Illustration, and Evaluation," presentation at Winter Educator's Conference, American Marketing Association, February 3–6, 1996, Hilton Head, South Carolina.
32. Ibid.
33. Margaret R. Roller, "Virtual Research Exists, But How Real Is It?" *Marketing News, 1996 Business Report on the Marketing Research Industry,* June 3, 1996, p. H32.
34. Strauss, "Early Survey Research."
35. John Peebles, "On-Line Technology Creates Research Tools," *Marketing News,* March 11, 1996, p. 5.
36. Debra Aho Williamson, "Web Searching for a Yardstick," *Advertising Age,* October 9, 1995, p. 21.
37. Michael R. Czinkota and Ilkka A. Ronkainen, "Market Research for Your Export Operations," *International Trade Forum* (1995), pp. 16–21.
38. Angela R. D'Auria, Earl D. Honeycutt Jr., and Wilbur W. Stanton, "A Guide for Improving Global Marketing Research," *Proceedings of the Annual Meeting of the Southern Marketing Association,* November 8–11, 1995, pp. 404–407.
39. Czinkota and Ronkainen, "Research for Export."
40. Ibid.
41. D'Auria, Honeycutt, and Stanton, "Guide for Improving."
42. O'Brien, Schoenbachler, and Gordon, "Marketing Information Systems."
43. "Famous AMOS: Cutting-Edge Promotion Selection System Helps Direct Marketer Cut Costs and Boost Profits," *Stores,* January 1996, pp. RR5–RR6.
44. Janet Novack, "The Data-Miners," *Forbes,* February 12, 1996, pp. 96–97.
45. Ibid.
46. Rose Aguilar, "Is the Net Worth It?"*CNET* September 9, 1996, downloaded from http:/www.news.com/, October 26, 1996 and Cybercitizens Study, Yankelovich Partners Web site, http://www.yankelovich.com/ downloaded on October 24, 1996.

CHAPTER 7

1. "Exploring the World Wide Web Population's Other Half," *SRI International World Wide Web Report on the Psychographics of Internet Users,* http://www.sri.com/, downloaded September 24, 1996; Margaret Mannix, Amy Berstein, and Mary Kathleen Flynn, "Welcome, Women!" *U.S. News & World Report,* July 1, 1996, pp. 58–60; "Increasing Diversity Is Detected among Web Clients," *San Diego Union-Tribune's ComputerLink,* June 16, 1996, p. 9; Hillary Rosner, "Trapping Students in the Web," *Brandweek,* April 15, 1996, p. 50; Jane Hodges, "It's Becoming a Small World Wide Web after All," *Advertising Age,* February 12, 1996, p. 26; and Cyndee Miller, "Targeting the Wired," *Marketing News,* October 23, 1995, p. 1.
2. This story is told in Richard S. Tedlown, *New and Improved: The Story of Mass Marketing in America* (New York: Basic Books, 1990), and elsewhere.
3. Pam Weisz, "The New Boom Is Colored Gray," *Brandweek,* January 22, 1996, p. 28.
4. "Publishers Tap Latino Market," *San Diego Union-Tribune,* June 23, 1996, p. B-1.
5. Catherine Dressler, "Holy Socks! This Line Sends a Christian Message," *Marketing News,* February 12, 1996, p. 5.
6. Zachary Schiller, "Make It Simple," *Business Week,* September 9, 1996, p. 96.
7. Haya El Nasser, "Immigration to Level Population Boom in West," *USA Today,* October 23, 1996, p. 7A; Diane Crispell, "The Hottest Metros," *American Demographics Marketing Power Supplement,* June 1996, pp. 14–16.
8. U.S. Bureau of the Census, International Data Base, 1995.
9. Kristian Helse, Kamel Jedidi, and Wayne S. DeSarbo, "A New Approach to County Segmentation Utilizing Multinational Diffusion Patterns," *Journal of Marketing,* October 1993, p. 60.
10. Crispell, "Hottest Metros."
11. Ibid.
12. David Greissing and Kate Murphy, "The Boomies Are Booming," *Business Week,* October 9, 1995, p. 104.
13. Erwin Ephron, "The Best Way to Target," *Advertising Age,* September 1994, p. T-3.
14. Bruce Horovitz, "Coke Aims to Reverse Cool Trend in Southern California," *USA Today,* March 5, 1996, p. B1.
15. Kasumi Tanaka, "Putting Your Business on the Map," *Inc., Technology Supplement No. 2* (1996), pp. 94–99.
16. Michael Garry, "GIS: Finding Opportunity in Data," *Progressive Grocer,* June 1996, pp. 61–69.

17. Tony Seidman, "You Gotta Know the Territory," *Profit,* November/December 1994, pp. 21–24.
18. Michele Meyer, "No Sex and Violence," *U.S. News & World Report,* March 18, 1996, p. 69.
19. Maria Mallory, Dan McGraw, and Jill Jordan Dieder, "Women on a Fast Track," *U.S. News & World Report,* November 6, 1995, p. 60.
20. Faye Rice, "Making Generational Marketing Come of Age," *Fortune,* June 26, 1995, pp. 110–114.
21. Cyndee Miller, "Liz Claiborne Throws a Curve with New Brand for Gen Xers," *Marketing News,* July 1, 1996, p. 1.
22. Richard Thau, "So-Called Generation X: How Do You Target a Market That Wants to Be Left Alone?" *Vital Speeches of the Day,* August 15, 1996, pp. 647–667.
23. Ibid.
24. Monika Guttman, "Facing the Facts of Life," *U.S. News & World Report,* April 22, 1996, p. 57.
25. Bradley Inman, "As Usual, Boomers Aren't Behaving as They Should," *San Diego Union-Tribune,* September 29, 1996, p. H-9.
26. Tanya Wenman Steel, "As Boomers Age, Wrinkle-Reducing Products Come of Age," *San Diego Union-Tribune,* September 5, 1996, p. E-3.
27. Pam Weisz, "The New Boom Is Colored Gray," *Brandweek,* January 22, 1996, p. 28.
28. Ibid.
29. Carolyn Shea, "The New Face of America," *PROMO,* January 1996, pp. 53–60.
30. Cliff Edwards, "Study Says Blacks Spend More on Big-Ticket Items than Whites," *Marketing News,* September 23, 1996, p. 27; and "Ethnic Profiles," *Brandweek,* July 17, 1995, p. 28.
31. "Face of the Nation," *U.S. News & World Report,* October 21, 1996, p. 30; and "Ethnic Profiles," *Brandweek,* July 17, 1995, p. 28.
32. Melissa Campanelli, "Asian Studies," *Sales & Marketing Management,* March 1995, p. 51; and "Ethnic Profiles," *Brandweek,* July 17, 1995, p. 28.
33. Fleming Marks, "Catering to Indulgent Parents," *Forbes,* October 23, 1995, p. 148.
34. *Information Please World Almanac and Atlas* (Boston: Houghton Mifflin, 1996), p. 432.
35. Leonard Lewis, "Catering to the Carriage Trade," *Frozen Food Age,* July 1996, pp. 53–55.
36. Ginger Conlon, "Where the Money Is," *Sales & Marketing Management,* August 1996, p. 90.
37. Rice, "Generational Marketing."
38. Judith Waldrop, "Markets with Attitude," *American Demographics,* July 1994, p. 22.
39. Rebecca Piirto Heath, "Psychographics: Q'est-ce-que C'est?" *American Demographics, Marketing Tools Supplement,* November/December 1995, pp. 74–79.
40. Information on the Japan VALS Segmentation System for SRI's Web Site, http://www.future.sri.com/, downloaded September 25, 1996.
41. Allana Sullivan, "Mobil Bets Drivers Pick Cappuccino over Low Prices," *Wall Street Journal,* January 30, 1995, p. B1.
42. Karen Blumenthal, "Compaq Is Segmenting Home-Computer Market," *Wall Street Journal,* July 16, 1996, p. A3.
43. Heath, "Psychographics: Q'est-ce-que C'est?"
44. "Know Your Best Customers," *Success,* December 1995, p. 25.
45. These segmentation techniques are suggested in Michael D. Hutt and Thomas W. Speh, *Business Marketing Management* (Fort Worth, Tex.: The Dryden Press, 1998), pp. 164–166.
46. William R. Swinyard, "The Hard Core and Zen Riders of Harley Davidson: A Market-Driven Segmentation Analysis," *Journal of Targeting, Measurement, and Analysis for Marketing,* June 1996, p. 338.
47. Fisher, "The Elusive American Grandparent."
48. Jerry Flint, "The Magazine Factory," *Forbes,* May 22, 1995, pp. 160–161.
49. Christopher Caggino, "A Brew Apart," *Inc.,* March 1996, pp. 62–69.
50. Richard L. Papiernik, "Where's the Beef? At McDonald's, Latest Data Hard to Come By," *Nation's Restaurant News,* August 12, 1996, p. 11.
51. Miller, "Liz Claiborne."
52. Joyce M. Rosenberg, "Cosmetics Line Designed for Asian Women," *Marketing News,* October 21, 1996, p. 15; "Face Value," *Entrepreneur,* May 1996, p. 220.
53. Alex Taylor III, "Speed! Power! Status!" *Fortune,* June 10, 1996, pp. 46–50.
54. Fisher, "Elusive Grandparent."
55. Kelly Shermach, "Niche Malls: Innovation for Industry in Decline," *Marketing News,* February 26, 1996, pp. 1, 2.

CHAPTER 8

1. Based on "Cybercitizen, A Profile of Online Users," Yankelovich Partners' Web page, http://www.yankelovich.com/cyber, downloaded August 22, 1996; "Cybercitizen II," http://www.yankelovich.com/cyber_ii, downloaded September 25, 1996; and Randall Rothenberg, "Life in Cyburbia," *Esquire,* February 1996, pp. 56–63.
2. Lynn Woods, "Women's Travel Challenge," *USA Today,* May 7, 1996, p. 4E.
3. Kathleen A. Hughes, "Kids, Cabins, and Free Time Say Status in Understated '90s," *Wall Street Journal,* September 30, 1996, pp. B1, B16.
4. Ellen Graham, "How to Sell More to Those Who Think It's Cool to Be Frugal," *Wall Street Journal,* September 30, 1996, pp. B1, B15.
5. Marcia Berss, "Whirlpool's Bloody Nose," *Forbes,* March 11, 1996, p. 90.
6. Leah Rickard, "Ex-Soviet States Lead World in Ad Cynicism," *Advertising Age,* June 5, 1995, p. 3.
7. "Face the Nation," *U.S. News & World Report,* October 21, 1996, p. 30; Carolyn Shea, "The New Face of America," *PROMO,* January 1996, pp. 55, 57.
8. Jack Schmid, "Ethnic Niche Catalogs," *Target Marketing,* November 1995, pp. 18–20.
9. Ronald E. Goldsmith, "A Study of Black/White Consumption Differences," *Developments in Marketing Science* 18 (1995), pp. 70–74.
10. "Ethnicity-Based Differences in Coupon Use: Anglo-Americans vs. African-Americans," *Stores,* January 1996, p. RR7.
11. James F. Engel, Roger D. Blackwell, and Paul W. Miniard, *Consumer Behavior,* 8th ed. (Fort Worth, Tex.: The Dryden Press, 1995), pp. 651–657.

12. Katherine Morrall, "Appealing to the African-American Market," *Bank Marketing,* May 1996, pp. 18–21.
13. Elaine Santoro, "Direct Mail Is Top Media to Reach African Americans," *Direct Marketing,* December 1995, p. 10.
14. Morrall, "Appealing to the African-American Market."
15. Ibid.
16. Shea, "New Face," p. 57.
17. Ibid.
18. Sydney Roslow and J. A. F. Nicholls, "Hispanic Mall Customers Outshop Non-Hispanics," *Marketing News,* May 6, 1996, p. 14.
19. Isabel M. Valdes and Marta H. Seoane, "Hispanic Buying Power," *American Demographics,* Marketing Power Supplement, October 1995, p. 10.
20. "Face the Nation"; and Yumiko Ono, "Kraft Hopes Hispanic Market Says Cheese," *Wall Street Journal,* December 13, 1995, p. B1.
21. Ali Kara and R. Natasha, "Ethnicity and Consumer Choice: A Study of Hispanic Decision Processes across Different Acculturation Levels," *Journal of Applied Business Research,* spring 1996, pp. 22–34.
22. Mark Hamstra, "Que Bueno! Chains Learn the Lucrative Language of Courting Hispanic Consumers," *Nation's Restaurant News,* July 15, 1996, pp. 67–72.
23. Shea, "New Face," p. 59.
24. Ibid., p. 60.
25. John Steere, "How Asian-Americans Make Purchase Decisions," *Marketing News,* March 13, 1995, p. 9.
26. Ibid.
27. Ibid.
28. Henry Assael, *Consumer Behavior and Marketing Action* (Boston: Southwest-ITP, 1995), p. 416.
29. David Leonhardt, "Grabbing Bargains and a $2 Cup of Coffee," *Business Week,* March 17, 1997, p. 90; and Engel, Blackwell, and Miniard, *Consumer Behavior,* pp. 682–683, 706–707.
30. Bradley Johnson, "Widening the Sanctum of Advice-Givers," *Advertising Age,* November 13, 1995, pp. S-1, S-6.
31. Sonia Reyes, "Jackie O Jewelry Inspires New Fashion Collections," *San Diego Union-Tribune,* September 5, 1996, p. E-5.
32. Engel, Blackwell, and Miniard, *Consumer Behavior,* pp. 747–750.
33. "Consumers Adapting to Pressures of Time," *Marketing News,* July 1, 1996, p. 2.
34. Kelly Barron, "A Gift for the Child Who Does Everything," *Record-Bergen County,* June 6, 1996, p. SL3.
35. Carolyn Shea, "Tough Customers," *PROMO,* December 1995, p. 49.
36. "Kids Market Keeps Growing," *Advertising Age,* May 15, 1995, p. 3; and Shea, "Tough Customers," p. 50.
37. David Fischer, "Let the Good Times Roll," *U.S. News & World Report,* July 1, 1996, pp. 51–52.
38. Tim Ferguson and Josephine Lee, "Coin of the New Age," *Forbes,* September 9, 1996, p. 86.
39. Mary Kuntz and Joseph Weber, "The New Hucksterism," *Business Week,* July 1, 1996, pp. 76–84.
40. Ibid.
41. Bruce Horovitz, Melanie Wells, and Dottie Enrico, "Super Bowl Marketers Win with Witty Ads," *USA Today,* January 30, 1996, pp. 1B, 2B.
42. "Impact in the Aisles," *PROMO,* January 1996, p. 26.
43. Andy Cohen, "Introducing the Virtual Sales Call," *Sales & Marketing Management,* May 1996, pp. 44.
44. Ian P. Murphy, "Cruise Lines Float Hopes on First-Time Customers," *Marketing News,* January 1, 1996, p. 2.
45. Chad Rubel, "Uphill Battle for Marketer of Shelf-Stable Milk," *Advertising Age,* May 20, 1996, p. 19.
46. This section is based on Michael L. Rothschild and William C. Gaidis, "Behavioral Learning Theory: Its Relevance to Marketing and Promotions," *Journal of Marketing,* spring 1981, pp. 70–78.
47. Engel, Blackwell, and Miniard, *Consumer Behavior,* pp. 215–216.
48. Claudia Coates, "For Buyers, It's a Matter of Choice (and Choice and . . .)," *Mobile Register,* April 28, 1996, p. 6-F.
49. These categories were originally suggested in John A. Howard, *Marketing Management: Analysis and Planning* (Homewood, Ill.: Richard D. Irwin, 1963). This discussion is based on Donald R. Lehmann, William L. Moore, and Terry Elrod, "The Development of Distinct Choice Process Segments over Time: A Stochastic Modeling Approach," *Journal of Marketing,* spring 1982, pp. 48–50.

CHAPTER 9

1. Industry.Net Web site, http://www.industry.net/, information downloaded October 10, 1996; Raju Narisett, "Industry.net Customers to Be Offered On-Line Payment Services from PNC," *Wall Street Journal,* September 25, 1996, p. B10; based on "AT&T Business Network and Nets Inc. Launch Two New Marketing Services," *Business Wire,* July 22, 1996, downloaded from http://www.businesswire.com/, July 29, 1996; "AT&T's New Media Services Unit Will Merge with Industry.Net to Form New Business-to-Business Internet Company: Nets Inc.," *Business Wire,* June 24, 1996, downloaded from http://www.businesswire.com/, June 28, 1996; and John W. Verity, "Invoice? What's an Invoice?" *Business Week,* June 10, 1996, pp. 110–111.
2. Shawn Tully, "Purchasing's New Muscle," *Fortune,* February 20, 1995, p. 75.
3. Frederick E. Webster Jr. and Yoram Wind, "A General Model for Understanding Organizational Buying Behavior," *Marketing Management,* winter/spring 1996, pp. 52–57.
4. Andy Cohen, "Global Do's and Don'ts," *Sales & Marketing Management,* June 1996, p. 72.
5. Michael D. Hutt and Thomas W. Speh, *Business Marketing Management* (Fort Worth, Tex.: The Dryden Press, 1998), pp. 164–166.
6. I. Jeanne Dugan, "'Small Business Is Big Business,'" *Business Week,* September 30, 1996, p. 117.
7. Sam Zuckerman, "Mom and Pop, You Are Prequalified!" *Business Week,* April 15, 1996, pp. 98–99.
8. Hutt and Speh, *Business Marketing Management,* pp. 136–139.
9. Ibid., pp. 34–35, 166–167.
10. Marsha W. Johnston, "Buy Global, Skip Local," *CIO,* April 1996, p. 30.
11. John A. Byrne, "Has Outsourcing Gone Too Far?" *Business Week,* April 1, 1996, pp. 26–28.
12. "The Power of Purchasing," *Inbound Logistics,* May 1996, p. 26.

13. Johnston, "Buy Global."
14. Walter Hamilton, "No Safe Harbors for Wary Tech Investors," *Investor's Business Daily,* March 29, 1996, downloaded from America Online, July 6, 1996.
15. Laurie Joan Aron, "The New Age in Purchasing," *Inbound Logistics,* May 1996, pp. 28–31.
16. Drew Winter, "Suppliers on Board," *Ward's Auto World,* July 1996, pp. 63-66.
17. Scott McCartney, "America West Has Turned Nighttime into Flight Time," *Wall Street Journal,* January 16, 1996, p. B4.
18. Jeffrey Young, "The Outsourcer," *Forbes,* November 6, 1995, pp. 344–346.
19. Unless otherwise noted, sources for this section are Ira Sager, "Outsourcing the Outsourcing," *Business Week,* March 10, 1997, downloaded from America Online, March 19, 1997; John A. Byrne, "Has Outsourcing Gone Too Far?" *Business Week,* April 1, 1996, pp. 26–28; Sana Siwilop, "Outsourcing: Savings Are Just the Start," *Business Week,* May 13, 1996, pp. ENT 24–25; and John W. Verity, "Let's Order Out for Technology," *Business Week,* May 13, 1996, p. 47.
20. Rebecca Blumenstein and Gabriella Stern, "GM's Parts Purchases Fuel Labor Strife," *Wall Street Journal,* October 11, 1996, p. A2; and Paul A. Eisenstein, "Detroit's Efficiency Push," *Investor's Business Daily,* August 6, 1996, downloaded from America Online, September 19, 1996.
21. Eisenstein, "Detroit's Efficiency Push."
22. "Power of Purchasing," p. 21.
23. Hutt and Speh, *Business Marketing Management,* pp. 102–103.
24. Tully, "Purchasing's New Muscle," p. 82.
25. Johnston, "Buy Global," p. 38; "Marketing Briefs," *Marketing Management,* winter/spring 1996, p. 43.
26. Verity, "Let's Order Out."
27. Verity, "What's an Invoice?"
28. Jim Carbone, "Web Tool Cuts Search Time for Buyers," *Purchasing,* July 11, 1996, p. 117.
29. Hutt and Speh, *Business Marketing Management,* pp. 70–71.
30. Verity, "What's an Invoice?"
31. Fred R. Bleakley, "When Corporate Purchasing Goes Plastic," *Wall Street Journal,* June 14, 1995, p. B1.
32. Tully, "Purchasing's New Muscle," p. 79.
33. Bleakley, "When Corporate Purchasing."
34. Tim Smart, "E-Sourcing: 'A Cheaper Way of Doing Business,'" *Business Week,* August 5, 1996, pp. 82–83.
35. Hutt and Speh, *Business Marketing Management,* pp. 104–105.
36. Ibid., pp. 110–111.
37. J. Dana Clark, Catherine H. Price, and Suzanne K. Murrmann, "Buying Centers: Who Chooses Convention Sites?" *Cornell Hotel & Restaurant Administration Quarterly,* August 1996, pp. 72–76.
38. Webster and Wind, "General Model."
39. Tim Grace, "Getting into the Team Selling Spirit," *Computer Reseller News, Distributor Census Supplement,* October 30, 1995, pp. 37–38.
40. Winter, "Suppliers on Board."
41. Andy Cohen, "Small World, Big Challenge," *Sales & Marketing Management,* June 1996, p. 72.
42. Lisa Sanders, "Uncle Sam's PC Shopping Binge," *Business Week,* October 28, 1996, p. 8.
43. Karen D. Schwartz, "Message to Federal Resellers: Get Wired," *Computer Reseller News,* August 19, 1996, p. GR2A.
44. Based on information from the ECRC Web site, http://www.ecrc.ctc.com/, downloaded October 28, 1996.
45. John Verity, "Revolution in the Supply Closet," *Business Week,* June 10, 1996, p. 112.
46. Pete Engardio, "Global Tremors from an Unruly Giant," *Business Week,* March 4, 1996, pp. 60–61.
47. Hutt and Speh, *Business Marketing Management,* pp. 11–13.

CHAPTER 10

1. "Exploring New Research Opportunities via On-Line Shopping," presentation by Tim Dorgan, president of Peapod Interactive, American Marketing Association (AMA) Attitude and Behavior Conference, January 1996, text downloaded from AMA Web site (http://www.ama.org/gem/dorgan.htm/) on June 26, 1996; "Introduction to Peapod," "Kids," and "Mom" Quicktime videos downloaded from Peapod Web site (http://www.peapod.com/) on June 15 and 26, 1996; "Peapod Interactive Grocery Shopping and Delivery Service Expands to Columbus with Kroger," press release, Reuters News Service, June 10, 1996; and B. Joseph Pine II, Don Peppers, and Martha Rogers, "Do You Want to Keep Your Customers Forever?" *Harvard Business Review,* March/April 1995, p. 109.
2. Leon L. Berry, "Relationship Marketing of Services—Growing Interest, Emerging Perspectives," *Journal of the Academy of Marketing Science,* fall 1995, p. 238.
3. Jonathan R. Copulsky and Michael J. Wolf, "Relationship Marketing: Positioning for the Future," *Journal of Business Strategy,* July/August 1990, pp. 16–20.
4. Joseph P. Cannon and Jagdish N. Sheth, "Developing a Curriculum to Enhance Teaching of Relationship Marketing," *Journal of Marketing Education,* summer 1994, p. 5.
5. Pine, Peppers, and Rogers, "Do You Want to Keep Your Customers Forever?" p. 105.
6. Martin Christopher, Adrian Payne, and David Ballantyne, *Relationship Marketing* (Oxford: Butterworth-Heinemann, 1993), p. 4.
7. "Real Money," *MediaWeek,* March 4, 1996, pp. 34–35; Raymond Serafin and Julie Ralston, "Jeep Sets up Camp to Help Build Stronger Bonds with Owners," *Advertising Age,* June 26, 1995, p. 40.
8. Stan Rapp and Thomas L. Collins, "The New Marketing: Sell and Socialize," *New York Times,* February 20, 1994, Sec. 3, p. 11.
9. Mary Jo Bitner, "Building Service Relationships: It's All about Promises," *Journal of the Academy of Marketing Science,* fall 1995, pp. 246–251.
10. Agnes Roletti, "Were Employees at Fair Friendly? They're Graded by 'Mystery Shoppers,' " *San Diego Union-Tribune,* July 2, 1996, p. B-3.
11. Bitner, "Building Service Relationships," p. 248.
12. Michael B. Callaghan, Janelle McPhail, and Oliver H. M. Yau, "Dimensions of a Relationship Marketing Orientation,"

paper delivered at the Seventh Biannual World Marketing Congress, Melbourne, Australia, July 1995.

13. Robert M. Morgan and Shelby D. Hunt, "The Commitment-Trust Theory of Relationship Marketing," *Journal of Marketing,* July 1994, pp. 20–38; and Gerrald Macintosh, Kenneth A. Anglin, David M. Szymanski, and James W. Gentry, "Relationship Development in Selling: A Cognitive Analysis," *Journal of Personal Selling and Sales Management,* fall 1992, pp. 23–34.

14. Berry, "Relationship Marketing Services," p. 240.

15. Ibid., pp. 238–240.

16. Pine, Peppers, and Rogers, "Do You Want to Keep Your Customers Forever?" p. 107.

17. See Robert A. Peterson, "Relationship Marketing and the Consumer," *Journal of the Academy of Marketing Science,* fall 1995, pp. 278–281; and Jagdish N. Sheth and Atul Parvatiyar, "Relationship Marketing in Consumer Markets: Antecedents and Consequences," *Journal of the Academy of Marketing Science,* fall 1995, pp. 255–271.

18. Sheth and Parvatiyar, "Relationship Marketing in Consumer Markets."

19. Donna Rosato, "Unhappy News Travels Fast," *USA Today,* May 21, 1996, p. 10B.

20. Uri Berliner, "Innovative Credit-Card Fashions Take Hold," *San Diego Union-Tribune,* June 18, 1996, p. A1.

21. Alice C. Cuneo, "Savvy Frequent Buyer Plans Build on a Loyal Base," *Advertising Age,* March 20, 1995, p. S-10.

22. "Nordstrom Issues a Visa with Dividends," *Colloquy* 5, no. 2 (1995), p. 14.

23. Thomas Jaffe, "The Corn Is Green," *Forbes,* December 4, 1995, p. 92.

24. B. G. Yovovich, "High Tech Tools Build New Concept of 'Market,'" *Advertising Age,* October 23, 1995, p. 29.

25. Jagdish N. Sheth and Rajendra S. Sisodia, "Feeling the Heat—Part 2," *Marketing Management,* winter 1995, pp. 19–33.

26. Charles Siler, "For Consumers, Loyalty Is in the Cards," *Advertising Age,* October 16, 1995, pp. 1–10.

27. John Uppgren, "Internet Is Key to Successful Database Marketing," *Brandweek,* November 20, 1995, p. 17.

28. Peter L. Brooks, "The Sweet Smell of Access," *Webmaster,* March/April 1996, pp. 28–32; Metropolitan Museum of Art Web page (http://www.metmuseum.org/), downloaded July 2, 1996.

29. Peterson, "Relationship Marketing," p. 278.

30. P. Rajan Varadarajan and Margaret H. Cunningham, "Strategic Alliances: A Synthesis of Conceptual Foundations," *Journal of the Academy of Marketing Science,* fall 1995, pp. 282–296.

31. David T. Wilson, "An Integrated Model of Buyer-Seller Relationships," *Journal of the Academy of Marketing Science,* fall 1995, pp. 335–345.

32. Don Clark, "Microsoft, Casio Agree to Co-Develop Electronic Devices Linked to Windows," *Wall Street Journal,* April 25, 1996, p. B2.

33. Karen Benezra, "Marketers of the Year: Restaurants—Nancy Schneid," *Superbrands '96,* October 9, 1995, pp. 100–101.

34. Blair R. Fischer, "The Reel World: The Action Begins with Film and Video Tie-Ins," *PROMO,* August 1995, p. 43.

35. Stewart Ugelow, "Movie Tie-In's Impossible Mission: Find the Sponsor's Name on Screen," *Wall Street Journal,* July 1, 1996, p. B1.

36. Karen Benezra, "Hunchback Rings Up $150M Support," *Brandweek,* February 5, 1996, p. 4; and Richard Gibson and Thomas R. King, "Burger King Savors 'Toy Story' Tie-In, but McDonald's Plots Unhappy Ending," *Wall Street Journal,* December 7, 1995, p. B1.

37. "Nestlé Teams with NBA, Again," *PROMO,* December 1995, p. 14.

38. "Breyer's to Mix It Up," *Brandweek,* February 19, 1996, p. 15.

39. "The GM Card Leads the Pack," *Colloquy* 5, no. 2 (1995), p. 10.

40. John W. Verity, "Invoice? What's an Invoice?" *Business Week,* June 10, 1996, pp. 110–111.

41. Ibid.

42. Ibid.; and "Small Relief," *Webmaster,* March/April 1996, p. 16.

43. Martin Everett, "Know Why They Buy," *Sales & Marketing Management,* December 1994, pp. 70–71.

44. Joseph Weber, "Just Get It to the Stores on Time," *Business Week,* March 6, 1995, pp. 66–67.

45. Verity, "Invoice?"

46. Verity, "Invoice?"

47. "EDI Implementation Guide," Revision 004, February 20, 1996; downloaded from Premenos Web page (http://www.premenos.com/standards/staples/) on June 30, 1996.

48. Sandra J. Skrovan, "Partnering with Vendors: The Ties That Bind," *Chain Store Age Executive,* January 1994, p. 7MH.

49. Catherine Arnst, "The Networked Corporation," *Business Week,* June 26, 1995, pp. 86–89.

50. Weber, "Get It to the Stores."

51. P. Rajan Varadarajan and Margaret H. Cunningham, "Strategic Alliances: A Synthesis of Conceptual Foundations," *Journal of the Academy of Marketing Science,* fall 1995, pp. 282–296.

52. Audrey Choi and Don Clark, "MCI, Digital, Microsoft Plan Joint Venture," *Wall Street Journal,* April 8, 1996, p. B6; and Johnny K. Johansson, "International Alliances: Why Now?" *Journal of the Academy of Marketing Science,* fall 1995, pp. 301–304.

53. Scott McCartney, "Airline Alliances to Alter Overseas Travel," *Wall Street Journal,* June 11, 1996, p. B1.

54. Christopher, Payne, and Ballantyne, *Relationship Marketing,* pp. 135–137.

55. Sheth and Sisodia, "Feeling the Heat."

56. Christopher, Payne, and Ballantyne, *Relationship Marketing,* p. 150.

57. Don E. Schultz, "Maybe It's Time to Think of Customers as Assets," *Marketing News,* January 2, 1995, p. 30.

CHAPTER 11

1. "Plantronics Introduces Noise Cancelling Headsets," downloaded from Ahern Communication Corp. Web site, http://aherncorp.com/plantronics/plx.html, November 23, 1996; "1996 Idea Winners," *Business Week,* June 3, 1996, p. 85; and Damon Darlin, "Hands-Off Pitch," *Forbes,* October 9, 1995, pp. 98–101.

2. Anne Field, "Breaking into the Big Leagues," *Small Business Computing,* October 1996, pp. 63–67.
3. Andrew J. Parsons, "Nestlé: The Visions of Local Managers," *McKinsey Quarterly* no. 2 (1996) pp. 4–29.
4. This three-way classification system was first proposed by Melvin T. Copeland. See his *Principles of Merchandising* (New York: McGraw-Hill, 1924), Chapters 2 through 4.
5. Dagmar Mussey, "Selling Esteemed Watch with Limited Ad Budget," *Ad Age International,* February 12, 1996, p. i18.
6. Laurel Wentz, "Cache and Carry," *Ad Age International,* February 12, 1996, p. i15.
7. Ibid.
8. Michael D. Hutt and Thomas W. Speh, *Business Marketing Management,* 6th ed. (Fort Worth, Tex.: The Dryden Press, 1998), Chapter 1.
9. Erick Schonfeld, "Getting in Real Early on Digital Video," *Fortune,* February 5, 1996, p. 136.
10. Robin Madell, "Evergreening for Consumer Meaning," *Pharmaceutical Executive,* August 1996, pp. 36–46.
11. Robert La Franco, "Wanted: Newcomers with Bright Ideas," *Forbes,* October 21, 1996, pp. 272–274.
12. Madell, "Evergreening for Consumer Meaning."
13. Jeffrey A. Trachtenberg, "Sony, Unfazed by Flops, Rolls Out MiniDisc for Third Time in U.S.," *Wall Street Journal,* July 24, 1996, p. B10.
14. Gerard J. Tellis and Peter N. Golder, "First to Market, First To Fail? Real Causes of Enduring Market Leadership," *Sloan Management Review,* winter 1996, pp. 65–75.
15. Mindy Blodgett, "Hitachi, NEC Climb into Laptop Market," *Computerworld,* May 20, 1996, p. 46.
16. "These Creative Executions Take the Prize," *Advertising Age,* November 11, 1996, p. A26.
17. Raju Narisetti, "Smaller Diaper Makers Encounter a Maturing Market," *Wall Street Journal,* July 8, 1996, p. B4.
18. "Smith Corona Types in 'Chapter 11,'" *Business Week,* July 17, 1995, p. 42.
19. "Macarena Will Step into Fragrance Market," *Advertising Age,* November 11, 1996, p. 50.
20. Karen Benezra, "When We Say 'Always' . . . Coke Maps Holistic Strategy by Seasons," *Brandweek,* November 4, 1996, pp. 1–6.
21. Cyndee Miller, "Hush Puppies: All of a Sudden They're Cool," *Marketing News,* February 12, 1996, p. 10.
22. "AOL Mounts Campaign in U.K.," *Advertising Age,* November 11, 1996, p. 50.
23. Laura Petrecca, "New Domino's Product Adds to Its Hot Streak," *Advertising Age,* November 11, 1996, p. 4.
24. David S. Fondiller, "The Pizza Connection," *Forbes,* October 21, 1996, p. 202.
25. Suzanne Oliver, "I Love These Brands," *Forbes,* September 25, 1995, pp. 94–95.
26. "Make It Simple," *Business Week,* September 9, 1996, pp. 96–103.
27. Ibid.
28. Ibid.
29. Scott Woolley, "The Slipstream Strategy," *Forbes,* October 7, 1996, pp. 78–79.
30. Yumiko Ono, "Kraft Searches Its Cupboard for Old Brands to Remake," *Wall Street Journal,* March 12, 1996, p. B14.

CHAPTER 12

1. Monopoly Web site, http://www.monopoly.com/, downloaded December 17, 1996; Matt Krantz, "Hasbro Retools Classic Games for Computers," *Investor's Business Daily,* November 5, 1996; and Karen Benezra, "Brand Builders," *Brandweek,* November 20, 1995, pp. 20–21.
2. Betty Morris, "The Brand's the Thing," *Fortune,* March 4, 1996, pp. 72–86.
3. Ibid.
4. Daniel Roth, "Just Call Us Cockroaches," *Forbes,* August 26, 1996, pp. 58–60.
5. Gabriella Stern and Rebecca Blumenstein, "GM's Saturn Division Plans to Build a Midsize Car to Keep Customers Loyal," *Wall Street Journal,* August 6, 1996, p. A2.
6. "So, It's Not Just Cheapskate Americans Doing It," *Adweek,* February 12, 1996.
7. Morris, "The Brand's the Thing."
8. David A. Aaker, *Building Strong Brands* (New York: Free Press, 1996), pp. 309–312.
9. Ibid., pp. 307–308.
10. Louis E. Boone, C. M. Kochunny, and Dianne Wilkins, "Applying the Brand Equity Concept to Major League Baseball," *Sport Marketing Quarterly,* 4, no. 3 (1995), p. 39.
11. Michael Clements, "GM Focuses on Brand Management," *USA Today,* January 23, 1996, pp. 1B–2B; and Mike McKesson, "GM Planning to Emphasize Brands, Dealers," *Marketing News,* November 6, 1995, p. 3.
12. Maxine Lans Retsky, "Trademarks: Use 'Em or Lose 'Em," *Marketing News,* August 12, 1996, p. 15.
13. Parker H. Bagley, "Trade Mark Developments in the U.S.," *Managing Intellectual Property Trade Mark Yearbook,* (1996), pp. 16–18.
14. Jodi B. Cohen, "Nameplate Dispute Dissolved," *Editor & Publisher,* September 21, 1996, pp. 14–15.
15. "Avon Traps Internet Infringer in Pioneering Case," *Managing Intellectual Property,* May 1996, p. 4.
16. Chris Nerney, "Sun Lawyers Fight for Java," *Network World,* June 17, 1996, pp. 1, 84.
17. "25 Things You Didn't Know about the Pepsi Trade Mark," *Managing Intellectual Property,* May 1996, p. 9.
18. Ian Jones, "Pirates and Poor Planning," *World Trade,* July 1996, pp. 64–65.
19. "25 Things You Didn't Know."
20. Elaine Underwood, "Re-Store Brands," *Adweek's Marketing Week,* June 15, 1992, pp. 28–30.
21. Seth Lubove, "Salad in a Bag," *Forbes,* October 23, 1995, pp. 201–204.
22. R. Lee Sullivan, "Soup, Oil, What's the Difference?" *Forbes,* September 23, 1996, pp. 78–79.
23. "Package Redesign Brings Consistency to Frozen Foods," *Marketing News,* July 15, 1996, p. 10.
24. "Coke to Go Curvy," *Marketing News,* April 8, 1996, p. 1.
25. Kevin Morrissey, "Right Label Improves Brand's Shelf Presence," *Marketing News,* July 1, 1996, p. 6.
26. Mary Ann Falkman, "Consumers Buy Packaging Benefits: A Packaging Digest Exclusive Survey," *Packaging Digest,* July 1996, pp. 24–25.
27. Richard Gibson, "Can Betty Crocker Heat Up General Mills

Cereal Sales?" *Wall Street Journal,* July 19, 1996, pp. B1–B2.

28. Seanna Browder, "Starbucks Does Not Live by Coffee Alone," *Business Week,* August 5, 1996, p. 76.

29. Jeanne Dugan, "The Thing that Ate the Kids' Market," *Business Week,* November 4, 1996, pp. 174–175.

30. Morris, "The Brand's the Thing."

31. Yumiko Ono, "Kraft Searches Its Cupboards for Old Brands to Remake," *Wall Street Journal,* March 12, 1996, p. B14.

32. Tali Levine Kamis, "Tickling Chinese Taste Buds," *China Business Review,* January/February 1996, pp. 44–47.

33. Kathy Rebello, "Honey, What's on Microsoft?" *Business Week,* October 21, 1996, pp. 134–136.

34. Richard A. Melcher, "Is It Finally Miller Time?" *Business Week,* February 12, 1996, p. 37.

35. Ronald Henkoff, "P&G: New and Improved!" *Fortune,* October 14, 1996, pp. 151–161.

36. Everett M. Rogers and F. Floyd Shoemaker, *Communication of Innovation* (New York: Free Press, 1971), pp. 135–157. Rogers later relabeled his model as an *innovation-decision process.* He called the five steps *knowledge, persuasion, decision, implementation,* and *confirmation.* See Everett M. Rogers, *Diffusion of Innovations,* 3rd ed. (New York: Free Press, 1983), pp. 164–165.

37. Lois Geller, "What's Your Offer?" *Marketing Tools,* October 1996, pp. 4–8.

38. Gene Koprowski, "Bovine Inspiration," *Marketing Tools,* October 1996, p. 10.

39. Joseph Pereira, "Unknown Fruit Takes on Unfamiliar Markets," *Wall Street Journal,* November 9, 1995, pp. B1–B2.

40. Elaine Underwood, "Karan Sets Massive Sampling Blitz for Formula Skincare," *Brandweek,* May 1, 1995, p. 14.

41. Koprowski, "Bovine Inspiration."

42. Matthew Schifrin, "I Happen to Be Very Lucky," *Forbes,* November 4, 1996, pp. 176–177.

43. Steve Gelsi, "In a Marryin' Mood," *Brandweek,* September 2, 1996, pp. 22–23.

44. Robert G. Cooper, "Stage-Gate Systems: A New Tool For Managing New Products," *Business Horizons,* May/June 1990, pp. 47–49.

45. Anne Murphy, "The Missing Link," *Inc.,* June 1995, pp. 58–66.

46. Seth Lubove, "Okay, Call Me a Predator," *Forbes,* February 15, 1993, pp. 150–153.

47. Joan O. C. Hamilton, "A Rocket in Its Pocket," *Business Week,* September 9, 1996, pp. 111–112.

48. "Campbell Hopes to Market Frozen Foods by Mail," *Marketing News,* October 21, 1996, p. 16.

49. Murphy, "The Missing Link."

50. "CPSC to Miniblind Producers: Get the Lead Out," *Bobbin,* September 1996, p. 130.

51. Tim Cavanaugh, "Push Down While Turning," *American Demographics,* March 1996, pp. 18–20.

CHAPTER 13

1. Laura Koss-Feder, "How Technology Is Changing Your Hotel Room," *Investor's Business Daily,* downloaded from America Online, February 1, 1997; Janet Kornblum, "Hotels Go High-Tech," CNET News.Com, downloaded from http:/www.news.com/, December 27, 1996; Robin Taylor Parets, "Room at the Inn-Ternet," *Inc. Technology,* no. 3 (1996), downloaded from America Online, November 20, 1996; and Joe Brancatelli, "Put Your Hotel to Work," *Fortune,* November 1, 1996, pp. 279–280.

2. The concept of a goods-services continuum is suggested in G. Lynn Shostack, "Breaking Free from Product Marketing," *Journal of Marketing,* April 1977, p. 77; see also John M. Rathmell, "What Is Meant by Services?" *Journal of Marketing,* October 1980, pp. 32–36.

3. Harish C. Kapoor and Elise Truly Sautter, "Self Service: A Cross Cultural Perspective," *Proceedings of the 1995 Winter Marketing Theory Conference,* San Diego, 1996.

4. "Service Industry Starts on the Rise," *Inc.,* December 1994, p. 34.

5. Peter Huber, "The Economics of Waiting," *Forbes,* December 30, 1996, p. 150.

6. Jeffrey Marshall, "Where Image Is (Almost) Everything," *US Banker,* October 1996, pp. 33–39.

7. Frederick Schmitt, "One Niche Market: Two Approaches," *National Underwriter,* October 7, 1996, pp. 7, 14.

8. Kevin Lumsdon, "A Winning Market Strategy for HMOs," *Hospitals & Health Networks,* October 5, 1996, pp. 69–70.

9. Suzanne Oliver, "Upping the Ante," *Forbes,* November 4, 1996, pp. 186–189.

10. Anne Kelleher, "What a Concierge Can Do For You," *Car & Travel,* November 1996, pp. 88–100.

11. Martha Brannigan and Eleena De Lisser, "Ground Control: Cost Cutting at Delta Raises the Stock Price but Lowers the Service," *Wall Street Journal,* June 26, 1996, p. A1.

12. Neil Weinberg, "Can These Dinosaurs Adapt?" *Forbes,* September 9, 1996, pp. 74–78.

13. Valarie A. Zeithaml, Leonard L. Berry, and A. Parasuraman, "Communication and Control Processes in the Delivery of Service Quality," *Journal of Marketing,* April 1988, p. 46; some of the definitions come from A. Parasuraman, Valarie A. Zeithaml, and Leonard L. Berry, "A Conceptual Model of Service Quality and Its Implications for Future Research," *Journal of Marketing,* fall 1985, p. 47.

14. David L. Kurtz and Kenneth E. Clow, *Services Marketing* (New York: John Wiley & Sons, 1988), Chapter 2.

15. Julie Baker and Michaelle Cameron, "The Effects of the Service Environment on Affect and Consumer Perception of Waiting Time: An Integrative Review and Research Propositions," *Journal of the Academy of Marketing Science,* fall 1996, pp. 338–349.

16. Kim Girard and Thomas Hoffman, "Bells Lag on Service," *Computerworld,* September 30, 1996, p. 14.

17. Bruce Upbin, "Happy Drivers, Happy Customers," *Forbes,* November 4, 1996, pp. 165–167.

18. "Ryder Provides Integrated Logistics for Northern Telecom," *Forbes,* October 14, 1996, Special Advertising Section.

19. Christopher H. Lovelock, *Services Marketing,* 3rd ed. (Upper Saddle River, N.J.: Prentice-Hall 1996), pp. 33–34.

20. Nina Munk, "Can't Lift Boxes? Then Sweep the Floors," *Forbes,* November 4, 1996, pp. 167–168.

21. Patricia Braus, "The Mother Market," *American Demographics,* October 1996, pp. 36–41.

22. Daniel Roth, "It's a Nice Living," *Forbes,* December 2, 1996, p. 88.
23. "Europeans Dubious on British Air Alliance," *New York Times,* December 10, 1996, p. D6.
24. John A. Byrne, "Virtual B-Schools," *Business Week,* October 23, 1995, pp. 64–68.
25. Rosalind Resnick, "Service with a Modem," *Internet World,* September 1996, pp. 38–39.
26. Kris Aaron, "High Tech and High Touch," *Credit Union Management,* September 1996, pp. 20–21.
27. Janice Maloney, "Yahoo! Still Searching for Profits on the Internet," *Fortune,* December 9, 1996, pp. 174–182.
28. "TeleTech Provides Call Handling for AT&T Wireless Services," *Forbes,* October 14, 1996, Special Advertising Supplement.
29. Ernan Roman, "Customers for Life," *American Demographics Marketing Tools Supplement,* July/August 1996, p. 66.
30. Frank Go, Tat Choi, and Carole Chan, "Four Seasons-Regent: Building a Global Presence in the Luxury Market," *Cornell Hotel & Restaurant Administration Quarterly,* August 1996, pp. 58–65.
31. Gautum Naik, "Baby Bells Profit by Tapping Phone Paranoia," *Wall Street Journal,* September 3, 1996, p. B1.
32. John Case and Jerry Useem, "Six Characters in Search of a Strategy," *Inc.*, March 1996, downloaded from America Online, December 15, 1996.
33. Gene Koprowski, "AOL CEO Steve Case," *Forbes ASAP Supplement,* October 7, 1996, pp. 92–96.
34. David Rohde, "MCI Entices Business Customers With New Services," *Network World,* September 16, 1996, p. 14.
35. Seth Lubove, "Would You Rather Do Business with a Computer?" *Forbes,* December 2, 1996, pp. 118–120.
36. Chad Rubel, "Banks Go Mobile to Serve Low-Income Areas," *Marketing News,* November 20, 1995, p. 12.
37. "Hilton Hotels Opens 'Cyber-Resort' for No-Risk Trial of New Online Reservations," *Business Wire,* July 24, 1996, downloaded from http://www.businesswire.com/, July 31, 1996.
38. Andrew Tanser, "Citibank Blitzes Asia," *Forbes,* May 6, 1996, p. 44.
39. Randall Lane, "Shakeout in Skiing," *Forbes,* May 6, 1996, pp. 56–58.
40. Seth Lubove, "High-Tech Cops," *Forbes,* September 25, 1995, pp. 44–45.

CHAPTER 14

1. Adapted from Monica Young, "Electronic Distribution: Friend or Foe?" *Computer Reseller News,* January 19, 1997, pp. 129–130; David Bank, "Middlemen Find Ways to Survive Cyberspace Shopping," *Wall Street Journal,* December 12, 1996, downloaded from http://www.wsj.com/, January 6, 1997; "The Internet Shopping Network Launches New Downloadable Software Store," *Business Wire,* September 10, 1996, downloaded from http://www.businesswire.com/, September 10, 1996; and Joan E. Rigdon, "Microsoft to Sell Most Popular Software through Resellers Using the Internet," *Wall Street Journal,* October 16, 1995, p. B10.
2. Audrey Choi, "SoftKey Sells Software Just Like Other Commodities," *Wall Street Journal,* November 1, 1995, p. B4.
3. Carla Goodman, "The Natural," *Business Start-Ups,* October 1996, pp. 24–29.
4. Daniel Roth, "Card Sharks," *Forbes,* October 7, 1996, p. 14.
5. Juan B. Elizondo Jr., "In-Home Parties Latest Way to Buy PC," *San Diego Union-Tribune,* September 27, 1996, p. C-2.
6. William C. Taylor, "What Comes After Your Success," *Fast Company,* January 1997, pp. 82–85.
7. Bob Weinstein, "The Computer in the Dell," *Business Start-Ups,* June 1996, pp. 23–27.
8. Laura Loro, "New Ways to Reach Customers," *Ad Age International,* March 11, 1996, p. I30.
9. "World Codes of Conduct for Direct Selling," World Federation of Direct Selling Associates, 1994.
10. Courtney Young, "Coming Up Roses," *Inc. Technology* no. 4 (1995) p. 105.
11. *Foundations of Wholesaling: A Strategic and Financial Chart Book,* Distribution Research Program, The University of Oklahoma (1996).
12. Ibid.
13. Bank, "Middlemen Find Ways."
14. Jerry Rosa, "Apple Unveils Revitalized Channel Plan," *Computer Reseller News,* November 18, 1996, pp. 241, 251.
15. Frank Green, "Battling for Shelf Control: No Matter Who Wins, Consumers Pay Some Hidden Costs," *San Diego Union Tribune,* November 19, 1996, pp. C-1, C-6.
16. Gary L. Frazier and Walfried M. Lasar, "Determinants of Distribution Intensity," *Journal of Marketing,* October 1996, pp. 39–51.
17. Nick Christy, "With Dairy Packaging, Coke Foods Turn Juice Loose on New Channels," *Beverage World,* July 31, 1996, p. 17.
18. Christopher McEvoy and Leigh Gallagher, "Only Elite Invited to Nike's Party," *Sporting Goods Business,* August 1996, p. 8.
19. Christopher McEvoy, "Nautilus Launches Exclusive Attack," *Sporting Goods Business,* March 1996, p. 28.
20. Joseph Pereira and Bryan Gruley, "Relative Power of Toys 'R' Us Is Central to Suit," *Wall Street Journal,* May 24, 1996, pp. B1, B5.
21. Dorothy Giobbe, "Big Glitch in Delivery Switch," *Editor & Publisher,* August 17, 1996, pp. 12, 36.
22. Jakki J. Mohr and Robert E. Spekman, "Perfecting Partnerships," *Marketing Management,* winter/spring 1996, pp. 35–42.
23. "Has Power Shifted in the Grocery Channel?" *Stores,* January 1996, pp. RR3–RR4.
24. "Retailing's Dirty Little Secrets," *Time,* June 10, 1996, p. 63.
25. M. Sharon Baker, "Software Makers Say Egghead Charging New Fees," *Puget Sound Business Journal,* May 10, 1995, p. 5.
26. Matthew Schifrin, "The Big Squeeze," *Forbes,* March 11, 1996, pp. 45–46.
27. Bank, "Middlemen Find Ways."
28. Susan Jackson, Stephanie Anderson Frost, and Lori Bongiorno, "Can Cadbury Dodge Big Cola's Bullets?" *Business Week,* August 12, 1996, pp. 70–71.
29. Donald V. Fites, "Make Your Dealers Your Partners," *Harvard Business Review,* March/April 1996, p. 84.
30. David A. Aaker, *Strategic Marketing Management* (New York: John Wiley & Sons, 1992) pp. 257–263.

31. Dale D. Buss, "The Little Guys Strike Back," *Nation's Business,* July 1996, pp. 18–23.

32. Ibid.

33. Amy Dunkin, "Franchising: A Recipe for Your Second Career?" *Business Week,* March 4, 1996, pp. 128–129.

34. Ibid..

35. Richard Gibson, "Court Decides Franchisees Get Elbow Room," *Wall Street Journal,* August 14, 1996, p. B1; and Jack Hayes, "Carvel, Franchisees Lock Horns over Retail Program," *Nation's Restaurant News,* September 4, 1995, pp. 3, 82.

CHAPTER 15

1. Adapted from: Laurie J. Flynn, "Malls and Stores Find New Outlets in Cyberspace," *New York Times CyberTimes,* December 5, 1996, downloaded from http://www.nytimes.com/, January 13, 1997; Seth Schiesel, "Payoff Is Still Elusive in Internet Gold Rush," *New York Times CyberTimes,* January 2, 1997, downloaded from http://www.nytimes.com/, January 13, 1997; Michael H. Martin, "Why the Web Is Still a No-Shop Zone," *Fortune,* February 5, 1996, p. 127; "Who's David and Who's Goliath on the Internet?" *Internet Marketing & Technology Report,* February 2, 1996, p. 3; and Julie Schmit, "Virtual Stores Open Doors," *USA Today,* November 13, 1995, p. 4E.

2. Gretchen Morgenson, "Too Much of a Good Thing?" *Forbes,* June 3, 1996, pp. 114–119.

3. Matthew Schifrin, "Goofus and Gallant," *Forbes,* December 18, 1995, pp. 115–117.

4. David P. Schulz, "Smaller Chains Battle Back with Focus on Hardware," *Stores,* June 1996, pp. 46–47.

5. Stephanie Faul, "1996 Small Store Retailer of the Year: E. Diane White," *Stores,* January 1996, pp. 149–151.

6. Susan Reda, "Learning-Focused Chains Carve Out Niche in Tough Toy Business," *Stores,* April 1996, pp. 44–45.

7. Thomas G. Stemberg, "Shaking the Money Tree," *Success,* September 1996, pp. 49–54.

8. Richard Halverson, "PetsMart Seeks Growth from Within, Delves into New Lines, Services," *Discount Store News,* April 15, 1996, pp. 19–21.

9. Shelly M. Reese, "Need for More Space Spurs Laura Ashley Prototype," *Stores,* October 1996, pp. 98–100.

10. Seth Lubove, "Don't Listen to the Boss, Listen to the Customer," *Forbes,* December 4, 1995, pp. 45–46.

11. Nancy J. Kim, "Calla Bay Aims for a Splash with Fitted Swimsuits," *Puget Sound Business Journal,* November 11, 1996, p. 4.

12. Scott McMurray, "Sears Fashions a New Future for Itself," *U.S. News & World Report,* May 13, 1996, pp. 61–62.

13. "Assortment Management," *Chain Store Age,* September 1996, pp. 28–31; and Larry J. Fox, "Best Practices in Retailing: An Integrated View of Assortment Management," *Chain Store Age,* November 1995, pp. 62–68.

14. Michael Goldberg, "Extra Room on the Shelf," *Computerworld,* October 7, 1996, pp. 79, 84.

15. Steve Stecklow, "Some Stores Are Becoming Kid-Friendly," *Wall Street Journal,* June 18, 1996, p. B6.

16. Leonard Novarro, "Specialty Cookware Store Goes to School," *San Diego Union-Tribune,* January 1, 1997, pp. C1–C2.

17. Zina Moukheiber, "The Price Is Right," *Forbes,* December 16, 1996, pp. 52–54.

18. Phyllis Plitch, "Egghead Is Latest Chain to Bow to Tough Retail Climate," *Dow Jones Business News,* January 31, 1997, downloaded from http://www.wsj.com/, February 4, 1997; and "Retailers Debate Store Closing Strategies," *Stores,* August 1995, pp. 38–39.

19. Shelly Reese, "Toilet Paper and a Big Mac," *American Demographics,* July 1996, pp. 15–16.

20. Susan Reda, "Kiosk Pioneers Explore New Formats, Products," *Stores,* August 1996, pp. 51–54.

21. Mitchell Pacelle, "Malls Add Fun and Games to Attract Shoppers," *Wall Street Journal,* January 23, 1996, p. B1.

22. Ellen Ramano, "Rainbow Retailing: Marketing to Ethnic Trade Areas," *Journal of Property Management,* September/October 1996, pp. 40–44.

23. Kelly Shermach, "Niche Malls: Innovation for an Industry in Decline," *Marketing News,* February 26, 1996, pp. 1–2.

24. "Targeting Baby, Directly," *Brandweek,* March 25, 1996, p. 20.

25. Rebecca Piirto Heath, "Wake of the Flood," *Marketing Tools,* November/December 1996, downloaded from the *American Demographics* Web site at http://www.marketingtools.com/, January 12, 1997.

26. "Musicland Ties Music Web Site to In-Store Sales," *Discount Store News,* November 4, 1996, p. 52.

27. James Mammarella, "HomeImage: Ward's Gamble for Growth," *Discount Store News,* October 7, 1996, pp. H5–H7.

28. "Lee Gets in Touch with Retail Kiosk," *Brandweek,* June 12, 1995, p. 9.

29. Joseph Pereira, "A Small Toy Store Manages to Level the Playing Field," *Wall Street Journal,* December 26, 1996, pp. A1–A5.

30. Cheryl Kane Heimlich, "Rainforest Cafe Becoming the 'Disney World' of Eateries," *South Florida Business Journal,* November 15, 1996, p. 1.

31. Virginia Matthews, "POP's the Star in Stores," *Marketing,* October 24, 1996, p. 34.

32. "Repainting the Shack," *Brandweek,* September 11, 1995, p. 24.

33. Paul Cockerham, "Retailers Hear Sweet Music in Improved Store Acoustics," *Stores,* April 1996, pp. 77–78.

34. "Sportmart Pins Hopes on New Prototype," *Discount Store News,* November 4, 1996, pp. 3, 17.

35. Joyce M. Rosenberg, "That's Entertainment?" *San Diego Union-Tribune,* September 10, 1996, pp. C1, C6.

36. Morgenson, "Too Much of a Good Thing."

37. Bruce V. Bigelow, "Tandy to Close Doors on Incredible Universe," *San Diego Union-Tribune,* December 31, 1996, pp. C1–C4.

38. Pete Hisey, "A 10-Gallon Training Ground for Retail Concepts," *Discount Store News,* April 15, 1996, p. 27.

39. Susan Greco, "Selling the Superstores," *Inc.,* July 1995, pp. 55–61.

40. Ira Apfel, "What Is an Outlet Center?" *American Demographics,* July 1996, downloaded from http://www.marketingtools.com/, January 12, 1997.

41. Susan Reda, "Sports Court Adds the Athletic Dimension," *Stores,* May 1996, pp. 64–65.

42. Patricia Sellers, "Can Wal-Mart Get Back the Magic?" *Fortune,* April 29, 1996, pp. 130–136.
43. Jay L. Johnson, "Supercenters: An Evolving Saga," *Discount Merchandiser,* April 1995, pp. 26–30.
44. Michael P. Niemira, "Are Nonstore Sales a Threat to Traditional Store Business? A Look at Cyberspace and Catalog Sales," *Chain Store Age,* September 1996, p. 26.
45. Elaine Underwood, "Is There a Future for the TV Mall?" *Brandweek,* March 25, 1996, p. 24.
46. Renee Covino Rouland, "The Real Channel Changers," *Discount Merchandiser,* January 1996, pp. 60–61.
47. Niemira, "Nonstore Sales a Threat."
48. Michael H. Martin, "The Next Big Thing: A Bookstore?" *Fortune,* December 9, 1996, p. 170.
49. Pete Hisey, "Wal-Mart Seeks Shoppers with On-Line Service," *Discount Store News,* August 19, 1996, pp. 1, 54.
50. Rita Rousseau, "Age of the Automat (at Last)," *Restaurants & Institutions,* October 1, 1996, pp. 57–67; and "Consumers Demanding Healthier Food from Vending Machines," *Marketing News,* September 23, 1996, p. 39.
51. Haidee Allerton, "Vending Your Way," *Training & Development,* September 1996, p. 72.
52. "Wal-Mart Reports January Sales Increased by Nearly 15 Percent," *The Morning News,* February 7, 1997, p. A5, (Bloomberg News Service); and Chuck Bartels, "Wal-Mart to Launch 401K Plan for Workers," *The Morning News,* February 7, 1997, p. A3 (Associated Press story).
53. R. Lee Sullivan, "Exxonsafeway," *Forbes,* March 11, 1996, p. 106.
54. Mary Beth Grover, "The Odd Couple," *Forbes,* November 18, 1996, pp. 178–181.

CHAPTER 16

1. Todd Lapin, "The Airline of the Internet," *Wired,* December 1996, pp. 232–240, 282–290; James A. Narus and James C. Anderson, "Rethinking Distribution: Adaptive Channels," *Harvard Business Review,* July/August 1996, p. 112; Matt Krantz, "Why In-House Tech Experts Have an External Focus Now," *Investor's Business Daily,* April 23, 1996, downloaded from America Online, February 10, 1997; and Matt Krantz, "Will Fast Data Delivery Give Boost to Shippers' Margins?" *Investor's Business Daily,* December 20, 1995, downloaded from America Online, February 10, 1997.
2. Rebecca Blumenstein, "How Do You Get a Hot GMC Suburban? You Wait for a Computer to Dole One Out," *Wall Street Journal,* April 10, 1996, p. B1.
3. "The Future of Truck Transportation," *Fortune,* April 3, 1995.
4. Sarah A. Bergin, "Recognizing Excellence: In Logistics Strategies," *Transportation & Distribution,* October 1996, pp. 47–56.
5. Clyde E. Witt, "How to Spend Your Distribution Dollars," *Materials Handling Engineering,* November 1996, pp. 73–76.
6. Bergin, "Recognizing Excellence."
7. "Outsourcing: You've Got a Friend," *Beverage World,* October 1996, p. 118.
8. Witt, "How to Spend."
9. Witt, "How to Spend."
10. "Toro's Philosophy on Logistics Outsourcing," *Transportation & Distribution,* September 1996, p. H.
11. Damon Darlin, "Maquiladora-ville," *Forbes,* May 6, 1996, pp. 111–112.
12. Chris Gillis, "Georgia-Pacific's Logistics Overall," *Logistics Management,* February 1996, pp. 37–40.
13. Tom Andel, "Carrier Selection Tools: Open a Window to Service," *Transportation & Distribution,* July 1996, pp. 27–32.
14. Robert Mottley, "Wilson's Logistics Game Plan," *American Shipper,* February 1996, pp. 33–36.
15. "A Smoother Ride for Motor Vehicles," *Railway Age,* October 1996, pp. 31–32.
16. "Effects of Railroad Mergers," *Transportation & Distribution,* December 1996, p. 53.
17. "Big Voice for Short Lines," *Transportation & Distribution,* October 1996, p. 64.
18. "Potholes on the Iron Highway," *Distribution,* December 1996, p. 42.
19. "Smoother Ride."
20. Perry A. Trunick, "Tightening the Grip on LTL Costs," *Transportation & Distribution,* June 1996, pp. 25–26.
21. "Tracking Freight on the Internet," *Transportation & Distribution,* October 1996, p. 98.
22. Sarah Bergin, "Specialized Truckload Carriers Find Niche Markets," *Transportation & Distribution,* December 1996, pp. 37–43.
23. Lisa H. Harrington, "Private Fleets: Finding Their Niche," *Transportation & Distribution,* September 1996, pp. 55–60.
24. Amy Zuckerman, "Ocean Carriers Feel the Squeeze," *Inbound Logistics,* May 1995, pp. 18–24.
25. Perry Tunick, "Growth Ahead for Air Cargo," *Transportation & Distribution,* July 1996, pp. 49–52.
26. Helen Richardson, "Freight Forwarder Basics," *Transportation & Distribution,* May 1996, pp. 80–84.
27. "Future of Truck."
28. "Intermodal: Still Not Meeting Customer Needs," *Transportation & Distribution,* October 1996, p. 11.
29. "Future of Truck."
30. Laurie Joan Aron, "Delivery Speed Keeps Electronics Boutique at the Top of Its Game," *Inbound Logistics,* January 1996, pp. 31–40.
31. Deborah Catalano Ruriani, "Logistics: Where Do We Go from Here?" *Inbound Logistics,* August 1995, pp. 30–33.
32. L. Clinton Hoch, "Metro Areas Losing Allure," *Transportation & Distribution,* December 1996, pp. 56–58.
33. Lisa H. Harrington, "Learning from 1995's Inventory Buildup," *Transportation & Distribution,* July 1996, p. 80.
34. "Inventory Reduction: A Slow Process," *IIE Solutions,* January 1997, p. 8.
35. Robin Yale Bergstrom, "Seamless JIT Doesn't Just Happen," *Automotive Production,* September 1996, pp. 44–49.
36. Laura Bird, "High-Tech Inventory System Coordinates Retailer's Clothes with Customers' Taste," *Wall Street Journal,* June 12, 1996, p. B1.
37. Karen Abramic Dilger, "Electronic Evolution," *Manufacturing Systems,* November 1996, pp. 76–84.
38. "New System Keeps the Goods Flowing at Macy's," *Chain Store Age,* September 1996, pp. 42–48.

CHAPTER 17

1. "Reebok Leaves 'Planet' for New Ad Campaign," *Marketing News,* March 3, 1997, p. 36; Patrick M. Reilly, "Will Women's Sports Magazines Be Hits?" *Wall Street Journal,* June 26, 1996, p. B1; Kellee K. Harris, "Interactive Web Sites Get Repeat Business," *Sporting Goods Business,* April 1996, p. 16; Chuck Ross and Jeff Jensen, "TPP, Reebok Skate into In-line Pact," *Advertising Age,* March 11, 1996, pp. 3, 37; Kenneth Labich, "Nike vs. Reebok, A Battle for Hearts, Minds & Feet," *Fortune,* September 18, 1995, pp. 90–106; and Alyssa Lustigman, "Team Spirit," *Sporting Goods Business,* June 1995, pp. 44–45.
2. James G. Hutton, "Integrated Marketing Communications and the Evolution of Marketing Thought," *Journal of Business Research,* November 1996, pp. 155–162; see also Don E. Schultz, Stanley I. Tannenbaum, and Robert F. Lauterborn, *Integrated Marketing Communications* (Lincolnwood, Ill.: NTC Business Books, 1993).
3. "Virtual Cereal," *PROMO,* March 1996, pp. R6–8.
4. Regis McKenna, "Real-Time Marketing," *Harvard Business Review,* July/August 1995, pp. 87–95.
5. Kim Cleland, "Few Wed Marketing, Communications," *Advertising Age,* February 27, 1995, p. 10.
6. "Windows on the World," *PROMO,* March 1996, pp. 69–70.
7. Stan Rapp and Thomas Collings, "The New MaxiMarketing," *Success,* April 1996, pp. 39–46; and Don E. Schultz, "Be Careful Picking Database for IMC Efforts," *Marketing News,* March 11, 1996, pp. 14–15.
8. Jan Stafford, "Database Marketing Keeps a Grocer's Customers Loyal," *Investor's Business Daily,* March 20, 1996; downloaded from America Online, June 23, 1996.
9. Rapp and Collings, "The New MaxiMarketing."
10. Ibid.
11. Dottie Enrico and Alan Bash, "Pepsi Units Pull Carvey Sponsorship," *USA Today,* March 15, 1996, p. B1; Sally Goll Beatty, "Taco Bell Pulls Out of Sponsoring Dana Carvey Show," *Wall Street Journal,* March 14, 1996, p. B8; and Elizabeth Jensen, "ABC to Air Program Spoofing Sponsors," *Wall Street Journal,* February 27, 1996, p. B8.
12. Don Clark, "Hey, #!@*% Amigo, Can You Translate the Word 'Gaffe'?" *Wall Street Journal,* July 8, 1996, p. B2; and Michael Stott, "Microsoft Apologizes for Thesaurus's Slurs," *San Diego Union-Tribune,* July 6, 1996, p. C2.
13. Junu Bryan Kim, "Marketing with Video: The Cassette Is in the Mail," *Advertising Age,* May 22, 1995, pp. S1, S4.
14. "Have a Pint, Keep the Pub," *PROMO,* December 1995, pp. 70–71.
15. "Thanks a Bunch!" *PROMO,* December 1995, pp. 73–74.
16. Weld F. Royal, "Good Chemistry," *Sales & Marketing Management,* April 1995, pp. 111–114.
17. Blair R. Fischer, "Stand Up Comic Books," *PROMO,* March 1996, pp. 57–58, 75–82.
18. Ann Zella, "Economic Impact: Direct Marketing Today," presentation at the Direct Marketing Educational Foundation Authors' Seminar, New York, June 6, 1996.
19. Pete Williams, "Pepsi: The Choice of a New Generation in Arizona," *USA Today Baseball Weekly,* April 10–16, 1996, p. 19.
20. "Sponsor Growth Slows," *Brandweek,* January 27, 1997, p. 18.
21. Christie Brown, "Goya O'Boya," *Forbes,* February 26, 1996, p. 102.
22. Mark Lewyn, "See a Game, Shop for a Car, Surf the Net," *Business Week,* January 29, 1996, p. 53.
23. William L. Shanklin and John R. Kuzma, "Sports Marketing," *Marketing Management,* spring 1992, p. 58.
24. Jeff Jensen, "Sports Sponsorships Are Finding Web Tie-ins," *Advertising Age,* January 29, 1996, p. 26.
25. Bruce Horovitz, "New Breed of Sponsors Race to NASCAR," *USA Today,* April 5, 1996, pp. 1B, 2B; and Blair R. Fischer, "The Rules of the Game," *PROMO,* December 1995, pp. 53–57.
26. Data reported in WEFA Group, "Economic Impact: U.S. Direct Marketing Today," Direct Marketing Association, New York, October 1995.
27. Claire Mencke, "Using Database Power in Credit Card Market," *Investor's Business Daily,* May 7, 1996, downloaded from America Online, June 23, 1996.
28. Joan Throckmorton, "Pick Their Brains," *Direct,* March 1996, pp. 62–63.
29. "Levi's Involves Young Girls in Mailing," *PROMO,* March 1996, p. 21.
30. "Sears' Big Book Repositioned," *Investor's Business Daily,* February 6, 1996, downloaded from America Online, July 15, 1996.
31. Sam Bradley, "D. Mail Is Becoming E-Mail," *Brandweek,* April 15, 1996, pp. 44–46.
32. Alexandra Alger, "Whose Phone Is It, Anyway?" *Forbes,* July 29, 1996, pp. 104–105.
33. Stephanie Gruner, "Telemarketing Dos and Don'ts," *Inc.,* February 1996, p. 94; and "Telemarketers See Benefits in New Federal Regulations," *Investor's Business Daily,* December 19, 1995, downloaded from America Online, July 15, 1996.
34. Debra Lynn Stephens, Ronald Paul Hill, and Karyn Bergman, "Enhancing the Consumer-Product Relationship: Lessons from the QVC Home Shopping Channel," *Journal of Business Research,* November 1996, pp. 193–200; see also Marilyn Much, "Celebrity Connections Boost Sales for L. L. Knickerbocker," *Investor's Business Daily,* February 5, 1996, downloaded from America Online, July 15, 1996.
35. Section based on Kathy Haley, "In the Changing '90s Market, the Infomercial Is Here to Stay," *Advertising Age,* March 11, 1996, p. 2A; Melanie Wells, "Genre Moves Mainstream on Cable Networks," *USA Today,* January 24, 1996, pp. 1B, 2B; and "Microsoft Ad Gives Infomercials New Credibility," *Investor's Business Daily,* September 11, 1995, downloaded from America Online, July 15, 1996.
36. Throckmorton, "Pick Their Brains."
37. Edward C. Baig, "Surfing the Net for Better Returns," *Business Week,* March 18, 1996, p. 116.
38. Laura Loro, "Minority Promotions Pick Up the Pace," *Advertising Age,* March 20, 1996, pp. S4, S6.
39. Bob Garfield, "Polaroid Ads Show Flash of Brilliance," *Advertising Age,* March 11, 1996, p. 37.
40. Fischer, "Stand Up Comic Books."

41. Leah Haran, "Sears Promo Hoops It Up," *Advertising Age,* March 11, 1996, pp. 1, 35.
42. Betsey Spethmann, "Trade Promotion, Redefined," *BrandWeek,* March 13, 1995, pp. 25–34.
43. Don E. Schultz, "The Six Scariest Letters in the Marketing Alphabet," *Marketing News,* November 20, 1995, p. 6.
44. Spethmann, "Trade Promotion."
45. Mitch Wagner, "Custom Software Helps Web Users Follow 'Hit' Parade," *Computerworld,* March 4, 1996, p. 63.
46. Scott Young, "Taking Measure," *Internet World,* July 1996, pp. 66–67.
47. Kevin Goldman, "Nielsen, I/Pro Form Joint Venture to Measure the Internet's Activity," *Wall Street Journal,* September 6, 1995, p. B8; and I/Pro press kit, May 1, 1996.
48. Les Carlson, Stephen J. Grove, Russell N. Laczniak, and Norman Kangun, "Does Environmental Advertising Reflect Integrated Marketing Communications? An Empirical Investigation," *Journal of Business Research,* November 1996, pp. 225–232; see also Mary Kuntz and Jospeh Walker, "The New Hucksterism," *Business Week,* July 1, 1996, pp. 76–84.

CHAPTER 18

1. Jeff Dubois, "Selling Delight," *Interactive World,* September 1996, pp. 87–94; "Ikonic Personalizes the Internet with Cover Girl's Online Make-Up Consultant," Ikonic press release, August 12, 1996; and "Ikonic Uses Megasite Management Expertise for Pacific Bell's Revolutionary At Hand Service," Ikonic press release, August 12, 1996.
2. R. Craig Endicott, "Top Marketers Invest $47.3 Billion in '95 Ads," *Advertising Age,* September 30, 1996, p. 54.
3. Tara Parker-Pope, "British Budweiser Ads Rankle American Indians," *Wall Street Journal,* July 16, 1996, pp. B1, B3.
4. Norihiko Shirouzu, "Snapple in Japan: How a Splash Dried Up," *Wall Street Journal,* April 15, 1996, pp. B1, B3.
5. G. Pascal Zachary, "Major U.S. Companies Expand Efforts to Sell to Consumers Abroad," *Wall Street Journal,* June 13, 1996, pp. A1, A6.
6. "Baskin Robbins Launches Ultimate Birthday Center on the World Wide Web," *Business Wire,* downloaded July 7, 1996.
7. Jennifer deJong, "Are Pioneer Web Advertisers Getting Their Money's Worth?" *Investor's Business Daily,* May 15, 1996, downloaded from America Online, May 19, 1996; "Online Advertising Will Hit Nearly $2 Billion in 2000," *Business Wire,* downloaded July 18, 1996; and Gary Welz, "The Ad Game," *Internet World,* July 1996, p. 50.
8. Sally Goll Beatty, "Advil Escalates Its Battle against Tylenol," *Wall Street Journal,* June 28, 1996, p. B7.
9. Sally Goll Beatty, "FTC Sues Doan's Pill Maker over Claim," *Wall Street Journal,* June 28, 1996, p. B2.
10. Marco R. della Cava, "90s Ads Cast Celebrities in a New Light," *USA Today,* April 4, 1996, pp. 1D, 2D.
11. Jagdish Agrawal and Wagner A. Kamakura, "The Economic Worth of Celebrity Endorsers: An Event Study Analysis," *Journal of Marketing,* July 1995, pp. 56–62.
12. "Stick to the Singing Frogs," *Newsweek,* November 6, 1995, p. 10.
13. Skip Wollenberg, "Ads Draw on Cartoon Heroes," *San Diego Union-Tribune,* August 10, 1996, p. C2.
14. Joseph N. Fry and Gordon H. McDougall, "Consumer Appraisal of Retail Price Advertisements," *Journal of Marketing,* July 1974, pp. 64–67.
15. Bradley Johnson, "Intel Inside Program Expands Global Reach," *Advertising Age,* January 29, 1996, p. 9.
16. Dottie Enrico, "Computers Give Ads New Dimensions," *USA Today,* May 22, 1995, pp. 1B, 2B.
17. "Marketing Experts Advise Web Sites to Think beyond the Banner," *Interactive Marketing News,* August 2, 1996, pp. 1, 8.
18. Robert Brueckner, "Taking on TV," *Internet World,* July 1996, pp. 59–60.
19. "The Advertiser's Web Site," *Advertising Age,* October 7, 1996, p. C14.
20. "Avis Uses Radio in Rentals Push," *Marketing News,* July 11, 1996, p. 4.
21. Bethany McLean, "The Lost Art of Writing Meets the Black Art of Direct Mail," *Fortune,* February 5, 1996, p. 36.
22. Fara Warner and Karen Hsu, "Intel Gets a Free Ride in China by Sticking Its Name on Bicycles," *Wall Street Journal,* July 23, 1996, p. B5.
23. Sam Bradley, "D. Mail Is Becoming E-Mail," *Brandweek,* April 15, 1996, pp. 44–46.
24. Welz, "The Ad Game," p. 54.
25. Mary Kuntz, "Now Madison Avenue Really Has to Sing for Its Supper," *Business Week,* December 18, 1995, p. 43.
26. Mark Gleason and Debra Aho Williamson, "The New Interactive Agency," *Advertising Age,* February 26, 1996, pp. S1, S6, S8, and S11.
27. Raju Narisetti, "P&G, Seeing Shoppers Were Being Confused, Overhauls Marketing," *Wall Street Journal,* January 15, 1997, pp. A1, A8; "A Vote for Co-Marketing," *Advertising Age,* October 21, 1996, p. 28; and Raju Narisetti, "Joint Marketing with Retailers Spreads," *Wall Street Journal,* October 24, 1996, p. B6.
28. Kate Fitzgerald, "Survey: Consumers Prefer Sampling over Coupons," *Advertising Age,* January 29, 1996, p. 9.
29. Andrea Petersen, "Take 2 Ounces of Italian Dressing, Add 100 Sheets of Newspaper; Toss," *Wall Street Journal,* May 7, 1996, p. B1.
30. Carolyn Shea, "Going Mobile," *PROMO,* February 1996, pp. 41–46.
31. Terrence Shimp, *Advertising, Promotion, and Supplemental Aspects of Integrated Marketing Communications* (Fort Worth, Tex.: The Dryden Press, 1997), pp. 462–470.
32. Carolyn Shea, "Bang the Drum Loudly," *PROMO*, June 1996, pp. 117–120.
33. Earle Eldridge, "Trooper Sales Skid on 'CR' Report," *USA Today,* October 8, 1996, p. 2B; and Larry Armstrong, "Talk about Spin Control," *Business Week,* September 30, 1996, p. 44; and "Steering with Two Hands and Two Wheels," *U.S. News & World Report,* September 2, 1996, p. 14.
34. Shimp, *Advertising, Promotion,* pp. 554–556.
35. Bob Lamons, "Taco Bell Rings in New Age of Publicity Stunts," *Marketing News,* May 20, 1996, p. 15.
36. Judann Pollack, "New Marketing Spin: the PR 'Experience,'" *Advertising Age,* August 5, 1996, p. 33.
37. Lisa L. Brownlee, "'Goosebumps' Deal in the Doritos Bag," *Wall Street Journal,* July 10, 1996, p. B1.

38. "Pepsi Debuts 'Chat' on TM Online," *Business Wire,* July 11, 1996, downloaded July 16, 1996.
39. Eva Pomice, "Misery Loves Madison Ave.," *U.S. News & World Report,* June 11, 1990, p. 53.
40. Walter K. Lindenmann, "An 'Effectiveness' Yardstick to Measure Public Relations," *Public Relations Quarterly,* spring 1993, pp. 7–9.
41. "Hit Me: Tricks and Traps of Measuring Traffic on the WWW," *Online Media Planning Handbook,* downloaded from http://www.i-traffic.com/, June 24, 1996; deJong, "Pioneer Web Advertisers?" and Welz, "The Ad Game," p. 54.
42. "Psst . . . Wanna Buy a Web Site?" *Interactive Marketing News,* August 23, 1996, pp. 3, 6.
43. Sally Goll Beatty, "TV Beer Ads May Be Caught in a Backlash," *Wall Street Journal,* June 14, 1996, p. B1; and Sally Goll Beatty and Yumiko Ono, "Liquor Industry Is Divided over Use of TV Ads," *Wall Street Journal,* June 12, 1996, pp. B1, B9.
44. Bart Ziegler, "Old Fashioned Ethic of Separating Ads Is Lost in Cyberspace," *Wall Street Journal,* June 12, 1996, pp. B1, B9.
45. Chuck Ross, "Marketers Fend Off Shift in Rules for Ad Puffery," *Advertising Age,* February 19, 1996, p. 41; and Barry R. Shapiro, "Beyond Puffery," *Marketing Management,* winter 1995, pp. 60–62.

CHAPTER 19

1. Earle Eldridge, "Shoppers Soon Can Cyber-Kick the Car Tires," *USA Today,* October 9, 1996, p. B1; Lori Bongiorno, "Online Services: Info Highway to Heaven," *Business Week,* February 19, 1996, p. 74; Jeff Hoffman, "Cyberdealers: High Technology, Low Aggravation," *Business Week,* February 19, 1996, p. 73; and "Chrysler Cuts Car Dealers in on New 'Instant' Web Sites," *Interactive Marketing News,* September 6, 1995, pp. 1, 6.
2. Thomas N. Ingram and Raymond W. LaForge, *Sales Management: Analysis and Decision Making* (Hinsdale, Ill.: The Dryden Press, 1989), p. 21.
3. Alessandra Stanley, "Avon Rings the Bell in Russia," *San Diego Union-Tribune,* September 1, 1996, p. 13.
4. Brenda Rile, "An Introduction to Telemarketing," presentation at the Direct Marketing Institute for Professors, August 17, 1994, pp. 7, 8.
5. Jim Strutton, "Training Builds Sales Culture at Household Bank," *Telemarketing,* May 1995, pp. 81–82.
6. Marilyn Much, "Rewarding Ride of Direct-Marketing Wave," *Investor's Business Daily,* April 26, 1996, downloaded from America Online, July 7, 1996.
7. Michael Collins, "Breaking into the Big Leagues," *American Demographics,* January/February 1996.
8. Ibid.
9. Edward Forrest and Richard Mizerski, ed., *Interactive Marketing* (Lincolnwood, Ill.: NTC Business Books, 1995), p. 79.
10. Nancy Arnott, "It's a Woman's World," *Sales & Marketing Management,* March 1995, pp. 54–59.
11. Thomas N. Ingram, "Relationship Selling: Moving from Rhetoric to Reality," *Mid-American Journal of Business* II, no. 1, p. 8.
12. Roger L. Fetterman and H. Richard Byrne, *Interactive Selling in the '90s* (San Diego, Calif.: Ellipsys International Publications, 1995) pp. 64–65.
13. Jeffrey Young, "Can Computers Really Boost Sales?" *Forbes ASAP,* August 28, 1995, pp. 88, 93.
14. Steve Ditlea, "Managing Sales with Software," *Nation's Business,* March 1996, pp. 29–31.
15. Thayer C. Taylor, "Sales Automation Cuts the Cord," *Sales & Marketing Management,* July 1995, p. 111.
16. Sarah Schafer, "Sales Force Automation," *Inc.,* July 1996, downloaded from America Online, August 27, 1996.
17. Young, "Can Computers Really Boost Sales?" p. 93.
18. David W. Cravens, "The Changing Role of the Sales Force," *Marketing Management,* fall 1995, p. 55.
19. Jaclyn Fierman, "The Death and Rebirth of the Salesman," *Fortune,* July 25, 1994, p. 88.
20. Owen Edwards, "Bow Tech," *Forbes ASAP,* June 3, 1996, pp. 54–58.
21. Fierman, "Death and Rebirth," p. 88.
22. Fetterman and Byrne, *Interactive Selling,* p. 16.
23. Ditlea, "Managing Sales with Software."
24. Ginger Conlon, "Generating Electronic Sales Leads," *Sales & Marketing Management,* August 1996, p. 93.
25. "Asian Horizons," *Sales & Marketing Management,* August 1996, p. 93.
26. Melissa Campanelli, "Yikes!" *Sales & Marketing Management,* March 1995, p. 32.
27. "Survey: Sellers Giving Away the Store," *Sales & Marketing Management,* July 1994, p. 34.
28. Arnott, "Woman's World."
29. "A Shot in the Arm for Sales," *Investor's Business Daily,* May 9, 1996, downloaded from America Online, August 28, 1996; and Cravens, "Changing Role," p. 49.
30. Andy Cohen, "Small World, Big Challenge," *Sales & Marketing Management,* June 1996, pp. 69–72.
31. Andy Cohen, "Smooth Sailing," *Sales & Marketing Management,* March 1995, pp. 10–16.
32. "Shot in the Arm."
33. "HP Realigns Computer Sales around Customer Segments," *Business Wire,* June 18, 1996, downloaded on June 20, 1996.
34. Sally J. Silberman, "Going National," *Sales & Marketing Management,* March 1995, pp. 10–16.
35. Royal F. Weld, "Global Pricing and Other Hazards," *Sales & Marketing Management,* August 1996, p. 32.
36. Eugene M. Johnson, David L. Kurtz, and Eberhard Scheuing, *Sales Management* (New York: McGraw Hill, 1994).
37. "Follow the Leader," *Sales & Marketing Management,* April 1994, p. 34.
38. Andy Cohen, "Why Some Contests Are Losers," *Sales & Marketing Management,* July 1994, p. 34.
39. "How Often Do You Set Sales Goals?" *Sales & Marketing Management,* July 1994, p. 34.
40. Cohen, "Smooth Sailing," p. 16.
41. Bill O'Connell and Lisa Bush Hankin, "If You Pay Them, They Will Come," *Sales & Marketing Management,* September 1994, pp. 123–126.
42. "What Salespeople Are Paid," *Sales & Marketing Management,* February 1995, p. 32.

43. Michele Marchetti, "Motivating Telesales Reps," *Sales & Marketing Management,* August 1996, p. 38.
44. Ira Sager, Gary McWilliams, and Robert D. Hof, "IBM Leans on Its Sales Force," *Business Week,* February 7, 1994, p. 110.
45. Cravens, "Changing Role."
46. Alison Lucas, "The Wrong Kind of Meeting," *Sales & Marketing Management,* June 1996, p. 21.
47. Dana Ray, "The Ethical Dilemma," *Selling Power,* March 1996, pp. 32–34.

CHAPTER 20

1. Andrew Kupfer, "The Telecom Wars," *Fortune,* March 3, 1997, pp. 136–142; "Wireless a Way around Bells," CNET News.Com, February 26, 1997, downloaded from http://www.news.com/, February 26, 1997; adapted from John J. Keller, "Best Phone Discounts Go to Hardest Bargainers," *Wall Street Journal,* February 13, 1997, pp. B1, B12; and John J. Keller, "AT&T Discounts Signal a National Price War," *Wall Street Journal,* May 30, 1996, pp. B1, B14.
2. Damon Darlin, "The Avocado War," *Forbes,* December 4, 1995, p. 149.
3. Susan Greco, 'Pricing Pitfalls," *Inc.,* October 1994, p. 119.
4. Anthony J. Greco, "A Southern Revival: Predatory Pricing in American Drugs et al. v. Wal-Mart Stores, Inc.," *Southern Business & Economic Journal,* January 1995, pp. 95–110.
5. Joshua Mendes, "The Prince of Smart Pricing," *Fortune,* March 23, 1992, pp. 107–108.
6. Matthew Grimm, "BK's High Road Leads to Table Service," *Brandweek,* September 21, 1992, p. 5; and Matthew Grimm, "Could This Actually Be the End of the Price Wars?" *Superbrands,* 1992, pp. 72–73.
7. David M. Szymanski, Sundar G. Bharadwaj, and P. Rajan Varadarajan, "An Analysis of the Market Share-Profitability Relationship," *Journal of Marketing,* July 1993, pp. 1–18.
8. Robert D. Buzzell and Frederick D. Wiersema, "Successful Share Building Strategies," *Harvard Business Review,* January/February 1981, pp. 135–144.
9. Karen Benezra, "Beyond Value," *Brandweek,* October 7, 1996, p. 16.
10. Jonathan Dahl, "Tracking Travel," *Wall Street Journal,* February 19, 1993, p. B1.
11. James R. Healey, "Automakers Shifting to Value Pricing," *USA Today,* July 9, 1993, pp. B1, B2; and Joseph B. White and Oscar Suris, "GM, Pitching Value, Scores Cavalier Upset," *Wall Street Journal,* May 11, 1993, pp. B1, B8.
12. Jennifer Lawrence, "Laundry Soap Marketers See the Value of 'Value!,'" *Advertising Age,* September 21, 1992, pp. 3, 56.
13. Raymond Serafin, "Even Lamborghini Must Think Marketing," *Advertising Age,* May 1, 1995, p. 4.
14. Pat Sloan, "Recession Adds Price to Image Ads," *Advertising Age,* February 24, 1992, p. 45.
15. Greg Jaffe, "With ValuJet Absent, Fares Soar in Region," *Wall Street Journal,* September 18, 1996, p. SE1.
16. Kathy Heine, "Life on the High Wire," *Monsanto,* July 1991, pp. 6–13.
17. Brad Edmondson, "Snail Mail Is Losing Out," *Wall Street Journal,* January 31, 1997, p. A7A.
18. Andy Reinhardt, "Breaking the $1,000 Barrier," *Business Week,* February 17, 1997, p. 75.
19. Yumiko Ono, "Toys 'R' Us Learns Give-and-Take Game of Discounting with Japanese Suppliers," *Wall Street Journal,* October 8, 1991, p. A18.

CHAPTER 21

1. Adapted from Frank Green, "Lawyer Revs Up His Suit over Big Oil Pricing Policies," *San Diego Union-Tribune,* November 12, 1996, p. C1; Murray Weidenbaum, "The Oil Price Story: A Botched Job," *Christian Science Monitor,* June 20, 1996, p. 19; H. Josef Hebert, "A Close Look at Costly Gas," *Mobile Press Register,* May 3, 1996, p. 7B; and Anne Reifenberg and Allana Sullivan, "Rising Gasoline Prices: Everyone Else's Fault," *Wall Street Journal,* May 1, 1996, p. B1.
2. Robert J. Dolan, "How Do You Know When the Price Is Right?" *Harvard Business Review,* September/October 1995, pp. 174–183; see also David Wessel, "The Price Is Wrong and Economists Are in an Uproar," *Wall Street Journal,* January 2, 1991, p. B1.
3. Arsenio Oloroso Jr., "Searle on Hormones with Buyout Strategy," *Crain's Chicago Business,* March 18, 1996, pp. 1–2.
4. Robert McMath, "New Products: Innovative Product Packaging: The Pluses and Pitfalls," *Brandweek,* January 4, 1993, p. 26.
5. Halman W. Jenkins Jr., "Brand Managers Get Old-Time Religion," *Wall Street Journal,* April 23, 1996, p. A21.
6. H. Garrett DeYoung, "Politics and Pills," *Monsanto,* December 1992, pp. 34–37.
7. Paul Dvorak, "Saturn SL2: Compact and Quite Classy," *Machine Design,* March 7, 1996, p. 296.
8. John Greenwald, "Cereal Showdown," *Time,* April 29, 1996, p. 60; see also Kevin Helliker, "U.S. Discount Retailers Are Targeting Europe and Its Fat Margins," *Wall Street Journal,* September 20, 1993, pp. A1, A7.
9. Bruce Horovitz, "Value-Minded Consumers Call the shots," *USA Today,* September 19, 1996, pp. B1, B2; Tim Carvell, "Cereal Wars: A Tale of Bran, Oats, and Air," *Fortune,* May 13, 1996, p. 30; and Jack Neff "Diaper Price Wars Expand to Training Pants," *Advertising Age,* April 1, 1996, p. 16.
10. Ellen Neuborne, "Procter & Gamble Tactic May Put Lid on Prices," *USA Today,* February 20, 1996, p. B1.
11. Jeff Cole, "Boeing Is Offering Cuts in Prices of New Jets, Rattling the Industry," *Wall Street Journal,* April 24, 1995, p. A1; and Howard Banks, "Moment of Truth," *Forbes,* May 22, 1995, pp. 51–62.
12. Michael Selz, "Small Firms Use Variety of Ploys to Raise Prices," *Wall Street Journal,* June 17, 1993, pp. B1, B2.
13. Kimberly Wray, "A New Leader at Sealy," *HFN: The Weekly Newspaper for the Home Furnishing Network,* March 4, 1996, p. 1; see also Pam Schancupp, "Sealy Sets Consumer Rebate," *HFD—The Weekly Home Furnishings Newspaper,* June 15, 1992, p. 22.
14. Steven Kaye, "The No-Dicker Sticker," *U.S. News & World Report,* April 27, 1992, pp. 74–76.
15. Judann Pollack, "Pop Tarts Packs More Pastry for Same Price," *Advertising Age,* August 5, 1996, p. 6; see also James

Hirsch, "Airlines Bet that Pampering Passengers Will Build Loyalty, Soften Fare Increases," *Wall Street Journal,* February 17, 1993, pp. B1, B8.

16. Hirsch, "Airlines Pampering Passengers; see also "Continental Air Lowers Fares," *Wall Street Journal,* June 19, 1996, p. C2.

17. Advertisement, *Wall Street Journal,* February 11, 1993, p. B3.

18. Rustan Kosenko and Don Rahtz, "Buyer Market Price Knowledge Influence on Acceptable Price Range and Price Limits," in *Advances in Consumer Research,* ed. by Michael J. Houston (Association for Consumer Research, 1987); and Anthony D. Cox, "New Evidence Concerning Consumer Price Limits," in *Advances in Consumer Research,* ed. by Richard Lutz (Association for Consumer Research, 1986), pp. 268–271.

19. Neal Templin, "PC Price Wars Force Electronics Chain to Curb Expansion, Push Big Appliances," *Wall Street Journal,* June 4, 1996, p. B1; see also Richard Gibson, "Marketing: Store-Brand Pricing Has to Be Just Right," *Wall Street Journal,* February 14, 1992, p. B1.

20. Lawrence Aragon, "Apple-IRS Will Aribitrate Dispute," *The Business Journal—San Jose,* March 16, 1992, p. 1.

21. Michael Czinkota and Ilkka Ronkainen, *International Marketing,* 5th ed. (Fort Worth, Tex.: The Dryden Press, 1998), pp. 336–358.

APPENDIX

1. Melissa E. James, "Postcards from the Class of '95," *Sales & Marketing Management,* June 1995, pp. 73–77.

2. Malcolm Fitch, "Cruise the Web to Land the Job of Your Dreams," *Money,* May 1997, pp. 29–30. See also Del Jones, "Résumé Advice: It's as Simple as Black and White," *USA Today,* January 24, 1996, p. 4B.

3. A portion of the information in this section is adapted from the *Occupational Outlook Handbook* (Washington, D.C.: U.S. Department of Labor, 1996).

4. "Want a Job in One of the 10 Hottest Career Fields?" *Adweek,* April 8, 1996, p. 20.

5. Beth Belton, "Degree-Based Earnings Gap Grows Quickly," *USA Today,* February 16, 1996, p. B1.

GLOSSARY

Page numbers after the definition refer to the page in the text where the term's "Marketing Dictionary" appears.

accessory equipment A capital product, usually less expensive and shorter-lived than an installation, such as a laptop computer. (p. 379)

administered marketing system A VMS that achieves channel coordination when a dominant channel member exercises its power. (p. 489)

adoption process A series of stages through which consumers decide whether or not to become regular users of a new product, including awareness, interest, evaluation, trial, and rejection or adoption. (p. 415)

advertising Paid, nonpersonal communication through various media by a business firm, not-for-profit organization, or individual identified in the message with the hope of informing or persuading members of a particular audience. (pp. 573, 603)

advertising agency Marketing specialist firm that assists advertisers in planning and implementing advertising programs. (p. 623)

affinity program A marketing effort sponsored by an organization that solicits responses from individuals who share common interests and activities. (p. 343)

agents and brokers Independent wholesaling intermediaries who may or may not take possession of goods, but never take title to them. (p. 475)

AIDA concept Acronym for attention-interest-desire-action, the traditional explanation of the steps an individual must take to complete the purchase decision. (p. 565)

AIO statements Statements in a psychographic survey; choices reflect a respondent's activities, interests, and opinions. (p. 243)

approach Salesperson's initial contact with a prospective customer. (p. 661)

Asch phenomenon Effect of a reference group on individual decision making. (p. 273)

assortment management A retailer's effort to offer the right product, at the right time and place, to the right customer. (p. 503)

atmospherics The combination of physical characteristics and amenities that contribute to a store's image. (p. 511)

attitude A person's enduring favorable or unfavorable evaluation, emotional feeling, or action tendency toward a product. (p. 281)

auction house An establishment that gathers buyers and sellers in one location where buyers can examine merchandise before submitting competing purchase offers. (p. 477)

basing point system A pricing system common in some industries during the early twentieth century that incorporated transportation costs by quoting factory prices plus freight charges from the basing point cities nearest the buyers. (p. 727)

benchmarking Process in which an organization continuously compares and measures itself against business leaders anywhere in the world to learn how it could improve performance. (p. 65)

bid Written sales proposal from a vendor. (p. 323)

boundary-spanning role Sales manager's activities to link the sales force to other elements of the organization's internal and external environments. (p. 665)

brand A name, term, sign, symbol, design, or some combination that identifies the products of a firm. (p. 399)

brand dilution A loss in brand equity that results when a firm introduces too many brand extensions. (p. 411)

brand equity The added value that a certain brand name gives to a product. (p. 403)

brand extension Application of a popular brand name to a new product in an unrelated product category. (p. 409)

brand insistence The stage of brand acceptance at which the consumer refuses to accept alternatives and searches extensively for the desired good or service. (p. 401)

brand licensing The practice of allowing other companies to use a brand name in exchange for a payment. (p. 411)

brand manager A marketing professional charged with planning and implementing marketing strategies and tactics for a brand. (p. 403)

brand mark A symbol or pictorial design that identifies a product. (p. 403)

brand name The part of a brand consisting of words or letters that form a name to identify and distinguish a firm's offerings. (p. 403)

brand preference The stage of brand acceptance at which the consumer selects one brand over competing offerings based on previous experience with it. (p. 401)

brand recognition The stage of brand acceptance at which the consumer knows of a brand, but does not prefer it to competing brands. (p. 401)

breakeven analysis A pricing technique that determines the number of products that a firm must sell at a specified price in order to generate enough revenue to cover total cost. (p. 707)

broker An agent wholesaling intermediary who does not take title to or possession of goods in the course of its primary function-to bring together buyers and sellers. (p. 477)

business product Good or service purchased for use either directly or indirectly in the production of other goods and services for resale. (p. 229)

business service An intangible product purchased to facilitate a firm's production and operating processes. (p. 381)

business-to-business marketing Organizational purchase of goods and services to support production of other goods and services or daily company operations or for resale. (p. 299)

buyer behavior Process by which consumers and business buyers make purchase decisions. (p. 267)

buyer's market Marketplace characterized by an abundance of goods and/or services. (p. 13)

buying center Participants in an organizational buying action. (p. 319)

canned presentation Memorized sales talk that ensures uniform coverage of the points that management deems important. (p. 661)

cannibalization A loss of sales of a current product due to competition from a new product in the same line. (p. 413)

cash-and-carry wholesaler A limited-function merchant wholesaler who performs most wholesaling functions except financing and delivery. (p. 475)

cash discount A price reduction offered to a consumer, industrial user, or marketing intermediary in return for prompt payment. (p. 725)

category killer A retailer that combines huge selection and low prices within a single product line. (p. 515)

cause marketing Identification and marketing of a social issue, cause, or idea to selected target markets. (p. 21)

census Collection of data from all possible members of a population or universe. (p. 211)

chain store A group of stores that operate under central ownership and management to market essentially the same product line. (p. 522)

channel captain A dominant and controlling member of a distribution channel. (p. 485)

class rate A standard transportation rate established for shipments of a specific commodity between any pair of destinations. (p. 539)

closed sales territory An exclusive geographic selling region defined and enforced by a manufacturer for a distributor. (p. 483)

closing Stage of the personal selling process at which the salesperson asks the customer to make a purchase decision. (p. 663)

cluster sample Probability sample in which researchers select geographic areas or clusters, and all of them or chosen individuals within them become respondents. (p. 211)

co-branding Partnership between two or more companies to closely link their brand names together for a single product. (pp. 351, 411)

co-marketing Formal links between two or more businesses to jointly market each other's products. (p. 351)

cognitive dissonance Postpurchase anxiety that results from an imbalance among an individual's knowledge, beliefs, and attitudes. (p. 289)

cohort effect Tendency for members of a generation to be influenced by the same events. (p. 235)

commercial market Individuals and firms that acquire goods and services to support, directly or indirectly, production of other goods and services. (p. 299)

commission Incentive compensation directly related to the sales or profits created by a salesperson's orders. (p. 671)

commission merchant An agent wholesaling intermediary who takes possession of goods shipped to a central market for sale, acts as the producer's agent, and collects an agreed-upon fee at the time of the sale. (p. 475)

commodity rate A special, favorable transportation rate granted by a carrier to a selected shipper as a reward for either regular business or a large-quantity shipment. (p. 539)

comparative advertising Nonpersonal selling efforts that emphasize direct or indirect promotional comparisons between competing brands. (p. 609)

competitive environment The interactive exchange in the marketplace influenced by actions of marketers of directly competitive products, marketers of products that can substitute for one another, and other marketers competing for the same consumers' purchasing power. (p. 83)

competitive pricing strategy A pricing strategy designed to de-emphasize price as a competitive variable by pricing a good or service at the general level of comparable offerings. (p. 723)

component parts and materials Finished business products that become parts of buying firms' final products. Also known as fabricated parts and materials. (p. 379)

concentrated marketing Marketing strategy that commits all of a firm's marketing resources to serve a single market segment. (p. 249)

concept testing An initiative to measure consumer attitudes and perceptions of a product idea prior to actual development. (p. 419)

Consolidated Metropolitan Statistical Area (CMSA) Major population concentration, including the country's 25 or so urban giants. (p. 233)

consultative selling Meeting customer needs by listening to them, understanding-and caring about-their problems, paying attention to details, and following through after the sale. (p. 653)

consumer behavior Buyer behavior of ultimate consumers. (p. 267)

consumer innovator An initial purchaser of a new product. (p. 415)

consumer orientation Business philosophy incorporating the marketing concept that emphasizes first determining unmet consumer needs and then designing a system for satisfying them. (p. 13)

consumer product Good or service purchased by an ultimate consumer for personal use. (p. 229)

consumer rights As stated by President Kennedy in 1962, the consumer's right to choose freely, to be informed, to be heard, and to be safe. (p. 101)

consumerism A social force within the environment designed to aid and protect buyers by exerting legal, moral, and economic pressures on businesses and government. (p. 99)

containerization The process of combining several unitized loads into a single, well-protected load. (p. 548)

continuous improvement Process of constantly studying and making changes in work activities; called kaizen in Japan. (p. 67)

contractual marketing system A VMS that coordinates channel activities through formal agreements among channel members. (p. 489)

convenience product A good or service that consumers want to purchase frequently, immediately, and with minimal effort. (p. 375)

convenience sample Nonprobability sample selected from among readily available respondents. (p. 211)

cooperative advertising Sharing advertising costs between a retailer and a manufacturer of the advertised good or service. (p. 611)

corporate marketing system A VMS in which a single owner runs organizations at each stage in its distribution channel. (p. 489)

cost of quality The total of costs associated with poor quality such as scrap, rework, and loss of customers. (p. 67)

cost-plus pricing The practice of adding a percentage or specified dollar amount (markup) to the base cost of a product to cover unassigned costs and provide a profit. (p. 703)

countertrade A form of exporting in which sellers barter their goods and services rather than exchanging them for cash. (p. 147)

creative selling Personal selling situations in which buyers must complete considerable analytical decision making, creating a need for skillful proposals of solutions for customer needs. (p. 655)

critical success factor Product or process characteristic that most powerfully affects efforts to gain competitive advantage and achieve long-term success. (p. 65)

cross promotion A technique in which marketing partners share the cost of a promotional campaign that meets their mutual needs. (p. 633)

cross-functional team A group of employees from different departments who work together on a specific project. (p. 61)

cue Any object in the environment that determines the nature of a consumer's response to a drive. (p. 283)

culture Values, beliefs, preferences, and tastes handed down from one generation to the next. (p. 267)

customary price The traditional amount that customers expect to pay for a certain good or service. (p. 699)

customer satisfaction The result of a good or service meeting or exceeding the buyer's needs and expectations. (p. 47)

customer satisfaction measurement (CSM) program A set of ongoing procedures for measuring customer feedback against customer satisfaction goals and developing an action plan for improvement. (p. 53)

customer service standard A statement of goals and acceptable performance for the quality of service that a firm expects to deliver to its customers. (p. 537)

customer-based segmentation Dividing a business-to-business market into homogeneous groups based on buyers' product specifications. (p. 301)

cycle time The time required to complete a work process or activity from beginning to end. (p. 67)

data mining Process of searching through customer information files to detect patterns that guide marketing decision making. (p. 221)

database marketing The use of computers to identify and target messages toward specific groups of potential customers. (p. 345)

Delphi technique A qualitative sales forecasting method that gathers and redistributes several rounds of anonymous forecasts until the participants reach a consensus. (p. 179)

demand A schedule of the amounts of a firm's product that consumers will purchase at different prices during a specified time period. (p. 699)

demarketing The process of reducing consumer demand for a good or service to a level that the firm can supply. (p. 95)

demographic segmentation Dividing consumer groups according to characteristics such as sex, age, income, occupation, education, household size, and stage in the family life cycle. (p. 235)

department store A large store that handles a variety of merchandise, including clothing, household goods, appliances, and furniture. (p. 517)

derived demand Demand for a business product that results from demand for a consumer product of which it is a component. (p. 307)

differentiated marketing Marketing strategy to produce numerous products and promote them with different marketing mixes designed to satisfy smaller segments. (p. 249)

diffusion process The sequence of acceptance of new products by the members of a community or social system. (p. 415)

direct channel A distribution channel that moves goods directly from a producer to an ultimate user. (p. 467)

direct marketing Direct communications other than personal sales contacts between buyer and seller. (p. 573)

direct selling A strategy designed to establish direct sales contact between producer and final user. (p. 467)

discount house A store that charges low prices but may not offer services such as credit. (p. 517)

distribution channel An organized system of marketing institutions and their interrelationships that promotes the physical flow of goods and services, along with title that confers ownership, from producer to consumer or business user. (p. 465)

distribution intensity The number of intermediaries through which a manufacturer distributes its goods. (p. 481)

distribution strategy Element of marketing decision making concerned with activities and marketing institutions that get the right good or service to the firm's customers. (p. 25)

distribution warehouse A facility designed to assemble and then redistribute goods in a way that facilitates rapid movement to purchasers. (p. 545)

drive Strong stimulus that impels action. (p. 283)

drop shipper A limited-function merchant wholesaler who accepts orders from customers and forwards them to producers, which ship directly to the customers who place the orders. (p. 475)

dual adaptation An international product and promotional strategy that modifies both product and promotional strategies to suit individual foreign markets. (p. 145)

dual distribution A network that moves products to a firm's target market through more than one distribution channel. (p. 469)

dumping The controversial trade practice of selling a product in a foreign market at a lower price than it commands in the producer's domestic market. (p. 131)

economic environment Forces that influence consumer buying power and marketing strategies, including the state of the business cycle, inflation, unemployment, resource availability, and income. (p. 93)

80/20 principle Idea that a big percentage of a product's revenues-roughly 80 percent-comes from a relatively small percentage of total customers-around 20 percent. (p. 245)

elasticity A measure of the responsiveness of purchasers and suppliers to changes in price. (p. 701)

electronic data interchange (EDI) Computer-to-computer exchanges of invoices, orders, and other business documents. (p. 355)

embargo An administrative trade restriction that imposes a complete ban on imports of a specified product. (p. 131)

employee involvement Motivating employees to improve their job performance through internal marketing, empowerment, training, and teamwork. (p. 59)

empowerment Giving employees authority to make decisions about their work without supervisory approval. (p. 59)

end-use application segmentation Segmenting a business-to-business market based on how industrial purchasers will use the product. (p. 303)

Engel's laws Three general statements based on Ernst Engel's studies of the impact of household income changes on consumer spending behavior. As family income increases, (1) a smaller percentage of expenditures go for food, (2) the percentage spent on housing and household operations and clothing remains constant, and (3) the percentage spent on other items (such as recreation and education) increases. (p. 241)

environmental forecast A broad-based projection of economic activity that focuses on the impact of external events and influences on the firm's markets. (p. 185)

environmental management An effort to attain organizational objectives by predicting and influencing the firm's competitive, political-legal, economic, technological, and social-cultural environments. (p. 81)

environmental scanning The process of collecting information about the external marketing environment in order to identify and interpret potential trends. (p. 81)

evaluative criteria Features considered in a consumer's choice of alternatives. (p. 287)

event marketing The marketing of sporting, cultural, and charitable activities to selected target markets. (p. 23)

everyday low pricing (EDLP) A pricing strategy of continuously offering low prices rather than relying on short-term price-cutting tactics such as cents-off coupons, rebates, and special sales. (p. 723)

evoked set Number of brands that a consumer considers buying before making a purchasing decision. (p. 287)

exchange control An administrative trade restriction that controls access to foreign currencies. (p. 131)

exchange process Activity in which two or more parties give something of value to each other to satisfy perceived needs. (p. 11)

exchange rate The price of one nation's currency in terms of another country's currency. (p. 125)

exclusive distribution A channel policy in which a firm grants exclusive rights to a single wholesaler or retailer to sell its products in a particular geographic area. (p. 481)

exclusive-dealing agreement An arrangement between a manufacturer and a marketing intermediary that prohibits the intermediary from handling competing product lines. (p. 483)

expectancy theory Theory that motivation depends on an individual's expectations of his or her ability to perform a job and how that performance relates to attaining a desired reward. (p. 671)

experiment Scientific investigation in which a researcher manipulates a test group(s) and compares the results with those of a control group that did not receive the experimental controls or manipulations. (p. 219)

exploratory research Process of discussing a marketing problem with informed sources both within and outside the firm and examining information from secondary sources. (p. 203)

exponential smoothing A quantitative forecasting technique that assigns weights to historical sales data, giving the greatest weight to the most recent data. (p. 185)

exporting Marketing domestically produced goods and services in foreign countries. (p. 117)

external customer A person or organization that buys or uses another firm's goods or services. (p. 49)

fair-trade law A statute (enacted in most states) that permits manufacturers to stipulate minimum retail prices for their products. (p. 691)

family brand A brand name that identifies several related products. (p. 401)

family life cycle Process of family formation and dissolution, which affects market segmentation because life stage, not age, is the primary determinant of many consumer purchases. (p. 237)

field selling Face-to-face sales presentations made at prospective customers' homes or businesses. (p. 649)

fixed-sum-per-unit method Allocating promotional expenditures as a predetermined dollar amount for each sales or production unit. (p. 587)

FOB plant A "free on board" price that does not include shipping charges; also called *FOB origin.* (p. 727)

focus group Information-gathering procedure in marketing research that typically brings together 8 to 12 individuals to discuss a given subject. (p. 215)

follow-up Postsale activities that often determine whether a one-time purchase will lead a buyer to become a repeat customer. (p. 665)

foreign licensing A contractual agreement that grants foreign marketers the right to distribute a firm's merchandise or use its trademark, patent, or process in a specified geographic area for a specified time period. (p. 139)

franchise A contractual arrangement in which a wholesaler or retailer (the franchisee) agrees to make some payment and to meet the operating requirements of a manufacturer or other franchiser in exchange for the right to market the franchiser's goods or services under its brand name. (p. 139)

freight absorption A pricing system that incorporates transportation costs by allowing a buyer to deduct shipping expenses from the price paid for the goods. (p. 727)

frequency marketing Frequent buyer or user marketing program that rewards customers who purchase a good or service with cash, rebates, merchandise, or other premiums. (p. 345)

friendship, commerce, and navigation (FCN) treaty An international agreement that sets terms for many aspects of commercial relations among nations. (p. 127)

gap A difference between expected service quality and perceived service quality. (p. 439)

General Agreement on Tariffs and Trade (GATT) An international trade accord that has helped to reduce worldwide tariffs. (p. 131)

general merchandise retailer A store that carries a wide variety of product lines, stocking all of them in some depth. (p. 515)

generic name A brand name that has become a generally descriptive term for a class of products. (p. 405)

generic product An item characterized by a plain label, with no advertising and no brand name. (p. 401)

geographic information system (GIS) Computer technology that records several layers of data on a single map. (p. 235)

geographic segmentation Dividing an overall market into homogeneous groups on the basis of population locations. (p. 231)

global marketing strategy A standardized marketing mix with minimal modifications that guides marketing decisions in all of a firm's domestic and foreign markets. (p. 143)

global sourcing Contracting to purchase goods and services from suppliers worldwide. (p. 307)

goods-services continuum A device that helps marketers to visualize the differences and similarities between goods and services. (p. 433)

green marketing Production, promotion, and reclamation of environmentally sensitive products. (p. 107)

grey good A product manufactured abroad under license from a U.S. firm and then sold in the U.S. market in competition with that firm's own counterpart products. (p. 489)

home shopping A retailing method based on promotions through cable television networks to sell merchandise through telephone orders for home delivery. (p. 521)

hypermarket A giant mass merchandiser of soft goods and groceries that operates on a low-price, self-service strategy. (p. 517)

hypothesis Tentative explanation for some specific event. (p. 205)

import quota An administrative trade restriction that limits the number of units of a certain good that can enter a country for resale. (p. 131)

importing Domestic purchases of goods, services, and raw materials produced in foreign countries. (p. 117)

individual brand A unique brand name that identifies a specific offering within a firm's product line to avoid grouping it under a family brand. (p. 401)

industrial distributor A wholesaling marketing intermediary that handles purchases of small accessory equipment and operating supplies. (pp. 379, 469)

infomercial Commercial for a single product running 30 minutes or longer in a format that resembles a regular television program. (p. 581)

informative advertising Nonpersonal promotion that seeks to announce the availability of and develop initial demand for a new good, service, organization, person, place, idea, or cause. (p. 609)

infrastructure A nation's basic conditions in transportation networks, communication systems, and energy facilities. (p. 125)

installation A major capital investment by a business buyer that typically involves expensive and relatively long-lived products, such as a new factory or piece of heavy machinery. (p. 379)

institutional advertising Promoting a concept, an idea, a philosophy, or the goodwill of an industry, company, organization, place, person, or government agency. (p. 609)

integrated marketing communications (IMC) Coordination of all promotional activities-media advertising, direct mail, personal selling, sales promotion, and public relations-to produce a unified, customer-focused promotional message. (p. 561)

intensive distribution A channel policy in which a manufacturer of a convenience product attempts to saturate the market. (p. 481)

interactive marketing Buyer-seller communications in which the customer controls the amount and type of information received from a marketer through such channels as the Internet, CD-ROM disks, interactive 800 telephone numbers, and virtual reality kiosks. (p. 29)

interactive media Communication channels that induce message recipients to participate actively in the promotional effort. (p. 621)

internal customer An employee or department within an organization whose job performance depends on the work of another employee or department. (p. 51)

internal marketing Management actions that help all members of an organization to understand and accept their respective roles in implementing its marketing strategy. (p. 51)

Internet An all-purpose global network composed of some 48,000 different networks around the globe that, within limits, lets anyone with access to a personal computer send and receive images and data anywhere. (p. 31)

intranet An internal network that conforms to Internet standards in order to support two-way organizational communications. (p. 51)

ISO 9000 A set of standards for quality management and quality assurance developed by the International Standards Organization in Switzerland for countries in the European Union (EU). (p. 57)

joint demand Demand for a business product that depends on the demand for another business product that is necessary for the use of the first. (p. 309)

joint venture An agreement in which a firm shares the risks, costs, and management of a foreign operation with one or more partners, who are usually citizens of the host country. (p. 141)

jury of executive opinion A qualitative sales forecasting method that combines and averages the sales expectations of various executives. (p. 179)

just-in-time system A production control system designed to minimize manufacturing and inventory costs by providing essential inputs to production processes in a timely manner. (p. 547)

label The descriptive part of a product's package that lists the brand name or symbol, name and address of manufacturer or distributor, product composition and size, and recommended uses. (p. 409)

learning Immediate or expected change in behavior as a result of experience. (p. 283)

lifestyle People's decisions about how to live their daily lives, including family, job, social, and consumer activities. (p. 243)

lifetime value of a customer The revenues and intangible benefits (referrals, customer feedback, etc.) that a customer brings to the seller over an average lifetime, less the amount the company must spend to acquire, market to, and service the customer. (p. 360)

limited-line store A retailer who offers a large assortment within a single product line or a few related product lines. (p. 515)

line extension Introduction of a new product that is closely related to other products in the firm's existing line. (p. 391)

list price An established price normally quoted to potential buyers. (p. 723)

logistics The process of coordinating the flow of information, goods, and services among members of the distribution channel. (p. 531)

loss leader A product offered at a price below cost to attract customers to a store in the hope that they will also buy other merchandise at regular prices. (p. 731)

mail-order wholesaler A limited-function merchant wholesaler who distributes catalogs instead of sending sales representatives to contact customers. (p. 475)

manufacturer's agent An agent wholesaling intermediary who represents a number of manufacturers of related but noncompeting products, receiving a commission on each sale. (p. 477)

manufacturer's brand A brand name owned by a manufacturer or other producer. (p. 401)

maquiladora A Mexican assembly plant located near the U.S. border. (p. 535)

markdown An amount by which a retailer reduces the original selling price of a product. (p. 507)

market People or institutions with sufficient purchasing power, authority, and willingness to buy. (p. 229)

market attractiveness/business strength matrix A portfolio analysis technique that rates SBUs according to the attractiveness of their markets and their organizational strengths. (p. 175)

market price A price that a consumer or marketing intermediary actually pays for a product after subtracting any discounts, allowances, or rebates from the list price. (p. 725)

market segmentation Division of the total market into smaller, relatively homogeneous groups. (p. 231)

market share/market growth matrix A marketing planning tool that classifies a firm's products according to industry growth rates and market shares relative to competing products. (p. 173)

market test A quantitative forecasting method that introduces a new product, price, promotional campaign, or other marketing variable in a relatively small test market location in order to assess consumer reactions. (p. 181)

marketing Process of planning and executing the conception, pricing, promotion, and distribution of ideas, goods, services, organizations, and events to create and maintain relationships that satisfy individual and organizational objectives. (p. 9)

marketing audit A thorough, objective evaluation of an organization's marketing philosophy, goals, policies, tactics, practices, and results. (p. 63)

marketing communication Transmission from a sender to a receiver of a message dealing with the buyer-seller relationship. (p. 561)

marketing concept Companywide consumer orientation with the objective of achieving long-run success. (p. 13)

marketing cost analysis Evaluation of expenses for tasks like selling, billing, and advertising to determine the profitability of particular customers, territories, or product lines. (p. 205)

marketing decision support system (MDSS) Marketing information system component that links a decision maker with relevant databases and analysis tools. (p. 221)

marketing ethics Marketers' standards of conduct and moral values. (p. 103)

marketing information system (MIS) Planned, computer-based system designed to provide managers with a continuous flow of information relevant to their specific decisions and areas of responsibility. (p. 219)

marketing intermediary A business firm, either wholesaler or retailer, that operates between producers and consumers or business users; also called a middleman. (p. 467)

marketing mix Blending the four strategy elements of marketing decision making—product, price, distribution, and promotion—to satisfy chosen consumer segments. (p. 25)

marketing myopia Term coined by Theodore Levitt in his argument that executives in many industries fail to recognize the broad scope of their businesses. (According to Levitt, future growth is endangered when executives lack a marketing orientation.) (p. 15)

marketing planning The process of anticipating future events and conditions and determining the courses of action necessary to achieve marketing objectives. (p. 163)

marketing research Collection and use of information for marketing decision making. (p. 199)

marketing strategy A firm's overall program for selecting and satisfying a target market. (p. 173)

markup An amount that a retailer or wholesaler adds to the cost of a product to determine its selling price. (p. 505)

mass customization Providing high-quality, competitively priced goods and services tailor-made to customers' specifications or needs. (p. 69)

mass merchandiser A store that stocks a wider line of goods than a department store, usually without the same depth of assortment within each line. (p. 517)

materials handling The set of activities that move production inputs and other goods within plants, warehouses, and transportation terminals. (p. 548)

media scheduling Setting the timing and sequence of a series of advertisements. (p. 621)

meeting competition method Allocating promotional spending to match that of a competitor, either as an absolute amount or relative to the firms' market shares. (p. 587)

merchandise mart A permanent exhibition facility in which manufacturers display products for visiting retail and wholesale buyers. (p. 475)

merchant wholesaler An independently owned wholesaling intermediary who takes title to the goods that it handles. (p. 475)

Metropolitan Statistical Area (MSA) Free-standing urban population center. (p. 233)

micromarketing Marketing strategy to target potential customers at basic levels such as by ZIP codes. (p. 251)

middleman See marketing intermediary.

mission A general, enduring statement of overall organizational purpose. (p. 167)

missionary sales Indirect type of selling in which specialized salespeople promote the firm's goodwill among indirect customers, often by assisting in product use (p. 657)

modified breakeven analysis A pricing technique that evaluates consumer demand by comparing the quantities that a firm must sell at a variety of prices in order to cover total costs together with estimates of expected sales at those prices. (p. 709)

modified rebuy Purchase decision in which a purchaser is willing to reevaluate available options for repurchasing a good or service. (p. 317)

monopolistic competition A market structure in which large numbers of buyers and sellers exchange heterogeneous relatively well-differentiated products, so marketers exert some control over prices. (p. 699)

monopoly A market structure in which only one seller dominates trade in a good or service for which buyers can find no close substitutes. (p. 701)

motive Inner state that directs a person toward the goal of satisfying a felt need. (p. 277)

MRO item Part of business supplies categorized as a maintenance item, a repair item, or an element of operating supplies. (p. 381)

multidomestic marketing strategy A program of market segmentation that identifies specific foreign markets and tailors the marketing mix to match specific traits in each nation. (p. 143)

multinational corporation A firm with significant operations and marketing activities outside its home country. (p. 141)

multiple sourcing Spreading purchases among several vendors. (p. 315)

national accounts organization Organization scheme that assigns sales teams to a firm's largest accounts. (p. 669)

need Lack of something useful; an imbalance between a desired state and an actual state. (p. 277)

new-task buying First-time or unique purchase situation that requires considerable effort by the decision makers. (p. 317)

nonprobability sample Arbitrary grouping that produces data unsuited for most standard statistical tests. (p. 211)

norm Value, attitude, or behavior that a group deems appropriate for its members. (p. 271)

North American Free-Trade Agreement (NAFTA) An accord to remove trade barriers among Canada, Mexico, and the United States. (p. 133)

odd pricing A pricing policy that ends prices with odd numbers just under round numbers to make them seem low—for instance, $9.99 rather than $10.00. (p. 731)

off-price retailer A store that finds exceptional deals on well-known, brand-name clothing and resells it at unusually low prices. (p. 517)

oligopoly A market structure in which relatively few sellers compete, while high start-up costs form barriers to keep out new competitors. (p. 699)

opinion leader Trendsetter likely to purchase new products before others and then share the resulting experiences and opinions via word of mouth. (p. 275)

order processing Selling, mostly at the wholesale and retail levels, that involves identifying customer needs, pointing them out to customers, and completing orders. (p. 655)

organization marketing Marketing by mutual-benefit organizations, service organizations, and government organizations intended to influence others to accept their goals, receive their services, or contribute to them in some way. (p. 23)

outlet mall A shopping center that houses only off-price retailers. (p. 517)

outsourcing Acquiring inputs from outside vendors for goods and services formerly produced in-house. (p. 309)

over-the-counter selling Personal selling conducted in retail and some wholesale locations in which customers visit the seller's place of business on their own initiative. (p. 649)

parallel product development A project-management effort based on teams of design, manufacturing, marketing, sales, and service people who carry out the development process from idea generation to commercialization. (p. 419)

partnership Affiliation of two or more marketers to assist each other in the achievement of common goals. (p. 347)

PDCA cycle Continuous improvement sequence of planning, doing, checking, and acting. (p. 67)

penetration pricing strategy A pricing strategy involving the use of a relatively low entry price as compared with competing offerings to help secure initial market acceptance. (p. 721)

percentage-of-sales method Allocating funds for promotion during a given time period based on a specified percentage of either past or forecasted sales. (p. 587)

perception Meaning that an individual creates by interpreting a stimulus. (p. 279)

perceptual screen Consumers' mental filtering processes through which all marketing messages must pass to gain attention. (p. 279)

person marketing Marketing efforts designed to cultivate the attention, interest, and preference of a target market toward a person (typically a political candidate or celebrity). (p. 21)

personal selling Interpersonal promotional process involving a seller's person-to-person presentation to a prospective buyer. (p. 571, 647)

persuasive advertising Competitive, nonpersonal promotion that seeks to increase demand for an existing good, service, organization, person, place, idea, or cause. (p.609)

phased development A sequential pattern for product development through an orderly series of steps. (p. 419)

physical distribution Activities to achieve efficient movement of finished goods from the end of the production line to the consumer. (p. 531)

place marketing Marketing efforts to attract people and organizations to a particular geographic area. (p. 21)

planned shopping center A group of retail stores planned, coordinated, and marketed as a unit. (p. 507)

planning The process of anticipating future events and conditions and determining the courses of action necessary to achieve organizational objectives. (p. 163)

point-of-purchase (POP) advertising Display or other promotion located near the site of an actual buying decision. (p. 629)

political-legal environment A component of the marketing environment defined by laws and their interpretations that require firms to operate under certain competitive conditions and to protect consumer rights. (p. 85)

population (universe) Total group that researchers want to study. (p. 211)

positioning Marketing strategy that emphasizes serving a specific market segment by achieving a certain position in buyers' minds. (p. 251)

positioning map Graphic illustration that shows differences in consumers' perceptions of competing products. (p. 251)

posttesting Assessment of an advertisement's effectiveness after it has appeared in the appropriate medium. (p. 635)

precall planning Use of information collected during the prospecting and qualifying stages of the sales process and during previous contacts with the prospect to tailor the approach and presentation in a way that matches the customer's needs. (p. 661)

presentation Describing a product's major features and relating them to a customer's problems or needs. (p. 661)

pretesting Assessment of an advertisement's effectiveness before it actually appears in the chosen medium. (p. 635)

price The exchange value of a good or service. (p. 689)

price flexibility A pricing policy that permits variable prices for different customers. (p. 731)

pricing policy A set of general guidelines that reflect marketing objectives and influence specific pricing decisions. (p. 729)

pricing strategy Element of marketing decision making dealing with methods of setting profitable and justifiable prices. (p. 25)

primary data Data collected for the first time. (p. 205)

Primary Metropolitan Statistical Area (PMSA) Major urban area within a CMSA. (p. 235)

private brand A brand name placed on products marketed by wholesalers and retailers. (p. 401)

probability sample Sample that gives every member of the population a known chance of being selected. (p. 211)

product A bundle of physical, service, and symbolic attributes designed to enhance buyers' want satisfaction. (p. 373)

product adaptation An international product and promotional strategy that calls for product modifications to suit a foreign market, but no changes in promotional strategy. (p. 145)

product advertising Nonpersonal selling of a good or service. (p. 609)

product invention An international product and promotion strategy to develop a new product supported by a new promotional strategy to take advantage of a unique foreign opportunity. (p. 147)

product liability The responsibility of manufacturers and marketers for injuries and damages caused by their products. (p. 423)

product life cycle The four basic stages through which a successful product progresses—introduction, growth, maturity, and decline. (p. 383)

product line A series of related products. (p. 381)

product line pricing The practice of setting a limited number of prices for a selection of merchandise. (p. 731)

product manager A marketing professional who determines the objectives and marketing strategies for an individual product or product line. (p. 417)

product mix A company's assortment of product lines and individual offerings. (p. 389)

product positioning Consumers' perceptions of a product's attributes, uses, quality, and advantages and disadvantages in relation to those of competing brands. (p. 411)

product strategy Element of marketing decision making involved in developing the right good or service for the firm's customers, including package design, branding, trademarks, warranties, product life cycles, and new-product development. (p. 25)

product-related segmentation Dividing a consumer population into homogeneous groups based on characteristics of their relationships to a product. (p. 245)

production orientation Business philosophy stressing efficiency in producing a quality product, with the attitude toward marketing that "a good product will sell itself." (p. 13)

productivity The ratio of output to input of goods and services for a nation, industry, firm, or individual worker. (p. 445)

profit center Any part of an organization with responsibility for revenue and controllable costs. (p. 735)

Profit Impact of Market Strategies (PIMS) project A research program that discovered a strong positive relationship between a firm's market share and its return on investment. (p. 695)

profit maximization Point at which the additional revenue gained by increasing the price of a product equals the increase in total costs. (p. 695)

promotion Function of informing, persuading, and influencing the consumer's purchase decision. (p. 561)

promotion adaptation An international product and promotional strategy that introduces a product without changes to a foreign market supported by a unique promotional strategy targeted to that new market. (p. 145)

promotional allowance Part of a buyer's purchase price returned by a manufacturer as a cash payment to fund advertising or sales promotion by other channel members in an attempt to integrate promotional strategy within the channel. (p. 727)

promotional mix Blend of personal selling and nonpersonal selling (including advertising, sales promotion, direct marketing, and public relations) designed to achieve promotional objectives. (p. 571)

promotional pricing A technique that temporarily lowers prices below normal levels in a temporary marketing campaign. (p. 731)

promotional strategy Element of marketing decision making that involves appropriate blending of personal selling, advertising, and sales promotion to communicate with and seek to persuade potential customers. (p. 25)

prospecting Personal-selling function of identifying potential customers. (p. 659)

psychographic segmentation Dividing a population into homogeneous groups on the basis of psychological and lifestyle profiles. (p. 243)

psychological pricing A pricing policy based on the belief that certain prices or price ranges make a good or service more appealing than others to buyers. (p. 729)

public relations Firm's communications and relationships with its various publics. (pp. 573, 629)

publicity Stimulation of demand for a good, service, place, idea, person, or organization by unpaid placement of commercially significant news or favorable media presentations (pp. 573, 631)

puffery Exaggerated claims of a product's superiority or the use of subjective or vague statements that may not be literally true. (p. 639)

pulling strategy Promotional effort by a seller to stimulate demand among final users, who will then exert pressure on the distribution channel to carry the good or service, pulling it through the marketing channel. (p. 585)

pure competition A market structure in which many buyers and sellers exchange homogeneous products, so no single participant has a significant influence on price. (p. 699)

pushing strategy Promotional effort by a seller to members of the marketing channel intended to stimulate personal selling of the good or service, pushing it through the marketing channel. (p. 585)

qualifying Determining that a prospect has the needs, income, and purchase authority necessary to become a potential customer. (p. 659)

quality The degree of excellence or superiority of an organization's goods and services. (p. 47)

quality circle A small group of employees from one work area or department who meet regularly to identify and solve problems. (p. 61)

quantity discount A price reduction on a large-volume purchase. (p. 725)

quick response Strategies that reduce the time companies must hold merchandise in inventory, resulting in substantial cost savings. (p. 355)

quota sample Nonprobability sample divided to ensure representation of different segments or groups in the total sample. (p. 211)

rack jobber A full-function merchant wholesaler who markets specialized lines of merchandise to retail stores. (p. 475)

raw material A business product, such as a farm product (wheat, cotton, soybeans) or natural product (coal, lumber, iron ore) that becomes part of a final product. (p. 379)

rebate A refund of a portion of a product's purchase price, usually granted by its manufacturer. (p. 727)

reciprocity Policy to extend purchasing preference to suppliers who are also customers. (p. 317)

reference group Group with which an individual identifies strongly enough that it dictates a standard of behavior. (p. 273)

reinforcement Reduction in drive that results from an appropriate consumer response. (p. 285)

relationship marketing Development and maintenance of long-term, cost-effective **exchange** relationships with individual customers, suppliers, employees, and other partners for mutual benefit. (pp. 35, 333)

relationship quality The customer's trust in and satisfaction with the seller. (p. 451)

relationship selling Regular contacts over an extended period to establish a sustained seller-buyer relationship. (p. 651)

remanufacturing Production to restore worn-out products to like-new condition. (p. 325)

reminder advertising Nonpersonal promotion that seeks to reinforce previous promotional activity by keeping the name of a good, service, organization, person, place, idea, or cause in front of the public. (p. 609)

repositioning Marketing strategy to change the position of a product in consumers' minds relative to the positions of competing products. (p. 253)

research design Series of decisions that, taken together, comprise a master plan for conducting marketing research. (p. 205)

retail advertising Nonpersonal selling by stores that offer goods or services directly to the consuming public. (p. 611)

retail image Consumers' perception of a store and the shopping experience it provides. (p. 501)

retailing All activities involved in selling goods and services to ultimate consumers. (p. 499)

reverse channel A path that carries used goods from consumers back to a manufacturer. (p. 471)

Robinson-Patman Act A federal law prohibiting price discrimination that is not based on a cost differential as well as selling at unreasonably low prices to eliminate competitors. (p. 689)

role Behavior that members of a group expect of an individual who holds a specific position within it. (p. 271)

salary Fixed compensation payments made periodically to an employee. (p. 671)

sales analysis In-depth evaluation of a firm's sales. (p. 205)

sales branch A manufacturer-owned facility that carries inventory and processes orders for customers from available stock. (p. 473)

sales force automation (SFA) Applications of computers and other technologies to improve the efficiency and competitiveness of the sales function. (p. 653)

sales force composite A qualitative sales forecasting method that develops sales estimates based on the combined estimates of the firm's salespeople. (p. 179)

sales forecast An estimate of company sales for a specified future period. (p. 177)

sales management Activities of planning, organizing, staffing, motivating, compensating, evaluating, and controlling salespeople to ensure their effectiveness. (p. 665)

sales office A manufacturer's facility that serves as a regional office for salespeople, but does not carry inventory. (p. 475)

sales orientation Business assumption that consumers will resist purchasing nonessential goods and services with the attitude toward marketing that only creative advertising and personal selling can overcome consumers' resistance and convince them to buy. (p. 13)

sales promotion Marketing activities other than personal selling, advertising, and publicity that stimulate consumer purchasing and dealer effectiveness (includes displays, trade shows, coupons, premiums, contests, product demonstrations, and various nonrecurrent selling efforts). (pp. 573, 625)

sales quota Level of expected sales for a territory, product, customer, or salesperson against which evaluations compare actual results. (p. 673)

sampling The process of selecting survey respondents or other research participants. (p. 209)

scrambled merchandising A retailing practice of combining dissimilar product lines to boost sales volume. (p. 522)

secondary data Previously published data. (p. 205)

selective distribution A channel policy in which a firm chooses only a limited number of retailers to handle its product line. (p. 481)

self-concept Person's conception of himself or herself, composed of the real self, self-image, looking-glass self, and ideal self. (p. 285)

self-managed team A group of employees who work with little or no supervision. (p. 61)

seller's market Marketplace characterized by a shortage of goods and/or services. (p. 13)

selling agent An agent wholesaling intermediary responsible for the entire marketing program of another firm's product line. (p. 477)

selling up A retail sales technique that tries to convince a customer to buy a higher-priced item than he or she had originally intended. (p. 511)

service An intangible task that satisfies consumer or business user needs. (p. 433)

service encounter The actual interaction point between a customer and a service provider (p. 439).

service quality The expected and perceived quality of a service offering. (p. 437)

shopping product A good or service purchased only after the consumer compares competing offerings from competing vendors on such characteristics as price, quality, style, and color. (p. 375)

simple random sample Basic type of probability sample in which every individual in the relevant universe has an equal opportunity of selection. (p. 211)

skimming pricing strategy A pricing strategy involving the use of a high price relative to competitive offerings. (p. 719)

slotting allowance A fee paid by a manufacturer to a retailer to assure shelf space for its products. (p. 485)

social responsibility The collection of marketing philosophies, policies, procedures, and actions intended primarily to enhance society's welfare. (p. 105)

social-cultural environment The component of the marketing environment defined by the relationship of marketers to society and its culture. (p. 99)

sole sourcing Purchasing a firm's entire stock of a product from just one vendor. (p. 309)

specialty advertising Sales promotion technique in which marketers distribute articles such as key rings, calendars, and ballpoint pens bearing their firm's name or other advertising message. (p. 627)

specialty product A good or service with unique characteristics that cause the buyer to prize it and make a special effort to obtain it. (p. 377)

specialty store A retailer who typically handles only part of a single product line. (p. 513)

specifications Written description of a needed good or service. (p. 323)

sponsorship Provision of funds for a sporting or cultural event in exchange for a direct association with the event. (p. 573)

spreadsheet analysis A marketing planning tool that uses a decision-oriented computer program to answer what-if questions posed by marketing managers. (p. 177)

Standard Industrial Classification (SIC) U.S. government classification system that subdivides the business marketplace into detailed market segments. (p. 301)

statistical quality control A set of methods for applying statistical techniques to locate and measure quality problems in production and marketing activities. (p. 55)

status Relative prominence of any individual in a group. (p. 271)

stockout An order for a product that is unavailable for shipment or sale. (p. 547)

storage warehouse A warehouse that holds goods for moderate to long periods prior to shipment, usually to buffer seasonal demand. (p. 545)

straight extension An international product and promotional strategy that introduces the same product marketed in the home market to a foreign market using the same promotional strategy. (p. 145)

straight rebuy Recurring purchase decision in which a customer repurchases a good or service that has performed satisfactorily in the past. (p. 317)

strategic alliance Partnership between organizations that creates competitive advantages. (p. 37)

strategic business unit (SBU) A division within a multiproduct firm built around related product groupings or business activities with its own managers, resources, objectives, competitors, and structure for optimal, independent planning. (p. 173)

strategic planning The process of determining an organization's primary objectives, allocating funds, and then initiating actions designed to achieve those objectives. (p. 165)

strategic window A limited period with an optimal fit between the key requirements of a market and the particular competencies of a firm. (p. 171)

stratified sample Probability sample constructed to represent randomly selected subsamples of different groups within the total sample. (p. 211)

subculture Subgroup of a culture with its own, distinct modes of behavior. (p. 269)

subliminal perception Subconscious receipt of information. (p. 281)

suboptimization A condition that results when individual operations achieve their objectives but interfere with progress toward broader organizational goals. (p. 535)

suggestion selling A retail sales technique that attempts to broaden a customer's original purchase to add related items, special promotional products, or holiday or seasonal merchandise. (p. 511)

supercenter A large store, though still smaller than a hypermarket, that combines groceries with discount store merchandise. (p. 519)

supplies Products that represent regular expenses necessary to carry out a firm's daily operations, but not part of the final product. (p. 381)

supply A schedule of the amounts of a good or service that a firm will offer for sale at different prices during a specified time period. (p. 699)

supply (value) chain The sequence of suppliers that contribute to the creation and delivery of a good or service. (pp. 357, 531)

survey of buyer intentions A qualitative sales forecasting method that samples opinions among groups of present and potential customers concerning their purchase intentions. (p. 179)

SWOT analysis A method of studying organizational resources and capabilities to assess the firm's strengths and weaknesses and scanning its external environment to identify opportunities and threats. (p. 169)

system An organized group of components linked according to a plan for achieving specific objectives. (p. 535)

systems integration Centralization of the procurement function within an internal division or as a service of an external supplier. (p. 315)

tactical planning The process of defining implementation activities that the firm must carry out to achieve its objectives. (p. 165)

target market Group of people toward whom a firm markets its goods, services, or ideas with a strategy designed to satisfy their specific needs and preferences. (pp. 23, 229)

target market decision analysis Procedure for evaluating the relevant characteristics and the prospects for satisfying business objectives of potential market segments. (p. 249)

target return objective A short-run or long-run pricing practice intended to achieve a specified return on either sales or investment. (p. 695)

tariff A tax levied on imported goods. (p. 129)

task force An interdisciplinary group on temporary assignment to work through functional departments in examining new-product issues. (p. 417)

task-objective method Allocating promotional spending by defining goals and then determining the amount of promotional spending needed to achieve them. (p. 587)

team selling Combination of salespeople with specialists from other functional areas to promote a product. (p. 653)

technological environment The application to marketing of discoveries in science, inventions, and innovations. (p. 95)

technology Application to business of knowledge based on scientific discoveries, inventions, and innovations. (p. 27)

telemarketing Promotional presentation involving the use of the telephone for outbound contacts by salespeople or inbound contacts initiated by customers who want to obtain information and place orders. (pp. 581, 649)

tertiary industry An industry that rises to dominance in the third stage of an economy's development; service firms are considered components of tertiary industries. (p. 441)

test marketing A trial introduction of a new product supported by a complete marketing campaign to a selected city or television coverage area typical of the total market. (p. 421)

third-party (contract) logistics firm A company that specializes in handling logistics activities for other firms. (p. 533)

time-based competition A strategy of developing and distributing goods and services more quickly than competitors can achieve. (p. 85)

total quality management (TQM) An effort to involve all employees in a firm to continually improve products and work processes with the goal of achieving customer satisfaction and world-class performance. (p. 55)

trade allowance Deal offered to wholesalers and retailers for purchasing or promoting a specific product. (p. 629)

trade discount A payment to a channel member or buyer as compensation for performing marketing functions; also known as a *functional discount.* (p. 725)

trade fair A periodic show at which manufacturers in a particular industry display wares for visiting retail and wholesale buyers. (p. 475)

trade-in A credit toward the selling price of a new product offered in exchange for a used product, usually of the same kind. (p. 727)

trade industry Retailers or wholesalers that purchase products for resale to others. (p. 299)

trade promotion Sales promotion aimed at marketing intermediaries rather than ultimate consumers. (pp. 573, 629)

trademark A brand to which the owner legally claims exclusive access. (p. 405)

transaction-based marketing Buyer and seller exchanges characterized by limited communications and little or no ongoing relationship between the parties. (p. 335)

transfer price A cost assessed for a product exchanged between profit centers within a single firm. (p. 735)

trend analysis A quantitative sales forecasting method that estimates future sales through statistical analyses of historical sales patterns. (p. 181)

truck wholesaler A limited-function merchant wholesaler who markets perishable food items; also called a truck jobber. (p. 475)

tying agreement An arrangement that requires a marketing intermediary to carry a manufacturer's full product line in exchange for an exclusive dealership. (p. 483)

undifferentiated marketing Marketing strategy to produce only one product and market it to all customers using a single marketing mix. (p. 249)

unfair-trade law A state law requiring sellers to maintain minimum prices for comparable merchandise. (p. 691)

uniform delivered price A price-setting system that incorporates transportation costs by quoting all buyers the same price, including average transportation expenses for all shipments. (p. 727)

unitizing The process of combining individual materials into large loads for easy handling. (p. 548)

unit pricing A pricing policy that states prices in terms of recognized units of measurement or standard numerical counts. (p. 731)

Universal Product Code (UPC) A bar code on a product's package that provides information read by optical scanners. (p. 409)

utility Want-satisfying power of a good or service. (p. 7)

VALS™ 2 Commercially available system for psychographic segmentation of consumers. (p. 243)

value The customer's perception of the balance between the quality of goods or services that a firm provides and their prices. (p. 47)

value analysis Systematic study of the components of a purchase to determine the most cost-effective ways to acquire them. (p. 319)

value chain See supply chain.

value pricing A pricing strategy that emphasizes benefits a product provides in comparison to the price and quality levels of competing offerings. (p. 697)

value-added Increased worth of a good or service resulting from added features, lower price, enhanced customer service, a strengthened warranty, or other marketing mix improvements that increase customer satisfaction. (p. 47)

value-added service An improved or supplemental service that customers do not normally receive or expect. (p. 533)

variety store A retailer that offers an extensive range and assortment of low-priced merchandise. (p. 515)

vendor analysis Assessment of supplier performance in areas such as price, back orders, timely delivery, and attention to special requests. (p. 319)

vendor-managed inventory (VMI) Inventory-management system in which the seller determines how much product a buyer needs and automatically ships new supplies. (p. 357)

venture team A new-product development organization that brings together specialists from different functional areas. (p. 417)

vertical marketing system (VMS) A planned channel system designed to improve distribution efficiency and cost effectiveness by integrating various functions throughout the distribution chain. (p. 489)

virtual storefront Form of interactive media that allows customers to view and order merchandise. (p. 33)

wheel of retailing The hypothesis that each new type of retailer gains a competitive foothold by offering lower prices than current suppliers charge, maintaining profits by reducing or eliminating services. (p. 499)

wholesaler A marketing intermediary who takes title to goods and then distributes them further; also called a jobber or distributor. (p. 467)

wholesaling intermediary A comprehensive term that describes wholesalers as well as agents and brokers. (p. 471)

World Trade Organization (WTO) A 125-member organization that succeeds GATT in overseeing trade agreements, mediating disputes, and reducing trade barriers; unlike GATT provisions, WTO decisions are binding. (p. 133)

World Wide Web (WWW or Web) An interlinked collection of graphically rich information sources within the larger Internet. (p. 31)

zone pricing A price-setting system that incorporates transportation costs by dividing an overall market into geographic regions and setting a single price, including average freight charges, for purchases in each region. (p. 727)

SOLUTIONS FOR THE ACHIEVEMENT CHECK SUMMARY SECTIONS

Chapter 1

Objective 1.1
1. T
2. T
3. T

Objective 1.2
1. F
2. b
3. T

Objective 1.3
1. T
2. T
3. F

Objective 1.4
1. F
2. F
3. e

Objective 1.5
1. b
2. F
3. F

Objective 1.6
1. T
2. F
3. F

Objective 1.7
1. F
2. d
3. T

Objective 1.8
1. F
2. F

Objective 1.9
1. F
2. T

Chapter 2

Objective 2.1
1. T
2. F
3. F

Objective 2.2
1. T
2. T
3. c

Objective 2.3
1. F
2. T
3. T

Objective 2.4
1. T
2. F
3. T
4. T

Objective 2.5
1. F
2. T
3. b
4. F
5. T

Objective 2.6
1. T
2. F
3. F

Objective 2.7
1. T
2. F

Objective 2.8
1. a
2. T
3. F
4. T

Objective 2.9
1. T
2. F
3. F
4. b

Objective 2.10
1. b
2. a
3. T
4. T

Chapter 3

Objective 3.1
1. b
2. T
3. F

Objective 3.2
1. b
2. T
3. T

Objective 3.3
1. F
2. T
3. F

Objective 3.4
1. F
2. F
3. T

Objective 3.5
1. F
2. T
3. T

Objective 3.6
1. T
2. T
3. c

Objective 3.7
1. T
2. T
3. F

Chapter 4

Objective 4.1
1. T
2. F
3. F

Objective 4.2
1. T
2. F
3. c

Objective 4.3
1. T
2. d
3. F

Objective 4.4
1. T
2. T
3. a

Objective 4.5
1. F
2. c
3. F

Objective 4.6
1. F
2. T
3. F

Chapter 5

Objective 5.1
1. b
2. T
3. F

Objective 5.2
1. F
2. T
3. F

Objective 5.3
1. d
2. b
3. T

Objective 5.4
1. F
2. c
3. T

Objective 5.5
1. T
2. b
3. T

Objective 5.6
1. a
2. T
3. F

Objective 5.7
1. T
2. T
3. F

Chapter 6

Objective 6.1
1. F
2. b
3. F

Objective 6.2
1. T
2. b
3. T
4. T

Objective 6.3
1. F
2. a
3. T

Objective 6.4
1. T

2. T
3. F

Objective 6.5
1. T
2. T
3. c

Objective 6.6
1. F
2. T
3. T

Objective 6.7
1. a
2. T
3. T

Chapter 7

Objective 7.1
1. T
2. F
3. T
4. b

Objective 7.2
1. T
2. T
3. F

Objective 7.3
1. T
2. T
3. F

Objective 7.4
1. T
2. b
3. b
4. T
5. T

Objective 7.5
1. F
2. T
3. F

Objective 7.6
1. T
2. a
3. a
4. b

Objective 7.7
1. b
2. c
3. F

Chapter 8

Objective 8.1
1. T
2. T

Objective 8.2
1. c
2. F

Objective 8.3
1. T
2. F
3. F
4. b

Objective 8.4
1. T
2. a
3. T
4. b

Objective 8.5
1. F
2. T
3. b
4. d

Objective 8.6
1. T
2. b
3. T

Chapter 9

Objective 9.1
1. F
2. F
3. T

Objective 9.2
1. T
2. F
3. c

Objective 9.3
1. F
2. d
3. F

Objective 9.4
1. F
2. F

Objective 9.5
1. F
2. F
3. F

Objective 9.6
1. T
2. F
3. F

Objective 9.7
1. F
2. b
3. T

Objective 9.8
1. F
2. F
3. F

Objective 9.9
1. T
2. F
3. d

Chapter 10

Objective 10.1
1. F
2. c
3. F

Objective 10.2
1. T
2. d
3. T

Objective 10.3
1. b
2. F
3. F

Objective 10.4
1. F
2. T

Objective 10.5
1. F
2. T
3. c

Objective 10.6
1. T
2. F
3. F

Objective 10.7
1. T
2. F
3. T

Objective 10.8
1. T
2. T
3. F

Objective 10.9
1. T
2. T
3. T

Chapter 11

Objective 11.1
1. F
2. T

Objective 11.2
1. F
2. F
3. T

Objective 11.3
1. T
2. T
3. a

Objective 11.4
1. F
2. F
3. T

Objective 11.5
1. a
2. F
3. T

Objective 11.6
1. F
2. T
3. T
4. T

Objective 11.7
1. F
2. F
3. T
4. T
5. T

Chapter 12

Objective 12.1
1. T
2. c
3. F

Objective 12.2
1. F
2. b
3. F

Objective 12.3
1. b
2. T
3. T
4. T

Objective 12.4
1. T
2. b
3. b
4. T
5. T

Objective 12.5
1. b
2. c
3. T
4. F

Objective 12.6
1. F
2. a
3. F
4. T
5. F

Objective 12.7
1. F
2. T
3. T

Objective 12.8
1. T
2. T
3. F

Objective 12.9
1. F
2. T
3. F

Chapter 13

Objective 13.1
1. T
2. a
3. T

Objective 13.2
1. F
2. T
3. T

Objective 13.3
1. T
2. T
3. F

Objective 13.4
1. F
2. F
3. T

Objective 13.5
1. T
2. b
3. T

Objective 13.6
1. F
2. F
3. T
4. T

Objective 13.7
1. T
2. F
3. c

Chapter 14

Objective 14.1
1. T
2. b
3. T
4. F

Objective 14.2
1. c
2. a
3. d
4. a

Objective 14.3
1. T
2. T
3. b

Objective 14.4
1. T
2. T
3. T

Objective 14.5
1. a
2. T
3. b

Objective 14.6
1. b
2. a
3. b
4. T

Objective 14.7
1. F
2. T
3. b

Objective 14.8
1. a
2. b
3. b

Objective 14.9
1. a
2. e
3. a
4. a

Chapter 15

Objective 15.1
1. T
2. F
3. T

Objective 15.2
1. F
2. F
3. F

Objective 15.3
1. F
2. b
3. d

Objective 15.4
1. T
2. F
3. c
4. T

Objective 15.5
1. b
2. F
3. T

Objective 15.6
1. b
2. T

Chapter 16

Objective 16.1
1. T
2. b
3. T

Objective 16.2
1. F
2. T
3. T
4. F

Objective 16.3
1. F
2. F
3. T

Objective 16.4
1. T
2. T
3. T

Objective 16.5
1. b
2. F
3. F
4. T

Objective 16.6
1. b
2. b

Chapter 17

Objective 17.1
1. F
2. F
3. T

Objective 17.2
1. T
2. d
3. F

Objective 17.3
1. T
2. c
3. F

Objective 17.4
1. T
2. T
3. b

Objective 17.5
1. T
2. F
3. d

Objective 17.6
1. F
2. F
3. T

Objective 17.7
1. F
2. T
3. F

Objective 17.8
1. c

2. F
3. F

Objective 17.9
1. F
2. T
3. F

Chapter 18

Objective 18.1
1. F
2. F
3. T

Objective 18.2
1. T
2. F
3. T

Objective 18.3
1. T
2. T
3. b

Objective 18.4
1. F
2. T
3. F

Objective 18.5
1. F
2. T
3. T

Objective 18.6
1. F
2. T
3. T

Objective 18.7
1. F
2. T
3. T

Objective 18.8
1. T
2. F
3. F

Objective 18.9
1. T
2. T
3. F

Chapter 19

Objective 19.1
1. F
2. T
3. F

Objective 19.2
1. T
2. F
3. F

Objective 19.3
1. T
2. F
3. F
4. T

Objective 19.4
1. F
2. F
3. b
4. c

Objective 19.5
1. a
2. F
3. T
4. F
5. T

Objective 19.6
1. F
2. T
3. d

Objective 19.7
1. b
2. a
3. T

Objective 19.8
1. T
2. F
3. T

Chapter 20

Objective 20.1
1. T
2. F
3. F

Objective 20.2
1. d
2. c

Objective 20.3
1. F
2. T
3. T

Objective 20.4
1. F
2. T
3. F

Objective 20.5
1. T
2. F
3. T

Objective 20.6
1. b
2. d

Objective 20.7
1. F
2. T
3. T

Objective 20.8
1. F
2. T
3. T

Chapter 21

Objective 21.1
1. F
2. T
3. T

Objective 21.2
1. c
2. c
3. b

Objective 21.3
1. T
2. F
3. T

Objective 21.4
1. T
2. F
3. T

Objective 21.5
1. b
2. d

Objective 21.6
1. T
2. F
3. T

Objective 21.7
1. F
2. T
3. T

PHOTO AND FIGURE CREDITS

Page 10 Fallon McElligott/Dublin Productions.

Page 17 Poster created by FJCandN on behalf of Hogle Zoo in Salt Lake City.

Page 20 Courtesy of Pepsi-Cola Company

Page 22 Courtesy of SPOT Design, NYC.

Page 26 Courtesy of The Martin Agency

Page 49 Data reported in "Americans Are More Finicky Than Ever," *Fortune,* February 3, 1997, pp. 108–110.

Page 54 "W. Edwards Deming: On Mission to Revamp Workplace: Deming's Steps to Quality," USA Today, October 15, 1990, p. 48. Copyright USA Today. Reprinted with permission.

Page 58 Photo and information on the 1997 Malcolm Baldrige Award Criteria courtesy of the National Institute of Standards and Technology, Office of Quality Programs, Gaithersburg, Maryland, 20899.

Page 99 AP/Damian Dovarganes.

Page 103 Courtesy of the American Marketing Association.

Page 118 Data from *Statistical Abstract of the United States* (Washington, D.C.: U.S. Bureau of the Census, 1996), pp. 805–806.

Page 121 Courtesy of McDonald's Corporation.

Page 122 Copyright © Munshi Ahmed.

Page 134 U.S. Department of Commerce data and *Business Week* estimates, reported in Amy Borrus, "Singing the NAFTA Blues," *Business Week,* December 6, 1996, p. 55.

Page 135 Copyright © Leo Celano.

Page 136 Data reported in Gary Clyde Hufbauer and Kimberly Ann Elliot, *Measuring the Costs of Protection in the United States* (Washington, D.C.: Institute for International Economics), 1994, p. 13.

Page 141 "Hope for Suzhou Industrial Park," *Forbes,* January 27, 1997, pp. 80–81. Text reprinted by permission of *Forbes* Magazine, Copyright © Forbes Inc. 1997. Illustrations reprinted by permission of Slim Films. Photo of Future skyline of China-Singapore Suzhou Industrial Park courtesy of China-Singapore Suzhou Industrial Park Development Co., Ltd.

Page 142 Data reported in "The 100 Largest U.S. Multinationals," *Forbes,* July 15, 1996, p. 288.

Page 144 Adapted from Warren Keagan, *Multinational Marketing Management* (Englewood Cliffs, N.J.: Prentice-Hall, 1985).

Page 163 "Coke Pours into Asia." Reprinted from *Business Week,* October 28, 1996, p. 76 by special permission. Copyright © 1996 by The McGraw-Hill Companies, Inc.

Page 168 Chevron Corporation 1995 Annual Report, p. 6.

Page 170 Adapted from a discussion in Ramon J. Aldag and Timothy M. Stearns, *Management* (Cincinnati, Ohio: South-Western Publishing, 1991), pp. 199–201.

Page 197 Reprinted by permission of Raymond R. Burke.

Page 201 Adapted from: Gilbert A. Churchill Jr., *Basic Marketing Research* (Fort Worth, Tex: The Dryden Press), 1996, p. 12.

Page 209 From the collections of the Henry Ford Museum and Greenfield Village. Reprinted with permission.

Page 210 Compiled and developed by Marlene G. Bellamy and Carolyn Z. Lawrence, Writeline Associates, 1997.

Page 214 Copyright © Guy Aroch.

Page 231 Copyright © Ki Ho Park/Kistone.

Page 240 Data from the Department of Commerce. Reprinted from *Newsweek,* July 10, 1995, p. 21.

Page 243 Copyright © 1997 SRI Consulting. All rights reserved. Unauthorized reproduction prohibited. VALS™2 is a trademark of SRI International.

Page 247 M. Dale Beckman, Louis E. Boone, and David L. Kurtz, *Foundations of Marketing,* 6th ed., (Toronto: Harcourt Brace & Company Canada, 1997). All rights reserved. The figure was originally prepared by Professor J. D. Forbes of the University of British Columbia and is reprinted by permission of the authors and publisher.

Page 251 Peter R. Dickson, *Marketing Management,* 2nd ed. (Fort Worth, Tex.: The Dryden Press, 1997), p. 331.

Page 259 AP/Steve Castillo

Page 300 Copyright © Christopher Irion.

Page 314 Adapted from Michael Hutt and Thomas Speh, *Business Marketing Management,* 6th ed. (Fort Worth, Tex.: The Dryden Press, 1998), p. 71.

Page 318 Courtesy of McDonald's Corporation.

Page 319 Chrysler Corp.; Michael D. Hutt and Thomas J. Speh, *Business Marketing Management,* 6th ed. (Fort Worth, Tex.: The Dryden Press, 1998), p. 104.

Page 326 Based on Michael Hutt and Thomas Speh, *Business Marketing Management,* 6th ed. (Fort Worth, Tex.: The Dryden Press, 1998), pp. 11–12.

Page 331 Copyright © Ilene Ehrlich Photography.

Page 333 Based on Joseph P. Cannon and Jagdish N. Sheth, "Developing a Curriculum to Enhance Teaching of Relationship Marketing," Journal of Marketing Education, summer 1994, p. 5.

Page 335 Adapted from Martin Christopher, Adrian Payne, and David Ballantyne, *Relationship Marketing* (Oxford, UK: Butterworth-Heinemann Ltd., 1993), p. 4.

Page 341 Adapted from information in Leonard L. Berry, "Relationship Marketing of Services—Growing Interest, Emerging Perspectives," *Journal of the Academy of Marketing Sciences,* fall 1995, p. 240.

Page 342 Copyright © 1995 Larime Photographic.

Page 349 Copyright © Disney; Mr. Potato Head Copyright © 1995 Hasbro Inc. All rights reserved. Photo courtesy of *PROMO Magazine.*

Page 356 Adapted from Michael Hutt and Thomas Speh, *Business Marketing Management,* 6th ed. (Fort Worth, Tex.: The Dryden Press), 1998, p. 276.

Page 358 Adapted from P. Rajan Varadarajan and Margaret H. Cunningham, "Strategic Alliances: A Synthesis of Conceptual Foundations," *Journal of the Academy of Marketing Science,* fall 1995, p. 292.

Page 365 AP/Paul Sakuma

Page 371 Copyright © Philip Saltonstall, Photography. All rights reserved.

Page 385 Courtesy of Apple Computer, Inc.

Page 389 1996 Annual Report. Additional information downloaded from http://www.ambrands.com/portfolio, November 11, 1996.

Page 402 David A. Aaker, *Building Strong Brands* (New York: The Free Press, 1996), p. 306.

Page 438 Adapted from Valarie A. Zeithaml, Leonard L. Berry, and A. Parasuraman, "Communication and Control Processes and Delivery of Service Quality," *Journal of Marketing,* April 1988, p. 35; and A. Parasuraman, Valarie A. Zeithaml, and Leonard L Berry, "A Conceptual Model of Service Quality and its Indications for Future Research," *Journal of Marketing,* fall 1985, p. 48.

Page 439 Reprinted from Valarie A. Zeithaml, Leonard L. Berry, and A Parasuraman, "Communication and Control Processes and Delivery of Service Quality," *Journal of Marketing,* April 1988, p. 36. Used by permission of the American Marketing Association.

Page 456 AP/Dennis Cook

Page 468 Mamoru Tsukada/ARIA.

Page 470 Steche/Visum/SABA

Page 471 Copyright © Craig Preston/Black Star.

Page 478 Adapted from Malty Jacknis and Steve Kratz, "The Channel Empowerment Solution," *Sales & Marketing Management,* March 1993, pp. 44–49. Reprinted by permission of *Sales and Marketing Management.*

Page 500 Copyright © 1996 by David A. Peterson.

Page 504 Copyright © Steven Rubin/The Image Works.

Page 512 Copyright © Elizabeth Heyert.

Page 514 U.S. Bureau of the Census, 1984 and 1992 Census of Retail Trade in 1996 Statistical Abstract.

Page 521 David Kurtz.

Page 538 1996 Davis Database, Herbert W. Davis and Company, Fort Lee, NJ.

Page 553 AP/Adam Nadel

Page 562 Courtesy of *PROMO Magazine.*

Page 570 Courtesy of World Wildlife Fund, Inc. Renewal Video Copyright © 1994.

Page 572 Courtesy of *PROMO Magazine.*

Page 575 Courtesy of *PROMO Magazine.*

Page 577 Copyright © Jessica Inch.

Page 578 Data from WEFA Group, "Economic Impact: U.S. Direct Marketing Today," *Direct Marketing Association,* New York, October 1995, pp. 5, 7.

Page 582 Text, "What's in a 30-Minute Infomercial?" Reprinted with permission, *Inc.,* May 1995. Copyright 1995 by Goldhirsh Group, Inc., 38 Commercial Wharf, Boston, MA 02110.

Page 587 Adapted from Cannondale Associates in Betsey Spethmann, "Trade Promotion, Redefined," *BrandWeek,* March 13, 1995, p. 30.

Page 620 Courtesy of Chick-fil-A, Inc. "Eat Mor' Chikin'" is the trademark of Chick-fil-A, Inc.

Page 627 Courtesy of *PROMO Magazine.*

Page 628 Courtesy of *PROMO Magazine.*

Page 630 Copyright © 1997 Shonna Valeska.

Page 634 Courtesy of Roper Starch Worldwide.

Page 650 Copyright © Photo Disc.

Page 651 Thomas N. Ingram, "Improving Sales Force Productivity: A Critical Examination of the Personal Selling Process," *Review of Business,* summer 1990, p. 12; and copyright © Photo Disc.

Page 653 Copyright © David Graham.

Page 656 Copyright © Robert Holmgren. All righs reserved..

Page 662 Copyright © John Gurzinski.

Page 663 Allison Lucas, ed., "Portrait of a Salesperson," *Sales and Marketing Management,* June 1995, p. 13.

Page 666 Data taken from Inc., July 1993, p. 24; and *Sales & Marketing Management,* June 22, 1993, p. 85.

Page 680 AP/Steven Senne

Page 689 Copyright © Vince Streano/The Stock Market.

Page 729 Mike Theiler/Reuters/Corbis-Bettmann.

Page 731 Reported in "Dealers' Secret Profit," *USA Today,* February 16, 1996, p. 6B.

Page 735 Reprinted with permission from September 10, 1990 issue of *Business Week* by special permission. Copyright © 1990 by McGraw-Hill, Inc.

Page 741 AP/Bebeto Matthews

Figure A.1 Reprinted with permission from December 6, 1993 issue of *Advertising Age.* Copyright © Crain Communications Inc., 1993.

Page A-1 Copyright © 1997 Dwight Cendrowski

ADDITIONAL SOURCES FOR THE VIDEO CASES:

Video Case 2: Theodore Kinni, "Lofty Goals," *Industry Week,* September 4, 1995, pp. 63–65; Tim Stevens, "And Then There Were Three," *Industry Week,* January 23, 1995, p. 11; "Creating a Violence-Free Company Culture," *Nation's Business,* February 1995, p. 22; and "News Breaks," *Aviation Week & Space Technology,* October 24, 1994; p. 17; **Video Case 3:** *Annual Report,* 1995, AT&T; and Julia Flynn, Catherine Arnst, and Gail Edmondson, "Who'll Be the First Global Phone Company?" *Business Week,* March 27, 1995, pp. 176–80; **Video Case 5:** Photos Courtesy of Kropf Inc.; **Video Case 15:** Photos courtesy of Cherry Capital Airport and Detroit Zoological Institute.

SOURCES FOR THE MICROSOFT CONTINUING CASES:

David Kirkpatrick, "He Wants All Your Business—And He's Starting to Get It," *Fortune,* May 26, 1997, pp. 58–81; Robert Hof and Gary McWilliams, "Digital TV: What Will It Be?" *Business Week,* April 21, 1997, pp. 34–36; Steve Hamm, "The Gates Keepers," *PC Week,* March 3, 1997, p. A1; Walter Isaacson, "In Search of the Real Bill Gates," *Time,* January 13, 1997, pp. 45–57; Kathy Rebello, "Bill's Quiet Shopping Spree," *Business Week,* January 13, 1997, pp. 34–35; Bob Trott, "NT Provides Backbone for Microsoft Financial Success," *Infoworld,* January 27, 1997, p. 35; Jeffrey Young, "The George S. Patton of Software," *Forbes,* January 27, 1997, pp. 86–92; Randall E. Stross, *The Microsoft Way* (Reading, MA: Addison-Wesley), 1996, pp. 50–51, 102–105, 98–99; Gerry Khermouch, "Microsoft Works Magic into Kids Push; Kodak, Revlon Get up on Oscar Net," *Brandweek,* March 25, 1996, p. 37; Diane

Mermigs, "Bill Gates Mines Internet Gold," *Advertising Age,* April 1, 1996, p. 55; James Gleick, "Making Microsoft Safe for Capitalism," *New York Times Magazine,* April 14, 1996; Cara Chang Mutert, "Gates Predicts Internet's Future," *Sales and Marketing Strategy & News,* April/May 1996, pp. 1, 4–5, 9; Clinton Walker, "Microsoft to Deliver via the Web," *Information Week,* May 6, 1996, p. 42; Paul Judge, "Surviving the Age of the Internet," *Business Week,* June 3, 1996, pp. 114, 118; Steve Hamm, "Microsoft's Man in India," *PC Week,* June 17, 1996, p. A8; Pete Engardio and Dexter Roberts, "Microsoft's Long March," *Business Week,* June 24, 1996, pp. 52–54; Kathy Rebello, "Inside Microsoft," *Business Week,* July 15, 1996, pp. 56–70; Rick Marin, "Rebooting the News," *Newsweek,* July 29, 1996, p. 77; John Teresko, "Too Much Data, Too Little Information," *Industry Week,* August 19, 1996, p. 66; Joshua Cooper Ramo, "Winner Take All," *Time,* September 16, 1996, pp. 56-62; Brent Schlender, "Software Hardball," *Fortune,* September 30,1996, pp. 107–16; Kathy Rebello, "Honey, What's on Microsoft?" *Business Week,* October 21, 1996, pp. 134–36; Randall E. Stross, "Microsoft's Big Advantage—Hiring Only the Supersmart," *Fortune,* November 25, 1996, pp. 160–162; Bradley Johnson, "Microsoft's Office 97 to get $14 mil support," *Advertising Age,* November 25, 1996; Tad Szulc, "One of the Greatest Shows on Earth," *Forbes,* December 2, 1996, pp. 67–71; Doug Bartholomew, "Bill Gates Envisions the Enterprise," *Industry Week,* December 16, 1996, pp. 8–13; Joshua Quittner, "In the Belly of the Beast," *Time,* December 16, 1996; Julie Miller, "'Getting to Know You' via Promotions," *Advertising Age,* March 20, 1995, p. S-6; Michael A. Cusumano and Richard W. Selby, *Microsoft Secrets* (New York: The Free Press, 1995), pp. 73–85, 89, 127, 227–34, 309–313, 362–363, 400–20, 433–38; Bill Gates, *The Road Ahead,* (New York: Penguin Books, 1995), pp. 42–44, 49–54; Philip Elmer-Dewitt, "Mine, All Mine," *Time,* June 5, 1995, pp. 46–54; Laura DiDio, "Software Pricing Sizzles," *Computerworld,* July 10, 1995, pp. 1, 125; Kathy Rebello and Mary Kuntz, "Feel the Buzz: Windows 95's Marketing Blitz," *Business Week,* August 28, 1995, p. 31; Mary Anne Mather, "Family Computing Workshops Are the Latest Rage," *Technology and Learning,* September 1995, p. 60; Brent Schlender, "Bill Gates & Paul Allen Talk," *Fortune,* October 2, 1995, pp. 68–86; Kathy Rebello, "After Win95, What Do You Do for an Encore?" *Business Week,* October 16, 1995, pp. 68–74; Jamie Lewis, "Microsoft's Net Plan Is Clear, Albeit Late," *PC Week,* December 18, 1995, p. N12; Wayne Walley, "NBC, Microsoft Set Joint Ventures," *Advertising Age,* December 18, 1995, p. 4; Tim Clark, "Microsoft Heads Home," *Advertising Age,* May 16, 1994, pp. S1–S2; Larry Armstrong, Ira Sager, Kathy Rebello, and Peter Burrows, "Home Computers," *Business Week,* November 28, 1994, pp. 89–96; Bradley Johnson, "Microsoft's New World," *Advertising Age,* November 14, 1994, pp. 1, 8; Richard Brandt and Amy Cortese, "Microsoft Wants to Move into Your Family Room," *Business Week,* November 28, 1994, pp. 92–93; Bradley Johnson, "Marketer of the Year: Bill Gates' Vision of Microsoft in Every Home," *Advertising Age,* December 19, 1994, pp. 14–15.

Microsoft Corporation's 1994, 1995, and 1996 annual reports.

NAME AND COMPANY INDEX

SUBJECT INDEX

INTERNATIONAL INDEX

International Business Machines Corp.	http://www.ibm.com/
Internet Shopping Network	http://www.isn.com/
J. D. Power and Associates	http://www.jdpower.com/
J. M. Smucker Co.	http://www.smucker.com/
Joe Boxer	http://www.joeboxer.com/
Kellogg Co.	http://www.kelloggs.com/
Kmart Corp.	http://www.kmart.com/
Kropf Food Co.	http://www.kropf-inc.com/
L. L. Bean, Inc.	http://www.llbean.com/
Lands' End Direct Merchants	http://www.landsend.com/
Learjet, Inc.	http://www.learjet.com/
Learning Co.	http://www.softkey.com/
Levi Strauss and Co.	http://www.levi.com/
Mall of America	http://www.mallofamerica.com/
McDonald's Corp.	http://www.mcdonalds.com/
Mediamark Research, Inc.	http://www.mediamark.com/
Metropolitan Life Insurance Co.	http://www.metlife.org/
Metropolitan Museum of Art	http://www.metmuseum.org/
Microsoft Corp.	http://www.microsoft.com/
Monopoly	http://www.monopoly.com/
Mountain Travel-Sobek	http://www.mtsobek.com/
Mt. Bachelor Ski Resort	http://www.mtbachelor.com/
MTV Music Television Networks	http://www.mtv.com/
Nabisco	http://www.nabisco.com/
Nestlé S.A.	http://www.nestle.com/
Netscape Communications Corp.	http://www.netscape.com/
New Jersey Online	http://www.nj.com/
Nike, Inc.	http://www.nike.com/
Nordstrom Personal Touch America	http://www.nordstrom-pta.com/
Pacific Bell At Hand	http://www.athand.com/
pcOrder.com, Inc.	http://www.pcorder.com/
Peapod	http://www.peapod.com/
Pepsi Corp.	http://www.pepsi.com/
Plantronics, Inc.	http://www.plantronics.com/
Polygon, Inc.	http://www.polygon.com/
Praxair Technology, Inc.	http://www.praxair.com/
Procter & Gamble	http://www.pg.com/